Federal Courts

Federal Courts

Cases and Materials on Judicial Federalism and the Lawyering Process

FOURTH EDITION

Arthur D. Hellman
SALLY ANN SEMENKO ENDOWED CHAIR
UNIVERSITY OF PITTSBURGH SCHOOL OF LAW

David R. Stras
ASSOCIATE JUSTICE
MINNESOTA SUPREME COURT

Ryan W. Scott
PROFESSOR OF LAW
INDIANA UNIVERSITY MAURER SCHOOL OF LAW

F. Andrew Hessick
PROFESSOR OF LAW
UNIVERSITY OF NORTH CAROLINA SCHOOL OF LAW

CAROLINA ACADEMIC PRESS
Durham, North Carolina

ISBN 978-1-53100-149-0
eISBN 978-1-53100-150-6
LCCN 2017942688

Carolina Academic Press, LLC
700 Kent Street
Durham, North Carolina 27701
Telephone (919) 489-7486
Fax (919) 493-5668
www.cap-press.com

Printed in the United States of America

To Diana, Jeffrey, Matthew, and Melissa, ADH
To Heather, Brandon, and Benjamin, DRS
To Cameron, RWS
To Carissa, Hattie, and Dorothy, FAH

Contents

Part Five
Challenging State Official Action

Part Six
Systemic Issues in Federal Litigation

Preface to the Fourth Edition

In the Preface to the First Edition (reprinted immediately following), we explained our basic approach in writing a new Federal Courts casebook. We would build on the traditional model of the Federal Courts course — a model that focuses on issues of federalism, separation of powers, and institutional competency — but would place equal emphasis on a second component: giving students the grounding they need to be effective lawyer-litigators. In this Fourth Edition, we continue that approach, but we have made a number of changes in implementing it. These changes have been prompted by new decisions from the Supreme Court, a desire to fine-tune the book's organization, and a commitment to reduce the size of the casebook. The result, we think, is a leaner book that will be a more effective tool for teaching.

New decisions. In the four years that immediately preceded the Third Edition, the Supreme Court issued a number of decisions that changed or significantly clarified the law. The last four years have not been as eventful, but four decisions seemed important enough to include in this Fourth Edition. Each replaces a case in the Third Edition. In addition, we use a district court decision to illustrate the lower courts' application of the 2011 law establishing a "bad faith" exception to the one-year rule for removal of diversity cases.

Of the Supreme Court decisions, *Gunn v. Minton* (Chapter 10) stands out because it is the Court's most recent opinion on a basic and recurring issue of Federal Courts law: the scope of the statutory "arising under" jurisdiction. The case confirms a four-part test for "incorporated federal question" jurisdiction in the district court, and it largely displaces the controversial decision in *Merrell Dow v. Thompson*, a principal case in all prior editions of the casebook.

Gunn narrowed the scope of federal jurisdiction, but another new decision, *Sprint Communications v. Jacobs* (Chapter 12), moves in the opposite direction. The Court made clear that *Younger* abstention applies only in three "exceptional" circumstances, and that the pendency of an action in state court is generally "no bar to proceedings concerning the same matter in the Federal court having jurisdiction."

Two new decisions addressed the scope of Congress's power under Article III. In *Bank Markazi v. Peterson* (Chapter 20), the Court rejected arguments that Congress violated the separation of powers by purporting to change the law for, and directing a particular result in, a single pending case. And in *Wellness Int'l v. Sharif* (Chapter 22), the Court recognized Congress's power to assign a broad class of cases to non-Article III tribunals based on the parties' consent.

The small number of new principal cases may appear surprising, but we emphasize that we have not replaced older cases simply because a new decision has come down on the same topic. When an existing case presents the issues in a way that makes for an effective classroom experience, we have kept it, even though a more recent case might add an interesting new wrinkle.

Fine-tuning the book's organization. Federal Courts has a reputation as a difficult course. One way of combating this, as we suggested in the Preface to the First Edition, is through structure—a structure that organizes the various topics into larger, well-defined units of study. We think that the seven-part structure used in the first and subsequent editions of the casebook is sound, and we have retained it in this edition. But within that framework we have made three modest changes suggested by experience.

First, Part Two, dealing with the role of federal law in state-court litigation, has been divided into three chapters rather than two. Chapter 4 now presents an overview of the topic, including the foundational cases on Supreme Court review of state-court decisions and an introduction to removal jurisdiction. This arrangement permits greater flexibility in teaching this topic; it also calls attention to the different routes Congress has taken in vesting the Article III judicial power over diversity and federal-question cases. As part of the reorganization, we have taken the opportunity to make Chapter 5 a more manageable size. This was a very large chapter in prior editions; in this edition, we have omitted matters of detail and nuance that are out of sync with the casebook's basic approach.

Second, we have moved the materials on the Court's various abstention doctrines into a single chapter on parallel proceedings in state and federal courts, now Chapter 12. Thus, the Anti-Injunction Act, the abstention doctrines, *Colorado River*, and *Brillhart* are now all treated in the same chapter. This arrangement has the additional benefit of enabling students to assess how the various statutory and decisional limitations on federal jurisdiction affect the different classes of cases heard by federal courts.

Third, the materials on federal district courts as a forum for challenges to state official action now precede the chapters on systemic issues in federal litigation. This change facilitated the reorganization of the abstention materials in Chapter 12, but it also accords with the emphasis placed on this subcategory of federal-question cases by many Federal Courts teachers.

Streamlining and trimming. Federal Courts intersects and overlaps with many other courses in the law school curriculum—Constitutional Law, Civil Procedure, Remedies, and Civil Rights in particular. Partly because of this overlap, Federal Courts courses differ greatly in their coverage. Accommodating those differences requires a large casebook. Nevertheless, we concluded that we could reduce the size of the book considerably while continuing to offer a range of coverage options and maintaining the depth of treatment. We have done this primarily in three ways.

First, we have dropped or truncated some topics that few if any teachers covered—Supreme Court review of state-court decisions on "incorporated federal law," state courts as a forum for challenging state official action, and federal common law on "interstitial" issues in the litigation of federal causes of action.

Second, we eliminated principal cases in the Third Edition that have not led to continuing litigation and debate, and those that have not had the predicted impact on the evolution of federal courts doctrine. A good example is *Hein v. Freedom From Religion Foundation* (formerly in Chapter 3).

Third, we gave Note treatment to older cases that remain relevant but in limited ways that do not require principal-case treatment. Examples include *Jefferson v. City of Tarrant* (Chapter 5), *Stewart Organization, Inc. v. Ricoh Corp.* (Chapter 7), and *Caterpillar, Inc. v. Williams* (Chapter 10).

* * *

There has been only one change in the membership of the Supreme Court since publication of the Third Edition: Justice Antonin Scalia died unexpectedly early in the 2015 Term. At this writing, his seat remains vacant. Appendix B provides an updated table of the Justices.

* * *

The most significant changes in the casebook can be seen on the title page. Provost Lauren Robel (Indiana University-Bloomington), one of the two founding authors of the book (along with Professor Hellman), is no longer listed as an author, but her contributions to structure, content, and approach remain throughout the casebook, and all of the authors acknowledge her significant role in the design of the book. In another milestone, the Fourth Edition introduces two new authors who have infused new ideas and different perspectives into the casebook. Professor Hellman and Justice Stras welcome Professor Ryan Scott of Indiana University Maurer School of Law and Professor F. Andrew Hessick of the University of North Carolina School of Law and express appreciation for their substantial contributions to this Fourth Edition.

* * *

In preparing this new edition, we have continued the approach followed by the three prior editions. First, we have concentrated on the main lines of doctrinal development and their implications for future disputes. In doing so, we have emphasized elements of litigation strategy and the practical application of Federal Courts doctrines and rules as well as the underlying policy and institutional-competence issues.

Second, we have edited the cases with a relatively light hand. We have also attempted to keep the decisions readable; thus, some brackets and internal quotation marks have been omitted from quoted material within cases.

* * *

The authors express their appreciation to the staff of the University of Pittsburgh School of Law Document Technology Center for dedicated efforts in preparing the manuscript. Professor Hessick would like to thank Professor Carissa Hessick. Professor Scott thanks his research assistants, Kevin LeRoy and Trevor Waliszewski. Justice Stras would like to thank his law clerks for their assistance in keeping him fresh on developments in federal jurisdiction while he continues to serve as a state Supreme Court Justice.

Preface to the First Edition

This book is the product of our rethinking of what a Federal Courts course should accomplish in the twenty-first century. The traditional course focuses on issues of federalism, separation of powers, and institutional competency. That focus provides a powerful intellectual model for organizing the materials that make up the field of study, and we have built on its insights. But the traditional model falls short in giving students the grounding they need to be effective lawyer-litigators.

Lawyers are goal-oriented. From their perspective, the American system of judicial federalism is important because it sets up four possible goals: getting into federal court; staying out of federal court; gaining the benefit of federal law; or avoiding the detriment of federal law. This book concentrates on providing the doctrinal and practical education that will enable lawyers to identify and pursue these goals effectively in the service of their clients, while assuring that they understand the underlying tensions and issues that will shape the law in the future. The emphasis of the book as well as its organization flows from this principle.

Emphasis. As one would expect, there is a core of material that is common to all Federal Courts casebooks. However, there is also wide latitude for differences in emphasis. Two major themes set this book apart from others.

First, we provide a comprehensive and unified treatment of the litigation of federal questions in state courts. To appreciate the issues involved in choosing between federal and state court, a lawyer must have an understanding of how federal questions are litigated in a state judicial system. In Part Two, we give sustained and systematic attention to the role of state courts as a forum for litigation of federal issues.

Second, the book is grounded in the realities of litigation today, rather than the assumptions that prevailed during the Civil Rights Era. Of particular importance is the strong tendency of defendants in civil litigation to prefer federal over state court. As a consequence of this development, the statutory device of removal now occupies a central place in litigation strategy. It is no accident that during the last 20 years virtually all of the Supreme Court's decisions on district court jurisdiction have come in cases in which the plaintiff has challenged the defendant's removal of the suit from state to federal court. This casebook treats removal pervasively, with an emphasis on the issues that dominate litigation practice today.

Features. In many law schools, Federal Courts has a reputation as a difficult course. This is not surprising; to some degree, difficulty is inherent in the subject. But the authors believe that the law of Federal Courts can be made understandable without sacrificing either depth or the intellectual rigor that is the hallmark of this area of study. Three features of the book promote this goal.

First, the book concentrates on the main lines of development and their implications for future disputes rather than traveling down every byway of doctrinal refinement. Major cases are set forth in full or in extended excerpts. The note material is extensive, but without a proliferation of citations to lesser cases that would only distract students from the important points. Nor is there a profusion of bibliographic references to secondary sources. In short, the book aims for depth rather than detail.

Second, to enable students to understand difficult material, it is essential that the various topics be organized into larger, well-defined units of study. The organization of a Federal Courts casebook should not simply reflect considerations of convenience; it should serve a pedagogical purpose. To that end, the organization of this book reflects a functional, *task-oriented* approach. For example, one task lawyers undertake is that of litigating federal questions in a state court. Part Two of the book presents the material relevant to that task. Another task is that of persuading a federal court to apply a rule of decision other than state law — the default law in our system of limited national government. That is the subject of Part Three. Another task is that of using federal court as a forum for challenging state official action. In Part Six, that task receives unified treatment.

Third, in addition to cases, notes, and questions, the book makes use of problems. Not all topics lend themselves to the problem method, but many do. The problems in the various chapters have been carefully designed to zero in on (a) points settled by the cases students have read; and (b) questions left unanswered or falling between precedents. Many are based on recent cases that did not go to the Supreme Court.

The best way to get a feel for the book's approach is to peruse the Table of Contents. We particularly invite attention to the sequence of topics, which has been carefully designed to reinforce learning. At the same time, the material has been subdivided into numerous smaller units to allow for maximum flexibility in choice of coverage.

Editing of cases. Cases have been edited for readability and as teaching tools; they should not be used for research purposes. Omissions are indicated by brackets or ellipses; alterations are indicated by brackets. Most footnotes have been omitted; however, footnotes in opinions and other quoted material retain their original numbers. Citations to cases other than those in the Casebook have generally been deleted. Brackets and internal quotation marks have been omitted from quoted material within cases. Lengthy paragraphs have sometimes been broken up to promote readability. References to "petitioner" and "respondent" have sometimes been replaced with party names or positions in the lower court.

Part One

The Constitutional Framework and the Federal Courts

Chapter 1

The Federal Judicial System

A. Development of the System

[1] The Constitution

The starting point for study of the federal courts is the Constitution of the United States. All that the Constitution has to say about the structure and functions of the federal judicial system is found in four sentences in Article III and one clause in Article I. In addition, one sentence in Article III and two provisions of Article II deal with the selection and tenure of judges.

Article III begins by establishing the structure of the system. The first sentence of Article III section 1 provides:

> The judicial power of the United States shall be vested in one supreme court and in such inferior courts as the Congress may from time to time ordain and establish.

Article I section 8 confirms the power of Congress "[t]o constitute Tribunals inferior to the supreme Court."

Jurisdiction is treated in Article III section 2. The first sentence of section 2 defines the nine categories of "cases" and "controversies" to which "the judicial power of the United States" extends. The next two sentences define the "original" and the "appellate" jurisdiction of the Supreme Court. Nothing is said about the jurisdiction of the "inferior courts."

The selection of judges is provided for in Article II:

> The President ... shall nominate, and by and with the Advice and Consent of the Senate, shall appoint ... Judges of the supreme Court, and all other Officers of the United States, whose Appointments are not herein otherwise provided for, and which shall be established by Law ....

Tenure and compensation are dealt with in Article III section 1: "The Judges, both of the supreme and inferior Courts, shall hold their Offices during good Behaviour, and shall, at stated Times, receive for their Services a Compensation, which shall not be diminished during their Continuance in Office." Implicitly, this language is supplemented by Article II section 4:

> The President, Vice President and all civil Officers of the United States, shall be removed from Office on Impeachment for, and Conviction of, Treason, Bribery, or other high Crimes and Misdemeanors.

These provisions leave many questions unanswered. We might look for guidance in the records of the Convention that met in Philadelphia in the summer of 1789 to draft the Constitution, but there is frustratingly little there about the judiciary article. A useful compilation of the Convention proceedings dealing with the creation of a national judiciary can be found, with brief commentary, in DANIEL A. FARBER & SUSAN SHERRY, A HISTORY OF THE AMERICAN CONSTITUTION 69–105 (2d ed. 2005).

Other provisions of the Constitution also affect the work of the judiciary. Of particular importance is the Supremacy Clause of Article VI:

> This Constitution, and the Laws of the United States which shall be made in Pursuance thereof; and all Treaties made, or which shall be made, under the Authority of the United States, shall be the supreme Law of the Land; and the Judges in every State shall be bound thereby, any Thing in the Constitution or Laws of any State to the Contrary notwithstanding.

[2] The Judiciary Act of 1789

The Constitution was ratified in 1788, and one year later, the first Congress enacted the first Judiciary Act. Professor (later Justice) Felix Frankfurter once commented: "Great judiciary acts, unlike great poems, are not written for all time."[1] Perhaps not, but if the Judiciary Act of 1789 was not written "for all time," it came much closer than most legislation. Many of the provisions of that Act can be recognized in the Judicial Code today; others lasted well into the nineteenth and twentieth centuries.

Four features of the 1789 Act were of particular importance. The Act's "transcendent achievement," in Frankfurter's view, was the creation of a system of "inferior" federal courts. The Constitution, in one of its great compromises, had left to Congress the decision whether to create any federal courts other than the Supreme Court. The first Congress took up the option and established two sets of trial courts within the states: district courts and circuit courts.

No less "transcendent," from the perspective of history, was section 25 of the Act. Section 25 authorized the United States Supreme Court to review final judgments of state courts where federal questions were raised and the state court decided against the federal claim or defense. Section 25 thus gave life to the Supremacy Clause.

A third important feature of the 1789 Act was the grant of jurisdiction to the new trial courts over suits between citizens of different states. Chief Justice Taft thought that the availability of "diversity" jurisdiction (as we would now call it) was a major influence in encouraging out-of-state investment.

Finally—though perhaps of somewhat lesser importance—the 1789 Act introduced the device of removal: it authorized defendants in certain types of cases filed in state court to "remove the cause for trial" to the federal court in the state.

---

1. FELIX FRANKFURTER & JAMES LANDIS, THE BUSINESS OF THE SUPREME COURT 107 (1928). Frankfurter was speaking of the Circuit Court of Appeals Act of 1891.

The combined effect of these provisions was to create a national judiciary with significant jurisdiction over ordinary private litigation and the potential for a prominent role in the allocation of power between state and national governments. Subsequent legislation substantially reinforced the nationalizing tendencies of the 1789 Act. These later enactments can usefully be divided into two broad areas: structure and jurisdiction.

[3] Evolution of the Structure

The most remarkable thing about the structure of the federal judicial system is how little it has changed in more than 200 years. Until 1891, there were basically two tiers of federal courts: trial courts (the district courts and circuit courts) and the Supreme Court.[2] In 1891, with the passage of the Evarts Act, Congress created the Circuit Courts of Appeals—appellate courts intermediate between the trial courts and the Supreme Court. (The word "circuit" was later dropped from the name of these courts.)

The Evarts Act thus converted a two-tier system into a three-tier system. But that has been the only major structural alteration in the federal judicial system in its entire history. And in one important respect the 1891 legislation represented continuity rather than change: it retained the circuit as the basic unit of organization. Each circuit encompassed at least three states; each was organized geographically, respectful both of regional spirit and of state boundaries.[3]

Of course, there have been some changes of lesser magnitude. A few deserve mention here.

Starting in the early twentieth century, Congress passed legislation requiring that certain kinds of cases be heard by three-judge district courts, with direct appeal to the Supreme Court. In recent years, almost all of this legislation has been repealed. Still subject to the requirement are reapportionment cases and cases under the Voting Rights Act of 1965.

From time to time, Congress has created various specialized courts. Most of these tribunals are no longer with us. Commitment to generalist judges is very strong.

Twice in the twentieth century, Congress created new circuits on a regional basis. The Tenth Circuit was carved out of the old Eighth in 1929. (That explains why, on the map, the Tenth is located between the Eighth and the Ninth.) In 1980, Congress divided the former Fifth Circuit into two new circuits, creating an Eleventh Circuit composed of the three states that formerly constituted the eastern half of the Fifth (Florida, Georgia, and Alabama). There are now twelve regional circuits, including the District

---

2. The circuit courts had some appellate jurisdiction over the district courts, but they functioned primarily as trial courts.

3. Respect for state boundaries continues today, with one insignificant exception: the Tenth Circuit includes the District of Wyoming, which in turn includes the portions of Yellowstone National Park situated in Montana and Idaho—states that otherwise are part of the Ninth Circuit. *See* 28 U.S.C. §§ 41, 131.

of Columbia Circuit, which, not surprisingly, has a special role in Federal Government litigation.

Legislation in the 1970s, although not structural in a literal sense, had a major impact on the allocation of the work of the federal courts. In 1976 and again in the Federal Magistrates Act of 1979, Congress substantially expanded the authority of "magistrate judges" (as they are now called). Magistrate judges are appointed for eight-year terms by the district judges of the district in which they serve. They do not have Article III protections, but today much of their work is indistinguishable from that of a federal district judge. In particular, as long as the parties consent, magistrate judges may now "conduct any or all proceedings in a jury or nonjury civil matter and order the entry of judgment in the case." *See* 28 U.S.C. § 636(c).

In 1982, Congress created the Court of Appeals for the Federal Circuit. The Federal Circuit hears appeals from three national courts: the Court of Federal Claims, the Court of Appeals for Veterans Claims, and the Court of International Trade. The Court of International Trade is an Article III court, but the other two are tribunals established under Article I of the Constitution; the judges do not have the protections of Article III. (For discussion of "Article I" courts, see Chapter 22.) In addition, some district court cases—notably those arising under the patent laws—are appealed to the Federal Circuit, not to the regional court of appeals.

What does the future hold for the structure of the federal courts? Over the last few decades, numerous proposals for structural change have been made by blue-ribbon commissions and committees, some of them created by Congress. There was a proposal for a "National Court of Appeals" to help the Supreme Court screen certiorari petitions. There was a proposal for an "Intercircuit Tribunal" to resolve conflicts between circuits on issues not worthy of the Supreme Court's attention. There was a proposal for "District Court Appellate Panels" to take some of the burden off the courts of appeals. None of these ambitious ideas ever attracted widespread support.

Only one proposal has ever made substantial headway in Congress. Repeatedly, legislation has been offered to divide the Ninth Circuit—by far the largest of the federal judicial circuits—and create a new Twelfth Circuit. Circuit-splitting bills were the subject of three hearings in the 108th Congress alone (2003–2004). However, since then, interest has waned. Although a new proposal was introduced in the 114th Congress (2015–2016), no hearings were held. Overall, the likelihood is that 50 years from now the structure of the federal judicial system will look very much the way it does today.

[4] Evolution of the Jurisdictional Arrangements

When we turn to the jurisdiction and powers of the federal courts, the history is more complicated. Two parallel lines of development can be identified. One involves the appellate jurisdiction of the Supreme Court over state courts; the other, the original and removal jurisdiction of the trial courts.

When we think about "federal jurisdiction," we tend to focus on the jurisdiction of the district courts, but historically the appellate jurisdiction over state courts has been at least as important. The key point is that from the Judiciary Act of 1789 to the present day, the Supreme Court has had authority, subject to some restrictions, to review state-court judgments that have rejected federal claims or defenses. After 1789, there are only two landmarks. In 1914, Congress passed legislation authorizing the Supreme Court to review state court judgments that have *accepted* a federal claim or defense. And in 1988 Congress gave the Court complete discretion to grant or deny review in state-court cases that fall within its jurisdiction.

As for the federal trial courts, the areas of original and removal jurisdiction were quite small initially. The major elements of federal court business during most of the nineteenth century were diversity cases and admiralty cases. Strange as it may seem to modern ears, there was no grant of jurisdiction over cases "arising under" federal law.

The scope of the trial courts' jurisdiction was expanded from time to time during the first several decades of the nineteenth century in response to particular felt needs. The watershed was the period immediately following the Civil War. Legislation of the Reconstruction Congresses made fundamental changes in the relation between state and national governments and in the role of the federal courts. Three enactments were particularly important:

- The Act of 1875 that gave federal trial courts original and removal jurisdiction of cases "arising under" federal law.

- The Act of Feb. 5, 1867 authorizing federal habeas corpus for state prisoners.

- The Civil Rights Acts and accompanying jurisdictional statutes, notably section 1 of the 1871 Act, now codified as 42 U.S.C. § 1983.

During the next hundred years, change came only intermittently. In 1948, the present arrangement of the Judicial Code was adopted. From time to time, Congress tinkered with the provisions for removal. On three occasions (1887, 1911, and 1958) it increased the minimum amount in controversy for diversity cases. On the other hand, in 1980, Congress eliminated the jurisdictional amount requirement for cases arising under federal law.

In the last years of the twentieth century, the pace of change accelerated. In 1988, the 100th Congress enacted the most significant package of reforms in federal jurisdiction in many years. The jurisdictional amount in diversity cases was increased from $10,000 to $50,000. Provisions for corporate venue were significantly modified, and new rules were adopted for ascertaining diversity in suits brought by representatives of estates or incompetents.

Additional changes came with the Judicial Improvements Act of 1990, a product of the final hours of the 101st Congress. The new law further altered the venue statutes and amended the statute governing removal. But the most important provision of the 1990 Act was the one that gave statutory recognition to the judicially created doctrines of pendent and ancillary jurisdiction, both now designated as "supplemental jurisdiction." Unfortunately, this legislation was enacted hastily, with virtually no opportunity for discussion by the bench and bar. One major problem of interpretation generated years of disagreement among the courts of appeals; the question was not resolved until 2005, when the Supreme Court decided the issue by a vote of 5 to 4. (See Chapter 11.)

Since 1990, Congress has continued to take an active interest in the operations of the federal courts. Numerous measures have been considered by the Judiciary Committees in the House and Senate, and some have been enacted into law. The jurisdictional amount in diversity cases was increased once again; it is now $75,000. And Congress passed a very limited form of "multiparty multiforum" jurisdiction designed primarily for litigation growing out of airline crashes. See Chapter 2.

Three major pieces of judiciary legislation became law during the last 20 years. The first two dealt with particular areas of federal jurisdiction—habeas corpus and class actions, respectively. Only the third affects the general run of civil litigation.

In 1996, President Clinton signed the Antiterrorism and Effective Death Penalty Act (AEDPA). The bill included provisions that significantly restrict the availability of federal habeas corpus as a vehicle for challenging state criminal convictions. Major elements of the legislation are discussed in Chapter 15.

In 2005, after many years of controversy, Congress passed and President Bush signed the Class Action Fairness Act. The legislation authorizes original and removal jurisdiction over interstate class actions based on minimal diversity. For a brief discussion, see Chapter 2.

In 2011, President Obama signed the Federal Courts Jurisdiction and Venue Clarification Act of 2011. This legislation, initially drafted by the Judicial Conference of the United States (the administrative policy-making body of the federal judiciary), embodied the most far-reaching package of revisions to the basic jurisdictional statutes since the Judicial Improvements Act of 1990. It made substantial changes to the procedures governing removal based on diversity, and it entirely rewrote the provisions of Chapter 87 dealing with venue. It also revised the provisions of Title 28 that deal with alienage jurisdiction and the removal of "separate and independent" claims. The amendments to Chapter 89 on removal jurisdiction and procedure are particularly important; they are treated in detail in Chapter 12.

B. Selection of Judges

As many of the cases in this book illustrate, lawyers often go to great lengths to get a case into federal court—or to keep a case out. A wide variety of factors will influence a lawyer's choice of forum, but one consideration may be the differences (or perceived differences) between federal and state judges.

As we have seen, the Constitution deals with the appointment of federal judges in a single sentence:

> The President . . . shall nominate, and by and with the Advice and Consent of the Senate, shall appoint . . . Judges of the supreme Court, and all other Officers of the United States, whose Appointments are not herein otherwise provided for, and which shall be established by Law . . . .

Not surprisingly, the process by which federal judges are nominated and appointed is considerably more complex than the constitutional language alone might suggest. Here we look at the process from the perspective of two prominent participants: an Assistant Attorney General in the George W. Bush administration and a representative of the American Bar Association.

A Practical Look at Federal Judicial Selection

Rachel Brand

53 THE ADVOCATE (Texas) 82 (2010)*

[*Editorial note.* Rachel Brand served as Associate Counsel to President George W. Bush at the White House and later as Assistant Attorney General for Legal Policy at the U.S. Department of Justice. She handled judicial selection and confirmation issues in both capacities.]

From a constitutional perspective, there are two indispensable participants in federal judicial selection: The President, who has the constitutional authority to nominate and appoint federal judges, and the Senate, whose advice and consent is required prior to appointment.

Practically speaking, the President relies on a team of aides to help him select judicial nominees. Which individual officials are responsible for judicial selection varies from Administration to Administration, but they usually work in the White House Counsel's Office and the Justice Department. . . . White House and Justice Department lawyers vet candidates for judicial appointments, but they do not write on a clean slate—rather, the Senate's views influence the judicial appointment process even before the President makes a nomination.

The Senate has two distinct ways of participating in judicial selection. It participates as a body by considering the President's judicial nominees after nomination. But individual Senators also play a role in determining whom the President nominates in the first place. This is because, by tradition, selection of federal judges is a very local exercise. Senate procedure gives the "home-state senators" for each judgeship (the Senators representing the state in which the judgeship is located) the power to block the confirmation of a nominee to whom they object, even if that nominee could be overwhelmingly confirmed if given a vote in the full Senate. This power is exercised through the "blue slip" process, by which a home-state Senator informs the Senate Judiciary Committee whether or not he will allow a nomination to a judgeship in his

LOL not anymore

---

* Originally published in THE ADVOCATE (Texas Bar Association, Litigation Section), vol. 53, 2010. Reprinted with permission.

state to move forward. At least in recent years, Senate Judiciary Committee Chairman have required both home-state Senators to return positive blue slips for a nominee before scheduling a confirmation hearing.

In light of the home-state Senators' power to block objectionable nominations, Presidents tend to consult extensively with them before making nominations. In fact, with respect to District Court nominations (and, in some cases, Court of Appeals nominations), Senators often expect the President to nominate the person the Senator has recommended, or at least to choose from a short list of options provided by the Senator.

Partisan politics plays a role in all of this. Where one home-state Senator is from the President's party and the other is not, the Senator from the President's party is generally understood to have the prerogative to provide candidates to the President. However, that Senator likely will consult with his colleague from the other party before submitting names, and whether or not he does so, the President will seek the views of the opposite-party Senator or risk a negative blue slip after nomination. When both of a state's Senators are from the opposite party, Presidents sometimes designate an official in that State from the President's party—such as a senior member of the state's U.S. House delegation—to provide recommendations. Nevertheless, the Senators' views cannot be ignored, as they—not the Congressman—will exercise the blue-slip power.

In most Administrations, the President gives less deference to the home-state Senators with respect to U.S. Court of Appeals appointments. . . .

In light of the Senators' influence over the President's nominations, the likeliest way to become a judicial nominee is to be recommended to the President by a Senator. Unfortunately, there is no formula for becoming a Senator's recommended candidate—every state, every Senator, and every case is different. Some Senators conduct their own exhaustive searches of the state bar for the most qualified candidates. Other Senators rely on ad-hoc commissions to vet candidates and provide a slate of recommendations to the Senators, who choose from that slate which names to suggest to the President. In other cases, an individual candidate might be recommended to the President because he is the state bar chairman, because of her political influence in the state, or even because he was the Senator's law-school roommate.

Eventually, the President will narrow the field to one prospective nominee. Even then, that person must clear several additional hurdles before the President will nominate her. Nominees are required to complete a stack of forms asking for extensive information about personal history, professional qualifications, and financial assets.

Perhaps the most time-consuming of these is the Senate Judiciary Committee Questionnaire, which asks detailed questions about employment history, requests lists of cases litigated (or of opinions decided in the event that a current judge is being elevated), and requires specifics of the nominee's financial holdings and liabilities, among other things. Although this form is written by the Senate, not the President, the White House normally requires prospective nominees to complete it before nomination. Most of the information provided on this form will be made public by the Judiciary Committee after nomination.

Other forms are required for the Federal Bureau of Investigation's thorough background check, which inquires into everything from criminal history to tax compliance to mental stability. Simultaneously, Justice Department lawyers will undertake a searching "vet" of the nominee's legal qualifications, legal employment history, written record, and reputation in the legal community. Both the FBI and the Justice Department vetters conduct interviews of the prospective nominee's colleagues and acquaintances and members of the local legal community, including sitting judges, to discuss the candidate's background and qualifications.

Because federal judicial appointments are so-called "lifetime appointments," prospective nominees are asked to provide the results of a comprehensive medical examination.

Finally, in the Obama Administration and in many past Administrations, the White House has asked the American Bar Association to review and rate the qualifications of each of the President's prospective nominees.

If all of these tests are passed, the President will formally nominate the individual. At that point, the Senate gains control of the process, though White House and Justice Department officials work closely with the Senate in an attempt to move confirmations forward as quickly and smoothly as possible.

The first stop for a judicial nomination is the Senate Judiciary Committee. As mentioned above, the Committee usually will not take action on a nomination until both home-state Senators have returned positive blue slips to the Committee. Once that has happened, it is up to the Committee Chairman to schedule a confirmation hearing. There is no requirement that the Chairman sequence confirmation hearings in the order the nominations were received, and some nominees never receive confirmation hearings because of Senate opposition to their nominations.

When they are scheduled, confirmation hearings often combine multiple judicial nominees; a common scenario would be a joint hearing for one Court of Appeals nominee and two or three District Court nominees. If the nominations at issue are contentious, all or most of the Committee's 19 members might attend the hearing, and the hearing might last more than a day. In the case of uncontroversial nominees, as few as one Senator might attend, and each nominee might be asked only one or two questions. Typically, one or both home-state Senators (or occasionally a home-state Congressman) will appear before the Committee to introduce the nominee, after which the nominees will be sworn in to answer Senators' questions. After the hearing, Senators may submit written "Questions for the Record" (QFRs) to the nominees. Uncontroversial nominees may receive no questions, while controversial nominees may receive pages of questions, all of which must be answered in writing, under penalty of perjury, within a week.

The next necessary step toward confirmation is a vote by the Judiciary Committee. The first potential opportunity for a vote is normally a week after the hearing takes place, but these votes are routinely delayed for weeks or months and could be delayed indefinitely for political reasons. When a vote is held, a majority "aye" vote results in the nomination being forwarded to the Senate "floor" for consideration by the full Senate. A majority "nay" vote usually means the nomination is dead, although on rare occasions, the Judiciary Committee has forwarded a nomination to the full Senate with a negative recommendation.

At this point, the fate of the nominee is in the hands of the Senate Majority Leader, who controls the full Senate's schedule. As in the Judiciary Committee, the power to schedule is significant—nominations can be defeated by allowing them to languish indefinitely. When a floor vote on a nomination is scheduled, the procedure may be as simple as seeking "unanimous consent" for confirmation of an uncontroversial nominee or as complicated as scheduling hours of floor debate on a high-profile nominee, and may even involve threats of filibuster for particularly contentious nominees. Regardless of which of these scenarios unfolds, the last necessary step to confirmation is an affirmative vote by a majority of the full Senate.

Confirmation, however, is not yet the end of the process. The final stage is appointment, which the President accomplishes by signing the judge's commission.

Statement of Thomas Z. Hayward, Jr., on Behalf of the American Bar Association

Hearing of the Senate Judiciary Committee, Feb. 25, 2004

[*Editorial note.* On Feb. 25, 2004, the Senate Judiciary Committee held a hearing on the nomination of Roger T. Benitez to the United States District Court for the Southern District of California. Thomas Z. Hayward, Jr., presented the views of the American Bar Association (ABA). Mr. Hayward was the Chair of the ABA's Standing Committee on Federal Judiciary. Before discussing the specific nomination, he outlined the process followed by the Committee in its investigation of nominees generally.]

The ABA Standing Committee investigates and considers only the professional qualifications of a nominee—his or her competence, integrity and judicial temperament. Ideology or political considerations are not taken into account. Our processes and procedures are carefully structured to produce a fair, thorough and objective peer evaluation of each nominee. A number of factors are investigated, including intellectual capacity, judgment, writing and analytical ability, industry, knowledge of the law, breadth of professional experience, character, integrity, compassion, courtesy, open-mindedness, patience, freedom from bias, commitment to equal justice under the law, and general reputation in the legal community.

The investigation is ordinarily assigned to the Committee member residing in the judicial circuit in which the vacancy exists, although it may be conducted by another member or former member. . . .

The investigator starts his investigation by reviewing the candidate's responses to the public portion of the Senate Judiciary Committee Questionnaire. These responses provide the opportunity for the nominee to set forth his or her qualifications, such as professional experience, significant cases handled and major writings. The circuit member makes extensive use of the questionnaire during the course of the investigation. In addition, the circuit member examines the legal writings of the nominee and personally conducts extensive confidential interviews with those likely to have information regarding the integrity, professional competence, and judicial temperament of the nominee, including, where pertinent, federal and state judges, practicing lawyers in both private and government service, legal services and public interest lawyers, representatives of professional legal organizations, and others who are in a position to evaluate the nominee's professional qualifications. This process provides a unique "peer review" aspect to our investigation.

Interviews are conducted under an assurance of confidentiality. If information adverse to the nominee is uncovered, the circuit member will advise the nominee of such information if he or she can do so without breaching the promise of confidentiality. During the personal interview with the nominee, the nominee is given a full opportunity to rebut the adverse information and provide any additional information bearing on it. If the nominee does not have the opportunity to rebut certain adverse information because it cannot be disclosed without breaching the confidentiality, the investigator will not use that information in writing the formal report and the committee, therefore, will not consider those facts in its evaluation.

Sometimes a clear pattern emerges during the interviews, and the investigation can be briskly concluded. In other cases, conflicting evaluations over some aspect of the nominee's professional qualifications may arise. In those instances, the circuit member takes whatever additional steps are necessary to reach a fair and accurate assessment of the nominee.

Upon completion of the investigation, the circuit member submits an informal report on the nominee to the Chair, who reviews it for thoroughness. Once the Chair determines that the investigation is thorough and complete, the circuit member then prepares the formal investigative report, containing a description of the candidate's background, summaries of all interviews conducted (including the interview with the nominee) and an evaluation of the candidate's professional qualifications. This formal report, together with the public portions of the nominee's completed Senate Judiciary Committee questionnaire and copies of any other relevant materials, is circulated to the entire 15-member committee. After carefully considering the formal report and its attachments, each member submits his or her vote to the Chair, rating the nominee "Well Qualified," "Qualified," or "Not Qualified."

I would like to emphasize that an important concern of the Committee in carrying out its function is confidentiality. The Committee seeks information on a confidential basis and assures its sources that their identities and the information they provide will not be revealed outside of the Committee, unless they consent to disclosure or the information is so well known in the community that it has been repeated to the Committee members by multiple sources. It is the Committee's experience that only by assuring and maintaining such confidentiality can sources be persuaded to provide full and candid information. However, we are also alert to the potential for abuse of confidentiality. The substance of adverse information is shared with the nominee, who is given full opportunity to explain the matter and to provide any additional information bearing on it. If the information cannot be shared with the nominee, the information is not included in the formal report and is not considered by the Committee in reaching its evaluation.

Note: The Appointment of Federal Judges

1. The process described by Assistant Attorney General Brand does not vary greatly from one administration to another. However, one major change occurred under President George W. Bush: the American Bar Association was not given the names of nominees until the nomination was announced publicly. President Barack Obama reverted to the practice of allowing the ABA to conduct investigations at an earlier stage.

2. As Ms. Brand notes, home-state Senators, particularly those of the President's party, play a major role in the selection of district court judges. In another article, Ms. Brand has reported that "a senator held a press conference to announce his selection for a judgeship before even providing the name to the White House, stating erroneously that he had 'nominated' that person to the bench." Rachel Brand, *Judicial Appointments: Checks and Balances in Practice*, 33 HARV. J.L. & PUB. POL'Y 47, 49 (2010). How would you expect the outsized role of home-state Senators to affect the kind of people who become federal judges?

3. Ms. Brand describes the activities of the FBI and Justice Department "vetters." In an interview conducted in 1998, Eleanor Dean Acheson, Assistant Attorney General in the administration of President William J. Clinton, elaborated on the search process within the Executive Branch:

> [After] the senator makes a recommendation, we have a fairly elaborate and, we hope, comprehensive and thorough internal—and when I mean internal, I mean internal to the Administration—evaluation of the candidate. We review forms, we essentially develop a pretty three-dimensional profile of somebody's professional life, whether it's in practice or whether it's on the bench or whether it's as a law professor or whether it's something else.
>
> We read all the cases. We read as much as we can about the cases that they've been involved with, the opinions that they've written and all that, and we call a cross section of practitioners, judges, and others in the professional community that the person works in. And then beyond the professional community, we try to reach out to pro bono organizations, civic organizations with which a candidate has been active, all in an effort to determine the individual's abilities, intellectual and professional, and the regard in which the person is held in the community, the individual's—to the extent that you can judge it in this way—integrity and reputation for reliability and integrity in . . . whatever it is that they've been doing professionally.

Interview with Eleanor Dean Acheson, Assistant Attorney General, 35 COURT REV. 6 (1998).*

4. The comments by Ms. Brand, Ms. Acheson, and Mr. Hayward give a good picture of the selection process for federal judges. Judicial selection in the states is quite different. In a majority of the states, some or all appellate and/or general-jurisdiction trial judges are selected by popular election. The opinions in *Minnesota Republican Party v. White* give a sense of what this means in practice.

Republican Party of Minnesota v. White

Supreme Court of the United States, 2002.

536 U.S. 765.

JUSTICE SCALIA delivered the opinion of the Court.

The question presented in this case is whether the First Amendment permits the Minnesota Supreme Court to prohibit candidates for judicial election in that State from announcing their views on disputed legal and political issues.

I

Since Minnesota's admission to the Union in 1858, the State's Constitution has provided for the selection of all state judges by popular election. Since 1912, those elections have been nonpartisan. Since 1974, they have been subject to a legal restriction which states that a "candidate for a judicial office, including an incumbent judge," shall not "announce his or her views on disputed legal or political issues." This prohibition, promulgated by the Minnesota Supreme Court and based on Canon 7(B) of the 1972 American Bar Association (ABA) Model Code of Judicial Conduct, is known as the "announce clause." . . .

[The Court held that the Announce Clause violates the First Amendment. The Court's analysis is omitted. Our interest is not in the constitutional issue but rather in what the Justices have to say about state systems of selecting judges by popular election. The opinion of the Court concluded:]

There is an obvious tension between the article of Minnesota's popularly approved Constitution which provides that judges shall be elected, and the Minnesota Supreme Court's announce clause which places most subjects of interest to the voters off limits. (The candidate-speech restrictions of all the other States that have them are also the product of judicial fiat.) The disparity is perhaps unsurprising, since the ABA, which originated the announce clause, has long been an opponent of judicial elections. That opposition may be well taken (it certainly had the support of the Founders of the Federal Government), but the First Amendment does not permit it to achieve its goal by leaving the principle of elections in place while preventing candidates from discussing what the elections are about. "The greater power to dispense with elections altogether does not include the lesser power to conduct elections under conditions of state-imposed voter ignorance. If the State chooses to tap the energy and the legitimizing

---

power of the democratic process, it must accord the participants in that process . . . the First Amendment rights that attach to their roles." *Renne v. Geary*, 501 U.S. 312 (1991) (Marshall, J., dissenting).

The Minnesota Supreme Court's canon of judicial conduct prohibiting candidates for judicial election from announcing their views on disputed legal and political issues violates the First Amendment. . . .

JUSTICE O'CONNOR, concurring.

I join the opinion of the Court but write separately to express my concerns about judicial elections generally. Respondents claim that "the Announce Clause is necessary . . . to protect the State's compelling governmental interest in an actual and perceived . . . impartial judiciary." I am concerned that, even aside from what judicial candidates may say while campaigning, the very practice of electing judges undermines this interest.

We of course want judges to be impartial, in the sense of being free from any personal stake in the outcome of the cases to which they are assigned. But if judges are subject to regular elections they are likely to feel that they have at least some personal stake in the outcome of every publicized case. Elected judges cannot help being aware that if the public is not satisfied with the outcome of a particular case, it could hurt their reelection prospects. [For example, former California Supreme Court Justice Otto Kaus has been quoted as saying] that ignoring the political consequences of visible decisions is "like ignoring a crocodile in your bathtub."[1] [Commentators have cited] statistics indicating that judges who face elections are far more likely to override jury sentences of life without parole and impose the death penalty than are judges who do not run for election.[2] Even if judges were able to suppress their awareness of the potential electoral consequences of their decisions and refrain from acting on it, the public's confidence in the judiciary could be undermined simply by the possibility that judges would be unable to do so.

Moreover, contested elections generally entail campaigning. And campaigning for a judicial post today can require substantial funds. [One scholar reports that] that in 2000, the 13 candidates in a partisan election for 5 seats on the Alabama Supreme Court spent an average of $1,092,076 on their campaigns.[3] [According to an ABA task force,] in 1995, one candidate for the Pennsylvania Supreme Court raised $1,848,142 in campaign funds, and in 1986, $2,700,000 was spent on the race for Chief Justice of the Ohio Supreme Court.[4] Unless the pool of judicial candidates is limited to those wealthy enough to independently fund their campaigns, a limitation unrelated to

---

1. *See* Eule, *Crocodiles in the Bathtub: State Courts, Voter Initiatives and the Threat of Electoral Reprisal*, 65 U. COLO. L. REV. 733, 739 (1994).

2. Bright & Keenan, *Judges and the Politics of Death: Deciding Between the Bill of Rights and the Next Election in Capital Cases*, 75 B.U.L. REV. 759, 793–94 (1995).

3. *See* Schotland, *Financing Judicial Elections, 2000: Change and Challenge*, 2001 L. REV. MICH. STATE U. DETROIT COLLEGE OF LAW 849, 866.

4. American Bar Association, Report and Recommendations of the Task Force on Lawyers' Political Contributions, pt. 2 (July 1998).

judicial skill, the cost of campaigning requires judicial candidates to engage in fundraising. Yet relying on campaign donations may leave judges feeling indebted to certain parties or interest groups. [A study by the public interest group Texans for Public Justice found] that 40 percent of the $9,200,000 in contributions of $100 or more raised by seven of Texas' nine Supreme Court justices for their 1994 and 1996 elections "came from parties and lawyers with cases before the court or contributors closely linked to these parties."[5]

Even if judges were able to refrain from favoring donors, the mere possibility that judges' decisions may be motivated by the desire to repay campaign contributors is likely to undermine the public's confidence in the judiciary. [A report published in 2001 describes] survey results indicating that 76 percent of registered voters believe that campaign contributions influence judicial decisions. The same report indicates that two-thirds of registered voters believe [that] individuals and groups who give money to judicial candidates often receive favorable treatment. [A recent commentator relates] anecdotes of lawyers who felt that their contributions to judicial campaigns affected their chance of success in court.[7]

Despite these significant problems, 39 States currently employ some form of judicial elections for their appellate courts, general jurisdiction trial courts, or both.[8] Judicial elections were not always so prevalent. The first 29 States of the Union adopted methods for selecting judges that did not involve popular elections.[9] [However,] beginning with Georgia in 1812, States began adopting systems for judicial elections. From the 1830's until the 1850's, as part of the Jacksonian movement toward greater popular control of public office, this trend accelerated, and by the Civil War, 22 of the 34 States elected their judges. By the beginning of the 20th century, however, elected judiciaries increasingly came to be viewed as incompetent and corrupt, and criticism of partisan judicial elections mounted. In 1906, Roscoe Pound gave a speech to the American Bar Association in which he claimed that "compelling judges to become politicians, in many jurisdictions has almost destroyed the traditional respect for the bench."[10]

In response to such concerns, some States adopted a modified system of judicial selection that became known as the Missouri Plan (because Missouri was the first State to adopt it for most of its judicial posts). Under the Missouri Plan, judges are appointed by a high elected official, generally from a list of nominees put together by a

---

5. *See* Thomas, National L.J., Mar. 16, 1998, at A8, col. 1.

7. Barnhizer, *"On the Make": Campaign Funding and the Corrupting of the American Judiciary*, 50 Cath. U. L. Rev. 361, 379 (2001).

8. American Judicature Society (AJS), Judicial Selection in the States: Appellate and General Jurisdiction Courts (Apr. 2002).

9. [Here and in the remainder of her opinion, Justice O'Connor relies on Croley, The Majoritarian Difficulty: Elective Judiciaries and the Rule of Law, 62 U. Chi. L. Rev. 689 (1995); Goldschmidt, Merit Selection: Current Status, Procedures, and Issues, 49 U. Miami L. Rev. 1 (1994); and the AJS report cited above.]

10. *The Causes of Popular Dissatisfaction with the Administration of Justice*, 8 Baylor L. Rev. 1, 23 (1956) (reprinting Pound's speech).

nonpartisan nominating commission, and then subsequently stand for unopposed retention elections in which voters are asked whether the judges should be recalled. If a judge is recalled, the vacancy is filled through a new nomination and appointment. This system obviously reduces threats to judicial impartiality, even if it does not eliminate all popular pressure on judges. [For example, former Judge Joseph Grodin has admitted] that he cannot be sure that his votes as a California Supreme Court Justice in "critical cases" during 1986 were not influenced subconsciously by his awareness that the outcomes could affect his chances in the retention elections being conducted that year.[11] The Missouri Plan is currently used to fill at least some judicial offices in 15 States.

Thirty-one States, however, still use popular elections to select some or all of their appellate and/or general jurisdiction trial court judges, who thereafter run for reelection periodically. Of these, slightly more than half use nonpartisan elections, and the rest use partisan elections. Most of the States that do not have any form of judicial elections choose judges through executive nomination and legislative confirmation.

Minnesota has chosen to select its judges through contested popular elections instead of through an appointment system or a combined appointment and retention election system along the lines of the Missouri Plan. In doing so the State has voluntarily taken on the risks to judicial bias described above. As a result, the State's claim that it needs to significantly restrict judges' speech in order to protect judicial impartiality is particularly troubling. If the State has a problem with judicial impartiality, it is largely one the State brought upon itself by continuing the practice of popularly electing judges.

JUSTICE KENNEDY, concurring. [Omitted.]

JUSTICE GINSBURG, with whom JUSTICE STEVENS, JUSTICE SOUTER, and JUSTICE BREYER join, dissenting.

... The ability of the judiciary to discharge its unique role rests to a large degree on the manner in which judges are selected. The Framers of the Federal Constitution sought to advance the judicial function through the structural protections of Article III, which provide for the selection of judges by the President on the advice and consent of the Senate, generally for lifetime terms. Through its own Constitution, Minnesota, in common with most other States, has decided to allow its citizens to choose judges directly in periodic elections. But Minnesota has not thereby opted to install a corps of political actors on the bench; rather, it has endeavored to preserve the integrity of its judiciary by other means. Recognizing that the influence of political parties is incompatible with the judge's role, for example, Minnesota has designated all judicial elections nonpartisan. And it has adopted a provision, here called the Announce Clause, designed to prevent candidates for judicial office from "publicly making known how they would decide issues likely to come before them as judges."

---

11. Grodin, *Developing a Consensus of Constraint: A Judge's Perspective on Judicial Retention Elections*, 61 S. CAL. L. REV. 1969, 1980 (1988).

... [The] rationale underlying unconstrained speech in elections for political office—that representative government depends on the public's ability to choose agents who will act at its behest—does not carry over to campaigns for the bench. As to persons aiming to occupy the seat of judgment, the Court's unrelenting reliance on decisions involving contests for legislative and executive posts is manifestly out of place. In view of the magisterial role judges must fill in a system of justice, a role that removes them from the partisan fray, States may limit judicial campaign speech by measures impermissible in elections for political office. . . .

The Court sees in this conclusion, and in the Announce Clause that embraces it, "an obvious tension." The Minnesota electorate is permitted to select its judges by popular vote, but is not provided information on "subjects of interest to the voters,"— in particular, the voters are not told how the candidate would decide controversial cases or issues if elected. This supposed tension, however, rests on the false premise that by departing from the federal model with respect to who chooses judges, Minnesota necessarily departed from the federal position on the criteria relevant to the exercise of that choice.[1]

The Minnesota Supreme Court thought otherwise:

> The methods by which the federal system and other states initially select and then elect or retain judges are varied, yet the explicit or implicit goal of the constitutional provisions and enabling legislation is the same: to create and maintain an independent judiciary as free from political, economic and social pressure as possible so judges can decide cases without those influences.

Nothing in the Court's opinion convincingly explains why Minnesota may not pursue that goal in the manner it did. . . .

This Court has recognized in the past, as Justice O'Connor does today, a "fundamental tension between the ideal character of the judicial office and the real world of electoral politics." We have no warrant to resolve that tension, however, by forcing States to choose one pole or the other. Judges are not politicians, and the First Amendment does not require that they be treated as politicians simply because they are chosen by popular vote. Nor does the First Amendment command States that wish to promote the integrity of their judges in fact and appearance to abandon systems of judicial selection that the people, in the exercise of their sovereign prerogatives, have devised.

For more than three-quarters of a century, States like Minnesota have endeavored, through experiment tested by experience, to balance the constitutional interests in judicial integrity and free expression within the unique setting of an elected judiciary.

---

1. In the context of the federal system, how a prospective nominee for the bench would resolve particular contentious issues would certainly be "of interest" to the President and the Senate in the exercise of their respective nomination and confirmation powers, just as information of that type would "interest" a Minnesota voter. But in accord with a longstanding norm, every Member of this Court declined to furnish such information to the Senate, and presumably to the President as well. Surely the Court perceives no tension here; the line each of us drew in response to preconfirmation questioning, the Court would no doubt agree, is crucial to the health of the Federal Judiciary. . . .

The Announce Clause, borne of this long effort, "comes to this Court bearing a weighty title of respect." I would uphold it as an essential component in Minnesota's accommodation of the complex and competing concerns in this sensitive area.

Note: Federal and State Judicial Selection

1. Justice O'Connor considers the consequences of an elective judiciary from what might be called a "good government" perspective. From the perspective of a lawyer choosing between federal and state court, how might the knowledge that the state judge will have to run for reelection influence your thinking? Are there particular kinds of cases where the prospect of litigating before an elected judge would seem particularly welcome — or unwelcome?

2. How would you expect the different selection processes in the federal and state systems to affect (a) the kind of people who become judges, and (b) the operation of the judicial systems?

3. The opinions in *Minnesota Republican Party v. White* focus primarily on the election of appellate judges. But in 26 states, popular election is also the method for selecting judges for the trial court of general jurisdiction. Are the "concerns about judicial elections" that Justice O'Connor expresses applicable in the same degree to elections at the trial court level?

C. The "Province and Duty of the Judicial Department"

Marbury v. Madison

Supreme Court of the United States, 1803.

1 Cranch (5 U.S.) 137.

[*Editorial note.* The presidential election of 1800 resulted in a tie vote in the Electoral College between Thomas Jefferson and the incumbent President, John Adams. At that time, a new President did not take office until March 4 of the year following the election. On February 17, 1801, the House of Representatives selected Jefferson. On March 2, two days before leaving office, President Adams nominated William Marbury as a Justice of the Peace for the District of Columbia. Marbury was one of several "midnight judges." His nomination was confirmed by the Senate on March 3, but when Adams left office, Marbury's commission had not been delivered. The new secretary of state, James Madison, refused to honor the appointment. Marbury then filed a motion in the Supreme Court "for a rule to [Madison] to shew cause why a mandamus should not issue commanding him to cause" the commission to be delivered.

[Marbury's suit was a small part of the political struggle between Jefferson's party, the Republicans, and the Federalists led by Adams. For a useful account, see William A. Van Alstyne, *A Critical Guide to* Marbury v. Madison, 1969 Duke L.J. 1 (1969).]

On the 24th of February [1803] the following opinion of the court was delivered by the chief justice [Marshall].

Opinion of the court.

At the last term on the affidavits then read and filed with the clerk, a rule was granted in this case, requiring the secretary of state to shew cause why a mandamus should not issue, directing him to deliver to William Marbury his commission as a justice of the peace for the county of Washington, in the district of Columbia.

No cause has been shewn, and the present motion is for a mandamus. The peculiar delicacy of this case, the novelty of some of its circumstances, and the real difficulty attending the points which occur in it, require a complete exposition of the principles, on which the opinion to be given by the court, is founded. . . .

In the order in which the court has viewed this subject, the following questions have been considered and decided.

1st. Has the applicant a right to the commission he demands?

2dly. If he has a right, and that right has been violated, do the laws of his country afford him a remedy?

3dly. If they do afford him a remedy, is it a *mandamus* issuing from this court?

The first object of inquiry is,

1st. Has the applicant a right to the commission he demands?

[After a lengthy analysis, the Chief Justice concluded:]

Mr. Marbury, then, since his commission was signed by the President, and sealed by the secretary of state, was appointed; and as the law creating the office, gave the officer a right to hold for five years, independent of the executive, the appointment was not revocable; but vested in the officer legal rights, which are protected by the laws of this country.

To withhold his commission, therefore, is an act deemed by the court not warranted by law, but violative of a vested legal right.

This brings us to the second inquiry; which is,

2dly. If he has a right, and that right has been violated, do the laws of this country afford him a remedy?

The very essence of civil liberty certainly consists in the right of every individual to claim the protection of the laws, whenever he receives an injury. One of the first duties of government is to afford that protection. In Great Britain the king himself is sued in the respectful form of a petition, and he never fails to comply with the judgment of his court. . . .

The government of the United States has been emphatically termed a government of laws, and not of men. It will certainly cease to deserve this high appellation, if the laws furnish no remedy for the violation of a vested legal right.

If this obloquy is to be cast on the jurisprudence of our country, it must arise from the peculiar character of the case.

It behoves us then to enquire whether there be in its composition any ingredient which shall exempt it from legal investigation, or exclude the injured party from legal redress. In pursuing this inquiry the first question which presents itself, is, whether this can be arranged with that class of cases which come under the description of *damnum absque injuria*—a loss without an injury.

This description of cases never has been considered, and it is believed never can be considered, as comprehending offices of trust, of honor or of profit. The office of justice of peace in the district of Columbia is such an office; it is therefore worthy of the attention and guardianship of the laws. . . . It is not then on account of the worthlessness of the thing pursued, that the injured party can be alleged to be without remedy.

Is it in the nature of the transaction? Is the act of delivering or withholding a commission to be considered as a mere political act, belonging to the executive department alone, for the performance of which, entire confidence is placed by our constitution in the supreme executive; and for any misconduct respecting which, the injured individual has no remedy.

That there may be such cases is not to be questioned; but that every act of duty, to be performed in any of the great departments of government, constitutes such a case, is not to be admitted. . . .

[The] question, whether the legality of an act of the head of a department be examinable in a court of justice or not, must always depend on the nature of that act. . . .

[Where] the heads of departments are the political or confidential agents of the executive, merely to execute the will of the President, or rather to act in cases in which the executive possesses a constitutional or legal discretion, nothing can be more perfectly clear than that their acts are only politically examinable. But where a specific duty is assigned by law, and individual rights depend upon the performance of that duty, it seems equally clear that the individual who considers himself injured, has a right to resort to the laws of his country for a remedy.

If this be the rule, let us enquire how it applies to the case under the consideration of the court. . . .

It is [the] opinion of the court,

1st. That by signing the commission of Mr. Marbury, the president of the United States appointed him a justice of peace, for the county of Washington in the district of Columbia; and that the seal of the United States, affixed thereto by the secretary of state, is conclusive testimony of the verity of the signature, and of the completion of the appointment; and that the appointment conferred on him a legal right to the office for the space of five years.

2dly. That, having this legal title to the office, he has a consequent right to the commission; a refusal to deliver which, is a plain violation of that right, for which the laws of his country afford him a remedy.

It remains to be inquired whether,

3dly. He is entitled to the remedy for which he applies. This depends on,

1st. The nature of the writ applied for, and,

2dly. The power of this court.

1st. The nature of the writ. . . .

[The writ of mandamus,] if awarded, would be directed to an officer of government, and its mandate to him would be, to use the words of Blackstone, "to do a particular thing therein specified, which appertains to his office and duty and which the court has previously determined, or at least supposes, to be consonant to right and justice." Or, in the words of Lord Mansfield, the applicant, in this case, has a right to execute an office of public concern, and is kept out of possession of that right.

These circumstances certainly concur in this case.

Still, to render the mandamus a proper remedy, the officer to whom it is to be directed, must be one to whom, on legal principles, such writ may be directed; and the person applying for it must be without any other specific and legal remedy.

1st. With respect to the officer to whom it would be directed. The intimate political relation, subsisting between the president of the United States and the heads of departments, necessarily renders any legal investigation of the acts of one of those high officers peculiarly irksome, as well as delicate; and excites some hesitation with respect to the propriety of entering into such investigation. Impressions are often received without much reflection or examination, and it is not wonderful that in such a case as this, the assertion, by an individual, of his legal claims in a court of justice; to which claims it is the duty of that court to attend; should at first view be considered by some, as an attempt to intrude into the cabinet, and to intermeddle with the prerogatives of the executive.

It is scarcely necessary for the court to disclaim all pretensions to such a jurisdiction. An extravagance, so absurd and excessive, could not have been entertained for a moment. The province of the court is, solely, to decide on the rights of individuals, not to enquire how the executive, or executive officers, perform duties in which they have a discretion. Questions, in their nature political, or which are, by the constitution and laws, submitted to the executive, can never be made in this court.

But, if this be not such a question; if so far from being an intrusion into the secrets of the cabinet, it respects a paper, which, according to law, is upon record, and to a copy of which the law gives a right, on the payment of ten cents; if it be no intermeddling with a subject, over which the executive can be considered as having exercised any control; what is there in the exalted station of the officer, which shall bar a citizen from asserting, in a court of justice, his legal rights, or shall forbid a court to listen to the claim; or to issue a mandamus, directing the performance of a duty, not depending on executive discretion, but on particular acts of congress and the general principles of law?

If one of the heads of departments commits any illegal act, under color of his office, by which an individual sustains an injury, it cannot be pretended that his office alone exempts him from being sued in the ordinary mode of proceeding, and being compelled to obey the judgment of the law. How then can his office exempt him from this particular mode of deciding on the legality of his conduct, if the case be such a case as would, were any other individual the party complained of, authorize the process?

It is not by the office of the person to whom the writ is directed, but the nature of the thing to be done that the propriety or impropriety of issuing a mandamus, is to be determined. Where the head of a department acts in a case, in which executive discretion is to be exercised; in which he is the mere organ of executive will; it is again repeated, that any application to a court to control, in any respect, his conduct, would be rejected without hesitation.

But where he is directed by law to do a certain act affecting the absolute rights of individuals, in the performance of which he is not placed under the particular direction of the President, and the performance of which, the President cannot lawfully forbid, and therefore is never presumed to have forbidden; as for example, to record a commission, or a patent for land, which has received all the legal solemnities; or to give a copy of such record; in such cases, it is not perceived on what ground the courts of the country are further excused from the duty of giving judgment, that right be done to an injured individual, than if the same services were to be performed by a person not the head of a department. . . .

This, then, is a plain case for a mandamus, either to deliver the commission, or a copy of it from the record; and it only remains to be inquired,

Whether it can issue from this court.

The act to establish the judicial courts of the United States authorizes the supreme court "to issue writs of mandamus, in cases warranted by the principles and usages of law, to any courts appointed, or persons holding office, under the authority of the United States." [The language quoted is from Section 13 of the Judiciary Act of 1789.]

The secretary of state, being a person holding an office under the authority of the United States, is precisely within the letter of the description; and if this court is not authorized to issue a writ of mandamus to such an officer, it must be because the law is unconstitutional, and therefore absolutely incapable of conferring the authority, and assigning the duties which its words purport to confer and assign.

The constitution vests the whole judicial power of the United States in one supreme court, and such inferior courts as congress shall, from time to time, ordain and establish. This power is expressly extended to all cases arising under the laws of the United States; and consequently, in some form, may be exercised over the present case; because the right claimed is given by a law of the United States.

In the distribution of this power it is declared that "the supreme court shall have original jurisdiction in all cases affecting ambassadors, other public ministers and consuls, and those in which a state shall be a party. In all other cases, the supreme court shall have appellate jurisdiction."

It has been insisted, at the bar, that as the original grant of jurisdiction, to the supreme and inferior courts, is general, and the clause, assigning original jurisdiction to the supreme court, contains no negative or restrictive words; the power remains to the legislature, to assign original jurisdiction to that court in other cases than those specified in the article which has been recited; provided those cases belong to the judicial power of the United States. . . .

When an instrument organizing fundamentally a judicial system, divides it into one supreme, and so many inferior courts as the legislature may ordain and establish; then enumerates its powers, and proceeds so far to distribute them, as to define the jurisdiction of the supreme court by declaring the cases in which it shall take original jurisdiction, and that in others it shall take appellate jurisdiction; the plain import of the words seems to be, that in one class of cases its jurisdiction is original, and not appellate; in the other it is appellate, and not original. . . .

To enable this court then to issue a mandamus, it must be shewn to be an exercise of appellate jurisdiction, or to be necessary to enable them to exercise appellate jurisdiction. . . .

It is the essential criterion of appellate jurisdiction, that it revises and corrects the proceedings in a cause already instituted, and does not create that cause. Although, therefore, a mandamus may be directed to courts, yet to issue such a writ to an officer for the delivery of a paper, is in effect the same as to sustain an original action for that paper, and therefore seems not to belong to appellate, but to original jurisdiction. Neither is it necessary in such a case as this, to enable the court to exercise its appellate jurisdiction.

The authority, therefore, given to the supreme court, by the act establishing the judicial courts of the United States, to issue writs of mandamus to public officers, appears not to be warranted by the constitution; and it becomes necessary to enquire whether a jurisdiction, so conferred, can be exercised.

The question, whether an act, repugnant to the constitution, can become the law of the land, is a question deeply interesting to the United States; but, happily, not of an intricacy proportioned to its interest. It seems only necessary to recognize certain principles, supposed to have been long and well established, to decide it.

That the people have an original right to establish, for their future government, such principles as, in their opinion, shall most conduce to their own happiness, is the basis, on which the whole American fabric has been erected. The exercise of this original right is a very great exertion; nor can it, nor ought it to be frequently repeated. The principles, therefore, so established, are deemed fundamental. And as the authority, from which they proceed, is supreme, and can seldom act, they are designed to be permanent.

This original and supreme will organizes the government, and assigns, to different departments, their respective powers. It may either stop here; or establish certain limits not to be transcended by those departments.

The government of the United States is of the latter description. The powers of the legislature are defined, and limited; and that those limits may not be mistaken, or forgotten, the constitution is written. To what purpose are powers limited, and to what purpose is that limitation committed to writing, if these limits may, at any time, be passed by those intended to be restrained? The distinction, between a government with limited and unlimited powers, is abolished, if those limits do not confine the persons on whom they are imposed, and if acts prohibited and acts allowed, are of equal obligation. It is a proposition too plain to be contested, that the constitution controls any legislative act repugnant to it; or, that the legislature may alter the constitution by an ordinary act.

Between these alternatives there is no middle ground. The constitution is either a superior, paramount law, unchangeable by ordinary means, or it is on a level with ordinary legislative acts, and like other acts, is alterable when the legislature shall please to alter it.

If the former part of the alternative be true, then a legislative act contrary to the constitution is not law: if the latter part be true, then written constitutions are absurd attempts, on the part of the people, to limit a power, in its own nature illimitable.

Certainly all those who have framed written constitutions contemplate them as forming the fundamental and paramount law of the nation, and consequently the theory of every such government must be, that an act of the legislature, repugnant to the constitution, is void.

This theory is essentially attached to a written constitution, and is consequently to be considered, by this court, as one of the fundamental principles of our society. It is not therefore to be lost sight of in the further consideration of this subject.

If an act of the legislature, repugnant to the constitution, is void, does it, notwithstanding its invalidity, bind the courts, and oblige them to give it effect? Or, in other words, though it be not law, does it constitute a rule as operative as if it was a law? This would be to overthrow in fact what was established in theory; and would seem, at first view, an absurdity too gross to be insisted on. It shall, however, receive a more attentive consideration.

It is emphatically the province and duty of the judicial department to say what the law is. Those who apply the rule to particular cases, must of necessity expound and interpret that rule. If two laws conflict with each other, the courts must decide on the operation of each.

So if a law be in opposition to the constitution; if both the law and the constitution apply to a particular case, so that the court must either decide that case conformably to the law, disregarding the constitution; or conformably to the constitution, disregarding the law; the court must determine which of these conflicting rules governs the case. This is of the very essence of judicial duty.

If then the courts are to regard the constitution; and the constitution is superior to any ordinary act of the legislature; the constitution, and not such ordinary act, must govern the case to which they both apply.

Those then who controvert the principle that the constitution is to be considered, in court, as a paramount law, are reduced to the necessity of maintaining that courts must close their eyes on the constitution, and see only the law.

This doctrine would subvert the very foundation of all written constitutions. It would declare that an act, which, according to the principles and theory of our government, is entirely void; is yet, in practice, completely obligatory. It would declare, that if the legislature shall do what is expressly forbidden, such act, notwithstanding the express prohibition, is in reality effectual. It would be giving to the legislature a practical and real omnipotence, with the same breath which professes to restrict their powers within narrow limits. It is prescribing limits, and declaring that those limits may be passed at pleasure.

That it thus reduces to nothing what we have deemed the greatest improvement on political institutions—a written constitution—would of itself be sufficient, in America, where written constitutions have been viewed with so much reverence, for rejecting the construction. But the peculiar expressions of the constitution of the United States furnish additional arguments in favour of its rejection.

The judicial power of the United States is extended to all cases arising under the constitution.

Could it be the intention of those who gave this power, to say that, in using it, the constitution should not be looked into? That a case arising under the constitution should be decided without examining the instrument under which it arises?

This is too extravagant to be maintained.

In some cases then, the constitution must be looked into by the judges. And if they can open it at all, what part of it are they forbidden to read, or to obey?

There are many other parts of the constitution which serve to illustrate this subject.

It is declared that "no tax or duty shall be laid on articles exported from any state." Suppose a duty on the export of cotton, of tobacco, or of flour; and a suit instituted to recover it. Ought judgment to be rendered in such a case? ought the judges to close their eyes on the constitution, and only see the law.

The constitution declares that "no bill of attainder or *ex post facto* law shall be passed."

If, however, such a bill should be passed and a person should be prosecuted under it; must the court condemn to death those victims whom the constitution endeavors to preserve?

"No person," says the constitution, "shall be convicted of treason unless on the testimony of two witnesses to the same overt act, or on confession in open court."

Here the language of the constitution is addressed especially to the courts. It prescribes, directly for them, a rule of evidence not to be departed from. If the legislature should change that rule, and declare *one* witness, or a confession *out of* court, sufficient for conviction, must the constitutional principle yield to the legislative act?

From these, and many other selections which might be made, it is apparent, that the framers of the constitution contemplated that instrument, as a rule for the government of *courts*, as well as of the legislature.

Why otherwise does it direct the judges to take an oath to support it? This oath certainly applies, in an especial manner, to their conduct in their official character. How immoral to impose it on them, if they were to be used as the instruments, and the knowing instruments, for violating what they swear to support?

The oath of office, too, imposed by the legislature, is completely demonstrative of the legislative opinion on this subject. It is in these words, "I do solemnly swear that I will administer justice without respect to persons, and do equal right to the poor and to the rich; and that I will faithfully and impartially discharge all the duties incumbent on me as according to the best of my abilities and understanding, agreeably to *the constitution*, and laws of the United States."

Why does a judge swear to discharge his duties agreeably to the constitution of the United States, if that constitution forms no rule for his government? if it is closed upon him, and cannot be inspected by him?

If such be the real state of things, this is worse than solemn mockery. To prescribe, or to take this oath, becomes equally a crime.

It is also not entirely unworthy of observation, that in declaring what shall be the *supreme* law of the land, the *constitution* itself is first mentioned; and not the laws of the United States generally, but those only which shall be made in *pursuance* of the constitution, have that rank.

Thus, the particular phraseology of the constitution of the United States confirms and strengthens the principle, supposed to be essential to all written constitutions, that a law repugnant to the constitution is void; and that *courts*, as well as other departments, are bound by that instrument.

The rule must be discharged.

Note: Marbury *and the Federal Courts*

Marbury v. Madison is of course the cornerstone of American constitutional law. But the decision may also be relevant to a variety of issues concerning the jurisdiction and powers of the federal courts. For example, consider the possible implications of the *Marbury* opinion for these questions:

1. Are there some issues of constitutional law that are not within the province of the judiciary—issues that only the political branches have the authority to resolve? (Chapter 3.)

2. In deciding whether to grant habeas corpus relief to a state criminal defendant who raises a federal constitutional challenge to his conviction, may the federal court defer to the state court's interpretation of federal law? (Chapter 15.)

3. If Congress imposes a duty on a class of private actors, but provides no statutory remedy for persons injured by a breach of that duty, may the courts create a remedy if they believe that doing so will effectuate the Congressional purpose? (Chapter 8.)

4. If Congress disagrees with a line of Supreme Court decisions interpreting the Constitution, may Congress eliminate the Court's jurisdiction to hear cases involving that particular question? (Chapter 20.)

5. May Congress instruct the Supreme Court to consider — or not consider — particular sources in interpreting the Constitution? (Chapter 21.)

Chapter 2

The Judicial Power Under Article III

Article III, section 2, of the Constitution defines the scope of the federal judicial power by reference to nine categories of "Cases" and "Controversies":

> The judicial Power shall extend to all Cases, in Law and Equity, arising under this Constitution, the Laws of the United States, and Treaties made, or which shall be made, under their Authority;—to all Cases affecting Ambassadors, other public Ministers and Consuls;—to all Cases of admiralty and maritime Jurisdiction;—to Controversies to which the United States shall be a Party;—to Controversies between two or more States;—between a State and Citizens of another State;—between Citizens of different States;—between Citizens of the same State claiming Lands under Grants of different States, and between a State, or the Citizens thereof, and foreign States, Citizens or Subjects.

In *Cohens v. Virginia*, 6 Wheat. (19 U.S.) 264 (1821) [*infra* section B], Chief Justice Marshall divided these nine categories into two "classes":

> Jurisdiction is given to the Courts of the Union in two classes of cases. In the first, their jurisdiction depends on the character of the cause, whoever may be the parties. This class comprehends "all cases in law and equity arising under this constitution, the laws of the United States, and treaties made, or which shall be made, under their authority." This clause extends the jurisdiction of the Court to all the cases described, without making in its terms any exception whatever, and without any regard to the condition of the party. . . .

> In the second class, the jurisdiction depends entirely on the character of the parties. In this are comprehended "controversies between two or more States, between a State and citizens of another State," and "between a State and foreign States, citizens or subjects." If these be the parties, it is entirely unimportant what may be the subject of controversy.

In this chapter, we consider the scope of the judicial power authorized by Article III. We will use Marshall's taxonomy, starting with the heads of jurisdiction defined by "the character of the parties."

A. Party-Based Heads of Jurisdiction

Questions as to the constitutional scope of the "party-based" heads of jurisdiction have not arisen very often. However, two decisions by the Supreme Court in the mid-twentieth century warrant attention because of their practical importance. Although the decisions deal with entirely different issues, they have one feature in common: both have their roots in opinions by Chief Justice Marshall.

Note: The "Tidewater *Problem*"

Article III extends the federal judicial power to suits "between Citizens of different States." In the Judiciary Act of 1789, Congress created a system of federal trial courts and gave them jurisdiction over suits "between a citizen of the State where the suit is brought, and a citizen of another State." The question soon arose whether citizens of the District of Columbia were citizens of a "State" within the meaning of this provision. In *Hepburn & Dundas v. Ellzey*, 2 Cranch (6 U.S.) 445 (1805), the Court held that they were not. Chief Justice Marshall wrote the Court's brief opinion.

In 1940, Congress amended the Judicial Code to authorize federal district courts to hear suits "between . . . citizens of the District of Columbia, the Territory of Hawaii, or Alaska, and any State or Territory." The constitutionality of extending diversity jurisdiction to suits involving citizens of the District of Columbia came before the Supreme Court in *National Mutual Insurance Co. v. Tidewater Co.*, 337 U.S. 582 (1949), generally known as the *Tidewater* case.

Two distinct arguments were put forth in support of the constitutionality of Congress's action. First, it was argued that, under Article III, "a citizen of the District of Columbia has the standing of a citizen of one of the states of the Union." Seven Justices rejected that argument. Justice Jackson, speaking for a three-Justice plurality, wrote:

> We [decline] to overrule the opinion of Chief Justice Marshall, and we hold that the District of Columbia is not a state within Article III of the Constitution. In other words, cases between citizens of the District and those of the states were not included in the catalogue of controversies over which the Congress could give jurisdiction to the federal courts by virtue of Art. III.

> The second argument was that Congress could enact the legislation under its Article I power to legislate for the District of Columbia and the territories. A majority of the Court — six Justices — rejected that argument as well.

You might think that the statute was therefore held unconstitutional. But it was not. Although different majorities rejected each of the arguments in support of the law, two Justices voted to overrule *Hepburn*, and three others (including Justice Jackson) accepted the Article I theory. Justice Frankfurter, in dissent, aptly described the outcome:

> A substantial majority of the Court agrees that each of the two grounds urged in support of the attempt by Congress to extend diversity jurisdiction to cases involving citizens of the District of Columbia must be rejected — but not the same majority. And so, conflicting minorities in combination bring to pass a result — paradoxical as it may appear — which differing majorities of the Court find insupportable.

Paradoxical the result is—but the statute remains on the books, codified as section 1332(e) of Title 28.

Note: "Minimal" Diversity

You are probably familiar with the "complete diversity" rule that governs the scope of diversity jurisdiction under 28 U.S.C. § 1332. That rule derives from Chief Justice Marshall's opinion in *Strawbridge v. Curtiss*, 3 Cranch (7 U.S.) 267 (1806). However, as the Supreme Court noted in *State Farm Fire & Casualty Co. v. Tashire*, 386 U.S. 523 (1967), the *Strawbridge* decision construed only the language of the jurisdictional statute, "not the Constitution itself." The Court confirmed in *Tashire* what several decisions had assumed: "Article III poses no obstacle to the legislative extension of federal jurisdiction, founded on diversity, so long as *any two* adverse parties are not co-citizens." (Emphasis added.)

Tashire itself involved the federal interpleader statute, 28 U.S.C. § 1335. The general diversity statute, 28 U.S.C. § 1332, continues to be governed by the complete diversity rule. That rule is a substantial impediment to the availability of the federal courts for large cases involving numerous litigants from different states; it also furnishes a tool that enables plaintiffs to frustrate defendants' desires to remove diversity suits to federal court. (See Chapter 12.) Over the last decade and a half, Congress has acted to take advantage of the constitutional holding in *Tashire* to provide for federal jurisdiction in other situations in which the need for a federal forum is thought to be particularly great.

A. Multiparty, Multiforum Jurisdiction

In late 2002, Congress created a new head of district court jurisdiction under the name "multiparty, multiforum jurisdiction." The new provision, codified as section 1369 of the Judicial Code, is set forth below. Note the definition of "minimal diversity" in subsection (c)(1).

Sec. 1369. Multiparty, multiforum jurisdiction

(a) IN GENERAL—The district courts shall have original jurisdiction of any civil action involving minimal diversity between adverse parties that arises from a single accident, where at least 75 natural persons have died in the accident at a discrete location, if—

(1) a defendant resides in a State and a substantial part of the accident took place in another State or other location, regardless of whether that defendant is also a resident of the State where a substantial part of the accident took place;

(2) any two defendants reside in different States, regardless of whether such defendants are also residents of the same State or States; or

(3) substantial parts of the accident took place in different States.

(b) LIMITATION OF JURISDICTION OF DISTRICT COURTS—The district court shall abstain from hearing any civil action described in subsection (a) in which—

(1) the substantial majority of all plaintiffs are citizens of a single State of which the primary defendants are also citizens; and

(2) the claims asserted will be governed primarily by the laws of that State.

(c) SPECIAL RULES AND DEFINITIONS—For purposes of this section—

(1) minimal diversity exists between adverse parties if any party is a citizen of a State and any adverse party is a citizen of another State, a citizen or subject of a foreign state, or a foreign state as defined in section 1603(a) of this title;

(2) a corporation is deemed to be a citizen of any State, and a citizen or subject of any foreign state, in which it is incorporated or has its principal place of business, and is deemed to be a resident of any State in which it is incorporated or licensed to do business or is doing business;

(3) the term "injury" means—

(A) physical harm to a natural person; and

(B) physical damage to or destruction of tangible property, but only if physical harm described in subparagraph (A) exists;

(4) the term "accident" means a sudden accident, or a natural event culminating in an accident, that results in death incurred at a discrete location by at least 75 natural persons; and

(5) the term "State" includes the District of Columbia, the Commonwealth of Puerto Rico, and any territory or possession of the United States.

(d) INTERVENING PARTIES—In any action in a district court which is or could have been brought, in whole or in part, under this section, any person with a claim arising from the accident described in subsection (a) shall be permitted to intervene as a party plaintiff in the action, even if that person could not have brought an action in a district court as an original matter.

(e) NOTIFICATION OF JUDICIAL PANEL ON MULTIDISTRICT LITIGATION— A district court in which an action under this section is pending shall promptly notify the judicial panel on multidistrict litigation of the pendency of the action.

B. The Class Action Fairness Act

1. For many years, Congress considered legislation that would use "minimal diversity" to greatly expand the jurisdiction of the federal courts over class actions not involving federal questions. Finally, in early 2005, the "Class Action Fairness Act of 2005" passed both Houses and was signed into law as P.L. 109-2.

The Act establishes a new head of original jurisdiction and also a new basis for removal. The grant of original jurisdiction is codified in new subsection 1332(d). That subsection provides in part:

> The district courts shall have original jurisdiction of any civil action in which the matter in controversy exceeds the sum or value of $5,000,000, exclusive of interest and costs, and is a class action in which—
>
> (A) any member of a class of plaintiffs is a citizen of a State different from any defendant;
>
> (B) any member of a class of plaintiffs is a foreign state or a citizen or subject of a foreign state and any defendant is a citizen of a State; or
>
> (C) any member of a class of plaintiffs is a citizen of a State and any defendant is a foreign state or a citizen or subject of a foreign state.

The new removal provision (codified as 28 U.S.C. § 1453) explicitly rejects three important limitations on the removal of ordinary diversity cases. The "rule of unanimity" does not apply; the one-year limitation of 28 U.S.C. § 1446(b) does not apply; and the "forum defendant" rule of 28 U.S.C. § 1441(b) does not apply. (For discussion of these rules, see Chapter 12.)

Other provisions of the new law require or permit district courts to decline to exercise jurisdiction over class actions in which interstate elements do not predominate.

2. The Supreme Court's discussion of the constitutionality of "minimal diversity" consisted of the single sentence quoted in the first paragraph of this Note, supported by footnote citation to lower court decisions and commentaries. *Tashire* was an interpleader case. Should the decision be read as settling the constitutionality of the Class Action Fairness Act?

C. A Law to Combat "Libel Tourism"

In 2010, Congress added a new chapter (Chapter 181) to Title 28 aimed at the problem of "libel tourism." The sponsors of the legislation explained the problem as follows:

> Libel tourism is the name given to the practice of end running the first amendment by suing American authors and publishers for defamation in the courts of certain foreign countries. These countries have laws that often disfavor speech critical of public figures. [Often they are countries with] little or no connection to the allegedly defamatory statements that gave rise to the suits. (Rep. Steve Cohen)
>
> A typical scenario involves an author who writes a critical news story about a social or legal problem.... [The plaintiff sues in a forum known for its weak free speech laws, but he or she] is not really interested in obtaining a judgment to collect damages. Instead, the plaintiff's main goal is

to dissuade anyone from researching and publishing other negative accounts about his or her activities. (Rep. Trent Franks)

Chapter 181 addresses the problem by limiting enforcement of foreign defamation judgments by American courts. The centerpiece of the law is §4102, entitled "Recognition of foreign defamation judgments." Section 4102 provides that no federal or state court shall "recognize or enforce a foreign judgment for defamation" unless that judgment would satisfy the First Amendment and also the constitution and law of the state in which enforcement is sought. "Defamation" is defined in §4101 as "any action or other proceeding for defamation, libel, slander, or similar claim alleging that forms of speech are false, have caused damage to reputation or emotional distress, have presented any person in a false light, or have resulted in criticism, dishonor, or condemnation of any person."

The law also creates a new basis for removal. Section 4103 provides:

> In addition to removal allowed under section 1441, any action brought in a [State] court to enforce a foreign judgment for defamation in which—
>
> (1) any plaintiff is a citizen of a State different from any defendant;
>
> (2) any plaintiff is a foreign state or a citizen or subject of a foreign state and any defendant is a citizen of a State; or
>
> (3) any plaintiff is a citizen of a State and any defendant is a foreign state or citizen or subject of a foreign state,
>
> may be removed by any defendant to the district court of the United States for the district and division embracing the place where such action is pending without regard to the amount in controversy between the parties.

Note that the new removal provision invokes the party-based heads of jurisdiction in Article III. Is there any issue as to the constitutionality of the provision? Could the provision have been grounded in the "arising under" jurisdiction of Article III? How might such a provision have been drafted? Why might Congress have preferred to rely on party-based jurisdiction?

B. Federal Question Jurisdiction: Foundation Cases

Article III extends the judicial power to "all Cases, in Law and Equity, arising under this Constitution, the Laws of the United States, and Treaties made, or which shall be made, under their Authority." This is generally referred to as the "federal question" jurisdiction, and although that is something of a misnomer, it is a convenient label.

When does a case "aris[e] under" federal law within the meaning of Article III? To answer that question, we turn first to two landmark decisions by Chief Justice Marshall, *Cohens v. Virginia* and *Osborn v. Bank of the United States.* Although *Osborn* is cited far more often, *Cohens* is the earlier of the two cases, and it sets the stage for the issue that divided the Court in *Osborn*.

Cohens v. Virginia

Supreme Court of the United States, 1821.

6 Wheat. (19 U.S.) 264.

This was a writ of error to the Quarterly Session Court for the borough of Norfolk, in the State of Virginia, under the 25th section of the judiciary act of 1789, it being the highest Court of law or equity of that State having jurisdiction of the case.

[Section 25 of the Judiciary Act of 1789 authorized the Supreme Court to review final judgments of state courts in three categories of cases. These included cases in which the state court rejected a claim under the federal constitution or laws.]

Mr. Chief Justice Marshall delivered the opinion of the Court.

This is a writ of error to a judgment rendered in the Court of Hustings for the borough of Norfolk, on an information for selling lottery tickets, contrary to an act of the Legislature of Virginia. In the State Court, the defendant claimed the protection of an act of Congress. A case was agreed between the parties, which states the act of Assembly on which the prosecution was founded, and the act of Congress on which the defendant relied, and concludes in these words: "If upon this case the Court shall be of opinion that the acts of Congress before mentioned were valid, and, on the true construction of those acts, the lottery tickets sold by the defendants as aforesaid, might lawfully be sold within the State of Virginia, notwithstanding the act or statute of the general assembly of Virginia prohibiting such sale, then judgment to be entered for the defendants; And if the Court should be of opinion that the statute or act of the General Assembly of the State of Virginia, prohibiting such sale, is valid, notwithstanding the said acts of Congress, then judgment to be entered that the defendants are guilty, and that the Commonwealth recover against them one hundred dollars and costs."

Judgment was rendered against the defendants; and the Court in which it was rendered being the highest Court of the State in which the cause was cognizable, the record has been brought into this Court by writ of error. . . .

The defendant in error moves to dismiss this writ, for want of jurisdiction.

In support of this motion, three points have been made, and argued with the ability which the importance of the question merits. These points are—

1st. That a State is a defendant.

2d. That no writ of error lies from this Court to a State Court.

3d. The third point has been presented in different forms by the gentlemen who have argued it. The counsel who opened the cause said, that the want of jurisdiction was shown by the subject matter of the case. The counsel who followed him said, that jurisdiction was not given by the judiciary act. The Court has bestowed all its attention on the arguments of both gentlemen, and supposes that their tendency is to show that this Court has no jurisdiction of the case, or, in other words, has no right to review the judgment of the State Court, because neither the constitution nor any law of the United States has been violated by that judgment.

The questions presented to the Court by the two first points made at the bar are of great magnitude, and may be truly said vitally to affect the Union. They exclude the inquiry whether the constitution and laws of the United States have been violated by the judgment which the plaintiffs in error seek to review; and maintain that, admitting such violation, it is not in the power of the government to apply a corrective. They maintain that the nation does not possess a department capable of restraining peaceably, and by authority of law, any attempts which may be made, by a part, against the legitimate powers of the whole; and that the government is reduced to the alternative of submitting to such attempts, or of resisting them by force. They maintain that the constitution of the United States has provided no tribunal for the final construction of itself, or of the laws or treaties of the nation; but that this power may be exercised in the last resort by the Courts of every State in the Union. That the constitution, laws, and treaties, may receive as many constructions as there are States; and that this is not a mischief, or, if a mischief, is irremediable. These abstract propositions are to be determined; for he who demands decision without permitting inquiry, affirms that the decision he asks does not depend on inquiry.

If such be the constitution, it is the duty of the Court to bow with respectful submission to its provisions. If such be not the constitution, it is equally the duty of this Court to say so; and to perform that task which the American people have assigned to the judicial department.

1st. The first question to be considered is, whether the jurisdiction of this Court is excluded by the character of the parties, one of them being a State, and the other a citizen of that State?

The second section of the third article of the constitution defines the extent of the judicial power of the United States. Jurisdiction is given to the Courts of the Union in two classes of cases. In the first, their jurisdiction depends on the character of the cause, whoever may be the parties. This class comprehends "all cases in law and equity arising under this constitution, the laws of the United States, and treaties made, or which shall be made, under their authority." This clause extends the jurisdiction of the Court to all the cases described, without making in its terms any exception whatever, and without any regard to the condition of the party. If there be any exception, it is to be implied against the express words of the article.

In the second class, the jurisdiction depends entirely on the character of the parties. In this are comprehended "controversies between two or more States, between a State and citizens of another State," and "between a State and foreign States, citizens or subjects." If these be the parties, it is entirely unimportant what may be the subject of controversy. Be it what it may, these parties have a constitutional right to come into the Courts of the Union.

The counsel for the defendant in error have stated that the cases which arise under the constitution must grow out of those provisions which are capable of self-execution; examples of which are to be found in the 2d section of the 4th article, and in the 10th section of the 1st article.

A case which arises under a law of the United States must, we are likewise told, be a right given by some act which becomes necessary to execute the powers given in the constitution, of which the law of naturalization is mentioned as an example.

The use intended to be made of this exposition of the first part of the section, defining the extent of the judicial power, is not clearly understood. If the intention be merely to distinguish cases arising under the constitution, from those arising under a law, for the sake of precision in the application of this argument, these propositions will not be controverted. If it be to maintain that a case arising under the constitution, or a law, must be one in which a party comes into Court to demand something conferred on him by the constitution or a law, we think the construction too narrow. A case in law or equity consists of the right of the one party, as well as of the other, and may truly be said to arise under the constitution or a law of the United States, whenever its correct decision depends on the construction of either. Congress seems to have intended to give its own construction of this part of the constitution in the 25th section of the judiciary act; and we perceive no reason to depart from that construction.

The jurisdiction of the Court, then, being extended by the letter of the constitution to all cases arising under it, or under the laws of the United States, it follows that those who would withdraw any case of this description from that jurisdiction, must sustain the exemption they claim on the spirit and true meaning of the constitution, which spirit and true meaning must be so apparent as to overrule the words which its framers have employed.

[The Court then rejected the argument that the jurisdiction was excluded because one of the parties was a state. This aspect of the case is discussed in Chapter 13.]

Note: Cohens *and Federal Question Jurisdiction*

1. On the basis of the language alone, is Marshall's interpretation of the words "arising under" a persuasive one? Is the language of Article III the clearest or most obvious that the Framers might have chosen to achieve the results Marshall envisions? Consider the following possibilities, drawn from the records of the Constitutional Convention:

> "[T]he jurisdiction of the national judiciary shall extend to all cases of national revenue, impeachment of national officers, and questions which involve the national peace or harmony." [Resolution adopted by the Committee of the Whole, June 13, 1787.]

> "[T]he jurisdiction shall extend to all cases arising under the Natl. laws: And to such other questions as may involve the Natl. peace & harmony." [Resolution adopted by the Convention, July 18, 1787.]

But there is no indication in the records of the Convention that the Framers viewed the final language as diverging from the general principle agreed to on July 18.

2. After setting forth his interpretation of the language of Article III, Marshall refers to the construction that "Congress seems to have intended" by enacting section 25 of the Judiciary Act of 1789. In essence, section 25 authorized appellate review by the Supreme Court when a state court handed down a decision rejecting a claim under federal law. Section 25 did not use the phrase "arising under," and no provision of the 1789 Act conferred jurisdiction on federal trial courts to adjudicate cases based on the presence of a federal question.

What implications, if any, can be drawn from the jurisdictional arrangements established by the Act of 1789? Marshall apparently viewed section 25 as delineating a minimum scope for the federal question jurisdiction. Should section 25 also be read as defining the maximum? That question was debated by the Justices in *Osborn v. Bank of the United States.*

Osborn v. Bank of the United States

Supreme Court of the United States, 1824.

9 Wheat. (22 U.S.) 738.

[The second Bank of the United States was created by an Act of Congress in 1816. In February 1819, the Ohio legislature enacted a law imposing a tax on any bank doing business in Ohio "without being allowed to do so by the laws thereof." The Bank of the United States was identified by name in the Ohio statute as one such bank. In September 1819, the Bank filed a bill in equity in federal court in Ohio seeking an injunction to restrain Ralph Osborn, Auditor of the State of Ohio, from proceeding against the Bank under the February 1819 law.

[The federal court issued the injunction, but J.L. Harper, an agent of Osborn's, "proceeded by violence to the office of the Bank at Chilicothe" and took from it $100,000 of the bank's money. Harper delivered the money to the state treasurer. Ultimately the federal court issued a decree directing Harper and Osborn to restore the money to the Bank. Osborn appealed to the Supreme Court. He argued that the decree was improper on several grounds, one of which was the federal court erroneously held that the Ohio tax was unconstitutional.]

Mr. Chief Justice Marshall delivered the opinion of the Court . . .

At the close of the argument, a point was suggested, of such vital importance, as to induce the Court to request that it might be particularly spoken to. That point is, the right of the Bank to sue in the Courts of the United States. It has been argued, and ought to be disposed of, before we proceed to the actual exercise of jurisdiction, by deciding on the rights of the parties.

The appellants contest the jurisdiction of the Court on two grounds:

1st. That the act of Congress has not given it.

2d. That, under the constitution, Congress cannot give it.

1. The first part of the objection depends entirely on the language of the act. The words are, that the Bank shall be "made able and capable in law," "to sue and be sued, plead and be impleaded, answer and be answered, defend and be defended, in all State Courts having competent jurisdiction, and in any Circuit Court of the United States."

These words seem to the Court to admit of but one interpretation. They cannot be made plainer by explanation. They give, expressly, the right "to sue and be sued," "in every Circuit Court of the United States," and it would be difficult to substitute other terms which would be more direct and appropriate for the purpose. . . . The act of incorporation, then, confers jurisdiction on the Circuit Courts of the United States, if Congress can confer it.

2. We will now consider the constitutionality of the clause in the act of incorporation, which authorizes the Bank to sue in the federal Courts.

In support of this clause, it is said, that the legislative, executive, and judicial powers, of every well constructed government, are co-extensive with each other; that is, they are potentially co-extensive. The executive department may constitutionally execute every law which the Legislature may constitutionally make, and the judicial department may receive from the Legislature the power of construing every such law. All governments which are not extremely defective in their organization, must possess, within themselves, the means of expounding, as well as enforcing, their own laws. If we examine the constitution of the United States, we find that its framers kept this great political principle in view. The 2d article vests the whole executive power in the President; and the 3d article declares, "that the judicial power shall extend to all cases in law and equity arising under this constitution, the laws of the United States, and treaties made, or which shall be made, under their authority."

This clause enables the judicial department to receive jurisdiction to the full extent of the constitution, laws, and treaties of the United States, when any question respecting them shall assume such a form that the judicial power is capable of acting on it. That power is capable of acting only when the subject is submitted to it by a party who asserts his rights in the form prescribed by law. It then becomes a case, and the constitution declares, that the judicial power shall extend to all cases arising under the constitution, laws, and treaties of the United States.

The suit of *The Bank of the United States v. Osborn and others*, is a case, and the question is, whether it arises under a law of the United States?

The appellants contend, that it does not, because several questions may arise in it, which depend on the general principles of the law, not on any act of Congress.

If this were sufficient to withdraw a case from the jurisdiction of the federal Courts, almost every case, although involving the construction of a law, would be withdrawn; and a clause in the constitution, relating to a subject of vital importance to the government, and expressed in the most comprehensive terms, would be construed to mean almost nothing. There is scarcely any case, every part of which depends on the constitution, laws, or treaties of the United States. [If the existence of other questions] be sufficient to arrest the jurisdiction of the Court, words which seem intended to be as extensive as the constitution, laws, and treaties of the Union, which seem designed to give the Courts of the government the construction of all its acts, so far as they affect the rights of individuals, would be reduced to almost nothing. . . .

A cause may depend on several questions of fact and law. Some of these may depend on the construction of a law of the United States; others on principles unconnected with that law. If it be a sufficient foundation for jurisdiction, that the title or right set up by the party, may be defeated by one construction of the constitution or law of the United States, and sustained by the opposite construction, provided the facts necessary to support the action be made out, then all the other questions must be decided as incidental to this, which gives that jurisdiction. Those other questions cannot arrest the proceedings.

Under this construction, the judicial power of the Union extends effectively and beneficially to that most important class of cases, which depend on the character of the cause. On the opposite construction, the judicial power never can be extended to a whole case, as expressed by the constitution, but to those parts of cases only which present the particular question involving the construction of the constitution or the law. We say it never can be extended to the whole case, because, if the circumstance that other points are involved in it, shall disable Congress from authorizing the Courts of the Union to take jurisdiction of the original cause, it equally disables Congress from authorizing those Courts to take jurisdiction of the whole cause, on an appeal, and thus will be restricted to a single question in that cause; and words obviously intended to secure to those who claim rights under the constitution, laws, or treaties of the United States, a trial in the federal Courts, will be restricted to the insecure remedy of an appeal upon an insulated point, after it has received that shape which may be given to it by another tribunal, into which he is forced against his will.

We think, then, that when a question to which the judicial power of the Union is extended by the constitution, forms an ingredient of the original cause, it is in the power of Congress to give the Circuit Courts jurisdiction of that cause, although other questions of fact or of law may be involved in it.

The case of the Bank is, we think, a very strong case of this description. The charter of incorporation not only creates it, but gives it every faculty which it possesses. The power to acquire rights of any description, to transact business of any description, to make contracts of any description, to sue on those contracts, is given and measured by its charter, and that charter is a law of the United States. This being can acquire no right, make no contract, bring no suit, which is not authorized by a law of the United States. It is not only itself the mere creature of a law, but all its actions and all its rights are dependant on the same law. Can a being, thus constituted, have a case which does not arise literally, as well as substantially, under the law?

Take the case of a contract, which is put as the strongest against the Bank.

When a Bank sues, the first question which presents itself, and which lies at the foundation of the cause, is, has this legal entity a right to sue? Has it a right to come, not into this Court particularly, but into any Court? This depends on a law of the United

States. The next question is, has this being a right to make this particular contract? If this question be decided in the negative, the cause is determined against the plaintiff; and this question, too, depends entirely on a law of the United States. These are important questions, and they exist in every possible case. The right to sue, if decided once, is decided for ever; but the power of Congress was exercised antecedently to the first decision on that right, and if it was constitutional then, it cannot cease to be so, because the particular question is decided. It may be revived at the will of the party, and most probably would be renewed, were the tribunal to be changed. But the question respecting the right to make a particular contract, or to acquire a particular property, or to sue on account of a particular injury, belongs to every particular case, and may be renewed in every case. The question forms an original ingredient in every cause. Whether it be in fact relied on or not, in the defence, it is still a part of the cause, and may be relied on. The right of the plaintiff to sue, cannot depend on the defence which the defendant may choose to set up. His right to sue is anterior to that defence, and must depend on the state of things when the action is brought. The questions which the case involves, then, must determine its character, whether those questions be made in the cause or not.

The appellants say, that the case arises on the contract; but the validity of the contract depends on a law of the United States, and the plaintiff is compelled, in every case, to show its validity. The case arises emphatically under the law. The act of Congress is its foundation. The contract could never have been made, but under the authority of that act. The act itself is the first ingredient in the case, is its origin, is that from which every other part arises. That other questions may also arise, as the execution of the contract, or its performance, cannot change the case, or give it any other origin than the charter of incorporation. The action still originates in, and is sustained by, that charter. . . .

It is said, that a clear distinction exists between the party and the cause; that the party may originate under a law with which the cause has no connexion; and that Congress may, with the same propriety, give a naturalized citizen, who is the mere creature of a law, a right to sue in the Courts of the United States, as give that right to the Bank.

This distinction is not denied; and, if the act of Congress was a simple act of incorporation, and contained nothing more, it might be entitled to great consideration. But the act does not stop with incorporating the Bank. It proceeds to bestow upon the being it has made, all the faculties and capacities which that being possesses. Every act of the Bank grows out of this law, and is tested by it. To use the language of the constitution, every act of the Bank arises out of this law.

[*Editorial note.* Marshall's reference to the "faculties" and "capacities" of the Bank is drawn from an argument made by counsel for the Bank. Counsel for the state of Ohio responded: "So it might be said of an alien who is naturalized by the laws of the Union, that he derives his citizenship from those laws. But, could Congress, therefore, authorize all naturalized citizens to sue in the Courts of the Union?" Marshall rejected the analogy:]

A naturalized citizen is indeed made a citizen under an act of Congress, but the act does not proceed to give, to regulate, or to prescribe his capacities. He becomes a member of the society, possessing all the rights of a native citizen, and standing, in the view of the constitution, on the footing of a native. The constitution does not authorize Congress to enlarge or abridge those rights. The simple power of the national Legislature, is to prescribe a uniform rule of naturalization, and the exercise of this power exhausts it, so far as respects the individual. The constitution then takes him up, and, among other rights, extends to him the capacity of suing in the Courts of the United States, precisely under the same circumstances under which a native might sue. He is distinguishable in nothing from a native citizen, except so far as the constitution makes the distinction. The law makes none.

There is, then, no resemblance between the act incorporating the Bank, and the general naturalization law.

Upon the best consideration we have been able to bestow on this subject, we are of opinion, that the clause in the act of incorporation, enabling the Bank to sue in the Courts of the United States, is consistent with the constitution, and to be obeyed in all Courts.

We will now proceed to consider the merits of the cause.

[The Court held that, except for the award of interest, the there was no error in the decree awarded by the trial court in favor of the Bank of the United States.]

MR. JUSTICE JOHNSON [dissenting].

The argument in this cause presents three questions: 1. Has Congress granted to the Bank of the United States, an unlimited right of suing in the Courts of the United States? 2. Could Congress constitutionally grant such a right? and 3. Has the power of the Court been legally and constitutionally exercised in this suit?

I have very little doubt that the public mind will be easily reconciled to the decision of the Court here rendered; for, whether necessary or unnecessary originally, a state of things has now grown up, in some of the States, which renders all the protection necessary, that the general government can give to this Bank. The policy of the decision is obvious, that is, if the Bank is to be sustained; and few will bestow upon its legal correctness, the reflection, that it is necessary to test it by the constitution and laws, under which it is rendered. . . .

In the present instance, I cannot persuade myself, that the constitution sanctions the vesting of the right of action in this Bank, in cases in which the privilege is exclusively personal, or in any case, merely on the ground that a question might *possibly* be raised in it, involving the constitution, or constitutionality of a law, of the United States. . . .

[Counsel arguing against the jurisdiction] contended, that until a question involving the construction or administration of the laws of the United States did actually arise, the *casus federis* [federal case] was not presented, on which the constitution authorized the government to take to itself the jurisdiction of the cause. That until such a question actually arose, until such a case was actually presented, *non constat* [it does not appear], but the cause depended upon general principles, exclusively cognizable in the State Courts; that neither the letter nor the spirit of the constitution sanctioned the assumption of jurisdiction on the part of the United States at any previous stage.

And this doctrine has my hearty concurrence in its general application. . . . I attach much importance to the 25th section of the judiciary act, not only as a measure of policy, but as a contemporaneous exposition of the constitution on this subject; as an exposition of *the words* of the constitution, deduced from a knowledge of its views and policy. The object was, to secure a uniform construction and a steady execution of the laws of the Union. Except as far as this purpose might require, the general government had no interest in stripping the State Courts of their jurisdiction; their policy would rather lead to avoid incumbering themselves with it. Why then should it be vested with jurisdiction in a thousand causes, on a mere possibility of a question arising, which question, at last, does not occur in one of them? Indeed, I cannot perceive how such a reach of jurisdiction can be asserted, without changing the reading of the constitution on this subject altogether. The judicial power extends only to "cases arising," that is, actual, not potential cases. The framers of the constitution knew better, than to trust such a *quo minus* fiction in the hands of any government.

I have never understood any one to question the right of Congress to vest original jurisdiction in its inferior Courts, in cases coming properly within the description of "cases arising under the laws of the United States;" but surely it must first be ascertained, in some proper mode, that the cases are such as the constitution describes. By possibility, a constitutional question may be raised in any conceivable suit that may be instituted; but that would be a very insufficient ground for assuming universal jurisdiction; and yet, that a question has been made, as that, for instance, on the Bank charter, and may again be made, seems still worse, as a ground for extending jurisdiction. For, the folly of raising it again in every suit instituted by the Bank, is too great, to suppose it possible. Yet this supposition, and this alone, would seem to justify vesting the Bank with an unlimited right to sue in the federal Courts. Indeed, I cannot perceive how, with ordinary correctness, a question can be said to be involved in a cause, which only may possibly be made, but which, in fact, is the very last question that there is any probability will be made; or rather, how that can any longer be denominated a question, which has been put out of existence by a solemn decision. The constitution presumes, that the decisions of the supreme tribunal will be acquiesced in; and after disposing of the few questions which the constitution refers to it, all the minor questions belong properly to the State jurisdictions, and never were intended to be taken away in mass.

Efforts have been made to fix the precise sense of the constitution, when it vests jurisdiction in the general government, in "cases arising under the laws of the United States." To me, the question appears susceptible of a very simple solution; that all depends upon the identity of the case supposed; according to which idea, a case may be such in its very existence, or it may become such in its progress. An action may "live, move, and have its being," in a law of the United States; such is that given for the violation of a patent-right, . . . in all of which cases the plaintiff must count upon the law itself as the ground of his action. And of the other description, would have been an action of trespass, in this case, had remedy been sought for an actual levy of the tax imposed. Such was the case of the former Bank against *Deveaux*, and many others that have occurred in this Court, in which the suit, in its form, was such as occur in ordinary cases, but in which the pleadings or evidence raised the question on the law or constitution of the United States. In this class of cases, the occurrence of a question makes the case, and transfers it, as provided for under the twenty-fifth section of the Judiciary Act, to the jurisdiction of the United States. . . .

It is only when the case exhibits one or the other of these characteristics, that it is acted upon by the constitution. Where no question is raised, there can be no contrariety of construction; and what else had the constitution to guard against? As to cases of the first description, *ex necessitate rei*, the Courts of the United States must be susceptible of original jurisdiction; and as to all other cases, I should hold them, also, susceptible of original jurisdiction, if it were practicable, in the nature of things, to make out the definition of the case, so as to bring it under the constitution judicially, upon an original suit. But until the plaintiff can control the defendant in his pleadings, I see no practical mode of determining when the case does occur, otherwise than by permitting the cause to advance until the case for which the constitution provides shall actually arise. If it never occurs, there can be nothing to complain of; and such are the provisions of the twenty-fifth section. The cause might be transferred to the Circuit Court before an adjudication takes place; but I can perceive no earlier stage at which it can possibly be predicated of such a case, that it is one within the constitution; nor any possible necessity for transferring it then, or until the Court has acted upon it to the prejudice of the claims of the United States.

It is not, therefore, because Congress may not vest an *original* jurisdiction, where they can constitutionally vest in the Circuit Courts *appellate* jurisdiction, that I object to this general grant of the right to sue; but, because that the peculiar nature of this jurisdiction is such, as to render it impossible to exercise it in a strictly original form, and because the principle of a possible occurrence of a question as a ground of jurisdiction, is transcending the bounds of the constitution, and placing it on a ground which will admit of an *enormous accession*, if not an *unlimited assumption*, of jurisdiction. . . .

Note: Osborn, Planters Bank, *and Federal Question Jurisdiction*

1. In addition to the federal question jurisdiction, Article III provides for federal judicial power over "Controversies to which the United States shall be a party." But Chief Justice Marshall's opinion in *Osborn* makes no mention of this head of jurisdiction, and for good reason. Although the Bank of the United States was created by

an Act of Congress, it was not part of the United States Government. Today we would probably refer to it as a federal instrumentality.

2. In explaining why the Bank's suit against Osborn arises under federal law within the meaning of Article III, Marshall says that the case presents at least one federal question — the question of the Bank's right to sue. In this part of his opinion he makes no mention of the ground on which the Bank sought relief in federal court. But as already noted, the Bank argued that the Ohio state tax was invalid under the United States Constitution. And by the time the circuit court issued the injunction, that issue had been resolved in the Bank's favor in the great case of *McCulloch v. Maryland*, 4 Wheat. (19 U.S.) 316 (1819).

The constitutionality of the Ohio tax might seem like a much more substantial federal question than the Bank's capacity to sue, but Marshall had sound reasons for approaching *Osborn* in the way he did. For one thing, the statute authorizing the Bank to "sue and be sued" in federal courts was not limited to suits to enforce rights under federal law. For another, the broader question addressed by Marshall was actually presented in a companion case, *Bank of the United States v. Planters' Bank of Georgia*, 9 Wheat. (22 U.S.) 904 (1824).

In *Planters' Bank*, the Bank of the United States brought suit in federal court against Planters' to recover damages for the bank's refusal to redeem promissory notes it had issued under Georgia law. *Planters' Bank* was argued together with *Osborn* by the same counsel.[1] In his opinion for the Court in *Planters Bank*, Marshall said simply that the jurisdictional issue "was fully considered" in *Osborn* and that it required no further discussion.

3. Although Justice Johnson, in dissent, does not cite *Cohens*, he in effect turns Chief Justice Marshall's argument in that case against him. Recall that in *Cohens*, Marshall referred to the construction that "Congress seems to have intended" by enacting section 25 of the Judiciary Act of 1789. Now Justice Johnson says that section 25, "as a contemporaneous exposition of the constitution on this subject," shows that "cases arising" refers to "actual, not potential cases." He argues that Marshall's interpretation contradicts this contemporaneous exposition. Is he persuasive on this point?

4. Justice Johnson emphatically rejects the proposition that every suit brought by the Bank of the United States arises under federal law. What about the Bank's suit against Osborn? Does Justice Johnson agree with Marshall that Congress has power to provide for original jurisdiction over that case?

Note: Removal Based on a Federal Question

1. *Cohens* involved the appellate jurisdiction of the Supreme Court; *Osborn* dealt with original jurisdiction in the trial court. Justice Johnson, dissenting in *Osborn*, mentions a third possibility: removal from state to federal trial court "before an adjudication

---

1. For an account of the case, see 10 PAPERS OF JOHN MARSHALL 83 (Charles F. Hobson ed., 2000).

takes place." Does Justice Johnson view removal as more analogous to appellate or to original jurisdiction?

2. The constitutionality of removal based on the presence of a federal question was not squarely adjudicated until after the Civil War. In *The Mayor v. Cooper*, 6 Wall. (73 U.S.) 247 (1867), the plaintiffs brought suit in state court alleging trespass on real estate. The defendants removed the case to federal court, invoking an Act of Congress that allowed removal of civil and criminal cases, before or after judgment, when the defendant pleaded that his acts were carried out under the authority of federal law. The lower court held the removal statute unconstitutional, but the Supreme Court reversed. The Court relied heavily on *Cohens*:

> If [one federal question exists,] if there be a single such ingredient in the mass, it is sufficient. That element is decisive upon the subject of jurisdiction. "A case in law or equity consists of the right of the one party as well as the other, and may be truly said to arise under the Constitution or a law of the United States whenever its correct decision depends upon the right construction of either." [*Sic.*] The rule applies with equal force where the plaintiff claims a right, and where the defendant claims protection, by virtue of one or the other. *Martin v. Hunter's Lessee* [*infra* Chapter 4]; *Cohens; Osborn.* . . .
>
> The jurisdiction here in question involves the same principle, and rests upon the same foundation with that conferred by the twenty-fifth section of the Judiciary Act of 1789. The constitutionality of that provision has been uniformly sustained by the unanimous judgment of this court whenever the subject has been presented for adjudication.

Was the Court correct in treating removal before judgment as involving "the same principle" as appellate review under section 25 of the Judiciary Act of 1789?

3. Although the language of *Cooper* might seem definitive, the Court returned to the constitutional question in *Tennessee v. Davis*, 100 U.S. 257 (1880). Davis was a federal revenue officer whose duties included seizing illicit distilleries. In the course of one such effort "he was assaulted and fired upon by a number of armed men." He fired back, killing one of the men, and was prosecuted in state court for murder. Davis removed the case to federal court under an Act of Congress that allowed removal of any suit brought against a federal revenue officer on account of any act done "under color of" any revenue law. The state challenged the constitutionality of the removal statute, but the Supreme Court held that the statute was valid. The Court framed the issue as follows:

> Has the Constitution conferred upon Congress the power to authorize the removal, from a State court to a Federal court, of an indictment against a revenue officer for an alleged crime against the State, and to order its removal before trial, when it appears that a Federal question or a claim to a Federal right is raised in the case, and must be decided therein?

Again the Court relied on *Cohens* for its definition of federal question jurisdiction:

What constitutes a case thus arising was early defined in the case cited from 6 Wheaton [*Cohens*]. It is not merely one where a party comes into court to demand something conferred upon him by the Constitution or by a law or treaty. A case consists of the right of one party as well as the other, and may truly be said to arise under the Constitution or a law or a treaty of the United States whenever its correct decision depends upon the construction of either. Cases arising under the laws of the United States are such as grow out of the legislation of Congress, whether they constitute the right or privilege, or claim or protection, or defence of the party . . . by whom they are asserted.

The Court continued:

The constitutional right of Congress to authorize the removal before trial of civil cases arising under the laws of the United States has long since passed beyond doubt. It was exercised almost contemporaneously with the adoption of the Constitution, and the power has been in constant use ever since. The Judiciary Act of Sept. 24, 1789, was passed by the first Congress, many members of which had assisted in framing the Constitution; and though some doubts were soon after suggested whether cases could be removed from State courts before trial, those doubts soon disappeared. Whether removal from a State to a Federal court is an exercise of appellate jurisdiction, as laid down in Story's Commentaries on the Constitution, or an indirect mode of exercising original jurisdiction, as intimated in *Railway Company v. Whitton* (13 Wall. 270), we need not now inquire. Be it one or the other, it was ruled in the case last cited to be constitutional. . . .

If, whenever and wherever a case arises under the Constitution and laws or treaties of the United States, the national government cannot take control of it, whether it be civil or criminal, in any stage of its progress, its judicial power is, at least, temporarily silenced, instead of being at all times supreme. In criminal as well as in civil proceedings in State courts, cases under the Constitution and laws of the United States might have been expected to arise, as, in fact, they do. Indeed, the powers of the general government and the lawfulness of authority exercised or claimed under it, are quite as frequently in question in criminal cases in State courts as they are in civil cases, in proportion to their number. . . .

It ought, therefore, to be considered as settled that the constitutional powers of Congress to authorize the removal of criminal cases for alleged offences against State laws from State courts to the circuit courts of the United States, when there arises a Federal question in them, is as ample as its power to authorize the removal of a civil case.

4. Davis alleged in his petition for removal that "at the time the alleged act for which he was indicted was committed he was [an] officer of the United States, to wit, a deputy collector of internal revenue, and the act for which he was indicted was performed in his own necessary self-defence, while engaged in the discharge of the duties of his office . . . ." Suppose that the petition had alleged only that the act for which the defendant was indicted was performed in the course of his duties as a federal officer. Would that have been enough to justify removal under the holding of *Davis*?

C. The Boundaries of Federal Question Jurisdiction

Cohens and *Osborn*, in tandem, mark out a broad scope for the federal question jurisdiction under Article III. Even so, over the years numerous issues have arisen concerning the power of Congress to authorize federal courts to hear cases that implicate federal law in ways not squarely covered by either of Marshall's definitions. We look now at some of these controversies.

Verlinden B.V. v. Central Bank of Nigeria

Supreme Court of the United States, 1983.

461 U.S. 480.

CHIEF JUSTICE BURGER delivered the opinion of the Court.

We granted certiorari to consider whether the Foreign Sovereign Immunities Act of 1976, by authorizing a foreign plaintiff to sue a foreign state in a United States District Court on a non-federal cause of action, violates Article III of the Constitution.

I

[*Editorial note.* The background of this case was vividly described in a Second Circuit opinion involving a related dispute:

> An African nation, developing at breakneck speed by virtue of huge exports of high-grade oil, contracted to buy huge quantities of Portland cement, a commodity crucial to the construction of its infrastructure. It overbought, and the country's docks and harbors became clogged with ships waiting to unload. Imports of other goods ground to a halt. More vessels carrying cement arrived daily; still others were steaming toward the port. Unable to accept delivery of the cement it had bought, the nation repudiated its contracts. [a]

The African nation was the Federal Republic of Nigeria. One of the suppliers of cement was Verlinden B.V., a Dutch corporation with its principal offices in Amsterdam. The Central Bank of Nigeria, an instrumentality of Nigeria, issued a letter of credit to finance the purchase.

[When Nigeria realized that it had badly misjudged the market, it took steps to halt the shipment of cement under the contracts. Of relevance here, Central Bank of Nigeria instructed an intermediary bank to not to pay Verlinden unless Verlinden obtained, two months before sailing, Nigeria's permission to enter one of its ports.

---

a. Texas Trading & Milling Corp. v. Federal Republic of Nigeria, 647 F.2d 300, 302 (2d Cir. 1981).

Verlinden sued Central Bank in United States District Court for the Southern District of New York, alleging that Central Bank's actions constituted an anticipatory breach of the letter of credit. Verlinden alleged jurisdiction under § 2 of the Foreign Sovereign Immunities Act, 28 U.S.C. § 1330. That section provides:

(a) The district courts shall have original jurisdiction without regard to amount in controversy of any nonjury civil action against a foreign state as defined in section 1603(a) of this title as to any claim for relief in personam with respect to which the foreign state is not entitled to immunity either under sections 1605–1607 of this title or under any applicable international agreement.

(b) Personal jurisdiction over a foreign state shall exist as to every claim for relief over which the district courts have jurisdiction under subsection (a) where service has been made under section 1608 of this title.

[Central Bank moved to dismiss on several grounds including lack of subject matter jurisdiction and lack of personal jurisdiction. The District Court ultimately dismissed the complaint. It held that a foreign instrumentality is entitled to sovereign immunity unless one of the exceptions specified in the Act applies, and that none did. The Court of Appeals affirmed, but on the ground that section 1330 exceeded the scope of Article III of the Constitution.]

II

For more than a century and a half, the United States generally granted foreign sovereigns complete immunity from suit in the courts of this country. [This immunity was] a matter of grace and comity on the part of the United States, and not a restriction imposed by the Constitution. Accordingly, this Court consistently [deferred] to the decisions of the political branches—in particular, those of the Executive Branch—on whether to take jurisdiction over actions against foreign sovereigns and their instrumentalities.

[In 1952, the State Department] announced its adoption of the "restrictive" theory of foreign sovereign immunity. Under this theory, immunity is confined to suits involving the foreign sovereign's public acts, and does not extend to cases arising out of a foreign state's strictly commercial acts.

The restrictive theory was not initially enacted into law, however, and its application proved troublesome. . . . On occasion, political considerations led to suggestions of immunity in cases where immunity would not have been available under the restrictive theory. . . .

In 1976, Congress passed the Foreign Sovereign Immunities Act in order to free the Government from the case-by-case diplomatic pressures, to clarify the governing standards, and to "assur[e] litigants that . . . decisions are made on purely legal grounds and under procedures that insure due process." To accomplish these objectives, the Act contains a comprehensive set of legal standards governing claims of immunity in every civil action against a foreign state or its political subdivisions, agencies or instrumentalities.

For the most part, the Act codifies, as a matter of federal law, the restrictive theory of sovereign immunity. A foreign state is normally immune from the jurisdiction of federal and state courts, 28 U.S.C. § 1604, subject to a set of exceptions specified in §§ 1605 and 1607. Those exceptions include actions in which the foreign state has explicitly or impliedly waived its immunity, and actions based upon commercial activities of the foreign sovereign carried on in the United States or causing a direct effect in the United States. When one of these or the other specified exceptions applies, "the foreign state shall be liable in the same manner and to the same extent as a private individual under like circumstances."

The Act expressly provides that its standards control in "the courts of the United States and of the States," and thus clearly contemplates that such suits may be brought in either federal or state courts. However, "[i]n view of the potential sensitivity of actions against foreign states and the importance of developing a uniform body of law in this area," the Act guarantees foreign states the right to remove any civil action from a state court to a federal court. The Act also provides that any claim permitted under the Act may be brought from the outset in federal court. If one of the specified exceptions to sovereign immunity applies, a federal district court may exercise subject matter jurisdiction under § 1330(a); but if the claim does not fall within one of the exceptions, federal courts lack subject matter jurisdiction. In such a case, the foreign state is also ensured immunity from the jurisdiction of state courts by § 1604.

III

The District Court and the Court of Appeals both held that the Foreign Sovereign Immunities Act purports to allow a foreign plaintiff to sue a foreign sovereign in the courts of the United States, provided the substantive requirements of the Act are satisfied. We agree. [Discussion omitted.]

IV

We now turn to the core question presented by this case: whether Congress exceeded the scope of Article III of the Constitution by granting federal courts subject matter jurisdiction over certain civil actions by foreign plaintiffs against foreign sovereigns where the rule of decision may be provided by state law.

This Court's cases firmly establish that Congress may not expand the jurisdiction of the federal courts beyond the bounds established by the Constitution. Within Article III of the Constitution, we find two sources authorizing the grant of jurisdiction in the Foreign Sovereign Immunities Act: the diversity clause and the "arising under" clause.[17] The diversity clause, which provides that the judicial power extends to controversies between "a State, or the Citizens thereof, and foreign States," covers actions by citizens of states. Yet diversity jurisdiction is not sufficiently broad to support a grant of jurisdiction over actions by foreign plaintiffs, since a foreign plaintiff is not "a State, or [a] Citize[n] thereof." We conclude, however, that the "arising

---

17. In view of our conclusion that proper actions by foreign plaintiffs under the Foreign Sovereign Immunities Act are within Article III "arising under" jurisdiction, we need not consider petitioner's alternative argument that the Act is constitutional as an aspect of so-called "protective jurisdiction."

under" clause of Article III provides an appropriate basis for the statutory grant of subject matter jurisdiction to actions by foreign plaintiffs under the Act.

The controlling decision on the scope of Article III "arising under" jurisdiction is Chief Justice Marshall's opinion for the Court in *Osborn v. Bank of the United States*, 9 Wheat. 738 (1824).... [*Osborn* reflects] a broad conception of "arising under" jurisdiction, according to which Congress may confer on the federal courts jurisdiction over any case or controversy that might call for the application of federal law. The breadth of that conclusion has been questioned. It has been observed that, taken at its broadest, *Osborn* might be read as permitting "assertion of original federal jurisdiction on the remote possibility of presentation of a federal question." *Textile Workers Union v. Lincoln Mills*, 353 U.S. 448, 482 (1957) (Frankfurter, J., dissenting). We need not now resolve that issue or decide the precise boundaries of Article III jurisdiction, however, since the present case does not involve a mere speculative possibility that a federal question may arise at some point in the proceeding. Rather, a suit against a foreign state under this Act necessarily raises questions of substantive federal law at the very outset, and hence clearly "arises under" federal law, as that term is used in Article III.

By reason of its authority over foreign commerce and foreign relations, Congress has the undisputed power to decide, as a matter of federal law, whether and under what circumstances foreign nations should be amenable to suit in the United States. Actions against foreign sovereigns in our courts raise sensitive issues concerning the foreign relations of the United States, and the primacy of federal concerns is evident.

To promote these federal interests, Congress exercised its Article I powers by enacting a statute comprehensively regulating the amenability of foreign nations to suit in the United States. The statute must be applied by the District Courts in every action against a foreign sovereign, since subject matter jurisdiction in any such action depends on the existence of one of the specified exceptions to foreign sovereign immunity, 28 U.S.C. § 1330(a). At the threshold of every action in a District Court against a foreign state, therefore, the court must satisfy itself that one of the exceptions applies — and in doing so it must apply the detailed federal law standards set forth in the Act. Accordingly, an action against a foreign sovereign arises under federal law, for purposes of Article III jurisdiction....

In rejecting "arising under" jurisdiction, the Court of Appeals [noted] that §2 of the Foreign Sovereign Immunities Act, 28 U.S.C. § 1330, is a jurisdictional provision. Because of this, the court felt its conclusion compelled by prior cases in which this Court has rejected Congressional attempts to confer jurisdiction on federal courts simply by enacting jurisdictional statutes.... [But] the statutes at issue in these prior cases sought to do nothing more than grant jurisdiction over a particular class of cases....

In contrast, in enacting the Foreign Sovereign Immunities Act, Congress expressly exercised its power to regulate foreign commerce, along with other specified Article I powers. As the House Report clearly indicates, the primary purpose of the Act was to "set forth comprehensive rules governing sovereign immunity"; the jurisdictional provisions of the Act are simply one part of this comprehensive scheme. The Act thus does not merely concern access to the federal courts. Rather, it governs the types of actions for which foreign sovereigns may be held liable in a court in the United States, federal or state. The Act codifies the standards governing foreign sovereign immunity as an aspect of substantive federal law; and applying those standards will generally require interpretation of numerous points of federal law. Finally, if a court determines that none of the exceptions to sovereign immunity applies, the plaintiff will be barred from raising his claim in any court in the United States — manifestly, "the title or right set up by the party, may be defeated by one construction of the . . . laws of the United States, and sustained by the opposite construction." *Osborn.* That the inquiry into foreign sovereign immunity is labeled under the Act as a matter of jurisdiction does not affect the constitutionality of Congress' action in granting federal courts jurisdiction over cases calling for application of this comprehensive regulatory statute.

Congress, pursuant to its unquestioned Article I powers, has enacted a broad statutory framework governing assertions of foreign sovereign immunity. In so doing, Congress deliberately sought to channel cases against foreign sovereigns away from the state courts and into federal courts, thereby reducing the potential for a multiplicity of conflicting results among the courts of the 50 states. The resulting jurisdictional grant is within the bounds of Article III, since every action against a foreign sovereign necessarily involves application of a body of substantive federal law, and accordingly "arises under" federal law, within the meaning of Article III.

V

A conclusion that the grant of jurisdiction in the Foreign Sovereign Immunities Act is consistent with the Constitution does not end the case. An action must not only satisfy Article III but must also be supported by a statutory grant of subject matter jurisdiction. As we have made clear, deciding whether statutory subject matter jurisdiction exists under the Foreign Sovereign Immunities Act entails an application of the substantive terms of the Act to determine whether one of the specified exceptions to immunity applies.

[The Court remanded the case to the Second Circuit with instructions to undertake that inquiry.]

Note: The Implications of Verlinden

1. The Second Circuit Court of Appeals, in holding the grant of jurisdiction in the FSIA unconstitutional, relied heavily on decisions construing 28 U.S.C. § 1331, the statutory counterpart to the "arising under" clause of Article III. The Second Circuit placed particular emphasis on the so-called "well-pleaded complaint" rule, which provides that federal jurisdiction may not be based on anticipation of a federal defense. (See Chapter 10.) The Supreme Court, in reversing, chastised the Second Circuit for its approach:

Although the language of § 1331 parallels that of the "arising under" clause of Article III, this Court never has held that statutory "arising under" jurisdiction is identical to Article III "arising under" jurisdiction. Quite the contrary is true. [For example, in *Romero v. International Terminal Operating Co.*, 358 U.S. 354 (1958), we observed:] "Of course the many limitations which have been placed on jurisdiction under § 1331 are not limitations on the constitutional power of Congress to confer jurisdiction on the federal courts."

2. In a footnote (note 17), the Supreme Court says that it need not consider the plaintiff's argument based on "protective jurisdiction" because "proper actions by foreign plaintiffs under FSIA are within Article III 'arising under' jurisdiction." Indeed, the Court apparently views such actions as falling squarely within the core of the Article III power as defined in *Osborn*. Is the Court persuasive on this point?

3. What does the Court mean by "protective jurisdiction"? The concept was discussed at length in Justice Frankfurter's dissent in the *Lincoln Mills* case, cited later in the opinion. Justice Frankfurter quoted the theory advanced by Professor Paul Mishkin: where Congress has "an articulated and active federal policy regulating a field, the 'arising under' clause of Article III apparently permits the conferring of jurisdiction on the national courts of all cases in the area—including those substantively governed by state law." In such cases, Professor Mishkin said, the protection being offered is not to the suitor, as in diversity cases, but to the "congressional legislative program."

Does *Mesa*, the next principal case, stand as a rejection of the concept of protective jurisdiction in the form articulated by Professor Mishkin?

4. At the end of its opinion, the Supreme Court remanded the case to the Second Circuit to determine whether Verlinden's suit fell within any of the statutory exceptions to immunity. There is no report of any subsequent decision by the Second Circuit.

Note: Jurisdiction Based on Congressional Charters

1. In the *Pacific Railroad Removal Cases*, 115 U.S. 1 (1885), the Court held that suits by and against federally chartered railroad corporations were suits "arising under" federal law. Although the Court focused on the then-new statutory grant of federal question jurisdiction, the opinion leaves no doubt that the Court viewed the railroad corporations as equivalent to the Bank of the United States from an Article III perspective:

> If the case of *Osborn v. Bank* is to be adhered to as a sound exposition of the Constitution, there is no escape from the conclusion that these suits against the [railroads], considering [those railroads] as corporations created by and organized under the acts of Congress referred to in the several petitions for removal in these cases, were and are suits arising under the laws of the United States. An examination of those acts of Congress shows that the corporations now before us, not only derive their existence, but their

powers, their functions, their duties, and a large portion of their resources, from those acts, and, by virtue thereof, sustain important relations to the government of the United States.

Through legislation in 1915 and 1925, Congress overruled the statutory holding of the *Pacific Railroad Removal Cases*. Section 1349 of Title 28 now provides:

> The district courts shall not have jurisdiction of any civil action by or against any corporation upon the ground that it was incorporated by or under an Act of Congress, unless the United States is the owner of more than one-half of its capital stock.

But the import of section 1349 is solely to preclude the exercise of jurisdiction under the general federal question statute. Congress may confer jurisdiction though other legislation, as the *American National Red Cross* case of 1992 makes clear.

2. In *American National Red Cross v. S.G.*, 505 U.S. 247 (1992), the Supreme Court considered a modern-day counterpart to *Osborn*. The case began when the plaintiff filed a state-law tort action in state court against American National Red Cross. The complaint alleged that plaintiff had contracted AIDS from a transfusion of contaminated blood during surgery and that Red Cross had supplied the tainted blood. Red Cross removed the case to federal district court, asserting federal jurisdiction based on its charter. That charter, enacted by Congress in 1905, authorized the Red Cross "to sue and be sued in courts of law and equity, State or Federal, within the jurisdiction of the United States."

By a vote of 5-4, the Supreme Court held that the "sue and be sued" provision conferred original jurisdiction on federal courts "over all cases to which the Red Cross is a party, with the consequence that the organization is thereby authorized to remove from state to federal court any state-law action it is defending." The opinion dealt with Article III in a single brief paragraph:

> Our holding leaves the jurisdiction of the federal courts well within Article III's limits. As long ago as *Osborn*, this Court held that Article III's "arising under" jurisdiction is broad enough to authorize Congress to confer federal-court jurisdiction over actions involving federally chartered corporations. We have consistently reaffirmed the breadth of that holding. See [among other cases] *Pacific Railroad Removal Cases; Verlinden*. We would be loath to repudiate such a longstanding and settled rule, on which Congress has surely been entitled to rely, and this case gives us no reason to contemplate overruling it.

The dissenters argued that the "sue and be sued" language granted "only the capacity to 'sue or be sued' in a state or federal court of appropriate jurisdiction." The dissent did not address the constitutional question.

3. The *Pacific Railroad Removal Cases* and the *American Red Cross* case both assume that *Osborn* applies equally whether the federally chartered corporation is plaintiff or defendant. Is that assumption justified?

Mesa v. California

Supreme Court of the United States, 1989.

489 U.S. 121.

Justice O'Connor delivered the opinion of the Court.

We decide today whether United States Postal Service employees may, pursuant to 28 U.S.C. § 1442(a)(1), remove to Federal District Court state criminal prosecutions brought against them for traffic violations committed while on duty.

I

In the summer of 1985 petitioners Kathryn Mesa and Shabbir Ebrahim were employed as mailtruck drivers by the United States Postal Service in Santa Clara County, California. In unrelated incidents, the State of California issued criminal complaints against petitioners, charging Mesa with misdemeanor-manslaughter and driving outside a laned roadway after her mailtruck collided with and killed a bicyclist, and charging Ebrahim with speeding and failure to yield after his mailtruck collided with a police car. . . .

[Both cases were removed to the United States District Court for the Northern District of California by the United States on behalf of the defendants. In each case the removal petition (now designated as "notice of removal") asserted that removal was proper under 28 U.S.C. § 1442(a)(1) because Mesa and Ebrahim were federal employees at the time of the incidents and because "the state charges arose from an accident involving defendant which occurred while defendant was on duty and acting in the course and scope of her employment with the Postal Service."]

[The District Court denied the state's motion to remand the cases to state court, but the Ninth Circuit Court of Appeals issued a writ of mandamus ordering the District Court to do so. The Court of Appeals held that "federal postal workers may not remove state criminal prosecutions to federal court when they raise no colorable claim of federal immunity or other federal defense."] We granted the United States' petition for certiorari on behalf of Mesa and Ebrahim to resolve a conflict among the Courts of Appeals concerning the proper interpretation of § 1442(a)(1). We now affirm.

II

[At the time of this case, 28 U.S.C. § 1442(a) provided in relevant part:]

A civil action or criminal prosecution commenced in a State court against any of the following persons may be removed by them to the district court of the United States for the district and division embracing the place wherein it is pending:

(1) Any officer of the United States or any agency thereof, or person acting under him, for any act under color of such office or on account of any right, title or authority claimed under any Act of Congress for the apprehension or punishment of criminals or the collection of the revenue. . . .

The United States and California agree that Mesa and Ebrahim, in their capacity as employees of the United States Postal Service, were "person[s] acting under" an "officer of the United States or any agency thereof" within the meaning of § 1442(a) (1). Their disagreement concerns whether the California criminal prosecutions brought against Mesa and Ebrahim were "for act[s] under color of such office" within the meaning of that subsection. The United States [would read] "under color of office" to permit removal "whenever a federal official is prosecuted for the manner in which he has performed his federal duties. . . ." California [would] have us read the same phrase to impose a requirement that some federal defense be alleged by the federal officer seeking removal.

On numerous occasions in the last 121 years we have had the opportunity to examine § 1442(a) or one of its long line of statutory forebears. In *Willingham v. Morgan*, 395 U.S. 402, 405 (1969), we traced the "long history" of the federal officer removal statute from its origin in the Act of February 4, 1815, as a congressional response to New England's opposition to the War of 1812, through its expansion in response to South Carolina's 1833 threats of nullification, and its further expansion in the Civil War era as the need to enforce revenue laws became acute, to enactment of the Judicial Code of 1948 when the removal statute took its present form encompassing all federal officers. . . .

[The Court reviewed its precedents at length. It concluded:] In sum, an unbroken line of this Court's decisions extending back nearly a century and a quarter have understood all the various incarnations of the federal officer removal statute to require the averment of a federal defense.

In the face of all these decisions, the Government defends the proposition that § 1442(a)(1) permits removal without the assertion of a federal defense. It does so based on the plain language of the removal statute and on the substantial federal interests that would be protected by permitting universal removal of all civil actions and criminal prosecutions brought against any federal official "for the manner in which he has performed his federal duties. . . ."

[The Court rejected the Government's interpretation of the statute.]

The Government's view, which would eliminate the federal defense requirement, raises serious doubt whether, in enacting § 1442(a), Congress would not have "expand[ed] the jurisdiction of the federal courts beyond the bounds established by the Constitution." *Verlinden B.V. v. Central Bank of Nigeria*, 461 U.S. 480, 491 (1983). In *Verlinden*, we discussed the distinction between "jurisdictional statutes" and "the federal law under which [an] action arises, for Art. III purposes," and recognized that pure jurisdictional statutes which seek "to do nothing more than grant jurisdiction over a particular class of cases" cannot support Art. III "arising under" jurisdiction. . . .

Section 1442(a), in our view, is a pure jurisdictional statute, seeking to do nothing more than grant district court jurisdiction over cases in which a federal officer is a defendant. Section 1442(a), therefore, cannot independently support Art. III "arising under" jurisdiction. Rather, it is the raising of a federal question in the officer's removal petition that constitutes the federal law under which the action against the federal offi-cer arises for Art. III purposes. The removal statute itself merely serves to overcome the "well-pleaded complaint" rule which would otherwise preclude removal even if a federal defense were alleged. . . . Adopting the Government's view would eliminate the substantive Art. III foundation of § 1442(a)(1) and unnecessarily present grave constitutional problems. We are not inclined to abandon a longstanding reading of the officer removal statute that clearly preserves its constitutionality and adopt one which raises serious constitutional doubt. . . .

At oral argument the Government urged upon us a theory of "protective jurisdic-tion" to avoid these Art. III difficulties. In *Willingham*, we recognized that Congress' enactment of federal officer removal statutes since 1815 served "to provide a federal forum for cases where federal officials must raise defenses arising from their official duties . . . [and] to protect federal officers from interference by hostile state courts." The Government insists that the full protection of federal officers from interference by hostile state courts cannot be achieved if the averment of a federal defense must be a predicate to removal. More important, the Government suggests that this gener-alized congressional interest in protecting federal officers from state court interfer-ence suffices to support Art. III "arising under" jurisdiction.

We have, in the past, not found the need to adopt a theory of "protective jurisdic-tion" to support Art. III "arising under" jurisdiction, *Verlinden*, and we do not see any need for doing so here because we do not recognize any federal interests that are not protected by limiting removal to situations in which a federal defense is alleged. In these prosecutions, no state court hostility or interference has even been alleged by petitioners and we can discern no federal interest in potentially forcing local district attorneys to choose between prosecuting traffic violations hundreds of miles from the municipality in which the violations occurred or abandoning those prosecutions. . . . We have emphasized:

> [U]nder our federal system, it goes without saying that <u>preventing and dealing with crime is much more the business of the States</u> than it is of the Federal Government. Because the regulation of crime is pre-eminently a matter for the States, we have identified a strong judicial policy against fed-eral interference with state criminal proceedings. *Arizona v. Manypenny*, 451 U.S. 232, 243 (1981).

It is hardly consistent with this "strong judicial policy" to permit removal of state criminal prosecutions of federal officers and thereby impose potentially extraordinary burdens on the States when absolutely no federal question is even at issue in such pros-ecutions. We are simply unwilling to credit the Government's ominous intimations of hostile state prosecutors and collaborationist state courts interfering with federal officers by charging them with traffic violations and other crimes for which they would have no federal defense in immunity or otherwise. That is certainly not the case in the prosecutions of Mesa and Ebrahim, nor was it the case in the removal of the state prosecutions of federal revenue agents that confronted us in our early decisions. In those cases where true state hostility may have existed, it was specifically directed against federal officers' efforts to carry out their federally mandated duties. *E.g., Tennessee v. Davis*, 100 U.S. 257 (1880). As we said in *Maryland v. Soper (No. 2)*, 270 U.S. 36 (1926), with respect to Judicial Code § 33:

> In answer to the suggestion that our construction of § 33 and our failure to sustain the right of removal in the case before us will permit evilly minded persons to evade the useful operations of § 33, we can only say that, if prosecutions of this kind come to be used to obstruct seriously the enforcement of federal laws, it will be for Congress in its discretion to amend § 33 so that the words . . . shall be enlarged to mean that any prosecution of a federal officer for any state offense which can be shown by evidence to have had its motive in a wish to hinder him in the enforcement of federal law, may be removed for trial to the proper federal court. We are not now considering or intimating whether such an enlargement would be valid; but what we wish to be understood as deciding is that the present language of § 33 can not be broadened by fair construction to give it such a meaning. These were not prosecutions, therefore, commenced on account of acts done by these defendants solely in pursuance of their federal authority. With the statute as it is, they can not have the protection of a trial in the federal court. . . .

Chief Justice Taft's words of 63 years ago apply equally well today; the present language of § 1442(a) cannot be broadened by fair construction to give it the meaning which the Government seeks. Federal officer removal under 28 U.S.C. § 1442(a) must be predicated upon averment of a federal defense. Accordingly, the judgment of the Court of Appeals is affirmed.

JUSTICE BRENNAN, with whom JUSTICE MARSHALL joins, concurring.

While I concur in the judgment and opinion of the Court, I write separately to emphasize a point that might otherwise be overlooked. In most routine traffic-accident cases like those presented here, no significant federal interest is served by removal; it is, accordingly, difficult to believe that Congress would have intended the statute to reach so far. It is not at all inconceivable, however, that Congress' concern about local hostility to federal authority could come into play in some circumstances where the federal officer is unable to present any "federal defense." The days of widespread resistance by state and local governmental authorities to Acts of Congress and to decisions of this Court in the areas of school desegregation and voting rights are not so distant that we should be oblivious to the possibility of harassment of federal agents by local law enforcement authorities. Such harassment could well take the form of unjustified prosecution for traffic or other offenses, to which the federal officer would have no immunity or other federal defense. The removal statute, it would seem to me, might well have been intended to apply in such unfortunate and exceptional circumstances.

The Court today rightly refrains from deciding whether removal in such a situation is possible, since that is not the case before us. But the Court [in its discussion of one of the earlier cases] leaves open the possibility that where a federal officer is prosecuted because of local hostility to his function, "careful pleading, demonstrating the close connection between the state prosecution and the federal officer's performance of his duty, might adequately replace the specific averment of a federal defense." With the understanding that today's decision does not foreclose the possibility of removal in such circumstances even in the absence of a federal defense, I join the Court's opinion.

Note: Suits Against Federal Officers

1. The Court in *Mesa* is interpreting 28 U.S.C. § 1442(a), not deciding a constitutional question. But the Court says explicitly that the Government's interpretation of the statute would raise "grave constitutional problems." This Note focuses on the constitutional issues underlying the statutory question.

2. Echoing *Verlinden*, the Court in *Mesa* says that a "pure jurisdictional statute" cannot support Article III "arising under" jurisdiction; there must be some other "federal law under which [an] action arises." What was the "federal law" in the Bank statute involved in *Osborn* and *Planters' Bank*?

3. Justice Brennan reads the *Mesa* opinion as not foreclosing the possibility of removal by a federal officer who "is prosecuted because of local hostility to his function," even in the absence of a federal defense. Can you draft a statute that would allow removal in such circumstances? Do you agree with Justice Brennan that the *Mesa* decision does not resolve the constitutionality of such a statute?

Problem: Suits Against Diplomats' Insurers

Foreign diplomats are immune from suit in American courts. As a consequence, victims of traffic accidents may be left without compensation for serious personal injury or property damage. To remedy this situation, Congress passed the Diplomatic Relations Act of 1978. The statute requires members of foreign diplomatic missions and their families to obtain liability insurance in accordance with regulations established by the President. The statute also authorizes a "direct action" against the insurers of such individuals. The "direct action" provision is codified in section 1364 of Title 28:

> (a) The district courts shall have original and exclusive jurisdiction, without regard to the amount in controversy, of any civil action commenced by any person against an insurer who by contract has insured an individual, who is, or was at the time of the tortious act or omission, a member of a mission (within the meaning of section 2(3) of the Diplomatic Relations Act) . . . or a member of the family of such a member of a mission . . . , against liability for personal injury, death, or damage to property.

> (b) Any direct action brought against an insurer under subsection (a) shall be tried without a jury, but shall not be subject to the defense that the insured is immune from suit, that the insured is an indispensable party, or in the absence of fraud or collusion, that the insured has violated a term of the contract, unless the contract was cancelled before the claim arose.

The authoritative Senate Report on the 1978 legislation states: "The substantive tort law to be applied by Federal courts in direct actions against insurers will be state law (i.e., the law of the place where the tortious act or omission occurs)."

Gerald Walker, a citizen of Virginia, was seriously injured when he was hit by a vehicle driven by the spouse of a foreign diplomat. He has brought suit in federal district court under 28 U.S.C. § 1364 against Acme Insurance Co., the insurance company that contracted to provide liability insurance to the spouse. Acme is incorporated in Virginia. Assume that the spouse would not be an "Ambassador" or "other public Minister" within the meaning of Article III. May the district court constitutionally exercise jurisdiction over the suit?

Problem: Nuclear "Incidents" and Liability Claims

On March 28, 1979, the Three Mile Island Nuclear Station near Harrisburg, Pennsylvania, experienced a partial meltdown of its reactor core. About 2,000 plaintiffs filed civil suits asserting various claims based on alleged exposure to radiation released from the reactor. The defendants were the owners and operators of the Three Mile Island Station and various providers of equipment or services to the facility.

Many of the suits were filed in state court. The defendants sought to remove the cases to federal district court, asserting that the claims arose under the Price-Anderson Act, a 1957 federal statute that established a system of private insurance and government indemnity for injuries resulting from nuclear incidents. However, the Third Circuit held that the Price-Anderson Act created no private cause of action and was not intended to confer jurisdiction on federal district courts.

In 1988, Congress enacted the Price-Anderson Amendments Act. That statute created a federal cause of action for "public liability actions," which are defined as "any suit asserting public liability." "Public liability," in turn, encompasses "any legal liability arising out of or resulting from a nuclear incident." The definition of "public liability action" includes the following provision:

> A public liability action shall be deemed to be an action arising under section 2210 of this title ["Indemnification and Limitation of Liability"], and the substantive rules for decision in such action shall be derived from the law of the State in which the nuclear incident involved occurs, unless such law is inconsistent with the provisions of such section.

The statute also includes the following jurisdictional provision, codified as 42 U.S.C. § 2210(2):

> With respect to any public liability action arising out of or resulting from a nuclear incident, the United States district court in the district where the nuclear incident takes place, or in the case of a nuclear incident taking place outside the United States, the United States District Court for the District of Columbia, shall have original jurisdiction without regard to the citizenship of any party or the amount in controversy.

Is this jurisdictional grant constitutional?

Problem: Danger Invites Rescue — and Also Removal?

Richard Cunningham worked for 20 years as a Special Agent for the Bureau of Alcohol, Tobacco, Firearms and Explosives (ATF). Three years ago he was transferred to a supervisory position at the ATF regional office in the state of Oceana.

Cunningham lives in a condo in a suburb of Bayport, the largest city in Oceana. One evening early this year Cunningham was leaving his condo when he saw his neighbor Alice Markell trying to back up her car. Her boyfriend Gerald Hanley was blocking her car and yelling at her. Witnesses said Hanley and Markell had been drinking at brunch before returning to the apartment complex.

According to police reports, Hanley grabbed a heavy metal tire jack from Markell's car and was edging toward Markell when Markell caught sight of Cunningham. Markell got out of her car and moved away from it. She called out to Cunningham, asking him for a ride to the guard gate. Cunningham agreed, and Markell got into his SUV.

Witnesses tell conflicting stories about what happened next, but according to affidavits submitted by the prosecution, Hanley approached Cunningham, who was sitting in the SUV with the driver's door open. Hanley struck the SUV's door with the tire jack. Cunningham drew his service weapon, a .40 caliber Glock, and told Hanley to step back. The police affidavit continues: "Hanley stood there with his hands at his side when Richard Cunningham discharged his service weapon. He hit Hanley five times in the chest." Hanley died of his injuries.

After investigating, the State Attorney General concluded that the shooting was unjustified, and he charged Cunningham with second degree murder. The case was filed in the Oceana Superior Court, the state trial court of general jurisdiction.

Cunningham immediately removed the case to federal district court. He relied on 28 U.S.C. § 1442 as amended by Pub. L. No. 112-239, signed by President Obama on Jan. 2, 2013. The 2013 amendment was originally introduced as a stand-alone bill, the Officer Safety Act of 2012, and for convenience that name will be used here. The new law added two new sections to 28 U.S.C. § 1442. In relevant part, they are as follows:

(c) Solely for purposes of determining the propriety of removal under subsection (a), a law enforcement officer, who is the defendant in a criminal prosecution, shall be deemed to have been acting under the color of his office if the officer—

(1) protected an individual in the presence of the officer from a crime of violence;

(2) provided immediate assistance to an individual who suffered, or who was threatened with, bodily harm; or

(3) prevented the escape of any individual who the officer reasonably believed to have committed, or was about to commit, in the presence of the officer, a crime of violence that resulted in, or was likely to result in, death or serious bodily injury.

(d) In this section, the following definitions apply: . . .

(2) The term "crime of violence" has the meaning given that term in section 16 of title 18.

(3) The term "law enforcement officer" means any employee described in subparagraph (A), (B), or (C) of section 8401(17) of title 5 and any special agent in the Diplomatic Security Service of the Department of State.

(4) The term "serious bodily injury" has the meaning given that term in section 1365 of title 18.

The legislative history of the Officer Safety Act is sparse. The principal sponsor of the legislation, Sen. Chuck Grassley of Iowa, explained its purpose as follows: "This bill allows a Federal law enforcement agent, who stops a violent crime while off-duty and is indicted in a State court for those actions, to petition for the State criminal prosecution against him to be removed to Federal court." Sen. Grassley added:

> This bill does not provide immunity for law enforcement agents, and it does not grant them additional authority. It doesn't even guarantee that the case will be moved from State to Federal court: the State will be heard and its position will be weighed by the judge before deciding if removal is appropriate. It does allow a Federal law enforcement officer/agent, who is indicted in a State court for actions related to his protection of a victim of a violent crime that is committed in the officer's presence, to petition for that criminal case to be removed to Federal court, where the officer will be required to defend his actions.

(For the complete text of section 1442, see the Judicial Code Supplement.)

You are a new lawyer in the Office of the State Attorney General. The Attorney General tells you:

> I am preparing a motion to remand the case back to our state court. I will have to concede that Cunningham is a "law enforcement officer" within the meaning of the Officer Safety Act, but apart from that, is it clear that the statute covers this case?

> The main argument I would like to make, though, is that if the new law allows removal of the prosecution against Cunningham, it is unconstitutional under the Supreme Court's decisions. Cunningham's attorney has been quoted in the media as saying that under ATF regulations, agents are "always on duty" and are always armed. Assuming that that is correct, is it enough?

How would you answer the Attorney General's questions?

Chapter 3

Justiciability and the Case or Controversy Requirement

In the preceding chapter we considered the scope of the federal judicial power—the kinds of cases and controversies that can be heard by federal courts. Here we look at the consequences of the "case or controversy" language itself. That language has given rise to a complex set of doctrines that limit the ability and willingness of federal judges to hear cases that would otherwise appear to fall within the scope of the federal judicial power. As Chief Justice Warren explained in *Flast v. Cohen,* 392 U.S. 83, 94–95 (1968):

> Embodied in the words "cases" and "controversies" are two complementary but somewhat different limitations. In part those words limit the business of the federal courts to questions presented in an adversary context and in a form historically capable of resolution through the judicial process. And in part those words define the role assigned to the judiciary in a tripartite allocation of power to assure that the federal courts will not intrude into areas committed to the other branches of government. Justiciability is the term of art employed to give expression to this dual limitation placed upon federal courts by the case-and-controversy doctrine.

Justiciability doctrines provide a series of hurdles to federal litigants, and can be a major difference between federal-court litigation and litigation in the state courts.[1] Lawyer unfamiliarity with justiciability doctrines can also cost litigants a great deal of money. Like subject-matter jurisdiction problems, issues involving these limitations can arise late in the life of a case, and can lead to dismissal after years of litigation.

Justiciability limitations can take several forms. They forbid federal courts from issuing opinions outside of the context of a concrete dispute; limit the parties who may pursue a case otherwise properly within a federal court's jurisdiction; determine that a case is brought too early or too late; or find that a dispute can properly be resolved only by another branch of government.

The prohibition against advisory opinions, established as early as 1792, embodies most of the concerns expressed through justiciability doctrines. Unlike some state courts and the courts of many other countries, federal courts may not answer questions

---

1. *See* Helen Hershkoff, *State Courts and the "Passive Virtues": Rethinking the Judicial Function*, 114 Harv. L. Rev. 1834, 1841 (2001) (noting that state courts "undertake a wider range of functions than do federal courts in terms of advice-giving, administration, and policy-making").

posed to them in the abstract by litigants, or even by the other branches of government. Rather, the federal courts require that even quite important issues await a dispute between litigants, one of whom is injured by the actions of the other. *Flast v. Cohen* again provides an explanation:

> When the federal judicial power is invoked to pass upon the validity of actions by the Legislative and Executive Branches of government, the rule against advisory opinions implements the separation of powers prescribed by the Constitution and confines federal courts to the role assigned them by Article III. However, the rule against advisory opinions also recognizes that such suits often "are not pressed before the Court with that clear concreteness provided when a question emerges precisely framed and necessary for decision from a clash of adversary argument exploring every aspect of a multifaceted situation embracing conflicting and demanding interests." Consequently, the Article III prohibition against advisory opinions reflects the complementary constitutional considerations expressed by the justiciability doctrine: Federal judicial power is limited to those disputes which confine federal courts to a rule consistent with a system of separated powers and which are traditionally thought to be capable of resolution through the judicial process.

In this chapter, we examine each of the justiciability limitations in turn, starting with the question of whether the proper party is before the court.

A. Standing

As explained in *Flast*, the doctrine of standing "focuses on the party seeking to get his complaint before a federal court and not on the issues he wishes to have adjudicated. The gist of the question of standing is whether the party seeking relief has alleged such a personal stake in the outcome of the controversy as to assure that concrete adverseness which sharpens the presentation of issues upon which the court so largely depends." Stated thus, standing doctrine serves pragmatic ends associated with the adversary process. But as the next case demonstrates, standing has a constitutional component.

[1] The Basic Doctrine

Allen v. Wright

Supreme Court of the United States, 1984.

468 U.S. 737.

Justice O'Connor delivered the opinion of the Court.

Parents of black public school children allege in this nation-wide class action that the Internal Revenue Service (IRS) has not adopted sufficient standards and procedures to fulfill its obligation to deny tax-exempt status to racially discriminatory private schools. They assert that the IRS thereby harms them directly and interferes with the ability of their children to receive an education in desegregated public schools. The issue before us is whether plaintiffs have standing to bring this suit. We hold that they do not.

I

The IRS denies tax-exempt status—and hence eligibility to receive charitable contributions deductible from income taxes—to racially discriminatory private schools.[1] The IRS policy requires that a school applying for tax-exempt status show that it "admits the students of any race to all the rights, privileges, programs, and activities generally accorded or made available to students at that school and that the school does not discriminate on the basis of race in administration of its educational policies, admissions policies, scholarship and loan programs, and athletic and other school-administered programs." To carry out this policy, the IRS has established guidelines and procedures for determining whether a particular school is in fact racially nondiscriminatory. Failure to comply with the guidelines "will ordinarily result in the proposed revocation of" tax-exempt status.

The guidelines provide that "[a] school must show affirmatively both that it has adopted a racially nondiscriminatory policy as to students that is made known to the general public and that since the adoption of that policy it has operated in a bona fide manner in accordance therewith." The school must state its nondiscrimination policy in its organizational charter, and in all of its brochures, catalogs, and other advertisements to prospective students. The school must make its nondiscrimination policy known to the entire community served by the school and must publicly disavow any contrary representations made on its behalf once it becomes aware of them. The school must have nondiscriminatory policies concerning all programs and facilities, including scholarships and loans, and the school must annually certify, under penalty of perjury, compliance with these requirements.

The IRS rules require a school applying for tax-exempt status to give a breakdown along racial lines of its student body and its faculty and administrative staff, as well as of scholarships and loans awarded. They also require the applicant school to state the year of its organization and to list "incorporators, founders, board members, and donors of land or buildings," and state whether any of the organizations among these have an objective of maintaining segregated public or private school education. The rules further provide that, once given an exemption, a school must keep specified records to document the extent of compliance with the IRS guidelines. Finally, the rules announce that any information concerning discrimination at a tax-exempt school is officially welcomed.

---

1. [The] IRS announced this policy in 1970 and formally adopted it in 1971. This change in prior policy was prompted by litigation over tax exemptions for racially discriminatory private schools in the State of Mississippi, litigation that resulted in the entry of an injunction against the IRS largely if not entirely coextensive with the position the IRS had voluntarily adopted.

In 1976 respondents challenged these guidelines and procedures in a suit against the Secretary of the Treasury and the Commissioner of Internal Revenue. The plaintiffs named in the complaint are parents of black children who, at the time the complaint was filed, were attending public schools in seven States in school districts undergoing desegregation. They brought this nationwide class action "on behalf of themselves and their children, and . . . on behalf of all other parents of black children attending public school systems undergoing, or which may in the future undergo, desegregation pursuant to court order [or Department of Health, Education, and Welfare (HEW)] HEW regulations and guidelines, under state law, or voluntarily." They estimated that the class they seek to represent includes several million persons.

Respondents allege in their complaint that many racially segregated private schools were created or expanded in their communities at the time the public schools were undergoing desegregation. According to the complaint, many such private schools, including 17 schools or school systems identified by name in the complaint (perhaps some 30 schools in all), receive tax exemptions either directly or through the tax-exempt status of "umbrella" organizations that operate or support the schools. Respondents allege that, despite the IRS policy of denying tax-exempt status to racially discriminatory private schools and despite the IRS guidelines and procedures for implementing that policy, some of the tax-exempt racially segregated private schools created or expanded in desegregating districts in fact have racially discriminatory policies.[11] Respondents allege that the IRS grant of tax exemptions to such racially discriminatory schools is unlawful. Respondents allege that the challenged Government conduct harms them in two ways.

The challenged conduct

> (a) constitutes tangible federal financial aid and other support for racially segregated educational institutions, and

> (b) fosters and encourages the organization, operation and expansion of institutions providing racially segregated educational opportunities for white children avoiding attendance in desegregating public school districts and thereby interferes with the efforts of federal courts, HEW and local school authorities to desegregate public school districts which have been operating racially dual school systems.

Thus, respondents do not allege that their children have been the victims of discriminatory exclusion from the schools whose tax exemptions they challenge as unlawful. Indeed, they have not alleged at any stage of this litigation that their children have ever applied or would ever apply to any private school. Rather, respondents claim a direct injury from the mere fact of the challenged Government conduct and, as indicated by the restriction of the plaintiff class to parents of children in desegregating school districts, injury to their children's opportunity to receive a desegregated

---

11. Contrary to Justice Brennan's statement [in dissent], the complaint does not allege that each desegregating district in which they reside contains one or more racially discriminatory private schools unlawfully receiving a tax exemption.

education. The latter injury is traceable to the IRS grant of tax exemptions to racially discriminatory schools, respondents allege, chiefly because contributions to such schools are deductible from income taxes and the "deductions facilitate the raising of funds to organize new schools and expand existing schools in order to accommodate white students avoiding attendance in desegregating public school districts."

Respondents request only prospective relief. They ask for a declaratory judgment that the challenged IRS tax-exemption practices are unlawful. They also ask for an injunction requiring the IRS to deny tax exemptions to a considerably broader class of private schools than the class of racially discriminatory private schools. Under the requested injunction, the IRS would have to deny tax-exempt status to all private schools

> which have insubstantial or nonexistent minority enrollments, which are located in or serve desegregating public school districts, and which either—
>
> (1) were established or expanded at or about the time the public school districts in which they are located or which they serve were desegregating;
>
> (2) have been determined in adversary judicial or administrative proceedings to be racially segregated; or
>
> (3) cannot demonstrate that they do not provide racially segregated educational opportunities for white children avoiding attendance in desegregating public school systems. . . .

Finally, respondents ask for an order directing the IRS to replace its 1975 guidelines with standards consistent with the requested injunction. . . .

The United States Court of Appeals for the District of Columbia Circuit [concluded] that respondents have standing to maintain this lawsuit. . . . The court [remanded] the case to the District Court for further proceedings, enjoining the defendants meanwhile from granting tax-exempt status to any racially discriminatory school.

II

A

Article III of the Constitution confines the federal courts to adjudicating actual "cases" and "controversies." As the Court explained in *Valley Forge Christian College v. Americans United for Separation of Church and State, Inc.*, 454 U.S. 464 (1982), the "case or controversy" requirement defines with respect to the Judicial Branch the idea of separation of powers on which the Federal Government is founded. The several doctrines that have grown up to elaborate that requirement are "founded in concern about the proper—and properly limited—role of the courts in a democratic society." *Warth v. Seldin*, 422 U.S. 490 (1975) . . . . The case-or-controversy doctrines state fundamental limits on federal judicial power in our system of government.

The Art. III doctrine that requires a litigant to have "standing" to invoke the power of a federal court is perhaps the most important of these doctrines. "In essence the question of standing is whether the litigant is entitled to have the court decide the merits of the dispute or of particular issues." *Warth.* Standing doctrine embraces several judicially self-imposed limits on the exercise of federal jurisdiction, such as the general prohibition on a litigant's raising another person's legal rights, the rule barring adjudication of generalized grievances more appropriately addressed in the representative branches, and the requirement that a plaintiff's complaint fall within the zone of interests protected by the law invoked. The requirement of standing, however, has a core component derived directly from the Constitution. A plaintiff must allege personal injury fairly traceable to the defendant's allegedly unlawful conduct and likely to be redressed by the requested relief. *Valley Forge.*

Like the prudential component, the constitutional component of standing doctrine incorporates concepts concededly not susceptible of precise definition. The injury alleged must be distinct and palpable, and not abstract or conjectural or hypothetical. The injury must be fairly traceable to the challenged action, and relief from the injury must be likely to follow from a favorable decision. These terms cannot be defined so as to make application of the constitutional standing requirement a mechanical exercise.

The absence of precise definitions, however, as this Court's extensive body of case law on standing illustrates, hardly leaves courts at sea in applying the law of standing. Like most legal notions, the standing concepts have gained considerable definition from developing case law. In many cases the standing question can be answered chiefly by comparing the allegations of the particular complaint to those made in prior standing cases. More important, the law of Art. III standing is built on a single basic idea — the idea of separation of powers. It is this fact which makes possible the gradual clarification of the law through judicial application. Of course, both federal and state courts have long experience in applying and elaborating in numerous contexts the pervasive and fundamental notion of separation of powers.

Determining standing in a particular case may be facilitated by clarifying principles or even clear rules developed in prior cases. Typically, however, the standing inquiry requires careful judicial examination of a complaint's allegations to ascertain whether the particular plaintiff is entitled to an adjudication of the particular claims asserted. Is the injury too abstract, or otherwise not appropriate, to be considered judicially cognizable? Is the line of causation between the illegal conduct and injury too attenuated? Is the prospect of obtaining relief from the injury as a result of a favorable ruling too speculative? These questions and any others relevant to the standing inquiry must be answered by reference to the Art. III notion that federal courts may exercise power only "in the last resort, and as a necessity," and only when adjudication is "consistent with a system of separated powers and [the dispute is one] traditionally thought to be capable of resolution through the judicial process," *Flast v. Cohen.*

B

Respondents allege two injuries in their complaint to support their standing to bring this lawsuit. First, they say that they are harmed directly by the mere fact of Government financial aid to discriminatory private schools. Second, they say that the federal tax exemptions to racially discriminatory private schools in their communities impair their ability to have their public schools desegregated.

In the Court of Appeals, respondents apparently relied on the first injury. Thus, the court below asserted that "[t]he sole injury [respondents] claim is the denigration they suffer" as a result of the tax exemptions. In this Court, respondents have not focused on this claim of injury. Here they stress the effect of the tax exemptions on their "equal educational opportunities," the second injury described in their complaint.

Because respondents have not clearly disclaimed reliance on either of the injuries described in their complaint, we address both allegations of injury. We conclude that neither suffices to support respondents' standing. The first fails under clear precedents of this Court because it does not constitute judicially cognizable injury. The second fails because the alleged injury is not fairly traceable to the assertedly unlawful conduct of the IRS.[19]

1

Respondents' first claim of injury can be interpreted in two ways. It might be a claim simply to have the Government avoid the violation of law alleged in respondents' complaint. Alternatively, it might be a claim of stigmatic injury, or denigration, suffered by all members of a racial group when the Government discriminates on the basis of race. Under neither interpretation is this claim of injury judicially cognizable.

This Court has repeatedly held that an asserted right to have the Government act in accordance with law is not sufficient, standing alone, to confer jurisdiction on a federal court. In *Schlesinger v. Reservists Committee to Stop the War*, 418 U.S. 208 (1974), for example, the Court rejected a claim of citizen standing to challenge Armed Forces Reserve commissions held by Members of Congress as violating the Incompatibility Clause of Art. I, § 6, of the Constitution. As citizens, the Court held, plaintiffs alleged nothing but "the abstract injury in nonobservance of the Constitution...." More recently, in *Valley Forge*, we rejected a claim of standing to challenge a Government conveyance of property to a religious institution. Insofar as the plaintiffs relied simply on "'their shared individuated right'" to a Government that made no law respecting an establishment of religion, we held that plaintiffs had not alleged a judicially cognizable injury. "Assertion of a right to a particular kind of Government

---

19. The "fairly traceable" and "redressability" components of the constitutional standing inquiry were initially articulated by this Court as "two facets of a single causation requirement." To the extent there is a difference, it is that the former examines the causal connection between the assertedly unlawful conduct and the alleged injury, whereas the latter examines the causal connection between the alleged injury and the judicial relief requested. Cases such as this, in which the relief requested goes well beyond the violation of law alleged, illustrate why it is important to keep the inquiries separate if the "redressability" component is to focus on the requested relief. Even if the relief respondents request might have a substantial effect on the desegregation of public schools, whatever deficiencies exist in the opportunities for desegregated education for respondents' children might not be traceable to IRS violations of law—grants of tax exemptions to racially discriminatory schools in respondents' communities.

conduct, which the Government has violated by acting differently, cannot alone satisfy the requirements of Art. III without draining those requirements of meaning." Respondents here have no standing to complain simply that their Government is violating the law.

Neither do they have standing to litigate their claims based on the stigmatizing injury often caused by racial discrimination. There can be no doubt that this sort of noneconomic injury is one of the most serious consequences of discriminatory government action and is sufficient in some circumstances to support standing. Our cases make clear, however, that such injury accords a basis for standing only to "those persons who are personally denied equal treatment" by the challenged discriminatory conduct. [Respondents] do not allege a stigmatic injury suffered as a direct result of having personally been denied equal treatment.

The consequences of recognizing respondents' standing on the basis of their first claim of injury illustrate why our cases plainly hold that such injury is not judicially cognizable. If the abstract stigmatic injury were cognizable, standing would extend nationwide to all members of the particular racial groups against which the Government was alleged to be discriminating by its grant of a tax exemption to a racially discriminatory school, regardless of the location of that school. All such persons could claim the same sort of abstract stigmatic injury respondents assert in their first claim of injury. A black person in Hawaii could challenge the grant of a tax exemption to a racially discriminatory school in Maine. Recognition of standing in such circumstances would transform the federal courts into no more than a vehicle for the vindication of the value interests of concerned bystanders. Constitutional limits on the role of the federal courts preclude such a transformation.

2

It is in their complaint's second claim of injury that respondents allege harm to a concrete, personal interest that can support standing in some circumstances. The injury they identify—their children's diminished ability to receive an education in a racially integrated school—is, beyond any doubt, not only judicially cognizable [but] one of the most serious injuries recognized in our legal system. Despite the constitutional importance of curing the injury alleged by respondents, however, the federal judiciary may not redress it unless standing requirements are met. In this case, respondents' second claim of injury cannot support standing because the injury alleged is not fairly traceable to the Government conduct respondents challenge as unlawful.[22]

---

22. Respondents' stigmatic injury, though not sufficient for standing in the abstract form in which their complaint asserts it, is judicially cognizable to the extent that respondents are personally subject to discriminatory treatment. The stigmatic injury thus requires identification of some concrete interest with respect to which respondents are personally subject to discriminatory treatment. That interest must independently satisfy the causation requirement of standing doctrine. In this litigation, respondents identify only one interest that they allege is being discriminatorily impaired—their interest in desegregated public school education. Respondents' asserted stigmatic injury, therefore, is sufficient to support their standing in this litigation only if their school-desegregation injury independently meets the causation requirement of standing doctrine.

The illegal conduct challenged by respondents is the IRS's grant of tax exemptions to some racially discriminatory schools. The line of causation between that conduct and desegregation of respondents' schools is attenuated at best. From the perspective of the IRS, the injury to respondents is highly indirect and "results from the independent action of some third party not before the court." As the Court pointed out in *Warth v. Seldin*, "the indirectness of the injury . . . may make it substantially more difficult to meet the minimum requirement of Art. III. . . ."

The diminished ability of respondents' children to receive a desegregated education would be fairly traceable to unlawful IRS grants of tax exemptions only if there were enough racially discriminatory private schools receiving tax exemptions in respondents' communities for withdrawal of those exemptions to make an appreciable difference in public school integration. Respondents have made no such allegation. It is, first, uncertain how many racially discriminatory private schools are in fact receiving tax exemptions. Moreover, it is entirely speculative [whether] withdrawal of a tax exemption from any particular school would lead the school to change its policies. It is just as speculative whether any given parent of a child attending such a private school would decide to transfer the child to public school as a result of any changes in educational or financial policy made by the private school once it was threatened with loss of tax-exempt status. It is also pure speculation whether, in a particular community, a large enough number of the numerous relevant school officials and parents would reach decisions that collectively would have a significant impact on the racial composition of the public schools.

The links in the chain of causation between the challenged Government conduct and the asserted injury are far too weak for the chain as a whole to sustain respondents' standing. . . .

The idea of separation of powers that underlies standing doctrine explains why our cases preclude the conclusion that respondents' alleged injury "fairly can be traced to the challenged action" of the IRS. That conclusion would pave the way generally for suits challenging, not specifically identifiable Government violations of law, but the particular programs agencies establish to carry out their legal obligations. Such suits, even when premised on allegations of several instances of violations of law, are rarely if ever appropriate for federal-court adjudication.

> Carried to its logical end, [respondents'] approach would have the federal courts as virtually continuing monitors of the wisdom and soundness of Executive action; such a role is appropriate for the Congress acting through its committees and the "power of the purse;" it is not the role of the judiciary, absent actual present or immediately threatened injury resulting from unlawful governmental action. *Laird v. Tatum*, 408 U.S. 1 (1972).

. . . Animating this Court's holdings was the principle that "[a] federal court . . . is not the proper forum to press" general complaints about the way in which government goes about its business.

Case-or-controversy considerations [obviously] shade into those determining whether the complaint states a sound basis for equitable relief. The latter set of considerations should therefore inform our judgment about whether respondents have standing. Most relevant to this case is the principle articulated in *Rizzo v. Goode*, 423 U.S. 362 (1976):

> When a plaintiff seeks to enjoin the activity of a government agency, even within a unitary court system, his case must contend with the well-established rule that the Government has traditionally been granted the widest latitude in the dispatch of its own internal affairs.

When transported into the Art. III context, that principle, grounded as it is in the idea of separation of powers, counsels against recognizing standing in a case brought, not to enforce specific legal obligations whose violation works a direct harm, but to seek a restructuring of the apparatus established by the Executive Branch to fulfill its legal duties. The Constitution, after all, assigns to the Executive Branch, and not to the Judicial Branch, the duty to "take Care that the Laws be faithfully executed." U.S. Const. art. II, § 3. We could not recognize respondents' standing in this case without running afoul of that structural principle.

III

"The necessity that the plaintiff who seeks to invoke judicial power stand to profit in some personal interest remains an Art. III requirement." Respondents have not met this fundamental requirement. The judgment of the Court of Appeals is accordingly reversed, and the injunction issued by that court is vacated.

Justice Marshall took no part in the decision of [this case].

Justice Brennan, dissenting. . . .

One could hardly dispute the proposition that Art. III of the Constitution, by limiting the judicial power to "Cases" or "Controversies," embodies the notion that each branch of our National Government must confine its actions to those that are consistent with our scheme of separated powers. But simply stating that unremarkable truism provides little, if any, illumination of the standing inquiry that must be undertaken by a federal court faced with a particular action filed by particular plaintiffs. "The question whether a particular person is a proper party to maintain the action does not, by its own force, raise separation of powers problems related to improper judicial interference in areas committed to other branches of the Federal Government." *Flast v. Cohen*, 392 U.S. 83 (1968).

The Court's attempt to obscure the standing question must be seen, therefore, as no more than a cover for its failure to recognize the nature of the specific claims raised by the respondents in these cases. By relying on generalities concerning our tripartite system of government, the Court is able to conclude that the respondents lack standing to maintain this action without acknowledging the precise nature of the injuries they have alleged. In so doing, the Court displays a startling insensitivity to the historical role played by the federal courts in eradicating race discrimination from our Nation's schools. Because I cannot join in such misguided decision making, I dissent.

I

The respondents, suing individually and on behalf of their minor children, are parents of black children attending public schools in various school districts across the Nation. Each of these school districts, the respondents allege, was once segregated and is now in the process of desegregating pursuant to court order, federal regulations or guidelines, state law, or voluntary agreement. Moreover, each contains one or more private schools that discriminate against black schoolchildren and that operate with the assistance of tax exemptions unlawfully granted to them by the Internal Revenue Service.

To eliminate this federal financial assistance for discriminating schools, the respondents seek a declaratory judgment that current IRS practices are inadequate both in identifying racially discriminatory schools and in denying requested tax exemptions or revoking existing exemptions for any schools so identified. In particular, they allege that existing IRS guidelines permit schools to receive tax exemptions simply by adopting and certifying—but not implementing—a policy of nondiscrimination. Pursuant to these ineffective guidelines, many private schools that discriminate on the basis of race continue to benefit illegally from their tax-exempt status and the resulting charitable deductions granted to taxpayers who contribute to such schools. The respondents therefore seek a permanent injunction requiring the IRS to deny tax exemptions to any private schools [satisfying the criteria set forth in the respondents' complaint, which is reproduced in relevant part toward the end of Part I of the Court's opinion].

II

Persons seeking judicial relief from an Art. III court must have standing to maintain their cause of action. At a minimum, the standing requirement is not met unless the plaintiff has "such a personal stake in the outcome of the controversy as to assure that concrete adverseness which sharpens the presentation of issues upon which the court so largely depends...." Under the Court's cases, this "personal stake" requirement is satisfied if the person seeking redress has suffered, or is threatened with, some "distinct and palpable injury," *Warth v. Seldin*, and if there is some causal connection between the asserted injury and the conduct being challenged. *Valley Forge.*

In these cases, the respondents have alleged at least one type of injury that satisfies the constitutional requirement of "distinct and palpable injury." In particular, they claim that the IRS's grant of tax-exempt status to racially discriminatory private schools directly injures their children's opportunity and ability to receive a desegregated education. As the complaint specifically alleges, the IRS action being challenged "fosters and encourages the organization, operation and expansion of institutions providing racially segregated educational opportunities for white children avoiding attendance in desegregating public school districts and thereby interferes with the efforts of federal courts, HEW and local school authorities to desegregate public school districts which have been operating racially dual school systems." The Court acknowledges that this alleged injury is sufficient to satisfy constitutional standards. It does so only grudgingly, however, without emphasizing the significance of the harm alleged. Nonetheless, we have consistently recognized throughout the last 30 years that the deprivation of a child's right to receive an education in a desegregated school is a harm of special significance; surely, it satisfies any constitutional requirement of injury in fact. . . . "The right of a student not to be segregated on racial grounds in schools . . . is indeed so fundamental and pervasive that it is embraced in the concept of due process of law."

In the analogous context of housing discrimination, the Court has similarly recognized that the denial of an opportunity to live in an integrated community is injury sufficient to satisfy the constitutional requirements of standing. In particular, we have recognized that injury is properly alleged when plaintiffs claim a deprivation "of the social and professional benefits of living in an integrated society." Noting "the importance of the 'benefits obtained from interracial associations,'" as well as the oft-stated principle "that noneconomic injuries may suffice to provide standing," we have consistently concluded that such an injury is "sufficient to satisfy the constitutional standing requirement of actual or threatened harm."

There is, of course, no rational basis on which to treat children who seek to be educated in desegregated school districts any differently for purposes of standing than residents who seek to live in integrated housing communities. . . . It is therefore beyond peradventure that the denial of the benefits of an integrated education alleged by the respondents in these cases constitutes "distinct and palpable injury." . . .

Viewed in light of the injuries they claim, the respondents have alleged a direct causal relationship between the Government action they challenge and the injury they suffer: their inability to receive an education in a racially integrated school is directly and adversely affected by the tax-exempt status granted by the IRS to racially discriminatory schools in their respective school districts. Common sense alone would recognize that the elimination of tax-exempt status for racially discriminatory private schools would serve to lessen the impact that those institutions have in defeating efforts to desegregate the public schools.

The Court admits that "[t]he diminished ability of respondents' children to receive a desegregated education would be fairly traceable to unlawful IRS grants of tax exemptions . . . if there were enough racially discriminatory private schools receiving tax exemptions in respondents' communities for withdrawal of those exemptions to make an appreciable difference in public school integration," but concludes that "[r]espondents have made no such allegation." With all due respect, the Court has either misread the complaint or is improperly requiring the respondents to prove their case on the merits in order to defeat a motion to dismiss. . . .

III

More than one commentator has noted that the causation component of the Court's standing inquiry is no more than a poor disguise for the Court's view of the merits of the underlying claims. The Court today does nothing to avoid that criticism. What is most disturbing about today's decision, therefore, is not the standing analysis applied, but the indifference evidenced by the Court to the detrimental effects that racially segregated schools, supported by tax-exempt status from the Federal Government, have on the respondents' attempt to obtain an education in a racially integrated school system. I cannot join such indifference, and would give the respondents a chance to prove their case on the merits.

JUSTICE STEVENS, with whom JUSTICE BLACKMUN joins, dissenting.

Three propositions are clear to me: (1) respondents have adequately alleged "injury in fact"; (2) their injury is fairly traceable to the conduct that they claim to be unlawful; and (3) the "separation of powers" principle does not create a jurisdictional obstacle to the consideration of the merits of their claim.

Respondents, the parents of black school-children, have alleged that their children are unable to attend fully desegregated schools because large numbers of white children in the areas in which respondents reside attend private schools which do not admit minority children. The Court, Justice Brennan, and I all agree that this is an adequate allegation of "injury in fact." . . .

In final analysis, the wrong respondents allege that the Government has committed is to subsidize the exodus of white children from schools that would otherwise be racially integrated. The critical question in these cases, therefore, is whether respondents have alleged that the Government has created that kind of subsidy.

In answering that question, we must of course assume that respondents can prove what they have alleged. Furthermore, at this stage of the litigation we must put to one side all questions about the appropriateness of a nationwide class action. The controlling issue is whether the causal connection between the injury and the wrong has been adequately alleged.

An organization that qualifies for preferential treatment under § 501(c)(3) of the Internal Revenue Code, because it is "operated exclusively for . . . charitable . . . purposes," is exempt from paying federal income taxes, and under § 170 of the Code, persons who contribute to such organizations may deduct the amount of their contributions when calculating their taxable income. . . .

The purpose of this scheme, like the purpose of any subsidy, is to promote the activity subsidized; the statutes "seek to achieve the same basic goal of encouraging the development of certain organizations through the grant of tax benefits." If the granting of preferential tax treatment would "encourage" private segregated schools to conduct their "charitable" activities, it must follow that the withdrawal of the treatment would "discourage" them, and hence promote the process of desegregation.

We have held that when a subsidy makes a given activity more or less expensive, injury can be fairly traced to the subsidy for purposes of standing analysis because of the resulting increase or decrease in the ability to engage in the activity. Indeed, we have employed exactly this causation analysis in the same context at issue here — subsidies given private schools that practice racial discrimination. . . .

This causation analysis is nothing more than a restatement of elementary economics: when something becomes more expensive, less of it will be purchased.

Sections 170 and 501(c)(3) are premised on that recognition. If racially discriminatory private schools lose the "cash grants" that flow from the operation of the statutes, the education they provide will become more expensive and hence less of their services will be purchased. Conversely, maintenance of these tax benefits makes an education in segregated private schools relatively more attractive, by decreasing its cost. Accordingly, without tax-exempt status, private schools will either not be competitive in terms of cost, or have to change their admissions policies, hence reducing their competitiveness for parents seeking "a racially segregated alternative" to public schools, which is what respondents have alleged many white parents in desegregating school districts seek. In either event the process of desegregation will be advanced— [the] withdrawal of the subsidy for segregated schools means the incentive structure facing white parents who seek such schools for their children will be altered. Thus, the laws of economics, not to mention the laws of Congress embodied in §§ 170 and 501(c)(3), compel the conclusion that the injury respondents have alleged—the increased segregation of their children's schools because of the ready availability of private schools that admit whites only—will be redressed if these schools' operations are inhibited through the denial of preferential tax treatment.

III

Considerations of tax policy, economics, and pure logic all confirm the conclusion that respondents' injury in fact is fairly traceable to the Government's allegedly wrongful conduct. The Court therefore is forced to introduce the concept of "separation of powers" into its analysis. The Court writes that the separation of powers "explains why our cases preclude the conclusion" that respondents' injury is fairly traceable to the conduct they challenge.

The Court could mean one of three things by its invocation of the separation of powers. First, it could simply be expressing the idea that if the plaintiff lacks Art. III standing to bring a lawsuit, then there is no "case or controversy" within the meaning of Art. III and hence the matter is not within the area of responsibility assigned to the Judiciary by the Constitution. . . . While there can be no quarrel with this proposition, in itself it provides no guidance for determining if the injury respondents have alleged is fairly traceable to the conduct they have challenged.

Second, the Court could be saying that it will require a more direct causal connection when it is troubled by the separation of powers implications of the case before it. That approach confuses the standing doctrine with the justiciability of the issues that respondents seek to raise. The purpose of the standing inquiry is to measure the plaintiff's stake in the outcome, not whether a court has the authority to provide it with the outcome it seeks. . . . Thus, the "'fundamental aspect of standing' is that it focuses primarily on the party seeking to get his complaint before the federal court rather than 'on the issues he wishes to have adjudicated.'" The strength of the plaintiff's interest in the outcome has nothing to do with whether the relief it seeks would intrude upon the prerogatives of other branches of government; the possibility that the relief might be inappropriate does not lessen the plaintiff's stake in obtaining that relief.

If a plaintiff presents a nonjusticiable issue, or seeks relief that a court may not award, then its complaint should be dismissed for those reasons, and not because the plaintiff lacks a stake in obtaining that relief and hence has no standing. Imposing an undefined but clearly more rigorous standard for redressability for reasons unrelated to the causal nexus between the injury and the challenged conduct can only encourage undisciplined, ad hoc litigation, a result that would be avoided if the Court straightforwardly considered the justiciability of the issues respondents seek to raise, rather than using those issues to obfuscate standing analysis.

Third, the Court could be saying that it will not treat as legally cognizable injuries that stem from an administrative decision concerning how enforcement resources will be allocated. This surely is an important point. Respondents do seek to restructure the IRS's mechanisms for enforcing the legal requirement that discriminatory institutions not receive tax-exempt status. Such restructuring would dramatically affect the way in which the IRS exercises its prosecutorial discretion. The Executive requires latitude to decide how best to enforce the law, and in general the Court may well be correct that the exercise of that discretion, especially in the tax context, is unchallengeable.

However, as the Court also recognizes, this principle does not apply when suit is brought "to enforce specific legal obligations whose violation works a direct harm. . . ." Here, respondents contend that the IRS is violating a specific constitutional limitation on its enforcement discretion. There is a solid basis for that contention. . . . [As we wrote in a prior case, the] constitutional obligation of the State "requires it to steer clear, not only of operating the old dual system of racially segregated schools, but also of giving significant aid to institutions that practice racial or other invidious discrimination."

Respondents contend that these [principles] limit the enforcement discretion enjoyed by the IRS. They establish, respondents argue, that the IRS cannot provide "cash grants" to discriminatory schools through preferential tax treatment without running afoul of a constitutional duty to refrain from "giving significant aid" to these institutions. Similarly, respondents claim that the Internal Revenue Code itself constrains enforcement discretion. It has been clear since *Marbury v. Madison*, 1 Cranch 137 (1803), that "[i]t is emphatically the province and duty of the judicial department to say what the law is." Deciding whether the Treasury has violated a specific legal limitation on its enforcement discretion does not intrude upon the prerogatives of the Executive, for in so deciding we are merely saying "what the law is." Surely the question whether the Constitution or the Code limits enforcement discretion is one within the Judiciary's competence, and I do not believe that the question whether the [law] imposes such an obligation upon the IRS is so insubstantial that respondents' attempt to raise it should be defeated for lack of subject-matter jurisdiction on the ground that it infringes the Executive's prerogatives.

In short, I would deal with the question of the legal limitations on the IRS's enforcement discretion on its merits, rather than by making the untenable assumption that the granting of preferential tax treatment to segregated schools does not make those schools more attractive to white students and hence does not inhibit the process of desegregation. I respectfully dissent.

Note: Standing and Allen

1. "Standing" has not always been part of the lexicon of federal jurisdiction. As Professor William A. Fletcher has written, "current standing law is a relatively recent creation." He explains:

> In the late nineteenth and early twentieth centuries, a plaintiff's right to bring suit was determined by reference to a particular common law, statutory, or constitutional right, or sometimes to a mixture of statutory or constitutional prohibitions and common law remedial principles. Friendly suits were prohibited, and on one occasion general pleading requirements were read in conjunction with a jurisdictional statute to deny an appeal to the United States Supreme Court on the ground that appellant had alleged insufficient personal interest. But no general doctrine of standing existed. Nor, indeed, was the term "standing" used as the doctrinal heading under which a person's right to sue was determined. . . .

> The creation of a separately articulated and self-conscious law of standing can be traced to two overlapping developments in the last half-century: the growth of the administrative state and an increase in litigation to articulate and enforce public, primarily constitutional, values. As private entities increasingly came to be controlled by statutory and regulatory duties, as government increasingly came to be controlled by statutory and constitutional commands, and as individuals sought to control the greatly augmented power of the government through the judicial process, many kinds of plaintiffs and would-be plaintiffs sought the articulation and enforcement of new and existing rights in the federal courts. Beginning in earnest in the 1930's, the Supreme Court began to develop a new doctrine, or perhaps more accurately, a new set of loosely linked protodoctrines, to replace the relatively stable formulations that had previously been used to decide who could sue to enforce various rights.

William A. Fletcher, *The Structure of Standing*, 98 YALE L.J. 221, 224–25 (1988).* Whatever its pedigree, the doctrine is firmly established, and *Allen v. Wright* is one of the leading decisions articulating and applying it.

2. As described in *Allen*, standing involves several components. The plaintiff must allege "personal injury fairly traceable to the defendant's allegedly unlawful conduct and likely to be redressed by the requested relief." Put simply, plaintiffs must demonstrate injury, causation, and redressability. Which aspects of standing were the *Allen* plaintiffs unable to meet? Could their complaint have been redrafted to satisfy those requirements?

---

* Reprinted by permission of the Yale Law Journal Company and William S. Hein Company from the Yale Law Journal, Volume 98, pages 221–91.

3. Why didn't the fact that the plaintiffs sought class action certification address some of the Court's concerns? Note that the Court believes that the plaintiffs sufficiently alleged injury "to the extent that respondents are personally subject to the discriminatory treatment." Given the scope of the class that plaintiffs sought to certify, surely some of the class members would have been within this description. In *Simon v. Eastern Kentucky Welfare Rights Organization*, 426 U.S. 26, 40 n.20 (1976), the Court made it clear that class action status is irrelevant for purposes of standing analysis: "Even named plaintiffs who represent a class must allege and show that they personally have been injured, not that injury has been suffered by other, unidentified members of the class to which they belong and which they purport to represent." What policies behind standing would such a requirement reinforce?

4. The connection between standing analysis and separation of powers was central to the majority opinion in *Allen*. That connection has not always been so clear. Compare *Flast v. Cohen*, 392 U.S. 83, 94–95 (1968). In that case, federal taxpayers challenged the use of federal funds to provide books and materials for parochial schools. The government argued that, in challenging the use to which tax funds were put, the plaintiffs were intruding into decisions properly vested in other branches of government, and that standing to present such an argument should be denied on separation-of-powers grounds. The Court disagreed:

> The question whether a particular person is a proper party to maintain the action does not, by its own force, raise separation of powers problems related to improper judicial interference in areas committed to other branches of the Federal Government. Such problems arise, if at all, only from the substantive issues the individual seeks to have adjudicated. Thus, in terms of Article III limitations on federal court jurisdiction, the question of standing is related only to whether the dispute sought to be adjudicated will be presented in an adversary context and in a form historically viewed as capable of judicial resolution. It is for that reason that the emphasis in standing problems is on whether the party invoking federal court jurisdiction has "a personal stake in the outcome of the controversy," and whether the dispute touches upon "the legal relations of parties having adverse legal interests."

5. The *Allen* Court's discussion of causation bears close analysis, particularly in the relationship between the asserted injury and separation-of-powers concerns. If the plaintiffs were correct in their assertion that the IRS's failure to enforce its policy effectively led to racially stigmatic injury, then "that conclusion would pave the way generally for suits challenging, not specifically identifiable Government violations of law, but the particular programs agencies establish to carry out their legal obligations. Such suits, even when premised on allegations of several instances of violations of law, are rarely if ever appropriate for federal-court adjudication."

What concerns are implicated by this statement? Does the Court mean to say that recognition of injury in a constitutional sense hinges on a preliminary determination that the scope of relief requested does not intrude too deeply into executive responsibilities? Or does it mean instead that prudential concerns about intrusion into decisions committed to the executive should counsel denying a remedy?

6. Justice Stevens makes a straightforward economic argument that tax breaks create a subsidy for private schools engaging in prohibited conduct by making "an education in segregated private schools relatively more attractive, by decreasing its cost." As a result, Justice Stevens would conclude that "considerations of tax policy, economics and pure logic" supported the plaintiffs' standing in *Allen*. Is Justice Stevens's argument persuasive? Under Justice Stevens's logic, would the size of the tax exemption matter in the standing analysis?

7. Justice O'Connor notes in passing that the causation and redressability components of the standing inquiry were originally "two facets of a single causation requirement." She explains, however, that when the relief requested "goes well beyond the violation of the law alleged," it is important to keep the two elements separate. Why? Should the scope of relief requested by the plaintiffs matter for purposes of the standing inquiry? Why or why not? As a matter of litigation strategy, would plaintiffs be wise to limit the scope of their requested relief? What would be the downside to this tactic?

Note: Taxpayer Standing

1. *Allen v. Wright* unequivocally rejects the proposition that *citizens* have standing to sue based solely on an interest in preventing the government from violating the law. The Court refers to "the rule barring adjudication of generalized grievances more appropriately addressed in the representative branches." Could the plaintiffs in *Allen v. Wright* have pursued their claims by invoking their interest as federal *taxpayers* in not supporting racially-discriminatory tax exemptions? For nearly a century, the Supreme Court has tackled similar cases of so-called taxpayer standing, wherein citizens challenge the constitutionality of federal taxing statutes, based purely on the theory that if the statute is declared unconstitutional, citizens' tax burden will diminish. The Court has permitted taxpayer standing under only the most limited circumstances.

2. In *Flast v. Cohen*, 392 U.S. 83 (1968), a taxpayer objected on Establishment Clause grounds to the use of federal funds to provide materials to religious schools. The Court found that Article III did not present "an absolute bar" to federal taxpayers "challenging allegedly unconstitutional federal taxing and spending programs." However, the Court noted, a federal taxpayer must still "have the personal stake and interest that impart the necessary concrete adverseness to such litigation so that standing can be conferred on the taxpayer qua taxpayer consistent with the constitutional limitations of Article III." That personal stake can be determined by examining the "logical nexus" between "the status asserted by the litigant and the claim he presents. Thus, our point of reference in this case is the standing of individuals who assert only the status of federal taxpayers and who challenge the constitutionality of a federal spending program." The Court explained:

> The nexus demanded of federal taxpayers has two aspects to it. First, the taxpayer must establish a logical link between that status and the type of legislative enactment attacked. Thus, a taxpayer will be a proper party to

allege the unconstitutionality only of exercises of congressional power under the taxing and spending clause of Art. I, § 8, of the Constitution. It will not be sufficient to allege an incidental expenditure of tax funds in the administration of an essentially regulatory statute. . . . Secondly, the taxpayer must establish a nexus between that status and the precise nature of the constitutional infringement alleged. Under this requirement, the taxpayer must show that the challenged enactment exceeds specific constitutional limitations imposed upon the exercise of the congressional taxing and spending power and not simply that the enactment is generally beyond the powers delegated to Congress by Art. I, § 8. When both nexuses are established, the litigant will have shown a taxpayer's stake in the outcome of the controversy and will be a proper and appropriate party to invoke a federal court's jurisdiction.

3. The Court addressed the continued viability of *Flast* in *Hein v. Freedom from Religion Found., Inc.*, 551 U.S. 587 (2007). Justice Alito, writing for a plurality, stated that taxpayers challenging the constitutionality of federal expenditures on Establishment Clause grounds have standing only when the specific appropriation is authorized by an express congressional grant, rather than generalized appropriations to the Executive Branch.

A majority of the Court, however, was not persuaded by the distinction between specific appropriations and generalized expenditures. Justice Scalia wrote separately to argue that "*Flast* is *indistinguishable* from [*Hein*] for purposes of Article III. Whether the challenged government expenditure is expressly allocated by a specific congressional enactment *has absolutely no relevance* to the Article III criteria of injury in fact, traceability, and redressability." Justice Souter, dissenting in *Hein*, saw "no basis for the distinction in either logic or precedent." Did the *Hein* plurality draw a principled distinction? Is the manner in which Congress appropriates money to the Executive Branch relevant to any of the three prongs of the standing inquiry?

4. The Supreme Court further narrowed *Flast* in *Arizona Christian School Tuition Organization v. Winn*, 563 U.S. 125 (2011). The Court held that taxpayer standing is permitted only when the government "extracts and spends" money in violation of the Establishment Clause, not when it provides tax credits that encourage spending in favor of religion. The Court reasoned:

Even assuming the tax credit [to individuals who contribute to schools, some of which are religious,] has an adverse effect on Arizona's annual budget, problems would remain. To conclude there is a particular injury in fact would require speculation that Arizona lawmakers react to revenue shortfalls by increasing [plaintiffs'] tax liability. A finding of causation would depend on the additional determination that any tax increase would be traceable to the tax credits, as distinct from other governmental expenditures or other tax benefits. [Plaintiffs] have not established that an injunction against application of the tax credit would prompt Arizona legislators to "pass along the supposed increased revenue in the form of tax reductions."

Justice Kagan's dissent argued that there is little left of *Flast* now that governments have a "roadmap" for insulating the "financing of religious activity from legal challenge." Is Justice Kagan right?

5. What is the objection to taxpayer standing? In his concurring opinion in *United States v. Richardson*, 418 U.S. 166 (1974), Justice Powell argued that taxpayer and citizen standing are essentially indistinguishable. The recognition of either "would significantly alter the allocation of power at the national level away from a democratic form of government," presumably by allowing losers in the political process free access to the courts to second-guess the choices of the executive and Congress. The imperatives of the judicial role require the courts to determine the legality of the actions of another branch in order to redress an injury. However, to do so when the injury is attenuated, as Justice Powell believed it to be when a litigant sues to enjoin a government action solely on the basis of the litigant's share of the tax burden, would involve the "life-tenured branch and the representative branches of government" in "repeated and essentially head-on confrontations."

6. All of the cases discussed thus far involved federal taxpayers challenging federal expenditures. What about state and municipal taxpayers? In *DaimlerChrysler Corp. v. Cuno*, 547 U.S. 332 (2006), the Court considered whether Ohio citizens had standing as taxpayers to challenge the constitutionality of property tax and franchise tax credits that the city of Toledo and the state of Ohio granted to the DaimlerChrysler Corporation. The plaintiffs filed suit in state court based on their status as state and municipal taxpayers against various government officials, alleging that the tax credits were repugnant to the Constitution's Commerce Clause.

DaimlerChrysler removed the action to federal court, but the taxpayer citizens filed a motion to remand the case to state court in part because of their doubts about meeting Article III standing requirements. The District Court declined to remand the case, concluding that, "at a bare minimum, the Plaintiffs who are taxpayers have standing to object to the property tax exemption and franchise tax credit statutes under the 'municipal taxpayer standing' rule articulated in *Massachusetts v. Mellon*, 262 U.S. 447 (1923)." The District Court then held that neither tax benefit violated the Commerce Clause. Without addressing standing, the United States Court of Appeals for the Sixth Circuit agreed with the District Court with respect to the municipal property tax exemption, but held that the state franchise tax credit violated the Commerce Clause.

DaimlerChrysler appealed the Sixth Circuit's decision to the Supreme Court. The Court addressed the issue the Sixth Circuit did not: whether the Ohio taxpayers possessed Article III standing to challenge the tax credits.

Without addressing the constitutionality of the municipal tax credit, the Supreme Court unanimously held that the Ohio taxpayers lacked standing to bring their Commerce Clause challenge. Emphasizing that taxpayers' injuries are not "concrete and particularized," and instead are akin to generalized grievances, the Court reasoned that the injury and redressability components of the standing inquiry were too speculative in the plaintiffs' case to grant them Article III standing. As the Court stated: "Establishing injury requires speculating that elected officials will increase a taxpayer-plaintiff's tax bill to make up a deficit; establishing redressability requires speculating that abolishing the challenged credit will redound to the benefit of the taxpayer because legislators will pass along the supposed increased revenue in the form of tax reductions. Neither sort of speculation suffices to support standing."

Responding to the plaintiffs' argument that state taxes were different because of the "disproportionate burden" imposed upon Ohio citizens, the Court noted that the same rationale for rejecting federal taxpayer standing "applies with undiminished force to state taxpayers," because state policymakers, like their federal counterparts, "retain broad discretion to make 'policy decisions' concerning state spending 'in different ways depending on their perceptions of wise state fiscal policy.'"

The Court also rejected the plaintiffs' *Flast* argument, noting that "whatever rights plaintiffs have under the Commerce Clause, they are fundamentally unlike the right not to 'contribute three pence ... for the support of any one religious establishment.'" Therefore, the analogy the plaintiffs attempted to draw between the Commerce Clause and the Establishment Clause was inapposite, according to the Court.

The Court appears to have firmly closed the door on cases of so-called state taxpayer standing. *Cuno* does, however, leave open the possibility of standing based on municipal taxpayer status. The Court failed to address the question of municipal taxpayer status because, in its view, the *Cuno* plaintiffs did not properly identify any "municipal action contributing to any claimed injury."

7. As *Cuno* suggests, the Court has been more generous in conferring standing based on municipal taxpayer status. The opinion in *Massachusetts v. Mellon* suggests why:

> The interest of a taxpayer of a municipality in the application of its moneys is direct and immediate and the remedy by injunction to prevent their misuse is not appropriate. It is upheld by a large number of state cases and is the rule of this court.... The reasons which support the extension of the equitable remedy to a single taxpayer in such cases are based upon the peculiar relation of the corporate taxpayer to the corporation, which is not without some resemblance to that subsisting between stockholder and private corporation.

Is the Court's distinction between municipal and state taxpayers convincing?

8. The Court's opinion in *Cuno* continued the pattern of limiting the instances in which taxpayer standing is permitted. The Court, however, did not modify the two-pronged nexus test from *Flast*.

[2] Standing Under Congressional Statutes

Allen v. Wright grounds standing doctrine in limitations found in Article III, coupled with concerns about separation of powers. As the following cases suggest, however, Congress has had a role in defining standing as well, typically by creating new statutory rights that, when violated, lead to injury. How is Congress's power to expand standing by statute limited by the Constitution?

Lujan v. Defenders of Wildlife

Supreme Court of the United States, 1992.

504 U.S. 555.

Justice Scalia delivered the opinion of the Court with respect to Parts I, II, III-A, and IV, and an opinion with respect to Part III-B, in which The Chief Justice, Justice White, and Justice Thomas join.

This case involves a challenge to a rule promulgated by the Secretary of the Interior interpreting §7 of the Endangered Species Act of 1973 (ESA), in such fashion as to render it applicable only to actions within the United States or on the high seas. The preliminary issue, and the only one we reach, is whether respondents here, plaintiffs below, have standing to seek judicial review of the rule.

I

The ESA seeks to protect species of animals against threats to their continuing existence caused by man. The ESA instructs the Secretary of the Interior to promulgate by regulation a list of those species which are either endangered or threatened under enumerated criteria, and to define the critical habitat of these species. Section 7(a)(2) of the Act then provides, in pertinent part:

> Each Federal agency shall, in consultation with and with the assistance of the Secretary [of the Interior], insure that any action authorized, funded, or carried out by such agency . . . is not likely to jeopardize the continued existence of any endangered species or threatened species or result in the destruction or adverse modification of habitat of such species which is determined by the Secretary, after consultation as appropriate with affected States, to be critical.

[In 1986, the Secretary of the Interior issued a regulation restricting the application of §7(a)(2) to actions taken in the United States or on the high seas.] Shortly thereafter, respondents, organizations dedicated to wildlife conservation and other environmental causes, filed this action against the Secretary of the Interior, seeking a declaratory judgment that the new regulation is in error as to the geographic scope of §7(a)(2) and an injunction requiring the Secretary to promulgate a new regulation restoring the initial interpretation. [The Secretary moved for summary judgment on the question whether the respondents had] standing, and respondents moved for summary judgment on the merits. The District Court denied the Secretary's motion [and] ordered the Secretary to publish a revised regulation. The Eighth Circuit affirmed.

II

. . . Over the years, our cases have established that the irreducible constitutional minimum of standing contains three elements. First, the plaintiff must have suffered an "injury in fact"—an invasion of a legally protected interest which is (a) concrete and particularized,[1] and (b) "actual or imminent, not 'conjectural' or 'hypothetical.'"

---

1. By particularized, we mean that the injury must affect the plaintiff in a personal and individual way.

Second, there must be a causal connection between the injury and the conduct complained of—the injury has to be "fairly . . . trace[able] to the challenged action of the defendant, and not . . . th[e] result [of] the independent action of some third party not before the court." Third, it must be "likely," as opposed to merely "speculative," that the injury will be "redressed by a favorable decision."

The party invoking federal jurisdiction bears the burden of establishing these elements. Since they are not mere pleading requirements but rather an indispensable part of the plaintiff's case, each element must be supported in the same way as any other matter on which the plaintiff bears the burden of proof, i.e., with the manner and degree of evidence required at the successive stages of the litigation. At the pleading stage, general factual allegations of injury resulting from the defendant's conduct may suffice, for on a motion to dismiss we "presum[e] that general allegations embrace those specific facts that are necessary to support the claim." In response to a summary judgment motion, however, the plaintiff can no longer rest on such "mere allegations," but must "set forth" by affidavit or other evidence "specific facts," Fed. Rule Civ. Proc. 56(e), which for purposes of the summary judgment motion will be taken to be true. And at the final stage, those facts (if controverted) must be "supported adequately by the evidence adduced at trial."

When the suit is one challenging the legality of government action or inaction, the nature and extent of facts that must be averred (at the summary judgment stage) or proved (at the trial stage) in order to establish standing depends considerably upon whether the plaintiff is himself an object of the action (or forgone action) at issue. If he is, there is ordinarily little question that the action or inaction has caused him injury, and that a judgment preventing or requiring the action will redress it. When, however, as in this case, a plaintiff's asserted injury arises from the government's allegedly unlawful regulation (or lack of regulation) of *someone else*, much more is needed. In that circumstance, causation and redressability ordinarily hinge on the response of the regulated (or regulable) third party to the government action or inaction—and perhaps on the response of others as well. The existence of one or more of the essential elements of standing "depends on the unfettered choices made by independent actors not before the courts and whose exercise of broad and legitimate discretion the courts cannot presume either to control or to predict;" and it becomes the burden of the plaintiff to adduce facts showing that those choices have been or will be made in such manner as to produce causation and permit redressability of injury. Thus, when the plaintiff is not himself the object of the government action or inaction he challenges, standing is not precluded, but it is ordinarily "substantially more difficult" to establish.

III

We think the Court of Appeals failed to apply the foregoing principles in denying the Secretary's motion for summary judgment. Respondents had not made the requisite demonstration of (at least) injury and redressability.

A

Respondents' claim to injury is that the lack of consultation with respect to certain funded activities abroad "increas[es] the rate of extinction of endangered and threatened species." Of course, the desire to use or observe an animal species, even for purely esthetic purposes, is undeniably a cognizable interest for purpose of standing. But the "injury in fact" test requires more than an injury to a cognizable interest. It requires that the party seeking review be himself among the injured. To survive the Secretary's summary judgment motion, respondents had to submit affidavits or other evidence showing, through specific facts, not only that listed species were in fact being threatened by funded activities abroad, but also that one or more of respondents' members would thereby be "directly" affected apart from their "'special interest' in th[e] subject."

[The Court here considered the assertion that two of respondent's members had suffered injury in fact based on their affidavits that they had traveled to Egypt and Sri Lanka to observe endangered species in the vicinity of projects funded by the United States, and that they hoped to do so again at some unspecified point in the future.]

We shall assume for the sake of argument that these affidavits contain facts showing that certain agency-funded projects threaten listed species—though that is questionable. They plainly contain no facts, however, showing how damage to the species will produce "imminent" injury to [the two affiants]. That [the affiants] "had visited" the areas of the projects before the projects commenced proves nothing. As we have said in a related context, "'Past exposure to illegal conduct does not in itself show a present case or controversy regarding injunctive relief . . . if unaccompanied by any continuing, present adverse effects.'" And the affiants' profession of an "inten[t]" to return to the places they had visited before—where they will presumably, this time, be deprived of the opportunity to observe animals of the endangered species—is simply not enough. Such "some day" intentions—without any description of concrete plans, or indeed even any specification of when the some day will be—do not support a finding of the "actual or imminent" injury that our cases require.

Besides relying upon [the] affidavits, respondents propose a series of novel standing theories. The first, inelegantly styled "ecosystem nexus," proposes that any person who uses any part of a "contiguous ecosystem" adversely affected by a funded activity has standing even if the activity is located a great distance away. This approach [is] inconsistent with [a prior case] which held that a plaintiff claiming injury from environmental damage must use the area affected by the challenged activity and not an area roughly "in the vicinity" of it. It makes no difference that the general-purpose section of the ESA states that the Act was intended in part "to provide a means whereby the ecosystems upon which endangered species and threatened species depend may be conserved." To say that the Act protects ecosystems is not to say that the Act creates (if it were possible) rights of action in persons who have not been injured in fact, that is, persons who use portions of an ecosystem not perceptibly affected by the unlawful action in question.

Respondents' other theories are called, alas, the "animal nexus" approach, whereby anyone who has an interest in studying or seeing the endangered animals anywhere on the globe has standing; and the "vocational nexus" approach, under which anyone with a professional interest in such animals can sue. Under these theories, anyone who goes to see Asian elephants in the Bronx Zoo, and anyone who is a keeper of Asian elephants in the Bronx Zoo, has standing to sue because the Director of the Agency for International Development (AID) did not consult with the Secretary regarding the AID-funded project in Sri Lanka. This is beyond all reason. Standing is not "an ingenious academic exercise in the conceivable," but as we have said requires, at the summary judgment stage, a factual showing of perceptible harm. It is clear that the person who observes or works with a particular animal threatened by a federal decision is facing perceptible harm, since the very subject of his interest will no longer exist. It is even plausible—though it goes to the outermost limit of plausibility—to think that a person who observes or works with animals of a particular species in the very area of the world where that species is threatened by a federal decision is facing such harm, since some animals that might have been the subject of his interest will no longer exist. It goes beyond the limit, however, and into pure speculation and fantasy, to say that anyone who observes or works with an endangered species, anywhere in the world, is appreciably harmed by a single project affecting some portion of that species with which he has no more specific connection.

B

Besides failing to show injury, respondents failed to demonstrate redressability. Instead of attacking the separate decisions to fund particular projects allegedly causing them harm, respondents chose to challenge a more generalized level of Government action (rules regarding consultation), the invalidation of which would affect all overseas projects. This programmatic approach has obvious practical advantages, but also obvious difficulties insofar as proof of causation or redressability is concerned. As we have said in another context, "suits challenging, not specifically identifiable Government violations of law, but the particular programs agencies establish to carry out their legal obligations . . . [are], even when premised on allegations of several instances of violations of law, . . . rarely if ever appropriate for federal-court adjudication." *Allen.*

The most obvious problem in the present case is redressability. Since the agencies funding the projects were not parties to the case, the District Court could accord relief only against the Secretary: He could be ordered to revise his regulation to require consultation for foreign projects. But this would not remedy respondents' alleged injury unless the funding agencies were bound by the Secretary's regulation, which is very much an open question. Whereas in other contexts the ESA is quite explicit as to the Secretary's controlling authority, with respect to consultation the initiative, and hence arguably the initial responsibility for determining statutory necessity, lies with the agencies. When the Secretary promulgated the regulation at issue here, he thought it was binding on the agencies. The Solicitor General, however, has repudiated that position here, and the agencies themselves apparently deny the Secretary's authority. . . .

Respondents assert that this legal uncertainty did not affect redressability (and hence standing) because the District Court itself could resolve the issue of the Secretary's authority as a necessary part of its standing inquiry. Assuming that it is appropriate to resolve an issue of law such as this in connection with a threshold standing inquiry, resolution by the District Court would not have remedied respondents' alleged injury anyway, because it would not have been binding upon the agencies. They were not parties to the suit, and there is no reason they should be obliged to honor an incidental legal determination the suit produced. . . . The short of the matter is that redress of the only injury in fact respondents complain of requires action (termination of funding until consultation) by the individual funding agencies; and any relief the District Court could have provided in this suit against the Secretary was not likely to produce that action.

A further impediment to redressability is the fact that the agencies generally supply only a fraction of the funding for a foreign project. . . . Respondents have produced nothing to indicate that the projects they have named will either be suspended, or do less harm to listed species, if that fraction is eliminated. [It] is entirely conjectural whether the nonagency activity that affects respondents will be altered or affected by the agency activity they seek to achieve. There is no standing.

IV

The Court of Appeals found that respondents had standing for an additional reason: because they had suffered a "procedural injury." The so-called "citizen-suit" provision of the ESA provides, in pertinent part, that "any person may commence a civil suit on his own behalf (A) to enjoin any person, including the United States and any other governmental instrumentality or agency . . . who is alleged to be in violation of any provision of this chapter." The court held that, because § 7(a)(2) requires interagency consultation, the citizen-suit provision creates a "procedural righ[t]" to consultation in all "persons"—so that anyone can file suit in federal court to challenge the Secretary's (or presumably any other official's) failure to follow the assertedly correct consultative procedure, notwithstanding his or her inability to allege any discrete injury flowing from that failure. To understand the remarkable nature of this holding one must be clear about what it does not rest upon: This is not a case where plaintiffs are seeking to enforce a procedural requirement the disregard of which could impair a separate concrete interest of theirs (e.g., the procedural requirement for a hearing prior to denial of their license application, or the procedural requirement for an environmental impact statement before a federal facility is constructed next door to them). Nor is it simply a case where concrete injury has been suffered by many persons, as in mass fraud or mass tort situations. Nor, finally, is it the unusual case in which Congress has created a concrete private interest in the outcome of a suit against a private party for the government's benefit, by providing a cash bounty for the victorious plaintiff. Rather, the court held that the injury-in-fact requirement had been satisfied by congressional conferral upon all persons of an abstract, self-contained, noninstrumental "right" to have the Executive observe the procedures required by law. We reject this view.

We have consistently held that a plaintiff raising only a generally available grievance about government—claiming only harm to his and every citizen's interest in proper application of the Constitution and laws, and seeking relief that no more directly and tangibly benefits him than it does the public at large—does not state an Article III case or controversy. . . .

To be sure, our generalized-grievance cases have typically involved Government violation of procedures assertedly ordained by the Constitution rather than the Congress. But there is absolutely no basis for making the Article III inquiry turn on the source of the asserted right. Whether the courts were to act on their own, or at the invitation of Congress, in ignoring the concrete injury requirement described in our cases, they would be discarding a principle fundamental to the separate and distinct constitutional role of the Third Branch—one of the essential elements that identifies those "Cases" and "Controversies" that are the business of the courts rather than of the political branches. "The province of the court," as Chief Justice Marshall said in *Marbury v. Madison*, 5 U.S. (1 Cranch) 137, 170 (1803), "is, solely, to decide on the rights of individuals." Vindicating the public interest (including the public interest in Government observance of the Constitution and laws) is the function of Congress and the Chief Executive.

The question presented here is whether the public interest in proper administration of the laws (specifically, in agencies' observance of a particular, statutorily prescribed procedure) can be converted into an individual right by a statute that denominates it as such, and that permits all citizens (or, for that matter, a subclass of citizens who suffer no distinctive concrete harm) to sue. If the concrete injury requirement has the separation-of-powers significance we have always said, the answer must be obvious: To permit Congress to convert the undifferentiated public interest in executive officers' compliance with the law into an "individual right" vindicable in the courts is to permit Congress to transfer from the President to the courts the Chief Executive's most important constitutional duty, to "take Care that the Laws be faithfully executed," Art. II, §3. It would enable the courts, with the permission of Congress, "to assume a position of authority over the governmental acts of another and co-equal department," and to become "'virtually continuing monitors of the wisdom and soundness of Executive action.'" *Allen*. We have always rejected that vision of our role:

> When Congress passes an Act empowering administrative agencies to carry on governmental activities, the power of those agencies is circumscribed by the authority granted. This permits the courts to participate in law enforcement entrusted to administrative bodies only to the extent necessary to protect justiciable individual rights against administrative action fairly beyond the granted powers. . . . This is very far from assuming that the courts are charged more than administrators or legislators with the protection of the rights of the people. Congress and the Executive supervise the acts of administrative agents. . . . But under Article III, Congress established courts to adjudicate cases and controversies as to claims of infringement of individual

rights whether by unlawful action of private persons or by the exertion of unauthorized administrative power. *Stark v. Wickard*, 321 U.S. 288 (1944).

"Individual rights," within the meaning of this passage, do not mean public rights that have been legislatively pronounced to belong to each individual who forms part of the public.

Nothing in this contradicts the principle that "[t]he . . . injury required by Art. III may exist solely by virtue of 'statutes creating legal rights, the invasion of which creates standing.'" . . . "[Statutory] broadening [of] the categories of injury that may be alleged in support of standing is a different matter from abandoning the requirement that the party seeking review must himself have suffered an injury." [It] is clear that in suits against the Government, at least, the concrete injury requirement must remain.

We hold that respondents lack standing to bring this action and that the Court of Appeals erred in denying the summary judgment motion filed by the United States. The opinion of the Court of Appeals is hereby reversed, and the cause is remanded for proceedings consistent with this opinion.

JUSTICE KENNEDY, with whom JUSTICE SOUTER joins, concurring in part and concurring in the judgment.

Although I agree with the essential parts of the Court's analysis, I write separately to make several observations.

I agree with the Court's conclusion in Part III-A that, on the record before us, respondents have failed to demonstrate that they themselves are "among the injured." . . . While it may seem trivial to require that [the affiants] acquire airline tickets to the project sites or announce a date certain upon which they will return, this is not a case where it is reasonable to assume that the affiants will be using the sites on a regular basis, nor do the affiants claim to have visited the sites since the projects commenced. With respect to the Court's discussion of respondents' "ecosystem nexus," "animal nexus," and "vocational nexus" theories, I agree that on this record respondents' showing is insufficient to establish standing on any of these bases. I am not willing to foreclose the possibility, however, that in different circumstances a nexus theory similar to those proffered here might support a claim to standing.

In light of the conclusion that respondents have not demonstrated a concrete injury here sufficient to support standing under our precedents, I would not reach the issue of redressability that is discussed by the plurality in Part III-B.

I also join Part IV of the Court's opinion with the following observations. As Government programs and policies become more complex and farreaching, we must be sensitive to the articulation of new rights of action that do not have clear analogs in our common-law tradition. Modern litigation has progressed far from the paradigm of Marbury suing Madison to get his commission, *Marbury v. Madison*, 5 U.S. (1 Cranch) 137 (1803), or Ogden seeking an injunction to halt Gibbons' steamboat operations, *Gibbons v. Ogden*, 22 U.S. (9 Wheat.) 1 (1824). In my view, Congress has the power to define injuries and articulate chains of causation that will give rise to a case or controversy where none existed before, and I do not read the Court's opinion to suggest a contrary view. In exercising this power, however, Congress must at the very least identify the injury it seeks to vindicate and relate the injury to the class of persons entitled to bring suit. The citizen-suit provision of the Endangered Species Act does not meet these minimal requirements, because while the statute purports to confer a right on "any person . . . to enjoin . . . the United States and any other governmental instrumentality or agency . . . who is alleged to be in violation of any provision of this chapter," it does not of its own force establish that there is an injury in "any person" by virtue of any "violation."

The Court's holding that there is an outer limit to the power of Congress to confer rights of action is a direct and necessary consequence of the case and controversy limitations found in Article III. I agree that it would exceed those limitations if, at the behest of Congress and in the absence of any showing of concrete injury, we were to entertain citizen suits to vindicate the public's nonconcrete interest in the proper administration of the laws. While it does not matter how many persons have been injured by the challenged action, the party bringing suit must show that the action injures him in a concrete and personal way. This requirement is not just an empty formality. It preserves the vitality of the adversarial process by assuring both that the parties before the court have an actual, as opposed to professed, stake in the outcome, and that "the legal questions presented . . . will be resolved, not in the rarified atmosphere of a debating society, but in a concrete factual context conducive to a realistic appreciation of the consequences of judicial action." In addition, the requirement of concrete injury confines the Judicial Branch to its proper, limited role in the constitutional framework of Government.

An independent judiciary is held to account through its open proceedings and its reasoned judgments. In this process it is essential for the public to know what persons or groups are invoking the judicial power, the reasons that they have brought suit, and whether their claims are vindicated or denied. The concrete injury requirement helps assure that there can be an answer to these questions; and, as the Court's opinion is careful to show, that is part of the constitutional design.

With these observations, I concur in Parts I, II, III-A, and IV of the Court's opinion and in the judgment of the Court.

JUSTICE STEVENS, concurring in the judgment.

Because I am not persuaded that Congress intended the consultation requirement in § 7(a)(2) of the Endangered Species Act of 1973 (ESA), to apply to activities in foreign countries, I concur in the judgment of reversal. I do not, however, agree with the Court's conclusion that respondents lack standing because the threatened injury to their interest in protecting the environment and studying endangered species is not "imminent." Nor do I agree with the plurality's additional conclusion that respondents' injury is not "redressable" in this litigation.

I

In my opinion a person who has visited the critical habitat of an endangered species, has a professional interest in preserving the species and its habitat, and intends to revisit them in the future has standing to challenge agency action that threatens their destruction. Congress has found that a wide variety of endangered species of fish, wildlife, and plants are of "aesthetic, ecological, educational, historical, recreational, and scientific value to the Nation and its people." Given that finding, we have no license to demean the importance of the interest that particular individuals may have in observing any species or its habitat, whether those individuals are motivated by esthetic enjoyment, an interest in professional research, or an economic interest in preservation of the species. Indeed, this Court has often held that injuries to such interests are sufficient to confer standing, and the Court reiterates that holding today.

The Court nevertheless concludes that respondents have not suffered "injury in fact" because they have not shown that the harm to the endangered species will produce "imminent" injury to them. I disagree. An injury to an individual's interest in study-ing or enjoying a species and its natural habitat occurs when someone (whether it be the Government or a private party) takes action that harms that species and habitat. In my judgment, therefore, the "imminence" of such an injury should be measured by the timing and likelihood of the threatened environmental harm, rather than—as the Court seems to suggest—by the time that might elapse between the present and the time when the individuals would visit the area if no such injury should occur.

To understand why this approach is correct and consistent with our precedent, it is necessary to consider the purpose of the standing doctrine. Concerned about "the proper—and properly limited—role of the courts in a democratic society," we have long held that "Art. III judicial power exists only to redress or otherwise to protect against injury to the complaining party." The plaintiff must have a "personal stake in the outcome" sufficient to "assure that concrete adverseness which sharpens the presentation of issues upon which the court so largely depends for illumination of difficult . . . questions." For that reason, "[a]bstract injury is not enough. It must be alleged that the plaintiff 'has sustained or is immediately in danger of sustaining some direct injury' as the result of the challenged statute or official conduct. . . . The injury or threat of injury must be both 'real and immediate,' not 'conjectural,' or 'hypothetical.'"

Consequently, we have denied standing to plaintiffs whose likelihood of suffering any concrete adverse effect from the challenged action was speculative. In this case, however, the likelihood that respondents will be injured by the destruction of the endangered species is not speculative. If respondents are genuinely interested in the preservation of the endangered species and intend to study or observe these animals in the future, their injury will occur as soon as the animals are destroyed. Thus the only potential source of "speculation" in this case is whether respondents' intent to study or observe the animals is genuine. In my view, [affiants] have introduced suf-ficient evidence to negate petitioner's contention that their claims of injury are "specu-lative" or "conjectural." . . .

The plurality also concludes that respondents' injuries are not redressable in this litigation for two reasons. First, respondents have sought only a declaratory judg-ment that the Secretary of the Interior's regulation interpreting §7(a)(2) to require con-sultation only for agency actions in the United States or on the high seas is invalid and an injunction requiring him to promulgate a new regulation requiring consultation for agency actions abroad as well. But, the plurality opines, even if respondents succeed and a new regulation is promulgated, there is no guarantee that federal agencies that are not parties to this case will actually consult with the Secretary. Furthermore, the plurality continues, respondents have not demonstrated that federal agencies can influence the behavior of the foreign governments where the affected projects are located. Thus, even if the agencies consult with the Secretary and terminate funding for foreign projects, the foreign governments might nonetheless pursue the projects and jeopardize the endangered species. Neither of these reasons is persuasive.

We must presume that if this Court holds that §7(a)(2) requires consultation, all affected agencies would abide by that interpretation and engage in the requisite consultations. Certainly the Executive Branch cannot be heard to argue that an authoritative construction of the governing statute by this Court may simply be ignored by any agency head. Moreover, if Congress has required consultation between agencies, we must presume that such consultation will have a serious purpose that is likely to produce tangible results. As Justice Blackmun explains, it is not mere speculation to think that foreign governments, when faced with the threatened withdrawal of United States assistance, will modify their projects to mitigate the harm to endangered species.

II

Although I believe that respondents have standing, I nevertheless concur in the judgment of reversal because I am persuaded that the Government is correct in its submission that §7(a)(2) does not apply to activities in foreign countries. [Discussion omitted.]

JUSTICE BLACKMUN, with whom JUSTICE O'CONNOR joins, dissenting.

I part company with the Court in this case in two respects. First, I believe that respondents have raised genuine issues of fact — sufficient to survive summary judgment — both as to injury and as to redressability. Second, I question the Court's breadth of language in rejecting standing for "procedural" injuries. I fear the Court seeks to impose fresh limitations on the constitutional authority of Congress to allow citizen suits in the federal courts for injuries deemed "procedural" in nature. I dissent.

[In Part I of his opinion, Justice Blackmun concluded that the affidavits raised questions of fact about the likelihood of injury sufficient to withstand a motion for summary judgment. He also disagreed with the Court's rejection of the plaintiffs' "ecosystem nexus" theory, because he rejected the conclusion that the plaintiffs should be required to show geographic proximity to the areas where the harm to endangered species occurs. Finally, he rejected the plurality's view that the plaintiffs could not show redressibility.]

II

The Court concludes that any "procedural injury" suffered by respondents is insufficient to confer standing. . . .

The Court expresses concern that allowing judicial enforcement of "agencies' observance of a particular, statutorily prescribed procedure" would "transfer from the President to the courts the Chief Executive's most important constitutional duty, to 'take Care that the Laws be faithfully executed,' Art. II, §3." In fact, the principal effect of foreclosing judicial enforcement of such procedures is to transfer power into the hands of the Executive at the expense — not of the courts — but of Congress, from which that power originates and emanates.

Under the Court's anachronistically formal view of the separation of powers, Congress legislates pure, substantive mandates and has no business structuring the procedural manner in which the Executive implements these mandates. To be sure, in the ordinary course, Congress does legislate in black-and-white terms of affirmative commands or negative prohibitions on the conduct of officers of the Executive Branch. In complex regulatory areas, however, Congress often legislates, as it were, in procedural shades of gray. That is, it sets forth substantive policy goals and provides for their attainment by requiring Executive Branch officials to follow certain procedures, for example, in the form of reporting, consultation, and certification requirements.

The consultation requirement of §7 of the Endangered Species Act is [an] action-forcing statute. Consultation is designed as an integral check on federal agency action, ensuring that such action does not go forward without full consideration of its effects on listed species. Once consultation is initiated, the Secretary is under a duty to provide to the action agency "a written statement setting forth the Secretary's opinion, and a summary of the information on which the opinion is based, detailing how the agency action affects the species or its critical habitat." The Secretary is also obligated to suggest "reasonable and prudent alternatives" to prevent jeopardy to listed species. The action agency must undertake as well its own "biological assessment for the purpose of identifying any endangered species or threatened species" likely to be affected by agency action. After the initiation of consultation, the action agency "shall not make any irreversible or irretrievable commitment of resources" which would foreclose the "formulation or implementation of any reasonable and prudent alternative measures" to avoid jeopardizing listed species.

These action-forcing procedures are "designed to protect some threatened concrete interest" of persons who observe and work with endangered or threatened species. That is why I am mystified by the Court's unsupported conclusion that "[t]his is not a case where plaintiffs are seeking to enforce a procedural requirement the disregard of which could impair a separate concrete interest of theirs."

Congress legislates in procedural shades of gray not to aggrandize its own power but to allow maximum Executive discretion in the attainment of Congress' legislative goals. Congress could simply impose a substantive prohibition on Executive conduct; it could say that no agency action shall result in the loss of more than 5% of any listed species. Instead, Congress sets forth substantive guidelines and allows the Executive, within certain procedural constraints, to decide how best to effectuate the ultimate goal. The Court never has questioned Congress' authority to impose such procedural constraints on Executive power. Just as Congress does not violate separation of powers by structuring the procedural manner in which the Executive shall carry out the laws, surely the federal courts do not violate separation of powers when, at the very instruction and command of Congress, they enforce these procedures.

To prevent Congress from conferring standing for "procedural injuries" is another way of saying that Congress may not delegate to the courts authority deemed "executive" in nature. Here Congress seeks not to delegate "executive" power but only to strengthen the procedures it has legislatively mandated. "We have long recognized that the nondelegation doctrine does not prevent Congress from seeking assistance, within proper limits, from its coordinate Branches." "Congress does not violate the Constitution merely because it legislates in broad terms, leaving a certain degree of discretion to executive or judicial actors." . . .

In short, determining "injury" for Article III standing purposes is a fact-specific inquiry. "Typically . . . the standing inquiry requires careful judicial examination of a complaint's allegations to ascertain whether the particular plaintiff is entitled to an adjudication of the particular claims asserted." *Allen v. Wright.* There may be factual circumstances in which a congressionally imposed procedural requirement is so insubstantially connected to the prevention of a substantive harm that it cannot be said to work any conceivable injury to an individual litigant. But, as a general matter, the courts owe substantial deference to Congress' substantive purpose in imposing a certain procedural requirement. . . .

Note: Congress's Role in Standing

1. Congress has typically been involved in creating standing by prescribing new statutory rights, the violation of which leads to injury in the traditional sense. *Lujan* represents a major limitation on Congress's freedom to define what counts as an injury for constitutional purposes. Can you define exactly how Congress is limited? Is Justice Kennedy correct that the opinion does not limit Congress's "power to define injuries and articulate chains of causation that will give rise to a case or controversy where none has existed before"?

2. *Lujan* is also important for the points it makes about the plaintiff's burden of demonstrating standing at various points in the litigation. Note that the Court here is considering standing at the time of a motion for summary judgment. At this point, plaintiffs are required to demonstrate with actual evidence that they have standing. What more could the plaintiffs here have done?

3. In *Allen, Lujan*, and many other standing cases, the Court repeatedly emphasizes that the standing requirements protect the separation of powers. As the Court states:

> To permit Congress to convert the undifferentiated public interest in executive officers' compliance with the law into an "individual right" vindicable in the courts is to permit Congress to transfer from the President to the courts the Chief Executive's most important constitutional duty, to "take Care that the Laws be faithfully executed."

Does the Court weigh the interests of each branch equally in its separation-of-powers analysis? Or is Justice Blackmun correct in arguing that the majority's analysis effectively "transfer[s] power into the hands of the Executive at the expense—not of the courts—but of Congress, from which that power originates and emanates"?

4. Under the False Claims Act (FCA), a private person (the relator) may bring what is known as a "qui tam" civil action "in the name of the [Federal] Government" against "[a]ny person" who "knowingly presents . . . to . . . the . . . Government . . . a false or fraudulent claim for payment." The relator receives a share of any proceeds from the action. In *Vermont Agency of Natural Resources v. United States ex rel. Stevens*, 529 U.S. 765 (2000), in an opinion by Justice Scalia, the Supreme Court held that the relator had standing to bring such an action:

> Respondent Jonathan Stevens brought this qui tam action in the United States District Court [against] petitioner Vermont Agency of Natural Resources, his former employer, alleging that it had submitted false claims to the Environmental Protection Agency (EPA) in connection with various federal grant programs administered by the EPA. Specifically, he claimed that petitioner had overstated the amount of time spent by its employees on the federally funded projects, thereby inducing the Government to disburse more grant money than petitioner was entitled to receive. The United States declined to intervene in the action.
>
> Petitioner then moved to dismiss, arguing that a State (or state agency) is not a "person" subject to liability under the FCA and that a *qui tam* action in federal court against a State is barred by the Eleventh Amendment. [The Court of Appeals rejected both arguments.]
>
> We first address the jurisdictional question whether respondent Stevens has standing under Article III of the Constitution to maintain this suit.
>
> As we have frequently explained, a plaintiff must meet three requirements in order to establish Article III standing. First, he must demonstrate "injury in fact"—a harm that is both "concrete" and "actual or imminent, not conjectural or hypothetical." Second, he must establish causation—a "fairly . . . trace[able]" connection between the alleged injury in fact and the alleged conduct of the defendant. And third, he must demonstrate redressability—a "substantial likelihood" that the requested relief will remedy the alleged injury in fact. These requirements together constitute the "irreducible constitutional minimum" of standing, *Lujan v. Defenders of Wildlife*, 504 U.S. 555 (1992), which is an "essential and unchanging part" of Article III's case-or-controversy requirement and a key factor in dividing the power of government between the courts and the two political branches.
>
> Respondent Stevens contends that he is suing to remedy an injury in fact suffered by the United States. It is beyond doubt that the complaint asserts an injury to the United States—both the injury to its sovereignty arising from violation of its laws (which suffices to support a criminal lawsuit by the

Government) and the proprietary injury resulting from the alleged fraud. But "[t]he Art. III judicial power exists only to redress or otherwise to protect against injury *to the complaining party.*" It would perhaps suffice to say that the relator here is simply the statutorily designated agent of the United States, in whose name (as the statute provides) the suit is brought—and that the relator's bounty is simply the fee he receives out of the United States' recovery for filing and/or prosecuting a successful action on behalf of the Government. This analysis is precluded, however, by the fact that the statute gives the relator himself an interest in the lawsuit, and not merely the right to retain a fee out of the recovery. Thus, it provides that "[a] person may bring a civil action for a violation of section 3729 *for the person and for the United States Government,*" (emphasis added); gives the relator "the right to continue as a party to the action" even when the Government itself has assumed "primary responsibility" for prosecuting it; entitles the relator to a hearing before the Government's voluntary dismissal of the suit; and prohibits the Government from settling the suit over the relator's objection without a judicial determination of "fair[ness], adequa[cy] and reasonable[ness]." For the portion of the recovery retained by the relator, therefore, some explanation of standing other than agency for the Government must be identified.

There is no doubt, of course, that as to this portion of the recovery—the bounty he will receive if the suit is successful—a qui tam relator has a "concrete private interest in the outcome of [the] suit." *Lujan.* But the same might be said of someone who has placed a wager upon the outcome. An interest unrelated to injury in fact is insufficient to give a plaintiff standing. The interest must consist of obtaining compensation for, or preventing, the violation of a legally protected right. A qui tam relator has suffered no such invasion— indeed, the "right" he seeks to vindicate does not even fully materialize until the litigation is completed and the relator prevails. This is not to suggest that Congress cannot define new legal rights, which in turn will confer standing to vindicate an injury caused to the claimant. As we have held in another context, however, an interest that is merely a "byproduct" of the suit itself cannot give rise to a cognizable injury in fact for Article III standing purposes.

We believe, however, that adequate basis for the relator's suit for his bounty is to be found in the doctrine that the assignee of a claim has standing to assert the injury in fact suffered by the assignor. The FCA can reasonably be regarded as effecting a partial assignment of the Government's damages claim. Although we have never expressly recognized "representational standing" on the part of assignees, we have routinely entertained their suits, and also suits by subrogees, who have been described as "equitable assign[ees]." We conclude, therefore, that the United States' injury in fact suffices to confer standing on respondent Stevens.

The Court went on to hold that the False Claims Act does not subject a state (or state agency) to liability in qui tam actions.

5. In *Lujan*, Justice Kennedy emphasizes in his concurrence that "Congress has the power to define injuries and articulate chains of causation that will give rise to a case or controversy where none existed before." Thus, when Congress identifies an injury it seeks to vindicate and relates that injury to the class of persons entitled to bring suit, the ordinary Article III standing requirements may be relaxed.

6. In 2007, the Supreme Court decided *Massachusetts v. Environmental Protection Agency*, 549 U.S. 497 (2007), which implicated the framework articulated by Justice Kennedy in *Lujan*. In that case, the Court appeared to relax the standing requirements for the state of Massachusetts, stressing its "special position and interest" as a sovereign. The Court stated that it was "of considerable relevance that the party seeking review here is a sovereign State and not, as it was in *Lujan*, a private individual." The dissent argues in response that the Court has "devised a new doctrine of state standing."

In *Massachusetts*, the majority explained that when Congress affords procedural rights to a litigant, the litigant can "assert those rights without meeting all the normal standards for redressability and immediacy." All that is required in such circumstances is the existence of "some possibility" that the requested relief will prompt the injury-causing party to reconsider the decision that allegedly harms the litigant. How different is the "some possibility" language of *Massachusetts* from *Lujan*'s articulation of the Article III requirement that a litigant's requested relief be "likely" to redress an injury? Does the majority's relaxed standing analysis render Article III standing limitations as described in *Lujan* "utterly toothless," as the *Massachusetts* dissent argued?

7. Although *Lujan* dealt with lawsuits filed against the government, the injury-in-fact requirement for Article III standing extends to other suits as well. In *Spokeo, Inc. v. Robins*, 136 S. Ct. 1540 (2016), the Court applied the standing requirements to a plaintiff who sued a consumer reporting agency for violating the Fair Credit Reporting Act of 1970 (FCRA), concluding that the plaintiff could not show sufficient injury in fact merely by alleging a bare procedural violation of the FCRA.

8. In *Summers v. Earth Island Institute*, 555 U.S. 488 (2009), the Supreme Court concluded that the plaintiffs—various environmental organizations—lacked standing to challenge the U.S. Forest Service's enforcement of regulations that exempt small fire-rehabilitation and timber-salvage projects from notice, comment, and appeal requirements under the Forest Service Decisionmaking and Appeals Reform Act. The Court's analysis echoed *Lujan* in addressing the sufficiency of an affidavit submitted by an individual member of an environmental organization to establish standing:

> [The affiant] asserts that he has visited many National Forests and plans to visit several unnamed National Forests in the future. [Plaintiffs] describe this as a mere failure to "provide the name of each timber sale that affected [his] interests." It is much more (or much less) than that. It is a failure to allege that *any* particular timber sale or other project claimed to be unlawfully subject to the regulations will impede a specific and concrete plan of

[the affiant] to enjoy the National Forests. . . . Here we are asked to assume not only that [the affiant] will stumble across a project tract unlawfully subject to the regulations, but also that the tract is about to be developed by the Forest Service in a way that harms his recreational interests, and that he would have commented on the project but for the regulation. Accepting an intention to visit the National Forests as adequate to confer standing to challenge any Government action affecting any portion of those forests would be tantamount to eliminating the requirement of concrete, particularized injury in fact.

In his majority opinion in *Summers*, Justice Scalia focused in particular on whether the U.S. Forest Service's regulations made the plaintiffs the "object of governmental action or inaction." Because the plaintiffs failed to "allege that *any* particular timber sale or other project" would "impede" any of their specific and concrete interests, the Court held that they lacked standing. What more could these plaintiffs have done? Given that the U.S. Forest Service had not announced every specific location where it planned to exempt timber sales from notice, comment, and appeal procedures, must the plaintiffs wait until such sales occur to bring a suit? Should the plaintiffs be required to wait when, as Justice Breyer argued in his dissent, it is extremely likely that at least one member of one of the organizations will be harmed because the Forest Service admitted that it will conduct "thousands of further [exempted] salvage-timber sales" in the near future?

Problems: Standing

1. Bovine spongiform encephalopathy, commonly known as "mad cow" disease, is a progressive and incurable neuro-degenerative disease that affects the central nervous system of adult cattle. Some scientific evidence suggests that "downed" cattle — cattle too ill to walk or stand prior to slaughter — may be at particular risk of infection with BSE, which causes animals to lose coordination and the ability to stand upright. A fatal variant of BSE can be transmitted to humans through the consumption of meat from contaminated animals.

James Larson has filed suit in federal court against the Secretary of Agriculture, seeking to ban the use of downed cattle for human consumption. Under current regulations of the Department of Agriculture, downed cattle may be used for human consumption after they pass a veterinary post-mortem examination. Larson claims that this policy violates the Federal Meat Inspection Act, 21 U.S.C. §§ 601–605 and the Federal Food, Drug, and Cosmetic Act, 21 U.S.C. §§ 301–399, both of which prohibit the sale of adulterated meat, because current observational post-mortems are not sufficient to detect BSE-infected cattle.

Larson asserts standing to pursue his claims as "a regular consumer of meat products who is concerned about eating adulterated meat." He alleges in his complaint that each time he eats meat, he is at risk of contracting mad cow disease. He claims injury in the increased risk that he may consume meat that is the product of a downed animal, and by his apprehension and concern arising from that risk. However, Larson is unable to allege that any BSE-infected cattle have entered the food supply in the United States. Does Larson have standing?

2. A city includes Christian religious symbols in its city seal and emblem. The seal is visible on all city vehicles and is on the city's tax sticker, which all automobile owners are required to affix to their windshields. The seal is prominently displayed on the city's water tower. The Society for Separation of Church and State sues on First Amendment grounds to enjoin the use of the seal. Its members, who object to religious symbolism in government, allege that they alter their travel routes to avoid the water tower, and that they object to having to view the seal on their windshields and in other places. Does the Society have standing?

3. A state provides financial support to a private treatment facility for those suffering from drug addiction. The funds are allocated from tax revenues through a specific appropriation made by the state legislature. Part of the rehabilitation program involves a twelve-step program modeled on Alcoholics Anonymous. The program steps include "making a decision to turn our will and lives over to the care of God" and "asking God to remove our shortcomings." A taxpayer sues to enjoin the use of tax revenues for support of the program. Does the taxpayer have standing?

[3] Prudential Standing

Note: Prudential Limitations on Standing

1. *Allen* and *Lujan* are concerned with constitutional limitations on standing. However, as the Court noted in *Allen*, standing doctrine also embraces "several judicially self-imposed limits on the exercise of federal jurisdiction" that may authorize a court to deny standing to a litigant who satisfies the requirements of Article III. Although these "prudential" limitations on standing have a long pedigree, they appear to conflict with the often-stated "heavy obligation to exercise jurisdiction" that Congress or the Constitution has conferred on the federal courts. *See, e.g., Colorado River Water Conservation Dist. v. United States*, 424 U.S. 800 (1976) (Chapter 16).

In *Elk Grove Unified Sch. Dist. v. Newdow*, 542 U.S. 1 (2004), the Court said the prudential limitations on standing include "the general prohibition on a litigant's raising another person's legal rights, the rule barring adjudication of generalized grievances more appropriately addressed in the representative branches, and the requirement that a plaintiff's complaint fall within the zone of interests protected by the law invoked." Yet, more recently, in *Lexmark International, Inc. v. Static Control Components, Inc.*, 134 S. Ct. 1377 (2014), the Court suggested that two of the items on that list — the rule barring adjudication of generalized grievances and the zone-of-interests test — may not fall within the rubric of prudential limitations at all.

2. In *Newdow*, the Court explained the policies underlying the prudential-standing requirements as follows:

Without such limitations — closely related to Art. III concerns but essentially matters of judicial self-governance — the courts would be called upon to decide abstract questions of wide public significance even though other governmental institutions may be more competent to address the questions and even though judicial intervention may be unnecessary to protect individual rights.

As you read the materials that follow, consider whether you find these policy concerns compelling.

3. Prudential limitations on standing have often been invoked when a litigant seeks to have a federal court consider the interests or determine the rights of someone not before the court. This situation can occur in numerous contexts. First, and always unsuccessfully, a litigant without Article III standing might seek to protect others' rights. An example is *Tileston v. Ullman*, 318 U.S. 44 (1943), where a doctor sought to invoke the constitutional interests of his patients to receive contraceptives. The doctor did not, however, invoke any interest of his own — not even his financial interest in practicing medicine. The Court found no standing.

Second, a litigant properly before the court could seek to have the court consider the effect of the challenged acts on others. Sometimes called "*jus tertii*," this form of standing can be successful. In *Craig v. Boren*, 429 U.S. 190 (1976), a vendor of 3.2 percent beer brought an equal protection challenge to an Oklahoma statute that allowed the sale of beer to women at age 18 but to men only at age 21. The suit had originally included an 18-year-old male plaintiff, but he had reached the age of 21 by the time the case reached the Court. The Court found that the vendor had standing to raise the equal protection challenge:

> Our decisions have settled that limitations on a litigant's assertion of *jus tertii* are not constitutionally mandated, but rather stem from a salutary "rule of self-restraint" designed to minimize unwarranted intervention into controversies where the applicable constitutional questions are ill-defined and speculative. These prudential objectives, thought to be enhanced by restrictions on third-party standing, cannot be furthered here, where the lower court already has entertained the relevant constitutional challenge and the parties have sought or at least have never resisted an authoritative constitutional determination. In such circumstances, a decision by us to forgo consideration of the constitutional merits in order to await the initiation of a new challenge to the statute by injured third parties would be impermissibly to foster repetitive and time-consuming litigation under the guise of caution and prudence. Moreover, insofar as the applicable constitutional questions have been and continue to be presented vigorously and "cogently," the denial of *jus tertii* standing in deference to a direct class suit can serve no functional purpose. It may be that a class could be assembled, whose fluid membership always included some males with live claims. But if the assertion of the right is to be "representative" to such an extent anyway, there seems little loss in terms of effective advocacy from allowing its assertion by the present *jus tertii* champion.
>
> In any event, we conclude that appellant has established independently her claim to assert *jus tertii* standing. The operation of [the Oklahoma statute]

plainly has inflicted "injury in fact" upon appellant sufficient to guarantee her "concrete adverseness," and to satisfy the constitutionally based standing requirements imposed by Art. III. The legal duties created by the statutory sections under challenge are addressed directly to vendors such as appellant. She is obliged either to heed the statutory discrimination, thereby incurring a direct economic injury through the constriction of her buyers' market, or to disobey the statutory command and suffer, in the words of Oklahoma's Assistant Attorney General, "sanctions and perhaps loss of license." This Court repeatedly has recognized that such injuries establish the threshold requirements of a "case or controversy" mandated by Art. III.

As a vendor with standing to challenge the lawfulness of [the statute], appellant is entitled to assert those concomitant rights of third parties that would be "diluted or adversely affected" should her constitutional challenge fail and the statutes remain in force. Otherwise, the threatened imposition of governmental sanctions might deter her and other similarly situated vendors from selling 3.2% beer to young males, thereby ensuring that "enforcement of the challenged restriction against the (vendor) would result indirectly in the violation of third parties' rights." Accordingly, vendors and those in like positions have been uniformly permitted to resist efforts at restricting their operations by acting as advocates of the rights of third parties who seek access to their market or function.

Should the Court have permitted vendors of 3.2% beer in Oklahoma to assert the rights of men between the ages of 18 and 21? Taken literally, does the standard articulated by the Court in *Craig*—requiring only the dilution or an adverse effect upon the rights of third parties—provide any meaningful limit on the type or number of cases in which third parties can assert the constitutional rights of others?

4. The policies behind the general prohibition on asserting the rights of others are discussed at length in *Singleton v. Wulff*, 428 U.S. 106 (1976), and *Kowalski v. Tesmer*, 543 U.S. 125 (2004), the next two principal cases.

Singleton v. Wulff

Supreme Court of the United States, 1976.

428 U.S. 106.

Mr. Justice Blackmun delivered the opinion of the Court (Parts I, II-A, and III) together with an opinion (Part II-B), in which Mr. Justice Brennan, Mr. Justice White, and Mr. Justice Marshall joined.

[Doctors challenged a Missouri statute that excluded certain abortions from reimbursement coverage under Medicaid. The doctors asserted not only their own interest in reimbursement for performing abortions, but also the constitutional interest of their patients, not parties to the suit, to terminate their pregnancies. The Court had no difficulty in determining that the doctors met Article III requirements for standing, because they suffered concrete injury from the operation of the challenged statute.]

II

B

The question of what rights the doctors may assert in seeking to resolve [the controversy between the parties] is more difficult. The Court of Appeals adverted to what it perceived to be the doctor's own "constitutional rights to practice medicine." We have no occasion to decide whether such rights exist. Assuming that they do, the doctors, of course, can assert them. It appears, however, that the Court of Appeals also accorded the doctors standing to assert, and indeed granted them relief based partly upon, the rights of their patients. We must decide whether this assertion of *jus tertii* was a proper one.

Federal courts must hesitate before resolving a controversy, even one within their constitutional power to resolve, on the basis of the rights of third persons not parties to the litigation. The reasons are two. First, the courts should not adjudicate such rights unnecessarily, and it may be that in fact the holders of those rights either do not wish to assert them, or will be able to enjoy them regardless of whether the in-court litigant is successful or not. Second, third parties themselves usually will be the best proponents of their own rights. The courts depend on effective advocacy, and therefore should prefer to construe legal rights only when the most effective advocates of those rights are before them. The holders of the rights may have a like preference, to the extent they will be bound by the courts' decisions under the doctrine of stare decisis. These two considerations underlie the Court's general rule: Ordinarily, one may not claim standing in this Court to vindicate the constitutional rights of some third party.

Like any general rule, however, this one should not be applied where its underlying justifications are absent. With this in mind, the Court has looked primarily to two factual elements to determine whether the rule should apply in a particular case. The first is the relationship of the litigant to the person whose right he seeks to assert. If the enjoyment of the right is inextricably bound up with the activity the litigant wishes to pursue, the court at least can be sure that its construction of the right is not unnecessary in the sense that the right's enjoyment will be unaffected by the outcome of the suit. Furthermore, the relationship between the litigant and the third party may be such that the former is fully, or very nearly, as effective a proponent of the right as the latter. Thus in *Griswold v. Connecticut*, 381 U.S. 479 (1965), where two persons had been convicted of giving advice on contraception, the Court permitted the defendants, one of whom was a licensed physician, to assert the privacy rights of the married persons whom they advised. The Court pointed to the "confidential" nature of the relationship between the defendants and the married persons, and reasoned that the rights of the latter were "likely to be diluted or adversely affected" if they could not be asserted in such a case. *See also Eisenstadt v. Baird*, 405 U.S. 438, 445–46 (1972) (stressing "advocate" relationship and "impact of the litigation on the third-party interests"); *Barrows v. Jackson*, 346 U.S. 249, 259 (1953) (owner of real estate subject to racial covenant granted standing to challenge such covenant in part because she was "the one in whose charge and keeping repose[d] . . . the power to continue to use her property to discriminate or to discontinue such use"). . . .

The other factual element to which the Court has looked is the ability of the third party to assert his own right. Even where the relationship is close, the reasons for requiring persons to assert their own rights will usually still apply. If there is some genuine obstacle to such assertion, however, the third party's absence from court loses its tendency to suggest that his right is not truly at stake, or truly important to him, and the party who is in court becomes by default the right's best available proponent. Thus, in *NAACP v. Alabama*, 357 U.S. 449 (1958), the Court held that the National Association for the Advancement of Colored People, in resisting a court order that it divulge the names of its members, could assert the First and Fourteenth Amendments rights of those members to remain anonymous. The Court reasoned that "[t]o require that [the right] be claimed by the members themselves would result in nullification of the right at the very moment of its assertion."

Application of these principles to the present case quickly yields its proper result. The closeness of the relationship is patent, as it was in *Griswold* and in *Doe v. Bolton*, 410 U.S. 179 (1973). A woman cannot safely secure an abortion without the aid of a physician, and an impecunious woman cannot easily secure an abortion without the physician's being paid by the State. The woman's exercise of her right to an abortion, whatever its dimension, is therefore necessarily at stake here. Moreover, the constitutionally protected abortion decision is one in which the physician is intimately involved. Aside from the woman herself, therefore, the physician is uniquely qualified to litigate the constitutionality of the State's interference with, or discrimination against, that decision.

As to the woman's assertion of her own rights, there are several obstacles. For one thing, she may be chilled from such assertion by a desire to protect the very privacy of her decision from the publicity of a court suit. A second obstacle is the imminent mootness, at least in the technical sense, of any individual woman's claim. Only a few months, at the most, after the maturing of the decision to undergo an abortion, her right thereto will have been irrevocably lost, assuming, as it seems fair to assume, that unless the impecunious woman can establish Medicaid eligibility she must forgo abortion. It is true that these obstacles are not insurmountable. Suit may be brought under a pseudonym, as so frequently has been done. A woman who is no longer pregnant may nonetheless retain the right to litigate the point because it is "'capable of repetition yet evading review.'" *Roe v. Wade*, 410 U.S. 113 (1973). And it may be that a class could be assembled, whose fluid membership always included some women with live claims. But if the assertion of the right is to be "representative" to such an extent anyway, there seems little loss in terms of effective advocacy from allowing its assertion by a physician.

For these reasons, we conclude that it generally is appropriate to allow a physician to assert the rights of women patients as against governmental interference with the abortion decision. . . .

Mr. Justice Stevens, concurring in part.

In this case (1) the plaintiff-physicians have a financial stake in the outcome of the litigation, and (2) they claim that the statute impairs their own constitutional rights. They therefore clearly have standing to bring this action.

Because these two facts are present, I agree that the analysis in Part II-B of Mr. Justice Blackmun's opinion provides an adequate basis for considering the arguments based on the effect of the statute on the constitutional rights of their patients. Because I am not sure whether the analysis in Part II-B would, or should, sustain the doctors' standing, apart from those two facts, I join only Parts I, II-A, and III of the Court's opinion.

JUSTICE POWELL, with whom THE CHIEF JUSTICE, MR. JUSTICE STEWART, and MR. JUSTICE REHNQUIST join, concurring in part and dissenting in part.

I

As the Court notes, respondents by complaint and affidavit established their Art. III standing to invoke the judicial power of the District Court. They have performed abortions for which Missouri's Medicaid system would compensate them directly if the challenged statutory section did not preclude it. Respondents allege an intention to continue to perform such abortions, and that the statute deprives them of compensation. These arguments, if proved, would give respondents a personal stake in the controversy over the statute's constitutionality.

II

[T]he Art. III standing inquiry often is only the first of two inquiries necessary to determine whether a federal court should entertain a claim at the instance of a particular party. The Art. III question is one of power within our constitutional system, as courts may decide only actual cases and controversies between the parties who stand before the court. Beyond this question, however, lies the further and less easily defined inquiry of whether it is prudent to proceed to decision on particular issues even at the instance of a party whose Art. III standing is clear. This inquiry has taken various forms, including the one presented by this case: whether, in defending against or anticipatorily attacking state action, a party may argue that it contravenes someone else's constitutional rights.

This second inquiry is a matter of judicial self-governance. The usual and wise stance of the federal courts when policing their own exercise of power in this manner is one of cautious reserve. This caution has given rise to the general rule that a party may not defend against or attack governmental action on the ground that it infringes the rights of some third party, and to the corollary that any exception must rest on specific factors outweighing the policies behind the rule itself.[3]

---

3. I agree with the plurality that a fundamental policy behind the general rule is a salutary desire to avoid unnecessary constitutional adjudication. The plurality perceives a second basis for the rule in the courts' need for effective advocacy. While this concern is relevant, it should receive no more emphasis in this context than in the context of Art. III standing requirements. There the need for effective advocacy or a factual sharpening of issues long was the touchstone of discussion. Perhaps a more accurate formulation of the Art. III limitation — one consistent with the concerns underlying the constitutional provision — is that the plaintiff's stake in a controversy must insure that exercise of the court's remedial powers is both necessary and sufficient to give him relief. The Court today uses this formulation. A similar focus upon the proper judicial role, rather than quality of advocacy, is preferable in the area of prudential limitations upon judicial power.

The plurality acknowledges this general rule, but identifies "two factual elements" thought to be derived from prior cases that justify the adjudication of the asserted third-party rights: (i) obstacles to the assertion by the third party of her own rights, and (ii) the existence of some "relationship" such as the one between physician and patient. In my view these factors do not justify allowing these physicians to assert their patients' rights.

A

Our prior decisions are enlightening. In *Barrows v. Jackson*, a covenantor who breached a racially restrictive covenant was permitted to set up the buyers' rights to equal protection in defense against a damages action by the covenantees. The Court considered the general rule outweighed by "the need to protect (these) fundamental rights" in a situation "in which it would be difficult if not impossible for the persons whose rights are asserted to present their grievance before any court." It would indeed have been difficult if not impossible for the rightholders to assert their own rights: the operation of the restrictive covenant and the threat of damages actions for its breach tended to insure they would not come into possession of the land, and there was at the time little chance of a successful suit based on a covenantor's failure to sell to them. In a second case, *NAACP v. Alabama*, an organization was allowed to resist an order to produce its membership list by asserting the associational rights of its members to anonymity because the members themselves would have had to forgo the rights in order to assert them. And in *Eisenstadt v. Baird*, the Court considered it necessary to relax the rule and permit a distributor of contraceptives to assert the constitutional rights of the recipients because the statutory scheme operating to deny the contraceptives to the recipients appeared to offer them no means of challenge.

The plurality purports to derive from these cases the principle that a party may assert another's rights if there is "some genuine obstacle" to the third party's own litigation. But this understates the teaching of those cases: On their facts they indicate that such an assertion is proper, not when there is merely some "obstacle" to the rightholder's own litigation, but when such litigation is in all practicable terms impossible. Thus, in its framing of this principle, the plurality has gone far beyond our major precedents.

Moreover, on the plurality's own statement of this principle and on its own discussion of the facts, the litigation of third-party rights cannot be justified in this case. The plurality virtually concedes, as it must, that the two alleged "obstacles" to the women's assertion of their rights are chimerical. Our docket regularly contains cases in which women, using pseudonyms, challenge statutes that allegedly infringe their right to exercise the abortion decision. Nor is there basis for the "obstacle" of incipient mootness when the plurality itself quotes from the portion of *Roe v. Wade*, 410 U.S. 113 (1973), that shows no such obstacle exists. . . .

Congress by statute may foreclose any inquiry into competing policy considerations and give a party with Art. III standing the right to assert the interests of third parties or even the public interest.

B

The plurality places primary reliance on a second element, the existence of a "confidential relationship" between the rightholder and the party seeking to assert her rights.[5] Focusing on the professional relationships present in *Griswold*, *Doe* and *Planned Parenthood of Missouri v. Danforth*, the plurality suggests that allowing the physicians in this case to assert their patients' rights flows naturally from those three. Indeed, its conclusion is couched in terms of the general appropriateness of allowing physicians to assert the privacy interests of their patients in attacks on "governmental interference with the abortion decision."

With all respect, I do not read these cases as merging the physician and his patient for constitutional purposes. The principle they support turns not upon the confidential nature of a physician-patient relationship but upon the nature of the State's impact upon that relationship. In each instance the State directly interdicted the normal functioning of the physician-patient relationship by criminalizing certain procedures. In the circumstances of direct interference, I agree that one party to the relationship should be permitted to assert the constitutional rights of the other, for a judicial rule of self-restraint should not preclude an attack on a State's proscription of constitutionally protected activity. But Missouri has not directly interfered with the abortion decision — neither the physicians nor their patients are forbidden to engage in the procedure. The only impact of [the statute] is that, because of the way Missouri chose to structure its Medicaid payments, it causes these doctors financial detriment. This affords them Art. III standing because they aver injury in fact, but it does not justify abandonment of the salutary rule against assertion of third-party rights.

C

The physicians have offered no special reason for allowing them to assert their patients' rights in an attack on this welfare statute, and I can think of none. Moreover, there are persuasive reasons not to permit them to do so. It seems wholly inappropriate, as a matter of judicial self-governance, for a court to reach unnecessarily to decide a difficult constitutional issue in a case in which nothing more is at stake than remuneration for professional services. And second, this case may well set a precedent that will prove difficult to cabin. No reason immediately comes to mind, after today's holding, why any provider of services should be denied standing to assert his client's or customer's constitutional rights, if any, in an attack on a welfare statute that excludes from coverage his particular transaction.

---

5. The plurality's primary emphasis upon this relationship is in marked contrast to the Court's previous position that the relationship between litigant and rightholder was subordinate in importance to "the impact of the litigation on the third-party interests." *Eisenstadt v. Baird*. I suspect the plurality's inversion of the previous order results from the weakness of the argument that this litigation is necessary to protect third-party interests. I would keep the emphasis where it has been before, and would consider the closeness of any "relationship" only as a factor imparting confidence that third-party interests will be represented adequately in a case in which allowing their assertion is justified on other grounds.

Putting it differently, the Court's holding invites litigation by those who perhaps have the least legitimate ground for seeking to assert the rights of third parties. Before today I certainly would not have thought that an interest in being compensated for professional services, without more, would be deemed a sufficiently compelling reason to justify departing from a rule of restraint that well serves society and our judicial system. The Court quite recently stated, with respect to the rule against assertion of third-party rights as well as certain other doctrines of judicial self-restraint, that "[t]hese principles rest on more than the fussiness of judges. They reflect the conviction that under our constitutional system courts are not roving commissions assigned to pass judgment on the validity of the Nation's laws. . . . Constitutional judgments . . . are justified only out of the necessity of adjudicating rights in particular cases between the litigants brought before the Court." Today's holding threatens to make just such "roving commissions" of the federal courts.

Kowalski v. Tesmer

Supreme Court of the United States, 2004.

543 U.S. 125.

CHIEF JUSTICE REHNQUIST delivered the opinion of the Court.

This case involves a constitutional challenge to Michigan's procedure for appointing appellate counsel for indigent defendants who plead guilty. The only challengers before us are two attorneys who seek to invoke the rights of hypothetical indigents to challenge the procedure. We hold that the attorneys lack standing and therefore do not reach the question of the procedure's constitutionality.

[Michigan amended its Constitution to abolish appeal as of right in criminal cases where a defendant has pleaded guilty or nolo contendere. As a result, Michigan state judges began to deny appointed appellate counsel to indigents who pleaded guilty, and the Michigan Legislature subsequently codified this practice. Two attorneys who represented indigents filed a federal suit for injunctive and declaratory relief on due process and equal protection grounds. They were joined by three indigents who were denied appellate counsel after pleading guilty. A day before the statute was to take effect, the District Court issued an order holding the practice and statute unconstitutional and enjoining Michigan state judges from denying appellate counsel to any indigent who pleaded guilty. The Court of Appeals for the Sixth Circuit ultimately held that abstention doctrines barred the indigent defendants' suit, but that the attorneys had third-party standing to assert the rights of the indigents.]

[We] shall assume the attorneys have satisfied Article III and address the alternative threshold question whether they have standing to raise the rights of others.[2]

---

2. To satisfy Article III, a party must demonstrate an "injury in fact"; a causal connection between the injury and the conduct of which the party complains; and that it is "likely" a favorable decision will provide redress. *Lujan v. Defenders of Wildlife*, 504 U.S. 555, 560–61 (1992). In this case, the attorneys alleged "injury in fact" flows from their contention that the Michigan system "has reduced the number of cases in which they could be appointed and paid as assigned appellate counsel." This

We have adhered to the rule that a party "generally must assert his own legal rights and interests, and cannot rest his claim to relief on the legal rights or interests of third parties." This rule assumes that the party with the right has the appropriate incentive to challenge (or not challenge) governmental action and to do so with the necessary zeal and appropriate presentation. It represents a "healthy concern that if the claim is brought by someone other than one at whom the constitutional protection is aimed," the courts might be "called upon to decide abstract questions of wide public significance even though other governmental institutions may be more competent to address the questions and even though judicial intervention may be unnecessary to protect individual rights."

We have not treated this rule as absolute, however, recognizing that there may be circumstances where it is necessary to grant a third party standing to assert the rights of another. But we have limited this exception by requiring that a party seeking third-party standing make two additional showings. First, we have asked whether the party asserting the right has a "close" relationship with the person who possesses the right. Second, we have considered whether there is a "hindrance" to the possessor's ability to protect his own interests.

We have been quite forgiving with these criteria in certain circumstances. "Within the context of the First Amendment," for example, "the Court has enunciated other concerns that justify a lessening of prudential limitations on standing." And "in several cases, this Court has allowed standing to litigate the rights of third parties when enforcement of the challenged restriction *against the litigant* would result indirectly in the violation of third parties' rights." *Warth v. Seldin* (emphasis added), citing [among other cases] *Griswold v. Connecticut*, 381 U.S. 479 (1965); see *Craig v. Boren*, 429 U.S. 190 (1976). Beyond these examples—none of which is implicated here—we have not looked favorably upon third-party standing. With this in mind, we turn to apply our "close relationship" and "hindrance" criteria to the facts before us.

The attorneys in this case invoke the attorney-client relationship to demonstrate the requisite closeness. Specifically, they rely on a future attorney-client relationship with as yet unascertained Michigan criminal defendants "who will request, but be denied, the appointment of appellate counsel, based on the operation" of the statute. In two cases, we have recognized an attorney-client relationship as sufficient to confer third-party standing. See *Caplin & Drysdale, Chartered v. United States*, 491 U.S. 617 (1989); *Department of Labor v. Triplett*, 494 U.S. 715 (1990). In *Caplin & Drysdale*, we granted a law firm third-party standing to challenge a drug forfeiture statute by invoking the rights of an existing client. This *existing* attorney-client relationship is, of course, quite distinct from the *hypothetical* attorney-client relationship posited here.

In *Department of Labor v. Triplett*, we dealt with the Black Lung Benefits Act of 1972, which prohibited attorneys from accepting fees for representing claimants,

---

harm, they allege, would be remedied by declaratory and injunctive relief aimed at the system. Again, we assume, without deciding, that these allegations are sufficient. See *Ruhrgas AG v. Marathon Oil Co.*, 526 U.S. 574, 585 (1999).

unless such fees were approved by the appropriate agency or court. An attorney, George Triplett, violated the Act and its implementing regulations by agreeing to represent claimants for 25% of any award obtained and then collecting those fees without the required approval. The state bar disciplined Triplett, and we allowed Triplett third-party standing to invoke the due process rights of the claimants to challenge the fee restriction that resulted in his punishment. *Triplett* is different from this case on two levels. First, *Triplett* falls within that class of cases where we have "allowed standing to litigate the rights of third parties when enforcement of the challenged restriction *against the litigant* would result indirectly in the violation of third parties' rights." Second, and similar to *Caplin & Drysdale*, *Triplett* involved the representation of known claimants. The attorneys before us do not have a "close relationship" with their alleged "clients"; indeed, they have no relationship at all.

We next consider whether the attorneys have demonstrated that there is a "hindrance" to the indigents' advancing their own constitutional rights against the Michigan scheme. It is uncontested that an indigent denied appellate counsel has open avenues to argue that denial deprives him of his constitutional rights. He may seek leave to challenge that denial in the Michigan Court of Appeals and, if denied, seek leave in the Michigan Supreme Court. He then may seek a writ of certiorari in this Court. Beyond that, there exists both state and federal collateral review.

The attorneys argue that, without counsel, these avenues are effectively foreclosed to indigents. They claim that unsophisticated, *pro se* criminal defendants could not satisfy the necessary procedural requirements, and, if they did, they would be unable to coherently advance the substance of their constitutional claim.

That hypothesis, however, was disproved in the Michigan courts and this Court. [Here the Court cited Michigan cases and Supreme Court certiorari petitions by *pro se* defendants raising this issue.] While we agree that an attorney would be valuable to a criminal defendant challenging the constitutionality of the scheme, we do not think that the lack of an attorney here is the type of hindrance necessary to allow another to assert the indigent defendants' rights.

We also are unpersuaded by the attorneys' "hindrance" argument on a more fundamental level. If an attorney is all that the indigents need to perfect their challenge in state court and beyond, one wonders why the attorneys asserting this § 1983 action did not attend state court and assist them. We inquired into this question at oral argument but did not receive a satisfactory answer. It is a fair inference that the attorneys and the three indigent plaintiffs that filed this § 1983 action did not want to allow the state process to take its course. Rather, they wanted a federal court to short-circuit the State's adjudication of this constitutional question. That is precisely what they got.

"[F]ederal and state courts are complementary systems for administering justice in our Nation. Cooperation and comity, not competition and conflict, are essential to the federal design." The doctrine of *Younger v. Harris*, 401 U.S. 37 (1971), reinforces our federal scheme by preventing a state criminal defendant from asserting ancillary challenges to ongoing state criminal procedures in federal court.

In this case, the three indigent criminal defendants who were originally plaintiffs in this § 1983 action were appropriately dismissed under *Younger*. As the Court of Appeals unanimously recognized, they had ongoing state criminal proceedings and ample avenues to raise their constitutional challenge in those proceedings.[3] There also was no extraordinary circumstance requiring federal intervention. An unwillingness to allow the *Younger* principle to be thus circumvented is an additional reason to deny the attorneys third-party standing.

In sum, we hold that the attorneys do not have third-party standing to assert the rights of Michigan indigent defendants denied appellate counsel. We agree with the dissenting opinion in the Court of Appeals that "it would be a short step from the . . . grant of third-party standing in this case to a holding that lawyers generally have third-party standing to bring in court the claims of future unascertained clients."[5]

The judgment of the Court of Appeals is therefore reversed, and the case is remanded for further proceedings consistent with this opinion.

JUSTICE THOMAS, concurring.

That this case is even remotely close demonstrates that our third-party standing cases have gone far astray. We have granted third-party standing in a number of cases to litigants whose relationships with the directly affected individuals were at best remote. We have held, for instance, that beer vendors have standing to raise the rights of their prospective young male customers, see *Craig v. Boren*; that criminal defendants have standing to raise the rights of jurors excluded from service, see *Powers v. Ohio*; that sellers of mail-order contraceptives have standing to assert the rights of potential customers, see *Carey v. Population Services Int'l*; that distributors of contraceptives to unmarried persons have standing to litigate the rights of the potential recipients, *Eisenstadt v. Baird*; and that white sellers of land have standing to litigate the constitutional rights of potential black purchasers, see *Barrows v. Jackson*. I agree with the Court that "[t]he attorneys before us do not have a 'close relationship' with their alleged 'clients'; indeed, they have no relationship at all." The Court of Appeals understandably could have thought otherwise, given how generously our precedents have awarded third-party standing.

It is doubtful whether a party who has no personal constitutional right at stake in a case should ever be allowed to litigate the constitutional rights of others. . . . Litigants who have no personal right at stake may have very different interests from the individuals whose rights they are raising. Moreover, absent a personal right, a litigant has

---

3. The Court of Appeals suggested, however, that adverse Michigan precedent on the merits of the constitutional claim made any resort to the state courts futile and thus justified the attorneys' sally into federal court. But forum-shopping of this kind is not a basis for third-party standing.

5. As [the dissent] explained, the lawyer would have to make a credible claim that a challenged regulation would affect his income to satisfy Article III; after that, however, the possibilities would be endless. A medical malpractice attorney could assert an abstract, generalized challenge to tort reform statutes by asserting the rights of some hypothetical malpractice victim (or victims) who might sue. An attorney specializing in Social Security cases could challenge implementation of a new regulation by asserting the rights of some hypothetical claimant (or claimants). And so on.

no cause of action (or defense), and thus no right to relief. It may be too late in the day to return to this traditional view. But even assuming it makes sense to grant litigants third-party standing in at least some cases, it is more doubtful still whether third-party standing should sweep as broadly as our cases have held that it does.

Because the Court's opinion is a reasonable application of our precedents, I join it in full.

Justice Ginsburg, with whom Justice Stevens and Justice Souter join, dissenting.

Plaintiffs . . . are Michigan attorneys who have routinely received appointments to represent defendants in state-court criminal appeals, including appeals from plea-based convictions. They assert third-party standing to challenge a state law limiting an indigent's right to counsel: . . . [The] challenged law prescribes that most indigents

> who plead guilty, guilty but mentally ill, or nolo contendere shall not have appellate counsel appointed for review of the defendant's conviction or sentence.

The attorneys before us emphasize that indigent defendants generally are unable to navigate the appellate process *pro se*. In view of that reality, the attorneys brought this action under 42 U.S.C. § 1983, to advance indigent defendants' constitutional right to counsel's aid in pursuing appeals from plea-based convictions.

The Court has recognized exceptions to the general rule [against third-party standing] when certain circumstances combine: (1) "The litigant [has] suffered an 'injury in fact,' . . . giving him or her a 'sufficiently concrete interest' in the outcome of the issue in dispute"; (2) "the litigant [has] a close relation to the third party"; and (3) "there [exists] some hindrance to the third party's ability to protect his or her own interests." The first requirement is of a different order than the second and third, for whether a litigant meets the constitutional prescription of injury in fact determines whether his suit is "a case or controversy subject to a federal court's Art. III jurisdiction." By contrast, the close relation and hindrance criteria are "prudential considerations."

[Justice Ginsburg noted that the attorneys' injury in fact was conceded.]

Nor, under our precedent, should [the] attorneys encounter a "close relation" shoal. Our prior decisions do not warrant the distinction between an "*existing*" relationship and a "*hypothetical*" relationship that the Court advances today. *See, e.g., Carey v. Population Services Int'l; Griswold v. Connecticut*, 381 U.S. 479, 481 (1965) (noting that in *Pierce v. Society of Sisters*, 268 U.S. 510 (1925), "the owners of private schools were entitled to assert the rights of *potential* pupils and their parents," and in *Barrows*, "a white defendant . . . was allowed to raise . . . the rights of *prospective* Negro purchasers" (emphases added)).

Without suggesting that the timing of a relationship is key, the Court's decisions have focused on the character of the relationship between the litigant and the right-holder. *Singleton*, for example, acknowledged the significant bond between physician and patient. Similarly, this Court has twice recognized, in the third-party standing context, that the attorney-client relationship is of "special consequence." Moreover, the Court has found an adequate "relation" between litigants alleging third-party standing and those whose rights they seek to assert when nothing more than a buyer-seller connection was at stake. See *Carey; Craig v. Boren*.

Thus, as I see it, this case turns on the last of the three third-party standing inquiries, here, the existence of an impediment to the indigent defendants' effective assertion of their own rights through litigation. I note first that the Court has approached this requirement with a degree of elasticity. [Thus, in *Craig v. Boren*, Chief Justice Burger, dissenting, noted that] males between the ages of 18 and 21 who sought to purchase 3.2% beer faced no serious obstacle to asserting their own rights. The hindrance faced by a rightholder need only be "genuine," not "insurmountable." Even assuming a requirement with more starch than the Court has insisted upon in prior decisions, this case satisfies the "impediment" test.

To determine whether the indigent defendants are impeded from asserting their own rights, one must recognize the incapacities under which these defendants labor and the complexity of the issues their cases may entail. According to the Department of Justice, approximately eight out of ten state felony defendants use court-appointed lawyers. Approximately 70% of indigent defendants represented by appointed counsel plead guilty, and 70% of those convicted are incarcerated. It is likely that many of these indigent defendants, in common with 68% of the state prison population, did not complete high school, and many lack the most basic literacy skills. A Department of Education study found that about seven out of ten inmates fall in the lowest two out of five levels of literacy—marked by an inability to do such basic tasks as write a brief letter to explain an error on a credit card bill, use a bus schedule, or state in writing an argument made in a lengthy newspaper article. An inmate so handicapped surely does not possess the skill necessary to pursue a competent *pro se* appeal.

These indigent and poorly educated defendants face appeals from guilty pleas often no less complex than other appeals. An indigent defendant who pleads guilty may still raise on appeal

> constitutional defects that are irrelevant to his factual guilt, double jeopardy claims requiring no further factual record, jurisdictional defects, challenges to the sufficiency of the evidence at the preliminary examination, preserved entrapment claims, mental competency claims, factual basis claims, claims that the state had no right to proceed in the first place, including claims that a defendant was charged under an inapplicable statute, and claims of ineffective assistance of counsel.

The indigent defendant pursuing his own appeal must also navigate Michigan's procedures for seeking leave to appeal after sentencing on a guilty plea. Michigan's stated Rule requires a defendant to file an application for appeal within 21 days after entry of the judgment. The defendant must submit five copies of the application "stating the date and nature of the judgment or order appealed from; concisely reciting the appellant's allegations of error and the relief sought; [and] setting forth a concise argument . . . in support of the appellant's position on each issue." The State Court Administrative Office has furnished a three-page form application accompanied by two pages of instructions for defendants seeking leave to appeal after sentencing on a guilty plea. But this form is unlikely to provide adequate aid to an indigent and poorly educated defendant. The form requires entry of such information as "charge code(s), MCL citation/PACC Code," asks the applicant to state the issues and facts relevant to the appeal, and then requires the applicant to "state the law that supports your position and explain how the law applies to the facts of your case." This last task would not be onerous for an applicant familiar with law school examinations, but it is a tall order for a defendant of marginal literacy.[4]

The Court ... writes that recognizing third-party standing here would allow lawyers generally to assert standing to champion their potential clients' rights. For example, a medical malpractice attorney could challenge a tort reform statute on behalf of a future client or a Social Security lawyer could challenge new regulations. In such cases, however, in marked contrast to the instant case, the persons directly affected—malpractice plaintiffs or benefits claimants—would face no unusual obstacle in securing the aid of counsel to attack the disadvantageous statutory or regulatory change. There is no cause, therefore, to allow an attorney to challenge the benefit- or award-reducing provision in a suit brought in the attorney's name. The party whose interests the provision directly impacts can instead mount the challenge with the aid of counsel.

This case is "unusual because it is the deprivation of counsel itself that prevents indigent defendants from protecting their right to counsel." The challenged statute leaves indigent criminal defendants without the aid needed to gain access to the appellate forum and thus without a viable means to protect their rights.

The Court is "unpersuaded by the attorneys' 'hindrance' argument," in the main, because it sees a clear path for [the plaintiffs]: They could have "attend[ed] state court and assist[ed] [indigent defendants]." Had the attorneys taken this course, hundreds, perhaps thousands, of criminal defendants would have gone uncounseled while the attorneys afforded assistance to a few individuals. In order to protect the rights of *all* indigent defendants, the attorneys sought prospective classwide relief to prevent the statute from taking effect. . . .

In sum, this case presents an unusual if not unique case of defendants facing near-insurmountable practical obstacles to protecting their rights in the state forum: First, it is the deprivation of counsel itself that prevents indigent defendants, many of whom are likely to be unsophisticated and poorly educated, from protecting their rights; second, the substantive issues that such defendants could raise in an appeal are myriad and often complicated; and third, the procedural requirements for an appeal after a guilty plea are not altogether indigent-user friendly. The exposure of impecunious defendants to these access-to-appeal blockages in state court makes the need for this suit all the more compelling.

---

4. The rare case of an unusually effective *pro se* defendant is the exception that proves the rule: The Court identifies three Michigan defendants who pursued right-to-counsel claims. The fact that a handful of *pro se* defendants has brought claims shows neither that the run-of-the-mine defendant can successfully navigate state procedures nor that he can effectively represent himself on the merits.

For the reasons stated, I would affirm the en banc Sixth Circuit decision that [the] attorneys have standing to maintain the instant action and would proceed to the merits of the controversy.

Note: More on Third-Party Standing

1. *Singleton* and *Kowalski* articulate several justifications for the court's general rule that a party "must assert his own legal rights and interests, and cannot rest his claim to relief on the legal rights or interests of third parties." Among them are: (1) the need to avoid unnecessary adjudication of constitutional issues; (2) a preference for a sharp presentation of the issues by those who "will be the best proponents of their own rights"; and (3) deference to other institutions that "may be more competent" to address questions of "wide public significance."

Both cases also explain, however, that when there is both a "close relationship" between the litigant and the third party and a "genuine obstacle" or "hindrance" to the third party bringing the action, the normal bar on third-party standing does not apply. As the two decisions suggest, however, applying these criteria consistently has proven difficult.

Consider the instances in which the Court has granted litigants standing to bring constitutional challenges on behalf of third parties. The Court has found sufficiently close relationships between doctors and patients (*Griswold v. Connecticut*, 381 U.S. 479 (1965)), lawyers and clients (*Caplin & Drysdale, Chartered v. United States*, 491 U.S. 617 (1989)), covenantors and prospective buyers of real estate (*Barrows v. Jackson*, 346 U.S. 249 (1953)), and even beer vendors and prospective 18-year-old male clients (*Craig v. Boren*, 429 U.S. 190 (1976)). What, if anything, do these relationships have in common? Under the Court's case law, why can beer vendors bring an Equal Protection challenge to an Oklahoma law prohibiting prospective clients from purchasing 3.2% beer, while attorneys are prohibited from raising Due Process and Equal Protection challenges to a Michigan statute denying the right to appointed appellate counsel to prospective indigent clients who plead guilty? Is the Court's case law consistent on what constitutes a sufficiently close relationship?

2. Justice Powell complains in *Singleton* that the Court's description of the "genuine obstacle" criterion is "chimerical." In his view, neither the privacy nor mootness considerations in *Singleton* are "genuine obstacles" because a woman can proceed under a pseudonym and the "capable of repetition, yet evading review" doctrine overcomes any mootness concerns.

In *Kowalski*, by contrast, the Court dismisses the attorneys' hindrance argument, primarily because an indigent denied appellate counsel "has open avenues to argue that [the] denial deprives him of his constitutional rights." Justice Ginsburg responds by arguing that the Court's reference to three cases of indigents bringing successful *pro se* appeals is the "exception that proves the rule," because of the "complex" procedural requirements for bringing an appeal and the "marginal literacy" of most indigents. Is the majority callously overlooking the hard reality that indigent defendants who plead guilty are unlikely to be successful on appeal? Or is their likelihood of success irrelevant in making the determination of whether the obstacle is "genuine"?

More fundamentally, in which case, *Singleton* or *Kowalski*, are the obstacles more compelling? After these two cases, how "genuine" must an obstacle be for a litigant to bring a constitutional challenge on behalf of a third party?

3. Under the majority's view in *Kowalski*, the proper plaintiffs to assert claims regarding the constitutionality of the Michigan statute are the indigent criminal defendants who were denied appointed appellate counsel. In *Halbert v. Michigan*, 545 U.S. 605 (2005), decided approximately six months after *Kowalski*, the Court held in a challenge brought by an indigent criminal defendant that Michigan's statute and practice of denying appointed appellate counsel was unconstitutional. Does the relative speed with which the Supreme Court heard the *Halbert* case support the majority's view in *Kowalski* that indigent criminal defendants did not face an obstacle in asserting their own constitutional rights?

4. The Court briefly mentions in *Kowalski* that "[w]ithin the context of the First Amendment . . . the Court has enunciated other concerns that justify a lessening of prudential limitations on standing." As the Court stated in *Secretary of State of Maryland v. Joseph H. Munson Co.*, 467 U.S. 947, 956–57 (1984):

> Even where a First Amendment challenge could be brought by [a person] actually engaged in protected activity, there is a possibility that, rather than risk punishment for his conduct in challenging the statute, he will refrain from engaging further in the protected activity. Society as a whole then would be the loser. Thus, when there is a danger of chilling free speech, the concern that constitutional adjudication be avoided whenever possible may be outweighed by society's interest in having the statute challenged. Litigants, therefore, are permitted to challenge a statute not because their own rights of free expression are violated, but because of a judicial prediction or assumption that the statute's very existence may cause others not before the court to refrain from constitutionally protected speech or expression.

The overbreadth doctrine, as it is commonly called, is another exception to the general prohibition against litigants bringing suits on behalf of third parties. As the Court has explained, overbreadth claims typically arise when a person to whom a statute is constitutionally applied seeks to challenge the statute on the grounds that its hypothetical application to others would deter constitutionally-protected conduct (typically, speech). In one sense, then, a litigant alleging overbreadth is seeking to assert the rights of others not before the court. But as Richard Fallon has observed, the litigant in a third-party standing claim differs from a litigant asserting overbreadth in that one asserting third-party standing

> typically presents a thoroughly concrete, not hypothetical, set of facts. There is indeed an underlying affinity between doctrines that invite facial challenges (such as the First Amendment "overbreadth" test) and third-party standing doctrines, but only one that is exceedingly abstract: Both are governed by

rules reflecting judicial judgments about the doctrinal structure that is appropriate to achieve effective implementation of constitutional norms and not about the moral deserts of particular litigants.

Richard H. Fallon, Jr., *As Applied and Facial Challenges and Third-Party Standing*, 113 HARV. L. REV. 1321, 1359 (2000).

Problem: A Lawsuit by a Non-Custodial Parent

Mark Ford and his wife Carrie, unable to resolve their marital differences, divorced in 2011. Carrie fought for, and ultimately won, sole custody of their only child, George, in part because Carrie convinced the family court judge that Mark's atheism was harmful to George's upbringing. Other than their differences about religion, however, Mark and Carrie are on amicable terms, and both play a part in George's life. George attends school in the Capital City School District, where the students recite the pledge of allegiance on a daily basis.

Mark believes that the words "under God" in the pledge violate the First Amendment's Establishment and Free Exercise Clauses. Accordingly, Mark brought suit in United States District Court against the Capital City School District, alleging that recitation of the pledge violated his and his son's constitutional rights. Carrie, as George's mother, intervened, and sought dismissal of the complaint on the grounds that she had sole legal custody and thus the sole right to decide questions regarding George's religion and education. She argued that neither she nor George objected to the religious language in the pledge.

Mark also alleged in his complaint that he had in the past and would again attend school with George on occasion; that he had attended school board meetings at which the pledge was recited; that he had "considered teaching elementary school" in the district; and that his child support payments formed part of the tax support for the district. Thus, Mark argued that he had standing to bring his own First Amendment challenge to the pledge of allegiance or, in the alternative, to represent the interests of his son George in the litigation. Capital City responded by filing a motion to dismiss for lack of subject matter jurisdiction.

How should the district court rule on the City's motion to dismiss?

Note: The "Zone of Interests" Test

In *Lujan*, the Court considered Congress's role in creating standing from an Article III perspective. But there is another strand of doctrine that falls into the prudential realm. This is the requirement (as summarized in *Allen*) that a plaintiff's complaint fall "within the zone of interests protected by the law invoked."

Early cases discussing the idea of a "zone of interests" were based on invocation of Section 10 of the Administrative Procedure Act (APA), which states:

A person suffering a legal wrong because of agency action, or adversely affected or aggrieved by agency action within the meaning of a relevant statute, is entitled to judicial review thereof.

Data Processing Service Organizations v. Camp, 397 U.S. 150 (1970), is the landmark case. The Bank Services Corporation Act of 1962 limits the activities in which banks may engage. The Comptroller of the Currency interpreted the Act to permit banks to provide data processing services to their customers, and that interpretation was challenged by firms that provided such services commercially. These firms met the Article III requirements for injury, because the decision would inevitably increase competition for their customers. The Court then determined as a separate matter that the firms were within the "zone of interests" that Congress intended to protect with the Act.

After *Data Processing*, which treated this question of statutory interpretation as a prudential limit on standing, the Court decided a number of cases in which the zone-of-interests analysis appeared dead. More recently, it has made a return. In *Federal Election Commission v. Akins*, 524 U.S. 11 (1998), the Court held that a group of voters had standing to challenge the Commission's determination that the American Israel Public Affairs Committee (AIPAC) was not a "political committee" as defined by the Federal Election Campaign Act of 1971 (FECA), and thus not subject to disclosure requirements. The voter group opposed AIPAC's positions and sought to have the FEC declare it a political committee and regulate its finances. FECA provided that "[a]ny person who believes a violation of this Act . . . has occurred may file a complaint with the Commission," and added that "[a]ny party aggrieved by an order of the Commission dismissing a complaint filed by such party . . . may file a petition" in district court seeking review of that dismissal.

The Court stated:

> History associates the word "aggrieved" with a congressional intent to cast the standing net broadly—beyond the common-law interests and substantive statutory rights upon which "prudential" standing traditionally rested. Moreover, prudential standing is satisfied when the injury asserted by a plaintiff "'arguably [falls] within the zone of interests to be protected or regulated by the statute . . . in question.'" The injury of which respondents complain—their failure to obtain relevant information—is injury of a kind that FECA seeks to address. We have found nothing in the Act that suggests Congress intended to exclude voters from the benefits of these provisions, or otherwise to restrict standing, say, to political parties, candidates, or their committees. Given the language of the statute and the nature of the injury, we conclude that Congress, intending to protect voters such as respondents from suffering the kind of injury here at issue, intended to authorize this kind of suit. Consequently, respondents satisfy "prudential" standing requirements.

The Court then concluded that the voter group also met constitutional standing requirements.

Justice Scalia, joined by Justice O'Connor and Justice Thomas, dissented from the constitutional holding. The dissent made no mention of the "zone of interests" test.

In *Match-E-Be-Nash-She-Wish Band of Pottowatomi Indians v. Patchak*, 132 S. Ct. 2199 (2012), the Court clarified the low bar created by the zone-of-interests test:

The prudential standing test . . . is not meant to be especially demanding. We apply the test in keeping with Congress's "evident intent" when enacting the APA to make agency action presumptively reviewable. We do not require any indication of congressional purpose to benefit the would-be plaintiff. And we have always conspicuously included the word "arguably" in the test to indicate that the benefit of the doubt goes to the plaintiff. The rest forecloses suit only when a plaintiff's interests are so marginally related to or inconsistent with the purposes implicit in the statute that it cannot reasonably be assumed that Congress intended to permit the suit.

B. Ripeness

Ripeness and mootness are complementary doctrines that focus on the timing of the injury. The doctrine of ripeness asks whether there is a controversy between the parties that requires adjudication, or whether there are contingencies that might avoid the need for the courts to intervene. Mootness asks whether the controversy between the parties has ended in such a manner that there remains no useful relief that a court could give. Ripeness and mootness have both constitutional and prudential aspects. We look at ripeness first.

Doe v. Bush

United States Court of Appeals for the First Circuit, 2003.

323 F. 3d 133.

Before LYNCH, CIRCUIT JUDGE, CYR and STAHL, SENIOR CIRCUIT JUDGES.

LYNCH, CIRCUIT JUDGE.

Plaintiffs are active-duty members of the military, parents of military personnel, and members of the U.S. House of Representatives. They filed a complaint in district court seeking a preliminary injunction to prevent the defendants, President George W. Bush and Secretary of Defense Donald Rumsfeld, from initiating a war against Iraq. They assert that such an action would violate the Constitution. The district court dismissed the suit, and plaintiffs appeal. We affirm the dismissal.

In October 2002, Congress passed the Authorization for Use of Military Force Against Iraq Resolution of 2002 (the "October Resolution"). Plaintiffs argue that the October Resolution is constitutionally inadequate to authorize the military offensive that defendants are now planning against Iraq. See U.S. Const. art. I, § 8, cl. 11 (granting Congress the power "[t]o declare war"). They base this argument on two theories. They argue that Congress and the President are in collision — that the President is about to act in violation of the October Resolution. They also argue that Congress and the President are in collusion — that Congress has handed over to the President its exclusive power to declare war.

In either case, plaintiffs argue, judicial intervention is necessary to preserve the principle of separation of powers which undergirds our constitutional structure. Only the judiciary, they argue, has the constitutionally assigned role and the institutional competence to police the boundaries of the constitutional mandates given to the other branches: Congress alone has the authority to declare war and the President alone has the authority to make war.

The plaintiffs argue that important and increasingly vital interests are served by the requirement that it be Congress which decides whether to declare war. Quoting Thomas Jefferson, they argue that congressional involvement will slow the "dogs of war"; that Congress, the voice of the people, should make this momentous decision, one which will cost lives; and that congressional support is needed to ensure that the country is behind the war, a key element in any victory. They also argue that, absent an attack on this country or our allies, congressional involvement must come prior to war, because once war has started, Congress is in an uncomfortable default position where the use of its appropriations powers to cut short any war is an inadequate remedy.

The defendants are equally eloquent about the impropriety of judicial intrusion into the "extraordinarily delicate foreign affairs and military calculus, one that could be fatally upset by judicial interference." Such intervention would be all the worse here, defendants say, because Congress and the President are in accord as to the threat to the nation and the legitimacy of a military response to that threat.

The case before us is a somber and weighty one. We have considered these important concerns carefully, and we have concluded that the circumstances call for judicial restraint. The theory of collision between the legislative and executive branches is not suitable for judicial review, because there is not a ripe dispute concerning the President's acts and the requirements of the October Resolution passed by Congress. By contrast, the theory of collusion, by its nature, assumes no conflict between the political branches, but rather a willing abdication of congressional power to an emboldened and enlarged presidency. That theory is not fit for judicial review for a different, but related, reason: Plaintiffs' claim that Congress and the President have transgressed the boundaries of their shared war powers, as demarcated by the Constitution, is presently insufficient to present a justiciable issue. Common to both is our assessment that, before courts adjudicate a case involving the war powers allocated to the two political branches, they must be presented with a case or controversy that clearly raises the specter of undermining the constitutional structure.

I.

Tensions between the United States and Iraq have been high at least since Iraq invaded neighboring Kuwait in 1990. In 1991, the United States led an international coalition in the Persian Gulf War, which drove Iraqi forces from Kuwait. Before that conflict, Congress passed a resolution quite similar to the October Resolution. As part of the ceasefire ending the Gulf War, Iraq agreed to United Nations Security Council Resolution 687, which required that Iraq end the development of nuclear, biological, and chemical weapons, destroy all existing weapons of this sort and their delivery systems, and allow United Nations weapons inspections to confirm its compliance with these terms. Since that time, Iraq has repeatedly been in breach of this agreement by, among other things, blocking inspections and hiding banned weapons. Iraq ended cooperation with the weapons inspection program in 1998. Since 1991, the United States and other nations have enforced a no-fly zone near the Kuwaiti border and on several occasions have launched missile strikes against Iraq.

Congress has been engaged in the American response to Iraqi noncompliance throughout this period. It was well-informed about ongoing American military activities, enforcement of the no-fly zone, and the missile strikes. In 1998, Congress passed a joint resolution which chronicled Iraqi noncompliance and declared that "the Government of Iraq is in material and unacceptable breach of its international obligations, and therefore the President is urged to take appropriate action, in accordance with the Constitution and relevant laws of the United States, to bring Iraq into compliance with its international obligations." Later that year, Congress also passed the Iraq Liberation Act of 1998. This statute authorized assistance, including military equipment and training, for "Iraqi democratic opposition organizations," and declared that it should be United States policy to remove Iraqi leader Saddam Hussein from power.

The United Nations has also remained engaged in the dispute ever since the Persian Gulf War. It supervised weapons inspections, supported economic sanctions against Iraq, and, through the Security Council, repeatedly passed resolutions declaring that Iraq was not fulfilling the conditions of Resolution 687. On September 12, 2002, President Bush addressed the United Nations General Assembly. There he called for a renewed effort to demand Iraqi disarmament and indicated that he thought military force would be necessary if diplomacy continued to fail. In response, Iraq agreed to allow inspectors back into the country, but it has failed to comply fully with the earlier Security Council resolutions.

The week after his September 12 speech at the United Nations, President Bush proposed language for a congressional resolution supporting the use of force against Iraq. Detailed and lengthy negotiations between and among congressional leaders and the Administration hammered out a revised and much narrower version of the resolution. The House of Representatives passed this measure by a vote of 296 to 133 on October 10, 2002; the Senate followed suit on October 11 by a vote of 77 to 23.

On November 8, 2002, the Security Council passed Resolution 1441, which declared that Iraq remained in material breach of its obligations and offered "a final opportunity to comply with its disarmament obligations." It also noted that "the Council has repeatedly warned Iraq that it will face serious consequences as a result of its continued violations of its obligations." In diplomatic parlance, the phrase "serious consequences" generally refers to military action. More than 200,000 United States troops are now deployed around Iraq, preparing for the possibility of an invasion. . . .

II.

The Constitution reserves the war powers to the legislative and executive branches. This court has declined the invitation to become involved in such matters once before. Over thirty years ago, the First Circuit addressed a war powers case challenging the constitutionality of the Vietnam War on the basis that Congress had not declared war.

Massachusetts v. Laird, 451 F.2d 26 (1st Cir. 1971). The court found that other actions by Congress, such as continued appropriations to fund the war over the course of six years, provided enough indication of congressional approval to put the question beyond the reach of judicial review:

> The war in Vietnam is a product of the jointly supportive actions of the two branches to whom the congeries of the war powers have been committed. Because the branches are not in opposition, there is no necessity of determining boundaries. Should either branch be opposed to the continuance of hostilities, however, and present the issue in clear terms, a court might well take a different view. This question we do not face.

Applying this precedent to the case at hand today, the district court concluded, "[T]here is a day to day fluidity in the situation that does not amount to resolute conflict between the branches — but that does argue against an uninformed judicial intervention."

The lack of a fully developed dispute between the two elected branches, and the consequent lack of a clearly defined issue, is exactly the type of concern which causes courts to find a case unripe. In his concurring opinion in *Goldwater v. Carter*, 444 U.S. 996 (1979), Justice Powell stated that courts should decline, on ripeness grounds, to decide "issues affecting the allocation of power between the President and Congress until the political branches reach a constitutional impasse." (Powell, J., concurring). A number of courts have adopted Justice Powell's ripeness reasoning in cases involving military powers. [Citations omitted.]

Ripeness doctrine involves more than simply the timing of the case. It mixes various mutually reinforcing constitutional and prudential considerations. One such consideration is the need "to prevent the courts, through avoidance of premature adjudication, from entangling themselves in abstract disagreements." Another is to avoid unnecessary constitutional decisions. A third is the recognition that, by waiting until a case is fully developed before deciding it, courts benefit from a focus sharpened by particular facts. The case before us raises all three of these concerns.

These rationales spring, in part, from the recognition that the scope of judicial power is bounded by the Constitution. "It is a principle of first importance that the federal courts are courts of limited jurisdiction." C.A. Wright & M.K. Kane, Law of Federal Courts 27 (6th ed. 2002). Article III of the Constitution limits jurisdiction to "cases" and "controversies," and prudential doctrines may counsel additional restraint. . . .

Ripeness is dependent on the circumstances of a particular case. Two factors are used to evaluate ripeness: "the fitness of the issues for judicial decision and the hardship to the parties of withholding court consideration." Ordinarily, both factors must be present.

The hardship prong of this test is most likely satisfied here; the current mobilization already imposes difficulties on the plaintiff soldiers and family members, so that they suffer "present injury from a future contemplated event." Plaintiffs also lack a realistic opportunity to secure comparable relief by bringing the action at a later time.

The fitness inquiry here presents a greater obstacle. Fitness "typically involves subsidiary queries concerning finality, definiteness, and the extent to which resolution of the challenge depends upon facts that may not yet be sufficiently developed." The baseline question is whether allowing more time for development of events would "significantly advance our ability to deal with the legal issues presented [or] aid us in their resolution." "[T]he question of fitness does not pivot solely on whether a court is capable of resolving a claim intelligently, but also involves an assessment of whether it is appropriate for the court to undertake the task." These prudential considerations are particularly strong in this case, which presents a politically-charged controversy involving momentous issues, both substantively (war and peace) and constitutionally (the powers of coequal branches).

One thrust of the plaintiffs' argument is that the October Resolution only permits actions sanctioned by the Security Council. In plaintiffs' view, the Resolution's authorization is so narrow that, even with Security Council approval of military force, Congress would need to pass a new resolution before United States participation in an attack on Iraq would be constitutional. At a minimum, according to plaintiffs, the October Resolution authorizes no military action "outside of a United Nations coalition."

For various reasons, this issue is not fit now for judicial review. For example, should there be an attack, Congress may take some action immediately. The purported conflict between the political branches may disappear. "That the future event may never come to pass augurs against a finding of fitness."

Many important questions remain unanswered about whether there will be a war, and, if so, under what conditions. Diplomatic negotiations, in particular, fluctuate daily. The President has emphasized repeatedly that hostilities still may be averted if Iraq takes certain actions. The Security Council is now debating the possibility of passing a new resolution that sets a final deadline for Iraqi compliance. United Nations weapons inspectors continue their investigations inside Iraq. Other countries ranging from Canada to Cameroon have reportedly pursued their own proposals to broker a compromise. As events unfold, it may become clear that diplomacy has either succeeded or failed decisively. The Security Council, now divided on the issue, may reach a consensus. To evaluate this claim now, the court would need to pile one hypothesis on top of another. We would need to assume that the Security Council will not authorize war, and that the President will proceed nonetheless.

Thus, even assuming that plaintiffs correctly interpret the commands of the legislative branch, it is impossible to say yet whether or not those commands will be obeyed. As was the situation in *Goldwater*, "[i]n the present posture of this case, we do not know whether there will ever be an actual confrontation between the Legislative and Executive Branches."

[The court's discussion of the plaintiffs' "collusion" theory is omitted.]

Note: Ripeness

1. As the *Doe* case makes clear, judgments involving whether a dispute has reached a point requiring or permitting resolution can be exceedingly difficult, and the costs of an inaccurate prediction can be high. Return to *Doe* after the section on political questions, *infra*. What impediments will plaintiffs face if they attempt to return to court after the invasion of Iraq became a reality?

2. In *Susan B. Anthony List v. Driehaus*, 134 S. Ct. 2334 (2014), the Court cryptically suggested that the fitness and hardship elements of ripeness may be prudential, and that the constitutional component of ripeness may be the same as the imminence requirement for standing. The Court stated:

> In concluding that petitioners' claims were not justiciable, the Sixth Circuit separately considered two other factors: whether the factual record was sufficiently developed, and whether hardship to the parties would result if judicial relief is denied at this stage in the proceedings. Respondents contend that these "prudential ripeness" factors confirm that the claims at issue are nonjusticiable. But we have already concluded that petitioners have alleged a sufficient Article III injury. To the extent respondents would have us deem petitioners' claims nonjusticiable "on grounds that are 'prudential,' rather than constitutional," "[t]hat request is in some tension with our recent reaffirmation of the principle that 'a federal court's obligation to hear and decide' cases within its jurisdiction 'is virtually unflagging.'"

Is ripeness more prudential than constitutional, or vice versa?

3. The policies and costs of a decision on ripeness grounds are discussed at length in *Poe v. Ullman*, the next principal case. *Poe* is best known today as the precursor of *Griswold v. Connecticut*, 381 U.S. 479 (1965), in which the Court finally decided the constitutionality of the Connecticut birth control statute.

4. *Doe v. Bush* and *Poe v. Ullman* were both suits for declaratory judgments. (*Doe* was litigated in federal court; *Poe* was litigated initially in state court.) This is no coincidence; declaratory judgment suits are prime candidates for ripeness problems. The declaratory judgment mechanism exists to permit resolution of rights between parties at a point where neither side has initiated coercive action.

Poe v. Ullman

United States Supreme Court, 1961.

367 U.S. 497.

MR. JUSTICE FRANKFURTER announced the judgment of the Court and an opinion in which THE CHIEF JUSTICE, MR. JUSTICE CLARK and MR. JUSTICE WHITTAKER join.

These appeals challenge the constitutionality, under the Fourteenth Amendment, of Connecticut statutes which, as authoritatively construed by the Connecticut Supreme Court of Errors, prohibit the use of contraceptive devices and the giving of medical advice in the use of such devices. In proceedings seeking declarations of law, not on review of convictions for violation of the statutes, that court has ruled that these statutes would be applicable in the case of married couples and even under claim that conception would constitute a serious threat to the health or life of the female spouse.

[There were three lawsuits involved in this case. The first involved a married couple; the wife had given birth to three children with genetic defects who died shortly after birth. The second involved a married woman who had barely survived a disastrous pregnancy. The third was brought by Dr. Buxton, who claimed that Connecticut law interfered with his practice of medicine. The other plaintiffs had sought medical advice from Buxton, whose advice was for them to avoid further pregnancies. Under Connecticut law, however, he was forbidden to give advice about or prescribe contraceptives.]

Appellants' complaints in these declaratory judgment proceedings do not clearly, and certainly do not in terms, allege that appellee Ullman [the State's Attorney] threatens to prosecute them for use of, or for giving advice concerning, contraceptive devices. The allegations are merely that, in the course of his public duty, he intends to prosecute any offenses against Connecticut law, and that he claims that use of and advice concerning contraceptives would constitute offenses. The lack of immediacy of the threat described by these allegations might alone raise serious questions of non-justiciability of appellants' claims. But even were we to read the allegations to convey a clear threat of imminent prosecutions, we are not bound to accept as true all that is alleged on the face of the complaint and admitted, technically, by demurrer, any more than the Court is bound by stipulation of the parties. Formal agreement between parties that collides with plausibility is too fragile a foundation for indulging in constitutional adjudication.

The Connecticut law prohibiting the use of contraceptives has been on the State's books since 1879. During the more than three-quarters of a century since its enactment, a prosecution for its violation seems never to have been initiated, save in *State v. Nelson*. The circumstances of that case, decided in 1940, only prove the abstract character of what is before us. There, a test case was brought to determine the constitutionality of the Act as applied against two doctors and a nurse who had allegedly disseminated contraceptive information. After the Supreme Court of Errors sustained the legislation on appeal from a demurrer to the information, the State moved to dismiss the information. Neither counsel nor our own researchers have discovered any other attempt to enforce the prohibition of distribution or use of contraceptive devices by criminal process.

The unreality of these law suits is illumined by another circumstance. We were advised by counsel for appellants that contraceptives are commonly and notoriously sold in Connecticut drug stores. Yet no prosecutions are recorded; and certainly such ubiquitous, open, public sales would more quickly invite the attention of enforcement officials than the conduct in which the present appellants wish to engage—the giving of private medical advice by a doctor to his individual patients, and their private use of the devices prescribed. The undeviating policy of nullification by Connecticut of its anti-contraceptive laws throughout all the long years that they have been on the statute books bespeaks more than prosecutorial paralysis. . . .

The restriction of our jurisdiction to cases and controversies within the meaning of Article III of the Constitution is not the sole limitation on the exercise of our appellate powers, especially in cases raising constitutional questions. The policy reflected in numerous cases and over a long period was thus summarized in the oft-quoted statement of Mr. Justice Brandeis: "The Court [has] developed, for its own governance in the cases confessedly within its jurisdiction, a series of rules under which it has avoided passing upon a large part of all the constitutional questions pressed upon it for decision." *Ashwander v. Tennessee Valley Authority*, 297 U.S. 288, 341, 346 (concurring opinion). In part the rules summarized in the *Ashwander* opinion have derived from the historically defined, limited nature and function of courts and from the recognition that, within the framework of our adversary system, the adjudicatory process is most securely founded when it is exercised under the impact of a lively conflict between antagonistic demands, actively pressed, which make resolution of the controverted issue a practical necessity. In part they derive from the fundamental federal and tripartite character of our National Government and from the role — restricted by its very responsibility — of the federal courts, and particularly this Court, within that structure.

These considerations press with special urgency in cases challenging legislative action or state judicial action as repugnant to the Constitution. "The best teaching of this Court's experience admonishes us not to entertain constitutional questions in advance of the strictest necessity." The various doctrines of "standing," "ripeness," and "mootness," which this Court has evolved with particular, though not exclusive, reference to such cases are but several manifestations — each having its own "varied application" — of the primary conception that federal judicial power is to be exercised to strike down legislation, whether state or federal, only at the instance of one who is himself immediately harmed, or immediately threatened with harm, by the challenged action. "This court can have no right to pronounce an abstract opinion upon the constitutionality of a State law. Such law must be brought into actual or threatened operation upon rights properly falling under judicial cognizance, or a remedy is not to be had here." The party who invokes the power [to annul legislation on grounds of its unconstitutionality] must be able to show not only that the statute is invalid, but that he has sustained or is immediately in danger of sustaining some direct injury as the result of its enforcement. . . .

The requirement for adversity was classically expounded in *Chicago & Grand Trunk R. Co. v. Wellman*, 143 U.S. 339 (1892):

> Whenever, in pursuance of an honest and actual antagonistic assertion of rights by one individual against another, there is presented a question involving the validity of any act of any legislature, State or Federal, and the decision necessarily rests on the competency of the legislature to so enact, the court must, in the exercise of its solemn duties, determine whether the act be constitutional or not; but such an exercise of power is the ultimate

and supreme function of courts. It is legitimate only in the last resort, and as a necessity in the determination of real, earnest and vital controversy between individuals. It never was the thought that, by means of a friendly suit, a party beaten in the legislature could transfer to the courts an inquiry as to the constitutionality of the legislative act.

. . . It is clear that the mere existence of a state penal statute would constitute insufficient grounds to support a federal court's adjudication of its constitutionality in proceedings brought against the State's prosecuting officials if real threat of enforcement is wanting. If the prosecutor expressly agrees not to prosecute, a suit against him for declaratory and injunctive relief is not such an adversary case as will be reviewed here. Eighty years of Connecticut history demonstrate a similar, albeit tacit agreement. The fact that Connecticut has not chosen to press the enforcement of this statute deprives these controversies of the immediacy which is an indispensable condition of constitutional adjudication. This Court cannot be umpire to debates concerning harmless, empty shadows. To find it necessary to pass on these statutes now, in order to protect appellants from the hazards of prosecution, would be to close our eyes to reality.

We cannot agree that if Dr. Buxton's compliance with these statutes is uncoerced by the risk of their enforcement, his patients are entitled to a declaratory judgment concerning the statutes' validity. And, with due regard to Dr. Buxton's standing as a physician and to his personal sensitiveness, we cannot accept, as the basis of constitutional adjudication, other than as chimerical the fear of enforcement of provisions that have during so many years gone uniformly and without exception unenforced.

Justiciability is of course not a legal concept with a fixed content or susceptible of scientific verification. Its utilization is the resultant of many subtle pressures, including the appropriateness of the issues for decision by this Court and the actual hardship to the litigants of denying them the relief sought. Both these factors justify withholding adjudication of the constitutional issue raised under the circumstances and in the manner in which they are now before the Court.

Dismissed.

MR. JUSTICE BLACK dissents because he believes that the constitutional questions should be reached and decided.

MR. JUSTICE BRENNAN, concurring in the judgment.

I agree that this appeal must be dismissed for failure to present a real and substantial controversy which unequivocally calls for adjudication of the rights claimed in advance of any attempt by the State to curtail them by criminal prosecution. I am not convinced, on this skimpy record, that these appellants as individuals are truly caught in an inescapable dilemma. The true controversy in this case is over the opening of birth-control clinics on a large scale; it is that which the State has prevented in the past, not the use of contraceptives by isolated and individual married couples. It will be time enough to decide the constitutional questions urged upon us when, if ever, that real controversy flares up again. Until it does, or until the State makes a definite and concrete threat to enforce these laws against individual married couples—a threat which it has never made in the past except under the provocation of litigation—this Court may not be compelled to exercise its most delicate power of constitutional adjudication.

Mr. Justice Douglas, dissenting.

These cases are dismissed because a majority of the members of this Court conclude, for varying reasons, that this controversy does not present a justiciable question. That conclusion is too transparent to require an extended reply. The device of the declaratory judgment is an honored one. Its use in the federal system is restricted to "cases" or "controversies" within the meaning of Article III. The question must be "appropriate for judicial determination," not hypothetical, abstract, academic or moot. . . .

The need for this remedy in the federal field was summarized in a Senate Report as follows: ". . . it is often necessary, in the absence of the declaratory judgment procedure, to violate or purport to violate a statute in order to obtain a judicial determination of its meaning or validity."

If there is a case where the need for this remedy in the shadow of a criminal prosecution is shown, it is this one. Plaintiffs in No. 60 are two sets of husband and wife. One wife is pathetically ill, having delivered a stillborn fetus. If she becomes pregnant again, her life will be gravely jeopardized. This couple have been unable to get medical advice concerning the "best and safest" means to avoid pregnancy from their physician, plaintiff in No. 61, because if he gave it he would commit a crime. The use of contraceptive devices would also constitute a crime. And it is alleged—and admitted by the State—that the State's Attorney intends to enforce the law by prosecuting offenses under the laws.

A public clinic dispensing birth-control information has indeed been closed by the State. Doctors and a nurse working in that clinic were arrested by the police and charged with advising married women on the use of contraceptives. That litigation produced *State v. Nelson*, which upheld these statutes. That same police raid on the clinic resulted in the seizure of a quantity of the clinic's contraception literature and medical equipment and supplies. . . .

The Court refers to the *Nelson* prosecution as a "test case" and implies that it had little impact. Yet its impact was described differently by a contemporary observer who concluded his comment with this sentence: "This serious setback to the birth control movement [the *Nelson* case] led to the closing of all the clinics in the state, just as they had been previously closed in the state of Massachusetts." At oral argument, counsel for appellants confirmed that the clinics are still closed. In response to a question from the bench, he affirmed that "no public or private clinic" has dared give birth-control advice since the decision in the *Nelson* case.

These, then, are the circumstances in which the Court feels that it can, contrary to every principle of American or English common law, go outside the record to conclude that there exists a "tacit agreement" that these statutes will not be enforced. No lawyer, I think, would advise his clients to rely on that "tacit agreement." No police official, I think, would feel himself bound by that "tacit agreement." After our national experience during the prohibition era, it would be absurd to pretend that all criminal statutes are adequately enforced. But that does not mean that bootlegging was the less a crime.

. . . Nor is the need lacking because the dispensing of birth-control information is by a single doctor rather than by birth-control clinics. The nature of the controversy would not be changed one iota had a dozen doctors, representing a dozen birth-control clinics, sued for remedial relief.

What are these people—doctor and patients—to do? Flout the law and go to prison? Violate the law surreptitiously and hope they will not get caught? By today's decision we leave them no other alternatives. It is not the choice they need have under the regime of the declaratory judgment and our constitutional system. It is not the choice worthy of a civilized society. A sick wife, a concerned husband, a conscientious doctor seek a dignified, discrete, orderly answer to the critical problem confronting them. We should not turn them away and make them flout the law and get arrested to have their constitutional rights determined. They are entitled to an answer to their predicament here and now.

Mr. Justice Harlan, dissenting.

There can be no quarrel with the plurality opinion's statement that "Justiciability is of course not a legal concept with a fixed content or susceptible of scientific verification," but, with deference, the fact that justiciability is not precisely definable does not make it ineffable. Although a large number of cases are brought to bear on the conclusion that is reached, I think it is fairly demonstrable that the authorities fall far short of compelling dismissal of these appeals. Even so, it is suggested that the cases do point the way to a "rigorous insistence on exigent adversity" and a "policy against premature constitutional decision," which properly understood does indeed demand that result.

The policy referred to is one to which I unreservedly subscribe. Without undertaking to be definitive, I would suppose it is a policy the wisdom of which is woven of several strands: (1) Due regard for the fact that the source of the Court's power lies ultimately in its duty to decide, in conformity with the Constitution, the particular controversies which come to it, and does not arise from some generalized power of supervision over state and national legislatures; (2) therefore it should insist that litigants bring to the Court interests and rights which require present recognition and controversies demanding immediate resolution; (3) also it follows that the controversy must be one which is in truth and fact the litigant's own, so that the clash of adversary contest which is needed to sharpen and illuminate issues is present and gives that aid on which our adjudicatory system has come to rely; (4) finally, it is required that other means of redress for the particular right claimed be unavailable, so that the process of the Court may not become overburdened and conflicts with other courts or departments of government may not needlessly be created, which might come about if either those truly affected are not the ones demanding relief, or if the relief we can give is not truly needed.

In particularization of this composite policy the Court, in the course of its decisions on matters of justiciability, has developed and given expression to a number of important limitations on the exercise of its jurisdiction, the presence or absence of which here should determine the justiciability of these appeals. Since all of them are referred to here in one way or another, it is well to proceed to a disclosure of those which are *not* involved in the present appeals, thereby focusing attention on the one factor on which reliance appears to be placed by both the plurality and concurring opinions in this instance.

First: It should by now be abundantly clear that the fact that only Constitutional claims are presented in proceedings seeking anticipatory relief against state criminal statutes does not for that reason alone make the claims premature. Whatever general pronouncements may be found to the contrary must, in context, be seen to refer to considerations quite different from anything present in these cases. . . .

Second: I do not think these appeals may be dismissed for want of "ripeness" as that concept has been understood in its "varied applications." . . . In all of [the cases cited by the Court], the lack of ripeness inhered in the fact that the need for some further procedure, some further contingency of application or interpretation, whether judicial, administrative or executive, or some further clarification of the intentions of the claimant, served to make remote the issue which was sought to be presented to the Court. Certainly the appellants have stated in their pleadings fully and unequivocally what it is that they intend to do; no clarifying or resolving contingency stands in their way before they may embark on that conduct. Thus there is no circumstance besides that of detection or prosecution to make remote the particular controversy. And it is clear beyond cavil that the mere fact that a controversy such as this is rendered still more unavoidable by an actual prosecution, is not alone sufficient to make the case too remote, not ideally enough "ripe" for adjudication, at the prior stage of anticipatory relief. . . .

I cannot see what further elaboration is required to enable us to decide the appellants' claims, and indeed neither the plurality opinion nor the concurring opinion — not-withstanding the latter's characterization of this record as "skimpy" — suggests what mere grist is needed before the judicial mill could turn.

Third: This is not a feigned, hypothetical, friendly or colorable suit such as discloses "a want of a truly adversary contest." . . . [There] is nothing to suggest that the parties by their conduct of this litigation have cooperated to force an adjudication of a Constitutional issue which — were the parties interested solely in winning their cases rather than obtaining a Constitutional decision — might not arise in an arm's-length contested proceeding. . . .

In the present appeals no more is alleged or conceded than is consistent with undisputed facts and with ordinary practice in deciding a case for anticipatory relief on demurrer. I think it is unjustifiably stretching things to assume that appellants are not deterred by the threat of prosecution from engaging in the conduct in which they assert a right to engage, or to assume that appellee's demurrer to the proposition that he asserts the right to enforce the statute against appellants at any time he chooses is anything but a candid one. . . .

Fourth: The doctrine of the cases dealing with a litigant's lack of standing to raise a Constitutional claim is said to justify the dismissal of these appeals. The precedents put forward as examples of this doctrine, do indeed stand for the proposition that a legal claim will not be considered at the instance of one who has no real and concrete interest in its vindication. . . . But this doctrine in turn needs further particularization lest it become a catchall for an unarticulated discretion on the part of this Court to decline to adjudicate appeals involving Constitutional issues.

There is no question but that appellants here are asserting rights which are peculiarly their own, and which, if they are to be raised at all, may be raised most appropriately by them. Nor do I understand the argument to be that this is the sort of claim which is too remote ever to be pressed by anyone, because no one is ever sufficiently involved. Thus, in truth, it is not the parties pressing this claim but the occasion chosen for pressing it which is objected to. But as has been shown the fact that it is anticipatory relief which is asked cannot of itself make the occasion objectionable.

We are brought, then, to the precise failing in these proceedings which is said to justify refusal to exercise our mandatory appellate jurisdiction: that there has been but one recorded Connecticut case dealing with a prosecution under the statute. The significance of this lack of recorded evidence of prosecutions is said to make the presentation of appellants' rights too remote, too contingent, too hypothetical for adjudication in the light of the policies already considered. In my view it is only as a result of misconceptions both about the purport of the record before us and about the nature of the rights appellants put forward that this conclusion can be reached.

As far as the record is concerned, I think it is pure conjecture, and indeed conjecture which to me seems contrary to realities, that an open violation of the statute by a doctor (or more obviously still by a birth-control clinic) would not result in a substantial threat of prosecution. Crucial to the opposite conclusion is the description of the 1940 prosecution instituted in *State v. Nelson*, 126 Conn. 412, 11 A.2d 856, as a "test case" which, as it is viewed, scarcely even punctuates the uniform state practice of nonenforcement of this statute. I read the history of Connecticut enforcement in a very different light. The *Nelson* case, as appears from the state court's opinion, was a prosecution of two doctors and a nurse for aiding and abetting violations of this statute by married women in prescribing and advising the use of contraceptive materials by them. It is true that there is evidence of a customary unwillingness to enforce the statute prior to *Nelson*, for in that case the prosecutor stated to the trial court in a later motion to discontinue the prosecutions that "When this Waterbury clinic [operated by the defendants] was opened there were in open operation elsewhere in the State at least eight other contraceptive clinics which had been in existence for a long period of time and no questions as to their right to operate had been raised. . . ."

What must also be noted is that the prosecutor followed this statement with an explanation that the primary purpose of the prosecution was to provide clear warning to all those who, like Nelson, might rely on this practice of nonenforcement. He stated that the purpose of the prosecution was:

> the establishment of the constitutional validity and efficacy of the statutes under which these accused are informed against. Henceforth any person, whether a physician or layman, who violates the provisions of these statutes, must expect to be prosecuted and punished in accordance with the literal provisions of the law.

Thus the respect in which *Nelson* was a test case is only that it was brought for the purpose of making entirely clear the State's power and willingness to enforce against "any person, whether a physician or layman," the statute and to eliminate from future cases the very doubt about the existence of these elements which had resulted in eight open birth-control clinics, and which would have made unfair the conviction of Nelson.

The plurality opinion now finds, and the concurring opinion must assume, that the only explanation of the absence of recorded prosecutions subsequent to the *Nelson* case is that Connecticut has renounced that intention to prosecute and punish "any person . . . in accordance with the literal provisions of the law" which it announced in *Nelson*. But if renunciation of the purposes of the *Nelson* prosecution is consistent with a lack of subsequent prosecutions, success of that purpose is no less consistent with this lack. I find it difficult to believe that doctors generally—and not just those operating specialized clinics—would continue openly to disseminate advice about contraceptives after *Nelson* in reliance on the State's supposed unwillingness to prosecute, or to consider that high-minded members of the profession would in consequence of such inaction deem themselves warranted in disrespecting this law so long as it is on the books. Nor can I regard as "chimerical" the fear of enforcement of these provisions that seems to have caused the disappearance of at least nine birth-control clinics.

In short, I fear that the Court has indulged in a bit of sleight of hand to be rid of this case. It has treated the significance of the absence of prosecutions during the twenty years since *Nelson* as identical with that of the absence of prosecutions during the years before *Nelson*. It has ignored the fact that the very purpose of the *Nelson* prosecution was to change defiance into compliance. It has ignored the very possibility that this purpose may have been successful. The result is to postulate a security from prosecution for open defiance of the statute which I do not believe the record supports. . . .

The Court's disposition assumes that to decide the case now, in the absence of any consummated prosecutions, is unwise because it forces a difficult decision in advance of any exigent necessity therefor. Of course it is abundantly clear that this requisite necessity can exist prior to any actual prosecution, for that is the theory of anticipatory relief, and is by now familiar law. What must be relied on, therefore, is that the historical absence of prosecutions in some way leaves these appellants free to violate the statute without fear of prosecution, whether or not the law is Constitutional, and thus absolves us from the duty of deciding if it is. Despite the suggestion of a "tougher and truer law" of immunity from criminal prosecution and despite speculation as to a "tacit agreement" that this law will not be enforced, there is, of course, no suggestion of an estoppel against the State if it should attempt to prosecute appellants. Neither the plurality nor the concurring opinion suggests that appellants have some legally cognizable right not to be prosecuted if the statute is Constitutional. What is meant is simply that the appellants are more or less free to act without fear of prosecution because the prosecuting authorities of the State, in their discretion and at their whim, are, as a matter of prediction, unlikely to decide to prosecute.

Here is the core of my disagreement with the present disposition. [The] most substantial claim which these married persons press is their right to enjoy the privacy of their marital relations free of the enquiry of the criminal law, whether it be in a prosecution of them or of a doctor whom they have consulted. And I cannot agree that their enjoyment of this privacy is not substantially impinged upon, when they are told that if they use contraceptives, indeed whether they do so or not, the only thing which stands between them and being forced to render criminal account of their marital privacy is the whim of the prosecutor. Connecticut's highest court has told us in the clearest terms that, given proof, the prosecutor will succeed if he decides to bring a proceeding against one of the appellants for taking the precise actions appellants have announced they intend to take.... Prosecution and conviction for the clearly spelled-out actions the appellants wish to take is not made unlikely by any fortuitous factor outside the control of the parties, nor is it made uncertain by possible variations in the actions appellants actually take from those the state courts have already passed upon. All that stands between the appellants and jail is the legally unfettered whim of the prosecutor and the Constitutional issue this Court today refuses to decide....

[Justice Harlan went on to discuss the merits of the appellants' constitutional claims. He concluded: "I would adjudicate these appeals and hold this statute unconstitutional, insofar as it purports to make criminal the conduct contemplated by these married women."]

MR. JUSTICE STEWART, dissenting.

For the reasons so convincingly advanced by both Mr. Justice Douglas and Mr. Justice Harlan, I join them in dissenting from the dismissal of these appeals....

Problem: A Preenforcement Challenge to Voter Registration Laws

The Help America Vote Act of 2002 (HAVA) was passed after the November 2000 presidential election in order to reform the administration of federal elections. HAVA, among other things, requires states to adopt and implement new voter registration requirements. Under HAVA, each state must create a centralized, periodically-updated database for registration rolls that separately links each voter with a unique identification number. When a voter registers, he must provide either the last four digits of his Social Security number or a driver's license number on his application. Finally, HAVA mandates that each state determine according to its own laws whether the information provided by each registrant is sufficient to meet the federal requirements.

Pursuant to HAVA, the state of Bedford Falls enacted the Bedford Falls Voter Registration Act (the Act), which contains many of the same provisions as HAVA: each voter must provide either his Social Security number or driver's license number (or other state identification number) when registering. The Act also requires that before an application is accepted and the voter listed as registered, the Bedford Falls Department of State must first verify or match the number provided by the applicant with the number assigned to the applicant's name by the Bedford Falls Department of Highway Safety (DHS) or the federal Social Security Administration (SSA).

The Act also provides that when the information from a prospective voter does not match the information held by DHS or SSA, the applicant receives a brief and generic notification through the mail alerting him to the discrepancy. What must be done to correct the mistake depends on the nature of the error: if an error was made by the state or federal agency, then the applicant must present documentary proof to the Supervisor of Elections that the identification number submitted on his application was correct. The voter can do this before registration day, or can vote provisionally on election day and then present this information within two days after the election. If, however, the error was made by the applicant, such as when the digits in a driver's license number are transposed or an applicant's nickname is placed on the application, then the only way to cure the defect is by filing a new application with the correct information prior to the deadline imposed by the Act. In the event that a voter makes an error in his application and receives notification of the error after the deadline, he would be ineligible to vote.

Stewart James, an illiterate prospective voter, brought a suit prior to the voter registration deadline against the Bedford Falls Secretary of State requesting a preliminary injunction to enjoin enforcement of the Act. James alleges that the Act is unenforceable because: (1) it violates the Due Process and Equal Protection Clauses of the Fourteenth Amendment; and (2) various federal statutes, including HAVA and the Voting Rights Act of 1965, preempt the Act.

The Bedford Falls Secretary of State, Ned Potter, moved to dismiss James's claims on ripeness grounds. You are a judge on the United States District Court for the District of Bedford Falls. How would you rule on Potter's motion to dismiss? Would it affect your analysis if Potter stated that he would not enforce the Act against voters who had made mistakes on their voter registration applications?

C. Mootness

Mootness is the doctrine that assures that standing and ripeness continue to exist from the time the lawsuit is filed until its final resolution. Like other justiciability doctrines, mootness conserves the courts' resources and assures that decisions are actually necessary to resolve live disputes. Mootness problems can arise in numerous contexts, and are among the most common justiciability issues that the federal courts face. They typically arise because events have intervened that make the usefulness of court action questionable. Perhaps the plaintiff no longer seeks a remedy; perhaps the defendant has voluntarily complied with the plaintiff's demands or settled the case to the plaintiff's satisfaction; or perhaps other events—legislative for instance—have undermined any need for judicial relief.

More difficult questions arise when the defendant has voluntarily ceased the offending activity, or the claim of a putative named plaintiff in a class action has been satisfied but the claims of other potential class members have not. The following case deals with the first of these issues; the next case deals with the second.

Friends of the Earth, Inc. v. Laidlaw Environmental Services (TOC), Inc.

United States Supreme Court, 2000.

528 U.S. 167.

JUSTICE GINSBURG delivered the opinion of the Court.

[Laidlaw Environmental Services (TOC), Inc., operated a hazardous waste incinerator facility that included a wastewater treatment plant. Shortly after Laidlaw acquired the facility, it received a National Pollutant Discharge Elimination System (NPDES) permit under the Federal Clean Water Act authorizing the company to discharge treated water into the North Tyger River. The permit placed limits on Laidlaw's discharge of several pollutants into the river, including mercury, an extremely toxic pollutant. Once it received its permit, Laidlaw began to discharge various pollutants into the waterway; repeatedly, Laidlaw's discharges exceeded the limits set by the permit. In particular, Laidlaw consistently failed to meet the permit's stringent daily average limit on mercury discharges. The District Court later found that Laidlaw had violated the mercury limits on 489 occasions between 1987 and 1995.

[Friends of the Earth (FOE) brought a citizen suit against Laidlaw under the Clean Water Act, alleging noncompliance with the permit and seeking declaratory and injunctive relief and an award of civil penalties. The Court of Appeals for the Fourth Circuit held that the case became moot once the defendant fully complied with the terms of its permit and the plaintiff failed to appeal the denial of equitable relief.]

We reverse the judgment of the Court of Appeals. The appellate court erred in concluding that a citizen suitor's claim for civil penalties must be dismissed as moot when the defendant, albeit after commencement of the litigation, has come into compliance. In directing dismissal of the suit on grounds of mootness, the Court of Appeals incorrectly conflated our case law on initial standing to bring suit with our case law on post-commencement mootness. A defendant's voluntary cessation of allegedly unlawful conduct ordinarily does not suffice to moot a case. The Court of Appeals also misperceived the remedial potential of civil penalties. Such penalties may serve, as an alternative to an injunction, to deter future violations and thereby redress the injuries that prompted a citizen suitor to commence litigation. . . .

II

A

The Constitution's case-or-controversy limitation on federal judicial authority, Art. III, § 2, underpins both our standing and our mootness jurisprudence, but the two inquiries differ in respects critical to the proper resolution of this case, so we address them separately. Because the Court of Appeals was persuaded that the case had become moot and so held, it simply assumed without deciding that FOE had initial standing. See *Arizonans for Official English v. Arizona*, 520 U.S. 43, 66–67 (1997) (court may assume without deciding that standing exists in order to analyze mootness). But because we hold that the Court of Appeals erred in declaring the case moot, we have an obligation to assure ourselves that FOE had Article III standing at the outset of the litigation. We therefore address the question of standing before turning to mootness.

In *Lujan v. Defenders of Wildlife*, 504 U.S. 555 (1992), we held that, to satisfy Article III's standing requirements, a plaintiff must show (1) it has suffered an "injury in fact" that is (a) concrete and particularized and (b) actual or imminent, not conjectural or hypothetical; (2) the injury is fairly traceable to the challenged action of the defendant; and (3) it is likely, as opposed to merely speculative, that the injury will be redressed by a favorable decision. An association has standing to bring suit on behalf of its members when its members would otherwise have standing to sue in their own right, the interests at stake are germane to the organization's purpose, and neither the claim asserted nor the relief requested requires the participation of individual members in the lawsuit.

Laidlaw contends first that FOE lacked standing from the outset even to seek injunctive relief, because the plaintiff organizations failed to show that any of their members had sustained or faced the threat of any "injury in fact" from Laidlaw's activities. In support of this contention Laidlaw points to the District Court's finding, made in the course of setting the penalty amount, that there had been "no demonstrated proof of harm to the environment" from Laidlaw's mercury discharge violations.

The relevant showing for purposes of Article III standing, however, is not injury to the environment but injury to the plaintiff. To insist upon the former rather than the latter as part of the standing inquiry is to raise the standing hurdle higher than the necessary showing for success on the merits in an action alleging noncompliance with an NPDES permit. Focusing properly on injury to the plaintiff, the District Court found that FOE had demonstrated sufficient injury to establish standing.

[The Court summarized affidavits and depositions that demonstrated that association members lived near the river and that these individuals were deterred from using the river for recreation because it looked and smelled polluted.]

These sworn statements, as the District Court determined, adequately documented injury in fact. We have held that environmental plaintiffs adequately allege injury in fact when they aver that they use the affected area and are persons "for whom the aesthetic and recreational values of the area will be lessened" by the challenged activity. *See Lujan*. . . . [The remainder of the Court's discussion of standing is omitted.]

B

Satisfied that FOE had standing under Article III to bring this action, we turn to the question of mootness. The only conceivable basis for a finding of mootness in this case is Laidlaw's voluntary conduct — either its achievement by August 1992 of substantial compliance with its NPDES permit or its more recent shutdown of the Roebuck facility. It is well settled that "a defendant's voluntary cessation of a challenged practice does not deprive a federal court of its power to determine the legality of the practice." "[I]f it did, the courts would be compelled to leave '[t]he defendant . . . free to return to his old ways.'" *City of Mesquite v. Aladdin's Castle, Inc.*, 455 U.S. 283 (1982). In accordance with this principle, the standard we have announced for determining whether a case has been mooted by the defendant's voluntary conduct is stringent: "A case might become moot if subsequent events made it absolutely clear that the allegedly wrongful behavior could not reasonably be expected to recur." The "heavy burden of persua[ding]" the court that the challenged conduct cannot reasonably be expected to start up again lies with the party asserting mootness.

The Court of Appeals justified its mootness disposition by reference to *Steel Co. v. Citizens for a Better Environment*, 523 U.S. 83 (1998), which held that citizen plaintiffs lack standing to seek civil penalties for wholly past violations. In relying on *Steel Co.*, the Court of Appeals confused mootness with standing. The confusion is understandable, given this Court's repeated statements that the doctrine of mootness can be described as "the doctrine of standing set in a time frame: The requisite personal interest that must exist at the commencement of the litigation (standing) must continue throughout its existence (mootness)." *Arizonans for Official English*, 520 U.S. at 68 n.22 (quoting *United States Parole Comm'n v. Geraghty*, 445 U.S. 388, 397 (1980), in turn quoting Monaghan, *Constitutional Adjudication: The Who and When*, 82 YALE L.J. 1363, 1384 (1973)).

Careful reflection on the long-recognized exceptions to mootness, however, reveals that the description of mootness as "standing set in a time frame" is not comprehensive. As just noted, a defendant claiming that its voluntary compliance moots a case bears the formidable burden of showing that it is absolutely clear the allegedly wrongful behavior could not reasonably be expected to recur. By contrast, in a lawsuit brought to force compliance, it is the plaintiff's burden to establish standing by demonstrating that, if unchecked by the litigation, the defendant's allegedly wrongful behavior will likely occur or continue, and that the "threatened injury [is] certainly impending." Thus, in *Los Angeles v. Lyons*, 461 U.S. 95 (1983), we held that a plaintiff lacked initial standing to seek an injunction against the enforcement of a police chokehold policy because he could not credibly allege that he faced a realistic threat arising from the policy. Elsewhere in the opinion, however, we noted that a citywide moratorium on police chokeholds — an action that surely diminished the already slim likelihood that any particular individual would be choked by police — would not have mooted an otherwise valid claim for injunctive relief, because the moratorium by its terms was not permanent. The plain lesson of these cases is that there are circumstances in which the prospect that a defendant will engage in (or resume) harmful conduct may be too speculative to support standing, but not too speculative to overcome mootness.

Furthermore, if mootness were simply "standing set in a time frame," the exception to mootness that arises when the defendant's allegedly unlawful activity is "capable of repetition, yet evading review," could not exist. When, for example, a mentally disabled patient files a lawsuit challenging her confinement in a segregated institution, her postcomplaint transfer to a community-based program will not moot the action, despite the fact that she would have lacked initial standing had she filed the complaint after the transfer. Standing admits of no similar exception; if a plaintiff lacks standing at the time the action commences, the fact that the dispute is capable of repetition yet evading review will not entitle the complainant to a federal judicial forum. See *Steel Co.*, 523 U.S. at 109 ("'[T]he mootness exception for disputes capable of repetition yet evading review . . . will not revive a dispute which became moot before the action commenced.'").

We acknowledged the distinction between mootness and standing most recently in *Steel Co.*:

> The United States . . . argues that the injunctive relief does constitute remediation because "there is a presumption of [future] injury when the defendant has voluntarily ceased its illegal activity in response to litigation," even if that occurs before a complaint is filed. . . . This makes a sword out of a shield. The "presumption" the Government refers to has been applied to refute the assertion of mootness by a defendant who, when sued in a complaint that alleges present or threatened injury, ceases the complained-of activity. . . . It is an immense and unacceptable stretch to call the presumption into service as a substitute for the allegation of present or threatened injury upon which initial standing must be based.

Standing doctrine functions to ensure, among other things, that the scarce resources of the federal courts are devoted to those disputes in which the parties have a concrete stake. In contrast, by the time mootness is an issue, the case has been brought and litigated, often (as here) for years. To abandon the case at an advanced stage may prove more wasteful than frugal. This argument from sunk costs[5] does not license courts to retain jurisdiction over cases in which one or both of the parties plainly lack a continuing interest, as when the parties have settled or a plaintiff pursuing a non-surviving claim has died. *See, e.g., DeFunis v. Odegaard*, 416 U.S. 312 (1974) (*per curiam*) (non-class-action challenge to constitutionality of law school admissions process mooted when plaintiff, admitted pursuant to preliminary injunction, neared graduation and defendant law school conceded that, as a matter of ordinary school policy, plaintiff would be allowed to finish his final term); *Arizonans* (non-class-action

---

5. Of course we mean sunk costs to the judicial system, not to the litigants. *Lewis v. Continental Bank Corp.*, 494 U.S. 472 (1990) (cited by the dissent), dealt with the latter, noting that courts should use caution to avoid carrying forward a moot case solely to vindicate a plaintiff's interest in recovering attorneys' fees.

challenge to state constitutional amendment declaring English the official language of the State became moot when plaintiff, a state employee who sought to use her bilingual skills, left state employment). But the argument surely highlights an important difference between the two doctrines. . . .

Laidlaw also [asserts] that the closure of its Roebuck facility, which took place after the Court of Appeals issued its decision, mooted the case. The facility closure, like Laidlaw's earlier achievement of substantial compliance with its permit requirements, might moot the case, but—we once more reiterate—only if one or the other of these events made it absolutely clear that Laidlaw's permit violations could not reasonably be expected to recur. The effect of both Laidlaw's compliance and the facility closure on the prospect of future violations is a disputed factual matter. FOE points out, for example—and Laidlaw does not appear to contest—that Laidlaw retains its NPDES permit. These issues have not been aired in the lower courts; they remain open for consideration on remand. . . .

For the reasons stated, the judgment of the United States Court of Appeals for the Fourth Circuit is reversed, and the case is remanded for further proceedings consistent with this opinion.

JUSTICE STEVENS, concurring.

Although the Court has identified a sufficient reason for rejecting the Court of Appeals' mootness determination, it is important also to note that the case would not be moot even if it were absolutely clear that respondent had gone out of business and posed no threat of future permit violations. The District Court entered a valid judgment requiring respondent to pay a civil penalty of $405,800 to the United States. No postjudgment conduct of respondent could retroactively invalidate that judgment. A record of voluntary postjudgment compliance that would justify a decision that injunctive relief is unnecessary, or even a decision that any claim for injunctive relief is now moot, would not warrant vacation of the valid money judgment.

Furthermore, petitioners' claim for civil penalties would not be moot even if it were absolutely clear that respondent's violations could not reasonably be expected to recur because respondent achieved substantial compliance with its permit requirements after petitioners filed their complaint but before the District Court entered judgment. As the Courts of Appeals (other than the court below) have uniformly concluded, a polluter's voluntary postcomplaint cessation of an alleged violation will not moot a citizen-suit claim for civil penalties even if it is sufficient to moot a related claim for injunctive or declaratory relief. This conclusion is consistent with the structure of the Clean Water Act, which attaches liability for civil penalties at the time a permit violation occurs. It is also consistent with the character of civil penalties, which, for purposes of mootness analysis, should be equated with punitive damages rather than with injunctive or declaratory relief. No one contends that a defendant's postcomplaint conduct could moot a claim for punitive damages; civil penalties should be treated the same way.

The cases cited by the Court in its discussion of the mootness issue all involved requests for injunctive or declaratory relief. In only one, *Los Angeles v. Lyons*, 461 U.S.

95 (1983), did the plaintiff seek damages, and in that case the opinion makes it clear that the inability to obtain injunctive relief would have no impact on the damages claim. There is no precedent, either in our jurisprudence, or in any other of which I am aware, that provides any support for the suggestion that postcomplaint factual developments that might moot a claim for injunctive or declaratory relief could either moot a claim for monetary relief or retroactively invalidate a valid money judgment.

JUSTICE SCALIA, with whom JUSTICE THOMAS joins, dissenting.

[In Parts I and II of his opinion, Justice Scalia argued that plaintiffs lacked standing. He said, *inter alia*:]

The Court cites affiants' testimony asserting that their enjoyment of the North Tyger River has been diminished due to "concern" that the water was polluted, and that they "believed" that Laidlaw's mercury exceedances had reduced the value of their homes. These averments alone cannot carry the plaintiffs' burden of demonstrating that they have suffered a "concrete and particularized" injury. *Lujan.* General allegations of injury may suffice at the pleading stage, but at summary judgment plaintiffs must set forth "specific facts" to support their claims. And where, as here, the case has proceeded to judgment, those specific facts must be "'supported adequately by the evidence adduced at trial.'" In this case, the affidavits themselves are woefully short on "specific facts," and the vague allegations of injury they do make are undermined by the evidence adduced at trial. . . .

III

Finally, I offer a few comments regarding the Court's discussion of whether FOE's claims became moot by reason of Laidlaw's substantial compliance with the permit limits. I do not disagree with the conclusion that the Court reaches. Assuming that the plaintiffs had standing to pursue civil penalties in the first instance (which they did not), their claim might well not have been mooted by Laidlaw's voluntary compliance with the permit, and leaving this fact-intensive question open for consideration on remand, as the Court does, seems sensible. In reaching this disposition, however, the Court engages in a troubling discussion of the purported distinctions between the doctrines of standing and mootness. I am frankly puzzled as to why this discussion appears at all. Laidlaw's claimed compliance is squarely within the bounds of our "voluntary cessation" doctrine, which is the basis for the remand. There is no reason to engage in an interesting academic excursus upon the differences between mootness and standing in order to invoke this obviously applicable rule.

Because the discussion is not essential—indeed, not even relevant—to the Court's decision, it is of limited significance. Nonetheless, I am troubled by the Court's too-hasty retreat from our characterization of mootness as "the doctrine of standing set in a time frame." We have repeatedly recognized that what is required for litigation to continue is essentially identical to what is required for litigation to begin: There must be a justiciable case or controversy as required by Article III. "Simply stated, a case is moot when the issues presented are no longer 'live' or the parties lack a legally cognizable interest in the outcome." A court may not proceed to hear an action if, subsequent to its initiation, the dispute loses "its character as a present, live controversy of the kind that must exist if [the court is] to avoid advisory opinions on abstract propositions of law." Because the requirement of a continuing case or controversy derives from the Constitution, it may not be ignored when inconvenient, or, as the Court suggests, to save "sunk costs."

It is true that mootness has some added wrinkles that standing lacks. One is the "voluntary cessation" doctrine to which the Court refers. But it is inaccurate to regard this as a reduction of the basic requirement for standing that obtained at the beginning of the suit. A genuine controversy must exist at both stages. And just as the initial suit could be brought (by way of suit for declaratory judgment) before the defendant actually violated the plaintiff's alleged rights, so also the initial suit can be continued even though the defendant has stopped violating the plaintiff's alleged rights. The "voluntary cessation" doctrine is nothing more than an evidentiary presumption that the controversy reflected by the violation of alleged rights continues to exist. Similarly, the fact that we do not find cases moot when the challenged conduct is "capable of repetition, yet evading review" does not demonstrate that the requirements for mootness and for standing differ. "Where the conduct has ceased for the time being but there is a demonstrated probability that it will recur, a real-life controversy between parties with a personal stake in the outcome continues to exist."

Part of the confusion in the Court's discussion is engendered by the fact that it compares standing, on the one hand, with mootness *based on voluntary cessation*, on the other hand. The required showing that it is "absolutely clear" that the conduct "could not reasonably be expected to recur" is *not* the threshold showing required for mootness, but the heightened showing required in a particular category of cases where we have sensibly concluded that there is reason to be skeptical that cessation of violation means cessation of live controversy. For claims of mootness based on changes in circumstances other than voluntary cessation, the showing we have required is less taxing, and the inquiry is indeed properly characterized as one of "'standing set in a time frame.'"

In sum, while the Court may be correct that the parallel between standing and mootness is imperfect due to realistic evidentiary presumptions that are by their nature applicable only in the mootness context, this does not change the underlying principle that "'[t]he requisite personal interest that must exist at the commencement of the litigation . . . must continue throughout its existence. . . .'"

Note: Laidlaw *and the Voluntary Cessation Exception*

1. *Laidlaw* discusses the relationship between standing and mootness. The Court has frequently described mootness as "the doctrine of standing set in a time frame." Writing for the majority, however, Justice Ginsburg notes three "critical" differences between standing and mootness. First is the allocation of the burden to prove that a case is justiciable when a defendant voluntarily ceases the offending behavior: "a defendant claiming that its voluntary compliance moots a case bears the formidable burden of showing that it is absolutely clear the allegedly wrongful behavior could not reasonably be expected to recur," while normally the plaintiff bears the burden "to establish standing by demonstrating that, if unchecked by the litigation, the defendant's allegedly wrongful behavior will likely occur or continue." Second, while mootness doctrine permits the Court to hear some cases that have become moot—such as those "capable of repetition, yet evading review"—"standing admits of no similar exception[s]." Finally, the purposes behind the doctrines differ: while standing doctrine exists to ensure that "scarce resources of the federal courts are devoted to those disputes in which the parties have a concrete stake," mootness doctrine considers whether "sunk costs" license courts to "retain jurisdiction over cases" when not to do so would be "more wasteful than frugal." To what extent does the dissent in *Laidlaw* reject the distinctions drawn by the majority between standing and mootness? What is at stake in the disagreement?

2. It is generally agreed that a defendant cannot moot a case simply by stopping illegal activity. But suppose that defendant is a government. In several cases, the Supreme Court has faced challenges to municipal ordinances that were amended or repealed during the litigation. In *City of Mesquite v. Aladdin's Castle*, 455 U.S. 283, 288–89 (1982), the district court struck down a city's licensing ordinance as unconstitutionally vague. The city repealed the ordinance while the case was pending on appeal. The Supreme Court rejected a suggestion of mootness:

> It is well settled that a defendant's voluntary cessation of a challenged practice does not deprive a federal court of its power to determine the legality of the practice. Such abandonment is an important factor bearing on the question whether a court should exercise its power to enjoin the defendant from renewing the practice, but that is a matter relating to the exercise rather than the existence of judicial power. In this case, the city's repeal of the objectionable language would not preclude it from reenacting precisely the same provision if the District Court decision were vacated.

Justice O'Connor objected to this line of reasoning in dissent in *Northeastern Florida Chapter of Associated General Contractors v. City of Jacksonville*, 508 U.S. 656 (1993), at least where the legislature had made changes in the law being challenged:

> In *City of Mesquite*, we decided to reach the merits of the plaintiff's claim because "the city's repeal of the objectionable language would not preclude it from reenacting precisely the same provision if the District Court's judgment were vacated." We expressly noted that the city in fact had announced an intention to do exactly that, just as it already had eliminated and then reinstated another aspect of the same ordinance in the course of the same litigation, obviously in response to prior judicial action. These circumstances made it virtually impossible to say that there was "no reasonable expectation" that the city would reenact the challenged language.
>
> *City of Mesquite* did not purport to overrule the long line of cases in which we have found repeal of a challenged statute to moot the case. Significantly, we have not referred to the voluntary-cessation doctrine in any other case involving a statute repealed or materially altered pending review. The

reason seems to me obvious. Unlike in *City of Mesquite*, in the ordinary case it is not at all reasonable to suppose that the legislature has repealed or amended a challenged law simply to avoid litigation and that it will reinstate the original legislation if given the opportunity. This is especially true where, as here, the law has been replaced—no doubt at considerable effort and expense—with a more narrowly drawn version designed to cure alleged legal infirmities. We ordinarily do not presume that legislative bodies act in bad faith. That is why, other than in *City of Mesquite*, we have not required the government to establish that it cannot be expected to reenact repealed legislation before we will dismiss the case as moot.

At most, I believe *City of Mesquite* stands for the proposition that the Court has discretion to decide a case in which the statute under review has been repealed or amended. The Court appropriately may render judgment where circumstances demonstrate that the legislature likely will reinstate the old law—which would make a declaratory judgment or an order enjoining the law's enforcement worthwhile. But such circumstances undoubtedly are rare.

Problem: Injunctive Relief Under the ADA

Jeff Brenton, a legally blind citizen of the state of New Avalon, scheduled an appointment at Radiology Associates (RA) to receive a computer axial tomography scan (CAT scan) ordered by his physician. Brenton brought his eighty-pound Labrador Retriever guide dog, Sam, to the appointment. When Brenton checked in, he informed the receptionist that Sam was a service animal trained to guide him.

When it came time for the CAT scan, the receptionist informed Brenton that his dog was to remain in the waiting room, rather than accompany him to the CAT scan imaging suite down the hall. When Brenton asked why his dog was not permitted beyond the main waiting room, the receptionist gave various reasons, including ensuring the dog's safety, avoiding traffic jams in the hallway due to the dog's size, and promoting compliance with applicable procedures for entry into the imaging suite. Despite Brenton's protests that such action violated the Americans with Disabilities Act (ADA), RA employees maintained that the office was a private facility not subject to the ADA. Brenton called the President of RA, David Cooper, who informed Brenton that office policy dictated that dogs and other service animals were not permitted beyond the waiting room for the safety of the animal, other patients, and the imaging equipment.

Brenton left the facility without receiving the CAT scan, and subsequently filed an action in the United States District Court for the District of New Avalon, seeking injunctive and declaratory relief under the ADA. Almost nine months into the lawsuit and after eight months of discovery, RA moved for summary judgment, announcing that it had implemented a new, written Service Animal Policy that rendered Brenton's claims moot. According to the Policy, RA would follow all applicable federal, state, and local laws with respect to permitting access to service animals accompanying clients with disabilities. The President of RA, David Cooper, emailed the new policy to all employees, who were required to print and sign a form indicating that they had received the policy and understood that it contained "very important information." Cooper explained that the purpose of the policy was to inform RA employees of rules related to service animal access and to comply with all requirements of the ADA and New Avalon law so as to avoid future disputes. Cooper also submitted an affidavit to the court attesting to the fact that the day after the policy was implemented, a patient with a service animal entered RA's New Avalon office and was permitted access in accordance with the policy.

How should the district court rule on RA's summary judgment motion?

Note: The Exception for Cases "Capable of Repetition, Yet Evading Review"

1. *Laidlaw* refers to another major exception to the mootness doctrine. This exception encompasses cases that are "capable of repetition, yet evading review." A famous application of this exception came in *Roe v. Wade*, 410 U.S. 113 (1973). In *Roe*, the state argued that the plaintiff's challenge to the Texas abortion statute had become moot because the plaintiff's pregnancy had long terminated since the beginning of the litigation. Justice Blackmun, writing for the majority, rejected that conclusion:

> The usual rule in federal cases is that an actual controversy must exist at stages of appellate or certiorari review, and not simply at the date the action is initiated. But when, as here, pregnancy is a significant fact in the litigation, the normal 266-day human gestation period is so short that the pregnancy will come to term before the usual appellate process is complete. If that termination makes a case moot, pregnancy litigation seldom will survive much beyond the trial stage, and appellate review will be effectively denied. Our law should not be that rigid. Pregnancy often comes more than once to the same woman, and in the general population, if man is to survive, it will always be with us. Pregnancy provides a classic justification for a conclusion of nonmootness. It truly could be "capable of repetition, yet evading review." *Southern Pacific Terminal Co. v. ICC*, 219 U.S. 498, 515 (1911). We, therefore, agree with the District Court that Jane Roe had standing to undertake this litigation, that she presented a justiciable controversy, and that the termination of her 1970 pregnancy has not rendered her case moot.

2. The exception for controversies "capable of repetition, yet evading review" is often invoked in relation to cases involving elections and limitations on speech. In *The Irish Lesbian and Gay Organization v. Giuliani*, 143 F.3d 638 (2d Cir. 1998), an Irish lesbian and gay organization sued New York City officials for violating the organization's free speech and equal protection rights by denying its application to conduct a protest parade before the annual St. Patrick's Day parade from which it had been traditionally excluded. New York officials argued that the dispute became moot when the parade date passed. The court, relying on an often-stated test, found that the controversy fit the exception for cases capable of repetition, yet evading review:

To show that a case falls within this exception, a party must demonstrate that "'(1) the challenged action was in duration too short to be fully litigated prior to its cessation or expiration, and (2) there was a reasonable expectation that the same complaining party would be subjected to the same action again.'" ILGO's claims fall within the "capable of repetition, yet evading review" exception. In the last two years, ILGO has had only a few weeks between being notified that its application for a permit was denied and the date of the Parade in which to obtain judicial review. This time period is clearly insufficient for full litigation of ILGO's claims. Given the annual nature of the Parade, and ILGO's repeated attempts to stage a march prior to it, the conduct complained of is almost certain to be repeated. Accordingly, we find that ILGO's claims for declaratory and injunctive relief are not moot.

In *Majors v. Abell*, 317 F.3d 719 (7th Cir. 2003), Judge Posner questioned the proposition that the challenged regulation must affect "the same complaining party." Political candidates and their supporters brought an action challenging the constitutionality, on First Amendment grounds, of a state statute requiring that political advertising expressly advocating the election or defeat of an identified candidate include the identity of the persons who paid for the advertisements. The trial court held that the candidate's claims had become moot by the passing of the election, since the candidate, who was defeated, showed no indication that he would run for public office again. Judge Posner, speaking for the court of appeals panel, disagreed:

A candidate plaintiff no more has a duty to run in every election in order to keep his suit alive than an abortion plaintiff has a duty to become pregnant again at the earliest possible opportunity in order to keep her suit alive. Politicians who are defeated in an election will often wait years before running again; obviously this doesn't show they're not serious about their political career.

Furthermore, while canonical statements of the exception to mootness for cases capable of repetition but evading review require that the dispute giving rise to the case be capable of repetition by the same plaintiff, the courts, perhaps to avoid complicating lawsuits with incessant interruptions to assure the continued existence of a live controversy, do not interpret the requirement literally, at least in abortion and election cases—and possibly more generally. If a suit attacking an abortion statute has dragged on for several years after the plaintiff's pregnancy terminated, the court does not conduct a hearing on whether she may have fertility problems or may have decided that she doesn't want to become pregnant again. And similarly in an election case the court will not keep interrogating the plaintiff to assess the likely trajectory of his political career.

3. As one might expect, the "capable of repetition, yet evading review" exception arises in certain categories of cases, which, by nature, can rarely be resolved during the normal course of litigation in federal courts. As suggested above, cases raising issues relating to pregnancy and elections are areas in which the capable of repetition, yet evading review exception is often invoked. *See, e.g., Davis v. Federal Election Comm'n,* 128 S. Ct. 2759, 2769 (2008); *Roe v. Wade,* 410 U.S. 113 (1973).

The exception can also arise in cases where a plaintiff is seeking educational entitlements. In *Honig v. Doe,* 484 U.S. 305 (1988), for example, the parents of students with disabilities brought a challenge under what is now the Individuals with Disabilities Education Act, alleging that their emotionally-disturbed children were unlawfully excluded from receiving a "free appropriate public education" under the statute. During the pendency of the lawsuit, the students either became too old to qualify for protection under the statute or moved out of the district from which they were seeking injunctive relief. Despite the fact that these changed circumstances would ordinarily moot the case, the Supreme Court noted that the case would be justiciable if the students continued to qualify for services under the statute and could reasonably be expected to bring a similar challenge in the future:

> Given [the student's] continued eligibility for educational services under the [Act], the nature of his disability, and petitioner's insistence that all local school districts retain residual authority to exclude disabled children for dangerous conduct, we have little difficulty concluding that there is a "reasonable expectation," that [the student] would once again be subjected to a unilateral "change in placement" for conduct growing out of his disabilities. . . .

The Court accordingly held that the case was not moot because it was capable of repetition, yet evading review.

Note: Mootness and the Class Action Exception

1. Can filing a case as a class action protect it from mootness even when the named plaintiff's claims have become moot? In two important cases decided on the same day, the Supreme Court expanded the possibilities of avoiding mootness through class certification. In *Deposit Guaranty National Bank v. Roper,* 445 U.S. 326 (1980), credit card holders brought a class action against a national bank on behalf of all other Mississippi holders of credit cards issued by the bank, alleging that certain charges were usurious under Mississippi law. The district court denied class certification, and the court of appeals denied an interlocutory appeal. The bank then offered the named plaintiffs a settlement of the maximum amount they could have hoped to obtain individually. When the plaintiffs refused, the district court entered judgment for them over their objection, and the bank deposited its settlement amount with the court. The bank subsequently argued that the controversy had become moot.

The Supreme Court disagreed:

> Neither the rejected tender nor the dismissal of the action over plaintiffs' objections mooted the plaintiffs' claim on the merits so long as they retained an economic interest in class certification. Although a case or controversy is mooted in the Art. III sense upon payment and satisfaction of a final, unappealable judgment, a decision that is "final" for purposes of appeal does not absolutely resolve a case or controversy until the time for appeal has run. Nor

does a confession of judgment by defendants on less than all the issues moot an entire case; other issues in the case may be appealable. We can assume that a district court's final judgment fully satisfying named plaintiffs' private substantive claims would preclude their appeal on that aspect of the final judgment; however, it does not follow that this circumstance would terminate the named plaintiffs' right to take an appeal on the issue of class certification.

... [To] deny the right to appeal simply because the defendant has sought to "buy off" the individual private claims of the named plaintiffs would be contrary to sound judicial administration. Requiring multiple plaintiffs to bring separate actions, which effectively could be "picked off" by a defendant's tender of judgment before an affirmative ruling on class certification could be obtained, obviously would frustrate the objectives of class actions; moreover it would invite waste of judicial resources by stimulating successive suits brought by others claiming aggrievement. It would be in the interests of a class-action defendant to forestall any appeal of denial of class certification if that could be accomplished by tendering the individual damages claimed by the named plaintiffs.

2. Chief Justice Burger wrote for the Court in *Roper*. Only Justice Powell, joined by Justice Stewart, dissented. However, in the companion case, *United States Parole Comm'n v. Geraghty*, 445 U.S. 388 (1980), the Chief Justice joined the dissenters.

Geraghty presented the question whether the denial of class certification can be appealed after the named plaintiff's claim has become moot. While serving time in a federal prison, a prisoner filed suit to challenge federal parole guidelines. He sought to represent a class composed of "all federal prisoners who are or who will become eligible for release on parole." After the district court denied certification of the class, the plaintiff was unconditionally released, and the Parole Commission argued that the case had become moot. An earlier case, *Sosna v. Iowa*, 419 U.S. 393 (1975), had held that a certified class action does not become moot when the named plaintiff loses a personal stake in the litigation.

Writing for the Court, Justice Blackmun stated:

Mootness has two aspects: "when the issues presented are no longer 'live' or the parties lack a legally cognizable interest in the outcome." It is clear that the controversy over the validity of the Parole Release Guidelines is still a "live" one between petitioners and at least some members of the class respondent seeks to represent. This is demonstrated by the fact that prisoners currently affected by the guidelines have moved to be substituted, or to intervene, as "named" respondents in this Court. We therefore are concerned here with the second aspect of mootness, that is, the parties' interest in the litigation. The Court has referred to this concept as the "personal stake" requirement.

The personal-stake requirement relates to the first purpose of the case-or-controversy doctrine—limiting judicial power to disputes capable of judicial resolution. ... The "personal stake" aspect of mootness doctrine also serves primarily the purpose of assuring that federal courts are presented with disputes they are capable of resolving. . . .

We therefore hold that an action brought on behalf of a class does not become moot upon expiration of the named plaintiff's substantive claim, even though class certification has been denied. The proposed representative retains a "personal stake" in obtaining class certification sufficient to assure that Art. III values are not undermined. If the appeal results in reversal of the class certification denial, and a class subsequently is properly certified, the merits of the class claim then may be adjudicated pursuant to the holding in *Sosna*.

Note: The Collateral Consequences Exception

In *Geraghty*, Justice Powell's dissent mentioned in passing that "[c]ollateral consequences of the original wrong may supply [an] individual" with a sufficient interest in the case to satisfy the personal stake requirement of the mootness inquiry. The collateral consequences exception primarily arises when a prisoner or parolee challenges the legality of his or her conviction, and is subsequently released before the challenge can be concluded. As the Supreme Court explained in *Spencer v. Kemna*, 523 U.S. 1, 8 (1998):

> An incarcerated convict's (or a parolee's) challenge to the validity of his conviction always satisfies the case-or-controversy requirement, because the incarceration (or the restriction imposed by the terms of the parole) constitutes a concrete injury, caused by the conviction and redressable by invalidation of the conviction. Once the convict's sentence has expired, however, some concrete and continuing injury other than the now-ended incarceration or parole—some "collateral consequence" of the conviction—must exist if the suit is to be maintained.

In many states, criminal convictions carry these "collateral consequences"—such as the permanent loss of voting privileges and the inability to obtain certain occupational licenses. Accordingly, even when the primary injury—incarceration—no longer exists, the related harms that normally accompany a conviction can prevent courts from dismissing the case as moot.

The collateral consequences exception also applies, though less frequently, in the civil context. In several labor and employment cases, for example, the Supreme Court has held that future, continuing injuries are sufficient to prevent a case from being dismissed as moot, even when a plaintiff's primary injury has been eliminated. *See, e.g., Firefighter's Local 1784 v. Stotts*, 467 U.S. 561 (1984) (holding that a plaintiff seeking both reimbursement and back pay can continue to pursue the case notwithstanding the plaintiff's reinstatement, in part because, "[w]hen collateral effects of a dispute remain and continue to affect the relationship of litigants, the case is not moot"); *Super Tire Engineering Co. v. McCorkle*, 416 U.S. 115 (1974) (holding that employers who challenged a state law permitting strikers to receive public assistance could still continue their case, even after the strike ended, because a federal court decision could still affect future labor-management negotiations).

Problem: A Settlement—with a Contingent Payment

Thrasher Boards is a distributor of skateboards, surfboards, and snow boards located in Honolulu, Hawaii. It sells most of its products through an internet site. Digital Discounts (DD) is a California company that created a software program that allows computer users to store personal information, such as credit card numbers and passwords, in a program. When a website asks for such information, DD's program automatically puts it in. The program also provides users with discount coupons that automatically "pop up" on the computer screen when the user visits certain websites that DD has selected.

Thrasher Boards discovered that when people who used DD's program visited its website, a discount coupon for Thrasher's competitor, Wiki Boards, popped up. After negotiations with DD failed, DD filed suit in a federal district court in California for a declaratory judgment that its action did not constitute trademark dilution, unfair competition, or false advertising. Recognizing that it would have been forced to litigate its intellectual property claims against DD as compulsory counterclaims in California, Thrasher moved to dismiss, alleging it was not subject to personal jurisdiction in that state. The district court dismissed the action on that ground, and DD appealed.

While the appeal was pending, the parties entered into a settlement agreement. Under its terms, DD agreed to discontinue placing coupons on Thrasher's site, and agreed to make monetary payment to Thrasher. Thrasher renounced all claims against DD. However, the parties stipulated that if the appellate court found that Thrasher was subject to personal jurisdiction in California, DD would be required to pay Thrasher $25,000.

When the appellate court discovered the agreement, it asked the parties to brief the question whether the agreement rendered the appeal moot. Does it?

D. The Political Question Doctrine

The political question doctrine serves as an enforcement mechanism for separation of powers concerns that can be traced back to *Marbury v. Madison*, 1 Cranch (5 U.S.) 137, 177 (1803). While Chief Justice Marshall was adamant that it is "emphatically the province and duty of the judicial department to say what the law is," he also recognized that the Constitution made other governmental functions just as emphatically the province of other branches: "The province of the court is, solely, to decide on the rights of individuals, not to enquire how the executive, or executive officers, perform duties in which they have a discretion. Questions, in their nature political, or which are, by the constitution and laws, submitted to the executive, can never be made in this court."

For more than 150 years after *Marbury*, the Court struggled with the scope of the political question doctrine. In *Baker v. Carr*, 369 U.S. 186, 217 (1962), the Court made its most significant attempt to define the precise contours of the doctrine. The question in *Baker* was whether legislative schemes resulting in malapportionment of state legislative districts could be challenged in federal court. In holding that the question of legislative districting did not raise a political question, Justice Brennan, writing for the majority, stated the understanding of the political question doctrine that has controlled since:

> Prominent on the surface of any case held to involve a political question is found a textually demonstrable constitutional commitment of the issue to a coordinate political department; or a lack of judicially discoverable and manageable standards for resolving it; or the impossibility of deciding without an initial policy determination of a kind clearly for nonjudicial discretion; or the impossibility of a court's undertaking independent resolution without expressing lack of the respect due coordinate branches of government; or an unusual need for unquestioning adherence to a political decision already made; or the potentiality of embarrassment from multifarious pronouncements by various departments on one question.

An application of Justice Brennan's formulation follows.

Nixon v. United States

Supreme Court of the United States, 1993.

506 U.S. 224.

CHIEF JUSTICE REHNQUIST delivered the opinion of the Court.

Petitioner Walter L. Nixon, Jr., asks this Court to decide whether Senate Rule XI, which allows a committee of Senators to hear evidence against an individual who has been impeached and to report that evidence to the full Senate, violates the Impeachment Trial Clause, Art. I, § 3, cl. 6. That Clause provides that the "Senate shall have the sole Power to try all Impeachments." But before we reach the merits of such a claim, we must decide whether it is "justiciable," that is, whether it is a claim that may be resolved by the courts. We conclude that it is not.

Nixon, a former Chief Judge of the United States District Court for the Southern District of Mississippi, was convicted by a jury of two counts of making false statements before a federal grand jury and sentenced to prison. The grand jury investigation stemmed from reports that Nixon had accepted a gratuity from a Mississippi businessman in exchange for asking a local district attorney to halt the prosecution of the businessman's son. Because Nixon refused to resign from his office as a United States District Judge, he continued to collect his judicial salary while serving out his prison sentence.

On May 10, 1989, the House of Representatives adopted three articles of impeachment for high crimes and misdemeanors. The first two articles charged Nixon with giving false testimony before the grand jury and the third article charged him with bringing disrepute on the Federal Judiciary.

After the House presented the articles to the Senate, the Senate voted to invoke its own Impeachment Rule XI, under which the presiding officer appoints a committee of Senators to "receive evidence and take testimony." The Senate committee held four days of hearings, during which 10 witnesses, including Nixon, testified. Pursuant to Rule XI, the committee presented the full Senate with a complete transcript of the proceeding and a Report stating the uncontested facts and summarizing the evidence on the contested facts. Nixon and the House impeachment managers submitted extensive final briefs to the full Senate and delivered arguments from the Senate floor during the three hours set aside for oral argument in front of that body. Nixon himself gave a personal appeal, and several Senators posed questions directly to both parties. The Senate voted by more than the constitutionally required two-thirds majority to convict Nixon on the first two articles. The presiding officer then entered judgment removing Nixon from his office as United States District Judge.

Nixon thereafter commenced the present suit, arguing that Senate Rule XI violates the constitutional grant of authority to the Senate to "try" all impeachments because it prohibits the whole Senate from taking part in the evidentiary hearings. See Art. I, § 3, cl. 6. Nixon sought a declaratory judgment that his impeachment conviction was void and that his judicial salary and privileges should be reinstated. The District Court held that his claim was nonjusticiable, and the Court of Appeals for the District of Columbia Circuit agreed.

A controversy is nonjusticiable—i.e., involves a political question—where there is "a textually demonstrable constitutional commitment of the issue to a coordinate political department; or a lack of judicially discoverable and manageable standards for resolving it...." *Baker v. Carr*, 369 U.S. 186, 217 (1962). But the courts must, in the first instance, interpret the text in question and determine whether and to what extent the issue is textually committed. *Powell v. McCormack*, 395 U.S. 486, 519 (1969). As the discussion that follows makes clear, the concept of a textual commitment to a coordinate political department is not completely separate from the concept of a lack of judicially discoverable and manageable standards for resolving it; the lack of judicially manageable standards may strengthen the conclusion that there is a textually demonstrable commitment to a coordinate branch.

In this case, we must examine Art. I, § 3, cl. 6, to determine the scope of authority conferred upon the Senate by the Framers regarding impeachment. It provides:

> The Senate shall have the sole Power to try all Impeachments. When sitting for that Purpose, they shall be on Oath or Affirmation. When the President of the United States is tried, the Chief Justice shall preside: And no Person shall be convicted without the Concurrence of two thirds of the Members present.

The language and structure of this Clause are revealing. The first sentence is a grant of authority to the Senate, and the word "sole" indicates that this authority is reposed in the Senate and nowhere else. The next two sentences specify requirements to which the Senate proceedings shall conform: The Senate shall be on oath or affirmation, a two-thirds vote is required to convict, and when the President is tried the Chief Justice shall preside.

Petitioner argues that the word "try" in the first sentence imposes by implication an additional requirement on the Senate in that the proceedings must be in the nature of a judicial trial. From there petitioner goes on to argue that this limitation precludes the Senate from delegating to a select committee the task of hearing the testimony of witnesses, as was done pursuant to Senate Rule XI. "'[T]ry' means more than simply 'vote on' or 'review' or 'judge.' In 1787 and today, trying a case means hearing the evidence, not scanning a cold record." Petitioner concludes from this that courts may review whether or not the Senate "tried" him before convicting him.

There are several difficulties with this position which lead us ultimately to reject it. The word "try," both in 1787 and later, has considerably broader meanings than those to which petitioner would limit it. Older dictionaries define try as "[t]o examine" or "[t]o examine as a judge." In more modern usage the term has various meanings. For example, try can mean "to examine or investigate judicially," "to conduct the trial of," or "to put to the test by experiment, investigation, or trial." Petitioner submits that "try," as contained in T. Sheridan, Dictionary of the English Language (1796), means "to examine as a judge; to bring before a judicial tribunal." Based on the variety of definitions, however, we cannot say that the Framers used the word "try" as an implied limitation on the method by which the Senate might proceed in trying impeachments. "As a rule the Constitution speaks in general terms, leaving Congress to deal with subsidiary matters of detail as the public interests and changing conditions may require. . . ."

The conclusion that the use of the word "try" in the first sentence of the Impeachment Trial Clause lacks sufficient precision to afford any judicially manageable standard of review of the Senate's actions is fortified by the existence of the three very specific requirements that the Constitution does impose on the Senate when trying impeachments: The Members must be under oath, a two-thirds vote is required to convict, and the Chief Justice presides when the President is tried. These limitations are quite precise, and their nature suggests that the Framers did not intend to impose additional limitations on the form of the Senate proceedings by the use of the word "try" in the first sentence.

Petitioner devotes only two pages in his brief to negating the significance of the word "sole" in the first sentence of Clause 6. As noted above, that sentence provides that "[t]he Senate shall have the sole Power to try all Impeachments." We think that the word "sole" is of considerable significance. Indeed, the word "sole" appears only one other time in the Constitution—with respect to the House of Representatives' "*sole* Power of Impeachment." Art. I, § 2, cl. 5 (emphasis added). The commonsense meaning of the word "sole" is that the Senate alone shall have authority to determine whether an individual should be acquitted or convicted. The dictionary definition bears this out. "Sole" is defined as "having no companion," "solitary," "being the only one," and "functioning . . . independently and without assistance or interference." WEBSTER'S THIRD NEW INTERNATIONAL DICTIONARY 2168 (1971). If the courts may review the actions of the Senate in order to determine whether that body "tried" an impeached official, it is difficult to see how the Senate would be "functioning . . . independently and without assistance or interference." . . .

Petitioner also contends that the word "sole" should not bear on the question of justiciability because Art. II, § 2, cl. 1, of the Constitution grants the President pardon authority "except in Cases of Impeachment." He argues that such a limitation on the President's pardon power would not have been necessary if the Framers thought that the Senate alone had authority to deal with such questions. But the granting of a pardon is in no sense an overturning of a judgment of conviction by some other tribunal; it is "[a]ny executive action that mitigates or sets aside *punishment* for a crime." BLACK's LAW DICTIONARY 1113 (6th ed. 1990) (emphasis added). Authority in the Senate to determine procedures for trying an impeached official, unreviewable by the courts, is therefore not at all inconsistent with authority in the President to grant a pardon to the convicted official. The exception from the President's pardon authority of cases of impeachment was a separate determination by the Framers that executive clemency should not be available in such cases.

Petitioner finally argues that even if significance be attributed to the word "sole" in the first sentence of the Clause, the authority granted is to the Senate, and this means that "the Senate — not the courts, not a lay jury, not a Senate Committee — shall try impeachments." It would be possible to read the first sentence of the Clause this way, but it is not a natural reading. Petitioner's interpretation would bring into judicial purview not merely the sort of claim made by petitioner, but other similar claims based on the conclusion that the word "Senate" has imposed by implication limitations on procedures which the Senate might adopt. Such limitations would be inconsistent with the construction of the Clause as a whole, which, as we have noted, sets out three express limitations in separate sentences.

The history and contemporary understanding of the impeachment provisions support our reading of the constitutional language. The parties do not offer evidence of a single word in the history of the Constitutional Convention or in contemporary commentary that even alludes to the possibility of judicial review in the context of the impeachment powers. This silence is quite meaningful in light of the several explicit references to the availability of judicial review as a check on the Legislature's power with respect to bills of attainder, ex post facto laws, and statutes.

The Framers labored over the question of where the impeachment power should lie. Significantly, in at least two considered scenarios the power was placed with the Federal Judiciary. 1 THE RECORDS OF THE FEDERAL CONVENTION OF 1787, at 21–22 (Max Farrand ed., 1911); *id.* at 244 (New Jersey Plan). Indeed, James Madison and the Committee of Detail proposed that the Supreme Court should have the power to determine impeachments. See 2 *id.* at 551 (Madison); *id.* at 178–179, 186 (Committee of Detail). Despite these proposals, the Convention ultimately decided that the Senate would have "the sole Power to try all Impeachments." Art. I, § 3, cl. 6. According to Alexander Hamilton, the Senate was the "most fit depositary of this important trust" because its Members are representatives of the people. See The Federalist No. 65, p. 440 (J. Cooke ed. 1961). The Supreme Court was not the proper body because the Framers "doubted whether the members of that tribunal would, at all times, be endowed with so eminent a portion of fortitude as would be called for in the execution of so difficult a task" or whether the Court "would possess the degree of credit and authority" to carry out its judgment if it conflicted with the accusation brought by the Legislature—the people's representative. In addition, the Framers believed the Court was too small in number: "The awful discretion, which a court of impeachments must necessarily have, to doom to honor or to infamy the most confidential and the most distinguished characters of the community, forbids the commitment of the trust to a small number of persons."

There are two additional reasons why the Judiciary, and the Supreme Court in particular, were not chosen to have any role in impeachments. First, the Framers recognized that most likely there would be two sets of proceedings for individuals who commit impeachable offenses—the impeachment trial and a separate criminal trial. In fact, the Constitution explicitly provides for two separate proceedings. See Art. I, §3, cl. 7. The Framers deliberately separated the two forums to avoid raising the specter of bias and to ensure independent judgments:

> Would it be proper that the persons, who had disposed of his fame and his most valuable rights as a citizen in one trial, should in another trial, for the same offence, be also the disposers of his life and his fortune? Would there not be the greatest reason to apprehend, that error in the first sentence would be the parent of error in the second sentence? That the strong bias of one decision would be apt to overrule the influence of any new lights, which might be brought to vary the complexion of another decision?

The Federalist No. 65, 442 (J. Cooke ed. 1961). Certainly judicial review of the Senate's "trial" would introduce the same risk of bias as would participation in the trial itself.

Second, judicial review would be inconsistent with the Framers' insistence that our system be one of checks and balances. In our constitutional system, impeachment was designed to be the only check on the Judicial Branch by the Legislature. On the topic of judicial accountability, Hamilton wrote:

> The precautions for their responsibility are comprised in the article respecting impeachments. They are liable to be impeached for mal-conduct by the house of representatives, and tried by the senate, and if convicted, may be dismissed from office and disqualified for holding any other. *This is the only provision on the point, which is consistent with the necessary independence of the judicial character, and is the only one which we find in our own constitution in respect to our own judges. Id.* No. 79 (emphasis added).

Judicial involvement in impeachment proceedings, even if only for purposes of judicial review, is counterintuitive because it would eviscerate the "important constitutional check" placed on the Judiciary by the Framers. See *id.* No. 81, at 545. Nixon's argument would place final reviewing authority with respect to impeachments in the hands of the same body that the impeachment process is meant to regulate.

Nevertheless, Nixon argues that judicial review is necessary in order to place a check on the Legislature. Nixon fears that if the Senate is given unreviewable authority to interpret the Impeachment Trial Clause, there is a grave risk that the Senate will usurp judicial power. The Framers anticipated this objection and created two constitutional safeguards to keep the Senate in check. The first safeguard is that the whole of the impeachment power is divided between the two legislative bodies, with the House given the right to accuse and the Senate given the right to judge. *Id.* No. 66, at 446. This split of authority "avoids the inconvenience of making the same persons both accusers and judges; and guards against the danger of persecution from the prevalency of a factious spirit in either of those branches." The second safeguard is the two-thirds supermajority vote requirement. Hamilton explained that "[a]s the concurrence of two-thirds of the senate will be requisite to a condemnation, the security to innocence, from this additional circumstance, will be as complete as itself can desire."

In addition to the textual commitment argument, we are persuaded that the lack of finality and the difficulty of fashioning relief counsel against justiciability. See *Baker v. Carr.* We agree with the Court of Appeals that opening the door of judicial review to the procedures used by the Senate in trying impeachments would "expose the political life of the country to months, or perhaps years, of chaos." This lack of finality would manifest itself most dramatically if the President were impeached. The legitimacy of any successor, and hence his effectiveness, would be impaired severely, not merely while the judicial process was running its course, but during any retrial that a differently constituted Senate might conduct if its first judgment of conviction were invalidated. Equally uncertain is the question of what relief a court may give other than simply setting aside the judgment of conviction. Could it order the reinstatement of a convicted federal judge, or order Congress to create an additional judgeship if the seat had been filled in the interim?

Petitioner finally contends that a holding of nonjusticiability cannot be reconciled with our opinion in *Powell v. McCormack*, 395 U.S. 486 (1969). The relevant issue in *Powell* was whether courts could review the House of Representatives' conclusion that Powell was "unqualified" to sit as a Member because he had been accused of misappropriating public funds and abusing the process of the New York courts. We stated that the question of justiciability turned on whether the Constitution committed authority to the House to judge its Members' qualifications, and if so, the extent of that commitment. Article I, § 5, provides that "Each House shall be the Judge of the Elections, Returns and Qualifications of its own Members." In turn, Art. I, § 2, specifies three requirements for membership in the House: The candidate must be at least 25 years of age, a citizen of the United States for no less than seven years, and an inhabitant of the State he is chosen to represent. We held that, in light of the three requirements specified in the Constitution, the word "qualifications"—of which the House was to be the Judge—was of a precise, limited nature.

Our conclusion in *Powell* was based on the fixed meaning of "[q]ualifications" set forth in Art. I, § 2. The claim by the House that its power to "be the Judge of the Elections, Returns and Qualifications of its own Members" was a textual commitment of unreviewable authority was defeated by the existence of this separate provision specifying the only qualifications which might be imposed for House membership. The decision as to whether a Member satisfied these qualifications was placed with the House, but the decision as to what these qualifications consisted of was not.

In the case before us, there is no separate provision of the Constitution that could be defeated by allowing the Senate final authority to determine the meaning of the word "try" in the Impeachment Trial Clause. We agree with Nixon that courts possess power to review either legislative or executive action that transgresses identifiable textual limits. As we have made clear, "whether the action of [either the Legislative or Executive Branch] exceeds whatever authority has been committed, is itself a delicate exercise in constitutional interpretation, and is a responsibility of this Court as ultimate interpreter of the Constitution." *Baker v. Carr.* But we conclude, after exercising that delicate responsibility, that the word "try" in the Impeachment Trial Clause does not provide an identifiable textual limit on the authority which is committed to the Senate.

For the foregoing reasons, the judgment of the Court of Appeals is

Affirmed.

JUSTICE STEVENS, concurring.

For me, the debate about the strength of the inferences to be drawn from the use of the words "sole" and "try" is far less significant than the central fact that the Framers decided to assign the impeachment power to the Legislative Branch. The disposition of the impeachment of Samuel Chase in 1805 demonstrated that the Senate is fully conscious of the profound importance of that assignment, and nothing in the subsequent history of the Senate's exercise of this extraordinary power suggests otherwise. Respect for a coordinate branch of the Government forecloses any assumption that improbable hypotheticals like those mentioned by Justice White and Justice Souter will ever occur. Accordingly, the wise policy of judicial restraint, coupled with the potential anomalies associated with a contrary view, provide a sufficient justification for my agreement with the views of The Chief Justice.

JUSTICE WHITE, with whom JUSTICE BLACKMUN joins, concurring in the judgment.

Petitioner contends that the method by which the Senate convicted him on two articles of impeachment violates Art. I, § 3, cl. 6, of the Constitution, which mandates that the Senate "try" impeachments. The Court is of the view that the Constitution forbids us even to consider his contention. I find no such prohibition and would therefore reach the merits of the claim. I concur in the judgment because the Senate fulfilled its constitutional obligation to "try" petitioner.

I

It should be said at the outset that, as a practical matter, it will likely make little difference whether the Court's or my view controls this case. This is so because the Senate has very wide discretion in specifying impeachment trial procedures and because it is extremely unlikely that the Senate would abuse its discretion and insist on a procedure that could not be deemed a trial by reasonable judges. Even taking a wholly practical approach, I would prefer not to announce an unreviewable discretion in the Senate to ignore completely the constitutional direction to "try" impeachment cases. When asked at oral argument whether that direction would be satisfied if, after a House vote to impeach, the Senate, without any procedure whatsoever, unanimously found the accused guilty of being "a bad guy," counsel for the United States answered that the Government's theory "leads me to answer that question yes." Especially in light of this advice from the Solicitor General, I would not issue an invitation to the Senate to find an excuse, in the name of other pressing business, to be dismissive of its critical role in the impeachment process.

Practicalities aside, however, since the meaning of a constitutional provision is at issue, my disagreement with the Court should be stated.

II

The majority states that the question raised in this case meets two of the criteria for political questions set out in *Baker v. Carr*, 369 U.S. 186 (1962). It concludes first that there is "'a textually demonstrable constitutional commitment of the issue to a coordinate political department.'" It also finds that the question cannot be resolved for "'a lack of judicially discoverable and manageable standards.'"

Of course the issue in the political question doctrine is not whether the constitutional text commits exclusive responsibility for a particular governmental function to one of the political branches. There are numerous instances of this sort of textual commitment, e.g., Art. I, § 8, and it is not thought that disputes implicating these provisions are nonjusticiable. Rather, the issue is whether the Constitution has given one of the political branches final responsibility for interpreting the scope and nature of such a power.

Although *Baker* directs the Court to search for "a textually demonstrable constitutional commitment" of such responsibility, there are few, if any, explicit and unequivocal instances in the Constitution of this sort of textual commitment. Conferral on Congress of the power to "Judge" qualifications of its Members by Art. I, § 5, may, for example, preclude judicial review of whether a prospective member in fact meets those qualifications. See *Powell v. McCormack*, 395 U.S. 486, 548 (1969). The courts therefore are usually left to infer the presence of a political question from the text and structure of the Constitution. In drawing the inference that the Constitution has committed final interpretive authority to one of the political branches, courts are sometimes aided by textual evidence that the Judiciary was not meant to exercise judicial review—a coordinate inquiry expressed in *Baker*'s "lack of judicially discoverable and manageable standards" criterion.

A.

The majority finds a clear textual commitment in the Constitution's use of the word "sole" in the phrase "[t]he Senate shall have the sole Power to try all Impeachments." Art. I, § 3, cl. 6. It attributes "considerable significance" to the fact that this term appears in only one other passage in the Constitution. The Framers' sparing use of "sole" is thought to indicate that its employment in the Impeachment Trial Clause demonstrates a concern to give the Senate exclusive interpretive authority over the Clause. . . .

The significance of the Constitution's use of the term "sole" lies not in the infrequency with which the term appears, but in the fact that it appears exactly twice, in parallel provisions concerning impeachment. That the word "sole" is found only in the House and Senate Impeachment Clauses demonstrates that its purpose is to emphasize the distinct role of each in the impeachment process. As the majority notes, the Framers, following English practice, were very much concerned to separate the prosecutorial from the adjudicative aspects of impeachment. Giving each House "sole" power with respect to its role in impeachments effected this division of labor. While the majority is thus right to interpret the term "sole" to indicate that the Senate ought to "'functio[n] independently and without assistance or interference,'" it wrongly identifies the Judiciary, rather than the House, as the source of potential interference with which the Framers were concerned when they employed the term "sole."

Even if the Impeachment Trial Clause is read without regard to its companion clause, the Court's willingness to abandon its obligation to review the constitutionality of legislative acts merely on the strength of the word "sole" is perplexing. Consider, by comparison, the treatment of Art. I, § 1, which grants "All legislative powers" to the House and Senate. As used in that context "all" is nearly synonymous with "sole"— both connote entire and exclusive authority. Yet the Court has never thought it would unduly interfere with the operation of the Legislative Branch to entertain difficult and important questions as to the extent of the legislative power. Quite the opposite, we have stated that the proper interpretation of the Clause falls within the province of the Judiciary. Addressing the constitutionality of the legislative veto, for example, the Court found it necessary and proper to interpret Art. I, § 1, as one of the "[e]xplicit and unambiguous provisions of the Constitution [that] prescribe and define the respective functions of the Congress and of the Executive in the legislative process." *INS v. Chadha*, 462 U.S. 919, 945 (1983).

The majority also claims support in the history and early interpretations of the Impeachment Clauses, noting the various arguments in support of the current system made at the Constitutional Convention and expressed powerfully by Hamilton in The Federalist Nos. 65 and 66. In light of these materials there can be little doubt that the Framers came to the view that the trial of officials' public misdeeds should be conducted by representatives of the people; that the fledgling Judiciary lacked the wherewithal to adjudicate political intrigues; that the Judiciary ought not to try both impeachments and subsequent criminal cases emanating from them; and that the impeachment power must reside in the Legislative Branch to provide a check on the largely unaccountable Judiciary.

The majority's review of the historical record thus explains why the power to try impeachments properly resides with the Senate. It does not explain, however, the sweeping statement that the Judiciary was "not chosen to have any role in impeachments." Not a single word in the historical materials cited by the majority addresses judicial review of the Impeachment Trial Clause. And a glance at the arguments surrounding the Impeachment Clauses negates the majority's attempt to infer nonjusticiability from the Framers' arguments in support of the Senate's power to try impeachments.

What the relevant history mainly reveals is deep ambivalence among many of the Framers over the very institution of impeachment, which, by its nature, is not easily reconciled with our system of checks and balances. As they clearly recognized, the branch of the Federal Government which is possessed of the authority to try impeachments, by having final say over the membership of each branch, holds a potentially unanswerable power over the others. In addition, that branch, insofar as it is called upon to try not only members of other branches, but also its own, will have the advantage of being the judge of its own members' causes. . . .

The historical evidence reveals above all else that the Framers were deeply concerned about placing in any branch the "awful discretion, which a court of impeachments must necessarily have." The Federalist No. 65, p. 441 (J. Cooke ed. 1961). Viewed against this history, the discord between the majority's position and the basic principles of checks and balances underlying the Constitution's separation of powers is clear. In essence, the majority suggests that the Framers' conferred upon Congress a potential tool of legislative dominance yet at the same time rendered Congress' exercise of that power one of the very few areas of legislative authority immune from any judicial review. While the majority rejects petitioner's justiciability argument as espousing a view "inconsistent with the Framers' insistence that our system be one of checks and balances," it is the Court's finding of nonjusticiability that truly upsets the Framers' careful design. In a truly balanced system, impeachments tried by the Senate would serve as a means of controlling the largely unaccountable Judiciary, even as judicial review would ensure that the Senate adhered to a minimal set of procedural standards in conducting impeachment trials.

III

The majority's conclusion that "try" is incapable of meaningful judicial construction is not without irony. One might think that if any class of concepts would fall within the definitional abilities of the Judiciary, it would be that class having to do with procedural justice. Examination of the remaining question—whether proceedings in accordance with Senate Rule XI are compatible with the Impeachment Trial Clause—confirms this intuition.

Petitioner bears the rather substantial burden of demonstrating that, simply by employing the word "try," the Constitution prohibits the Senate from relying on a fact-finding committee. It is clear that the Framers were familiar with English impeachment practice and with that of the States employing a variant of the English model at the time of the Constitutional Convention. Hence there is little doubt that the term "try" as used in Art. I, § 3, cl. 6, meant that the Senate should conduct its proceedings in a manner somewhat resembling a judicial proceeding. Indeed, it is safe to assume that Senate trials were to follow the practice in England and the States, which contemplated a formal hearing on the charges, at which the accused would be represented by counsel, evidence would be presented, and the accused would have the opportunity to be heard.

Petitioner argues, however, that because committees were not used in state impeachment trials prior to the Convention, the word "try" cannot be interpreted to permit their use. It is, however, a substantial leap to infer from the absence of a particular device of parliamentary procedure that its use has been forever barred by the Constitution.

In short, textual and historical evidence reveals that the Impeachment Trial Clause was not meant to bind the hands of the Senate beyond establishing a set of minimal procedures. Without identifying the exact contours of these procedures, it is sufficient to say that the Senate's use of a factfinding committee under Rule XI is entirely compatible with the Constitution's command that the Senate "try all impeachments." Petitioner's challenge to his conviction must therefore fail.

JUSTICE SOUTER, concurring in the judgment.

I agree with the Court that this case presents a nonjusticiable political question. Because my analysis differs somewhat from the Court's, however, I concur in its judgment by this separate opinion.

As we cautioned in *Baker v. Carr*, 369 U.S. 186 (1962), "the 'political question' label" tends "to obscure the need for case-by-case inquiry." The need for such close examination is nevertheless clear from our precedents, which demonstrate that the functional nature of the political question doctrine requires analysis of "the precise facts and posture of the particular case," and precludes "resolution by any semantic cataloguing":

> Prominent on the surface of any case held to involve a political question is found a textually demonstrable constitutional commitment of the issue to a coordinate political department; or a lack of judicially discoverable and manageable standards for resolving it; or the impossibility of deciding without an initial policy determination of a kind clearly for nonjudicial discretion; or the impossibility of a court's undertaking independent resolution without expressing lack of the respect due coordinate branches of government; or an unusual need for unquestioning adherence to a political decision already made; or the potentiality of embarrassment from multifarious pronouncements by various departments on one question.

Whatever considerations feature most prominently in a particular case, the political question doctrine is "essentially a function of the separation of powers," existing to restrain courts "from inappropriate interference in the business of the other branches of Government," and deriving in large part from prudential concerns about the respect we owe the political departments. Not all interference is inappropriate or disrespectful, however, and application of the doctrine ultimately turns, as Learned Hand put it, on "how importunately the occasion demands an answer." L. HAND, THE BILL OF RIGHTS 15 (1958).

This occasion does not demand an answer. The Impeachment Trial Clause commits to the Senate "the sole Power to try all Impeachments," subject to three procedural requirements: the Senate shall be on oath or affirmation; the Chief Justice shall preside when the President is tried; and conviction shall be upon the concurrence of two-thirds of the Members present. It seems fair to conclude that the Clause contemplates that the Senate may determine, within broad boundaries, such subsidiary issues as the procedures for receipt and consideration of evidence necessary to satisfy its duty to "try" impeachments. Other significant considerations confirm a conclusion that this case presents a nonjusticiable political question: the "unusual need for unquestioning adherence to a political decision already made," as well as "the potentiality of embarrassment from multifarious pronouncements by various departments on one question." *Baker*. As the Court observes, judicial review of an impeachment trial would under the best of circumstances entail significant disruption of government.

One can, nevertheless, envision different and unusual circumstances that might justify a more searching review of impeachment proceedings. If the Senate were to act in a manner seriously threatening the integrity of its results, convicting, say, upon a coin toss, or upon a summary determination that an officer of the United States was simply "'a bad guy,'" judicial interference might well be appropriate. In such circumstances, the Senate's action might be so far beyond the scope of its constitutional authority, and the consequent impact on the Republic so great, as to merit a judicial response despite the prudential concerns that would ordinarily counsel silence. "The political question doctrine, a tool for maintenance of governmental order, will not be so applied as to promote only disorder."

Note: The Political Question Doctrine

1. In *Zivotofsky v. Clinton*, 566 U.S. 189 (2012), the Court may have narrowed the political question doctrine to some degree. In that case, the parents of a child born in Jerusalem brought suit against the Secretary of State to have "Israel" listed as the child's place of birth on his passport. A statute provided that Americans born in Jerusalem may elect to have "Israel" listed as the place of birth on their passports, but the State Department did not follow that directive due to its long-standing policy of not taking a position on the status of Jerusalem. Noting that the political question doctrine is a "narrow exception" to the obligation of courts to decide cases properly before them, the Court declined to apply it. The Court stated that it was not being asked to decide the political status of Jerusalem, but rather to determine which interpretation of the statute was correct and whether the statute was constitutional, both of which involved "familiar judicial exercises."

2. In *Doe v. Bush*, a principal case in the ripeness section of this chapter, the First Circuit declined to use the political question doctrine to avoid decision on the question of the legality of the Iraq war:

> Our analysis is based on ripeness rather than the political question doctrine. The political question doctrine—that courts should not intervene in questions that are the province of the legislative and executive branches— is a famously murky one. It has also been used fairly infrequently to block judicial review. The modern definition of the doctrine was established in the landmark case of *Baker v. Carr*, 369 U.S. 186. In the forty years since that case, the Supreme Court has found a case nonjusticiable on the basis of the political question doctrine only twice. *See Nixon v. United States*, 506 U.S. 224 (1993) (Senate procedures for impeachment of a federal judge); *Gilligan*

v. Morgan, 413 U.S. 1, 12, 93 (1973) (training, weaponry, and orders of Ohio National Guard). Our court has been similarly sparing in its reliance on the political question doctrine.

What might account for the federal courts' reluctance to employ this doctrine?

3. The Court has employed the political question doctrine in several categories of cases. The first concerns Article IV, § 4's Guarantee Clause, which provides: "The United States shall guarantee to every State in this Union a Republican Form of Government." Dating back to the seminal case of *Luther v. Borden*, 48 U.S. (7 How.) 1 (1849), the Supreme Court has consistently rejected Guarantee Clause challenges as nonjusticiable political questions. As the Court said in *Luther*, "it rests with Congress to decide what government is the established one in a State. For as the United States guarantee to each State a republican government, Congress must necessarily decide what government is established in the State before it can determine whether it is republican or not." More recently, however, the Court has suggested, in dicta, that an inflexible rule in the Guarantee Clause context may not be appropriate. *See New York v. United States*, 505 U.S. 144, 185 (1992) ("[P]erhaps not all claims under the Guarantee Clause present nonjusticiable political questions.").

The Court has been even less clear about whether suits challenging the redistricting decisions of state legislatures are justiciable. In a 2004 decision, a plurality of the Court stated that a dispute about partisan gerrymandering of legislative districts in Pennsylvania was a nonjusticiable political question because of a lack of judicially manageable standards in such cases. *See Vieth v. Jubelirer*, 541 U.S. 267 (2004); *accord League of United Latin American Citizens v. Perry*, 548 U.S. 399 (2006) (Scalia, J., concurring in the judgment in part and dissenting in part). Although there was no majority opinion in *Vieth*, the Court appears to be retreating from its earlier conclusion in *Davis v. Bandemer*, 478 U.S. 109 (1986), that partisan gerrymandering claims should be reviewed on the merits. The Court has consistently held, by contrast, that claims of racial gerrymandering are justiciable. *See, e.g., White v. Regester*, 412 U.S. 755 (1973); *Whitcomb v. Chavis*, 403 U.S. 124 (1971). Therefore, the Court has hardly been clear about application of the political question doctrine to redistricting cases.

The Court has also vacillated on the application of the political question doctrine to challenges to the ratification of constitutional amendments by states. In *Coleman v. Miller*, 307 U.S. 433 (1937), the Court held that Kansas's late approval of a proposed amendment prohibiting the use of child labor was not reviewable because of the political question doctrine. Yet, in several previous cases, the Court had adjudicated on the merits challenges to procedures for amending the Constitution. *See, e.g., Dillon v. Gloss*, 256 U.S. 368 (1921) (reviewing the validity of the Eighteenth Amendment in light of a time constraint imposed by Congress); *Hollingsworth v. Virginia*, 3 U.S. (3 Dall.) 378 (1798) (holding that the Eleventh Amendment was adopted under procedures consistent with the Constitution).

The lower court opinion in *Nixon* extensively discussed another category of cases subject to the political question doctrine: determinations by the House of Representatives and the Senate regarding the eligibility and qualifications of their respective members. *See Nixon v. United States*, 938 F.2d 239 (D.C. Cir. 1991). With respect to those qualifications found in Art. 1, § 2 of the Constitution, such as age, period of citizenship of the United States, and residence when elected, the House and the Senate have the final authority to determine the eligibility of members. *See Powell v. McCormack*, 395 U.S. 486 (1969). The Court has also made clear, however, that refusals by the Senate and House to seat a member based on grounds other than those expressly stated in the Constitution are justiciable. *See Roudebush v. Hartke*, 405 U.S. 15 (1972). As the Court stated in *Powell* with respect to the latter type of case: "Our system of government requires that federal courts on occasion interpret the Constitution in a manner at variance with the construction given the document by another branch. The alleged conflict that such an adjudication may cause cannot justify the courts' avoiding their constitutional responsibilities."

Even these relatively discrete categories of cases demonstrate that the Court's adherence to the political question doctrine ebbs and flows over time. While Guarantee Clause challenges have always been held to be nonjusticiable, more recently the Court has suggested that such a categorical rule may be inappropriate. Similarly, the Court has announced decisions in other categories of political question cases — challenges to the constitutional amendment process, for example — where it reaches the merits in some instances and dismisses in others. Given the indeterminancy in this area, how can attorneys and litigants avoid the costly mistake of bringing a challenge that is later held to be a nonjusticiable political question? More fundamentally, are there particular attributes that each of these categories of cases have in common?

4. Perhaps the most important category of political question cases, and one in which it historically has had some teeth, is in the context of foreign affairs. Although the *Doe* court declined to use the doctrine to avoid a decision on the legality of the use of force in Iraq, many courts have rejected challenges to United States foreign policy, particularly in the context of military actions, through resort to the political question doctrine. *See, e.g., Goldwater v. Carter*, 444 U.S. 996 (1979) (plurality opinion) (rejecting a challenge on political question grounds to President Carter's rescission of a treaty with Taiwan); *Atlee v. Richardson*, 411 U.S. 911 (1973) (summarily affirming the dismissal of a challenge to the Vietnam War on political question grounds).

In *Boumediene v. Bush*, 553 U.S. 723 (2008), however, the Supreme Court arguably retreated from its use of the political question doctrine in cases involving foreign affairs. The question in *Boumediene* was whether the Military Commissions Act of 2006 (MCA), which stripped federal courts of jurisdiction over cases involving "enemy combatants" detained in Guantanamo Bay, Cuba, violated the Suspension Clause of the Constitution. In a 5-4 decision, the Court held that federal courts could entertain detainees' petitions for writs of habeas corpus because the MCA violated the Suspension Clause. (For a brief discussion of the Court's holding on the merits, see Chapter 15.) However, because the case involved the powers of the President and Congress over foreign affairs and the determination of sovereignty in particular, the Court first responded to the government's contention that the case should be dismissed as a political question.

The Court explained that though the President's declarations on sovereignty were entitled to "great respect," such judgments were not the "end of the analysis":

> Our cases do not hold it is improper for us to inquire into the objective degree of control the Nation asserts over foreign territory. As commentators have noted, "'[s]overeignty' is a term used in many senses and is much abused." When we have stated that sovereignty is a political question, we have referred not to sovereignty in the general, colloquial sense, meaning the exercise of dominion or power, but sovereignty in the narrow, legal sense of the term, meaning a claim of right. Indeed, it is not altogether uncommon for a territory to be under the *de jure* sovereignty of one nation, while under the plenary control, or practical sovereignty, of another. This condition can occur when the territory is seized during war, as Guantanamo was during the Spanish-American war. Accordingly, for purposes of our analysis, we accept the Government's position that Cuba, and not the United States, retains *de jure* sovereignty over Guantanamo Bay. As we did [in a previous case], however, we take notice of the obvious and uncontested fact that the United States, by virtue of its complete jurisdiction and control over the base, maintains *de facto* sovereignty over this territory.

Boumediene's truncated discussion of the scope of the political question doctrine raises more questions than it answers. For instance, by authorizing courts to hear cases raising certain types of sovereignty questions, did the Court narrow the scope of the political question doctrine, at least as it pertains to foreign affairs? Moreover, does the Court's distinction between claims of *de facto* and *de jure* sovereignty make sense? Is there reason to believe that the Court has greater expertise or more of a constitutional obligation to decide questions involving a claim of *de facto* sovereignty?

Consider the Court's decision six decades before *Boumediene* in *Chicago & Southern Air Lines, Inc. v. Waterman Steamship Corporation*, 333 U.S. 103, 111 (1948), in which the Court noted that:

> [T]he very nature of executive decisions as to foreign policy is political, not judicial. Such decisions are wholly confided by our Constitution to the political departments of the government, Executive and Legislative. They are delicate, complex, and involve large elements of prophecy. They are and should be undertaken only by those directly responsible to the people whose welfare they advance or imperil. They are decisions of a kind for which the Judiciary has neither aptitude, facilities, nor responsibility, and have long been held to belong in the domain of political power not subject to judicial intrusion or inquiry.

Does the Court's decision in *Boumediene* fall into the class of cases that are so "delicate" and "complex" as to preclude judicial inquiry? If so, is it still true that the political question doctrine has teeth in the context of foreign affairs?

5. Since *Baker v. Carr* was decided in 1962, the Court has only twice refused to decide a case because of the political question doctrine. *See Nixon v. United States*; *Gilligan v. Morgan*, 413 U.S. 1 (1973). One explanation for the Court's reticence to

use the doctrine is that the growth of judicial supremacy over the past forty years has made resort to the political question doctrine unnecessary, possibly even antagonistic to expanding notions of judicial power. *See, e.g.*, Rachel E. Barkow, *More Supreme Than the Court? The Fall of the Political Question Doctrine and the Rise of Judicial Supremacy*, 102 Colum. L. Rev. 237, 237 (2002). Other scholars suggest that courts are hesitant to find political questions because the *Baker* criteria are highly manipulable. *See, e.g.*, Robert J. Pushaw, Jr., *Judicial Review and the Political Question Doctrine: Reviving the Federalist "Rebuttable Presumption" Analysis*, 80 N.C. L. Rev. 1165, 1182 (2002). Still others have asserted that the function once served by the political question doctrine is now being filled by standing doctrine. *See, e.g.*, Mark Tushnet, *Law and Prudence in the Law of Justiciability: The Transformation and Disappearance of the Political Question Doctrine*, 80 N.C. L. Rev. 1203 (2002). Whatever the reason, scholars generally agree that the political question doctrine has been narrowed considerably in recent years.

Problem: A Suit Against a Terrorist Organization

Mark and Ellen Todd were traveling in Israel with their infant son when they were killed by members of Hamas Islamic Resistance Movement, a group designated as a terrorist organization by the United States. The administrator of their estate brought an action in federal district court against the Palestine Authority (PA) and the Palestine Liberation Organization (PLO), under the federal Anti-Terrorism Act, which provides a cause of action in favor of any "national of the United States injured . . . by any act of international terrorism [and] his or her estate, survivors, or heirs." The administrator alleges that the PA and the PLO had engaged in acts of terrorism within the meaning of the Act that led to the Todds' deaths.

The defendants argue that they are protected by sovereign immunity. To determine the question of sovereign immunity, the district court would be required to interpret a number of United Nations resolutions and Israeli-Palestinian agreements. The defendants move to dismiss, alleging that the case presents a non-justiciable political question. Does it?

Part Two

The Role of Federal Law in State-Court Litigation

Chapter 4

State Courts in a Federal System

It may seem odd that a casebook on "Federal Courts" devotes so much attention to state courts. But there are good reasons for doing so. To begin with, the vast bulk of litigation in this country takes place in state courts. Much of that litigation involves federal questions, and when it does, Congress has the power not only to alter the governing law, but also to designate the forum in which the dispute will or may be resolved.

Many provisions of the Constitution give Congress the authority to affect practice in state courts. Our focus in this and the next two chapters is on Article III and its grant of judicial power over cases "arising under" federal law. As outlined in Chapter 2, decisions by the Supreme Court established that Congress can "take control" of such cases in state courts "at any stage of [their] progress." *Tennessee v. Davis*, 100 U.S. 257 (1880). Congress has exercised that power in two ways. It has provided for *review* by the Supreme Court of final judgments rendered by state courts, and it has authorized *removal* to federal district court of cases initiated in a state trial court. But Congress has defined the appellate and removal jurisdictions in very different ways, and the differences have been widened by the constructions the Supreme Court has given to the governing statutes over the years.

In this chapter we examine the foundational cases defining the Supreme Court's jurisdiction over state court cases; we also introduce the law governing the removal jurisdiction. In Chapter 5 we study in some detail the doctrines that govern the availability and scope of Supreme Court review of state-court decisions. In Chapter 6, we consider the ways in which federal law affects the litigation of federal claims that are filed in state court and not removed.

Two other aspects of the relationship between federal and state courts deserve mention here. The modern-day descendant of section 25 of the Judiciary Act of 1789 — 28 U.S.C. § 1257 — has been interpreted as precluding review of state-court decisions by any federal court other than the Supreme Court. This prohibition is known as the *Rooker-Feldman* doctrine. See Chapter 17 section B. However, Congress has carved out an exception: it has authorized the use of federal habeas corpus as a vehicle for challenging state criminal convictions on the basis of federal law. See Chapter 15.

A. Supreme Court Review: Foundations

As we have seen in Chapter 2, section 25 of the Judiciary Act of 1789 authorized the Supreme Court to review decisions of state courts that rejected claims under federal law. More precisely, section 25 provided for review of "a final judgment or decree in any suit, in the highest court of law or equity of a State in which a decision in the suit could be had," in three categories of cases:

[1] where is drawn in question the validity of a treaty or statute of, or an authority exercised under the United States, and the decision is against their validity; or

[2] where is drawn in question the validity of a statute of, or an authority exercised under any State, on the ground of their being repugnant to the constitution, treaties or laws of the United States, and the decision is in favour of such their validity, or

[3] where is drawn in question the construction of any clause of the constitution, or of a treaty, or statute of, or commission held under the United States, and the decision is against the title, right, privilege or exemption specially set up or claimed by either party, under such clause of the said Constitution, treaty, statute or commission.

The constitutionality of section 25 was challenged in the great case of *Martin v. Hunter's Lessee.*

Martin v. Hunter's Lessee
Supreme Court of the United States, 1816.
1 Wheat. (14 U.S.) 304.

Story, J., delivered the opinion of the court.

[*Editorial note.* The decision in *Martin v. Hunter's Lessee* arose out of lengthy and complex litigation involving competing claims of ownership to the Northern Neck, a large tract of land in Virginia. On one side, Denny (and later Philip) Martin claimed under a devise from Lord Fairfax. Lord Fairfax was the only peer of the realm to have emigrated to the American colonies. At his death in 1781 he was a citizen of Virginia; however, Denny Martin was a subject of Great Britain. On the other side, Hunter and his successors claimed under a grant from Virginia. They relied on various laws passed by the Virginia legislature in the 1780s that provided for the forfeiture to the state of lands held by aliens like Martin, who under the common law were incapable of holding lands in the state.

[The Martin claimants argued that the purported forfeitures were invalid by reason of federal treaties — the Treaty of Peace of 1783 and the Jay Treaty of 1794. In an earlier phase of the litigation, the Virginia Court of Appeals, the highest court of the state, rejected these arguments. Martin took the case to the United States Supreme Court by writ of error under section 25 of the Judiciary Act of 1789. The Supreme Court held that the treaty of 1794 "completely protect[ed] and confirm[ed] the title" of Denny Martin. It reversed the judgment of the Virginia Court of Appeals. *Fairfax's Devisee v. Hunter's Lessee*, 7 Cranch (11 U.S.) 603 (1813).

[When the case returned to the Virginia court, the judges of that court refused to obey the Supreme Court's mandate. Martin again brought the case to the United States Supreme Court.]

This is a writ of error from the court of appeals of Virginia, founded upon the refusal of that court to obey the mandate of this court, requiring the judgment rendered in this very cause, at February term, 1813, to be carried into due execution. The following is the judgment of the court of appeals rendered on the mandate: "The court is unanimously of opinion, that the appellate power of the supreme court of the United States does not extend to this court, under a sound construction of the constitution of the United States; that so much of the 25th section of the act of congress to establish the judicial courts of the United States, as extends the appellate jurisdiction of the supreme court to this court, is not in pursuance of the constitution of the United States; that the writ of error, in this cause, was improvidently allowed under the authority of that act; that the proceedings thereon in the supreme court were, *coram non judice*, in relation to this court, and that obedience to its mandate be declined by the court." . . .

Jud. Act of 1789

[After laying out general principles of constitutional interpretation, Justice Story turned to Article III. In this part of his opinion he argued that it is the duty of Congress to vest the whole of the federal judicial power. That issue is discussed in Chapter 19.]

[Appellate jurisdiction] is given by the constitution to the supreme court in all cases where it has not original jurisdiction; subject, however, to such exceptions and regulations as congress may prescribe. It is, therefore, capable of embracing every case enumerated in the constitution, which is not exclusively to be decided by way of original jurisdiction. . . .

[W]hat is there to restrain its exercise over state tribunals in the enumerated cases? The appellate power is not limited by the terms of the third article to any particular courts. The words are, "the judicial power (which includes appellate power) shall extend *to all cases*," &c., and "in all other cases before mentioned the supreme court shall have appellate jurisdiction." It is the *case*, then, and not *the court*, that gives the jurisdiction. . . .

[It] is plain that the framers of the constitution did contemplate that cases within the judicial cognizance of the United States not only might but would arise in the state courts, in the exercise of their ordinary jurisdiction. [Here Justice Story quoted the Supremacy Clause.] . . .

A moment's consideration will show us the necessity and propriety of this provision in cases where the jurisdiction of the state courts is unquestionable. Suppose a contract for the payment of money is made between citizens of the same state, and performance thereof is sought in the courts of that state; no person can doubt that the jurisdiction completely and exclusively attaches, in the first instance, to such courts. Suppose at the trial the defendant sets up in his defence . . . a state law, impairing the obligation of such contract, which law, if binding, would defeat the suit. The constitution of the United States has declared that no state [shall pass] a law impairing the obligation of contracts. If congress shall not have passed a law providing for the removal of such a suit to the courts of the United States, must not the state court proceed to hear and determine it? . . . Suppose an indictment for a crime in a state court, and the defendant should allege in his defence that the crime was created by an *ex post facto* act of the state, must not the state court, in the exercise of a jurisdiction which has already rightfully attached, have a right to pronounce on the validity and sufficiency of the defence? Innumerable instances of the same sort might be stated, in illustration of the position; and unless the state courts could sustain jurisdiction in such cases, [the Supremacy Clause] would be without meaning or effect, and public mischiefs, of a most enormous magnitude, would inevitably ensue.

It must, therefore, be conceded that the constitution not only contemplated, but meant to provide for cases within the scope of the judicial power of the United States, which might yet depend before state tribunals. It was foreseen that in the exercise of their ordinary jurisdiction, state courts would incidentally take cognizance of cases arising under the constitution, the laws, and treaties of the United States. Yet to all these cases the judicial power, by the very terms of the constitution, is to extend. It cannot extend by original jurisdiction if that was already rightfully and exclusively attached in the state courts, which (as has been already shown) may occur; it must, therefore, extend by appellate jurisdiction, or not at all. It would seem to follow that the appellate power of the United States must, in such cases, extend to state tribunals; and if in such cases, there is no reason why it should not equally attach upon all others within the purview of the constitution.

It has been argued that such an appellate jurisdiction over state courts is inconsistent with the genius of our governments, and the spirit of the constitution. That the latter was never designed to act upon state sovereignties, but only upon the people, and that if the power exists, it will materially impair the sovereignty of the states, and the independence of their courts. We cannot yield to the force of this reasoning; it assumes principles which we cannot admit, and draws conclusions to which we do not yield our assent.

It is a mistake, that the constitution was not designed to operate upon states, in their corporate capacities. It is crowded with provisions which restrain or annul the sovereignty of the states in some of the highest branches of their prerogatives. [For example Article I, § 10] contains a long list of disabilities and prohibitions imposed upon the states. . . . [When] the states are stripped of some of the highest attributes of sovereignty, and the same are given to the United States; when the legislatures of the states are, in some respects, under the control of congress, and in every case are, under the constitution, bound by the paramount authority of the United States; it is certainly difficult to support the argument that the appellate power over the decisions of state courts is contrary to the genius of our institutions. The courts of the United States can, without question, revise the proceedings of the executive and legislative authorities of the states, and if they are found to be contrary to the constitution, may declare them to be of no legal validity. Surely the exercise of the same right over judicial tribunals is not a higher or more dangerous act of sovereign power.

Nor can such a right be deemed to impair the independence of state judges. It is assuming the very ground in controversy to assert that they possess an absolute independence of the United States. In respect to the powers granted to the United States, they are not independent; they are expressly bound to obedience by the letter of the constitution. . . .

It is further argued, that no great public mischief can result from a construction which shall limit the appellate power of the United States to cases in their own courts: first, because state judges are bound by an oath to support the constitution of the United States, and must be presumed to be men of learning and integrity; and, secondly, because congress must have an unquestionable right to remove all cases within the scope of the judicial power from the state courts to the courts of the United States, at any time before final judgment, thought not after final judgment.

As to the first reason — admitting that the judges of the state courts are, and always will be, of as much learning, integrity, and wisdom, as those of the courts of the United States, (which we very cheerfully admit,) it does not aid the argument. It is manifest that the constitution has proceeded upon a theory of its own, and given or withheld powers according to the judgment of the American people, by whom it was adopted. We can only construe its powers, and cannot inquire into the policy or principles which induced the grant of them. The constitution has presumed (whether rightly or wrongly we do not inquire) that state attachments, state prejudices, state jealousies, and state interests, might some times obstruct, or control, or be supposed to obstruct or control, the regular administration of justice. Hence, in controversies between states; between citizens of different states; between citizens claiming grants under different states; between a state and its citizens, or foreigners, and between citizens and foreigners, it enables the parties, under the authority of congress, to have the controversies heard, tried, and determined before the national tribunals. No other reason than that which has been stated can be assigned, why some, at least, of those cases should not have been left to the cognizance of the state courts.

This is not all. A motive of another kind, perfectly compatible with the most sincere respect for state tribunals, might induce the grant of appellate power over their decisions. That motive is the importance, and even necessity of *uniformity* of decisions throughout the whole United States, upon all subjects within the purview of the constitution. Judges of equal learning and integrity, in different states, might differently interpret a statute, or a treaty of the United States, or even the constitution itself: If there were no revising authority to control these jarring and discordant judgments, and harmonize them into uniformity, the laws, the treaties, and the constitution of the United States would be different in different states, and might, perhaps, never have precisely the same construction, obligation, or efficacy, in any two states. . . .

There is an additional consideration, which is entitled to great weight. The [judicial power] of the United States was designed for the common and equal benefit of all the people of the United States. It was not to be exercised exclusively for the benefit of parties who might be plaintiffs, and would elect the national forum, but also for the protection of defendants who might be entitled to try their rights, or assert their privileges, before the same forum. Yet, if the construction contended for be correct, it will follow, that as the plaintiff may always elect the state court, the defendant may be deprived of all the security which the constitution intended in aid of his rights. Such a state of things can, in no respect, be considered as giving equal rights. To obviate this difficulty, we are referred to the power which it is admitted congress possess to remove suits from state courts to the national courts; and this forms the second ground upon which the argument we are considering has been attempted to be sustained.

This power of removal . . . presupposes an exercise of original jurisdiction to have attached elsewhere. But [removal is always deemed] an exercise of appellate, and not of original jurisdiction. If, then, the right of removal be included in the appellate jurisdiction, it is only because it is one mode of exercising that power, and as congress is not limited by the constitution to any particular mode, or time of exercising it, it may authorize a removal either before or after judgment. . . .

A writ of error is, indeed, but a process which removes the record of one court to the possession of another court, and enables the latter to inspect the proceedings, and give such judgment as its own opinion of the law and justice of the case may warrant. There is nothing in the nature of the process which forbids it from being applied by the legislature to interlocutory as well as final judgments. And if the right of removal from state courts exist before judgment, because it is included in the appellate power, it must, for the same reason, exist after judgment. And if the appellate power by the constitution does not include cases pending in state courts, the right of removal, which is but a mode of exercising that power, cannot be applied to them. Precisely the same objections, therefore, exist as to the right of removal before judgment, as after, and both must stand or fall together. Nor, indeed, would the force of the arguments on either side materially vary, if the right of removal were an exercise of original jurisdiction. It would equally trench upon the jurisdiction and independence of state tribunals. . . .

On the whole, the court are of opinion, that the appellate power of the United States does extend to cases pending in the state courts; and that the 25th section of the judiciary act, which authorizes the exercise of this jurisdiction in the specified cases, by a writ of error, is supported by the letter and spirit of the constitution. We find no clause in that instrument which limits this power; and we dare not interpose a limitation where the people have not been disposed to create one.

Strong as this conclusion stands upon the general language of the constitution, it may still derive support from other sources. It is an historical fact, that this exposition of the constitution, extending its appellate power to state courts, was, previous to its adoption, uniformly and publicly avowed by its friends, and admitted by its enemies, as the basis of their respective reasonings, both in and out of the state conventions. It is an historical fact, that at the time when the judiciary act was submitted to the deliberations of the first congress, composed, as it was, not only of men of great learning and ability, but of men who had acted a principal part in framing, supporting, or opposing that constitution, the same exposition was explicitly declared and admitted by the friends and by the opponents of that system. It is an historical fact, that the supreme court of the United States have, from time to time, sustained this appellate jurisdiction in a great variety of cases, brought from the tribunals of many of the most important states in the union, and that no state tribunal has ever breathed a judicial doubt on the subject, or declined to obey the mandate of the supreme court, until the present occasion. This weight of contemporaneous exposition by all parties, this acquiescence of enlightened state courts, and these judicial decisions of the supreme court through so long a period, do, as we think, place the doctrine upon a foundation of authority which cannot be shaken, without delivering over the subject to perpetual and irremediable doubts. . . .

JOHNSON, J. [concurring].

. . . I view this question as one of the most momentous importance; as one which may affect, in its consequences, the permanence of the American union. It presents an instance of collision between the judicial powers of the union, and one of the greatest states in the union, on a point the most delicate and difficult to be adjusted. On the one hand, the general government must cease to exist whenever it loses the power of protecting itself in the exercise of its constitutional powers. . . .

On the other hand, so firmly am I persuaded that the American people can no longer enjoy the blessings of a free government, whenever the state sovereignties shall be prostrated at the feet of the general government, nor the proud consciousness of equality and security, any longer than the independence of judicial power shall be maintained consecrated and intangible, that I could borrow the language of a celebrated orator, and exclaim, "I rejoice that Virginia has resisted."

Yet here I must claim the privilege of expressing my regret, that the opposition of the high and truly respected tribunal of that state had not been marked with a little more moderation. . . .

. . . [In cases like this one,] the legislature of the union evince their confidence in the state tribunals; for they do not attempt to give original cognizance to their own circuit courts of such cases, or to remove them by petition and order; but still believing that their decisions will be generally satisfactory, a writ of error is not given immediately as a question within the jurisdiction of the United States shall occur, but only in case the decision shall finally, in the court of the last resort, be against the title set up under the constitution, treaty, &c.

In this act I can see nothing which amounts to an assertion of the inferiority or dependence of the state tribunals. . . .

Note: Martin *and the Constitutionality of Section 25*

1. From today's perspective, Justice Story's painstaking defense of the constitutionality of section 25 may seem like an exposition of the obvious. But the situation was quite different in 1816. The highest court of a state had unanimously declared that section 25 was "not in pursuance of the constitution." And this was not just any state. Virginia was the home of Washington, Jefferson, and Madison—but it was also a state

in which the Constitution had been ratified by a narrow margin less than 30 years earlier. Justice Story saw it as his task to construct a chain of reasoning that would make section 25 invulnerable to further challenge.

2. As Justice Story points out, counsel for the Hunter claimants acknowledged that Congress has the power to provide for the *removal* of cases from state to federal courts. If removal is permissible, it is difficult to see why appellate review is not. But why was removal so readily accepted? (Recall that Justice Johnson, dissenting in *Osborn* (Chapter 2), did not question the legitimacy of removal "before an adjudication takes place.")

3. Justice Johnson dissented in *Fairfax's Devisee v. Hunter's Lessee*, but here he joins in upholding the constitutionality of section 25.

The "celebrated orator" whom he paraphrases was William Pitt the Elder. In 1766, Pitt electrified the House of Commons with an extemporaneous speech in opposition to the tax imposed by the Stamp Act. Responding to the Prime Minister's defense of the tax, Pitt declared, "The gentleman tells us, America is obstinate; America is almost in open rebellion. I rejoice that America has resisted. Three million of people so dead to all feelings of liberty, as voluntarily to submit to be slaves, would have been fit instruments to make slaves of the rest."

4. The tension described by Justice Johnson at the outset of his opinion is a recurring one in American history and American law. Many of the doctrines we study in this book reflect the Supreme Court's efforts to assure that the national government can "protect[] itself in the exercise of its constitutional powers" without "prostrat[ing]" state sovereignty.

5. Notwithstanding Justice Story's efforts, the decision in *Martin* did not put an end to challenges to the constitutionality of section 25. In the decades that followed, issues relating to Supreme Court review of state courts continued to arise, often as part of the metastasizing conflicts over federal and state power centered on slavery. Ultimately, as Justice Black bluntly stated in *Testa v. Katt*, 330 U.S. 386 (1947) [Chapter 6 Note], "the fundamental issues over the extent of federal supremacy [were] resolved by [the Civil War]."

Note: The Judiciary Act Amendments of 1867

The Civil War and Reconstruction opened a new chapter in the history of the federal courts and their relation to the courts of the states. One manifestation of the new regime was the Act of Feb. 5, 1867, designated as an act to amend the Judiciary Act of 1789.

The Act had two sections. Section 1 is often referred to as the Habeas Corpus Act of 1867. For the first time, it authorized federal courts to issue writs of habeas corpus on behalf of persons held in custody by *state* officials in violation of the federal constitution. This section laid the foundation for the system of collateral review of state criminal judgments that we will study in Chapter 15.

Our interest here is in section 2 of the Act. Section 2 reproduced section 25 of the Judiciary Act of 1789 — but with some changes. One of these changes was the omission of the final sentence of section 25. That sentence read:

But no other error shall be assigned or regarded as a ground of reversal in any such case as aforesaid than such as appears on the face of the record and immediately respects the before-mentioned questions of validity or construction of the said Constitution, treaties, statutes, commissions, or authorities in dispute.

The final sentence of section 25 thus limited the Supreme Court's jurisdiction over state-court cases to federal questions. The question soon arose: did the omission of that sentence in the 1867 law expand the Court's jurisdiction? In *Murdock v. City of Memphis*, an otherwise unremarkable case from the state courts of Tennessee, the Supreme Court took the opportunity to resolve that question.

Murdock v. City of Memphis

Supreme Court of the United States, 1875.

20 Wall. (87 U.S.) 590.

Error to the Supreme Court of Tennessee; the case being thus:

Murdock filed a bill in one of the courts of chancery of Tennessee, against the city of Memphis, in that State. The bill and its exhibits made this case:

[In 1844, Congress authorized the expenditure of $100,000 to construct a naval depot in Memphis, Tennessee. Murdock's family owned land in Memphis and arranged to sell it to the City. By deed in July 1844, the family executed a deed conveying the land to the City of Memphis "for the location of the naval depot," with the further provision that the land would be held in trust for the grantors and their heirs "in case the [land] shall not be appropriated by the United States for that purpose." In September 1844, the City in turn conveyed the land to the United States, unconditionally, for the sum of $20,000.

[The United States made some improvements to the land, but the Navy soon soured on the project, and in 1854 an Act of Congress transferred the land back to the City: "All the grounds and appurtenances thereunto belonging, known as the Memphis Navy Yard, in Shelby County, Tennessee, be, and the same is hereby, ceded to the mayor and aldermen of the city of Memphis, for the use and benefit of said city."

[Murdock sued the City of Memphis in Tennessee chancery court, seeking a judgment in equity that the land was now held in trust for his benefit. He advanced two legal theories: one grounded in state law, the other in federal law. The primary basis for the suit was state property law. Under the original deed, he argued, once the United States abandoned the land, the property was to be conveyed in trust for his benefit. The chancery court rejected that contention, and the Tennessee Supreme Court affirmed, holding that "perpetual occupation" by the United States was not a condition subsequent, and thus no breach of the deed had occurred. In the alternative, Murdock argued that federal law—the Act of Congress in 1854—itself operated to convey the property for his benefit. The state courts also rejected that contention, holding that the Act by its terms ceded the property to the mayor and aldermen of Memphis, solely for the use of the City.]

The complainant thereupon sued out a writ of error to this court.

Mr. Justice Miller (now, January 11th, 1875) delivered the opinion of the court.

. . . The second section [of the Act of Feb. 5, 1867] was a reproduction, with some changes, of the twenty-fifth section of the act of 1789, to which, by its title, the act of 1867 was an amendment, and it related to the appellate jurisdiction of this court over judgments and decrees of State courts.

The difference between the twenty-fifth section of the act of 1789 and the second section of the act of 1867 did not attract much attention, if any, for some time after the passage of the latter. . . . But in several cases argued within the last two or three years the proposition has been urged upon the court that the latter act worked a total repeal of the twenty-fifth section of the former, and introduced a rule for the action of this court in the class of cases to which they both referred, of such extended operation and so variant from that which had governed it heretofore that the subject received the serious consideration of the court. . . .

The proposition is that by a fair construction of the act of 1867 this court must, when it obtains jurisdiction of a case decided in a State court, by reason of one of the questions stated in the act, proceed to decide every other question which the case presents which may be found necessary to a final judgment on the whole merits. . . .

The questions propounded by the court for discussion by counsel were these:

1. Does the second section of the act of February 5th, 1867, repeal all or any part of the twenty-fifth section of the act of 1789, commonly called the Judiciary Act?

2. Is it the true intent and meaning of the act of 1867, above referred to, that when this court has jurisdiction of a case, by reason of any of the questions therein mentioned, it shall proceed to decide all the questions presented by the record which are necessary to a final judgment or decree?

3. If this question be answered affirmatively, does the Constitution of the United States authorize Congress to confer such a jurisdiction on this court?

[The Court first held that the Act of 1867 repealed the original section 25 and that section 2 of the Act of 1867 took its place.]

2. The affirmative of the second question propounded above is founded upon the effect of the omission or repeal of the last sentence of the twenty- fifth section of the act of 1789. That clause in express terms limited the power of the Supreme Court in reversing the judgment of a State court, to errors [which] respected questions, that for the sake of brevity, though not with strict verbal accuracy, we shall call Federal questions, namely, those in regard to the validity or construction of the Constitution, treaties, statutes, commissions, or authority of the Federal government.

The argument may be thus stated: 1. That the Constitution declares that the judicial power of the United States shall extend to *cases* of a character which includes the questions described in the section, and that by the word *case*, is to be understood all of the case in which such a question arises. 2. That by the fair construction of the act of 1789 in regard to removing those cases to this court, the power and the duty of re-examining the whole case would have been devolved on the court, but for the restriction of the clause omitted in the act of 1867; and that the same language is used in the latter act regulating the removal, but omitting the restrictive clause. And, 3. That by re-enacting the statute in the same terms as to the removal of cases from the State courts, without the restrictive clause, Congress is to be understood as conferring the power which that clause prohibited.

We will consider the last proposition first.

[The Court began by determining that, despite its omission of the final clause of the statute, Congress did not intend to authorize the Supreme Court to re-examine the entire case when reviewing state-court judgments by writ of error. Congress may have believed the final clause was unnecessary, the Court explained, either because the language of Section 25 does not authorize review of all issues, even without the final clause, or because the Constitution imposes that limit regardless of any statutory language. But in the Court's view, "the most important part of the statute" was its careful restrictions on the types of questions that authorize Supreme Court review: only federal questions, only those actually and finally decided by the state courts, and only where the federal claim or defense was rejected.]

Is it consistent with this extreme caution to suppose that Congress intended, when those cases came here, that this court should not only examine those questions, but all others found in the record?—questions of common law, of State statutes, of controverted facts, and conflicting evidence. Or is it the more reasonable inference that Congress intended that the cases should be brought here that *those questions* might be decided and *finally* decided by the court established by the Constitution of the Union, and the court which has always been supposed to be not only the most appropriate but the only proper tribunal for their final decision? No such reason nor any necessity exists for the decision by this court of other questions in those cases. The jurisdiction has been exercised for nearly a century without serious inconvenience to the due administration of justice. The State courts are the appropriate tribunals, as this court has repeatedly held, for the decision of questions arising under their local law, whether statutory or otherwise. And it is not lightly to be presumed that Congress acted upon a principle which implies a distrust of their integrity or of their ability to construe those laws correctly.

Let us look for a moment into the effect of the proposition contended for upon the cases as they come up for consideration in the conference-room. If it is found that no such question is raised or decided in the court below, then all will concede that it must be dismissed for want of jurisdiction. But if it is found that the Federal question was raised and was decided against the plaintiff in error, then the first duty of the court obviously is to determine whether it was correctly decided by the State court. Let us suppose that we find that the court below was right in its decision on that question. What, then, are we to do? Was it the intention of Congress to say that while you can only bring the case here on account of this question, yet when it is here, though it may turn out that the plaintiff in error was wrong on that question, and the judgment of the court below was right, though he has wrongfully dragged the defendant into this court by the allegation of an error which did not exist, and without which the case could not rightfully be here, he can still insist on an inquiry into all the other matters which were litigated in the case? This is neither reasonable nor just.

In such case both the nature of the jurisdiction conferred and the nature and fitness of things demand that, no error being found in the matter which authorized the re-examination, the judgment of the State court should be affirmed, and the case remitted to that court for its further enforcement. . . .

We are of opinion that upon a fair construction of the whole language of the section the jurisdiction conferred is limited to the decision of the questions mentioned in the statute, and, as a necessary consequence of this, to the exercise of such powers as may be necessary to cause the judgment in that decision to be respected.

We will now advert to one or two considerations apart from the mere language of the statute, which seem to us to give additional force to this conclusion. . . .

Very many cases are brought here now [where] the moment the Federal question is stated by counsel we all know that there is nothing in it. This has become such a burden and abuse that we either refuse to hear, or hear only one side of many such, and stop the argument, and have been compelled to adopt a rule that when a motion is made to dismiss it shall only be heard on printed argument. If the temptation to do this is so strong under the rule of this court for over eighty years to hear only the Federal question, what are we to expect when, by merely *raising* one of those questions in any case, the party who does it can bring it here for decision on all the matters of law and fact involved in it. It is to be remembered that there is not even a limitation as to the value in controversy in writs to the State courts as there is to the Circuit Courts; and it follows that there is no conceivable case so insignificant in amount or unimportant in principle that a perverse and obstinate man may not bring it to this court by the aid of a sagacious lawyer raising a Federal question in the record—a point which he may be wholly unable to support by the facts, or which he may well know will be decided against him the moment it is stated. But he obtains his object, if this court, when the case is once open to re examination on account of that question, must decide all the others that are to be found in the record.

It is impossible to believe that Congress intended this result, and equally impossible that they did not see that it would follow if they intended to open the cases that are brought here under this section to re-examination on all the points involved in them and necessary to a final judgment on the merits.

The twenty-fifth section of the act of 1789 has been the subject of innumerable decisions. These form a system of appellate jurisprudence relating to the exercise of the appellate power of this court over the courts of the States. That system has been based upon the fundamental principle that this jurisdiction was limited to the correction of errors relating solely to Federal law. And though it may be argued with some plausibility that the reason of this is to be found in the restrictive clause of the act of 1789, which is omitted in the act of 1867, yet an examination of the cases will show that it rested quite as much on the conviction of this court that without that clause and on general principles the jurisdiction extended no further. It requires a very bold reach of thought, and a readiness to impute to Congress a radical and hazardous change of a policy vital in its essential nature to the independence of the State courts, to believe that that body contemplated, or intended, what is claimed, by the mere omission of a clause in the substituted statute, which may well be held to have been superfluous, or nearly so, in the old one.

Another consideration, not without weight in seeking after the intention of Congress, is found in the fact that where that body has clearly shown an intention to bring the whole of a case which arises under the constitutional provision as to its subject-matter under the jurisdiction of a Federal court, it has conferred its cognizance on Federal courts of original jurisdiction and not on the Supreme Court. . . .

It is not difficult to discover what the purpose of Congress in the passage of [section 25] was. The highest courts of the States were sufficiently numerous, even in 1789, to cause it to be feared that, with the purest motives, [the construction given to federal law] in different courts would be various and conflicting. It was desirable, however, that whatever conflict of opinion might exist in those courts on other subjects, the rights which depended on the Federal laws should be the same everywhere, and that their construction should be uniform. This could only be done by conferring upon the Supreme Court of the United States . . . the right to decide these questions finally and in a manner which would be conclusive on all other courts. . . . This was the first purpose of the statute, and it does not require that, in a case involving a variety of questions, any other should be decided than those described in the act.

Secondly. It was no doubt the purpose of Congress to secure to every litigant whose rights depended on any question of Federal law that that question should be decided for him by the highest Federal tribunal if he desired it, when the decisions of the State courts were against him on that question. That rights of this character, guaranteed to him by the Constitution and laws of the Union, should not be left to the exclusive and final control of the State courts.

There may be some plausibility in the argument that these rights cannot be protected in all cases unless the Supreme Court has final control of the whole case. But the experience of eighty-five years of the administration of the law under the opposite theory would seem to be a satisfactory answer to the argument. It is not to be presumed that the State courts, where the rule is clearly laid down to them on the Federal question, and its influence on the case fully seen, will disregard or overlook it, and this is all that the rights of the party claiming under it require. Besides, by the very terms of this statute, when the Supreme Court is of opinion that the question of Federal law is of such relative importance to the whole case that it should control the final judgment, that court is authorized to render such judgment and enforce it by its own process. It cannot, therefore, be maintained that it is in any case necessary for the security of the rights claimed under the Constitution, laws, or treaties of the United States that the Supreme Court should examine and decide other questions not of a Federal character.

And we are of opinion that the act of 1867 does not confer such a jurisdiction.

This renders unnecessary a decision of the question whether, if Congress had conferred such authority, the act would have been constitutional. It will be time enough for this court to inquire into the existence of such a power when that body has attempted to exercise it in language which makes such an intention so clear as to require it.

[Here the Court explained how it would deal with cases in which the state court decided both federal and state questions. The Court emphasized that in such cases it would not attempt to determine whether the state court correctly decided the nonfederal issues, but it would examine them for the purpose of ascertaining whether the state court's disposition of these questions was sufficient to support the judgment. The opinion thus prefigured the "adequate state ground" doctrine, explored in the next chapter.]

Applying the principles here laid down to the case now before the court, we are of opinion that this court has jurisdiction, and that the judgment of the Supreme Court of Tennessee must be affirmed. . . .

It may be very true that it is not easy to see anything in the deed by which the United States received the title from the city, or the act by which they ceded it back, which raises such a trust, but the complainants claimed a right under this act of the United States, which was decided against them by the Supreme Court of Tennessee, and this claim gives jurisdiction of that question to this court.

But we need not consume many words to prove that neither by the deed of the city to the United States, . . . nor from anything found in the act of 1854, is there any such trust to be inferred. The act, so far from recognizing or implying any such trust, cedes the property to the mayor and aldermen *for the use of the city*. We are, therefore, of opinion that this, the only Federal question in the case, was rightly decided by the Supreme Court of Tennessee.

[The claim under the deed] is one to be determined by the general principles of equity jurisprudence, and is unaffected by anything found in the Constitution, laws, or treaties of the United States. Whether decided well or otherwise by the State court, we have no authority to inquire. According to the principles we have laid down as applicable to this class of cases, the judgment of the Supreme Court of Tennessee must be

Affirmed.

[Chief Justice Waite, who was not appointed until after the reargument, took no part in the decision of the case.]

MR. JUSTICE CLIFFORD, with whom concurred MR. JUSTICE SWAYNE, dissenting:

I dissent from so much of the opinion of the court as denies the jurisdiction of this court to determine the whole case, where it appears that the record presents a Federal question and that the Federal question was erroneously decided to the prejudice of the plaintiff in error; as in that state of the record it is, in my judgment, the duty of this court, under the recent act of Congress, to decide the whole merits of the controversy, and to affirm or reverse the judgment of the State court. . . .

Mr. Justice Bradley, dissenting:

[Justice Bradley first argued that Murdock based his claim entirely on the deed, so the Court did not have jurisdiction over the case.]

But supposing, as the majority of the court holds, that it has jurisdiction, I cannot concur in the conclusion that we can only decide the Federal question raised by the record. If we have jurisdiction at all, in my judgment we have jurisdiction of the *case*, and not merely of a *question* in it. . . .

[The final clause of section 25] meant something, and effected something. It had the effect of restricting the consideration of the court to a certain class of question as a ground of reversal, which restriction would not have existed without it. The omission of the clause, according to a well-settled rule of construction, must necessarily have the effect of removing the restriction which it effected in the old law.

In my judgment, therefore, if the court had jurisdiction of the case, it was bound to consider not only the Federal question raised by the record, but the whole case. . . .

Note: Murdock, *The Act of 1867, and the Constitution*

1. The Court finds it "impossible to believe that Congress intended" an interpretation of the 1867 Act that would allow the Court to reexamine "all of the points . . . necessary to a final judgment on the merits" in cases from state courts. But is it so implausible? The Reconstruction Congress deeply distrusted the state courts of the south. In the same statute that reenacted section 25 without its final sentence, Congress authorized federal courts to grant writs of habeas corpus to persons in state custody. Soon afterward, Congress voted to send the Fourteenth Amendment to the states for ratification.

On the other hand, as the Court points out, if Congress did want the Court to consider all issues in cases from state courts, it could easily have said so. Is that a sufficient answer to the argument for extended jurisdiction? *Compare* Jonathan F. Mitchell, *Reconsidering* Murdock: *State-Law Reversals as Constitutional Avoidance,* 77 U. Chi. L. Rev. 1335 (2010) (arguing that *Murdock* was wrongly decided as a matter of statutory interpretation); *with* Michael G. Collins, *Reconstructing* Murdock v. Memphis, 98 Va. L. Rev. 1439 (2012) (defending the result in *Murdock* as consistent with Congress's intent).

2. Because the Court finds that the 1867 Act did not change the scope of review, there is no need to consider the third of the questions posed on reargument: if the Act did authorize the Court "to decide all the questions . . . which are necessary to a final judgment or decree," does the Constitution authorize such a jurisdiction? How should that question be answered? Does the decision in *Erie Railroad Co. v. Tompkins* (Chapter 7) offer any guidance?

3. What would the effect have been on the American legal system if *Murdock* had come out the other way?

B. Removal of Cases from State to Federal Court

In defending the constitutionality of section 25, Justice Story says "it is admitted" that Congress has power "to remove suits from state courts to the national courts." But Justice Story does not say that Martin could have removed the Northern Neck land litigation to federal court, and indeed he could not have done so. Nor could he do so under current law.

The framework for removal today is found in Chapter 89 of the Judicial Code, encompassing sections 1441 through 1455. The general rule is set forth in section 1441(a). Unless Congress provides otherwise, any civil case within the original jurisdiction of the federal district courts can be removed by the defendant:

> Except as otherwise expressly provided by Act of Congress, any civil action brought in a State court of which the district courts of the United States have original jurisdiction, may be removed by the defendant or the defendants, to the district court of the United States for the district and division embracing the place where such action is pending.

The two principal grants of original jurisdiction are § 1331, which grants jurisdiction over "all civil actions arising under [federal law]," and § 1332(a)(1), which grants jurisdiction over "all civil actions where the matter in controversy exceeds the sum or value of $75,000, exclusive of interest and costs, and is between . . . citizens of different States." In common parlance, these are referred to, respectively, as "federal question" and "diversity" jurisdiction.

Three sections of Chapter 89 authorize removal of criminal prosecutions as well as civil actions. The most important of these is 28 U.S.C. § 1442, which authorizes removal of suits instituted in state court against federal officers for acts committed under color of their federal office. Section 1442a is a similar provision that can be invoked by members of the armed forces of the United States. Finally, 28 U.S.C. § 1443 authorizes removal by a defendant "who is denied . . . a right under any law providing for . . . equal civil rights." This "civil rights removal" provision has been construed so narrowly by the Supreme Court that it is almost never invoked successfully.

The procedure for removal in civil actions is set forth in section 1446. A striking feature of the system is that once the defendant takes the steps required by section 1446, removal is accomplished. The case is no longer pending in the state court; it is a case in the federal district court. It will remain in the federal court unless the district court issues an order of remand.

The removal jurisdiction is governed by complex rules that often coexist uneasily with other doctrines and other provisions of the Judicial Code. That body of law is explored in detail in later chapters of this book. Here we briefly introduce the law governing removal based on the presence of a federal question.

The Judiciary Act of 1789 contained no provisions authorizing removal based on the presence of a federal question. That authorization came in 1875, with a law providing for the removal of "all suits of a civil nature at common law or in equity . . .

arising under [the Constitution, laws, or treaties of the United States]." But the law was amended in 1887, and by 1894 the Supreme Court had definitively established that the amended law did not authorize removal by a defendant based on a federal *defense*. In doctrinal terms, the Court held that the "well pleaded complaint rule" (as it came to be called) limited removal jurisdiction in the same way that it limited original jurisdiction.

That interpretation continues to control today. For example, in *Rivet v. Regions Bank*, 522 U.S 470 (1998) (Chapter 10), the Court noted that "a case may not be removed to federal court on the basis of a federal defense, . . . even if the defense is anticipated in the plaintiff's complaint, and even if both parties admit that the defense is the only question truly at issue in the case."

Note: Federal-Question and Diversity Jurisdiction

The opinions in *Martin* and *Murdock* discuss the policy considerations that underlie Congress's decision to use the "arising under" jurisdiction of Article III to authorize Supreme Court review of state-court decisions rejecting federal claims or defenses. But Justice Story in *Martin* also invokes the party-based heads of jurisdiction of Article III and the "state prejudices" that they are designed to redress. Yet both historically and under current law, Congress has taken very different approaches to implementing the party-based heads and the "arising under" jurisdiction.

What accounts for the differences between Congress's treatment of diversity cases and its treatment of federal-question cases? Consider:

Diversity cases: From the beginning of the Nation's history, an out-of-state defendant sued in state court by a citizen of the forum state has had the right to remove the case to federal court, provided that the case satisfied an amount-in-controversy requirement. But if the defendant does not remove (or is unable to do so because of limitations on diversity removal, discussed in Chapter 12) and the defendant loses on the merits, there is no possibility of Supreme Court review of the state-court decision. Indeed, Congress has never extended the appellate jurisdiction of the Supreme Court to state-court cases based on any of the party-based heads of jurisdiction.

Federal-question cases: If the *plaintiff* in a civil action in state court asserts a federal *claim*, current law generally allows the defendant to remove to federal court, although the Judiciary Act of 1789 did not. If the case stays in state court and the state court rests its judgment on federal law, Supreme Court review is available (and was available under the Judiciary Act of 1789 if the state court rejected the federal claim or defense).

On the other hand, if a defendant in state court asserts a federal defense to a state-law claim, the defense does *not* provide a basis for removal to federal court. That was true in Justice Story's time, and it is true today. But if the state court rejects the defense, the defendant can (subject to limitations discussed in Chapter 5) secure Supreme Court review of the state-court judgment.

Why would Congress have thought that removal (but not appellate review) is the cure for state-court bias against non-citizens, but that appellate review (but not removal) is the cure for state-court bias against federal rights? Consider the examples of federal questions that Justice Story hypothesizes would be adjudicated in "cases where the jurisdiction of the state courts is unquestionable."

C. Federal Claims and State-Court Standing

Note: ASARCO *and Constitutional Litigation*

1. In *DaimlerChrysler Corp. v. Cuno*, 547 U.S. 332 (2006) (discussed in Chapter 3), the plaintiffs — residents of Toledo, Ohio — filed suit in Ohio state court asserting that a state tax credit offered under Ohio law violated the Commerce Clause. The defendants removed the case to the federal district court. The Sixth Circuit agreed with plaintiffs that the tax credit was unconstitutional, but the Supreme Court held that, under Article III, the plaintiffs did not have standing to pursue their claim in federal court.

Suppose that the plaintiffs now pursue their challenge in the state court. May the state court consider the plaintiffs' federal constitutional claim? If it does, would the United States Supreme Court have jurisdiction to review its judgment?

2. The first question was resolved (from the perspective of federal law) in *ASARCO, Inc. v. Kadish*, 490 U.S. 605 (1989). In *ASARCO*, state taxpayers brought suit in state court asserting that a state statute governing mineral leases on state lands violated federal law. As *DaimlerChrysler* later made clear, the taxpayers would not have had standing to bring suit in federal court. But the Supreme Court in *ASARCO* reaffirmed precedents holding that state courts may follow their own rules of justiciability even in cases involving federal law:

> [The state judiciary here] took no account of federal standing rules in letting the case go to final judgment in the Arizona courts. That result properly follows from the allocation of authority in the federal system. We have recognized often that the constraints of Article III do not apply to state courts, and accordingly the state courts are not bound by the limitations of a case or controversy or other federal rules of justiciability even when they address issues of federal law, as when they are called upon to interpret the Constitution or, in this case, a federal statute. . . .

> Although the state courts are not bound to adhere to federal standing requirements, they possess the authority, absent a provision for exclusive federal jurisdiction, to render binding judicial decisions that rest on their own interpretations of federal law.

3. Suppose, then, that the Ohio Supreme Court rules on the Commerce Clause claim raised by the *DaimlerChrysler* plaintiffs. May the United States Supreme Court review that determination? *ASARCO* suggests that the answer may depend on how the Ohio Supreme Court resolves the federal question. In *ASARCO*, the Arizona Supreme Court held that the state leasing statute did violate federal law. Lessees (who had intervened as defendants in the state court) sought review in the United States Supreme Court. The Court found that it had jurisdiction:

At this juncture, petitioners allege a specific injury stemming from the state-court decree, a decree which rests on principles of federal law. Petitioners insist that, as a result of the state-court judgment, the case has taken on such definite shape that they are under a defined and specific legal obligation, one which causes them direct injury.

We agree. Although respondents [plaintiffs in the state court] would not have had standing to commence suit in federal court based on the allegations in the complaint, they are not the party attempting to invoke the federal judicial power. Instead it is petitioners, the defendants in the case and the losing parties below, who bring the case here and thus seek entry to the federal courts for the first time in the lawsuit. We determine that petitioners have standing to invoke the authority of a federal court and that this dispute now presents a justiciable case or controversy for resolution here.

Petitioners hold mineral leases that were granted under the state law the Arizona Supreme Court invalidated. Although no accounting of sums due under these leases remains at issue in this particular case, it is undisputed that the decision to be reviewed poses a serious and immediate threat to the continuing validity of those leases by virtue of its holding that they were granted under improper procedures and an invalid law. The state proceedings ended in a declaratory judgment adverse to petitioners, an adjudication of legal rights which constitutes the kind of injury cognizable in this Court on review from the state courts. . . .

[We] adopt the following rationale for our decision on this jurisdictional point: When a state court has issued a judgment in a case where plaintiffs in the original action had no standing to sue under the principles governing the federal courts, we may exercise our jurisdiction on certiorari if the judgment of the state court causes direct, specific, and concrete injury to the parties who petition for our review, where the requisites of a case or controversy are also met.

In *DaimlerChrysler*, the defendants were state and local officials as well as the DaimlerChrysler Corporation. Under *ASARCO*, could the United States Supreme Court review a determination by the Ohio Supreme Court that the Ohio tax credit violates the Commerce Clause? How about a decision that the credit does not violate the Federal Constitution?

4. In the *DaimlerChrysler* litigation, the plaintiffs opposed the removal to federal court. Among other arguments, they expressed "substantial doubts about their ability to satisfy either the constitutional or the prudential limitations on standing in the federal court," and they urged the District Court to avoid the issue entirely by remanding.

Why would plaintiffs challenging a state tax scheme under the Commerce Clause prefer state court to federal court? Putting aside any special features of the Ohio court system, would you expect a state court or a federal court to be more sympathetic to such a challenge?

Chapter 5

Supreme Court Review of State-Court Decisions

The decision in *Martin v. Hunter's Lessee* (Chapter 4) broadly confirmed that Article III authorizes the United States Supreme Court to review state-court judgments. At the same time, however, the Court recognized that Congress has power to set limits on the scope of Supreme Court review. *See* Art. III, § 2 (providing that the Supreme Court shall have appellate jurisdiction "with such exceptions, and under such regulations as the Congress shall make").

In this chapter, we begin by tracing the development of Supreme Court review of state-court judgments over time, from mandatory review by writ of error under the Judiciary Act of 1789 to discretionary review by writ of certiorari today. We then discuss two important and long-standing limits on the scope of that review. First, the Supreme Court lacks jurisdiction to review federal questions when the judgment of the state court rests on an "adequate and independent state ground." *See Fox Film Corp. v. Muller*, 296 U.S. 207 (1935), discussed *infra* section B. Second, the Supreme Court has the power to review only "[f]inal judgments or decrees rendered by the highest court of a State in which a decision could be had," 28 U.S.C. § 1257(a), and the Court has developed a complex body of case law defining what qualifies as a "final judgment." *See Cox Broadcasting Corp. v. Cohn*, 420 U.S. 469 (1975), discussed *infra* section C.

A. Evolution of the Statutory Jurisdiction

From 1789 through 1914, two features characterized the statutory scheme governing Supreme Court review of state-court decisions. First, the Court's jurisdiction was limited to cases in which the state court rejected the federal claim or defense. Justice Miller emphasized this point in *Murdock v. City of Memphis*, 87 U.S. 590 (1875) (Chapter 4): "It may be quite apparent to this court that a wrong construction has been given to the Federal law, but if the right claimed under it by plaintiff in error has been conceded to him, this court cannot entertain jurisdiction of the case."

Second, the procedural device used to invoke the jurisdiction was the writ of error. (Hence the party seeking review was the "plaintiff in error.") The writ of error was a form of mandatory jurisdiction. If a case came within the ambit of the statute, the Court had no choice but to decide whether the state court erred in rejecting the federal claim.

An Act of Congress in 1914 made two major changes in these arrangements. For the first time, Congress authorized the Supreme Court to review cases in which the state court *upheld* a litigant's claim under federal law. The impetus for this change came from a 1911 decision in which the New York Court of Appeals struck down the first American workers' compensation act as a denial of due process under the federal as well as the state constitution.

The second change involved the mode of review. In cases where the state court upheld the federal claim, the Court's jurisdiction was to be invoked by writ of certiorari rather than writ of error. Certiorari, as the Court has said, "is not a matter of right, but of judicial discretion." And the Court could deny certiorari without determining whether the state court's decision was erroneous.

In the decade and a half that followed the 1914 Act, Congress made additional, less important changes in the statute governing the Supreme Court's jurisdiction over state courts. It made the jurisdiction discretionary rather than mandatory in some cases where the state court had rejected the federal claim. And it substituted the "appeal" for the "writ of error" in the remaining cases that were subject to review as of right.

For the next six decades, the statutory scheme distinguished between two classes of state-court cases. In the overwhelming majority, review was available only by certiorari. But in a small class of cases the jurisdiction was mandatory. This class principally encompassed cases in which a state court upheld the validity of a state statute against a claim of unconstitutionality under federal law.

Finally, in 1988, after several unsuccessful attempts, Congress eliminated the remaining elements of the mandatory jurisdiction in state-court cases. Today, judgments of state courts can be brought to the Supreme Court only by certiorari, and there are no statutory constraints on the Court's discretion to grant or deny review in cases that fall within the jurisdiction.

Note: Operation of the Certiorari Jurisdiction

To seek review by the Supreme Court, the party who lost in the state court files a petition for writ of certiorari. The Court's rules emphasize that certiorari jurisdiction is discretionary and that the writ "will be granted only for compelling reasons." The most "compelling reason" the petitioner can offer is that the state court's decision conflicts with a decision of another appellate court or with a decision of the Supreme Court. The petitioner may also attempt to show that the state court's decision presents an important and unresolved issue of federal law.

The opposing party (designated as the respondent) may file a brief in opposition that explains why the petition should be denied. One provision of the Supreme Court's rules is of particular importance to respondents at the certiorari stage:

> Counsel are admonished that they have an obligation to the Court to point out in the brief in opposition, and not later, any perceived misstatement made in the petition. Any objection to consideration of a question presented based

on what occurred in the proceedings below, if the objection does not go to jurisdiction, may be deemed waived unless called to the Court's attention in the brief in opposition.

Under the "Rule of Four," the Court will grant certiorari if four Justices vote to do so. After a case has been accepted, the parties file briefs on the merits and the Court hears oral argument.

Although the overwhelming majority of petitions are denied without recorded dissent, state-court cases constitute a surprisingly large proportion of the Supreme Court's plenary docket. In the 2015 Term, for example, the Court heard a total of 68 cases; 12 came from state courts.

In addition, the Court sometimes grants certiorari and reverses the state-court judgment on the basis of the petition and response, without waiting for full briefing or oral argument. Several of the cases in this chapter, including *Pennsylvania v. Labron*, fall into this category.

Note: Dismissals "For Want of a Substantial Federal Question"

During the era of mandatory jurisdiction, lawyers and the Court itself often struggled to determine whether a particular case could be brought by appeal or only by certiorari. Happily, that body of law is now obsolete. But one remnant of the mandatory jurisdiction remains with us.

When a case was properly brought to the Court on appeal, the Court could not avoid deciding the merits. But that did not mean that the Court was required to invite full briefing and hear oral argument. Rather, the Court developed a practice of dismissing state-court appeals "for want of a substantial federal question" when it determined, on the basis of the initial filings, that the decision below was plainly correct. These dismissals were decisions on the merits, albeit without explanation. And their import was narrow. As the Court explained in *Mandel v. Bradley*, 432 U.S. 173 (1977) (per curiam):

> [D]ismissals for want of a substantial federal question [reject] the specific challenges presented in the [application for review]. . . . They [prevent] lower courts from coming to opposite conclusions on the precise issues presented and necessarily decided by those actions. . . . Summary actions, however, [should] not be understood as breaking new ground but as applying principles established by prior decisions to the particular facts involved.

From time to time, summary dismissals become relevant in current litigation. Over the course of the last decade, for example, same-sex couples seeking the right to marry filed dozens of lawsuits in federal court seeking to invalidate state laws that define marriage as a union between members of the opposite sex. State officials defending those laws frequently argued, however, that the Supreme Court had already decided that question. They cited *Baker v. Nelson*, 409 U.S. 810 (1972) (mem.), in which the plaintiffs, two men whose application for a marriage license was denied, urged that state laws prohibiting same-sex marriage violated the Equal Protection Clause of the Fourteenth Amendment. The Minnesota Supreme Court upheld the statute, and the Supreme Court dismissed the appeal for want of a substantial federal question.

More than 40 years later, a number of lower federal courts likewise rejected equal protection challenges to state marriage laws, relying on the dismissal in *Baker* as binding precedent. *See, e.g.*, *DeBoer v. Snyder*, 772 F.2d 388 (6th Cir. 2014) ("Only the Supreme Court may overrule its own precedents, and we remain bound even by its summary decisions until such time as the Court informs us that we are not."). In *Obergefell v. Hodges*, 135 S. Ct. 2584 (2015), the Court reversed *DeBoer*, overruling *Baker* and holding that the Equal Protection Clause prohibits states from denying same-sex couples the right to marry. Characterizing *Baker* as "a one-line summary decision issued in 1972," the Court relied instead on "other, more instructive precedents."

Note: "The Highest Court of a State"

In defining the Supreme Court's jurisdiction over state-court cases, section 25 of the Judiciary Act of 1789 specified that review was available only for "a final judgment or decree . . . in the highest court of law or equity of a State in which a decision in the suit could be had." Although the wording has been simplified, the statute now in force retains the two requirements of the original Act: to be reviewable, the judgment of a state court must be final, and it must have been rendered "by the highest court of a State in which a decision could be had."

The requirement of finality might seem straightforward, but it is not. The reason is that the Supreme Court has construed the statute to allow review of some judgments that are not final in a literal sense. This body of law will be considered in section C, *infra*.

The "highest court" requirement has not often posed difficulty, but one issue requires attention. It is the subject of the Problem that follows.

Problem: Discretionary Review in the State's Highest Court

California, like most states, has a two-tier appellate system. The Court of Appeal is the intermediate appellate court; the Supreme Court is the highest court. Except in limited circumstances, the jurisdiction of the Supreme Court is discretionary. The California Supreme Court denies review in most of the cases presented to it, and it does not give reasons for the denial.

Charles Vickers was convicted of child sex abuse in the Superior Court of Los Angeles County. He appealed as of right to the Court of Appeal, which affirmed the conviction, rejecting his argument that his conviction violated the Ex Post Facto clause of the United States Constitution. Must Vickers seek discretionary review in the California Supreme Court before filing a petition for certiorari in the United States Supreme Court?

If your answer is "yes," would the result be different if the California Supreme Court rejected an identical constitutional argument in a case decided a week earlier?

B. The Relation Between State and Federal Law

Martin v. Hunter's Lessee upheld the authority of the Supreme Court to review state-court judgments that decide federal questions. *Murdock v. City of Memphis* disclaimed power to review state-court rulings on issues that are not federal. The two decisions in tandem might seem to establish a simple pair of rules: in cases from state courts, issues of federal law are open for review; issues of state law are not.

But the interplay of federal and state law can take many forms, and it should come as no surprise that the role of the Supreme Court in balancing the competing values of supremacy and federalism cannot be reduced to a simple dichotomy. The foundational rules must be qualified in three important respects.

First, a state court's ruling on a federal question, which plainly would be subject to review by the Supreme Court if it stood alone, may become unreviewable if the state court's judgment is adequately supported by a holding on an issue of state law. The point is illustrated by *Fox Film Corp. v. Muller*, the next principal case.

Second, contrary to what one might deduce from *Murdock*, the Supreme Court does not necessarily accept state-court determinations on matters of state law. When the resolution of a federal question depends in some way on the interpretation or application of state law, the Court in some circumstances will re-examine the state court's holding on the state-law issue. Leading cases include *Indiana ex rel. Anderson v. Brand* and *James v. Kentucky*.

Third, state court decisions may be ambiguous as to whether they are based on federal or state law. Over the years, the Court has taken a variety of approaches to ambiguous opinions. Today the Court takes the position that "when [a] state court decision fairly appears to rest primarily on federal law, or to be interwoven with the federal law, and when the adequacy and independence of any possible state law ground is not clear from the face of the opinion," the Court will presume that the decision is based on federal law. The leading case is *Michigan v. Long*, from which this language is quoted.

In this section we explore the interplay between federal and state law in the decisions of state courts and the consequences for reviewability by the United States Supreme Court.

[1] The Basic Doctrine

Fox Film Corp. v. Muller

Supreme Court of the United States, 1935.

296 U.S. 207.

MR. JUSTICE SUTHERLAND delivered the opinion of the Court.

This is an action brought in a Minnesota state court of first instance by the Film Corporation against Muller, to recover damages for an alleged breach of two contracts by which Muller was licensed to exhibit certain moving-picture films belonging to the corporation. Muller answered, setting up the invalidity of the contracts under the Sherman Anti-trust Act. It was and is agreed that these contracts are substantially the same as the one involved in [*Paramount Famous Lasky Corp. v. United States*, 282 U.S. 30 (1930)]; that petitioner was one of the defendants in that action; and that the "arbitration clause," paragraph 18 of each of the contracts sued upon, is the same as that held in that case to be invalid. In view of the disposition which we are to make of this writ, it is not necessary to set forth the terms of the arbitration clause or the other provisions of the contract.

The court of first instance held that each contract sued upon violated the Sherman Anti-trust Act, and dismissed the action. In a supplemental opinion that court put its decision upon the grounds, first, that the arbitration plan is so connected with the remainder of the contract that the entire contract is tainted, and, second, that the contract violates the Sherman Anti-trust law. The state supreme court affirmed. We granted certiorari. . . .

In its opinion, the state supreme court, after a statement of the case, said:

> The question presented on this appeal is whether the arbitration clause is severable from the contract, leaving the remainder of the contract enforceable, or not severable, permeating and tainting the whole contract with illegality and making it void.

That court then proceeded to refer to and discuss a number of decisions of state and federal courts, some of which took the view that the arbitration clause was severable, and others that it was not severable, from the remainder of the contract. After reviewing the opinion and decree of the federal district court in the *Paramount* case, the lower court reached the conclusion that the holding of the federal court was that the entire contract was illegal; and upon that view and upon what it conceived to be the weight of authority, held the arbitration plan was inseparable from the other provisions of the contract. Whether this conclusion was right or wrong we need not determine. It is enough that it is, at least, not without fair support.

Respondent contends that the question of severability was alone decided and that no federal question was determined by the lower court. This contention petitioner challenges, and asserts that a federal question was involved and decided. We do not attempt to settle the dispute; but, assuming for present purposes only that petitioner's view is the correct one, the case is controlled by the settled rule that where the judgment of a state court rests upon two grounds, one of which is federal and the other non-federal in character, our jurisdiction fails if the non-federal ground is independent of the federal ground and adequate to support the judgment. This rule had become firmly fixed at least as early as *Klinger v. Missouri*, 80 U.S. 257 (1871), and has been reiterated in a long line of cases since that time. It is enough to cite, in addition to the *Klinger* case, the following: *Enterprise Irrigation District v. Canal Co.*, 243 U.S. 157 (1917); *Petrie v. Nampa Irrigation District*, 248 U.S. 154 (1918); *McCoy v. Shaw*, 277 U.S. 302 (1928); *Eustis v. Bolles*, 150 U.S. 361 (1893).

Whether the provisions of a contract are non-severable, so that if one be held invalid the others must fall with it, is clearly a question of general and not of federal law. The invalidity of the arbitration clause which the present contracts embody is conceded. It was held invalid by the federal district court in the *Paramount* case, and its judgment was affirmed here. The question, therefore, was foreclosed; and was not the subject of controversy in the state courts. In that situation, the primary question to be determined by the court below was whether the concededly invalid clause was separable from the other provisions of the contract. The ruling of the state supreme court that it was not, is sufficient to conclude the case without regard to the determination, if, in fact, any was made, in respect of the federal question. It follows that the non-federal ground is adequate to sustain the judgment.

The rule announced in *Enterprise Irrigation District v. Canal Co.* and other cases, to the effect that our jurisdiction attaches where the non-federal ground is so interwoven with the other as not to be an independent matter, does not apply. The construction put upon the contracts did not constitute a preliminary step which simply had the effect of bringing forward for determination the federal question, but was a decision which automatically took the federal question out of the case if otherwise it would be there. The non-federal question in respect of the construction of the contracts, and the federal question in respect of their validity under the Anti-trust Act, were clearly independent of one another. See *Allen v. Southern Pacific R. Co.*, 173 U.S. 479 (1899). The case, in effect, was disposed of before the federal question said to be involved was reached. A decision of that question then became unnecessary; and whether it was decided or not, our want of jurisdiction is clear.

Writ dismissed for want of jurisdiction.

The CHIEF JUSTICE [HUGHES] took no part in the consideration or decision of this case.

Note: The Adequate and Independent State Ground Doctrine

1. In *Fox Film*, the Court states and applies what it describes as "the settled rule": "where the judgment of a state court rests upon two grounds, one of which is federal and the other nonfederal in character, [the Supreme Court's] jurisdiction fails if the nonfederal ground is independent of the federal ground and adequate to support the judgment." This is referred to today as the adequate and independent state ground doctrine.

What is the rationale for the doctrine? The Court in *Fox Film* takes the rule as established and does not discuss its derivation or justification. Later cases have offered two principal rationales.

In *Herb v. Pitcairn*, 324 U.S. 117 (1945), the Court, speaking through Justice Jackson, indicated that the rule derives primarily from the case-and-controversy limitations of Article III:

> This Court from the time of its foundation has adhered to the principle that it will not review judgments of state courts that rest on adequate and

independent state grounds. [The Court cited *Fox Film, Enterprise Irrigation District* (also cited in *Fox Film*), and *Murdock*.] The reason is so obvious that it has rarely been thought to warrant statement. It is found in the partitioning of power between the state and federal judicial systems and in the limitations of our own jurisdiction. Our only power over state judgments is to correct them to the extent that they incorrectly adjudge federal rights. And our power is to correct wrong judgments, not to revise opinions. We are not permitted to render an advisory opinion, and if the same judgment would be rendered by the state court after we corrected its views of federal laws, our review could amount to nothing more than an advisory opinion.

Two decades later, Justice Harlan, in a dissenting opinion in a case involving federal habeas corpus for a state prisoner, offered a more complex explanation. In *Fay v. Noia*, 372 U.S. 391 (1963), he wrote:

What is the reason for the rule that an adequate and independent state ground of decision bars Supreme Court review of that decision—a rule which, of course, is as applicable to procedural as to substantive grounds? . . . [As the Court in *Murdock*] strongly implied, and as emphasized in subsequent decisions, the adequate state ground rule has roots far deeper than the statutes governing our jurisdiction, and rests on fundamentals that touch this Court's habeas corpus jurisdiction equally with its direct reviewing power. An examination of the alternatives that might conceivably be followed [will confirm] that the rule is one of constitutional dimensions going to the heart of the division of judicial powers in a federal system.

In his "examination of the alternatives," Justice Harlan argued that there are basically two other possible approaches that the Court might take. The first "would be for the Court to review and decide any federal questions in [a] case, even if the determination of nonfederal questions were adequate to sustain the judgment below, and then to send the case back to the state court for further consideration. But it needs no extended analysis to demonstrate that such action would exceed this Court's powers under Article III." Here Justice Harlan relied on Justice Jackson's rationale in *Herb v. Pitcairn*.

The second possibility "would be [for the Court] to take the entire case and to review on the merits the state court's decision of every question in it." This would avoid the problem of advisory opinions, but it would be unacceptable for a different reason. That reason, Justice Harlan said, "was perhaps most articulately expressed in a different but closely related context by Mr. Justice Field in his opinion in *Baltimore & O.R. Co. v. Baugh*, 149 U.S. 368 (1893)." Justice Field wrote:

[T]he constitution of the United States . . . recognizes and preserves the autonomy and independence of the states, independence in their legislative and independence in their judicial departments. Supervision over either the legislative or the judicial action of the states is in no case permissible except as to matters by the constitution specifically authorized or delegated to the United States. Any interference with either, except as thus permitted, is an invasion of the authority of the state, and, to that extent, a denial of its independence.

As Justice Harlan noted, this passage was "quoted with approval by the Court in the historic decision in *Erie R. Co. v. Tompkins*, 304 U.S. 64 (1938)."

This analysis suggests that the Article III and federalism rationales are not competing but complementary. As you read the cases in the remainder of this chapter, consider whether Justice Harlan's explanation adequately captures the justification for the doctrine.

2. Justice Harlan takes care to emphasize that "a state ground, to be of sufficient breadth to support the judgment, must be both 'adequate' and 'independent.'" Further, the Supreme Court makes its own determination of adequacy and independence. Both elements can be problematic, as the cases that follow demonstrate.

Note: The Federal and Non-Federal Grounds in Fox Film

1. As the Court explains, when Fox Film filed its complaint in Minnesota state court, "Muller answered, setting up the invalidity of the contracts under the Sherman Anti-Trust Act." If that was Muller's only basis for challenging Fox Film's breach of contract claim, why didn't he remove the case to federal district court?

2. The Court says that the issue of severability "is clearly a question of general and not of federal law." *Fox Film* predates the Court's landmark decision in *Erie R. Co. v. Tompkins*, 304 U.S. 64 (1938), which held that "[t]here is no federal general common law." We will examine *Erie* at length in Chapter 7, but cases like *Fox Film* make clear that the Court has long viewed some legal questions as fundamentally nonfederal. What did the Court mean by "general" law? And why did the Court assume that a question of "general" law would be beyond its power to review?

3. In *Fox Film* as in *Murdock*, one of the parties claimed under both federal and state law. Was *Murdock* an adequate state ground case? Can you explain why the Supreme Court had jurisdiction to review the federal question in *Murdock*, but not in *Fox Film*?

4. The Court in *Fox Film* says that the case before it is not one in which "the non-federal ground is so interwoven with the other as not to be an independent matter" or where the non-federal ground constitutes "a preliminary step which [has] the effect of bringing forward for determination the federal question." For a discussion of what makes a state-law ground "independent," see section B[4].

[2] Adequacy of State "Substantive" Grounds

As *Fox Film* illustrates, the effect of the adequate state ground doctrine is to prevent the Supreme Court from considering federal questions that would otherwise be within its jurisdiction. When is a state ground "adequate"? And by what standard is that determination to be made? We turn now to those questions.

Indiana ex rel. Anderson v. Brand

Supreme Court of the United States, 1938.

303 U.S. 95.

MR. JUSTICE ROBERTS delivered the opinion of the Court.

The petitioner sought a writ of mandate to compel the respondent to continue her in employment as a public school teacher. Her complaint alleged that as a duly licensed teacher she entered into a contract in September, 1924, to teach in the township schools and, pursuant to successive contracts, taught continuously to and including the school year 1932–1933; that her contracts for the school years 1931–1932 and 1932–1933 contained this clause: "It is further agreed by the contracting parties that all of the provisions of the Teachers' Tenure Law, approved March 8, 1927, shall be in full force and effect in this contract"; and that by force of that act she had a contract, indefinite in duration, which could be canceled by the respondent only in the manner and for the causes specified in the act.

Petitioner charged that in July, 1933, the respondent notified her he proposed to cancel her contract for cause; that, after a hearing, he adhered to his decision and the county superintendent affirmed his action; that, despite what occurred in July, 1933, the petitioner was permitted to teach during the school year 1933–1934 and the respondent was presently threatening to terminate her employment at the end of that year. The complaint alleged the termination of her employment would be a breach of her contract with the school corporation.

The respondent demurred on the grounds that (1) [the county superintendent's determination was binding on Anderson]; and (2) the Teachers' Tenure Law had been repealed in respect of teachers in township schools. The demurrer was sustained and the petitioner appealed to the state Supreme Court which affirmed the judgment. The Court did not discuss the first ground of demurrer . . . but rested its decision upon the second, that, by an act of 1933, the Teachers' Tenure Law had been repealed as respects teachers in township schools; and held that the repeal did not deprive the petitioner of a vested property right and did not impair her contract within the meaning of [Article I § 10 of the] Constitution. In its original opinion the court said: "The relatrix contends * * * that, having become a permanent teacher under the Teachers' Tenure Law before the amendment, she had a vested property right in her indefinite contract, which may not be impaired under the Constitution. The question is whether there is a vested right in a permanent teacher's contract; whether, under the tenure law, there is a grant which cannot lawfully be impaired by a repeal of the statute."

Where the state court does not decide against a petitioner or appellant upon an independent state ground, but deeming the federal question to be before it, actually entertains and decides that question adversely to the federal right asserted, this Court has jurisdiction to review the judgment if, as here, it is a final judgment. [Here the Court cited *Murdock* and several subsequent cases.] We cannot refuse jurisdiction because the state court might have based its decision, consistently with the record, upon an independent and adequate nonfederal ground. And since the amendment of the judiciary act of 1789 by the act of February 5, 1867 it has always been held this Court may examine the opinion of the state court to ascertain whether a federal question was raised and decided, and whether the court rested its judgment on an adequate nonfederal ground. [Again the Court cited *Murdock*, along with *Fox Film* and several other cases.] . . .

The court below holds that in Indiana teachers' contracts are made for but 1 year; that there is no contractual right to be continued as a teacher from year to year; that the law grants a privilege to one who has taught 5 years and signed a new contract to continue in employment under given conditions; [and] that the statute is directed merely to the exercise of their powers by the school authorities and the policy therein expressed may be altered at the will of the Legislature. . . .

As in most cases brought to this court under the contract clause of the Constitution, the question is as to the existence and nature of the contract and not as to the construction of the law which is supposed to impair it. The principal function of a legislative body is not to make contracts but to make laws which declare the policy of the state and are subject to repeal when a subsequent Legislature shall determine to alter that policy. Nevertheless, it is established that a legislative enactment may contain provisions which, when accepted as the basis of action by individuals, become contracts between them and the State or its subdivisions within the protection of article 1, § 10. If the people's representatives deem it in the public interest they may adopt a policy of contracting in respect of public business for a term longer than the life of the current session of the Legislature. This the petitioner claims has been done with respect to permanent teachers. The Supreme Court has decided, however, that it is the state's policy not to bind school corporations by contract for more than 1 year.

On such a question, one primarily of state law, we accord respectful consideration and great weight to the views of the state's highest court but, in order that the constitutional mandate may not become a dead letter, we are bound to decide for ourselves whether a contract was made, what are its terms and conditions, and whether the State has, by later legislation, impaired its obligation. This involves an appraisal of the statutes of the State and the decisions of its courts.

The courts of Indiana have long recognized that the employment of school teachers was contractual and have afforded relief in actions upon teachers' contracts. [The Court cited 8 decisions of the Indiana courts.]

In 1927 the State adopted the Teachers' Tenure Act under which the present controversy arises. . . . By this act it was provided that a teacher who has served under contract for 5 or more successive years, and thereafter enters into a contract for further service with the school corporation, shall become a permanent teacher and the contract, upon the expiration of its stated term, shall be deemed to continue in effect for an indefinite period, shall be known as an indefinite contract, and shall remain in force unless succeeded by a new contract or canceled as provided in the act. . . .

By an amendatory act of 1933 township school corporations were omitted from the provisions of the act of 1927. The court below construed this act as repealing the act of 1927 so far as township schools and teachers are concerned and as leaving the respondent free to terminate the petitioner's employment. But we are of opinion that the petitioner had a valid contract with the respondent, the obligation of which would be impaired by the termination of her employment.

Where the claim is that the state's policy embodied in a statute is to bind its instrumentalities by contract, the cardinal inquiry is as to the terms of the statute supposed to create such a contract. The State long prior to the adoption of the act of 1927 required the execution of written contracts between teachers and school corporations, specified certain subjects with which such contracts must deal, and required that they be made a matter of public record. These were annual contracts, covering a single school term. The act of 1927 announced a new policy that a teacher who had served for 5 years under successive contracts, upon the execution of another was to become a permanent teacher and the last contract was to be indefinite as to duration and terminable by either party only upon compliance with the conditions set out in the statute. The policy which induced the legislation evidently was that the teacher should have protection against the exercise of the right, which would otherwise inhere in the employer, of terminating the employment at the end of any school term without assigned reasons and solely at the employer's pleasure. The state courts in earlier cases so declared.

The title of the act is couched in terms of contract. It speaks of the making and canceling of indefinite contracts. In the body the word "contract" appears ten times in section 1, defining the relationship; eleven times in section 2, relating to the termination of the employment by the employer, and four times in section 4, stating the conditions of termination by the teacher.

The tenor of the act indicates that the word "contract" was not used inadvertently or in other than its usual legal meaning. By section 6 it is expressly provided that the act is a supplement to that of March 7, 1921, requiring teachers' employment contracts to be in writing. By section 1 it is provided that the written contract of a permanent teacher "shall be deemed to continue in effect for an indefinite period and shall be known as an indefinite contract." Such an indefinite contract is to remain in force unless succeeded by a new contract signed by both parties or canceled as provided in section 2. No more apt language could be employed to define a contractual relationship. . . . Examination of the entire act convinces us that the teacher was by it assured of the possession of a binding and enforceable contract against school districts.

Until its decision in the present case the Supreme Court of the State had uniformly held that the teacher's right to continued employment by virtue of the indefinite contract created pursuant to the act was contractual.

[The Court quoted from 4 decisions of the Indiana Supreme Court. These included *School City of Elwood v. State ex rel. Griffin et al.*, 180 N.E. 471 (Ind. 1932), in which the court said: "The position of a teacher in the public schools is not a public office, but an employment by contract between the teacher and the school corporation. The relation remains contractual after the teacher has, under the provisions of a Teachers' Tenure Law, become a permanent teacher—but the terms and conditions of the contract are thereafter governed primarily by the statute."]

We think the decision in this case runs counter to the policy evinced by the act of 1927, to its explicit mandate and to earlier decisions construing its provisions. . . .

The respondent urges that every contract is subject to the police power and that in repealing the Teachers' Tenure Act the Legislature validly exercised that reserved power of the State. The sufficient answer is found in the statute. By section 2 of the act of 1927 power is given to the school corporation to cancel a teacher's indefinite contract for incompetency, insubordination (which is to be deemed to mean willful refusal to obey the school laws of the State or reasonable rules prescribed by the employer), neglect of duty, immorality, justifiable decrease in the number of teaching positions, or other good and just cause. . . . [The Legislature also stated] that the contract shall not be canceled for political or personal reasons. . . .

It is significant that the act of 1933 left the system of permanent teachers and indefinite contracts untouched as respects school corporations in cities and towns of the State. It is not contended, nor can it be thought, that the Legislature of 1933 determined that it was against public policy for school districts in cities and towns to terminate the employment of teachers of 5 or more years' experience for political or personal reasons and to permit cancellation, for the same reasons, in townships.

Our decisions recognize that every contract is made subject to the implied condition that its fulfillment may be frustrated by a proper exercise of the police power but we have repeatedly said that, in order to have this effect, the exercise of the power must be for an end which is in fact public and the means adopted must be reasonably adapted to that end, and the Supreme Court of Indiana has taken the same view in respect of legislation impairing the obligation of the contract of a state instrumentality. The causes of cancellation provided in the act of 1927 and the retention of the system of indefinite contracts in all municipalities except townships by the act of 1933 are persuasive that the repeal of the earlier act by the later was not an exercise of the police power for the attainment of ends to which its exercise may properly be directed.

As the court below has not passed upon one of the grounds of demurrer which appears to involve no federal question, and may present a defense still open to the respondent, we reverse the judgment and remand the cause for further proceedings not inconsistent with this opinion.

MR. JUSTICE CARDOZO took no part in the consideration or decision of this case.

MR. JUSTICE BLACK, dissenting.

In my opinion this reversal unconstitutionally limits the right of Indiana to control Indiana's public school system. . . .

The Indiana Supreme Court has consistently held, even before its decision in this case, that the right of teacher, under the 1927 act, to serve until removed for cause, was not given by contract, but by statute. [Justice Black said that in *Elwood* the state court rejected the argument that the teacher's rights were fixed by contract. The state court said:]

> *It is because of appellees' rights under this statute* * * * that mandamus is the proper remedy in this case. * * * A public school teacher who, *under a*

positive provision of the statute, has a fixed tenure of employment or can be removed only in a certain manner prescribed by the statute, is entitled to reinstatement if he has been removed from his position in violation of his statutory rights.

These cases demonstrate that the Supreme Court of Indiana has uniformly held that teachers did not hold their "indefinite" tenure under contract, but by grant of a repealable statute. In order to hold in this case that a contract was impaired, it is necessary to create a contract unauthorized by the Indiana Legislature and declared to be nonexistent by the Indiana Supreme Court. . . .

Note: State and Federal Law in Anderson

1. In *Fox Film*, the Court said that the state court's ruling on the severability issue "was a decision which automatically took the federal question out of the case if otherwise it would be there." The Court distinguished cases in which the state-law ruling would "constitute a preliminary step which simply had the effect of bringing forward for determination the federal question." In *Anderson*, precisely that situation is presented: the state court's ruling on the nature of the obligation created by the 1927 statute is a "preliminary step" that brings forward the federal question under the Contract Clause. This "preliminary step" would probably be referred to today as an antecedent state-law issue.

2. The Court says that questions as to the existence and nature of the contract are "primarily" questions of state law. What does the Court mean? Isn't an issue either an issue of federal law or an issue of state law?

3. In more recent Contracts Clause cases, the Court has taken a different view of the threshold question. For example, in *General Motors Corp. v. Romein*, 503 U.S. 181 (1992), the Court said: "The question whether a contract was made is a federal question for purposes of Contract Clause analysis, and 'whether it turns on issues of general or purely local law, we can not surrender the duty to exercise our own judgment.'" To the extent that the Court follows that rule, the issue of adequacy disappears. We shall assume, as the Court did in *Anderson*, that the issue is "primarily one of state law."

4. The Court in *Anderson* says that it gives "respectful consideration and great weight to the views of the state's highest court" on the question of whether a contract was made. Does the Court's treatment of Indiana statutes and precedents in its opinion reflect a high measure of deference?

Note: Antecedent and Remedial State-Law Grounds

Contract Clause cases do not arise frequently today, but the problem of the antecedent state-law ground can surface in other contexts. Here we consider: by what standard should the Supreme Court review a state-court decision on an issue of state law that provides the predicate for resolution of a federal question?

The Court may also confront cases in which the state court holds or assumes that the federal claim is meritorious but rules against the claimant by denying a particular *remedy* as a matter of state law. In that situation, too, the Court must consider whether the decision is reviewable and, if so, by what standard.

A. The Antecedent Issue in *Martin*

The litigation that yielded the landmark decision in *Martin v. Hunter's Lessee* (Chapter 4) itself involved an antecedent issue of state law. Recall that Denny and Philip Martin argued that federal treaties invalidated the purported forfeiture of the Northern Neck lands to the state of Virginia. This argument would be defeated if the lands were validly confiscated by the state before the treaties took effect. The opposing litigant, Hunter's Lessee, insisted that under section 25 the Supreme Court "[could] not inquire into the title [to the lands], but simply into the correctness of the construction put upon the treaty by the [state] court of appeals." The Supreme Court rejected this position:

> If this be the true construction of the section, it will be wholly inadequate for the purposes which it professes to have in view, and may be evaded at pleasure. But we see no reason for adopting this narrow construction. . . . How, indeed, can it be possible to decide whether a title be within the protection of a treaty, until it is ascertained what that title is, and whether it have a legal validity? From the very necessity of the case, there must be a preliminary inquiry into the existence and structure of the title, before the court can construe the treaty in reference to that title. If the court below should decide, that the title was bad, and, therefore, not protected by the treaty, must not this court have a power to decide the title to be good, and, therefore, protected by the treaty?

Does this go further than *Anderson*? Or is it just a different way of expressing the same approach?

B. *Broad River*

In *Broad River Power Co. v. South Carolina*, 281 U.S. 537 (1930), the state sought to compel a railroad company to resume operation of a railway system which it had abandoned. The company argued that because the railway system was being operated at a loss, any such order would deprive it of property without due process of law in violation of the Fourteenth Amendment. The state court held that operation of the railway system was part of a unified franchise that also included the electric power system. Therefore, under state law, as long as the company continued to operate the power system, it could not abandon the railway line.

The Supreme Court granted certiorari to consider the due process claim. Justice Stone, writing for a unanimous Court, began by defining the Court's reviewing authority:

> Whether the state court has denied to rights asserted under local law the protection which the Constitution guarantees is a question upon which the petitioners are entitled to invoke the judgment of this Court. Even though the constitutional protection invoked be denied on nonfederal grounds, it is

the province of this Court to inquire whether the decision of the state court rests upon a fair or substantial basis. If unsubstantial, constitutional obligations may not be thus evaded. But if there is no evasion of the constitutional issue, and the nonfederal ground of decision has fair support, this Court will not inquire whether the rule applied by the state court is right or wrong, or substitute its own view of what should be deemed the better rule for that of the state court.

Turning to the case before it, the Court reviewed the South Carolina statutes, the history of the corporation, and the South Carolina court's interpretation. It concluded:

In the light of the familiar rule that franchises are to be strictly construed, and that construction adopted which works the least harm to the public, we cannot say that this interpretation of statutes of the state of South Carolina, by its highest court, so departs from established principles as to be without substantial basis, or presents any ground for the protection, under the Constitution, of rights or immunities which the state court has found to be non-existent. It follows that it was within the constitutional power of the state to refuse to permit any partial abandonment of the consolidated franchise.

Having concluded that the South Carolina court's judgment was "supported by a state ground which we may rightly accept as substantial," the Court dismissed the writ of certiorari.[1]

How does the *Broad River* standard differ from asking "whether the rule applied by the state court is right or wrong"—a standard that the Court disclaims? Recall that the Court used similar language in *Fox Film*: "Whether [the state court's] conclusion was right or wrong we need not determine. It is enough that it is, at least, not without fair support."

In *Anderson*, the Court did not cite *Broad River*. Did the Court apply the same standard?

C. *Lucas* and the Takings Clause

In *Lucas v. South Carolina Coastal Council*, 505 U.S. 1003 (1992), Lucas owned two residential lots on a South Carolina barrier island. The state legislature enacted a law that barred him from erecting any permanent habitable structures on his lots. Lucas sued the responsible state agency, contending that the ban on construction deprived him of all "economically viable use" of his property and therefore effected a "taking" in violation of the Fifth and Fourteenth Amendments that required the payment of "just compensation." The state court rejected his claim, but the United States Supreme Court reversed.

The Court held that "when the owner of real property has been called upon to sacrifice *all* economically beneficial uses [by state regulation], he has suffered a taking."

---

1. The Court later granted rehearing. Although it reached the same result, only four of the eight participating Justices endorsed the reasoning quoted above.

The state "may resist compensation only if the logically antecedent inquiry into the nature of the owner's estate shows that the proscribed use interests were not part of his title to begin with."

The federal claim under the Takings Clause thus depends on "the nature of the owner's estate" under state law. The Court elaborated on this "logically antecedent inquiry":

> [Our Takings jurisprudence has] traditionally been guided by the understandings of our citizens regarding the content of, and the State's power over, the "bundle of rights" that they acquire when they obtain title to property. . . . [The question] is one of state law to be dealt with on remand. We emphasize that to win its case South Carolina must do more than proffer the legislature's declaration that the uses Lucas desires are inconsistent with the public interest. . . . As we have said, a "State, by *ipse dixit*, may not transform private property into public property without compensation. . . ." *Webb's Fabulous Pharmacies, Inc. v. Beckwith*, 449 U.S. 155 (1980). Instead, as it would be required to do if it sought to restrain Lucas in a common-law action for public nuisance, South Carolina must identify background principles of nuisance and property law that prohibit the uses he now intends in the circumstances in which the property is presently found. Only on this showing can the State fairly claim that, in proscribing all such beneficial uses, the Beachfront Management Act is taking nothing.

In a footnote, the Court offered brief additional guidance:

> There is no doubt some leeway in a [state] court's interpretation of what existing state law permits—but not remotely as much, we think, as in a legislative crafting of the reasons for its confiscatory regulation. We stress that an affirmative decree eliminating all economically beneficial uses may be defended only if an *objectively reasonable application* of relevant precedents would exclude those beneficial uses in the circumstances in which the land is presently found. [Emphasis in original.]

Are these formulations more helpful than those in *Anderson* and *Broad River*? Consider the Problems below.

Problem: Property on a Tidal Canal

In the late 1960s, Richard McGee purchased a tract of land located on an artificially created saltwater canal in Surf City in the state of Oceana. The property has remained undeveloped. Three years ago, McGee applied to the Oceana State Coastal Council for a permit to build bulkheads on the property. The Council denied the permit, based on its determination that the property encompassed "predominantly critical area wetlands."

McGee then brought suit in state court seeking compensation for a regulatory taking under *Lucas*. The trial court found that McGee had been deprived of all economically beneficial use of his property and awarded compensation. The Coastal Council appealed to the Oceana Supreme Court. The Oceana Supreme Court reversed, finding that no taking had occurred. The court said:

> We accept as uncontested that McGee's property retains no value and that there has been a total deprivation of all economically beneficial use. However, we conclude that under background principles of Oceana property law, the proscribed use was not part of McGee's title to begin with.
>
> As a coastal state, Oceana has a long line of cases regarding the public trust doctrine in the context of land bordering navigable waters. Under that doctrine, the State holds presumptive title to land below the high water mark, and it cannot permit activity that substantially impairs the public interest in marine life, water quality, or public access. McGee's property borders a man-made tidal canal. At the time the permit was denied, the property had reverted to tidelands with only irregular portions of highland remaining. This reversion to tidelands effected a restriction on McGee's property rights inherent in the ownership of property bordering tidal water.
>
> McGee argues that our cases on the public trust doctrine have all involved land bordering "*navigable* tidal" water. That is true, but under Oceana law tidal water is presumed navigable unless shown to be incapable of navigation *in fact*, a showing not made here. Nor is it relevant that the waterway is artificial. Although we have never squarely decided the point, our decisions have assumed that artificial waterways are the functional equivalent of natural waterways.

You are an associate in the firm representing McGee. The senior partner asks you: "Our client's federal claim has been denied by the Oceana Supreme Court. Is that court's decision reviewable by the United States Supreme Court? If so, by what standard?"

How would you answer the senior partner?

Problem: Anderson *on Remand*

The Supreme Court's opinion in *Anderson* noted that the state court had "not passed on one of the grounds of demurrer that involved no federal question." The Court remanded the case so that Indiana court could consider that defense. However, that court did not do so. Instead, it affirmed the sustaining of the demurrer on a different ground:

> This action is brought in the name of the State, on the relation of Dorothy Anderson. It seeks to mandate the school authorities to reinstate the relatrix as a teacher and continue her in employment. It is not an action by Dorothy Anderson to enforce her contract, but an action to require a public officer to perform a duty required of him by law, which can be maintained only in the name of the State.
>
> It was thought by this court when [this case] was decided, that the enforcement of tenure rights depended entirely upon the statutory duty of the school

officers to continue the teacher in employment, and that the teacher's only protection was an action in mandate in the name of the State to enforce the performance of a statutory duty by the school officers. . . . The United States Supreme Court has [held] the repeal of the statute to be ineffectual [under the Contracts Clause] to strike down the teacher's contractual tenure rights. We conclude that the repeal of the statute is otherwise valid in all respects, and therefore there is no longer any statutory duty which requires the school officers to continue the teacher in employment. The school officers therefore cannot be mandated. The teacher's rights under her contract must be enforced in a civil action upon the contract in her own name. See *City of Peru v. State ex rel. McGuire*, 199 N.E. 151 (Ind. 1935), and *State ex rel. Ham v. Hulley*, 137 N.E. 177 (Ind. 1922). . . .

We must still conclude therefore that the complaint in the name of the State for mandate does not state a cause of action.

State ex rel. Anderson v. Brand, 13 N.E.2d 955 (Ind. 1938).

Is this decision open to review by the United States Supreme Court? If so, by what standard is the holding of the Indiana Supreme Court to be judged? Would it matter if, by the time of the Indiana Supreme Court's second decision, a breach-of-contract claim by Anderson would be barred by a statute of limitations? Should state-court rulings on these issues be treated as "procedural" grounds, to be viewed through the lens of cases like *James v. Kentucky*, set forth in the next section?

[3] Adequacy of State Procedural Grounds

Every American court system has rules of procedure that tell litigants how and when to present their claims and defenses. Failure to follow the rules will ordinarily result in forfeiture, even if the claim or defense might otherwise have carried the day.

Familiar examples are found in the Federal Rules of Civil Procedure. Under Rule 12(h)(1), various defenses, including lack of personal jurisdiction, are waived if not made in accordance with other provisions of the Rule. Under Rule 16, orders entered after a pretrial conference control the subsequent course of the action, and a litigant will be foreclosed from raising new contentions unless he or she can show "manifest injustice." Rule 51 provides the framework for objecting to jury instructions, and objections not raised in accordance with the Rule can be considered only if they involve "plain error . . . affecting substantial rights."

In state courts, litigants must follow the state's procedural rules. Contentions grounded in federal law are no exception. And when the highest state court refuses to consider a federal claim or defense because of failure to comply with state procedural requirements, the judgment may be deemed to rest on an adequate and independent state ground that bars Supreme Court review of the federal question.

"May be"—because the Supreme Court will not necessarily accept the state court's view of the procedural barrier. In the next principal case, for example, the Court delved deeply into Kentucky treatises and case law to make its own determination of the adequacy of the proffered state ground.

James v. Kentucky

Supreme Court of the United States, 1984.

466 U.S. 341.

Justice White delivered the opinion of the Court.

In *Carter v. Kentucky*, 450 U.S. 288 (1981), we held that a trial judge must, if requested to do so, instruct the jury not to draw an adverse inference from the defendant's failure to take the stand. In this case, the Kentucky Supreme Court found that the trial judge was relieved of that obligation because defense counsel requested an "admonition" rather than an "instruction."

I

Petitioner Michael James was indicted for receipt of stolen property, burglary, and rape. James had been convicted of two prior felonies—forgery and murder—and the prosecution warned that were James to take the stand it would use the forgery conviction to impeach his testimony. During *voir dire*, defense counsel asked the prospective jurors how they would feel were James not to testify. After a brief exchange between counsel and one member of the venire, the trial judge interrupted, stating: "They have just said they would try the case solely upon the law and the evidence. That excludes any other consideration." With that, *voir dire* came to a close. James did not testify at trial.

At the close of testimony, counsel and the judge had an off-the-record discussion about instructions. When they returned on the record, James' lawyer noted that he objected to several of the instructions being given, and that he "requests that an admonition be given to the jury that no emphasis be given to the defendant's failure to testify which was overruled." The judge then instructed the jury, which returned a verdict of guilty on all counts. At a subsequent persistent felony offender proceeding, the jury sentenced James to life imprisonment in light of his two previous convictions.

On appeal, James argued that the trial judge's refusal to tell the jury not to draw an adverse inference from his failure to testify violated *Carter v. Kentucky*. The Kentucky Supreme Court conceded that *Carter* requires the trial judge, upon request, to instruct the jury not to draw an adverse inference. The court noted, however, that James had requested an admonition rather than an instruction, and there is a "vast difference" between the two under state law. He "was entitled to the instruction, but did not ask for it. The trial court properly denied the request for an admonition." We granted certiorari to determine whether petitioner's asserted procedural default adequately supports the result below. We now reverse.

II

In *Carter* we held that, in order fully to effectuate the right to remain silent, a trial judge must instruct the jury not to draw an adverse inference from the defendant's failure to testify if requested to do so. James argues that the essence of the holding in *Carter* is that the judge must afford some form of guidance to the jury, and that the admonition he sought was the "functional equivalent" of the instruction required by *Carter*. The State responds that the trial judge was under no obligation to provide an admonition when under Kentucky practice James should have sought an instruction. An examination of the state-law background is necessary to understand these arguments.

A

Kentucky distinguishes between "instructions" and "admonitions." The former tend to be statements of black-letter law, the latter cautionary statements regarding the jury's conduct. Thus, "admonitions" include statements to the jury requiring it to disregard certain testimony, to consider particular evidence for purposes of evaluating credibility only, and to consider evidence as to one codefendant only. [On each of these points, the Court cited one or more Kentucky cases.] The State Rules of Criminal Procedure provide that at each adjournment the jury is to be "admonished" not to discuss the case.

Instructions, on the other hand, set forth the legal rules governing the outcome of a case. They "state what the jury must believe from the evidence . . . in order to return a verdict in favor of the party who bears the burden of proof." The judge reads the instructions to the jury at the end of the trial, and provides it a written copy. After *Carter*, Kentucky amended its Criminal Rules to provide that, if the defendant so requests, the instructions must state that he is not compelled to testify and that the jury shall not draw an adverse inference from his election not to.

The substantive distinction between admonitions and instructions is not always clear or closely hewn to. Kentucky's highest court has recognized that the content of admonitions and instructions can overlap. In a number of cases, for example, it has referred to a trial court's failure either to instruct or to admonish the jury on a particular point, indicating that either was a possibility. E.g., *Caldwell v. Commonwealth*, 503 S.W.2d 485 (Ky. 1972) ("instructions" did not contain a particular "admonition," but the "failure to admonish or instruct" was harmless); *Reeves v. Commonwealth*, 462 S.W.2d 926 (Ky. 1971). The court has acknowledged that "sometimes matters more appropriately the subject of admonition are included with or as a part of the instructions." *Webster v. Commonwealth*, 508 S.W.2d 33 (Ky. App. 1974).

In pre-*Carter* cases holding that a defendant had no right to have the jury told not to draw an adverse inference, Kentucky's highest court did not distinguish admonitions from instructions. [Here the Court cited 7 cases from 1933 through 1977.] A statement to the jury not to draw an adverse inference from the defendant's failure to testify would seem to fall more neatly into the admonition category than the instruction category. Cautioning the jury against considering testimony not given differs little from cautioning it not to consider testimony that was. However, the Kentucky Criminal Rules treat it as an instruction.

One procedural difference between admonitions and instructions is that the former are normally oral, while the latter, though given orally, are also provided to the jury in writing. *See generally* [J. Palmore & R. Lawson, *Instructions to Juries in Kentucky* (1975).] However, this distinction is not strictly adhered to. As the cases cited above indicate, "admonitions" frequently appear in the written instructions. Conversely, instructions may be given only orally if the defendant waives the writing requirement. The State contends, though without citing any authority, that the instructions must be all in writing or all oral, and that it would have been reversible error for the trial judge to have given this "instruction" orally. Yet the Kentucky Court of Appeals has held, for example, that there was no error where the trial court, after reading the written instructions, told the jury orally that its verdict must be unanimous, a statement normally considered an "instruction." *Freeman v. Commonwealth*, 425 S.W.2d 575 (1968). And in several cases the Court of Appeals has found no error where the trial court gave oral explanations of its written instructions. [Citing 2 cases.] Finally, given Kentucky's strict contemporaneous-objection rule, it would be odd if it were reversible error for the trial court to have given a *Carter* instruction orally at the defendant's request.

B

There can be no dispute that, for federal constitutional purposes, James adequately invoked his substantive right to jury guidance. See *Douglas v. Alabama*, 380 U.S. 415 (1965). The question is whether counsel's passing reference to an "admonition" is a fatal procedural default under Kentucky law adequate to support the result below and to prevent us from considering petitioner's constitutional claim. In light of the state-law background described above, we hold that it is not. Kentucky's distinction between admonitions and instructions is not the sort of firmly established and regularly followed state practice that can prevent implementation of federal constitutional rights. *Cf. Barr v. City of Columbia*, 378 U.S. 146 (1964). *Carter* holds that if asked to do so the trial court must tell the jury not to draw the impermissible inference. To insist on a particular label for this statement would "force resort to an arid ritual of meaningless form," *Staub v. City of Baxley*, 355 U.S. 313 (1958), and would further no perceivable state interest, *Henry v. Mississippi*, 379 U.S. 443 (1965). *See also NAACP v. Alabama ex rel. Flowers*, 377 U.S. 288 (1964). "Admonition" is a term that both we and the State Supreme Court have used in this context and which is reasonable under state law and normal usage. As Justice Holmes wrote 60 years ago: "Whatever springes the State may set for those who are endeavoring to assert rights that the State confers, the assertion of federal rights, when plainly and reasonably made, is not to be defeated under the name of local practice." *Davis v. Wechsler*, 263 U.S. 22 (1923).

C

The State argues that this is more than a case of failure to use the required magic word, however. It considers James' request for an admonition to have been a deliberate strategy. He sought an oral statement only in order to put "less emphasis on this particular subject, not before the jury, not in writing to be read over and over, but to have been commented upon and passed by." James, now represented by his third attorney, seems to concede that the first attorney did seek an oral admonition. He does not argue that the trial court had to include the requested statement in the instructions, though he suggests that it could have done so, and that he would have been happy with either a written or an oral statement.

We would readily agree that the State is free to require that all instructions be in writing; and to categorize a no-adverse-inference statement as an instruction. The Constitution obliges the trial judge to tell the jury, in an effective manner, not to draw the inference if the defendant so requests; but it does not afford the defendant the right to dictate, inconsistent with state practice, how the jury is to be told. . . . [We] do not think that a State would impermissibly infringe the defendant's right not to testify by requiring that if the jury is to be alerted to it, it be alerted in writing.

This is not a case, however, of a defendant attempting to circumvent such a firm state procedural rule. For one thing, as the discussion in Part II-A, *supra*, indicates, the oral/written distinction is not as solid as the State would have us believe. Admonitions can be written and instructions oral, and the Kentucky Supreme Court has itself used the term "admonition" in referring to instructions that "admonish." In addition, our own examination of the admittedly incomplete record reveals little to support the State's view of petitioner's request. The single passing reference to an "admonition" is far too slender a reed on which to rest the conclusion that petitioner insisted on an oral statement and nothing but. . . .

Where it is inescapable that the defendant sought to invoke the substance of his federal right, the asserted state-law defect in form must be more evident than it is here. In the circumstances of this case, we cannot find that petitioner's constitutional rights were respected or that the result below rests on independent and adequate state grounds.

III

Respondent argues that even if there was error, it was harmless. It made the same argument below, but the Kentucky Supreme Court did not reach it in light of its conclusion that no error had been committed. We have not determined whether *Carter* error can be harmless, and we do not do so now. Even if an evaluation of harmlessness is called for, it is best made in state court before it is made here. The case is remanded for further proceedings not inconsistent with this opinion.

JUSTICE MARSHALL took no part in the decision of this case.

JUSTICE REHNQUIST dissents for the reasons stated in his dissenting opinion in *Carter v. Kentucky*, 450 U.S. 288 (1981).

Note: James v. Kentucky *and Its Antecedents*

Justice White's opinion for the Court in *James v. Kentucky* cites some of the leading decisions on state procedural grounds. This Note examines a few of the precedents in greater detail.

A. State Procedure and Federal Due Process

A procedural ruling that constitutes a denial of due process cannot, of course, serve as a state ground that will bar Supreme Court review of other federal constitutional claims. The case that is often cited for this proposition is *Brinkerhoff-Faris Trust & Savings Co. v. Hill*, 281 U.S. 673 (1930).

In *Brinkerhoff-Faris*, a bank sued in Missouri state court challenging a township tax assessment as a violation of the Equal Protection Clause of the Fourteenth Amendment. The state supreme court affirmed the dismissal of the suit on the ground that the bank had not filed a complaint with the State Tax Commission. The court overruled a decision (*Laclede*) holding that the Commission had no power to grant relief from discrimination similar to that alleged by the bank. But the time had passed for the bank to avail itself of the newly recognized remedy.

The United States Supreme Court reversed, holding that the judgment of the state court was a denial of due process. The Court explained:

> The state court refused to hear the plaintiff's complaint and denied it relief, not because of lack of power or because of any demerit in the complaint, but because, assuming power and merit, the plaintiff did not first seek an administrative remedy which in fact was never available and which is not now open to it. . . .
>
> We are not now concerned with the rights of the plaintiff on the merits, although [the] plaintiff's claim is one arising under the federal Constitution and, consequently, one on which the opinion of the state court is not final; or with the accuracy of the state court's construction of the statute in either the *Laclede* Case or in the case at bar. Our present concern is solely with the question whether the plaintiff has been accorded due process in the primary sense — whether it has had an opportunity to present its case and be heard in its support.
>
> Undoubtedly, the state court had the power to construe the statute dealing with the state tax commission; and to re-examine and overrule the *Laclede* Case. Neither of these matters raises a federal question; neither is subject to our review. But, while it is for the state courts to determine the adjective as well as the substantive law of the state, they must, in so doing, accord the parties due process of law. Whether acting through its judiciary or through its Legislature, a state may not deprive a person of all existing remedies for the enforcement of a right, which the state has no power to destroy, unless there is, or was, afforded to him some real opportunity to protect it.

A few early cases were sometimes read as saying that a state ground can be inadequate *only* when, as in *Brinkerhoff-Faris*, it violates due process. That plainly is not the law today. At least two themes can be found in the Court's opinions.

B. "Firmly Established and Regularly Followed"?

The Court holds in *James* that the distinction between "admonitions" and "instructions" "is not the sort of firmly established and regularly followed state practice that can prevent implementation of federal constitutional rights." Although the formulation is new, the idea it encapsulates is one with deep roots in the Court's precedents.

Indeed, the doctrine can be viewed as no more than a step removed from the one applied in *Brinkerhoff-Faris*.

The connection can be seen in an often-cited case from the 1950s, *NAACP v. Alabama ex rel. Patterson*, 357 U.S. 449 (1958). The Alabama trial court entered a judgment of civil contempt against the NAACP for refusing to comply fully with an order requiring the production of membership lists. The NAACP claimed that the order violated its federal constitutional rights. The Alabama Supreme Court held that it could not consider the constitutional issues underlying the contempt judgment because the NAACP had pursued the wrong appellate remedy under state law by applying for certiorari rather than mandamus. The NAACP brought the case to the United States Supreme Court, which granted certiorari.

State officials argued that the Alabama Supreme Court ruling rested on an adequate independent nonfederal ground, but the Supreme Court disagreed. In a unanimous opinion by Justice Harlan, the Court said:

> We are unable to reconcile the procedural holding of the Alabama Supreme Court in the present case with its past unambiguous holdings as to the scope of review available upon a writ of certiorari addressed to a contempt judgment. [Here the Court cited six decisions of the Alabama Supreme Court extending from 1909 through 1949.] . . . . The Alabama cases do indicate, as was said in the opinion below, that an order requiring production of evidence ". . . *may* be reviewed on petition for mandamus." (Italics added.) But we can discover nothing in the prior state cases which suggests that mandamus is the *exclusive* remedy for reviewing court orders after disobedience of them has led to contempt judgments. . . . Novelty in procedural requirements cannot be permitted to thwart review in this Court applied for by those who, in justified reliance upon prior decisions, seek vindication in state courts of their federal constitutional rights. *Cf. Brinkerhoff-Faris Co. v. Hill.*

The Court then found that the contempt judgment violated the NAACP's rights under the Fourteenth Amendment.

Seven years later, in a decision cited in *James*, the Court considered another phase of the same dispute. This was *NAACP v. Alabama ex rel. Flowers*, 377 U.S. 288 (1964). Once again the Alabama Supreme Court ruled against the NAACP on procedural grounds. This time the Alabama court relied on "a rule of long standing and frequent application that where unrelated assignments of error are argued together and one is without merit, the others will not be considered."

The state attorney general argued that this procedural ruling was an adequate nonfederal ground that barred review of the NAACP's constitutional claims, but the Supreme Court unanimously found that position "wholly unacceptable." As it did in the earlier case, the Court carefully canvassed the Alabama precedents. Again speaking through Justice Harlan, the Court said: "The Alabama courts have not heretofore applied their rules respecting the preparation of briefs with the pointless severity shown here." In support of this proposition, the Court cited or quoted a dozen Alabama appellate decisions. The Court then considered another dozen cases that were cited in the Alabama Supreme Court's opinion and in the attorney general's brief. These cases, the Court said, "quite evidently do not support the State's position."

The state attorney general urged the Court to give the Alabama court an opportunity to consider the merits, but in view of the long history of the case, the Court declined. It reversed the Alabama court's judgment.

C. "An Arid Ritual of Meaningless Form"?

The Court in *James* also says that for the state to insist that the defendant request an "instruction" rather than an "admonition" would be to "force resort to an arid ritual of meaningless form." This striking phrase comes from *Staub v. City of Baxley*, 355 U.S. 313 (1958), another leading precedent on the adequacy of state procedural grounds.

Staub came to the Supreme Court on appeal from the Georgia state courts under the now-repealed mandatory jurisdiction. The appellant was convicted of violating a city ordinance that prohibited soliciting members for an organization without a permit. She appealed her conviction to the intermediate appellate court, asserting (among other contentions) that the ordinance violated her rights under the First Amendment. The court declined to consider any of her constitutional arguments. It said that her attack "should have been made against specific sections of the ordinance and not against the ordinance as a whole." The Georgia Supreme Court denied review.

In the United States Supreme Court, the city argued that the appeal should be dismissed because the state court decision rested on an adequate state procedural ground. The Court rejected this contention by a vote of 7 to 2. In an opinion by Justice Whittaker, the Court said:

> The several sections of the ordinance are interdependent in their application to one in appellant's position and constitute but one complete act for the licensing and taxing of her described activities. For that reason, no doubt, she challenged the constitutionality of the whole ordinance, and in her objections used language challenging the constitutional effect of all its sections. She did, thus, challenge all sections of the ordinance, though not by number. To require her, in these circumstances, to count off, one by one, the several sections of the ordinance would be to force resort to an arid ritual of meaningless form.

The Court cited decisions of the Georgia Supreme Court to show that that court "seems to have recognized the arbitrariness of such exaltation of form." Turning to the merits, the Court reversed.

Justice Frankfurter, joined by Justice Clark, dissented from the jurisdictional holding in *Staub*:

> The cases relied upon by the Georgia court in this case are part of a long line of decisions holding a comprehensive, all-inclusive challenge to the constitutionality of a statute inadequate and requiring explicit particularity in

pleadings in order to raise constitutional questions. Those cases rest essentially on a recognition of the gravity of judicial invalidation of legislation. They require the pleader to allege the specific portion of the challenged legislation. . . .

There is nothing frivolous or futile (though it may appear "formal") about a rule insisting that parties specify with arithmetic particularity those provisions in a legislative enactment they would ask a court to strike down. This is so, because such exactitude helps to make concrete the plaintiffs' relation to challenged provisions. [Among other things,] where the parties identify particular language in a statute as allegedly violating a constitutional provision, the court will often be able to construe the words in such a way as to render them inoffensive. . . .

Of course, even if the Georgia rule is intrinsically reasonable and thus entitled to respect by this Court, we must be sure that it has not been applied arbitrarily in the case before us. . . . There is no indication whatever in the case before us that the Georgia Court of Appeals applied this well-established rule of pleading arbitrarily or inadvisedly; this case cannot be said to stand out, among the many cases in which the rule has been applied, as a deviation from the norm.

Is *Staub* based on the same rationale as the *NAACP* cases? Or does it rely on a different reason for rejecting the adequacy of the state procedural ground?

D. Adequacy of State Procedural Grounds "As Applied"

It is no coincidence that two prominent decisions on the adequacy of state procedural grounds grew out of the NAACP's battle with Alabama authorities over membership lists in the decade following the school desegregation case, *Brown v. Board of Education*, 357 U.S. 483 (1954). In the 1950s and early 1960s, the development of the doctrine was closely associated with cases from southern states that involved black criminal defendants or civil rights organizations. In many such cases, where the state courts invented novel procedural rules or relied on dubious applications of existing rules, the Court deemed the state-law ground inadequate because the rules were not "firmly established" and "regularly followed."

But what if the state procedural rule *is* firmly established, regularly followed, and serves a legitimate interest? Does that suffice, without more, to show the state ground is adequate? Or should the Supreme Court evaluate state procedural grounds on a case-by-case basis, disregarding violations when it considers the rule inadequate as applied in particular circumstances?

The Court's answers to these questions have been controversial, beginning with the Warren Court's decision in *Henry v. Mississippi*, 379 U.S. 443 (1965). In that case, civil rights leader and Mississippi NAACP president Aaron Henry was convicted of disturbing the peace, based on an accusation that he had solicited sex from an 18-year-old white man who was hitchhiking. *See* Minion K.C. Morrison, Aaron Henry of Mississippi: Inside Agitator 61–63 (2015) (calling the allegations against

Henry a "fabricated morals charge, albeit a spectacular failure," that seemed "suspicious from the start"). Henry argued that certain evidence should have been excluded at trial as the fruit of an unlawful search in violation of the Fourth Amendment. But counsel raised the issue after the evidence was already admitted, as part of a motion for a directed verdict. The jury found Henry guilty and the Mississippi Supreme Court affirmed the conviction, refusing to consider the Fourth Amendment claim in light of the "long established procedural rule in this State" that parties must lodge a contemporaneous objection to the admissibility of evidence. *Henry v. State*, 154 So. 2d 289 (Miss. 1963).

The United States Supreme Court vacated the judgment and remanded for further proceedings. It acknowledged that state rules "requiring a contemporaneous objection to the introduction of illegal evidence clearly do[] serve a legitimate state interest." Nonetheless, the Court said:

> [O]n the record before us it appears that this purpose of the contemporaneous-objection rule may have been substantially served by petitioner's motion at the close of the State's evidence asking for a directed verdict because of the erroneous admission of the officer's testimony. . . . [If] enforcement of the rule here would serve no substantial state interest, then settled principles would preclude treating the state ground as adequate; giving effect to the contemporaneous-objection rule for its own sake "would be to force resort to an arid ritual of meaningless form." *Staub*.

No one disputed that Henry had a full and fair opportunity to raise his federal claim in the state courts, nor that his default of that claim followed from a well-established and legitimate state procedural requirement. In a departure from the Court's earlier cases, however, the decision in *Henry* suggested that the adequacy of a state-law procedural rule depends on the particular circumstances in which it is applied.

That approach has been roundly criticized. In dissent, Justice Harlan called the Court's analysis "little short of fanciful" in its understanding of the dynamics of the courtroom, and warned that it portended "a severe dilution, if not complete abolition, of the concept of 'adequacy' as pertaining to state procedural grounds." Many scholars have echoed those concerns. *See* 16B WRIGHT & MILLER, FEDERAL PRACTICE AND PROCEDURE § 4028 (3d ed. 1998) (arguing that *Henry*'s approach "unduly subordinates state interests"); RICHARD H. FALLON, DANIEL J. MELTZER & DAVID L. SHAPIRO, HART AND WECHSLER'S THE FEDERAL COURTS AND THE FEDERAL SYSTEM 584–85 (4th ed. 1996) (calling *Henry* "radical" for suggesting "that failure to comply with a rule that undoubtedly serves a legitimate interest should be overlooked because, in the particular case, that interest could have been 'substantially served' by some *other* procedure").

Perhaps because of those criticisms, over the next 40 years the Court rarely followed *Henry*'s lead by suggesting that particular applications of generally legitimate rules were "inadequate." In *Camp v. Arkansas*, 404 U.S. 69 (1971) (per curiam), the defendant raised a Fifth Amendment self-incrimination claim for the first time on appeal, and the state supreme court rejected the claim based on the failure to make a contemporaneous objection. The Supreme Court summarily reversed, stating without elaboration that the "alleged procedural default does not bar consideration of his constitutional claim in the circumstances of this case," and (indirectly) citing *Henry*. Similarly, in *Osborne v. Ohio*, 495 U.S. 103 (1990), counsel for a criminal defendant failed to request a jury instruction on "lewdness," as required by a well-established procedural rule that "serves the State's important interest in ensuring that counsel do their part in preventing trial courts from providing juries with erroneous instructions." But the Court noted that immediately *before* trial, Osborne's attorney had moved to dismiss the case on similar grounds, and the trial that followed was brief. Based on that sequence of events, the Court reasoned, "we are convinced that Osborne's attorney pressed the issue of the State's failure of proof on lewdness before the trial court and, under the circumstances, nothing would be gained by requiring Osborne's lawyer to object a second time, specifically to the jury instructions." Both *Camp* and *Osborne* appeared to recognize case-specific exceptions to the adequacy of generally legitimate state procedural rules. Yet neither case attracted much attention; in both, the Court unanimously concluded that no adequate state ground precluded its jurisdiction.

Does that mean the "as applied" approach to adequacy is well settled and uncontroversial? Hardly, as evidenced by the sharp division within the Court in *Lee v. Kemna*, 534 U.S. 362 (2002). In that case, the defendant in a murder trial planned to introduce an alibi defense, but on the day the witnesses were scheduled to testify, they left the courthouse and could not be found. Lee's counsel moved for a continuance, but the trial judge denied the request because the witnesses "in effect abandoned the defendant" and in any event the judge's schedule could not accommodate the change. On appeal following his conviction, Lee challenged the denial of the continuance as a denial of due process. The Missouri Court of Appeals rejected that claim based on a state procedural rule "not relied upon or even mentioned in the trial court," requiring that continuance motions must be submitted in writing and accompanied by an affidavit setting out the grounds. Lee later filed a petition for habeas corpus. (As discussed in Chapter 15, the adequate state ground doctrine also applies in federal habeas cases brought by state prisoners.)

By a 6-to-3 vote, in an opinion by Justice Ginsburg, the Court found the state procedural ground inadequate. It did not dispute that, ordinarily, the violation of "firmly established and regularly followed" state rules is adequate to foreclose review of a federal claim. It also acknowledged that the state procedural rule "serves a governmental interest of undoubted legitimacy" by "arm[ing] trial judges with the information needed to rule reliably on a motion to delay a scheduled criminal trial." Nonetheless, the Court explained, there are "exceptional cases in which exorbitant application of a generally sound rule renders the state ground inadequate to stop consideration of a federal question." It relied on "[t]hree considerations, in combination," to conclude that those exceptional circumstances were present. First, even if counsel had complied with the rule, the motion would have been denied because of the trial judge's schedule. Second, "no published Missouri decision directs flawless compliance with [the state procedural rule] in the unique circumstances this case presents—the sudden, unanticipated, and at the time unexplained disappearance of critical, subpoenaed witnesses on what became the trial's last day." Third, counsel had "substantially complied" with the rule because the reasons for the continuance "were either covered by the oral continuance motion or otherwise conspicuously apparent on the record." With the rule's "essential requirements" satisfied, nothing would have been gained "by requiring Lee's counsel to recapitulate in (a), (b), (c), (d) order the showings the Rule requires." *Lee* (citing *Osborne* and *Staub*).

Justice Kennedy, joined by Justices Scalia and Thomas, dissented. In part, the dissenters were troubled by the Court's "quite novel" reliance on the lack of "published decisions directing flawless compliance" with the rule in identical circumstances. "If the Court means what it says on this point," the dissent argued, "few procedural rules will give rise to an adequate state ground" because "[a]lmost every case presents unique circumstances that cannot be foreseen and articulated by prior decisions." The whole point of general rules is to "eliminate second-guessing about the rule's applicability in special cases." More broadly, the dissent saw *Lee* as reviving the "discredited rationale" of *Henry*:

> [In the majority's view,] the Rule's essential purposes were substantially served by other procedural devices, such as opening statement, *voir dire*, and Lee's testimony on the stand. These procedures, it is said, provided the court with the information the Rule requires the motion itself to contain. So viewed, the Court's substantial-compliance terminology . . . . simply paraphrases the flawed analytical approach first proposed by the Court in *Henry v. Mississippi*, 379 U.S. 443 (1965), but not further ratified or in fact used to set aside a procedural rule until today. . . .
>
> *Henry* was troubling, and much criticized, because it injected an as-applied factor into the equation. . . . For all *Henry* possessed in mischievous potential, however, it lacked significant precedential effect. . . . Subsequent cases maintained the pre-*Henry* focus on the general validity of the challenged state practice, either declining to cite *Henry* or framing its holding in innocuous terms. See, e.g., *James*; see also Hart & Wechsler, *supra* (describing the "[d]emise of *Henry*").
>
> There is no meaningful distinction between the *Henry* Court's analysis and the standard the Court applies today, and this surprising reinvigoration of the case-by-case approach is contrary to the principles of federalism underlying our habeas corpus jurisprudence. Procedural rules, like the substantive laws they implement, are the products of sovereignty and democratic processes. The States have weighty interests in enforcing rules that protect the integrity and uniformity of trials, even when "the reason for a rule does not clearly apply." *Staub* (Frankfurter, J., dissenting). . . . Yet [under the majority's approach], the State's sound judgment on these matters can now be overridden by a federal court, which may determine for itself, given its own understanding of the rule's purposes, whether a requirement was essential or compliance was substantial in the unique circumstances of any given case.

In response, the majority disavowed any reliance on *Henry* and faulted the dissent for its "vigorous attack on an imaginary opinion." The majority saw its decision as a straightforward application of precedent: "We chart no new course.... If the dissent's shrill prediction that today's decision will disrupt our federal system were accurate, we would have seen clear signals of such disruption in the 11 years since *Osborne*." In a footnote, the majority acknowledged that *Henry* has been called "radical," but "not for pursuing an 'as applied' approach, as the dissent states." The questionable aspect of *Henry*, according to the majority, was its suggestion "that the failure to comply with an anterior procedure was cured by compliance with some subsequent procedure." This case, the majority said, involved "[n]othing of the sort."

Is the Court persuasive in saying that the default in *Lee* was different in kind from the one involved in *Henry*? Does *Lee* signal a major change, obligating the Court to "comb through the full transcript and trial record, searching for ways in which the defendant might have substantially complied with the essential requirements of an otherwise broken rule"? *Lee* (Kennedy, J., dissenting). Or does the scarcity of cases like *Lee* and the unique combination of factors on which the Court relied suggest that it is a one-off, unlikely to have a major influence?

Note: Discretionary State Procedural Rules

The opinion in *James v. Kentucky* appears to say that state procedural default will serve as an adequate state ground only when the state procedural rule is not only "firmly established" but also "regularly followed." But many state procedural rules incorporate an element of discretion. How does the *James* standard apply when a state court invokes a discretionary rule in declining to consider a federal claim? This Note considers three Supreme Court decisions that shed light on that question.

A. *Jimmy Swaggart Ministries*

One of the last cases to come to the Supreme Court under the mandatory jurisdiction was *Jimmy Swaggart Ministries v. Board of Equalization of California*, 493 U.S. 378 (1990). The appellant Ministries raised several constitutional challenges to a state law that imposed a generally applicable sales and use tax on the distribution of religious materials by a religious organization. The Court rejected the Ministries' argument based on the Religion Clauses of the First Amendment, but it declined to consider the Ministries' challenge based on lack of "nexus." The Court explained:

> Appellant also contends that the State's imposition of use tax liability on it violates the Commerce and Due Process Clauses because, as an out-of-state distributor, it had an insufficient "nexus" to the State. We decline to reach the merits of this claim, however, because the courts below ruled that the claim was procedurally barred.
>
> California law provides that an administrative claim for a tax refund "shall state the specific grounds upon which the claim is founded," and that [suit may] thereafter be brought only "on the grounds set forth in the claim." ...

The record in this case makes clear that appellant, in its refund claim before the Board, failed even to cite the Commerce Clause or the Due Process Clause, much less articulate legal arguments contesting the nexus issue. . . . Accordingly, both the trial court and the Court of Appeal declined to rule on the nexus issue . . . . This unambiguous application of state procedural law makes it unnecessary for us to review the asserted claim.

Appellant nevertheless urges that the state procedural ground relied upon by the courts below is inadequate because the procedural rule is not "'strictly or regularly followed.'" *Hathorn v. Lovorn*, 457 U.S. 255 (1982). Appellant asserts that state courts in California retain the authority to hear claims "involving important questions of public policy" notwithstanding the parties' failure to raise those claims before an administrative agency. [Appellant cited California cases from 1978 and 1986.] Appellant observes, for example, that although the Court of Appeal in this case found appellant's nexus claim to be procedurally barred, it ignored the procedural bar and ruled on the merits of appellant's Ninth and Tenth Amendment arguments, even though those arguments were likewise not raised in appellant's refund claim.

The Court of Appeal, however, specifically rejected appellant's claim that the nexus issue raised "important questions of public policy," noting that the issue instead "raised factual questions, the determination of which is not a matter of 'public policy' but a matter of evidence." Even if the Court of Appeal erred as a matter of state law in declining to rule on appellant's nexus claim, appellant has failed to substantiate any claim that the California courts in general apply this exception in an irregular, arbitrary, or inconsistent manner. Accordingly, we conclude that appellant's Commerce Clause and Due Process Clause argument is not properly before us.

Although the Court does not cite *James v. Kentucky*, it does acknowledge other cases stating that a state ground is not adequate unless the procedural rule is "regularly followed." Does the Court say that the state rule satisfies the *James* standard? If not, is there justification for treating the cases differently?

B. The habeas cases

Although the adequate state ground doctrine was initially developed in cases involving Supreme Court review of state-court decisions, it also applies in a second context—in determining whether federal district courts should address the federal constitutional claims of state prisoners in habeas corpus actions. (See Chapter 15.) In two recent habeas cases, the Court considered whether a discretionary state rule could serve as an adequate state ground.

The first of the cases was *Beard v. Kindler*, 558 U.S. 53 (2009). Kindler, convicted of capital murder, escaped from prison while his post-verdict motions were pending. The state supreme court held that his escape forfeited all claims challenging his conviction and sentence that he might once have been entitled to bring. On federal habeas, the Third Circuit held that the state's fugitive forfeiture rule was not an adequate state ground because the state courts "had discretion to hear an appeal filed by a fugitive who had been returned to custody before an appeal was initiated or dismissed."

The Supreme Court granted certiorari to consider the question "whether discretionary procedural rulings are automatically inadequate to bar federal court review on habeas." The Court unanimously held that the answer was "No." Chief Justice Roberts, writing for the Court, began by quoting the familiar language from *James v. Kentucky*. He continued:

> We hold that a discretionary state procedural rule can serve as an adequate ground to bar federal habeas review. Nothing inherent in such a rule renders it inadequate for purposes of the adequate state ground doctrine. To the contrary, a discretionary rule can be "firmly established" and "regularly followed"— even if the appropriate exercise of discretion may permit consideration of a federal claim in some cases but not others.
>
> A contrary holding would pose an unnecessary dilemma for the States: States could preserve flexibility by granting courts discretion to excuse procedural errors, but only at the cost of undermining the finality of state court judgments. Or States could preserve the finality of their judgments by withholding such discretion, but only at the cost of precluding any flexibility in applying the rules.

As the Court noted in *Kindler*, the procedural default in that case was "hardly typical." Two years later, in *Walker v. Martin*, 562 U.S. 307 (2011), the Court considered the doctrine in a more representative setting. Under California practice, a state prisoner may be barred from collaterally attacking his conviction when he has "substantially delayed" filing his habeas petition. The Ninth Circuit held that this standard was not "sufficiently clear and certain to be an adequate state bar." The Supreme Court disagreed. Justice Ginsburg, writing for a unanimous Court, explained:

> California's time rule, although discretionary, meets the "firmly established" criterion, as *Kindler* comprehended that requirement. The California Supreme Court ... framed the timeliness requirement ... in a trilogy of cases [that] instruct habeas petitioners to "allege with specificity" the absence of substantial delay, good cause for delay, or eligibility for one of four exceptions to the time bar. . . .
>
> The Ninth Circuit concluded that California's time bar is not consistently applied because outcomes under the rule vary from case to case. For example, in [one case] a one-year delay was found substantial, while in [another], a delay of 14 months was determined to be insubstantial. [But a] discretionary rule ought not be disregarded automatically upon a showing of seeming inconsistencies. Discretion enables a court to home in on case-specific considerations and to avoid the harsh results that sometimes attend consistent application of an unyielding rule. [Moreover, closer inspection] may reveal that "seeming inconsistencies ... are not necessarily arbitrary or irrational."

If the Court had taken this approach in *James v. Kentucky*, might the result have been different?

Problem: A "Lynch Mob Atmosphere?"

William Bonnie was convicted of attempted murder in Oceana state court for shooting and gravely wounding an off-duty police officer. Under Oceana law, the jury fixes the sentence in all felony cases, and Bonnie was sentenced to life imprisonment.

Bonnie appealed to the Oceana Supreme Court. He raised six assignments of error, five of which were based on state law. Point 6 asserted that the totality of circumstances surrounding the sentencing phase of the proceedings violated Bonnie's Sixth Amendment right to a fair trial. Specifically, Bonnie alleged that the trial was conducted in a "lynch mob atmosphere," because numerous uniformed police officers were conspicuously present in the courtroom throughout the trial, and because the prosecutor, in his closing remarks to the jury during the sentencing phase, directed the jury's attention to the officers.

The Oceana Supreme Court found no merit in any of the state-law arguments. With respect to the Sixth Amendment argument, the court said:

> Rule 52(a) of the Oceana Rules of Appellate Procedure requires that to preserve a complaint for appellate review, the party must have presented to the trial court "a timely request, objection, or motion, stating the specific grounds for the ruling desired. . . ." Defendant failed to object either to the presence of the officers or to the prosecutor's remarks. We therefore do not consider his "fair trial" argument. The conviction and sentence are affirmed.

Bonnie has now filed a petition for certiorari in the United States Supreme Court, asserting the Sixth Amendment fair trial claim. The state argues that the judgment rests on an adequate independent state procedural ground. It cites more than a dozen cases from the last 10 years in which the Oceana Supreme Court has refused to consider a criminal defendant's argument on appeal because of failure to comply with Rule 52(a).

In his reply brief, Bonnie acknowledges that the Oceana Supreme Court has invoked Rule 52(a) in numerous cases, but he also points to *State v. Harkins* (2000), *State v. Miller* (2007), and *State v. Langham* (2015). In *Harkins*, the defendant argued that certain expert testimony was improperly admitted. The Oceana Supreme Court said:

> There was no objection to Dr. Grandison's testimony, and therefore nothing was preserved for review. And even if the matter were properly before us, we see no reversible error. [This was followed by one paragraph of discussion.]

In *Miller*, the defendant argued that the trial court abused its discretion by allowing the state to call a witness without giving proper notice. The Oceana Supreme Court said:

> Appellant did not make an objection when the witness was called to testify. His complaint is therefore not properly preserved for review. However, in the interest of justice and due to the severity of the attending punishment

we address appellant's claim. We find it to be without merit. [This was followed by several paragraphs of discussion.]

Langham is similar to *Miller.*

Does the state-court judgment in Bonnie's case rest on an adequate state-law ground that will bar Supreme Court review?

Note: Laying the Groundwork for Supreme Court Review

In each of the cases in this subsection, the state court ruled that the petitioner's federal claim was procedurally barred because of failure to present it in accordance with state rules. What happens if the petitioner seeks Supreme Court review of a federal claim that was never presented to the state courts at all? You would probably think that Supreme Court review would be precluded, and you would be right.

In *Howell v. Mississippi*, 543 U.S. 440 (2005), the certiorari petition presented a claim that the Mississippi courts had violated petitioner's rights under the Eighth and Fourteenth Amendments to the United States Constitution by refusing to require a jury instruction about a lesser included offense in his capital case. The petition relied on the Supreme Court's decision in *Beck v. Alabama*, 447 U.S. 625 (1980). But *Howell* had not presented that claim to the Mississippi Supreme Court, "which unsurprisingly did not address it."

In an ordinary case, the Supreme Court probably would have denied certiorari without worrying about whether the case was properly before it. But Howell had been sentenced to death. The Court granted his petition — and asked the parties to address the following additional question: "Was petitioner's federal constitutional claim properly raised before the Mississippi Supreme Court for purposes of 28 U.S.C. § 1257?" After reviewing the briefing in the state court, the Supreme Court concluded that the answer was "No."

The Court noted that 28 U.S.C. § 1257 itself authorizes review of state-court judgments only "where any . . . right . . . is *specially set up or claimed* under the Constitution or the treaties or statutes of . . . the United States." (Emphasis by the Court.) Howell offered two arguments in support of his assertion that he had "specially set up or claimed" his rights under the federal Constitution.

First, he argued that he presented his federal claim by citing a state-court decision, which cited (among other cases) an earlier state-court decision, which in turn cited *Beck*, but only by way of acknowledging that Mississippi's general rule requiring lesser-included-offense instructions "takes on constitutional proportions" in capital cases. The Supreme Court said that this "daisy chain" was "too lengthy to meet this Court's standards for proper presentation of a federal claim." Quoting from a decision in the context of federal habeas corpus (see Chapter 15), the Court said:

> A litigant wishing to raise a federal issue can easily indicate the federal law basis for his claim in a state-court petition or brief . . . by citing in conjunction with the claim the federal source of law on which he relies or a case

deciding such a claim on federal grounds, or by simply labeling the claim "federal."

Howell had not done any of those things.

Howell also argued that he raised his federal claim by implication because the state-law rule on which he relied was "identical" (or "virtually identical") to the constitutional rule articulated in *Beck*. The Supreme Court responded: "Assuming, without deciding, that identical standards might overcome a petitioner's failure to identify his claim as federal, Mississippi's rule regarding lesser-included-offense instructions is not identical to *Beck*— or at least not identical to the Mississippi Supreme Court's interpretation of *Beck*."

If federal law offers any possibility of relief for a state-court litigant, is there any justification for counsel's failure to cite it? Consider the Problem that follows.

Problem: "Inadequate" Assistance of Counsel

Harry Graham pled guilty in West Fremont state court to one count of rape and one count of sex abuse. He was sentenced to 15 years imprisonment on the rape count and two years imprisonment on the sex abuse count, to be served consecutively. He appealed to the state intermediate court, asserting (among other claims) a denial of his right to counsel under the state and federal constitutions. The state intermediate court affirmed. Graham then appealed to the state supreme court. His brief claimed a violation of the right to counsel in the following language:

> Failure of trial defense counsel to specifically advise a defendant that a letter he proposes to submit to the Court as a part of the sentencing process contains admissions of facts constituting irrefutable evidence of aggravating factors justifying an upward departure sentence is not adequate assistance of counsel, within the meaning of Article 1, Section 11 of the West Fremont Constitution. See *People v. Garland*, 441 W.F. 289 (1995); *People v. Stannard*, 456 W.F. 302 (2000).

The West Fremont Supreme Court affirmed in a per curiam order that stated in its entirety: "The conviction is affirmed. The defendant's arguments were adequately answered by the court of appeals opinion."

Graham has now filed a petition for certiorari in the United States Supreme Court, asserting a claim of ineffective assistance of counsel under the Sixth Amendment. The state moves to dismiss the petition, arguing that Graham did not raise the Sixth Amendment claim in the West Fremont Supreme Court. The state notes that the term usually employed by West Fremont courts in applying the right to counsel provision of the West Fremont Constitution is "*inadequate* assistance of counsel," not "*ineffective* assistance." The state acknowledges that the *Garland* and *Stannard* decisions cited in Graham's state supreme court brief analyzed right-to-counsel claims under both the state and the federal constitution, but it points out that the brief itself made no mention of the Sixth Amendment and did not cite any federal cases.

Did Graham properly raise his federal constitutional claim in the West Fremont Supreme Court for purposes of 28 U.S.C. § 1257?

[4] Independence of State Grounds and the Rule of *Michigan v. Long*

In *Anderson v. Brand* and *James v. Kentucky*, the state court ruled *against* the litigant claiming under federal law, and the question was whether a purported non-federal ground was *adequate* to support the judgment. That is the posture in which the adequate state ground doctrine was litigated for most of the twentieth century. (*Fox Film* was an exception.) Starting in the 1970s, the Supreme Court increasingly confronted cases in which the state court had ruled *in favor of* the litigant asserting a federal right. In these cases, when the doctrine is invoked, the jurisdiction typically depends on whether the asserted non-federal ground is *independent*.

Consider, for example, the Court's decision in *Delaware v. Prouse*, 440 U.S. 648 (1979). After being convicted on drug charges, Prouse appealed on the ground that the "spot check" protective search of a vehicle he was driving was unlawful, and key evidence therefore should have been excluded. He argued that the search was "unreasonable" under both the Fourth Amendment to the United States Constitution and an analogous provision of the Delaware Constitution. The state supreme court held that the search violated the Fourth Amendment, but its opinion also contained two references to the state constitution (one in a footnote, the other in the conclusion of the opinion). When the State filed a petition for certiorari seeking United States Supreme Court review, Prouse contended that the Court lacked jurisdiction because the state constitution provided an adequate state ground. The Court disagreed:

> Because the Delaware Supreme Court held that the stop at issue not only violated the Federal Constitution but also was impermissible under Art. I, § 6, of the Delaware Constitution, it is urged that the judgment below was based on an independent and adequate state ground and that we therefore have no jurisdiction in this case. *Fox Film Corp. v. Muller.* . . . Based on our reading of the opinion, however, we are satisfied that even if the State Constitution would have provided an adequate basis for the judgment, the Delaware Supreme Court did not intend to rest its decision independently on the State Constitution and that we have jurisdiction of this case.

> As we understand the opinion below, Art. I, § 6, of the Delaware Constitution will automatically be interpreted at least as broadly as the Fourth Amendment; that is, every police practice authoritatively determined to be contrary to the Fourth and Fourteenth Amendments will, without further analysis, be held to be contrary to Art. I, § 6. This approach, which is consistent with previous opinions of the Delaware Supreme Court, was followed in this case. The court analyzed the various decisions interpreting the Federal Constitution, concluded that the Fourth Amendment foreclosed spot checks of automobiles, and summarily held that the State Constitution was

therefore also infringed. This is one of those cases where "at the very least, the [state] court felt compelled by what it understood to be federal constitutional considerations to construe . . . its own law in the manner it did." *Zacchini v. Scripps-Howard Broadcasting Co.*, 433 U.S. 562 (1977). Had state law not been mentioned at all, there would be no question about our jurisdiction, even though the State Constitution might have provided an independent and adequate state ground. The same result should follow here where the state constitutional holding depended upon the state court's view of the reach of the Fourth and Fourteenth Amendments. If the state court misapprehended federal law, "[i]t should be freed to decide . . . these suits according to its own local law." *Missouri ex rel. Southern R. Co. v. Mayfield*, 340 U.S. 1 (1950).

Over time, the Court confronted an increasing number of cases like *Prouse*, in which an ambiguous state-court opinion did not explicitly distinguish between federal and state-law grounds, leaving the Court's jurisdiction unclear. In *Michigan v. Long*, the Court adopted a new approach for dealing with that situation.

Michigan v. Long

Supreme Court of the United States, 1983.

463 U.S. 1032.

Justice O'Connor delivered the opinion of the Court.

In *Terry v. Ohio*, 392 U.S. 1 (1968), we upheld the validity of a protective search for weapons in the absence of probable cause to arrest because it is unreasonable to deny a police officer the right "to neutralize the threat of physical harm," when he possesses an articulable suspicion that an individual is armed and dangerous. We did not, however, expressly address whether such a protective search for weapons could extend to an area beyond the person in the absence of probable cause to arrest. . . .

I

[David Long was convicted for possession of marijuana found by police in the passenger compartment and trunk of the automobile that he was driving. The police searched the passenger compartment after a *Terry* stop because they had reason to believe that the vehicle contained weapons potentially dangerous to the officers. The Michigan Supreme Court reversed the conviction. It held that "the sole justification of the *Terry* search, protection of the police officers and others nearby, cannot justify the search in this case." The marijuana found in Long's trunk was considered by the court below to be the "fruit" of the illegal search of the interior, and was also suppressed.]

We granted certiorari in this case to consider the important question of the authority of a police officer to protect himself by conducting a *Terry*-type search of the passenger compartment of a motor vehicle during the lawful investigatory stop of the occupant of the vehicle.

II

Before reaching the merits, we must consider Long's argument that we are without jurisdiction to decide this case because the decision below rests on an adequate and independent state ground. The court below referred twice to the state constitution in its opinion, but otherwise relied exclusively on federal law.

[In a footnote, the Court explained:] On the first occasion, the [Michigan] court merely cited in a footnote both the state and federal constitutions. On the second occasion, at the conclusion of the opinion, the court stated: "We hold, therefore, that the deputies' search of the vehicle was proscribed by the Fourth Amendment to the United States Constitution and art. 1, § 11 of the Michigan Constitution."

Long argues that the Michigan courts have provided greater protection from searches and seizures under the state constitution than is afforded under the Fourth Amendment, and the references to the state constitution therefore establish an adequate and independent ground for the decision below.

It is, of course, "incumbent upon this Court . . . to ascertain for itself . . . whether the asserted non-federal ground independently and adequately supports the judgment." Although we have announced a number of principles in order to help us determine whether various forms of references to state law constitute adequate and independent state grounds,[4] we openly admit that we have thus far not developed a satisfying and consistent approach for resolving this vexing issue. In some instances, we have taken the strict view that if the ground of decision was at all unclear, we would dismiss the case. See, *e.g.*, *Lynch v. New York*, 293 U.S. 52 (1934). In other instances, we have vacated, see, *e.g.*, *Minnesota v. National Tea Co.*, 309 U.S. 551 (1940), or continued a case, see, *e.g.*, *Herb v. Pitcairn*, 324 U.S. 117 (1945), in order to obtain clarification about the nature of a state court decision. In more recent cases, we have ourselves examined state law to determine whether state courts have used federal law to guide their application of state law or to provide the actual basis for the decision that was reached. . . .

This *ad hoc* method of dealing with cases that involve possible adequate and independent state grounds is antithetical to the doctrinal consistency that is required when sensitive issues of federal-state relations are involved. Moreover, none of the various methods of disposition that we have employed thus far recommends itself as the preferred method that we should apply to the exclusion of others, and we therefore

---

4. For example, we have long recognized that "where the judgment of a state court rests upon two grounds, one of which is federal and the other non-federal in character, our jurisdiction fails if the non-federal ground is independent of the federal ground and adequate to support the judgment." *Fox Film Corp. v. Muller.* We may review a state case decided on a federal ground even if it is clear that there was an available state ground for decision on which the state court could properly have relied. *Beecher v. Alabama*, 389 U.S. 35 (1967). Also, if, in our view, the state court "'felt compelled by what it understood to be federal constitutional considerations to construe . . . its own law in the manner that it did,'" then we will not treat a normally adequate state ground as independent, and there will be no question about our jurisdiction. *Delaware v. Prouse.* Finally, "where the non-federal ground is so interwoven with the [federal ground] as not to be an independent matter, or is not of sufficient breadth to sustain the judgment without any decision of the other, our jurisdiction is plain." *Enterprise Irrigation District v. Farmers Mutual Canal Company*, 243 U.S. 157 (1917).

determine that it is appropriate to reexamine our treatment of this jurisdictional issue in order to achieve the consistency that is necessary.

The process of examining state law is unsatisfactory because it requires us to interpret state laws with which we are generally unfamiliar, and which often, as in this case, have not been discussed at length by the parties. Vacation and continuance for clarification have also been unsatisfactory both because of the delay and decrease in efficiency of judicial administration, and, more important, because these methods of disposition place significant burdens on state courts to demonstrate the presence or absence of our jurisdiction. Finally, outright dismissal of cases is clearly not a panacea because it cannot be doubted that there is an important need for uniformity in federal law, and that this need goes unsatisfied when we fail to review an opinion that rests primarily upon federal grounds and where the *independence* of an alleged state ground is not apparent from the four corners of the opinion. We have long recognized that dismissal is inappropriate "where there is strong indication . . . that the federal constitution as judicially construed controlled the decision below." *National Tea Co.*

Respect for the independence of state courts, as well as avoidance of rendering advisory opinions, have been the cornerstones of this Court's refusal to decide cases where there is an adequate and independent state ground. It is precisely because of this respect for state courts, and this desire to avoid advisory opinions, that we do not wish to continue to decide issues of state law that go beyond the opinion that we review, or to require state courts to reconsider cases to clarify the grounds of their decisions. Accordingly, when, as in this case, a state court decision fairly appears to rest primarily on federal law, or to be interwoven with the federal law, and when the adequacy and independence of any possible state law ground is not clear from the face of the opinion, we will accept as the most reasonable explanation that the state court decided the case the way it did because it believed that federal law required it to do so.

If a state court chooses merely to rely on federal precedents as it would on the precedents of all other jurisdictions, then it need only make clear by a plain statement in its judgment or opinion that the federal cases are being used only for the purpose of guidance, and do not themselves compel the result that the court has reached. In this way, both justice and judicial administration will be greatly improved. If the state court decision indicates clearly and expressly that it is alternatively based on bona fide separate, adequate, and independent grounds, we, of course, will not undertake to review the decision.

This approach obviates in most instances the need to examine state law in order to decide the nature of the state court decision, and will at the same time avoid the danger of our rendering advisory opinions.[6] It also avoids the unsatisfactory and intrusive practice of requiring state courts to clarify their decisions to the satisfaction of this Court. We believe that such an approach will provide state judges with a clearer

---

6. There may be certain circumstances in which clarification is necessary or desirable, and we will not be foreclosed from taking the appropriate action.

opportunity to develop state jurisprudence unimpeded by federal interference, and yet will preserve the integrity of federal law. . . .

The principle that we will not review judgments of state courts that rest on adequate and independent state grounds is based, in part, on "the limitations of our own jurisdiction." *Herb v. Pitcairn.*[7] The jurisdictional concern is that we not "render an advisory opinion, and if the same judgment would be rendered by the state court after we corrected its views of federal laws, our review could amount to nothing more than an advisory opinion." Our requirement of a "plain statement" that a decision rests upon adequate and independent state grounds does not in any way authorize the rendering of advisory opinions. Rather, in determining, as we must, whether we have jurisdiction to review a case that is alleged to rest on adequate and independent state grounds, we merely assume that there are no such grounds when it is not clear from the opinion itself that the state court relied upon an adequate and independent state ground and when it fairly appears that the state court rested its decision primarily on federal law.[8]

Our review of the decision below under this framework leaves us unconvinced that it rests upon an independent state ground. Apart from its two citations to the state constitution, the court below relied *exclusively* on its understanding of *Terry* and other federal cases. Not a single state case was cited to support the state court's holding that the search of the passenger compartment was unconstitutional. Indeed, the court declared that the search in this case was unconstitutional because "[t]he Court of Appeals erroneously applied the principles of *Terry v. Ohio* . . . to the search of the interior of the vehicle in this case." The references to the state constitution in no way indicate that the decision below rested on grounds in any way *independent* from the state court's interpretation of federal law. Even if we accept that the Michigan constitution has been interpreted to provide independent protection for certain rights also secured under the Fourth Amendment, it fairly appears in this case that the Michigan Supreme Court rested its decision primarily on federal law.

Rather than dismissing the case, or requiring that the state court reconsider its decision on our behalf solely because of a mere possibility that an adequate and independent ground supports the judgment, we find that we have jurisdiction in the

---

7. In *Herb v. Pitcairn*, the Court also wrote that it was desirable that state courts "be asked rather than told what they have intended." It is clear that we have already departed from that view in those cases in which we have examined state law to determine whether a particular result was guided or compelled by federal law. Our decision today departs further from *Herb* insofar as we disfavor further requests to state courts for clarification, and we require a clear and express statement that a decision rests on adequate and independent state grounds. However, the "plain statement" rule protects the integrity of state courts for the reasons discussed above. The preference for clarification expressed in *Herb* has failed to be a completely satisfactory means of protecting the state and federal interests that are involved.

8. It is not unusual for us to employ certain presumptions in deciding jurisdictional issues. For instance, although the petitioner bears the burden of establishing our jurisdiction, we have held that the party who alleges that a controversy before us has become moot has the "heavy burden" of establishing that we lack jurisdiction. *County of Los Angeles v. Davis*, 440 U.S. 625 (1979). That is, we presume in those circumstances that we have jurisdiction until some party establishes that we do not for reasons of mootness. . . .

absence of a plain statement that the decision below rested on an adequate and independent state ground. It appears to us that the state court "felt compelled by what it understood to be federal constitutional considerations to construe . . . its own law in the manner it did."[10]

III

[The Court held that "the protective search of the passenger compartment was reasonable under the principles articulated in *Terry* and other decisions of this Court." It remanded the case to the Michigan Supreme Court to determine whether the search of the trunk was permissible as a valid inventory search or under other Fourth Amendment doctrines.]

JUSTICE BLACKMUN, concurring in part and concurring in the judgment.

. . . While I am satisfied that the Court has jurisdiction in this particular case, I do not join the Court, in Part II of its opinion, in fashioning a new presumption of jurisdiction over cases coming here from state courts. Although I agree with the Court that uniformity in federal criminal law is desirable, I see little efficiency and an increased danger of advisory opinions in the Court's new approach.

JUSTICE BRENNAN, with whom Justice Marshall joins, dissenting.

[Justice Brennan, joined by Justice Marshall, disagreed with the Court's holding on the Fourth Amendment issue, but he agreed that the Court had jurisdiction to decide the case. His dissent cited footnote 10 of the Court's opinion.]

JUSTICE STEVENS, dissenting.

The jurisprudential questions presented in this case are far more important than the question whether the Michigan police officer's search of respondent's car violated the Fourth Amendment. The case raises profoundly significant questions concerning the relationship between two sovereigns — the State of Michigan and the United States of America.

The Supreme Court of the State of Michigan expressly held "that the deputies' search of the vehicle was proscribed by the Fourth Amendment of the United States Constitution and *art. 1, § 11 of the Michigan Constitution.*" (Emphasis added). The state law ground is clearly adequate to support the judgment, but the question whether it is independent of the Michigan Supreme Court's understanding of federal law is

---

10. There is nothing unfair about requiring a plain statement of an independent state ground in this case. Even if we were to rest our decision on an evaluation of the state law relevant to Long's claim, as we have sometimes done in the past, our understanding of Michigan law would also result in our finding that we have jurisdiction to decide this case. Under state search and seizure law, a "higher standard" is imposed under art. 1, § 11 of the 1963 Michigan Constitution. See *People v. Secrest*, 321 N.W.2d 368 (Mich. 1982). If, however, the item seized is, *inter alia*, a "narcotic drug . . . seized by a peace officer outside the curtilage of any dwelling house in this state," art. 1, § 11 of the 1963 Michigan Constitution, then the seizure is governed by a standard identical to that imposed by the Fourth Amendment.

. . . In the light of our holding in *Delaware v. Prouse*, that an interpretation of state law in our view compelled by federal constitutional considerations is not an independent state ground, we would have jurisdiction to decide the case.

more difficult. Four possible ways of resolving that question present themselves: (1) asking the Michigan Supreme Court directly, (2) attempting to infer from all possible sources of state law what the Michigan Supreme Court meant, (3) presuming that adequate state grounds are independent unless it clearly appears otherwise, or (4) presuming that adequate state grounds are *not* independent unless it clearly appears otherwise. This Court has, on different occasions, employed each of the first three approaches; never until today has it even hinted at the fourth. In order to "achieve the consistency that is necessary," the Court today undertakes a reexamination of all the possibilities. It rejects the first approach as inefficient and unduly burdensome for state courts, and rejects the second approach as an inappropriate expenditure of our resources. Although I find both of those decisions defensible in themselves, I cannot accept the Court's decision to choose the fourth approach over the third—to presume that adequate state grounds are intended to be dependent on federal law unless the record plainly shows otherwise. I must therefore dissent.

If we reject the intermediate approaches, we are left with a choice between two presumptions: one in favor of our taking jurisdiction, and one against it. Historically, the latter presumption has always prevailed. The rule, as succinctly stated in *Lynch v. New York*, 293 U.S. 52 (1934), was as follows:

> Where the judgment of the state court rests on two grounds, one involving a federal question and the other not, or if it does not appear upon which of two grounds the judgment was based, and the ground independent of a federal question is sufficient in itself to sustain it, this Court will not take jurisdiction. [Citing 5 cases].

The Court today points out that in several cases we have weakened the traditional presumption by using the other two intermediate approaches identified above. Since those two approaches are now to be rejected, however, I would think that *stare decisis* would call for a return to historical principle. Instead, the Court seems to conclude that because some precedents are to be rejected, we must overrule them all.

Even if I agreed with the Court that we are free to consider as a fresh proposition whether we may take presumptive jurisdiction over the decisions of sovereign states, I could not agree that an expansive attitude makes good sense. It appears to be common ground that any rule we adopt should show "respect for state courts, and [a] desire to avoid advisory opinions." And I am confident that all members of this Court agree that there is a vital interest in the sound management of scarce federal judicial resources. All of those policies counsel against the exercise of federal jurisdiction. They are fortified by my belief that a policy of judicial restraint—one that allows other decisional bodies to have the last word in legal interpretation until it is truly necessary for this Court to intervene—enables this Court to make its most effective contribution to our federal system of government.

The nature of the case before us hardly compels a departure from tradition. These are not cases in which an American citizen has been deprived of a right secured by the United States Constitution or a federal statute. Rather, they are cases in which a state court has upheld a citizen's assertion of a right, finding the citizen to be protected under both federal and state law. The complaining party is an officer of the state itself, who asks us to rule that the state court interpreted federal rights too broadly and "overprotected" the citizen.

Such cases should not be of inherent concern to this Court. The reason may be illuminated by assuming that the events underlying this case had arisen in another country, perhaps the Republic of Finland. If the Finnish police had arrested a Finnish citizen for possession of marijuana, and the Finnish courts had turned him loose, no American would have standing to object. If instead they had arrested an American citizen and acquitted him, we might have been concerned about the arrest but we surely could not have complained about the acquittal, even if the Finnish Court had based its decision on its understanding of the United States Constitution. That would be true even if we had a treaty with Finland requiring it to respect the rights of American citizens under the United States Constitution. We would only be motivated to intervene if an American citizen were unfairly arrested, tried, and convicted by the foreign tribunal.

In this case the State of Michigan has arrested one of its citizens and the Michigan Supreme Court has decided to turn him loose. The respondent is a United States citizen as well as a Michigan citizen, but since there is no claim that he has been mistreated by the State of Michigan, the final outcome of the state processes offended no federal interest whatever. Michigan simply provided greater protection to one of its citizens than some other State might provide or, indeed, than this Court might require throughout the country.

I believe that in reviewing the decisions of state courts, the primary role of this Court is to make sure that persons who seek to *vindicate* federal rights have been fairly heard. That belief resonates with statements in many of our prior cases. . . .

Until recently we had virtually no interest in cases of this type. Thirty years ago, this Court reviewed only one. *Nevada v. Stacher*, 346 U.S. 907 (1953). Indeed, that appears to have been the only case during the entire 1952 Term in which a state even sought review of a decision by its own judiciary. Fifteen years ago, we did not review any such cases, although the total number of requests had mounted to three. Some time during the past decade, perhaps about the time of the 5-to-4 decision in *Zacchini v. Scripps-Howard Broadcasting Co.*, 433 U.S. 562 (1977), our priorities shifted. The result is a docket swollen with requests by states to reverse judgments that their courts have rendered in favor of their citizens.[3] I am confident that a future Court will recognize the error of this allocation of resources. When that day comes, I think it likely that the Court will also reconsider the propriety of today's expansion of our jurisdiction.

The Court offers only one reason for asserting authority over cases such as the one presented today: "an important need for uniformity in federal law [that] goes

---

3. This year, we devoted argument time to [12 other cases] as well as this case. And a cursory survey of the United States Law Week index reveals that so far this Term at least 80 petitions for certiorari to state courts were filed by the states themselves.

unsatisfied when we fail to review an opinion that rests primarily upon federal grounds and where the independence of an alleged state ground is not apparent from the four corners of the opinion." Of course, the supposed need to "review an opinion" clashes directly with our oft-repeated reminder that "our power is to correct wrong judgments, not to revise opinions." *Herb v. Pitcairn*. The clash is not merely one of form: the "need for uniformity in federal law" is truly an ungovernable engine. That same need is no less present when it is perfectly clear that a state ground is both independent and adequate. In fact, it is equally present if a state prosecutor announces that he believes a certain policy of nonenforcement is commanded by federal law. Yet we have never claimed jurisdiction to correct such errors, no matter how egregious they may be, and no matter how much they may thwart the desires of the state electorate. We do not sit to expound our understanding of the Constitution to interested listeners in the legal community; we sit to resolve disputes. If it is not apparent that our views would affect the outcome of a particular case, we cannot presume to interfere.

Finally, I am thoroughly baffled by the Court's suggestion that it must stretch its jurisdiction and reverse the judgment of the Michigan Supreme Court in order to show "[r]espect for the independence of state courts." Would we show respect for the Republic of Finland by convening a special sitting for the sole purpose of declaring that its decision to release an American citizen was based upon a misunderstanding of American law?

I respectfully dissent.

Note: "Over-Reading" by State Courts

1. Justice Stevens, dissenting alone in *Michigan v. Long*, does not simply dispute the Court's new approach to ambiguous state-court decisions. He appears to argue that the Court should not review state-court decisions that uphold federal claims even when those decisions rest squarely and solely on the Federal Constitution. The Court responds to this point in a footnote:

> In dissent, Justice Stevens proposes the novel view that this Court should never review a state court decision unless the Court wishes to vindicate a federal right that has been endangered. The rationale of the dissent is not restricted to cases where the decision is arguably supported by adequate and independent state grounds. Rather, Justice Stevens appears to believe that even if the decision below rests exclusively on federal grounds, this Court should not review the decision as long as there is no federal right that is endangered.

> The state courts handle the vast bulk of all criminal litigation in this country. In 1982, more than twelve million criminal actions (excluding juvenile and traffic charges) were filed in the 50 state court systems and the District of Columbia. By comparison, approximately 32,700 criminal suits were filed in federal courts during that same year. The state courts are required to apply federal constitutional standards, and they necessarily create a considerable body of "federal law" in the process. It is not surprising that this Court has become more interested in the application and development of federal law

by state courts in the light of the recent significant expansion of federally created standards that we have imposed on the States.

Is this the best answer to Justice Stevens's point? Is the question solely a matter of policy for the Court to decide?

2. Professor Preble Stolz used the term "over-reading" to describe cases in which state courts "invalidate state statutes or official action on federal grounds when the Supreme Court itself would not do so." Writing before the Supreme Court's docket began to be "swollen with requests by states to reverse judgments that their courts have rendered in favor of their citizens," he said:

> By definition, no federal interest is damaged by such a decision, but it does needlessly restrict state power and thus damages the values inherent in a federalism which presupposes that state governments should be free to act as they wish within constitutional boundaries. When a state court draws those boundaries too narrowly it impinges upon the freedom of choice of co-ordinate branches of state government (typically the legislature); although the injury may be regarded as self-inflicted, it is nonetheless real.

Preble Stolz, *Federal Review of State Court Decisions of Federal Questions: The Need for Additional Appellate Capacity*, 64 CAL. L. REV. 943, 971 (1976). Why should the Supreme Court be concerned about a "self-inflicted" harm?

3. Justice Stevens says that the flood of petitions filed by states came about because "our priorities shifted" sometime during the 1970s. Was the Supreme Court alone responsible for the change in the makeup of the docket that Justice Stevens describes?

4. Debate about "over-reading" cases continues. In *Kansas v. Carr*, 136 S. Ct. 633 (2016), the Kansas Supreme Court vacated two death sentences on Eighth Amendment grounds. When the State sought certiorari, the prisoners urged that the judgments also rested on an adequate state constitutional ground. The Court disagreed and reversed, holding that the state supreme court's opinion "leaves no room for doubt that it was relying on the Federal Constitution."

Justice Sotomayor cast the lone dissenting vote, echoing Justice Stevens' concerns in *Long*:

> I respectfully dissent because I do not believe these cases should ever have been reviewed by the Supreme Court. I see no reason to intervene in cases like these — and plenty of reasons not to. Kansas has not violated any federal constitutional right. If anything, the State has overprotected its citizens based on its interpretation of state and federal law. . . .
>
> Even where a state court has wrongly decided an "important question of federal law," Sup. Ct. Rule 10, we often decline to grant certiorari, instead reserving such grants for instances where the benefits of hearing a case outweigh the costs of so doing. My colleagues and predecessors have effectively set forth many of the costs of granting certiorari in cases where state courts grant relief to criminal defendants: We risk issuing opinions that, while not strictly advisory, may have little effect if a lower court is able to

reinstate its holding as a matter of state law. *Florida v. Powell*, 559 U.S. 50 (2010) (Stevens, J., dissenting). We expend resources on cases where the only concern is that a State has "overprotected" its citizens. *Long* (Stevens, J., dissenting). We intervene in an intrastate dispute between the State's executive and its judiciary rather than entrusting the State's structure of government to sort it out. *See Coleman v. Thompson*, 501 U.S. 722 (1991) (Blackmun, J., dissenting). And we lose valuable data about the best methods of protecting constitutional rights—a particular concern in cases like these, where the federal constitutional question turns on ... an empirical question best answered with evidence from many state courts. *Cf. Arizona v. Evans*, 514 U.S. 1 (1995) (Ginsburg, J., dissenting). . . .

The cases here demonstrate yet another cost of granting certiorari to correct a state court's overprotection of federal rights: In explaining that the Federal Constitution does not protect some particular right, it is natural to buttress the conclusion by explaining why that right is not very important. In so doing, the Court risks discouraging States from adopting valuable procedural protections even as a matter of their own state law. . . . State experimentation with how best to guarantee a fair trial to criminal defendants is an essential aspect of our federalism scheme. The Federal Constitution guarantees only a minimum slate of protections; States can and do provide individual rights above that constitutional floor. That role is particularly important in the criminal arena because state courts preside over many millions more criminal cases than their federal counterparts and so are more likely to identify protections important to a fair trial. . . .

Though the Court pretends that it sends back cases like this one with a clean slate, it rarely fully erases its thoughts on the virtues of the procedural protection at issue. By placing a thumb on the scale against a State adopting— even as a matter of state law—procedural protections the Constitution does not require, the Court risks turning the Federal Constitution into a ceiling, rather than a floor, for the protection of individual liberties.

Writing for the majority, Justice Scalia—in one of the last opinions he authored before his death—responded to that contention:

[T]he criticism leveled by the dissent is misdirected. It generally would have been "none of our business" had the Kansas Supreme Court vacated [these] death sentences on state-law grounds. *Kansas v. Marsh*, 548 U.S. 163 (2006) (Scalia, J., concurring). But it decidedly did not. And when the Kansas Supreme Court time and again invalidates death sentences because it says the Federal Constitution requires it, "review by this Court, far from undermining state autonomy, is the only possible way to vindicate it." *Id.* "When we correct a state court's federal errors, we return power to the State, and to its people." The state courts may experiment all they want with their own constitutions, and often do in the wake of this Court's decisions. But what a state court cannot do is experiment with our Federal Constitution and expect to elude this Court's review so long as victory goes to the criminal defendant. "Turning a blind eye" in such cases "would change the uniform 'law of the land' into a crazy quilt." And it would enable state courts to blame the unpopular death-sentence reprieve of the most horrible criminals upon the Federal Constitution when it is in fact their own doing.

Note: The Long Presumption

1. The decision in *Michigan v. Long* has been highly controversial among commentators, but it is solidly entrenched at the Supreme Court. In the 12 years after the decision was handed down, six new Justices were appointed; all but one joined an opinion reaffirming the *Long* presumption.

In *Arizona v. Evans*, 514 U.S. 1 (1995), the state supreme court held that the exclusionary rule required suppression of evidence seized under a warrant when the warrant was based on erroneous information in a computer record resulting from carelessness by a court clerk. The United States Supreme Court determined that it had jurisdiction under *Long*, and it reversed the suppression order. Justice Ginsburg, joined in dissent by Justice Stevens, argued that the writ should have been dismissed. She said that the *Long* presumption "impedes the States' ability to serve as laboratories for testing solutions to novel legal problems," and she urged the Court to abandon it. The dissent explained:

> The debate over the efficacy of an exclusionary rule reveals that deterrence is an empirical question, not a logical one. "It is one of the happy incidents of the federal system that a single courageous State may, if its citizens choose, serve as a laboratory; and try novel social and economic experiments without risk to the rest of the country." *New State Ice Co. v. Liebmann*, 285 U.S. 262 (1932) (Brandeis, J., dissenting). With that facet of our federalism in mind, this Court should select a jurisdictional presumption that encourages States to explore different means to secure respect for individual rights in modern times.
>
> Historically, state laws were the source, and state courts the arbiters, of individual rights. . . . State courts interpreting state law remain particularly well situated to enforce individual rights against the States. . . . [One reason is that this] Court is reluctant to intrude too deeply into areas traditionally regulated by the States. . . .
>
> The [*Long*] presumption is an imperfect barometer of state courts' intent. Although it is easy enough for a state court to say the requisite magic words, the court may not recognize that its opinion triggers *Long*'s plain statement requirement. . . .
>
> Application of the *Long* presumption has increased the incidence of non-dispositive United States Supreme Court determinations — instances in which state courts, on remand, have reinstated their prior judgments after clarifying their reliance on state grounds. . . . Even if these reinstatements do not render the Supreme Court's opinion technically "advisory," they do suggest that the Court unnecessarily spent its resources on cases better left, at

the time in question, to state-court solution. . . . Most critically, as this case shows, the *Long* presumption interferes prematurely with state-court endeavors to explore different solutions to new problems facing modern society.

Restoring a main rule denying jurisdiction where there is uncertainty would stop this Court from asserting authority in matters belonging, or at least appropriately left, to the States' domain. *Cf. Erie R. Co. v. Tompkins*, 304 U.S. 64 (1938).

The Court, in an opinion by Chief Justice Rehnquist joined by the other six Justices, emphatically rejected the call to overrule *Long*:

We believe that *Michigan v. Long* properly serves its purpose and should not be disturbed. Under it, state courts are absolutely free to interpret state constitutional provisions to accord greater protection to individual rights than do similar provisions of the United States Constitution. They also are free to serve as experimental laboratories, in the sense that Justice Brandeis used that term in his dissenting opinion in *New State Ice Co. v. Liebmann*. Under our decision today, the State of Arizona remains free to seek whatever solutions it chooses to problems of law enforcement posed by the advent of computerization. Indeed, it is freer to do so because it is disabused of its erroneous view of what the United States Constitution requires.

State courts, in appropriate cases, are not merely free to—they are bound to—interpret the United States Constitution. In doing so, they are *not* free from the final authority of this Court. This principle was enunciated in *Cohens v. Virginia*, and presumably Justice Ginsburg does not quarrel with it. In *Minnesota v. National Tea Co.*, 309 U.S. 551 (1940), we recognized that our authority as final arbiter of the United States Constitution could be eroded by a lack of clarity in state-court decisions.

The Court then quoted from *National Tea*:

It is fundamental that state courts be left free and unfettered by us in interpreting their state constitutions. But it is equally important that ambiguous or obscure adjudications by state courts do not stand as barriers to a determination by this Court of the validity under the federal constitution of state action. Intelligent exercise of our appellate powers compels us to ask for the elimination of the obscurities and ambiguities from the opinions in such cases. . . . For no other course assures that important federal issues, such as have been argued here, will reach this Court for adjudication; that state courts will not be the final arbiters of important issues under the federal constitution; and that we will not encroach on the constitutional jurisdiction of the states.

2. Justice Ginsburg invokes *Erie* (see Chapter 7); the Court responds by invoking *Cohens* (see Chapter 2). Is either citation apt?

3. Justice Ginsburg acknowledges that "it is easy enough for a state court to say the requisite magic words." Why do state courts continue to hand down decisions that are ambiguous?

4. A few months after *Long* was decided, the Supreme Court of New Hampshire stated in a search and seizure case: "We hereby make clear that when this court cites federal or other State court opinions in construing provisions of the New Hampshire Constitution or statutes, we rely on those precedents merely for guidance and do not consider our results bound by those decisions." *State v. Ball*, 471 A.2d 347, 352 (N.H. 1983). Is a blanket disclaimer of this kind sufficient to satisfy the "plain statement" rule of *Long* for subsequent cases?

Pennsylvania v. Labron

Supreme Court of the United States, 1996.

518 U.S. 938.

PER CURIAM.

In these two cases, the Supreme Court of Pennsylvania held that the Fourth Amendment, as applied to the States through the Fourteenth, requires police to obtain a warrant before searching an automobile unless exigent circumstances are present. Because the holdings rest on an incorrect reading of the automobile exception to the Fourth Amendment's warrant requirement, we grant the petitions for certiorari and reverse.

In *Labron*, police observed respondent Labron and others engaging in a series of drug transactions on a street in Philadelphia. The police arrested the suspects, searched the trunk of a car from which the drugs had been produced, and found bags containing cocaine. The Pennsylvania Supreme Court [held] that this evidence should be suppressed. After surveying our precedents on the automobile exception as well as some of its own decisions, the court "conclude[d] that this Commonwealth's jurisprudence of the automobile exception has long required both the existence of probable cause and the presence of exigent circumstances to justify a warrantless search." Satisfied the police had time to secure a warrant, the court held that "the warrantless search of this stationary vehicle violated constitutional guarantees."

[In *Kilgore*, the Supreme Court of Pennsylvania held that the search of a pickup truck violated the Fourth Amendment because no exigent circumstances justified the failure to obtain a warrant.]

The Supreme Court of Pennsylvania held the rule permitting warrantless searches of automobiles is limited to cases where "'unforeseen circumstances involving the search of an automobile [are] coupled with the presence of probable cause.'" 543 Pa. at 100, quoting *Commonwealth v. White*, 669 A.2d 896 (Pa. 1995) (emphasis deleted). This was incorrect. . . . We conclude the searches of the automobiles in these cases did not violate the Fourth Amendment.

Respondent Labron claims we have no jurisdiction to review the judgment in his case because the Pennsylvania Supreme Court's opinion rests on an adequate and independent state ground, viz., "this Commonwealth's jurisprudence of the automobile exception." We disagree. The language we have quoted is not a "plain statement" sufficient to tell us "the federal cases [were] being used only for the purpose of guidance, and d[id] not themselves compel the result that the court ha[d] reached." *Michigan v. Long*, 463 U.S. 1032 (1983). The Pennsylvania Supreme Court did discuss several of its own decisions; as it noted, however, some of those cases relied on an analysis of our cases on the automobile exception, see, *e.g.*, *Labron* (observing *Commonwealth v. Holzer*, 480 Pa. 93 (1978), cited *Coolidge v. New Hampshire*, 403 U.S. 443 (1971)); *id.* (stating *Commonwealth v. White, supra*, rested in part upon the Pennsylvania Supreme Court's analysis of *Chambers v. Maroney*, 399 U.S. 42 (1970)). The law of the Commonwealth thus appears to us "interwoven with the federal law, and . . . the adequacy and independence of any possible state law ground is not clear from the face of the opinion." Our jurisdiction in Labron's case is secure. The opinion in respondent Kilgore's case, meanwhile, rests on an explicit conclusion that the officers' conduct violated the Fourth Amendment; we have jurisdiction to review this judgment as well.

The petitions for writs of certiorari are granted, the judgments of the Supreme Court of Pennsylvania are reversed, and the cases are remanded for further proceedings not inconsistent with this opinion.

JUSTICE STEVENS, with whom JUSTICE GINSBURG joins, dissenting.

The decisions that the Court summarily reverses today are two of a trilogy of cases decided by the Pennsylvania Supreme Court within three days of each other. In each case, that court concluded that citizens of Pennsylvania are protected from warrantless searches and seizures of their automobiles absent exigent circumstances. But a fair reading of both *White* (the holding of which the Commonwealth has not challenged in this Court) and *Labron* (which the Court reverses today) demonstrates that their judgments almost certainly rested upon the Pennsylvania court's independent consideration of its own Constitution. For that reason, I do not believe that we have jurisdiction over the decision in *Labron*, just as we would not have jurisdiction in *White*. See 28 U.S.C. § 1257(a).[2] Furthermore, when considered in light of those two more carefully reasoned decisions, there is no reason for this Court to disturb the state court's finding in *Kilgore*, since the result will almost certainly be affirmed on remand.

In its per curiam decision, this Court concludes that because the decision in *Labron* cited state decisions which in turn referred to two 25-year-old cases of this Court, any reference to state law is "'interwoven with the federal law.'" These references, however, seem to me a rather short thread with which to weave — let alone upon which to hang — our jurisdiction.

In my opinion, the best reading of *Labron*'s plain language is that it relied on adequate and independent state grounds. The majority decision below includes references to four sources of federal law: the Federal Constitution and three federal cases. None of the references demonstrates that the decision rested upon anything other than state law.

---

2. Even if, as the Court concludes, some element of residual doubt suggests that Pennsylvania's Supreme Court drew inspiration from our interpretations of the Federal Constitution, I do not think that reliance sufficient to justify expending this Court's time — or that of the Pennsylvania Supreme Court — simply to scour the state decisions of all references to the Federal Constitution.

The decision begins with the proposition, not at issue here, that "the Fourth Amendment to the United States Constitution and Article I, § 8 of the Pennsylvania Constitution generally require that searches be predicated upon a warrant issued by a neutral and detached magistrate." It then reviews the history of the so-called "automobile exception" to the warrant requirement by quoting several passages from our decision in *Carroll v. United States*, 267 U.S. 132 (1925), which first established the exception, and then quotes a passage from *Chambers v. Maroney*, 399 U.S. 42, 52 (1970), which appears to support the proposition under federal law that the Court emphasizes here today (that the existence of probable cause is sufficient in and of itself to justify a search of a vehicle).

Rather than follow the developments of federal law, however, the decision then specifically and immediately notes that "[w]hen reviewing warrantless automobile searches *in this Commonwealth*, we have constantly held that 'there is no "automobile exception" as such and [that] the constitutional protections are applicable to searches and seizures of a person's car.'" (Emphasis added.) From that point onward, the only reference to federal law in the decision's remaining 30 citations is a recognition that *White*, the sole decision of this trio of "exigent circumstance" cases that is not before our Court, was "based upon" that Court's analysis of *Chambers*. Every other citation in *Labron* is to Pennsylvania law. . . .

Notably, the Commonwealth has not asked this Court to review the Pennsylvania court's decision in *White*, even though the search in that case would be affirmed under the Commonwealth's and this Court's understanding of Pennsylvania's holding regarding exigent circumstances. I also note that lower state courts have explicitly read *White* as establishing a state constitutional right, not a federal right. . . .

Given the explicit and nearly exclusive references to state law that I review above, it seems to me that the Court's decision to take jurisdiction in *Labron* not only extends *Michigan v. Long* beyond its original scope, but stands its rationale on its head. *Labron* does not rest "primarily" on federal law; . . . every indication is that the rule adopted in *Labron* and *White* rests primarily on state law. Nor are these holdings "interwoven" with federal law: Both *Labron* and *White* cite only two federal cases, both over a quarter-century old; rather than implicitly conclude that the absence of any reference to more recent decisions is due to poor legal research, I would trust the Pennsylvania courts' ability to understand and choose to deviate from our federal law. Certainly it would be a more respectful approach, in a case where the question is as close as it is in this case, to conclude that the State had made a conscious decision to depart from the jurisprudence of this Court rather than an error of law. . . .

While *Kilgore* relies more explicitly on the Federal Constitution than the other two decisions, it decided the identical issue that was decided in *Labron* and *White* only three days before those decisions issued. The reference to the Federal Constitution upon which the Court rests its jurisdiction—only one of two references to federal law—must be read in the context of the other two decisions, each of which relied heavily upon the Commonwealth's own Constitution. In light of *Labron* and *White*, the judgment in *Kilgore* will almost certainly remain the same on remand. In such a circumstance, the rationales supporting the rule of *Michigan v. Long* simply do not support the decision to reverse. The petition in *Kilgore* should simply be denied.

On many prior occasions, I have noted the unfortunate effects of the rule of *Michigan v. Long*. Because the state-law ground supporting these judgments is so much clearer than has been true on most prior occasions, these decisions exacerbate those effects to a nearly intolerable degree. Particularly in light of my understanding of this Court's primary role—"to protect the rights of the individual that are embodied in the Federal Constitution"—the decision to summarily reverse state decisions resting tenuously at best on federal grounds is imprudent and entirely inconsistent "with the sound administration of this Court's discretionary docket."

The Pennsylvania court has in these and other cases expressly indicated its intent to extend the protections of its Constitution beyond those available under the Federal Constitution. The per curiam decision that the Court issues today merely makes that task harder by requiring the Commonwealth to purge its decisions of any reliance on the latter, despite the value of the insights that our decisions can provide on related issues of law. . . .

These harms are particularly unnecessary given the likely result on remand. To reinvigorate the privacy protections extended to Pennsylvania citizens under *Labron*, *Kilgore*, and *White*, the Pennsylvania Supreme Court need only set forth the appropriate talismanic language and state, even more clearly than it already has, that the "*Commonwealth*'s jurisprudence of the automobile exception [requires] both the existence of probable cause and the presence of exigent circumstances to justify a warrantless search." (Emphasis added.) While the result will be identical, resources and respect will have been unnecessarily lost.

I respectfully dissent.

Note: Labron *and* Kilgore *on Remand*

Justice Stevens' prediction proved to be correct as to *Labron*, but incorrect as to *Kilgore*.

In *Labron* the Pennsylvania Supreme Court adhered to its decision holding that the evidence was properly suppressed. The court said, "We now reaffirm our holding in *Labron*, and explicitly note that it was, in fact, decided upon independent state grounds." 690 A.2d 228 (Pa. 1997). The court added, "Although we cited United States Supreme Court cases in our discussion of the automobile exception [in the opinion reversed by the United States Supreme Court], we continually referred to our Court's prior interpretation of the exception to the warrant requirement."

On the other hand, in *Kilgore*, the court reversed its ruling in favor of the defendant. 690 A.2d 229 (1997). The court explained:

> Appellant here . . . did not adequately preserve a state constitutional claim. The record establishes that Appellant's first reference to Article I, Section 8 of the Pennsylvania Constitution appears in his brief to our Court. He did not raise a claim under the Pennsylvania Constitution in the lower courts.

Matters not raised in the trial court cannot be considered on appeal. [Citations omitted.]

Accordingly, since Appellant has failed to preserve a state constitutional claim and the United States Supreme Court reversed our previous decision as an improper interpretation of federal law, we vacate our order which reversed the Superior Court's affirmance of Appellant's judgment of sentence.

What lesson can be drawn from the contrary results in the two cases?

Problem: "Squarely Within State Law"?

Acme Energy, Inc., is incorporated in the State of Anadarko, where its principal place of business is located. Acme contracts with operators of oil and gas wells in several southwestern states to provide specialized services known as "geo-tech." A few years ago, Acme hired Jett Rink, a citizen of Anadarko, to work out of its office in Oil City in Anadarko. Rink had approximately 20 years' experience in the oil and gas industry.

Upon being hired, Rink signed a confidentiality and noncompetition agreement with Acme. The agreement provided that for a period of two years following separation from Acme, Rink would not be employed by any business engaged in geo-tech activities within the United States. The agreement also contained an arbitration clause that read as follows:

Any dispute, difference or unresolved question between Acme and the Employee (collectively the "Disputing Parties") shall be settled by arbitration by a single arbitrator mutually agreeable to the Disputing Parties in an arbitration proceeding conducted in Oil City, Anadarko, in accordance with the rules existing at the date hereof of the American Arbitration Association.

Rink worked for Acme for two years, but disputes arose over compensation paid and hours worked, and Rink resigned.

A few months later, Acme learned that Rink had taken a job with Excelsior, Inc., a competing company that provides geo-tech services. Claiming that Rink had breached the noncompetition agreement, Acme served him with a demand for arbitration. Rink did not respond; instead, he filed suit in the trial court of general jurisdiction of Anadarko asking the court to declare the non-competition agreement null and void and to enjoin its enforcement. Rink relied on the Anadarko Freedom of Contract Act, which severely limits covenants not to compete.

Acme moved to dismiss Rink's complaint on the ground that any dispute as to the enforceability of the contract was a question for the arbitrator. In its supporting memorandum, Acme relied on the Federal Arbitration Act (FAA) and United States Supreme Court decisions interpreting the FAA.

The FAA provides that a "written provision in . . . a contract evidencing a transaction involving commerce to settle by arbitration a controversy thereafter arising out of such contract or transaction ... shall be valid, irrevocable, and enforceable, save upon such grounds as exist at law or in equity for the revocation of any contract." 9 U.S.C. § 2. As Acme pointed out, the United States Supreme Court has said that the FAA declares "a national policy favoring arbitration." The Court's decisions have also established two more specific propositions: first, that the FAA applies in state as well as federal courts; and second, that "when parties commit to arbitrate contractual disputes, it is a mainstay of the Act's substantive law that attacks on the validity of the contract, as distinct from attacks on the validity of the arbitration clause itself, are to be resolved by the arbitrator in the first instance, not by a federal or state court."

Acme asserted, in reliance on this line of cases, that because the contract contained a valid arbitration clause, federal law required that the arbitrator, and not the court, settle the parties' disagreement. The state trial court agreed with Acme and dismissed Rink's complaint.

Rink appealed, and the Anadarko Supreme Court reversed. The court held that the noncompetition clause was void as against public policy under the Anadarko Freedom of Contract Act. The state supreme court opinion read as follows:

> Acme argues that the issue of the validity of the covenant not to compete is for the arbitrator. In doing so, Acme relies upon United States Supreme Court jurisprudence. Rink asserts that jurisdiction lies in this Court based on our pronouncements addressing the issue. We agree with Rink.
>
> Our jurisprudence controls this issue. First, this court held in *Harmon v. Utex, Inc.*, 205 Ana. 356 (2007), that the Federal Arbitration Act does not prohibit an Anadarko court from reviewing a contract submitted to arbitration where one party asserts that the underlying agreement is void and unenforceable. We reaffirmed our precedents establishing that the public right to be free from restraint of trade "cannot be waived by the parties' agreement to submit the issue of the validity of a contract provision to arbitration. A void provision provides no legal basis for enforcement whether through arbitration or judicial pronouncement."
>
> Second, we rely on the well-established principle in Anadarko law that where two statutes address the same subject, one specific and one general, the specific will govern over the general. Two years ago, we held in *Pratt v. Hospicecare, Inc.*, 212 Ana. 402 (2011), that the specific statute in the Nursing Home Care Act addressing the right to commence an action and to have a jury trial would govern over the more general statute favoring arbitration. Here, we are presented with similar circumstances. The Anadarko Legislature has enacted a specific statute addressing noncompetition agreements. Here, as in *Pratt*, the more specific statute addressing the validity of covenants not to compete must govern over the more general statute favoring arbitration.
>
> Most instructive on Acme's arguments is *Biddle v. Gruner Co.*, 200 Ana. 347 (2005). *Biddle* contains an exhaustive overview of the United States Supreme Court decisions construing the Federal Arbitration Act and state arbitration

law. The Supreme Court decisions discussed therein, and relied upon by Acme here, were found not to inhibit our review of the underlying contract's validity. We therefore hold that the existence of an arbitration agreement in an employment contract does not prohibit judicial review of the underlying agreement.

[Here the court dropped a footnote: "In reaching our decision today, we consider extant federal and state precedent. Nevertheless, our determinations rest squarely within Anadarko law, which provides bona fide, separate, adequate, and independent grounds for our decision. *Michigan v. Long*, 463 U.S. 1032 (1983)."]

We turn now to the question of the validity of the covenant not to compete. Acme argues that the covenant is reasonable and necessary to protect the confidential information and technical knowledge imparted to Rink during training. We reject that argument.

Although the prohibition in the Freedom of Contract Act is not absolute, the non-competition provisions in the Acme contract go well beyond the bounds of what is allowable under the statute and therefore violate the legislatively expressed public policy. [Extensive discussion omitted.]

The judgment of the trial court is reversed, and case is remanded with directions to grant the relief requested by the plaintiff.

You are an associate in the law firm that represents Acme. The senior partner says, "It looks to me as though the Anadarko Supreme Court decision violates federal law. But the decision says it's based on state law. I would like to take the case to the United States Supreme Court if it's possible, but I don't want to waste our client's money if the Court doesn't have jurisdiction. You've studied this stuff recently; I'd like to know if this case is reviewable by the Supreme Court and, if so, what issues it can decide."

Please write a memorandum that answers the partner's question.

C. The Requirement of a "Final Judgment"

From 1789 until the present day, Supreme Court review of state-court decisions has been limited to "final judgments or decrees" of the highest court of the state in which a decision could be had. But the Supreme Court has not interpreted the finality requirement literally. In *Cox Broadcasting Co. v. Cohn*, the Court took the opportunity to synthesize its jurisprudence on the final-judgment rule of 28 U.S.C. § 1257.

Cox Broadcasting Corporation v. Cohn

Supreme Court of the United States, 1975.

420 U.S. 469.

Mr. Justice White delivered the opinion of the Court.

The issue before us in this case is whether, consistently with the First and Fourteenth Amendments, a State may extend a cause of action for damages for invasion of privacy caused by the publication of the name of a deceased rape victim which was publicly revealed in connection with the prosecution of the crime.

I

In August 1971, appellee's 17-year-old daughter was the victim of a rape and did not survive the incident. Six youths were soon indicted for murder and rape. Although there was substantial press coverage of the crime and of subsequent developments, the identity of the victim was not disclosed pending trial, perhaps because of Ga. Code Ann. § 26-9901 (1972), which makes it a misdemeanor to publish or broadcast the name or identity of a rape victim. . . .

[While criminal proceedings were pending, a reporter covering the incident for Cox Broadcasting learned the name of the victim from an examination of the indictments, which were made available for his inspection in the courtroom. A television station owned by Cox broadcast a report that named the victim.]

[The victim's father] brought an action for money damages against appellants, relying on § 26-9901 and claiming that his right to privacy had been invaded by the television broadcasts giving the name of his deceased daughter. Appellants admitted the broadcasts but claimed that they were privileged under both state law and the First and Fourteenth Amendments. The trial court, rejecting appellants' constitutional claims and holding that the Georgia statute gave a civil remedy to those injured by its violation, granted summary judgment to appellee as to liability, with the determination of damages to await trial by jury.

[On appeal, the Georgia Supreme Court held that the statute did not violate the First Amendment. However, the court also held that the public disclosure "did not establish liability on the part of the [broadcaster] as a matter of law." The court remanded the case to the lower courts to determine whether the invasion of privacy was willful and whether the disclosure actually invaded the plaintiff's zone of privacy.

[Before reaching the merits, the United States Supreme Court considered whether the Georgia Supreme Court decision was a "[f]inal judgment or decree."]

Since 1789, Congress has granted this Court appellate jurisdiction with respect to state litigation only after the highest state court in which judgment could be had has rendered a "[f]inal judgment or decree." Title 28 U.S.C. § 1257 retains this limitation on our power to review cases coming from state courts. The Court has noted that "[c]onsiderations of English usage as well as those of judicial policy" would justify an interpretation of the final-judgment rule to preclude review "where anything further remains to be determined by a State court, no matter how dissociated from the only federal issue that has finally been adjudicated by the highest court of the State." *Radio Station WOW, Inc. v. Johnson*, 326 U.S. 120 (1945). But the Court there observed that the rule had not been administered in such a mechanical fashion and that there were circumstances in which there has been "a departure from this requirement of finality for federal appellate jurisdiction."

These circumstances were said to be "very few," but as the cases have unfolded, the Court has recurringly encountered situations in which the highest court of a State has finally determined the federal issue present in a particular case, but in which there are further proceedings in the lower state courts to come. There are now at least four categories of such cases in which the Court has treated the decision on the federal issue as a final judgment for the purposes of 28 U.S.C. § 1257 and has taken jurisdiction without awaiting the completion of the additional proceedings anticipated in the lower state courts. In most, if not all, of the cases in these categories, these additional proceedings would not require the decision of other federal questions that might also require review by the Court at a later date, and immediate rather than delayed review would be the best way to avoid "the mischief of economic waste and of delayed justice," as well as precipitate interference with state litigation. [In a footnote, the Court cited *Gillespie v. United States Steel Corp.*, 379 U.S. 148 (1964), as taking a "practical rather than a technical approach" to finality. For further discussion of *Gillespie*, see the Note that follows this case.]

In the cases in the first two categories considered below, the federal issue would not be mooted or otherwise affected by the proceedings yet to be had because those proceedings have little substance, their outcome is certain, or they are wholly unrelated to the federal question. In the other two categories, however, the federal issue would be mooted if the petitioner or appellant seeking to bring the action here prevailed on the merits in the later state-court proceedings, but there is nevertheless sufficient justification for immediate review of the federal question finally determined in the state courts.

In the first category are those cases in which there are further proceedings — even entire trials — yet to occur in the state courts but where for one reason or another the federal issue is conclusive or the outcome of further proceedings preordained. In these circumstances, because the case is for all practical purposes concluded, the judgment of the state court on the federal issue is deemed final. In *Mills v. Alabama*, 384 U.S. 214 (1966), for example, a demurrer to a criminal complaint was sustained on federal constitutional grounds by a state trial court. The State Supreme Court reversed, remanding for jury trial. This Court took jurisdiction on the reasoning that the appellant had no defense other than his federal claim and could not prevail at trial on the facts or any nonfederal ground. To dismiss the appeal "would not only be an inexcusable delay of the benefits Congress intended to grant by providing for appeal to this Court, but it would also result in a completely unnecessary waste of time and energy in judicial systems already troubled by delays due to congested dockets."

Second, there are cases such as *Radio Station WOW* and *Brady v. Maryland*, 373 U.S. 83 (1963), in which the federal issue, finally decided by the highest court in the State, will survive and require decision regardless of the outcome of future state-court proceedings. In *Radio Station WOW*, the Nebraska Supreme Court directed the transfer of the properties of a federally licensed radio station and ordered an accounting, rejecting the claim that the transfer order would interfere with the federal license. The federal issue was held reviewable here despite the pending accounting on the "presupposition . . . that the federal questions that could come here have been adjudicated by the State court, and that the accounting which remains to be taken could not remotely give rise to a federal question . . . that may later come here. . . ." Nothing that could happen in the course of the accounting, short of settlement of the case, would foreclose or make unnecessary decision on the federal question. . . .

In *Brady v. Maryland*, the Maryland courts had ordered a new trial in a criminal case but on punishment only, and the petitioner asserted here that he was entitled to a new trial on guilt as well. We entertained the case, saying that the federal issue was separable and would not be mooted by the new trial on punishment ordered in the state courts.

In the third category are those situations where the federal claim has been finally decided, with further proceedings on the merits in the state courts to come, but in which later review of the federal issue cannot be had, whatever the ultimate outcome of the case. Thus, in these cases, if the party seeking interim review ultimately prevails on the merits, the federal issue will be mooted; if he were to lose on the merits, however, the governing state law would not permit him again to present his federal claims for review. The Court has taken jurisdiction in these circumstances prior to completion of the case in the state courts. *California v. Stewart*, 384 U.S. 436 (1966) (decided with *Miranda v. Arizona*), epitomizes this category. There the state court reversed a conviction on federal constitutional grounds and remanded for a new trial. Although the State might have prevailed at trial, we granted its petition for certiorari and affirmed, explaining that the state judgment was "final" since an acquittal of the defendant at trial would preclude, under state law, an appeal by the State. . . .

Lastly, there are those situations where the federal issue has been finally decided in the state courts with further proceedings pending in which the party seeking review here might prevail on the merits on nonfederal grounds, thus rendering unnecessary review of the federal issue by this Court, and where reversal of the state court on the federal issue would be preclusive of any further litigation on the relevant cause of action rather than merely controlling the nature and character of, or determining the admissibility of evidence in, the state proceedings still to come. In these circumstances, if a refusal immediately to review the state court decision might seriously erode federal policy, the Court has entertained and decided the federal issue, which itself has been finally determined by the state courts for purposes of the state litigation.

In *Construction Laborers v. Curry*, 371 U.S. 542 (1963), the state courts temporarily enjoined labor union picketing over claims that the National Labor Relations Board had exclusive jurisdiction of the controversy. The Court took jurisdiction for two independent reasons. First, the power of the state court to proceed in the face of the preemption claim was deemed an issue separable from the merits and ripe for review in this Court, particularly "when postponing review would seriously erode the national labor policy requiring the subject matter of respondents' cause to be heard by the . . . Board, not by the state courts." Second, the Court was convinced that in any event the union had no defense to the entry of a permanent injunction other than the preemption claim that had already been ruled on in the state courts. Hence the case was for all practical purposes concluded in the state tribunals.

In *Mercantile National Bank v. Langdeau*, 371 U.S. 555 (1963), two national banks were sued, along with others, in the courts of Travis County, Tex. The claim asserted was conspiracy to defraud an insurance company. The banks as a preliminary matter asserted that a special federal venue statute immunized them from suit in Travis County and that they could properly be sued only in another county. Although trial was still to be had and the banks might well prevail on the merits, the Court, relying on *Curry*, entertained the issue as a "separate and independent matter, anterior to the merits and not enmeshed in the factual and legal issues comprising the plaintiff's cause of action." Moreover, it would serve the policy of the federal statute "to determine now in which state court appellants may be tried rather than to subject them . . . to long and complex litigation which may all be for naught if consideration of the preliminary question of venue is postponed until the conclusion of the proceedings."

Miami Herald Publishing Co. v. Tornillo, 418 U.S. 241 (1974), is the latest case in this category. There a candidate for public office sued a newspaper for refusing, allegedly contrary to a state statute, to carry his reply to the paper's editorial critical of his qualifications. The trial court held the act unconstitutional, denying both injunctive relief and damages. The State Supreme Court reversed, sustaining the statute against the challenge based upon the First and Fourteenth Amendments and remanding the case for a trial and appropriate relief, including damages. The newspaper brought the case here. We sustained our jurisdiction, . . . observing:

> Whichever way we were to decide on the merits, it would be intolerable to leave unanswered, under these circumstances, an important question of freedom of the press under the First Amendment; an uneasy and unsettled constitutional posture of § 104.38 could only further harm the operation of a free press.

[In a footnote the Court added:] The import of the Court's holding in *Tornillo* is underlined by its citation of the concurring opinion in *Mills v. Alabama*. There, Mr. Justice Douglas, joined by Mr. Justice Brennan, stated that even if the appellant had a defense and might prevail at trial, jurisdiction was properly noted in order to foreclose unwarranted restrictions on the press should the state court's constitutional judgment prove to be in error.

In light of the prior cases, we conclude that we have jurisdiction to review the judgment of the Georgia Supreme Court rejecting the challenge under the First and Fourteenth Amendments to the state law authorizing damage suits against the press for publishing the name of a rape victim whose identity is revealed in the course of a public prosecution. The Georgia Supreme Court's judgment is plainly final on the federal issue and is not subject to further review in the state courts. Appellants will be liable for damages if the elements of the state cause of action are proved. They may prevail at trial on nonfederal grounds, it is true, but if the Georgia court erroneously upheld the statute, there should be no trial at all.

Moreover, even if appellants prevailed at trial and made unnecessary further consideration of the constitutional question, there would remain in effect the unreviewed decision of the State Supreme Court that a civil action for publishing the name of a rape victim disclosed in a public judicial proceeding may go forward despite the First and Fourteenth Amendments. Delaying final decision of the First Amendment claim until after trial will "leave unanswered . . . an important question of freedom of the press under the First Amendment," "an uneasy and unsettled constitutional posture [that] could only further harm the operation of a free press." *Tornillo*. On the other hand, if we now hold that the First and Fourteenth Amendments bar civil liability for broadcasting the victim's name, this litigation ends. Given these factors—that the litigation could be terminated by our decision on the merits[13] and that a failure to decide the question now will leave the press in Georgia operating in the shadow of the civil and criminal sanctions of a rule of law and a statute the constitutionality of which is in serious doubt—we find that reaching the merits is consistent with the pragmatic approach that we have followed in the past in determining finality. See *Gillespie*; *Radio Station WOW*; *Mills v. Alabama* (Douglas, J., concurring).

The author of the dissent, a member of the majority in *Tornillo*, does not disavow that decision. He seeks only to distinguish it by indicating that the First Amendment issue at stake there was more important and pressing than the one here. This seems to embrace the thesis of that case and of this one as far as the approach to finality is concerned, even though the merits and the avoidance doctrine are to some extent involved.

[On the merits, the Court held that under the circumstances of the case, "the protection of freedom of the press provided by the First and Fourteenth Amendments bars the State of Georgia from making appellants' broadcast the basis of civil liability." Justice Powell, who joined the Court's opinion, noted his agreement that the *Tornillo* case "supports the conclusion that the issue presented in this appeal is final for review."]

Mr. Justice Rehnquist, dissenting.

Because I am of the opinion that the decision which is the subject of this appeal is not a "final" judgment or decree, as that term is used in 28 U.S.C. §1257, I would dismiss this appeal for want of jurisdiction.

---

13. Mr. Justice Rehnquist is correct in saying that this factor involves consideration of the merits in determining jurisdiction. But it does so only to the extent of determining that the issue is substantial and only in the context that if the state court's final decision on the federal issue is incorrect, federal law forecloses further proceedings in the state court. That the petitioner who protests against the state court's decision on the federal question might prevail on the merits on nonfederal grounds in the course of further proceedings anticipated in the state court and hence obviate later review of the federal issue here is not preclusive of our jurisdiction. *Curry*, *Langdeau*, . . . and *Tornillo* make this clear. In those cases, the federal issue having been decided, arguably wrongly, and being determinative of the litigation if decided the other way, the finality rule was satisfied.

Radio Station WOW, Inc. v. Johnson, 326 U.S. 120 (1945), established that in a "very few" circumstances review of state-court decisions could be had in this Court even though something "further remain[ed] to be determined by a State court." Over the years, however, and despite vigorous protest by Mr. Justice Harlan, this Court has steadily discovered new exceptions to the finality requirement, such that they can hardly any longer be described as "very few." Whatever may be the unexpressed reasons for this process of expansion, it has frequently been the subject of no more formal an express explanation than cursory citations to preceding cases in the line. Especially is this true of cases in which the Court, as it does today, relies on *Construction Laborers v. Curry*, 371 U.S. 542 (1963). Although the Court's opinion today does accord detailed consideration to this problem, I do not believe that the reasons it expresses can support its result.

I

... I consider § 1257 finality to be but one of a number of congressional provisions reflecting concern that uncontrolled federal judicial interference with state administrative and judicial functions would have untoward consequences for our federal system.... [As Mr. Justice Harlan said in his dissent in *Mercantile National Bank v. Langdeau*, 371 U.S. 555 (1963)], one basis of the finality rule was that it foreclosed "this Court from passing on constitutional issues that may be dissipated by the final outcome of a case, thus helping to keep to a minimum undesirable federal-state conflicts." One need cast no doubt on the Court's decision in such cases as *Langdeau* to recognize that Mr. Justice Harlan was focusing on a consideration which should be of significance in the Court's disposition of this case....

II

But quite apart from the considerations of federalism which counsel against an expansive reading of our jurisdiction under § 1257, the Court's holding today enunciates a virtually formless exception to the finality requirement, one which differs in kind from those previously carved out. By contrast, *Construction Laborers v. Curry* and *Mercantile National Bank v. Langdeau* are based on the understandable principle that where the proper forum for trying the issue joined in the state courts depends on the resolution of the federal question raised on appeal, sound judicial administration requires that such a question be decided by this Court, if it is to be decided at all, sooner rather than later in the course of the litigation. *Organization for a Better Austin v. Keefe*, 402 U.S. 415 (1971), and *Mills v. Alabama*, 384 U.S. 214 (1966), rest on the premise that where as a practical matter the state litigation has been concluded by the decision of the State's highest court, the fact that in terms of state procedure the ruling is interlocutory should not bar a determination by this Court of the merits of the federal question.

Still other exceptions, as noted in the Court's opinion, have been made where the federal question decided by the highest court of the State is bound to survive and be presented for decision here regardless of the outcome of future state-court proceedings, *Radio Station WOW; Brady v. Maryland*, and for the situation in which later review of the federal issue cannot be had, whatever the ultimate outcome of the subsequent proceedings directed by the highest court of the State, *California v. Stewart*.

While the totality of these exceptions certainly indicates that the Court has been willing to impart to the language "final judgment or decree" a great deal of flexibility, each of them is arguably consistent with the intent of Congress in enacting § 1257, if not with the language it used, and each of them is relatively workable in practice.

To those established exceptions is now added one so formless that it cannot be paraphrased, but instead must be quoted:

> Given these factors—that the litigation could be terminated by our decision on the merits and that a failure to decide the question now will leave the press in Georgia operating in the shadow of the civil and criminal sanctions of a rule of law and a statute the constitutionality of which is in serious doubt—we find that reaching the merits is consistent with the pragmatic approach that we have followed in the past in determining finality.

There are a number of difficulties with this test. One of them is the Court's willingness to look to the merits. . . .

Another problem is that in applying the second prong of its test, the Court has not engaged in any independent inquiry as to the consequences of permitting the decision of the Supreme Court of Georgia to remain undisturbed pending final state-court resolution of the case. This suggests that in order to invoke the benefit of today's rule, the "shadow" in which an appellant must stand need be neither deep nor wide. In this case nothing more is at issue than the right to report the name of the victim of a rape. No hindrance of any sort has been imposed on reporting the fact of a rape or the circumstances surrounding it. Yet the Court unquestioningly places this issue on a par with the core First Amendment interest involved in *Tornillo* and *Mills v. Alabama*, that of protecting the press in its role of providing uninhibited political discourse.

[In a footnote, Justice Rehnquist added:] As pointed out in *Tornillo*, not only did uncertainty about Florida's "right of reply" statute interfere with this important press function, but delay by this Court would have left the matter unresolved during the impending 1974 elections. In *Mills*, the Court observed that "there is practically universal agreement that a major purpose of [the First] Amendment was to protect the free discussion of governmental affairs."

But the greatest difficulty with the test enunciated today is that it totally abandons the principle that constitutional issues are too important to be decided save when absolutely necessary, and are to be avoided if there are grounds for decision of lesser dimension. The long line of cases which established this rule makes clear that it is a principle primarily designed, not to benefit the lower courts, or state-federal relations, but rather to safeguard this Court's own process of constitutional adjudication.

In this case there has yet to be an adjudication of liability against appellants, and unlike the appellant in *Mills v. Alabama*, they do not concede that they have no nonfederal defenses. Nonetheless, the Court rules on their constitutional defense. Far from eschewing a constitutional holding in advance of the necessity for one, the Court construes § 1257 so that it may virtually rush out and meet the prospective constitutional litigant as he approaches our doors. . . .

Note: Finality in Section 1257 and Section 1291

In the course of its opinion in *Cox Broadcasting*, the Court cites precedents holding that "the requirement of finality is to be given a 'practical rather than a technical construction.'" Among the cases the Court relies on are *Gillespie v. United States Steel Corp.*, 379 U.S. 148 (1964), and *Cohen v. Beneficial Industrial Loan Corp.*, 337 U.S. 541 (1949). However, as the Court acknowledges, these were cases that "arose in the federal courts and involved the requirement of 28 U.S.C. § 1291 that judgments of district courts be final if they are to be appealed to the courts of appeals."

Justice Rehnquist, in dissent, challenged the Court's reliance on § 1291 jurisprudence:

> Although acknowledging [the distinction between the two contexts], the Court accords it no importance and adopts *Gillespie*'s approach without any consideration of whether the finality requirement for this Court's jurisdiction over a "judgment or decree" of a state court is grounded on more serious concerns than is the limitation of court of appeals jurisdiction to final "decisions" of the district courts. I believe that the underlying concerns are different, and that the difference counsels a more restrictive approach when § 1257 finality is at issue.

> According to *Gillespie*, the finality requirement is imposed as a matter of minimizing "the inconvenience and costs of piecemeal review." This proposition is undoubtedly sound so long as one is considering the administration of the federal court system. Were judicial efficiency the only interest at stake there would be less inclination to challenge the Court's resolution in this case.... The case before us, however, is an appeal from a state court, and this fact introduces additional interests which must be accommodated in fashioning any exception to the literal application of the finality requirement. I consider § 1257 finality to be but one of a number of congressional provisions reflecting concern that uncontrolled federal judicial interference with state administrative and judicial functions would have untoward consequences for our federal system.

> ... Because [concerns about comity and federalism] are important, and because they provide "added force" to § 1257's finality requirement, I believe that the Court has erred by simply importing the approach of cases in which the only concern is efficient judicial administration.

Later decisions on finality under § 1257 have seldom relied on *Gillespie* or other cases construing § 1291. Finality within the federal system under § 1291 is discussed in Chapter 18.

Note: The First, Second, and Third *Cox* Categories

The Court's decision in *Cox* identifies four categories of cases in which a state-court judgment is considered "final." In each of them, the highest court of the state has conclusively resolved a federal issue, but further proceedings are expected in the state courts. The Court treats those decisions as final if:

1. the federal issue is conclusive, or the outcome of further proceedings in state court is preordained;

2. the federal issue will survive and require decision regardless of the outcome of further state-court proceedings;

3. later review of the federal issue cannot be had, whatever the ultimate outcome of the case; or

4. the party seeking review of the federal issue might ultimately prevail on nonfederal grounds in state court, rendering the Court's review unnecessary, but reversal on the federal issue would be preclusive of any further litigation, and a refusal immediately to review the state-court decision might seriously erode federal policy.

Few cases have fallen within the ambit of the first two categories, and none of the first three categories has proven controversial.

1. In *Duquesne Light Co. v. Barasch*, 488 U.S. 299 (1989), the Pennsylvania Public Utility Commission (PUC) issued an order allowing a utility to increase its rates to recover its expenditures for certain electrical generating facilities that were planned but never built. The Pennsylvania Supreme Court held that Act 335, a recent amendment to the Pennsylvania Utility Code, prohibited recovery of the costs in question either by inclusion in the rate base or by amortization. The court rejected the utility's argument that this interpretation resulted in a taking of the utility's property without just compensation in violation of the Fifth Amendment. The court remanded to the PUC for further proceedings to correct its rate order, giving effect to the exclusion required by Act 335.

The United States Supreme Court granted review. Chief Justice Rehnquist, writing for the Court, began by addressing the Court's appellate jurisdiction:

> Although this case has been remanded for further proceedings to revise the relevant rate orders, we hold that for purposes of our appellate jurisdiction the judgment of the Pennsylvania Supreme Court is final. . . . [The] case falls into the first of the four [*Cox*] categories. The Pennsylvania Supreme Court has finally adjudicated the constitutionality of Act 335 in the context of otherwise completed rate proceedings and so has left "the outcome of further proceedings preordained."

> We do not think that the PUC might undo the effects of Act 335 on remand by allowing recovery of the disputed costs in some other way consistent with state law. The Pennsylvania Supreme Court's interpretation of the Act does not leave its effect in doubt. . . . We are satisfied that we are presented with the State's last word on the constitutionality of Act 335 and that all that remains is the straightforward application of its clear directive to otherwise complete rate orders. We therefore have jurisdiction.

Justice Blackmun dissented alone on the jurisdictional issue.

2. In *NAACP v. Claiborne Hardware Co.*, 458 U.S. 886 (1982), the Mississippi Supreme Court affirmed a judgment imposing damages liability on the NAACP for a boycott of

white merchants. The court rejected the NAACP's argument that the boycott was protected by the First Amendment. It remanded for a computation of damages.

The United States Supreme Court granted review. Without elaboration, it relied on the second *Cox* category in holding that the Mississippi Supreme Court's judgment was "final for purposes of our jurisdiction." Can you explain why the judgment in *Claiborne Hardware* was "final" under the second *Cox* category?

3. The third *Cox* category involves situations where "later review of the federal issue cannot be had, whatever the ultimate outcome of the case." This category has its primary application in criminal cases where state courts have ruled in favor of the defendant. For example, in *New York v. Quarles*, 467 U.S. 649 (1984), the trial court suppressed evidence based on a *Miranda* violation. The highest state court affirmed. The Supreme Court granted certiorari to consider the correctness of the *Miranda* ruling. The Court explained why the state-court judgment was "final" for purposes of § 1257:

> Although respondent has yet to be tried in state court, the suppression ruling challenged herein is a "final judgment" within the meaning of 28 U.S.C. § 1257 ... [The case] falls within the category which includes "those situations where the federal claim has been finally decided ... but in which later review of the federal issue cannot be had, whatever the ultimate outcome of the case." In this case should the State convict respondent at trial, its claim that certain evidence was wrongfully suppressed will be moot. Should respondent be acquitted at trial, the State will be precluded from pressing its federal claim again on appeal [because of the Double Jeopardy Clause of the Fifth Amendment].

Does the third *Cox* category allow review in any case in which the state's highest court has ruled in favor of a defendant in a criminal prosecution? Consider the Problem below.

4. On the other hand, the Court found no exception applicable in *Jefferson v. City of Tarrant*, 522 U.S. 75 (1997). In that case, the Court granted certiorari to review the Alabama Supreme Court's decision that the state's Wrongful Death Act, which limits recovery to punitive damages, is controlling when a decedent's estate brings suit under 42 U.S.C. § 1983, claiming that the death resulted from a deprivation of federal rights. The trial court had denied the city's motion for judgment on the pleadings, rejecting the applicability of the state statute to the § 1983 claims, but the Alabama Supreme Court, on an interlocutory appeal, reversed. For the first time in its brief on the merits, the City pointed out a jurisdictional problem. As the Court explained:

> The Alabama Supreme Court's decision was not a "final judgment." It was avowedly interlocutory. Far from terminating the litigation, the court answered a single certified question that affected only two of the four counts in petitioners' complaint. The court then remanded the case for further proceedings. Absent settlement or further dispositive motions, the proceedings on remand will include a trial on the merits of the state-law claims. ...

> Petitioners contend that this case comes within the "limited set of situations in which we have found finality as to the federal issue despite the

ordering of further proceedings in the lower state courts." *O'Dell v. Espinoza*, 456 U.S. 430 (1982) (per curiam). We do not agree. This is not a case in which "the federal issue, finally decided by the highest court in the State, will survive and require decision regardless of the outcome of future state-court proceedings." *Cox* [second category]. Resolution of the state-law claims could effectively moot the federal-law question raised here. . . . If the City prevails on [its] account of the facts, then any § 1983 claim will necessarily fail, however incorrect the Alabama Supreme Court's ruling . . . .

Nor is this an instance "where the federal claim has been finally decided, with further proceedings on the merits in the state courts to come, but in which later review of the federal issue cannot be had, whatever the ultimate outcome of the case." *Cox* [third category]. If the Alabama Supreme Court's decision on the federal claim ultimately makes a difference to the Jeffersons—in particular, if they prevail on their state claims but recover less than they might have under federal law, or if their state claims fail for reasons that do not also dispose of their federal claims—they will be free to seek our review once the state-court litigation comes to an end. Even if the Alabama Supreme Court adheres to its interlocutory ruling as "law of the case," that determination will in no way limit our ability to review the issue on final judgment. . . .

This case fits within no exceptional category. It presents the typical situation in which the state courts have resolved some but not all of petitioners' claims. Our jurisdiction therefore founders on the rule that a state-court decision is not final unless and until it has effectively determined the entire litigation. Because the Alabama Supreme Court has not yet rendered a final judgment, we lack jurisdiction to review its decision. . . .

In rejecting the applicability of the third *Cox* exception, the Court notes that if the Alabama Supreme Court's ruling on the federal question "ultimately makes a difference to the Jeffersons, . . . they will be free to seek our review once the state-court litigation comes to an end." But in rejecting the applicability of the *second* exception, the Court points out that if the Jeffersons lose on their state-law claims, or if the facts are resolved against them, the federal question will be effectively mooted. Under this rationale, what role is left for the third category in civil litigation?

5. In explaining why the third *Cox* category does not apply, the Court in *Jefferson* noted that even if the Alabama Supreme Court were to adhere to its interlocutory ruling on the damages issue as "law of the case," that determination "will in no way limit [the United States Supreme Court's] ability to review the issue on final judgment." The "law of the case" doctrine, followed by state as well as federal courts, "generally provides that when a court decides upon a rule of law, that decision should continue to govern the same issues in subsequent stages in the same case." *Musacchio v. United States*, 136 S. Ct. 709 (2016) (internal quotation marks omitted). According to the Court's statement in *Jefferson*, if the case reaches final resolution and the state courts refuse to reconsider the federal question on law-of-the-case grounds, that ruling will not be an adequate state-law ground that bars Supreme Court review. Is there any reason the Court would not reach a similar result in any civil case where a state court has rejected a federal claim in an interlocutory ruling?

6. Note that *Jefferson* is a case in which the interlocutory ruling *rejected* the position of the litigant raising a federal claim or defense. Suppose the state court had ruled that federal law barred application of the Wrongful Death Act limitation to §1983 claims, and the *defendant* sought review in the United States Supreme Court. Would the analysis be the same?

Problem: The Fruits of a Backpack Search

Illiana State police officers were investigating the sale of marijuana at a residence when Roy Davenport walked up to the house carrying a heavy backpack. A check of Davenport's license revealed an outstanding warrant for his arrest. The officers arrested Davenport, handcuffed him, and placed him in the back of a police cruiser. They then searched the backpack and discovered narcotics. Charged with possession of a controlled substance, Davenport moved to suppress the evidence, asserting that it was seized in violation of the Fourth Amendment.

The state trial court granted the motion to suppress, but an intermediate appellate court reversed, finding the search valid under *United States v. Robinson*, 414 U.S. 218 (1973). That case established a "bright-line" rule permitting a law enforcement officer who has made a lawful custodial arrest to search the person of the arrestee as a contemporaneous incident of the arrest. The Illiana Supreme Court in turn reversed, holding that *Robinson* did not apply. The court reasoned that *Robinson*'s bright-line rule is limited to a search of the arrestee's person, and has no application once the arrestee is secured. *See Arizona v. Gant*, 556 U.S. 332 (2009). The court directed the trial court to determine "whether the factors set forth in *Chimel v. California*, 395 U.S. 752 (1969), justify the search of Davenport's backpack." *Chimel* allows searches "incident to arrest" under some circumstances. But the state supreme court explained that "based on the record, we are unable to ascertain whether the officer's safety was endangered or whether the preservation of the evidence was in jeopardy, as is necessary to justify the search under *Chimel*."

The state has filed a petition for certiorari in the United States Supreme Court, presenting a single question: "Is the rule of *United States v. Robinson* limited to situations in which the law enforcement officer searches the person of the arrestee, rather than any bags or other containers in the arrestee's possession?" The respondent argues that the state-court judgment is not final. How should that question be resolved?

Note: The Fourth Cox Category

1. The decision in *Cox* itself relied on the fourth category. The state-court proceedings had not ended, as the case was set for trial on remand. The Court nonetheless deemed the judgment final. Although the defendants may yet have prevailed on non-federal grounds, the federal issue was conclusively decided, and "if the Georgia court erroneously upheld the statute, there should be no trial at all." Moreover, any delay would "leave unanswered . . . an important question of freedom of the press under the First Amendment," which "could only further harm the operation of a free press." *Cox* (quoting *Miami Herald Publishing Co. v. Tornillo*, 418 U.S. 241 (1974)).

The fourth *Cox* category has played an important role in the Court's jurisdiction over First Amendment claims. *See, e.g., Fort Wayne Books, Inc. v. Indiana*, 489 U.S. 46 (1989); *Flynt v. Ohio*, 451 U.S. 619 (1981); *National Socialist Party of America v. Skokie*, 432 U.S. 43 (1977). But the Court has also invoked the fourth category in a wide variety of other contexts in both civil and criminal litigation. Two examples will suffice.

2. *Belknap, Inc. v. Hale*, 463 U.S. 491 (1983), involved a labor dispute. Belknap had entered into a collective bargaining agreement with its employees under the National Labor Relations Act (NLRA). When Belknap and the union reached an impasse, 400 members of the bargaining unit went out on strike. Belknap advertised for permanent employees to replace the striking workers. A large number of people responded to the offer and were hired. After the strike was settled, however, Belknap laid off the replacements to make room for the returning strikers.

The replacement workers sued in state court for misrepresentation and breach of contract. The trial court granted summary judgment to Belknap, agreeing with Belknap that the plaintiffs' state-law claims were preempted by the NLRA. The state appellate court reversed, holding that the suit was not preempted. The United States Supreme Court granted Belknap's petition for certiorari, but upon plenary review it affirmed the judgment. In explaining why the Kentucky appellate court's decision was "final" within the meaning of § 1257, the Court invoked the fourth of *Cox*'s categories:

> [The state-court judgment] finally disposed of the federal preemption issue; a reversal here would terminate the state court action; and to permit the proceedings to go forward in the state court without resolving the preemption issue would involve a serious risk of eroding the federal statutory policy of "'requiring the subject matter of respondents' cause to be heard by the . . . Board, not by the state courts.'" Or as Justice Rehnquist put it, our jurisdiction in *Curry* rested on the "understandable principle that where the proper forum for trying the issue joined in the state court depends on the resolution of the federal question raised on appeal, sound judicial administration requires that such a question be decided by this Court, if it is to be decided at all, sooner rather than later in the course of the litigation."

But how could it be said that allowing the proceedings to go forward in state court "would involve a serious risk of eroding the federal statutory policy" when the Court concluded that the state claims were *not* preempted? Here is the Court's answer:

> [Our] jurisdiction to affirm or reverse the Kentucky Court of Appeals on the preemption issue, an issue which is not by any means frivolous, is clear. That we affirm rather than reverse, thereby holding that federal policy would not be subverted by the Kentucky proceedings, is not tantamount to a holding that we are without power to render such a judgment; nor does it require us to dismiss this case for want of a final judgment.

3. In *Southland Corp. v. Keating*, 465 U.S. 1 (1984), Keating filed a class action in California state court against Southland, the owner and franchisor of the 7-Eleven convenience stores, on behalf of a class of California franchisees. The suit asserted common-law claims and also claims under the California Franchise Investment Law. Southland moved to compel arbitration of all of the plaintiffs' claims, invoking a provision in the standard franchise agreement that required any controversy arising out of the agreement to be settled by arbitration. The trial court granted the motion except as to claims based on the state statute.

The case went to the California Supreme Court. That court interpreted the Franchise Investment Law to require judicial consideration, rather than arbitration, of claims brought under that statute. It rejected Southland's argument that under this interpretation the statute contravened the Federal Arbitration Act. The court also remanded the case to the trial court for consideration of the plaintiffs' request for class-wide arbitration.

The United States Supreme Court granted review to consider Southland's preemption argument. The plaintiffs contended that the California Supreme Court's action was not a "final judgment or decree" within the meaning of § 1257, but the Supreme Court disagreed, relying on the fourth *Cox* exception:

> Here Southland challenged the California Franchise Investment Law as it was applied to invalidate a contract for arbitration made pursuant to the Federal Arbitration Act. . . . The judgment of the California Supreme Court with respect to this claim is reviewable under *Cox Broadcasting*. Without immediate review of the California holding by this Court there may be no opportunity to pass on the federal issue and as a result "there would remain in effect the unreviewed decision of the State Supreme Court" holding that the California statute does not conflict with the Federal Arbitration Act. On the other hand, reversal of a state court judgment in this setting will terminate litigation of the merits of this dispute.

> Finally, the failure to accord immediate review of the decision of the California Supreme Court might "seriously erode federal policy." Plainly the effect of the judgment of the California court is to nullify a valid contract made by private parties under which they agreed to submit all contract disputes to final, binding arbitration. The federal Act permits "parties to an arbitrable dispute [to move] out of court and into arbitration as quickly and easily as possible."

> . . . Contracts to arbitrate are not to be avoided by allowing one party to ignore the contract and resort to the courts. Such a course could lead to prolonged litigation, one of the very risks the parties, by contracting for arbitration, sought to eliminate. . . . For us to delay review of a state judicial decision denying enforcement of the contract to arbitrate until the state court litigation has run its course would defeat the core purpose of a contract to arbitrate.

4. Not all important federal questions, however, implicate the fourth *Cox* category. In *Johnson v. California*, 541 U.S. 428 (2004) (per curiam), the state court of appeals vacated a criminal conviction based on *Batson v. Kentucky*, 476 U.S. 79 (1986), in which the Court held that a prosecutor violates the Equal Protection Clause by using peremptory challenges to exclude potential jurors on the basis of race. That court therefore did not reach the defendant's separate evidentiary and prosecutorial misconduct claims. The California Supreme Court reversed, rejecting the *Batson* claim and remanding "for further proceedings consistent with [its] opinion."

The Supreme Court granted the defendant's petition for certiorari, the case was fully briefed and argued, and the Court seemed poised to announce a decision on the merits. Instead it ordered post-argument supplemental briefing and ultimately dismissed for want of jurisdiction:

> [P]etitioner argues that the fourth of the[] [*Cox*] categories fits this case. . . .

> [But] petitioner can make no convincing claim of erosion of federal policy that is not common to all decisions rejecting a defendant's *Batson* claim. The fourth category therefore does not apply. *See Florida v. Thomas*, 532 U.S. 774 (2001). "A contrary conclusion would permit the fourth exception to swallow the rule." *Flynt v. Ohio*, 451 U.S. 619 (1981) (per curiam).

How did the Court miss the jurisdictional issue until such a late stage in the case? Part of the problem was that the state court of appeals certified its decision for "partial publication," addressing the *Batson* claim in the published portion but discussing the remaining claims in the unpublished portion. The Supreme Court admonished counsel in the future to append all "relevant opinions . . . entered in the case" to a petition for certiorari, *see* Supreme Court Rule 14.1(i), and appealed more broadly for greater attention to the finality of state-court judgments, to "avoid the expenditure of resources of both counsel and this Court on an abortive proceeding such as the present one."

5. Is the final judgment rule required by the Constitution? If not, why is the Court obliged "to raise any question of . . . compliance on [its] own motion," as the Court stated in *Johnson*?

6. In *Florida v. Thomas*, 532 U.S. 774 (2001), the Court said that none of the *Cox* categories fit the judgment of the Florida Supreme Court, "and we *therefore* conclude that its judgment is not final." (Emphasis added.) The implication—confirmed by *Johnson*—is that the four categories define the outer limits of finality under § 1257. But *Cox* itself spoke of "*at least* four categories." Is the Court justified in treating the four categories as a closed set?

Consider a case like *Johnson*, in which the question presented was important and recurring, implicated the fundamental constitutional right to equal protection, and had been fully briefed on the merits. *Cox Broadcasting* makes clear that the Court has not administered the finality requirement in a "mechanical fashion." Should the Court extend the rationale of *Cox* by identifying new, additional types of "final judgments" under § 1257? Or should the Court abandon categories altogether and accept state-court cases as long as the federal issue has been finally decided in the state court, and failure to review immediately would frustrate a significant federal policy?

Problem: Objection to Territorial Jurisdiction

Apex Corporation, a Florida corporation with its principal place of business in Florida, was sued in Ohio state court. Apex moved to dismiss for want of personal jurisdiction, arguing that under *International Shoe* and its progeny, the exercise of jurisdiction over Apex by the state court would violate Apex's rights under the due process clause of the Fourteenth Amendment. The trial court denied the motion. State law allows a nonresident defendant to challenge an adverse jurisdictional ruling by filing a writ of mandamus in the state supreme court. Apex did so. The state supreme court heard oral argument and denied the writ, ruling that the exercise of jurisdiction over Apex did not violate Apex's rights under the United States Constitution.

Apex has filed a writ of certiorari in the United States Supreme Court. Is the judgment of the state supreme court "final" for purposes of 28 U.S.C. § 1257?

In *Calder v. Jones*, 465 U.S. 783 (1984), the Supreme Court considered a case in which the state court had rejected the defendant's objections to the exercise of territorial jurisdiction. The Court said:

> Although there has not yet been a trial on the merits in this case, the judgment of the California appellate court "is plainly final on the federal issue and is not subject to further review in the state courts." *Cox Broadcasting*. Accordingly, as in several past cases presenting jurisdictional issues in this posture, "we conclude that the judgment below is final within the meaning of [28 U.S.C.] § 1257." *Shaffer v. Heitner*, 433 U.S. 186 (1977).

Is this merely an application of the *Cox Broadcasting* doctrine, or does it expand the exceptions to finality outlined there?

Chapter 6

Litigating Federal Claims in State Courts

In the preceding chapter, we examined the law that governs review by the United States Supreme Court of state-court decisions that involve federal questions. In the vast majority of the cases we studied, federal law was invoked as a *defense* to a claim or prosecution under state law. We now look at the law that governs when federal *claims* are filed in state court and not removed.

A. The Power of State Courts to Hear Federal Claims

Tafflin v. Levitt

Supreme Court of the United States, 1990.

493 U.S. 455.

Justice O'Connor delivered the opinion of the Court.

[The Racketeer Influenced and Corrupt Organizations Act (RICO) was enacted as part of the Organized Crime Control Act of 1970. As the name suggests, RICO is primarily a criminal statute, but it also creates a private civil remedy for any person "injured in his business or property by reason of a violation of" its substantive provisions. These substantive provisions prohibit certain conduct involving "racketeering activity," which is defined to mean any of numerous acts "chargeable" or "indictable" under enumerated federal and state criminal laws.

[Initially the civil remedy lay dormant, but in the mid-1980s, civil suits under RICO began to proliferate. One of the questions that arose was whether civil RICO suits could be brought in state as well as federal courts.]

... To resolve a conflict among the federal appellate courts and state supreme courts, we granted certiorari limited to the question whether state courts have concurrent jurisdiction over civil RICO claims. [We hold that they do.]

II

We begin with the axiom that, under our federal system, the States possess sovereignty concurrent with that of the Federal Government, subject only to limitations imposed by the Supremacy Clause. Under this system of dual sovereignty, we have consistently held that state courts have inherent authority, and are thus presumptively competent, to adjudicate claims arising under the laws of the United States. As we noted in *Claflin v. Houseman*, 93 U.S. 130 (1876), "if exclusive jurisdiction be neither express nor implied, the State courts have concurrent jurisdiction whenever, by their own constitution, they are competent to take it." [Similarly, in *Charles Dowd Box Co. v. Courtney*, 368 U.S. 502 (1962), we said:] "We start with the premise that nothing in the concept of our federal system prevents state courts from enforcing rights created by federal law. Concurrent jurisdiction has been a common phenomenon in our judicial history, and exclusive federal court jurisdiction over cases arising under federal law has been the exception rather than the rule."

This deeply rooted presumption in favor of concurrent state court jurisdiction is, of course, rebutted if Congress affirmatively ousts the state courts of jurisdiction over a particular federal claim. As we stated in *Gulf Offshore Co. v. Mobil Oil Corp.*, 453 U.S. 473 (1981):

> In considering the propriety of state-court jurisdiction over any particular federal claim, the Court begins with the presumption that state courts enjoy concurrent jurisdiction. Congress, however, may confine jurisdiction to the federal courts either explicitly or implicitly. Thus, the presumption of concurrent jurisdiction can be rebutted by an explicit statutory directive, by unmistakable implication from legislative history, or by a clear incompatibility between state-court jurisdiction and federal interests.

[Earlier, in *Claflin*, we said] that state courts have concurrent jurisdiction "where it is not excluded by express provision, or by incompatibility in its exercise arising from the nature of the particular case." The parties agree that these principles, which have remained unmodified through the years, provide the analytical framework for resolving this case.

III

The precise question presented, therefore, is whether state courts have been divested of jurisdiction to hear civil RICO claims "by an explicit statutory directive, by unmistakable implication from legislative history, or by a clear incompatibility between state-court jurisdiction and federal interests." Because we find none of these factors present with respect to civil claims arising under RICO, we hold that state courts retain their presumptive authority to adjudicate such claims.

At the outset, petitioners concede that there is nothing in the language of RICO — much less an "explicit statutory directive" — to suggest that Congress has, by affirmative enactment, divested the state courts of jurisdiction to hear civil RICO claims. The statutory provision authorizing civil RICO claims provides in full:

> Any person injured in his business or property by reason of a violation of section 1962 of this chapter *may* sue therefor in any appropriate United States district court and shall recover threefold the damages he sustains and the cost of the suit, including a reasonable attorney's fee.

18 U.S.C. § 1964(c) (emphasis added).

This grant of federal jurisdiction is plainly permissive, not mandatory, for "[t]he statute does not state nor even suggest that such jurisdiction shall be exclusive. It provides that suits of the kind described 'may' be brought in the federal district courts, not that they must be." *Charles Dowd Box*. Indeed, "it is black letter law . . . that the mere grant of jurisdiction to a federal court does not operate to oust a state court from concurrent jurisdiction over the cause of action." *Gulf Offshore*.

Petitioners thus rely solely on the second and third factors suggested in *Gulf Offshore*, arguing that exclusive federal jurisdiction over civil RICO actions is established "by unmistakable implication from legislative history, or by a clear incompatibility between state-court jurisdiction and federal interests."

Our review of the legislative history, however, reveals no evidence that Congress even considered the question of concurrent state court jurisdiction over RICO claims, much less any suggestion that Congress affirmatively intended to confer exclusive jurisdiction over such claims on the federal courts. As the Courts of Appeals that have considered the question have concluded, "[t]he legislative history contains no indication that Congress ever expressly considered the question of concurrent jurisdiction; indeed, as the principal draftsman of RICO has remarked, 'no one even thought of the issue.' . . ." Petitioners nonetheless insist that if Congress had considered the issue, it would have granted federal courts exclusive jurisdiction over civil RICO claims. This argument, however, is misplaced, for even if we could reliably discern what Congress' intent might have been had it considered the question, we are not at liberty to so speculate; the fact that Congress did not even *consider* the issue readily disposes of any argument that Congress unmistakably intended to divest state courts of concurrent jurisdiction.

Sensing this void in the legislative history, petitioners rely, in the alternative, on our decisions in [previous RICO cases], in which we noted that Congress modeled § 1964(c) after § 4 of the Clayton Act, 15 U.S.C. § 15(a). Petitioners assert that, because we have interpreted § 4 of the Clayton Act to confer exclusive jurisdiction on the federal courts, see, *e.g.*, *General Investment Co. v. Lake Shore & M.S.R. Co.*, 260 U.S. 261 (1922), and because Congress may be presumed to have been aware of and incorporated those interpretations when it used similar language in RICO, Congress intended, by implication, to grant exclusive federal jurisdiction over claims arising under § 1964(c).

This argument is also flawed. To rebut the presumption of concurrent jurisdiction, the question is not whether any intent at all may be divined from legislative silence on the issue, but whether Congress in its deliberations may be said to have affirmatively or unmistakably intended jurisdiction to be exclusively federal. In the instant case, the lack of any indication in RICO's legislative history that Congress either considered or assumed that the importing of remedial language from the Clayton Act into RICO had any jurisdictional implications is dispositive. The "mere borrowing of statutory language does not imply that Congress also intended to incorporate all of the baggage that may be attached to the borrowed language." . . .

Petitioners finally urge that state court jurisdiction over civil RICO claims would be clearly incompatible with federal interests. We noted in *Gulf Offshore* that factors indicating clear incompatibility "include the desirability of uniform interpretation, the expertise of federal judges in federal law, and the assumed greater hospitality of federal courts to peculiarly federal claims." Petitioners' primary contention is that concurrent jurisdiction is clearly incompatible with the federal interest in uniform interpretation of federal criminal laws, because state courts would be required to construe the federal crimes that constitute predicate acts defined as "racketeering activity." Petitioners predict that if state courts are permitted to interpret federal criminal statutes, they will create a body of precedent relating to those statutes and that the federal courts will consequently lose control over the orderly and uniform development of federal criminal law.

We perceive no "clear incompatibility" between state court jurisdiction over civil RICO actions and federal interests. . . . [Our] decision today creates no significant danger of inconsistent application of federal criminal law. Although petitioners' concern with the need for uniformity and consistency of federal criminal law is well taken, federal courts would retain full authority and responsibility for the interpretation and application of federal criminal law, for they would not be bound by state court interpretations of the federal offenses constituting RICO's predicate acts. State courts adjudicating civil RICO claims will, in addition, be guided by federal court interpretations of the relevant federal criminal statutes, just as federal courts sitting in diversity are guided by state court interpretations of state law. State court judgments misinterpreting federal criminal law would, of course, also be subject to direct review by this Court. Thus, we think that state court adjudication of civil RICO actions will, in practice, have at most a negligible effect on the uniform interpretation and application of federal criminal law, and will not, in any event, result in any more inconsistency than that which a multimembered, multi-tiered federal judicial system already creates.

Moreover, contrary to petitioners' fears, we have full faith in the ability of state courts to handle the complexities of civil RICO actions, particularly since many RICO cases involve asserted violations of state law, such as state fraud claims, over which state courts presumably have greater expertise. To hold otherwise would not only denigrate the respect accorded coequal sovereigns, but would also ignore our "consistent history of hospitable acceptance of concurrent jurisdiction." . . .

Finally, we note that, far from disabling or frustrating federal interests, "[p]ermitting state courts to entertain federal causes of action facilitates the enforcement of federal rights." *Gulf Offshore*. Thus, to the extent that Congress intended RICO to serve broad remedial purposes, concurrent state court jurisdiction over civil RICO claims will advance rather than jeopardize federal policies underlying the statute.

For all of the above reasons, we hold that state courts have concurrent jurisdiction to consider civil claims arising under RICO. Nothing in the language, structure, legislative history, or underlying policies of RICO suggests that Congress intended otherwise. The judgment of the Court of Appeals is accordingly

Affirmed.

JUSTICE WHITE, concurring.

. . . RICO is an unusual federal criminal statute. It borrows heavily from state law; racketeering activity is defined in terms of numerous offenses chargeable under state law, as well as various federal offenses. To the extent that there is any danger under RICO of nonuniform construction of criminal statutes, it is quite likely that the damage will result from federal misunderstanding of the content of state law—a problem, to be sure, but not one to be solved by exclusive federal jurisdiction. Many of the federal offenses named as racketeering activity under RICO have close, though perhaps not exact, state-law analogues, and it is unlikely that the state courts will be incompetent to construe those federal statutes. Nor does incorrect state-court construction of those statutes present as significant a threat to federal interests as that posed by improper interpretation of the federal antitrust laws, which could have a disastrous effect on interstate commerce, a particular concern of the Federal Government. Racketeering activity as defined by RICO includes other federal offenses without state-law analogues, but given the history as written until now of civil RICO litigation, I doubt that state-court construction of these offenses will be greatly disruptive of important federal interests. . . .

JUSTICE SCALIA, with whom JUSTICE KENNEDY joins, concurring.

I join the opinion of the Court, addressing the issues before us on the basis argued by the parties, which has included acceptance of the dictum in *Gulf Offshore Co. v. Mobil Oil Corp.* that "'the presumption of concurrent jurisdiction can be rebutted by an explicit statutory directive, by unmistakable implication from legislative history, or by a clear incompatibility between state-court jurisdiction and federal interests.'" Such dicta, when repeatedly used as the point of departure for analysis, have a regrettable tendency to acquire the practical status of legal rules. I write separately, before this one has become too entrenched, to note my view that in one respect it is not a correct statement of the law, and in another respect it may not be.

State courts have jurisdiction over federal causes of action not because it is "conferred" upon them by the Congress; nor even because their inherent powers permit them to entertain transitory causes of action arising under the laws of foreign sovereigns, but because "[t]he laws of the United States are laws in the several States, and just as much binding on the citizens and courts thereof as the State laws are. . . . The two together form one system of jurisprudence, which constitutes the law of the land for the State; and the courts of the two jurisdictions are not foreign to each other. . . ." *Claflin v. Houseman*, 93 U.S. 130 (1876).

It therefore takes an affirmative act of power under the Supremacy Clause to oust the States of jurisdiction—an exercise of what one of our earliest cases referred to as "the power of congress to *withdraw*" federal claims from state-court jurisdiction. *Houston v. Moore*, 5 Wheat. 1 (1820) (emphasis added).

As an original proposition, it would be eminently arguable that depriving state courts of their sovereign authority to adjudicate the law of the land must be done, if not with the utmost clarity, at least *expressly*. That was the view of Alexander Hamilton:

> When . . . we consider the State governments and the national governments, as they truly are, in the light of kindred systems, and as parts of ONE WHOLE, the inference seems to be conclusive that the State courts would have a concurrent jurisdiction in all cases arising under the laws of the Union, where it was not expressly prohibited.

THE FEDERALIST No. 82 (E. Bourne ed., 1947).

Although as early as *Claflin*, and as late as *Gulf Offshore*, we have *said* that the exclusion of concurrent state jurisdiction could be achieved by implication, the only cases in which to my knowledge we have acted upon such a principle are those relating to the Sherman Act and the Clayton Act—where the full extent of our analysis was the less than compelling statement that provisions giving the right to sue in United States District Court "show that [the right] is to be exercised *only* in a 'court of the United States.'" *General Investment Co. v. Lake Shore & Michigan Southern R. Co.*, 260 U.S. 261 (1922) (emphasis added). In the standard fields of exclusive federal jurisdiction, the governing statutes specifically recite that suit may be brought "only" in federal court (Investment Company Act of 1940); that the jurisdiction of the federal courts shall be "exclusive" (Securities Exchange Act of 1934, Natural Gas Act of 1938, and Employee Retirement Income Security Act of 1974); or indeed even that the jurisdiction of the federal courts shall be "exclusive of the courts of the States." [The last-quoted language can be found in] 18 U.S.C. § 3231 (criminal cases); 28 U.S.C. §§ 1333 (admiralty, maritime, and prize cases), 1334 (bankruptcy cases), 1338 (patent, plant variety protection, and copyright cases), 1351 (actions against consuls or vice consuls of foreign states), 1355 (actions for recovery or enforcement of fine, penalty, or forfeiture incurred under Act of Congress), and 1356 (seizures on land or water not within admiralty and maritime jurisdiction).

Assuming, however, that exclusion by implication is possible, surely what is required is implication in the text of the statute, and not merely, as the second part of the *Gulf Offshore* dictum would permit, through "unmistakable implication from legislative history." . . . We have never found state jurisdiction excluded by "unmistakable implication" from legislative history. It is perhaps harmless enough to say that it can be, since one can hardly imagine an "implication from legislative history" that is "unmistakable"—*i.e.*, that demonstrates agreement to a proposition by a majority of both Houses and the President—unless the proposition is embodied in statutory text to which those parties have given assent. But harmless or not, it is simply wrong in principle to assert that Congress can effect this affirmative legislative act by simply talking about it with unmistakable clarity. What is needed to oust the States of jurisdiction is congressional *action* (*i.e.*, a provision of law), not merely congressional discussion.

It is perhaps also true that implied preclusion can be established by the fact that a statute expressly mentions only federal courts, plus the fact that state-court jurisdiction would plainly disrupt the statutory scheme. That is conceivably what was meant by the third part of the *Gulf Offshore* dictum, "clear incompatibility between state-court jurisdiction and federal interests." If the phrase is interpreted more broadly than that, however — if it is taken to assert some power on the part of this Court to exclude state-court jurisdiction when systemic federal interests make it undesirable — it has absolutely no foundation in our precedent. . . .

In sum: As the Court holds, the RICO cause of action meets none of the three tests for exclusion of state-court jurisdiction recited in *Gulf Offshore*. Since that is so, the proposition that meeting any one of the tests would have sufficed is dictum here, as it was there. In my view meeting the second test is assuredly not enough, and meeting the third may not be.

Note: Rebutting the Presumption of Concurrent Jurisdiction

1. Justice Scalia's concurring opinion in *Tafflin* provides a useful catalogue of statutes that explicitly make federal-court jurisdiction exclusive. One of the most important of these is 28 U.S.C. § 1338 (patent, plant variety protection, and copyright cases). That statute is the subject of the Note below.

2. In the absence of "an explicit statutory directive," what kind of showing would rebut the presumption of concurrent jurisdiction? Shortly after the decision in *Tafflin*, the Court handed down a similar ruling involving civil actions under Title VII of the Civil Rights Act of 1964, which prohibits discrimination in employment on the basis of race, sex, and other specified characteristics. The Court said:

> Petitioner has called our attention to a number of passages in the legislative history indicating that many participants in the complex process that finally produced the law fully expected that all Title VII cases would be tried in federal court. That expectation, even if universally shared, is not an adequate substitute for a legislative decision to overcome the presumption of concurrent jurisdiction. Like its plain text, the legislative history of the Act affirmatively describes the jurisdiction of the federal courts, but is completely silent on any role of the state courts over Title VII claims.

Yellow Freight System, Inc. v. Donnelly, 494 U.S. 820 (1990). Justice Stevens wrote for a unanimous Court. There were no separate opinions.

3. After *Tafflin* and *Yellow Freight*, what is left of the statement in *Gulf Offshore* that the presumption of concurrent jurisdiction could be rebutted "by unmistakable implication from legislative history"?

4. As Justice Scalia notes in his *Tafflin* concurrence, the only decisions actually rejecting state-court jurisdiction without an explicit statement from Congress are those involving the federal antitrust laws. Justice White endorses this line of cases, saying that "improper interpretation of the federal antitrust laws [by state courts could] have a disastrous effect on interstate commerce, a particular concern of the Federal Government."

How persuasive is this argument? States have their own antitrust laws, and these laws may be invoked in state courts against national corporations even when the suit would be barred under federal law. For example, the Supreme Court has construed the Clayton Act as not authorizing recovery under federal antitrust laws by indirect purchasers. At the same time, the Court has held that states may allow indirect purchasers to sue under state antitrust laws. *California v. ARC America Corp.*, 490 U.S. 93 (1990). In accordance with *ARC America*, the Arizona Supreme Court has allowed indirect purchasers to bring suit against various manufacturers of flat glass and tobacco. *See Bunker's Glass Co. v. Pilkington PLC*, 75 P.3d 99 (Ariz. 2003).

In this light, and taking into account the rationale of *Tafflin*, would the United States Supreme Court reach the same result today if the question of antitrust exclusivity were to arise as a matter of first impression?

Note: Exclusive Jurisdiction and Intellectual Property Rights

1. As Justice Scalia notes in his concurring opinion in *Tafflin*, one statute that explicitly makes federal jurisdiction exclusive is 28 U.S.C. § 1338. At the time of the *Tafflin* decision, § 1338(a) read as follows:

> The district courts shall have original jurisdiction of any civil action arising under any Act of Congress relating to patents, plant variety protection, copyrights and trademarks. *Such jurisdiction shall be exclusive of the courts of the states* in patent, plant variety protection and copyright cases.

(Emphasis added.) It has never been questioned that if a patent or copyright holder sues for infringement in state court, § 1338(a) requires that the state court dismiss the action. But suppose litigation is initiated in state court by the alleged infringer, claiming solely under state law, and a patent or copyright claim is asserted by the defendant in a responsive pleading—for example, a counterclaim. May the state court adjudicate the patent or copyright counterclaim?

Until 2002, most courts would probably have said "no," relying on 28 U.S.C. § 1338 for the proposition that state courts may not entertain a counterclaim asserting a claim that would be within § 1338 if filed as a complaint. However, in *Holmes Group, Inc. v. Vornado Air Circulation Systems, Inc.*, 535 U.S. 826 (2002), the Supreme Court held that § 1338 must be interpreted in accordance with the "face of the complaint" rule that has long governed the interpretation of 18 U.S.C. § 1331. *See, e.g.*, the familiar case of *Louisville & Nashville R. Co. v. Mottley* (Chapter 10). Under this interpretation, the court said, a counterclaim "cannot serve as a basis for 'arising under' jurisdiction." As a result, state courts suddenly found themselves with jurisdiction to hear patent and copyright infringement claims—provided they were raised by defendants. *See Green v. Hendrickson Publishers, Inc.*, 770 N.E.2d 784 (Ind. 2002) (acknowledging that this result was contrary to Congress's intent, but: "[*Holmes Group*] teaches that what Congress said—not what it intended—is controlling here").

The intellectual property bar was already concerned about the consequences of the *Holmes Group* decision for appellate jurisdiction in the federal system. The prospect that patent and copyright claims would now be heard by state courts aroused additional apprehension. In response to those concerns, Rep. Lamar Smith of Texas introduced legislation generally known as the "*Holmes Group* fix."[1]

In 2011, a modified version of the "*Holmes Group* fix" was enacted into law as part of the Leahy-Smith America Invents Act (AIA). The AIA replaces the second sentence of 28 U.S.C. § 1338(a) with the following new language: "No State court shall have jurisdiction over any claim for relief arising under any Act of Congress relating to patents, plant variety protection, or copyrights." The AIA also added a new provision to the Judicial Code authorizing removal of a case in which "*any* party asserts a claim for relief arising under any Act of Congress relating to patents, plant variety protection, or copyrights." *See* 28 U.S.C. § 1454(a) (emphasis added).

2. Exclusive federal jurisdiction over patent and copyright *claims* does not foreclose state courts from considering patent and copyright *issues*. In *Gunn v. Minton*, 133 S. Ct. 1059 (2014), for example, the plaintiff filed an action in Texas state court against his former attorneys, alleging legal malpractice during earlier patent litigation in federal court. Proving causation, an essential element of that state-law cause of action, required a "case within a case" analysis of the likely outcome of the earlier patent dispute in the absence of the alleged attorney errors. Because the case would "necessarily require application of patent law to the facts of [the] case," the Texas Supreme Court concluded that federal jurisdiction was exclusive. The Supreme Court reversed, stressing that federal courts "have exclusive jurisdiction of all cases arising under the patent laws, but not of all questions in which a patent may be the subject-matter of the controversy." The Court held that legal malpractice—the "claim for relief"—did not "arise[] under" the patent laws as required by § 1338(a), allowing state courts to exercise concurrent jurisdiction. *Gunn* is discussed further in Chapter 10.

Note: Reverse Exclusivity?

1. The Telephone Consumer Protection Act of 1991 (TCPA) makes it unlawful "to send an unsolicited advertisement to a telephone facsimile machine." A section of the Act entitled "Private right of action," 47 U.S.C. § 227(b)(3), provides:

> A person or entity may, if otherwise permitted by the laws or rules of court of a State, bring in an appropriate court of that State—
>
> (A) an action based on a violation of this subsection or the regulations prescribed under this subsection to enjoin such violation,
>
> (B) an action to recover for actual monetary loss from such a violation, or to receive $500 in damages for each such violation, whichever is greater, or
>
> (C) both such actions.

---

1. The senior author of this casebook worked on drafting the legislation. For a detailed legislative history, see H. Rep. 109-407 (2006).

If the court finds that the defendant willfully or knowingly violated this subsection or the regulations prescribed under this subsection, the court may, in its discretion, increase the amount of the award to an amount equal to not more than 3 times the amount available under subparagraph (B) of this paragraph.

Note that the statute authorizes individuals and entities to bring suit for violation of the Act "*in an appropriate court of [a] State,*" "if [such an action is] otherwise permitted by the laws or rules of court of [that] State." Does this mean that suits under the TCPA may *not* be brought in federal court? Is this a rare instance where Congress has created a federal right of action but has vested exclusive jurisdiction in *state* courts?

When that question first came before the federal courts of appeals, the courts generally answered "yes." One dissenting voice was that of then-Judge Samuel A. Alito. Judge Alito relied heavily on the Supreme Court's decision in *Tafflin v. Levitt*. He wrote: "In light of the longstanding and explicit grant of federal question jurisdiction in 28 U.S.C. § 1331, I would ... conclude that a divestment of district court jurisdiction should be as reluctantly found as a divestment of state court jurisdiction." *ErieNet, Inc. v. Velocity Net, Inc.*, 156 F.3d 513 (3d Cir. 1998) (Alito, J., dissenting).

In 2012, the Supreme Court unanimously agreed with Judge Alito. The case was *Mims v. Arrow Financial Services, LLC*, 132 S. Ct. 740 (2012). The Court held, in essence, that actions under the TCPA fall within the general federal-question jurisdiction statute, 28 U.S.C. § 1331, and nothing in the TCPA divested that jurisdiction. Justice Ginsburg wrote for the Court:

> [When] federal law creates a private right of action and furnishes the substantive rules of decision, the claim arises under federal law, and district courts possess federal-question jurisdiction under § 1331. That principle endures unless Congress divests federal courts of their § 1331 adjudicatory authority. ... Accordingly, the District Court retains § 1331 jurisdiction over Mims's complaint unless the TCPA, expressly or by fair implication, excludes federal-court adjudication.

Applying that test, the Court began by analyzing the statutory language. Said Justice Ginsburg: "Nothing in the permissive language of [the TCPA] makes state-court jurisdiction exclusive, or otherwise purports to oust federal courts of their 28 U.S.C. § 1331 jurisdiction over federal claims." The Court then examined the "structure, purpose, [and] legislative history." It found "[nothing that called] for displacement of the federal-question jurisdiction U.S. district courts ordinarily have under 28 U.S.C. § 1331."

2. Could a state decline to allow TCPA suits to be brought in its courts? Reconsider this question in light of the material in section B, *infra*.

Note: Suits Against Federal Officers

During the nineteenth century, the Supreme Court handed down several decisions on the power of state courts to entertain suits against federal officers challenging conduct carried out under the authority of federal law. The best known of these decisions is *Tarble's Case*, 80 U.S. 397 (1872). The Court held there that a state court has no jurisdiction to issue a writ of habeas corpus "for the discharge of a person held under the authority . . . of the United States, by an officer of that government." Earlier, in *McClung v. Silliman*, 6 Wheat. (19 U.S.) 598 (1821), the Court held that a state court could not issue a writ of mandamus against the register of a federal land office to require him to convey land that the plaintiff claimed under federal law. On the other hand, the Court has sustained the power of state courts to entertain actions for damages and actions at law for specific relief against federal officers.

Scholars have questioned whether the distinctions drawn by these holdings make sense. *See, e.g.*, Richard S. Arnold, *The Power of State Courts to Enjoin Federal Officers*, 73 YALE L.J. 1385 (1964). In any event, the cases are of little practical importance today, because any such suit would almost certainly be removed to federal district court. *See* Chapter 4, section B.

B. The Duty of State Courts to Hear Federal Claims

Cases like *Tafflin* lay down a clear default rule: unless Congress provides otherwise, state courts are *permitted* to hear federal claims. Does it follow that state courts are *required* to hear such claims when litigants choose the state forum?

Haywood v. Drown

Supreme Court of the United States, 2009.

556 U.S. 729.

JUSTICE STEVENS delivered the opinion of the Court.

In our federal system of government, state as well as federal courts have jurisdiction over suits brought pursuant to 42 U.S.C. § 1983, the statute that creates a remedy for violations of federal rights committed by persons acting under color of state law. While that rule is generally applicable to New York's supreme courts—the State's trial courts of general jurisdiction—New York's Correction Law § 24 divests those courts of jurisdiction over § 1983 suits that seek money damages from correction officers. New York thus prohibits the trial courts that generally exercise jurisdiction over § 1983 suits brought against other state officials from hearing virtually all such suits brought against state correction officers. The question presented is whether that exceptional treatment of a limited category of § 1983 claims is consistent with the Supremacy Clause of the United States Constitution.

I

Petitioner, an inmate in New York's Attica Correctional Facility, commenced two § 1983 actions against several correction employees alleging that they violated his civil rights in connection with three prisoner disciplinary proceedings and an altercation.

Proceeding *pro se*, petitioner filed his claims in State Supreme Court and sought punitive damages and attorney's fees. The trial court dismissed the actions on the ground that, under N.Y. Correct. Law Ann. §24 (West 1987) [hereinafter Correction Law §24], it lacked jurisdiction to entertain any suit arising under state or federal law seeking money damages from correction officers for actions taken in the scope of their employment. . . .

The New York Court of Appeals, by a 4-to-3 vote, [affirmed] the dismissal of petitioner's damages action. The Court of Appeals rejected petitioner's argument that Correction Law §24's jurisdictional limitation interfered with §1983 and therefore ran afoul of the Supremacy Clause of the United States Constitution. The majority reasoned that, because Correction Law §24 treats state and federal damages actions against correction officers equally (that is, neither can be brought in New York courts), the statute should be properly characterized as a "neutral state rule regarding the administration of the courts" and therefore a "valid excuse" for the State's refusal to entertain the federal cause of action. The majority understood our Supremacy Clause precedents to set forth the general rule that so long as a State does not refuse to hear a federal claim for the "sole reason that the cause of action arises under federal law," its withdrawal of jurisdiction will be deemed constitutional. So read, discrimination *vel non* is the focal point of Supremacy Clause analysis. . . .

Recognizing the importance of the question decided by the New York Court of Appeals, we granted certiorari. We now reverse.

II

Motivated by the belief that damages suits filed by prisoners against state correction officers were by and large frivolous and vexatious, New York passed Correction Law §24. The statute employs a two-step process to strip its courts of jurisdiction over such damages claims and to replace those claims with the State's preferred alternative. The provision states in full:

> 1. No civil action shall be brought in any court of the state, except by the attorney general on behalf of the state, against any officer or employee of the department, in his personal capacity, for damages arising out of any act done or the failure to perform any act within the scope of employment and in the discharge of the duties by such officer or employee.

> 2. Any claim for damages arising out of any act done or the failure to perform any act within the scope of employment and in the discharge of the duties of any officer or employee of the department shall be brought and maintained in the court of claims as a claim against the state.

Thus, under this scheme, a prisoner seeking damages from a correction officer will have his claim dismissed for want of jurisdiction and will be left, instead, to pursue a claim for damages against an entirely different party (the State) in the Court of Claims — a court of limited jurisdiction.[4]

---

4. Although the State has waived its sovereign immunity from liability by allowing itself to be sued in the Court of Claims, a plaintiff seeking damages against the State in that court cannot use §1983 as

For prisoners seeking redress, pursuing the Court of Claims alternative comes with strict conditions. In addition to facing a different defendant, plaintiffs in that Court are not provided with the same relief, or the same procedural protections, made available in § 1983 actions brought in state courts of general jurisdiction. Specifically, under New York law, plaintiffs in the Court of Claims must comply with a 90-day notice requirement, are not entitled to a jury trial, have no right to attorney's fees, and may not seek punitive damages or injunctive relief.

We must decide whether Correction Law § 24, as applied to § 1983 claims, violates the Supremacy Clause.

III

This Court has long made clear that federal law is as much the law of the several States as are the laws passed by their legislatures. Federal and state law "together form one system of jurisprudence, which constitutes the law of the land for the State; and the courts of the two jurisdictions are not foreign to each other, nor to be treated by each other as such, but as courts of the same country, having jurisdiction partly different and partly concurrent." *Claflin v. Houseman*, 93 U.S. 130 (1876). Although § 1983, a Reconstruction-era statute, was passed "to interpose the federal courts between the States and the people, as guardians of the people's federal rights," *Mitchum v. Foster*, 407 U.S. 225 (1972), state courts as well as federal courts are entrusted with providing a forum for the vindication of federal rights violated by state or local officials acting under color of state law.

So strong is the presumption of concurrency that it is defeated only in two narrowly defined circumstances: first, when Congress expressly ousts state courts of jurisdiction, see *Claflin*, and second, "[w]hen a state court refuses jurisdiction because of a neutral state rule regarding the administration of the courts," *Howlett v. Rose*, 496 U.S. 356 (1990). Focusing on the latter circumstance, we have emphasized that only a neutral jurisdictional rule will be deemed a "valid excuse" for departing from the default assumption that "state courts have inherent authority, and are thus presumptively competent, to adjudicate claims arising under the laws of the United States." *Tafflin v. Levitt*, 493 U.S. 455 (1990).

In determining whether a state law qualifies as a neutral rule of judicial administration, our cases have established that a State cannot employ a jurisdictional rule "to dissociate [itself] from federal law because of disagreement with its content or a refusal to recognize the superior authority of its source." *Howlett*. In other words, although States retain substantial leeway to establish the contours of their judicial systems, they lack authority to nullify a federal right or cause of action they believe is inconsistent with their local policies. "The suggestion that [an] act of Congress is not in harmony with the policy of the State, and therefore that the courts of the State are free to decline jurisdiction, is quite inadmissible, because it presupposes what in legal contemplation does not exist." *Second Employers' Liability Cases*, 223 U.S. 1 (1912).

---

a vehicle for redress because a State is not a "person" under § 1983. See *Will v. Michigan Dept. of State Police*, 491 U.S. 58 (1989).

It is principally on this basis that Correction Law § 24 violates the Supremacy Clause. In passing Correction Law § 24, New York made the judgment that correction officers should not be burdened with suits for damages arising out of conduct performed in the scope of their employment. Because it regards these suits as too numerous or too frivolous (or both), the State's longstanding policy has been to shield this narrow class of defendants from liability when sued for damages.[5] The State's policy, whatever its merits, is contrary to Congress' judgment that *all* persons who violate federal rights while acting under color of state law shall be held liable for damages. As we have unanimously recognized, "[a] State may not . . . relieve congestion in its courts by declaring a whole category of federal claims to be frivolous. Until it has been proved that the claim has no merit, that judgment is not up to the States to make." *Howlett*. That New York strongly favors a rule shielding correction officers from personal damages liability and substituting the State as the party responsible for compensating individual victims is irrelevant. The State cannot condition its enforcement of federal law on the demand that those individuals whose conduct federal law seeks to regulate must nevertheless escape liability.

IV

While our cases have uniformly applied the principle that a State cannot simply refuse to entertain a federal claim based on a policy disagreement, we have yet to confront a statute like New York's that registers its dissent by divesting its courts of jurisdiction over a disfavored federal claim in addition to an identical state claim. The New York Court of Appeals' holding was based on the misunderstanding that this equal treatment of federal and state claims rendered Correction Law § 24 constitutional. To the extent our cases have created this misperception, we now make clear that equality of treatment does not ensure that a state law will be deemed a neutral rule of judicial administration and therefore a valid excuse for refusing to entertain a federal cause of action.

Respondents correctly observe that, in the handful of cases in which this Court has found a valid excuse, the state rule at issue treated state and federal claims equally. In *Douglas v. New York, N.H. & H.R. Co.*, 279 U.S. 377 (1929), we upheld a state law that granted state courts discretion to decline jurisdiction over state and federal claims alike when neither party was a resident of the State. Later, in *Herb v. Pitcairn*, 324 U.S.

---

5. In many respects, Correction Law § 24 operates more as an immunity-from-damages provision than as a jurisdictional rule. Indeed, the original version of the statute gave correction officers qualified immunity, providing that no officer would be "liable for damages if he shall have acted in good faith, with reasonable care and upon probable cause." . . .

In *Howlett v. Rose*, 496 U.S. 356 (1990), we considered the question whether a Florida school board could assert a state-law immunity defense in a § 1983 action brought in state court when the defense would not have been available if the action had been brought in federal court. We unanimously held that the State's decision to extend immunity "over and above [that which is] already provided in § 1983 . . . directly violates federal law," and explained that the "elements of, and the defenses to, a federal cause of action are defined by federal law." Thus, if Correction Law § 24 were understood as offering an immunity defense, *Howlett* would compel the conclusion that it violates the Supremacy Clause.

117 (1945), a city court dismissed an action brought under the Federal Employers' Liability Act (FELA), for want of jurisdiction because the cause of action arose outside the court's territorial jurisdiction. We upheld the dismissal on the ground that the State's venue laws were not being applied in a way that discriminated against the federal claim. In a third case, *Missouri ex rel. Southern R. Co. v. Mayfield*, 340 U.S. 1 (1950), we held that a State's application of the *forum non conveniens* doctrine to bar adjudication of a FELA case brought by nonresidents was constitutionally sound as long as the policy was enforced impartially. And our most recent decision finding a valid excuse, *Johnson v. Fankell*, 520 U.S. 911 (1997), rested largely on the fact that Idaho's rule limiting interlocutory jurisdiction did not discriminate against § 1983 actions.

Although the absence of discrimination is necessary to our finding a state law neutral, it is not sufficient. A jurisdictional rule cannot be used as a device to undermine federal law, no matter how evenhanded it may appear. As we made clear in *Howlett*, "[t]he fact that a rule is denominated jurisdictional does not provide a court an excuse to avoid the obligation to enforce federal law if the rule does not reflect the concerns of power over the person and competence over the subject matter that jurisdictional rules are designed to protect." Ensuring equality of treatment is thus the beginning, not the end, of the Supremacy Clause analysis.

In addition to giving too much weight to equality of treatment, respondents mistakenly treat this case as implicating the "great latitude [States enjoy] to establish the structure and jurisdiction of their own courts." Although Correction Law § 24 denies state courts authority to entertain damages actions against correction officers, this case does not require us to decide whether Congress may compel a State to offer a forum, otherwise unavailable under state law, to hear suits brought pursuant to § 1983. The State of New York has made this inquiry unnecessary by creating courts of general jurisdiction that routinely sit to hear analogous § 1983 actions. New York's constitution vests the state supreme courts with general original jurisdiction, and the "inviolate authority to hear and resolve all causes in law and equity." For instance, if petitioner had attempted to sue a police officer for damages under § 1983, the suit would be properly adjudicated by a state supreme court. Similarly, if petitioner had sought declaratory or injunctive relief against a correction officer, that suit would be heard in a state supreme court. It is only a particular species of suits — those seeking damages relief against correction officers — that the State deems inappropriate for its trial courts.

We therefore hold that, having made the decision to create courts of general jurisdiction that regularly sit to entertain analogous suits, New York is not at liberty to shut the courthouse door to federal claims that it considers at odds with its local policy. A State's authority to organize its courts, while considerable, remains subject to the strictures of the Constitution. See, *e.g., McKnett v. St. Louis & San Francisco R. Co.*, 292 U.S. 230 (1934). We have never treated a State's invocation of "jurisdiction" as a trump that ends the Supremacy Clause inquiry, and we decline to do so in this case. Because New York's supreme courts generally have personal jurisdiction over the parties in § 1983 suits brought by prisoners against correction officers and because they hear the lion's share of all other § 1983 actions, we find little concerning "power over the person and competence over the subject matter" in Correction Law § 24.

Accordingly, the dissent's fear that "no state jurisdictional rule will be upheld as constitutional" is entirely unfounded. Our holding addresses only the unique scheme adopted by the State of New York—a law designed to shield a particular class of defendants (correction officers) from a particular type of liability (damages) brought by a particular class of plaintiffs (prisoners). Based on the belief that damages suits against correction officers are frivolous and vexatious, Correction Law § 24 is effectively an immunity statute cloaked in jurisdictional garb. Finding this scheme unconstitutional merely confirms that the Supremacy Clause cannot be evaded by formalism.[9]

V

The judgment of the New York Court of Appeals is reversed, and the case is remanded to that court for further proceedings not inconsistent with this opinion.

JUSTICE THOMAS, with whom THE CHIEF JUSTICE, JUSTICE SCALIA, and JUSTICE ALITO join as to Part III, dissenting.

The Court holds that New York Correction Law Annotated § 24, which divests New York's state courts of subject-matter jurisdiction over suits seeking money damages from correction officers, violates the Supremacy Clause of the Constitution, Art. VI, cl. 2, because it requires the dismissal of federal actions brought in state court under 42 U.S.C. § 1983. I disagree. Because neither the Constitution nor our precedent requires New York to open its courts to § 1983 federal actions, I respectfully dissent.

I

Although the majority decides this case on the basis of the Supremacy Clause, the proper starting point is Article III of the Constitution. . . . The history of the drafting and ratification of this Article establishes that it leaves untouched the States' plenary authority to decide whether their local courts will have subject-matter jurisdiction over federal causes of action.

[Lengthy discussion omitted. Justice Thomas concluded:]

Under our federal system, therefore, the States have unfettered authority to determine whether their local courts may entertain a federal cause of action. Once a State exercises its sovereign prerogative to deprive its courts of subject-matter jurisdiction over a federal cause of action, it is the end of the matter as far as the Constitution is concerned.

II

[In Part II, Justice Thomas argued that "[t]here is no textual or historical support for the Court's incorporation of [an] antidiscrimination principle into the Supremacy Clause." He agreed with the results in *Claflin, Douglas,* and *Testa v. Katt* (all discussed in the Note *infra*), but strongly criticized *McKnett,* both for its result and for

---

9. A contrary conclusion would permit a State to withhold a forum for the adjudication of any federal cause of action with which it disagreed as long as the policy took the form of a jurisdictional rule. That outcome, in turn, would provide a roadmap for States wishing to circumvent our prior decisions.

its declaration "that state jurisdictional statutes must be policed for antifederal discrimination."]

III

Even accepting the entirety of the Court's precedent in this area of the law, however, I still could not join the majority's resolution of this case as it mischaracterizes and broadens this Court's decisions. The majority concedes not only that NYCLA § 24 is jurisdictional, but that the statute is neutral with respect to federal and state claims. Nevertheless, it concludes that the statute violates the Supremacy Clause because it finds that "equality of treatment does not ensure that a state law will be deemed a neutral rule of judicial administration and therefore a valid excuse for refusing to entertain a federal cause of action." This conclusion is incorrect in light of Court precedent for several reasons.

A

The majority mischaracterizes this Court's precedent when it asserts that jurisdictional neutrality is "the beginning, not the end, of the Supremacy Clause analysis." As [Justice Frankfurter said in his concurring opinion in *Brown v. Gerdes*, 321 U.S. 178 (1944),] "subject to only one limitation, each State of the Union may establish its own judicature, distribute judicial power among the courts of its choice, [and] define the conditions for the exercise of their jurisdiction and the modes of their proceeding, to the same extent as Congress is empowered to establish a system of inferior federal courts within the limits of federal judicial power." That "one limitation" is the neutrality principle that the Court has . . . found in the Supremacy Clause. Here, it is conceded that New York has deprived its courts of subject-matter jurisdiction over a particular class of claims on terms that treat federal and state actions equally.

The majority's assertion that jurisdictional neutrality is not the touchstone because "[a] jurisdictional rule cannot be used as a device to undermine federal law, no matter how even-handed it may appear," reflects a misunderstanding of the law. A jurisdictional statute simply deprives the relevant court of the power to decide the case altogether. Such a statute necessarily operates without prejudice to the adjudication of the matter in a competent forum. Jurisdictional statutes therefore by definition are incapable of undermining federal law. NYCLA § 24 no more undermines § 1983 than the amount-in-controversy requirement for federal diversity jurisdiction undermines state law. The relevant law (state or federal) remains fully operative in both circumstances. The sole consequence of the jurisdictional barrier is that the law cannot be enforced in one particular judicial forum. . . .

It may be true that it was "Congress' judgment that *all* persons who violate federal rights while acting under color of state law shall be held liable for damages." But Congress has not enforced that judgment by statutorily requiring the States to open their courts to all § 1983 claims. And this Court has "never held that state courts must entertain § 1983 suits." *National Private Truck Council, Inc. v. Oklahoma Tax Comm'n*, 515 U.S. 582 (1995). Our decisions have held only that the States cannot use jurisdictional statutes to discriminate against federal claims. Because NYCLA § 24 does not violate this command, any policy-driven reasons for depriving jurisdiction over a "federal claim in addition to an identical state claim" are irrelevant for purposes of the Supremacy Clause.

This Court's decision in *Howlett* is not to the contrary. . . .

[That case] stands for the unremarkable proposition that States may not add immunity defenses to § 1983. A state law is not jurisdictional just because the legislature has "denominated" it as such. . . . The majority [is] correct that a state court's decision "to nullify a federal right or cause of action [that it] believe[s] is inconsistent with [its] local policies" cannot evade the Supremacy Clause by hiding behind a jurisdictional label. . . . Rather, a state statute must in fact *operate* jurisdictionally: It must deprive the court of the power to hear the claim and it must not preclude relitigation of the action in a proper forum. *Howlett* proved the point by striking down a state-law immunity rule that bore the jurisdictional label but operated as a defense on the merits and provided for the dismissal of the state court action with prejudice.

But the majority's axiomatic refrain about jurisdictional labels is entirely unresponsive to the issue before the Court — *i.e.*, whether NYCLA § 24 operates jurisdictionally. Unlike the Florida immunity rule in *Howlett*, NYCLA § 24 is not a defense to a federal claim and the dismissal it authorizes is without prejudice. For this reason, NYCLA § 24 is not merely "denominated" as jurisdictional — it actually is jurisdictional. The New York courts, therefore, have not declared a "category" of § 1983 claims to be "frivolous" or to have "no merit" in order to "relieve congestion" in the state-court system. These courts have simply recognized that they lack the power to adjudicate this category of claims regardless of their merit. . . .

The majority's principal response is that NYCLA § 24 "is effectively an immunity statute cloaked in jurisdictional garb." But this curious rejoinder resurrects an argument that the majority abandons earlier in its own opinion. [See footnote 5 of the majority opinion.] The majority needs to choose. Either it should definitively commit to making the impossible case that a statute denying state courts the power to entertain a claim without prejudice to its reassertion in federal court is an immunity defense in disguise, or it should clearly explain why some other aspect of *Howlett* controls the outcome of this case. This Court has required Congress to speak clearly when it intends to "upset the usual constitutional balance of federal and state powers." It should require no less of itself.

At bottom, the majority's warning that upholding New York's law "would permit a State to withhold a forum for the adjudication of any federal cause of action with which it disagreed as long as the policy took the form of a jurisdictional rule" is without any basis in fact. This Court's jurisdictional neutrality command already guards against antifederal discrimination. A decision upholding NYCLA § 24, which fully adheres to that rule, would not "circumvent our prior decisions." It simply would adhere to them.

B

The majority also incorrectly concludes that NYCLA § 24 is not a neutral jurisdictional statute because it applies to a "narrow class of defendants," and because New

York courts "hear the lion's share of all other § 1983 actions." A statute's jurisdictional status does not turn on its narrowness or on its breadth. Rather, as explained above, a statute's jurisdictional status turns on the grounds on which the state-law dismissal rests and the consequences that follow from such rulings. No matter how narrow the majority perceives NYCLA § 24 to be, it easily qualifies as jurisdictional under this established standard. Accordingly, it is immaterial that New York has chosen to allow its courts of general jurisdiction to entertain § 1983 actions against certain categories of defendants but not others (such as correction officers), or to entertain § 1983 actions against particular defendants for only certain types of relief. . . .

[T]he majority's novel approach breaks the promise that the States still enjoy "great latitude . . . to establish the structure and jurisdiction of their own courts." *Ante* (quoting *Howlett*). It cannot be that New York has forsaken the right to withdraw a particular class of claims from its courts' purview simply because it has created courts of general jurisdiction that would otherwise have the power to hear suits for damages against correction officers. The Supremacy Clause does not fossilize the jurisdiction of state courts in their original form. Under this Court's precedent, States remain free to alter the structure of their judicial system even if that means certain federal causes of action will no longer be heard in state court, so long as States do so on nondiscriminatory terms. See *Johnson v. Fankell*, 520 U.S. 911 (1997) ("We have made it quite clear that it is a matter for each State to decide how to structure its judicial system"). Today's decision thus represents a dramatic and unwarranted expansion of this Court's precedent.

IV

. . . [By] declaring unconstitutional even those laws that divest state courts of jurisdiction over federal claims on a non-discriminatory basis, the majority has silently overturned this Court's unbroken line of decisions upholding state statutes that are materially indistinguishable from the New York law under review. And it has transformed a single exception to the rule of state judicial autonomy into a virtually iron-clad obligation to entertain federal business. I respectfully dissent.

Note: The Obligation to Hear Federal Claims

The majority and the dissent in *Haywood* debate the import of the Court's precedents governing the obligation of state courts to hear federal claims. This Note explores some of the important earlier cases and raises questions about the breadth of the doctrine. A separate Note explores the implications of the *Haywood* decision.

A. *Claflin, Testa,* and the Issues "Resolved by War"

In *Testa v. Katt*, 330 U.S. 386 (1947), the state courts of Rhode Island refused jurisdiction over claims under a federal statute that called for treble damages against defendants, reasoning that the statute was "penal" in nature and thus non-binding. The Court unanimously rejected that contention, and in doing so placed the debate over the duty of state courts to hear federal claims in historical perspective. Writing for the Court, Justice Black said:

[We] cannot accept the basic premise . . . that [a state court] has no more obligation to enforce a valid penal law of the United States than it has to enforce a penal law of another state or a foreign country. Such a broad assumption flies in the face of the fact that the States of the Union constitute a nation. It disregards the purpose and effect of Article VI, § 2 of the Constitution which provides: "This Constitution, and the Laws of the United States which shall be made in Pursuance thereof . . . shall be the supreme Law of the Land; and the Judges in every State shall be bound thereby, any Thing in the Constitution or Laws of any State to the Contrary notwithstanding."

It cannot be assumed, the supremacy clause considered, that the responsibilities of a state to enforce the laws of a sister state are identical with its responsibilities to enforce federal laws. Such an assumption represents an erroneous evaluation of the statutes of Congress and the prior decisions of this Court in their historic setting. Those decisions establish that state courts do not bear the same relation to the United States that they do to foreign countries. The first Congress that convened after the Constitution was adopted conferred jurisdiction upon the state courts to enforce important federal civil laws, and succeeding Congresses conferred on the states jurisdiction over federal crimes and actions for penalties and forfeitures.

Enforcement of federal laws by state courts did not go unchallenged. Violent public controversies existed throughout the first part of the Nineteenth Century until the 1860's concerning the extent of the constitutional supremacy of the Federal Government. During that period there were instances in which this Court and state courts broadly questioned the power and duty of state courts to exercise their jurisdiction to enforce United States civil and penal statutes or the power of the Federal Government to require them to do so. But after the fundamental issues over the extent of federal supremacy had been resolved by war, this Court took occasion in 1876 to review the phase of the controversy concerning the relationship of state courts to the Federal Government. *Claflin v. Houseman*, 93 U.S. 130.

The opinion of a unanimous court in that case was strongly buttressed by historic references and persuasive reasoning. . . . It asserted that the obligation of states to enforce [federal] laws is not lessened by reason of the form in which they are cast or the remedy which they provide. And the Court stated that "If an act of Congress gives a penalty to a party aggrieved, without specifying a remedy for its enforcement, there is no reason why it should not be enforced, if not provided otherwise by some act of Congress, by a proper action in a state court."

Justice Black said that *Claflin* "answered most of the arguments theretofore advanced against the power *and duty* of state courts to enforce federal penal laws." (Emphasis added.) But the issue in *Claflin* was whether the state court had *authority* to hear the federal claim. The Court did not consider whether a state court is *obligated* to entertain a federal claim if it objects to doing so.

B. The FELA cases

That issue came into focus in a series of cases involving the Federal Employers Liability Act (FELA). This was not happenstance. Until well into the twentieth century, Congress passed few laws that authorized private individuals to go into court to enforce federal rights. (Indeed, there were not many federal rights to be enforced.) There were some civil rights laws, like the predecessor of § 1983, that created private remedies, but they were little used. Thus, questions as to whether state courts were obliged to hear federal claims did not arise very often.

The Federal Employers Liability Act was one of the first federal statutes to authorize a federal cause of action that was available to a large class of potential plaintiffs. FELA was enacted in 1908, with amendments in 1910. The statute created a remedy in damages for employees of interstate railroads who were injured or killed as a result of negligence on the part of the railroad. FELA also abolished the common-law "fellow servant" rule, under which an employee could not recover damages from his employer if his injuries resulted from the negligence of a "fellow servant."

Challenges to FELA came to the Supreme Court quickly. One of the landmark decisions was *Mondou v. New York, N.H. & H.R. Co.*, 223 U.S. 1 (1912) (sometimes cited as *Second Employers' Liability Cases*). The *Mondou* case arose in Connecticut, one of the states that adhered to the fellow-servant rule. The Connecticut court believed that the rule was founded upon considerations of justice as well as policy. It held that Congress could not require a state court to entertain FELA actions and thus "to enforce what [the state] deemed injustice." The Supreme Court rejected that proposition in the language quoted in part by Justice Stevens:

> The suggestion that the act of Congress is not in harmony with the policy of the state, and therefore that the courts of the state are free to decline jurisdiction, is quite inadmissible, because it presupposes what in legal contemplation does not exist. When Congress, in the exertion of the power confided to it by the Constitution, adopted that act, it spoke for all the people and all the states, and thereby established a policy for all. That policy is as much the policy of Connecticut as if the act had emanated from its own legislature, and should be respected accordingly in the courts of the state.

But how far did *Mondou* go? The *Mondou* opinion referred to "the duty of [a state] court, when its ordinary jurisdiction as prescribed by local laws is appropriate to the occasion and is invoked *in conformity with those laws*." (Emphasis added.) This language certainly implied that the Court did not contemplate an absolute obligation on the part of state courts to hear federal claims. A few years later, in *Douglas v. New York, N.H. & H.R. Co.*, 279 U.S. 377 (1929), the Court confirmed this interpretation. The Court indicated, in a characteristically terse opinion by Justice Holmes, that state courts could refuse to entertain federal claims if they had "an otherwise valid excuse."

What is an otherwise valid excuse? To date, there are only three cases in which the Court has excused a state court's refusal to entertain a federal cause of action. All three arose under FELA. All three involved rules permitting or requiring courts to dismiss claims based on extraterritoriality. And in all three cases the rule applied equally to state and federal claims. *See Missouri ex rel. Southern R. Co. v. Mayfield*, 340 U.S. 1 (1950) (dismissal based on *forum non conveniens*); *Herb v. Pitcairn*, 324 U.S. 117 (1945) (dismissal of claims arising outside the state's territorial jurisdiction); *Douglas* (discretionary dismissal of claims where neither the plaintiff nor the defendant was a resident of the state).

The Court has also made clear, however, that no "excuse" can be valid if it applies to federal claims but not to claims under state law. That was the holding of *McKnett v. St. Louis & S.F.R. Co.*, 292 U.S. 230 (1934). Justice Brandeis wrote for the Court:

> While Congress has not attempted to compel states to provide courts for the enforcement of the Federal Employers' Liability Act [citing *Douglas*], the Federal Constitution prohibits state courts of general jurisdiction from refusing to do so solely because the suit is brought under a federal law. The denial of jurisdiction by the Alabama court is based solely upon the source of law sought to be enforced. The plaintiff is cast out because he is suing to enforce a federal act. A state may not discriminate against rights arising under federal laws.

C. *Howlett v. Rose*

Section 1 of the Civil Rights Act of 1871, now codified as 42 U.S.C. § 1983, creates a remedy for violations of federal rights committed by any "person" acting under color of state law. In *Howlett v. Rose*, 496 U.S. 356 (1990), the plaintiff sued the local school board under § 1983 seeking damages for an allegedly unconstitutional search of his car by an assistant principal. The state appellate court held that the suit was properly dismissed because Florida's statutory waiver of sovereign immunity did not apply to § 1983 cases. The United States Supreme Court unanimously reversed. Justice Stevens, writing for the Court, said:

> [Whether] the question is framed in pre-emption terms, as petitioner would have it, or in the obligation to assume jurisdiction over a "federal" cause of action, as respondents would have it, the Florida court's refusal to entertain one discrete category of § 1983 claims, when the court entertains similar state-law actions against state defendants, violates the Supremacy Clause.

> If the District Court of Appeal meant to hold that governmental entities subject to § 1983 liability enjoy an immunity over and above those already provided in § 1983, that holding directly violates federal law. The elements of, and the defenses to, a federal cause of action are defined by federal law. . . . [Since] the Court has held that municipal corporations and similar governmental entities are "persons" [subject to suit under § 1983], see *Monell v. New York City Dept. of Social Services*, 436 U.S. 658 (1978), a state court entertaining a § 1983 action must adhere to that interpretation. . . .

> If, on the other hand, the District Court of Appeal meant that § 1983 claims are excluded from the category of tort claims that the Circuit Court could

hear against a school board, its holding was no less violative of federal law. . . . [The Circuit Court] exercises jurisdiction over tort claims by private citizens against state entities (including school boards), of the size and type of petitioner's claim here, and it can enter judgment against them. . . . Respondents have offered no neutral or valid excuse for the Circuit Court's refusal to hear § 1983 actions against state entities.

Note: Haywood *and Its Implications*

1. Justice Stevens, writing for the Court in *Haywood*, acknowledges that the Court's prior decisions may have created the "misperception" that "equal treatment of federal and state claims . . . [ensures] that a state law will be deemed a neutral rule of judicial administration and therefore a valid excuse for refusing to entertain a federal cause of action." One source of that "misperception" might have been Justice Stevens' own opinion for the Court in *Howlett*, which as noted above stated that "the Florida court's refusal to entertain one discrete category of § 1983 claims, *when the court entertains similar state-law actions against state defendants*, violates the Supremacy Clause." (Emphasis added.)

As long as the state court does not discriminate against federal claims, why should the Supremacy Clause require more? As Justice Thomas noted in dissent, the federal court will be open to the federal claim in any event.

2. In *National Private Truck Council., Inc. v. Oklahoma Tax Commission*, 515 U.S. 582 (1995), the Court said in a footnote: "We have never held that state courts must entertain § 1983 suits." The Court cited two earlier cases in which it noted that the question was an open one. In *Howlett*, the Court implied that federal law might not impose such a requirement. Justice Stevens wrote:

> When a state court refuses jurisdiction because of a neutral state rule regarding the administration of the courts, we must act with utmost caution before deciding that it is obligated to entertain the claim. The requirement that a state court of competent jurisdiction treat federal law as the law of the land does not necessarily include within it a requirement that the State create a court competent to hear the case in which the federal claim is presented. The general rule, "bottomed deeply in belief in the importance of state control of state judicial procedure, is that federal law takes the state courts as it finds them." Hart, *The Relations Between State and Federal Law*, 54 COLUM. L. REV. 489 (1954). The States thus have great latitude to establish the structure and jurisdiction of their own courts. In addition, States may apply their own neutral procedural rules to federal claims, unless those rules are preempted by federal law.

After *Haywood*, does the question remain open? Has the Court now held that "state courts must entertain § 1983 suits?"

3. In *Haywood*, all members of the Court agree that, as stated in *Howlett*, the "elements of, and the defenses to, a federal cause of action are defined by federal law." So if Corrections Law § 24 creates an immunity defense to § 1983 claims, it would be

invalid even under the dissent's view. Is § 24 such a law? Toward the end of its opinion, the Court says that § 24 "is effectively an immunity statute cloaked in jurisdictional garb." But in footnote 5, the Court seems to disclaim that position. And Justice Thomas, in dissent, says that it is "impossible" to make the case "that a statute denying state courts the power to entertain a claim without prejudice to its reassertion in federal court is an immunity defense in disguise."

Does the Court's decision rest on a determination that New York has attempted to establish an immunity defense to a federal claim? If not, what is the basis for the decision?

4. The Court says that a jurisdictional rule "cannot be used as a device to undermine federal law, no matter how evenhanded it may appear." Justice Thomas responds by saying that § 24 "no more undermines § 1983 than the amount-in-controversy requirement for federal diversity jurisdiction undermines state law." Does the majority respond? Is the analogy persuasive?

5. A plaintiff who wishes to pursue a claim under § 1983 can always sue in federal district court. Why might a plaintiff prefer state court?

6. Consider the Problem below. Does *Haywood* provide the answer? Or is the case distinguishable?

Problem: A Title VII Claim in State Court

Robert Johnson has filed suit in the state court of New Harmony against his former employer, Acme Packaging Co. (Acme), asserting that Acme discharged him on the basis of his race in violation of Title VII of the Civil Rights Act of 1964. He seeks damages and reinstatement. Acme has moved to dismiss the action for lack of subject-matter jurisdiction. Acme invokes section 203 of the New Harmony Human Rights Act (HRA).

The HRA is a comprehensive statute that prohibits discrimination on the basis of race, color, sex, and various other characteristics. Section 203 of the Act provides: "Except as otherwise provided by law, no court of this state shall have jurisdiction over the subject of an alleged civil rights violation other than as set forth in this Act." The New Harmony courts have consistently held that the HRA is the exclusive vehicle for resolution of employment discrimination cases. They have also held that the initial limiting phrase ("[e]xcept as otherwise provided by law") must be construed narrowly.

Section 103 of the HRA requires that before bringing an action in state court for an alleged violation of civil rights, the claimant must file a complaint with the New Harmony Human Rights Commission (HRC) and exhaust state administrative remedies. In particular, the HRC must review the complaint and attempt to resolve the dispute "by informal methods of conciliation, conference, and persuasion." If the plaintiff is not satisfied, he or she can seek redress in court. Under the HRA, a dismissal for failure to exhaust is without prejudice to filing an action after remedies have been exhausted. Johnson did not file a complaint with the HRC before instituting his action in state court.

Johnson argues that federal law allows him to bring his claim in state court notwithstanding section 203 of the HRA. Is he correct?

C. State Law and the Enforcement of Federal Rights

Haywood emphasizes the supremacy of federal law when a litigant seeks to pursue a federal claim in state court. How far does the principle carry? Does federal law govern all of the issues that may arise in the course of litigation? If not, under what circumstances may state courts apply their own law?

One answer to these questions came from Professor Henry M. Hart, a great scholar of the mid-twentieth century. Professor Hart said the general rule, "bottomed deeply in belief in the importance of state control of state judicial procedure, is that federal law takes the state courts as it finds them." (The Court quoted this language in *Howlett*.) But in *Felder v. Casey*, 487 U.S. 131 (1988), the Court, speaking through Justice Brennan, qualified Professor Hart's statement, saying, "Federal law takes state courts as it finds them only insofar as those courts employ rules that do not 'impose unnecessary burdens upon rights of recovery authorized by federal laws.'" As you study the materials in this section, consider whether either of these two statements accurately encapsulates the doctrines that delineate the role of state law when a litigant seeks to enforce federal rights in state court.

Johnson v. Fankell

Supreme Court of the United States, 1997.

520 U.S. 911.

JUSTICE STEVENS delivered the opinion of the Court.

The question presented is whether defendants in an action brought under 42 U.S.C. § 1983 in state court have a federal right to an interlocutory appeal from a denial of qualified immunity. We hold that they do not.

I

Petitioners are officials of the Idaho Liquor Dispensary. Respondent, a former liquor store clerk, brought this action for damages under § 1983 in the District Court for the County of Bonner, Idaho. She alleged that petitioners deprived her of property without due process of law in violation of the Fourteenth Amendment to the Federal Constitution when they terminated her employment. Petitioners moved to dismiss the complaint on the ground that they were entitled to qualified immunity. They contended that, at the time of respondent's dismissal, they reasonably believed that she was a probationary employee who had no property interest in her job. Accordingly, petitioners argued, her termination did not violate clearly established law. The trial court denied the motion, and petitioners filed a timely notice of appeal to the Supreme Court of the State of Idaho.

The State Supreme Court entered an order dismissing the appeal. The court explained that an order denying a motion for summary judgment is not appealable under Idaho Appellate Rule 11(a)(1) "for the reason it is not from a final order or Judgment." [The court also rejected petitioners' argument that they had a right to appeal as a matter of federal law.]

Petitioners then filed a petition in this Court seeking either a writ of certiorari or a writ of mandamus. They pointed out that some state courts, unlike the Idaho Supreme Court, allow interlocutory appeals of orders denying qualified immunity on the theory that such review is necessary to protect a substantial federal right. We granted certiorari to resolve the conflict, and now affirm.

II

We have recognized a qualified immunity defense for both federal officials sued under the implied cause of action asserted in *Bivens v. Six Unknown Fed. Narcotics Agents*, 403 U.S. 388 (1971), and state officials sued under 42 U.S.C. § 1983. In both situations, "officials performing discretionary function[s], generally are shielded from liability for civil damages insofar as their conduct does not violate clearly established statutory or constitutional rights of which a reasonable person would have known." *Harlow v. Fitzgerald*, 457 U.S. 800 (1982).

This "qualified immunity" defense is valuable to officials asserting it for two reasons. First, if it is found applicable at any stage of the proceedings, it determines the outcome of the litigation by shielding the official from damages liability. Second, when the complaint fails to allege a violation of clearly established law or when discovery fails to uncover evidence sufficient to create a genuine issue whether the defendant committed such a violation, it provides the defendant with an immunity from the burdens of trial as well as a defense to liability. Indeed, one reason for adopting the objective test announced in *Harlow* was to "permit the resolution of many insubstantial claims on summary judgment."

Consistent with that purpose, we held in *Mitchell v. Forsyth*, 472 U.S. 511 (1985), that a Federal District Court order rejecting a qualified immunity defense on the ground that the defendant's actions — if proved — would have violated clearly established law may be appealed immediately as a "final decision" within the meaning of the general federal appellate jurisdiction statute, 28 U.S.C. § 1291. If this action had been brought in a federal court, therefore, petitioners would have had a right to take an appeal from the trial court's order denying their motion for summary judgment.

Relying on the facts (a) that respondent has asserted a federal claim under a federal statute, and (b) that they are asserting a defense provided by federal law, petitioners submit that the Idaho courts must protect their right to avoid the burdens of trial by allowing the same interlocutory appeal that would be available in a federal court. They support this submission with two different arguments: First, that when the Idaho courts construe their own rules allowing appeals from final judgments, they must accept the federal definition of finality in cases brought under § 1983; and second, that if those rules do not authorize the appeal, they are pre-empted by federal law. We find neither argument persuasive.

III

We can easily dispense with petitioners' first contention that Idaho must follow the federal construction of a "final decision." Even if the Idaho and federal statutes contained identical language—and they do not—the interpretation of the Idaho statute by the Idaho Supreme Court would be binding on federal courts. Neither this Court nor any other federal tribunal has any authority to place a construction on a state statute different from the one rendered by the highest court of the State. This proposition, fundamental to our system of federalism, is applicable to procedural as well as substantive rules.

The definition of the term "final decision" that we adopted in *Mitchell* was an application of the "collateral order" doctrine first recognized in *Cohen v. Beneficial Industrial Loan Corp.*, 337 U.S. 541 (1949). In that case, as in all of our cases following it, we were construing the federal statutory language of 28 U.S.C. § 1291. . . . Idaho could, of course, place the same construction on its Appellate Rule 11(a)(1) as we have placed on § 1291. But that is clearly a choice for that court to make, not one that we have any authority to command.

IV

Petitioners also contend that, to the extent that Idaho Appellate Rule 11(a)(1) does not allow an interlocutory appeal, it is pre-empted by § 1983. Relying heavily on *Felder v. Casey*, 487 U.S. 131 (1988), petitioners first assert that pre-emption is necessary to avoid "different outcomes in § 1983 litigation based solely on whether the claim is asserted in state or federal court." Second, they argue that the state procedure "impermissibly burden[s]" the federal immunity from suit because it does not adequately protect their right to prevail on the immunity question in advance of trial.

For two reasons, petitioners have a heavy burden of persuasion in making this argument. First, our normal presumption against pre-emption is buttressed by the fact that the Idaho Supreme Court's dismissal of the appeal rested squarely on a neutral state Rule regarding the administration of the state courts.[9] As we explained in *Howlett v. Rose*, 496 U.S. 356 (1990):

> When a state court refuses jurisdiction because of a neutral state rule regarding the administration of the courts, we must act with utmost caution before deciding that it is obligated to entertain the claim. . . . The general rule, "bottomed deeply in belief in the importance of state control of state judicial procedure, is that federal law takes the state courts as it finds them." Hart, *The*

---

9. Unlike the notice-of-claim rule at issue in *Felder v. Casey*, Idaho Appellate Rule 11(a)(1) does not target civil rights claims against the State. See also *Howlett v. Rose*, 496 U.S. 356 (1990). Instead, it generally permits appeals only of "[j]udgments, orders and decrees which are final," without regard to the identity of the party seeking the appeal or the subject matter of the suit. Petitioners claim that the rule is not neutral because it permits interlocutory appeals in certain limited circumstances but denies an appeal here. But we have never held that a rule must be monolithic to be neutral. Absent evidence that Appellate Rule 11(a)(1) discriminates against interlocutory appeals of § 1983 qualified immunity determinations by defendants—as compared with other types of appeals—we must deem the state procedure neutral.

Relations Between State and Federal Law, 54 COLUM. L. REV. 489 (1954). The States thus have great latitude to establish the structure and jurisdiction of their own courts.

A second barrier to petitioners' argument arises from the nature of the interest protected by the defense of qualified immunity. Petitioners' argument for pre-emption is bottomed on their claims that the Idaho rules are interfering with their federal rights. While it is true that the defense has its source in a federal statute (§ 1983), the ultimate purpose of qualified immunity is to protect the State and its officials from overenforcement of federal rights. The Idaho Supreme Court's application of the State's procedural rules in this context is thus less an interference with *federal* interests than a judgment about how best to balance the competing *state* interests of limiting interlocutory appeals and providing state officials with immediate review of the merits of their defense.

Petitioners' arguments for pre-emption are not strong enough to overcome these considerable hurdles. Contrary to petitioners' assertions, Idaho's decision not to provide appellate review for the vast majority of interlocutory orders—including denials of qualified immunity in § 1983 cases—is not "outcome determinative" in the sense that we used that term when we held that Wisconsin's notice-of-claim statute could not be applied to defeat a federal civil rights action brought in state courts under § 1983. The failure to comply with the Wisconsin statute in *Felder* resulted in a judgment dismissing a complaint that would not have been dismissed—at least not without a judicial determination of the merits of the claim—if the case had been filed in a federal court. One of the primary grounds for our decision was that, because the notice-of-claim requirement would "frequently and predictably produce different outcomes" depending on whether § 1983 claims were brought in state or federal court, it was inconsistent with the federal interest in uniformity.[11]

Petitioners' reliance on *Felder* is misplaced because "outcome," as we used the term there, referred to the ultimate disposition of the case. If petitioners' claim to qualified immunity is meritorious, there is no suggestion that the application of the Idaho rules of procedure will produce a final result different from what a federal ruling would produce. Petitioners were able to argue their immunity from suit claim to the trial court, just as they would to a federal court. And the claim will be reviewable by the Idaho Supreme Court after the trial court enters a final judgment, thus providing petitioners with a further chance to urge their immunity. Consequently, the postponement of the appeal until after final judgment will not affect the ultimate outcome of the case.

Petitioners' second argument for pre-emption of the state procedural Rule is that the Rule does not adequately protect their right to prevail in advance of trial. In evaluating this contention, it is important to focus on the precise source and scope of the

---

11. See also *Brown v. Western R. Co. of Ala.*, 338 U.S. 294 (1949) (Federal Employers' Liability Act (FELA) pre-empted different state pleading requirements when effect was to defeat plaintiff's cause of action); *Garrett v. Moore-McCormack Co.*, 317 U.S. 239 (1942) (federal Jones Act pre-empted different state burden of proof regarding releases when effect was to defeat plaintiff's cause of action).

federal right at issue. The right to have the trial court rule on the merits of the qualified immunity defense presumably has its source in § 1983, but the right to immediate appellate review of that ruling in a federal case has its source in § 1291. The former right is fully protected by Idaho. The latter right, however, is a federal procedural right that simply does not apply in a nonfederal forum.[12]

. . . When pre-emption of state law is at issue, we must respect the "principles [that] are fundamental to a system of federalism in which the state courts share responsibility for the application and enforcement of federal law." *Howlett.* This respect is at its apex when we confront a claim that federal law requires a State to undertake something as fundamental as restructuring the operation of its courts. We therefore cannot agree with petitioners that § 1983's recognition of the defense of qualified immunity pre-empts a State's consistent application of its neutral procedural rules, even when those rules deny an interlocutory appeal in this context.

The judgment of the Supreme Court of the State of Idaho dismissing petitioners' appeal is therefore affirmed.

Note: Preemption of State Law and the FELA Cases

In *Fankell*, the Court reiterates Professor Hart's assertion that "federal law takes state courts as it finds them." The Court's opinion distinguishes and perhaps downplays several important decisions that qualify this proposition. Prominent among these are cases involving the Federal Employers Liability Act (FELA). The Court also distinguishes *Felder v. Casey*; that case is discussed in the Note that follows.

A. *Dice*

In footnote 12, Justice Stevens distinguishes *Dice v. Akron, Canton & Youngstown R. Co.*, 342 U.S. 359 (1952). In that case, a difficult choice-of-law question arose because Ohio maintained "the old division between law and equity as to the mode of trying issues." As part of this allocation of functions, the judge rather than the jury would determine the factual questions relating to the validity of a release when the release was challenged on the ground of fraud. A bare majority of the Court held that this rule could not be applied in FELA cases:

> We have previously held that "The right to trial by jury is a basic and fundamental feature of our system of federal jurisprudence" and that it is "part and parcel of the remedy afforded railroad workers under the Employers' Liability Act." *Bailey v. Central Vermont R. Co.*, 319 U.S. 350 (1943). We also recognized in that case that to deprive railroad workers of the benefit of a jury trial where there is evidence to support negligence "is to take away a

---

12. Petitioners' reliance on *Dice v. Akron, C. & Y.R. Co.*, 342 U.S. 359 (1952), is therefore misplaced. In *Dice* we held that the FELA pre-empted a state rule denying a right to a jury trial. In that case, however, we made clear that Congress had provided in FELA that the jury trial procedure was to be part of claims brought under the Act. In this case, by contrast, Congress has mentioned nothing about interlocutory appeals in § 1983; rather, the right to an immediate appeal in the federal court system is found in § 1291, which obviously has no application to state courts.

goodly portion of the relief which Congress has afforded them." It follows that the right to trial by jury is too substantial a part of the rights accorded by the Act to permit it to be classified as a mere "local rule of procedure" for denial in the manner that Ohio has here used. *Brown v. Western R. Co.*, 338 U.S. 294 (1949).

Justice Frankfurter, joined by three other Justices, dissented on this point:

> Although a State must entertain negligence suits brought under the Federal Employers' Liability Act if it entertains ordinary actions for negligence, it need conduct them only in the way in which it conducts the run of negligence litigation. . . . Ohio and her sister States with a similar division of functions between law and equity are not trying to evade their duty under the Federal Employers' Liability Act; nor are they trying to make it more difficult for railroad workers to recover, than for those suing under local law. The States merely exercise a preference in adhering to historic ways of dealing with a claim of fraud; they prefer the traditional way of making unavailable through equity an otherwise valid defense.
>
> The State judges and local lawyers who must administer the Federal Employers' Liability Act in State courts are trained in the ways of local practice; it multiplies the difficulties and confuses the administration of justice to require, on purely theoretical grounds, a hybrid of State and Federal practice in the State courts as to a single class of cases. Nothing in the Employers' Liability Act or in the judicial enforcement of the Act for over forty years forces such judicial hybridization upon the States. The fact that Congress authorized actions under the Federal Employers' Liability Act to be brought in State as well as in Federal courts seems a strange basis for the inference that Congress overrode State procedural arrangements controlling all other negligence suits in a State, by imposing upon State courts to which plaintiffs choose to go the rules prevailing in the Federal courts regarding juries.

The dissenters in *Dice* placed heavy reliance on the venerable case of *Minneapolis & St. Louis R. Co. v. Bombolis*, 241 U.S. 211 (1916). In *Bombolis*, state law permitted nonunanimous jury verdicts in certain circumstances. The Supreme Court held that this rule could be applied to FELA cases. The dissenters in *Dice* said that the import of *Bombolis* was "to leave to States the choice of the fact-finding tribunal in all negligence actions, including those arising under [FELA]." The majority responded by saying that *Bombolis* "might be more in point had Ohio abolished trial by jury in all negligence cases including those arising under the federal Act." But *Bombolis* did not allow the state to "single out one phase of the question of fraudulent releases for determination by a judge rather than a jury."

Can the Court really mean that the state could abolish trial by jury altogether in negligence cases (including suits under the FELA) but cannot allow one particular issue in FELA cases to be determined by the judge?

B. The "clinker" case (*Brown v. Western Railway*)

Footnote 11 in *Fankell* implicitly distinguishes another FELA case, *Brown v. Western Railway of Alabama*, 338 U.S. 294 (1949). *Brown* is sometimes referred to as "the clinker case."

Brown sued the railroad in Georgia state court. His complaint asserted that he was injured while in the performance of his duties when he stepped on a large "clinker" lying alongside the track in the railroad yards. (A "clinker" is a hard fragment of incombustible matter that remains after wood or charcoal has been burned.) The trial court dismissed the suit, saying that the complaint was insufficient as a matter of law. The state appellate court affirmed. The court followed a state rule of practice to construe pleading allegations "most strongly against the pleader." The court said: "The mere presence of a large clinker in a railroad yard can not be said to constitute an act of negligence."

The United States Supreme Court held first that it was not bound by the Georgia court's construction of the complaint. The Court then held that "the allegations of the complaint do set forth a cause of action which should not have been dismissed." After quoting the allegations at length, the Court continued:

> These allegations, fairly construed, are much more than a charge that petitioner "stepped on a large clinker lying alongside the track in the railroad yards." They also charge that the railroad permitted clinkers and other debris to be left along the tracks, "well knowing" that this was dangerous to workers; that petitioner was compelled to "cross over" the clinkers and debris; that in doing so he fell and was injured; and that all of this was in violation of the railroad's duty to furnish petitioner a reasonably safe place to work. Certainly these allegations are sufficient to permit introduction of evidence from which a jury might infer that petitioner's injuries were due to the railroad's negligence in failing to supply a reasonably safe place to work. . . .

> Strict local rules of pleading cannot be used to impose unnecessary burdens upon rights of recovery authorized by federal laws. . . . Should this Court fail to protect federally created rights from dismissal because of over-exacting local requirements for meticulous pleadings, desirable uniformity in adjudication of federally created rights could not be achieved.

Justice Frankfurter (joined by Justice Jackson) dissented, but on narrow grounds. The question, as he saw it, was "whether the Georgia courts have merely enforced a local requirement of pleading, however finicky, applicable to all such litigation in Georgia," or whether those court had qualified "the basis of recovery under FELA" or had weighted the scales against the plaintiff. In his reading of the decision, the Georgia court had done no more than to "conscientiously apply . . . the local requirement of particularity" for setting forth a claim of negligence.

Does *Brown* mean that state courts, when adjudicating federal claims, must apply federal rules of pleading? Note the *Fankell* Court's summary: FELA "pre-empted different state pleading requirements *when [the] effect was to defeat plaintiff's cause of action*." (Emphasis added.)

C. The import of the FELA cases

Do the FELA decisions establish rules of preemption applicable to all federal claims, or are they sui generis? In an earlier FELA case, *Bailey v. Central Vermont Ry., Inc.*, 319 U.S. 350 (1943), the Court said:

> The right to trial by jury . . . is part and parcel of the remedy afforded rail-road workers under the Employers' Liability Act. Reasonable care and cause and effect are as elusive here as in other fields. But the jury has been chosen as the appropriate tribunal to apply those standards to the facts of these personal injuries. That method of determining the liability of the carriers and of placing on them the cost of these industrial accidents may be crude, archaic, and expensive as compared with the more modern systems of workmen's compensation. But however inefficient and backward it may be, it is the system which Congress has provided. To deprive these workers of the benefit of a jury trial in close or doubtful cases is to take away a goodly portion of the relief which Congress has afforded them.

Why does denying trial by jury "in close or doubtful cases . . . take away a goodly portion of the relief which Congress has afforded" to railroad workers? Is the Court assuming that juries will decide all such cases in favor of the injured employee?

Justice Roberts, joined by Justice Frankfurter, said that the Court should never have granted review in the case. He added:

> I cannot concur in the intimation, which I think the opinion gives, that, as Congress has seen fit not to enact a workmen's compensation law, this court will strain the law of negligence to accord compensation where the employer is without fault. I yield to none in my belief in the wisdom and equity of workmen's compensation laws, but I do not conceive it to be within our judicial function to write the policy which underlies compensation laws into acts of Congress when Congress has not chosen that policy but, instead, has adopted the common law doctrine of negligence.

Justice Roberts and Justice Frankfurter were not alone in thinking that the Court in cases like *Brown* and *Dice* was bending the law to create the equivalent of a workers' compensation system for railroad employees. But the more recent decision in *Felder v. Casey* suggests that a broader principle may be at work.

Note: Preemption of State Law and Section 1983

1. The defendants in *Johnson v. Fankell* relied heavily on another § 1983 case, *Felder v. Casey*, 487 U.S. 131 (1988). The plaintiff in *Felder* sued the city of Milwaukee and certain of its police officers, asserting claims of excessive force in an arrest. The defendants invoked the Wisconsin notice-of-claim statute. As the Supreme Court explained:

> [The notice-of-claim statute] provides that no action may be brought or maintained against any state governmental subdivision, agency, or officer unless the claimant either provides written notice of the claim within 120 days of the alleged injury, or demonstrates that the relevant subdivision, agency,

or officer had actual notice of the claim and was not prejudiced by the lack of written notice. The statute further provides that the party seeking redress must also submit an itemized statement of the relief sought to the governmental subdivision or agency, which then has 120 days to grant or disallow the requested relief. Finally, claimants must bring suit within six months of receiving notice that their claim has been disallowed.

The Wisconsin Supreme Court held that this statute applied to federal civil rights actions brought in state court under § 1983. The United States Supreme Court, in an opinion by Justice Brennan, framed the issue as follows:

> No one disputes the general and unassailable proposition relied upon by the Wisconsin Supreme Court below that States may establish the rules of procedure governing litigation in their own courts. By the same token, however, where state courts entertain a federally created cause of action, the "federal right cannot be defeated by the forms of local practice." *Brown v. Western R. Co. of Alabama*, 338 U.S. 294 (1949). The question before us today, therefore, is essentially one of pre-emption: is the application of the State's notice-of-claim provision to § 1983 actions brought in state courts consistent with the goals of the federal civil rights laws, or does the enforcement of such a requirement instead "stand as an obstacle to the accomplishment and execution of the full purposes and objectives of Congress"?

The Court held that Wisconsin could not apply the notice-of-claim rule to § 1983 cases:

> [The] central purpose of the Reconstruction-Era laws is to provide compensatory relief to those deprived of their federal rights by state actors. Section 1983 accomplishes this goal by creating a form of liability that, by its very nature, runs only against a specific class of defendants: government bodies and their officials. Wisconsin's notice-of-claim statute undermines this uniquely federal remedy in several interrelated ways.

> First, it conditions the right of recovery that Congress has authorized, and does so for a reason manifestly inconsistent with the purposes of the federal statute: to minimize governmental liability. Nor is this condition a neutral and uniformly applicable rule of procedure; rather, it is a substantive burden imposed only upon those who seek redress for injuries resulting from the use or misuse of governmental authority.

> Second, the notice provision discriminates against the federal right. While the State affords the victim of an intentional tort two years to recognize the compensable nature of his or her injury, the civil rights victim is given only four months to appreciate that he or she has been deprived of a federal constitutional or statutory right.

> Finally, the notice provision operates, in part, as an exhaustion requirement, in that it forces claimants to seek satisfaction in the first instance from the governmental defendant. We think it plain that Congress never intended

that those injured by governmental wrongdoers could be required, as a condition of recovery, to submit their claims to the government responsible for their injuries.

In what sense did the state statute "discriminate against the federal right?" Here is the Supreme Court's explanation:

> Although it is true that the notice-of-claim statute does not discriminate between state and federal causes of action against local governments, the fact remains that the law's protection extends only to governmental defendants and thus conditions the right to bring suit against the very persons and entities Congress intended to subject to liability. We therefore cannot accept the suggestion [in an amicus brief] that this requirement is simply part of "the vast body of procedural rules, rooted in policies unrelated to the definition of any particular substantive cause of action, that forms no essential part of 'the cause of action' as applied to any given plaintiff." On the contrary, the notice-of-claim provision is imposed only upon a specific class of plaintiffs — those who sue governmental defendants — and [is] firmly rooted in policies very much related to, and to a large extent directly contrary to, the substantive cause of action provided those plaintiffs.

> This defendant-specific focus of the notice requirement serves to distinguish it, rather starkly, from rules uniformly applicable to all suits, such as rules governing service of process or substitution of parties, which respondents cite as examples of procedural requirements that penalize noncompliance through dismissal. That state courts will hear the entire § 1983 cause of action once a plaintiff complies with the notice-of-claim statute, therefore, in no way alters the fact that the statute discriminates against the precise type of claim Congress has created.

Justice O'Connor, joined by Chief Justice Rehnquist, dissented at length. She said:

> [The Wisconsin statute] erects no barrier at all to a plaintiff's right to bring a § 1983 suit against anyone. Every plaintiff has the option of proceeding in federal court, and the Wisconsin statute has not the slightest effect on that right. Second, if a plaintiff chooses to proceed in the Wisconsin state courts, those courts stand ready to hear the entire federal cause of action, as the majority concedes. Thus, the Wisconsin statute "discriminates" only against a right that Congress has never created: the right of a plaintiff to have the benefit of selected federal court procedures after the plaintiff has rejected the federal forum and chosen a state forum instead. The majority's "discrimination" theory is just another version of its unsupported conclusion that Congress intended to force the state courts to adopt procedural rules from the federal courts.

2. In *Mitchell v. Forsyth*, 472 U.S. 511 (1985), the Court held that the denial of qualified immunity in federal court should be immediately appealable because immunity from suit is "an entitlement [that is] effectively lost if a case is erroneously permitted to go to trial." In *Fankell*, the Court acknowledges that the "qualified immunity" defense "provides the defendant with an immunity from the burdens of trial as well as a defense to liability." Why, then, does federal law not preempt a state rule that results in the effective loss of the immunity that federal law establishes?

Note: "Substance" Versus "Procedure"?

Justice Frankfurter, dissenting in *Brown v. Western Railway*, and Justice Brennan, writing for the Court in *Felder v. Casey*, both invoked the distinction between "substance" and "procedure" drawn in the *Erie* line of cases (Chapter 7). In *Brown*, Justice Frankfurter said:

> [The terms "substance" and "procedure"] are not meaningless even though they do not have fixed undeviating meanings. They derive content from the functions they serve here in precisely the same way in which we have applied them in reverse situations — when confronted with the problem whether the Federal courts respected the substance of State-created rights, as required by the rule in *Erie R. Co. v. Tompkins*, 304 U.S. 64 (1938), or impaired them by professing merely to enforce them by the mode in which the Federal courts do business. Review on this aspect of State court judgments in Federal Employers' Liability cases presents essentially the same kind of problem as that with which this Court dealt in *Guaranty Trust Co. v. York*, 326 U.S. 99 (1945) . . . Congress has authorized State courts to enforce Federal rights, and Federal courts State-created rights. Neither system of courts can impair these respective rights, but both may have their own requirements for stating claims (pleading) and conducting litigation (practice).

In *Felder*, Justice Brennan invoked the *Erie* analogy in responding to the assertion that "federal law takes the state courts as it finds them." He said:

> In a State that demands compliance with [a notice-of-claim] statute before a §1983 action may be brought or maintained in its courts, the outcome of federal civil rights litigation will frequently and predictably depend on whether it is brought in state or federal court. Thus, the very notions of federalism upon which respondents rely dictate that the State's outcome-determinative law must give way when a party asserts a federal right in state court.
>
> Under *Erie R. Co. v. Tompkins*, 304 U.S. 64 (1938), when a federal court exercises diversity or pendent jurisdiction over state-law claims, "the outcome of the litigation in the federal court should be substantially the same, so far as legal rules determine the outcome of a litigation, as it would be if tried in a State court." *Guaranty Trust Co. v. York*, 326 U.S. 99 (1945). Accordingly, federal courts entertaining state-law claims against Wisconsin municipalities are obligated to apply the notice-of-claim provision. Just as federal courts are constitutionally obligated to apply state law to state claims, see *Erie*, so too the Supremacy Clause imposes on state courts a constitutional duty "to proceed in such manner that all the substantial rights of the parties under controlling federal law [are] protected." *Garrett v. Moore-McCormack, Co.*, 317 U.S. 239 (1942).

Civil rights victims often do not appreciate the constitutional nature of their injuries, and thus will fail to file a notice of injury or claim within the requisite time period, which in Wisconsin is a mere four months. Unless such claimants can prove that the governmental defendant had actual notice of the claim . . . , and unless they also file an itemized claim for damages, they must bring their § 1983 suits in federal court or not at all. Wisconsin, however, may not alter the outcome of federal claims it chooses to entertain in its courts by demanding compliance with outcome-determinative rules that are inapplicable when such claims are brought in federal court. . . .

The state notice-of-claim statute is more than a mere rule of procedure: . . . the statute is a substantive condition on the right to sue governmental officials and entities, and the federal courts have therefore correctly recognized that the notice statute governs the adjudication of state-law claims in diversity actions. In *Guaranty Trust*, we held that, in order to give effect to a State's statute of limitations, a federal court could not hear a state-law action that a state court would deem time barred. Conversely, a state court may not decline to hear an otherwise properly presented federal claim because that claim would be barred under a state law requiring timely filing of notice. State courts simply are not free to vindicate the substantive interests underlying a state rule of decision at the expense of the federal right.

Are Justice Frankfurter and Justice Brennan suggesting that any state rule that would be deemed "substantive" under *Erie* may not be applied to the litigation of federal claims in state courts? Justice O'Connor, dissenting in *Felder* (joined by Chief Justice Rehnquist), said:

[The suggested parallel to *Erie* cases] seems to be based on a sort of upside-down theory of federalism, which the Court attributes to Congress on the basis of no evidence at all. Nor are the implications of this "reverse-*Erie*" theory quite clear. If the Court means the theory to be taken seriously, it should follow that defendants, as well as plaintiffs, are entitled to the benefit of all federal court procedural rules that are "outcome determinative." If, however, the Court means to create a rule that benefits only plaintiffs, then the discussion of *Erie* principles is simply an unsuccessful effort to find some analogy, no matter how attenuated, to today's unprecedented holding.

Problem: A Prisoner's Medical Claim

The Supreme Court has held that "deliberate indifference to serious medical needs of prisoners" constitutes "cruel and unusual punishment" in violation of the Eighth Amendment. Claims of "deliberate indifference to a prisoner's serious illness or injury" can be brought under 42 U.S.C. § 1983 against prison doctors and other prison officials.

William Walker, an inmate of the State Prison of New Harmony, has brought a § 1983 action in New Harmony state court against Dr. James Finlay, the prison physician. The complaint alleges that Dr. Finlay was "deliberately indifferent" to Walker's serious medical needs when he delayed obtaining specialized treatment for a severed finger that was decaying following surgery. Walker asserts that the delay caused the permanent loss of the finger.

The finger was accidentally severed when it was caught in Walker's cell door. The complaint alleges that Dr. Finlay was not qualified to perform an emergency re-attachment of the finger but refused to obtain outside specialized medical assistance both before performing the surgery and after Walker's injury exhibited signs of significant worsening in the weeks following the surgery.

Section 8-180 of the New Harmony Revised Statutes, enacted as part of the Medical Malpractice Reform Act, provides: "No cause of action involving medical malpractice may be filed until the medical malpractice case has been submitted to an appropriate screening panel and a determination made by such panel as provided in this Act, and any action filed without satisfying the requirements of those sections is subject to dismissal without prejudice for failure to comply with this section." The screening panel must consider "all the documentary material," after which it issues a finding as to whether or not there is a "reasonable probability of medical malpractice." Once the panel issues its finding, the complainant may initiate a court action for malpractice. Another section of the Reform Act defines "medical malpractice" as any claim, irrespective of the legal theory, based on the alleged failure of a physician, hospital or hospital employee, in rendering services, "to use the reasonable care, skill or knowledge ordinarily used under similar circumstances."

Walker did not submit his claim to a screening panel before filing suit, and Dr. Finlay has moved to dismiss the § 1983 action for failure to comply with § 8-180. Walker argues that federal law preempts application of § 8-180 to § 1983 claims in state court. Should his argument prevail?

Problem: Forum Selection Strategy

In an often-cited article published in 1977, Professor Burt Neuborne, a prominent civil liberties lawyer, articulated the assumptions that underlie his litigation strategy. He said: "persons advancing federal constitutional claims against local officials will fare better, as a rule, in a federal, rather than a state, trial court." Burt Neuborne, *The Myth of Parity*, 90 HARV. L. REV. 1105, 1115-16 (1977). Yet in each of the civil rights cases discussed in this chapter, the plaintiff filed suit in state trial court. Why might a civil rights plaintiff today prefer state to federal court?

The defendants in each of these cases could have removed to federal court. Why might they not have done so?

Part Three

The Power of the Federal Courts to Formulate Rules of Decision

Chapter 7

The *Erie* Doctrine and the Obligation of Federal Courts to Follow State Law

A. Foundations of the Doctrine

In Part Two, we examined the role of federal law in cases litigated in state courts. We turn now to a topic that is in a sense the converse: the power of federal courts to formulate rules of decision that deviate from those that state courts have followed in similar cases. Our starting-point is section 34 of the Judiciary Act of 1789, known as the Rules of Decision Act:

> *And be it further enacted*, That the laws of the several states, except where the constitution, treaties or statutes of the United States shall otherwise require or provide, shall be regarded as rules of decision in trials at common law in the courts of the United States in cases where they apply.

Section 34 has been codified, with minor changes, as 28 U.S.C. § 1652:

> The laws of the several states, except where the Constitution or treaties of the United States or Acts of Congress otherwise require or provide, shall be regarded as rules of decision in civil actions in the courts of the United States, in cases where they apply.

The Court's first detailed exposition of the meaning of section 34 came in *Swift v. Tyson*, a commercial dispute that was litigated in federal court in New York.[1]

Swift v. Tyson
Supreme Court of the United States, 1842.

16 Pet. (41 U.S.) 1.

STORY, JUSTICE, delivered the opinion of the court.

This cause comes before us from the circuit court of the southern district of New York, upon a certificate of division of the judges of that court. The action was brought by the plaintiff, Swift, as indorsee, against the defendant, Tyson, as acceptor, upon a bill of exchange [for] the sum of $1540.30, payable six months after date, and grace,

---

1. For a detailed account of the case, see TONY FREYER, HARMONY & DISSONANCE: THE SWIFT & ERIE CASES IN AMERICAN FEDERALISM 1–17 (1981).

drawn by one Nathaniel Norton and one Jairus S. Keith upon and accepted by Tyson, at the city of New York, in favor of the order of Nathaniel Norton, and by Norton indorsed to the plaintiff. The bill was dishonored at maturity. . . .

In the present case, the plaintiff is a *bonâ fide* holder, without notice, for what the law deems a good and valid consideration, that is, for a preexisting debt; and the only real question in the cause is, whether, under the circumstances of the present case, such a pre-existing debt constitutes a valuable consideration, in the sense of the general rule applicable to negotiable instruments. We say, under the circumstances of the present case, for the acceptance having been made in New York, the argument on behalf of the defendant is, that the contract is to be treated as a New York contract, and therefore, to be governed by the laws of New York, as expounded by its courts, as well upon general principles, as by the express provisions of the 34th section of the judiciary act of 1789. And then it is further contended, that by the law of New York, as thus expounded by its courts, a pre-existing debt does not constitute, in the sense of the general rule, a valuable consideration applicable to negotiable instruments.

In the first place, then, let us examine into the decisions of the courts of New York upon this subject. [Detailed discussion omitted. Justice Story concluded:] So that, to say the least of it, it admits of serious doubt, whether any doctrine upon this question can, at the present time, be treated as finally established; and it is certain that the court of errors [the highest New York law court] have not pronounced any positive opinion upon it.

But, admitting the doctrine to be fully settled in New York, it remains to be considered, whether it is obligatory upon this court, if it differs from the principles established in the general commercial law. It is observable, that the courts of New York do not found their decisions upon this point, upon any local statute, or positive, fixed or ancient local usage; but they deduce the doctrine from the general principles of commercial law. It is, however, contended, that the 34th section of the judiciary act of 1789 furnishes a rule obligatory upon this court to follow the decisions of the state tribunals in all cases to which they apply. . . . In order to maintain the argument, it is essential [to] hold, that the word "laws," in this section, includes within the scope of its meaning, the decisions of the local tribunals. In the ordinary use of language, it will hardly be contended, that the decisions of courts constitute laws. They are, at most, only evidence of what the laws are, and are not, of themselves, laws. They are often re-examined, reversed and qualified by the courts themselves, whenever they are found to be either defective, or ill-founded, or otherwise incorrect.

The laws of a state are more usually understood to mean the rules and enactments promulgated by the legislative authority thereof, or long-established local customs having the force of laws. In all the various cases, which have hitherto come before us for decision, this court have uniformly supposed, that the true interpretation of the 34th section limited its application to state laws, strictly local, that is to say, to the positive statutes of the state, and the construction thereof adopted by the local tribunals, and to rights and titles to things having a permanent locality, such as the rights and titles to real estate, and other matters immovable and intra-territorial in their nature and character. It never has been supposed by us, that the section did apply, or was designed to apply, to questions of a more general nature, not at all dependent upon local statutes or local usages of a fixed and permanent operation, as, for example, to the construction of ordinary contracts or other written instruments, and especially to questions of general commercial law, where the state tribunals are called upon to perform the like functions as ourselves, that is, to ascertain, upon general reasoning and legal analogies, what is the true exposition of the contract or instrument, or what is the just rule furnished by the principles of commercial law to govern the case.

And we have not now the slightest difficulty in holding, that this section, upon its true intendment and construction, is strictly limited to local statutes and local usages of the character before stated, and does not extend to contracts and other instruments of a commercial nature, the true interpretation and effect whereof are to be sought, not in the decisions of the local tribunals, but in the general principles and doctrines of commercial jurisprudence. Undoubtedly, the decisions of the local tribunals upon such subjects are entitled to, and will receive, the most deliberate attention and respect of this court; but they cannot furnish positive rules, or conclusive authority, by which our own judgments are to be bound up and governed. The law respecting negotiable instruments may be truly declared in the language of Cicero, adopted by Lord Mansfield in *Luke* v. *Lyde*, 2 Burr. 883, 887, to be in a great measure, not the law of a single country only, but of the commercial world. . . .

It becomes necessary for us, therefore, upon the present occasion, to express our own opinion of the true result of the commercial law upon the question now before us. And we have no hesitation in saying, that a pre-existing debt does constitute a valuable consideration, in the sense of the general rule already stated, as applicable to negotiable instruments. . . . It is for the benefit and convenience of the commercial world, to give as wide an extent as practicable to the credit and circulation of negotiable paper, that it may pass not only as security for new purchases and advances, made upon the transfer thereof, but also in payment of, and as security for, pre-existing debts. The creditor is thereby enabled to realize or to secure his debt, and thus may safely give a prolonged credit, or forbear from taking any legal steps to enforce his rights. The debtor also has the advantage of making his negotiable securities of equivalent value to cash. But establish the opposite conclusion, that negotiable paper cannot be applied in payment of, or as security for, pre-existing debts, without letting in all the equities between the original and antecedent parties, and the value and circulation of such securities must be essentially diminished, and the debtor driven to the embarrassment of making a sale thereof, often at a ruinous discount, to some third person, and then, by circuit, to apply the proceeds to the payment of his debts. . . .

This question has been several times before this court, and it has been uniformly held, that it makes no difference whatsoever, as to the rights of the holder, whether the debt, for which the negotiable instrument is transferred to him, is a pre-existing debt, or is contracted at the time of the transfer. . . .

In the American courts, so far as we have been able to trace the decisions, the same doctrine seems generally, but not universally, to prevail. [We] entertain no doubt, that a *bonâ fide* holder, for a pre-existing debt, of a negotiable instrument, is not affected by any equities between the antecedent parties, where he has received the same, before it became due, without notice of any such equities. We are all, therefore, of opinion, that the question on this point, propounded by the circuit court for our consideration, ought to be answered in the negative; and we shall, accordingly, direct it so to be certified to the circuit court.

[Separate opinion of Justice Catron omitted.]

Note: Section 34 and Swift v. Tyson

1. Early in his discussion of section 34, Justice Story rejects the proposition that the word "laws" in the statute includes "the decisions of the local [i.e., state] tribunals." But does the Court take the position that state-court decisions are never binding on federal courts?

2. Justice Story's interpretation of section 34 was challenged by historian Charles Warren in an article published in 1923. *See* Charles Warren, *New Light on the History of the Federal Judiciary Act of 1789*, 37 HARV. L. REV. 49 (1923). Warren discovered a manuscript with an alternative text of section 34 in the handwriting of Oliver Ellsworth, a leading member of the Senate subcommittee that drafted the Judiciary Act of 1789. In the alternative text, section 34 would have read:

> And be it further enacted, That the statute law of the several States in force for the time being and their unwritten or common law now in use, whether by adoption from the common law of England, the ancient statutes of the same or otherwise, except where the constitution, Treaties or Statutes of the United States shall otherwise require or provide, shall be regarded as the rules of decision in the trials at common law in the courts of the United States in cases where they apply.

Warren believed that the phrase "laws of the several states" "was intended to be a more concise expression and a summary of the more detailed enumeration of the different forms of State law, set forth in the original draft." He thus concluded that Justice Story's interpretation was erroneous. However, more recent research has largely discredited Warren's reading of the evidence. *See, e.g.*, Patrick J. Borchers, *The Origins of Diversity Jurisdiction, The Rise of Legal Positivism, and a Brave New World for* Erie *and* Klaxon, 72 TEX. L. REV. 79, 105 (1993).

3. Professor William Fletcher, after a careful examination of early nineteenth century decisions, concluded that "the early understanding of section 34 was closer to the holding in *Swift* than is currently supposed." He wrote:

> [L]awyers and judges in the early nineteenth century did not categorize all nonfederal law as state law within the meaning of section 34. There was a "local" state law, to which the section applied, and a "general" law, to which it did not. The specific command of section 34 was relatively narrow: federal courts in trials at common law were required to follow local state law in cases where it applied. Section 34 was also the partial embodiment of a larger lex

loci principle under which the federal courts . . . followed local law in all cases to which it applied. But the lex loci principle, like section 34 itself, had no application to questions of general law. . . . This general common law provided the rule of decision in the federal courts in all cases to which it applied, and no one thought section 34 required otherwise.

William A. Fletcher, *The General Common Law and Section 34 of the Judiciary Act of 1789: The Example of Marine Insurance*, 97 Harv. L. Rev. 1513, 1514–15 (1984).

4. The most far-reaching reexamination of the meaning of section 34 came in a posthumously published book by Professor Wilfrid J. Ritz. Ritz pointed out that modern systems of reporting appellate decisions were not established until the nineteenth century. (Indeed, there were no published reports of American cases until 1789.) Nor had states codified their statutes. Thus, there was "no . . . authoritative source for the law of a state," and "Congress could not have required the national courts to look to the opinions of state courts to ascertain what state law was . . . ." Wilfrid Ritz, Rewriting the History of the Judiciary Act of 1789 at 51 (Wythe Holt & Lewis H. LaRue eds., 1990).

What then was the meaning of section 34? Ritz concludes:

> Section 34 is a direction to the national courts to apply American law, as distinguished from English law. American law is to be found in the "laws of the several states" viewed as a group of eleven states in 1789, and not viewed separately and individually. It is not a direction to apply the law of a particular state, for if it had been so intended, the section would have referred to the "laws of the *respective* states."

Id. at 148 (emphasis added).

5. During the first third of the twentieth century, dissatisfaction with the doctrine of *Swift v. Tyson* grew. Although Charles Warren's historical research received some attention, the primary focus of concern was the practical effects of allowing federal courts to exercise an independent judgment on the rules of decision applied in ordinary private litigation. Against that background, the Supreme Court granted certiorari in *Erie Railroad Co. v. Tompkins*.

Erie R. Co. v. Tompkins

Supreme Court of the United States, 1938.

304 U.S. 64.

Mr. Justice Brandeis delivered the opinion of the Court.

The question for decision is whether the oft-challenged doctrine of *Swift v. Tyson*, 16 Pet. 1 (1842), shall now be disapproved.

Tompkins, a citizen of Pennsylvania, was injured on a dark night by a passing freight train of the Erie Railroad Company while walking along its right of way at Hughestown in that state. He claimed that the accident occurred through negligence in the operation, or maintenance, of the train; that he was rightfully on the premises as licensee because on a commonly used beaten footpath which ran for a short distance along-side the tracks; and that he was struck by something which looked like a door projecting from one of the moving cars. To enforce that claim he brought an action in the federal court for Southern New York, which had jurisdiction because the company is a corporation of that state. It denied liability; and the case was tried by a jury.

The Erie insisted that its duty to Tompkins was no greater than that owed to a trespasser. It contended, among other things, that its duty to Tompkins, and hence its liability, should be determined in accordance with the Pennsylvania law; that under the law of Pennsylvania, as declared by its highest court, persons who use pathways along the railroad right of way—that is, a longitudinal pathway as distinguished from a crossing—are to be deemed trespassers; and that the railroad is not liable for injuries to undiscovered trespassers resulting from its negligence, unless it be wanton or willful. Tompkins denied that any such rule had been established by the decisions of the Pennsylvania courts; and contended that, since there was no statute of the state on the subject, the railroad's duty and liability is to be determined in federal courts as a matter of general law.

The trial judge refused to rule that the applicable law precluded recovery. The jury brought in a verdict of $30,000; and the judgment entered thereon was affirmed by the Circuit Court of Appeals, which held, that it was unnecessary to consider whether the law of Pennsylvania was as contended, because the question was one not of local, but of general, law, and that "upon questions of general law the federal courts are free, in absence of a local statute, to exercise their independent judgment as to what the law is; and it is well settled that the question of the responsibility of a railroad for injuries caused by its servants is one of general law. * * * Where the public has made open and notorious use of a railroad right of way for a long period of time and without objection, the company owes to persons on such permissive pathway a duty of care in the operation of its trains. * * * It is likewise generally recognized law that a jury may find that negligence exists toward a pedestrian using a permissive path on the railroad right of way if he is hit by some object projecting from the side of the train."

The Erie had contended that application of the Pennsylvania rule was required, among other things, by section 34 of the Federal Judiciary Act of September 24, 1789, which provides: "The laws of the several States, except where the Constitution, treaties, or statutes of the United States otherwise require or provide, shall be regarded as rules of decision in trials at common law, in the courts of the United States, in cases where they apply."

Because of the importance of the question whether the federal court was free to disregard the alleged rule of the Pennsylvania common law, we granted certiorari.

First. Swift v. Tyson held that federal courts exercising jurisdiction on the ground of diversity of citizenship need not, in matters of general jurisprudence, apply the unwritten law of the state as declared by its highest court; that they are free to exercise an independent judgment as to what the common law of the state is—or should be . . .

The Court in applying the rule of section 34 to equity cases, in *Mason v. United States*, 260 U.S. 545, 559, said: "The statute, however, is merely declarative of the rule which would exist in the absence of the statute." The federal courts assumed, in the broad field of "general law," the power to declare rules of decision which Congress was confessedly without power to enact as statutes. Doubt was repeatedly expressed as to the correctness of the construction given section 34, and as to the soundness of the rule which it introduced. But it was the more recent research of a competent scholar, who examined the original document, which established that the construction given to it by the Court was erroneous; and that the purpose of the section was merely to make certain that, in all matters except those in which some federal law is controlling, the federal courts exercising jurisdiction in diversity of citizenship cases would apply as their rules of decision the law of the state, unwritten as well as written. Charles Warren, *New Light on the History of the Federal Judiciary Act of 1789* (1923) 37 HARV. L. REV. 49, 51–52, 81–88, 108.

Criticism of the doctrine became widespread after the decision of *Black & White Taxicab & Transfer Co. v. Brown & Yellow Taxicab & Transfer Co.*, 276 U.S. 518. There, Brown & Yellow, a Kentucky corporation owned by Kentuckians, and the Louisville & Nashville Railroad, also a Kentucky corporation, wished that the former should have the exclusive privilege of soliciting passenger and baggage transportation at the Bowling Green, Ky., Railroad station; and that the Black & White, a competing Kentucky corporation, should be prevented from interfering with that privilege. Knowing that such a contract would be void under the common law of Kentucky, it was arranged that the Brown & Yellow reincorporate under the law of Tennessee, and that the contract with the railroad should be executed there. The suit was then brought by the Tennessee corporation in the federal court for Western Kentucky to enjoin competition by the Black & White; an injunction issued by the District Court was sustained by the Court of Appeals; and this Court, citing many decisions in which the doctrine of Swift & Tyson had been applied, affirmed the decree.

Second. Experience in applying the doctrine of *Swift v. Tyson*, had revealed its defects, political and social; and the benefits expected to flow from the rule did not accrue. Persistence of state courts in their own opinions on questions of common law prevented uniformity; and the impossibility of discovering a satisfactory line of demarcation between the province of general law and that of local law developed a new well of uncertainties.[8]

On the other hand, the mischievous results of the doctrine had become apparent. Diversity of citizenship jurisdiction was conferred in order to prevent apprehended discrimination in state courts against those not citizens of the state. *Swift v. Tyson* introduced grave discrimination by noncitizens against citizens. It made rights enjoyed under the unwritten "general law" vary according to whether enforcement was sought

---

8. *Compare* 2 Warren, *The Supreme Court in United States History*, rev. ed. 1935, 89: "Probably no decision of the Court has ever given rise to more uncertainty as to legal rights; and though doubtless intended to promote uniformity in the operation of business transactions, its chief effect has been to render it difficult for business men to know in advance to what particular topic the Court would apply the doctrine. * * *" *The Federal Digest* through the 1937 volume, lists nearly 1,000 decisions involving the distinction between questions of general and of local law.

in the state or in the federal court; and the privilege of selecting the court in which the right should be determined was conferred upon the noncitizen.[9] Thus, the doctrine rendered impossible equal protection of the law. In attempting to promote uniformity of law throughout the United States, the doctrine had prevented uniformity in the administration of the law of the state.

The discrimination resulting became in practice far-reaching. This resulted in part from the broad province accorded to the so-called "general law" as to which federal courts exercised an independent judgment. In addition to questions of purely commercial law, "general law" was held to include the obligations under contracts entered into and to be performed within the state, the extent to which a carrier operating within a state may stipulate for exemption from liability for his own negligence or that of his employee; the liability for torts committed within the state upon persons resident or property located there, even where the question of liability depended upon the scope of a property right conferred by the state; and the right to exemplary or punitive damages. Furthermore, state decisions construing local deeds, mineral conveyances, and even devises of real estate, were disregarded.

In part the discrimination resulted from the wide range of persons held entitled to avail themselves of the federal rule by resort to the diversity of citizenship jurisdiction. Through this jurisdiction individual citizens willing to remove from their own state and become citizens of another might avail themselves of the federal rule. And, without even change of residence, a corporate citizen of the state could avail itself of the federal rule by reincorporating under the laws of another state, as was done in the *Taxicab Case*.

The injustice and confusion incident to the doctrine of *Swift v. Tyson* have been repeatedly urged as reasons for abolishing or limiting diversity of citizenship jurisdiction. Other legislative relief has been proposed. If only a question of statutory construction were involved, we should not be prepared to abandon a doctrine so widely applied throughout nearly a century. But the unconstitutionality of the course pursued has now been made clear, and compels us to do so.

Third. Except in matters governed by the Federal Constitution or by acts of Congress, the law to be applied in any case is the law of the state. And whether the law of the state shall be declared by its Legislature in a statute or by its highest court in a decision is not a matter of federal concern. There is no federal general common law. Congress has no power to declare substantive rules of common law applicable in a state whether they be local in their nature or "general," be they commercial law or a part of the law of torts. And no clause in the Constitution purports to confer such a power upon the federal courts. As stated by Mr. Justice Field when protesting in *Baltimore & Ohio R.R. Co. v. Baugh*, 149 U.S. 368, 401, against ignoring the Ohio common law of fellow-servant liability:

---

9. It was even possible for a nonresident plaintiff defeated on a point of law in the highest court of a State nevertheless to win out by taking a nonsuit and renewing the controversy in the federal court.

I am aware that what has been termed the general law of the country—which is often little less than what the judge advancing the doctrine thinks at the time should be the general law on a particular subject—has been often advanced in judicial opinions of this court to control a conflicting law of a state. I admit that learned judges have fallen into the habit of repeating this doctrine as a convenient mode of brushing aside the law of a state in conflict with their views. And I confess that, moved and governed by the authority of the great names of those judges, I have, myself, in many instances, unhesitatingly and confidently, but I think now erroneously, repeated the same doctrine. But, notwithstanding the great names which may be cited in favor of the doctrine, and notwithstanding the frequency with which the doctrine has been reiterated, there stands, as a perpetual protest against its repetition, the constitution of the United States, which recognizes and preserves the autonomy and independence of the states,—independence in their legislative and independence in their judicial departments. Supervision over either the legislative or the judicial action of the states is in no case permissible except as to matters by the constitution specifically authorized or delegated to the United States. Any interference with either, except as thus permitted, is an invasion of the authority of the state, and, to that extent, a denial of its independence.

The fallacy underlying the rule declared in *Swift v. Tyson* is made clear by Mr. Justice Holmes.[23] The doctrine rests upon the assumption that there is "a transcendental body of law outside of any particular State but obligatory within it unless and until changed by statute," that federal courts have the power to use their judgment as to what the rules of common law are; and that in the federal courts "the parties are entitled to an independent judgment on matters of general law":

> But law in the sense in which courts speak of it today does not exist without some definite authority behind it. The common law so far as it is enforced in a State, whether called common law or not, is not the common law generally but the law of that State existing by the authority of that State without regard to what it may have been in England or anywhere else. * * *

> The authority and only authority is the State, and if that be so, the voice adopted by the State as its own (whether it be of its Legislature or of its Supreme Court) should utter the last word.

Thus the doctrine of *Swift v. Tyson* is, as Mr. Justice Holmes said, "an unconstitutional assumption of powers by the Courts of the United States which no lapse of time or respectable array of opinion should make us hesitate to correct." In disapproving that doctrine we do not hold unconstitutional section 34 of the Federal Judiciary Act of 1789 or any other act of Congress. We merely declare that in applying the doctrine

---

23. *Kuhn v. Fairmont Coal Co.*, 215 U.S. 349, 370–72; *Black & White Taxicab, Co. v. Brown & Yellow Taxicab, Co.*, 276 U.S. 518, 532–36.

this Court and the lower courts have invaded rights which in our opinion are reserved by the Constitution to the several states.

Fourth. The defendant contended that by the common law of Pennsylvania as declared by its highest court in *Falchetti v. Pennsylvania R. Co.*, 307 Pa. 203, 160 A. 859, the only duty owed to the plaintiff was to refrain from willful or wanton injury. The plaintiff denied that such is the Pennsylvania law.[24] In support of their respective contentions the parties discussed and cited many decisions of the Supreme Court of the state. The Circuit Court of Appeals ruled that the question of liability is one of general law; and on that ground declined to decide the issue of state law. As we hold this was error, the judgment is reversed and the case remanded to it for further proceedings in conformity with our opinion.

MR. JUSTICE CARDOZO took no part in the consideration or decision of this case.

MR. JUSTICE BUTLER.

. . . Defendant's petition for writ of certiorari presented two questions: Whether its duty toward plaintiff should have been determined in accordance with the law as found by the highest court of Pennsylvania, and whether the evidence conclusively showed plaintiff guilty of contributory negligence. . . .

No constitutional question was suggested or argued below or here. And as a general rule, this Court will not consider any question not raised below and presented by the petition. Here it does not decide either of the questions presented, but, changing the rule of decision in force since the foundation of the government, remands the case to be adjudged according to a standard never before deemed permissible. . . .

The doctrine of [*Swift v. Tyson*] has been followed by this Court in an unbroken line of decisions. So far as appears, it was not questioned until more than 50 years later, and then by a single judge. *Baltimore & O. Railroad Co. v. Baugh*, 149 U.S. 368, 390. [In a footnote, Justice Butler added:] Mr. Justice Field filed a dissenting opinion, several sentences of which are quoted in the decision just announced. The dissent failed to impress any of his associates. It assumes that adherence to section 34 as construed involves a supervision over legislative or judicial action of the states. There is no foundation for that suggestion. Clearly, the dissent of the learned Justice rests upon misapprehension of the rule. He joined in applying the doctrine for more than a quarter of a century before his dissent. The reports do not disclose that he objected to it in any later case.

So far as appears, no litigant has ever challenged the power of Congress to establish the rule as construed. It has so long endured that its destruction now without appropriate deliberation cannot be justified. . . . Against the protest of those joining in this opinion, the Court declines to assign the case for reargument. . . .

---

24. Tompkins also contended that the alleged rule of the *Falchetti Case* is not in any event applicable here because he was struck at the intersection of the longitudinal pathway and a transverse crossing. The court below found it unnecessary to consider this contention, and we leave the question open.

The course pursued by the Court in this case is repugnant to the Act of Congress of August 24, 1937 ... If defendant had applied for and obtained the writ of certiorari upon the claim that, as now held, Congress has no power to prescribe the rule of decision, section 34 as construed, it would have been the duty of this Court to issue the prescribed certificate to the Attorney General in order that the United States might intervene and be heard on the constitutional question. ...

... [Plainly] through the form of words employed, the substance of the decision appears; it strikes down as unconstitutional section 34 as construed by our decisions; it divests the Congress of power to prescribe rules to be followed by federal courts when deciding questions of general law. In that broad field it compels this and the lower federal courts to follow decisions of the courts of a particular state.

I am of opinion that the constitutional validity of the rule need not be considered, because under the law, as found by the courts of Pennsylvania and generally throughout the country, it is plain that the evidence required a finding that plaintiff was guilty of negligence that contributed to cause his injuries, and that the judgment below should be reversed upon that ground.

Mr. Justice McReynolds, concurs in this opinion.

Mr. Justice Reed (concurring in part).

I concur in the conclusion reached in this case, in the disapproval of the doctrine of *Swift v. Tyson*, and in the reasoning of the majority opinion, except in so far as it relies upon the unconstitutionality of the "course pursued" by the federal courts.

The "doctrine of *Swift v. Tyson*," as I understand it, is that the words "the laws," as used in section 34, line 1, of the Federal Judiciary Act of September 24, 1789, do not included in their meaning "the decisions of the local tribunals. . . ."

To decide the case now before us and to "disapprove" the doctrine of *Swift v. Tyson* requires only that we say that the words "the laws" include in their meaning the decisions of the local tribunals. As the majority opinion shows, by its reference to Mr. Warren's researches and the first quotation from Mr. Justice Holmes, that this Court is now of the view that "laws" includes "decisions," it is unnecessary to go further and declare that the "course pursued" was "unconstitutional," instead of merely erroneous.

The "unconstitutional" course referred to in the majority opinion is apparently the ruling in *Swift v. Tyson* that the supposed omission of Congress to legislate as to the effect of decisions leaves federal courts free to interpret general law for themselves. I am not at all sure whether, in the absence of federal statutory direction, federal courts would be compelled to follow state decisions. There was sufficient doubt about the matter in 1789 to induce the first Congress to legislate. No former opinions of this Court have passed upon it. Mr. Justice Holmes evidently saw nothing "unconstitutional" which required the overruling of *Swift v. Tyson*, for he said in the very opinion quoted by the majority, "I should leave *Swift v. Tyson* undisturbed, as I indicated in *Kuhn v. Fairmont Coal Co.*, but I would not allow it to spread the assumed dominion into new fields." *Black & White Taxicab Co. v. Brown & Yellow Taxicab Co.*, 276 U.S. 518, 535. If the opinion commits this Court to the position that the Congress is without power to declare what rules of substantive law shall govern the federal courts, that conclusion also seems questionable. The line between procedural and substantive law is hazy, but no one doubts federal power over procedure. *Wayman v. Southard*, 10 Wheat. 1. The Judiciary Article, § 3, and the "necessary and proper" clause of article 1, § 8, may fully authorize legislation, such as this section of the Judiciary Act.

In this Court, stare decisis, in statutory construction, is a useful rule, not an inexorable command. It seems preferable to overturn an established construction of an act of Congress, rather than, in the circumstances of this case, to interpret the Constitution.

There is no occasion to discuss further the range or soundness of these few phrases of the opinion. It is sufficient now to call attention to them and express my own non-acquiescence.

Note: The Decision in Erie

1. The opinion in *Erie* opens with the sentence: "The question for decision is whether the oft-challenged doctrine of *Swift v. Tyson* shall now be disapproved." But that was not the way the parties saw the case — least of all the Erie Railroad Co. When the Second Circuit affirmed the jury verdict in favor of Tompkins, the Erie filed a certiorari petition arguing that the federal courts were bound to apply the Pennsylvania decisions "repudiating the doctrine of Permissive Pathways" because those decisions "relate to a matter local in nature." The Erie's brief said, "We do not question the finality of the holding of this Court in *Swift v. Tyson* that the 'laws of the several states' referred to in the Rules of Decision Act do not include state court decisions as such."

Was it appropriate for the Supreme Court to decide whether the *Swift* doctrine "shall now be disapproved" when the issue was not raised by either party?

2. As Justice Brandeis makes clear in the *Erie* opinion, the doctrine of *Swift v. Tyson* had been widely challenged both within and without the Court. Yet not only did the Erie Railroad refrain from asking the Court to overrule *Swift*; it explicitly endorsed the continuing validity of the doctrine. Why might the railroad have adopted this strategy? (The Taxicab Case, cited in the opinion, may give a clue.)

3. The separate opinion of Justice Butler says that the course pursued by the Court violates the federal statute (now codified at 28 U.S.C. § 2403) requiring federal courts "to give the United States the right to be heard in every case involving constitutionality of an act [of Congress] affecting the public interest." Is this objection well taken?

Note: The Opinion in Erie

1. Examine the structure of the *Erie* opinion. What function is served by each of the numbered parts?

2. In Part "First" of the opinion, Justice Brandeis states that the research of Charles Warren "established that the construction given to [section 34] by the Court [in *Swift*] was erroneous." As already noted, Warren's research has been largely discredited. Does this cast doubt on the soundness of the result in *Erie*?

3. In Part "Second," Justice Brandeis says that "*Swift v. Tyson* introduced grave discrimination by noncitizens against citizens." This passage requires some elucidation. It is clear from the context that Justice Brandeis is referring to "citizens" and "noncitizens" of the forum state. What is not so clear is that Brandeis is also making a second assumption: that in a diversity suit the forum state will be the defendant's home state.

Certainly we would not make that assumption today. For example, in the well-known case of *Burger King v. Rudzewicz*, 471 U.S. 462 (1985), the plaintiff, a Florida corporation, sued the defendant, a Michigan resident, in federal district court in Florida. But Brandeis assumed that such a suit would have been brought in Michigan. Why was this a natural assumption in 1938?

And what was the nature of the discrimination? Justice Brandeis says that only the noncitizen had "the privilege of selecting the court" and, along with it, the rule of decision. Why couldn't a "citizen" select the federal forum if decisions of the state court on an issue of "general" law were unfavorable?

4. Does the "discrimination" described in Part "Second" furnish the Court's rationale for overruling *Swift*?

The Court says that the doctrine of *Swift v. Tyson* "rendered impossible equal protection of the law." Is the holding in *Erie* based on a violation of the Equal Protection clause of the Constitution?

5. Justice Butler, in his opinion dissenting from the overruling of *Swift*, says:

> So far as appears, no litigant has ever challenged the power of Congress to establish the rule as construed. . . . By way of reasoning, [the Court's opinion] contains nothing that requires the conclusion reached. Admittedly, there is no authority to support that conclusion.

Does Justice Brandeis cite any authority to support "the conclusion reached"? Why not?

6. In Part "Third," the Court says: "Congress has no power to declare substantive rules of common law applicable in a state whether they be local in their nature or 'general.'" The Erie was an interstate railroad, and long before 1938 it was established that Congress could enact legislation regulating the tort liability of interstate railroads. (Recall the FELA cases discussed in Chapter 6.) Why doesn't the Court consider that body of law?

Justice Stone, after considering Justice Brandeis's draft of the *Erie* opinion, sent him the following comments:

> One part of your opinion in *Erie Railroad v. Tompkins* gives me some concern. You say in effect that there is no constitutional power in Congress to require federal courts to apply rules of law inconsistent with those in force in the state, unless Congress is acting under one of the substantive powers granted to the national government. This may be so, but I hesitate to say it, partly because it is unnecessary to do so, and the matter is not, in my mind, entirely free from doubt—the power may be implicit in the judicial sections.

(Stone's letter is quoted in Alpheus T. Mason, Harlan Fiske Stone: Pillar of the Law 478 (1956).)

Does the final version of the opinion deal adequately with this point? How persuasive is the argument that "implicit in the judicial sections" of the Constitution is a power in Congress "to require federal courts to apply rules of law inconsistent with those in force in the states"? If the argument has merit, does it suggest that the decision in *Erie* is wrong?

7. Tompkins' suit against the Erie Railroad was litigated in federal court in New York. In Part Fourth, the Court assumes that the controlling state law is the law of Pennsylvania. On what basis does the Court make that assumption?

8. *Erie* began a new era in the history of the federal courts. The decision gave rise to at least four important questions.

First, the Court says that the law to be applied is "the law of the state." How does a federal court determine which state's law is to be applied?

Second, suppose the parties disagree as to what state law is, and there is no statute or decision of the highest state court that is on point. How does a federal court determine what rule of decision to apply?

Third, Justice Reed, in his concurring opinion, states that "no one doubts federal power over procedure." To what extent are issues of "procedure" outside the rule of *Erie*?

Fourth, the Court says unequivocally, "There is no federal general common law." Yet, on the same day, in another opinion by Justice Brandeis, the Court applied "federal common law" to reverse a state court decision on apportioning the waters of an interstate stream. *See Hinderliter v. La Plata River & Cherry Creek Ditch Co.*, 304 U.S. 92, 110 (1938). What is the difference between "federal general common law," which the Court says does not exist, and "federal common law," which does?

These issues are considered in this chapter and Chapter 8.

B. Identifying and Ascertaining the Applicable State Law

The *Erie* opinion declares: "Except in matters governed by the Federal Constitution or by acts of Congress, the law to be applied in any case is the law of the state." But which state's law is to be applied? And what should a federal court do if state law on point is unclear or absent? We turn now to those questions.

In *Erie* itself, the Court assumed without discussion that the federal courts should look to the law of Pennsylvania. Three years later, the Court explained how federal courts should identify the applicable law.

Klaxon Co. v. Stentor Electric Mfg. Co.

Supreme Court of the United States, 1941.

313 U.S. 487.

Mr. Justice Reed delivered the opinion of the Court.

The principal question in this case is whether in diversity cases the federal courts must follow conflict of laws rules prevailing in the states in which they sit. The frequent recurrence of the problem, as well as the conflict of approach to the problem between the Third Circuit's opinion here and that of the First Circuit in *Sampson v. Channell*, 110 F.2d 754, led us to grant certiorari.

[Respondent instituted this action in the United States District Court for the District of Delaware for breach of contract.] Jurisdiction rested on diversity of citizenship. In 1939 respondent recovered a jury verdict of $100,000, upon which judgment was entered. Respondent then moved to correct the judgment by adding interest at the rate of six percent from June 1, 1929, the date the action had been brought. The basis of the motion was the provision in section 480 of the New York Civil Practice Act directing that in contract actions interest be added to the principal sum "whether theretofore liquidated or unliquidated." The District Court granted the motion, taking the view that the rights of the parties were governed by New York law and that under New York law the addition of such interest was mandatory. The Circuit Court of Appeals affirmed, and we granted certiorari, limited to the question whether section 480 of the New York Civil Practice Act is applicable to an action in the federal court in Delaware.

The Circuit Court of Appeals was of the view that under New York law the right to interest before verdict under section 480 went to the substance of the obligation, and that proper construction of the contract in suit fixed New York as the place of performance. It then concluded that section 480 was applicable to the case because "it is clear by what we think is undoubtedly the better view of the law that the rules for ascertaining the measure of damages are not a matter of procedure at all, but are matters of substance which should be settled by reference to the law of the appropriate state according to the type of case being tried in the forum. The measure of damages for breach of a contract is determined by the law of the place of performance; Restatement, Conflict of Laws § 413." . . . Application of the New York statute apparently followed from the court's independent determination of the "better view" without regard to Delaware law, for no Delaware decision or statute was cited or discussed.

We are of opinion that the prohibition declared in *Erie Railroad v. Tompkins*, 304 U.S. 64, against such independent determinations by the federal courts extends to the field of conflict of laws. The conflict of laws rules to be applied by the federal court in Delaware must conform to those prevailing in Delaware's state courts. Otherwise the accident of diversity of citizenship would constantly disturb equal administration of justice in coordinate state and federal courts sitting side by side. Any other ruling would do violence to the principle of uniformity within a state upon which the *Tompkins* decision is based. Whatever lack of uniformity this may produce between federal courts in different states is attributable to our federal system, which leaves to a state, within the limits permitted by the Constitution, the right to pursue local policies diverging from those of its neighbors. It is not for the federal courts to thwart such local policies by enforcing an independent "general law" of conflict of laws. Subject only to review by this Court on any federal question that may arise, Delaware is free to determine whether a given matter is to be governed by the law of the forum or some other law. This Court's views are not the decisive factor in determining the applicable conflicts rule. And the proper function of the Delaware federal court is to ascertain what the state law is, not what it ought to be. . . .

Looking then to the Delaware cases, petitioner relies on one group to support his contention that the Delaware state courts would refuse to apply section 480 of the New York Civil Practice Act, and respondent on another to prove the contrary. We make no analysis of these Delaware decisions, but leave this for the Circuit Court of Appeals when the case is remanded.

Respondent makes the further argument that the judgment must be affirmed because, under the full faith and credit clause of the Constitution, Art. 4, § 1, the state courts of Delaware would be obliged to give effect to the New York statute. . . . Nothing in the Constitution ensures unlimited extraterritorial recognition of all statutes or of any statute under all circumstances. The full faith and credit clause does not go so far as to compel Delaware to apply section 480 if such application would interfere with its local policy.

Accordingly, the judgment is reversed and the case remanded to the Circuit Court of Appeals for decision in conformity with the law of Delaware.

Note: The Klaxon *Rule*

1. The holding in *Klaxon* is that federal courts must follow the conflict of law rules that would be followed by the courts of the state in which the federal court sits. "Any other ruling," says the Court, "would do violence to the principle of uniformity within a state upon which the *Tompkins* decision is based." Has the Court correctly stated the principle that was the basis for the decision in *Erie*?

2. *Erie* held that federal courts have no power to declare rules of general common law. Does it follow that federal courts also lack power to choose among state rules?

3. In *Griffin v. McCoach*, 313 U.S. 498 (1941), decided on the same day as *Klaxon*, the Court applied the *Klaxon* rule to an interpleader action filed in a federal district court in Texas. Commentators have pointed out that some of the claimants "were made party to a suit in federal court in Texas only by virtue of the nationwide service authorized by the Federal Interpleader Act," and that these claimants "could not have been made parties to an action in a Texas state court against their will." CHARLES ALAN WRIGHT & MARY KAY KANE, FEDERAL COURTS § 57 at 390 (6th ed. 2001). But there is no mention of that fact in the Court's opinion.

4. At the time of *Klaxon*, most American jurisdictions followed the "lex loci" approach to choice of law. Thus, on issues of tort law, the courts would apply the law of the place where the injury occurred; on issues of contract law, courts would apply the law of the place where the contract was made. Starting in the 1950s, many courts abandoned "lex loci" doctrines and adopted more flexible approaches to choice of law. The American Law Institute encouraged this development; thus, the *Restatement (Second) of Conflict of Laws* urged courts to look to "the local law of the state which, as to [the particular] issue, has the most significant relationship to the occurrence and the parties." One consequence of these more flexible approaches is that state courts are much more likely to apply their own law rather than the law of some other jurisdiction. Moreover, plaintiffs today have a wider choice of forum than they did when *Klaxon* was decided.

In light of these developments, commentators have suggested that the *Klaxon* rule should be abandoned or modified. *See, e.g.*, Borchers, *supra*, at 120–33. However, the Supreme Court has shown no interest whatever in rethinking *Klaxon*, and the doctrine remains as firmly embedded as any in the law of the federal courts.

5. The Supreme Court's unwillingness to reconsider *Klaxon* was made clear in *Day & Zimmerman, Inc. v. Challoner*, 423 U.S. 3 (1975). Plaintiffs brought suit in federal district court in Texas seeking to recover damages for death and personal injury resulting from the premature explosion of a 105-mm. howitzer round in Cambodia. Federal jurisdiction was based on diversity of citizenship.

At that time, the Texas courts adhered to the lex loci doctrine. Thus, as the Fifth Circuit Court of Appeals acknowledged, under Texas choice of law rules, "the substantive law of Cambodia would control." Nevertheless, the Fifth Circuit held that "as a matter of federal choice of law" it would not apply "the law of a jurisdiction that had no interest in the case, no policy at stake." (In modern conflicts parlance, the court found a "false conflict.") The court affirmed a judgment in favor of the plaintiffs based on "strict liability principles enunciated by Texas law."

The Supreme Court granted certiorari and summarily reversed. In a brusque opinion, the Court sharply reprimanded the Fifth Circuit for deviating from *Klaxon*:

> We are of the opinion that *Klaxon* is by its terms applicable here and should have been adhered to by the Court of Appeals. . . . By parity of reasoning [with *Klaxon*], the conflict-of-laws rules to be applied by a federal court in Texas must conform to those prevailing in the Texas state courts. A federal court in a diversity case is not free to engraft onto those state rules exceptions or modifications which may commend themselves to the federal court, but which have not commended themselves to the State in which the federal court sits. The Court of Appeals in this case should identify and follow the Texas conflicts rule.

Note: Ascertaining State Law

1. The *Erie* doctrine requires the court to apply "the law of the state," but sometimes there is no state statute or authoritative judicial decision on point. As a general matter, the task of the federal court is to determine how the highest court of the state would rule if it were confronted with the question. But the relevant indicia may be sparse — or may point in different directions.

2. Consider, for example, *Hakimoglu v. Trump Taj Mahal Assocs.*, 70 F.3d 291 (3d Cir. 1995), in which the Third Circuit had to decide whether to recognize a tort that the New Jersey Supreme Court had not yet created. Dissenting, Judge Becker argued that the federal courts should recognize the new tort, reasoning, *inter alia*, that the New Jersey Supreme Court "has long been a leader in expanding tort liability." Would that alone be sufficient to justify a federal court in recognizing a novel tort claim?

3. In contrast to Judge Becker's approach, some judges take the position that federal courts should be particularly reluctant to adopt innovative theories that would expand liability under state law. This view has often been expressed in the Seventh Circuit. For example, in one case involving claims against tobacco companies, the court said:

> [The] plaintiffs ask us to recognize a tort claim of "intentional exposure to a hazardous substance" or, alternatively, to certify the issue to the Wisconsin Supreme Court. Federal courts are loathe to fiddle around with state law. Though district courts may try to determine how the state courts would rule on an unclear area of state law, district courts are encouraged to dismiss actions based on novel state law claims. When confronted with a state law question that could go either way, the federal courts usually choose the narrower interpretation that restricts liability. Innovative state law claims should be brought in state court.

Insolia v. Philip Morris, Inc., 216 F.3d 596, 607 (7th Cir. 2000). Is this approach sound?

Suppose that the plaintiff files suit in state court, but the defendant removes to federal court based on diversity. Should the court still "choose the narrower interpretation that restricts liability"? The Seventh Circuit in *Insolia* said:

> The plaintiffs say they tried to litigate this in state court, but the tobacco companies — as they generally do in cases like this — removed the case to federal court. The plaintiffs are in a predicament because state law in this area is stunted by the ability of tobacco companies to remove cases under diversity jurisdiction. Some tobacco litigation, however, has taken place in state courts. [The court cited cases from six states.] And even if the plaintiffs are in something of a bind, that does not justify the federal courts imposing a new tort claim on Wisconsin.

4. What if a state's supreme court has not addressed the issue before the federal court? Typically, federal courts take the position that, in the absence of a ruling by the state supreme court, "decisions of the state appellate courts control, unless there are persuasive indications that the state supreme court would decide the issue differently." *Much v. Pacific Mutual Life Ins. Co.*, 266 F.3d 637, 643 (7th Cir. 2001). What might those indications be?

5. The requirement that federal courts follow state law as interpreted by the state's highest court, together with *Klaxon*'s rule that a federal court in a diversity case must "identify and follow [the] conflicts rule" of the state in which the court sits, can lead to situations requiring substantial speculation by the federal courts. As Judge Friendly once observed when facing that problem, "Our principal task [in this case] is to determine what the New York courts would think the California courts would think on an issue about which neither has thought." *Nolan v. Transocean Air Lines*, 276 F.2d 280, 281 (2d Cir. 1960).

Problem: An "Open and Obvious" Hazard

→ May be an exam question

Greta Burnside has brought suit in federal district court against Home Station, Inc., a retail store chain, seeking damages for personal injuries. The complaint alleges that the plaintiff was injured when she tripped over a pallet resting on a forklift in the aisle of a store owned by the defendant. Jurisdiction is based on diversity, and Oceana law controls.

The defendant has moved for summary judgment. It argues that under Oceana law, the owner of a place of business has no duty to protect or warn a visitor who encounters an open and obvious hazard, even if the owner has created the hazard and has reason to foresee that a customer might be distracted from observing it. The defendant acknowledges that the highest court of Oceana, the Oceana Supreme Court, has never decided this question, but the brief in support of the motion points to several decisions by the Oceana intermediate appellate court. That court has ruled in three cases (decided in 2005, 2008, and 2009) that a property owner "owes no duty to warn of conditions that are in plain view, easily discoverable by those employing reasonable use of their senses." Under these decisions, "a threshold finding that a dangerous condition is open and obvious discharges any duty to warn, and precludes a finding of landowner liability."

The plaintiff argues that these decisions do not reflect how the Oceana Supreme Court is likely to rule when it confronts this issue. First, she notes that the Second Restatement of Torts states that there are cases in which a possessor of land can and should anticipate harm from a dangerous condition notwithstanding its obvious nature, "for example, where the possessor has reason to expect that the invitee's attention may be distracted, so that he will not discover what is obvious." In the past, the Oceana Supreme Court has relied on the Second Restatement of Torts to clarify ambiguous points of tort law.

Second, the plaintiff points out that in the analogous area of products liability, the Oceana Supreme Court abandoned the established rule that an open and obvious danger in a *product* absolved the manufacturer from a duty to protect a plaintiff from such a patent defect. In 2000, that court held that a manufacturer, because of its superior ability to recognize and cure defects, is obligated to exercise the degree of care required "to avoid any unreasonable risk of harm to anyone who is likely to be exposed to the danger," notwithstanding the patent nature of the defect.

Should the district court accept the interpretation of Oceana law put forward by the defendant?

Note: Certification of State-Law Issues

Every state except North Carolina has enacted laws or rules permitting federal courts, under specified circumstances, to certify open questions of state law to the state's highest court. Federal courts are not obliged to certify open questions of state law, but these certification procedures provide a way for federal courts to obtain definitive answers to those questions of state law. Even when certification is permitted, there may be reasons not to use the procedure. In *Kremen v. Cohen*, 325 F.3d 1035 (9th Cir. 2003), a Ninth Circuit panel requested the California Supreme Court "to exercise its discretion to adjudicate a question of California law related to Internet domain names and the tort of conversion." Judge Kozinski dissented vigorously:

> When a federal court certifies a case to a state supreme court, it draws from a limited reservoir of comity. Certifying the case shifts the difficult work of deciding it to the state court, which is often so busy keeping its own house in order that it scarcely has time for our overflow laundry. Certification also burdens litigants, forcing them to reargue the case in a different forum—a process that is costly and full of delay. . . .

> I am aware of the prevailing infatuation with this procedural device— the "sacred cow in our modern judicial barnyard." But we have a duty to use it sparingly and sensibly; that a case raises difficult legal questions is not enough. Certification is justified only when the state supreme court has provided no authoritative guidance, other courts are in serious disarray and the question cries out for a definitive ruling.

> These circumstances are not present here. We are perfectly capable of answering both questions ourselves, and there is no indication that courts are overrun with lawsuits raising the issue. Cyberspace will not implode if the supreme court confronts the majority's questions at some point in the future rather than today; the issues may well be sharpened by common law development in the meantime. . . .

> The crowded California docket also means that certification is a less efficient mechanism for ascertaining state law. The cases we send to the California Supreme Court are beset by the same delays that plague the rest of its caseload.

> Certification burdens litigants, who foot the bill while their lawyers reargue the controversy in a different forum. . . .

> The California Supreme Court is always free to overrule any decision we render on the subject. It may even benefit from the insights we are able to offer, just as it benefits from prior consideration by state court judges. In this sense, we are just like another state court of appeal. We do California no favors by asking its supreme court to solve our problems while we stand mutely by.

Judge Kozinski's misgivings proved to be justified. The California Supreme Court denied the certification, and the Ninth Circuit panel decided the case without the benefit of its views. *Kremen v. Cohen*, 337 F.3d 1024 (9th Cir. 2003). Does this outcome vindicate Judge Kozinski's criticisms of the procedure?

C. State Law and Federal-Court Procedure

Part "Third" of the *Erie* opinion begins with an unequivocal declaration: "Except in matters governed by the Federal Constitution or by acts of Congress, the law to be applied in any case is the law of the state." The opinion does not carve out an exception for matters of "procedure," though it does say that "Congress has no power to declare substantive rules of common law applicable in a state." Justice Reed, in his concurring opinion, adds: "The line between procedural and substantive law is hazy, but no one doubts federal power over procedure."

Partly in reliance on these meager indicia, lawyers and judges concluded rather quickly that the rule of *Erie* does not apply to matters of "procedure." And courts began to confront the task of determining "what law, for *this* purpose, is 'procedural,' what 'substantive.'" Note, *After* Erie Railroad v. Tompkins: *Some Problems in "Substance" and "Procedure*," 39 COLUM. L. REV. 1472, 1473–34 (1939). That problem continues to confront courts today. This section explores the issues raised by the tension between the *Erie* doctrine and "federal power over procedure."

[1] "Substance" and "Procedure": Foundations

Note: The Rules Enabling Act

1. When Justice Reed said that "no one doubts federal power over procedure," he was not speaking in the abstract. A few months earlier, in December 1937, the Court had given its approval to the first set of Federal Rules of Civil Procedure. The Court acted under the authority given it by Congress in the Rules Enabling Act of 1934. This Note examines the Enabling Act and its relation to the substance-procedure distinction suggested by Justice Reed.

2. Prior to 1938, procedure in the federal district courts generally conformed to the practice in state courts in actions at law, with distinct federal rules for suits in equity. The Rules Enabling Act was designed to bring nationwide uniformity to federal procedure. It also authorized the Supreme Court to "unite" the rules for equity cases with those applicable to actions at law. The Act provided:

> Be it enacted . . . That the Supreme Court of the United States shall have the power to prescribe, by general rules, for the district courts of the United States and for the courts of the District of Columbia, the forms of process, writs, pleadings, and motions, and the practice and procedure in civil actions at law. Said rules shall neither abridge, enlarge, nor modify the substantive rights of

any litigant. They shall take effect six months after their promulgation, and thereafter all laws in conflict therewith shall be of no further force or effect.

Sec. 2. The court may at any time unite the general rules prescribed by it for cases in equity with those in actions at law so as to secure one form of civil action and procedure for both: Provided, however, That in such union of rules the right of trial by jury as at common law and declared by the seventh amendment to the Constitution shall be preserved to the parties inviolate. Such united rules shall not take effect until they shall have been reported to Congress by the Attorney General at the beginning of a regular session thereof and until after the close of such session.

In June 1935, Chief Justice Hughes appointed an Advisory Committee to draw up a unified set of rules that would govern procedure in both actions at law and suits in equity in all federal district courts. Drafts were circulated for comment, and ultimately the Supreme Court promulgated the rules in accordance with the Act. The rules took effect on September 16, 1938.

3. The authority conferred by the Enabling Act was limited to "the forms of process, writs, pleadings, and motions, and the practice and procedure" in civil actions. The Act also provided that the rules "shall neither abridge, enlarge, nor modify the substantive rights of any litigant." Thus, quite apart from *Erie*, the Enabling Act drew a distinction between "substantive rights" and matters of "practice and procedure." How was that line to be drawn? The Court soon confronted the issue.

4. The new Federal Rules included broad-ranging provisions allowing discovery. In particular, Rule 35 authorized a federal court to require a party "to submit to a physical or mental examination by a physician" when "the mental or physical condition of [the] party is in controversy." Rule 37 provided for sanctions for failure to comply with a discovery order.

In *Sibbach v. Wilson & Co.*, 312 U.S. 1 (1941), the plaintiff challenged the validity of Rule 35 and Rule 37 under the Enabling Act. Justice Roberts, writing for a bare majority of the Court, rejected her arguments:

> Congress has undoubted power to regulate the practice and procedure of federal courts, and may exercise that power by delegating to this or other federal courts authority to make rules not inconsistent with the statutes or Constitution of the United States; but it has never essayed to declare the substantive state law, or to abolish or nullify a right recognized by the substantive law of the state where the cause of action arose, save where a right or duty is imposed in a field committed to Congress by the Constitution. On the contrary it has enacted that the state law shall be the rule of decision in the federal courts.

> Hence we conclude that the [Enabling Act] was purposely restricted in its operation to matters of pleading and court practice and procedure. . . .

> [The plaintiff] admits, and, we think, correctly, that Rules 35 and 37 are rules of procedure. She insists, nevertheless, that by the prohibition against abridging substantive rights, Congress has banned the rules here challenged.

In order to reach this result she translates "substantive" into "important" or "substantial" rights. And she urges that if a rule affects such a right, albeit the rule is one of procedure merely, its prescription is not within the statutory grant of power embodied in the [Enabling Act]. She contends that our decisions and recognized principles require us so to hold.

The Court rejected the plaintiff's arguments based on precedent. The opinion continued:

We are thrown back, then, to the arguments drawn from the language of the [Enabling Act]. . . . [The plaintiff argues that by using the phrase "substantive rights"] Congress intended that in regulating procedure this court should not deal with important and substantial rights theretofore recognized. Recognized where and by whom? The state courts are divided as to the power in the absence of statute to order a physical examination. In a number such an order is authorized by statute or rule. . . .

The asserted right, moreover, is no more important than many others enjoyed by litigants in District Courts sitting in the several states, before the Federal Rules of Civil Procedure altered and abolished old rights or privileges and created new ones in connection with the conduct of litigation. . . . If we were to adopt the suggested criterion of the importance of the alleged right we should invite endless litigation and confusion worse confounded. The test must be whether a rule really regulates procedure,—the judicial process for enforcing rights and duties recognized by substantive law and for justly administering remedy and redress for disregard or infraction of them. That the rules in question are such is admitted.

Justice Frankfurter wrote for the four dissenters. He said:

[It] does not seem to me that the answer to our question is to be found by an analytic determination whether the power of examination here claimed is a matter of procedure or a matter of substance, even assuming that the two are mutually exclusive categories with easily ascertainable contents. . . .

So far as national law is concerned, a drastic change in public policy in a matter deeply touching the sensibilities of people or even their prejudices as to privacy, ought not to be inferred from a general authorization to formulate rules for the more uniform and effective dispatch of business on the civil side of the federal courts. I deem a requirement as to the invasion of the person to stand on a very different footing from questions pertaining to the discovery of documents, pre-trial procedure and other devices for the expeditious, economic and fair conduct of litigation.

5. It is noteworthy that Justice Frankfurter did not cite *Erie* in his *Sibbach* dissent, nor did he view the case as raising issues of federalism. His argument, rather, was that the particular rule—a rule authorizing physical examinations—intruded on the "historic immunity of the privacy of the person." Such a drastic change, he contended, requires "explicit legislation."

Can we infer from this that Justice Frankfurter believed that the rule in question was plainly outside the domain of *Erie*? Compare Justice Frankfurter's opinion for the Court in *Guaranty Trust Co. v. York*, summarized in the Note that follows.

6. The Enabling Act has been amended since 1934, and the process for formulating and promulgating rules is considerably more elaborate today than it was under the original Act. For further discussion, see section C[2] *infra*.

Note: Guaranty Trust *and the "Outcome Determinative" Test*

1. Two days after the *Erie* decision came down, then-Professor Felix Frankfurter wrote to Justice Harlan Fiske Stone: "Whhew [sic]!!! What will your Court do next? I haven't yet caught my breath over the Tompkins case."[1] Less than a year later, Professor Frankfurter was appointed to Justice Stone's Court and became Justice Frankfurter. But it was not until 1945 that he had the opportunity to put his stamp on the *Erie* doctrine. The occasion came with *Guaranty Trust Co. v. York*, 326 U.S. 99 (1945).

The case arose when holders of notes in a failing corporation brought suit for breach of trust against Guaranty Trust, the trustee for the noteholders. The suit was filed in federal district court in New York, with jurisdiction based on diversity of citizenship. The defendant argued that, under *Erie*, the court was required to apply the New York statute of limitations as construed by the New York courts, and that under New York law the suit was time-barred. The Second Circuit disagreed. The court first held that *Erie* "did not . . . in any way alter the wholly distinct doctrine relating to equitable 'remedial rights.'" Under that doctrine, the statute of limitations would be tolled if the defendant was guilty of "inequitable conduct" that caused the plaintiff to be ignorant of his rights. The court reversed the summary judgment granted by the district court and remanded for a determination of whether the defendant's conduct was inequitable.

The Supreme Court in turn reversed the Second Circuit. Justice Frankfurter, writing for the Court, began by emphasizing that when jurisdiction is based on diversity of citizenship, federal courts must respect "substantive rights" as defined by the states, and that this obligation extends to suits in equity as much as to actions at law:

> In giving federal courts "cognizance" of equity suits in cases of diversity jurisdiction, Congress never gave, nor did the federal courts ever claim, the power to deny substantive rights created by State law or to create substantive rights denied by State law. . . .
>
> And so this case reduces itself to the narrow question whether, when no recovery could be had in a State court because the action is barred by the statute of limitations, a federal court in equity can take cognizance of the suit because there is diversity of citizenship between the parties. Is the outlawry, according to State law, of a claim created by the States a matter of "substantive rights" to be respected by a federal court of equity when that court's jurisdiction is dependent on the fact that there is a State created right,

---

1. Quoted in EDWARD A. PURCELL, JR., BRANDEIS AND THE PROGRESSIVE CONSTITUTION 195 (2000).

or is such statute of "a mere remedial character" which a federal court may disregard?

Justice Frankfurter answered his question in an analysis that dominated *Erie* jurisprudence for two decades and continues to be influential today. He wrote:

> Matters of "substance" and matters of "procedure" are much talked about in the books as though they defined a great divide cutting across the whole domain of law. But, of course, "substance" and "procedure" are the same keywords to very different problems. Neither "substance" nor "procedure" represents the same invariants. Each implies different variables depending upon the particular problem for which it is used. . . .

> Here we are dealing with a right to recover derived not from the United States but from one of the States. When, because the plaintiff happens to be a nonresident, such a right is enforceable in a federal as well as in a State court, the forms and mode of enforcing the right may at times, naturally enough, vary because the two judicial systems are not identic. But since a federal court adjudicating a state-created right solely because of the diversity of citizenship of the parties is for that purpose, in effect, only another court of the State, it cannot afford recovery if the right to recover is made unavailable by the State nor can it substantially affect the enforcement of the right as given by the State.

> And so the question is not whether a statute of limitations is deemed a matter of "procedure" in some sense. The question is whether such a statute concerns merely the manner and the means by which a right to recover, as recognized by the State, is enforced, or whether such statutory limitation is a matter of substance in the aspect that alone is relevant to our problem, namely, does it significantly affect the result of a litigation for a federal court to disregard a law of a State that would be controlling in an action upon the same claim by the same parties in a State court?

> It is therefore immaterial whether statutes of limitation are characterized either as "substantive" or "procedural" in State court opinions in any use of those terms unrelated to the specific issue before us. *Erie R. Co. v. Tompkins* was not an endeavor to formulate scientific legal terminology. It expressed a policy that touches vitally the proper distribution of judicial power between State and federal courts. In essence, the intent of that decision was to insure that, in all cases where a federal court is exercising jurisdiction solely because of the diversity of citizenship of the parties, the outcome of the litigation in the federal court should be substantially the same, so far as legal rules determine the outcome of a litigation, as it would be if tried in a State court.

> The nub of the policy that underlies *Erie R. Co. v. Tompkins* is that for the same transaction the accident of a suit by a non-resident litigant in a federal court instead of in a State court a block away, should not lead to a substantially different result. . . . *Erie R. Co. v. Tompkins* has been applied with an eye

alert to essentials in avoiding disregard of State law in diversity cases in the federal courts. A policy so important to our federalism must be kept free from entanglements with analytical or terminological niceties.

Plainly enough, a statute that would completely bar recovery in a suit if brought in a State court bears on a State created right vitally and not merely formally or negligibly. As to consequences that so intimately affect recovery or non-recovery a federal court in a diversity case should follow State law. . . .

[Congress] afforded out-of-State litigants another tribunal, not another body of law. . . . The source of substantive rights enforced by a federal court under diversity jurisdiction, it cannot be said too often, is the law of the States. Whenever that law is authoritatively declared by a State, whether its voice be the legislature or its highest court, such law ought to govern in litigation founded on that law, whether the forum of application is a State or a federal court and whether the remedies be sought at law or may be had in equity.

Justice Rutledge, joined by Justice Murphy, dissented. They relied on "the long tradition, both federal and state, which regards statutes of limitations as falling within the category of remedial rather than substantive law." Justice Roberts and Justice Douglas took no part in the consideration of the case.

2. Justice Frankfurter says that *Erie* was based on "policy" and that the "intent" of the decision "was to insure that [in diversity cases] the outcome of the litigation in the federal court should be substantially the same, so far as legal rules determine the outcome of a litigation, as it would be if tried in a State court." Is that an accurate description of the rationale of *Erie*?

3. Justice Frankfurter says that the obligation to follow state law depends on whether the choice between state and federal law "concerns merely the manner and the means by which a right to recover, as recognized by the State, is enforced" or whether the choice "significantly affect[s] the result of a litigation." Are the two characterizations mutually exclusive? If not, what does this suggest about the *Guaranty Trust* test?

Note: "Only Another Court of the State"

In the decade that followed *Guaranty Trust*, the Court made clear that it fully embraced the proposition that "a federal court adjudicating a state-created right solely because of the diversity of citizenship of the parties is for that purpose, in effect, only another court of the State." This approach reached its zenith in three decisions handed down on the same day in 1949.

1. In *Ragan v. Merchants Transfer & Warehouse Co.*, 337 U.S. 530 (1949), the plaintiff filed his suit within the limitations period but did not serve process on the defendant until later. Under state law, an action was not "deemed commenced" within the meaning of the statute of limitation until process was served. The plaintiff nevertheless argued that the suit was timely by reason of Rule 3 of the Federal Rules of Civil Procedure, which provides: "A civil action is commenced by filing a complaint with the court."

The Court rejected the plaintiff's argument and held that when the cause of action is created by state law, the claim "accrues and comes to an end when local law so declares." The Court added: "We cannot give [the cause of action] longer life in the federal court than it would have had in the state court without adding something to the cause of action. We may not do that consistently with *Erie R. Co. v. Tompkins.*"

Ragan is further discussed in *Walker v. Armco Steel Co., infra.*

2. In *Woods v. Interstate Realty Co.*, 337 U.S. 535 (1949), a Mississippi statute required "foreign" corporations (i.e., corporations not incorporated in Mississippi) to designate an agent for service of process. The statute further provided: "Any foreign corporation failing to comply with the above provisions shall not be permitted to bring or maintain any action or suit in any of the courts of this state." The Supreme Court held that the statute also barred suit by a non-complying foreign corporation in federal court in Mississippi. The Court's analysis was brief:

> The *York* case was premised on the theory that a right which local law creates but which it does not supply with a remedy is no right at all for purposes of enforcement in a federal court in a diversity case; that where in such cases one is barred from recovery in the state court, he should likewise be barred in the federal court. The contrary result would create discriminations against citizens of the State in favor of those authorized to invoke the diversity jurisdiction of the federal courts. It was that element of discrimination that *Erie R. Co. v. Tompkins* was designed to eliminate.

3. In *Cohen v. Beneficial Loan Corp.*, 337 U.S. 541 (1949), the plaintiff brought a shareholder's derivative action in federal district court in New Jersey. The suit alleged that corporate insiders had engaged in a conspiracy to enrich themselves at the expense of the corporation. A New Jersey statute provided that when a plaintiff who has only a small interest in a corporation brings a shareholder's derivative suit that proves unsuccessful, the plaintiff will be liable for the reasonable expenses of the defense, including attorney's fees. The statute also required the plaintiff to post security for the payment of these expenses. The question was whether this statute was binding on a federal court in a diversity case. The Supreme Court held that it was. The Court said:

> [In] diversity cases the federal court administers the state system of law in all except details related to its own conduct of business. *Guaranty Trust.* The only substantial argument that this New Jersey statute is not applicable here is that its provisions are mere rules of procedure rather than rules of substantive law.
>
> Even if we were to agree that the New Jersey statute is procedural, it would not determine that it is not applicable. Rules which lawyers call procedural do not always exhaust their effect by regulating procedure. But this statute is not merely a regulation of procedure. With it or without it the main action takes the same course. However, it creates a new liability where none existed before, for it makes a stockholder who institutes a derivative action liable for the expense to which he puts the corporation and other defendants, if he does

not make good his claims. Such liability is not usual and it goes beyond payment of what we know as "costs."

> If all the Act did was to create this liability, it would clearly be substantive. But this new liability would be without meaning and value in many cases if it resulted in nothing but a judgment for expenses at or after the end of the case. Therefore, a procedure is prescribed by which the liability is insured by entitling the corporate defendant to a bond of indemnity before the outlay is incurred. We do not think a statute which so conditions the stockholder's action can be disregarded by the federal court as a mere procedural device.

The Court considered and rejected the argument that the statute conflicted with Rule 23 of the Federal Rules of Civil Procedure, which regulates class actions. The Court concluded: "We see no reason why the policy stated in *Guaranty Trust* should not apply."

Interestingly, Justice Frankfurter joined Justice Douglas's brief dissent. The dissent said that state statutes "do not fall under the principle of *Erie* unless they define, qualify or delimit the cause of action or otherwise relate to it. This New Jersey statute, like statutes governing security for costs, regulates only the procedure for instituting a particular cause of action and hence need not be applied in this diversity suit in the federal court." Justice Rutledge dissented separately.

Note: **Byrd v. Blue Ridge**

The Court began to pull back from the single-mindedness of the *Guaranty Trust* approach in *Byrd v. Blue Ridge Rural Electric Cooperative, Inc.*, 356 U.S. 525 (1958).

Byrd did not come to the Court as an *Erie* case. Plaintiff Byrd was injured while working as a lineman in the construction crew of a construction contractor. The contractor was building power lines for Blue Ridge. Byrd (a citizen of North Carolina) brought a negligence suit in federal district court against Blue Ridge (a South Carolina corporation) to recover damages for the injuries. Jurisdiction was based on diversity and South Carolina law controlled.

As an affirmative defense, Blue Ridge asserted that under the South Carolina Workmen's Compensation Act, Byrd had the status of a statutory employee of Blue Ridge. That meant that Byrd's exclusive remedy was under the workers' compensation act; he could not recover damages in tort.

Byrd won a jury verdict, but the Fourth Circuit reversed and directed the entry of judgment for Blue Ridge on the ground that Byrd was indeed a statutory employee. Byrd then filed a certiorari petition asserting that the Fourth Circuit, by entering judgment rather than ordering a new trial, deprived him of the opportunity to introduce relevant evidence on the "statutory employee" issue.

Today, it is highly unlikely that the Supreme Court would hear such a case, but in the 1950s the Court's attitude was different, and the Court granted certiorari. Blue Ridge now raised the point that under South Carolina law the court, not the jury, would decide whether the defendant was a statutory employer. Byrd countered by saying that in federal court "the procedural question of whether factual issues are triable by a jury" is controlled by federal law.

Neither side's briefs made any mention of *Erie*. However, after oral argument the Court ordered the parties to address "the application of *Erie* in connection with" the question of Byrd's status as a statutory employee. Shortly after the reargument, the Court handed down its decision. Justice Brennan wrote the Court's opinion.

The Court first held that the Fourth Circuit erred in denying Byrd the opportunity to introduce further evidence on the "statutory employee" issue. The Court then said: "A question is also presented as to whether on remand the factual issue is to be decided by the judge or by the jury." The Court acknowledged that the South Carolina Supreme Court had recently held "that it was for the judge and not the jury to decide on the evidence whether the [defendant] was a statutory employer." The Court also acknowledged that, under *Erie*, "the federal courts in diversity cases must respect the definition of state-created rights and obligations by the state courts." However, the Court concluded that *Erie* did not require application of the state rule. The Court gave three reasons for this conclusion.

First, the Court said that the state rule was not "bound up with [state] rights and obligations in such a way that its application in the federal court is required." The Court explained:

> [The state-court] holding is grounded in the practical consideration that the question had theretofore come before the South Carolina courts from the Industrial Commission and the courts had become accustomed to deciding the factual issue of immunity without the aid of juries. We find nothing to suggest that this rule was announced as an integral part of the special relationship created by the statute. Thus the requirement appears to be merely a form and mode of enforcing the immunity, *Guaranty Trust*, and not a rule intended to be bound up with the definition of the rights and obligations of the parties.

That, however, was not the end of the matter. The Court continued:

> But cases following *Erie* have evinced a broader policy to the effect that the federal courts should conform as near as may be—in the absence of other considerations—to state rules even of form and mode where the state rules may bear substantially on the question whether the litigation would come out one way in the federal court and another way in the state court if the federal court failed to apply a particular local rule. *E.g.*, *Guaranty Trust*. Concededly the nature of the tribunal which tries issues may be important in the enforcement of the parcel of rights making up a cause of action or defense, and bear significantly upon achievement of uniform enforcement of the right. It may well be that in the instant personal-injury case the outcome would be substantially affected by whether the issue of immunity is decided by a judge or a jury. Therefore, were "outcome" the only consideration, a strong case might appear for saying that the federal court should follow the state practice.

But there are affirmative countervailing considerations at work here. The federal system is an independent system for administering justice to litigants who properly invoke its jurisdiction. An essential characteristic of that system is the manner in which, in civil common-law actions, it distributes trial functions between judge and jury and, under the influence—if not the command—of the Seventh Amendment, assigns the decisions of disputed questions of fact to the jury. The policy of uniform enforcement of state-created rights and obligations, see, *e.g.*, *Guaranty Trust Co.*, cannot in every case exact compliance with a state rule—not bound up with rights and obligations—which disrupts the federal system of allocating functions between judge and jury. *Herron v. Southern Pacific Co.*, 283 U.S. 91. Thus the inquiry here is whether the federal policy favoring jury decisions of disputed fact questions should yield to the state rule in the interest of furthering the objective that the litigation should not come out one way in the federal court and another way in the state court.

We think that in the circumstances of this case the federal court should not follow the state rule. It cannot be gainsaid that there is a strong federal policy against allowing state rules to disrupt the judge-jury relationship in the federal courts. . . . [In] light of the influence of the Seventh Amendment, the function assigned to the jury "is an essential factor in the process for which the Federal Constitution provides."

Finally, the Court said that the choice of decision-maker might not be outcome-determinative after all. "The trial judge in the federal system has powers denied the judges of many States to comment on the weight of evidence and credibility of witnesses, and discretion to grant a new trial if the verdict appears to him to be against the weight of the evidence. We do not think the likelihood of a different result is so strong as to require the federal practice of jury determination of disputed factual issues to yield to the state rule in the interest of uniformity of outcome."

Only Justice Whittaker disagreed with the Court's *Erie* analysis. Justice Frankfurter, joined by Justice Harlan, would have affirmed without reaching the *Erie* issue.

Byrd is an opaque decision in several respects, not the least of which is the Court's ambiguous invocation of the Seventh Amendment. In a footnote, the Court insisted that it was not deciding "the constitutional question whether the right of jury trial protected in federal courts by the Seventh Amendment embraces the factual issue of statutory immunity when asserted, as here, as an affirmative defense in a common-law negligence action." But the Court twice referred to the "influence" of the Seventh Amendment. How can a constitutional provision "influence" a decision if it does not apply?

[2] The *Hanna* Bifurcation

Hanna v. Plumer

Supreme Court of the United States, 1965.

380 U.S. 460.

Mr. Chief Justice Warren delivered the opinion of the Court.

The question to be decided is whether, in a civil action where the jurisdiction of the United States district court is based upon diversity of citizenship between the parties, service of process shall be made in the manner prescribed by state law or that set forth in Rule 4(d)(1) of the Federal Rules of Civil Procedure.

On February 6, 1963, petitioner, a citizen of Ohio, filed her complaint in the District Court for the District of Massachusetts, claiming damages in excess of $10,000 for personal injuries resulting from an automobile accident in South Carolina, allegedly caused by the negligence of one Louise Plumer Osgood, a Massachusetts citizen deceased at the time of the filing of the complaint. Respondent, Mrs. Osgood's executor and also a Massachusetts citizen, was named as defendant. On February 8, service was made by leaving copies of the summons and the complaint with respondent's wife at his residence, concededly in compliance with Rule 4(d)(1), which provides:

> The summons and complaint shall be served together. The plaintiff shall furnish the person making service with such copies as are necessary. Service shall be made as follows:
>
> (1) Upon an individual other than an infant or an incompetent person, by delivering a copy of the summons and of the complaint to him personally or by leaving copies thereof at his dwelling house or usual place of abode with some person of suitable age and discretion then residing therein * * *.

Respondent filed his answer on February 26, alleging, inter alia, that the action could not be maintained because it had been brought "contrary to and in violation of the provisions of Massachusetts General Laws (Ter. Ed.) Chapter 197, Section 9." That section provides:

> Except as provided in this chapter, an executor or administrator shall not be held to answer to an action by a creditor of the deceased which is not commenced within one year from the time of his giving bond for the performance of his trust, or to such an action which is commenced within said year unless before the expiration thereof the writ in such action has been served by delivery in hand upon such executor or administrator or service thereof accepted by him or a notice stating the name of the estate, the name and address of the creditor, the amount of the claim and the court in which the action has been brought has been filed in the proper registry of probate. * * *

Mass. Gen. Laws Ann., c. 197, § 9 (1958).

On October 17, 1963, the District Court granted respondent's motion for summary judgment, citing *Ragan v. Merchants Transfer & Warehouse Co.*, 337 U.S. 530, and

Guaranty Trust Co. of New York v. York, 326 U.S. 99, in support of its conclusion that the adequacy of the service was to be measured by §9, with which, the court held, petitioner had not complied. On appeal, petitioner admitted noncompliance with §9, but argued that Rule 4(d)(1) defines the method by which service of process is to be effected in diversity actions. The Court of Appeals for the First Circuit, finding that "[r]elatively recent amendments [to §9] evince a clear legislative purpose to require personal notification within the year,"[1] concluded that the conflict of state and federal rules was over "a substantive rather than a procedural matter," and unanimously affirmed. Because of the threat to the goal of uniformity of federal procedure posed by the decision below, we granted certiorari.

We conclude that the adoption of Rule 4(d)(1), designed to control service of process in diversity actions, neither exceeded the congressional mandate embodied in the Rules Enabling Act nor transgressed constitutional bounds, and that the Rule is therefore the standard against which the District Court should have measured the adequacy of the service. Accordingly, we reverse the decision of the Court of Appeals.

The Rules Enabling Act, 28 U.S.C. §2072 (1958 ed.), provides, in pertinent part:

> The Supreme Court shall have the power to prescribe, by general rules, the forms of process, writs, pleadings, and motions, and the practice and procedure of the district courts of the United States in civil actions.

> Such rules shall not abridge, enlarge or modify any substantive right and shall preserve the right of trial by jury * * *.

Under the cases construing the scope of the Enabling Act, Rule 4(d)(1) clearly passes muster. Prescribing the manner in which a defendant is to be notified that a suit has been instituted against him, it relates to the "practice and procedure of the district courts."

> The test must be whether a rule really regulates procedure, — the judicial process for enforcing rights and duties recognized by substantive law and for justly administering remedy and redress for disregard or infraction of them. *Sibbach v. Wilson & Co.*, 312 U.S. 1, 14.

---

1. Section 9 is in part a statute of limitations, providing that an executor need not "answer to an action * * * which is not commenced within one year from the time of his giving bond * * *." This part of the statute, the purpose of which is to speed the settlement of estates, is not involved in this case, since the action clearly was timely commenced. (Respondent filed bond on March 1, 1962; the complaint was filed February 6, 1963; and the service — the propriety of which is in dispute — was made on February 8, 1963.)

Section 9 also provides for the manner of service. Generally, service of process must be made by "delivery in hand," although there are two alternatives: acceptance of service by the executor, or filing of a notice of claim, the components of which are set out in the statute, in the appropriate probate court. The purpose of this part of the statute, which is involved here, is, as the court below noted, to insure that executors will receive actual notice of claims. Actual notice is of course also the goal of Rule 4(d)(1); however, the Federal Rule reflects a determination that this goal can be achieved by a method less cumbersome than that prescribed in §9. In this case the goal seems to have been achieved; although the affidavit filed by respondent in the District Court asserts that he had not been served in hand nor had he accepted service, it does not allege lack of actual notice.

In *Mississippi Pub. Corp. v. Murphree*, 326 U.S. 438, this Court upheld Rule 4(f), which permits service of a summons anywhere within the State (and not merely the district) in which a district court sits:

> We think that Rule 4(f) is in harmony with the Enabling Act * * *. Undoubtedly most alterations of the rules of practice and procedure may and often do affect the rights of litigants. Congress' prohibition of any alteration of substantive rights of litigants was obviously not addressed to such incidental effects as necessarily attend the adoption of the prescribed new rules of procedure upon the rights of litigants who, agreeably to rules of practice and procedure, have been brought before a court authorized to determine their rights. *Sibbach v. Wilson & Co.*, 312 U.S. 1. The fact that the application of Rule 4(f) will operate to subject petitioner's rights to adjudication by the district court for northern Mississippi will undoubtedly affect those rights. But it does not operate to abridge, enlarge or modify the rules of decision by which that court will adjudicate its rights.

Thus were there no conflicting state procedure, Rule 4(d)(1) would clearly control. However, respondent, focusing on the contrary Massachusetts rule, calls to the Court's attention another line of cases, a line which—like the Federal Rules—had its birth in 1938. *Erie R. Co. v. Tompkins* held that federal courts sitting in diversity cases, when deciding questions of "substantive" law, are bound by state court decisions as well as state statutes. The broad command of *Erie* was therefore identical to that of the Enabling Act: federal courts are to apply state substantive law and federal procedural law. However, as subsequent cases sharpened the distinction between substance and procedure, the line of cases following *Erie* diverged markedly from the line construing the Enabling Act. *Guaranty Trust Co. of New York v. York,* 326 U.S. 99, made it clear that *Erie*-type problems were not to be solved by reference to any traditional or common-sense substance-procedure distinction:

> And so the question is not whether a statute of limitations is deemed a matter of "procedure" in some sense. The question is * * * does it significantly affect the result of a litigation for a federal court to disregard a law of a State that would be controlling in an action upon the same claim by the same parties in a State court?"

Respondent, by placing primary reliance on *York* and *Ragan*, suggests that the *Erie* doctrine acts as a check on the Federal Rules of Civil Procedure, that despite the clear command of Rule 4(d)(1), *Erie* and its progeny demand the application of the Massachusetts rule. Reduced to essentials, the argument is: (1) *Erie*, as refined in *York*, demands that federal courts apply state law whenever application of federal law in its stead will alter the outcome of the case. (2) In this case, a determination that the Massachusetts service requirements obtain will result in immediate victory for respondent. If, on the other hand, it should be held that Rule 4(d)(1) is applicable, the litigation will continue, with possible victory for petitioner. (3) Therefore, *Erie* demands application of the Massachusetts rule. The syllogism possesses an appealing simplicity, but is for several reasons invalid.

In the first place, it is doubtful that, even if there were no Federal Rule making it clear that in-hand service is not required in diversity actions, the *Erie* rule would have obligated the District Court to follow the Massachusetts procedure. "Outcome-determination" analysis was never intended to serve as a talisman. *Byrd v. Blue Ridge Rural Elec. Cooperative.* Indeed, the message of *York* itself is that choices between state and federal law are to be made not by application of any automatic, "litmus paper" criterion, but rather by reference to the policies underlying the *Erie* rule.

The *Erie* rule is rooted in part in a realization that it would be unfair for the character of result of a litigation materially to differ because the suit had been brought in a federal court.

> Diversity of citizenship jurisdiction was conferred in order to prevent apprehended discrimination in state courts against those not citizens of the state. *Swift v. Tyson* introduced grave discrimination by noncitizens against citizens. It made rights enjoyed under the unwritten "general law" vary according to whether enforcement was sought in the state or in the federal court; and the privilege of selecting the court in which the right should be determined was conferred upon the noncitizen. Thus, the doctrine rendered impossible equal protection of the law. *Erie R. Co. v. Tompkins.*

The decision was also in part a reaction to the practice of "forum-shopping" which had grown up in response to the rule of *Swift v. Tyson.* That the *York* test was an attempt to effectuate these policies is demonstrated by the fact that the opinion framed the inquiry in terms of "substantial" variations between state and federal litigation. Not only are nonsubstantial, or trivial, variations not likely to raise the sort of equal protection problems which troubled the Court in *Erie*; they are also unlikely to influence the choice of a forum. The "outcome-determination" test therefore cannot be read without reference to the twin aims of the *Erie* rule: discouragement of forum-shopping and avoidance of inequitable administration of the laws.[9]

The difference between the conclusion that the Massachusetts rule is applicable, and the conclusion that it is not, is of course at this point "outcome-determinative" in the sense that if we hold the state rule to apply, respondent prevails, whereas if we hold that Rule 4(d)(1) governs, the litigation will continue. But in this sense every

---

9. The Court of Appeals seemed to frame the inquiry in terms of how "important" § 9 is to the State. In support of its suggestion that § 9 serves some interest the State regards as vital to its citizens, the court noted that something like § 9 has been on the books in Massachusetts a long time, that § 9 has been amended a number of times and that § 9 is designed to make sure that executors receive actual notice. The apparent lack of relation among these three observations is not surprising, because it is not clear to what sort of question the Court of Appeals was addressing itself. One cannot meaningfully ask how important something is without first asking "important for what purpose?" *Erie* and its progeny make clear that when a federal court sitting in a diversity case is faced with a question of whether or not to apply state law, the importance of a state rule is indeed relevant, but only in the context of asking whether application of the rule would make so important a difference to the character or result of the litigation that failure to enforce it would unfairly discriminate against citizens of the forum State, or whether application of the rule would have so important an effect upon the fortunes of one or both of the litigants that failure to enforce it would be likely to cause a plaintiff to choose the federal court.

procedural variation is "outcome-determinative." For example, having brought suit in a federal court, a plaintiff cannot then insist on the right to file subsequent pleadings in accord with the time limits applicable in state courts, even though enforcement of the federal timetable will, if he continues to insist that he must meet only the state time limit, result in determination of the controversy against him. So it is here. Though choice of the federal or state rule will at this point have a marked effect upon the outcome of the litigation, the difference between the two rules would be of scant, if any, relevance to the choice of a forum. Petitioner, in choosing her forum, was not presented with a situation where application of the state rule would wholly bar recovery; rather, adherence to the state rule would have resulted only in altering the way in which process was served. Moreover, it is difficult to argue that permitting service of defendant's wife to take the place of in-hand service of defendant himself alters the mode of enforcement of state-created rights in a fashion sufficiently "substantial" to raise the sort of equal protection problems to which the *Erie* opinion alluded.

There is, however, a more fundamental flaw in respondent's syllogism: the incorrect assumption that the rule of *Erie R. Co. v. Tompkins* constitutes the appropriate test of the validity and therefore the applicability of a Federal Rule of Civil Procedure. The *Erie* rule has never been invoked to void a Federal Rule. It is true that there have been cases where this Court has held applicable a state rule in the face of an argument that the situation was governed by one of the Federal Rules. [The Court cited *Ragan* and *Cohen* as examples of this proposition.] But the holding of each such case was not that *Erie* commanded displacement of a Federal Rule by an inconsistent state rule, but rather that the scope of the Federal Rule was not as broad as the losing party urged, and therefore, there being no Federal Rule which covered the point in dispute, Erie commanded the enforcement of state law. . . . (Here, of course, the clash is unavoidable; Rule 4(d)(1) says—implicitly, but with unmistakable clarity—that in-hand service is not required in federal courts.) At the same time, in cases adjudicating the validity of Federal Rules, we have not applied the *York* rule or other refinements of *Erie*, but have to this day continued to decide questions concerning the scope of the Enabling Act and the constitutionality of specific Federal Rules in light of the distinction set forth in *Sibbach*.

Nor has the development of two separate lines of cases been inadvertent. The line between "substance" and "procedure" shifts as the legal context changes. "Each implies different variables depending upon the particular problem for which it is used." *Guaranty Trust*. It is true that both the Enabling Act and the *Erie* rule say, roughly, that federal courts are to apply state "substantive" law and federal "procedural" law, but from that it need not follow that the tests are identical. For they were designed to control very different sorts of decisions. When a situation is covered by one of the Federal Rules, the question facing the court is a far cry from the typical, relatively unguided *Erie* choice: the court has been instructed to apply the Federal Rule, and can refuse to do so only if the Advisory Committee, this Court, and Congress erred in their prima facie judgment that the Rule in question transgresses neither the terms of the Enabling Act nor constitutional restrictions.

We are reminded by the *Erie* opinion that neither Congress nor the federal courts can, under the guise of formulating rules of decision for federal courts, fashion rules which are not supported by a grant of federal authority contained in Article I or some other section of the Constitution; in such areas state law must govern because there can be no other law. But the opinion in *Erie*, which involved no Federal Rule and dealt with a question which was "substantive" in every traditional sense (whether the railroad owed a duty of care to Tompkins as a trespasser or a licensee), surely neither said nor implied that measures like Rule 4(d)(1) are unconstitutional. For the constitutional provision for a federal court system (augmented by the Necessary and Proper Clause) carries with it congressional power to make rules governing the practice and pleading in those courts, which in turn includes a power to regulate matters which, though falling within the uncertain area between substance and procedure, are rationally capable of classification as either. Cf. *M'Culloch v. State of Maryland*, 4 Wheat. 316, 421. Neither *York* nor the cases following it ever suggested that the rule there laid down for coping with situations where no Federal Rule applies is coextensive with the limitation on Congress to which *Erie* had adverted. Although this Court has never before been confronted with a case where the applicable Federal Rule is in direct collision with the law of the relevant State, courts of appeals faced with such clashes have rightly discerned the implications of our decisions. . . .

Erie and its offspring cast no doubt on the long-recognized power of Congress to prescribe housekeeping rules for federal courts even though some of those rules will inevitably differ from comparable state rules. "When, because the plaintiff happens to be a non-resident, such a right is enforceable in a federal as well as in a State court, the forms and mode of enforcing the right may at times, naturally enough, vary because the two judicial systems are not identic." *Guaranty Trust Co.* Thus, though a court, in measuring a Federal Rule against the standards contained in the Enabling Act and the Constitution, need not wholly blind itself to the degree to which the Rule makes the character and result of the federal litigation stray from the course it would follow in state courts, *Sibbach v. Wilson & Co.*, it cannot be forgotten that the *Erie* rule, and the guidelines suggested in *York*, were created to serve another purpose altogether. To hold that a Federal Rule of Civil Procedure must cease to function whenever it alters the mode of enforcing state-created rights would be to disembowel either the Constitution's grant of power over federal procedure or Congress' attempt to exercise that power in the Enabling Act. Rule 4(d)(1) is valid and controls the instant case.

Reversed.

Mr. Justice Black concurs in the result.

Mr. Justice Harlan, concurring [omitted].

Note: The Opinion in Hanna

1. Although the Court in *Hanna* says that the defendant's argument is invalid "for several reasons," there are really only two. The first is that the *Erie* doctrine, even as "refined" in *Guaranty Trust*, does not compel application of the Massachusetts rule. The second is that the *Erie* line of cases does not apply at all.

2. Consider first the Court's discussion of "the typical, relatively unguided *Erie* choice." The Court says that *Guaranty Trust*, in addressing "*Erie*-type problems," did not apply a "traditional or common-sense substance-procedure distinction." But look at the block quotation from *Guaranty Trust*, and compare it with the original. What has the Chief Justice omitted, and what is the significance of the omission?

3. In *Byrd*, the Court seemed to say that a "substantive" rule, for *Erie* purposes, is one that is "bound up" with the definition of rights and obligations under state law. The Massachusetts rule requiring in-hand service was part of the same statutory provision—indeed, the same sentence—that established the limitations period for actions against an executor. Does *Hanna* repudiate this aspect of *Byrd*?

The First Circuit Court of Appeals—the court that was reversed by the Supreme Court in *Hanna*—commented in a later case that the Supreme Court misinterpreted the Massachusetts statute:

> [Perhaps] because of the way in which issue was joined, the Court misconstrued the state statute that it struck down. . . . In our view section 9 [of the Massachusetts statute] does not purport to be, and is not, a restriction on methods of service so far as process is concerned, but leaves extant the full Massachusetts service procedure, which includes last and usual service, precisely in accord with the provisions of Rule 4. Rather, in addition to bringing the executor into court, the Massachusetts legislature felt it so important that he be free to make distributions at the earliest possible moment, that it afforded him the protection of affirmative personal notice within the year during which suit must be commenced, and specified three permissible means of notification so as to leave no room for dispute. . . . Massachusetts regards compliance with the statutory terms so important that the defense of inadequate notice cannot even be claimed to be waived.

Marshall v. Mulrenin, 508 F.2d 39, 42–43 (1st Cir. 1974). If this is correct, does it cast doubt on the holding of *Hanna*?

4. The Court faults the First Circuit for its misunderstanding of the *Erie* doctrine, but the Chief Justice never states the correct test in the text of his opinion. For that one must look to footnote 9.

5. Technically, the Court's discussion of the "typical, unguided *Erie* choice" is dictum, because the Court goes on to hold that the *Erie* line of cases is irrelevant to the question before it. In a separate concurrence in *Hanna*, Justice Harlan summarized the Court's approach as "arguably procedural, ergo constitutional." He elaborated:

> So long as a reasonable man could characterize any duly adopted federal rule as "procedural," the Court, unless I misapprehend what is said, would have it apply no matter how seriously it frustrated a State's substantive regulation of the primary conduct and affairs of its citizens.

Is this an accurate statement of *Hanna*'s holding? Reconsider this question after reading *Walker v. Armco Steel Corp.*, the next principal case.

Walker v. Armco Steel Corporation

Supreme Court of the United States, 1980.

446 U.S. 740.

MR. JUSTICE MARSHALL delivered the opinion of the Court.

This case presents the issue whether in a diversity action the federal court should follow state law or, alternatively, Rule 3 of the Federal Rules of Civil Procedure in determining when an action is commenced for the purpose of tolling the state statute of limitations.

I

According to the allegations of the complaint, petitioner, a carpenter, was injured on August 22, 1975, in Oklahoma City, Okla., while pounding a Sheffield nail into a cement wall. Respondent was the manufacturer of the nail. Petitioner claimed that the nail contained a defect which caused its head to shatter and strike him in the right eye, resulting in permanent injuries. The defect was allegedly caused by respondent's negligence in manufacture and design.

Petitioner is a resident of Oklahoma, and respondent is a foreign corporation having its principal place of business in a State other than Oklahoma. Since there was diversity of citizenship, petitioner brought suit in the United States District Court for the Western District of Oklahoma. The complaint was filed on August 19, 1977. Although summons was issued that same day, service of process was not made on respondent's authorized service agent until December 1, 1977. On January 5, 1978, respondent filed a motion to dismiss the complaint on the ground that the action was barred by the applicable Oklahoma statute of limitations. Although the complaint had been filed within the 2-year statute of limitations, state law does not deem the action "commenced" for purposes of the statute of limitations until service of the summons on the defendant, Okla. Stat., tit. 12, § 97 (1971).[4] If the complaint is filed within the limitations period, however, the action is deemed to have commenced from that date of filing if the plaintiff serves the defendant within 60 days, even though that service may occur outside the limitations period. In this case, service was not effectuated until long after this 60-day period had expired. Petitioner in his reply brief to the motion to dismiss admitted that his case would be foreclosed in state court, but he argued that Rule 3 of the Federal Rules of Civil Procedure governs the manner in which an action is commenced in federal court for all purposes, including the tolling of the state statute of limitations.

---

4. OKLAHOMA STAT., tit. 12, § 97 (1971), provides in pertinent part: "An action shall be deemed commenced, within the meaning of this article [the statute of limitations], as to each defendant, at the date of the summons which is served on him, or on a codefendant, who is a joint contractor or otherwise united in interest with him. . . . An attempt to commence an action shall be deemed equivalent to the commencement thereof, within the meaning of this article, when the party faithfully, properly and diligently endeavors to procure a service; but such attempt must be followed by the first publication or service of the summons, . . . within sixty (60) days."

The District Court dismissed the complaint as barred by the Oklahoma statute of limitations. The court concluded that Okla. Stat., tit. 12, § 97 (1971) was "an integral part of the Oklahoma statute of limitations," and therefore, under *Ragan v. Merchants Transfer & Warehouse Co.*, 337 U.S. 530 (1949), state law applied. The court rejected the argument that *Ragan* had been implicitly overruled in *Hanna v. Plumer*, 380 U.S. 460 (1965).

The United States Court of Appeals for the Tenth Circuit affirmed. That court concluded that Okla. Stat., tit. 12, § 97 (1971), was in "direct conflict" with Rule 3. However, the Oklahoma statute was "indistinguishable" from the statute involved in *Ragan*, and the court felt itself "constrained" to follow *Ragan*.

We granted certiorari because of a conflict among the Courts of Appeals. We now affirm.

II

The question whether state or federal law should apply on various issues arising in an action based on state law which has been brought in federal court under diversity of citizenship jurisdiction has troubled this Court for many years. [The Court reviewed the decisions in *Erie* and *Guaranty Trust*.]

The decision in [*Guaranty Trust*] led logically to our holding in *Ragan*. . . . [In *Ragan*, we rejected] the argument that Rule 3 of the Federal Rules of Civil Procedure governed the manner in which an action was commenced in federal court for purposes of tolling the state statute of limitations. Instead, we held that the service of summons statute controlled because it was an integral part of the state statute of limitations, and under [*Guaranty Trust*] that statute of limitations was part of the state-law cause of action. . . .

III

The present case is indistinguishable from *Ragan*. . . . In both cases the suit would concededly have been barred in the applicable state court, and in both instances the state service statute was held to be an integral part of the statute of limitations by the lower court more familiar than we with state law. Accordingly, as the Court of Appeals held below, the instant action is barred by the statute of limitations unless *Ragan* is no longer good law.

Petitioner argues that the analysis and holding of *Ragan* did not survive our decision in *Hanna*. Petitioner's position is that Okla. Stat., tit. 12, § 97 (1971), is in direct conflict with the Federal Rule. Under *Hanna*, petitioner contends, the appropriate question is whether Rule 3 is within the scope of the Rules Enabling Act and, if so, within the constitutional power of Congress. In petitioner's view, the Federal Rule is to be applied unless it violates one of those two restrictions. This argument ignores both the force of stare decisis and the specific limitations that we carefully placed on the *Hanna* analysis. . . .

This Court in *Hanna* distinguished *Ragan* rather than overruled it, and for good reason. Application of the *Hanna* analysis is premised on a "direct collision" between the Federal Rule and the state law. In *Hanna* itself the "clash" between Rule 4(d)(1) and the state in-hand service requirement was "unavoidable." The first question must therefore be whether the scope of the Federal Rule in fact is sufficiently broad to control the issue before the Court. It is only if that question is answered affirmatively that the *Hanna* analysis applies.[9]

[We] recognized in *Hanna* that the present case is an instance where "the scope of the Federal Rule [is] not as broad as the losing party urge[s], and therefore, there being no Federal Rule which cover[s] the point in dispute, *Erie* command[s] the enforcement of state law." Rule 3 simply states that "[a] civil action is commenced by filing a complaint with the court." There is no indication that the Rule was intended to toll a state statute of limitations, much less that it purported to displace state tolling rules for purposes of state statutes of limitations. In our view, in diversity actions[11] Rule 3 governs the date from which various timing requirements of the Federal Rules begin to run, but does not affect state statutes of limitations.

In contrast to Rule 3, the Oklahoma statute is a statement of a substantive decision by that State that actual service on, and accordingly actual notice by, the defendant is an integral part of the several policies served by the statute of limitations. See *C & C Tile Co. v. Independent School District No. 7 of Tulsa County*, 503 P.2d 554, 559 (Okl. 1972). The statute of limitations establishes a deadline after which the defendant may legitimately have peace of mind; it also recognizes that after a certain period of time it is unfair to require the defendant to attempt to piece together his defense to an old claim. A requirement of actual service promotes both of those functions of the statute. It is these policy aspects which make the service requirement an "integral" part of the statute of limitations both in this case and in *Ragan*. As such, the service rule must be considered part and parcel of the statute of limitations. Rule 3 does not replace such policy determinations found in state law. Rule 3 and Okla. Stat., tit. 12, § 97 (1971), can exist side by side, therefore, each controlling its own intended sphere of coverage without conflict.

Since there is no direct conflict between the Federal Rule and the state law, the *Hanna* analysis does not apply.[14] Instead, the policies behind *Erie* and *Ragan* control the issue whether, in the absence of a federal rule directly on point, state service requirements which are an integral part of the state statute of limitations should control in an action based on state law which is filed in federal court under diversity jurisdiction.

---

9. This is not to suggest that the Federal Rules of Civil Procedure are to be narrowly construed in order to avoid a "direct collision" with state law. The Federal Rules should be given their plain meaning. If a direct collision with state law arises from that plain meaning, then the analysis developed in *Hanna v. Plumer* applies.

11. The Court suggested in *Ragan* that in suits to enforce rights under a federal statute Rule 3 means that filing of the complaint tolls the applicable statute of limitations. . . . We do not here address the role of Rule 3 as a tolling provision for a statute of limitations, whether set by federal law or borrowed from state law, if the cause of action is based on federal law.

14. Since we hold that Rule 3 does not apply, it is unnecessary for us to address the second question posed by the *Hanna* analysis: whether Rule 3, if it applied, would be outside the scope of the Rules Enabling Act or beyond the power of Congress under the Constitution.

The reasons for the application of such a state service requirement in a diversity action in the absence of a conflicting federal rule are well explained in *Erie* and *Ragan*, and need not be repeated here. It is sufficient to note that although in this case failure to apply the state service law might not create any problem of forum shopping, the result would be an "inequitable administration" of the law. There is simply no reason why, in the absence of a controlling federal rule, an action based on state law which concededly would be barred in the state courts by the state statute of limitations should proceed through litigation to judgment in federal court solely because of the fortuity that there is diversity of citizenship between the litigants. The policies underlying diversity jurisdiction do not support such a distinction between state and federal plaintiffs, and *Erie* and its progeny do not permit it.

The judgment of the Court of Appeals is

Affirmed.

Note: Walker *and* West

1. Recall Justice Harlan's summary of the Enabling Act holding in *Hanna*: "So long as a reasonable man could characterize any duly adopted federal rule as 'procedural,' the Court [would] would have it apply no matter how seriously it frustrated a State's substantive regulation of the primary conduct and affairs of its citizens." Many others read *Hanna* similarly. After all, the Court itself said:

> When a situation is covered by one of the Federal Rules, [the court can refuse to apply the Rule] only if the Advisory Committee, this Court, and Congress erred in their prima facie judgment that the Rule in question transgresses neither the terms of the Enabling Act nor constitutional restrictions.

It would have been difficult to argue that Rule 3 transgressed the terms of the Enabling Act or constitutional restrictions. Why then didn't it apply in *Walker*?

2. Two footnotes in *Walker* raised questions about the scope of the holding. In footnote 9, the Court insisted that it was not construing Rule 3 narrowly "to avoid a 'direct collision' with state law"; on the contrary, the Court said, the Federal Rules "should be given their plain meaning." However, in footnote 11, the Court said that it was leaving open "the role of Rule 3 as a tolling provision for a statute of limitations [if] the cause of action is based on federal law." If the "plain meaning" of Rule 3 did not encompass the tolling of the statute of limitations in a diversity case, how could the Rule have a different meaning in a suit based on federal law?

3. The Court gave its answer to that question a few years later in *West v. Conrail*, 481 U.S. 35 (1987). West was an employee of Conrail. Conrail had signed a collective bargaining agreement with a union under the Railway Labor Act. West brought a "hybrid" suit against Conrail, the union, and his union representative alleging that Conrail had breached the collective-bargaining agreement and that the union and its representative had breached their duty of fair representation.

Congress had not enacted a federal statute of limitations for claims like West's, but in *DelCostello v. Teamsters*, 462 U.S. 151 (1983), the Supreme Court held that the six-month period prescribed in § 10(b) of the Labor Management Relations Act should be applied to hybrid claims invoking § 301 of the LMRA. The parties in West's case agreed that the *DelCostello* holding applied as well to hybrid claims under the Railway Labor Act.

West filed his complaint within the six-month period, but the summonses and complaints were not mailed to the defendants until more than six months after the statute began to run. The Supreme Court held that the suit was timely. The Court said:

> Rule 3 of the Federal Rules of Civil Procedure provides that a civil action is commenced by filing a complaint with the court, and Rule 4 governs the procedure for effecting service and the period within which service must be made. . . . Service must normally be made within 120 days. See Rule 4(j). Although we have not expressly so held before, we now hold that when the underlying cause of action is based on federal law and the absence of an express federal statute of limitations makes it necessary to borrow a limitations period from another statute, the action is not barred if it has been "commenced" in compliance with Rule 3 within the borrowed period.

This certainly seems at odds with the interpretation of Rule 3 in *Walker*. The Court responded in a footnote (footnote 4):

> When the underlying cause of action is based on state law, and federal jurisdiction is based on diversity of citizenship, state law not only provides the appropriate period of limitations but also determines whether service must be effected within that period. *Walker.* Respect for the State's substantive decision that actual service is a component of the policies underlying the statute of limitations requires that the service rule in a diversity suit "be considered part and parcel of the statute of limitations." This requirement, naturally, does not apply to federal-question cases.

4. *West* explains the result in *Walker* by saying that "[r]espect for the State's substantive decision that actual service is a component of the policies underlying the statute of limitations requires that the service rule in a diversity suit 'be considered part and parcel of the statute of limitations.'" What about the "service rule" in *Hanna*? Under the *Walker/West* rationale, was *Hanna* wrongly decided?

5. The *West* footnote suggested that, notwithstanding the disclaimer in footnote 9, the Court in *Walker* did construe Rule 3 narrowly to avoid a collision with state law. In other contexts, the Court has emphasized that "Congress should make its intention 'clear and manifest' if it intends to pre-empt the historic powers of the States." *Gregory v. Ashcroft*, 501 U.S. 452, 461 (1991). Is the Court's apparent decision in *Walker* to construe Rule 3 narrowly simply an application of this principle?

6. In *Hanna* and *Walker*, the federal law that arguably "covered the situation" was found in an Enabling Act Rule. The Court has applied a similar approach in considering the application of federal procedural *statutes*. For example, in *Stewart Organization, Inc. v. Ricoh Corp.*, 487 U.S. 22 (1988), a suit was brought in federal court involving a contract containing a forum-selection clause. The Court concluded that

the federal statute on transfer of venue, 28 U.S.C. § 1404(a), required a federal district court to give effect to a forum-selection clause even though state law would not have enforced the clause.

Note: Rulemaking Under the Enabling Act

1. The Rules Enabling Act was substantially amended in 1988 and 1990. Section 2072 of Title 28 now provides:

> (a) The Supreme Court shall have the power to prescribe general rules of practice and procedure and rules of evidence for cases in the United States district courts (including proceedings before magistrate judges thereof) and courts of appeals.

> (b) Such rules shall not abridge, enlarge or modify any substantive right. All laws in conflict with such rules shall be of no further force or effect after such rules have taken effect.

> (c) Such rules may define when a ruling of a district court is final for the purposes of appeal under section 1291 of this title.

(Subsection (c) was added in 1990.) In addition, the statute (in 28 U.S.C. § 2073) now requires an extensive process for drafting and circulation of proposed rules. The Judicial Conference of the United States has provided the following description:

> The pervasive and substantial impact of the rules on the practice of law in the federal courts demands exacting and meticulous care in drafting rule changes. The rulemaking process is time-consuming and involves a minimum of seven stages of formal comment and review. From beginning to end, it usually takes two to three years for a suggestion to be enacted as a rule. . . .

> All interested individuals and organizations are provided an opportunity to comment on proposed rules amendments and to recommend alternative proposals. The comments received from this extensive and thorough public examination are studied very carefully by the committees and generally improve the amendments. The committees actively encourage the submission of comments, both positive and negative, to ensure that proposed amendments have been considered by a broad segment of the bench and bar.

A detailed description of the various stages of the process can be found at http://www.uscourts.gov/rules/proceduresum.htm, from which the preceding extract is taken.

Should the current process, with its numerous opportunities for comment by judges and lawyers, be taken into account when federal courts consider whether an Enabling Act Rule "occupies [a state rule's] field of occupation"?

2. In *Hanna*, the Court says that when a Rule is promulgated under the Enabling Act, this represents a prima facie judgment by "the Advisory Committee, this Court, *and Congress* [that] the Rule in question transgresses neither the terms of the Enabling Act nor constitutional restrictions." (Emphasis added.) But is it accurate to say that Congress has made a "judgment" about the Rule? Under the Enabling Act, the Chief

Justice transmits proposed rules to Congress by May 1. The rules take effect "no earlier than December 1 of [that year] *unless otherwise provided by law.*" *See* 28 U.S.C. § 2074 (emphasis added).

What this means is that if Congress does not pass countermanding legislation within seven months of receiving the Chief Justice's letter, the rules will become law in the form proposed by the Supreme Court. But the realities of the legislative process today make it a virtual impossibility that Congress could act that quickly, especially if the subject is at all controversial. As a lawyer active in tort reform commented in testimony some years ago, "Apart from matters of urgent national concern, it is rare in 2004 that a bill can be passed by the Congress within seven months. Often, significant legislation that impacts the courts requires debate that can span one or more Congresses in order to reach consensus."[1]

In this light, it would be quite unrealistic to attribute to Congress any sort of judgment about the validity (or soundness) of an Enabling Act Rule. Should that fact be taken into account in considering whether a Rule should be interpreted as overriding a contrary directive in state law?

Note: *Enabling Act Rules and Federalism Concerns*

1. In *Hanna*, the Supreme Court rejected the application of state law on the ground that a provision of federal law controlled the issue before the court. The decision did not mention the idea that (as summarized in *West*) "[r]espect for [a] State's substantive decision" embodied in state law might influence the choice-of-law determination. However, two subsequent decisions invoked federalism concerns as relevant to the interpretation of an Enabling Act Rule.

2. The first of the decisions was *Gasperini v. Center for Humanities, Inc.*, 518 U.S. 415 (1996). *Gasperini* was a diversity case litigated in federal court in New York. The New York legislature, as part of a series of tort reform measures, had enacted a law that authorized appellate courts to review the size of jury verdicts and to order a new trial when the jury's award "deviates materially from what would be reasonable compensation." The question was whether this law applied in federal court and, if so, how.

Justice Ginsburg, writing for the Court, acknowledged that classification of a law as "substantive" or "procedural" for *Erie* purposes "is sometimes a challenging endeavor." But in the Enabling Act context, the challenge generally disappears, as Justice Ginsburg explained in footnote 7 of her opinion:

> Concerning matters covered by the Federal Rules of Civil Procedure, the characterization [of a law as "substantive" or "procedural"] is usually unproblematic: It is settled that if the Rule in point is consonant with the Rules Enabling Act, 28 U.S.C. § 2072, and the Constitution, the Federal Rule applies regardless of contrary state law. See *Hanna*. Federal courts have

---

1. Hearing Before the House Judiciary Committee on *Safeguarding Americans from a Legal Culture of Fear: Approaches to Limiting Lawsuit Abuse* (June 22, 2004) (Statement of Victor E. Schwartz).

interpreted the Federal Rules, however, with sensitivity to important state interests and regulatory policies. See, *e.g., Walker.*

A dissenting opinion in *Gasperini* argued that the issue was indeed controlled by a Federal Rule—Rule 59 of the Federal Rules of Civil Procedure. At that time (before the stylistic revision), Rule 59 provided that "[a] new trial may be granted . . . for any of the reasons for which new trials have heretofore been granted in actions at law *in the courts of the United States.*" (Emphasis added by the dissent.) The dissent argued that Rule 59 supplied a federal standard that left no room for the application of the New York law. The majority disagreed. Justice Ginsburg wrote for the Court (in footnote 22):

> It is indeed "Hornbook" law that a most usual ground for a Rule 59 motion is that "the damages are excessive." Whether damages are excessive for the claim-in-suit must be governed by some law. And there is no candidate for that governance other than the law that gives rise to the claim for relief—here, the law of New York.

The Court then quoted commentators who observed that the Court "has continued since [*Hanna*] to interpret the federal rules to avoid conflict with important state regulatory policies." The Court noted that the commentators cited *Walker.*

3. Five years after *Gasperini*, the Court decided *Semtek International Inc. v. Lockheed Martin Corp.*, 531 U.S. 497 (2001). In *Semtek* the Court confronted the question: whose law determines the claim-preclusive effect of a judgment by a federal court dismissing a diversity suit? The defendant argued that the issue was controlled by Rule 41(b) of the Federal Rules of Civil Procedure, which says (roughly) that unless the court's order specifies otherwise, a dismissal "operates as an adjudication on the merits."

In a unanimous opinion by Justice Scalia, the Court held that Rule 41(b) did not address the preclusion issue. After discussing the changing meaning of the term "judgment on the merits," the Court turned to more general considerations in the choice of law analysis:

> [Even] apart from the purely default character of Rule 41(b), it would be peculiar to find a rule governing the effect that must be accorded federal judgments by other courts ensconced in rules governing the internal procedures of the rendering court itself. Indeed, such a rule would arguably violate the jurisdictional limitation of the Rules Enabling Act: that the Rules "shall not abridge, enlarge or modify any substantive right." In the present case, for example, if California law left petitioner free to sue on this claim in Maryland even after the California statute of limitations had expired, the federal court's extinguishment of that right (through Rule 41(b)'s mandated claim-preclusive effect of its judgment) would seem to violate this limitation.
>
> Moreover, as so interpreted, the Rule would in many cases violate the federalism principle of *Erie R. Co. v. Tompkins*, by engendering "'substantial' variations [in outcomes] between state and federal litigation" which would

"[l]ikely . . . influence the choice of a forum," *Hanna v. Plumer*. See also *Guaranty Trust Co. v. York*. Cf. *Walker v. Armco Steel Corp*. With regard to the claim-preclusion issue involved in the present case, for example, the traditional rule is that expiration of the applicable statute of limitations merely bars the remedy and does not extinguish the substantive right, so that dismissal on that ground does not have claim-preclusive effect in other jurisdictions with longer, unexpired limitations periods. Out-of-state defendants sued on stale claims in California and in other States adhering to this traditional rule would systematically remove state-law suits brought against them to federal court—where, unless otherwise specified, a statute-of-limitations dismissal would bar suit everywhere.

4. As the extract above indicates, the *Semtek* Court said that if Rule 41(b) were interpreted to govern the preclusive effects of federal-court judgments in diversity suits, "the Rule would in many cases violate the federalism principle of *Erie*" because the resulting variations in outcomes "would likely influence the choice of forum." But in *Hanna* the Court emphatically rejected "the incorrect assumption that the rule of *Erie R. Co. v. Tompkins* constitutes the appropriate test of the validity and therefore the applicability of a Federal Rule of Civil Procedure." Was the Court now saying that the applicability of Enabling Act Rules must, after all, be tested under *Erie* as well as the Enabling Act itself? What light does *Shady Grove*, the next principal case, shed on this question?

5. Because the Court in both *Gasperini* and *Semtek* found that no Enabling Act Rule addressed the question in dispute, the Court was faced with an "unguided *Erie* choice." That aspect of the opinions is considered in subsection [4] *infra*.

Problem: Evidence Rule 402 and State Law

Grafton v. Larch Aircraft Co. is a products liability action brought by the estate of a pilot killed in the crash of an airplane. The defendant is the manufacturer of the airplane. The suit has been brought in federal district court in the state of Upland on the basis of diversity of citizenship. The gist of the claim is that the aircraft was designed negligently and that this negligence was a proximate cause of the decedent's death, giving rise to a wrongful death cause of action under Upland law.

Defendant has moved to exclude evidence that the plaintiff would like to present at trial. The evidence consists of extracts from the Larch Aircraft Co. Engineering Manual, which plaintiff would like to offer on the issues of industry standard for safe flight control design, alternative design feasibility, and Larch's knowledge of industry standards. Plaintiff has invoked Rule 402 of the Federal Rules of Evidence, which provides:

> All relevant evidence is admissible, except as otherwise provided by the Constitution of the United States, by Act of Congress, by these rules, or by other rules prescribed by the Supreme Court pursuant to statutory authority. Evidence which is not relevant is not admissible.

The Federal Rules of Evidence were enacted by Congress. The federal courts have generally interpreted Rule 402 to mean that all relevant evidence is admissible unless some specific rule of evidence excludes it. The defendant does not argue that any specific rule of exclusion in the Federal Rules of Evidence or other federal law has any bearing on this case. However, the defendant does invoke a rule found in the decisions of the Upland courts. Upland courts have held that, as a matter of public policy, the internal rules of a party "are not admissible to prove negligence or set a standard against which a party's duties are to be assessed."

The rule was first articulated in 1915 by the Supreme Court of Upland in *Halker v. Upland Railway Co.*, 254 Upl. 405 (1915). The court held that "a person cannot, by the adoption of private rules, fix the standard of his duties to others. That is fixed by law, either statutory or common. Private rules of a corporation or other enterprise may require of its employees less or more than is required by law. But whether a given course of conduct is negligent, or the exercise of reasonable care, must be determined by the standard fixed by law, without regard to any private rules of the party." In *Halker* the court held that the safety rules of a street car company were inadmissible as evidence in a personal injury action initiated against the company by a passenger.

Since 1915, a majority of the states have held, contrary to *Halker*, that such documents are admissible. However, the Upland Supreme Court has recently re-evaluated the *Halker* rule and reaffirmed its soundness.

Assume that under the *Halker* rule, the court would have to exclude the Larch Engineering Manual. Is the federal district court sitting in diversity required to follow the *Halker* rule?

[3] Renewed Controversy: *Shady Grove*

Shady Grove Orthopedic Associates v. Allstate Insurance Co.

Supreme Court of the United States, 2010.

559 U.S. 393.

JUSTICE SCALIA announced the judgment of the Court and delivered the opinion of the Court with respect to Parts I and II-A, an opinion with respect to Parts II-B and II-D, in which THE CHIEF JUSTICE, JUSTICE THOMAS, and JUSTICE SOTOMAYOR join, and an opinion with respect to Part II-C, in which THE CHIEF JUSTICE and JUSTICE THOMAS join.

New York law prohibits class actions in suits seeking penalties or statutory minimum damages. [Section 901(b) of the New York Civil Practice Law provides:]

> Unless a statute creating or imposing a penalty, or a minimum measure of recovery specifically authorizes the recovery thereof in a class action, an action to recover a penalty, or minimum measure of recovery created or imposed by statute may not be maintained as a class action.

We consider whether this precludes a federal district court sitting in diversity from entertaining a class action under Federal Rule of Civil Procedure 23.

I

The petitioner's complaint alleged the following: Shady Grove Orthopedic Associates, P.A., provided medical care to Sonia E. Galvez for injuries she suffered in an automobile accident. As partial payment for that care, Galvez assigned to Shady Grove her rights to insurance benefits under a policy issued in New York by Allstate Insurance Co. Shady Grove tendered a claim for the assigned benefits to Allstate, which under New York law had 30 days to pay the claim or deny it. Allstate apparently paid, but not on time, and it refused to pay the statutory interest that accrued on the overdue benefits (at two percent per month).

Shady Grove filed this diversity suit in the Eastern District of New York to recover the unpaid statutory interest. Alleging that Allstate routinely refuses to pay interest on overdue benefits, Shady Grove sought relief on behalf of itself and a class of all others to whom Allstate owes interest.

[The district court applied § 901(b) and dismissed the suit for lack of jurisdiction. The Second Circuit affirmed. Its reasoning is discussed below.]

II

The framework for our decision is familiar. We must first determine whether Rule 23 answers the question in dispute. *Burlington Northern R. Co. v. Woods*, 480 U.S. 1 (1987). If it does, it governs—New York's law notwithstanding—unless it exceeds statutory authorization or Congress's rulemaking power. See *Hanna v. Plumer*, 380 U.S. 460 (1965). We do not wade into *Erie*'s murky waters unless the federal rule is inapplicable or invalid.

A

The question in dispute is whether Shady Grove's suit may proceed as a class action. Rule 23 provides an answer. It states that "[a] class action may be maintained" if two conditions are met: The suit must satisfy the criteria set forth in subdivision (a) (i.e., numerosity, commonality, typicality, and adequacy of representation), and it also must fit into one of the three categories described in subdivision (b). By its terms this creates a categorical rule entitling a plaintiff whose suit meets the specified criteria to pursue his claim as a class action. (The Federal Rules regularly use "may" to confer categorical permission, as do federal statutes that establish procedural entitlements.) Thus, Rule 23 provides a one-size-fits-all formula for deciding the class-action question. Because § 901(b) attempts to answer the same question—i.e., it states that Shady Grove's suit "may *not* be maintained as a class action" (emphasis added) because of the relief it seeks—it cannot apply in diversity suits unless Rule 23 is ultra vires.

The Second Circuit believed that § 901(b) and Rule 23 do not conflict because they address different issues. Rule 23, it said, concerns only the criteria for determining whether a given class can and should be certified; section 901(b), on the other hand, addresses an antecedent question: whether the particular type of claim is eligible for class treatment in the first place—a question on which Rule 23 is silent. Allstate embraces this analysis.

We disagree. To begin with, the line between eligibility and certifiability is entirely artificial. Both are preconditions for maintaining a class action. Allstate suggests that eligibility must depend on the "particular cause of action" asserted, instead of some other attribute of the suit. But that is not so. Congress could, for example, provide that only claims involving more than a certain number of plaintiffs are "eligible" for class treatment in federal court. In other words, relabeling Rule 23(a)'s prerequisites "eligibility criteria" would obviate Allstate's objection — a sure sign that its eligibility-certifiability distinction is made-to-order.

There is no reason, in any event, to read Rule 23 as addressing only whether claims made eligible for class treatment by some *other* law should be certified as class actions. Allstate asserts that Rule 23 neither explicitly nor implicitly empowers a federal court "to certify a class in each and every case" where the Rule's criteria are met. But that is *exactly* what Rule 23 does: It says that if the prescribed preconditions are satisfied "[a] class action *may be maintained*" (emphasis added) — not "*a class action may be permitted.*" Courts do not maintain actions; litigants do. The discretion suggested by Rule 23's "may" is discretion residing in the plaintiff: He may bring his claim in a class action if he wishes. And like the rest of the Federal Rules of Civil Procedure, Rule 23 *automatically* applies "in all civil actions and proceedings in the United States district courts," Fed. Rule Civ. Proc. 1. . . .

The dissent argues that § 901(b) has nothing to do with whether Shady Grove may maintain its suit as a class action, but affects only the *remedy* it may obtain if it wins. Whereas "Rule 23 governs procedural aspects of class litigation" by "prescrib[ing] the considerations relevant to class certification and postcertification proceedings," § 901(b) addresses only "the size of a monetary award a class plaintiff may pursue." Accordingly, the dissent says, Rule 23 and New York's law may coexist in peace.

We need not decide whether a state law that limits the remedies available in an existing class action would conflict with Rule 23; that is not what § 901(b) does. By its terms, the provision precludes a plaintiff from "maintain[ing]" a class action seeking statutory penalties. Unlike a law that sets a ceiling on damages (or puts other remedies out of reach) in properly filed class actions, § 901(b) says nothing about what remedies a court may award; it prevents the class actions it covers from coming into existence at all.[4] Consequently, a court bound by § 901(b) could not certify a class action seeking both statutory penalties and other remedies even if it announces in advance that it will refuse to award the penalties in the event the plaintiffs prevail; to do so would violate the statute's clear prohibition on "maintain[ing]" such suits as class actions. . . .

---

4. Contrary to the dissent's implication, we express no view as to whether state laws that set a ceiling on damages recoverable in a single suit are pre-empted. Whether or not those laws conflict with Rule 23, § 901(b) does conflict because it addresses not the remedy, but the procedural right to maintain a class action. As Allstate and the dissent note, several federal statutes also limit the recovery available in class actions. See, *e.g.*, 12 U.S.C. § 2605(f)(2)(B); 15 U.S.C. § 1640(a)(2)(B); 29 U.S.C. § 1854(c)(1). But Congress has plenary power to override the Federal Rules, so its enactments, unlike those of the States, prevail even in case of a conflict.

The dissent all but admits that the literal terms of § 901(b) address the same subject as Rule 23 — i.e., whether a class action may be maintained — but insists the provision's *purpose* is to restrict only remedies. Unlike Rule 23, designed to further procedural fairness and efficiency, § 901(b) (we are told) "responds to an entirely different concern": the fear that allowing statutory damages to be awarded on a classwide basis would "produce overkill." . . .

This evidence of the New York Legislature's purpose is pretty sparse. But even accepting the dissent's account of the Legislature's objective at face value, it cannot override the statute's clear text. Even if its aim is to restrict the remedy a plaintiff can obtain, § 901(b) achieves that end by limiting a plaintiff's power to maintain a class action. The manner in which the law "could have been written" has no bearing; what matters is the law the Legislature *did* enact. We cannot rewrite that to reflect our perception of legislative purpose. The dissent's concern for state prerogatives is frustrated rather than furthered by revising state laws when a potential conflict with a Federal Rule arises; the state-friendly approach would be to accept the law as written and test the validity of the Federal Rule.

The dissent's approach of determining whether state and federal rules conflict based on the subjective intentions of the state legislature is an enterprise destined to produce "confusion worse confounded," *Sibbach v. Wilson & Co.*, 312 U.S. 1, 14 (1941). It would mean, to begin with, that one State's statute could survive pre-emption (and accordingly affect the procedures in federal court) while another State's identical law would not, merely because its authors had different aspirations. It would also mean that district courts would have to discern, in every diversity case, the purpose behind any putatively pre-empted state procedural rule, even if its text squarely conflicts with federal law. That task will often prove arduous. Many laws further more than one aim, and the aim of others may be impossible to discern.

Moreover, to the extent the dissent's purpose-driven approach depends on its characterization of § 901(b)'s aims as substantive, it would apply to many state rules ostensibly addressed to procedure. Pleading standards, for example, often embody policy preferences about the types of claims that should succeed — as do rules governing summary judgment, pretrial discovery, and the admissibility of certain evidence. Hard cases will abound. It is not even clear that a state supreme court's pronouncement of the law's purpose would settle the issue, since existence of the factual predicate for avoiding federal pre-emption is ultimately a federal question. Predictably, federal judges would be condemned to poring through state legislative history — which may be less easily obtained, less thorough, and less familiar than its federal counterpart.

But while the dissent does indeed artificially narrow the scope of § 901(b) by finding that it pursues only substantive policies, that is not the central difficulty of the dissent's position. The central difficulty is that even artificial narrowing cannot render § 901(b) compatible with Rule 23. *Whatever* the policies they pursue, they flatly contradict each other. Allstate asserts (and the dissent implies) that we can (and must) *interpret* Rule 23 in a manner that avoids overstepping its authorizing statute. If the

Rule were susceptible of two meanings—one that would violate §2072(b) and another that would not—we would agree. But it is not. Rule 23 unambiguously authorizes *any* plaintiff, in *any* federal civil proceeding, to maintain a class action if the Rule's prerequisites are met. We cannot contort its text, even to avert a collision with state law that might render it invalid. See *Walker v. Armco Steel Corp.*, n.9.[8] What the dissent's approach achieves is not the avoiding of a "conflict between Rule 23 and §901(b)," but rather the invalidation of Rule 23 (pursuant to §2072(b) of the Rules Enabling Act) to the extent that it conflicts with the substantive policies of §901. There is no other way to reach the dissent's destination. We must therefore confront head-on whether Rule 23 falls within the statutory authorization.

B

Erie involved the constitutional power of federal courts to supplant state law with judge-made rules. In that context, it made no difference whether the rule was technically one of substance or procedure; the touchstone was whether it "significantly affect[s] the result of a litigation." *Guaranty Trust Co.* That is not the test for either the constitutionality or the statutory validity of a Federal Rule of Procedure. Congress has undoubted power to supplant state law, and undoubted power to prescribe rules for the courts it has created, so long as those rules regulate matters "rationally capable of classification" as procedure. *Hanna.* In the Rules Enabling Act, Congress authorized this Court to promulgate rules of procedure subject to its review, 28 U.S.C. §2072(a), but with the limitation that those rules "shall not abridge, enlarge or modify any substantive right," §2072(b).

We have long held that this limitation means that the Rule must "really regulat[e] procedure,—the judicial process for enforcing rights and duties recognized by substantive law and for justly administering remedy and redress for disregard or infraction of them," *Sibbach*; *Hanna*; *Burlington.* The test is not whether the rule affects a litigant's substantive rights; most procedural rules do. *Mississippi Publishing Corp. v. Murphree*, 326 U.S. 438 (1946). What matters is what the rule itself regulates: If it governs only "the manner and the means" by which the litigants' rights are "enforced," it is valid; if it alters "the rules of decision by which [the] court will adjudicate [those] rights," it is not. *Id.*

Applying that test, we have rejected every statutory challenge to a Federal Rule that has come before us. We have found to be in compliance with §2072(b) rules prescribing methods for serving process, see *id.* (Fed. Rule Civ. Proc. 4(f)); *Hanna* (Fed. Rule Civ. Proc. 4(d)(1)), and requiring litigants whose mental or physical condition is in dispute to submit to examinations, see *Sibbach* (Fed. Rule Civ. Proc. 35). Likewise, we have upheld rules authorizing imposition of sanctions upon those who file frivolous appeals, see *Burlington* (Fed. Rule App. Proc. 38), or who sign court papers without a reasonable inquiry into the facts asserted, see *Business Guides, Inc. v. Chromatic*

---

8. The cases chronicled by the dissent each involved a Federal Rule that we concluded could fairly be read not to "control the issue" addressed by the pertinent state law, thus avoiding a "direct collision" between federal and state law. *Walker.* But here, as in *Hanna*, a collision is "unavoidable."

Communications Enterprises, Inc., 498 U.S. 533 (1991) (Fed. Rule Civ. Proc. 11). Each of these rules had some practical effect on the parties' rights, but each undeniably regulated only the process for enforcing those rights; none altered the rights themselves, the available remedies, or the rules of decision by which the court adjudicated either.

Applying that criterion, we think it obvious that rules allowing multiple claims (and claims by or against multiple parties) to be litigated together are also valid. See, *e.g.*, Fed. Rules Civ. Proc. 18 (joinder of claims), 20 (joinder of parties), 42(a) (consolidation of actions). Such rules neither change plaintiffs' separate entitlements to relief nor abridge defendants' rights; they alter only how the claims are processed. For the same reason, Rule 23 — at least insofar as it allows willing plaintiffs to join their separate claims against the same defendants in a class action — falls within § 2072(b)'s authorization. A class action, no less than traditional joinder (of which it is a species), merely enables a federal court to adjudicate claims of multiple parties at once, instead of in separate suits. And like traditional joinder, it leaves the parties' legal rights and duties intact and the rules of decision unchanged.

Allstate contends that the authorization of class actions is not substantively neutral: Allowing Shady Grove to sue on behalf of a class "transform[s] [the] dispute over a five *hundred* dollar penalty into a dispute over a five *million* dollar penalty." Allstate's aggregate liability, however, does not depend on whether the suit proceeds as a class action. Each of the 1,000-plus members of the putative class could (as Allstate acknowledges) bring a freestanding suit asserting his individual claim. It is undoubtedly true that some plaintiffs who would not bring individual suits for the relatively small sums involved will choose to join a class action. That has no bearing, however, on Allstate's or the plaintiffs' legal rights. The likelihood that some (even many) plaintiffs will be induced to sue by the availability of a class action is just the sort of "incidental effec[t]" we have long held does not violate § 2072(b). *Mississippi Publishing.*

Allstate argues that Rule 23 violates § 2072(b) because the state law it displaces, § 901(b), creates a right that the Federal Rule abridges — namely, a "substantive right . . . not to be subjected to aggregated class-action liability" in a single suit. To begin with, we doubt that that is so. Nothing in the text of § 901(b) (which is to be found in New York's procedural code) confines it to claims under New York law; and of course New York has no power to alter substantive rights and duties created by other sovereigns. As we have said, the *consequence* of excluding certain class actions may be to cap the damages a defendant can face in a single suit, but the law itself alters only procedure. In that respect, § 901(b) is no different from a state law forbidding simple joinder. As a fallback argument, Allstate argues that even if § 901(b) is a procedural provision, it was enacted "for *substantive reasons*" (emphasis added). Its end was not to improve "the conduct of the litigation process itself" but to alter "the outcome of that process."

The fundamental difficulty with both these arguments is that the substantive nature of New York's law, or its substantive purpose, *makes no difference.* A Federal Rule of Procedure is not valid in some jurisdictions and invalid in others — or valid in some cases and invalid in others — depending upon whether its effect is to frustrate a state substantive law (or a state procedural law enacted for substantive purposes). . . . *Hanna* unmistakably expressed the same understanding that compliance of a Federal Rule with the Enabling Act is to be assessed by consulting the Rule itself, and not its effects in individual applications. . . .

In sum, it is not the substantive or procedural nature or purpose of the affected state law that matters, but the substantive or procedural nature of the Federal Rule. We have held since *Sibbach*, and reaffirmed repeatedly, that the validity of a Federal Rule depends entirely upon whether it regulates procedure. See *Sibbach*; *Hanna*; *Burlington*. If it does, it is authorized by § 2072 and is valid in all jurisdictions, with respect to all claims, regardless of its incidental effect upon state-created rights.

C

A few words in response to the concurrence. We understand it to accept the framework we apply—which requires first, determining whether the federal and state rules can be reconciled (because they answer different questions), and second, if they cannot, determining whether the Federal Rule runs afoul of § 2072(b). The concurrence agrees with us that Rule 23 and § 901(b) conflict and departs from us only with respect to the second part of the test, i.e., whether application of the Federal Rule violates § 2072(b). Like us, it answers no, but for a reason different from ours.

The concurrence would decide this case on the basis, not that Rule 23 is procedural, but that the state law it displaces is procedural, in the sense that it does not "function as a part of the State's definition of substantive rights and remedies." A state procedural rule is not preempted, according to the concurrence, so long as it is "so bound up with," or "sufficiently intertwined with," a substantive state-law right or remedy "that it defines the scope of that substantive right or remedy."

This analysis squarely conflicts with *Sibbach*, which established the rule we apply. . . . Recognizing the impracticability of a test that turns on the idiosyncrasies of state law, *Sibbach* adopted and applied a rule with a single criterion: whether the Federal Rule "really regulates procedure. . . ."

In reality, the concurrence seeks not to apply *Sibbach*, but to overrule it (or, what is the same, to rewrite it). Its approach, the concurrence insists, gives short shrift to the statutory text forbidding the Federal Rules from "abridg[ing], enlarg[ing], or modify[ing] any substantive right," § 2072(b). There is something to that. It is possible to understand how it can be determined whether a Federal Rule "enlarges" substantive rights without consulting State law: If the Rule creates a substantive right, even one that duplicates some state-created rights, it establishes a new *federal* right. But it is hard to understand how it can be determined whether a Federal Rule "abridges" or "modifies" substantive rights without knowing what state-created rights would obtain if the Federal Rule did not exist. *Sibbach*'s exclusive focus on the challenged Federal Rule—driven by the very real concern that Federal Rules which vary from State to State would be chaos—is hard to square with § 2072(b)'s terms.[11]

---

11. The concurrence's approach, however, is itself unfaithful to the statute's terms. Section 2072(b) bans abridgement or modification only of "substantive rights," but the concurrence would prohibit

Sibbach has been settled law, however, for nearly seven decades. Setting aside any precedent requires a "special justification" beyond a bare belief that it was wrong. And a party seeking to overturn a *statutory* precedent bears an even greater burden, since Congress remains free to correct us, and adhering to our precedent enables it do so. We do Congress no service by presenting it a moving target. In all events, Allstate has not even asked us to overrule *Sibbach*, let alone carried its burden of persuading us to do so. Why we should cast aside our decades-old decision escapes us, especially since (as the concurrence explains) that would not affect the result.

The concurrence also contends that applying *Sibbach* and assessing whether a Federal Rule regulates substance or procedure is not always easy. Undoubtedly some hard cases will arise (though we have managed to muddle through well enough in the 69 years since *Sibbach* was decided). But as the concurrence acknowledges, the basic difficulty is unavoidable: The statute itself refers to "substantive right[s]," so there is no escaping the substance-procedure distinction. What is more, the concurrence's approach does nothing to diminish the difficulty, but rather magnifies it many times over. Instead of a single hard question of whether a Federal Rule regulates substance or procedure, that approach will present hundreds of hard questions, forcing federal courts to assess the substantive or procedural character of countless state rules that may conflict with a single Federal Rule. And it still does not sidestep the problem it seeks to avoid. At the end of the day, one must come face to face with the decision whether or not the state policy (with which a putatively procedural state rule may be "bound up") pertains to a "substantive right or remedy"—that is, whether it is substance or procedure. The more one explores the alternatives to *Sibbach*'s rule, the more its wisdom becomes apparent.

D

We must acknowledge the reality that keeping the federal-court door open to class actions that cannot proceed in state court will produce forum shopping. That is unacceptable when it comes as the consequence of judge-made rules created to fill supposed "gaps" in positive federal law. See *Hanna*. For where neither the Constitution, a treaty, nor a statute provides the rule of decision or authorizes a federal court to supply one, "state law must govern because there can be no other law." *Ibid.* But divergence from state law, with the attendant consequence of forum shopping, is the inevitable (indeed, one might say the intended) result of a uniform system of federal procedure. Congress itself has created the possibility that the same case may follow a different course if filed in federal instead of state court. The short of the matter is that a Federal Rule governing procedure is valid whether or not it alters the outcome of the case in a way that induces forum shopping. To hold otherwise would be to "disembowel either the Constitution's grant of power over federal procedure" or Congress's exercise of it.

*   *   *

---

pre-emption of "procedural rules that are intimately bound up in the scope of a substantive right or remedy." This would allow States to force a wide array of parochial procedures on federal courts so long as they are "sufficiently intertwined with a state right or remedy."

The judgment of the Court of Appeals is reversed, and the case is remanded for further proceedings.

It is so ordered.

Justice Stevens, concurring in part and concurring in the judgment.

The New York law at issue . . . is a procedural rule that is not part of New York's substantive law. Accordingly, I agree with Justice Scalia that Federal Rule of Civil Procedure 23 must apply in this case and join Parts I and II-A of the Court's opinion. But I also agree with Justice Ginsburg that there are some state procedural rules that federal courts must apply in diversity cases because they function as a part of the State's definition of substantive rights and remedies.

I

. . . The Enabling Act . . . instructs only that federal rules cannot "abridge, enlarge or modify any substantive right." The Enabling Act's limitation does not mean that federal rules cannot displace state policy judgments; it means only that federal rules cannot displace a State's definition of its own rights or remedies.

Congress has thus struck a balance: "[H]ousekeeping rules for federal courts" will generally apply in diversity cases, notwithstanding that some federal rules "will inevitably differ" from state rules. *Hanna*. But not every federal "rul[e] of practice or procedure," § 2072(a), will displace state law. To the contrary, federal rules must be interpreted with some degree of "sensitivity to important state interests and regulatory policies," *Gasperini*, and applied to diversity cases against the background of Congress' command that such rules not alter substantive rights and with consideration of "the degree to which the Rule makes the character and result of the federal litigation stray from the course it would follow in state courts," *Hanna*. This can be a tricky balance to implement.

It is important to observe that the balance Congress has struck turns, in part, on the nature of the state law that is being displaced by a federal rule. And in my view, the application of that balance does not necessarily turn on whether the state law at issue takes the *form* of what is traditionally described as substantive or procedural. Rather, it turns on whether the state law actually is part of a State's framework of substantive rights or remedies.

Applying this balance, therefore, requires careful interpretation of the state and federal provisions at issue. . . . A "state procedural rule, though undeniably 'procedural' in the ordinary sense of the term," may exist "to influence substantive outcomes," and may in some instances become so bound up with the state-created right or remedy that it defines the scope of that substantive right or remedy. Such laws, for example, may be seemingly procedural rules that make it significantly more difficult to bring or to prove a claim, thus serving to limit the scope of that claim. See, *e.g.*, *Cohen*; *Guaranty Trust Co.* Such "procedural rules" may also define the amount of recovery.

In our federalist system, Congress has not mandated that federal courts dictate to state legislatures the form that their substantive law must take. And were federal courts to ignore those portions of substantive state law that operate as procedural devices, it could in many instances limit the ways that sovereign States may define their rights and remedies. When a State chooses to use a traditionally procedural vehicle as a means of defining the scope of substantive rights or remedies, federal courts must recognize and respect that choice.

II

When both a federal rule and a state law appear to govern a question before a federal court sitting in diversity, our precedents have set out a two-step framework for federal courts to negotiate this thorny area. At both steps of the inquiry, there is a critical question about what the state law and the federal rule mean.

The court must first determine whether the scope of the federal rule is "'sufficiently broad'" to "'control the issue'" before the court, "thereby leaving no room for the operation" of seemingly conflicting state law. See *Burlington Northern*; *Walker*. If the federal rule does not apply or can operate alongside the state rule, then there is no "Ac[t] of Congress" governing that particular question, 28 U.S.C. § 1652, and the court must engage in the traditional Rules of Decision Act inquiry under *Erie* and its progeny. . . .

If, on the other hand, the federal rule is "sufficiently broad to control the issue before the Court," such that there is a "direct collision," *Walker*, the court must decide whether application of the federal rule "represents a valid exercise" of the "rulemaking authority . . . bestowed on this Court by the Rules Enabling Act." *Burlington Northern*. That Act requires, *inter alia*, that federal rules "not abridge, enlarge or modify *any* substantive right." 28 U.S.C. § 2072(b) (emphasis added). Unlike Justice Scalia, I believe that an application of a federal rule that effectively abridges, enlarges, or modifies a state-created right or remedy violates this command. Congress may have the constitutional power "to supplant state law" with rules that are "rationally capable of classification as procedure," but we should generally presume that it has not done so. . . .

Thus, the second step of the inquiry may well bleed back into the first. When a federal rule appears to abridge, enlarge, or modify a substantive right, federal courts must consider whether the rule can reasonably be interpreted to avoid that impermissible result. See, *e.g.*, *Semtek* (avoiding an interpretation of Federal Rule of Civil Procedure 41(b) that "would arguably violate the jurisdictional limitation of the Rules Enabling Act" contained in § 2072(b)). And when such a "saving" construction is not possible and the rule would violate the Enabling Act, federal courts cannot apply the rule. A federal rule, therefore, cannot govern a particular case in which the rule would displace a state law that is procedural in the ordinary use of the term but is so intertwined with a state right or remedy that it functions to define the scope of the state-created right. And absent a governing federal rule, a federal court must engage in the traditional Rules of Decision Act inquiry, under the *Erie* line of cases. . . .

Justice Scalia believes that the sole Enabling Act question is whether the federal rule "really regulates procedure," which means, apparently, whether it regulates "the manner and the means by which the litigants' rights are enforced." I respectfully disagree.

This interpretation of the Enabling Act is consonant with the Act's first limitation to "general rules of practice and procedure," § 2072(a). But it ignores the second limitation that such rules also "not abridge, enlarge or modify *any* substantive right," § 2072(b) (emphasis added), and in so doing ignores the balance that Congress struck between uniform rules of federal procedure and respect for a State's construction of its own rights and remedies. It also ignores the separation-of-powers presumption and federalism presumption that counsel against judicially created rules displacing state substantive law.

Although the plurality appears to agree with much of my interpretation of § 2072, it nonetheless rejects that approach for two reasons, both of which are mistaken. First, Justice Scalia worries that if federal courts inquire into the effect of federal rules on state law, it will enmesh federal courts in difficult determinations about whether application of a given rule would displace a state determination about substantive rights. I do not see why an Enabling Act inquiry that looks to state law necessarily is more taxing than Justice Scalia's. But in any event, that inquiry is what the Enabling Act requires. . . .

Second, the plurality argues that its interpretation of the Enabling Act is dictated by this Court's decision in *Sibbach*, which applied a Federal Rule about when parties must submit to medical examinations. But the plurality misreads that opinion. . . .

[The matter at issue in *Sibbach*], requiring medical exams for litigants, did not pertain to "substantive rights" under the Enabling Act. Although most state rules bearing on the litigation process are adopted for some policy reason, few seemingly "procedural" rules define the scope of a substantive right or remedy. The matter at issue in *Sibbach* reflected competing federal and state judgments about privacy interests. Those privacy concerns may have been weighty and in some sense substantive; but they did not pertain to the scope of any state right or remedy at issue in the litigation. . . .

III

Justice Ginsburg views the basic issue in this case as whether and how to apply a federal rule that dictates an answer to a traditionally procedural question (whether to join plaintiffs together as a class), when a state law that "defines the dimensions" of a state-created claim dictates the opposite answer. As explained above, I readily acknowledge that if a federal rule displaces a state rule that is "'procedural' in the ordinary sense of the term," but sufficiently interwoven with the scope of a substantive right or remedy, there would be an Enabling Act problem, and the federal rule would have to give way. In my view, however, this is not such a case.

Rule 23 Controls Class Certification

When the District Court in the case before us was asked to certify a class action, Federal Rule of Civil Procedure 23 squarely governed the determination whether the court should do so. That is the explicit function of Rule 23. Rule 23, therefore, must apply unless its application would abridge, enlarge, or modify New York rights or remedies. . . .

At bottom, the dissent's interpretation of Rule 23 seems to be that Rule 23 covers only those cases in which its application would create no *Erie* problem. . . . Although it reflects a laudable concern to protect "state regulatory policies," Justice Ginsburg's approach would, in my view, work an end run around Congress' system of uniform federal rules and our decision in *Hanna*. Federal courts can and should interpret federal rules with sensitivity to "state prerogatives"; but even when "state interests . . . warrant our respectful consideration," federal courts cannot rewrite the rules. If my dissenting colleagues feel strongly that § 901(b) is substantive and that class certification should be denied, then they should argue within the Enabling Act's framework. Otherwise, "the Federal Rule applies regardless of contrary state law." *Gasperini*; *accord Hanna*.

Applying Rule 23 Does Not Violate the Enabling Act

As I have explained, in considering whether to certify a class action such as this one, a federal court must inquire whether doing so would abridge, enlarge, or modify New York's rights or remedies, and thereby violate the Enabling Act. This inquiry is not always a simple one because "[i]t is difficult to conceive of any rule of procedure that cannot have a significant effect on the outcome of a case." WRIGHT ET AL., FEDERAL PRACTICE AND PROCEDURE. . . . Faced with a federal rule that dictates an answer to a traditionally procedural question and that displaces a state rule, one can often argue that the state rule was *really* some part of the State's definition of its rights or remedies.

In my view, however, the bar for finding an Enabling Act problem is a high one. The mere fact that a state law is designed as a procedural rule suggests it reflects a judgment about how state courts ought to operate and not a judgment about the scope of state-created rights and remedies. And for the purposes of operating a federal court system, there are costs involved in attempting to discover the true nature of a state procedural rule and allowing such a rule to operate alongside a federal rule that appears to govern the same question. The mere possibility that a federal rule would alter a state-created right is not sufficient. There must be little doubt.

The text of CPLR § 901(b) expressly and unambiguously applies not only to claims based on New York law but also to claims based on federal law or the law of any other State. And there is no interpretation from New York courts to the contrary. It is therefore hard to see how § 901(b) could be understood as a rule that, though procedural in form, serves the function of defining New York's rights or remedies. . . .

The legislative history, moreover, does not clearly describe a judgment that § 901(b) would operate as a limitation on New York's statutory damages. In evaluating that legislative history, it is necessary to distinguish between procedural rules adopted for *some* policy reason and seemingly procedural rules that are intimately bound up in the scope of a substantive right or remedy. Although almost every rule is adopted for some reason and has some effect on the outcome of litigation, not every state rule "defines the dimensions of [a] claim itself." . . .

The legislative history of § 901 . . . reveals a classically procedural calibration of making it easier to litigate claims in New York courts (under any source of law) only when it is necessary to do so, and not making it *too* easy when the class tool is not required. This is the same sort of calculation that might go into setting filing fees or deadlines for briefs. There is of course a difference of degree between those examples and class certification, but not a difference of kind; the class vehicle may have a greater practical effect on who brings lawsuits than do low filing fees, but that does not transform it into a damages "proscription," or "limitation."[18]

The difference of degree is relevant to the forum shopping considerations that are part of the Rules of Decision Act or *Erie* inquiry. If the applicable federal rule did not govern the particular question at issue (or could be fairly read not to do so), then those considerations would matter, for precisely the reasons given by the dissent. But that is not *this* case. . . .

Because Rule 23 governs class certification, the only decision is whether certifying a class in this diversity case would "abridge, enlarge or modify" New York's substantive rights or remedies. § 2072(b). Although one can argue that class certification would enlarge New York's "limited" damages remedy, such arguments rest on extensive speculation about what the New York Legislature had in mind when it created § 901(b). But given that there are two plausible competing narratives, it seems obvious to me that we should respect the plain textual reading of § 901(b), a rule in New York's procedural code about when to certify class actions brought under any source of law, and respect Congress' decision that Rule 23 governs class certification in federal courts. In order to displace a federal rule, there must be more than just a possibility that the state rule is different than it appears.

Accordingly, I concur in part and concur in the judgment.

JUSTICE GINSBURG, with whom JUSTICE KENNEDY, JUSTICE BREYER, and JUSTICE ALITO join, dissenting.

The Court today approves Shady Grove's attempt to transform a $500 case into a $5,000,000 award, although the State creating the right to recover has proscribed this alchemy. If Shady Grove had filed suit in New York state court, the 2% interest payment authorized by New York Ins. Law Ann. § 5106(a) as a penalty for overdue benefits would, by Shady Grove's own measure, amount to no more than $500. By instead filing in federal court based on the parties' diverse citizenship and requesting class certification, Shady Grove hopes to recover, for the class, statutory damages of more than $5,000,000. The New York Legislature has barred this remedy, instructing that, unless specifically permitted, "an action to recover a penalty, or minimum measure of recovery created or imposed by statute may not be maintained as a class action." N.Y. Civ. Prac. Law Ann. (CPLR) § 901(b). The Court nevertheless holds that Federal

---

18. Justice Ginsburg asserts that class certification in this matter would "transform a $500 case into a $5,000,000 award." But in fact, class certification would transform 10,000 $500 cases into one $5,000,000 case. It may be that without class certification, not all of the potential plaintiffs would bring their cases. But that is true of any procedural vehicle; without a lower filing fee, a conveniently located courthouse, easy-to-use federal procedural rules, or many other features of the federal courts, many plaintiffs would not sue.

Rule of Civil Procedure 23, which prescribes procedures for the conduct of class actions in federal courts, preempts the application of § 901(b) in diversity suits.

The Court reads Rule 23 relentlessly to override New York's restriction on the availability of statutory damages. Our decisions, however, caution us to ask, before undermining state legislation: Is this conflict really necessary? Had the Court engaged in that inquiry, it would not have read Rule 23 to collide with New York's legitimate interest in keeping certain monetary awards reasonably bounded. I would continue to interpret Federal Rules with awareness of, and sensitivity to, important state regulatory policies. Because today's judgment radically departs from that course, I dissent.

I

[Justice Ginsburg reviewed the decisions interpreting and applying the Rules of Decision Act and the Rules Enabling Act.]

In sum, both before and after *Hanna*, the above-described decisions show, federal courts have been cautioned by this Court to "interpre[t] the Federal Rules . . . with sensitivity to important state interests," *Gasperini* n.7, and a will "to avoid conflict with important state regulatory policies" *id*. The Court veers away from that approach — and conspicuously, its most recent reiteration in *Gasperini* — in favor of a mechanical reading of Federal Rules, insensitive to state interests and productive of discord.

C

Our decisions instruct over and over again that, in the adjudication of diversity cases, state interests — whether advanced in a statute, *e.g.*, *Cohen*, or a procedural rule, *e.g.*, *Gasperini* — warrant our respectful consideration. Yet today, the Court gives no quarter to New York's limitation on statutory damages and requires the lower courts to thwart the regulatory policy at stake: To prevent excessive damages, New York's law controls the penalty to which a defendant may be exposed in a single suit. The story behind § 901(b)'s enactment deserves telling.

[Justice Ginsburg recounted the history, beginning with a proposal by the Judicial Conference of the State of New York for a class-action statute that would provide "an effective, but controlled group remedy." The ultimate product was described by the state's highest court as "the result of a compromise among competing interests."]

. . . Section 901(a) allows courts leeway in deciding whether to certify a class, but § 901(b) rejects the use of the class mechanism to pursue the particular remedy of statutory damages. The limitation was not designed with the fair conduct or efficiency of litigation in mind. Indeed, suits seeking statutory damages are arguably *best* suited to the class device because individual proof of actual damages is unnecessary. New York's decision instead to block class-action proceedings for statutory damages therefore makes scant sense, except as a means to a manifestly substantive end: Limiting a defendant's liability in a single lawsuit in order to prevent the exorbitant inflation of penalties — remedies the New York Legislature created with individual suits in mind.

D

Shady Grove contends—and the Court today agrees—that Rule 23 unavoidably preempts New York's prohibition on the recovery of statutory damages in class actions....

The Court, I am convinced, finds conflict where none is necessary. Mindful of the history behind § 901(b)'s enactment, the thrust of our precedent, and the substantive-rights limitation in the Rules Enabling Act, I conclude, as did the Second Circuit and every District Court to have considered the question in any detail, that Rule 23 does not collide with § 901(b). As the Second Circuit well understood, Rule 23 prescribes the considerations relevant to class certification and postcertification proceedings—but it does not command that a particular remedy be available when a party sues in a representative capacity. Section 901(b), in contrast, trains on that latter issue. Sensibly read, Rule 23 governs procedural aspects of class litigation, but allows state law to control the size of a monetary award a class plaintiff may pursue.

In other words, Rule 23 describes a method of enforcing a claim for relief, while § 901(b) defines the dimensions of the claim itself. In this regard, it is immaterial that § 901(b) bars statutory penalties in wholesale, rather than retail, fashion. The New York Legislature could have embedded the limitation in every provision creating a cause of action for which a penalty is authorized; § 901(b) operates as shorthand to the same effect. It is as much a part of the delineation of the claim for relief as it would be were it included claim by claim in the New York Code.

The Court single-mindedly focuses on whether a suit "may" or "may not" be maintained as a class action. Putting the question that way, the Court does not home in on the reason *why*. Rule 23 authorizes class treatment for suits satisfying its prerequisites because the class mechanism generally affords a fair and efficient way to aggregate claims for adjudication. Section 901(b) responds to an entirely different concern; it does not allow class members to recover statutory damages because the New York Legislature considered the result of adjudicating such claims en masse to be exorbitant. The fair and efficient *conduct* of class litigation is the legitimate concern of Rule 23; the *remedy* for an infraction of state law, however, is the legitimate concern of the State's lawmakers and not of the federal rulemakers.

Suppose, for example, that a State, wishing to cap damages in class actions at $1,000,000, enacted a statute providing that "a suit to recover more than $1,000,000 may not be maintained as a class action." Under the Court's reasoning—which attributes dispositive significance to the words "may not be maintained"—Rule 23 would preempt this provision, nevermind that Congress, by authorizing the promulgation of rules of procedure for federal courts, surely did not intend to displace state-created ceilings on damages. The Court suggests that the analysis might differ if the statute "limit[ed] the remedies available in an existing class action," such that Rule 23 might not conflict with a state statute prescribing that "no more than $1,000,000 may be recovered in a class action." There is no real difference in the purpose and intended effect of these two hypothetical statutes. The notion that one directly impinges on

Rule 23's domain, while the other does not, fundamentally misperceives the office of Rule 23. . . .

Any doubt whether Rule 23 leaves § 901(b) in control of the remedial issue at the core of this case should be dispelled by our *Erie* jurisprudence, including *Hanna*, which counsels us to read Federal Rules moderately and cautions against stretching a rule to cover every situation it could conceivably reach. The Court states that "[t]here is no reason . . . to read Rule 23 as addressing only whether claims made eligible for class treatment by some *other* law should be certified as class actions." To the contrary, *Ragan, Cohen, Walker, Gasperini,* and *Semtek* provide good reason to look to the law that creates the right to recover. That is plainly so on a more accurate statement of what is at stake: Is there any reason to read Rule 23 as authorizing a claim for relief when the State that created the remedy disallows its pursuit on behalf of a class? None at all is the answer our federal system should give. . . .

By finding a conflict without considering whether Rule 23 rationally should be read to avoid any collision, the Court unwisely and unnecessarily retreats from the federalism principles undergirding *Erie*. Had the Court reflected on the respect for state regulatory interests endorsed in our decisions, it would have found no cause to interpret Rule 23 so woodenly — and every reason not to do so.

II

Because I perceive no unavoidable conflict between Rule 23 and § 901(b), I would decide this case by inquiring "whether application of the [state] rule would have so important an effect upon the fortunes of one or both of the litigants that failure to [apply] it would be likely to cause a plaintiff to choose the federal court." *Hanna* n.9.

Seeking to pretermit that inquiry, Shady Grove urges that the class-action bar in § 901(b) must be regarded as "procedural" because . . . "nothing in [the statute] suggests that it is limited to rights of action based on New York state law, as opposed to federal law or the law of other states"; instead it "applies to actions seeking penalties under *any* statute."

It is true that § 901(b) is not specifically *limited* to claims arising under New York law. But neither is it expressly *extended* to claims arising under foreign law. . . . Shady Grove overlooks the most likely explanation for the absence of limiting language: New York legislators make law with New York plaintiffs and defendants in mind, i.e., as if New York were the universe. . . .

In short, Shady Grove's effort to characterize § 901(b) as simply "procedural" cannot successfully elide this fundamental norm: When no federal law or rule is dispositive of an issue, and a state statute is outcome affective in the sense our cases on *Erie* (pre- and post-*Hanna*) develop, the Rules of Decision Act commands application of the State's law in diversity suits. *Gasperini; Hanna; York.* As this case starkly demonstrates, if federal courts exercising diversity jurisdiction are compelled by Rule 23 to award statutory penalties in class actions while New York courts are bound by § 901(b)'s proscription, "substantial variations between state and federal [money judgments] may be expected." *Gasperini* (quoting *Hanna*). The "variation" here is indeed "substantial."

Shady Grove seeks class relief that is *ten thousand times* greater than the individual remedy available to it in state court. As the plurality acknowledges, forum shopping will undoubtedly result if a plaintiff need only file in federal instead of state court to seek a massive monetary award explicitly barred by state law.

It is beyond debate that "a statutory cap on damages would supply substantive law for *Erie* purposes." *Gasperini*. See also *id.* (Scalia, J., dissenting) ("State substantive law controls what injuries are compensable and in what amount."). In *Gasperini*, we determined that New York's standard for measuring the alleged excessiveness of a jury verdict was designed to provide a control analogous to a damages cap. The statute was framed as "a procedural instruction," we noted, "but the State's objective [wa]s manifestly substantive."

Gasperini's observations apply with full force in this case. By barring the recovery of statutory damages in a class action, § 901(b) controls a defendant's maximum liability in a suit seeking such a remedy. The remedial provision could have been written as an explicit cap: "In any class action seeking statutory damages, relief is limited to the amount the named plaintiff would have recovered in an individual suit." That New York's Legislature used other words to express the very same meaning should be inconsequential. . . .

III

The Court's erosion of *Erie*'s federalism grounding impels me to point out the large irony in today's judgment. Shady Grove is able to pursue its claim in federal court only by virtue of the recent enactment of the Class Action Fairness Act of 2005 (CAFA), 28 U.S.C. § 1332(d). In CAFA, Congress opened federal-court doors to state-law-based class actions so long as there is minimal diversity, at least 100 class members, and at least $5,000,000 in controversy. By providing a federal forum, Congress sought to check what it considered to be the overreadiness of some state courts to certify class actions. In other words, Congress envisioned fewer — not more — class actions overall. Congress surely never anticipated that CAFA would make federal courts a mecca for suits of the kind Shady Grove has launched: class actions seeking state-created penalties for claims arising under state law-claims that would be barred from class treatment in the State's own courts.

* * *

I would continue to approach *Erie* questions in a manner mindful of the purposes underlying the Rules of Decision Act and the Rules Enabling Act, faithful to precedent, and respectful of important state interests. I would therefore hold that the New York Legislature's limitation on the recovery of statutory damages applies in this case, and would affirm the Second Circuit's judgment.

Note: The Implications of Shady Grove

1. After *Gasperini* (1996) and *Semtek* (2001), it appeared that the Court was moving toward a regime of giving priority to what *Semtek* called "the federalism principle of *Erie*," even when Enabling Act Rules were arguably controlling. *Shady Grove* is a distinct turnabout from that trend, but the Court is deeply divided, with only a plurality joining most of Justice Scalia's opinion.

2. Both Justice Scalia and Justice Stevens devote extensive attention to the venerable precedent of *Sibbach v. Wilson* (1941). Justice Scalia insists that *Sibbach* "established the rule we apply," namely that if an Enabling Act rule "really regulates procedure," it is valid "with respect to all claims, regardless of its incidental effect on state-created rights." Justice Stevens, in contrast, maintains that the *Sibbach* Court "had no occasion to consider whether the particular application of the Federal Rules in question would offend the Enabling Act."

Does Justice Stevens make the most effective argument against the majority's reliance on *Sibbach*? As noted earlier in this chapter, the dissent in *Sibbach*—by Justice Frankfurter, the author of *Guaranty Trust*—made no mention of *Erie*. Indeed, Justice Frankfurter noted that "Rule 35 applies to all civil litigation in the federal courts, and thus concerns the enforcement of federal rights and not merely of state law in the federal courts."

3. Justice Ginsburg, in dissent, relies on two footnotes in *Gasperini* for the proposition that courts should interpret the Federal Rules "with sensitivity to important state interests" and "to avoid conflict with important state regulatory policies." (Both footnotes are quoted in the Note preceding the *Shady Grove* opinion.) Justice Scalia responds (in a footnote that is part of his opinion for the Court):

> The search for state interests and policies that are "important" is just as standardless as the "important or substantial" criterion we rejected in *Sibbach*, to define the state-created rights a Federal Rule may not abridge.

> If all the dissent means is that we should read an ambiguous Federal Rule to avoid "substantial variations [in outcomes] between state and federal litigation," *Semtek*, we entirely agree. We should do so not to avoid doubt as to the Rule's validity—since a Federal Rule that fails *Erie*'s forum-shopping test is not *ipso facto* invalid, see *Hanna*—but because it is reasonable to assume that "Congress is just as concerned as we have been to avoid significant differences between state and federal courts in adjudicating claims," *Stewart Organization, Inc.* (Scalia, J., dissenting). The assumption is irrelevant here, however, because there is only one reasonable reading of Rule 23.

How much is left of *Gasperini* as a guide to interpreting Enabling Act Rules that appear to conflict with state law?

4. What happens to *Walker*? Justice Ginsburg, in dissent, relies on *Walker* as illustrating how, after *Hanna*, the Court "continued to 'interpret the federal rules to avoid conflict with state regulatory policies.'" She explains (in a footnote):

> Just as we read Federal Rule 3 in *Walker* not to govern when a suit commences for purposes of tolling a state statute of limitations (although the Rule indisputably controls when an action commences for federal procedural purposes), so too we could read Rule 23 not to direct when a class action may be maintained for purposes of recovering statutory damages prescribed

by state law. On this reading of Rule 23, no rewriting of § 901(b) is necessary to avoid a conflict.

The Court responds:

> [In *Walker* the state statute provided] that "'[a]n action shall be deemed commenced, *within the meaning of this article [the statute of limitations]*, as to each defendant, at the date of the summons which is served on him....'" Rule 3, we explained, "governs the date from which various timing requirements of the Federal Rules begin to run, but does not affect state statutes of limitations" or tolling rules, which it did not "purpor[t] to displace." The texts were therefore not in conflict. While our opinion observed that the State's actual-service rule was (in the State's judgment) an "integral part of the several policies served by the statute of limitations," nothing in our decision suggested that a federal court may resolve an obvious conflict between the texts of state and federal rules by resorting to the state law's ostensible objectives.

Reread *Walker*. Who has the better of this argument?

5. Justice Stevens — who as noted above casts the deciding vote — emphasizes that the New York law "expressly and unambiguously applies not only to claims based on New York law but also to claims based on federal law or the law of any other State." Thus the law cannot be viewed "as a rule that, though procedural in form, serves the function of defining New York's rights or remedies."

Suppose that the New York Legislature were to enact a law similar to § 901(b) applicable only to "statutes of the State of New York creating or imposing a penalty or a minimum measure of recovery." Would the Court hold that a statute of that kind must be applied in diversity cases heard in federal court?

Problem: State Antitrust Actions in Federal Court

Like many states, Hawaii has a "little Sherman Act" that provides remedies for antitrust violations. (See Chapter 6.) Hawaii's statute, HAW. REV. STAT. § 480-13(a), states: "Except as provided in subsections (b) and (c), any person who is injured in the person's business or property" due to an antitrust violation "may sue for damages sustained by the person, and, if the judgment is for the plaintiff, the plaintiff shall be awarded a sum not less than $1,000." One of the specified exceptions — contained in paragraph (c)(1) — states that "[t]he minimum $1,000 recovery provided in" subsection (a) "shall not apply in a class action or a de facto class action lawsuit."

In its brief to the Supreme Court in *Shady Grove*, Allstate contended that New York's § 901(b), like Hawaii's § 480-13(c)(1), is a state law that "caps a defendant's liability in a particular lawsuit." (Brief for Respondent at 28.) Allstate thus suggested that if the Court held that § 901(b) was preempted in federal court by Rule 23, then statutes like § 480-13 would also be preempted. Is that argument persuasive? How might you distinguish § 480-13(c)(1) from § 901(b)?

Problem: Summary Judgment and the Standard of Care

Rory Parker was badly injured during a bicycle race when several of the racers collided with a trailer driving in the opposite direction. Parker brought suit in state court against the race's organizers and the entities responsible for overseeing and promoting the race. He asserted claims of negligence and gross negligence. The case was removed to federal court on the basis of diversity of citizenship. There is no dispute that removal was proper and that, under *Klaxon*, Illiana law controls. Under Illiana law, it is part of the plaintiff's burden of proof to establish the standard of care.

After some discovery, the defendants moved for summary judgment on all of the plaintiffs' claims. Under Rule 56 of the Federal Rules of Civil Procedure, summary judgment must be granted if the moving party "is entitled to judgment as a matter of law." Decisions of the federal courts of appeals have established that when the defendant presents facts showing a lack of negligence, the burden is on the plaintiff to proffer evidence that would create an issue of material fact on the standard of care. However, Illiana law is different. Under Illiana law, as stated in the leading case of *Pierson v. Smith* (1998), "summary judgment in negligence cases, including gross negligence cases, is inappropriate unless the applicable standard of care is *fixed by law*." As the Supreme Court of Illiana has explained, "identification of the proper standard of care is a necessary precondition to assessing the degree to which conduct deviates, if at all, from the standard of care—the core test in any claim of negligence or gross negligence." The court has further explained that "the applicable standard of care in a given case may be established, as a matter of law, by legislative enactment or prior judicial decision." But if the standard has not been so established, "the determination of the appropriate standard is a factual issue to be resolved by the finder of fact."

It is undisputed that no statute or precedent provides a standard of care for bicycle races such as the one involved here. Plaintiff argues that under Illiana law, this means that the defendants' motion for summary judgment must be denied. The defendants contend that Rule 56 provides the sole standard and the Illiana rule has no application in federal court. Is this argument well taken?

[4] "Unguided *Erie*" Choices

Chambers v. NASCO, Inc.

Supreme Court of the United States, 1991.

501 U.S. 32.

JUSTICE WHITE delivered the opinion of the Court.

This case requires us to explore the scope of the inherent power of a federal court to sanction a litigant for bad-faith conduct. Specifically, we are asked to determine whether the District Court, sitting in diversity, properly invoked its inherent power in assessing as a sanction for a party's bad-faith conduct attorney's fees and related expenses paid by the party's opponent to its attorneys. We hold that the District Court acted within its discretion, and we therefore affirm the judgment of the Court of Appeals. . . .

Chambers asserts that even if federal courts can use their inherent power to assess attorney's fees as a sanction in some cases, they are not free to do so when they sit in diversity, unless the applicable state law recognizes the "bad-faith" exception to the general rule against fee shifting. He relies on footnote 31 in *Alyeska Pipeline Service Co. v. Wilderness Society*, 421 U.S. 240 (1975), in which we stated with regard to the exceptions to the American Rule that "[a] very different situation is presented when a federal court sits in a diversity case. '[I]n an ordinary diversity case where the state law does not run counter to a valid federal statute or rule of court, and usually it will not, state law denying the right to attorney's fees or giving a right thereto, which reflects a substantial policy of the state, should be followed.' 6 J. MOORE, FEDERAL PRACTICE. . . ."

We agree with NASCO that Chambers has misinterpreted footnote 31. The limitation on a court's inherent power described there applies only to fee-shifting rules that embody a substantive policy, such as a statute which permits a prevailing party in certain classes of litigation to recover fees. . . .

Only when there is a conflict between state and federal substantive law are the concerns of *Erie R. Co. v. Tompkins* at issue. As we explained in *Hanna v. Plumer*, the "outcome determinative" test of *Erie* and *Guaranty Trust Co. v. York* "cannot be read without reference to the twin aims of the *Erie* rule: discouragement of forum-shopping and avoidance of inequitable administration of the laws." Despite Chambers' protestations to the contrary, neither of these twin aims is implicated by the assessment of attorney's fees as a sanction for bad-faith conduct before the court which involved disobedience of the court's orders and the attempt to defraud the court itself. In our recent decision in *Business Guides, Inc. v. Chromatic Communications Enterprises, Inc.*, 498 U.S. 533 (1991), we stated, "Rule 11 sanctions do not constitute the kind of fee shifting at issue in Alyeska [because they] are not tied to the outcome of litigation; the relevant inquiry is whether a specific filing was, if not successful, at least well founded." Likewise, the imposition of sanctions under the bad-faith exception depends not on which party wins the lawsuit, but on how the parties conduct themselves during the litigation. Consequently, there is no risk that the exception will lead to forum-shopping. Nor is it inequitable to apply the exception to citizens and noncitizens alike, when the party, by controlling his or her conduct in litigation, has the power to determine whether sanctions will be assessed. As the Court of Appeals expressed it, "*Erie* guarantees a litigant that if he takes his state law cause of action to federal court, and abides by the rules of that court, the result in his case will be the same as if he had brought it in state court. It does not allow him to waste the court's time and resources with cantankerous conduct, even in the unlikely event a state court would allow him to do so." . . .

Here the District Court did not attempt to sanction petitioner for breach of contract,[16] but rather imposed sanctions for the fraud he perpetrated on the court and the bad faith he displayed toward both his adversary and the court throughout the course of the litigation. We agree with the Court of Appeals that "[w]e do not see how

---

16. We therefore express no opinion as to whether the District Court would have had the inherent power to sanction Chambers for conduct relating to the underlying breach of contract, or whether such sanctions might implicate the concerns of *Erie*.

the district court's inherent power to tax fees for that conduct can be made subservient to any state policy without transgressing the boundaries set out in *Erie*, *Guaranty Trust Co.*, and *Hanna*," for "[f]ee-shifting here is not a matter of substantive remedy, but of vindicating judicial authority."

JUSTICE KENNEDY, with whom THE CHIEF JUSTICE [REHNQUIST], and JUSTICE SOUTER join, dissenting.

Today's decision effects a vast expansion of the power of federal courts, unauthorized by rule or statute. I have no doubt petitioner engaged in sanctionable conduct that warrants severe corrective measures. But our outrage at his conduct should not obscure the boundaries of settled legal categories.

With all respect, I submit the Court commits two fundamental errors. First, it permits the exercise of inherent sanctioning powers without prior recourse to controlling rules and statutes, thereby abrogating to federal courts Congress' power to regulate fees and costs. Second, the Court upholds the wholesale shift of respondent's attorney's fees to petitioner, even though the District Court opinion reveals that petitioner was sanctioned at least in part for his so-called bad faith breach of contract. The extension of inherent authority to sanction a party's prelitigation conduct subverts the American Rule and turns the *Erie* doctrine upside down by punishing petitioner's primary conduct contrary to Louisiana law. Because I believe the proper exercise of inherent powers requires exhaustion of express sanctioning provisions and much greater caution in their application to redress prelitigation conduct, I dissent. . . .

The District Court's own candid and extensive opinion reveals that the bad faith for which petitioner was sanctioned extended beyond the litigation tactics and comprised as well what the District Court considered to be bad faith in refusing to perform the underlying contract three weeks before the lawsuit began. . . . The District Court makes the open and express concession that it is sanctioning petitioner for his breach of contract: "[T]he balance of . . . fees and expenses included in the sanctions, would not have been incurred by NASCO if Chambers had not defaulted and forced NASCO to bring this suit. There is absolutely no reason why Chambers should not reimburse in full all attorney's fees and expenses that NASCO, by Chambers' action, was forced to pay." The trial court also explained that "[t]he attorney's fees and expenses charged to NASCO by its attorneys . . . flowed from and were a direct result of this suit. We shall include them in the attorney's fees sanctions."

Despite the Court's equivocation on the subject, ante, at n. 16, it is impermissible to allow a District Court acting pursuant to its inherent authority to sanction such prelitigation primary conduct. A Court's inherent authority extends only to remedy abuses of the judicial process. By contrast, awarding damages for a violation of a legal norm, here the binding obligation of a legal contract, is a matter of substantive law, . . . which must be defined either by Congress (in cases involving federal law), or by the States (in diversity cases).

The American Rule recognizes these principles. It bars a federal court from shifting fees as a matter of substantive policy, but its bad faith exception permits fee shifting as a sanction to the extent necessary to protect the judicial process. . . . When a federal court, through invocation of its inherent powers, sanctions a party for bad-faith prelitigation conduct, it goes well beyond the exception to the American Rule and violates the Rule's careful balance between open access to the federal court system and penalties for the willful abuse of it.

By exercising inherent power to sanction prelitigation conduct, the District Court exercised authority where Congress gave it none. The circumstance that this exercise of power occurred in a diversity case compounds the error. . . . The inherent power exercised here violates the fundamental tenet of federalism announced in *Erie* by regulating primary behavior that the Constitution leaves to the exclusive province of States.

The full effect of the District Court's encroachment on State prerogatives can be appreciated by recalling that the rationale for the bad faith exception is punishment. To the extent that the District Court imposed sanctions by reason of the so-called bad-faith breach of contract, its decree is an award of punitive damages for the breach. Louisiana prohibits punitive damages "unless expressly authorized by statute," and no Louisiana statute authorizes attorney's fees for breach of contract as a part of damages in an ordinary case [citing cases]. . . . If respondent had brought this suit in state court he would not have recovered extra damages for breach of contract by reason of the so-called willful character of the breach. Respondent's decision to bring this suit in federal rather than state court resulted in a significant expansion of the substantive scope of his remedy. This is the result prohibited by *Erie* and the principles that flow from it.

As the Court notes, there are some passages in the District Court opinion suggesting its sanctions were confined to litigation conduct. . . . The ambiguity of the scope of the sanctionable conduct cannot be resolved against petitioner alone, who, despite the conceded bad-faith conduct of his attorneys, has been slapped with all of respondent's not inconsiderable attorney's fees. At the very least, adherence to the rule of law requires the case to be remanded to the District Court for clarification on the scope of the sanctioned conduct.

[Justice Scalia dissented separately.]

Note: Chambers *and Unguided* Erie *Choices*

1. Several federal rules and statutes deal with attorney misconduct, but none applied in *Chambers*. The Court was thus faced with an "unguided *Erie* choice."

2. There are not many Supreme Court opinions that analyze unguided *Erie* choices. One opinion that does, however, is Justice Scalia's dissent in *Stewart Org., Inc. v. Ricoh Corp.*, 487 U.S. 22 (1988). There, the plaintiff brought a breach of contract action under diversity jurisdiction in the United States District Court for the Northern District of Alabama. The contract contained a forum-selection clause providing that any dispute arising out of the contract could be brought only in a court located in Manhattan. Relying on this clause, the defendant sought to transfer the case to the Southern District of Manhattan. The district court denied the motion, concluding that Alabama

law applied and that Alabama looks unfavorably on forum-selection clauses. The Eleventh Circuit reversed, holding that the federal venue law, 28 U.S.C. § 1404, applied and that the clause was enforceable under that federal law. The Supreme Court affirmed, concluding that § 1404 "covered the situation" in the case.

Dissenting, Justice Scalia argued that § 1404 did not cover the situation. He therefore applied the twin-aims test articulated in *Hanna* to determine whether to follow state law:

> Under the twin-aims test, I believe state law controls the question of the validity of a forum-selection clause between the parties. The Eleventh Circuit's rule clearly encourages forum shopping. Venue is often a vitally important matter, as is shown by the frequency with which parties contractually provide for and litigate the issue. Suit might well not be pursued, or might not be as successful, in a significantly less convenient forum. Transfer to such a less desirable forum is, therefore, of sufficient import that plaintiffs will base their decisions on the likelihood of that eventuality when they are choosing whether to sue in state or federal court. With respect to forum-selection clauses, in a State with law unfavorable to validity, plaintiffs who seek to avoid the effect of a clause will be encouraged to sue in state court, and nonresident defendants will be encouraged to shop for more favorable law by removing to federal court. In the reverse situation—where a State has law favorable to enforcing such clauses—plaintiffs will be encouraged to sue in federal court. This significant encouragement to forum shopping is alone sufficient to warrant application of state law.

> I believe creating a judge-made rule fails the second part of the twin-aims test as well, producing inequitable administration of the laws. The best explanation of what constitutes inequitable administration of the laws is that found in *Erie* itself: allowing an unfair discrimination between noncitizens and citizens of the forum state. Whether discrimination is unfair in this context largely turns on how important is the matter in question. The decision of an important legal issue should not turn on the accident of diversity of citizenship or the presence of a federal question unrelated to that issue. It is difficult to imagine an issue of more importance, other than one that goes to the very merits of the lawsuit, than the validity of a contractual forum-selection provision. Certainly, the *Erie* doctrine has previously been held to require the application of state law on subjects of similar or obviously lesser importance. See, *e.g.*, *Walker* (whether filing of complaint or service tolls statute of limitations); *Cohen* (indemnity bond for litigation expenses). Nor can or should courts ignore that issues of contract validity are traditionally matters governed by state law.

3. Justice Kennedy, dissenting in *Chambers*, says that the exercise of inherent power in that case "violates the fundamental tenet of federalism announced in *Erie* by regulating primary behavior that the Constitution leaves to the exclusive province of States." What is the relationship between that "tenet" and the "twin aims" test of *Hanna*?

Note: Gasperini, Semtek, *and the* "*Unguided* Erie *Choice*"

1. Recall that in *Gasperini* (1996) and again in *Semtek* (2001) (both summarized in subsection [2]), the Court rejected arguments that an Enabling Act Rule "cover[ed] the point in dispute." Thus, in both cases, the Court was confronted with an "unguided *Erie* choice." But the two decisions took different approaches to making that choice.

2. *Gasperini*, as already noted, was a diversity case litigated in federal court in New York. The New York legislature, as part of a series of tort reform measures, had enacted a law that authorized appellate courts to review the size of jury verdicts and to order a new trial when the jury's award "deviates materially from what would be reasonable compensation." The primary question in *Gasperini* was whether this law could be applied in federal court without violating the Seventh Amendment right of trial by jury in civil cases. But before dealing with the Seventh Amendment, the Court addressed the *Erie* doctrine.

The opinion, by Justice Ginsburg, began by observing that the New York law, viewed from an *Erie* perspective, "is both 'substantive' and 'procedural': 'substantive' in that § 5501(c)'s 'deviates materially' standard controls how much a plaintiff can be awarded; 'procedural' in that § 5501(c) assigns decisionmaking authority to New York's Appellate Division." The opinion continued:

> Under the *Erie* doctrine, federal courts sitting in diversity apply state substantive law and federal procedural law. Classification of a law as "substantive" or "procedural" for *Erie* purposes is sometimes a challenging endeavor. [The Court summarized the treatment of the substance-procedure distinction in *Guaranty Trust*, *Ragan*, and *Hanna*.]

> Informed by these decisions, we address the question whether New York's "deviates materially" standard, codified in CPLR § 5501(c), is outcome affective in this sense: Would "application of the [standard] . . . have so important an effect upon the fortunes of one or both of the litigants that failure to [apply] it would [unfairly discriminate against citizens of the forum State, or] be likely to cause a plaintiff to choose the federal court"? *Hanna* n.9.

> We start from a point the parties do not debate. Gasperini acknowledges that a statutory cap on damages would supply substantive law for *Erie* purposes. . . . Although CPLR § 5501(c) is less readily classified, it was designed to provide an analogous control.

> New York's Legislature codified in § 5501(c) a new standard, one that requires closer court review than the common-law 'shock the conscience' test. . . . [Although] § 5501(c) contains a procedural instruction, [the] State's objective is manifestly substantive.

> It thus appears that if federal courts ignore the change in the New York standard and persist in applying the "shock the conscience" test to damage awards on claims governed by New York law, "'substantial' variations between state and federal [money judgments]" may be expected. See *Hanna*.

We therefore agree with the Second Circuit that New York's check on excessive damages implicates what we have called *Erie*'s "twin aims." Just as the *Erie* principle precludes a federal court from giving a state-created claim "longer life . . . than [the claim] would have had in the state court," *Ragan*, so *Erie* precludes a recovery in federal court significantly larger than the recovery that would have been tolerated in state court.

The Court then turned to the Seventh Amendment issue — and also to the import of *Byrd v. Blue Ridge*, discussed in the Note preceding *Hanna*. The Court quoted the passage from *Byrd* describing the federal judicial system as "an independent system for administering justice to litigants who properly invoke the jurisdiction." One characteristic of that system, the *Gasperini* Court said, involves the "proper role of the trial and appellate courts in the federal system in reviewing the size of jury verdicts."

What did federal law have to say about the matter? The Court first endorsed lower court decisions holding that the Reexamination Clause of the Seventh Amendment does not preclude appellate review of the trial judge's denial of a motion to set aside a jury verdict as excessive. As for the New York statute, the Court held that "the principal state and federal interests [could] be accommodated" without the need for an either-or choice:

> New York's dominant interest can be respected, without disrupting the federal system, once it is recognized that the federal district court is capable of performing the checking function, *i.e.*, that court can apply the State's "deviates materially" standard in line with New York case law evolving under CPLR § 5501(c).

Justice Scalia, joined by Chief Justice Rehnquist and Justice Thomas, dissented strongly. On the Seventh Amendment issue he said:

> Today the Court overrules a longstanding and well-reasoned line of precedent that has for years prohibited federal appellate courts from reviewing refusals by district courts to set aside civil jury awards as contrary to the weight of the evidence. Such unreasoned capitulation to the nullification of what was long regarded as a core component of the Bill of Rights — the Seventh Amendment's prohibition on appellate reexamination of civil jury awards — is wrong. It is not for us . . . to decide that the Seventh Amendment's restriction on federal-court review of jury findings has outlived its usefulness.

The dissent also argued that the Court was wrong in holding "that a state practice that relates to the division of duties between state judges and juries must be followed by federal courts in diversity cases." The dissent relied heavily on *Byrd*.

3. Five years after *Gasperini* came *Semtek*. The question in *Semtek* was: whose law determines the claim-preclusive effect of a federal judgment dismissing a diversity action on statute-of-limitations grounds? Justice Scalia wrote for a unanimous Court.

After concluding that the situation was not covered by Rule 41(a) of the Federal Rules of Civil Procedure, the Court "turn[ed] to consideration of what determines the issue." The Court surveyed its old decisions and derived from them the rule that "federal common law governs the claim-preclusive effect of a dismissal by a federal court sitting in diversity." The Court continued:

> It is left to us, then, to determine the appropriate federal rule. And despite the sea change that has occurred in the background law since *Dupasseur v. Rochereau*, 21 Wall. (87 U.S.) 130 (1875), was decided—not only repeal of the Conformity Act but also the watershed decision of this Court in *Erie*—we think the result decreed by *Dupasseur* continues to be correct for diversity cases. Since state, rather than federal, substantive law is at issue there is no need for a uniform federal rule. And indeed, nationwide uniformity in the substance of the matter is better served by having the same claim-preclusive rule (the state rule) apply whether the dismissal has been ordered by a state or a federal court. This is, it seems to us, a classic case for adopting, as the federally prescribed rule of decision, the law that would be applied by state courts in the State in which the federal diversity court sits. See, *e.g.*, *Gasperini*; *Walker; Klaxon*. As we have alluded to above [in the discussion of Rule 41(b)], any other rule would produce the sort of "forum-shopping ... and ... inequitable administration of the laws" that *Erie* seeks to avoid, *Hanna*, since filing in, or removing to, federal court would be encouraged by the divergent effects that the litigants would anticipate from likely grounds of dismissal. See *Guaranty Trust*.

The Court then added one qualification:

> This federal reference to state law will not obtain, of course, in situations in which the state law is incompatible with federal interests. If, for example, state law did not accord claim-preclusive effect to dismissals for willful violation of discovery orders, federal courts' interest in the integrity of their own processes might justify a contrary federal rule.

4. Note that in applying the "twin aims" test of *Hanna*, the Court observes that if federal courts do not follow the state rule, "filing in, *or removing to*, federal court would be encouraged." But *Hanna* was very specific in asking whether the difference in rules "would ... be likely to cause *a plaintiff* to choose the federal court." (Emphasis added in both quotations.) Is the *Semtek* Court justified in equating forum shopping by plaintiffs and by defendants for purposes of applying the "twin aims" test?

5. Another curious aspect of *Semtek* is the holding that the source of the appropriate preclusion rule is to be found in "federal common law." Until *Semtek*, the "substance-procedure" distinction and the "federal common law" doctrines had developed independently. The "federal common law" line of cases is treated in Chapter 8.

6. Note, though, that after stating that it is adopting state law "as the federally prescribed rule of decision," the Court cites *Gasperini*, *Walker*, and *Klaxon*. Perhaps *Gasperini* fits that description. But did *Walker* and *Klaxon* adopt state law "as the federally prescribed rule of decision"? Or did they hold that state law applied of its own force? (And why might it make a difference?)

Problems: Asbestos Litigation Reform Measures

In June 2004, the Governor of Ohio signed a bill aimed at reforming asbestos litigation. The intent of the legislation, as stated in the bill, is to:

(1) give priority to those asbestos claimants who can demonstrate actual physical harm or illness caused by exposure to asbestos; (2) fully preserve the rights of claimants who were exposed to asbestos to pursue compensation should those claimants become impaired in the future as a result of such exposure; (3) enhance the ability of the state's judicial systems and federal judicial systems to supervise and control litigation and asbestos-related bankruptcy proceedings; and (4) conserve the scarce resources of the defendants to allow compensation of cancer victims and others who are physically impaired by exposure to asbestos while securing the right to similar compensation for those who may suffer physical impairment in the future.

1. One provision of the law asks the Ohio Supreme Court "to adopt a rule that requires that an asbestos claim meet specific nexus requirements, including the requirement that the plaintiff be domiciled in Ohio or that Ohio is the state in which the plaintiff's exposure to asbestos is a substantial contributing factor."

Assume that the Ohio Supreme Court, in response to this request, adopts a rule (Rule 1005) providing that no suit based on asbestos exposure shall be brought in any court in Ohio "unless the plaintiff is domiciled in Ohio or Ohio is the state in which the plaintiff's exposure to asbestos is a substantial contributing factor."

After the effective date of the rule, Matt Renton, a citizen of Pennsylvania, brings suit in federal district court in Ohio against Acme Corp., alleging injury based on exposure to asbestos allegedly manufactured by the defendant. Acme is incorporated in Ohio. Assume that diversity jurisdiction is properly based on 28 U.S.C. § 1332. Defendant moves to dismiss under Rule 1005. Plaintiff makes no claim that he was exposed to asbestos in Ohio, but he argues that Rule 1005 should not apply in federal court.

Should the court grant the defendant's motion?

2. The new law also provides: "No person shall bring or maintain a tort action alleging an asbestos claim based on a nonmalignant condition" unless the plaintiff satisfies the statutory requirement of a "prima facie showing." The prima facie showing includes physical impairment and causation.

Within 30 days of filing an asbestos claim, the plaintiff is required to file a written report and supporting test results that satisfy the prima facie standard. If the defendant challenges the prima facie showing, the court must determine if the requirement has been satisfied. If the court finds that the plaintiff has failed to make the prima facie showing, the court is required to "administratively dismiss the plaintiff's claim without prejudice." The court retains jurisdiction over such cases, and the claim can be reinstated if the plaintiff makes the required prima facie showing.

Jack Williams has filed an asbestos suit in federal district court in Ohio. Jurisdiction is properly based on 28 U.S.C. § 1332. Must Williams file the written report and supporting test results required by the new law?

3. Federal law has no provisions for administrative dismissals. Dismissals are governed by Rule 41 of the Federal Rules of Civil Procedure and are "voluntary" or "involuntary." Do the administrative dismissal procedures under the new law apply in federal court?

Chapter 8

Federal Common Law

In his opinion for the Court in *Erie*, Justice Brandeis famously said, "There is no federal general common law." Yet, on the same day, the Court applied "federal common law" to reverse a state-court decision on apportioning the waters of an interstate stream. *See Hinderliter v. La Plata River & Cherry Creek Ditch Co.*, 304 U.S. 92 (1938). That opinion, too, was by Justice Brandeis. The Court thus made clear that *Erie* did not signal the demise of "federal common law"—something different from "federal *general* common law."

Scholars dispute the boundaries of the "federal common law" that remains alive notwithstanding *Erie*. In one decision the Court itself defined "what one might call 'federal common law' in the strictest sense": "a rule of decision that amounts, not simply to an interpretation of a federal statute or a properly promulgated administrative rule, but, rather, to the judicial 'creation' of a special federal rule of decision." *Atherton v. FDIC*, 519 U.S. 213, 218 (1997). Here we will examine the principal contexts in which federal courts have created federal rules of decision that go beyond interpreting a federal statute. As we will see, federal common law has also been developed in the realm of constitutional adjudication.

A. Rights and Duties of the United States

Clearfield Trust Co. v. United States

Supreme Court of the United States, 1943.

318 U.S. 363.

Mr. Justice Douglas delivered the opinion of the Court.

On April 28, 1936, a check was drawn on the Treasurer of the United States through the Federal Reserve Bank of Philadelphia to the order of Clair A. Barner in the amount of $24.20. It was dated at Harrisburg, Pennsylvania and was drawn for services rendered by Barner to the Works Progress Administration. The check was placed in the mail addressed to Barner at his address in Mackeyville, Pa. Barner never received the check. Some unknown person obtained it in a mysterious manner and presented it to the J.C. Penney Co. store in Clearfield, Pa., representing that he was the payee and identifying himself to the satisfaction of the employees of J.C. Penney Co. He endorsed the check in the name of Barner and transferred it to J.C. Penney Co. in exchange for cash and merchandise. Barner never authorized the endorsement nor participated in the proceeds of the check. J.C. Penney Co. endorsed the check over to the Clearfield Trust Co. which accepted it as agent for the purpose of collection and endorsed it as follows: "Pay to the order of Federal Reserve Bank of Philadelphia, Prior Endorsements Guaranteed." Clearfield Trust Co. collected the check from the United States through the Federal Reserve Bank of Philadelphia and paid the full amount thereof to J.C. Penney Co.

Neither the Clearfield Trust Co. nor J.C. Penney Co. had any knowledge or suspicion of the forgery. Each acted in good faith. On or before May 10, 1936, Barner advised the timekeeper and the foreman of the W.P.A. project on which he was employed that he had not received the check in question. This information was duly communicated to other agents of the United States and on November 30, 1936, Barner executed an affidavit alleging that the endorsement of his name on the check was a forgery. No notice was given the Clearfield Trust Co. or J.C. Penney Co. of the forgery until January 12, 1937, at which time the Clearfield Trust Co. was notified. The first notice received by Clearfield Trust Co. that the United States was asking reimbursement was on August 31, 1937.

This suit was instituted in 1939 by the United States against the Clearfield Trust Co., the jurisdiction of the federal District Court being invoked pursuant to the provisions of § 24(1) of the Judicial Code [now 28 U.S.C. § 1345]. The cause of action was based on the express guaranty of prior endorsements made by the Clearfield Trust Co. J.C. Penney Co. intervened as a defendant. The case was heard on complaint, answer and stipulation of facts. The District Court held that the rights of the parties were to be determined by the law of Pennsylvania and that since the United States unreasonably delayed in giving notice of the forgery to the Clearfield Trust Co., it was barred from recovery under the rule of *Market Street Title & Trust Co. v. Chelten T. Co.*, 296 Pa. 230, 145 A. 848. It accordingly dismissed the complaint. On appeal the Circuit Court of Appeals reversed. . . .

We agree with the Circuit Court of Appeals that the rule of *Erie R. Co. v. Tompkins*, 304 U.S. 64, does not apply to this action. The rights and duties of the United States on commercial paper which it issues are governed by federal rather than local law. When the United States disburses its funds or pays its debts, it is exercising a constitutional function or power. This check was issued for services performed under the Federal Emergency Relief Act of 1935. The authority to issue the check had its origin in the Constitution and the statutes of the United States and was in no way dependent on the laws of Pennsylvania or of any other state. The duties imposed upon the United States and the rights acquired by it as a result of the issuance find their roots in the same federal sources.[2] In absence of an applicable Act of Congress it is for the federal courts to fashion the governing rule of law according to their own standards. . . .

---

2. Various Treasury Regulations govern the payment and endorsement of government checks and warrants and the reimbursement of the Treasurer of the United States by Federal Reserve banks and member bank depositories on payment of checks or warrants bearing a forged endorsement. Forgery of the check was an offense against the United States.

In our choice of the applicable federal rule we have occasionally selected state law. But reasons which may make state law at times the appropriate federal rule are singularly inappropriate here. The issuance of commercial paper by the United States is on a vast scale and transactions in that paper from issuance to payment will commonly occur in several states. The application of state law, even without the conflict of laws rules of the forum, would subject the rights and duties of the United States to exceptional uncertainty. It would lead to great diversity in results by making identical transactions subject to the vagaries of the laws of the several states. The desirability of a uniform rule is plain. And while the federal law merchant developed for about a century under the regime of *Swift v. Tyson*, 16 Pet. 1, represented general commercial law rather than a choice of a federal rule designed to protect a federal right, it nevertheless stands as a convenient source of reference for fashioning federal rules applicable to these federal questions.

United States v. National Exchange Bank, 214 U.S. 302, falls in that category. The Court held that the United States could recover as drawee from one who presented for payment a pension check on which the name of the payee had been forged, in spite of a protracted delay on the part of the United States in giving notice of the forgery. . . .

The *National Exchange Bank* case went no further than to hold that prompt notice of the discovery of the forgery was not a condition precedent to suit. It did not reach the question whether lack of prompt notice might be a defense. We think it may. If it is shown that the drawee on learning of the forgery did not give prompt notice of it and that damage resulted, recovery by the drawee is barred. The fact that the drawee is the United States and the laches those of its employees are not material. The United States as drawee of commercial paper stands in no different light than any other drawee. . . . But the damage occasioned by the delay must be established and not left to conjecture. . . . No such damage has been shown by Clearfield Trust Co. who so far as appears can still recover from J.C. Penney Co. . . . It is [stipulated] that when J.C. Penney Co. was notified of the forgery in the present case none of its employees was able to remember anything about the transaction or check in question. The inference is that the more prompt the notice the more likely the detection of the forger. But that falls short of a showing that the delay caused a manifest loss. It is but another way of saying that mere delay is enough.

Affirmed.

Mr. Justice Murphy and Mr. Justice Rutledge did not participate in the consideration or decision of this case.

Note: The Law Governing the Rights and Obligations of the United States

1. Three decades after *Clearfield*, Chief Justice Burger, writing for the Court, said:

The federal jurisdictional grant over suits brought by the United States is not in itself a mandate for applying federal law in all circumstances. This principle follows from *Erie* itself, where, although the federal courts had jurisdiction over diversity cases, we held that the federal courts did not possess the power to develop a concomitant body of general federal law.

United States v. Little Lake Misere Co., 412 U.S. 580, 591 (1973).

Is the Chief Justice persuasive in his reliance on *Erie*? The Court has taken a different view of the constitutional grant of judicial power over "all cases of admiralty and maritime jurisdiction." For example, in *The Lottawanna*, 21 Wall. (88 U.S.) 558, 575 (1874), the Court said:

> That we have a maritime law of our own, operative throughout the United States, cannot be doubted. The general system of maritime law which was familiar to the lawyers and statesmen of the country when the Constitution was adopted, was most certainly intended and referred to when it was declared in that instrument that the judicial power of the United States shall extend "to all cases of admiralty and maritime jurisdiction."

How might you argue that the federal jurisdictional grant over suits by the United States provides a closer analogy, in this context, than the grant over diversity suits?

2. Although the Court has rejected the proposition that federal law applies to transactions involving the United States "in all circumstances," it has recognized a broad lawmaking power for the federal courts in Federal Government litigation. In support of this power, the Court has often cited an influential article by Professor Paul J. Mishkin. Thus, in *Little Lake Misere*, after the passage quoted above, Chief Justice Burger continued:

> Since *Erie*, and as a corollary of that decision, we have consistently acted on the assumption that dealings which may be "ordinary" or "local" as between private citizens raise serious questions of national sovereignty when they arise in the context of a specific constitutional or statutory provision; particularly is this so when transactions undertaken by the Federal Government are involved, as in this case. In such cases, the Constitution or Acts of Congress "require" otherwise than that state law govern of its own force.
>
> There will often be no specific federal legislation governing a particular transaction to which the United States is a party; here, for example, no provision of the Migratory Bird Conservation Act guides us to choose state or federal law in interpreting federal land acquisition agreements under the Act. But silence on that score in federal legislation is no reason for limiting the reach of federal law, as the Court of Appeals [believed]. To the contrary, the inevitable incompleteness presented by all legislation means that interstitial federal lawmaking is a basic responsibility of the federal courts. "At the very least, effective Constitutionalism requires recognition of power in the federal courts to declare, as a matter of common law or 'judicial legislation,' rules which may be necessary to fill in interstitially or otherwise effectuate the statutory patterns enacted in the large by Congress. In other words, it must mean recognition of federal judicial competence to declare the governing law in an area comprising issues substantially related to an

established program of government operation." Mishkin, *The Variousness of "Federal Law": Competence and Discretion in the Choice of National and State Rules for Decision*, 105 U. Pa. L. Rev. 797, 800 (1957).

Note that the Chief Justice refers to judicial competence to declare the law for "transaction[s] to which the United States is a party." Professor Mishkin speaks more broadly about "the statutory patterns enacted in the large by Congress." As you study the materials in the remainder of this chapter, consider whether the Court has recognized (or should recognize) greater lawmaking power when the United States is a party than in private litigation involving federal programs.

3. Another influential commentary is an article published by Judge Henry J. Friendly. Judge Friendly wrote:

> *Clearfield* decided not one issue but two. The first, to which most of the opinion was devoted and on which it is undeniably sound, is that the right of the United States to recover for conversion of a Government check is a federal right, so that the courts of the United States may formulate a rule of decision. The second, over which the Supreme Court jumped rather quickly and not altogether convincingly, is whether, having this opportunity, the federal courts should adopt a uniform nation-wide rule or should follow state law. Noting that "In our choice of the applicable federal rule we have occasionally selected state law," the opinion said that reasons for following that course "are singularly inappropriate here" since application of state law "would subject the rights and duties of the United States to exceptional uncertainty." The next sentence descended to the more apt and moderate phase, "diversity in results," and the question persists why it is more important that federal fiscal officials rather than Pennsylvanians dealing in commercial paper should have the solace of uniformity.

Henry J. Friendly, *In Praise of* Erie — *And of the New Federal Common Law*, 39 N.Y.U. L. Rev. 383, 430. Judge Friendly's description of the two issues in *Clearfield* has been widely accepted. And, as the next principal case illustrates, the Supreme Court has taken heed of Judge Friendly's criticism of the second step in the *Clearfield* opinion.

4. Judge Friendly pointed out another problem with the decision in *Clearfield*:

> Although the direct consequence of the Government's victory in *Clearfield* was to impose liability on the paying bank in accordance with the "uniform" federal rule, this would necessarily lead to an action by the bank against the endorser. If that action were held to be governed by state law, which would excuse the endorser because of the delay, this would destroy the whole substantive basis of the *Clearfield* decision, namely, that the bank did not suffer from the delay since, under federal law, it could recover from the endorser, and as Mishkin notes, "the burden of financial loss will merely be shifted from the Government to the particular endorser whom it chooses to sue."

To avoid this outcome, as Judge Friendly observed, the Court could hold that the federal rule would also apply in the action by the bank against the endorser. But that would further federalize the domain of state commercial law. Several years after *Clearfield*, the Court refused to take that step in an analogous setting. In *Bank of America National Trust & Savings Ass'n v. Parnell*, 352 U.S. 29 (1956), the plaintiff brought a diversity suit alleging that the defendants had converted federal bonds that belonged to the plaintiff. The principal issue at trial was whether the defendants took the bonds in good faith, without knowledge or notice of a defect in title. The Third Circuit held that, under *Clearfield*, federal law controlled on the burden of proof as to good faith. The Supreme Court reversed. Justice Frankfurter, writing for the Court, said:

> Securities issued by the Government generate immediate interests of the Government. These were dealt with in *Clearfield Trust* . . . But they also radiate interests in transactions between private parties. The present litigation is purely between private parties and does not touch the rights and duties of the United States. The only possible interest of the United States in a situation like the one here, exclusively involving the transfer of Government paper between private persons, is that the floating of securities of the United States might somehow or other be adversely affected by the local rule of a particular State regarding the liability of a converter. This is far too speculative, far too remote a possibility to justify the application of federal law to transactions essentially of local concern.

Justice Black, joined by Justice Douglas (the author of the Court's opinion in *Clearfield*) dissented:

> The virtue of a uniform law governing bonds, notes, and other paper issued by the United States is that it provides a certain and definite guide to the rights of all parties rather than subjecting them to the vagaries of the law of many States. The business of the United States will go on without that uniformity. But the policy surrounding our choice of laws is concerned with the convenience, certainty, and definiteness in having one set of rules governing the rights of all parties to government paper, as contrasted to multiple rules. If the rule of the *Clearfield Trust* case is to be abandoned as to some parties, it should be abandoned as to all and we should start afresh on this problem.

United States v. Kimbell Foods, Inc.

United States Supreme Court, 1979.

440 U.S. 715.

Mr. Justice Marshall delivered the opinion of the Court.

We granted certiorari in these cases to determine whether contractual liens arising from certain federal loan programs take precedence over private liens, in the absence of a federal statute setting priorities. To resolve this question, we must decide first whether federal or state law governs the controversies; and second, if federal law applies, whether this Court should fashion a uniform priority rule or incorporate state commercial law. We conclude that the source of law is federal, but that a national rule is unnecessary to protect the federal interests underlying the loan programs. Accordingly, we adopt state law as the appropriate federal rule for establishing the relative priority of these competing federal and private liens.

I

A

[The *Kimbell Foods* case] involves two contractual security interests in the personal property of O. K. Super Markets, Inc. Both interests were perfected pursuant to Texas' Uniform Commercial Code (UCC). The United States' lien secures a loan guaranteed by the Small Business Administration (SBA). The private lien, which arises from security agreements that preceded the federal guarantee, secures advances respondent Kimbell Foods made after the federal guarantee.

[Detailed account omitted.]

II

This Court has consistently held that federal law governs questions involving the rights of the United States arising under nationwide federal programs. As the Court explained in *Clearfield Trust Co. v. United States*:

> When the United States disburses its funds or pays its debts, it is exercising a constitutional function or power. . . . The authority [to do so] had its origin in the Constitution and the statutes of the United States and was in no way dependent on the laws [of any State]. The duties imposed upon the United States and the rights acquired by it . . . find their roots in the same federal sources. In absence of an applicable Act of Congress it is for the federal courts to fashion the governing rule of law according to their own standards.

Guided by these principles, we think it clear that the priority of liens stemming from federal lending programs must be determined with reference to federal law. The SBA and FHA unquestionably perform federal functions within the meaning of *Clearfield*. Since the agencies derive their authority to effectuate loan transactions from specific Acts of Congress passed in the exercise of a "constitutional function or power," their rights, as well, should derive from a federal source. When Government activities "aris[e] from and bea[r] heavily upon a federal . . . program," the Constitution and Acts of Congress "'require' otherwise than that state law govern of its own force." *United States v. Little Lake Misere Land Co.*, 412 U.S. 580, 592, 593 (1973). In such contexts, federal interests are sufficiently implicated to warrant the protection of federal law. [Here, the Court cited Mishkin, *The Variousness of "Federal Law": Competence and Discretion in the Choice of National and State Rules for Decision*, 105 U. PA. L. REV. 797, 800, and n.15 (1957) [hereinafter Mishkin].]

That the statutes authorizing these federal lending programs do not specify the appropriate rule of decision in no way limits the reach of federal law. It is precisely when Congress has not spoken "'in an area comprising issues substantially related to an established program of government operation,'" *id.*, quoting Mishkin, that *Clearfield* directs federal courts to fill the interstices of federal legislation "according to their own standards." *Clearfield*.

Federal law therefore controls the Government's priority rights. The more difficult task, to which we turn, is giving content to this federal rule.

III

Controversies directly affecting the operations of federal programs, although governed by federal law, do not inevitably require resort to uniform federal rules. See *Clearfield; Little Lake Misere*. Whether to adopt state law or to fashion a nationwide federal rule is a matter of judicial policy "dependent upon a variety of considerations always relevant to the nature of the specific governmental interests and to the effects upon them of applying state law." *United States v. Standard Oil Co.*, 332 U.S. 301, 310 (1947). As explained by [Professor Mishkin:]

> Whether state law is to be incorporated as a matter of federal common law . . . involves the . . . problem of the relationship of a particular issue to a going federal program. The question of judicial incorporation can only arise in an area which is sufficiently close to a national operation to establish competence in the federal courts to choose the governing law, and yet not so close as clearly to require the application of a single nationwide rule of substance.

Undoubtedly, federal programs that "by their nature are and must be uniform in character throughout the Nation" necessitate formulation of controlling federal rules. *United States v. Yazell*, 382 U.S. 341, 354 (1966). Conversely, when there is little need for a nationally uniform body of law, state law may be incorporated as the federal rule of decision. Apart from considerations of uniformity, we must also determine whether application of state law would frustrate specific objectives of the federal programs. If so, we must fashion special rules solicitous of those federal interests. Finally, our choice-of-law inquiry must consider the extent to which application of a federal rule would disrupt commercial relationships predicated on state law.

The Government argues that effective administration of its lending programs requires uniform federal rules of priority. It contends further that resort to any rules other than first in time, first in right and choateness would conflict with protectionist fiscal policies underlying the programs.

[Under the first of these rules, the lien "first in time" is "first in right." However, to be considered first in time, the nonfederal lien must be "choate," that is, sufficiently specific, when the federal lien arises. A state-created lien is not choate until the "identity of the lienor, the property subject to the lien, and the amount of the lien are established." Failure to meet any one of these conditions forecloses priority over the federal lien, even if under state law the nonfederal lien was enforceable for all purposes when the federal lien arose.]

We are unpersuaded that, in the circumstances presented here, nationwide standards favoring claims of the United States are necessary to ease program administration or to safeguard the Federal Treasury from defaulting debtors. Because the state commercial codes "furnish convenient solutions in no way inconsistent with adequate protection of the federal interest[s]," *United States v. Standard Oil Co.*, we decline to override intricate state laws of general applicability on which private creditors base their daily commercial transactions.

A

Incorporating state law to determine the rights of the United States as against private creditors would in no way hinder administration of the SBA and FHA loan programs. In *United States v. Yazell*, 382 U.S. 341 (1966), this Court rejected the argument, similar to the Government's here, that a need for uniformity precluded application of state coverture rules to an SBA loan contract. Because SBA operations were "specifically and in great detail adapted to state law," the federal interest in supplanting "important and carefully evolved state arrangements designed to serve multiple purposes" was minimal. Our conclusion that compliance with state law would produce no hardship on the agency was also based on the SBA's practice of "individually negotiat [ing] in painfully particularized detail" each loan transaction. These observations apply with equal force here and compel us again to reject generalized pleas for uniformity as substitutes for concrete evidence that adopting state law would adversely affect administration of the federal programs.

Although the SBA Financial Assistance Manual on which this Court relied in *Yazell* is no longer "replete with admonitions to follow state law carefully," SBA employees are still instructed to, and indeed do, follow state law. In fact, a fair reading of the *SBA Financial Assistance Manual* indicates that the agency assumes its security interests are controlled to a large extent by the commercial law of each State. Similarly, FHA regulations expressly incorporate state law. They mandate compliance with state procedures for perfecting and maintaining valid security interests, and highlight those rules that differ from State to State. To ensure that employees are aware of new developments, the FHA also issues "State supplements" to "reflect any State statutory changes in its version of the UCC." . . .

Thus, the agencies' own operating practices belie their assertion that a federal rule of priority is needed to avoid the administrative burdens created by disparate state commercial rules. The programs already conform to each State's commercial standards. By using local lending offices and employees who are familiar with the law of their respective localities, the agencies function effectively without uniform procedures and legal rules.

Nevertheless, the Government maintains that requiring the agencies to assess security arrangements under local law would dictate close scrutiny of each transaction and thereby impede expeditious processing of loans. We disagree. Choosing responsible debtors necessarily requires individualized selection procedures, which the agencies have already implemented in considerable detail. Each applicant's financial condition is evaluated under rigorous standards in a lengthy process. . . . In addition, they adapt the terms of every loan to the parties' needs and capabilities. Because each application currently receives individual scrutiny, the agencies can readily adjust loan transactions to reflect state priority rules, just as they consider other factual and legal matters before disbursing Government funds. As we noted in *United States v. Yazell*, these lending programs are distinguishable from "nationwide act[s] of the Federal Government, emanating in a single form from a single source." Since there is no indication that variant state priority schemes would burden current methods of loan processing, we conclude that considerations of administrative convenience do not warrant adoption of a uniform federal law.

B

[The Government points out that the Court has imposed the first-in-time and choateness doctrines in the context of federal tax liens, and it argues that] the federal interest in recovering on loans compels similar legal protection of the agencies' consensual liens. However, we believe significant differences between federal tax liens and consensual liens counsel against unreflective extension of rules that immunize the United States from the commercial law governing all other voluntary secured creditors. . . .

. . . The importance of securing adequate revenues to discharge national obligations justifies the extraordinary priority accorded federal tax liens through the choateness and first-in-time doctrines. By contrast, when the United States operates as a moneylending institution under carefully circumscribed programs, its interest in recouping the limited sums advanced is of a different order. Thus, there is less need here than in the tax lien area to invoke protective measures against defaulting debtors in a manner disruptive of existing credit markets.

To equate tax liens with these consensual liens also misperceives the principal congressional concerns underlying the respective statutes. The overriding purpose of the tax lien statute obviously is to ensure prompt revenue collection. The same cannot be said of the SBA and FHA lending programs.[34] They are a form of social welfare legislation, primarily designed to assist farmers and businesses that cannot obtain funds from private lenders on reasonable terms. We believe that had Congress intended the private commercial sector, rather than taxpayers in general, to bear the risks of default entailed by these public welfare programs, it would have established a priority scheme displacing state law. Far from doing so, both Congress and the agencies have expressly recognized the priority of certain private liens over the agencies' security interests, thereby indicating that the extraordinary safeguards applied in the tax lien area are unnecessary to maintain the lending programs.

The Government's ability to safeguard its interests in commercial dealings further reveals that the rules developed in the tax lien area are unnecessary here, and that state priority rules would not conflict with federal lending objectives. The United States is an involuntary creditor of delinquent taxpayers, unable to control the factors that make tax collection likely. In contrast, when the United States acts as a lender or

---

34. Congress did not delineate specific priority rules in either the tax lien statute prior to 1966, the insolvency statute, or the statutes authorizing these lending programs. Accordingly, the Government urges that we establish identical priority rules for all three situations. This argument overlooks the evident distinction between lending programs for needy farmers and businesses and statutes created to guarantee receipt of debts due the United States. We, of course, express no view on the proper priority rules to govern federal consensual liens in the context of statutes other than those at issue here.

guarantor, it does so voluntarily, with detailed knowledge of the borrower's financial status. The agencies evaluate the risks associated with each loan, examine the interests of other creditors, choose the security believed necessary to assure repayment, and set the terms of every agreement. By carefully selecting loan recipients and tailoring each transaction with state law in mind, the agencies are fully capable of establishing terms that will secure repayment. . . .

C

In structuring financial transactions, businessmen depend on state commercial law to provide the stability essential for reliable evaluation of the risks involved. However, subjecting federal contractual liens to the doctrines developed in the tax lien area could undermine that stability. Creditors who justifiably rely on state law to obtain superior liens would have their expectations thwarted whenever a federal contractual security interest suddenly appeared and took precedence.

Because the ultimate consequences of altering settled commercial practices are so difficult to foresee, we hesitate to create new uncertainties, in the absence of careful legislative deliberation. Of course, formulating special rules to govern the priority of the federal consensual liens in issue here would be justified if necessary to vindicate important national interests. But neither the Government nor the Court of Appeals advanced any concrete reasons for rejecting well-established commercial rules which have proven workable over time. Thus, the prudent course is to adopt the readymade body of state law as the federal rule of decision until Congress strikes a different accommodation.

IV

Accordingly, we hold that, absent a congressional directive, the relative priority of private liens and consensual liens arising from these Government lending programs is to be determined under nondiscriminatory state laws. [The] Court of Appeals found that Texas law gave preference to respondent Kimbell's lien. We therefore affirm the judgment in that case. . . .

Note: Uniformity or Borrowing?

1. *Kimbell Foods* states without qualification that in litigation involving the rights of the United States under nationwide federal programs, "federal law governs." The only question is whether the "federal law" will be a uniform federal rule fashioned by federal courts or a rule borrowed from state law.

2. At one end of the spectrum, federal law will not borrow from state law if the state rule is aberrant or hostile to the interests of the United States. In *United States v. Little Lake Misere Land Co.*, 412 U.S. 580 (1973), the United States brought suit to quiet title to two parcels of land in Louisiana that the Government had acquired under the Migratory Bird Conservation Act. The defendants claimed mineral rights in the property under Act 315, a Louisiana law that limited mineral reservations in land acquired "by the United States of America, or any of its subdivisions or agencies." The Supreme Court held that Act 315 would not be applied to the mineral reservations in the case before it. The Court said:

The Court in the past has been careful to state that, even assuming in general terms the appropriateness of "borrowing" state law, specific aberrant or hostile state rules do not provide appropriate standards for federal law. . . .

Under Louisiana's Act 315, land acquisitions of the United States, explicitly authorized by the Migratory Bird Conservation Act, are made subject to a rule of retroactive imprescriptibility, a rule that is plainly hostile to the interests of the United States. As applied to a consummated land transaction under a contract which specifically defined conditions for prolonging the vendor's mineral reservation, retroactive application of Act 315 to the United States deprives it of bargained-for contractual interests.

To permit state abrogation of the explicit terms of a federal land acquisition would deal a serious blow to the congressional scheme contemplated by the Migratory Bird Conservation Act and indeed all other federal land acquisition programs. These programs are national in scope. They anticipate acute and active bargaining by officials of the United States charged with making the best possible use of limited federal conservation appropriations. Certainty and finality are indispensable in any land transaction, but they are especially critical when, as here, the federal officials carrying out the mandate of Congress irrevocably commit scarce funds. . . .

We are not unsympathetic to Louisiana's concern for the consequences of a continuing, substantial, even if contingent, federal interest in Louisiana minerals. Congress, however, could scarcely have viewed that concern as a proper justification for retroactive application of state legislation which effectively deprives the Government of its bargained-for contractual interests. Our Federal Union is a complicated organism, but its legal processes cannot legitimately be simplified through the inviting expedient of special legislation which has the effect of confiscating interests of the United States.

Justice Rehnquist, concurring in the judgment, saw not only hostility to federal interests but also discrimination:

Act 315 enacted by Louisiana by its terms applies only to transactions in which "the United States of America, or any of its subdivisions or agencies" is a party. While it is argued that Louisiana by other legislation made the same principle applicable to the state government, this proposition is, as the Court's opinion points out, by no means demonstrated. And in any event the change in the period of prescriptibility was not made applicable to nongovernmental grantees.

Implicit in the holdings of a number of our cases dealing with state taxation and regulatory measures applied to the Federal Government is that such measures must be nondiscriminatory. The doctrine of intergovernmental immunity . . . requires at least that the United States be immune from discriminatory treatment by a State which in some manner interferes with the execution of federal laws.

3. In contrast, the Court's opinion in *Kimbell Foods* emphatically rejects all of the Government's numerous arguments for applying a federal rule of decision. This might suggest that the Court will seldom find such arguments persuasive. However, in *West Virginia v. United States*, 479 U.S. 305 (1987), the Government's position prevailed. The question was whether the State of West Virginia was liable for prejudgment interest on a debt arising from a contractual obligation to reimburse the United States for services rendered by the Army Corps of Engineers under the Disaster Relief Act of 1970 (DRA). The Court held, with only brief discussion, that federal law controlled. The Court said:

> "[T]he rule governing the interest to be recovered as damages for delayed payment of a contractual obligation to the United States is not controlled by state statute or local common law. In the absence of an applicable federal statute, it is for the federal courts to determine, according to their own criteria, the appropriate measure of damage, expressed in terms of interest, for nonpayment of the amount found to be due." *Royal Indemnity Co. v. United States*, 313 U.S. 289, 296 (1941); *see also Clearfield Trust Co.* While there are instances in which state law may be adopted as the federal rule of decision, see *United States v. Yazell*, 382 U.S. 341 (1966), this case presents no compelling reason for doing so. A single nationwide rule would be preferable to one turning on state law, and the incorporation of state law would not give due regard to the federal interest in maintaining the apportionment of responsibility Congress devised in the DRA. Finally, application of a federal rule would not "disrupt commercial relationships predicated on state law," *Kimbell Foods*, since state law would not of its own force govern contracts between a State and the Federal Government.

In *West Virginia* as in *Kimbell Foods*, Justice Marshall wrote for a unanimous Court.

4. Has the Court drawn a clear line between the situations in which state law will be borrowed and those in which the Court will fashion a uniform federal rule? Consider the problem that follows.

Problem: *Ejecting the Post Office*

The United States Postal Service is "an independent establishment of the executive branch of the Government of the United States." It was created by an Act of Congress in 1971, replacing the Post Office Department.

In 1995, the Postal Service leased a building (with an adjoining parking lot) in the City of Bayport in the State of Oceana for use as a post office. The owner of the property is Nicholas Forsyte. The lease was for ten years at an annual rent of $20,000, with an option to the tenant to renew through 2014 at the same rent. The option has been exercised in each succeeding year.

Last year, the Postal Service notified Forsyte that the post office needed to be painted—at his expense. But the lease is silent on whether the landlord's maintenance obligation includes painting, and Forsyte refused to paint. The Service then hired someone to do it, at a cost of $2,000, and deducted this amount from the rent. For-syte then served written notice on the Postal Service that unless it paid the full rent within 10 days he would exercise his rights under Oceana law and terminate the lease. When the Service refused either to pay up or to quit the premises, Forsyte brought suit in federal district court in Oceana for the rent due and for ejectment. He based federal jurisdiction on 39 U.S.C. § 409(a), which gives the federal courts, concurrently with the state courts, jurisdiction over suits by or against the Postal Service.

Under Oceana law, painting is not a part of the landlord's maintenance obligation; thus, the Postal Service's withholding of rent was wrongful. Further, under Oceana law, a lessor may eject a tenant for failure to pay rent, even if the default is only partial.

The Postal Service argues that federal common law rather than Oceana law should govern the parties' rights under the lease, and that the district court should adopt a rule that would not allow ejectment when the tenant has failed to pay only a small portion of the rent due.

How should the district court rule?

Note: The Standard Oil Case

1. Four years after *Clearfield*, the Supreme Court decided *United States v. Standard Oil Co. of California*, 332 U.S. 301 (1947). The case arose out of an accident in California. A soldier was hit and injured by a truck of the Standard Oil Company. The United States sued Standard in federal district court to recover the amounts it had expended for hospitalization and for the soldier's pay during the period of his disability. The Supreme Court's response was signaled in the opening paragraph of its opinion:

> Not often since the decision in *Erie R. Co. v. Tompkins* is this Court asked to create a new substantive legal liability without legislative aid and as at the common law. This case of first impression here seeks such a result.

Ironically, the Court began by holding that "the creation or negation of liability" was *not* to be governed by the rule in *Erie* but by the rule of *Clearfield*. The Court elaborated on this point at length, saying in part:

> Perhaps no relation between the Government and a citizen is more distinctively federal in character than that between it and members of its armed forces. To whatever extent state law may apply to govern the relations between soldiers or others in the armed forces and persons outside them or nonfederal governmental agencies, the scope, nature, legal incidents and consequences of the relation between persons in service and the Government are fundamentally derived from federal sources and governed by federal authority. So also we think are interferences with that relationship such as the facts of this case involve. For, as the Federal Government has the exclusive power to establish and define the relationship by virtue of its military and other powers, equally clearly it has power in execution of the same functions to protect the relation once formed from harms inflicted by others. . . .

Not only is the government-soldier relation distinctively and exclusively a creation of federal law, but we know of no good reason why the Government's right to be indemnified in these circumstances, or the lack of such a right, should vary in accordance with the different rulings of the several states, simply because the soldier marches or today perhaps as often flies across state lines. . . . The question [is] chiefly one of federal fiscal policy, not of special or peculiar concern to the states or their citizens.

The Court then turned to "consideration of the policy properly to be applied concerning the wrongdoer, whether of liability or of continued immunity as in the past." The Government offered several analogies from the common law in support of its claim. It pointed out, for example, that the common law recognized "the master's rights of recovery for loss of the services of his servant or apprentice" and "the parent's right to indemnity for loss of a child's services." But the Court refused to consider the validity of the analogies or the merits of the policy considerations. Instead, it declared:

[We] have not here simply a question of creating a new liability in the nature of a tort. . . . Whatever the merits of the policy, its conversion into law is a proper subject for congressional action, not for any creative power of ours. Congress, not this Court or the other federal courts, is the custodian of the national purse. By the same token it is the primary and most often the exclusive arbiter of federal fiscal affairs. And these comprehend . . . securing the treasury or the government against financial losses however inflicted, including requiring reimbursement for injuries creating them, as well as filling the treasury itself. . . .

When Congress has thought it necessary to take steps to prevent interference with federal funds, property or relations, it has taken positive action to that end. . . . Until [Congress] acts to establish the liability, this Court and others should withhold creative touch.

2. Is the Court persuasive in saying that matters involving the protection of "the national purse" should be outside the scope of federal common law? Justice Jackson, who dissented alone in *Standard Oil*, said:

I cannot see why the principles of tort law that allow a husband or parent to recover do not logically sustain the right of the United States to recover in this case. . . . If there is one function which I should think we would feel free to exercise under a Constitution which vests in us judicial power, it would be to apply well established common law principles to a case whose only novelty is in facts.

Note that the Court's disavowal of the "creative power" of federal courts comes after the Court has held that state rules can not be applied in cases of this kind. Professor Henry M. Hart commented: "The result is to thrust upon Congress a burden of exclusive responsibility for the interstitial development of legal doctrine — a burden which it is wholly unequipped to bear."[1] Do you agree that this task is beyond Congress's capacity?

---

1. Henry M. Hart, *The Relations Between State and Federal Law*, 54 Colum. L. Rev. 489, 534 (1954).

3. Fifteen years after the decision in *Standard Oil*, Congress enacted the Federal Medical Care Recovery Act.[2] The Act gives the United States the right to recover from third-party tortfeasors "the reasonable value of the care and treatment" that the Government provided to victims of the tort. The language of the Act was modified several times during the course of its consideration in Congress.[3] And the law has been amended twice since its enactment. Does this history vindicate the Court's reluctance to recognize liability as a matter of federal common law?

B. Implied Remedies for Statutory Violations

Title IX of the Education Amendments of 1972 provides: "No person . . . shall, on the basis of sex, be excluded from participation in, be denied the benefits of, or be subjected to discrimination under any education program or activity receiving Federal financial assistance." The statute has no provisions authorizing a person who believes that she has been wrongfully excluded from a federally funded program to seek damages or other remedies in court. Does the lawmaking power recognized in cases like *Clearfield* and *Kimbell Foods* include the power to create a private right of action (or "cause of action") for would-be Title IX plaintiffs?

To place this question in perspective, it is useful to begin by looking at rights of action expressly created by Congress. The paradigm of the statutory cause of action is the one created by the Federal Employers Liability Act, 45 U.S.C. § 51:

> Every common carrier by railroad while engaging in [interstate commerce] shall be liable in damages to any person suffering injury while he is employed by such carrier in such commerce, or, in case of the death of such employee, to his or her personal representative, for the benefit of the surviving widow or husband and children [or other survivors] of such employee . . . for such injury or death resulting in whole or in part from the negligence of any of the officers, agents, or employees of such carrier, or by reason of any defect or insufficiency, due to its negligence, in its cars, engines, appliances, machinery, track, roadbed, works, boats, wharves, or other equipment.

Another example of an expressly created cause of action is Section 4 of the Clayton Act (15 U.S.C. § 15). That statute provides:

> (a) Amount of recovery . . .
>
> Except as provided in subsection (b) of this section, any person who shall be injured in his business or property by reason of anything forbidden in the antitrust laws may sue therefor in any district court of the United States in the district in which the defendant resides or is found or has an agent, without respect to the amount in controversy, and shall recover threefold the

---

2. The Act is codified at 42 U.S.C. §§ 2651–53.

3. *See* Eli P. Bernzweig, *Public Law 87-693: An Analysis and Interpretation of the Federal Medical Care Recovery Act*, 64 Colum. L. Rev. 1257, 1259–61 (1964).

damages by him sustained, and the cost of suit, including a reasonable attorney's fee.

Yet another example is the civil rights statute, 42 U.S.C. § 1983:

> Every person who, under color of any statute, ordinance, regulation, custom, or usage, of any State or Territory or the District of Columbia, subjects, or causes to be subjected, any citizen of the United States or other person within the jurisdiction thereof to the deprivation of any rights, privileges, or immunities secured by the Constitution and laws, shall be liable to the party injured in an action at law, suit in equity, or other proper proceeding for redress . . .

Note that three elements are common to all of these statutes. First, each statute specifies a class of wrongful acts; thus, FELA refers to "negligence"; the Clayton Act, to "anything forbidden in the antitrust laws"; section 1983, to "the deprivation of rights . . . secured by the Constitution and laws [of the United States]." Second, each statute authorizes a judicial proceeding or a judicially cognizable remedy. FELA provides for liability "in damages"; the Clayton Act creates a right to "sue" for injuries; section 1983 allows for liability "in an action at law, suit in equity, or other proper proceeding for redress." Third, each statute defines the class of persons who may bring suit. FELA creates a cause of action for any person who suffers injury while employed by an interstate railroad in interstate commerce. The Clayton Act authorizes suit by "any person injured in his business or property" by an antitrust violation. Section 1983 extends its remedy to "any citizen of the United States or other person within the jurisdiction thereof."

Sometimes a cause of action statute will also specify the class of defendants who may be sued. For example, a FELA claim may be brought only against a railroad engaging in interstate commerce. A section 1983 suit may be brought only against a "person" who acts "under color of" state law.

Other Acts of Congress make conduct wrongful without creating a private cause of action. The question is whether federal courts may fill the gap and, if so, under what circumstances. Over the years, the Court has taken different approaches to that question.

Note: The Rigsby Era

1. The Federal Employers Liability Act, quoted above, provides a cause of action for "any person suffering injury while he is employed by [the carrier] in [interstate] commerce." But suppose the person was injured while engaged in intrastate commerce. Or suppose that the person injured was a passenger on the train. Is a federal cause of action available to such plaintiffs?

Almost a century ago, in *Texas & Pacific Railway Co. v. Rigsby*, 241 U.S. 33 (1916), the Court considered a suit by a railroad worker who was injured in the course of his employment by the defendant railroad. The plaintiff's suit was "based on" the Federal Safety Appliance Act (FSAA), a federal statute that requires railroads to provide safe brakes and couplings. As the Court explained, the plaintiff's injury was "directly attributable to a defect in an appliance which, by the [FSAA as amended in 1910], was required to be secure."

The railroad argued that even if the FSAA covered the plaintiff's employment, an employee injured through a violation of the FSAA did not have a right of action "unless he was engaged in interstate commerce." The Supreme Court rejected the argument, saying:

> None of the [Safety Acts] contains express language conferring a right of action for the death or injury of an employee; but the safety of employees and travelers is their principal object, and the right of private action by an injured employee, even without the Employers' Liability Act, has never been doubted. [Here the Court cited numerous cases.] A disregard of the command of the statute is a wrongful act, and where it results in damage to one of the class for whose especial benefit the statute was enacted, the right to recover the damages from the party in default is implied, according to a doctrine of the common law expressed in 1 Comyn's Dig. title, "Action upon Statute" (f), in these words: "So, in every case, where a statute enacts or prohibits a thing for the benefit of a person, he shall have a remedy upon the same statute for the thing enacted for his advantage, or for the recompense of a wrong done to him contrary to the said law." (*Per* Holt, Ch. J., Anonymous, 6 Mod. 26, 27.) This is but an application of the maxim, *Ubi jus ibi remedium*.

2. The Court in *Rigsby* invoked "a doctrine of the common law." Could that rationale survive the decision in *Erie*?

3. The Court says that the "principal object" of the Safety Acts is "the safety of employees and *travelers*." Does this mean that the right of action recognized in *Rigsby* would also be available to passengers on interstate railroads? That might seem like a logical conclusion, but the courts never took the doctrine that far. *See, e.g., Jacobson v. New York, New Haven, & Hartford R. Co.*, 206 F.2d 153 (1st Cir. 1953).

4. Modern-day Justices have offered sharply divergent perspectives on *Rigsby*. At one end of the spectrum, Justice Stevens has treated *Rigsby* as a foundational case ratifying the authority of federal courts to recognize implied private remedies. Writing for the Court in *Merrill Lynch, Pierce, Fenner & Smith, Inc. v. Curran*, 456 U.S. 353 (1982), he said:

> When federal statutes were less comprehensive, the Court applied a relatively simple test to determine the availability of an implied private remedy. If a statute was enacted for the benefit of a special class, the judiciary normally recognized a remedy for members of that class. *Texas & Pacific R. Co. v. Rigsby*. Under this approach, federal courts, following a common-law tradition, regarded the denial of a remedy as the exception rather than the rule.

> Because the *Rigsby* approach prevailed throughout most of our history [here Justice Stevens cited *Marbury v. Madison*], there is no merit to the argument . . . that the judicial recognition of an implied private remedy violates the separation-of-powers doctrine. . . .

During the years prior to 1975, the Court occasionally refused to recognize an implied remedy, either because the statute in question was a general regulatory prohibition enacted for the benefit of the public at large, or because there was evidence that Congress intended an express remedy to provide the exclusive method of enforcement. While the *Rigsby* approach prevailed, however, congressional silence or ambiguity was an insufficient reason for the denial of a remedy for a member of the class a statute was enacted to protect.

In contrast, Justice Powell read *Rigsby* as a narrow decision on the standard of care applicable to a state tort action. In his dissent in *Cannon v. University of Chicago* [summarized in the Note *infra*], he said:

> The origin of implied private causes of actions in the federal courts is said to date back to *Texas & Pacific R. Co. v. Rigsby*. A close look at the facts of that case and the contemporary state of the law indicates, however, that *Rigsby*'s reference to the "inference of a private right of action," carried a far different connotation than the isolated passage quoted [above] might suggest. The narrow question presented for decision was whether the standards of care defined by the Federal Safety Appliance Act's penal provisions applied to a tort action brought against an interstate railroad by an employee not engaged in interstate commerce at the time of his injury. The jurisdiction of the federal courts was not in dispute, the action having been removed from state court on the ground that the defendant was a federal corporation. Under the regime of *Swift v. Tyson* then in force, the Court was free to create the substantive standards of liability applicable to a common-law negligence claim brought in federal court. The practice of judicial reference to legislatively determined standards of care was a common expedient to establish the existence of negligence. See Thayer, *Public Wrong and Private Action*, 27 HARV. L. REV. 317 (1914). *Rigsby* did nothing more than follow this practice, and cannot be taken as authority for the judicial creation of a cause of action not legislated by Congress.

A careful study of "the contemporary state of the law" at the time of *Rigsby* would be required to determine who has the better of this argument. But how important is it to establish a historical pedigree for the practice of implying private rights of action? Consider this question as you read the cases that follow.

J. I. Case Co. v. Borak

Supreme Court of the United States, 1964.

377 U.S. 426.

MR. JUSTICE CLARK delivered the opinion of the Court.

This is a civil action brought by respondent, a stockholder of petitioner J. I. Case Company, charging deprivation of the pre-emptive rights of respondent and other shareholders by reason by a merger between Case and the American Tractor Corporation. It is alleged that the merger was effected through the circulation of a false and misleading proxy statement by those proposing the merger. The complaint was in two counts, the first based on diversity and claiming a breach of the directors' fiduciary duty to the stockholders. The second count alleged a violation of § 14(a) of the Securities Exchange Act of 1934 with reference to the proxy solicitation material. [Section 14 makes it "unlawful" to solicit proxies in violation of rules prescribed by the Securities and Exchange Commission (SEC) for the protection of investors. The SEC's Rule 14a-9, promulgated under the authority of this section, prohibits the use of false or misleading statements in the solicitation of proxies.]

We consider only the question of whether § 27 of the Act authorizes a federal cause of action for rescission or damages to a corporate stockholder with respect to a consummated merger which was authorized pursuant to the use of a proxy statement alleged to contain false and misleading statements violative of § 14(a) of the Act. . . .

I.

[Respondent's complaint] alleged: that petitioners, or their predecessors, solicited or permitted their names to be used in the solicitation of proxies of Case stockholders for use at a special stockholders' meeting at which the proposed merger with ATC was to be voted upon; that the proxy solicitation material so circulated was false and misleading in violation of § 14(a) of the Act and Rule 14a-9 which the Commission had promulgated thereunder; that the merger was approved at the meeting by a small margin of votes and was thereafter consummated; that the merger would not have been approved but for the false and misleading statements in the proxy solicitation material; and that Case stockholders were damaged thereby. The respondent sought judgment holding the merger void and damages for himself and all other stockholders similarly situated, as well as such further relief "as equity shall require." [The Court of Appeals held that the district court had power under § 27 "to award damages or such other retrospective relief to the plaintiff as the merits of the controversy may require."]

II.

It appears clear that private parties have a right under § 27 to bring suit for violation of § 14(a) of the Act. Indeed, this section specifically grants the appropriate District Courts jurisdiction over "all suits in equity and actions at law brought to enforce any liability or duty created" under the Act. The petitioners make no concessions, however, emphasizing that Congress made no specific reference to a private right of action in § 14(a); that, in any event, the right would not extend to derivative suits and should be limited to prospective relief only. . . .

III.

While the respondent contends that his Count 2 claim is not a derivative one, we need not embrace that view, for we believe that a right of action exists as to both derivative and direct causes.

The purpose of § 14(a) is to prevent management or others from obtaining authorization for corporate action by means of deceptive or inadequate disclosure in proxy solicitation. . . . [The statute's] broad remedial purposes are evidenced in the language of the section which makes it "unlawful for any person * * * to solicit or to permit the use of his name to solicit any proxy or consent or authorization in respect of any security * * * registered on any national securities exchange in contravention of such rules and regulations as the Commission may prescribe as necessary or appropriate in the public interest *or for the protection of investors*." (Italics supplied.) While this language makes no specific reference to a private right of action, among its chief purposes is "the protection of investors," which certainly implies the availability of judicial relief where necessary to achieve that result.

The injury which a stockholder suffers from corporate action pursuant to a deceptive proxy solicitation ordinarily flows from the damage done the corporation, rather than from the damage inflicted directly upon the stockholder. The damage suffered results not from the deceit practiced on him alone but rather from the deceit practiced on the stockholders as a group. To hold that derivative actions are not within the sweep of the section would therefore be tantamount to a denial of private relief. Private enforcement of the proxy rules provides a necessary supplement to Commission action.

As in anti-trust treble damage litigation, the possibility of civil damages or injunctive relief serves as a most effective weapon in the enforcement of the proxy requirements. The Commission advises that it examines over 2,000 proxy statements annually and each of them must necessarily be expedited. Time does not permit an independent examination of the facts set out in the proxy material and this results in the Commission's acceptance of the representations contained therein at their face value, unless contrary to other material on file with it. Indeed, on the allegations of respondent's complaint, the proxy material failed to disclose alleged unlawful market manipulation of the stock of ATC, and this unlawful manipulation would not have been apparent to the Commission until after the merger.

We, therefore, believe that under the circumstances here it is the duty of the courts to be alert to provide such remedies as are necessary to make effective the congressional purpose. . . .

Affirmed.

Note: "To Make Effective the Congressional Purpose"

1. *Borak* represents the high-water mark of the Supreme Court's willingness to infer a private cause of action from a federal statute that does not explicitly provide for one. In contrast to *Rigsby*, the Court does not invoke "a doctrine of the common law"; rather, the Court looks to "the congressional purpose." Does this approach avoid any collision with the decision in *Erie*?

2. The Court acknowledges that § 14(a) of the 1934 Act "makes no specific reference to a private right of action," but it says that one of the chief purposes of the Act is "the protection of investors," and that this "certainly implies the availability of judicial relief where necessary to achieve that result." Assume that the Court is correct in identifying a chief purpose of the 1934 Act. Does the Court's conclusion follow?

3. In explaining why it recognizes a private cause of action for derivative claims by shareholders, the Court says: "Private enforcement of the proxy rules provides a necessary supplement to [SEC] action." If this is so, why didn't Congress itself provide for private enforcement? Why might Congress have foregone "a most effective weapon in the enforcement of the proxy requirements"?

4. The Court also says that the SEC does not have time to independently examine the facts set out in proxy materials; thus the agency misses some instances of "unlawful manipulation." The Court therefore concludes that private enforcement is "necessary to make effective the congressional purpose." How might one respond to this line of argument?

Note: Cort v. Ash *and the Four-Factor Test*

1. A decade after *Borak*, the Court began to pull back from the approach taken in that case. A key precedent in the development of the law was *Cort v. Ash*, 422 U.S. 66 (1975). In *Cort*, a federal criminal statute prohibited corporations from making campaign contributions in connection with a presidential election. The Third Circuit Court of Appeals, partly in reliance on *Borak*, held that a corporate shareholder has an implied cause of action for damages against corporate directors for violation of the statute. The Supreme Court reversed. In a unanimous opinion by Justice Brennan, the Court set forth a four-part test:

> In determining whether a private remedy is implicit in a statute not expressly providing one, several factors are relevant. First, is the plaintiff "one of the class for whose *especial* benefit the statute was enacted," *Rigsby*, (emphasis supplied)—that is, does the statute create a federal right in favor of the plaintiff? Second, is there any indication of legislative intent, explicit or implicit, either to create such a remedy or to deny one? Third, is it consistent with the underlying purposes of the legislative scheme to imply such a remedy for the plaintiff? And finally, is the cause of action one traditionally relegated to state law, in an area basically the concern of the States, so that it would be inappropriate to infer a cause of action based solely on federal law?

Is this an improvement over the approach taken in *Borak*?

2. The Court applied the four-factor test in *Cannon v. University of Chicago*, 441 U.S. 677 (1979), to determine whether Title IX of the Education Amendments of 1972 supports a private cause of action. Title IX provides: "No person . . . shall, on the basis of sex, be excluded from participation in, be denied the benefits of, or be subjected to discrimination under any education program or activity receiving Federal financial assistance." Applying the four factors identified in *Cort*, the Court concluded that Title IX did support a private right of action.

Regarding the first factor—whether the plaintiff is "one of the class for whose *especial* benefit the statute was enacted"—the Court noted that Title IX had not been written "simply as a ban on discriminatory conduct by recipients of federal funds or as a prohibition against the disbursement of public funds to educational institutions engaged in discriminatory practices." Instead, "Title IX explicitly confers a benefit on persons discriminated against on the basis of sex, and petitioner is clearly a member of that class for whose special benefit the statute was enacted."

Regarding the second factor—whether there is any indication of legislative intent to create or deny a remedy—the Court concluded that "the history of Title IX rather plainly indicates that Congress intended to create such a remedy." The Court explained:

> Title IX was patterned after Title VI of the Civil Rights Act of 1964. Except for the substitution of the word "sex" in Title IX to replace the words "race, color, or national origin" in Title VI, the two statutes use identical language to describe the benefited class. . . . Neither statute expressly mentions a private remedy for the person excluded from participation in a federally funded program. The drafters of Title IX explicitly assumed that it would be interpreted and applied as Title VI had been during the preceding eight years.

> In 1972 when Title IX was enacted, the critical language in Title VI had already been construed [by lower courts] as creating a private remedy. . . . It was *after* 1972 that this Court decided *Cort v. Ash* and the other cases cited by the Court of Appeals in support of its strict construction of the remedial aspect of the statute. We, of course, adhere to the strict approach followed in our recent cases, but our evaluation of congressional action in 1972 must take into account its contemporary legal context.

As for the third factor—whether implying a remedy is consistent with the underlying purposes of the legislative scheme—the Court identified two interests underlying Title IX: to avoid the use of federal resources to support discriminatory practices, and to provide individual citizens effective protection against those practices. According to the Court, recognizing a private action would serve both interests:

> The first purpose is generally served by the statutory procedure for the termination of federal financial support for institutions engaged in discriminatory practices. That remedy is, however, severe and often may not provide an appropriate means of accomplishing the second purpose if merely an isolated violation has occurred. In that situation, the violation might be remedied more efficiently by an order requiring an institution to accept an applicant who had been improperly excluded. Moreover, in that kind of situation it makes little sense to impose on an individual, whose only interest is in obtaining a benefit for herself . . . the burden of demonstrating that an institution's practices are so pervasively discriminatory that a complete cut-off of federal funding is appropriate. The award of individual relief to a private litigant who has prosecuted her own suit is not only sensible but is also fully consistent with—and in some cases even necessary to—the orderly enforcement of the statute. . . .

Addressing the fourth factor—whether the subject matter involves an area traditionally relegated to state law—the Court concluded that preventing discrimination on the basis of sex is a matter of federal concern. The Court wrote:

> Since the Civil War, the Federal Government and the federal courts have been the "'*primary* and powerful reliances'" in protecting citizens against such discrimination. Moreover, it is the expenditure of federal funds that provides the justification for this particular statutory prohibition.

The Court accordingly concluded that all of the *Cort* factors supported "implication of a cause of action in favor of private victims of discrimination."

3. Justice Powell dissented in *Cannon*. He launched a broadside attack on "judicial implication of private causes of action," writing:

> *Cort* allows the Judicial Branch to assume policymaking authority vested by the Constitution in the Legislative Branch. It also invites Congress to avoid resolution of the often controversial question whether a new regulatory statute should be enforced through private litigation. Rather than confronting the hard political choices involved, Congress is encouraged to shirk its constitutional obligation and leave the issue to the courts to decide. When this happens, the legislative process with its public scrutiny and participation has been bypassed, with attendant prejudice to everyone concerned. Because the courts are free to reach a result different from that which the normal play of political forces would have produced, the intended beneficiaries of the legislation are unable to ensure the full measure of protection their needs may warrant. For the same reason, those subject to the legislative constraints are denied the opportunity to forestall through the political process potentially unnecessary and disruptive litigation. Moreover, the public generally is denied the benefits that are derived from the making of important societal choices through the open debate of the democratic process.

How persuasive are Justice Powell's arguments?

4. In *Borak*, the Court said that private enforcement is "a most effective weapon" in the enforcement of the requirements Congress has imposed. In his dissent in *Cannon*, Justice Powell disputed the benefits of broader enforcement through private actions. In his view, recognizing private actions not conferred by Congress raises the threat of overenforcement. He noted that the defendants in *Cannon* had "been forced to use their scarce resources to defend against this suit at three levels of our federal judicial system, and in light of the Court's holding today they must contend with at least one more round of proceedings." How persuasive is this argument?

5. In its 2003–2004 sessions, Congress considered legislation that would prohibit insurance companies and employers from discriminating on the basis of a person's genetic makeup. One such measure "sailed through the Senate . . . by a 95-0 vote after concessions were made to the U.S. Chamber of Commerce and a coalition of other business lobbies on remedies and penalties." *CongressDaily*, July 19, 2004. Does this suggest an additional argument in support of Justice Powell's position? (The measure, in different form, became law in 2008.)

Note: From Cannon *to* Sandoval

1. Although no other member of the Court joined Justice Powell's dissent in *Cannon*, later decisions moved toward his position. Only a few weeks after *Cannon*, in *Touche Ross & Co. v. Redington*, 442 U.S. 560 (1979), the Court considered "whether customers of securities brokerage firms that are required to file certain financial reports with regulatory authorities by § 17(a) of the Securities Exchange Act of 1934 have an implied cause of action for damages under § 17(a) against accountants who audit such reports, based on misstatements contained in the reports." The court of appeals, applying the four-factor test of *Cort v. Ash*, held in favor of the plaintiffs, but the Supreme Court reversed. Justice Rehnquist, writing for the Court, said:

> It is true that in *Cort v. Ash* the Court set forth four factors that it considered "relevant" in determining whether a private remedy is implicit in a statute not expressly providing one. But the Court did not decide that each of these factors is entitled to equal weight. The central inquiry remains whether Congress intended to create, either expressly or by implication, a private cause of action. Indeed, the first three factors discussed in *Cort*—the language and focus of the statute, its legislative history, and its purpose—are ones traditionally relied upon in determining legislative intent.
>
> Here, the statute by its terms grants no private rights to any identifiable class and proscribes no conduct as unlawful. And the parties as well as the Court of Appeals agree that the legislative history of the 1934 Act simply does not speak to the issue of private remedies under § 17(a). At least in such a case as this, the inquiry ends there: The question whether Congress, either expressly or by implication, intended to create a private right of action, has been definitely answered in the negative.

Only Justice Marshall dissented. (Ironically, Justice Powell took no part in the decision of the case because of illness.)

2. *Touche Ross* strongly implies that when a statute "by its terms grants no private rights to any identifiable class and proscribes no conduct as unlawful," the Court will not create an implied right of action. But suppose that a statute does make certain conduct unlawful. Might the Court still be willing to recognize an implied right of action?

In *Transamerica Mortgage Advisers, Inc. (TAMA) v. Lewis*, 444 U.S. 11 (1979), decided a few months after *Touche Ross*, the Court considered a claim invoking the Investment Advisers Act of 1940. Section 206 of the Act broadly proscribes fraudulent practices by investment advisers, making it unlawful for any investment adviser "to employ any device, scheme, or artifice to defraud . . . [or] to engage in any transaction, practice, or course of business which operates as a fraud or deceit upon any client or prospective client," or to engage in specified transactions with clients without making required disclosures. Section 215 of the Act provides that contracts whose formation or performance would violate the Act "shall be void . . . as regards the rights of" the violator and knowing successors in interest.

Based on the language of section 215, the Court held that the plaintiff could maintain an action to void a contract that violated the Act. But the Court refused to allow a claim for damages or other monetary relief. The Court said:

> Unlike § 215, § 206 simply proscribes certain conduct, and does not in terms create or alter any civil liabilities. If monetary liability to a private plaintiff is to be found, it must be read into the Act. Yet it is an elemental canon of statutory construction that where a statute expressly provides a particular remedy or remedies, a court must be chary of reading others into it.

The plaintiff, the SEC, and a dissenting opinion joined by four Justices relied on *Cort v. Ash*, but the Court looked instead to *Touche Ross*:

> We rejected the same contentions last Term in *Touche Ross*. . . . The statute in *Touche Ross* by its terms neither granted private rights to the members of any identifiable class, nor proscribed any conduct as unlawful. In those circumstances it was evident to the Court that no private remedy was available. Section 206 of the Act here involved concededly was intended to protect the victims of the fraudulent practices it prohibited. But the mere fact that the statute was designed to protect advisers' clients does not require the implication of a private cause of action for damages on their behalf. The dispositive question remains whether Congress intended to create any such remedy. Having answered that question in the negative, our inquiry is at an end.

3. You might think that *TAMA* marked the end of the line for implied private rights of action, but it did not. In *Merrill Lynch, Pierce, Fenner & Smith, Inc. v. Curran*, 456 U.S. 353 (1982), the Court held that a private party may maintain an action for damages for violation of the Commodity Exchange Act (CEA). The Court relied primarily on the fact that Congress amended the CEA in 1974, after several lower federal courts had recognized an implied cause of action under the statute. In an opinion by Justice Stevens for a bare majority, the Court said:

> Our cases subsequent to *Cort v. Ash* have plainly stated that our focus must be on "the intent of Congress." The key to [this case] is our understanding of the intent of Congress in 1974 when it comprehensively reexamined and strengthened the federal regulation of futures trading.
>
> In determining whether a private cause of action is implicit in a federal statutory scheme when the statute by its terms is silent on that issue, the initial focus must be on the state of the law at the time the legislation was enacted. More precisely, we must examine Congress' perception of the law that it was shaping or reshaping. When Congress enacts new legislation, the question is whether Congress intended to create a private remedy as a supplement to the express enforcement provisions of the statute. When Congress acts in a statutory context in which an implied private remedy has already been recognized by the courts, however, the inquiry logically is different. Congress need not have intended to create a new remedy, since one already existed; the question is whether Congress intended to preserve the pre-existing remedy. . . .

Prior to the comprehensive amendments to the CEA enacted in 1974, the federal courts routinely and consistently had recognized an implied private cause of action on behalf of plaintiffs seeking to enforce and to collect damages for violation of provisions of the CEA or rules and regulations promulgated pursuant to the statute.

In view of the absence of any dispute about the proposition prior to the decision of *Cort v. Ash* in 1975, it is abundantly clear that an implied cause of action under the CEA was a part of the "contemporary legal context" in which Congress legislated in 1974. *Cf. Cannon.* In that context, the fact that a comprehensive reexamination and significant amendment of the CEA left intact the statutory provisions under which the federal courts had implied a cause of action is itself evidence that Congress affirmatively intended to preserve that remedy. A review of the legislative history of the statute persuasively indicates that preservation of the remedy was indeed what Congress actually intended.

Four dissenters, in an opinion by Justice Powell, emphatically rejected this approach:

First, the Court relies on fewer than a dozen cases in which the lower federal courts *erroneously* upheld private rights of action in the years prior to the 1974 amendments to the CEA. Reasoning that these mistaken decisions constituted "the law" in 1974, the Court holds that Congress must be assumed to have endorsed this path of error when it *failed to amend* certain sections of the CEA in that year. This theory is incompatible with our constitutional separation of powers, and in my view it is without support in logic or in law. Additionally—whether alternatively or cumulatively is unclear—the Court finds that Congress in 1974 "affirmatively" manifested its intent to "preserve" private rights of action by adopting particular amendments to the CEA. This finding is reached without even token deference to established tests for discerning congressional intent.

4. At some point an implied right of action can become sufficiently well established that it will be accepted even by those who oppose the concept. In *Herman & MacLean v. Huddleston*, 459 U.S. 375 (1983), the Court reiterated its approval of the implied private right of action under § 10(b) of the 1934 Securities Act and the SEC rule that implements it, Rule 10b-5. The statute and rule prohibit fraud in connection with the purchase and sale of securities.

The right of action under § 10(b) was first recognized by a federal district court in 1946. By 1969, it had been accepted by ten of the eleven federal courts of appeals. The Supreme Court itself, in a footnote in a 1971 decision, had said, "It is now established that a private right of action is implied under § 10(b)."

In *Huddleston*, the Court summarized this history and concluded: "The existence of this implied remedy is simply beyond peradventure." The opinion was unanimous. Although Justice Powell did not participate, he accepted the outcome. *See* A.C. Pritchard, *Justice Lewis F. Powell, Jr., and the Counterrevolution in the Federal Securities Laws*, 52 DUKE L.J. 841, 890–91 (2003).

5. In *Cort*, the Court made clear that Congress's intent in enacting a statute dictates whether the court should infer a private cause of action. In *Cannon*, the Court stated that, in ascertaining Congress's intent, it would consider the contemporary legal context under which Congress enacted the statute. Thus, the Court inferred a private right of action under Title IX because its text was nearly identical to statutory text that courts had previously interpreted to create a private right of action. Should courts consider contemporary legal context in evaluating Congress's intent, or should they limit their inquiry to the text and structure of the statute in question? In answering that question, consider the next case.

Alexander v. Sandoval

Supreme Court of the United States, 2001.

532 U.S. 275.

JUSTICE SCALIA delivered the opinion of the Court.

This case presents the question whether private individuals may sue to enforce disparate-impact regulations promulgated under Title VI of the Civil Rights Act of 1964.

I

The Alabama Department of Public Safety (Department), of which petitioner James Alexander is the director, accepted grants of financial assistance from the United States Department of Justice (DOJ) and Department of Transportation (DOT) and so subjected itself to the restrictions of Title VI of the Civil Rights Act of 1964. Section 601 of that Title provides that no person shall, "on the ground of race, color, or national origin, be excluded from participation in, be denied the benefits of, or be subjected to discrimination under any program or activity" covered by Title VI. Section 602 authorizes federal agencies "to effectuate the provisions of [§ 601] . . . by issuing rules, regulations, or orders of general applicability," and the DOJ in an exercise of this authority promulgated a regulation forbidding funding recipients to "utilize criteria or methods of administration which have the effect of subjecting individuals to discrimination because of their race, color, or national origin. . . ."

The State of Alabama amended its Constitution in 1990 to declare English "the official language of the state of Alabama." Pursuant to this provision and, petitioners have argued, to advance public safety, the Department decided to administer state driver's license examinations only in English. Respondent Sandoval, as representative of a class, brought suit in the United States District Court for the Middle District of Alabama to enjoin the English-only policy, arguing that it violated the DOJ regulation because it had the effect of subjecting non-English speakers to discrimination based on their national origin. The District Court agreed. It enjoined the policy and ordered the Department to accommodate non-English speakers. Petitioners appealed to the Court of Appeals for the Eleventh Circuit, which affirmed. Both courts rejected petitioners' argument that Title VI did not provide respondents a cause of action to enforce the regulation.

We do not inquire here whether the DOJ regulation was authorized by § 602, or whether the courts below were correct to hold that the English-only policy had the effect of discriminating on the basis of national origin. The petition for writ of certiorari raised, and we agreed to review, only the question posed in the first paragraph of this opinion: whether there is a private cause of action to enforce the regulation.

II

Although Title VI has often come to this Court, it is fair to say (indeed, perhaps an understatement) that our opinions have not eliminated all uncertainty regarding its commands. For purposes of the present case, however, it is clear from our decisions, from Congress's amendments of Title VI, and from the parties' concessions that three aspects of Title VI must be taken as given. First, private individuals may sue to enforce § 601 of Title VI and obtain both injunctive relief and damages. In *Cannon v. University of Chicago*, 441 U.S. 677 (1979), the Court held that a private right of action existed to enforce Title IX of the Education Amendments of 1972. The reasoning of that decision embraced the existence of a private right to enforce Title VI as well. . . . Congress has since ratified *Cannon's* holding. It is thus beyond dispute that private individuals may sue to enforce § 601.

Second, it is similarly beyond dispute—and no party disagrees—that § 601 prohibits only intentional discrimination. [The Court cited *Regents of Univ. of Cal. v. Bakke*, 438 U.S. 265 (1978), and *Guardians Assn. v. Civil Serv. Comm'n of New York City*, 463 U.S. 582 (1983).]

Third, we must assume for purposes of deciding this case that regulations promulgated under § 602 of Title VI may validly proscribe activities that have a disparate impact on racial groups, even though such activities are permissible under § 601. Though no opinion of this Court has held that, five Justices in *Guardians* voiced that view of the law at least as alternative grounds for their decisions, and dictum in *Alexander v. Choate*, 469 U.S. 287 (1985), is to the same effect. These statements are in considerable tension with the rule of *Bakke* and *Guardians* that § 601 forbids only intentional discrimination, but petitioners have not challenged the regulations here. We therefore assume for the purposes of deciding this case that the DOJ and DOT regulations proscribing activities that have a disparate impact on the basis of race are valid.

Respondents assert that the issue in this case, like the first two described above, has been resolved by our cases. [The Court rejected this interpretation of its precedents, including *Lau v. Nichols*, 414 U.S. 563 (1974).]

We must face now the question avoided by *Lau*, because we have since rejected *Lau's* interpretation of § 601 as reaching beyond intentional discrimination. It is clear now that the disparate-impact regulations do not simply apply § 601—since they indeed forbid conduct that § 601 permits—and therefore clear that the private right of action to enforce § 601 does not include a private right to enforce these regulations. [As we said in *Bank of Denver, N.A. v. First Interstate Bank of Denver, N.A.*, 511 U.S. 164, 173 (1994),] a "private plaintiff may not bring a [suit based on a regulation] against a defendant for acts not prohibited by the text of [the statute]." [The private right of action] must come, if at all, from the independent force of § 602. As stated earlier, we assume for purposes of this decision that § 602 confers the authority to promulgate disparate-impact regulations; the question remains whether it confers a private right of action to enforce them. If not, we must conclude that a failure to comply with regulations promulgated under § 602 that is not also a failure to comply with § 601 is not actionable.

Implicit in our discussion thus far has been a particular understanding of the genesis of private causes of action. Like substantive federal law itself, private rights of action to enforce federal law must be created by Congress. *Touche Ross & Co. v. Redington*, 442 U.S. 560, 578 (1979) (remedies available are those "that Congress enacted into law"). The judicial task is to interpret the statute Congress has passed to determine whether it displays an intent to create not just a private right but also a private remedy. *Transamerica Mortgage Advisors, Inc. v. Lewis*, 444 U.S. 11, 15 (1979). Statutory intent on this latter point is determinative. Without it, a cause of action does not exist and courts may not create one, no matter how desirable that might be as a policy matter, or how compatible with the statute. "Raising up causes of action where a statute has not created them may be a proper function for common-law courts, but not for federal tribunals."

Respondents would have us revert in this case to the understanding of private causes of action that held sway 40 years ago when Title VI was enacted. That understanding is captured by the Court's statement in *J.I. Case Co. v. Borak*, 377 U.S. 426, 433 (1964), that "it is the duty of the courts to be alert to provide such remedies as are necessary to make effective the congressional purpose" expressed by a statute. We abandoned that understanding in *Cort v. Ash*, 422 U.S. 66, 78 (1975)—which itself interpreted a statute enacted under the *ancien regime*—and have not returned to it since. Not even when interpreting the same Securities Exchange Act of 1934 that was at issue in *Borak* have we applied *Borak's* method for discerning and defining causes of action. [*E.g.,*] *Touche Ross*. Having sworn off the habit of venturing beyond Congress's intent, we will not accept respondents' invitation to have one last drink.

Nor do we agree with the Government that our cases interpreting statutes enacted prior to *Cort v. Ash* have given "dispositive weight" to the "expectations" that the enacting Congress had formed "in light of the 'contemporary legal context.'" Only three of our legion of implied-right-of-action cases have found this sort of "contemporary legal context" relevant, and two of those involved Congress's enactment (or reenactment) of the verbatim statutory text that courts had previously interpreted to create a private right of action. See *Merrill Lynch, Pierce, Fenner & Smith, Inc. v. Curran*, 456 U.S. 353 (1982); *Cannon v. University of Chicago*. In the third case, this sort of "contemporary legal context" simply buttressed a conclusion independently supported by the text of the statute. See *Thompson v. Thompson*, 484 U.S. 174 (1988). We have never accorded dispositive weight to context shorn of text. In determining whether statutes create private rights of action, as in interpreting statutes generally, legal context matters only to the extent it clarifies text.

We therefore begin (and find that we can end) our search for Congress's intent with the text and structure of Title VI.[7] Section 602 authorizes federal agencies "to effectuate the provisions of [§ 601] . . . by issuing rules, regulations, or orders of general applicability." It is immediately clear that the "rights-creating" language so critical to the Court's analysis in *Cannon* of § 601 is completely absent from § 602. Whereas § 601 decrees that "[n]o person . . . shall . . . be subjected to discrimination," the text of § 602 provides that "[e]ach Federal department and agency . . . is authorized and directed to effectuate the provisions of [§ 601]."

Far from displaying congressional intent to create new rights, § 602 limits agencies to "effectuat[ing]" rights already created by § 601. And the focus of § 602 is twice removed from the individuals who will ultimately benefit from Title VI's protection. Statutes that focus on the person regulated rather than the individuals protected create "no implication of an intent to confer rights on a particular class of persons." *California v. Sierra Club*, 451 U.S. 287, 294 (1981). Section 602 is yet a step further removed: It focuses neither on the individuals protected nor even on the funding recipients being regulated, but on the agencies that will do the regulating. Like the statute found not to create a right of action in *Universities Research Assn., Inc. v. Coutu*, 450 U.S. 754 (1981), § 602 is "phrased as a directive to federal agencies engaged in the distribution of public funds." When this is true, "[t]here [is] far less reason to infer a private remedy in favor of individual persons." *Cannon.* So far as we can tell, this authorizing portion of § 602 reveals no congressional intent to create a private right of action.

Nor do the methods that § 602 goes on to provide for enforcing its authorized regulations manifest an intent to create a private remedy; if anything, they suggest the opposite. Section 602 empowers agencies to enforce their regulations either by terminating funding to the "particular program, or part thereof," that has violated the regulation or "by any other means authorized by law." No enforcement action may be taken, however, "until the department or agency concerned has advised the appropriate person or persons of the failure to comply with the requirement and has determined that compliance cannot be secured by voluntary means." And every agency enforcement action is subject to judicial review. If an agency attempts to terminate program funding, still more restrictions apply. . . .

Whatever these elaborate restrictions on agency enforcement may imply for the private enforcement of rights created *outside* of § 602, . . . they tend to contradict a congressional intent to create privately enforceable rights through § 602 itself. The express provision of one method of enforcing a substantive rule suggests that Congress intended to preclude others. *See, e.g., TAMA v. Lewis.* Sometimes the suggestion is so strong that it precludes a finding of congressional intent to create a private right of

---

7. Although the dissent claims that we "adop[t] a methodology that blinds itself to important evidence of congressional intent," our methodology is not novel, but well established in earlier decisions (including one authored by Justice Stevens, see *Northwest Airlines, Inc. v. Transport Workers*, 451 U.S. 77, 94 n.31 (1981)), which explain that the interpretive inquiry begins with the text and structure of the statute, and ends once it has become clear that Congress did not provide a cause of action.

action, even though other aspects of the statute (such as language making the would-be plaintiff "a member of the class for whose benefit the statute was enacted") suggest the contrary. And as our 42 U.S.C. § 1983 cases show, some remedial schemes foreclose a private cause of action to enforce even those statutes that admittedly create substantive private rights. *See, e.g., Middlesex County Sewerage Authority v. National Sea Clammers Assn.*, 453 U.S. 1, 19–20 (1981).

In the present case, the claim of exclusivity for the express remedial scheme does not even have to overcome such obstacles. The question whether § 602's remedial scheme can overbear other evidence of congressional intent is simply not presented, since we have found no evidence anywhere in the text to suggest that Congress intended to create a private right to enforce regulations promulgated under § 602.

Both the Government and respondents argue that the *regulations* contain rights-creating language and so must be privately enforceable, but that argument skips an analytical step. Language in a regulation may invoke a private right of action that Congress through statutory text created, but it may not create a right that Congress has not. Thus, when a statute has provided a general authorization for private enforcement of regulations, it may perhaps be correct that the intent displayed in each regulation can determine whether or not it is privately enforceable. But it is most certainly incorrect to say that language in a regulation can conjure up a private cause of action that has not been authorized by Congress. Agencies may play the sorcerer's apprentice but not the sorcerer himself.

The last string to respondents' and the Government's bow is their argument that two amendments to Title VI [in 1986 and 1987] "ratified" this Court's decisions finding an implied private right of action to enforce the disparate-impact regulations. One problem with this argument is that, as explained above, none of our decisions establishes (or even assumes) the private right of action at issue here. . . . Incorporating our cases in the amendments would thus not help respondents. . . .

Respondents point to *Merrill Lynch, Pierce, Fenner & Smith, Inc. v. Curran*, which inferred congressional intent to ratify lower court decisions regarding a particular statutory provision when Congress comprehensively revised the statutory scheme but did not amend that provision. But we recently criticized *Curran's* reliance on congressional inaction, saying that "[a]s a general matter . . . [the] argumen[t] deserve[s] little weight in the interpretive process." *Central Bank of Denver, N.A. v. First Interstate Bank of Denver, N.A.* And when, as here, Congress has not comprehensively revised a statutory scheme but has made only isolated amendments, we have spoken more bluntly: "It is 'impossible to assert with any degree of assurance that congressional failure to act represents' affirmative congressional approval of the Court's statutory interpretation."

Neither as originally enacted nor as later amended does Title VI display an intent to create a freestanding private right of action to enforce regulations promulgated under § 602.[8] We therefore hold that no such right of action exists. . . .

---

8. The dissent complains that we "offe[r] little affirmative support" for this conclusion. But as Justice Stevens has previously recognized in an opinion for the Court, "affirmative" evidence of

The judgment of the Court of Appeals is reversed.

JUSTICE STEVENS, with whom JUSTICE SOUTER, JUSTICE GINSBURG, and JUSTICE BREYER join, dissenting.

In 1964, as part of a groundbreaking and comprehensive civil rights Act, Congress prohibited recipients of federal funds from discriminating on the basis of race, ethnicity, or national origin. Pursuant to powers expressly delegated by that Act, the federal agencies and departments responsible for awarding and administering federal contracts immediately adopted regulations prohibiting federal contractees from adopting policies that have the "effect" of discriminating on those bases. At the time of the promulgation of these regulations, prevailing principles of statutory construction assumed that Congress intended a private right of action whenever such a cause of action was necessary to protect individual rights granted by valid federal law. Relying both on this presumption and on independent analysis of Title VI, this Court has repeatedly and consistently affirmed the right of private individuals to bring civil suits to enforce rights guaranteed by Title VI. A fair reading of those cases, and coherent implementation of the statutory scheme, requires the same result under Title VI's implementing regulations.

In separate lawsuits spanning several decades, we have endorsed an action identical in substance to the one brought in this case, see *Lau v. Nichols*, 414 U.S. 563 (1974); demonstrated that Congress intended a private right of action to protect the rights guaranteed by Title VI, see *Cannon v. University of Chicago*, 441 U.S. 677 (1979); and concluded that private individuals may seek declaratory and injunctive relief against state officials for violations of regulations promulgated pursuant to Title VI, see *Guardians Assn. v. Civil Serv. Comm'n of New York City*, 463 U.S. 582 (1983). Giving fair import to our language and our holdings, every Court of Appeals to address the question has concluded that a private right of action exists to enforce the rights guaranteed both by the text of Title VI and by any regulations validly promulgated pursuant to that Title, and Congress has adopted several statutes that appear to ratify the status quo.

Today, in a decision unfounded in our precedent and hostile to decades of settled expectations, a majority of this Court carves out an important exception to the right of private action long recognized under Title VI. In so doing, the Court makes three distinct, albeit interrelated, errors. First, the Court provides a muddled account of both the reasoning and the breadth of our prior decisions endorsing a private right of action under Title VI, thereby obscuring the conflict between those opinions and today's decision. Second, the Court offers a flawed and unconvincing analysis of the relationship between §§ 601 and 602 of the Civil Rights Act of 1964, ignoring more plausible and persuasive explanations detailed in our prior opinions. Finally, the Court badly misconstrues the theoretical linchpin of our decision in *Cannon v. University of Chicago*,

---

congressional intent must be provided *for* an implied remedy, not against it, for without such intent "the essential predicate for implication of a private remedy simply does not exist," *Northwest Airlines, Inc. . . .*

441 U.S. 677 (1979), mistaking that decision's careful contextual analysis for judicial fiat.

[In Parts I and II of his dissent, Justice Stevens reviewed the Court's Title VI precedents at length.]

III

The majority couples its flawed analysis of the structure of Title VI with an uncharitable understanding of the substance of the divide between those on this Court who are reluctant to interpret statutes to allow for private rights of action and those who are willing to do so if the claim of right survives a rigorous application of the criteria set forth in *Cort v. Ash*, 422 U.S. 66 (1975). As the majority narrates our implied right of action jurisprudence, the Court's shift to a more skeptical approach represents the rejection of a common-law judicial activism in favor of a principled recognition of the limited role of a contemporary "federal tribuna[l]." According to its analysis, the recognition of an implied right of action when the text and structure of the statute do not absolutely compel such a conclusion is an act of judicial self-indulgence. As much as we would like to help those disadvantaged by discrimination, we must resist the temptation to pour ourselves "one last drink." To do otherwise would be to "ventur[e] beyond Congress's intent."

Overwrought imagery aside, it is the majority's approach that blinds itself to congressional intent. While it remains true that, if Congress intends a private right of action to support statutory rights, "the far better course is for it to specify as much when it creates those rights," *Cannon*, its failure to do so does not absolve us of the responsibility to endeavor to discern its intent. In a series of cases since *Cort v. Ash*, we have laid out rules and developed strategies for this task.

The very existence of these rules and strategies assumes that we will sometimes find manifestations of an implicit intent to create such a right. Our decision in *Cannon* represents one such occasion. As the *Cannon* opinion iterated and reiterated, the question whether the plaintiff had a right of action that could be asserted in federal court was a "question of statutory construction," not a question of policy for the Court to decide. Applying the *Cort v. Ash* factors, we examined the nature of the rights at issue, the text and structure of the statute, and the relevant legislative history.[21] Our conclusion was that Congress unmistakably intended a private right of action to enforce both Title IX and Title VI. Our reasoning—and, as I have demonstrated, our holding—was equally applicable to intentional discrimination and disparate-impact claims.[22]

---

21. The text of the statute contained "an unmistakable focus on the benefited class," its legislative history "rather plainly indicates that Congress intended to create such a remedy," the legislators' repeated references to private enforcement of Title VI reflected "their intent with respect to Title IX," and the absence of legislative action to change the prevailing view with respect to Title VI left us with "no doubt that Congress intended to create Title IX remedies comparable to those available under Title VI and that it understood Title VI as authorizing an implied private cause of action for victims of prohibited discrimination."

22. We should not overlook the fact that *Cannon* was decided after the *Bakke* majority had concluded that the coverage of Title VI was co-extensive with the coverage of the Equal Protection Clause.

Underlying today's opinion is the conviction that *Cannon* must be cabined because it exemplifies an "expansive rights-creating approach." *Franklin v. Gwinnett County Public Schools*, 503 U.S. 60, 77 (1992) (Scalia, J., concurring in judgment). But, as I have taken pains to explain, it was Congress, not the Court, that created the cause of action, and it was the Congress that later ratified the *Cannon* holding in 1986 and again in 1988.

In order to impose its own preferences as to the availability of judicial remedies, the Court today adopts a methodology that blinds itself to important evidence of congressional intent. It is one thing for the Court to ignore the import of our holding in *Cannon*, as the breadth of that precedent is a matter upon which reasonable jurists may differ. It is entirely another thing for the majority to ignore the reasoning of that opinion and the evidence contained therein, as those arguments and that evidence speak directly to the question at issue today. . . . *Cannon* carefully explained that both Title VI and Title IX were intended to benefit a particular class of individuals, that the purposes of the statutes would be furthered rather than frustrated by the implication of a private right of action, and that the legislative histories of the statutes support the conclusion that Congress intended such a right. Those conclusions and the evidence supporting them continue to have force today.

Similarly, if the majority is genuinely committed to deciphering congressional intent, its unwillingness to even consider evidence as to the context in which Congress legislated is perplexing. Congress does not legislate in a vacuum. As the respondents and the Government suggest, and as we have held several times, the objective manifestations of congressional intent to create a private right of action must be measured in light of the enacting Congress' expectations as to how the judiciary might evaluate the question.

At the time Congress was considering Title VI, it was normal practice for the courts to infer that Congress intended a private right of action whenever it passed a statute designed to protect a particular class that did not contain enforcement mechanisms which would be thwarted by a private remedy. See *Merrill Lynch* (discussing this history). Indeed, the very year Congress adopted Title VI, this Court specifically stated that "it is the duty of the courts to be alert to provide such remedies as are necessary to make effective the congressional purpose." *J.I. Case Co. v. Borak*, 377 U.S. 426 (1964). Assuming, as we must, that Congress was fully informed as to the state of the law, the contemporary context presents important evidence as to Congress' intent—evidence the majority declines to consider.

Ultimately, respect for Congress' prerogatives is measured in deeds, not words. Today, the Court coins a new rule, holding that a private cause of action to enforce a statute does not encompass a substantive regulation issued to effectuate that statute unless the regulation does nothing more than "authoritatively construe the statute itself." This rule might be proper if we were the kind of "common-law court" the majority decries, inventing private rights of action never intended by Congress. For if we are not construing a statute, we certainly may refuse to create a remedy for violations of federal regulations. But if we are faithful to the commitment to discerning congressional intent that all Members of this Court profess, the distinction is untenable. There is simply no reason to assume that Congress contemplated, desired, or adopted a distinction between regulations that merely parrot statutory text and broader regulations that are authorized by statutory text.

IV

Beyond its flawed structural analysis of Title VI and an evident antipathy toward implied rights of action, the majority offers little affirmative support for its conclusion that Congress did not intend to create a private remedy for violations of the Title VI regulations. The Court offers essentially two reasons for its position. First, it attaches significance to the fact that the "rights-creating" language in § 601 that defines the classes protected by the statute is not repeated in § 602. But, of course, there was no reason to put that language in § 602 because it is perfectly obvious that the regulations authorized by § 602 must be designed to protect precisely the same people protected by § 601. Moreover, it is self-evident that, linguistic niceties notwithstanding, any statutory provision whose stated purpose is to "effectuate" the eradication of racial and ethnic discrimination has as its "focus" those individuals who, absent such legislation, would be subject to discrimination.

Second, the Court repeats the argument advanced and rejected in *Cannon* that the express provision of a fund cutoff remedy "suggests that Congress intended to preclude others." In *Cannon*, we carefully explained why the presence of an explicit mechanism to achieve one of the statute's objectives (ensuring that federal funds are not used "to support discriminatory practices") does not preclude a conclusion that a private right of action was intended to achieve the statute's other principal objective ("to provide individual citizens effective protection against those practices"). In support of our analysis, we offered policy arguments, cited evidence from the legislative history, and noted the active support of the relevant agencies. In today's decision, the Court does not grapple with—indeed, barely acknowledges—our rejection of this argument in *Cannon*.

Like much else in its opinion, the present majority's unwillingness to explain its refusal to find the reasoning in *Cannon* persuasive suggests that today's decision is the unconscious product of the majority's profound distaste for implied causes of action rather than an attempt to discern the intent of the Congress that enacted Title VI of the Civil Rights Act of 1964. Its colorful disclaimer of any interest in "venturing beyond Congress's intent" has a hollow ring.

V

The question the Court answers today was only an open question in the most technical sense. Given the prevailing consensus in the Courts of Appeals, the Court should have declined to take this case. Having granted certiorari, the Court should have answered the question differently by simply according respect to our prior decisions. But most importantly, even if it were to ignore all of our post-1964 writing, the Court should have answered the question differently on the merits.

I respectfully dissent.

Note: The Implications of Sandoval

1. The majority and dissent in *Sandoval* engage in a debate that goes well beyond the Title VI issue that is immediately before the Court. The Court's opinion leaves little room for recognizing implied rights of action in future cases, but the vote is 5-4, and the dissent's approach may yet prevail.

2. It is hardly surprising that the Court disdains the approach of *Borak*; at least as early as *Touche Ross* (1979), the Court made clear that it no longer adhered to the standard employed in that case. Even Justice Stevens, in dissent, relies on "a rigorous application of the criteria set forth in *Cort v. Ash*," not *Borak*.

3. More significant is the Court's rejection of the argument that when interpreting a statute enacted prior to *Cort v. Ash* (1975), the Court should look at "the contemporary legal context" to determine the expectations that the enacting Congress had formed. Rather, the Court determines Congress's intent based only on "the text and structure" of the statute. The dissenters, in contrast, would consider "the enacting Congress' expectations as to how the judiciary might evaluate the question." That, of course, would depend on the standard applied at the time of enactment, even if the Court later repudiated it.

4. The Court distinguishes among three types of statutes: those that focus on "the individuals protected"; those that focus on "the person regulated"; and those that focus on "the agencies that will do the regulating." Are there any circumstances in which the Court would recognize a right of action under a statute in the second or third category?

Note: Sandoval *and Section 1983*

The defendant in *Sandoval* was acting under color of state law, and the plaintiffs asserted that his actions violated their rights under a federal statute. Could they have brought suit under 42 U.S.C. § 1983 — the Congressionally created cause of action — even if, as the Court held, they had no private right of action under Title VI?

Soon after *Sandoval* was decided, a federal district court allowed a similar suit to go forward under § 1983, but a divided panel of the Third Circuit reversed. *South Camden Citizens in Action v. New Jersey Dep't of Environmental Protection*, 274 F.3d 771 (3d Cir. 2001).

The plaintiffs in that case sought an injunction against state environmental officials who had issued an air pollution permit to a cement processing facility. They alleged that the facility would have an adverse disparate racial impact upon them in violation of Title VI and regulations promulgated by the Environmental Protection Agency. The Third Circuit held that the suit could not be maintained under § 1983. The court said that "a federal regulation alone may not create a right enforceable through section 1983 not already found in the enforcing statute." The court also rejected the argument "that enforceable rights may be found in any valid administrative implementation of a statute that in itself creates some enforceable right." The court concluded:

Applying these rules here, it is clear that, particularly in light of *Sandoval*, Congress did not intend by adoption of Title VI to create a federal right to be free from disparate impact discrimination and that while the EPA's regulations on the point may be valid, they nevertheless do not create rights enforceable under section 1983.

The dissent noted that the Third Circuit had previously held that "§ 1983 provides an independent avenue to enforce disparate impact regulations promulgated under § 602 of Title VI." The dissent insisted that the *holding* in *Sandoval* did not overrule that decision.

For further discussion of section 1983 as a vehicle for statutory claims, see Chapter 14, section C.

Problem: Unordered Merchandise

Plaintiff Michael Trask brought suit in federal district court against Bodoni Books, Inc., a book publishing corporation, alleging that Bodoni violated section 3009 of the Postal Reorganization Act, known as the "unordered merchandise statute." Trask moved to certify the case as a class action on behalf of all those to whom Bodoni had sent unsolicited products and payment demands, with a subclass consisting of those who had paid in whole or in part for the unsolicited products.

Section 3009 provides as follows:

(a) [With exceptions not relevant here,] the mailing of unordered merchandise or of communications prohibited by subsection (c) of this section constitutes an unfair method of competition and an unfair trade practice in violation of section 45(a)(1) of title 15.

(b) Any merchandise mailed in violation of subsection (a) of this section ... may be treated as a gift by the recipient, who shall have the right to retain, use, discard, or dispose of it in any manner he sees fit without any obligation whatsoever to the sender. All such merchandise shall have attached to it a clear and conspicuous statement informing the recipient that he may treat the merchandise as a gift to him and has the right to retain, use, discard, or dispose of it in any manner he sees fit without any obligation whatsoever to the sender.

(c) No mailer of any merchandise mailed in violation of subsection (a) of this section ... shall mail to any recipient of such merchandise a bill for such merchandise or any dunning communications.

(d) For the purposes of this section, "unordered merchandise" means merchandise mailed without the prior expressed request or consent of the recipient.

The complaint alleges that Bodoni sent Trask books that he had never ordered and demanded payment for them, and that he paid Bodoni for one of the books to avoid damage to his credit rating.

Section 3009 became law as part of the Postal Reorganization Act of 1970. That Act effected a major reorganization of the federal postal service. Section 3009 was included as part of the newly created Chapter 30 ("Nonmailable Matter"), positioned between the prohibition on pandering advertisements in § 3008 and the regulations governing the mailing of sexually oriented advertisements in § 3010. The legislative history has nothing relevant about section 3009.

Section 45(a)(1) of Title 15, which is referenced in § 3009(a), is part of the Federal Trade Commission Act (FTC Act). Section 45(a)(1) provides: "Unfair methods of competition in or affecting commerce, and unfair or deceptive acts or practices in or affecting commerce, are hereby declared unlawful." Other provisions of the FTC Act authorize the FTC to obtain a variety of remedies for violations of § 45(a)(1), including injunctions and civil penalties.

Bodoni has moved to dismiss Trask's claim on the ground that there is no private right of action for violation of § 3009. Should the motion be granted?

Note: Interstitial Issues

1. Even when Congress creates a federal cause of action to enforce a federal right, it may not specify all of the elements of the liability scheme. *A fortiori*, when the cause of action is judicially created, Congress will not have addressed such issues as the period of limitations, the availability of contribution or indemnity, or other incidents of the cause of action. Where should the courts look for rules of decision?

2. Traditionally, when faced with a federal cause of action that does not contain a limitations period, courts have borrowed a limitations period from an analogous cause of action under state law. An important example is *Wilson v. Garcia*, 471 U.S. 261 (1985), involving civil rights actions under 42 U.S.C. § 1983. Section 1983 does not contain a statute of limitations. The Court concluded that the best analogy for § 1983 actions was found in the limitations period for "the tort action for the recovery of damages for personal injuries" under state law. The Court explained:

> The specific historical catalyst for the Civil Rights Act of 1871 [the genesis of § 1983] was the campaign of violence and deception in the South, fomented by the Ku Klux Klan, which was denying decent citizens their civil and political rights. . . . The atrocities that concerned Congress in 1871 plainly sounded in tort. . . . Had the 42d Congress expressly focused on the issue decided today, we believe it would have characterized § 1983 as conferring a general remedy for injuries to personal rights.

3. The Court has not always drawn statutes of limitations from analogous state actions; instead, it has sometimes adopted statutes of limitations from other *federal* statutes. An example comes from *Agency Holding Corp. v. Malley-Duff & Assocs.*, 483 U.S. 143 (1987), which presented the question of what statute of limitations should apply to private civil actions under the Racketeer Influenced and Corrupt Organizations Act (RICO), 18 U.S.C. § 1964. The Court explained that it would adopt a federal statute of limitations if state law does not provide a good analogy and if adopting a limitations period from another federal statute would protect federal interests. The Court wrote:

[T]here is not always an obvious state-law choice for application to a given federal cause of action; yet resort to state law remains the norm for borrowing of limitations periods. Nevertheless, when a rule from elsewhere in federal law clearly provides a closer analogy than available state statutes, and when the federal policies at stake and the practicalities of litigation make that rule a significantly more appropriate vehicle for interstitial lawmaking, we have not hesitated to turn away from state law.

The Court then concluded that it would not adopt a state statute of limitations for RICO but instead would adopt the statute of limitations from the Clayton Act, another federal statute. The Court gave two reasons. First, pointing out that the language in the RICO cause of action is nearly identical to the language in the Clayton Act cause of action, the Court stated that "[e]ven a cursory comparison of the two statutes reveals that the civil action provision of RICO was patterned after the Clayton Act." Second, the Court noted that the two acts served similar purposes:

Both RICO and the Clayton Act are designed to remedy economic injury by providing for the recovery of treble damages, costs, and attorney's fees. Both statutes bring to bear the pressure of "private attorneys general" on a serious national problem for which public prosecutorial resources are deemed inadequate; the mechanism chosen to reach the objective in both the Clayton Act and RICO is the carrot of treble damages. Moreover, both statutes aim to compensate the same type of injury; each requires that a plaintiff show injury "in his business or property by reason of" a violation.

Based on the similarity of purpose and text between the two acts, the Court concluded that the Clayton Act's limitations period should apply to civil RICO actions.

4. Judicially created causes of action pose special problems with regard to statutes of limitations. The Supreme Court confronted such an issue in *Lampf, Pleva, Lipkind, Prupis & Petigrow v. Gilbertson*, 501 U.S. 350 (1991), which addressed the question of what statute of limitations should apply to a private securities fraud suit brought pursuant to § 10(b) of the Securities Exchange Act of 1934 and Securities and Exchange Commission Rule 10b-5. Neither § 10(b) nor Rule 10b-5 creates a cause of action; instead, federal courts created that cause of action.

The Court concluded that, when determining which statute of limitations to apply, courts should not immediately turn to analogous state statutes. Instead, it stated, "where, as here, the claim asserted is one implied under a statute that also contains an express cause of action with its own time limitation, a court should look first to the statute of origin to ascertain the proper limitations period. . . . Only where no analogous counterpart is available should a court then proceed to apply state-borrowing principles."

Applying that rule to the § 10(b) cause of action, the Court looked to "the express causes of action contained in the 1933 and 1934 [Securities] Acts." The Court explained:

In the present litigation, there can be no doubt that the contemporaneously enacted express remedial provisions represent "a federal statute of limitations actually designed to accommodate a balance of interests very similar to that at stake here—a statute that is, in fact, an analogy to the present lawsuit more apt than any of the suggested state-law parallels." The 1934 Act contained a number of express causes of action, each with an explicit limitations period. With only one more restrictive exception, each of these includes some variation of a 1-year period after discovery combined with a 3-year period of repose. In adopting the 1934 Act, the 73d Congress also amended the limitations provision of the 1933 Act, adopting the 1-and-3-year structure for each cause of action contained therein.

In 2002, as part of the Sarbanes-Oxley Act, Congress finally enacted a statute of limitations for securities fraud claims. Under 28 U.S.C. § 1658(b), a securities fraud action must be brought "not later than the earlier of 2 years after the discovery of the facts constituting the violation or 5 years after such violation."

5. As one might expect, judges and justices have often disagreed about which statute provides the most appropriate analogy in creating a statute of limitations for federal actions. To obviate these difficulties, Congress enacted the Judicial Improvements Act of 1990. That Act added what is now 29 U.S.C. § 1658(a):

> Except as otherwise provided by law, a civil action arising under an Act of Congress enacted after the date of the enactment of this section may not be commenced later than 4 years after the cause of action accrues.

Although this fallback provision substantially simplifies the question of what limitations period applies to federal actions that do not contain their own limitations periods, the solution is incomplete. In particular, this fallback provision applies only to civil actions "arising under an Act of Congress enacted after the date of the enactment of this section." Thus, the 1990 law has no effect on causes of action based solely on pre-1990 statutes.

6. Section 1658(a) seems straightforward, but it proved to have one major ambiguity. Suppose that the plaintiff brings suit based on a post-1990 amendment to a statute enacted before 1990. Does section 1658 supply the limitations period?

In *Jones v. R.R. Donnelley & Sons Co.*, 541 U.S. 369 (2004), the Court gave its answer. It held that a cause of action "aris[es] under an Act of Congress enacted" after December 1, 1990—and therefore "is governed by § 1658's four-year statute of limitations—if the plaintiff's claim against the defendant was made possible by a post-1990 enactment."

7. Identifying an appropriate statute of limitations is not the only interstitial issue that arises in private litigation to enforce federal statutory rights. Another question is whether contribution or indemnity is available among joint wrongdoers.

In *Texas Industries, Inc. v. Radcliffe Materials, Inc.*, 451 U.S. 630 (1981), the Court considered a suit under the federal antitrust laws. The question was whether these laws "allow a defendant, against whom civil damages, costs, and attorney's fees have been assessed, a right to contribution from other participants in the unlawful conspiracy on which recovery was based." The Court held unanimously that no right of contribution exists.

The Court first determined that Congress did not create a right of contribution either expressly or by implication. It then asked whether a right of contribution could be recognized as a matter of federal common law. The Court found nothing in the statutes that authorized courts "to alter or supplement the remedies enacted." Nor did contribution "implicate 'uniquely federal interests' of the kind that oblige courts to formulate federal common law." On the latter point the Court explained:

> Admittedly, there is a federal interest in the sense that vindication of rights arising out of these congressional enactments supplements federal enforcement and fulfills the objects of the statutory scheme. Notwithstanding that nexus, contribution among antitrust wrongdoers does not involve the duties of the Federal Government, the distribution of powers in our federal system, or matters necessarily subject to federal control even in the absence of statutory authority.

The Court concluded that the matter was one "for Congress, not the courts, to resolve."

8. The Court in *Texas Industries* made no mention of state law. Does that suggest that when the issue is whether to allow contribution or indemnity, the option of borrowing state law is not available? Why should it not be?

9. In contrast, the Court held that in a suit based on the implied private right of action under § 10(b) of the Securities Exchange Act of 1934 and Rule 10b-5 of the Securities and Exchange Commission, defendants do have a right to seek contribution from other joint tortfeasors. The case was *Musick, Peeler & Garrett v. Employers Insurance of Wausau*, 508 U.S. 286 (1993), and the Court relied heavily on its decision in *Lampf Pleva*, the limitations case discussed above.

The Court first explained why arguments based on *Texas Industries* were not persuasive: "Having implied the underlying liability in the first place, to now disavow any authority to allocate it on the theory that Congress has not addressed the issue would be most unfair to those against whom damages are assessed." The Court then turned to the question "whether a right to contribution is within the contours of the 10b-5 action." The Court said:

> Our task is not to assess the relative merits of the competing rules, but rather to attempt to infer how the 1934 Congress would have addressed the issue had the 10b-5 action been included as an express provision in the 1934 Act. . . .
>
> Inquiring about what a given Congress might have done, though not a promising venture as a general proposition, does in this case yield an answer we find convincing. . . . There [are] two sections of the 1934 Act, §§ 9 and 18, that, as we have noted, are close in structure, purpose, and intent to the 10b-5 action. *Lampf Pleva*. Each confers an explicit right of action in favor of private parties and, in so doing, discloses a congressional intent regarding the definition and apportionment of liability among private parties.

For two distinct reasons, these express causes of action are of particular significance in determining how Congress would have resolved the question of contribution had it provided for a private cause of action under § 10(b). First, §§ 9 and 18 are instructive because both "target the precise dangers that are the focus of § 10(b)," *Lampf Pleva*, and the intent motivating all three sections is the same—"to deter fraud and manipulative practices in the securities markets, and to ensure full disclosure of information material to investment decisions."

Second, of the eight express liability provisions contained in the 1933 and 1934 Acts, §§ 9 and 18 impose liability upon defendants who stand in a position most similar to 10b-5 defendants for the sake of assessing whether they should be entitled to contribution.... Sections 9 and 18 contain nearly identical express provisions for a right to contribution, each permitting a defendant to "recover contribution as in cases of contract from any person who, if joined in the original suit, would have been liable to make the same payment."

In view of this unique history, *Musick Peeler* is not likely to be a generative precedent, and we can look to *Texas Industries* as stating the dominant approach.

Note: Remedies and Standards of Liability

1. Once the federal courts recognize an implied cause of action, questions may arise as to the remedies available and the standard of liability. Thus, over the years, the Supreme Court has dealt with several issues involving the implied cause of action for securities fraud. More recently, the Court has confronted issues generated by the holding in *Cannon* that there is an implied right of action under Title IX of the Education Amendments of 1972. This Note focuses on the Title IX cases.

2. In *Franklin v. Gwinnett County Public Schools*, 503 U.S. 60 (1992), the Court considered whether the implied right of action recognized in *Cannon* supports a claim for monetary damages. The Court held that it does.

The Court began by observing that "the question of what remedies are available under a statute that provides a private right of action is 'analytically distinct' from the issue of whether such a right exists in the first place." However, the "general rule" is that "absent clear direction to the contrary by Congress, the federal courts have the power to award any appropriate relief in a cognizable cause of action brought pursuant to a federal statute."

The next question was "whether Congress intended to limit application of this general principle in the enforcement of Title IX." The Court said that "the same contextual approach used to justify an implied right of action more than amply demonstrates the lack of any legislative intent to abandon the traditional presumption in favor of all available remedies." Further, two amendments to Title IX enacted after *Cannon* pointed in the same direction. The Court thus concluded that "a damages remedy is available for an action brought to enforce Title IX."

3. In reliance on *Franklin*, the Eighth Circuit held that "appropriate relief" in an action under section 202 of the Americans with Disabilities Act of 1990 (ADA) includes punitive damages. In *Barnes v. Gorman*, 536 U.S. 181 (2002), the Supreme Court reversed. The Court held that punitive damages may not be awarded under statutes that invoke Congress's power under the Spending Clause to place conditions on the grant of federal funds. This is because Spending Clause legislation is "in the nature of a *contract.*" The Court explained:

> [A] remedy is "appropriate relief" only if the funding recipient is on *notice* that, by accepting federal funding, it exposes itself to liability of that nature. A funding recipient is generally on notice that it is subject not only to those remedies explicitly provided in the relevant legislation, but also to those remedies traditionally available in suits for breach of contract.... [But punitive] damages are generally not available for breach of contract....

This holding applies directly to Title IX of the Education Amendments; it also applies to section 202 of the ADA, because the ADA incorporates the remedial provision of Spending Clause legislation.

4. *Franklin* also held, with little discussion, that Title IX's prohibition of discrimination on the basis of sex is violated "when a teacher sexually harasses and abuses a student." Six years later, in *Gebser v. Lago Vista Independent School District*, 524 U.S. 274 (1998), the Court confronted the question: *when* may a school board be held liable in damages for sexual harassment of a student by one of the district's teachers? The Court concluded that "damages may not be recovered in those circumstances unless an official of the school district who at a minimum has authority to institute corrective measures on the district's behalf has actual notice of, and is deliberately indifferent to, the teacher's misconduct." Of particular interest is the method used by the Court to reach this conclusion. The Court said:

> Because the private right of action under Title IX is judicially implied, we have a measure of latitude to shape a sensible remedial scheme that best comports with the statute. That endeavor inherently entails a degree of speculation, since it addresses an issue on which Congress has not specifically spoken. To guide the analysis, we generally examine the relevant statute to ensure that we do not fashion the scope of an implied right in a manner at odds with the statutory structure and purpose....

> [In *Franklin*, we] recognized "the general rule that all appropriate relief is available in an action brought to vindicate a federal right," but indicated that the rule must be reconciled with congressional purpose. The "general rule," that is, "yields where necessary to carry out the intent of Congress or to avoid frustrating the purposes of the statute involved."

> Applying those principles here, we conclude that it would "frustrate the purposes" of Title IX to permit a damages recovery against a school district for a teacher's sexual harassment of a student based on principles of *respondeat superior* or constructive notice, *i.e.*, without actual notice to a school district official....

Title IX's contractual nature has implications for our construction of the scope of available remedies. When Congress attaches conditions to the award of federal funds under its spending power, as it has in Title IX and Title VI, we examine closely the propriety of private actions holding the recipient liable in monetary damages for noncompliance with the condition. Our central concern in that regard is with ensuring that "the receiving entity of federal funds [has] notice that it will be liable for a monetary award." . . . If a school district's liability for a teacher's sexual harassment rests on principles of constructive notice or *respondeat superior*, it will [be] the case that the recipient of funds was unaware of the discrimination. It is sensible to assume that Congress did not envision a recipient's liability in damages in that situation.

The Court concluded:

The issue in this case [is] whether the independent misconduct of a teacher is attributable to the school district that employs him under a specific federal statute designed primarily to prevent recipients of federal financial assistance from using the funds in a discriminatory manner. . . . Until Congress speaks directly on the subject, [we] will not hold a school district liable in damages under Title IX for a teacher's sexual harassment of a student absent actual notice and deliberate indifference.

Four Justices dissented in an opinion by Justice Stevens. They emphatically rejected the Court's premise that "because the private cause of action under Title IX is 'judicially implied,' the Court has 'a measure of latitude' to use its own judgment in shaping a remedial scheme." They said:

Because [the constructions of Title IX in *Cannon* and *Franklin*] have been accepted by Congress and are unchallenged here, they have the same legal effect as if the private cause of action seeking damages had been explicitly, rather than implicitly, authorized by Congress. We should therefore seek guidance from the text of the statute and settled legal principles rather than from our views about sound policy.

The dissenters also disagreed with the Court's rejection of respondeat superior liability:

That holding is at odds with settled principles of agency law, under which the district is responsible for [the teacher's] misconduct because "he was aided in accomplishing the tort by the existence of the agency relation." . . . The reason why the common law imposes liability on the principal in such circumstances is the same as the reason why Congress included the prohibition against discrimination on the basis of sex in Title IX: to induce school boards to adopt and enforce practices that will minimize the danger that vulnerable students will be exposed to such odious behavior. The rule that the Court has crafted creates the opposite incentive.

5. Recall the language of Title IX: "No person . . . shall, on the basis of sex, . . . be subjected to discrimination under any education program or activity receiving

Federal financial assistance. . . ." After *Cannon, Franklin,* and *Gebser,* a school board can be held liable under Title IX for compensatory (but not punitive) damages for sexual harassment of a student by a teacher if the plaintiff can show "actual notice and deliberate indifference." How can we determine whether this set of rules is (in Justice Stevens' words) "faithful to [the Court's] duty to interpret, rather than to revise, congressional commands"?

C. Other Matters of National Concern

In a commentary frequently quoted by the Court, Professor Paul Mishkin argued that there must be "federal judicial competence to declare the governing law in an area comprising issues substantially related to an established program of government operation."[a] Thus far we have seen how the Court has exercised this authority in litigation involving the United States as a party and in suits to enforce rights created by federal law. Do those situations define the boundaries of "federal judicial competence to declare the governing law"? Or does the power also extend to some situations involving private litigation and state-created rights? Consider the cases that follow.

Kohr v. Allegheny Airlines

United States Court of Appeals for the Seventh Circuit, 1974.

504 F.2d 400.

Before SWYGERT, CHIEF JUDGE, KILEY,[1] SENIOR CIRCUIT JUDGE, and HOFFMAN,[2] SENIOR DISTRICT JUDGE.

SWYGERT, CHIEF JUDGE.

Defendants-appellants Allegheny Airlines, Inc. and the United States appeal from the dismissal of their cross-claims and third-party complaints for indemnity and contribution against defendants-appellees Brookside Corporation (Brookside), Forth Corporation (Forth is a wholly-owned subsidiary of Brookside), and the estate of Robert W. Carey. The instant actions arise out of a mid-air collision on September 9, 1969, in the airspace over Fairland, Indiana between an Allegheny Airlines DC-9-31 jet aircraft and a Piper Cherokee aircraft piloted by Robert W. Carey and owned by Forth. . . .

The Allegheny aircraft was operated as Flight No. 853 en route from Cincinnati, Ohio to Indianapolis, Indiana. At the time of the collision Flight No. 853 was flying under an instrument flight rules clearance from Cincinnati to Indianapolis and was

---

a. Paul Mishkin, *The Variousness of "Federal Law": Competence and Discretion in the Choice of National and State Rules for Decision,* 105 U. PA. L. REV. 797, 800 (1957).

1. Judge Kiley heard oral argument in these appeals, but he died on September 6, 1974 before he considered this opinion.

2. Senior Judge Julius J. Hoffman of the United States District Court for the Northern District of Illinois is sitting by designation.

receiving and adhering to air traffic control radar directions from an air traffic controller employed by the Federal Aviation Administration [at the Indianapolis airport]. The Piper Cherokee aircraft was operated by Carey, a student pilot, under visual flight rules. At the time of the collision Carey was engaged in a solo cross-country flight from Brookside Airport, McCordsville, Indiana to Bakalar Air Force Base, Columbus, Indiana. As a result of the mid-air collision both aircraft were totally destroyed and all eighty-three occupants were killed.

Subsequent to the accident, wrongful death actions were commenced on behalf of the estates of all the deceased passengers save one, the estates of three of the four Allegheny crew members, and the estate of Robert W. Carey. In addition, property damages suits were initiated to recover for the destruction of the two aircraft. All of these suits were commenced in various federal district courts on the basis of diversity of citizenship as to defendants Allegheny, Brookside, Forth, and the estate of Carey, and the Federal Tort Claims Act as to the defendant United States.

The Judicial Panel on Multidistrict Litigation assumed jurisdiction over the various actions commenced outside of Indiana and pursuant to 28 U.S.C. 1407 transferred them to the United States District Court for the Southern District of Indiana for the purpose of supervision of the pretrial discovery. Subsequent to the section 1407 transfer, the district court judge issued orders pursuant to 28 U.S.C. 1404 transferring cases from respective transferor forums to the United States District Court for the Southern District of Indiana and consolidated those cases with other companion cases that had been initially commenced in the Indiana district court. By the time of trial Allegheny and the United States had filed cross-claims and third-party complaints against Brookside, Forth, and the estate of Carey seeking indemnity and contribution.

[Eventually] an agreement was arrived at between the United States and the liability insurers of Allegheny for a pro-rata formula to be utilized between them in disposing of all cases, whether by settlement or judgment. The defendants Forth, Brookside, and estate of Carey were not parties to, and did not contribute anything to or under the agreement. . . . The district court found the compromise to be reasonable and accordingly Allegheny's insurers and the United States proceeded to settle the remaining passenger cases. [The plaintiffs' complaints were then dismissed.]

[Forth, Brookside, and the estate of Carey filed motions to dismiss the claims by Allegheny and the United States on the ground that no right to indemnity and contribution existed under Indiana law. The district court, applying Indiana law, granted the motion.]

Allegheny contends that it was error for the district court to dismiss its cross-claims and third-party complaints for indemnity and contribution. The district court held that Indiana law was controlling on these claims and that under Indiana law there could be no contribution and indemnity under that state's law. Allegheny urges that a federal rule of contribution and indemnity should govern in the instant action. Failing the application of a federal law of contribution Allegheny contends that in view of the multiplicity of state jurisdictions involved, [the trial judge] should have conducted an evidentiary hearing to facilitate a proper choice of law analysis. . . . In addition, Allegheny contends that even assuming Indiana law controls, the district court misapplied the rules on contribution and indemnity.

Were it necessary, we would be inclined to agree with Allegheny that the district judge failed to engage in an adequate conflict of law analysis and that he erred on the application of Indiana law on contribution and indemnity. We need not reach these issues, however, for we agree with Allegheny that there should be a federal law of contribution and indemnity governing mid-air collisions such as the one here.

III

The basis for imposing a federal law of contribution and indemnity is what we perceive to be the predominant, indeed almost exclusive, interest of the federal government in regulating the affairs of the nation's airways. Moreover, the imposition of a federal rule of contribution and indemnity serves a second purpose of eliminating inconsistency of result in similar collision occurrences as well as within the same occurrence due to the application of differing state laws on contribution and indemnity. Given the prevailing federal interest in uniform air law regulation, we deem it desirable that a federal rule of contribution and indemnity be applied.

That the federal interest in regulating airways is predominant was long ago recognized by Justice Jackson in *Northwest Airlines v. Minnesota*, 322 U.S. 292 (1944):

> Students of our legal evolution know how this Court interpreted the commerce clause of the Constitution to lift navigable waters of the United States out of local controls and into the domain of federal control. Air as an element in which to navigate is even more inevitably federalized by the commerce clause then is navigable water. Local exactions and barriers to free transit in the air would neutralize its indifference to space and its conquest of time.

> Congress has recognized the national responsibility for regulating air commerce. Federal control is intensive and exclusive. Planes do not wander about in the sky like vagrant clouds. They move only by federal permission, subject to federal inspection, in the hands of federally certified personnel and under an intricate system of federal commands. The moment a ship taxis onto a runway it is caught up in an elaborate and detailed system of controls. It takes off only by instruction from the control tower, it travels on prescribed beams, it may be diverted from its intended landing, and it obeys signals and order. Its privileges, rights, and protection, so far as transit is concerned, it owes to the Federal Government alone and not to any state government.

With the passage of the Federal Aviation Act of 1958, Congress expressed the view that the control of aviation should rest exclusively in the hands of the federal government. In section 1108 of the Act, it is clearly provided that:

> (a) The United States of America is declared to possess and exercise complete and exclusive national sovereignty in the airspace of the United States, including the airspace above all inland waters and the airspace above those

portions of the adjacent marginal high seas, bays, and lakes, over which by international law or treaty or convention the United States exercises national jurisdiction. Aircraft of the armed forces of any foreign nation shall not be navigated in the United States, including the Canal Zone, except in accordance with an authorization granted by the Secretary of State.

The explicit objective of the Act is to foster the development of air commerce. 49 U.S.C. § 1346. To that end, it has been recognized that the principal purpose of the Act is to create one unified system of flight rules and to centralize in the Administrator of the Federal Aviation Administration the power to promulgate rules for the safe and efficient use of the country's airspace. [The court cited 2 cases from other circuits.]

When the notion of federal preemption over aviation is viewed in combination with the fact that this litigation ensues from a mid-air collision occurring in national airspace, that the Government is a party to the action pursuant to the Federal Tort Claims Act (28 U.S.C. § 1346(b) *et seq.*), and that this litigation has since its inception been subject to the supervision of the Judicial Panel created by the Multidistrict Litigation Act, there is no perceptible reason why federal law should not be applied to determine the rights and liabilities of the parties involved. The interest of the state wherein in the fortuitous event of the collision occurred is slight as compared to the dominant federal interest. Accordingly, the rights and liabilities of Allegheny and the United States are peculiarly federal in nature and are to be governed by a federal rule of contribution and indemnity.

[At this point the court added the following footnote:] In view of the aforementioned predominant federal interest in formulating a rule of contribution and indemnity we are of the view that the Federal Tort Claims Act is not an obstacle to the application of such a rule to the United State's claims.

IV

Having determined that a federal rule of contribution and indemnity among joint tort-feasors should control in aviation collisions, we reject as being outmoded and entirely unsatisfactory, the contention that the federal rule should be one of "no contribution." We agree that "there is an obvious lack of sense and justice in a rule which permits the entire burden of a loss, for which two defendants were equally, unintentionally responsible, to be shouldered on to one alone, according to the accident of a successful levy of execution, the existence of liability insurance, the plaintiffs' whim or spite, or his collusion with the other wrongdoer, while the latter goes scot free." PROSSER, LAW OF TORTS, 50 (4th ed. 1971).

In our judgment the better rule is that of contribution and indemnity on a comparative negligence basis. Under such an approach the trier of fact will determine on a percentage basis the degree of negligent involvement of each party in the collision. The loss will then be distributed in proportion to the allocable concurring fault. In allocating the loss where as here that amount involves a settlement and not a judgment, the trier of fact must also establish what amount would be a reasonable settlement under the circumstances. On reaching such an amount each party contributes according to his degree of fault. . . .

. . . Reversed in part and remanded for a new trial.

Note: The "Predominant" Federal Interest in "Aviation"

1. The Seventh Circuit in *Kohr* applies a federal rule of contribution and indemnity based on its perception of "the predominant, indeed almost exclusive, interest of the federal government in regulating the affairs of the nation's airways." Is that enough? Note that the court does not cite *Erie*. Can the decision be reconciled with *Erie*'s rejection of "federal general common law"?

2. The court relies on "the prevailing federal interest in *uniform* air law regulation." (Emphasis added.) Recall that the desirability of a uniform set of rules was also one of the justifications for the doctrine of *Swift v. Tyson*. Did *Erie* reject that line of reasoning as a basis for creating a rule of federal common law?

3. The court gives weight to the fact that "the [United States] Government is a party to the action pursuant to the Federal Tort Claims Act." Does that aspect of the case support the court's creation of a special federal rule of decision? Look carefully at the Federal Tort Claims Act, 28 U.S.C. § 1346(b)(1), particularly the last clause.

4. The court quotes from the Federal Aviation Act and from Justice Jackson's concurring opinion in *Northwest Airlines*, a case involving the constitutional limitations on state power to tax airplanes. How strongly do these authorities support the decision to apply federal law to the issue in *Kohr*?

5. How would *Kohr* be decided under the analysis in *Miree v. DeKalb County*, the next principal case?

Miree v. DeKalb County

Supreme Court of the United States, 1977.

433 U.S. 25.

MR. JUSTICE REHNQUIST delivered the opinion of the Court.

These consolidated cases arise out of the 1973 crash of a Lear Jet shortly after takeoff from the DeKalb-Peachtree Airport. The United States Court of Appeals for the Fifth Circuit, en banc, affirmed the dismissal of petitioners' complaint against respondent DeKalb County (hereafter respondent), holding that principles of federal common law were applicable to the resolution of petitioners' breach-of-contract claim. We granted certiorari to consider whether federal or state law should have been applied to that claim; we conclude that the latter should govern.

I

Petitioners are, respectively, the survivors of deceased passengers, the assignee of the jet aircraft owner, and a burn victim. They brought separate lawsuits, later consolidated, against respondent in the United States District Court for the Northern

District of Georgia.[1] The basis for federal jurisdiction was diversity of citizenship, and the complaints asserted that respondent was liable on three independent theories: negligence, nuisance, and breach of contract. The District Court granted respondent's motion to dismiss each of these claims. The courts below have unanimously agreed that the negligence and nuisance theories are without merit; only the propriety of the dismissal of the contract claims remains in the cases.

Petitioners seek to impose liability on respondent as third-party beneficiaries of contracts between it and the Federal Aviation Administration (FAA). Their complaints allege that respondent entered into six grant agreements with the FAA. Under the terms of the contracts respondent agreed to "take action to restrict the use of land adjacent to or in the immediate vicinity of the Airport to activities and purposes compatible with normal airport operations including landing and takeoff of aircraft." Petitioners assert that respondent breached the FAA contracts by owning and maintaining a garbage dump adjacent to the airport, and that the cause of the crash was the ingestion of birds swarming from the dump into the jet engines of the aircraft.

Applying Georgia law, the District Court found that petitioners' claims as third-party beneficiaries under the FAA contracts were barred by the county's governmental immunity, and dismissed the complaints under Fed. Rule Civ. Proc. 12(b)(6). A divided panel of the Court of Appeals decided that under state law petitioners could sue as third-party beneficiaries and that governmental immunity would not bar the suit. The dissenting judge argued that the court should have applied federal rather than state law; he concluded that under the principles of federal common law the petitioners in this case did not have standing to sue as third-party beneficiaries of the contracts. Sitting en banc, the Court of Appeals reversed the panel on the breach-of-contract issue and adopted the panel dissent on this point as its opinion. Judge Morgan, who had written the panel opinion, argued for five dissenters that there was no identifiable federal interest in the outcome of this diversity case, and thus that federal common law had no applicability.

II

Since the only basis of federal jurisdiction alleged for petitioners' claim against respondent is diversity of citizenship, the case would unquestionably be governed by Georgia law, *Erie Railroad Co. v. Tompkins*, 304 U.S. 64 (1938), but for the fact that the United States is a party to the contracts in question, entered into pursuant to federal statute [the Airport and Airway Development Act of 1970]. The en banc majority of the Court of Appeals adopted, by reference, the view that, given these factors, application of federal common law was required: "Although jurisdiction here is based upon diversity, the contract we are interpreting is one in which the United States is a party, and one which is entered into pursuant to authority conferred by federal statute.

---

1. Petitioners also sued the United States under the Federal Tort Claims Act. The litigation before us arises out of the District Court's granting of respondent DeKalb County's motion to dismiss and the entry of final judgment under Fed. Rule Civ. Proc. 54(b). The United States has made no similar motion, and is not a party to the cases in this Court.

The necessity of uniformity of decision demands that federal common law, rather than state law, control the contract's interpretation."

We do not agree with the conclusion of the Court of Appeals. The litigation before us raises no question regarding the liability of the United States or the responsibilities of the United States under the contracts. The relevant inquiry is a narrow one: whether petitioners as third-party beneficiaries of the contracts have standing to sue respondent. While federal common law may govern even in diversity cases where a uniform national rule is necessary to further the interests of the Federal Government, *Clearfield Trust Co. v. United States*, 318 U.S. 363 (1943), the application of federal common law to resolve the issue presented here would promote no federal interests even approaching the magnitude of those found in *Clearfield Trust*:

> The issuance of commercial paper by the United States is on a vast scale and transactions in that paper from issuance to payment will commonly occur in several states. The application of state law, even without the conflict of laws rules of the forum, would subject the rights and duties of the United States to exceptional uncertainty. It would lead to great diversity in results by making identical transactions subject to the vagaries of the laws of the several states. The desirability of a uniform rule is plain.

But, in this case, the resolution of petitioners' breach-of-contract claim against respondent will have no direct effect upon the United States or its Treasury.[4] The Solicitor General, waiving his right to respond in these cases advised us:

> In the course of the proceedings below, the United States determined that its interests would not be directly affected by the resolution of these issue[s] and therefore did not participate in briefing or argument in the court of appeals. In view of these considerations, the United States does not intend to respond to the petitions unless it is requested to do so by the Court.

The operations of the United States in connection with FAA grants such as these are undoubtedly of considerable magnitude. However, we see no reason for concluding that these operations would be burdened or subjected to uncertainty by variant state-law interpretations regarding whether those with whom the United States contracts might be sued by third-party beneficiaries to the contracts. Since only the rights of private litigants are at issue here, we find the *Clearfield Trust* rationale inapplicable.

We think our conclusion that these cases do not fit within the *Clearfield Trust* rule follows from the Court's later decision in *Bank of America National Trust & Savings Assn. v. Parnell*, 352 U.S. 29 (1956), in which the Court declined to apply that rule in a fact situation analogous to this one. *Parnell* was a diversity action between private parties involving United States bonds. The Bank of America had sued Parnell to

---

4. There is no indication that petitioners' tort claim against the United States will be affected by the resolution of this issue. Indeed, the Federal Tort Claims Act itself looks to state law in determining liability. 28 U.S.C. § 1346(b).

recover funds that he had obtained by cashing the bonds, which had been stolen from the bank. There were two issues: whether the bonds were "overdue" and whether Parnell had taken the bonds in good faith. The Court of Appeals, over a dissent, applied federal law to resolve both issues; this Court reversed with respect to the good-faith issue. After stressing that the basis for the *Clearfield Trust* decision was that the application of state law in that case would "subject the rights and duties of the United States to exceptional uncertainty," the Court rejected the application of the *Clearfield Trust* rationale: "Securities issued by the Government generate immediate interests of the Government. These were dealt with in *Clearfield Trust*. . . . But they also radiate interests in transactions between private parties. The present litigation is purely between private parties and does not touch the rights and duties of the United States."

The Court recognized, as we do here, that the application of state law to the issue of good faith did not preclude the application of federal law to questions directly involving the rights and duties of the Federal Government, and found: "Federal law of course governs the interpretation of the nature of the rights and obligations created by the Government bonds themselves. A decision with respect to the 'overdueness' of the bonds is therefore a matter of federal law, which, in view of our holding, we need not elucidate."

The parallel between *Parnell* and these cases is obvious. The question of whether petitioners may sue respondent does not require decision under federal common law since the litigation is among private parties and no substantial rights or duties of the United States hinge on its outcome. On the other hand, nothing we say here forecloses the applicability of federal common law in interpreting the rights and duties of the United States under federal contracts.

Nor is the fact that the United States has a substantial interest in regulating aircraft travel and promoting air travel safety sufficient, given the narrow question before us, to call into play the rule of *Clearfield Trust*. In *Wallis v. Pan American Petroleum Corporation*, 384 U.S. 63, 68 (1966), the Court discussed the nature of a federal interest sufficient to bring forth the application of federal common law:

> In deciding whether rules of federal common law should be fashioned, normally the guiding principle is that *a significant conflict between some federal policy or interest and the use of state law in the premises must first be specifically shown*. It is by no means enough that, as we may assume, Congress could under the Constitution readily enact a complete code of law governing transactions in federal mineral leases among private parties. Whether latent federal power should be exercised to displace state law is primarily a decision for Congress. (Emphasis added.)

The question of whether private parties may, as third-party beneficiaries, sue a municipality for breach of the FAA contracts involves this federal interest only insofar as such lawsuits might be thought to advance federal aviation policy by inducing compliance with FAA safety provisions. However, even assuming the correctness of this notion, we adhere to the language in *Wallis*, cited above, stating that the issue of whether to displace state law on an issue such as this is primarily a decision for Congress. Congress has chosen not to do so in this case.[5]

Actually the application of federal common law, as interpreted by the Court of Appeals here would frustrate this federal interest *pro tanto*, since that court held that this breach-of-contract lawsuit would not lie under federal law. On the other hand, at least in the opinion of the majority of the panel below, Georgia law would countenance the action. Even assuming that a different result were to be reached under federal common law, we think this language from *Wallis* all but forecloses its application to these cases: "Apart from the highly abstract nature of [the federal] interest, there has been no showing that state law is not adequate to achieve it." We conclude that any federal interest in the outcome of the question before us "is far too speculative, far too remote a possibility to justify the application of federal law to transactions essentially of local concern." *Parnell*.

Although we have determined that Georgia law should be applied to the question raised by respondent's motion to dismiss, we shall not undertake to decide the correct outcome under Georgia law. . . . [We] vacate the judgment and remand to the Court of Appeals for consideration of the claim under applicable Georgia law.

III

Petitioners have argued in this Court that the Airport and Airway Development Act of 1970 provides an implied civil right of action to recover for death or injury due to violation of the Act.[6] Petitioners, however, allege only diversity of citizenship as the basis for federal jurisdiction of their lawsuits; they do not rely upon federal-question jurisdiction, 28 U.S.C. § 1331, which would be more consistent with a theory of an implied federal cause of action under that Act. . . . There is no indication that petitioners alleged a violation of a federal statute and a right to recovery for such a violation. The fact that this asserted basis of liability is so obviously an afterthought may be some indication of its merit, but since it was neither pleaded, argued, nor briefed either in the District Court or in the Court of Appeals, we will not consider it.

The judgment is vacated, and the cases are remanded to the Court of Appeals for further proceedings consistent with this opinion.

Mr. Chief Justice Burger, concurring in the judgment.

There is language in the Court's opinion which might be misinterpreted as rigidly limiting the application of "federal common law" to only those situations where the rights and obligations of the Federal Government are at issue. I do not agree with such a restrictive approach.

---

5. The Congress has considered, but not passed, a bill to provide for a federal cause of action arising out of aircraft disasters.

6. In language similar to that used in the FAA grant agreements, §§ 1718(3) and (4) require, as a condition precedent to approval of an airport development project, written assurances that the airport approaches will be safely maintained and that the use of land adjacent to the airport will be restricted to uses compatible with aircraft takeoff and landing.

I cannot read *Clearfield Trust Co. v. United States*, 318 U.S. 363 (1943), and *Bank of America National Trust and Savings Assn. v. Parnell*, 352 U.S. 29 (1956) as, in all circumstances, precluding the application of "federal common law" to all matters involving only the rights of private citizens. Certainly, in a diversity action, state substantive law should not be ousted on the basis of "'an amorphous doctrine of national sovereignty' divorced from any specific constitutional or statutory provision and premised solely on the argument 'that every authorized activity of the United States represents an exercise of its governmental power.'" However, I am not prepared to foreclose, at this point, the possibility that there may be situations where the rights and obligations of private parties are so dependent on a specific exercise of congressional regulatory power that "the Constitution or Acts of Congress 'require' otherwise than that state law govern of its own force."

In such a situation, I would not read *Wallis v. Pan American Petroleum Corporation*, 384 U.S. 63, 68 (1966), to preclude a choice of "federal common law" simply because there is no specific federal legislation governing the particular transaction at issue. Once it has been determined that it would be inappropriate to apply state law and that federal law must govern, "the inevitable incompleteness presented by all legislation means that interstitial federal lawmaking is a basic responsibility of the federal courts." *United States v. Little Lake Misere Land Co.*, 412 U.S. 580, 593 (1973). In short, although federal courts will be called upon to invoke it infrequently, there must be "'federal judicial competence to declare the governing law in an area comprising issues substantially related to an established program of government operation.'" *Ibid.*, quoting Mishkin, *The Variousness of "Federal Law": Competence and Discretion in the Choice of National and State Rules for Decision*, 105 U. Pa. L. Rev. 797, 800 (1957).

Although in my view the issue is close, I conclude, on balance, that the cause of action asserted by the plaintiffs is not so intimately related to the purpose of the Airport and Airway Development Act of 1970, as to require the application of federal law in this case. Accordingly, the rule of *Erie R. Co. v. Tompkins*, 304 U.S. 64 (1938), applies, and I join the judgment of the Court remanding the cases for a determination of the correct outcome under Georgia law.

Note: The "Radiations" of Federal Government Transactions

1. In *Miree*, Chief Justice Burger declines to join the Court's opinion because he finds language that "might be misinterpreted as rigidly limiting the application of 'federal common law' to only those situations where the rights and obligations of the Federal Government are at issue." Certainly there is language in the Court's opinion that points in that direction. But does the opinion foreclose the possibility that federal common law might be applied to some "matters involving only the rights of private citizens"? If not, under what circumstances?

2. The Court finds "no reason for concluding that [the operations of the United States in connection with FAA grants] would be burdened or subjected to uncertainty by variant state-law interpretations regarding" suits by third-party beneficiaries. Does this suggest that if "variant state-law interpretations" did impose burdens on the

Government, the Court would apply federal common law? Is that the thrust of the *Wallis* case, quoted by the Court?

3. The Court acknowledges that "the United States has a substantial interest in regulating aircraft travel and promoting air travel safety," but says that that fact is not enough to bring into play the rule of *Clearfield Trust*. Is this tantamount to rejecting the rationale and holding of *Kohr*?

4. The Court also states that "the issue of whether to displace state law on an issue such as this is primarily a decision for Congress." It notes that "Congress has considered, but not passed, legislation to provide for a federal cause of action arising out of aircraft disasters." In support of that proposition, the Court cites Senate Judiciary Committee hearings in 1969 — five years before the decision in Kohr. Should the Kohr court have taken account of those hearings?

Boyle v. United Technologies Corporation

Supreme Court of the United States, 1988.

487 U.S. 500.

JUSTICE SCALIA delivered the opinion of the Court.

This case requires us to decide when a contractor providing military equipment to the Federal Government can be held liable under state tort law for injury caused by a design defect.

I

On April 27, 1983, David A. Boyle, a United States Marine helicopter copilot, was killed when the CH-53D helicopter in which he was flying crashed off the coast of Virginia Beach, Virginia, during a training exercise. Although Boyle survived the impact of the crash, he was unable to escape from the helicopter and drowned. Boyle's father, petitioner here, brought this diversity action in Federal District Court against the Sikorsky Division of United Technologies Corporation (Sikorsky), which built the helicopter for the United States.

At trial, petitioner presented two theories of liability under Virginia tort law that were submitted to the jury. First, petitioner alleged that Sikorsky had defectively repaired a device called the servo in the helicopter's automatic flight control system, which allegedly malfunctioned and caused the crash. Second, petitioner alleged that Sikorsky had defectively designed the copilot's emergency escape system: the escape hatch opened out instead of in (and was therefore ineffective in a submerged craft because of water pressure), and access to the escape hatch handle was obstructed by other equipment. The jury returned a general verdict in favor of petitioner and awarded him $725,000. The District Court denied Sikorsky's motion for judgment notwithstanding the verdict.

The Court of Appeals reversed and remanded with directions that judgment be entered for Sikorsky. It found, as a matter of Virginia law, that Boyle had failed to meet his burden of demonstrating that the repair work performed by Sikorsky, as opposed to work that had been done by the Navy, was responsible for the alleged malfunction of the flight control system. It also found, as a matter of federal law, that Sikorsky could not be held liable for the allegedly defective design of the escape hatch because, on the evidence presented, it satisfied the requirements of the "military contractor defense," which the court had recognized the same day in *Tozer v. LTV Corp.*, 792 F.2d 403 (CA4 1986).

Petitioner sought review here, challenging the Court of Appeals' decision on three levels: First, petitioner contends that there is no justification in federal law for shielding Government contractors from liability for design defects in military equipment. Second, he argues in the alternative that even if such a defense should exist, the Court of Appeals' formulation of the conditions for its application is inappropriate. Finally, petitioner contends that the Court of Appeals erred in not remanding for a jury determination of whether the elements of the defense were met in this case.

II

Petitioner's broadest contention is that, in the absence of legislation specifically immunizing Government contractors from liability for design defects, there is no basis for judicial recognition of such a defense. We disagree. In most fields of activity, to be sure, this Court has refused to find federal pre-emption of state law in the absence of either a clear statutory prescription or a direct conflict between federal and state law. But we have held that a few areas, involving "uniquely federal interests," *Texas Industries, Inc. v. Radcliff Materials, Inc.*, 451 U.S. 630 (1981), are so committed by the Constitution and laws of the United States to federal control that state law is pre-empted and replaced, where necessary, by federal law of a content prescribed (absent explicit statutory directive) by the courts—so-called "federal common law." *See, e.g., United States v. Kimbell Foods, Inc.*, 440 U.S. 715 (1979); *Banco Nacional v. Sabbatino*, 376 U.S. 398 (1964); *Howard v. Lyons*, 360 U.S. 593 (1959); *Clearfield Trust Co. v. United States*, 318 U.S. 363 (1943); *D'Oench, Duhme & Co. v. FDIC*, 315 U.S. 447 (1942).

The dispute in the present case borders upon two areas that we have found to involve such "uniquely federal interests." We have held that obligations to and rights of the United States under its contracts are governed exclusively by federal law. *See, e.g., United States v. Little Lake Misere Land Co.*, 412 U.S. 580 (1973); *Clearfield Trust*. The present case does not involve an obligation to the United States under its contract, but rather liability to third persons. That liability may be styled one in tort, but it arises out of performance of the contract—and traditionally has been regarded as sufficiently related to the contract that until 1962 Virginia would generally allow design defect suits only by the purchaser and those in privity with the seller.

Another area that we have found to be of peculiarly federal concern, warranting the displacement of state law, is the civil liability of federal officials for actions taken in the course of their duty. We have held in many contexts that the scope of that liability is controlled by federal law. *See, e.g., Westfall v. Erwin*, 484 U.S. 292, 295 (1988); *Howard v. Lyons; Barr v. Matteo*, 360 U.S. 564 (1959). The present case involves an independent contractor performing its obligation under a procurement contract, rather than an official performing his duty as a federal employee, but there is obviously implicated the same interest in getting the Government's work done.[1]

We think the reasons for considering these closely related areas to be of "uniquely federal" interest apply as well to the civil liabilities arising out of the performance of federal procurement contracts. We have come close to holding as much. In *Yearsley v. W.A. Ross Construction Co.*, 309 U.S. 18 (1940), we rejected an attempt by a landowner to hold a construction contractor liable under state law for the erosion of 95 acres caused by the contractor's work in constructing dikes for the Government. We said that "if [the] authority to carry out the project was validly conferred, that is, if what was done was within the constitutional power of Congress, there is no liability on the part of the contractor for executing its will." The federal interest justifying this holding surely exists as much in procurement contracts as in performance contracts; we see no basis for a distinction.

Moreover, it is plain that the Federal Government's interest in the procurement of equipment is implicated by suits such as the present one—even though the dispute is one between private parties. It is true that where "litigation is purely between private parties and does not touch the rights and duties of the United States," *Bank of America Nat. Trust & Sav. Assn. v. Parnell*, 352 U.S. 29 (1956), federal law does not govern. Thus, for example, in *Miree v. DeKalb County*, 433 U.S. 25 (1977), which involved the question whether certain private parties could sue as third-party beneficiaries to an agreement between a municipality and the Federal Aviation Administration, we found that state law was not displaced because "the operations of the United States in connection with FAA grants such as these . . . would [not] be burdened" by allowing state law to determine whether third-party beneficiaries could sue, and because "any federal interest in the outcome of the [dispute] before us '[was] far too speculative, far too remote a possibility to justify the application of federal law to transactions essentially of local concern.'" *Id.*, quoting *Parnell; see also Wallis v. Pan American Petroleum Corp.*, 384 U.S. 63 (1966).[2] But the same is not true here. The imposition of liability on Government contractors will directly affect the terms of Government contracts: either the contractor will decline to manufacture the design specified by the Government, or it will raise its price. Either way, the interests of the United States will be directly affected.

That the procurement of equipment by the United States is an area of uniquely federal interest does not, however, end the inquiry. That merely establishes a

---

1. Justice Brennan's dissent misreads our discussion here to "intimat[e] that the immunity [of federal officials] . . . might extend . . . [to] nongovernment employees" such as a Government contractor. But we do not address this issue, as it is not before us. We cite these cases merely to demonstrate that the liability of independent contractors performing work for the Federal Government, like the liability of federal officials, is an area of uniquely federal interest.

2. As this language shows, Justice Brennan's dissent is simply incorrect to describe *Miree* and other cases as declining to apply federal law despite the assertion of interests "comparable" to those before us here.

necessary, not a sufficient, condition for the displacement of state law.[3] Displacement will occur only where, as we have variously described, a "significant conflict" exists between an identifiable "federal policy or interest and the [operation] of state law," *Wallis*, or the application of state law would "frustrate specific objectives" of federal legislation, *Kimbell Foods*. The conflict with federal policy need not be as sharp as that which must exist for ordinary pre-emption when Congress legislates "in a field which the States have traditionally occupied." *Rice v. Santa Fe Elevator Corp.*, 331 U.S. 218 (1947). Or to put the point differently, the fact that the area in question *is* one of unique federal concern changes what would otherwise be a conflict that cannot produce pre-emption into one that can. But conflict there must be.

In some cases, for example where the federal interest requires a uniform rule, the entire body of state law applicable to the area conflicts and is replaced by federal rules. *See, e.g., Clearfield Trust* (rights and obligations of United States with respect to commercial paper must be governed by uniform federal rule). In others, the conflict is more narrow, and only particular elements of state law are superseded. *See, e.g., Little Lake Misere Land Co.* (even assuming state law should generally govern federal land acquisitions, particular state law at issue may not); *Howard v. Lyons* (state defamation law generally applicable to federal official, but federal privilege governs for statements made in the course of federal official's duties).

In *Miree*, the suit was not seeking to impose upon the person contracting with the Government a duty contrary to the duty imposed by the Government contract. Rather, it was the contractual duty *itself* that the private plaintiff (as third-party beneficiary) sought to enforce. Between *Miree* and the present case, it is easy to conceive of an intermediate situation, in which the duty sought to be imposed on the contractor is not identical to one assumed under the contract, but is also not contrary to any assumed. If, for example, the United States contracts for the purchase and installation of an air conditioning-unit, specifying the cooling capacity but not the precise manner of construction, a state law imposing upon the manufacturer of such units a duty of care to include a certain safety feature would not be a duty identical to anything promised the Government, but neither would it be contrary. The contractor could comply with both its contractual obligations and the state-prescribed duty of care. No one suggests that state law would generally be pre-empted in this context.

The present case, however, is at the opposite extreme from *Miree*. Here the state-imposed duty of care that is the asserted basis of the contractor's liability (specifically, the duty to equip helicopters with the sort of escape-hatch mechanism

---

3. We refer here to the displacement of state law, although it is possible to analyze it as the displacement of federal-law reference to state law for the rule of decision. Some of our cases appear to regard the area in which a uniquely federal interest exists as being entirely governed by federal law, with federal law deigning to "borro[w]," *United States v. Little Lake Misere Land Co.*, or "incorporat[e]" or "adopt" *United States v. Kimbell Foods, Inc.*, state law except where a significant conflict with federal policy exists. We see nothing to be gained by expanding the theoretical scope of the federal pre-emption beyond its practical effect, and so adopt the more modest terminology. If the distinction between displacement of state law and displacement of federal law's incorporation of state law ever makes a practical difference, it at least does not do so in the present case.

petitioner claims was necessary) is precisely contrary to the duty imposed by the Government contract (the duty to manufacture and deliver helicopters with the sort of escape-hatch mechanism shown by the specifications). Even in this sort of situation, it would be unreasonable to say that there is always a "significant conflict" between the state law and a federal policy or interest. If, for example, a federal procurement officer orders, by model number, a quantity of stock helicopters that happen to be equipped with escape hatches opening outward, it is impossible to say that the Government has a significant interest in that particular feature. That would be scarcely more reasonable than saying that a private individual who orders such a craft by model number cannot sue for the manufacturer's negligence because he got precisely what he ordered.

In its search for the limiting principle to identify those situations in which a "significant conflict" with federal policy or interests does arise, the Court of Appeals [identified] as the source of the conflict the *Feres* doctrine, under which the Federal Tort Claims Act (FTCA) does not cover injuries to Armed Services personnel in the course of military service. See *Feres v. United States*, 340 U.S. 135 (1950). [The Court rejected this approach.]

There is, however, a statutory provision that demonstrates the potential for, and suggests the outlines of, "significant conflict" between federal interests and state law in the context of Government procurement. In the FTCA, Congress authorized damages to be recovered against the United States for harm caused by the negligent or wrongful conduct of Government employees, to the extent that a private person would be liable under the law of the place where the conduct occurred. 28 U.S.C. § 1346(b). It excepted from this consent to suit, however,

> "[a]ny claim . . . based upon the exercise or performance or the failure to exercise or perform a discretionary function or duty on the part of a federal agency or an employee of the Government, whether or not the discretion involved be abused." 28 U.S.C. § 2680(a).

We think that the selection of the appropriate design for military equipment to be used by our Armed Forces is assuredly a discretionary function within the meaning of this provision. It often involves not merely engineering analysis but judgment as to the balancing of many technical, military, and even social considerations, including specifically the trade-off between greater safety and greater combat effectiveness. And we are further of the view that permitting "second-guessing" of these judgments through state tort suits against contractors would produce the same effect sought to be avoided by the FTCA exemption. The financial burden of judgments against the contractors would ultimately be passed through, substantially if not totally, to the United States itself, since defense contractors will predictably raise their prices to cover, or to insure against, contingent liability for the Government-ordered designs. To put the point differently: It makes little sense to insulate the Government against financial liability for the judgment that a particular feature of military equipment is necessary when the Government produces the equipment itself, but not when it contracts for the production. In sum, we are of the view that state law which holds Government contractors liable for design defects in military equipment does in some circumstances present a "significant conflict" with federal policy and must be displaced.

We agree with the scope of displacement adopted by the Fourth Circuit here. Liability for design defects in military equipment cannot be imposed, pursuant to state law, when (1) the United States approved reasonably precise specifications; (2) the equipment conformed to those specifications; and (3) the supplier warned the United States about the dangers in the use of the equipment that were known to the supplier but not to the United States. The first two of these conditions assure that the suit is within the area where the policy of the "discretionary function" would be frustrated—i.e., they assure that the design feature in question was considered by a Government officer, and not merely by the contractor itself. The third condition is necessary because, in its absence, the displacement of state tort law would create some incentive for the manufacturer to withhold knowledge of risks, since conveying that knowledge might disrupt the contract but withholding it would produce no liability. We adopt this provision lest our effort to protect discretionary functions perversely impede them by cutting off information highly relevant to the discretionary decision.

We have considered the alternative formulation of the Government contractor defense, urged upon us by petitioner. . . . That would preclude suit only if (1) the contractor did not participate, or participated only minimally, in the design of the defective equipment; or (2) the contractor timely warned the Government of the risks of the design and notified it of alternative designs reasonably known by it, and the Government, although forewarned, clearly authorized the contractor to proceed with the dangerous design. While this formulation may represent a perfectly reasonable tort rule, it is not a rule designed to protect the federal interest embodied in the "discretionary function" exemption. The design ultimately selected may well reflect a significant policy judgment by Government officials whether or not the contractor rather than those officials developed the design. In addition, it does not seem to us sound policy to penalize, and thus deter, active contractor participation in the design process, placing the contractor at risk unless it identifies all design defects.

III

. . . It is somewhat unclear from the Court of Appeals' opinion [whether] it was in fact deciding that no reasonable jury could, under the properly formulated defense, have found for the petitioner on the facts presented, or rather was assessing on its own whether the defense had been established. The latter, which is what petitioner asserts occurred, would be error, since whether the facts establish the conditions for the defense is a question for the jury. . . . If the Court of Appeals was saying that no reasonable jury could find, under the principles it had announced and on the basis of the evidence presented, that the Government contractor defense was inapplicable, its judgment shall stand, since petitioner did not seek from us, nor did we grant, review of the sufficiency-of-the-evidence determination. If the Court of Appeals was not saying that, it should now undertake the proper sufficiency inquiry.

Accordingly, the judgment is vacated and the case is remanded.

JUSTICE BRENNAN, with whom JUSTICE MARSHALL and JUSTICE BLACKMUN join, dissenting.

Lieutenant David A. Boyle died when the CH-53D helicopter he was copiloting spun out of control and plunged into the ocean. We may assume, for purposes of this case, that Lt. Boyle was trapped under water and drowned because respondent United Technologies negligently designed the helicopter's escape hatch. We may further assume that any competent engineer would have discovered and cured the defects, but that they inexplicably escaped respondent's notice. Had respondent designed such a death trap for a commercial firm, Lt. Boyle's family could sue under Virginia tort law and be compensated for his tragic and unnecessary death. But respondent designed the helicopter for the Federal Government, and that, the Court tells us today, makes all the difference: Respondent is immune from liability so long as it obtained approval of "reasonably precise specifications"—perhaps no more than a rubber stamp from a federal procurement officer who might or might not have noticed or cared about the defects, or even had the expertise to discover them.

If respondent's immunity "bore the legitimacy of having been prescribed by the people's elected representatives," we would be duty bound to implement their will, whether or not we approved. *United States v. Johnson*, 481 U.S. 681, 703 (1987) (dissenting opinion of Scalia, J.). Congress, however, has remained silent—and conspicuously so, having resisted a sustained campaign by Government contractors to legislate for them some defense. [Justice Brennan cited six bills that failed of enactment.] The Court—unelected and unaccountable to the people—has unabashedly stepped into the breach to legislate a rule denying Lt. Boyle's family the compensation that state law assures them. This time the injustice is of this Court's own making.

Worse yet, the injustice will extend far beyond the facts of this case, for the Court's newly discovered Government contractor defense is breathtakingly sweeping. It applies not only to military equipment like the CH-53D helicopter, but (so far as I can tell) to any made-to-order gadget that the Federal Government might purchase after previewing plans—from NASA's Challenger space shuttle to the Postal Service's old mail cars. The contractor may invoke the defense in suits brought not only by military personnel like Lt. Boyle, or Government employees, but by anyone injured by a Government contractor's negligent design, including, for example, the children who might have died had respondent's helicopter crashed on the beach. It applies even if the Government has not intentionally sacrificed safety for other interests like speed or efficiency, and, indeed, even if the equipment is not of a type that is typically considered dangerous; thus, the contractor who designs a Government building can invoke the defense when the elevator cable snaps or the walls collapse. And the defense is invocable regardless of how blatant or easily remedied the defect, so long as the contractor missed it and the specifications approved by the Government, however unreasonably dangerous, were "reasonably precise."

In my view, this Court lacks both authority and expertise to fashion such a rule, whether to protect the Treasury of the United States or the coffers of industry. Because I would leave that exercise of legislative power to Congress, where our Constitution places it, I would reverse the Court of Appeals and reinstate petitioner's jury award.

I

Before our decision in *Erie R. Co. v. Tompkins*, 304 U.S. 64 (1938), federal courts sitting in diversity were generally free, in the absence of a controlling state statute, to fashion rules of "general" federal common law. *Erie* renounced the prevailing scheme.... [*Erie* was] deeply rooted in notions of federalism, and is most seriously implicated when, as here, federal judges displace the state law that would ordinarily govern with their own rules of federal common law.[2]

In pronouncing that "[t]here is no federal general common law," *Erie* put to rest the notion that the grant of diversity jurisdiction to federal courts is itself authority to fashion rules of substantive law. See *United States v. Little Lake Misere Land Co.*, 412 U.S. 580, 591 (1973). As the author of today's opinion for the Court pronounced for a unanimous Court just two months ago, "we start with the assumption that the historic police powers of the States were not to be superseded ... unless that was the clear and manifest purpose of Congress." *Puerto Rico Dept. of Consumer Affairs v. Isla Petroleum Corp.*, 485 U.S. 495, 500 (1988). Just as "[t]here is no federal pre-emption *in vacuo*, without a constitutional text or a federal statute to assert it," federal common law cannot supersede state law *in vacuo* out of no more than an idiosyncratic determination by five Justices that a particular area is "uniquely federal."

Accordingly, we have emphasized that federal common law can displace state law in "few and restricted" instances. *Wheeldin v. Wheeler*, 373 U.S. 647, 651 (1963). "[A]bsent some congressional authorization to formulate substantive rules of decision, federal common law exists only in such narrow areas as those concerned with the rights and obligations of the United States, interstate and international disputes implicating conflicting rights of States or our relations with foreign nations, and admiralty cases." *Texas Industries, Inc. v. Radcliff Materials, Inc.*, 451 U.S. 630 (1981). "The enactment of a federal rule in an area of national concern, and the decision whether to displace state law in doing so, is generally made not by the federal judiciary, purposefully insulated from democratic pressures, but by the people through their elected representatives in Congress." *Milwaukee v. Illinois*, 451 U.S. 304 (1981). *See also Wallis v. Pan American Petroleum Corp.*, 384 U.S. 63, 68 (1966); *Miree v. DeKalb County*, 433 U.S. 25, 32 (1977). State laws "should be overridden by the federal courts only where clear and substantial interests of the National Government, which cannot be served

---

2. Not all exercises of our power to fashion federal common law displace state law in the same way. For example, our recognition of federal causes of action based upon either the Constitution, *see, e.g.*, *Bivens v. Six Unknown Fed. Narcotics Agents*, 403 U.S. 388 (1971), or a federal statute, see *Cort v. Ash*, 422 U.S. 66 (1975), supplements whatever rights state law might provide, and therefore does not implicate federalism concerns in the same way as does pre-emption of a state-law rule of decision or cause of action. Throughout this opinion I use the word "displace" in the latter sense.

consistently with respect for such state interests, will suffer major damage if the state law is applied." *United States v. Yazell*, 382 U.S. 341, 352 (1966).

II

Congress has not decided to supersede state law here (if anything, it has decided not to, see n.1, *supra*) and the Court does not pretend that its newly manufactured "Government contractor defense" fits within any of the handful of "narrow areas" of "uniquely federal interests" in which we have heretofore done so. Rather, the Court creates a new category of "uniquely federal interests" out of a synthesis of two whose origins predate *Erie* itself: the interest in administering the "obligations to and rights of the United States under its contracts," and the interest in regulating the "civil liability of federal officials for actions taken in the course of their duty." This case is, however, simply a suit between two private parties. We have steadfastly declined to impose federal contract law on relationships that are collateral to a federal contract, or to extend the federal employee's immunity beyond federal employees. And the Court's ability to list 2, or 10, inapplicable areas of "uniquely federal interest" does not support its conclusion that the liability of Government contractors is so "clear and substantial" an interest that this Court must step in lest state law does "major damage." *Yazell.*

A

The proposition that federal common law continues to govern the "obligations to and rights of the United States under its contracts" is nearly as old as *Erie* itself. . . . Any such transaction necessarily "radiate[s] interests in transactions between private parties." *Parnell.* But it is by now established that our power to create federal common law controlling the *Federal Government's* contractual rights and obligations does not translate into a power to prescribe rules that cover all transactions or contractual relationships collateral to Government contracts.

In *Miree*, for example, . . . we held that state law should govern the claim because "only the rights of private litigants are at issue here," and the claim against the county "will have *no direct effect upon the United States or its Treasury*" (emphasis added).

Miree relied heavily on *Parnell* and *Wallis* . . . Here, as in *Miree, Parnell*, and *Wallis*, a Government contract governed by federal common law looms in the back ground. But here, too, the United States is not a party to the suit and the suit neither "touch[es] the rights and duties of the United States," *Parnell*, nor has a "direct effect upon the United States or its Treasury," *Miree*. The relationship at issue is at best collateral to the Government contract.[3] We have no greater power to displace state law governing the collateral relationship in the Government procurement realm than we had to

---

3. True, in this case the collateral relationship is the relationship between victim and tortfeasor, rather than between contractors, but that distinction makes no difference. We long ago established that the principles governing application of federal common law in "contractual relations of the Government . . . are equally applicable . . . where the relations affected are noncontractual or tortious in character." *United States v. Standard Oil Co.*, 332 U.S. 301, 305 (1947).

dictate federal rules governing equally collateral relationships in the areas of aviation, Government-issued commercial paper, or federal lands.

That the Government might have to pay higher prices for what it orders if delivery in accordance with the contract exposes the seller to potential liability does not distinguish this case. Each of the cases just discussed declined to extend the reach of federal common law despite the assertion of comparable interests that would have affected the terms of the Government contract—whether its price or its substance—just as "directly" (or indirectly). Third-party beneficiaries can sue under a county's contract with the FAA, for example, even though—as the Court's focus on the absence of "*direct* effect on the United States or its Treasury" (emphasis added), suggests—counties will likely pass on the costs to the Government in future contract negotiations. Similarly, we held that state law may govern the circumstances under which stolen federal bonds can be recovered, notwithstanding Parnell's argument that "the value of bonds to the first purchaser and hence their salability by the Government would be materially affected." As in each of the cases declining to extend the traditional reach of federal law of contracts beyond the rights and duties of the *Federal Government*, "any federal interest in the outcome of the question before us 'is far too speculative, far too remote a possibility to justify the application of federal law to transactions essentially of local concern.'" *Miree*, quoting *Parnell*.

B

Our "uniquely federal interest" in the tort liability of affiliates of the Federal Government is equally narrow. The immunity we have recognized has extended no further than a subset of "officials of the Federal Government" and has covered only "discretionary" functions within the scope of their legal authority. Never before have we so much as intimated that the immunity (or the "uniquely federal interest" that justifies it) might extend beyond that narrow class to cover also nongovernment employees whose authority to act is independent of any source of federal law and that are as far removed from the "functioning of the Federal Government" as is a Government contractor . . .

The historical narrowness of the federal interest and the immunity is hardly accidental. A federal officer exercises statutory authority, which not only provides the necessary basis for the immunity in positive law, but also permits us confidently to presume that interference with the exercise of discretion undermines congressional will. In contrast, a Government contractor acts independently of any congressional enactment. Thus, immunity for a contractor lacks both the positive law basis and the presumption that it furthers congressional will. . . .

C

Yearsley v. W. A. Ross Construction Co., 309 U.S. 18 (1940), the sole case cited by the Court immunizing a Government contractor, is a slender reed on which to base so drastic a departure from precedent. In *Yearsley* we barred the suit of landowners against a private Government contractor alleging that its construction of a dam eroded their land without just compensation in violation of the Takings Clause of the Fifth Amendment. We relied in part on the observation that the plaintiffs failed to state a Fifth Amendment claim since just compensation had never been requested, much less denied) and at any rate the cause of action lay against the Government, not the contractor. . . . It is therefore unlikely that the Court intended *Yearsley* to extend anywhere beyond the takings context, and we have never applied it elsewhere.

Even if *Yearsley* were applicable beyond the unique context in which it arose, it would have little relevance here. The contractor's work "was done pursuant to a contract with the United States Government, and under the direction of the Secretary of War and the supervision of the Chief of Engineers of the United States, . . . as authorized by an Act of Congress." . . . In other words, unlike respondent here, the contractor in *Yearsley* was following, not formulating, the Government's specifications, and (so far as is relevant here) followed them correctly. Had respondent merely manufactured the CH-53D helicopter, following minutely the Government's own in-house specifications, it would be analogous to the contractor in *Yearsley*. . . . But respondent's participation in the helicopter's design distinguishes this case from *Yearsley*, which has never been read to immunize the discretionary acts of those who perform service contracts for the Government.

III

In a valiant attempt to bridge the analytical canyon between what *Yearsley* said and what the Court wishes it had said, the Court invokes the discretionary function exception of the Federal Tort Claims Act (FTCA), 28 U.S.C. § 2680(a). The Court does not suggest that the exception has any direct bearing here, for petitioner has sued a private manufacturer (not the Federal Government) under Virginia law (not the FTCA). Perhaps that is why respondent has three times disavowed any reliance on the discretionary function exception, [as] has the Government.

Notwithstanding these disclaimers, the Court invokes the exception, reasoning that federal common law must immunize Government contractors from state tort law to prevent erosion of the discretionary function exception's *policy* of foreclosing judicial "second-guessing" of discretionary governmental decisions. The erosion the Court fears apparently is rooted not in a concern that suits against Government contractors will prevent them from designing, or the Government from commissioning the design of, precisely the product the Government wants, but in the concern that such suits might preclude the Government from purchasing the desired product at the price it wants: "The financial burden of judgments against the contractors," the Court fears, "would ultimately be passed through, substantially if not totally, to the United States itself."

Even granting the Court's factual premise, which is by no means self-evident, the Court cites no authority for the proposition that burdens imposed on Government contractors, but passed on to the Government, burden the Government in a way that justifies extension of its immunity. However substantial such indirect burdens may be, we have held in other contexts that they are legally irrelevant.

IV

At bottom, the Court's analysis is premised on the proposition that any tort liability indirectly absorbed by the Government so burdens governmental functions as to compel us to act when Congress has not. That proposition is by no means uncontroversial. The tort system is premised on the assumption that the imposition of liability encourages actors to prevent any injury whose expected cost exceeds the cost of prevention. If the system is working as it should, Government contractors will design equipment to avoid certain injuries (like the deaths of soldiers or Government employees), which would be certain to burden the Government. The Court therefore has no basis for its assumption that tort liability will result in a net burden on the Government (let alone a clearly excessive net burden) rather than a net gain.

Perhaps tort liability is an inefficient means of ensuring the quality of design efforts, but "[w]hatever the merits of the policy" the Court wishes to implement, "its conversion into law is a proper subject for congressional action, not for any creative power of ours." . . . If Congress shared the Court's assumptions and conclusion it could readily enact "A BILL [t]o place limitations on the civil liability of government contractors to ensure that such liability does not impede the ability of the United States to procure necessary goods and services," H.R. 4765, 99th Cong., 2d Sess. (1986). It has not.

Were I a legislator, I would probably vote against any law absolving multibillion dollar private enterprises from answering for their tragic mistakes, at least if that law were justified by no more than the unsupported speculation that their liability might ultimately burden the United States Treasury. Some of my colleagues here would evidently vote otherwise (as they have here), but that should not matter here. We are judges not legislators, and the vote is not ours to cast.

I respectfully dissent.

Justice Stevens, dissenting.

When judges are asked to embark on a lawmaking venture, I believe they should carefully consider whether they, or a legislative body, are better equipped to perform the task at hand. There are instances of so-called interstitial lawmaking that inevitably become part of the judicial process. But when we are asked to create an entirely new doctrine — to answer "questions of policy on which Congress has not spoken," we have a special duty to identify the proper decisionmaker before trying to make the proper decision.

When the novel question of policy involves a balancing of the conflicting interests in the efficient operation of a massive governmental program and the protection of the rights of the individual — whether in the social welfare context, the civil service context, or the military procurement context — I feel very deeply that we should defer to the expertise of the Congress. . . .

Note: The Implications of Boyle

1. Justice Brennan, dissenting in *Boyle*, relies heavily on *Miree*. Does the Court adequately explain why *Miree* is not controlling?

2. In *Miree*, the Court said that there was no need to apply federal common law "since the litigation is among private parties and *no substantial rights or duties of the United States* hinge on its outcome." (Emphasis added.) Does the Court in *Boyle* say that the outcome of the case *will* affect substantial rights or duties of the United States? Or does the Court hold that there can be other justifications for applying federal common law to suits between private parties?

3. In distinguishing *Miree* and *Wallis*, the Court in *Boyle* says: "The imposition of liability on Government contractors will directly affect the terms of Government contracts: either the contractor will decline to manufacture the design specified by the Government, or it will raise its price. Either way, the interests of the United States will be directly affected." Later in the opinion, the Court says that if state tort suits were allowed to "second-guess" procurement decisions, "[t]he financial burden of judgments against the contractors would ultimately be passed through [to the United States itself]."

Six years after *Boyle*, in *O'Melveny & Myers v. FDIC*, 512 U.S. 79 (1994), the Court confronted the question "whether, in a suit by the Federal Deposit Insurance Corporation (FDIC) as receiver of a federally insured bank, it is a federal-law or rather a state-law rule of decision that governs the tort liability of attorneys who provided services to the bank." The Court held that state law controlled. Justice Scalia—the author of *Boyle*—wrote for the Court. He said:

> The closest [the FDIC] comes to identifying a specific, concrete federal policy or interest that is compromised by California law is its contention that state rules regarding the imputation of knowledge might "deplete the deposit insurance fund." But [no federal statute] sets forth any anticipated level for the fund, so what [the FDIC] must mean by "depletion" is simply the forgoing of *any* money which, under any *conceivable* legal rules, might accrue to the fund. That is a broad principle indeed, which would support not just elimination of the defense at issue here, but judicial creation of new, "federal-common-law" causes of action to enrich the fund. Of course we have no authority to do that, because there is no federal policy that the fund should always win. Our cases have previously rejected "more money" arguments remarkably similar to the one made here.

In support of the last-quoted sentence, Justice Scalia cited *Kimbell Foods* and two other cases. He made no mention of *Boyle*.

Doesn't the Court opinion in *Boyle* rely heavily on a "more money" argument? Why should the argument prevail in *Boyle* but not in *O'Melveny* or *Kimbell Foods*?

4. In *Miree*, the Court quoted with approval from *Wallis*: "Whether latent federal power should be exercised to displace state law is primarily a decision for Congress."

As Justice Brennan points out in his dissent in *Boyle*, several bills had been introduced in Congress to legislate a "government contractor" defense, but none had been enacted. Does Justice Scalia adequately explain why the Court, rather than Congress, was exercising the "latent federal power . . . to displace state law"?

5. Justice Stevens, dissenting, says: "When judges are asked to embark on a lawmaking venture, I believe they should carefully consider whether they, or a legislative body, are better equipped to perform the task at hand." Is the approach of the *Boyle* dissent consistent with Justice Stevens's opinions in *Cannon, Sandoval,* and other cases involving implied rights of action?

Problems: Suits Against Government Contractors

1. Frank Pulver has brought suit in federal district court on behalf of a class of plaintiffs against various manufacturers of asbestos. Jurisdiction is based on diversity. The complaint asserts that the plaintiffs were exposed to asbestos dust while serving in the United States Navy and that they suffered asbestosis or cancer as a result. The defendants are companies who manufactured and supplied asbestos products that were used as insulation materials in Navy ships. The plaintiffs seek recovery on various state-law theories including strict liability. The defendants have filed a motion in limine seeking to assert the government contractor defense recognized in *Boyle*. Does the defense apply to the plaintiffs' claims?

2. Virginia Houser is an emergency medical technician employed by Magruder Hospital in the District of Columbia. She has filed suit in United States District Court for the District of Columbia to recover for injuries received in an accident late last year. The defendant is Acme Ambulance Manufacturing Co. (Acme), a New Jersey corporation, and jurisdiction is based on diversity.

The accident occurred while Houser was on duty and riding as a passenger in a 1997 Type II 6.9 liter diesel-powered ambulance manufactured by Acme. While the ambulance was en route to the scene of an emergency, an automobile failed to properly yield the right-of-way. The ambulance made an evasive maneuver and flipped over. Houser suffered injuries to her knee and back, including a herniated disk. A police officer who witnessed the accident reported that the ambulance was driven in a reasonable and safe manner for an emergency situation.

The ambulance was manufactured by Acme pursuant to a contract with the United States General Services Administration ("GSA"). The GSA solicited bids for the manufacture of the ambulance in compliance with the Federal Specification for Ambulance KKK-A-1822B, dated June 1, 1995, which was incorporated into the contract. After Acme completed the ambulance, a GSA quality assurance inspector examined it, concluded that it complied with contract specifications, and released it for shipment.

Houser's complaint asserts claims of strict products liability and breach of warranty arising from the manufacture and sale of an ambulance with a design defect. The complaint states that the ambulance was unreasonably prone to turn over during intended use because of an excessively high center of gravity.

Acme has filed a motion for summary judgment asserting that it is immune from liability because it built the ambulance in the performance of its obligations under a contract with the United States Government. Houser argues that the motion should be denied because the government contractor defense as defined in *Boyle* is not available to Acme.

How should the court rule?

Atherton v. FDIC

Supreme Court of the United States, 1997.

519 U.S. 213.

JUSTICE BREYER delivered the opinion of the Court.

The Resolution Trust Corporation (RTC) sued several officers and directors of City Federal Savings Bank, claiming that they had violated the legal standard of care they owed that federally chartered, federally insured institution. The case here focuses upon the legal standard for determining whether or not their behavior was improper. It asks where courts should look to find the standard of care to measure the legal propriety of the defendants' conduct — to state law, to federal common law, or to a special federal statute (12 U.S.C. § 1821(k)) that speaks of "gross negligence"?

We conclude that state law sets the standard of conduct as long as the state standard (such as simple negligence) is stricter than that of the federal statute. The federal statute nonetheless sets a "gross negligence" floor, which applies as a substitute for state standards that are more relaxed.

I

In 1989, City Federal Savings Bank (City Federal), a federal savings association, went into receivership. The RTC, as receiver, brought this action in the bank's name against officers and directors. (Throughout this opinion, we use the more colloquial term "bank" to refer to a variety of institutions such as "federal savings associations.") The complaint said that the defendants had acted (or failed to act) in ways that led City Federal to make various bad development, construction, and business acquisition loans. It claimed that these actions (or omissions) were unlawful because they amounted to gross negligence, simple negligence, and breaches of fiduciary duty.

The defendants moved to dismiss. They pointed to a federal statute, 12 U.S.C. § 1821(k), that says in part that a "director or officer" of a federally insured bank "may be held personally liable for monetary damages" in an RTC-initiated "civil action . . . for *gross negligence*" or "similar conduct . . . that demonstrates a greater disregard of a duty of care (than gross negligence). . . ." (Emphasis added.) They argued that, by authorizing actions for gross negligence or more seriously culpable conduct, the statute intended to forbid actions based upon less seriously culpable conduct, such as conduct that rose only to the level of simple negligence. The District Court agreed and dismissed all but the gross negligence claims.

The Third Circuit, providing an interlocutory appeal, reversed. It interpreted the federal statute as simply offering a safeguard against state legislation that had watered down applicable state standards of care—below a gross negligence benchmark. As so interpreted, the statute did not prohibit actions resting upon stricter standard of care rules—whether those stricter standard of care rules originated in state law (which the Circuit found applicable in the case of state-chartered banks) or in federal common law (which the Circuit found applicable in the case of federally chartered banks). Noting that City Federal is a federally chartered savings institution, the Circuit concluded that the RTC was free "to pursue any claims for negligence or of breach of fiduciary duty available as a matter of federal common law."

The defendants, pointing to variations in the Circuits' interpretations of the "gross negligence" statute, sought certiorari. And we granted review.

II

We begin by temporarily setting the federal "gross negligence" statute to the side, and by asking whether, were there no such statute, federal common law would provide the applicable legal standard. We recognize, as did the Third Circuit, that this Court did once articulate federal common-law corporate governance standards, applicable to federally chartered banks. *Briggs v. Spaulding*, 141 U.S. 132 (1891). But the Court found its rules of decision in federal common law long before it held, in *Erie R. Co. v. Tompkins*, 304 U.S. 64 (1938), that "[t]here is no federal general common law." The Third Circuit, while considering itself bound by *Briggs*, asked whether relevant federal common-law standards could have survived *Erie*. We conclude that they did not and that (except as modified in Part III, *infra*) state law, not federal common law, provides the applicable rules for decision.

This Court has recently discussed what one might call "federal common law" in the strictest sense, i.e., a rule of decision that amounts, not simply to an interpretation of a federal statute or a properly promulgated administrative rule, but, rather, to the judicial "creation" of a special federal rule of decision. The Court has said that "cases in which judicial creation of a special federal rule would be justified . . . are . . . 'few and restricted.'" *O'Melveny & Myers v. FDIC*, 512 U.S. 79, 87 (1994). "Whether latent federal power should be exercised to displace state law is primarily a decision for Congress," not the federal courts. *Wallis v. Pan American Petroleum Corp.*, 384 U.S. 63 (1966). Nor does the existence of related federal statutes automatically show that Congress intended courts to create federal common-law rules, for "'Congress acts . . . against the background of the total corpus juris of the states. . . .'" *Id.* (quoting H. Hart & H. Wechsler, *The Federal Courts and the Federal System* 435 (1953)). Thus, normally, when courts decide to fashion rules of federal common law, "the guiding principle is that a significant conflict between some federal policy or interest and the use of state law . . . must first be specifically shown." *Ibid.* Indeed, such a "conflict" is normally a "precondition." *O'Melveny. See also United States v. Kimbell Foods, Inc.*, 440 U.S. 715 (1979); *Kamen v. Kemper Financial Services, Inc.*, 500 U.S. 90 (1991).

No one doubts the power of Congress to legislate rules for deciding cases like the one before us. Indeed, Congress has enacted related legislation. . . . No one argues, however, that either these statutes, or federal regulations validly promulgated pursuant to statute, set forth general corporate governance standards of the sort at issue applicable to a federally chartered savings association such as City Federal. *Cf.* 12 C.F.R. § 7.2000 (1996) (describing governance procedures applicable to federally chartered national banks, but not federal savings associations). Consequently, we must decide whether the application of state-law standards of care to such banks would conflict with, and thereby significantly threaten, a federal policy or interest.

We have examined each of the basic arguments that the respondent implicitly or explicitly raises. In our view, they do not point to a conflict or threat that is significant, and we shall explain why. (The respondent, by the way, is now the Federal Deposit Insurance Corporation—the FDIC—which has replaced the Resolution Trust Corporation pursuant to a new federal statute.)

First, the FDIC invokes the need for "uniformity." Federal common law, it says, will provide uniformity, but "[s]uperimposing state standards of fiduciary responsibility over standards developed by a federal chartering authority would ... 'upset the balance' that the federal chartering authority 'may strike. ...'" Brief for Respondent 23 (quoting *Kamen*). To invoke the concept of "uniformity," however, is not to prove its need. *Cf. Kimbell Foods* (rejecting "generalized pleas for uniformity"); *O'Melveny* (same).

For one thing, the number of federally insured banks is about equally divided between federally chartered and state-chartered banks, ... and a federal standard that increases uniformity among the former would increase disparity with the latter.

For another, our Nation's banking system has thrived despite disparities in matters of corporate governance. Consider, for example, the divergent state law governance standards applicable to banks chartered in different States. ... Indeed, the Comptroller of the Currency, acting through regulation, permits considerable disparity in the standard of care applicable to federally chartered banks other than savings banks (which are under the jurisdiction of the Office of Thrift Supervision). ...

Second, the FDIC at times suggests that courts must apply a federal common-law standard of care simply because the banks in question are federally chartered. This argument, with little more, might have seemed a strong one during most of the first century of our Nation's history, for then state-chartered banks were the norm and federally chartered banks an exception—and federal banks often encountered hostility and deleterious state laws. ...

[In 1933, Congress provided for the federal chartering of savings banks. In 1870 and thereafter this Court held that federally chartered banks are subject to state law. The Court subsequently found numerous state laws applicable to federally chartered banks.]

For present purposes, the consequence is the following: To point to a federal charter by itself shows no conflict, threat, or need for "federal common law." It does not answer the critical question ....

* * *

Finally, we note that here, as in *O'Melveny*, the FDIC is acting only as a receiver of a failed institution; it is not pursuing the interest of the Federal Government as a bank insurer—an interest likely present whether the insured institution is state, or federally, chartered.

In sum, we can find no significant conflict with, or threat to, a federal interest. The federal need is far weaker than was present in what the Court has called the "few and restricted instances," in which this Court has created a federal common law. Consider, for example, *Hinderlider v. La Plata River & Cherry Creek Ditch Co.*, 304 U.S. 92 (1938) (controversy between two States regarding apportionment of streamwater); *Boyle v. United Technologies Corp.*, 487 U.S. 500 (1988) (Federal Government contractors and civil liability of federal officials); *United States v. Standard Oil Co. of Cal.*, 332 U.S. 301, 305 (1947) (relationship between Federal Government and members of its armed forces); *Howard v. Lyons*, 360 U.S. 593, 597 (1959) (liability of federal officers in the course of official duty); *Banco Nacional de Cuba v. Sabbatino*, 376 U.S. 398, 425 (1964) (relationships with other countries). *See also Texas Industries, Inc. v. Radcliff Materials, Inc.*, 451 U.S. 630, 641 (1981) ("[A]bsent some congressional authorization to formulate substantive rules of decision, federal common law exists only in such narrow areas as those concerned with the rights and obligations of the United States, interstate and international disputes implicating the conflicting rights of States or our relations with foreign nations, and admiralty cases"). Indeed, the interests in many of the cases where this Court has declined to recognize federal common law appear at least as strong as, if not stronger than, those present here. *E.g., Wallis v. Pan American Petroleum Corp.*, 384 U.S. 63 (1966) (applying state law to claims for land owned and leased by the Federal Government); *Kimbell Foods*, 440 U.S. at 726, 732–38 (applying state law to priority of liens under federal lending programs).

We conclude that the federal common-law standards enunciated in cases such as *Briggs* did not survive this Court's later decision in *Erie R. Co. v. Tompkins*. There is no federal common law that would create a general standard of care applicable to this case.

III

We now turn to a further question: Does federal statutory law (namely, the federal "gross negligence" statute), supplant any state-law standard of care? . . .

In our view, the statute's "gross negligence" standard provides only a floor—a guarantee that officers and directors must meet at least a gross negligence standard. It does not stand in the way of a stricter standard that the laws of some States provide. [Detailed discussion omitted.]

For these reasons, the judgment of the Court of Appeals is vacated, and the case is remanded for proceedings consistent with this opinion.

[Concurring opinion omitted.]

Note: Federal Common Law after Atherton

1. In *Miree*, Chief Justice Burger expressed concern that the Court was foreclosing the application of federal common law "to all matters involving only the rights of private citizens." *Boyle* made clear that that was not the Court's position. *Atherton* appears to bring the law back to about where *Miree* left it, but it does not overrule *Boyle*. This note surveys the current state of the doctrine.

2. In contrast to *Miree*, the opinion in *Atherton* intermingles citations to cases involving the Federal Government as a party and cases involving only private litigants. But the two-step approach of *Clearfield* and *Kimbell Foods* for Federal Government litigation is so well established that we would not expect the Court to abandon it without saying so.

3. The Court in *Atherton* quotes with approval from *Texas Industries, Inc. v. Radcliffe Materials, Inc.*, 451 U.S. 630 (1981): "[A]bsent some congressional authorization to formulate substantive rules of decision, federal common law exists *only in such narrow areas* as those concerned with the rights and obligations of the United States, interstate and international disputes implicating the conflicting rights of States or our relations with foreign nations, and admiralty cases." (Emphasis added.) This is sometimes referred to as the "enclave" approach to federal common law. Was that the approach taken in *Boyle*?

4. One of the "narrow areas" encompasses "relationships with other countries." The leading case is *Banco Nacional de Cuba v. Sabbatino*, 376 U.S. 398 (1964). *Sabbatino* involved the "act of state" doctrine. As the Court explained, that doctrine "in its traditional formulation precludes the courts of this country from inquiring into the validity of the public acts a recognized foreign sovereign power committed within its own territory." (The doctrine was later modified by an Act of Congress.)

5. How would *Kohr* be analyzed today? Do the decisions in *Miree, Boyle*, and *Atherton* allow the use of federal common law in the circumstances of that case?

D. Implied Remedies for Violation of Constitutional Rights

As we have seen, section 1 of the Civil Rights Act of 1871, codified as 42 U.S.C. § 1983, provides a remedy to individuals who have suffered a deprivation of federal constitutional rights by persons acting under color of state law. But Congress has not authorized a remedy for the violation of constitutional rights by agents of the Federal Government. To what extent may the federal courts do so? The Supreme Court addressed that question in the context of a Fourth Amendment claim in the landmark case of *Bivens v. Six Unknown Named Agents*.

Bivens v. Six Unknown Named Agents
of Federal Bureau of Narcotics

Supreme Court of the United States, 1971.

403 U.S. 388.

MR. JUSTICE BRENNAN delivered the opinion of the Court.

The Fourth Amendment provides that:

> The right of the people to be secure in their persons, houses, papers, and effects, against unreasonable searches and seizures, shall not be violated. * * *

In *Bell v. Hood*, 327 U.S. 678 (1946), we reserved the question whether violation of that command by a federal agent acting under color of his authority gives rise to a cause of action for damages consequent upon his unconstitutional conduct. Today we hold that it does.

This case has its origin in an arrest and search carried out on the morning of November 26, 1965. Petitioner's complaint alleged that on that day respondents, agents of the Federal Bureau of Narcotics acting under claim of federal authority, entered his apartment and arrested him for alleged narcotics violations. The agents manacled petitioner in front of his wife and children, and threatened to arrest the entire family. They searched the apartment from stem to stern. Thereafter, petitioner was taken to the federal courthouse in Brooklyn, where he was interrogated, booked, and subjected to a visual strip search.

On July 7, 1967, petitioner brought suit in Federal District Court. In addition to the allegations above, his complaint asserted that the arrest and search were effected without a warrant, and that unreasonable force was employed in making the arrest; fairly read, it alleges as well that the arrest was made without probable cause. Petitioner claimed to have suffered great humiliation, embarrassment, and mental suffering as a result of the agents' unlawful conduct, and sought $15,000 damages from each of them. The District Court, on respondents' motion, dismissed the complaint on the ground, *inter alia*, that it failed to state a cause of action.[2] The Court of Appeals [affirmed] on that basis. We granted certiorari [and now] reverse.

I

Respondents do not argue that petitioner should be entirely without remedy for an unconstitutional invasion of his rights by federal agents. In respondents' view, however, the rights that petitioner asserts—primarily rights of privacy—are creations of state and not of federal law. Accordingly, they argue, petitioner may obtain money damages to redress invasion of these rights only by an action in tort, under state law, in the state courts. In this scheme the Fourth Amendment would serve merely to limit the extent to which the agents could defend the state law tort suit by asserting that their actions were

---

2. The agents were not named in petitioner's complaint, and the District Court ordered that the complaint be served upon "those federal agents who it is indicated by the records of the United States Attorney participated in the November 25, 1965, arrest of the [petitioner]." Five agents were ultimately served.

a valid exercise of federal power: if the agents were shown to have violated the Fourth Amendment, such a defense would be lost to them and they would stand before the state law merely as private individuals. Candidly admitting that it is the policy of the Department of Justice to remove all such suits from the state to the federal courts for decision, respondents nevertheless urge that we uphold dismissal of petitioner's complaint in federal court, and remit him to filing an action in the state courts in order that the case may properly be removed to the federal court for decision on the basis of state law.

We think that respondents' thesis rests upon an unduly restrictive view of the Fourth Amendment's protection against unreasonable searches and seizures by federal agents, a view that has consistently been rejected by this Court. Respondents seek to treat the relationship between a citizen and a federal agent unconstitutionally exercising his authority as no different from the relationship between two private citizens. In so doing, they ignore the fact that power, once granted, does not disappear like a magic gift when it is wrongfully used. An agent acting—albeit unconstitutionally—in the name of the United States possesses a far greater capacity for harm than an individual trespasser exercising no authority other than his own. Accordingly, as our cases make clear, the Fourth Amendment operates as a limitation upon the exercise of federal power regardless of whether the State in whose jurisdiction that power is exercised would prohibit or penalize the identical act if engaged in by a private citizen. It guarantees to citizens of the United States the absolute right to be free from unreasonable searches and seizures carried out by virtue of federal authority. And "where federally protected rights have been invaded, it has been the rule from the beginning that courts will be alert to adjust their remedies so as to grant the necessary relief." *Bell v. Hood.*

First. Our cases have long since rejected the notion that the Fourth Amendment proscribes only such conduct as would, if engaged in by private persons, be condemned by state law. . . . In light of these cases, respondents' argument that the Fourth Amendment serves only as a limitation on federal defenses to a state law claim, and not as an independent limitation upon the exercise of federal power, must be rejected.

Second. The interests protected by state laws regulating trespass and the invasion of privacy, and those protected by the Fourth Amendment's guarantee against unreasonable searches and seizures, may be inconsistent or even hostile. . . . A private citizen, asserting no authority other than his own, will not normally be liable in trespass if he demands, and is granted, admission to another's house. But one who demands admission under a claim of federal authority stands in a far different position. The mere invocation of federal power by a federal law enforcement official will normally render futile any attempt to resist an unlawful entry or arrest by resort to the local police; and a claim of authority to enter is likely to unlock the door as well. "In such cases there is no safety for the citizen, except in the protection of the judicial tribunals, for rights which have been invaded by the officers of the government, professing to act in its name. There remains to him but the alternative of resistance, which may amount to crime." *United States v. Lee,* 106 U.S. 196, 219 (1882). . . .

Third. That damages may be obtained for injuries consequent upon a violation of the Fourth Amendment by federal officials should hardly seem a surprising proposition. Historically, damages have been regarded as the ordinary remedy for an invasion of personal interests in liberty. Of course, the Fourth Amendment does not in so many words provide for its enforcement by an award of money damages for the consequences of its violation. But "it is * * * well settled that where legal rights have been invaded, and a federal statute provides for a general right to sue for such invasion, federal courts may use any available remedy to make good the wrong done." *Bell v. Hood.* The present case involves no special factors counseling hesitation in the absence of affirmative action by Congress. We are not dealing with a question of "federal fiscal policy," as in *United States v. Standard Oil Co.*, 332 U.S. 301 (1947). In that case we refused to infer from the Government-soldier relationship that the United States could recover damages from one who negligently injured a soldier and thereby caused the Government to pay his medical expenses and lose his services during the course of his hospitalization. Noting that Congress was normally quite solicitous where the federal purse was involved, we pointed out that "the United States [was] the party plaintiff to the suit. And the United States has power at any time to create the liability." Nor are we asked in this case to impose liability upon a congressional employee for actions contrary to no constitutional prohibition, but merely said to be in excess of the authority delegated to him by the Congress. *Wheeldin v. Wheeler*, 373 U.S. 647 (1963).

Finally, we cannot accept respondents' formulation of the question as whether the availability of money damages is necessary to enforce the Fourth Amendment. For we have here no explicit congressional declaration that persons injured by a federal officer's violation of the Fourth Amendment may not recover money damages from the agents, but must instead be remitted to another remedy, equally effective in the view of Congress. The question is merely whether petitioner, if he can demonstrate an injury consequent upon the violation by federal agents of his Fourth Amendment rights, is entitled to redress his injury through a particular remedial mechanism normally available in the federal courts. *Cf. J.I. Case Co. v. Borak*, 377 U.S. 426 (1964). "The very essence of civil liberty certainly consists in the right of every individual to claim the protection of the laws, whenever he receives an injury." *Marbury v. Madison*, 1 Cranch 137, 163 (1803). Having concluded that petitioner's complaint states a cause of action under the Fourth Amendment, we hold that petitioner is entitled to recover money damages for any injuries he has suffered as a result of the agents' violation of the Amendment.

II

In addition to holding that petitioner's complaint had failed to state facts making out a cause of action, the District Court ruled that in any event respondents were immune from liability by virtue of their official position. This question was not passed upon by the Court of Appeals, and accordingly we do not consider it here. The judgment of the Court of Appeals is reversed and the case is remanded for further proceedings consistent with this opinion.

Mr. Justice Harlan, concurring in the judgment.

My initial view of this case was that the Court of Appeals was correct in dismissing the complaint, but for reasons stated in this opinion I am now persuaded to the contrary. Accordingly, I join in the judgment of reversal. . . .

For the reasons set forth below, I am of the opinion that federal courts do have the power to award damages for violation of "constitutionally protected interests" and I agree with the Court that a traditional judicial remedy such as damages is appropriate to the vindication of the personal interests protected by the Fourth Amendment.

II

The contention that the federal courts are powerless to accord a litigant damages for a claimed invasion of his federal constitutional rights until Congress explicitly authorizes the remedy cannot rest on the notion that the decision to grant compensatory relief involves a resolution of policy considerations not susceptible of judicial discernment. Thus, in suits for damages based on violations of federal statutes lacking any express authorization of a damage remedy, this Court has authorized such relief where, in its view, damages are necessary to effectuate the congressional policy underpinning the substantive provisions of the statute. *J.I. Case Co. v. Borak*, 377 U.S. 426 (1964).

If it is not the nature of the remedy which is thought to render a judgment as to the appropriateness of damages inherently "legislative," then it must be the nature of the legal interest offered as an occasion for invoking otherwise appropriate judicial relief. But I do not think that the fact that the interest is protected by the Constitution rather than statute or common law justifies the assertion that federal courts are powerless to grant damages in the absence of explicit congressional action authorizing the remedy. Initially, I note that it would be at least anomalous to conclude that the federal judiciary—while competent to choose among the range of traditional judicial remedies to implement statutory and common-law policies, and even to generate substantive rules governing primary behavior in furtherance of broadly formulated policies articulated by statute or Constitution, see *Textile Workers Union v. Lincoln Mills*, 353 U.S. 448 (1957); *United States v. Standard Oil Co.*, 332 U.S. 301 (1947); *Clearfield Trust Co. v. United States*, 318 U.S. 363 (1943)—is powerless to accord a damages remedy to vindicate social policies which, by virtue of their inclusion in the Constitution, are aimed predominantly at restraining the Government as an instrument of the popular will.

More importantly, the presumed availability of federal equitable relief against threatened invasions of constitutional interests appears entirely to negate the contention that the status of an interest as constitutionally protected divests federal courts of the power to grant damages absent express congressional authorization. . . .

If explicit congressional authorization is an absolute prerequisite to the power of a federal court to accord compensatory relief regardless of the necessity or appropriateness of damages as a remedy simply because of the status of a legal interest as constitutionally protected, then it seems to me that explicit congressional authorization is similarly prerequisite to the exercise of equitable remedial discretion in favor of constitutionally protected interests. Conversely, if a general grant of jurisdiction to the federal courts by Congress is thought adequate to empower a federal court to grant equitable relief for all areas of subject-matter jurisdiction enumerated therein, see 28 U.S.C. § 1331(a), then it seems to me that the same statute is sufficient to empower a federal court to grant a traditional remedy at law. Of course, the special historical traditions governing the federal equity system, might still bear on the comparative appropriateness of granting equitable relief as opposed to money damages. That possibility, however, relates, not to whether the federal courts have the power to afford one type of remedy as opposed to the other, but rather to the criteria which should govern the exercise of our power. To that question, I now pass.

[Justice Harlan then concluded that damages were appropriate for this violation of the Fourth Amendment.]

MR. CHIEF JUSTICE BURGER, dissenting. [Omitted.]

MR. JUSTICE BLACK, dissenting.

. . . There can be no doubt that Congress could . . . create a remedy against federal officials who violate the Fourth Amendment in the performance of their duties. But the point of this case and the fatal weakness in the Court's judgment is that neither Congress nor the State of New York has enacted legislation creating such a right of action. For us to do so is, in my judgment, an exercise of power that the Constitution does not give us.

Even if we had the legislative power to create a remedy, there are many reasons why we should decline to create a cause of action where none has existed since the formation of our Government. The courts of the United States as well as those of the States are choked with lawsuits. . . . A majority of these cases are brought by citizens with substantial complaints. . . . Unfortunately, there have also been a growing number of frivolous lawsuits, particularly actions for damages against law enforcement officers whose conduct has been judicially sanctioned by state trial and appellate courts and in many instances even by this Court. My fellow Justices on this Court and our brethren throughout the federal judiciary know only too well the time-consuming task of conscientiously poring over hundreds of thousands of pages of factual allegations of misconduct by police, judicial, and corrections officials. Of course, there are instances of legitimate grievances, but legislators might well desire to devote judicial resources to other problems of a more serious nature.

We sit at the top of a judicial system accused by some of nearing the point of collapse. Many criminal defendants do not receive speedy trials and neither society nor the accused are assured of justice when inordinate delays occur. Citizens must wait years to litigate their private civil suits. Substantial changes in correctional and parole systems demand the attention of the lawmakers and the judiciary. If I were a legislator I might well find these and other needs so pressing as to make me believe that the resources of lawyers and judges should be devoted to them rather than to civil damage actions against officers who generally strive to perform within constitutional bounds. There is also a real danger that such suits might deter officials from the proper and honest performance of their duties.

All of these considerations make imperative careful study and weighing of the arguments both for and against the creation of such a remedy under the Fourth Amendment. I would have great difficulty for myself in resolving the competing policies, goals, and priorities in the use of resources, if I thought it were my job to resolve those questions. But that is not my task. The task of evaluating the pros and cons of creating judicial remedies for particular wrongs is a matter for Congress and the legislatures of the States. Congress has not provided that any federal court can entertain a suit against a federal officer for violations of Fourth Amendment rights occurring in the performance of his duties. A strong inference can be drawn from creation of such actions against state officials that Congress does not desire to permit such suits against federal officials. Should the time come when Congress desires such lawsuits, it has before it a model of valid legislation, 42 U.S.C. § 1983, to create a damage remedy against federal officers. Cases could be cited to support the legal proposition which I assert, but it seems to me to be a matter of common understanding that the business of the judiciary is to interpret the laws and not to make them.

I dissent.

MR. JUSTICE BLACKMUN, dissenting. [Omitted.]

Note: The Bivens *Cause of Action*

1. Justice Black, dissenting in *Bivens*, argues that the Court's creation of a damages remedy against federal officials for violation of Fourth Amendment rights is "an exercise of power that the Constitution does not give us." A few years earlier, Justice Black joined the Court's opinion in *J.I. Case Co. v. Borak*, 377 U.S. 426 (1964), in which the Court authorized a damages remedy for violations of a federal statute. Justice Harlan, in his concurring opinion in *Bivens*, relies heavily on *Borak*:

> The *Borak* case is an especially clear example of the exercise of federal judicial power to accord damages as an appropriate remedy in the absence of a federal cause statutory authorization of a federal cause of action. There we "implied" ... a private cause of action for damages for violation of § 14(a) of the Securities Exchange Act of 1934. We did so in an area where federal regulation has been singularly comprehensive and elaborate administrative enforcement machinery had been provided. The exercise of judicial power involved in *Borak* simply cannot be justified in terms of statutory construction, nor did the *Borak* Court purport to do so. The notion of "implying" a remedy, therefore, as applied to cases like *Borak*, can only refer to a process whereby the federal judiciary exercises a choice among traditionally available judicial remedies according to reasons related to the substantive social policy embodied in an act of positive law.

On what basis might Justice Black have argued that the Court has power to create remedies for violations of federal statutes but not for violations of the Federal Constitution?

2. The Court sends Bivens' case back to the lower courts for consideration of the defendants' argument that they were "immune from liability by virtue of their official position." In later decisions, the Court developed an elaborate jurisprudence of "qualified immunity." Under this doctrine, state and federal officials performing discretionary functions generally are "shielded from liability for civil damages insofar as their conduct does not violate clearly established statutory or constitutional rights of which a reasonable person would have known." *Harlow v. Fitzgerald*, 457 U.S. 800, 818 (1982). For further discussion of qualified immunity, see Chapter 14.

3. The majority opinion in *Bivens* is narrowly focused on the Fourth Amendment. Would the *Bivens* remedy be limited to Fourth Amendment violations? The Court did not address that question until 1979. In *Davis v. Passman*, 442 U.S. 228 (1979), the Court extended *Bivens* by recognizing an implied remedy for damages under the Due Process Clause of the Fifth Amendment. A year later, in *Carlson v. Green*, 446 U.S. 14 (1980), the Court issued a similar ruling on the Cruel and Unusual Punishments Clause of the Eighth Amendment.

Those, however, were the last cases in which the Court broadened the availability of the *Bivens* remedy. In a series of decisions starting with *Bush v. Lucas*, 462 U.S. 367 (1983), the Court declined to extend *Bivens* to new classes of claims or new categories of defendants. The most recent of these cases is *Minneci v. Pollard*.

Minneci v. Pollard

Supreme Court of the United States, 2012.

132 S. Ct. 617.

Justice Breyer delivered the opinion of the Court.

The question is whether we can imply the existence of an Eighth Amendment-based damages action (a *Bivens* action) against employees of a privately operated federal prison. Because we believe that in the circumstances present here state tort law authorizes adequate alternative damages actions — actions that provide both significant deterrence and compensation — we cannot do so. See *Wilkie v. Robbins*, 551 U.S. 537 (2007) (no *Bivens* action where "alternative, existing" processes provide adequate protection).

I

Richard Lee Pollard was a prisoner at a federal facility operated by a private company, the Wackenhut Corrections Corporation. In 2002 he filed a *pro se* complaint in federal court against several Wackenhut employees, who (now) include a security officer, a food-services supervisor, and several members of the medical staff. As the Federal Magistrate Judge interpreted Pollard's complaint, he claimed that these employees had deprived him of adequate medical care, had thereby violated the Eighth Amendment's prohibition against "cruel and unusual" punishment, and had caused him injury. He sought damages.

Pollard said that a year earlier he had slipped on a cart left in the doorway of the prison's butcher shop. The prison medical staff took x rays, thought he might have fractured both elbows, brought him to an outside clinic for further orthopedic evaluation, and subsequently arranged for surgery. In particular, Pollard claimed:

(1) Despite his having told a prison guard that he could not extend his arm, the guard forced him to put on a jumpsuit (to travel to the outside clinic), causing him "the most excruciating pain";

(2) During several visits to the outside clinic, prison guards made Pollard wear arm restraints that were connected in a way that caused him continued pain;

(3) Prison medical (and other) personnel failed to follow the outside clinic's instructions to put Pollard's left elbow in a posterior splint, failed to provide necessary physical therapy, and failed to conduct necessary studies, including nerve conduction studies;

(4) At times when Pollard's arms were in casts or similarly disabled, prison officials failed to make alternative arrangements for him to receive meals, with the result that (to avoid "being humiliated" in the general food service area) Pollard had to auction off personal items to obtain funds to buy food at the commissary;

(5) Prison officials deprived him of basic hygienic care to the point where he could not bathe for two weeks;

(6) Prison medical staff provided him with insufficient medicine, to the point where he was in pain and could not sleep; and

(7) Prison officials forced him to return to work before his injuries had healed.

[The] Ninth Circuit found that the Eighth Amendment provided Pollard with a *Bivens* action. . . . The defendants sought certiorari. And, in light of a split among the Courts of Appeals, we granted the petition.

II

Recently, in *Wilkie v. Robbins*, we rejected a claim that the Fifth Amendment impliedly authorized a *Bivens* action that would permit landowners to obtain damages from government officials who unconstitutionally interfere with their exercise of property rights. After reviewing the Court's earlier *Bivens* cases, the Court stated:

> [T]he decision whether to recognize a *Bivens* remedy may require two steps. In the first place, there is the question whether any alternative, existing process for protecting the [constitutionally recognized] interest amounts to a convincing reason for the Judicial Branch to refrain from providing a new and freestanding remedy in damages. . . . But even in the absence of an alternative, a *Bivens* remedy is a subject of judgment: "the federal courts must make the kind of remedial determination that is appropriate for a common-law tribunal, paying particular heed, however, to any special factors counselling hesitation before authorizing a new kind of federal litigation." *Wilkie* (quoting *Bush v. Lucas*, 462 U.S. 367 (1983)).

These standards seek to reflect and to reconcile the Court's reasoning set forth in earlier cases. In *Bivens* itself the Court held that the Fourth Amendment implicitly authorized a court to order federal agents to pay damages to a person injured by the agents' violation of the Amendment's constitutional strictures. . . .

In *Davis v. Passman*, 442 U.S. 228 (1979), the Court considered a former congressional employee's claim for damages suffered as a result of her employer's unconstitutional discrimination based on gender. The Court found a damages action implicit in the Fifth Amendment's Due Process Clause. In doing so, the Court emphasized the unavailability of "other alternative forms of judicial relief." And the Court noted that there was "no evidence" that Congress (or the Constitution) intended to foreclose such a remedy.

In *Carlson v. Green*, 446 U.S. 14 (1980), the Court considered a claim for damages brought by the estate of a federal prisoner who (the estate said) had died as the result of government officials' "deliberate indifference" to his medical needs—indifference that violated the Eighth Amendment. *Id.* (citing *Estelle v. Gamble*, 429 U.S. 97 (1976)). The Court implied an action for damages from the Eighth Amendment. It noted that state law offered the particular plaintiff no meaningful damages remedy. Although the estate might have brought a damages claim under the Federal Tort Claims Act, the defendant in any such lawsuit was the employer, namely the United States, not the individual officers who had committed the violation. A damages remedy against an individual officer, the Court added, would prove a more effective deterrent. And, rather than leave compensation to the "vagaries" of state tort law, a federal *Bivens* action would provide "uniform rules."

Since *Carlson*, the Court has had to decide in several different instances whether to imply a *Bivens* action. And in each instance it has decided against the existence of such an action. These instances include:

(1) A federal employee's claim that his federal employer dismissed him in violation of the First Amendment, *Bush v. Lucas*, 462 U.S. 367 (1983) (congressionally created federal civil service procedures provide meaningful redress);

(2) A claim by military personnel that military superiors violated various constitutional provisions, *Chappell v. Wallace*, 462 U.S. 296 (1983) (special factors related to the military counsel against implying a *Bivens* action); see also *United States v. Stanley*, 483 U.S. 669 (1987) (similar);

(3) A claim by recipients of Social Security disability benefits that benefits had been denied in violation of the Fifth Amendment, *Schweiker v. Chilicky*, 487 U.S. 412 (1988) (elaborate administrative scheme provides meaningful alternative remedy);

(4) A former bank employee's suit against a federal banking agency, claiming that he lost his job due to agency action that violated the Fifth Amendment's Due Process Clause, *FDIC v. Meyer*, 510 U.S. 471 (1994) (no *Bivens* actions against government agencies rather than particular individuals who act unconstitutionally);

(5) A prisoner's Eighth Amendment-based suit against a private corporation that managed a federal prison, *Correctional Services Corp. v. Malesko*,

534 U.S. 61 (2001) (to permit suit against the employer-corporation would risk skewing relevant incentives; at the same time, the ability of a prisoner to bring state tort law damages action against *private* individual defendants means that the prisoner does not "lack effective remedies").

Although the Court, in reaching its decisions, has not always similarly emphasized the same aspects of the cases, *Wilkie* fairly summarizes the basic considerations that underlie those decisions. We consequently apply its approach here. And we conclude that Pollard cannot assert a *Bivens* claim.

That is primarily because Pollard's Eighth Amendment claim focuses upon a kind of conduct that typically falls within the scope of traditional state tort law. And in the case of a privately employed defendant, state tort law provides an "alternative, existing process" capable of protecting the constitutional interests at stake. The existence of that alternative here constitutes a "convincing reason for the Judicial Branch to refrain from providing a new and freestanding remedy in damages." Our reasoning is best understood if we set forth and explain why we reject Pollard's arguments to the contrary.

III

Pollard (together with supporting *amici*) asks us to imply a *Bivens* action for four basic reasons—none of which we find convincing. First, Pollard argues that this Court has already decided in *Carlson* that a federal prisoner may bring an Eighth Amendment-based *Bivens* action against prison personnel; and we need do no more than simply apply *Carlson*'s holding here. *Carlson*, however, was a case in which a federal prisoner sought damages from personnel employed by the *government*, not personnel employed by a *private* firm. And for present purposes that fact—of employment status—makes a critical difference.

For one thing, the potential existence of an adequate "alternative, existing process" differs dramatically in the two sets of cases. Prisoners ordinarily cannot bring state-law tort actions against employees of the Federal Government. See 28 U.S.C. §§ 2671, 2679(b)(1) (Westfall Act) (substituting United States as defendant in tort action against federal employee); *Osborn v. Haley*, 549 U.S. 225 (2007) (Westfall Act immunizes federal employee through removal and substitution of United States as defendant). But prisoners ordinarily can bring state-law tort actions against employees of a private firm.

For another thing, the Court specifically rejected Justice Stevens' somewhat similar suggestion in his dissenting opinion in *Malesko*, namely that a prisoner's suit against a private prison-management firm should fall within *Carlson*'s earlier holding because such a firm, like a federal employee, is a "federal agent." In rejecting the dissent's suggestion, the Court explained that the context in *Malesko* was "fundamentally different" from the contexts at issue in earlier cases, including *Carlson*. That difference, the Court said, reflected in part the nature of the defendant, *i.e.*, a corporate employer rather than an individual employee, and in part reflected the existence of alternative "effective" state tort remedies. This last-mentioned factor makes it difficult to square Pollard's argument with *Malesko*'s reasoning.

Second, Pollard argues that, because of the "vagaries" of state tort law, *Carlson*, we should consider only whether *federal* law provides adequate alternative remedies. This argument flounders, however, on the fact that the Court rejected it in *Malesko*. State tort law, after all, can help to deter constitutional violations as well as to provide compensation to a violation's victim. And it is consequently unsurprising that several cases have considered the adequacy or inadequacy of state-law remedies when determining whether to imply a *Bivens* remedy. See, *e.g.*, *Bivens* (state tort law "inconsistent or even hostile" to Fourth Amendment); *Davis* (noting no state-law remedy available); cf. *Malesko* (noting that the Court has implied *Bivens* action only where any alternative remedy against individual officers was "nonexistent" or where plaintiff "lacked *any alternative remedy*" at all).

Third, Pollard argues that state tort law does not provide remedies *adequate* to protect the constitutional interests at issue here. Pollard's claim, however, is a claim for physical or related emotional harm suffered as a result of aggravated instances of the kind of conduct that state tort law typically forbids. That claim arose in California, where state tort law provides for ordinary negligence actions, for actions based upon "want of ordinary care or skill," for actions for "negligent failure to diagnose or treat," and for actions based upon the failure of one with a custodial duty to care for another to protect that other from "'unreasonable risk of physical harm.'" California courts have specifically applied this law to jailers, including private operators of prisons.

Moreover, California's tort law basically reflects general principles of tort law present, as far as we can tell, in the law of every State. See Restatement (Second) of Torts §§ 314A(4), 320 (1963–1964). We have found specific authority indicating that state law imposes general tort duties of reasonable care (including medical care) on prison employees in every one of the eight States where privately managed secure federal facilities are currently located.

We note, as Pollard points out, that state tort law may sometimes prove less generous than would a *Bivens* action, say, by capping damages, or by forbidding recovery for emotional suffering unconnected with physical harm, or by imposing procedural obstacles, say, initially requiring the use of expert administrative panels in medical malpractice cases. But we cannot find in this fact sufficient basis to determine state law inadequate.

State-law remedies and a potential *Bivens* remedy need not be perfectly congruent. See *Bush* (administrative remedies adequate even though they "do not provide complete relief"). Indeed, federal law as well as state law contains limitations. Prisoners bringing federal lawsuits, for example, ordinarily may not seek damages for mental or emotional injury unconnected with physical injury. See 42 U.S.C. § 1997e(e). And *Bivens* actions, even if more generous to plaintiffs in some respects, may be less generous in others. For example, to show an Eighth Amendment violation a prisoner must typically show that a defendant acted, not just negligently, but with "deliberate indifference." *Farmer v. Brennan*, 511 U.S. 825 (1994). And a *Bivens* plaintiff, unlike a state tort law plaintiff, normally could not apply principles of *respondeat superior* and thereby obtain recovery from a defendant's potentially deep-pocketed employer. See *Ashcroft v. Iqbal*, 556 U.S. 662 (2009).

Rather, in principle, the question is whether, in general, state tort law remedies provide roughly similar incentives for potential defendants to comply with the Eighth Amendment while also providing roughly similar compensation to victims of violations. The features of the two kinds of actions just mentioned suggest that, in practice, the answer to this question is "yes." And we have found nothing here to convince us to the contrary.

Fourth, Pollard argues that there "may" be similar kinds of Eighth Amendment claims that state tort law does not cover. But Pollard does not convincingly show that there are such cases. Compare Brief for Respondent Pollard (questioning the availability of state tort remedies for "prisoners [who] suffer attacks by other inmates, preventable suicides, or the denial of heat, ventilation or movement"), with [a California case stating that courts have long held that prison officials must protect, e.g., transgender inmate from foreseeable harm by other inmates].

Regardless, we concede that we cannot prove a negative or be totally certain that the features of state tort law relevant here will universally prove to be, or remain, as we have described them. Nonetheless, we are certain enough about the shape of present law as applied to the kind of case before us to leave different cases and different state laws to another day. That is to say, we can decide whether to imply a *Bivens* action in a case where an Eighth Amendment claim or state law differs significantly from those at issue here when and if such a case arises. The possibility of such a different future case does not provide sufficient grounds for reaching a different conclusion here.

For these reasons, where, as here, a federal prisoner seeks damages from privately employed personnel working at a privately operated federal prison, where the conduct allegedly amounts to a violation of the Eighth Amendment, and where that conduct is of a kind that typically falls within the scope of traditional state tort law (such as the conduct involving improper medical care at issue here), the prisoner must seek a remedy under state tort law. We cannot imply a *Bivens* remedy in such a case.

The judgment of the Ninth Circuit is reversed.

So ordered.

JUSTICE SCALIA, with whom JUSTICE THOMAS joins, concurring.

I join the opinion of the Court because I agree that a narrow interpretation of the rationale of *Bivens v. Six Unknown Fed. Narcotics Agents*, 403 U.S. 388 (1971), would not cause the holding of that case to apply to the circumstances of this case. Even if the narrowest rationale of *Bivens* did apply here, however, I would decline to extend its holding. *Bivens* is "a relic of the heady days in which this Court assumed common-law powers to create causes of action" by constitutional implication. *Correctional Services Corp. v. Malesko*, 534 U.S. 61 (2001) (Scalia, J., concurring). We have abandoned that power in the statutory field, see *Alexander v. Sandoval*, 532 U.S. 275 (2001), and we should do the same in the constitutional field, where (presumably) an imagined "implication" cannot even be repudiated by Congress. As I have previously stated, see *Malesko*, I would limit *Bivens* and its two follow-on cases (*Davis v. Passman*, 442 U.S.

228 (1979), and *Carlson v. Green*, 446 U.S. 14 (1980)) to the precise circumstances that they involved.

JUSTICE GINSBURG, dissenting.

Were Pollard incarcerated in a federal- or state-operated facility, he would have a federal remedy for the Eighth Amendment violations he alleges. See *Carlson v. Green*, 446 U.S. 14 (1980) (*Bivens* action); *Estelle v. Gamble*, 429 U.S. 97 (1976) (42 U.S.C. § 1983 action). For the reasons stated in the dissenting opinion I joined in *Correctional Services Corp. v. Malesko*, 534 U.S. 61 (2001) (opinion of Stevens, J.), I would not deny the same character of relief to Pollard, a prisoner placed by federal contract in a privately operated prison. Pollard may have suffered "aggravated instances" of conduct state tort law forbids, but that same aggravated conduct, when it is engaged in by official actors, also offends the Federal Constitution, see *Estelle*. Rather than remitting Pollard to the "vagaries" of state tort law, *Carlson*, I would hold his injuries, sustained while serving a federal sentence, "compensable according to uniform rules of federal law," *Bivens v. Six Unknown Fed. Narcotics Agents*, 403 U.S. 388 (1971) (Harlan, J., concurring in judgment).

Indeed, there is stronger cause for providing a federal remedy in this case than there was in *Malesko*. There, the question presented was whether a *Bivens* action lies against a private corporation that manages a facility housing federal prisoners. Suing a corporate employer, the majority observed in *Malesko*, would not serve to deter individual officers from conduct transgressing constitutional limitations on their authority. Individual deterrence, the Court reminded, was the consideration central to the *Bivens* decision. Noting the availability of state tort remedies, the majority in *Malesko* declined to "exten[d] *Bivens* beyond [that decision's] core premise," *i.e.*, deterring individual officers. Pollard's case, in contrast, involves *Bivens'* core concern: His suit seeking damages directly from individual officers would have precisely the deterrent effect the Court found absent in *Malesko*.

For the reasons stated, I would hold that relief potentially available under state tort law does not block Pollard's recourse to a federal remedy for the affront to the Constitution he suffered. Accordingly, I would affirm the Ninth Circuit's judgment.

Note: Minneci *and the Future of* Bivens

1. Justice Breyer, writing for the Court in *Minneci*, gives only a cursory account of the Court's post-1980 decisions refusing to imply the existence of a *Bivens* remedy. Chief Justice Rehnquist, writing for the Court in *Malesko* (2001), provided a somewhat more detailed summary of the precedents as of that time. He wrote:

> Since *Carlson v. Green* (1980) we have consistently refused to extend *Bivens* liability to any new context or new category of defendants. In *Bush v. Lucas*, 462 U.S. 367 (1983), we declined to create a *Bivens* remedy against individual Government officials for a First Amendment violation arising in the context of federal employment. Although the plaintiff had no opportunity to fully remedy the constitutional violation, we held that administrative

review mechanisms crafted by Congress provided meaningful redress and thereby foreclosed the need to fashion a new, judicially crafted cause of action. [The *Bush* opinion noted: "Federal civil servants are now protected by an elaborate, comprehensive scheme that . . . provides meaningful remedies for employees who may have been unfairly disciplined for making critical comments about their agencies."] We further recognized Congress' institutional competence in crafting appropriate relief for aggrieved federal employees as a "special factor counseling hesitation in the creation of a new remedy." [We also noted] that "Congress is in a far better position than a court to evaluate the impact of a new species of litigation between federal employees." We have reached a similar result in the military context, *Chappell v. Wallace*, 462 U.S. 296 (1983), even where the defendants were alleged to have been civilian personnel, *United States v. Stanley*, 483 U.S. 669 (1987).

In *Schweiker v. Chilicky*, 487 U.S. 412 (1988), we declined to infer a damages action against individual Government employees alleged to have violated due process in their handling of Social Security applications. . . . We [rejected] the claim that a *Bivens* remedy should be implied simply for want of any other means for challenging a constitutional deprivation in federal court. It did not matter, for example, that "[t]he creation of a *Bivens* remedy would obviously offer the prospect of relief for injuries that must now go unredressed. . . ." So long as the plaintiff had an avenue for some redress, bedrock principles of separation of powers foreclosed judicial imposition of a new substantive liability.

Most recently, in *FDIC v. Meyer*, 510 U.S. 471 (1994), we unanimously declined an invitation to extend *Bivens* to permit suit against a federal agency, even though the agency—because Congress had waived sovereign immunity—was otherwise amenable to suit. Our opinion emphasized that "the purpose of *Bivens* is to deter *the officer*," not the agency. (Emphasis in original.) We reasoned that if given the choice, plaintiffs would sue a federal agency instead of an individual who could assert qualified immunity as an affirmative defense. To the extent aggrieved parties had less incentive to bring a damages claim against individuals, "the deterrent effects of the *Bivens* remedy would be lost." Accordingly, to allow a *Bivens* claim against federal agencies "would mean the evisceration of the *Bivens* remedy, rather than its extension." We noted further that "special factors" counseled hesitation in light of the "potentially enormous financial burden" that agency liability would entail.

The pattern continued in *Malesko*; the Court declined to recognize a *Bivens* remedy against a private corporation operating a halfway house under contract with the Federal Bureau of Prisons.

2. Six years after *Malesko*, the Supreme Court again rejected an attempt to assert a cause of action under *Bivens*. The case was *Wilkie v. Robbins*, 551 U.S. 537 (2007), and it grew out of complex facts succinctly summarized in Justice Ginsburg's dissent:

[Federal] Bureau of Land Management (BLM) officials in Wyoming made a careless error. They failed to record an easement obtained for the United States along a stretch of land on the privately owned High Island Ranch. Plaintiff-respondent Frank Robbins purchased the ranch knowing nothing about the easement granted by the prior owner. Under Wyoming law, Robbins took title to the land free of the easement.

BLM officials, realizing their mistake, demanded from Robbins an easement—for which they did not propose to pay—to replace the one they carelessly lost. Their demand, one of them told Robbins, was nonnegotiable. Robbins was directed to provide the easement, or else. When he declined to follow that instruction, the BLM officials mounted a seven-year campaign of relentless harassment and intimidation to force Robbins to give in. They refused to maintain the road providing access to the ranch, trespassed on Robbins' property, brought unfounded criminal charges against him, canceled his special recreational use permit and grazing privileges, interfered with his business operations, and invaded the privacy of his ranch guests on cattle drives.

Robbins brought suit in federal district court against the BLM officials seeking compensatory and punitive damages. He argued that the Fifth Amendment forbids government officials from using harassment and intimidation to acquire private property cost-free, and that *Bivens* provides a cause of action. The Tenth Circuit agreed, but the Supreme Court reversed. Justice Souter, writing for the Court, laid out the two-step approach quoted by Justice Breyer in *Minneci*.

With respect to the first step (unavailability of alternative remedies), the Court appeared to accept "the force of the metaphor Robbins invoke[d], 'death by a thousand cuts'":

> It is one thing to be threatened with the loss of grazing rights, or to be prosecuted, or to have one's lodge broken into, but something else to be subjected to this in combination over a period of six years, by a series of public officials bent on making life difficult. Agency appeals, lawsuits, and criminal defense take money, and endless battling depletes the spirit along with the purse. The whole here is greater than the sum of its parts.

Nevertheless, the Court concluded that Robbins' claim failed at "*Bivens* step two" ("special factors counselling hesitation"):

> The point [is] not to deny that Government employees sometimes overreach, for of course they do, and they may have done so here if all the allegations are true. The point is the reasonable fear that a general *Bivens* cure would be worse than the disease. . . . A judicial standard to identify illegitimate pressure going beyond legitimately hard bargaining would be endlessly knotty to work out, and a general provision for tortlike liability when Government employees are unduly zealous in pressing a governmental interest affecting property would invite an onslaught of *Bivens* actions.

3. In *Malesko*, the vote was 5-4. In *Wilkie v. Robbins*, only Justice Ginsburg, joined by Justice Stevens, dissented. In *Minneci* (decided after Justice Stevens retired from the Court), Justice Ginsburg dissents alone. What does this suggest about the prospects for extending *Bivens* liability to new contexts or new categories of defendants?

4. In *Minneci*, Justice Scalia, joined by Justice Thomas, reiterates his view that *Bivens* and its two follow-on cases (*Davis* and *Carlson*) should be limited "to the precise circumstances that they involved." After *Minneci*, *Wilkie*, and the other cases summarized above, how much difference is there between Justice Scalia's position and that of the Court? Consider the Problem below.

Problem: Bivens *and Religious Discrimination*

1. In *Ashcroft v. Iqbal*, 556 U.S. 662 (2009), the plaintiff brought a *Bivens* action against former federal officials, alleging that the officials adopted an unconstitutional policy that subjected him to harsh conditions of confinement on the basis of his religion (as well as his race and national origin). The Court held that the plaintiff's complaint "fail[ed] to plead sufficient facts to state a claim for purposeful and unlawful discrimination" by the defendants. But before reaching that conclusion, the Court suggested that the claim might not have been actionable at all under *Bivens*. Justice Kennedy wrote for a 5-4 majority:

> Because implied causes of action are disfavored, the Court has been reluctant to extend *Bivens* liability "to any new context or new category of defendants." *Malesko*; see also *Wilkie*. That reluctance might well have disposed of [plaintiff's] First Amendment claim of religious discrimination. For while we have allowed a *Bivens* action to redress a violation of the equal protection component of the Due Process Clause of the Fifth Amendment, see *Davis v. Passman*, 442 U.S. 228 (1979), we have not found an implied damages remedy under the Free Exercise Clause. Indeed, we have declined to extend *Bivens* to a claim sounding in the First Amendment. *Bush v. Lucas*, 462 U.S. 367 (1983).

2. Review the summary of *Bush v. Lucas* in the preceding Note. The Court in *Iqbal* implies that the same considerations would lead to rejecting the availability of a *Bivens* remedy for a claim of religious discrimination such as Iqbal's. Do you agree? Consider the allegations of the complaint, as summarized by the Court:

> The complaint contends that [defendants] designated [plaintiff] a person of high interest on account of his race, religion, or national origin, in contravention of the First and Fifth Amendments to the Constitution. The complaint alleges that "the [FBI], under the direction of Defendant MUELLER, arrested and detained thousands of Arab Muslim men . . . as part of its investigation of the events of September 11." It further alleges that "[t]he policy of holding post-September-11th detainees in highly restrictive conditions of confinement until they were 'cleared' by the FBI was approved by Defendants ASHCROFT and MUELLER in discussions in the weeks after September 11, 2001." Lastly, the complaint posits that [defendants] "each

knew of, condoned, and willfully and maliciously agreed to subject" respondent to harsh conditions of confinement "as a matter of policy, solely on
account of [his] religion, race, and/or national origin and for no legitimate
penological interest."

3. In *Bivens* itself, the Court created a damages remedy for violation of Fourth
Amendment rights. In *Minneci* and *Wilkie* (and in the intervening decisions discussed
in *Minneci* and the Note above), the Court declined to allow liability. On which side
of the line do Iqbal's allegations fall? What additional facts might you need to know
to answer that question?

Part Four

The Jurisdiction of the Federal District Courts

Chapter 9

Challenges to Jurisdiction

An elaborate body of doctrine governs the original and removal jurisdiction of the federal district courts. In Chapters 10 through 12 we will examine that law in some detail. First, however, we look at the rules governing challenges to subject-matter jurisdiction. These rules can lay traps for the unwary, and they require vigilance at every stage of litigation. To complicate matters, it is not always clear when an issue is to be treated as "jurisdictional."

A. The "*Mansfield* Rule"

Mansfield, Coldwater & Lake Michigan Ry. Co. v. Swan

Supreme Court of the United States, 1884.

111 U.S. 379.

MR. JUSTICE MATTHEWS delivered the opinion of the court.

This was an action at law originally brought in the Court of Common Pleas of Fulton County, Ohio, by John Swan, S. C. Rose, F. M. Hutchinson, and Robert McMann, as partners under the name of Swan, Rose & Co., against the plaintiffs in error. The object of the suit was the recovery of damages for alleged breaches of a contract for the construction of the railroad of the defendants below. It was commenced June 10th, 1874.

Afterwards on October 28th, 1879, the cause being at issue, the defendants below filed a petition for its removal to the Circuit Court of the United States. They aver therein that one of the petitioners is a corporation created by the laws of Ohio alone, and the other, a corporation consolidated under the laws of Michigan and Ohio, the constituent corporations having been organized under the laws of those States respectively, and that they are, consequently, citizens, one of Ohio, and one of both Michigan and Ohio. It is also alleged, in the petition for removal, "that the plaintiffs, John Swan and Frank M. Hutchinson, at the time of the commencement of this suit, were, and still are, citizens of the State of Pennsylvania; that the said Robert H. McMann was then (according to your petitioners' recollection) a citizen of the State of Ohio, but that he is not now a citizen of that State, but where he now resides or whereof he is now a citizen (except that he is a citizen of one of the States or Territories comprising the United States), your petitioners are unable to state; that he went into bankruptcy in the bankruptcy court held at Cleveland, in the State of Ohio, several years since, and since the alleged claim of the plaintiffs arose, but your petitioners cannot now state whether he has now an assignee in bankruptcy or not, but they are informed and believe that he has not; that the said Stephen C. Rose, at the time of the commencement of this suit, was a citizen of the State of Michigan; that he died therein during the pendency of this suit, and the said Lester E. Rose is the administrator of the estate of the said Stephen C. Rose in the State of Michigan, he holding such office under and by virtue of the laws of that State only, the said Lester E. Rose being a citizen of the State of Michigan when so appointed and now, but that he is not a necessary party as plaintiff in this suit, for the reason, that the suit being prosecuted by the plaintiffs as partners under the firm name and style of Swan, Rose & Co., and for the collection of an alleged debt or claim due to them as such partners, and which arose wholly out of their dealings as partners, if it exists at all, upon the death of the said Stephen C. Rose the cause of action survived to the other partners."

The petition, being accompanied with a satisfactory bond, was allowed, and an order made for the removal of the cause.

The plaintiffs below afterwards, on December 13th, 1879, moved to remand the cause on the ground, among others, that the Circuit Court had no jurisdiction, because the "real and substantial controversy in the cause is between real and substantial parties who are citizens of the same State and not of different States." But the motion was denied.

Subsequently a trial took place upon the merits, which resulted in a verdict and judgment in favor of the plaintiffs, the defendants in error, for $238,116.18 against the defendants jointly, and the further sum of $116,468.32 against one of them.

Many exceptions to the rulings of the court during the trial were taken and are embodied in a bill of exceptions, on which errors have been assigned, and the writ of error is prosecuted by the defendants below to reverse this judgment.

An examination of the record, however, discloses that the Circuit Court had no jurisdiction to try the action; and as, for this reason, we are constrained to reverse the judgment, we have not deemed it within our province to consider any other questions involved in it.

It appears from the petition for removal, and not otherwise by the record elsewhere, that, at the time the action was first brought in the State court, one of the plaintiffs, and a necessary party, McMann, was a citizen of Ohio, the same State of which the defendants were citizens. It does not affirmatively appear that at the time of the removal he was a citizen of any other State. The averment is, that he was not then a citizen of Ohio, and that his actual citizenship was unknown, except that he was a citizen of one of the States or Territories. It is consistent with this statement, that he was not a citizen of any State. He may have been a citizen of a Territory, and, if so, the requisite citizenship would not exist. *New Orleans v. Winter*, 1 Wheat. 91. According to the decision in *Gibson v. Bruce*, 108 U. S. 561, the difference of citizenship on which the right of removal depends must have existed at the time when the suit was begun, as well as at the time of the removal. And according to the uniform decisions of this court, the jurisdiction of the Circuit Court fails, unless the necessary citizenship affirmatively appears in the pleadings or elsewhere in the record. *Grace v. American Central Insurance Company*, 109 U.S. 278, 283; *Robertson v. Cease*, 97 U.S. 646. It was error, therefore, in the Circuit Court to assume jurisdiction in the case, and not to remand it, on the motion of the plaintiffs below.

It is true that the plaintiffs below, against whose objection the error was committed, do not complain of being, prejudiced by it; and it seems to be an anomaly and a hardship that the party at whose instance it was committed should be permitted to derive an advantage from it; but the rule, springing, from the nature and limits of the judicial power of the United States, is inflexible and without exception, which requires this court, of its own motion, to deny its own jurisdiction, and, in the exercise of its appellate power, that of all other courts of the United States, in all cases where such jurisdiction does not affirmatively appear in the record on which, in the exercise of that power, it is called to act.

On every writ of error or appeal, the first and fundamental question is that of jurisdiction, first, of this court, and then of the court from which the record comes. This question the court is bound to ask and answer for itself, even when not otherwise suggested, and without respect to the relation of the parties to it. This rule was adopted in *Capron v. Van Noorden*, 2 Cranch, 126, decided in 1804, where a judgment was reversed, on the application of the party against whom it had been rendered in the Circuit Court, for want of the allegation of his own citizenship, which he ought to have made to establish the jurisdiction which he had invoked. . . .

In the *Dred Scott Case*, 19 How. 393–400, it was decided that a judgment of the Circuit Court, upon the sufficiency of a plea in abatement denying its jurisdiction, was open for review upon a writ of error sued out by the party in whose favor the plea had been overruled. And in this view Mr. Justice Curtis, in his dissenting opinion, concurred; and we adopt from that opinion the following statement of the law on the point: "It is true," he said, "as a general rule, that the court will not allow a party to rely on anything as cause for reversing a judgment, which was for his advantage. In this, we follow an ancient rule of the common law. But so careful was that law of the preservation of the course of its courts, that it made an exception out of that general rule, and allowed a party to assign for error that which was for his advantage, if it were a departure by the court itself from its settled course of procedure. . . .

"[I]t is not necessary to determine whether the defendant can be allowed to assign want of jurisdiction as an error in a judgment in his own favor. The true question is, not what either of the parties may be allowed to do, but whether this court will affirm or reverse a judgment of the Circuit Court on the merits, when it appears on the record, by a plea to the jurisdiction, that it is a case to which the judicial power of the United States does not extend. The course of the court is, where no motion is made by either party on its own motion, to reverse such a judgment for want of jurisdiction, not only in cases where it is shown negatively, by a plea to the jurisdiction, that jurisdiction does not exist, but even when it does not appear affirmatively that it does exist. It acts upon the principle that the judicial power of the United States must not be exerted in a case to which it does not extend, even if both parties desire to have it exerted.

"I consider, therefore, that when there was a plea to the jurisdiction of the Circuit Court in a case brought here by a writ of error, the first duty of this court is, *sua sponte*, if not moved to it by either party, to examine the sufficiency of that plea, and thus to take care that neither the Circuit Court nor this court shall use the judicial power of the United States in a case to which the Constitution and laws of the United States have not extended that power."

This is precisely applicable to the present case, for the motion of the plaintiffs below to remand the cause was equivalent to a special plea to the jurisdiction of the court; but the doctrine applies equally in every case where the jurisdiction does not appear from the record. . . .

For these reasons the judgment of the Circuit Court must be reversed, and the cause remanded with directions to remand the same to the Court of Common Pleas of Fulton County, Ohio.

Note: The "Mansfield *Rule*"

1. What were the obstacles to the exercise of jurisdiction in the *Mansfield* case? Which of them would still exist under current law? What circumstance, not mentioned in the Court's opinion, would plainly preclude removal today?

2. *Mansfield* is still good law today, and the rule applies at every level of the federal judiciary. For example, Rule 12(h)(3) of the Federal Rules of Civil Procedure (as revised in 2007) provides: "If the court determines at any time that it lacks subject-matter jurisdiction, the court must dismiss the action."

3. Suppose that a case proceeds to judgment even though, at the time of filing (or removal), the requirements of subject-matter jurisdiction were not met. Perhaps no one noticed the problem, or perhaps the district court erroneously denied a motion to dismiss or remand. However, by the time judgment is entered, the jurisdictional defect is cured. Can the judgment stand? The answer is generally "yes" — but determining whether a jurisdictional defect has been cured can raise difficult issues. In *Caterpillar, Inc. v. Lewis*, 519 U.S. 61 (1996), the Supreme Court held that dismissal of the party that destroyed diversity cured the jurisdictional defect, so that the judgment could stand. But in *Grupo Dataflux v. Atlas Global Group, L.P.*, 541 U.S. 567 (2004), the Court ruled, by a vote of 5 to 4, that a change in the citizenship of a continuing party did not cure the defect. The Court ordered the dismissal of a case in which judgment had been entered by the district court after nearly three years of pretrial activity (motions and discovery) and a six-day jury trial.

4. Should Congress modify the *Mansfield* rule? If so, under what circumstances should a court be permitted to adjudicate a case after it has become aware that it lacks subject-matter jurisdiction?

Note: Appellate Scrutiny and Collateral Attack

1. In *Mansfield*, the plaintiffs argued from the outset that the federal court lacked jurisdiction over the case. In *Capron v. Van Noorden* (cited in the *Mansfield* opinion), the losing party in the trial court urged the Supreme Court to reverse for lack of subject-matter jurisdiction. But limits on the subject-matter jurisdiction of district courts will be policed by appellate courts even if the parties do not raise the issue at all. Thus, defects that escape notice in the district court may prove fatal if they are caught by the court of appeals or even by the United States Supreme Court.

Consider, for example, *Simon v. Wal-Mart Stores, Inc.*, 193 F.3d 848 (5th Cir. 1999). Simon filed a tort action in Louisiana state court against Wal-Mart. In accordance with Louisiana law, Simon did not plead a monetary amount of damages, but asserted that he "suffered bodily injuries and damages including but not limited to a severely injured shoulder, soft-tissue injuries throughout her body, bruises, abrasions and other injuries to be shown more fully at trial, and has incurred or will incur medical expenses."

Wal-Mart removed the action to federal district court. The notice of removal alleged that the parties were diverse and that "the matter in controversy herein exceeds the sum of $75,000, exclusive of interests and costs." The plaintiff did not contest the removal, and the case went to trial. The jury found Wal-Mart liable and awarded the plaintiff compensatory damages of $30,000.

Wal-Mart appealed the damages award to the Fifth Circuit, but the court of appeals did not consider any of Wal-Mart's arguments. Instead, it vacated the judgment of the district court and ordered that the action be remanded to the state court. The court explained that under Fifth Circuit precedent, removal was proper only if the jurisdictional amount was either "facially apparent" from the complaint or supported by a statement of facts. In this instance Wal-Mart had not provided a statement of facts, and the jurisdictional amount was not "facially apparent." Thus, the court was required to wipe out the judgment, even though: (a) neither the district court nor either party ever questioned the court's jurisdiction; (b) the parties' Uniform Pretrial Order stated: "Plaintiff's injuries, if causally related, could well exceed the $75,000 threshold amount"; and (c) at oral argument the plaintiff's counsel asserted that he believed the case was worth much more than $75,000 and thus had no basis to object.

What can a lawyer do to protect his or her client against such an outcome?

2. As the *Simon* case illustrates, challenges to subject-matter jurisdiction may be raised at any time during the pendency of a case, even by the court of appeals on its own initiative. But what happens after final judgment is entered? Is a federal-court judgment vulnerable to collateral attack on the ground that the court did not have jurisdiction to enter it?

No recent Supreme Court decisions have addressed this question, and the older decisions do not speak with a single voice. At least if the jurisdictional issue was actually litigated and decided, it seems unlikely that a party would be allowed to renew the challenge in a later proceeding. *See Stoll v. Gottlieb*, 305 U.S. 165 (1938).

Problem: What's Wrong with this Picture?

You are a new associate in the law firm representing Euclid Market Place, L.L.C. (Euclid), an upscale shopping center located in the state of Illinois. Suit has been filed against Euclid in the United States District Court for the Central District of Illinois. The plaintiffs are Parkside Catering Co. (Parkside), a former tenant of the shopping center, and five individuals (guarantors of the corporate plaintiff's obligations). The complaint alleges that Parkside is incorporated in Missouri and has its principal place of business there and that the five individual plaintiffs are citizens of Missouri. It also alleges that the defendant is a "Delaware Limited Liability Company, with its principal place of business in the State of Illinois." The complaint asserts state-law claims for breach of contract and seeks damages in excess of $200,000.

The senior partner who is handling the case asks you to draft an answer to the complaint. In addition to the complaint, the partner gives you a copy of the lease that gave rise to the dispute. The lease refers to Parkside as "a Missouri corporation."

Is there anything you should do before starting to draft the answer to the complaint?

Problem: Deliberate Concealment of Jurisdictional Facts

Edna Holcomb, a citizen of Iowa, brought suit in United States District Court for the District of Nebraska against Midland Ethanol Corp. (Midland). The complaint alleged that Midland "is a Nebraska corporation with its principal place of business in Nebraska." Midland's answer admitted that Midland "is a Nebraska corporation with its principal place of business in Nebraska" and denied every other allegation in the complaint. After some discovery and motions proceedings, the case went to trial.

At trial, Holcomb's witnesses presented an unusually strong case. On the third day of the trial, Midland disclosed that its state of incorporation is Iowa, not Nebraska. This of course destroyed diversity of citizenship, and Midland moved to dismiss the complaint for lack of jurisdiction. The District Court held a hearing and determined that Midland deliberately concealed its Iowa citizenship until the middle of trial when its case was going badly.

Should the District Court dismiss the case? Would it make a difference if the statute of limitations has run on the plaintiff's claim and state law would not allow tolling?

In *Owen Equipment & Erection Co. v. Kroger*, 437 U.S. 365 (1978), the Supreme Court considered a similar situation involving mid-trial disclosure of corporate citizenship. The original defendant was no longer part of the case, and the opposing parties at trial were the plaintiff and a third-party defendant over whom there was no independent basis of jurisdiction. The Eighth Circuit held that the plaintiff's claim against the third-party defendant came within the district court's supplemental jurisdiction (then called "ancillary jurisdiction"), but the Supreme Court rejected that holding. (See Chapter 11.) The Court added in a footnote (footnote 21):

> Our holding is that the District Court lacked power to entertain the respondent's lawsuit against the petitioner. Thus, the asserted inequity in the respondent's alleged concealment of its citizenship is irrelevant. Federal judicial power does not depend upon "prior action or consent of the parties."

The jurisdictional defect in *Kroger* was statutory, not constitutional. Is it so clear that "the asserted inequity" is irrelevant? The Eighth Circuit offered this analysis:

> By subtle and adroit pleading the defendant has gained a substantial advantage. If the trial goes well, it can keep the jurisdictional point hidden. If the trial seems to be going badly or, indeed, if it loses on the merits, it asserts that it can even then challenge jurisdiction and successfully, so it argues, since it insists that it is clear to all that jurisdiction may be challenged by anyone at any time....

> The District Court had judicial power over the case initially and we find no abuse of its discretion in the continued exercise of that power. But beyond that, whether the court's discretion was abused or not in its retention of the cause, defendant's conduct estops it from asserting abuse of discretion, not only under the teachings of [a lower-court case], but also under the most elementary considerations of judicial fairness.

Did the Supreme Court's footnote adequately address these arguments?

B. Jurisdiction and Merits

Note: Threshold Requirements and Subject-Matter Jurisdiction

1. When Congress creates a federal cause of action, the legislation will generally specify the necessary ingredients of a claim for relief. Until 2006, courts sometimes assumed that if the plaintiff failed to establish one or more of those ingredients, the effect was to negate the court's subject-matter jurisdiction. In *Arbaugh v. Y & H Corp.*, 546 U.S. 500 (2006), the Supreme Court repudiated that approach. The Court held that limits on the scope of a federal statute should be treated as jurisdictional only if Congress has "clearly" commanded that treatment.

Arbaugh was a suit for employment discrimination under Title VII of the Civil Rights Act of 1964. Title VII makes it unlawful for an "employer" to discriminate on the basis of sex, and the statute limits the definition of "employer" to include only those having "fifteen or more employees." The plaintiff won a jury verdict against Y & H, but two weeks after the trial court entered judgment on the verdict, Y & H moved to dismiss the entire action for want of federal subject-matter jurisdiction. Y & H asserted—for the first time in the litigation—that it had fewer than 15 employees on its payroll and therefore was not amenable to suit under Title VII. In support of its assertion, Y & H argued that eight delivery drivers and four owners did not qualify as "employees" for Title VII purposes.

The trial court, after reviewing the parties' submissions, agreed with Y & H and vacated its prior judgment in favor of Arbaugh. The court dismissed Arbaugh's Title VII claim with prejudice and her state-law claims without prejudice. The Fifth Circuit affirmed, relying on circuit precedents holding that a defendant's "failure to qualify as an 'employer' under Title VII deprives a district court of subject matter jurisdiction."

The Supreme Court reversed. The Court acknowledged that its own decisions had been "less than meticulous" in distinguishing between subject-matter jurisdiction and the ingredients of a claim. By way of example, the Court cited another Title VII case, *EEOC v. Arabian American Oil Co.*, 499 U.S. 244 (1991). The plaintiff, Ali Boureslan, was employed in Saudi Arabia by an American corporation. The defendant filed a motion for summary judgment on the ground that the district court lacked subject-matter jurisdiction over Boureslan's claim. It argued that the protections of Title VII did not extend to United States citizens employed abroad by American employers. The district court agreed and granted the motion; the court of appeals and ultimately the United States Supreme Court affirmed the dismissal. In the course of its opinion, the Court referred to "the jurisdictional language of Title VII."

In *Arbaugh*, the Court repudiated "drive-by jurisdictional rulings" such as the one in the *Boureslan* case. Instead, it laid down a "readily administrable bright line" rule:

> If [Congress] clearly states that a threshold limitation on a statute's scope shall count as jurisdictional, then courts and litigants will be duly instructed and will not be left to wrestle with the issue. But when Congress does not rank a statutory limitation on coverage as jurisdictional, courts should treat the restriction as nonjurisdictional in character.

Applying that rule to the case before it, the Court held that the threshold number of employees for application of Title VII is an element of a plaintiff's claim for relief, not a jurisdictional issue. The Court explained:

> Arbaugh invoked federal-question jurisdiction under § 1331, but her case "aris[es]" under a federal law, Title VII, that specifies, as a prerequisite to its application, the existence of a particular fact, i.e., 15 or more employees. . . . Of course, Congress could make the employee-numerosity requirement "jurisdictional," just as it has made an amount-in-controversy threshold an ingredient of subject-matter jurisdiction in delineating diversity-of-citizenship jurisdiction under 28 U.S.C. § 1332. But neither § 1331, nor Title VII's jurisdictional provision, 42 U.S.C. § 2000e-5(f)(3) (authorizing jurisdiction over actions "brought under" Title VII), specifies any threshold ingredient akin to 28 U.S.C. § 1332's monetary floor. Instead, the 15-employee threshold appears in a separate provision that "does not speak in jurisdictional terms or refer in any way to the jurisdiction of the district courts."

2. The most important consequence of classifying a statutory limitation as jurisdictional is, of course, that jurisdictional limitations are subject to the *Mansfield* rule. As the Court explained in *Arbaugh*:

If the [15-employee minimum] conditions subject-matter jurisdiction, as the lower courts held it did, then a conclusion that Y & H had fewer than 15 employees would require erasure of the judgment for Arbaugh entered on the jury verdict. But if the lower courts' subject-matter jurisdiction characterization is incorrect, and the issue, instead, concerns the merits of Arbaugh's case, then Y & H raised the employee-numerosity requirement too late. Its pretrial stipulations and its failure to speak to the issue prior to the conclusion of the trial on the merits, see Fed. Rule Civ. Proc. 12(h)(2), would preclude vacation of the $40,000 judgment in Arbaugh's favor.

3. Section 501(b) of the Copyright Act provides that when a copyright is infringed, the copyright owner "is entitled, *subject to the requirements of section 411*, to institute an action" for infringement. (Emphasis added.) Section 411 in turn provides that with certain exceptions, "no civil action for infringement of the copyright in any United States work shall be instituted until preregistration or registration of the copyright claim has been made in accordance with this title."

Prior to *Arbaugh*, there was widespread agreement among the circuits that the registration requirement under section 411(a) is a "jurisdictional prerequisite" to an infringement suit. However, in *Reed Elsevier, Inc. v. Muchnick*, 559 U.S. 154 (2010), the Supreme Court rejected this view. The Court applied the "same approach" it had taken in *Arbaugh* and reached a similar conclusion:

> [Section 411(a)'s] registration requirement, like Title VII's numerosity requirement, is located in a provision "separate" from those granting federal courts subject-matter jurisdiction over those respective claims. Federal district courts have subject-matter jurisdiction over copyright infringement actions based on 28 U.S.C. §§ 1331 and 1338. But [neither § 1331 nor § 1338(a)] conditions its jurisdictional grant on whether copyright holders have registered their works before suing for infringement.

> Nor does any other factor suggest that section 411(a)'s registration requirement can be read to "speak in jurisdictional terms or refer in any way to the jurisdiction of the district courts." First, and most significantly, § 411(a) expressly allows courts to adjudicate infringement claims involving unregistered works in three circumstances .... It would be at least unusual to ascribe jurisdictional significance to a condition subject to these sorts of exceptions.

The Court acknowledged one possible distinction: "the numerosity requirement in *Arbaugh* could be considered an element of a Title VII claim, rather than a prerequisite to initiating a lawsuit." But that did not change the Court's conclusion.

> A statutory condition that requires a party to take some action before filing a lawsuit is not automatically "a *jurisdictional* prerequisite to suit." Rather, the jurisdictional analysis must focus on the "legal character" of the requirement, which we [discern] by looking to the condition's text, context, and relevant historical treatment. ...

Section 411(a) imposes a precondition to filing a claim that is not clearly labeled jurisdictional, is not located in a jurisdiction-granting provision, and admits of congressionally authorized exceptions. Section 411(a) thus imposes a type of precondition to suit that supports nonjurisdictional treatment under our precedents.

4. The Sherman Act provides: "Every contract, combination in the form of trust or otherwise, or conspiracy, in restraint of *trade or commerce among the several States*, or with foreign nations, is declared to be illegal." (Emphasis added.) The Clayton Act (15 U.S.C. § 15) creates a cause of action for anyone "injured in his business or property" by an antitrust violation. In the past, the Court has often referred to the commerce nexus as "the jurisdictional requirement of the Sherman Act." *E.g., McLain v. Real Estate Board of New Orleans*, Inc., 444 U.S. 232 (1980). After *Arbaugh* and *Reed Elsevier*, should the commerce nexus be treated as a jurisdictional requirement, or only as an element of the plaintiff's claim? Is it relevant that the statutory language echoes the language of Article I of the Constitution?

Problem: "But He Wasn't a Participant!"

James Martel is a former employee of Acme Co. While employed there, he participated in Acme's long-term disability income plan (LTD Plan or Plan). The LTD Plan is an employee benefit plan within the meaning of the Employee Retirement Income Security Act (ERISA). The Plan is administered by Fiduciary Insurance Co. (Fidco).

In 2010, Martel was in an automobile accident that resulted in injury to his neck and caused him to suffer severe headaches. He continued to work until June 2013, at which time he took a leave of absence due to his deteriorating physical condition. Shortly thereafter, he timely applied for LTD benefits under the Plan. Fidco determined that Martel was eligible for LTD benefits and approved his application subject to "continuing evaluation of his claim."

The Plan paid LTD benefits to Martel until July 2, 2015, when Fidco determined that he was no longer disabled within the meaning of the Plan. Martel challenged that determination, invoking the administrative remedies that are part of the Plan, but his challenges were rejected. Martel then filed a civil action against Fidco under ERISA. The suit was based on § 502(a)(1)(B) [29 U.S.C. § 1132(a)(1)(B)] and invoked federal court jurisdiction pursuant to 29 U.S.C. § 1132(e)(1). The former provides that "a participant or beneficiary" may bring a civil action "to recover benefits due to him under the terms of his plan [or] to enforce his rights under the terms of the plan." The latter provides for district court jurisdiction over such actions. The complaint asserted that Martel was a "participant" in the LTD Plan under the definitional section of ERISA [29 U.S.C. § 1002(7)].

After considering the administrative record, the district court granted Fidco's motion for summary judgment on the ground that the termination of benefits did not constitute an abuse of discretion. Martel appealed, and the court of appeals held that under a recent en banc ruling of the circuit, the Plan's decision should have been reviewed de novo. The panel remanded the case to the district court for further consideration under the de novo standard. The case is now back in the district court.

Fidco never asserted in the administrative process, in the original district court proceeding, or in the appeal to the court of appeals, that Martel was not a plan "participant" within the meaning of 29 U.S.C. § 1002(7). However, Fidco has now filed a motion under FRCP 12(h)(3) to dismiss for lack of subject matter jurisdiction on the ground that Martel did not qualify as a plan participant and therefore lacked statutory standing to sue under ERISA.

In support of the motion, Fidco explains that after the remand, its newly retained counsel located relevant plan documents that govern Martel's eligibility for benefits. Under these documents, Fidco argues, Martel was not a plan "participant" because he was on an unpaid leave of absence when he applied for benefits. Fidco cites Section 3.3.4 of the Plan, which expressly provides that "if an Eligible Employee is on an unpaid leave of absence, his or her status as a Long-Term Participant shall be suspended and he or she shall be ineligible for Long-Term Disability Benefits."

Recognizing that it had not previously raised this standing issue, Fidco argues that because the issue ultimately relates to the district court's subject matter jurisdiction it can, under Rule 12(h)(3), raise the issue at any time. Fidco relies on a 2005 decision by the court of appeals for the governing circuit which expressly held that "federal courts lack subject matter jurisdiction if the plaintiff in an action for benefits owed under an ERISA plan lacks standing to bring a civil suit enforcing ERISA under 29 U.S.C. § 1132(a)(1)(B)."

Ordinarily, of course, a district court must follow on-point precedent of the court of appeals for its circuit. However, there is an exception for situations "where intervening Supreme Court authority is clearly irreconcilable with our prior circuit authority."

Should the district court allow Fidco to raise the standing issue?

Note: The Frivolous Federal Claim

Suppose that the plaintiff's complaint asserts a federal cause of action, but fails to adequately allege one or more elements of the claim. Ordinarily, the complaint would be dismissed under Rule 12(b)(6) for failure to state a claim on which relief can be granted. But a complaint may be so inadequate that the court will dismiss for want of subject matter jurisdiction.

An interesting illustration is *Williams v. Aztar Indian Gaming Corp.*, 351 F.3d 294 (7th Cir. 2003). Williams was a compulsive gambler who gambled away his life savings at a riverboat casino. He brought suit against the operators of the casino in federal district court. There was no diversity, and most of his claims were grounded in state law, but he also asserted a civil violation of the federal RICO statute.

Although RICO is part of the federal criminal code (Title 18), the statute also creates a civil cause of action. (See *Tafflin v. Levitt* in Chapter 6.) An essential element of a RICO claim is a pattern of racketeering activity. This element in turn requires the plaintiff to plead "predicate acts." Williams alleged that certain mailings by the casino constituted predicate acts of mail fraud.

The district court took jurisdiction of the case. It dismissed the RICO claim, finding that Williams failed to allege acts that gave rise to mail fraud. It exercised supplemental jurisdiction over the state-law claims and granted summary judgment to the defendants on all of the remaining counts.

Williams appealed to the Seventh Circuit. The court of appeals held that Williams' entire complaint should have been dismissed for want of subject matter jurisdiction. The court said:

> A necessary element of a scheme to defraud is the making of a false statement or material misrepresentation, or the concealment of a material fact, and it is here that Williams's complaint fails. [Even if some of the statements in the casino's communications] could be considered "false" or "misrepresentations," it is clear that they are nothing more than sales puffery on which no person of ordinary prudence and comprehension would rely . . . .

> While in many circumstances Williams's failure to prove his contentions would not deprive a court of jurisdiction, it appears to us that his RICO theory "is *so* feeble, so transparent an attempt to move a state-law dispute to federal court . . . that it does not arise under federal law at all." At oral argument, Williams's counsel all but conceded that he lacked a good faith basis for bringing the RICO claim (he specifically noted that Williams was not appealing the district court's resolution of that issue). When confronted by the apparent inadequacy of the claim, Williams's counsel could not point to one RICO case on which he relied before filing this lawsuit (much less an analogous case). Instead, he stated that "gambling is new in our country," and simply reiterated the facts pled in his complaint to substantiate how this is a "new" or "novel" invocation of RICO. We are unpersuaded by his rhetoric and do not find this to be a "nonfrivolous argument for the extension [or] modification . . . of existing law or the establishment of new law." Fed. R. Civ. P. 11(b)(2). Rather, we find this case to be exactly the type of bootstrapping use of RICO that federal courts abhor.

What difference does it make if the court dismisses for want of subject matter jurisdiction or for failure to state a claim? Under what circumstances should a defendant respond to a weak "federal" complaint with a motion to dismiss for want of jurisdiction?

C. Choosing Among Threshold Grounds

Note: "Hypothetical Jurisdiction" and the Steel Co. Case

Consider the following case. Plaintiff brings suit in federal district court seeking to enjoin alleged violations of federal environmental laws by the defendant. The defendant challenges the plaintiff's standing under Article III to bring the suit. The district court finds that the standing issue is novel and difficult. But the court also concludes that the plaintiff's claim must fail under the governing federal environmental laws. May the court assume *arguendo* that the plaintiff has standing and enter judgment rejecting the claim on the merits?

Until 1998, many courts viewed this as a permissible course of action. The doctrine was sometimes referred to as "hypothetical jurisdiction," and it rested on grounds of practicality: why wrestle with a difficult jurisdictional issue when the court can reach the same result by deciding an easy "merits" question? However, in *Steel Co. v. Citizens for a Better Environment*, 523 U.S. 83 (1998), the Supreme Court appeared to reject this approach. Justice Scalia wrote the Court's opinion:

> Several Courts of Appeals [find] it proper to proceed immediately to [a merits] question, despite jurisdictional objections, at least where (1) the merits question is more readily resolved, and (2) the prevailing party on the merits would be the same as the prevailing party were jurisdiction denied. The Ninth Circuit has denominated this practice—which it characterizes as "assuming" jurisdiction for the purpose of deciding the merits—the "doctrine of hypothetical jurisdiction."

> We decline to endorse such an approach because it carries the courts beyond the bounds of authorized judicial action and thus offends fundamental principles of separation of powers. This conclusion should come as no surprise, since it is reflected in a long and venerable line of our cases. . . . The requirement that jurisdiction be established as a threshold matter "spring[s] from the nature and limits of the judicial power of the United States" and is "inflexible and without exception." *Mansfield*.

> [The Court then discussed cases cited by lower courts and by Justice Stevens in a concurring opinion that disputed the Court's rejection of "hypothetical jurisdiction."] While some of the above cases must be acknowledged to have diluted the absolute purity of the rule that Article III jurisdiction is always an antecedent question, none of them even approaches approval of a doctrine of "hypothetical jurisdiction" that enables a court to resolve contested questions of law when its jurisdiction is in doubt. Hypothetical jurisdiction produces nothing more than a hypothetical judgment—which comes to the same thing as an advisory opinion, disapproved by this Court from the beginning.

> The statutory and (especially) constitutional elements of jurisdiction are an essential ingredient of separation and equilibration of powers, restraining the courts from acting at certain times, and even restraining them from acting permanently regarding certain subjects. For a court to pronounce upon the meaning or the constitutionality of a state or federal law when it has no jurisdiction to do so is, by very definition, for a court to act ultra vires.

The Court's opinion certainly seems to put an end to any further resort to "hypothetical jurisdiction." However, that opinion garnered only five votes, and two of the votes came from Justice O'Connor and Justice Kennedy. Justice O'Connor, in a concurring opinion joined by Justice Kennedy, said:

> [I agree] with the Court's statement that federal courts should be certain of their jurisdiction before reaching the merits of a case. As the Court acknowledges, however, several of our decisions "have diluted the absolute purity of the rule that Article III jurisdiction is always an antecedent question." The opinion of the Court adequately describes why the assumption of jurisdiction was defensible in those cases, and why it is not in this case. I write separately to note that, in my view, the Court's opinion should not be read as cataloging an exhaustive list of circumstances under which federal courts may exercise judgment in "reserv[ing] difficult questions of . . . jurisdiction when the case alternatively could be resolved on the merits in favor of the same party."

Note: Personal and Subject-Matter Jurisdiction

Suppose that the defendant challenges personal jurisdiction (invoking *International Shoe Corp. v. Washington*, 326 U.S. 310 (1945), and its progeny) as well as subject-matter jurisdiction. The district court readily concludes that the defendant lacks "minimum contacts," but finds that the challenge to subject matter jurisdiction presents a novel and difficult issue. Does the decision in *Steel Co.* mean that the court may not dismiss for want of personal jurisdiction without first establishing that subject-matter jurisdiction exists? The Fifth Circuit, sitting en banc, thought so, but the Supreme Court unanimously held otherwise. In *Ruhrgas AG v. Marathon Oil Co.*, 526 U.S. 574 (1999), Justice Ginsburg explained:

> The particular civil action we confront was commenced in state court and removed to federal court. The specific question on which we granted certiorari asks "[w]hether a federal district court is absolutely barred in all circumstances from dismissing a removed case for lack of personal jurisdiction without first deciding its subject-matter jurisdiction."
>
> We hold that in cases removed from state court to federal court, as in cases originating in federal court, there is no unyielding jurisdictional hierarchy. Customarily, a federal court first resolves doubts about its jurisdiction over the subject matter, but there are circumstances in which a district court appropriately accords priority to a personal jurisdiction inquiry. The proceeding before us is such a case. . . .
>
> The Court of Appeals accorded priority to the requirement of subject-matter jurisdiction because it is nonwaivable and delimits federal-court power, while restrictions on a court's jurisdiction over the person are waivable and protect individual rights. The character of the two jurisdictional bedrocks unquestionably differs. Subject-matter limitations on federal jurisdiction serve institutional interests. They keep the federal courts within the bounds the Constitution and Congress have prescribed. Accordingly, subject-matter delineations must be policed by the courts on their own initiative even at the highest level.

Personal jurisdiction, on the other hand, "represents a restriction on judicial power . . . as a matter of individual liberty." *Insurance Corp. of Ireland v. Compagnie des Bauxites de Guinee*, 456 U.S. 694, 702 (1982). Therefore, a party may insist that the limitation be observed, or he may forgo that right, effectively consenting to the court's exercise of adjudicatory authority.

These distinctions do not mean that subject-matter jurisdiction is ever and always the more "fundamental." . . . While *Steel Co.* reasoned that subject-matter jurisdiction necessarily precedes a ruling on the merits, the same principle does not dictate a sequencing of jurisdictional issues. It is hardly novel for a federal court to choose among threshold grounds for denying audience to a case on the merits. Thus, as the Court observed in *Steel Co.*, district courts do not overstep Article III limits when they decline jurisdiction of state-law claims on discretionary grounds without determining whether those claims fall within their pendent jurisdiction or abstain under *Younger v. Harris*, 401 U.S. 37 (1971), without deciding whether the parties present a case or controversy.

. . . [In] most instances subject-matter jurisdiction will involve no arduous inquiry. In such cases, both expedition and sensitivity to state courts' coequal stature should impel the federal court to dispose of that issue first. . . . Where, as here, however, a district court has before it a straightforward personal jurisdiction issue presenting no complex question of state law, and the alleged defect in subject-matter jurisdiction raises a difficult and novel question, the court does not abuse its discretion by turning directly to personal jurisdiction.

Note: Other Threshold Issues

1. *Ruhrgas* made clear that, contrary to what might have been inferred from *Steel Co.*, federal courts are not invariably required to consider issues of subject-matter jurisdiction before all others. But *Ruhrgas* itself involved an issue of "jurisdiction." Does the qualification stated in *Ruhrgas* also apply to threshold issues that do not bear the "jurisdictional" label?

In *Tenet v. Doe*, 544 U.S. 1, 6 n.4 (2005), the Court indicated that the answer is "yes." The plaintiffs in this case alleged that they had conducted espionage for the United States during the Cold War and that the Government had reneged on its promise to provide assistance in return for their services. They asserted claims of estoppel and due process. The Government argued that the suit was barred by the rule announced in *Totten v. United States*, 92 U.S. 105 (1876). The *Totten* rule prohibits suits against the Government based on covert espionage agreements. The Ninth Circuit rejected the Government's argument, and the Supreme Court granted the Government's petition for certiorari on the *Totten* issue.

In the lower courts, the Government also argued that the Tucker Act, 28 U.S.C. § 1491(a)(1), required that plaintiffs' claims be brought in the Court of Federal Claims, rather than in the District Court. The lower courts rejected this argument, and the

Government did not pursue it in the Supreme Court. The Court assumed (but did not decide) that the Tucker Act question is "the kind of jurisdictional issue that *Steel Co.* directs must be resolved before addressing the merits of a claim." But it went on to hold that *Steel Co.* did not prevent it from resolving the case on the basis of the *Totten* issue. The Court relied on *Ruhrgas* for the proposition that a federal court may "choose among threshold grounds for denying audience to a case on the merits." The Court explained:

> It would be inconsistent with the unique and categorical nature of the *Totten* bar — a rule designed not merely to defeat the asserted claims, but to preclude judicial inquiry — to first allow discovery or other proceedings in order to resolve the jurisdictional question.

Justice Scalia, who concurred in the Court's opinion, also wrote separately to emphasize the distinction between the type of rule represented by *Totten* and "the run-of-the-mill, nonthreshold *merits* question whether a cause of action exists." He concluded: "As applied today, the bar of *Totten* is a jurisdictional one."

2. Suppose that the defendant in a civil case in federal district court moves to dismiss for lack of subject matter jurisdiction and also on the ground of *forum non conveniens*. May the district court dismiss on the latter ground without reaching the jurisdictional issue? In other words, is *forum non conveniens* another threshold issue that may be resolved prior to matters of jurisdiction?

The Supreme Court confronted this question in *Sinochem Int'l v. Malaysia Int'l Shipping*, 549 U.S. 422 (2007). The court below, the Third Circuit, held that the district court could not dismiss the case under the *forum non conveniens* doctrine unless and until it determined definitively that it had both subject-matter jurisdiction over the cause and personal jurisdiction over the defendant. The court relied on statements in a Supreme Court opinion to the effect that "the doctrine of *forum non conveniens* can never apply if there is absence of jurisdiction."

The Supreme Court reversed, holding that the prior statements did not address the question of sequence. The Court held that the doctrine of *forum non conveniens* falls within the category of non-merits grounds for dismissal that can be considered by a district court even though jurisdictional issues remain unresolved. Thus, a district court "may dispose of an action by a *forum non conveniens* dismissal, bypassing questions of subject-matter and personal jurisdiction, when considerations of convenience, fairness, and judicial economy so warrant." The Court quoted with approval the Seventh Circuit's summary of the governing doctrine: "Jurisdiction is vital only if the court proposes to issue a judgment on the merits."

3. Consider this scenario. Plaintiff brings suit in state court and loses. He then files the identical suit in federal district court. The defendant moves to dismiss for lack of subject-matter jurisdiction and also pleads res judicata (claim preclusion). The jurisdictional issue is a difficult one, but it seems plain that the suit is barred by the prior judgment. May the district court dismiss on res judicata grounds without deciding the jurisdictional issue?

Problem: The "Enrolled Bill Rule"

Last year, the President signed an omnibus budget bill known as the Deficit Reduction Act (Act). The Act amends a variety of federal statutes including the Medicare Act and the Federal Deposit Insurance Act. One of its provisions amends Title 28 to increase the filing fee for civil actions in federal district courts.

Almost immediately, Public Citizen, a consumer advocacy group, filed suit in federal district court against the Clerk of Court. The suit asked the court to declare the Act unconstitutional and to compel the Clerk to maintain the existing filing fee.

The complaint asserts that the Act is unconstitutional because the statute's enactment did not comport with the bicameral passage requirement of Article I, Section 7 of the Constitution. The Supreme Court has held that before a bill can become law, the identical text must be approved by both Houses and signed by the President. However, in this instance, the version of the legislation that was presented to the House contained a clerk's error with respect to one term in the section amending the Medicare Act. As a consequence, the House and Senate voted on slightly different versions of the bill, and the President signed the version passed by the Senate. Nevertheless, the Speaker of the House and the President pro tempore of the Senate both signed a version of the proposed legislation identical to the version signed by the President. These signatures attested that indistinguishable legislative text passed both Houses.

In response, the Clerk has asserted: (1) that the plaintiff cannot meet the irreducible constitutional minimum of standing; and (2) the bicameralism claim is foreclosed by the "enrolled bill rule" established by the Supreme Court decision in *Marshall Field & Co. v. Clark*, 143 U.S. 649 (1892). The defendant's argument on standing is that the putatively unconstitutional provision of the Act can be severed, so that Public Citizen's grievance about increased filing fees would not be redressed by a favorable decision.

In *Marshall Field*, the Court held that the judiciary must treat the attestations of "the two houses, through their presiding officers" as "conclusive evidence that [a bill] was passed by Congress." Under the Court's decision, a bill signed by the leaders of the House and Senate—an attested "enrolled bill"—establishes that Congress passed the text included therein "according to the forms of the Constitution," and it "should be deemed complete and unimpeachable." Thus "the judicial department [must] accept, as having passed congress, all bills authenticated in the manner stated."

Public Citizen takes the position that *Marshall Field* is distinguishable and that in any event subsequent decisions of the Supreme Court have narrowed the enrolled bill rule.

The district court found that the plaintiff "barely" satisfied the constitutional minimum for standing. It went to hold that even if Public Citizen's allegations were accepted as true, the bicameralism challenge still "must fail" under the enrolled bill rule. The court granted the defendant's motion to dismiss under 12(b)(6).

Public Citizen has appealed. The court of appeals believes that the standing question is difficult and close, but it is convinced that *Marshall Field* is squarely controlling and requires dismissal of the suit. May the court of appeals affirm without reaching the standing issue?

Problem: *A Doomed Claim and the* Steel Co. *Rule*

A domestic organization that advocates reproductive rights has brought suit in federal district court challenging a federal government policy that requires foreign organizations, as a condition of receiving government funds, to agree neither to perform abortions nor to promote abortion generally. The plaintiffs assert that these restrictions violate their First Amendment rights to freedom of speech and association. The government argues that the plaintiffs lack standing under Article III to pursue this claim. The government also points out that, five years ago, the court of appeals for the circuit in which the district is located rejected the same constitutional claim on the merits. No circuit or Supreme Court decision has questioned that ruling.

The standing issue is a difficult one. May the district court dismiss the First Amendment claim on the merits, and may the court of appeals affirm, without addressing the standing issue?

Chapter 10

The "Federal Question" Jurisdiction

As we saw in Chapter 2, the Supreme Court has given a broad construction to the clause in Article III authorizing federal courts to hear cases "arising under" the Constitution, laws, and treaties of the United States. The identical language in 28 U.S.C. § 1331 and other provisions of Title 28 has been construed much more narrowly. This chapter explores the doctrines that define the "federal question" jurisdiction of the federal district courts.

A. The "Well Pleaded Complaint" Rule

Louisville & Nashville Railroad Co. v. Mottley

Supreme Court of the United States, 1908.

211 U.S. 149.

[The Court stated the facts as follows:] The appellees (husband and wife), being residents and citizens of Kentucky, brought this suit in equity in the circuit court of the United States for the western district of Kentucky against the appellant, a railroad company and a citizen of the same state. The object of the suit was to compel the specific performance of the following contract:

> Louisville, Ky., Oct. 2d, 1871. The Louisville & Nashville Railroad Company, in consideration that E. L. Mottley and wife, Annie E. Mottley, have this day released company from all damages or claims for damages for injuries received by them on the 7th of September, 1871, in consequence of a collision of trains on the railroad of said company at Randolph's Station, Jefferson County, Kentucky, hereby agrees to issue free passes on said railroad and branches now existing or to exist, to said E. L. & Annie E. Mottley for the remainder of the present year, and thereafter to renew said passes annually during the lives of said Mottley and wife or either of them.

The bill alleged that in September, 1871, plaintiffs, while passengers upon the defendant railroad, were injured by the defendant's negligence, and released their respective claims for damages in consideration of the agreement for transportation during their lives, expressed in the contract. It is alleged that the contract was performed by the defendant up to January 1, 1907, when the defendant declined to renew the passes. The bill then alleges that the refusal to comply with the contract was based solely upon that part of the act of Congress of June 29, 1906 [the Hepburn Act], which forbids

491

the giving of free passes or free transportation. The bill further alleges: First, that the act of Congress referred to does not prohibit the giving of passes under the circumstances of this case; and, second, that, if the law is to be construed as prohibiting such passes, it is in conflict with the 5th Amendment of the Constitution, because it deprives the plaintiffs of their property without due process of law. The defendant demurred to the bill. The judge of the circuit court overruled the demurrer, entered a decree for the relief prayed for, and the defendant appealed directly to this court.

Mr. Justice Moody delivered the opinion of the court:

Two questions of law were raised by the demurrer to the bill, were brought here by appeal, and have been argued before us. They are, first, whether that part of the act of Congress of June 29, 1906, which forbids the giving of free passes or the collection of any different compensation for transportation of passengers than that specified in the tariff filed, makes it unlawful to perform a contract for transportation of persons who, in good faith, before the passage of the act, had accepted such contract in satisfaction of a valid cause of action against the railroad; and, second, whether the statute, if it should be construed to render such a contract unlawful, is in violation of the 5th Amendment of the Constitution of the United States. We do not deem it necessary, however, to consider either of these questions, because, in our opinion, the court below was without jurisdiction of the cause. Neither party has questioned that jurisdiction, but it is the duty of this court to see to it that the jurisdiction of the circuit court, which is defined and limited by statute, is not exceeded. This duty we have frequently performed of our own motion. *Mansfield, C. & L. M. R. Co. v. Swan*, 111 U. S. 379, 382 . . . .

There was no diversity of citizenship, and it is not and cannot be suggested that there was any ground of jurisdiction, except that the case was a "suit . . . arising under the Constitution or laws of the United States." It is the settled interpretation of these words, as used in this statute, conferring jurisdiction, that a suit arises under the Constitution and laws of the United States only when the plaintiff's statement of his own cause of action shows that it is based upon those laws or that Constitution. It is not enough that the plaintiff alleges some anticipated defense to his cause of action, and asserts that the defense is invalidated by some provision of the Constitution of the United States. Although such allegations show that very likely, in the course of the litigation, a question under the Constitution would arise, they do not show that the suit, that is, the plaintiff's original cause of action, arises under the Constitution.

In *Tennessee v. Union & Planters' Bank*, 152 U. S. 454, the plaintiff, the state of Tennessee, brought suit in the circuit court of the United States to recover from the defendant certain taxes alleged to be due under the laws of the state. The plaintiff alleged that the defendant claimed an immunity from the taxation by virtue of its charter, and that therefore the tax was void, because in violation of the [contracts clause of the United States Constitution]. The cause was held to be beyond the jurisdiction of the circuit court, the court saying, by Mr. Justice Gray (p. 464): "A suggestion of one party, that the other will or may set up a claim under the Constitution or laws of the United States, does not make the suit one arising under that Constitution or those laws." . . . The interpretation of the act which we have stated was first announced in *Metcalf v. Watertown*, 128 U.S. 586 (1888), and has since been repeated and applied in [many cases]. [The Court here cited 17 decisions.]

It is ordered that the judgment be reversed and the case remitted to the circuit court with instructions to dismiss the suit for want of jurisdiction.

Notes and Questions: The Aftermath of Mottley

1. After the dismissal of their suit in federal circuit court, the Mottleys brought suit in the state court of Kentucky. The state courts granted specific performance. In *Louisville & Nashville Railroad Co. v. Mottley*, 219 U.S. 467 (1911) [*Mottley II*], the Supreme Court reversed, saying:

> It is [said] that, as the contract of Mottley and wife with the railroad company was originally valid, it cannot be supposed that Congress intended by the act of 1906 to annul or prevent its enforcement. But the purpose of Congress was to cut up by the roots every form of discrimination, favoritism, and inequality, except in the cases of certain excepted classes to which Mottley and his wife did not belong, and which exceptions rested upon peculiar grounds. Manifestly, from the face of the commerce act itself, Congress, before taking final action, considered the question as to what exceptions, if any, should be made in respect of the prohibition of free tickets, free passes, and free transportation. It solved the question when, without making any exceptions of existing contracts, it forbade by broad, explicit words any carrier to charge, demand, collect, or receive a "greater or less or different compensation" for any services in connection with the transportation of passengers or property than was specified in its published schedules of rates. The court cannot add an exception based on equitable grounds when Congress forbore to make such an exception.

2. From beginning to end, the only questions in dispute between the Mottleys and the railroad were questions of federal law. What is the justification for a rule that kept the case out of the federal trial court and required the Mottleys to start over in the state court?

3. Suppose that when the Mottleys sued in the state court of Kentucky, the defendant acknowledged the validity of the contract and the breach but asserted that its refusal to comply was required by the Hepburn Act. Could the defendant have removed the case to the federal trial court? Consider the discussion of *Gully* in the Note that follows.

Note: Gully *and the "Merely Possible" Federal Question*

1. In *Gully v. First National Bank*, 299 U.S. 109 (1936), Justice Cardozo, speaking for the Court, attempted to define the scope of the statutory "arising under" jurisdiction. As described in *Franchise Tax Board* [Section D, *infra*], "*Gully* was a suit by Mississippi tax authorities, claiming that the First National Bank had failed to make good on a contract with its predecessor corporation whereby, according to the State, the bank had promised to pay the predecessor's tax liabilities." The predecessor bank was a national bank. The Fifth Circuit held that the case was properly removed to federal court on the theory (as summarized by the Supreme Court) that "the power to lay a tax upon the shares of national banks has its origin and measure in the provisions of a federal statute." The statute was one enacted by Congress to limit the immunity rule laid down by the Supreme Court in *McCulloch v. Maryland* (1819). The Supreme Court held that the case did not "arise under" federal law:

> Not every question of federal law emerging in a suit is proof that a federal law is the basis of the suit. The tax here in controversy, if valid as a tax at all, was imposed under the authority of a statute of Mississippi. The federal law did not attempt to impose it or to confer upon the tax collector authority to sue for it. True, the tax, though assessed through the action of the state, must be consistent with the federal statute consenting, subject to restrictions, that such assessments may be made. It must also be consistent with the Constitution of the United States.

> If there were no federal law permitting the taxation of shares in national banks, a suit to recover such a tax would not be one arising under the Constitution of the United States, though the bank would have the aid of the Constitution when it came to its defense. That there *is* a federal law permitting such taxation does not change the basis of the suit, which is still the statute of the state, though the federal law is evidence to prove the statute valid.

> The argument for the [defendant bank in support of removal] proceeds on the assumption that, because permission at times is preliminary to action, the two are to be classed as one. But the assumption will not stand. A suit does not arise under a law renouncing a defense, though the result of the renunciation is an extension of the area of legislative power which will cause the suitor to prevail.

> Here the right to be established is one created by the state. If that is so, it is unimportant that federal consent is the source of state authority. To reach the underlying law we do not travel back so far. By unimpeachable authority, a suit brought upon a state statute does not arise under an act of Congress or the Constitution of the United States because prohibited thereby. Louisville & Nashville R. Co. v. Mottley. With no greater reason can it be said to arise thereunder because permitted thereby.

That was enough to decide the case, was it not? But the Court did not stop there. Justice Cardozo continued:

> If we follow the ascent far enough, countless claims of right can be discovered to have their source or their operative limits in the provisions of a federal statute or in the Constitution itself with its circumambient restrictions upon legislative power. To set bounds to the pursuit, the courts have

formulated the distinction between controversies that are basic and those that are collateral, between disputes that are necessary and those that are merely possible. We shall be lost in a maze if we put that compass by.

Given *Mottley*, what obstacle does a court face in attempting to determine when a controversy over federal law is "necessary" and when it is "merely possible"?

2. *Gully* makes no mention of the Holmes test as stated and applied in *American Well Works*, the next principal case. Wouldn't the lack of jurisdiction be obvious under the Holmes test? What might account for the failure to cite *American Well Works*?

Problem: A Medical-Device Products Liability Suit

Robert Lydon brought suit in state court against Acme Medical Device Corp. seeking to recover for injuries allegedly resulting from the failure of a bone screw manufactured by Acme. A bone screw is a "medical device" within the meaning of the Medical Device Act (MDA), a federal statute.

Under the MDA, certain medical devices may not be lawfully marketed unless they comply with requirements established by the Food and Drug Administration, a federal agency. Bone screws fall within that category. The MDA provides in section 360k:

> No State may establish with respect to a [covered] device any state requirement which is different from, or in addition to, any federal requirement.

Assume that the Supreme Court has held that "requirements" under this statute include legal requirements that grow out of the application of state tort law to particular circumstances. Under these holdings, a plaintiff can recover in tort only if his claim is predicated on a breach of duties that are substantially identical to requirements imposed by federal law. May Acme remove the case to federal court on the basis of section 360k?

B. The State-Created Cause of Action with a Federal "Ingredient"

American Well Works Co. v. Layne & Bowler Co.

Supreme Court of the United States, 1916.

241 U.S. 257.

MR. JUSTICE HOLMES delivered the opinion of the court:

[The question presented was whether the case was one "arising under" the patent laws of the United States.]

Of course the question depends upon the plaintiff's declaration. That may be summed up in a few words. The plaintiff alleges that it owns, manufactures, and sells a certain pump, has or has applied for a patent for it, and that the pump is known as the best in the market. It then alleges that the defendants have falsely and maliciously libeled and slandered the plaintiff's title to the pump by stating that the pump and certain parts thereof are infringements upon the defendant's pump and certain parts thereof, and that without probable cause they have brought suits against some parties who are using the plaintiff's pump, and that they are threatening suits against all who use it. The allegation of the defendants' libel or slander is repeated in slightly varying form, but it all comes to statements to various people that the plaintiff was infringing the defendants' patent, and that the defendant would sue both seller and buyer if the plaintiff's pump was used. Actual damage to the plaintiff in its business is alleged to the extent of $50,000, and punitive damages to the same amount are asked.

It is evident that the claim for damages is based upon conduct; or, more specifically, language, tending to persuade the public to withdraw its custom from the plaintiff, and having that effect to its damage. . . . [It] is enough to allege and prove the conduct and effect, leaving the defendant to justify if he can. If the conduct complained of [is] a statement of fact, it may be justified, absolutely or with qualifications, by proof that the statement is true. But all such justifications are defenses, and raise issues that are no part of the plaintiff's case.

In the present instance it is part of the plaintiff's case that it had a business to be damaged; whether built up by patents or without them does not matter. It is no part of it to prove anything concerning the defendants' patent, or that the plaintiff did not infringe the same—still less to prove anything concerning any patent of its own. The material statement complained of is that the plaintiff infringes,—which may be true notwithstanding the plaintiff's patent. That is merely a piece of evidence. Furthermore, the damage alleged presumably is rather the consequence of the threat to sue than of the statement that the plaintiff's pump infringed the defendants' rights.

A suit for damages to business caused by a threat to sue under the patent law is not itself a suit under the patent law. And the same is true when the damage is caused by a statement of fact,—that the defendant has a patent which is infringed. What makes the defendants' act a wrong is its manifest tendency to injure the plaintiff's business; and the wrong is the same whatever the means by which it is accomplished. But whether it is a wrong or not depends upon the law of the state where the act is done, not upon the patent law, and therefore the suit arises under the law of the state. A suit arises under the law that creates the cause of action. The fact that the justification may involve the validity and infringement of a patent is no more material to the question under what law the suit is brought than it would be in an action of contract. If the state adopted for civil proceedings the saying of the old criminal law: the greater the truth, the greater the libel, the validity of the patent would not come in question at all. . . . The state is master of the whole matter, and if it saw fit to do away with actions of this type altogether, no one, we imagine, would suppose that they still could be maintained under the patent laws of the United States.

MR. JUSTICE MCKENNA dissents, being of opinion that the case involves a direct and substantial controversy under the patent laws.

Note: American Well Works *and the "Holmes Test"*

1. In the first part of his opinion in *American Well Works*, Justice Holmes appears to rely on the well pleaded complaint rule: "It is no part of [the plaintiff's case] to prove anything concerning the defendants' patent . . . still less to prove anything concerning any patent of its own." But the opinion does not end there. Instead, the Court goes on to give us what has become known as the "Holmes test": "A suit arises under the law that creates the cause of action."

2. Whatever its other merits, the "Holmes test" serves as a reliable rule of inclusion. Thus, if the plaintiff sues on a federal cause of action, there is jurisdiction under § 1331. And, as the Court said in *Merrell-Dow Pharmaceuticals v. Thompson*, 478 U.S. 804 (1986), "the vast majority of cases brought under the general federal-question jurisdiction of the federal courts are those in which federal law creates the cause of action."

3. Some writers have suggested that two old Supreme Court decisions, *Shulthis v. McDougal*, 225 U.S. 561 (1912), and *Shoshone Mining Co. v. Rutter*, 177 U.S. 505 (1900), are inconsistent with the Holmes test. Recent research by Professor John B. Oakley indicates that there is no inconsistency. *Shulthis*, Professor Oakley reports, was "a suit on a state-created claim for relief from interference with the plaintiff's alleged property rights." And "*Shoshone* did not involve a federally created right of suit to establish or defend federal title to the mining claim in question." John B. Oakley, *Federal Jurisdiction and the Problem of the Litigative Unit: When Does What "Arise Under" Federal Law?*, 76 Tex. L. Rev. 1829, 1841–42 n.63 (1998). In any event, these old cases have no modern progeny, and the Holmes test can safely be relied on as a rule of inclusion.

4. As Judge Henry J. Friendly pointed out in an oft-cited opinion, Holmes intended his test not as rule of inclusion but as a rule of exclusion. *See T.B. Harms Co. v. Eliscu*, 339 F.2d 823, 827 (2d Cir. 1964). However, only five years after *American Well Works*, in *Smith v. Kansas City Title Co.*, the Supreme Court appeared to reject that approach.

Smith v. Kansas City Title & Trust Co.

Supreme Court of the United States, 1921.

255 U.S. 180.

Mr. Justice Day delivered the opinion of the Court.

A bill was filed in the United States District Court for [the Western District of Missouri] by a shareholder in the Kansas City Title & Trust Company to enjoin the company [from] investing the funds of the company in farm loan bonds issued by Federal Land Banks or Joint-Stock Land Banks under authority of the Federal Farm Loan Act of July 17, 1916.

The relief was sought on the ground that these acts were beyond the constitutional power of Congress. The bill avers that the board of directors of the company are about to invest its funds in the bonds to the amount of $10,000 in each of the classes described, and will do so unless enjoined by the court in this action. . . . The bill prays that the acts of Congress authorizing the creation of the banks [shall] be adjudged and decreed to be unconstitutional, void and of no effect, and that the issuance of the farm loan bonds [shall] be adjudged and decreed to be invalid. . . .

No objection is made to the federal jurisdiction, either original or appellate, by the parties to this suit, but that question will be first examined. The company is authorized to invest its funds in legal securities only. The attack upon the proposed investment in the bonds described is because of the alleged unconstitutionality of the acts of Congress undertaking to organize the banks and authorize the issue of the bonds. No other reason is set forth in the bill as a ground of objection to the proposed investment by the board of directors acting in the company's behalf. As diversity of citizenship is lacking, the jurisdiction of the District Court depends upon whether the cause of action set forth arises under the Constitution or laws of the United States. Judicial Code, § 24 [now 28 U.S.C. § 1331].

The general rule is that, where it appears from the bill or statement of the plaintiff that the right to relief depends upon the construction or application of the Constitution or laws of the United States, and that such federal claim is not merely colorable, and rests upon a reasonable foundation, the District Court has jurisdiction under this provision. [The Court here quoted the definitions from *Osborn v. Bank of the United States* and *Cohens v. Virginia*.] . . .

In the instant case the averments of the bill show that the directors were proceeding to make the investments in view of the act authorizing the bonds about to be purchased, maintaining that the act authorizing them was constitutional and the bonds valid and desirable investments. The objecting shareholder avers in the bill that the securities were issued under an unconstitutional law, and hence of no validity. It is therefore apparent that the controversy concerns the constitutional validity of an act of Congress which is directly drawn in question. The decision depends upon the determination of this issue. . . .

[On the merits, the Court held that the Act was constitutional.]

MR. JUSTICE BRANDEIS took no part in the consideration or decision of this case.

MR. JUSTICE HOLMES, dissenting.

No doubt it is desirable that the question raised in this case should be set at rest, but that can be done by the Courts of the United States only within the limits of the jurisdiction conferred upon them by the Constitution and the laws of the United States. As this suit was brought by a citizen of Missouri against a Missouri corporation the single ground upon which the jurisdiction of the District Court can be maintained is that the suit "arises under the Constitution or laws of the United States" within the meaning of section 24 of the Judicial Code. I am of opinion that this case does not arise in that way and therefore that the bill should have been dismissed.

It is evident that the cause of action arises not under any law of the United States but wholly under Missouri law. The defendant is a Missouri corporation and the right claimed is that of a stockholder to prevent the directors from doing an act, that is, making an investment, alleged to be contrary to their duty. But the scope of their duty depends upon the charter of their corporation and other laws of Missouri. If those laws had authorized the investment in terms the plaintiff would have had no case, and this seems to me to make manifest what I am unable to deem even debatable, that, as I have said, the cause of action arises wholly under Missouri law. If the Missouri law authorizes or forbids the investment according to the determination of this Court upon a point under the Constitution or Acts of Congress, still that point is material only because the Missouri law saw fit to make it so. The whole foundation of the duty is Missouri law, which at its sole will incorporated the other law as it might incorporate a document. The other law or document depends for its relevance and effect not on its own force but upon the law that took it up, so I repeat once more the cause of action arises wholly from the law of the State.

But it seems to me that a suit cannot be said to arise under any other law than that which creates the cause of action. . . . The mere adoption by a State law of a United States law as a criterion or test, when the law of the United States has no force *proprio vigore*, does not cause a case under the State law to be also a case under the law of the United States, and so it has been decided by this Court again and again. . . .

[In *American Well Works*, the Court held that] "a suit arises under the law that creates the cause of action." I know of no decisions to the contrary and see no reason for overruling it now.

MR. JUSTICE MCREYNOLDS concurs in this dissent. In view of our opinion that this Court has no jurisdiction we express no judgment on the merits.

Note: Smith *and* Moore

1. The Court in *Smith* quotes the definitions of "arising under" jurisdiction from *Osborn* and *Cohens*. Were those precedents relevant?

2. The majority does not respond to Holmes's citation of *American Well Works*. Can the cases be distinguished?

3. What is the relationship between "*Smith* jurisdiction" and the well-pleaded complaint rule? Note that Justice Holmes does not rely on *Mottley*, and he does not say that Smith's complaint anticipated a federal defense. He says that state law has adopted federal law "as a criterion or test" for asserting the state-created claim, but that this is not enough because a suit arises *only* under "the law that creates the cause of action."

The Holmes dissent thus makes clear that *Smith* and *Mottley* address different issues. *Mottley* holds that a case does not arise under federal law, for purposes of the statutory jurisdiction, when the plaintiff anticipates a federal defense to his state-created cause of action. *Mottley* does not address the question that divides the Court in *Smith*: whether a case "arises under" federal law when state law creates the cause of action, but the plaintiff relies on federal law for one of the elements of the claim.

4. Although *Smith* suggests that state-law claims that depend on the interpretation of federal law "arise under" federal law for purposes of what is today § 1331, the subsequent decision in *Moore v. Chesapeake & Ohio R. Co.,* 291 U.S. 205 (1934), appears to cast doubt on that conclusion.

The plaintiff in *Moore* sued his employer, an interstate railroad, for injuries he sustained in the course of his employment. The question was whether a claim for injuries "received in *intra*state commerce" could be brought under the statutory "federal question" jurisdiction because the complaint (in its second paragraph) "invoked the Safety Appliance Acts enacted by the Congress."

The opinion of the Supreme Court does not specify how the complaint "invoked" the federal Safety Appliance Acts. The lower court opinion indicates that the complaint said only that the plaintiff brought the action "under and by virtue of . . . the Safety Appliance Acts." The lower court opinion also states that, according to the plaintiff, the second paragraph was not "founded on" the federal statute. Rather, the reference to the Safety Appliance Acts was only "to supply the negligence, with certainty, required by the Kentucky Employers' Liability Act."

The Supreme Court opinion (by Chief Justice Hughes) is unusually opaque, but the Court's conclusion is unambiguous: "the second paragraph of the complaint set forth a cause of action under the Kentucky statute, and, as to this cause of action, the suit is not to be regarded as one arising under the laws of the United States." Here are the relevant passages explaining how the Court reached this result:

> The Federal Safety Appliance Acts prescribed duties, and injured employees are entitled to recover for injuries sustained through the breach of these duties. [The Court cites, among other cases, *Rigsby*, discussed in Chapter 8.]

> Questions arising in actions in state courts to recover for injuries sustained by employees in intrastate commerce and relating to the scope or construction of the Federal Safety Appliance Acts are, of course, federal questions which may appropriately be reviewed in this Court. [Citations omitted.] But it does not follow that a suit brought under the state statute which defines liability to employees who are injured while engaged in intrastate commerce, and brings within the purview of the statute a breach of the duty imposed by the federal statute, should be regarded as a suit arising under the laws of the United States and cognizable in the federal court in the absence of diversity of citizenship. . . .

> With respect to injuries sustained in intrastate commerce, nothing in the Safety Appliance Acts precluded the state from incorporating in its legislation applicable to local transportation the paramount duty which the Safety Appliance Acts imposed as to the equipment of cars used on interstate railroads. . . .

> We are of the opinion that the second paragraph of the complaint set forth a cause of action under the Kentucky statute, and, as to this cause of action, the suit is not to be regarded as one arising under the laws of the United States.

Note: Franchise Tax Board *and* Merrell Dow

1. Despite *Moore*'s apparent departure from *Smith*, later decisions followed *Smith*'s lead in extending federal jurisdiction over state-law claims involving federal law. In

Franchise Tax Board v. Construction Laborers Vacation Trust, 463 U.S. 1 (1983), the Court summarized the law governing when a claim arises under federal law for purposes of § 1331:

> Under our interpretations, Congress has given the lower federal courts jurisdiction to hear, originally or by removal from a state court, only those cases in which a well-pleaded complaint establishes either [1] that federal law creates the cause of action or [2] that the plaintiff's right to relief necessarily depends on resolution of a substantial question of federal law.

Franchise Tax Board thus articulated a two-pronged test for "federal question" jurisdiction. Prong One corresponds to the Holmes test. Prong Two encapsulates "*Smith* jurisdiction*.*" Earlier in the opinion, the Court offered a slight variation on the second prong:

> Even though state law creates appellant's causes of action, its case might still "arise under" the laws of the United States if a well-pleaded complaint established that its right to relief under state law requires resolution of a substantial question of federal law in dispute between the parties.

Franchise Tax Board thus seemed to squarely affirm the continued availability of "*Smith* jurisdiction."

2. Only three years later, however, the Court made clear that the *Franchise Tax Board* dictum was not the clear "restatement" that it appeared to be. In *Merrell Dow Pharmaceuticals Inc. v. Thompson*, 478 U.S. 804 (1986), the Court held that a state law claim that asserted a violation of federal law did not arise under federal law under 28 U.S.C. § 1331.

In that case, the plaintiffs sued Merrell Dow, claiming that the ingestion of Bendectin, a drug produced by Merrell Dow, caused birth defects in the plaintiffs' children. One of the counts was a state-law claim for negligence. To establish Merrell Dow's negligence, the claim alleged that Merrell Dow had "misbranded" the Bendectin in violation of the Federal Food, Drug, and Cosmetic Act (FDCA), 21 U.S.C. § 301 *et seq.*, by failing to provide adequate warning that its use was potentially dangerous.

Although the state-law claim alleged a violation of federal law, the Supreme Court held that the claim did not arise under federal law under § 1331. Noting that the FDCA itself did not provide a private cause of action, the Court concluded that the absence of a federal action suggested Congress's intent not to extend federal jurisdiction over any claims alleging violations of the FDCA:

> The significance of the necessary assumption that there is no federal private cause of action thus cannot be overstated. For the ultimate import of such a conclusion, as we have repeatedly emphasized, is that it would flout congressional intent to provide a private federal remedy for the violation of the federal statute. We think it would similarly flout, or at least undermine, congressional intent to conclude that the federal courts might nevertheless exercise federal-question jurisdiction and provide remedies for violations of that federal statute solely because the violation of the federal statute is

said to be a "rebuttable presumption" or a "proximate cause" under state law, rather than a federal action under federal law.

The Court also addressed the tension between *Smith* and *Moore*. It stated that the two decisions were consistent with each other because they involved different federal interests. The Court wrote:

> Several commentators have suggested that our § 1331 decisions can best be understood as an evaluation of the nature of the federal interest at stake. *See, e.g.*, Shapiro, *Jurisdiction and Discretion*, 60 N.Y.U. L. REV. 543, 568 (1985); C. WRIGHT, FEDERAL COURTS 96 (4th ed. 1983); Cohen, *The Broken Compass: The Requirement That a Case Arise 'Directly' Under Federal Law*, 115 U. PA. L. REV. 890, 916 (1967). . . .

> Focusing on the nature of the federal interest, moreover, suggests that the widely perceived "irreconcilable" conflict between the finding of federal jurisdiction in *Smith* and the finding of no jurisdiction in *Moore* . . . is far from clear. For the difference in results can be seen as manifestations of the differences in the nature of the federal issues at stake. In *Smith*, as the Court emphasized, the issue was the constitutionality of an important federal statute. . . .

> In *Moore*, in contrast, the Court emphasized that the violation of the federal standard as an element of state tort recovery did not fundamentally change the state tort nature of the action. ("The action fell within the familiar category of cases involving the duty of a master to his servant. This duty is defined by the common law, except as it may be modified by legislation. The federal statute, in the present case, touched the duty of the master at a single point and, save as provided in the statute, the right of the plaintiff to recover was left to be determined by the law of the State").

Should the nature of the federal interest at stake determine whether a suit arises under federal law? Or does that test leave too much discretion to judges in determining whether a claim arises under federal law?

3. *Merrell Dow* concluded that *Smith* jurisdiction did not extend over the plaintiffs' state-law claims that turned on the violation of the FDCA because the FDCA itself did not provide a private cause of action for its violation. The Court clarified in the next case, however, that a federal cause of action is not a necessary prerequisite to *Smith* jurisdiction.

Grable & Sons Metal Products, Inc. v. Darue Engineering & Manufacturing

Supreme Court of the United States, 2005.

545 U.S. 308.

JUSTICE SOUTER delivered the opinion of the Court.

The question is whether want of a federal cause of action to try claims of title to land obtained at a federal tax sale precludes removal to federal court of a state action with non-diverse parties raising a disputed issue of federal title law. We answer no, and hold that the national interest in providing a federal forum for federal tax litigation is sufficiently substantial to support the exercise of federal question jurisdiction over the disputed issue on removal, which would not distort any division of labor between the state and federal courts, provided or assumed by Congress.

I

In 1994, the Internal Revenue Service seized Michigan real property belonging to petitioner Grable & Sons Metal Products, Inc., to satisfy Grable's federal tax delinquency. Title 26 U.S.C. § 6335 required the IRS to give notice of the seizure, and there is no dispute that Grable received actual notice by certified mail before the IRS sold the property to respondent Darue Engineering & Manufacturing. Although Grable also received notice of the sale itself, it did not exercise its statutory right to redeem the property within 180 days of the sale, § 6337(b)(1), and after that period had passed, the Government gave Darue a quitclaim deed.

Five years later, Grable brought a quiet title action in state court, claiming that Darue's record title was invalid because the IRS had failed to notify Grable of its seizure of the property in the exact manner required by § 6335(a), which provides that written notice must be "given by the Secretary to the owner of the property [or] left at his usual place of abode or business." Grable said that the statute required personal service, not service by certified mail.

Darue removed the case to Federal District Court as presenting a federal question, because the claim of title depended on the interpretation of the notice statute in the federal tax law. The District Court declined to remand the case at Grable's behest after finding that the "claim does pose a significant question of federal law," and ruling that Grable's lack of a federal right of action to enforce its claim against Darue did not bar the exercise of federal jurisdiction. On the merits, the court granted summary judgment to Darue, holding that although § 6335 by its terms required personal service, substantial compliance with the statute was enough.

The Court of Appeals for the Sixth Circuit affirmed. On the jurisdictional question, the panel thought it sufficed that the title claim raised an issue of federal law that had to be resolved, and implicated a substantial federal interest (in construing federal tax law). The court went on to affirm the District Court's judgment on the merits. We granted certiorari on the jurisdictional question alone,[1] to resolve a split within the Courts of Appeals on whether *Merrell Dow Pharmaceuticals Inc. v. Thompson*, 478 U.S. 804 (1986), always requires a federal cause of action as a condition for exercising federal-question jurisdiction.[2] We now affirm.

---

1. Accordingly, we have no occasion to pass upon the proper interpretation of the federal tax provision at issue here.

2. *Compare Seinfeld v. Austen*, 39 F.3d 761, 764 (CA7 1994) (finding that federal-question jurisdiction over a state-law claim requires a parallel federal private right of action), with *Ormet Corp. v. Ohio Power Co.*, 98 F.3d 799, 806 (CA4 1996) (finding that a federal private action is not required).

II

Darue was entitled to remove the quiet title action if Grable could have brought it in federal district court originally, 28 U.S.C. § 1441(a), as a civil action "arising under the Constitution, laws, or treaties of the United States," § 1331. This provision for federal-question jurisdiction is invoked by and large by plaintiffs pleading a cause of action created by federal law (*e.g.*, claims under 42 U.S.C. § 1983). There is, however, another longstanding, if less frequently encountered, variety of federal "arising under" jurisdiction, this Court having recognized for nearly 100 years that in certain cases federal question jurisdiction will lie over state-law claims that implicate significant federal issues. *E.g., Hopkins v. Walker*, 244 U.S. 486, 490–91 (1917). The doctrine captures the commonsense notion that a federal court ought to be able to hear claims recognized under state law that nonetheless turn on substantial questions of federal law, and thus justify resort to the experience, solicitude, and hope of uniformity that a federal forum offers on federal issues, see ALI, Study of the Division of Jurisdiction Between State and Federal Courts 164–66 (1968).

The classic example is *Smith v. Kansas City Title & Trust Co.*, 255 U.S. 180 (1921), a suit by a shareholder claiming that the defendant corporation could not lawfully buy certain bonds of the National Government because their issuance was unconstitutional. Although Missouri law provided the cause of action, the Court recognized federal-question jurisdiction because the principal issue in the case was the federal constitutionality of the bond issue. Smith thus held, in a somewhat generous statement of the scope of the doctrine, that a state-law claim could give rise to federal-question jurisdiction so long as it "appears from the [complaint] that the right to relief depends upon the construction or application of [federal law]."

The *Smith* statement has been subject to some trimming to fit earlier and later cases recognizing the vitality of the basic doctrine, but shying away from the expansive view that mere need to apply federal law in a state-law claim will suffice to open the "arising under" door. As early as 1912, this Court had confined federal-question jurisdiction over state-law claims to those that "really and substantially involve a dispute or controversy respecting the validity, construction or effect of [federal] law." *Shulthis v. McDougal*, 225 U.S. 561, 569 (1912). This limitation was the ancestor of Justice Cardozo's later explanation that a request to exercise federal-question jurisdiction over a state action calls for a "common-sense accommodation of judgment to [the] kaleidoscopic situations" that present a federal issue, in "a selective process which picks the substantial causes out of the web and lays the other ones aside." *Gully v. First Nat. Bank in Meridian*, 299 U.S. 109, 117–18 (1936). It has in fact become a constant refrain in such cases that federal jurisdiction demands not only a contested federal issue, but a substantial one, indicating a serious federal interest in claiming the advantages thought to be inherent in a federal forum. E.g., *Chicago v. International College of Surgeons*, 522 U.S. 156, 164 (1997); *Merrell Dow*, 478 U.S. at 814, and n.12; *Franchise Tax Bd. of Cal. v. Construction Laborers Vacation Trust for Southern Cal.*, 463 U.S. 1, 28 (1983).

But even when the state action discloses a contested and substantial federal question, the exercise of federal jurisdiction is subject to a possible veto. For the federal issue will ultimately qualify for a federal forum only if federal jurisdiction is consistent with congressional judgment about the sound division of labor between state and federal courts governing the application of § 1331. Thus, *Franchise Tax Bd.* explained that the appropriateness of a federal forum to hear an embedded issue could be evaluated only after considering the "welter of issues regarding the interrelation of federal and state authority and the proper management of the federal judicial system." Because arising-under jurisdiction to hear a state-law claim always raises the possibility of upsetting the state-federal line drawn (or at least assumed) by Congress, the presence of a disputed federal issue and the ostensible importance of a federal forum are never necessarily dispositive; there must always be an assessment of any disruptive portent in exercising federal jurisdiction. *See also Merrell Dow.*

These considerations have kept us from stating a "single, precise, all-embracing" test for jurisdiction over federal issues embedded in state-law claims between nondiverse parties. *Christianson v. Colt Industries Operating Corp.*, 486 U.S. 800, 821 (1988) (Stevens, J., concurring). We have not kept them out simply because they appeared in state raiment, as Justice Holmes would have done, see *Smith* (dissenting opinion), but neither have we treated "federal issue" as a password opening federal courts to any state action embracing a point of federal law. Instead, the question is, does a state-law claim necessarily raise a stated federal issue, actually disputed and substantial, which a federal forum may entertain without disturbing any congressionally approved balance of federal and state judicial responsibilities.

III

A

This case warrants federal jurisdiction. Grable's state complaint must specify "the facts establishing the superiority of [its] claim," Mich. Ct. Rule 3.411(B)(2)(c) (West 2005), and Grable has premised its superior title claim on a failure by the IRS to give it adequate notice, as defined by federal law. Whether Grable was given notice within the meaning of the federal statute is thus an essential element of its quiet title claim, and the meaning of the federal statute is actually in dispute; it appears to be the only legal or factual issue contested in the case. The meaning of the federal tax provision is an important issue of federal law that sensibly belongs in a federal court. The Government has a strong interest in the "prompt and certain collection of delinquent taxes," and the ability of the IRS to satisfy its claims from the property of delinquents requires clear terms of notice to allow buyers like Darue to satisfy themselves that the Service has touched the bases necessary for good title. The Government thus has a direct interest in the availability of a federal forum to vindicate its own administrative action, and buyers (as well as tax delinquents) may find it valuable to come before judges used to federal tax matters. Finally, because it will be the rare state title case that raises a contested matter of federal law, federal jurisdiction to resolve genuine disagreement over federal tax title provisions will portend only a microscopic effect on the federal-state division of labor. See n.3, *infra.*

This conclusion puts us in venerable company, quiet title actions having been the subject of some of the earliest exercises of federal-question jurisdiction over state-law claims. In *Hopkins*, the question was federal jurisdiction over a quiet title action based on the plaintiffs' allegation that federal mining law gave them the superior claim. Just as in this case, "the facts showing the plaintiffs' title and the existence and invalidity of the instrument or record sought to be eliminated as a cloud upon the title are essential parts of the plaintiffs' cause of action."[3] As in this case again, "it is plain that a controversy respecting the construction and effect of the [federal] laws is involved and is sufficiently real and substantial." This Court therefore upheld federal jurisdiction in *Hopkins*, as well as in the similar quiet title matters of *Northern Pacific R. Co. v. Soderberg*, 188 U.S. 526, 528 (1903), and *Wilson Cypress Co. v. Del Pozo y Marcos*, 236 U.S. 635, 643–44 (1915). Consistent with those cases, the recognition of federal jurisdiction is in order here.

B

Merrell Dow Pharmaceuticals Inc. v. Thompson, 478 U.S. 804 (1986), on which Grable rests its position, is not to the contrary. *Merrell Dow* considered a state tort claim resting in part on the allegation that the defendant drug company had violated a federal misbranding prohibition, and was thus presumptively negligent under Ohio law. The Court assumed that federal law would have to be applied to resolve the claim, but after closely examining the strength of the federal interest at stake and the implications of opening the federal forum, held federal jurisdiction unavailable. Congress had not provided a private federal cause of action for violation of the federal branding requirement, and the Court found "it would . . . flout, or at least undermine, congressional intent to conclude that federal courts might nevertheless exercise federal-question jurisdiction and provide remedies for violations of that federal statute solely because the violation . . . is said to be a . . . 'proximate cause' under state law."

Because federal law provides for no quiet title action that could be brought against Darue,[4] Grable argues that there can be no federal jurisdiction here, stressing some broad language in *Merrell Dow* (including the passage just quoted) that on its face supports Grable's position, see Note, *Mr. Smith Goes to Federal Court: Federal Question Jurisdiction over State Law Claims Post*-Merrell Dow, 115 Harv. L. Rev. 2272, 2280–82 (2002) (discussing split in Circuit Courts over private right of action requirement after *Merrell Dow*). But an opinion is to be read as a whole, and *Merrell Dow* cannot be read whole as overturning decades of precedent, as it would have done

---

3. The quiet title cases also show the limiting effect of the requirement that the federal issue in a state-law claim must actually be in dispute to justify federal-question jurisdiction. In *Shulthis v. McDougal*, 225 U.S. 561 (1912), this Court found that there was no federal question jurisdiction to hear a plaintiff's quiet title claim in part because the federal statutes on which title depended were not subject to "any controversy respecting their validity, construction, or effect." As the Court put it, the requirement of an actual dispute about federal law was "especially" important in "suits involving rights to land acquired under a law of the United States," because otherwise "every suit to establish title to land in the central and western states would so arise [under federal law], as all titles in those States are traceable back to those laws."

4. Federal law does provide a quiet title cause of action against the Federal Government. 28 U.S.C. § 2410. That right of action is not relevant here, however, because the federal government no longer has any interest in the property, having transferred its interest to Darue through the quitclaim deed.

by effectively adopting the Holmes dissent in *Smith* and converting a federal cause of action from a sufficient condition for federal-question jurisdiction[5] into a necessary one.

In the first place, *Merrell Dow* disclaimed the adoption of any bright-line rule, as when the Court reiterated that "in exploring the outer reaches of § 1331, determinations about federal jurisdiction require sensitive judgments about congressional intent, judicial power, and the federal system." The opinion included a lengthy footnote explaining that questions of jurisdiction over state-law claims require "careful judgments" about the "nature of the federal interest at stake" (emphasis deleted). And as a final indication that it did not mean to make a federal right of action mandatory, it expressly approved the exercise of jurisdiction sustained in *Smith*, despite the want of any federal cause of action available to Smith's shareholder plaintiff. *Merrell Dow* then, did not toss out, but specifically retained the contextual enquiry that had been *Smith*'s hallmark for over 60 years. At the end of *Merrell Dow*, Justice Holmes was still dissenting.

Accordingly, *Merrell Dow* should be read in its entirety as treating the absence of a federal private right of action as evidence relevant to, but not dispositive of, the "sensitive judgments about congressional intent" that § 1331 requires. The absence of any federal cause of action affected *Merrell Dow*'s result two ways. The Court saw the fact as worth some consideration in the assessment of substantiality. But its primary importance emerged when the Court treated the combination of no federal cause of action and no preemption of state remedies for misbranding as an important clue to Congress's conception of the scope of jurisdiction to be exercised under § 1331. The Court saw the missing cause of action not as a missing federal door key, always required, but as a missing welcome mat, required in the circumstances, when exercising federal jurisdiction over a state misbranding action would have attracted a horde of original filings and removal cases raising other state claims with embedded federal issues. For if the federal labeling standard without a federal cause of action could get a state claim into federal court, so could any other federal standard without a federal cause of action. And that would have meant a tremendous number of cases.

One only needed to consider the treatment of federal violations generally in garden variety state tort law. "The violation of federal statutes and regulations is commonly given negligence per se effect in state tort proceedings."[6] RESTATEMENT (THIRD) OF TORTS (proposed final draft) § 14, cmt. a. A general rule of exercising federal jurisdiction over state claims resting on federal mislabeling and other statutory violations would thus have heralded a potentially enormous shift of traditionally state cases into federal courts. Expressing concern over the "increased volume of federal litigation,"

---

5. For an extremely rare exception to the sufficiency of a federal right of action, see *Shoshone Mining Co. v. Rutter*, 177 U.S. 505, 507 (1900).

6. Other jurisdictions treat a violation of a federal statute as evidence of negligence or, like Ohio itself in *Merrell Dow Pharmaceuticals Inc. v. Thompson*, 478 U.S. 804 (1986), as creating a rebuttable presumption of negligence. RESTATEMENT (THIRD) OF TORTS (proposed final draft) § 14, cmt. c. Either approach could still implicate issues of federal law.

and noting the importance of adhering to "legislative intent," *Merrell Dow* thought it improbable that the Congress, having made no provision for a federal cause of action, would have meant to welcome any state-law tort case implicating federal law "solely because the violation of the federal statute is said to [create] a rebuttable presumption [of negligence] . . . under state law." In this situation, no welcome mat meant keep out. *Merrell Dow*'s analysis thus fits within the framework of examining the importance of having a federal forum for the issue, and the consistency of such a forum with Congress's intended division of labor between state and federal courts.

As already indicated, however, a comparable analysis yields a different jurisdictional conclusion in this case. Although Congress also indicated ambivalence in this case by providing no private right of action to Grable, it is the rare state quiet title action that involves contested issues of federal law, see n.3, *supra*. Consequently, jurisdiction over actions like Grable's would not materially affect, or threaten to affect, the normal currents of litigation. Given the absence of threatening structural consequences and the clear interest the Government, its buyers, and its delinquents have in the availability of a federal forum, there is no good reason to shirk from federal jurisdiction over the dispositive and contested federal issue at the heart of the state-law title claim.[7]

IV

The judgment of the Court of Appeals, upholding federal jurisdiction over Grable's quiet title action, is affirmed.

JUSTICE THOMAS, concurring.

The Court faithfully applies our precedents interpreting 28 U.S.C. § 1331 to authorize federal-court jurisdiction over some cases in which state law creates the cause of action but requires determination of an issue of federal law. In this case, no one has asked us to overrule those precedents and adopt the rule Justice Holmes set forth in *American Well Works Co. v. Layne & Bowler Co.*, 241 U.S. 257 (1916), limiting § 1331 jurisdiction to cases in which federal law creates the cause of action pleaded on the face of the plaintiff's complaint. In an appropriate case, and perhaps with the benefit of better evidence as to the original meaning of § 1331's text, I would be willing to consider that course.

Jurisdictional rules should be clear. Whatever the virtues of the *Smith* standard, it is anything but clear. . . .

Whatever the vices of the *American Well Works* rule, it is clear. Moreover, it accounts for the "'vast majority'" of cases that come within § 1331 under our current case law—further indication that trying to sort out which cases fall within the smaller *Smith*

---

7. At oral argument Grable's counsel espoused the position that after *Merrell Dow*, federal-question jurisdiction over state-law claims absent a federal right of action, could be recognized only where a constitutional issue was at stake. There is, however, no reason in text or otherwise to draw such a rough line. As *Merrell Dow* itself suggested, constitutional questions may be the more likely ones to reach the level of substantiality that can justify federal jurisdiction. But a flat ban on statutory questions would mechanically exclude significant questions of federal law like the one this case presents.

category may not be worth the effort it entails. Accordingly, I would be willing in appropriate circumstances to reconsider our interpretation of § 1331.

Note: Smith *and* Grable

1. In *Grable*, the Court attempts to synthesize its precedents on the availability of § 1331 jurisdiction for state-created causes of action that contain a federal ingredient. How successful is this effort?

2. Note first that the Court uses some new terminology: it refers to state-law claims with "embedded" federal issues. Is this new terminology helpful? Is there any substantive difference between an "embedded" federal question and an "incorporated" federal question?

3. *Grable* makes clear that *Smith* is still good law, and that "Justice Holmes [is] still dissenting." But what is the ambit of "*Smith* jurisdiction"? Justice Thomas, in his concurring opinion, notes that the *Smith* standard is "anything but clear." He quotes three formulations from the Court's opinion:

> (a) The standard "calls for a 'common-sense accommodation of judgment to [the] kaleidoscopic situations' that present a federal issue, in 'a selective process which picks the substantial causes out of the web and lays the other ones aside'" (quoting *Gully*).

> (b) "[T]he question is, does a state-law claim necessarily raise a stated federal issue, actually disputed and substantial, which a federal forum may entertain without disturbing any congressionally approved balance of federal and state judicial responsibilities."

> (c) "[D]eterminations about federal jurisdiction require sensitive judgments about congressional intent, judicial power, and the federal system"; "the absence of a federal private right of action [is] evidence relevant to, but not dispositive of, the 'sensitive judgments about congressional intent' that § 1331 requires" (quoting *Merrell Dow*).

Does the Court's opinion give greater content to these formulations?

4. One possible distinction between *Merrell Dow* on one side and *Smith* on the other was that the latter involved constitutional rather than statutory issues. The *Grable* opinion (in footnote 7) rejects that line of demarcation. Is there anything to be said for it?

5. The Court says that even if there is a "disputed federal issue," and even if the availability of the federal forum appears to be important, those features "are never necessarily dispositive." Rather, "there must always be an assessment of any *disruptive portent* in exercising federal jurisdiction." (Emphasis added.)

Presumably the Court is describing the task of the judiciary. But at what level of specificity is the assessment to be performed? Should the court look at the "disruptive portent" of exercising jurisdiction in the particular case? In all cases invoking the particular federal statute? Or should the focus be on the nature or elements of the state cause of action? Note that the Michigan court rule cited in the opinion (at the start of Part III(A)) is a rule governing "Civil Action[s] to Determine Interests in Land."

6. The *Grable* opinion explains at length why *Merrell Dow* is not controlling. What is the class of cases that *Merrell Dow*, as interpreted in *Grable*, excludes from § 1331 jurisdiction? Is *Merrell Dow* limited to tort claims? Does it exclude all cases in which violation of a federal statute is an element of a state tort claim?

7. Despite finding jurisdiction in *Grable*, the Court has described *Grable* as exemplifying a "special and small category" of cases that fall within § 1331 even though the plaintiff is suing on a state cause of action. The next principal case demonstrates how small the category is.

Gunn v. Minton

Supreme Court of the United States, 2013.

133 S. Ct. 1059.

CHIEF JUSTICE ROBERTS delivered the opinion of the Court.

Federal courts have exclusive jurisdiction over cases "arising under any Act of Congress relating to patents." 28 U.S.C. § 1338(a). The question presented is whether a state law claim alleging legal malpractice in the handling of a patent case must be brought in federal court.

I

In the early 1990s, respondent Vernon Minton developed a computer program and telecommunications network designed to facilitate securities trading. In March 1995, he leased the system—known as the Texas Computer Exchange Network, or TEXCEN—to R.M. Stark & Co., a securities brokerage. A little over a year later, he applied for a patent for an interactive securities trading system that was based substantially on TEXCEN. The U.S. Patent and Trademark Office issued the patent in January 2000.

Patent in hand, Minton filed a patent infringement suit in Federal District Court against the National Association of Securities Dealers, Inc. (NASD) and the NASDAQ Stock Market, Inc. He was represented by Jerry Gunn and the other petitioners. NASD and NASDAQ moved for summary judgment on the ground that Minton's patent was invalid under the "on sale" bar, 35 U.S.C. § 102(b). That provision specifies that an inventor is not entitled to a patent if "the invention was . . . on sale in [the United States], more than one year prior to the date of the application," and Minton had leased TEXCEN to Stark more than one year prior to filing his patent application. Rejecting Minton's argument that there were differences between TEXCEN and the patented system that precluded application of the on-sale bar, the District Court granted the summary judgment motion and declared Minton's patent invalid.

Minton then filed a motion for reconsideration in the District Court, arguing for the first time that the lease agreement with Stark was part of ongoing testing of

TEXCEN and therefore fell within the "experimental use" exception to the on-sale bar. The District Court denied the motion.

Minton appealed to the U.S. Court of Appeals for the Federal Circuit. That court affirmed, concluding that the District Court had appropriately held Minton's experimental-use argument waived.

Minton, convinced that his attorneys' failure to raise the experimental-use argument earlier had cost him the lawsuit and led to invalidation of his patent, brought this malpractice action in Texas state court. His former lawyers defended on the ground that the lease to Stark was not, in fact, for an experimental use, and that therefore Minton's patent infringement claims would have failed even if the experimental-use argument had been timely raised. The trial court agreed, holding that Minton had put forward "less than a scintilla of proof" that the lease had been for an experimental purpose. It accordingly granted summary judgment to Gunn and the other lawyer defendants.

On appeal, Minton raised a new argument: Because his legal malpractice claim was based on an alleged error in a patent case, it "aris[es] under" federal patent law for purposes of 28 U.S.C. § 1338(a). And because, under § 1338(a), "[n]o State court shall have jurisdiction over any claim for relief arising under any Act of Congress relating to patents," the Texas court—where Minton had originally brought his malpractice claim—lacked subject matter jurisdiction to decide the case. Accordingly, Minton argued, the trial court's order should be vacated and the case dismissed, leaving Minton free to start over in the Federal District Court.

A divided panel of the Court of Appeals of Texas rejected Minton's argument. Applying the test we articulated in *Grable & Sons Metal Products, Inc. v. Darue Engineering & Mfg.*, 545 U.S. 308 (2005), it held that the federal interests implicated by Minton's state law claim were not sufficiently substantial to trigger § 1338 "arising under" jurisdiction. It also held that finding exclusive federal jurisdiction over state legal malpractice actions would, contrary to *Grable*'s commands, disturb the balance of federal and state judicial responsibilities. Proceeding to the merits of Minton's malpractice claim, the Court of Appeals affirmed the trial court's determination that Minton had failed to establish experimental use and that arguments on that ground therefore would not have saved his infringement suit.

The Supreme Court of Texas reversed, relying heavily on a pair of cases from the U.S. Court of Appeals for the Federal Circuit, *Air Measurement Technologies, Inc. v. Akin Gump Strauss Hauer & Feld, L.L.P.*, 504 F.3d 1262 (2007), and *Immunocept, LLC v. Fulbright & Jaworski, LLP*, 504 F.3d 1281 (2007)). The Court concluded that Minton's claim involved "a substantial federal issue" within the meaning of *Grable* "because the success of Minton's malpractice claim is reliant upon the viability of the experimental use exception as a defense to the on-sale bar." Adjudication of Minton's claim in federal court was consistent with the appropriate balance between federal and state judicial responsibilities, it held, because "the federal government and patent litigants have an interest in the uniform application of patent law by courts well-versed in that subject matter."

Justice Guzman, joined by Justices Medina and Willett, dissented. The dissenting justices would have held that the federal issue was neither substantial nor disputed, and that maintaining the proper balance of responsibility between state and federal courts precluded relegating state legal malpractice claims to federal court.

We granted certiorari.

II

"Federal courts are courts of limited jurisdiction," possessing "only that power authorized by Constitution and statute." *Kokkonen v. Guardian Life Ins. Co. of America*, 511 U.S. 375 (1994). There is no dispute that the Constitution permits Congress to extend federal court jurisdiction to a case such as this one, see *Osborn v. Bank of United States*, 9 Wheat. 738 (1824) [Chapter 2]; the question is whether Congress has done so.

As relevant here, Congress has authorized the federal district courts to exercise original jurisdiction in "all civil actions arising under the Constitution, laws, or treaties of the United States," 28 U.S.C. § 1331, and, more particularly, over "any civil action arising under any Act of Congress relating to patents," § 1338(a). Adhering to the demands of "[l]inguistic consistency," we have interpreted the phrase "arising under" in both sections identically, applying our § 1331 and § 1338(a) precedents interchangeably. See *Christianson v. Colt Industries Operating Corp.*, 486 U.S. 800 (1988). For cases falling within the patent-specific arising under jurisdiction of § 1338(a), however, Congress has not only provided for federal jurisdiction but also eliminated state jurisdiction, decreeing that "[n]o State court shall have jurisdiction over any claim for relief arising under any Act of Congress relating to patents." § 1338(a). To determine whether jurisdiction was proper in the Texas courts, therefore, we must determine whether it would have been proper in a federal district court—whether, that is, the case "aris[es] under any Act of Congress relating to patents."

For statutory purposes, a case can "aris[e] under" federal law in two ways. Most directly, a case arises under federal law when federal law creates the cause of action asserted. See *American Well Works Co. v. Layne & Bowler Co.*, 241 U.S. 257 (1916) ("A suit arises under the law that creates the cause of action"). As a rule of inclusion, this "creation" test admits of only extremely rare exceptions, *see, e.g., Shoshone Mining Co. v. Rutter*, 177 U.S. 505 (1900), and accounts for the vast bulk of suits that arise under federal law. Minton's original patent infringement suit against NASD and NASDAQ, for example, arose under federal law in this manner because it was authorized by 35 U.S.C. §§ 271, 281.

But even where a claim finds its origins in state rather than federal law—as Minton's legal malpractice claim indisputably does—we have identified a "special and small category" of cases in which arising under jurisdiction still lies. *Empire Health-Choice Assurance, Inc. v. McVeigh*, 547 U.S. 677 (2006). In outlining the contours of this slim category, we do not paint on a blank canvas. Unfortunately, the canvas looks like one that Jackson Pollock got to first.

In an effort to bring some order to this unruly doctrine several Terms ago, we condensed our prior cases into the following inquiry: Does the "state-law claim necessarily raise a stated federal issue, actually disputed and substantial, which a federal forum may entertain without disturbing any congressionally approved balance of federal and state judicial responsibilities"? *Grable.* That is, federal jurisdiction over a state law claim will lie if a federal issue is: (1) necessarily raised, (2) actually disputed, (3) substantial, and (4) capable of resolution in federal court without disrupting the federal-state balance approved by Congress. Where all four of these requirements are met, we held, jurisdiction is proper because there is a "serious federal interest in claiming the advantages thought to be inherent in a federal forum," which can be vindicated without disrupting Congress's intended division of labor between state and federal courts.

III

Applying *Grable*'s inquiry here, it is clear that Minton's legal malpractice claim does not arise under federal patent law. Indeed, for the reasons we discuss, we are comfortable concluding that state legal malpractice claims based on underlying patent matters will rarely, if ever, arise under federal patent law for purposes of § 1338(a). Although such cases may necessarily raise disputed questions of patent law, those cases are by their nature unlikely to have the sort of significance for the federal system necessary to establish jurisdiction.

A

To begin, we acknowledge that resolution of a federal patent question is "necessary" to Minton's case. Under Texas law, a plaintiff alleging legal malpractice must establish four elements: (1) that the defendant attorney owed the plaintiff a duty; (2) that the attorney breached that duty; (3) that the breach was the proximate cause of the plaintiff's injury; and (4) that damages occurred. See *Alexander v. Turtur & Associates, Inc.*, 146 S.W.3d 113 (Tex. 2004). In cases like this one, in which the attorney's alleged error came in failing to make a particular argument, the causation element requires a "case within a case" analysis of whether, had the argument been made, the outcome of the earlier litigation would have been different. To prevail on his legal malpractice claim, therefore, Minton must show that he would have prevailed in his federal patent infringement case if only petitioners had timely made an experimental-use argument on his behalf. That will necessarily require application of patent law to the facts of Minton's case.

B

The federal issue is also "actually disputed" here — indeed, on the merits, it is the central point of dispute. Minton argues that the experimental-use exception properly applied to his lease to Stark, saving his patent from the on-sale bar; petitioners argue that it did not. This is just the sort of "'dispute . . . respecting the . . . effect of [federal] law'" that *Grable* envisioned.

C

Minton's argument founders on *Grable*'s next requirement, however, for the federal issue in this case is not substantial in the relevant sense. In reaching the opposite conclusion, the Supreme Court of Texas focused on the importance of the issue to the plaintiff's case and to the parties before it. [The court said that] "because the success of Minton's malpractice claim is reliant upon the viability of the experimental use exception as a defense to the on-sale bar, we hold that it is a substantial federal issue." As our past cases show, however, it is not enough that the federal issue be significant to the particular parties in the immediate suit; that will *always* be true when the state claim "necessarily raise[s]" a disputed federal issue, as *Grable* separately requires. The substantiality inquiry under *Grable* looks instead to the importance of the issue to the federal system as a whole.

In *Grable* itself, for example, the Internal Revenue Service had seized property from the plaintiff and sold it to satisfy the plaintiff's federal tax delinquency. Five years later, the plaintiff filed a state law quiet title action against the third party that had purchased the property, alleging that the IRS had failed to comply with certain federally imposed notice requirements, so that the seizure and sale were invalid. In holding that the case arose under federal law, we primarily focused not on the interests of the litigants themselves, but rather on the broader significance of the notice question for the Federal Government. We emphasized the Government's "strong interest" in being able to recover delinquent taxes through seizure and sale of property, which in turn "require[d] clear terms of notice to allow buyers . . . to satisfy themselves that the Service has touched the bases necessary for good title." The Government's "direct interest in the availability of a federal forum to vindicate its own administrative action" made the question "an important issue of federal law that sensibly belong[ed] in a federal court."

A second illustration of the sort of substantiality we require comes from *Smith v. Kansas City Title & Trust Co.*, 255 U.S. 180 (1921), which *Grable* described as "[t]he classic example" of a state claim arising under federal law. In *Smith*, the plaintiff argued that the defendant bank could not purchase certain bonds issued by the Federal Government because the Government had acted unconstitutionally in issuing them. We held that the case arose under federal law, because the "decision depends upon the determination" of "the constitutional validity of an act of Congress which is directly drawn in question." Again, the relevant point was not the importance of the question to the parties alone but rather the importance more generally of a determination that the Government "securities were issued under an unconstitutional law, and hence of no validity." *Ibid.*

Here, the federal issue carries no such significance. Because of the backward-looking nature of a legal malpractice claim, the question is posed in a merely hypothetical sense: *If* Minton's lawyers had raised a timely experimental-use argument, would the result in the patent infringement proceeding have been different? No matter how the state courts resolve that hypothetical "case within a case," it will not change the real-world result of the prior federal patent litigation. Minton's patent will remain invalid.

Nor will allowing state courts to resolve these cases undermine "the development of a uniform body of [patent] law." *Bonito Boats, Inc. v. Thunder Craft Boats, Inc.*, 489

U.S. 141 (1989). Congress ensured such uniformity by vesting exclusive jurisdiction over actual patent cases in the federal district courts and exclusive appellate jurisdiction in the Federal Circuit. See 28 U.S.C. §§ 1338(a), 1295(a)(1). In resolving the non-hypothetical patent questions those cases present, the federal courts are of course not bound by state court case-within-a-case patent rulings. See *Tafflin v. Levitt*, 493 U.S. 455 (1990) [Chapter 6]. In any event, the state court case-within-a-case inquiry asks what would have happened in the prior federal proceeding if a particular argument had been made. In answering that question, state courts can be expected to hew closely to the pertinent federal precedents. It is those precedents, after all, that would have applied had the argument been made. Cf. *ibid.* ("State courts adjudicating civil RICO claims will . . . be guided by federal court interpretations of the relevant federal criminal statutes, just as federal courts sitting in diversity are guided by state court interpretations of state law").

As for more novel questions of patent law that may arise for the first time in a state court "case within a case," they will at some point be decided by a federal court in the context of an actual patent case, with review in the Federal Circuit. If the question arises frequently, it will soon be resolved within the federal system, laying to rest any contrary state court precedent; if it does not arise frequently, it is unlikely to implicate substantial federal interests. The present case is "poles apart from *Grable*," in which a state court's resolution of the federal question "would be controlling in numerous other cases."

Minton also suggests that state courts' answers to hypothetical patent questions can sometimes have real-world effect on other patents through issue preclusion. Minton, for example, has filed what is known as a "continuation patent" application related to his original patent. He argues that, in evaluating this separate application, the patent examiner could be bound by the Texas trial court's interpretation of the scope of Minton's original patent. It is unclear whether this is true. . . . In fact, Minton has not identified any case finding such preclusive effect based on a state court decision. But even assuming that a state court's case-within-a-case adjudication may be preclusive under some circumstances, the result would be limited to the parties and patents that had been before the state court. Such "fact-bound and situation-specific" effects are not sufficient to establish federal arising under jurisdiction.

Nor can we accept the suggestion that the federal courts' greater familiarity with patent law means that legal malpractice cases like this one belong in federal court. It is true that a similar interest was among those we considered in *Grable*. But the possibility that a state court will incorrectly resolve a state claim is not, by itself, enough to trigger the federal courts' exclusive patent jurisdiction, even if the potential error finds its root in a misunderstanding of patent law.

There is no doubt that resolution of a patent issue in the context of a state legal malpractice action can be vitally important to the particular parties in that case. But something more, demonstrating that the question is significant to the federal system as a whole, is needed. That is missing here.

D

It follows from the foregoing that *Grable*'s fourth requirement is also not met. That requirement is concerned with the appropriate "balance of federal and state judicial responsibilities." We have already explained the absence of a substantial federal issue within the meaning of *Grable*. The States, on the other hand, have "a special responsibility for maintaining standards among members of the licensed professions." Their "interest . . . in regulating lawyers is especially great since lawyers are essential to the primary governmental function of administering justice, and have historically been officers of the courts." We have no reason to suppose that Congress—in establishing exclusive federal jurisdiction over patent cases—meant to bar from state courts state legal malpractice claims simply because they require resolution of a hypothetical patent issue.

* * *

As we recognized a century ago, "[t]he Federal courts have exclusive jurisdiction of all cases arising under the patent laws, but not of all questions in which a patent may be the subject-matter of the controversy." In this case, although the state courts must answer a question of patent law to resolve Minton's legal malpractice claim, their answer will have no broader effects. It will not stand as binding precedent for any future patent claim; it will not even affect the validity of Minton's patent. Accordingly, there is no "serious federal interest in claiming the advantages thought to be inherent in a federal forum," *Grable*. Section 1338(a) does not deprive the state courts of subject matter jurisdiction.

The judgment of the Supreme Court of Texas is reversed, and the case is remanded for further proceedings not inconsistent with this opinion.

It is so ordered.

Note: Clarifying Grable — and Narrowing It?

1. The Court in *Gunn* interpreted 28 U.S.C. § 1338, not § 1331. But the Court treats § 1331 and § 1338 precedents interchangeably. Note, too, that although the Court makes no mention of it, § 1338 was amended in 2011, and the second sentence—quoted in Part II of the Court's opinion—was changed. See Casebook Chapter 6, section A.

2. Although the *Grable* opinion did not explicitly say that it was establishing a four-part test, some courts and commentators read it that way. *Gunn* confirms that reading. Chief Justice Roberts, after quoting *Grable*, restates the "inquiry" as a set of four numbered requirements. But are the four requirements really that distinct? Consider the questions below.

3. The Court acknowledges that the federal patent issue is "necessary" to plaintiff Minton's legal-malpractice case and also that it is "actually disputed." In explaining its conclusion on the latter point, the Court says that Minton argues that the experimental-use exception properly applied to the lease; Gunn (the malpractice defendant) argues that it did not. But does the well-pleaded complaint rule allow the court to consider the defendant's argument? At the jurisdictional stage, how does a court know that the defendant is disputing the "experimental use" issue rather than, for example, conceding the point (at least for the sake of argument) and arguing that the malpractice claim fails because of some state-law rule?

4. Most of the Court's analysis is devoted to explaining why the "substantiality" prong is not met. "The substantiality inquiry under *Grable*," the Court explains, looks "to the importance of the issue *to the federal system as a whole*." (Emphasis added.) When does an issue meet that requirement?

5. In rejecting the argument that the "case within a case" might involve novel questions of federal law that would satisfy the "substantiality" requirement, the Court says, "If the question arises frequently, it will soon be resolved within the federal system, laying to rest any contrary state court precedent; if it does not arise frequently, it is unlikely to implicate substantial federal interests." Why doesn't that argument also apply in *Grable* and *Smith*?

6. After explaining at length why Minton's malpractice claim does not satisfy the "substantiality" prong, the Court continues: "It follows from the foregoing that *Grable*'s fourth requirement is also not met." What kind of case might satisfy the third requirement but not the fourth — or vice versa?

7. On June 11, 2015, the House Judiciary Committee voted to favorably report H.R. 9, the Innovation Act. Section 9(e) of the Act is titled "Clarification of Jurisdiction," and it provides as follows:

> (1) IN GENERAL.—An action or claim arises under an Act of Congress relating to patents if such action or claim—
>
> > (A) necessarily requires resolution of a disputed question as to the validity of a patent or the scope of a patent claim; or
> >
> > (B) is an action or claim for legal malpractice that arises from an attorney's conduct in relation to an action or claim arising under an Act of Congress relating to patents (including as described in paragraph (1)). [Sic; the reference probably should be to paragraph (1)(A).]

Would this provision completely override *Gunn*? Does the legislation cast doubt on the *Gunn* Court's conclusion that allowing Minton's legal malpractice claim to be heard in federal court under § 1338(a) would "disrupt[] the federal-state balance approved by Congress"?

Problem: A Wrongful Discharge Claim

William Walters was employed by Acme Manufacturing Co. for 10 years until he was terminated in May of last year. Walters has filed suit in Oceana state court asserting a claim for wrongful discharge. The nub of the claim is that Walters was terminated as a result of his refusal to acquiesce in the "cover up" of Acme's theft of trade secrets.

The complaint invokes a recent decision by the Oceana supreme court recognizing a "wrongful discharge exception" to the employment at will doctrine. As explained by the state court, to come within the exception, the discharge "(1) must be contrary to a fundamental and well-defined public policy as evidenced by existing law," and (2) "that policy must be evidenced by a constitutional or statutory provision."

Walters' complaint alleges that that his discharge was "contrary to public policy of this state and of the United States, including but not limited to the policies evidenced in the following statutes." The complaint then lists four federal criminal statutes: 18 U.S.C. § 1509 (Obstruction of court orders), 18 U.S.C. § 2314 (Transportation of stolen goods), 18 U.S.C. § 2315 (Sale or receipt of stolen goods), and 18 U.S.C. § 1621 (Perjury). The complaint elaborates on these allegations; for example, it asserts that Walters was terminated for his refusal to participate in Acme's theft of trade secrets ("stolen goods" under 18 U.S.C. §§ 2314, 2315), and its employees' perjury about concealing or destroying documents.

Acme removed the case to federal district court, asserting that Walters' claim is one "arising under" federal law. Walters has filed a motion to remand, asserting that the district court lacks subject-matter jurisdiction. Should the motion be granted?

Problem: Another *Smith* Case

In *Smith v. Industrial Valley Title Insurance Co.*, 957 F.2d 90 (3d Cir. 1992), the plaintiffs were home sellers who brought suit in Pennsylvania state court against several title insurance companies who provided services in connection with the sale of plaintiffs' homes. The defendant title insurance companies were "real estate reporting person[s]" as defined in section 6045 of the Internal Revenue Code.

Section 6045 imposes transactional reporting requirements on "real estate reporting person[s]." Paragraph (e)(3) of § 6045 makes it unlawful for any real estate reporting person "to *separately charge* any customer" for complying with the requirements. (Emphasis added.) The nub of plaintiffs' claims was that the defendants "separately charg[ed]" the homeowners for the information reporting required by section 6045, in violation of paragraph (e)(3).

Plaintiffs did not assert federal causes of action, and indeed all parties assumed that Congress had not provided a federal private cause of action for violation of 26 U.S.C. § 6045. Rather, the plaintiffs sought recovery of damages on state common law theories (including conversion and unjust enrichment) and for unfair or deceptive acts or practices within the meaning of Pennsylvania's Unfair Trade Practices and Consumer Protection Law. Each state law theory of recovery required proof of an unlawful or wrongful act by defendants; in each instance this element was supplied by plaintiffs' allegations that defendants violated § 6045. Further, the parties disputed the meaning of § 6045(e)(3)'s prohibition against "separate charge[s]"; thus, each of the plaintiffs' claims required judicial construction of a federal provision as well as a determination of whether the title insurance companies' alleged conduct fell within the statutory prohibition.

Defendants removed the suit to federal court, asserting that each of the claims arose under federal law within the meaning of section 1331. The district court denied plaintiffs' motion to remand and dismissed the claims on the merits.

The Third Circuit held that the district court did not have subject matter jurisdiction and should have remanded the case to the state court. The court held that under *Merrell-Dow*, the absence of a private federal cause of action was fatal to "arising under" jurisdiction. In the court's view, when Congress has determined that there should be no private federal remedy for violation of a federal statute, "a federal court is prohibited from finding federal question jurisdiction on the ground that such federal violation is a disputed and necessary element of a state cause of action."

If the same case were to arise today, would the district court have jurisdiction under *Grable* and *Gunn*?

Problem: Fiduciary Duty and Antitrust Law

In describing the split of authority that led to the grant of certiorari in *Grable*, the Supreme Court cites *Seinfeld v. Austin*, 39 F.3d 761 (7th Cir. 1994). In that case, shareholders of Abbott Laboratories, Inc., filed a shareholders derivative action in state court against Abbott's board of directors for breach of fiduciary duty. Specifically, the complaint alleged that (1) the defendants failed to properly monitor Abbott's most senior executives and prevent them from engaging in violations of federal antitrust laws; and (2) this failure caused the corporation to lose $140 million, the amount that the corporation paid to settle several alleged antitrust claims. The defendants removed the case to federal court, arguing that the plaintiffs' state law claims were inextricably dependent on a determination of substantial issues of federal antitrust law. The district court agreed, saying:

> Here, plaintiffs' claims for relief rest in large part on the premise that Abbott engaged in conduct violative of federal antitrust law. For example, in order to prove that the defendant directors failed to "cease violations of Federal Anti-Trust laws," . . . plaintiffs will first have to prove that such violations occurred. Likewise, in order to prove that the defendant directors participated in a "price fixing scheme," . . . plaintiffs will have to prove that the conduct alleged in the complaint constituted price fixing violative of federal law. It follows, therefore, that the success of plaintiffs' breach of fiduciary duty claims will depend on the application of federal antitrust law to the conduct alleged in the complaints. As such, we find the Supreme Court's rationale in *Franchise Tax* directly applicable . . . .

The Seventh Circuit reversed, holding that under *Merrell Dow*, "if federal law does not provide a private right of action, then a state law action based on its violation perforce does not raise a 'substantial' federal question." The Supreme Court in *Grable* rejects this proposition. But does *Grable* also require rejection of the Seventh Circuit's holding that the plaintiffs' claims did not "arise under" federal law within the meaning of § 1331?

Note: Christianson *and Claims versus Theories*

In *Grable*, Grable's quiet title action against Darue was based on the IRS's alleged failure to provide notice required by federal law when it seized Grable's land.

Suppose Grable had raised another argument in support of its quiet title action—that Darue had sold the land back to Grable. Grable would have presented two theories for its quiet title action—one that depended on federal law and one that did not. Would the existence of that alternative state-law theory affect whether Grable's claim arose under federal law?

In *Christianson v. Colt Industries Operating Corp.*, 486 U.S. 800 (1988), the Court answered that question in the affirmative, drawing a sharp distinction between a "claim" and the particular "theories" asserted in support of the claim. There, Christianson sued Colt in the federal District Court for the Central District of Illinois, claiming that Colt had violated various federal antitrust laws. At issue before the Supreme Court was whether the Seventh Circuit or the Federal Circuit had appellate jurisdiction over an appeal from the district court's decision.

Ordinarily, cases in the federal district courts may be appealed to the court of appeals for the geographically defined circuit that includes the particular district. See 28 U.S.C. § 1294. Under 28 U.S.C. § 1295(a)(1), however, the Federal Circuit has exclusive appellate jurisdiction of cases "arising under" a federal patent statute, and at that time the appellate jurisdiction was keyed to the "arising under" jurisdiction of 28 U.S.C. § 1338(a). In a unanimous opinion, the Court held that the plaintiff's antitrust claims did not arise under the patent laws. The analysis drew heavily upon the Court's decisions construing the "arising under" language in § 1331. The Court stated:

> A district court's federal-question jurisdiction, we recently explained, extends over "only those cases in which a well-pleaded complaint establishes either that federal law creates the cause of action or that the plaintiff's right to relief necessarily depends on resolution of a substantial question of federal law," *Franchise Tax Board*, in that "federal law is a necessary element of one of the well-pleaded . . . claims." Linguistic consistency, to which we have historically adhered, demands that § 1338(a) jurisdiction likewise extend only to those cases in which a well-pleaded complaint establishes either that federal patent law creates the cause of action or that the plaintiff's right to relief necessarily depends on resolution of a substantial question of federal patent law, in that patent law is a necessary element of one of the well-pleaded claims.

> [No one disputes] that patent law did not in any sense create Christianson's antitrust or intentional-interference claims. Since no one asserts that federal jurisdiction rests on Christianson's state-law claims, the dispute centers around whether patent law "is a necessary element of one of the well-pleaded [antitrust] claims."

> [It is not] necessarily sufficient that a well-pleaded claim alleges a single theory under which resolution of a patent-law question is essential. If "on the face of a well-pleaded complaint there are . . . reasons completely unrelated to the provisions and purposes of [the patent laws] why the [plaintiff] may or may not be entitled to the relief it seeks," *Franchise Tax Board*, then the claim does not "arise under" those laws. Thus, a claim supported by

alternative theories in the complaint may not form the basis for § 1338(a) jurisdiction unless patent law is essential to each of those theories.

Framed in these terms, our resolution of the jurisdictional issue in this case is straightforward. Christianson's antitrust count can readily be understood to encompass both a monopolization claim under § 2 of the Sherman Act and a group-boycott claim under § 1. The patent-law issue, while arguably necessary to at least one theory under each claim, is not necessary to the overall success of either claim.

. . . The thrust of Christianson's monopolization claim is that Colt has "embarked on a course of conduct to illegally extend its monopoly position with respect to the described patents and to prevent ITS [Christianson's company] from engaging in any business with respect to parts and accessories of the M-16." The complaint specifies several acts, most of which relate either to Colt's prosecution of the lawsuit against Christianson or to letters Colt sent to Christianson's potential and existing customers. . . . [Colt focuses entirely on what it perceives] to be "the only basis Christianson asserted in the complaint for the alleged antitrust violation"—namely, that Colt made false assertions in its letters and pleadings that [Christianson and ITS] were violating its trade secrets, when those trade secrets were not protected under state law because Colt's patents were invalid under § 112. Thus, Colt concludes, the validity of the patents is an essential element of Christianson's prima facie monopolization theory and the case "arises under" patent law.

We can assume without deciding that the invalidity of Colt's patents is an essential element of the foregoing monopolization theory rather than merely an argument in anticipation of a defense. The well-pleaded complaint rule, however, focuses on claims, not theories, see *Franchise Tax Board*, and just because an element that is essential to a particular theory might be governed by federal patent law does not mean that the entire monopolization claim "arises under" patent law.

Examination of the complaint reveals that the monopolization theory that Colt singles out (and on which Christianson ultimately prevailed in the District Court) is only one of several, and the only one for which the patent-law issue is even arguably essential. So far as appears from the complaint, for example, Christianson might have attempted to prove that Colt's accusations of trade-secret infringement were false not because Colt had no trade secrets, but because Colt authorized Christianson to use them. . . . In fact, most of the conduct alleged in the complaint could be deemed wrongful quite apart from the truth or falsity of Colt's accusations. [For example, according to the complaint, Colt's letters also contained "copies of inapplicable court orders" and "suggest[ed] that these court orders prohibited [the recipients] from doing business with" Christianson.] Since there are "reasons completely unrelated to the provisions and purposes" of federal patent law why [Christianson and ITS] "may or may not be entitled to the relief [they] seek" under their monopolization claim, the claim does not "arise under" federal patent law. The same analysis obtains as to Christianson's group-boycott claim under § 1 of the Sherman Act . . . [Omitted.]

As in *Gunn*, the Court in *Christianson* interpreted 28 U.S.C. § 1338, not 28 U.S.C. § 1331. Once again, the Court repeatedly cites and draws on various cases interpreting § 1331. Under *Christianson*, would Grable's quiet title claim arise under federal law if one of its theories was that Darue had resold the land to Grable?

C. Preemption, Removal, and "Artful Pleading"

As *Mottley* itself illustrates, preemption ordinarily is a federal defense that does not provide a basis for district court jurisdiction under section 1331. However, the Supreme Court has held that Congress may so *completely* preempt an area of state law that "any claim based on that preempted state law is considered, from its inception," a federal claim. Such claims "arise under" federal law and may be brought in federal court — or removed there — even though the complaint makes no reference to federal law. This section examines the "complete preemption" doctrine.

We begin with the 2003 decision in *Beneficial National Bank*, which provides an overview of the doctrine. We then look at the most important area in which the doctrine operates today — ERISA. We examine the often misunderstood distinction between "ordinary" preemption under § 514 of ERISA, which does not support removal, and "complete" preemption under § 502(a), which does. Finally, we look briefly at the "artful pleading" doctrine and its relation to the doctrine of complete preemption.

Beneficial National Bank v. Anderson

Supreme Court of the United States, 2003.

539 U.S. 1.

Justice Stevens delivered the opinion of the Court.

The question in this case is whether an action filed in a state court to recover damages from a national bank for allegedly charging excessive interest in violation of both "the common law usury doctrine" and an Alabama usury statute may be removed to a federal court because it actually arises under federal law. We hold that it may.

I

Respondents are 26 individual taxpayers who made pledges of their anticipated tax refunds to secure short-term loans obtained from petitioner Beneficial National Bank, a national bank chartered under the National Bank Act. Respondents brought suit in an Alabama court against the bank and the two other petitioners that arranged the loans, seeking compensatory and punitive damages on the theory, among others, that the bank's interest rates were usurious. Their complaint did not refer to any federal law.

Petitioners removed the case to the United States District Court for the Middle District of Alabama. In their notice of removal they asserted that the National Bank Act, 12 U.S.C. § 85, is the exclusive provision governing the rate of interest that a national bank may lawfully charge, that the rates charged to respondents complied with that provision, that § 86 provides the exclusive remedies available against a national bank charging excessive interest, and that the removal statute, 28 U.S.C. § 1441, therefore applied. The District Court denied respondents' motion to remand the case to state court but certified the question whether it had jurisdiction to proceed with the case to the Court of Appeals pursuant to 28 U.S.C. § 1292(b).

A divided panel of the Eleventh Circuit reversed. The majority held that under our "well-pleaded complaint" rule, removal is generally not permitted unless the complaint expressly alleges a federal claim and that the narrow exception from that rule known as the "complete preemption doctrine" did not apply because it could "find no clear congressional intent to permit removal under §§ 85 and 86." Because this holding conflicted with an Eighth Circuit decision we granted certiorari.

II

A civil action filed in a state court may be removed to federal court if the claim is one "arising under" federal law. § 1441(b). To determine whether the claim arises under federal law, we examine the "well pleaded" allegations of the complaint and ignore potential defenses: "a suit arises under the Constitution and laws of the United States only when the plaintiff's statement of his own cause of action shows that it is based upon those laws or that Constitution. It is not enough that the plaintiff alleges some anticipated defense to his cause of action and asserts that the defense is invalidated by some provision of the Constitution of the United States." Thus, a defense that relies on the preclusive effect of a prior federal judgment, *Rivet v. Regions Bank of La.*, 522 U.S. 470 (1998) [*infra* this section], or the pre-emptive effect of a federal statute, *Franchise Tax Bd.*, will not provide a basis for removal. As a general rule, absent diversity jurisdiction, a case will not be removable if the complaint does not affirmatively allege a federal claim.

Congress has, however, created certain exceptions to that rule. For example, the Price-Anderson Act contains an unusual pre-emption provision, 42 U.S.C. § 2014(hh), that not only gives federal courts jurisdiction over tort actions arising out of nuclear accidents but also expressly provides for removal of such actions brought in state court even when they assert only state-law claims.

We have also construed § 301 of the Labor Management Relations Act of 1947 as not only preempting state law but also authorizing removal of actions that sought relief only under state law. *Avco Corp. v. Machinists*, 390 U.S. 557 (1968). We later explained that holding as resting on the unusually "powerful" pre-emptive force of § 301:

> The Court of Appeals held, and we affirmed, that the petitioner's action "arose under" § 301, and thus could be removed to federal court, although the petitioner had undoubtedly pleaded an adequate claim for relief under

the state law of contracts and had sought a remedy available only under state law. The necessary ground of decision was that the pre-emptive force of § 301 is so powerful as to displace entirely any state cause of action "for violation of contracts between an employer and a labor organization." Any such suit is purely a creature of federal law, notwithstanding the fact that state law would provide a cause of action in the absence of § 301. Avco stands for the proposition that if a federal cause of action completely pre-empts a state cause of action any complaint that comes within the scope of the federal cause of action necessarily "arises under" federal law. *Franchise Tax Bd.*

Similarly, in *Metropolitan Life Ins. Co. v. Taylor*, 481 U.S. 58 (1987), we considered whether the "complete pre-emption" approach adopted in *Avco* also supported the removal of state common-law causes of action asserting improper processing of benefit claims under a plan regulated by the Employee Retirement Income Security Act of 1974 (ERISA). For two reasons, we held that removal was proper even though the complaint purported to raise only state-law claims. First, the statutory text in § 502(a), not only provided an express federal remedy for the plaintiffs' claims, but also in its jurisdiction subsection, § 502(f), used language similar to the statutory language construed in *Avco*, thereby indicating that the two statutes should be construed in the same way. Second, the legislative history of ERISA unambiguously described an intent to treat such actions "as arising under the laws of the United States in similar fashion to those brought under section 301 of the Labor-Management Relations Act of 1947."

Thus, a state claim may be removed to federal court in only two circumstances— when Congress expressly so provides, such as in the Price-Anderson Act, or when a federal statute wholly displaces the state-law cause of action through complete pre-emption.[3] When the federal statute completely pre-empts the state-law cause of action, a claim which comes within the scope of that cause of action, even if pleaded in terms of state law, is in reality based on federal law. This claim is then removable under 28 U.S.C. § 1441(b), which authorizes any claim that "arises under" federal law to be removed to federal court. In the two categories of cases[4] where this Court has found complete pre-emption—certain causes of action under the LMRA and ERISA—the federal statutes at issue provided the exclusive cause of action for the claim asserted and also set forth procedures and remedies governing that cause of action. See 29 U.S.C. § 1132 (setting forth procedures and remedies for civil claims under ERISA); § 185 (describing procedures and remedies for suits under the LMRA).

---

3. Of course, a state claim can also be removed through the use of the supplemental jurisdiction statute, 28 U.S.C. § 1367(a), provided that another claim in the complaint is removable.

4. This Court has also held that federal courts have subject-matter jurisdiction to hear possessory land claims under state law brought by Indian tribes because of the uniquely federal "nature and source of the possessory rights of Indian tribes." *Oneida Indian Nation of N.Y. v. County of Oneida*, 414 U.S. 661 (1974). Because that case turned on the special historical relationship between Indian tribes and the Federal Government, it does not assist the present analysis.

III

Count IV of respondents' complaint sought relief for "usury violations" and claimed that petitioners "charged . . . excessive interest in violation of the common law usury doctrine" and violated Alabama Code. § 8-8-1, *et seq.* by charging excessive interest." Respondents' complaint thus expressly charged petitioners with usury. *Metropolitan Life, Avco*, and *Franchise Tax Board* provide the framework for answering the dispositive question in this case: Does the National Bank Act provide the exclusive cause of action for usury claims against national banks? If so, then the cause of action necessarily arises under federal law and the case is removable. If not, then the complaint does not arise under federal law and is not removable.

Sections 85 and 86 serve distinct purposes. The former sets forth the substantive limits on the rates of interest that national banks may charge. The latter sets forth the elements of a usury claim against a national bank, provides for a 2-year statute of limitations for such a claim, and prescribes the remedies available to borrowers who are charged higher rates and the procedures governing such a claim. If, as petitioners asserted in their notice of removal, the interest that the bank charged to respondents did not violate § 85 limits, the statute unquestionably pre-empts any common-law or Alabama statutory rule that would treat those rates as usurious. The section would therefore provide the petitioners with a complete federal defense. Such a federal defense, however, would not justify removal. *Caterpillar Inc. v. Williams*, 482 U.S. 386 (1987). Only if Congress intended § 86 to provide the exclusive cause of action for usury claims against national banks would the statute be comparable to the provisions that we construed in the *Avco* and *Metropolitan Life* cases.[5]

In a series of cases decided shortly after the Act was passed, we endorsed that approach. [For example,] in *Evans v. National Bank of Savannah*, 251 U.S. 108 (1919), we stated that "federal law . . . completely defines what constitutes the taking of usury by a national bank, referring to the state law only to determine the maximum permitted rate." *See also Barnet v. National Bank*, 98 U.S. 555, 558 (1879) (the "statutes of Ohio and Indiana upon the subject of usury . . . cannot affect the case" because the Act "creates a new right" that is "exclusive"); *Haseltine v. Central Bank of Springfield*, 183 U.S. 132, 134 (1901) ("[T]he definition of usury and the penalties affixed thereto must be determined by the National Banking Act and not by the law of the State").

In addition to this Court's longstanding and consistent construction of the National Bank Act as providing an exclusive federal cause of action for usury against national banks, this Court has also recognized the special nature of federally chartered banks. Uniform rules limiting the liability of national banks and prescribing exclusive remedies for their overcharges are an integral part of a banking system that needed protection from "possible unfriendly State legislation." *Tiffany v. National Bank of*

---

5. Because the proper inquiry focuses on whether Congress intended the federal cause of action to be exclusive rather than on whether Congress intended that the cause of action be removable, the fact that these sections of the National Bank Act were passed in 1864, 11 years prior to the passage of the statute authorizing removal, is irrelevant, contrary to respondents' assertions.

Mo., 18 Wall. 409, 412 (1874). The same federal interest that protected national banks from the state taxation that Chief Justice Marshall characterized as the "power to destroy," *McCulloch v. Maryland*, 4 Wheat. 316, 431 (1819), supports the established interpretation of §§ 85 and 86 that gives those provisions the requisite pre-emptive force to provide removal jurisdiction. In actions against national banks for usury, these provisions supersede both the substantive and the remedial provisions of state usury laws and create a federal remedy for overcharges that is exclusive, even when a state complainant, as here, relies entirely on state law.

Because §§ 85 and 86 provide the exclusive cause of action for such claims, there is, in short, no such thing as a state-law claim of usury against a national bank. Even though the complaint makes no mention of federal law, it unquestionably and unambiguously claims that petitioners violated usury laws. This cause of action against national banks only arises under federal law and could, therefore, be removed under § 1441.

The judgment of the Court of Appeals is reversed.

JUSTICE SCALIA, with whom JUSTICE THOMAS joins, dissenting.

Today's opinion takes the view that because § 30 of the National Bank Act, 12 U.S.C. §§ 85, 86, provides the exclusive cause of action for claims of usury against a national bank, all such claims—even if explicitly pleaded under state law—are to be construed as "aris[ing] under" federal law for purposes of our jurisdictional statutes. This view finds scant support in our precedents and no support whatever in the National Bank Act or any other Act of Congress. I respectfully dissent. . . .

. . . [Today's holding] cannot be squared with bedrock principles of removal jurisdiction. One or another of two of those principles must be ignored: Either (1) the principle that merely setting forth in state court facts that would support a federal cause of action—indeed, even facts that would support a federal cause of action and would not support the claimed state cause of action—does not produce a federal question supporting removal, *Caterpillar* [the next principal case], or (2) the principle that a federal defense to a state cause of action does not support federal-question jurisdiction. . . .

In an effort to justify this shift, the Court explains that "[b]ecause §§ 85 and 86 [of the National Bank Act] provide the exclusive cause of action for such claims, there is . . . no such thing as a state-law claim of usury against a national bank." But the mere fact that a state-law claim is invalid no more deprives it of its character as a state-law claim which does not raise a federal question, than does the fact that a federal claim is invalid deprive it of its character as a federal claim which does raise a federal question. The proper response to the presentation of a nonexistent claim to a state court is dismissal, not the "federalize-and-remove" dance authorized by today's opinion. For even if the Court is correct that the National Bank Act obliterates entirely any state-created right to relief for usury against a national bank, that does not explain how or why the claim of such a right is transmogrified into the claim of a federal right. Congress's mere act of creating a federal right and eliminating all state-created rights in no way suggests an expansion of federal jurisdiction so as to wrest from state courts the authority to decide questions of pre-emption under the National Bank Act. . . .

There may well be good reasons to favor the expansion of removal jurisdiction that petitioners urge and that the Court adopts today. As the United States explains in its amicus brief:

> Absent removal, the state court would have only two legitimate options—to recharacterize the claim in federal-law terms or to dismiss the claim altogether. Any plaintiff who truly seeks recovery on that claim would prefer the first option, which would make the propriety of removal crystal clear. A third possibility, however, is that the state court would err and allow the claim to proceed under state law notwithstanding Congress's decision to make the federal cause of action exclusive. The complete pre-emption rule avoids that potential error.

True enough, but inadequate to render today's decision either rational or properly within the authority of this Court. Inadequate for rationality, because there is no more reason to fear state-court error with respect to federal pre-emption accompanied by creation of a federal cause of action than there is with respect to federal pre-emption unaccompanied by creation of a federal cause of action—or, for that matter, than there is with respect to any federal defense to a state-law claim. The rational response to the United States' concern is to eliminate the well-pleaded-complaint rule entirely. And inadequate for judicial authority, because it is up to Congress, not the federal courts, to decide when the risk of state-court error with respect to a matter of federal law becomes so unbearable as to justify divesting the state courts of authority to decide the federal matter. Unless and until we receive instruction from Congress that claims pre-empted under the National Bank Act—in contrast to almost all other claims that are subject to federal pre-emption—"arise under" federal law, we simply lack authority to "avoi[d] . . . potential errors," by permitting removal.

* * *

Today's opinion has succeeded in giving to our *Avco* decision a theoretical foundation that neither *Avco* itself nor *Taylor* provided. Regrettably, that theoretical foundation is itself without theoretical foundation. That is to say, the more general proposition that (1) the existence of a pre-emptive federal cause of action causes the invalid assertion of a state cause of action to raise a federal question, has no more logic or precedent to support it than the very narrow proposition that (2) the LMRA (*Avco*) and statutes modeled after the LMRA (*Taylor*) cause invalid assertions of state causes of action pre-empted by those particular statutes to raise federal questions. Since I believe that, as between an inexplicable narrow holding and an inexplicable broad one, the former is the lesser evil, I would adhere to the approach taken by *Taylor* and on the basis of stare decisis simply affirm, without any real explanation, that the LMRA and statutes modeled after it have a "unique pre-emptive force" that (quite illogically) suspends the normal rules of removal jurisdiction. Since no one asserts that the National Bank Act is modeled after the LMRA, the state-law claim pleaded here cannot be removed, and it is left to the state courts to dismiss it. From the Court's judgment to the contrary, I respectfully dissent.

Problem: Property Damages in an Interstate Move

Myrtle Gilman contracted with Acme Van Lines to move and temporarily store her personal belongings in a storage facility in Oil City, Anadarko, then later to ship her belongings to her new residence in Keswick, Oceana. Acme, a carrier subject to the Interstate Commerce Act (ICA), acted as the initial, connecting, and delivering carrier for Gilman's shipment of goods.

At the time of delivery in Oceana, Gilman noticed that many items were damaged or missing, including furniture and antique silverware. She filed claims with Acme for the missing or damaged items. Acme paid Gilman $70,000 on her claims, but Gilman asserts that she is entitled to at least an additional $108,437 in damages for repair and replacement of the damaged or missing goods.

Gilman filed suit against Acme in Anadarko state court. Her complaint alleged negligence, breach of contract, and violation of the Anadarko Deceptive Trade Practices Act. Among other things, Gilman sought damages, including exemplary damages, and attorney's fees. The complaint did not assert any federal claims.

Acme removed the case to federal district court based on 28 U.S.C. §§ 1331 and 1337 and 49 U.S.C. § 14706. The latter section is known as the "Carmack Amendment" to the Interstate Commerce Act. There is no diversity, and Gilman has filed a motion to remand on the ground that her suit does not arise under federal law.

Under the Carmack Amendment, a carrier subject to the ICA must issue a receipt or bill of lading for property received for transportation. Section 14706(a) imposes liability on the carrier "for the actual loss or injury to the property caused by (A) the receiving carrier, (B) the delivering carrier, or (C) another carrier over whose line or route the property is transported in the United States." Section 14706(d), entitled "Civil Actions," provides in part:

> A civil action under this section may be brought against a delivering carrier in a district court of the United States or in a State court.

The Carmack Amendment was adopted without discussion or debate. However, in a series of decisions in the first decades of the twentieth century, the Supreme Court attributed broad preemptive purposes to the statute. The Court said:

> With the enactment in 1906 of the Carmack Amendment, Congress superseded diverse state laws with a nationally uniform policy governing the liability of interstate carriers for loss or damage to interstate shipments. . . . State laws are pre-empted by the Carmack Amendment if they "in any way enlarge the responsibility of the carrier for loss or at all affect the ground of recovery or the measure of recovery." [However, state laws are not pre-empted if they do not in any way] either enlarge or limit the responsibility of the carrier for the loss of property entrusted to it in transportation, and [if they] only incidentally affect the remedy for enforcing that responsibility.

Should the motion to remand be granted?

Felix v. Lucent Technologies, Inc.

United States Court of Appeals for the Tenth Circuit, 2004.

387 F.3d 1146.

Before EBEL, ANDERSON, and McCONNELL, CIRCUIT JUDGES.

EBEL, CIRCUIT JUDGE.

Plaintiffs, a group of former employees of Defendant Lucent Technologies, Inc. ("Defendant"), sued Defendant in state court for fraud arising out of alleged misrepresentations made in encouraging Plaintiffs to take an early retirement benefits package. Defendant removed the case to federal court on the basis of complete preemption under the Employee Retirement Income Security Act ("ERISA") and the Labor Management Relations Act ("LMRA"), and then moved to dismiss. Plaintiffs filed a motion to remand, which was denied by the district court on the basis of ERISA complete preemption. Plaintiffs appealed this order, and Defendant now asserts the same grounds for removal jurisdiction as it did below . . . .

Exercising jurisdiction over the district court's order under 28 U.S.C. § 1291, we conclude that Plaintiffs' state law fraud claims are not completely preempted by ERISA. Accordingly, we REVERSE and REMAND with instructions to remand to state court.

BACKGROUND

Plaintiffs [worked] at a manufacturing facility in Oklahoma City known as the Oklahoma City Works ("OKCW"). In their Fourth Amended Petition, Plaintiffs alleged the following:

> Because of a series of substantial financial reversals Lucent determined to sell off its manufacturing facilities including OKCW. It communicated to its workforce at OKCW its intent to restructure and engaged in a series of highly-publicized attempts to sell its manufacturing plants or merge with other similar companies. In an effort to make it more attractive to purchasers/merging companies Lucent determined to reduce the number of long-term senior employees at the OKCW.
>
> On February 19, 2001, Lucent entered into a Memorandum of Agreement with the International Brotherhood of Electrical Workers ("IBEW") System Council EM-3 whereby OKCW employees that were retirement-eligible would retire in exchange for receipt of a payment equivalent to 110% of the amount of termination allowance to which the employee would be entitled if the employee was laid-off for lack of work up to a maximum of 32 years' service (under the applicable IBEW collective bargaining agreements) plus a "special pension benefit" in the amount of $11,000 which represented the amount to which the employee was otherwise entitled under a pending National Labor Relations Board award against Lucent. These payments were to be made out of the over-funded portion of the

Lucent pension plan funded by the employees at the OKCW. Additionally, for those OKCW employees that were not then retirement-eligible, Lucent proposed to provide a transitional leave of absence by adding 5 years to the age and/or service to make the employee pension-eligible and to reduce to the extent possible any pension discount for early retirement. Acceptance of Lucent's offer had to be made by May 29, 2001, and an employee accepting the offer would leave the OKCW roll on June 30, 2001.

Written material was distributed to the employees at the OKCW and meetings were held with Lucent representatives at which these benefits were outlined. Based upon information communicated to its officers and representatives by Lucent, the IBEW locals at the OKCW also provided information to the employees.

At each meeting attended by each individual plaintiff, it was stated by Lucent's authorized representatives that the offer being made by Lucent was a one-time, non-negotiable, final offer that was a take-it-or-leave-it proposal and that any delay by any employee in accepting the offer would not result in any additional benefit. To the contrary, it was emphasized at such meetings that failure to accept Lucent's offer was risking the benefits being offered since Lucent might file bankruptcy or merge with another company. . . .

In reliance upon the representations made by Lucent (and reiterated by union officials) that the offer being made was a take-it-or-leave-it . . . offer and that delaying retirement not only would not gain the employee additional benefits, but instead might jeopardize all of these benefits, over 1,000 eligible employees, including all of the plaintiffs herein, timely accepted the offer, retired, and left the OKCW roll on June 30, 2001.

Subsequently, Lucent entered into an agreement with Celestica, Inc., a Canadian corporation involved in the manufacture of computer and telecommunications equipment whereby Celestica, Inc. was to act as a contract manufacturer and take over the operation of the OKCW and hire as its employees certain remaining OKCW Lucent employees on November 30, 2001.

Contrary to the representations made by Lucent, on October 1, 2001, Lucent agreed to pay retirement-eligible (and those made eligible by the 5+5 transitional offer) employees still on the OKCW roll benefits identical to those paid to the plaintiffs **plus** an additional payment of a "special one-time pension benefit" by Lucent of $15,000. . . .

Lucent intentionally misrepresented to each plaintiff the nature of the offer as described . . . above with the intent to induce each plaintiff to rely upon such misrepresentations and to change their respective positions to their detriment. Rather than a "one-time offer," Lucent knew at the time such misrepresentations were made that additional "sweeteners" would be made to reduce the number of senior employees in the OKCW workforce.

Each plaintiff did rely upon such misrepresentations in making the decision to retire on June 30, 2001. No plaintiff had the opportunity or ability to discover the truth concerning such misrepresentations.

Plaintiffs requested as damages the additional $15,000 benefit that was later offered to the remaining employees, the value of an additional year of service that was lost by accepting the June 30 retirement date, and punitive damages.

Discussion

ERISA is a "comprehensive statute designed to promote the interests of employees and their beneficiaries in employee benefit plans." It covers both employee pension plans and welfare plans that meet its definitions under 29 U.S.C. § 1002(1)-(3). [See Judicial Code Supplement.]

ERISA "imposes participation, funding, and vesting requirements on pension plans. It also sets various uniform standards, including rules concerning reporting, disclosure, and fiduciary responsibility. . . . ERISA does not mandate that employers provide any particular benefits, and does not itself proscribe discrimination in the provision of employee benefits." The parties in the instant case do not dispute that Defendant's pension plan at issue is covered by ERISA.

. . . Plaintiffs argue that the district court erred in denying their motion to remand and dismissing the case for failure to state a claim. Specifically, Plaintiffs argue that, contrary to the district court's holding, their state fraud claim was not "completely preempted" by ERISA. We agree with Plaintiffs.

Important to understanding the propriety of removing the instant case is the distinction between "conflict preemption" under § 514 of ERISA and "complete preemption" under § 502(a) of ERISA. Because these two concepts are often confused, as they were in the instant case, we provide an explanation of both before we analyze the district court's denial of the motion to remand here.

A. ERISA § 514 Conflict Preemption

Section 514 of ERISA, codified at 29 U.S.C. § 1144, contains an express preemption provision that provides that ERISA "shall supersede any and all State laws insofar as they may now or hereafter relate to any employee benefit plan" covered by ERISA. The Supreme Court has "observed repeatedly that this broadly worded provision is 'clearly expansive.'" *Egelhoff v. Egelhoff*, 532 U.S. 141, 146 (2001). "But at the same time, [the Court has] recognized that the term 'relate to' cannot be taken 'to extend to the furthest stretch of its indeterminacy,' or else 'for all practical purposes pre-emption would never run its course.'"

The Court has held that a state law "relates to" an ERISA plan, and is thus preempted under § 514, "if it has a connection with or reference to such a plan." *Shaw v. Delta Air Lines, Inc.*, 463 U.S. 85, 97 (1983). Further, the Court has

> cautioned against an uncritical literalism that would make pre-emption turn on infinite connections. Instead, to determine whether a state law has the forbidden connection, we look both to the objectives of the ERISA statute as a

guide to the scope of the state law that Congress understood would survive, as well as to the nature of the effect of the state law on ERISA plans.

This preemption provision does not apply "if the state law has only a tenuous, remote, or peripheral connection with covered plans, as is the case with many laws of general applicability." *District of Columbia v. Greater Wash. Bd. of Trade*, 506 U.S. 125, 130 n.1 (1992).

B. "Complete Preemption" Under ERISA

[Here the court summarized the background law on preemption and removal, drawing primarily on the Supreme Court opinions in *Beneficial National Bank* and *Caterpillar*.]

. . . In *Metropolitan Life Ins. Co. v. Taylor*, 481 U.S. 58 (1987), the Court [held] that the complete preemption doctrine allows the removal of state actions that fall within the scope of § 502(a), ERISA's civil enforcement provision. Section 502(a)(1) provides a cause of action to any plan beneficiary or participant to recover benefits due under the terms of a pension plan, to enforce rights under the terms of the plan, or to clarify rights to future benefits under the terms of the plan. Noting that the "language of the jurisdictional subsection of ERISA's civil enforcement provisions closely parallels that of § 301 of the LMRA [at issue in *Avco*]," the *Taylor* Court found that ERISA manifested sufficient congressional intent to recharacterize state law claims that fall within the scope of § 502(a) as federal claims subject to removal.

The Court recently further refined the doctrine of complete preemption under ERISA in *Aetna Health Inc. v. Davila*, 542 U.S. 200 (2004), where it phrased the test as follows:

> [W]here the individual is entitled to such [claimed] coverage only because of the terms of an ERISA-regulated employee benefit plan, and where no legal duty (state or federal) independent of ERISA or the plan terms is violated, then the suit falls "within the scope of" ERISA § 502(a)(1)(B). In other words, if an individual, at some point in time, could have brought his claim under ERISA § 502(a)(1)(B), and where there is no other independent legal duty that is implicated by a defendant's actions, then the individual's cause of action is completely pre-empted by ERISA § 502(a)(1)(B).

In *Davila*, the Court held that a claim brought under a separate statute for drug benefits under an ERISA plan was completely preempted because the claim was not independent of the ERISA plan.

In sum, the preemptive force of § 502(a) of ERISA is so "extraordinary" that it converts a state claim into a federal claim for purposes of removal and the well-pleaded complaint rule.

C. Distinction Between Preemption and Complete Preemption in the Context of ERISA

Although courts and parties often confuse § 514 preemption with § 502(a) complete preemption, the Supreme Court has held that the two are distinct concepts, with only the latter supporting removal. In *Taylor*, the Court first explained that "federal pre-emption is ordinarily a federal defense to the plaintiff's suit," and thus is insufficient grounds for removal. The *Taylor* Court stated that there was no dispute that the plaintiff's state law claims were preempted under § 514 of ERISA in the case before it, but that the remaining question was "whether or not the *Avco* principle can be extended to statutes other than the LMRA in order to recharacterize a state law complaint displaced by *§ 502(a)(1)(B)* as an action arising under federal law." (Emphasis added.)

The Court next pointed out that it had previously held in *Franchise Tax Board* that "ERISA pre-emption [under § 514], without more, does not convert a state claim into an action arising under federal law." "The [*Franchise Tax Board*] court suggested, however, that a state action that was not only pre-empted by ERISA [under § 514], *but also* came within the scope of § 502(a) of ERISA might fall within the *Avco* rule [of complete preemption]." (Emphasis added.) The Court then found that state claims falling within the scope of § 502(a) (as contrasted with those state claims that merely "relate to" plans under § 514) were indeed completely preempted and thus removable. The Supreme Court recently affirmed this approach in *Beneficial National Bank*, where it held that a federal statute completely preempts a state law cause of action when the state claim "comes within the scope of that [federal] cause of action," discussing § 502(a) of ERISA.

We have explained that ERISA preemption under § 514 is not sufficient for removal jurisdiction and that a state law claim is only "completely preempted" under *Taylor* if it can be recharacterized as a claim under § 502(a). . . . This is true regardless of the strength of the defendant's argument for § 514 preemption. As the Supreme Court said in *Taylor*, "[E]ven an 'obvious' pre-emption defense does not . . . create removal jurisdiction."

D. Are Plaintiffs' state law fraud claims completely preempted so as to provide subject matter jurisdiction for removal?

The district court in the instant case found that Plaintiffs' state law claims were "related to" an ERISA plan and were thus preempted under the broad language in § 514. This finding may be correct. *See, e.g., Lee v. E.I. DuPont de Nemours & Co.*, 894 F.2d 755, 755–56, 758 (5th Cir. 1990) (finding § 514 preemption in similar case). However, as discussed above, § 514 preemption is merely a federal defense that cannot provide the basis for removal jurisdiction. We thus turn to the separate question of whether Plaintiffs' claims fell within the scope of § 502(a) and were thus completely preempted. We ultimately conclude in this section that Plaintiffs could not have brought these fraud claims under § 502(a) because their suit is not one to recover benefits due to them under the terms of their employee benefit plan. Accordingly, we reverse the district court's finding of complete preemption.

1. Standing to Sue under ERISA

A plaintiff must have standing to sue under § 502(a) before his or her state law claim can be recharacterized as arising under federal law subject to federal jurisdiction under the doctrine of complete preemption. *See, [e.g.,] Hobbs v. Blue Cross Blue Shield of Ala.*,

276 F.3d 1236, 1240–41 (11th Cir. 2001). Section 502(a)(1) of ERISA provides a cause of action to any "participant or beneficiary . . . to recover benefits due to him under the terms of his plan, to enforce his rights under the terms of the plan, or to clarify his rights to future benefits under the terms of the plan." Congress defined "participant" to mean:

> any employee or former employee of an employer, or any member or former member of an employee organization, who is or may become eligible to receive a benefit of any type from an employee benefit plan which covers employees of such employer or members of such organization, or whose beneficiaries may be eligible to receive any such benefit.

In *Firestone Tire and Rubber Co. v. Bruch*, 489 U.S. 101 (1989), the Supreme Court clarified that under the statute, a former employee with no reasonable expectation of returning to covered employment must have a "colorable claim to vested benefits" under the plan.

Here, Plaintiffs do not seek "to recover benefits due to [them] under the terms of [their] plan, to enforce [their] rights under the terms of the plan, or to clarify [their] rights to future benefits under the terms of the plan." Neither Plaintiffs nor Defendants contend that Plaintiffs are entitled to the additional benefits under the plan. Rather, Plaintiffs claim that they were fraudulently induced to take early retirement, to their financial detriment; they seek monetary damages from their employer (not from the pension plan) for that alleged fraud. That is not a claim "to recover benefits due to [them] under the terms of [their] plan," and therefore falls outside the scope of 29 U.S.C. § 1132(a)(1).

2. The "But For" Exception

Defendants contend, however, that Plaintiffs' claim is completely preempted because it is, in substance, a claim that "but for" Defendants' wrongful actions, they would have been entitled to the additional benefits under the plan. The circuits are split over whether plaintiffs have standing to sue under ERISA in such a case. Although the First, Second, Fifth, Sixth, and Eighth Circuits have held that former employees may sue under ERISA if they make a "but for" claim of this sort, we, along with the Fourth and Eleventh Circuits, have rejected this approach. . . .

In *Raymond v. Mobil Oil Corp.*, 983 F.2d 1258 (10th Cir. 1993), [we held] that former employees who had received the full extent of their vested benefits did not have the right to sue under ERISA for additional benefits that they might have received but for the wrongful conduct of their employers. This is because where a former employee has received all benefits entitled to him under his plan at the time of retirement, he has no "colorable claim" that additional benefits have "vested" or "will vest." The plaintiffs were not eligible or likely to become eligible to receive the additional benefit at the time they filed the suit. . . .

We pointed out that "the receipt of the 'full extent' of [plaintiffs'] vested benefits" was a "crucial" fact, because that meant that the plaintiffs "seek a damage award based upon their allegedly fraudulent discharge from their jobs; they do not seek 'vested benefits improperly withheld.'" We then explicitly rejected a "but for" test for ERISA standing. We stated, "To say that but for Mobil's conduct, plaintiffs would have standing is to admit that they lack standing and to allow those who merely *claim* to be participants to be deemed as such." Because there is no controlling case law or statutory language to support such a "but for" exception to find ERISA standing where the plaintiff is not technically entitled to the additional benefit under the pension plan, we declined to create an exception to *Firestone* and rejected the availability of any "but for" test. . . .

In sum, we have rejected a "but for" test for determining standing to sue under ERISA. We have found a lack of a "colorable claim to vested benefits" where the plaintiffs have already received full payment of all benefits entitled to them under their plan as it existed at the time of their retirement, where the plaintiff was not enrolled in the pension plan at issue, and where the plaintiff's medical condition was excluded by the terms of the ERISA health plan (notwithstanding defendant's misrepresentations to the contrary). . . .

3. Do Plaintiffs Have ERISA Standing in the Instant Case?

In the instant case, because no party disputes that Plaintiffs are "former employees," we may only find they have standing to sue under ERISA if they have either a "reasonable expectation of returning to covered employment" or "a colorable claim for vested benefits." Plaintiffs do not assert any statutory or contractual right to reinstatement, nor do they even request reinstatement. Thus, they do not have a "reasonable expectation" of returning to such employment.

Nor have Plaintiffs asserted a "colorable claim to vested benefits," as they do not claim that they are entitled to benefits under the terms of their plan as it existed at the time of their retirement. Rather, they claim that they should receive damages for the loss of the additional benefits under the later package (e.g., the $15,000 lump sum and the year of service) because they *would have been* participants under that package but for Defendant's misrepresentations. . . .

The terms of the later October package explicitly excluded Plaintiffs, and they do not argue that they have a colorable claim for those benefits. Plaintiffs are simply not claiming that, at the time of their suit, they were eligible or likely to become eligible for the additional benefits *under the terms of any welfare or pension plan*. The nature of their claim is not that Defendants improperly withheld vested benefits owed to them, but rather that they should receive damages for the fraud they suffered. As the Eleventh Circuit has held, ERISA provides no cause of action to non-participants who claim they were defrauded out of pension benefits in violation of common law fraud principles. Because Plaintiffs are not entitled to the additional benefits at issue "under the terms of [their] plain," their state law claims do not fall within the scope of ERISA § 502(a)(1), and our subject matter jurisdiction cannot be based upon the doctrine of complete preemption.

It is true that our opinion leaves open the uncomfortable possibility that Plaintiffs may lack standing to sue under ERISA, but will then be preempted in state court under

§ 514 from asserting a state claim, leaving them with no remedy. Although this is a valid concern, we have not found it to be a concern of the federal judiciary. "[W]e have noted the unavailability of a remedy under ERISA is not germane to preemption analysis." Congress intended the civil enforcement mechanisms of ERISA to be exclusive, and the "policy choices reflected in the inclusion of certain remedies and the exclusion of others under the federal scheme would be completely undermined if ERISA-plan participants . . . were free to obtain remedies under state law that Congress rejected in ERISA." *Pilot Life Ins. Co. v. Dedeaux*, 481 U.S. 41, 54 (1987).

We also point out that the policy gap here is smaller than it may first appear, as it is possible that some plaintiffs may be able to bring claims under other subsections of § 502 that are not at issue in the instant case. For example, there may be the possibility of claims, under proper factual circumstances, under § 510 of ERISA, or breach of fiduciary duty claims brought on behalf of the plan under § 502(a)(2), or claims for equitable relief brought under the catch-all provision of § 502(a)(3), *see Varity Corp. v. Howe*, 516 U.S. 489, 507–15 (1996).[16]

In conclusion, we refuse to second-guess Congress' policy choices in ERISA, and we hold that Plaintiffs are not "participants" so as to bring their fraud claims within the reach of § 502(a)(1). We thus hold that the district court erred in finding complete preemption. Upon remand, the state court will be free to consider dismissal under § 514's conflict preemption provision, but that issue is not properly before us. . . .

CONCLUSION

[The court also rejected the defendant's argument for "complete preemption" under the NLRA and the LMRA.]

For the foregoing reasons, we REVERSE and REMAND with instructions to remand this case to the state court.

Note: ERISA and Federal-Question Removal

1. The "complete preemption" doctrine originated in cases involving section 301 of the Labor Management Relations Act of 1947. The pathbreaking decision was *Avco Corp. v. Machinists*, 390 U.S. 557 (1968), but as the Court notes in *Beneficial National Bank*, the authoritative statement of the doctrine is found in the *Franchise Tax Board* opinion:

> The necessary ground of decision [in *Avco*] was that the pre-emptive force of § 301 is so powerful as to displace entirely any state cause of action "for violation of contracts between an employer and a labor organization." Any

---

16. No party in the instant case argues that Plaintiffs' fraud claims should be characterized as breach of fiduciary duty claims, nor are Plaintiffs' allegations in their complaint properly so construed. A claim for fraud requires different elements than does a claim for breach of fiduciary duty, and in any event, Plaintiffs do not request equitable relief as required by a § 502(a)(3) claim. We note that at least one court has held that § 502(a)(3) is not available under [Supreme Court case law] where § 502(a)(1) provides an available remedy, even if the particular plaintiffs end up lacking standing as "participants" under § 502(a)(1).

such suit is purely a creature of federal law, notwithstanding the fact that state law would provide a cause of action in the absence of § 301.

As noted in *Beneficial National Bank*, *Avco*'s reasoning was extended to ERISA claims in *Metropolitan Life Ins. Co. v. Taylor*, 481 U.S. 58 (1987). Thus, "causes of action within the scope of the civil enforcement provisions of § 502(a) are removable to federal court."

2. As *Felix* illustrates, the *Avco* and *Taylor* line of cases does not stand for the proposition that every suit brought by an employee relating to his benefits will be treated as a suit under § 502(a). Instead, only those claims seeking to recover benefits under an employee plan fall under § 502(a).

The holding in *Taylor* is simple to state, but the lower courts experienced great difficulty in applying it. One source of misunderstanding was the express preemption provision of ERISA, § 514(a). That section provides that, with exceptions not generally relevant in the context of disputes over removal, "the provisions of this subchapter . . . shall supersede any and all State laws insofar as they may now or hereafter *relate to* any employee benefit plan . . . ." (Emphasis added.)

3. It was easy to assume that any state-law claim that "related to" an employee benefit plan could be removed to federal district court. But this was not correct. A leading decision by the Third Circuit, *Dukes v. U.S. Healthcare, Inc.*, 57 F.3d 350 (3d Cir. 1995), explained why:

> Section 514 of ERISA defines the scope of ERISA preemption. . . . The [*Taylor*] complete-preemption exception, on the other hand, is concerned with a more limited set of state laws, those which fall within the scope of ERISA's civil enforcement provision, § 502. State law claims which fall outside of the scope of § 502, even if preempted by § 514(a), are still governed by the well-pleaded complaint rule and, therefore, are not removable under the complete-preemption principles established in [*Taylor*]. . . .
>
> The difference between preemption and complete preemption is important. When the doctrine of complete preemption does not apply, but the plaintiff's state claim is arguably preempted under § 514(a), the district court, being without removal jurisdiction, cannot resolve the dispute regarding preemption. It lacks power to do anything other than remand to the state court where the preemption issue can be addressed and resolved.

4. In the decade and a half that followed the *Taylor* decision, the Supreme Court handed down numerous opinions on conflict preemption under ERISA and on the scope of ERISA remedies. However, it was not until *Aetna Health Inc. v. Davila* in 2004—quoted by the Tenth Circuit in *Felix*—that the Court again addressed the complete preemption doctrine in the ERISA context. *Davila* appears to establish a two-part test for complete preemption:

> [If] an individual, at some point in time, could have brought his claim under ERISA § 502(a)(1)(B), and where there is no other independent legal duty that is implicated by a defendant's actions, then the individual's cause

of action is completely pre-empted by ERISA § 502(a)(1)(B) [and the suit can be removed even though it is pleaded as a state-law claim].

5. In *Davila*, the plaintiffs' suits were grounded in a state statute, the Texas Health Care Liability Act (THCLA), and the complaints asserted the breach of a duty that Texas law imposed specifically on managed care entities for health plans. The THCLA itself stated that the statutory standards "create no obligation on the . . . managed care entity to provide to an insured or enrollee treatment which is not covered by the health care plan of the entity." It was thus relatively easy to conclude that any potential liability under the THCLA derived "entirely from the particular rights and obligations established by the benefit plans." This in turn meant that "[plaintiffs'] THCLA causes of action [were] not entirely independent of the federally regulated contract itself." But most of the suits that defendants remove under § 502 involve common-law tort claims. Applying the *Davila* test to such claims requires careful consideration of the allegations of the complaint and the elements of the state-law cause of action.

6. The *Davila* opinion did clarify one aspect of the analysis in the course of rejecting the reasoning of the court below, the Fifth Circuit, which had held that the plaintiffs' claims were not completely preempted:

> [The] Court of Appeals found significant that [plaintiffs] "assert a tort claim for tort damages" rather than "a contract claim for contract damages," and that respondents "are not seeking reimbursement for benefits denied them." But, distinguishing between pre-empted and non-pre-empted claims based on the particular label affixed to them would "elevate form over substance and allow parties to evade" the pre-emptive scope of ERISA simply "by relabeling their contract claims as claims for tortious breach of contract." *Allis-Chalmers* [discussed *supra* in the Note on section 301 preemption].
>
> Nor can the mere fact that the state cause of action attempts to authorize remedies beyond those authorized by ERISA § 502(a) put the cause of action outside the scope of the ERISA civil enforcement mechanism. In [three prior cases], the plaintiffs all brought state claims that were labeled either tort or tort-like. . . . And, in all these cases, the plaintiffs' claims were pre-empted. The limited remedies available under ERISA are an inherent part of the "careful balancing" between ensuring fair and prompt enforcement of rights under a plan and the encouragement of the creation of such plans. . . .
>
> Congress' intent to make the ERISA civil enforcement mechanism exclusive would be undermined if state causes of action that supplement the ERISA § 502(a) remedies were permitted, even if the elements of the state cause of action did not precisely duplicate the elements of an ERISA claim.

7. Before *Davila*, some courts applied a three-part test for complete preemption under ERISA:

> [There are] three essential requirements for complete preemption: (1) the plaintiff must have standing under § 502(a) to pursue its claim; (2) its claim must "fall[ ] within the scope of an ERISA provision that [it] can enforce via

§ 502(a)"; and (3) the claim must not be capable of resolution "without an interpretation of the contract governed by federal law," i.e., an ERISA-governed employee benefit plan.

Sonoco Prods. Co. v. Physicians Health Plan, Inc., 338 F.3d 366 (4th Cir. 2003). The first and second prongs fit comfortably into the *Davila* test, but what about the third? The *Davila* opinion does not say much about the point, but it does note that "interpretation of the terms of [plaintiffs'] benefit plans forms an essential part of their THCLA claim, and THCLA liability would exist here only because of [the defendants'] administration of ERISA-regulated benefit plans." The Court thus concluded that the plaintiffs were bringing suit "only to rectify a wrongful denial of benefits promised under ERISA-regulated plans, and [were not attempting] to remedy any violation of a legal duty independent of ERISA."

Note: A Wrong Without a Remedy?

1. Because the district court in *Felix* granted the defendant's motion to dismiss, the Tenth Circuit accepts all of the allegations in the plaintiff's complaint as true. Thus, for purposes of analysis, we must assume that Lucent made intentional misrepresentations to the plaintiffs, that the plaintiffs took early retirement in reliance on those representations, and that the plaintiffs thereby lost out on the additional "sweeteners" they could have received if they had waited.

2. The Tenth Circuit acknowledges that "our opinion leaves open the uncomfortable possibility that Plaintiffs may lack standing to sue under ERISA, but will then be preempted in state court under § 514 from asserting a state claim, leaving them with no remedy." That is exactly what happened when the case returned to the Oklahoma courts. The trial court held that the plaintiffs' fraud claims were preempted by § 514, and the appellate court affirmed. The appellate opinion explained:

> Although there is authority otherwise, the vast majority of both state and federal courts hold that ERISA bars a state law fraud claim based on allegations of the employee's detrimental reliance on an employer's intentional misrepresentation of benefits available under an early retirement plan.

> Plaintiffs [attempt] to distinguish these cases, [arguing] that they did not seek benefits under their pension plan, but rather, damages for Defendant's fraudulent misrepresentation concerning the extent of benefits available or to be available to early retirees, a claim wholly separate and distinct from, and only tangentially related to, a claim to recover pension plan benefits.

> We are unpersuaded . . . . The tie between Plaintiffs' allegations of fraudulent misrepresentation and the ERISA plan is plain and substantial. To establish Defendant's liability, Plaintiffs would have to show the reasonableness of their reliance on the alleged misrepresentations regarding future early retirement benefits. [That] would require resort to the terms of the ERISA plan, and would necessarily include an examination of "the operation and funding of the retirement plan prior to the . . . changes, the language of the

amendments to the retirement plan, and Defendant's communication to Plaintiffs concerning the terms of the retirement plan amendments."

Felix v. Lucent Technologies, Inc., 157 P.3d 769 (Okla. Civ. App. 2006).

3. The Tenth Circuit notes that "some plaintiffs may be able to bring claims under other subsections of § 502 that are not at issue in the instant case." Does the discussion in the opinion suggest that the *Felix* plaintiffs might have been able to proceed with their lawsuit if they had sought relief under a different theory?

4. Many judges have lamented the "policy gap" described by the Tenth Circuit and have called upon Congress to amend the statute. However, thus far, Congress has not acted.

Problem: An On-the-Job Injury

New Harmony, like several other states, allows employers to opt out of the state-administered workers' compensation system. If an employer does so, its employees may sue their employer for work-related injuries or death, and the non-subscribing employer may not invoke common-law defenses such as contributory negligence or the fellow-servant rule.

Deer Creek Estates (Deer Creek) is an employer that does not participate in the New Harmony workers' compensation system. However, to compensate employees for on-the-job injuries, Deer Creek established an ERISA welfare benefits plan. The Plan provides no-fault benefits to employees in the event of an on-the-job injury; it also requires arbitration of any disputes regarding benefits. Deer Creek's employees are not required to enroll in the Plan.

Crystal Harper worked for Deer Creek as a landscaper for a two-year period. She enrolled in the company's employee injury benefit plan and signed an agreement that the Plan would provide the exclusive avenue of relief for on-the-job injuries.

Harper claims that she suffered a job-related injury late last year, when she tripped over a cement parking stop while using a grass cutter in a parking lot. She landed with her back on the grass cutter and was subsequently diagnosed with a herniated disk that required surgery. Harper did not report this injury to Deer Creek until several months later, which was after her employment with Deer Creek ended. At that time, Harper submitted an injury claim form to the Plan. The Plan administrator denied the claim because Harper did not timely report her injury, did not seek pre-approval for her treatment, and did not use a Plan-approved physician. The initial determination contained a notice of appeal rights, but Harper did not pursue an administrative appeal. Instead, she filed suit in New Harmony state court asserting a common law negligence claim alleging that Deer Creek was negligent in failing to provide a safe workplace.

Deer Creek timely removed the suit to federal district court, asserting that federal subject matter jurisdiction existed because ERISA completely preempts Harper's claim. Harper has filed a motion to remand, relying on a pre-*Davila* circuit precedent in a very similar case. The court of appeals in that case held that removal was improper because the plaintiff's claim did not " 'relate to' [the employer's] ERISA plan."

How should the district court rule on Harper's motion to remand the case to state court?

Problem: ERISA and Medical Negligence

Frederick Martin participates in an ERISA-governed employee welfare benefit plan that is administered by his HMO, QualityCare. Under the terms of this plan, Martin is entitled to certain "Covered Benefits." Unless there is a specific provision for a particular type of treatment, a benefit is covered only if, in the determination of QualityCare, it is "Medically Necessary." "Medically Necessary" is defined in the plan as meaning that the service or supply must be "care or treatment as likely to produce a significant positive outcome as, and no more likely to produce a negative outcome than, any alternative service or supply"; must be "related to diagnosis of an existing illness or injury"; may "include only those services and supplies that cannot be safely and satisfactorily provided at home"; and, "as to diagnosis, care and treatment, must be no more costly (taking into account all health expenses incurred in connection with the service or supply) than any equally effective service or supply."

Last March, Martin was diagnosed with "sleep apnea/upper airway obstruction," for which he required a tracheotomy tube. His doctor, Dr. Michael Draper, surgically inserted a tracheotomy tube to eliminate the obstruction, but the tube continually came out. Dr. Draper then placed an order for a specially designed tube. However, QualityCare instructed Dr. Draper that the special tube was "medically unnecessary." Instead of ordering the special tube, the doctor then inserted a different tube, which caused Martin severe pain and resulted in an infection. Martin was later admitted to a local hospital for treatment, but, the complaint avers, he was thereafter discharged "at QualityCare's insistence."

Martin filed a five-count complaint in state court against QualityCare, his treating physicians, and the hospital. In Count I, he alleged that QualityCare negligently interfered with his medical care by (a) instructing Dr. Draper that the specially designed tracheotomy tube he deemed necessary was medically unnecessary for Martin and (b) improperly interfering with Dr. Draper's medical decision concerning the tracheotomy tube and insisting on Martin's discharge from the hospital before his attending physician was planning on discharging him." The other counts involved claims against parties other than QualityCare.

QualityCare removed the case to the District Court on the ground that the claim against it was completely preempted under ERISA. Martin has moved to remand to state court. Should the motion be granted?

Rivet v. Regions Bank of Louisiana

Supreme Court of the United States, 1998.

522 U.S. 470.

JUSTICE GINSBURG delivered the opinion of the Court.

Congress has provided for removal of cases from state court to federal court when the plaintiff's complaint alleges a claim arising under federal law. Congress has not authorized removal based on a defense or anticipated defense federal in character. This case presents the question whether removal may be predicated on a defendant's assertion that a prior federal judgment has disposed of the entire matter and thus bars plaintiffs from later pursuing a state-law-based case. We reaffirm that removal is improper in such a case. In so holding we clarify and confine to its specific context the Court's second footnote in *Federated Department Stores, Inc. v. Moitie*, 452 U.S. 394, 397 n.2 (1981). The defense of claim preclusion, we emphasize, is properly made in the state proceeding, subject to this Court's ultimate review.

I

[After a partnership mortgaged its interest in the Louisiana equivalent of a leasehold estate to respondent Regions Bank of Louisiana (Bank), the partnership granted a second mortgage to petitioners, and later filed for bankruptcy. The Bankruptcy Court approved a sale of the leasehold estate to the Bank. Thereafter, the Bank acquired the underlying land and sold the entire property to respondent Fountainbleau Storage Associates (FSA). Petitioners then filed this action in Louisiana state court, alleging that transfer of the property without satisfying their rights under the second mortgage violated state law. Respondents removed the action to federal court, contending that federal-question jurisdiction existed because the prior Bankruptcy Court orders extinguished petitioners' rights. The District Court denied petitioners' motion to remand and granted summary judgment to the Bank and FSA. The Fifth Circuit affirmed.]

II

A

A state-court action may be removed to federal court if it qualifies as a "civil action . . . of which the district courts of the United States have original jurisdiction," unless Congress expressly provides otherwise. 28 U.S.C. § 1441(a). In this case, respondents invoked, in support of removal, the district courts' original federal-question jurisdiction over "[a]ny civil action . . . founded on a claim or right arising under the Constitution, treaties or laws of the United States." 28 U.S.C. § 1441(b); see also 28 U.S.C. § 1331.

We have long held that "[t]he presence or absence of federal-question jurisdiction is governed by the 'well-pleaded complaint rule,' which provides that federal jurisdiction exists only when a federal question is presented on the face of the plaintiff's properly pleaded complaint." *Caterpillar Inc. v. Williams*, 482 U.S. 386, 392 (1987). A defense is not part of a plaintiff's properly pleaded statement of his or her claim. . . . Thus, "a case may not be removed to federal court on the basis of a federal defense, . . . even if the defense is anticipated in the plaintiff's complaint, and even if both parties admit that the defense is the only question truly at issue in the case." *Franchise Tax Bd. of Cal. v. Construction Laborers Vacation Trust for Southern Cal.*, 463 U.S. 1, 14 (1983).

Allied as an "independent corollary" to the well-pleaded complaint rule is the further principle that "a plaintiff may not defeat removal by omitting to plead necessary federal questions." If a court concludes that a plaintiff has "artfully pleaded" claims in this fashion, it may uphold removal even though no federal question appears on the face of the plaintiff's complaint. The artful pleading doctrine allows removal where federal law completely preempts a plaintiff's state-law claim. . . . Although federal preemption is ordinarily a defense, "[o]nce an area of state law has been completely preempted, any claim purportedly based on that pre-empted state-law claim is considered, from its inception, a federal claim, and therefore arises under federal law." *Caterpillar.*

B

Petitioners' complaint sought recognition and enforcement of a mortgage. The dispute involved Louisiana parties only, and petitioners relied exclusively on Louisiana law. Respondents defended their removal of the case from state court to federal court on the ground that petitioners' action was precluded, as a matter of federal law, by the earlier Bankruptcy Court orders. We now explain why the removal was improper.

Under the doctrine of claim preclusion, "[a] final judgment on the merits of an action precludes the parties or their privies from relitigating issues that were or could have been raised in that action." *Moitie.* Claim preclusion (res judicata), as Rule 8(c) of the Federal Rules of Civil Procedure makes clear, is an affirmative defense.

A case blocked by the claim preclusive effect of a prior federal judgment differs from the standard case governed by a completely preemptive federal statute in this critical respect: The prior federal judgment does not transform the plaintiff's state-law claims into federal claims but rather extinguishes them altogether. See *Commissioner v. Sunnen*, 333 U.S. 591, 597 (1948) ("The judgment puts an end to the cause of action, which cannot again be brought into litigation between the parties upon any ground whatever, absent fraud or some other factor invalidating the judgment."). Under the well-pleaded complaint rule, preclusion thus remains a defensive plea involving no recasting of the plaintiff's complaint, and is therefore not a proper basis for removal.

In holding removal appropriate here, the Court of Appeals relied on a footnote—the second one—in our *Moitie* opinion. The Fifth Circuit is not alone in concluding from the *Moitie* footnote that removal properly may rest on the alleged preclusive effect of a prior federal judgment. The *Moitie* footnote, however, was a marginal comment and will not bear the heavy weight lower courts have placed on it.

We granted certiorari in *Moitie* principally to address the Ninth Circuit's "novel exception to the doctrine of res judicata." In that case, several actions alleging price fixing by department stores in California were consolidated in federal court and dismissed. Most of the plaintiffs appealed and obtained a reversal, but two chose instead to file separate claims in state court. The defendants removed the actions to Federal District Court, where plaintiffs unsuccessfully moved to remand and defendants successfully moved to dismiss the actions on preclusion grounds. The Court of Appeals for the Ninth Circuit agreed that removal was proper, but held that preclusion did not apply in the unique circumstances of the case.

In the course of reversing the Ninth Circuit's holding on preclusion, we noted, without elaboration, our agreement with the Court of Appeals that "at least some of the claims had a sufficient federal character to support removal." 452 U.S. at 397 n.2. In that case-specific context, we declined to "question ... [the District Court's] factual finding" that the plaintiffs "had attempted to avoid removal jurisdiction by artfully casting their essentially federal[-]law claims as state-law claims."

"*Moitie*'s enigmatic footnote," we recognize, has caused considerable confusion in the circuit courts. We therefore clarify today that *Moitie* did not create a preclusion exception to the rule, fundamental under currently governing legislation, that a defendant cannot remove on the basis of a federal defense.

In sum, claim preclusion by reason of a prior federal judgment is a defensive plea that provides no basis for removal under § 1441(b). Such a defense is properly made in the state proceedings, and the state courts' disposition of it is subject to this Court's ultimate review.[3]

For the foregoing reasons, the judgment of the Court of Appeals for the Fifth Circuit is reversed, and the case is remanded for further proceedings consistent with this opinion.

Note: Rivet *and "Artful Pleading"*

1. As we have seen, one "defense"—that of complete preemption—can serve as the basis for removal. Explain how the preemption issue differs from the preclusion issue in *Rivet*.

2. The "artful pleading" doctrine exists, as Justice Ginsburg notes, to prevent a plaintiff from thwarting removal "by omitting to plead necessary federal questions." She gives the example of complete preemption: "[o]nce an area of state law has been completely pre-empted, any claim purportedly based on that pre-empted state-law claim is considered, from its inception, a federal claim, and therefore arises under federal law." But are there any other applications of the artful pleading doctrine?

One possible example is *City of Chicago v. International College of Surgeons*, 522 U.S. 156 (1997). In that case, plaintiff, the International College of Surgeons (ICS), filed two suits in state court seeking judicial review of decisions by the Chicago Landmarks Commission designating its property as part of a landmark district. Both complaints raised a number of state and federal constitutional claims, including assertions that the city's landmarks ordinances, both on their face and as applied, violated the Due Process and Equal Protection Clauses and effected a taking of property without just compensation under the Fifth and Fourteenth Amendments.

---

3. We note also that under the relitigation exception to the Anti-Injunction Act, 28 U.S.C. § 2283, a federal court may enjoin state-court proceedings "where necessary ... to protect or effectuate its judgments."

The plaintiff's claims would appear to have been tailor-made for a cause of action under 42 U.S.C. § 1983, the federal civil rights statute. But the complaints conspicuously avoided pleading a claim under § 1983. Instead, the complaints alleged Illinois state-law actions for administrative review. The Supreme Court nevertheless held that the suit was properly removed to federal court under § 1331 and § 1441 because "[the plaintiffs'] well-pleaded complaint established that [their] right to relief under state law require[d] resolution of a substantial question of federal law."

3. ICS, in opposing removal of its suit against Chicago, relied heavily on the Court's decision in *Caterpillar Inc. v. Williams*, 482 U.S. 386 (1987). In that case, plaintiffs were employees at Caterpillar who started in managerial and weekly salaried positions but were downgraded to hourly positions covered by Caterpillar's collective bargaining agreement. When the plant closed and the plaintiffs were laid off, they filed an action in state court asserting state-law contract claims. Specifically, they alleged that Caterpillar breached individual employment agreements it had made with the plaintiffs while they served Caterpillar as managers or weekly salaried employees. Caterpillar removed the action to federal court, arguing that the plaintiffs' state-law contract claims were in reality completely pre-empted § 301 claims, which therefore arose under federal law. The Supreme Court rejected the argument, saying:

> Section 301 governs claims founded directly on rights created by collective-bargaining agreements, and also claims "substantially dependent on analysis of a collective-bargaining agreement." *Allis-Chalmers Corp. v. Lueck*, 471 U.S. 202 (1985). Plaintiffs allege that Caterpillar has entered into and breached individual employment contracts with them. Section 301 says nothing about the content or validity of individual employment contracts. It is true that plaintiffs, bargaining unit members at the time of the plant closing, possessed substantial rights under the collective agreement, and could have brought suit under § 301. As masters of the complaint, however, they chose not to do so.
>
> Caterpillar's basic error is its failure to recognize that a plaintiff covered by a collective-bargaining agreement is permitted to assert legal rights independent of that agreement, including state-law contract rights, so long as the contract relied upon is not a collective-bargaining agreement. Caterpillar impermissibly attempts to create the prerequisites to removal by ignoring the set of facts (i.e., the individual employment contracts) presented by plaintiffs, along with their legal characterization of those facts, and arguing that there are different facts plaintiffs might have alleged that would have constituted a federal claim. In sum, Caterpillar does not seek to point out that the contract relied upon by plaintiffs is in fact a collective agreement; rather it attempts to justify removal on the basis of facts not alleged in the complaint. The "artful pleading" doctrine cannot be invoked in such circumstances.
>
> [If] an employer wishes to dispute the continued legality or viability of a pre-existing individual employment contract because an employee has taken a position covered by a collective agreement, it may raise this question in state court. The employer may argue that the individual employment contract has

been pre-empted due to the principle of exclusive representation in §9(a) of the National Labor Relations Act (NLRA). Or the employer may contend that enforcement of the individual employment contract arguably would constitute an unfair labor practice under the NLRA, and is therefore pre-empted. The fact that a defendant might ultimately prove that a plaintiff's claims are pre-empted under the NLRA does not establish that they are removable to federal court.

4. In *ICS*, the Court distinguished *Caterpillar* as follows:

> ICS errs in relying on the established principle that a plaintiff, as master of the complaint, can "choose to have the cause heard in state court." *Caterpillar.* By raising several claims that arise under federal law, ICS subjected itself to the possibility that the City would remove the case to the federal courts.

Has the Court drawn a clear line in explaining when the artful pleading doctrine overrides the "master of the complaint" rule? Consider the Problem that follows.

Problem: Discharge of a Salesman

After many years of working as a salesman for the Acme Company, Willy Loman was fired. He is convinced that he was let go because the managers thought he was "too old to do the job well." He has therefore filed a suit in New Harmony state court alleging that Acme discharged him "because of his age, in violation of section 235 of the New Harmony Law Against Discrimination." Section 235 makes it unlawful for an employer to discriminate against an employee because of age.

The language of section 235 is identical to that of the Age Discrimination in Employment Act of 1972 (ADEA), a federal statute. Acme has removed the suit to federal district court on the theory that Loman's complaint has artfully pleaded a claim under ADEA. Loman has moved to remand the case to state court. Should the motion be granted?

D. Jurisdiction over Declaratory Judgment Actions

Congress enacted the Declaratory Judgment Act in 1934. The Act is now codified in sections 2201 and 2202 of the Judicial Code. Section 2201 creates the declaratory judgment remedy; it provides in relevant part:

> In a case of actual controversy within its jurisdiction, . . . any court of the United States, upon the filing of an appropriate pleading, may declare the rights and other legal relations of any interested party seeking such declaration, whether or not further relief is or could be sought.

As the opening clause makes clear, a federal court may issue a declaratory judgment only in a case of actual controversy "within its jurisdiction." This language signals that the Act is not itself a grant of subject-matter jurisdiction; rather, jurisdictional authorization must be found in some other statute. We turn now to the question: under what circumstances does a declaratory judgment action "arise under" federal law for purposes of the original and removal jurisdiction of the district courts?

This question has proved troublesome, in part because of the difficulty of integrating the declaratory judgment remedy with the well-pleaded complaint rule. In *Franchise Tax Board*, the next principal case, Justice Brennan essayed a comprehensive synthesis of the law. The most important of the earlier decisions is summarized in the Note that follows.

Note: The Skelly Oil *Case*

Skelly Oil Co. v. Phillips Petroleum Co., 339 U.S. 667 (1950), arose out of the following facts (as summarized in the *Franchise Tax Board* opinion):

> Skelly Oil and Phillips had a contract, for the sale of natural gas, that entitled the seller—Skelly Oil—to terminate the contract at any time after December 1, 1946, if the Federal Power Commission had not yet issued a certificate of convenience and necessity to a third party, a pipeline company to whom Phillips intended to resell the gas purchased from Skelly Oil. Their dispute began when the Federal Power Commission informed the pipeline company on November 30 that it would issue a conditional certificate, but did not make its order public until December 2. By this time Skelly Oil had notified Phillips of its decision to terminate their contract.

Phillips then brought an action in United States district court under the federal Declaratory Judgment Act. The complaint alleged that a certificate of public convenience and necessity "within the meaning of the Natural Gas Act and [the] contracts" had been issued prior to Skelly's attempt at termination of the contracts. It sought a declaration that the contracts were therefore still "in effect and binding upon the parties thereto."

The Supreme Court held that the case did not fall within the "arising under" jurisdiction. Justice Frankfurter wrote for the Court:

> "[T]he operation of the Declaratory Judgment Act is procedural only." Congress enlarged the range of remedies available in the federal courts but did not extend their jurisdiction. [In this context, "jurisdiction"] means the kinds of issues which give right of entrance to federal courts. Jurisdiction in this sense was not altered by the Declaratory Judgment Act. Prior to that Act, a federal court would entertain a suit on a contract only if the plaintiff asked for an immediately enforceable remedy like money damages or an injunction, but such relief could only be given if the requisites of jurisdiction, in the sense of a federal right or diversity, provided foundation for resort to the federal courts. The Declaratory Judgment Act allowed relief to be given by way of recognizing the plaintiff's right even though no immediate enforcement of it was asked. But the requirements of jurisdiction—the limited subject matters which alone Congress had authorized the District Courts to adjudicate—were not impliedly repealed or modified.

If Phillips sought damages from [Skelly] or specific performance of their contracts, it could not bring suit in a United States District Court on the theory that it was asserting a federal right. And for the simple reason that such a suit would 'arise' under the State law governing the contracts. Whatever federal claim Phillips may be able to urge would in any event be injected into the case only in anticipation of a defense to be asserted by petitioners. . . .

With exceptions not now relevant, Congress has narrowed the opportunities for entrance into the federal courts, and this Court has been more careful than in earlier days in enforcing these jurisdictional limitations. . . . To be observant of these restrictions is not to indulge in formalism or sterile technicality. It would turn into the federal courts a vast current of litigation indubitably arising under State law, in the sense that the right to be vindicated was State-created, if a suit for a declaration of rights could be brought into the federal courts merely because an anticipated defense derived from federal law. Not only would this unduly swell the volume of litigation in the District Courts but it would also embarrass those courts — and this Court on potential review — in that matters of local law may often be involved, and the District Courts may either have to decide doubtful questions of State law or hold cases pending disposition of such State issues by State courts.

To sanction suits for declaratory relief as within the jurisdiction of the District Courts merely because, as in this case, artful pleading anticipates a defense based on federal law would contravene the whole trend of jurisdictional legislation by Congress, disregard the effective functioning of the federal judicial system and distort the limited procedural purpose of the Declaratory Judgment Act. [The] matter in controversy as to which Phillips asked for a declaratory judgment is not one that 'arises under the * * * laws * * * of the United States,' and [the proceedings] should have been dismissed.

The Court thus viewed Phillips' complaint as an end run around the well pleaded complaint rule. But did the Court have to consider that issue? The complaint alleged that a certificate of public convenience and necessity "within the meaning of the Natural Gas Act *and [the] contracts*" had been issued. (Emphasis added.) Could the Court have rejected jurisdiction on the ground that, even accepting the *Smith* doctrine, a suit does not arise under federal law when federal law has been incorporated into a private contract? This seems to have been the view of Chief Justice Vinson. In a separate opinion, the Chief Justice expressed "real doubts as to whether there is a federal question here at all, even though interpretation of the contract between private parties requires an interpretation of a federal statute and the action of a federal regulatory body."

Franchise Tax Board of California v. Construction Laborers Vacation Trust for Southern California

Supreme Court of the United States, 1983.

463 U.S. 1.

JUSTICE BRENNAN delivered the opinion of the Court.

The principal question in dispute between the parties is whether the Employment Retirement Income Security Act of 1974 (ERISA), permits state tax authorities to collect unpaid state income taxes by levying on funds held in trust for the taxpayers under an ERISA-covered vacation benefit plan. The issue is an important one, which affects thousands of federally regulated trusts and all non-federal tax collection systems, and it must eventually receive a definitive, uniform resolution. Nevertheless, for reasons involving perhaps more history than logic, we hold that the lower federal courts had no jurisdiction to decide the question in the case before us, and we vacate the judgment and remand the case with instructions to remand it to the state court from which it was removed.

I

None of the relevant facts is in dispute. Appellee Construction Laborers Vacation Trust for Southern California (CLVT) is a trust established by an agreement between four associations of employers active in the construction industry in Southern California and [a union organization]. The purpose of the agreement and trust was to establish a mechanism for administering the provisions of a collective bargaining agreement that grants construction workers a yearly paid vacation.[2] The trust agreement expressly proscribes any assignment, pledge, or encumbrance of funds held in trust by CLVT. The plan that CLVT administers is unquestionably an "employee welfare benefit plan" within the meaning of §3 of ERISA, and CLVT and its individual trustees are thereby subject to extensive regulation under titles I and III of ERISA.

Appellant Franchise Tax Board is a California agency charged with enforcement of that State's personal income tax law. California law authorizes appellant to require any person in possession of "credits or other personal property belonging to a taxpayer" "to withhold . . . the amount of any tax, interest, or penalties due from the taxpayer . . . and to transmit the amount withheld to the Franchise Tax Board." Any person who, upon notice by the Franchise Tax Board, fails to comply with its request to withhold and to transmit funds becomes personally liable for the amounts identified in the notice.

In June 1980, the Franchise Tax Board filed a complaint in state court against CLVT and its trustees. Under the heading "First Cause of Action," appellant alleged that CLVT had failed to comply with three levies issued under §18817, concluding with the allegation that it had been "damaged in a sum . . . not to exceed $380.56 plus interest from

---

2. As part of the hourly compensation due bargaining unit members, employers pay a certain amount to CLVT, which places the money in an account for each employee. Once a year, CLVT distributes the money in each account to the employee for whom it is kept, provided the employee complies with CLVT's application procedures. . . .

June 1, 1980." Under the heading "Second Cause of Action," appellant incorporated its previous allegations and added:

> There was at the time of the levies alleged above and continues to be an actual controversy between the parties concerning their respective legal rights and duties. The Board [appellant] contends that defendants [CLVT] are obligated and required by law to pay over to the Board all amounts held . . . in favor of the Board's delinquent taxpayers. On the other hand, defendants contend that section 514 of ERISA preempts state law and that the trustees lack the power to honor the levies made upon them by the State of California.

> . . . [D]efendants will continue to refuse to honor the Board's levies in this regard. Accordingly, a declaration by this court of the parties' respective rights is required to fully and finally resolve this controversy.

In a prayer for relief, appellant requested damages for defendants' failure to honor the levies and a declaration that defendants are "legally obligated to honor all future levies by the Board."

[The complaint did not identify statutory authority for the relief requested; indeed, the only statute mentioned on the face of the complaint is ERISA.]

CLVT removed the case to the United States District Court for the Central District of California, and the court denied the Franchise Tax Board's motion for remand to the state court. On the merits, the District Court ruled that ERISA did not preempt the State's power to levy on funds held in trust by CLVT. CLVT appealed, and the Court of Appeals reversed. . . . We now hold that this case was not within the removal jurisdiction conferred by 28 U.S.C. § 1441, and therefore we do not reach the merits of the preemption question.

II

The jurisdictional structure at issue in this case has remained basically unchanged for the past century. [Justice Brennan summarized the doctrines explored in the preceding sections of this chapter.]

III

Simply to state these principles is not to apply them to the case at hand. Appellants' complaint sets forth two "causes of action," one of which expressly refers to ERISA; if either comes within the original jurisdiction of the federal courts, removal was proper as to the whole case. Although appellant's complaint does not specifically assert any particular statutory entitlement for the relief it seeks, the language of the complaint suggests (and the parties do not dispute) that appellant's "first cause of action" states a claim under Cal. Rev. & Tax. Code § 18818, and its "second cause of action" states a claim under California's Declaratory Judgment Act. As an initial proposition, then, the "law that creates the cause of action" is state law, and original federal jurisdiction is unavailable unless it appears that some substantial, disputed question of federal law is a necessary element of one of the well-pleaded state claims, or that one or the other claim is "really" one of federal law.

A

Even though state law creates appellant's causes of action, its case might still "arise under" the laws of the United States if a well-pleaded complaint established that its right to relief under state law requires resolution of a substantial question of federal law in dispute between the parties. For appellant's first cause of action—to enforce its levy, under §18818—a straightforward application of the well-pleaded complaint rule precludes original federal court jurisdiction. California law establishes a set of conditions, without reference to federal law, under which a tax levy may be enforced; federal law becomes relevant only by way of a defense to an obligation created entirely by state law, and then only if appellant has made out a valid claim for relief under state law. The well-pleaded complaint rule was framed to deal with precisely such a situation. [Since] 1887 it has been settled law that a case may not be removed to federal court on the basis of a federal defense, including the defense of preemption, even if the defense is anticipated in the plaintiff's complaint, and even if both parties admit that the defense is the only question truly at issue in the case.

Appellant's declaratory judgment action poses a more difficult problem. Whereas the question of federal preemption is relevant to appellant's first cause of action only as a potential defense, it is a necessary element of the declaratory judgment claim. Under Cal. Civ. Proc. Code §1060, a party with an interest in property may bring an action for a declaration of another party's legal rights and duties with respect to that property upon showing that there is an "actual controversy relating to the respective rights and duties" of the parties. The only questions in dispute between the parties in this case concern the rights and duties of CLVT and its trustees under ERISA. Not only does appellant's request for a declaratory judgment under California law clearly encompass questions governed by ERISA, but appellant's complaint identifies no other questions as a subject of controversy between the parties. Such questions must be raised in a well-pleaded complaint for a declaratory judgment. Therefore, it is clear on the face of its well-pleaded complaint that appellant may not obtain the relief it seeks in its second cause of action ("[t]hat the court declare defendants legally obligated to honor all future levies by the Board upon [CLVT]") without a construction of ERISA and/or an adjudication of its preemptive effect and constitutionality—all questions of federal law.

Appellant argues that original federal court jurisdiction over such a complaint is foreclosed by our decision in *Skelly Oil Co. v. Phillips Petroleum Co.*, 339 U.S. 667 (1950). As we shall see, however, *Skelly Oil* is not directly controlling. [The Court summarized the *Skelly Oil* case.]

[In *Skelly Oil*, we] observed that, under the well-pleaded complaint rule, an action by Phillips to enforce its contract would not present a federal question. *Skelly Oil* has come to stand for the proposition that "if, but for the availability of the declaratory judgment procedure, the federal claim would arise only as a defense to a state created action, jurisdiction is lacking." 10A C. Wright, A. Miller & M. Kane, *Federal Practice and Procedure* §2767, at 744–45 (2d ed. 1983). *Cf. Public Service Comm'n v. Wycoff*, 344 U.S. 237, 248 (1952) (dictum).

As an initial matter, we must decide whether the doctrine of *Skelly Oil* limits original federal court jurisdiction under § 1331—and by extension removal jurisdiction under § 1441—when a question of federal law appears on the face of a well-pleaded complaint for a state law declaratory judgment. Apparently, it is a question of first impression. As the passage quoted above makes clear, *Skelly Oil* relied significantly on the precise contours of the federal Declaratory Judgment Act as well as of § 1331. The Court's emphasis that the Declaratory Judgment Act was intended to affect only the remedies available in a federal district court, not the court's jurisdiction, was critical to the Court's reasoning. Our interpretation of the federal Declaratory Judgment Act in *Skelly Oil* does not apply of its own force to *state* declaratory judgment statutes, many of which antedate the federal statute.

Yet while *Skelly Oil* itself is limited to the federal Declaratory Judgment Act, fidelity to its spirit leads us to extend it to state declaratory judgment actions as well. If federal district courts could take jurisdiction, either originally or by removal, of state declaratory judgment claims raising questions of federal law, without regard to the doctrine of *Skelly Oil*, the federal Declaratory Judgment Act—with the limitations *Skelly Oil* read into it—would become a dead letter. For any case in which a state declaratory judgment action was available, litigants could get into federal court for a declaratory judgment despite our interpretation of § 2201, simply by pleading an adequate state claim for a declaration of federal law.

Having interpreted the Declaratory Judgment Act of 1934 to include certain limitations on the jurisdiction of federal district courts to entertain declaratory judgment suits, we should be extremely hesitant to interpret the Judiciary Act of 1875 and its 1887 amendments in a way that renders the limitations in the later statute nugatory. Therefore, we hold that under the jurisdictional statutes as they now stand[17] federal courts do not have original jurisdiction, nor do they acquire jurisdiction on removal, when a federal question is presented by a complaint for a state declaratory judgment, but *Skelly Oil* would bar jurisdiction if the plaintiff had sought a federal declaratory judgment.

The question, then, is whether a federal district court could take jurisdiction of appellant's declaratory judgment claim had it been brought under 28 U.S.C. § 2201.[18] The application of *Skelly Oil* to such a suit is somewhat unclear. Federal courts

---

17. It is not beyond the power of Congress to confer a right to a declaratory judgment in a case or controversy arising under federal law—within the meaning of the Constitution or of § 1331—without regard to *Skelly Oil's* particular application of the well-pleaded complaint rule. The 1969 ALI report strongly criticized the *Skelly Oil* doctrine: "If no other changes were to be made in federal question jurisdiction, it is arguable that such language, and the historical test it seems to embody, should be repudiated." ALI Study § 1311, at 170–171. Nevertheless, Congress has declined to make such a change. At this point, any adjustment in the system that has evolved under the *Skelly Oil* rule must come from Congress.

18. It may seem odd that, for purposes of determining whether removal was proper, we analyze a claim brought under state law, in state court, by a party who has continuously objected to district court jurisdiction over its case, as if that party had been trying to get original federal court jurisdiction all along. That irony, however, is a more-or-less constant feature of the removal statute, under which a case is removable if a federal district court could have taken jurisdiction had the same

have regularly taken original jurisdiction over declaratory judgment suits in which, if the declaratory judgment defendant brought a coercive action to enforce its rights, that suit would necessarily present a federal question.[19] Section 502(a)(3) of ERISA specifically grants trustees of ERISA-covered plans like CLVT a cause of action for injunctive relief when their rights and duties under ERISA are at issue, and that action is exclusively governed by federal law.[20] If CLVT could have sought an injunction under ERISA against application to it of state regulations that require acts inconsistent with ERISA,[21] does a declaratory judgment suit by the State "arise under" federal law?

We think not. We have always interpreted what *Skelly Oil* called "the current of jurisdictional legislation since the Act of March 3, 1875," with an eye to practicality and necessity. . . . There are good reasons why the federal courts should not entertain suits by the States to declare the validity of their regulations despite possibly conflicting federal law. States are not significantly prejudiced by an inability to come to federal court for a declaratory judgment in advance of a possible injunctive suit by a person subject to federal regulation. They have a variety of means by which they can enforce their own laws in their own courts, and they do not suffer if the preemption questions such enforcement may raise are tested there.[22] The express grant of federal jurisdiction in ERISA is limited to suits brought by certain parties, as to whom Congress

---

complaint been filed. See Wechsler, *Federal Jurisdiction and the Revision of the Judicial Code*, 13 Law & Contemp. Prob. 216, 234 (1948).

19. For instance, federal courts have consistently adjudicated suits by alleged patent infringers to declare a patent invalid, on the theory that an infringement suit by the declaratory judgment defendant would raise a federal question over which the federal courts have exclusive jurisdiction. See *E. Edelmann & Co. v. Triple-A Specialty Co.*, 88 F.2d 852 (CA7 1937); Hart & Wechsler 896–897. Taking jurisdiction over this type of suit is consistent with the dictum in *Public Service Comm'n of Utah v. Wycoff Co.*, 344 U.S. 237, 248 (1952), which we stated only that a declaratory judgment plaintiff could not get original federal jurisdiction if the anticipated lawsuit by the declaratory judgment defendant would *not* "arise under" federal law. It is also consistent with the nature of the declaratory remedy itself, which was designed to permit adjudication of either party's claims of right. See E. Borchard, *Declaratory Judgments* 15–18, 23–25 (1934).

20. . . . Even if ERISA did not expressly provide jurisdiction, CLVT might have been able to obtain federal jurisdiction under the doctrine applied in some cases that a person subject to a scheme of federal regulation may sue in federal court to enjoin application to him of conflicting state regulations, and a declaratory judgment action by the same person does not necessarily run afoul of the *Skelly Oil* doctrine. *See, e.g., Lake Carriers' Assn. v. MacMullan*, 406 U.S. 498, 506–508 (1972) . . . .

21. We express no opinion, however, whether a party in CLVT's position could sue under ERISA to enjoin or to declare invalid a state tax levy, despite the Tax Injunction Act, 28 U.S.C. §1341. See *California v. Grace Brethren Church*, 457 U.S. 393 (1982). To do so, it would have to show either that state law provided no "speedy and efficient remedy" or that Congress intended §502 of ERISA to be an exception to the Tax Injunction Act.

22. Indeed, as appellant's strategy in this case shows, they may often be willing to go to great lengths to avoid federal-court resolution of a preemption question. Realistically, there is little prospect that States will flood the federal courts with declaratory judgment actions; most questions will arise, as in this case, because a State has sought a declaration in state court and the defendant has removed the case to federal court. Accordingly, it is perhaps appropriate to note that considerations of comity make us reluctant to snatch cases which a State has brought from the courts of that State, unless some clear rule demands it.

presumably determined that a right to enter federal court was necessary to further the statute's purposes.[23] It did not go so far as to provide that any suit *against* such parties must also be brought in federal court when they themselves did not choose to sue. The situation presented by a State's suit for a declaration of the validity of state law is sufficiently removed from the spirit of necessity and careful limitation of district court jurisdiction that informed our statutory interpretation in *Skelly Oil* and *Gully* to convince us that, until Congress informs us otherwise, such a suit is not within the original jurisdiction of the United States district courts. Accordingly, the same suit brought originally in state court is not removable either.

B

CLVT also argues that appellant's "causes of action" are, in substance, federal claims. Although we have often repeated that "the party who brings the suit is master to decide what law he will rely upon," *The Fair v. Kohler Die & Specialty Co.*, 228 U.S. 22, 25 (1913), it is an independent corollary of the well-pleaded complaint rule that a plaintiff may not defeat removal by omitting to plead necessary federal questions in a complaint. [In *Avco*, the Court of Appeals held, and we affirmed,] that the petitioner's action "arose under" § 301, and thus could be removed to federal court, although the petitioner had undoubtedly pleaded an adequate claim for relief under the state law of contracts and had sought a remedy available *only* under state law. [See discussion in Section C.]

CLVT argues by analogy that ERISA, like § 301, was meant to create a body of federal common law, and that "any state court action which would require the interpretation or application of ERISA to a plan document 'arises under' the laws of the United States." ERISA contains provisions creating a series of express causes of action in favor of participants, beneficiaries, and fiduciaries of ERISA-covered plans, as well as the Secretary of Labor. § 502(a). It may be that, as with § 301 as interpreted in *Avco*, any state action coming within the scope of § 502(a) of ERISA would be removable to federal district court, even if an otherwise adequate state cause of action were pleaded without reference to federal law. It does not follow, however, that either of appellant's claims in this case comes within the scope of one of ERISA's causes of action.

The phrasing of § 502(a) is instructive. Section 502(a) specifies which persons—participants, beneficiaries, fiduciaries, or the Secretary of Labor—may bring actions for particular kinds of relief. It neither creates nor expressly denies any cause of action in favor of state governments, to enforce tax levies or for any other purpose. It does not purport to reach every question relating to plans covered by ERISA. Furthermore, § 514(b)(2)(A) of ERISA makes clear that Congress did not intend to preempt entirely every state cause of action relating to such plans. With important, but express

---

23. *Cf.* nn.19 and 20, *supra*. Alleged patent infringers, for example, have a clear interest in swift resolution of the federal issue of patent validity—they are liable for damages if it turns out they are infringing a patent, and they frequently have a delicate network of contractual arrangements with third parties that is dependent on their right to sell or license a product. Parties subject to conflicting state and federal regulatory schemes also have a clear interest in sorting out the scope of each government's authority, especially where they face a threat of liability if the application of federal law is not quickly made clear.

limitations, it states that "nothing in this subchapter shall be construed to relieve any person from any law of any State which regulates insurance, banking, or securities."

Against this background, it is clear that a suit by state tax authorities under a statute like § 18818 does not "arise under" ERISA. Unlike the contract rights at issue in *Avco*, the State's right to enforce its tax levies is not of central concern to the federal statute. For that reason, as in *Gully*, on the face of a well-pleaded complaint there are many reasons completely unrelated to the provisions and purposes of ERISA why the State may or may not be entitled to the relief it seeks. Furthermore, ERISA does not provide an alternative cause of action in favor of the State to enforce its rights, while § 301 expressly supplied the plaintiff in *Avco* with a federal cause of action to replace its preempted state contract claim. Therefore, even though the Court of Appeals may well be correct that ERISA precludes enforcement of the State's levy in the circumstances of this case, an action to enforce the levy is not itself preempted by ERISA.

Once again, appellant's declaratory judgment cause of action presents a somewhat more difficult issue. The question on which a declaration is sought—that of the CLVT trustees' "power to honor the levies made upon them by the State of California,"—is undoubtedly a matter of concern under ERISA. It involves the meaning and enforceability of provisions in CLVT's trust agreement forbidding the trustees to assign or otherwise to alienate funds held in trust, and thus comes within the class of questions for which Congress intended that federal courts create federal common law. Under § 502(a)(3)(B) of ERISA, a participant, beneficiary, or fiduciary of a plan covered by ERISA may bring a declaratory judgment action in federal court to determine whether the plan's trustees may comply with a state levy on funds held in trust. Nevertheless, CLVT's argument that appellant's second cause of action arises under ERISA fails for the second reason given above. ERISA carefully enumerates the parties entitled to seek relief under § 502; it does not provide anyone other than participants, beneficiaries, or fiduciaries with an express cause of action for a declaratory judgment on the issues in this case. A suit for similar relief by some other party does not "arise under" that provision.

IV

Our concern in this case is consistent application of a system of statutes conferring original federal court jurisdiction, as they have been interpreted by this Court over many years. Under our interpretations, Congress has given the lower federal courts jurisdiction to hear, originally or by removal from a state court, only those cases in which a well-pleaded complaint establishes either that federal law creates the cause of action or that the plaintiff's right to relief necessarily depends on resolution of a substantial question of federal law. We hold that a suit by state tax authorities both to enforce its levies against funds held in trust pursuant to an ERISA-covered employee benefit plan, and to declare the validity of the levies notwithstanding ERISA, is neither a creature of ERISA itself nor a suit of which the federal courts will take jurisdiction because it turns on a question of federal law. Accordingly, we vacate the judgment of the Court of Appeals and remand so that this case may be remanded to the Superior Court of the State of California for the County of Los Angeles.

It is so ordered.

Note: Declaratory Judgments, Franchise Tax Board, and the Shaw Footnote

1. Footnote 19 of *Franchise Tax Board* cites with apparent approval the lower-court decisions that "have consistently adjudicated suits by alleged patent infringers to declare a patent invalid, on the theory that an infringement suit by the declaratory judgment defendant would raise a federal question over which the federal courts have exclusive jurisdiction." The exclusive jurisdiction that the Court refers to derives from 28 U.S.C. § 1338, which confers exclusive federal jurisdiction over any claim "arising under any Act of Congress relating to patents, plant variety protection, copyrights and trademarks."

In *Medtronic, Inc. v. Mirowski Family Ventures, LLC*, 134 S. Ct. 843 (2014), the Supreme Court implicitly confirmed these lower court decisions. There, Mirowski licensed Medtronic to use Mirowski's patents in exchange for royalties. The license provided that if Medtronic concluded that its products did not infringe Mirowski's patents, Medtronic could refuse to pay royalties, at which point Mirowski could terminate the license and bring a patent infringement action. At some point, Medtronic stopped paying royalties and brought a declaratory judgment action against Mirowski, seeking a declaration that its products did not infringe Mirowski's patents.

The Supreme Court held that federal jurisdiction was proper over Medtronic's claim. Noting the provision in the licensing agreement that Mirowski could terminate the license and bring a patent infringement suit if Medtronic stopped paying royalties, the Court concluded that the coercive action Mirowski would have brought would have been for patent infringement. The Court wrote:

> Medtronic believes—and seeks to establish in this declaratory judgment suit—that it does not owe royalties because its products are noninfringing. If Medtronic were to act on that belief (by not paying royalties and not bringing a declaratory judgment action), Mirowski could terminate the license and bring an ordinary federal patent law action for infringement. Consequently this declaratory judgment action, which avoids that threatened action, also "arises under" federal patent law.

Accordingly, the Court concluded, Medtronic's claim properly fell within § 1338. Would *Medtronic*'s rationale lead to a different result in *Franchise Tax Board*?

2. On the same day that it handed down the decision in *Franchise Tax Board*, the Court also decided *Shaw v. Delta Airlines*, 463 U.S. 85 (1983). *Shaw* was a consolidation of two separate but similar lawsuits. The suits were brought in federal district court by employers and employees seeking a declaratory judgment that certain provisions of two New York laws (its Human Rights Law and its Disability Benefits Law) were preempted by ERISA. The Supreme Court, like the lower courts, decided the preemption issues on the merits. In footnote 14, the Court said:

> The Court's decision today in *Franchise Tax Board v. Construction Laborers Vacation Trust*, 463 U.S. 1 (1983), does not call into question the lower courts' jurisdiction to decide these cases. *Franchise Tax Board* was an action

seeking a declaration that state laws were *not* pre-empted by ERISA. Here, in contrast, companies subject to ERISA regulation seek injunctions against enforcement of state laws they claim *are* pre-empted by ERISA, as well as declarations that those laws are pre-empted.

It is beyond dispute that federal courts have jurisdiction over suits to enjoin state officials from interfering with federal rights. See *Ex parte Young*, 209 U.S. 123, 160–162 (1908). A plaintiff who seeks injunctive relief from state regulation, on the ground that such regulation is pre-empted by a federal statute which, by virtue of the Supremacy Clause of the Constitution, must prevail, thus presents a federal question which the federal courts have jurisdiction under 28 U.S.C. § 1331 to resolve. See *Smith v. Kansas City Title & Trust Co.*, 255 U.S. 180, 199–200 (1921); *Louisville & Nashville R. Co. v. Mottley*, 211 U.S. 149, 152 (1908); *see also Franchise Tax Board*, 463 U.S. at 18–20, and n.20; Note, Federal Jurisdiction over Declaratory Suits Challenging State Action, 79 Colum. L. Rev. 983, 996–1000 (1979). This Court, of course, frequently has resolved pre-emption disputes in a similar jurisdictional posture. *See, e.g., Ray v. Atlantic Richfield Co.*, 435 U.S. 151 (1978); *Jones v. Rath Packing Co.*, 430 U.S. 529 (1976); *Florida Lime & Avocado Growers, Inc. v. Paul*, 373 U.S. 132 (1963); *Hines v. Davidowitz*, 312 U.S. 52 (1941).

What is the doctrine that distinguishes *Shaw* from *Franchise Tax Board*? Does it make sense to allow jurisdiction in one case but not the other?

Note that the Court's footnote cites cases only for the proposition that section 1331 embraces suits for *injunctive* relief. (You are familiar with both cases. How strongly do they support the proposition?) On what basis do those cases translate into a holding that section 1331 also provides jurisdiction over suits seeking a declaratory judgment?

3. The opinion in *Franchise Tax Board* cites (with the notation "dictum") the decision in *Public Service Commission of Utah v. Wycoff*, 344 U.S. 237 (1952). In that case the Court said:

> Where the complaint in an action for declaratory judgment seeks in essence to assert a defense to an impending or threatened state court action, it is the character of the threatened action, and not of the defense, which will determine whether there is federal-question jurisdiction in the District Court. If the cause of action, which the declaratory defendant threatens to assert, does not itself involve a claim under federal law, it is doubtful if a federal court may entertain an action for a declaratory judgment establishing a defense to that claim. This is dubious even though the declaratory complaint sets forth a claim of federal right, if that right is in reality in the nature of a defense to a threatened cause of action.

In cases like *Shaw*, the "threatened cause of action" is clearly not federal. Does *Shaw* overrule the *Wycoff* "dictum," at least in cases where the plaintiff seeks a declaration that state law is preempted?

4. At the time of the *Mottley* litigation, the federal Declaratory Judgment Act had not been enacted. With the Act now on the books, could the Louisville & Nashville Railroad bring a declaratory judgment action in federal court against Mottleys seeking a declaration that the contract was not preempted by the Hepburn Act? Consider also the Problems that follow.

Problem: Adopting a Highway

Some years ago, the State of New Harmony initiated an Adopt-A-Highway program. The program is designed to reduce the State's litter-control expenses by enlisting volunteers to clean up highway rights-of-way. A brochure produced by the State represents that "any person, organization, club or governmental agency can adopt a section of state highway." The State erects a sign acknowledging the participation of each person or group that adopts a section of highway.

A few months ago, the New Harmony Chapter of the Knights of the Ku Klux Klan (the Klan) applied to participate in the Adopt-A-Highway program. Without approving or denying the Klan's application, the State authorized its attorneys to file a lawsuit in federal district court seeking a declaratory judgment that it is not required by the First Amendment to the United States Constitution to approve the Klan's application. The state's attorneys filed the lawsuit, with the Director of Highways as the named plaintiff.

Attached to the complaint were the official regulations governing the program. One regulation provides that the State may exclude "applicants whose participation would be counterproductive to the program; applicants that discriminate on the basis of race, religion, color, national origin, or disability; and applicants with a history of unlawfully violent or criminal behavior." Another regulation states: "This program is not intended as a means of providing a public forum under the First Amendment to the United States Constitution for the participants to use in promoting name recognition or political causes."

The Klan filed a counterclaim seeking a declaratory judgment and a writ of mandamus ordering the State to allow it to participate in the Adopt-A-Highway program. The counterclaim asserts that "any decision on the part of the State to exclude the Klan's participation in the New Harmony Adopt-A-Highway Program will be a violation of the Klan's First Amendment right to free speech."

You are the law clerk to the United States District Judge to whom the case has been assigned. The judge tells you: "Other states have tried to exclude the Klan from their Adopt-A-Highway programs, and the courts have generally ruled that these attempts violate the Klan's First Amendment rights. But as you know, my first task is to be sure that this court has jurisdiction over this action. The parties are not of diverse citizenship, so if I have jurisdiction, it must be on the basis of a 'federal question.'"

Does the district court have jurisdiction over this case?

Problem: A Medical Provider's Lien

Gerald Hamilton was seriously injured in an automobile accident. He was treated at Acme Medical Center. The expenses of his hospitalization and treatment were covered through Medicaid, a cooperative federal-state program authorized by the federal Medicaid Act.

Hamilton sued the driver of the car and obtained a substantial sum as settlement of his claim. The Oceana Medical Providers Protection Act (MPPA), a law passed by the Oceana legislature last year, authorizes medical providers to "file a lien for all fees for services provided to the beneficiary against any judgment, award or settlement obtained by the beneficiary [from a] third party." Acting under the authority of the MPPA, Acme Medical Center has placed a lien on the settlement that Hamilton received.

Section 1396a of the federal Medicaid Act provides that state Medicaid plans may not allow medical providers (such as Acme) to attempt to collect from a patient who has received payment from a liable third party. Hamilton has brought suit against Acme in federal district court seeking a declaratory judgment that the MPPA is pre-empted by section 1396a.

Acme has moved to dismiss for lack of subject matter jurisdiction. The Medicaid Act does not provide a private right of action. However, Hamilton asserts that the district court has § 1331 jurisdiction over his declaratory judgment suit.

Should the district court grant the motion to dismiss?

E. Supplemental Jurisdiction

Plaintiffs who file suit in federal court often bring both federal claims falling within § 1331 and state-law claims. Traditionally, federal courts could exercise "pendent jurisdiction" over those state-law claims, so long as they bore a sufficiently close relationship to the federal claims over which the court did have § 1331 jurisdiction.

"Pendent jurisdiction" was a judge-created doctrine that traced its lineage to Chief Justice Marshall's opinion in *Osborn v. Bank of United States* (Chapter 2). In the twentieth century, the Court reconfirmed that doctrine in *Mine Workers v. Gibbs*, 383 U.S. 715 (1966). *Gibbs* held that if a federal district court had jurisdiction over a case by reason of one or more federal claims, it could also hear state-law claims not otherwise within its jurisdiction if they bore a sufficiently close relationship to the federal claims.

In the Judicial Improvements Act of 1990, Congress codified the doctrine of pendent jurisdiction and gave it a new name: "supplemental jurisdiction." Section 1367(a) defines supplemental jurisdiction:

> Except as provided in subsections (b) and (c) or as expressly provided otherwise by Federal statute, in any civil action of which the district courts have original jurisdiction, the district courts shall have supplemental jurisdiction over all other claims that are so related to claims in the action within such original jurisdiction that they form part of the same case or controversy under Article III of the United States Constitution. Such supplemental

jurisdiction shall include claims that involve the joinder or intervention of additional parties.

The legislative history of § 1367 makes clear that Congress intended to ratify the approach to supplemental jurisdiction that the Supreme Court adopted in *Gibbs*. For that reason, we look at *Gibbs* before turning to decisions that interpret the 1990 statute.

Supplemental jurisdiction is not limited to cases in which original jurisdiction is based on a federal question; on the contrary, § 1367(a) applies to "any civil action of which the district courts have original jurisdiction," irrespective of the basis of that jurisdiction. However, the second part of the statute, § 1367(b), substantially cuts back on the availability of supplemental jurisdiction in diversity cases. The interplay of § 1367 and diversity jurisdiction doctrines is briefly discussed in Chapter 11, section B.

United Mine Workers of America v. Gibbs

Supreme Court of the United States, 1966.

383 U.S. 715.

MR. JUSTICE BRENNAN delivered the opinion of the Court.

Respondent Paul Gibbs was awarded compensatory and punitive damages in this action against petitioner United Mine Workers of America (UMW) for alleged violations of § 303 of the Labor Management Relations Act, 1947, and of the common law of Tennessee. [Section 303 provides a federal cause of action for persons injured by various coercive activities of labor unions, including secondary boycotts.] The case grew out of the rivalry between the United Mine Workers and the Southern Labor Union over representation of workers in the southern Appalachian coal fields. Tennessee Consolidated Coal Company, not a party here, laid off 100 miners of the UMW's Local 5881 when it closed one of its mines in southern Tennessee during the spring of 1960. Late that summer, Grundy Company, a wholly owned subsidiary of Consolidated, hired respondent as mine superintendent to attempt to open a new mine on Consolidated's property at nearby Gray's Creek through use of members of the Southern Labor Union. As part of the arrangement, Grundy also gave respondent a contract to haul the mine's coal to the nearest railroad loading point.

On August 15 and 16, 1960, armed members of Local 5881 forcibly prevented the opening of the mine, threatening respondent and beating an organizer for the rival union. [There was no further violence at the mine site, and the mine remained closed.]

Respondent lost his job as superintendent, and never entered into performance of his haulage contract. He testified that he soon began to lose other trucking contracts and mine leases he held in nearby areas. Claiming these effects to be the result of a concerted union plan against him, he sought recovery not against Local 5881 or its members, but only against petitioner, the international union. The suit was brought in the United States District Court for the Eastern District of Tennessee, and jurisdiction was premised on allegations of secondary boycotts under § 303. The state law claim, for which jurisdiction was based upon the doctrine of pendent jurisdiction, asserted "an unlawful conspiracy and an unlawful boycott aimed at him and [Grundy] to maliciously, wantonly and willfully interfere with his contract of employment and with his contract of haulage."

[The jury found a violation of both state and federal law, and Gibbs was awarded compensatory and punitive damages.]

I.

A threshold question is whether the District Court properly entertained jurisdiction of the claim based on Tennessee law. There was no need to decide a like question in [an earlier case] since the pertinent state claim there was based on peaceful secondary activities and we held that state law based on such activities had been preempted by § 303. But here respondent's claim is based in part on proofs of violence and intimidation. . . .

The fact that state remedies were not entirely pre-empted does not, however, answer the question whether the state claim was properly adjudicated in the District Court absent diversity jurisdiction. The Court held in *Hurn v. Oursler*, 289 U.S. 238, that state law claims are appropriate for federal court determination if they form a separate but parallel ground for relief also sought in a substantial claim based on federal law. . . .

[In the years following the decision in *Hurn*] there has been some tendency to limit its application to cases in which the state and federal claims are, as in *Hurn*, "little more than the equivalent of different epithets to characterize the same group of circumstances."

This limited approach is unnecessarily grudging. Pendent jurisdiction, in the sense of judicial power, exists whenever there is a claim "arising under [the] Constitution, the Laws of the United States, and Treaties made, or which shall be made, under their Authority * * *," U.S. Const., art. III, § 2, and the relationship between that claim and the state claim permits the conclusion that the entire action before the court comprises but one constitutional "case." The federal claim must have substance sufficient to confer subject matter jurisdiction on the court. The state and federal claims must derive from a common nucleus of operative fact. But if, considered without regard to their federal or state character, a plaintiff's claims are such that he would ordinarily be expected to try them all in one judicial proceeding, then, assuming substantiality of the federal issues, there is power in federal courts to hear the whole.

That power need not be exercised in every case in which it is found to exist. It has consistently been recognized that pendent jurisdiction is a doctrine of discretion, not of plaintiff's right. Its justification lies in considerations of judicial economy, convenience and fairness to litigants; if these are not present a federal court should hesitate to exercise jurisdiction over state claims, even though bound to apply state law to them. Needless decisions of state law should be avoided both as a matter of comity and to promote justice between the parties, by procuring for them a surer-footed reading of applicable law. Certainly, if the federal claims are dismissed before trial, even though not insubstantial in a jurisdictional sense, the state claims should be dismissed as well.

Similarly, if it appears that the state issues substantially predominate, whether in terms of proof, of the scope of the issues raised, or of the comprehensiveness of the remedy sought, the state claims may be dismissed without prejudice and left for resolution to state tribunals.

There may, on the other hand, be situations in which the state claim is so closely tied to questions of federal policy that the argument for exercise of pendent jurisdiction is particularly strong. In the present case, for example, the allowable scope of the state claim implicates the federal doctrine of pre-preemption; while this interrelationship does not create statutory federal question jurisdiction, *Louisville & N.R. Co. v. Mottley*, 211 U.S. 149, its existence is relevant to the exercise of discretion. Finally, there may be reasons independent of jurisdictional considerations, such as the likelihood of jury confusion in treating divergent legal theories of relief, that would justify separating state and federal claims for trial, Fed. Rule Civ. Proc. 42(b). If so, jurisdiction should ordinarily be refused.

The question of power will ordinarily be resolved on the pleadings. But the issue whether pendent jurisdiction has been properly assumed is one which remains open throughout the litigation. Pretrial procedures or even the trial itself may reveal a substantial hegemony of state law claims, or likelihood of jury confusion, which could not have been anticipated at the pleading stage. Although it will of course be appropriate to take account in this circumstance of the already completed course of the litigation, dismissal of the state claim might even then be merited. For example, it may appear that the plaintiff was well aware of the nature of his proofs and the relative importance of his claims; recognition of a federal court's wide latitude to decide ancillary questions of state law does not imply that it must tolerate a litigant's effort to impose upon it what is in effect only a state law case. Once it appears that a state claim constitutes the real body of a case, to which the federal claim is only an appendage, the state claim may fairly be dismissed.

We are not prepared to say that in the present case the District Court exceeded its discretion in proceeding to judgment on the state claim. . . .

Although § 303 limited recovery to compensatory damages based on secondary pressures, and state law allowed both compensatory and punitive damages, and allowed such damages as to both secondary and primary activity, the state and federal claims arose from the same nucleus of operative fact and reflected alternative remedies. Indeed, the verdict sheet sent in to the jury authorized only one award of damages, so that recovery could not be given separately on the federal and state claims. . . . Moreover, the question whether the permissible scope of the state claim was limited by the doctrine of pre-emption afforded a special reason for the exercise of pendent jurisdiction; the federal courts are particularly appropriate bodies for the application of pre-emption principles. We thus conclude that although it may be that the District Court might, in its sound discretion, have dismissed the state claim, the circumstances show no error in refusing to do so.

City of Chicago v. International College of Surgeons

Supreme Court of the United States, 1997.

522 U.S. 156.

JUSTICE O'CONNOR delivered the opinion of the Court.

The city of Chicago, like municipalities throughout the country, has an ordinance that provides for the designation and protection of historical landmarks. The city's Landmarks Ordinance is administered by the Commission on Chicago Historical and Architectural Landmarks (the Chicago Landmarks Commission or the Commission). Pursuant to the Illinois Administrative Review Law, judicial review of final decisions of a municipal landmarks commission lies in state circuit court. In this case, we are asked to consider whether a lawsuit filed in the Circuit Court of Cook County seeking judicial review of decisions of the Chicago Landmarks Commission may be removed to federal district court, where the case contains both federal constitutional and state administrative challenges to the Commission's decisions.

I

[Respondent International College of Surgeons owns] two properties on North Lake Shore Drive in the city of Chicago. In July 1988, the Chicago Landmarks Commission made a preliminary determination that seven buildings on Lake Shore Drive, including two mansions on ICS's properties, qualified for designation as a landmark district under the city's Landmarks Ordinance. In June 1989, the city council enacted an ordinance (the Designation Ordinance) designating the landmark district.

. . . In October 1990, ICS applied to the Landmarks Commission for the necessary permits to allow demolition of a designated landmark. The Commission denied the permit applications, finding that the proposed demolition would "adversely affect and destroy significant historical and architectural features of the [landmark] district." ICS then reapplied for the permits under a provision of the Landmarks Ordinance allowing for exceptions in cases of economic hardship. The Commission again denied the applications, finding that ICS did not qualify for the hardship exception.

Following each of the Commission's decisions, ICS filed actions for judicial review in the Circuit Court of Cook County pursuant to the Illinois Administrative Review Law. Both of ICS's complaints raised a number of federal constitutional claims, including that the Landmarks and Designation Ordinances, both on their face and as applied, violate the Due Process and Equal Protection Clauses and effect a taking of property without just compensation under the Fifth and Fourteenth Amendments, and that the manner in which the Commission conducted its administrative proceedings violated ICS's rights to due process and equal protection. The complaints also sought relief under the Illinois Constitution as well as administrative review of the Commission's decisions denying the permits.

The defendants (collectively the City), who are petitioners in this Court, removed both lawsuits to the District Court for the Northern District of Illinois on the basis of federal question jurisdiction. The District Court consolidated the cases. After dismissing some of the constitutional claims and exercising supplemental jurisdiction over the state law claims, the court granted summary judgment in favor of the City, ruling that the Landmarks and Designation Ordinances and the Commission's proceedings were consistent with the Federal and State Constitutions, and that the Commission's findings were supported by the evidence in the record and were not arbitrary and capricious.

The Court of Appeals for the Seventh Circuit reversed and remanded the case to state court, concluding that the District Court was without jurisdiction. . . .

* * *

We granted certiorari to address whether a case containing claims that local administrative action violates federal law, but also containing state law claims for on-the-record review of the administrative findings, is within the jurisdiction of federal district courts. Because neither the jurisdictional statutes nor our prior decisions suggest that federal jurisdiction is lacking in these circumstances, we now reverse.

II

A

We have reviewed on several occasions the circumstances in which cases filed initially in state court may be removed to federal court. [For this part of the opinion, *see* the Note in Section B of this chapter] . . . By raising several claims that arise under federal law, ICS subjected itself to the possibility that the City would remove the case to the federal courts.

As for ICS's accompanying state law claims, this Court has long adhered to principles of pendent and ancillary jurisdiction by which the federal courts' original jurisdiction over federal questions carries with it jurisdiction over state law claims that "derive from a common nucleus of operative fact," such that "the relationship between [the federal] claim and the state claim permits the conclusion that the entire action before the court comprises but one constitutional 'case.'" *Mine Workers v. Gibbs*, 383 U.S. 715, 725 (1966). Congress has codified those principles in the supplemental jurisdiction statute, which combines the doctrines of pendent and ancillary jurisdiction under a common heading. 28 U.S.C. § 1367. . . . That provision applies with equal force to cases removed to federal court as to cases initially filed there; a removed case is necessarily one "of which the district courts have original jurisdiction." See § 1441(a); *Carnegie-Mellon Univ. v. Cohill*, 484 U.S. 343, 350–51(1988) (discussing pendent claims removed to federal court).

Here, once the case was removed, the District Court had original jurisdiction over ICS's claims arising under federal law, and thus could exercise supplemental jurisdiction over the accompanying state law claims so long as those claims constitute "other claims that . . . form part of the same case or controversy." We think it clear that they do. The claims for review of the Commission's decisions are legal "claims," in the sense that that term is generally used in this context to denote a judicially cognizable cause of action. And the state and federal claims "derive from a common nucleus of operative fact," namely, ICS's unsuccessful efforts to obtain demolition permits from the

Chicago Landmarks Commission. That is all the statute requires to establish supplemental jurisdiction (barring an express statutory exception, see § 1367(a)). ICS seemed to recognize as much in the amended complaint it filed in the District Court following removal, stating that the nonfederal claims "are subject to this Court's pendent jurisdiction." We conclude, in short, that the District Court properly exercised federal question jurisdiction over the federal claims in ICS's complaints, and properly recognized that it could thus also exercise supplemental jurisdiction over ICS's state law claims.

B

ICS, urging us to adopt the reasoning of the Court of Appeals, argues that the District Court was without jurisdiction over its actions because they contain state law claims that require on-the-record review of the Landmarks Commission's decisions. A claim that calls for deferential judicial review of a state administrative determination, ICS asserts, does not constitute a "civil action ... of which the district courts of the United States have original jurisdiction" under 28 U.S.C. § 1441(a).

That reasoning starts with an erroneous premise. Because this is a federal question case, the relevant inquiry is not, as ICS submits, whether its state claims for on-the-record review of the Commission's decisions are "civil actions" within the "original jurisdiction" of a district court: The district court's original jurisdiction derives from ICS's federal claims, not its state law claims. Those federal claims suffice to make the actions "civil actions" within the "original jurisdiction" of the district courts for purposes of removal. § 1441(a). The Court of Appeals, in fact, acknowledged that ICS's federal claims, "if brought alone, would be removable to federal court." Nothing in the jurisdictional statutes suggests that the presence of related state law claims somehow alters the fact that ICS's complaints, by virtue of their federal claims, were "civil actions" within the federal courts' "original jurisdiction."

Having thus established federal jurisdiction, the relevant inquiry respecting the accompanying state claims is whether they fall within a district court's supplemental jurisdiction, not its original jurisdiction. And that inquiry turns, as we have discussed, on whether the state law claims "are so related to [the federal] claims ... that they form part of the same case or controversy." § 1367(a); see *Gibbs* (distinguishing between "the issue whether a claim for relief qualifies as a case 'arising under ... the Laws of the United States' and the issue whether federal and state claims constitute one 'case' for pendent jurisdiction purposes"). ICS's proposed approach—that we first determine whether its state claims constitute "civil actions" within a district court's "original jurisdiction"—would effectively read the supplemental jurisdiction statute out of the books: The whole point of supplemental jurisdiction is to allow the district courts to exercise pendent jurisdiction over claims as to which original jurisdiction is lacking. ...

III

Of course, to say that the terms of § 1367(a) authorize the district courts to exercise supplemental jurisdiction over state law claims for on-the-record review of administrative decisions does not mean that the jurisdiction must be exercised in all cases. Our decisions have established that pendent jurisdiction "is a doctrine of discretion, not of plaintiff's right," *Gibbs*, and that district courts can decline to exercise jurisdiction over pendent claims for a number of valid reasons. [In *Cohill* we observed:] "As articulated by *Gibbs*, the doctrine of pendent jurisdiction thus is a doctrine of flexibility, designed to allow courts to deal with cases involving pendent claims in the manner that most sensibly accommodates a range of concerns and values." Accordingly, we have indicated that "district courts [should] deal with cases involving pendent claims in the manner that best serves the principles of economy, convenience, fairness, and comity which underlie the pendent jurisdiction doctrine." *Cohill*.

The supplemental jurisdiction statute codifies these principles. After establishing that supplemental jurisdiction encompasses "other claims" in the same case or controversy as a claim within the district courts' original jurisdiction, § 1367(a), the statute confirms the discretionary nature of supplemental jurisdiction by enumerating the circumstances in which district courts can refuse its exercise:

> (c) The district courts may decline to exercise supplemental jurisdiction over a claim under subsection (a) if—

> (1) the claim raises a novel or complex issue of State law,

> (2) the claim substantially predominates over the claim or claims over which the district court has original jurisdiction,

> (3) the district court has dismissed all claims over which it has original jurisdiction, or

> (4) in exceptional circumstances, there are other compelling reasons for declining jurisdiction. 28 U.S.C. § 1367(c).

Depending on a host of factors, then—including the circumstances of the particular case, the nature of the state law claims, the character of the governing state law, and the relationship between the state and federal claims—district courts may decline to exercise jurisdiction over supplemental state law claims. The statute thereby reflects the understanding that, when deciding whether to exercise supplemental jurisdiction, "a federal court should consider and weigh in each case, and at every stage of the litigation, the values of judicial economy, convenience, fairness, and comity." *Cohill*. In this case, the District Court decided that those interests would be best served by exercising jurisdiction over ICS's state law claims.

In addition to their discretion under § 1367(c), district courts may be obligated not to decide state law claims (or to stay their adjudication) where one of the abstention doctrines articulated by this Court applies. Those doctrines embody the general notion that "federal courts may decline to exercise their jurisdiction, in otherwise exceptional circumstances, where denying a federal forum would clearly serve an important countervailing interest, for example where abstention is warranted by considerations of proper constitutional adjudication, regard for federal-state relations, or wise judicial administration." *Quackenbush v. Allstate Ins. Co.*, 517 U.S. 706 (1996) [Chapter 16]. We have recently outlined the various abstention principles, and need not elaborate them here except to note that there may be situations in which a district court should abstain from reviewing local administrative determinations even if the jurisdictional prerequisites are otherwise satisfied.

IV

The District Court properly recognized that it could exercise supplemental jurisdiction over ICS's state law claims, including the claims for on-the-record administrative review of the Landmarks Commission's decisions. ICS contends that abstention principles required the District Court to decline to exercise supplemental jurisdiction, and also alludes to its contention below that the District Court should have refused to exercise supplemental jurisdiction under 28 U.S.C. § 1367(c). We express no view on those matters, but think it the preferable course to allow the Court of Appeals to address them in the first instance. Accordingly, we reverse the judgment of the Court of Appeals and remand the case for further proceedings consistent with this opinion.

JUSTICE GINSBURG, with whom JUSTICE STEVENS joins, dissenting.

This now-federal case originated as an appeal in state court from a municipal agency's denials of demolition permits. The review that state law provides is classically appellate in character—on the agency's record, not de novo. Nevertheless, the court decides today that this standard brand of appellate review can be shifted from the appropriate state tribunal to a federal court of first instance at the option of either party—plaintiff originally or defendant by removal. The Court approves this enlargement of district court authority explicitly in federal-question cases, and by inescapable implication in diversity cases, satisfied that "neither the jurisdictional statutes nor our prior decisions suggest that federal jurisdiction is lacking."

The Court's authorization of cross-system appeals qualifies as a watershed decision. After today, litigants asserting federal-question or diversity jurisdiction may routinely lodge in federal courts direct appeals from the actions of all manner of local (county and municipal) agencies, boards, and commissions. Exercising this cross-system appellate authority, federal courts may now directly superintend local agencies by affirming, reversing, or modifying their administrative rulings.

The Court relies on the statutory words found in both 28 U.S.C. §§ 1331 and 1332: "The district courts shall have original jurisdiction of all civil actions. . . ." Then, as its linchpin, the Court emphasizes the 1990 codification and expansion, in § 1367, of what previously had been known as "ancillary jurisdiction" and "pendent jurisdiction." . . . [1] The bare words of §§ 1331, 1332, and 1367(a) permit the Court's construction. For the reasons advanced in this opinion, however, I do not construe these prescriptions, on allocation of judicial business to federal courts of first instance, to embrace the category of appellate business at issue here.

---

1. The Court assumes, although § 1367 does not expressly so provide, that the section covers cases originating in a state court and removed to a federal court. Although the point has not been briefed, I do not question that assumption.

The Court's expansive reading, in my judgment, takes us far from anything Congress conceivably could have meant. Cross-system appeals, if they are to be introduced into our federal system, should stem from the National Legislature's considered and explicit decision. In accord with the views of the large majority of federal judges who have considered the question, I would hold the cross-system appeal unauthorized by Congress, and affirm the Seventh Circuit's judgment.

[Remainder of lengthy dissent omitted.]

Lyon v. Whisman

United States Court of Appeals for the Third Circuit, 1995.

45 F.3d 758.

Before GREENBERG and McKEE, CIRCUIT JUDGES, and POLLAK, DISTRICT JUDGE.*

GREENBERG, CIRCUIT JUDGE.

I. Introduction

Patricia A. Lyon sued her employer, Whisman & Associates, an accounting firm which is a Delaware corporation, and its president James A. Whisman, in the United States District Court for the District of Delaware, charging that they failed to pay her overtime wages as required by the Fair Labor Standards Act ("FLSA"), 29 U.S.C. § 207(a). As a matter of convenience we will refer to both defendants as Whisman. Lyon's complaint also included Delaware contract and tort claims charging that Whisman failed to pay her a promised bonus on time or in full. At trial Lyon prevailed on all three grounds. Whisman then appealed, challenging only the judgment on the tort claim. We must vacate the judgments on both of the state law claims, however, because the claims did not share a "common nucleus of operative fact" with the FLSA claim, and thus the district court lacked subject matter jurisdiction over them supplemental to its federal question jurisdiction over the FLSA claim.

. . . Lyon began working as a bookkeeper for Whisman in January 1988 on an at-will basis for hourly wages. Lyon and Whisman soon became embroiled in a dispute over a bonus that Whisman promised to pay Lyon at the end of 1988; by 1989 Lyon planned to find a new job. Whisman, however, threatened to rescind the bonus if Lyon left its employment. Although Whisman eventually did pay Lyon a bonus, she charges that the payment was late and was for less than the promised amount.

After Lyon left Whisman's employment she filed a three-count complaint alleging that it had

> (1) violated the FLSA, 29 U.S.C. § 207(a), by failing to pay overtime wages;

> (2) violated Delaware contract law by paying a bonus smaller than promised; and

---

* Honorable Louis H. Pollak, Senior United States District Judge for the Eastern District of Pennsylvania, sitting by designation.

(3) violated Delaware tort law by threatening to withhold a vested bonus if she left its employ.

The district court had federal question jurisdiction over Lyon's FLSA claim under 28 U.S.C. § 1331, and Lyon asserted that it had "pendent" federal jurisdiction over the state law claims in counts two and three. Neither the district court nor Whisman questioned this assertion of pendent jurisdiction which, in accordance with 28 U.S.C. § 1367, we usually will call supplemental jurisdiction. Since the district court did not have diversity jurisdiction, it could entertain the state-law claims only by exercising supplemental jurisdiction.

At trial Lyon won on all three counts. She recovered $731.20 on the contract claim and $5,000 in compensatory damages and $20,000 in punitive damages on the tort claim.[3] We cannot ascertain what she recovered on the FLSA claim as the docket sheets do not reflect the amount and the parties make no reference to it in their briefs. Whisman appealed only from the judgment on count three, the Delaware law tort claim. We have jurisdiction pursuant to 28 U.S.C. § 1291.

II. Discussion

Although neither the parties nor the district court questioned the court's supplemental jurisdiction over Lyon's state law contract and tort claims, we inquire into that jurisdiction on our own initiative. See *Bender v. Williamsport Area Sch. Dist.*, 475 U.S. 534, 541 (1986). Consequently following oral argument we directed the parties to file briefs on this point and they have done so.

A. The Constitutional Test

Congress has authorized district courts to exercise jurisdiction supplemental to their federal question jurisdiction in 28 U.S.C. § 1367 . . . In *Sinclair v. Soniform, Inc.*, 935 F.2d 599, 603 (3d Cir. 1991), we treated section 1367 as codifying the jurisdictional standard established in *United Mine Workers v. Gibbs*, 383 U.S. 715 (1966).[4] *Gibbs* laid down three requirements for supplemental jurisdiction. First, "[t]he federal claim must have substance sufficient to confer subject matter jurisdiction on the court." *Gibbs*. Lyon's FLSA claim satisfies this standard.

The other two requirements before federal courts may exercise supplemental jurisdiction to hear state law claims are:

> [1] The state and federal claims must derive from a common nucleus of operative facts. [2] But if, considered without regard to their federal or state character, a plaintiff's claims are such that he would ordinarily be expected to try them all in one judicial proceeding, then, assuming substantiality of the federal issues, there is power in federal courts to hear the whole.

Despite the ambiguity of the language connecting [1] the "nexus" requirement with [2] the "one proceeding" standard, all judicial authority finds that they are cumulative: state claims must satisfy both before a district court may exercise supplemental

---

3. The punitive damages verdict was for $75,000 but Lyon accepted a remittitur reducing the damages to $20,000.

jurisdiction. Because we find that there was an insufficient factual nexus between the federal and state claims to establish a common nucleus of operative facts, we will not consider the "one proceeding" arm of *Gibbs*.

B. The Case-Specific Nature of the Inquiry

The test for a "common nucleus of operative facts" is not self-evident. Indeed, "[i]n trying to set out standards for supplemental jurisdiction and to apply them consistently, we observe that, like unhappy families, no two cases of supplemental jurisdiction are exactly alike." *Nanavati v. Burdette Tomlin Memorial Hosp.*, 857 F.2d 96, 105 (3d Cir. 1988).

We can illustrate the fact-sensitive nature of supplemental jurisdiction determinations by contrasting our treatment of state defamation claims in *Nanavati* with our treatment of similar claims in *PAAC v. Rizzo*, 502 F.2d 306 (3d Cir. 1974). In *Nanavati*, we found that the district court had the power to adjudicate a slander claim asserted by an antitrust defendant, noting that "a critical background fact (the enmity between the two physicians) is common to all claims." We concluded that the alleged slanders naturally would become part of the antitrust trial since the slander victim might use the slanderer's allegedly wrongful behavior to justify the victim's conduct which the other party contended was actionable under the antitrust laws. In *PAAC*, however, we ruled that the district court lacked jurisdiction over a state defamation claim in a suit brought under the Economic Opportunity Act charging the defendant with unlawfully interfering with the agency established under that law. In *PAAC* we recited the operative language of *Gibbs* and found that the state claims were not related sufficiently to the federal claim to permit the exercise of pendent jurisdiction.

The line that separates *Nanavati* and *PAAC* is Article III of the Constitution. Both cases fall near the line; one is on one side, the other is on the other side. In most instances the question whether Article III is satisfied is not that close. For example, when the same acts violate parallel federal and state laws, the common nucleus of operative facts is obvious and federal courts routinely exercise supplemental jurisdiction over the state law claims. *See, e.g., Pueblo Int'l, Inc. v. De Cardona*, 725 F.2d 823, 826 (1st Cir. 1984) (finding jurisdiction over claims under Puerto Rico constitution, civil rights laws, and antitrust laws where federal jurisdiction was established under parallel laws, observing that "[t]he facts necessary to prove a violation of one are practically the same as those needed to prove a violation of the other").

Thus, district courts will exercise supplemental jurisdiction if the federal and state claims "are merely alternative theories of recovery based on the same acts," *Lentino v. Fringe Employee Plans, Inc.*, 611 F.2d 474, 479 (3d Cir. 1979). In *Lentino*, for instance, we recognized that there was federal jurisdiction over a state legal malpractice claim joined with an ERISA claim because the alleged malpractice involved precisely the same acts that the plaintiffs charged constituted a breach of fiduciary duties under ERISA. In *White v. County of Newberry*, 985 F.2d 168 (4th Cir. 1993), landowners sued the county for "response costs" under CERCLA and for inverse condemnation, claiming that the county's discharge of toxic waste into groundwater and wells effectively took their property. In sustaining the exercise of supplemental jurisdiction over the state law inverse condemnation claim, the court said that "[b]oth claims share the common element of showing that the County engaged in an act—a release [CERCLA language] or an affirmative, positive, aggressive act [South Carolina inverse condemnation language]—that in this case would be the dumping or disposal of [a toxin] in a manner that caused contamination. . . ." Two areas in which the federal courts quite commonly exercise supplemental jurisdiction based on "alternative theories of recovery based on the same acts" are state fraud claims in securities cases and state assault claims in civil rights suits charging police abuses.

On the other hand, we have refused to exercise supplemental jurisdiction over state claims totally unrelated to a cause of action under federal law. For instance, in *Local No. 1 (ACA) v. International Bhd. of Teamsters*, 614 F.2d 846 (3d Cir. 1980), we found the district court powerless to try a state-law salary dispute when federal jurisdiction arose from a union merger dispute actionable under the Labor Management Relations Act ("LMRA"). We reasoned that "the merger and salary claims are factually distinct and do not meet the test enunciated in *United Mine Workers v. Gibbs*. . . . [The two are] not derived 'from a common nucleus of operative facts.'"

As might be expected there are closer cases than those we have described. Furthermore, the courts have not been consistent in defining the nexus between the federal and state claims necessary to support supplemental jurisdiction in these closer cases. Thus, some courts have stated that even a "loose" nexus is enough. . . . Numerous other decisions implicitly reject the loose nexus test. Here we see no need to define how close the nexus between the federal and state claims must be to support the exercise of supplemental jurisdiction for, as we will demonstrate, under any standard the nexus between the federal and state claims in this case is inadequate for that purpose.

C. Implications of the Employer/Employee Nexus

. . . The only link between Lyon's FLSA and state law claims is the general employer-employee relationship between the parties. In *Prakash v. American Univ.*, 727 F.2d 1174 (D.C. Cir. 1984), the court seemingly found such a relationship sufficient to confer supplemental jurisdiction over state claims. In *Prakash* a terminated professor sued his former employer, asserting FLSA claims as well as state law claims for breach of contract, interference with contractual relations, conversion, deceit, and defamation. In finding that the district court had jurisdiction over the state law claims, the court of appeals said that "[t]he federal and nonfederal claims [plaintiff] advances 'derive from a common nucleus of operative facts'—[the plaintiff's] contract dispute with the university. . . ."

Arguably *Prakash* is factually distinguishable from this case. Fairly read, however, we believe that *Prakash* stands for the proposition that FLSA plaintiffs can try all state law contract claims against their employers in a federal proceeding, as the employment relationship alone provides a factual nexus sufficient to confer supplemental jurisdiction.

Yet there is virtually no support for this broad reading of the reach of Article III and of *Gibbs*.[9] In *Hales v. Winn-Dixie Stores, Inc.*, 500 F.2d 836 (4th Cir. 1974), the court ruled that it could not entertain a state-law claim for failure to make payments from a profit-sharing plan despite the factual link to a federal claim under the Welfare and Pension Plans Disclosure Act, charging that a plan administrator failed to provide statutorily required information. The factual nexus in *Winn-Dixie*, where both claims revolved around a specific area of employer-employee relations, presents stronger grounds for jurisdiction than cases based solely on the general employment relationship. Nonetheless, the court found that:

> [t]he record establishes beyond doubt that the [two counts] do not grow out of a 'common nucleus of operative facts' [citing *Gibbs*]. . . . While plaintiffs may have sought [the federally mandated] information in order to consider and/or assert their [state law] claims, their causes of action under both Counts I and II are separately maintainable and determinable without any reference to the facts alleged or contentions stated in or with regard to the other count.

District courts have resisted expanding supplemental jurisdiction based merely on an employment contract in a variety of federal statutory settings. Thus, in both *Nicol v. Imagematrix, Inc.*, 767 F. Supp. 744 (E.D. Va. 1991), and *Benton v. Kroger Co.*, 635 F. Supp. 56 (S.D. Tex. 1986), the courts refused to permit plaintiffs to use Title VII discrimination suits, combined with their status as employees, to bootstrap state claims into federal court. In declining to entertain state contract and fraud claims in a sexual discrimination suit, *Nicol* pointedly noted that the sole common fact between the state and federal claims was the employment relationship. In *Benton*, the plaintiff contended that her employer fired her either as an act of sexual discrimination or in retaliation for her having filed a worker's compensation claim. The court refused to consider the state law retaliation claim, finding that "[a]lleged incidents of sexual harassment or gender bias were entirely separate from the circumstances surrounding plaintiff's back injury. These separate events can hardly be grouped as the 'common nucleus of operative facts. . . .'"

We find these precedents compelling. Lyon's FLSA claim involved very narrow, well-defined factual issues about hours worked during particular weeks. The facts relevant to her state law contract and tort claims, which involved Whisman's alleged underpayment of a bonus and its refusal to pay the bonus if Lyon started looking for another job, were quite distinct. In these circumstances it is clear that there is so little overlap between the evidence relevant to the FLSA and state claims, that there is no "common nucleus of operative fact" justifying supplemental jurisdiction over the state law

9. We note that even under the opinion of the *Prakash* court it might be found that the district court lacked jurisdiction over Lyon's state tort claim, inasmuch as the *Prakash* court predicated its finding that there was federal jurisdiction on the nexus between the federal and state claims created by the employment relationship. Nevertheless, because we find the *Prakash* decision unconvincing, we do not analyze the difference between supplemental jurisdiction based on the nature of the claim, be it tort or contract. In both cases, we question the existence of a sufficient factual nexus to confer jurisdiction.

claims. In fact, it would be charitable to characterize the relationship of the federal and state claims as involving even a "loose" nexus. Thus, Article III bars federal jurisdiction. . . .

We do not mean to imply that a district court never may exercise supplemental jurisdiction over state claims in an FLSA action. For example, an employee seeking to enforce an employment contract granting hourly wages in excess of the (statutorily required) time and a half probably could assert her state law contract claim on a supplemental jurisdictional basis along with her FLSA claim in a district court, since the "operative facts" in the two claims would be identical. But still, when a court exercises federal jurisdiction pursuant to a rather narrow and specialized federal statute it should be circumspect when determining the scope of its supplemental jurisdiction. Accordingly, Congressional intent may provide a second, non-constitutional ground for finding that the district court did not have jurisdiction over Lyon's state law claims.[10]

III. Conclusion

Because we find that the district court lacked subject matter jurisdiction over Lyon's state law contract and tort claims, we will vacate its judgments on those two counts and remand the matter with instructions to dismiss those claims without prejudice. Of course, the district court did have jurisdiction over Lyon's FLSA claim, and our decision does not disturb the judgment on that count.

Note: The Supplemental Jurisdiction Statute

1. In *Lyon*, as in *Mottley*, neither party raised the jurisdictional issue; nevertheless, the court did so and found jurisdiction wanting. As noted in Chapter 9, the subject-matter jurisdiction of a federal court cannot be waived, and objections can be raised at any time. *See* Fed. R. Civ. Pro. 12(h)(3).

2. The Third Circuit in *Lyon* rejects what it calls the "loose nexus test" for determining whether a state claim can be brought under supplemental jurisdiction. Could the court have upheld the jurisdiction here without embracing that test? The court says, "The only link between Lyon's FLSA and state law claims is the general employer-employee relationship between the parties." Is that a persuasive characterization?

3. The court declines to follow the D.C. Circuit decision in *Prakash*. The court says, "Fairly read, . . . *Prakash* stands for the proposition that FLSA plaintiffs can try *all* state law contract claims against their employers in a federal proceeding, as *the employment relationship alone* provides a factual nexus sufficient to confer supplemental jurisdiction." (Emphasis added.) Look again at the description of the two state-law claims in this case. Is it necessary to hold that plaintiffs can try *all* state law contract claims

---

10. While our result may seem harsh as this case was tried without jurisdictional objection in the district court, we point out that in all likelihood Lyon will be able to file her state law claims in the Delaware state courts without being barred by the statute of limitations. See *Frombach v. Gilbert Assocs., Inc.*, 236 A.2d 363 (Del. 1967); *Howmet Corp. v. City of Wilmington*, 285 A.2d 423 (Del. Super. Ct. 1971). However, our conclusion is not dependent on that belief.

against their employers in a federal proceedings in order to allow Lyon to pursue claims (2) and (3) in this proceeding? For example, might the court have allowed the jurisdiction in this case while rejecting it where the state-law claims involved conditions of employment or conditions in the workplace?

4. Because the court finds that the nexus requirement is not met, it does not address the "one proceeding" portion of the *Gibbs* test. How would you analyze the case under the "one proceeding" test?

5. *Lyon* was decided by the Third Circuit before the Supreme Court decision in *ICS*. Does *ICS* cast doubt on the holding or analysis in *Lyon*? Consider the Problem below.

6. The Supreme Court's opinion in *ICS* emphasizes that supplemental jurisdiction "is a doctrine of discretion." It quotes the language in *Mine Workers v. Gibbs* stating that "district courts [should] deal with cases involving pendent claims in the manner that best serves the principles of economy, convenience, fairness, and comity which underlie the pendent jurisdiction doctrine." The Court then says that that the supplemental jurisdiction statute "codifies these principles."

Compare the formulation in *Gibbs* with the language of § 1367(c). Is it persuasive to say that the statute "codifies" the *Gibbs* principles?

In a decision handed down before *ICS*, the Ninth Circuit said: "By providing that an exercise of discretion under subsection 1367(c)(4) ought to be made only in 'exceptional circumstances' Congress has sounded a note of caution that the bases for declining jurisdiction should be extended beyond the circumstances identified in subsections (c)(1)–(3) only if the circumstances are quite unusual." *Executive Software North America, Inc. v. U.S. District Court*, 24 F.3d 1545 (9th Cir. 1994). Should *ICS* be read as rejecting that conclusion? Or is the discussion too perfunctory to be treated as resolving the issue?

For a comprehensive discussion of the positions of the various circuits, see Rachel Ellen Hinkle, Comment, *The Revision of 28 U.S.C. § 1367(c) and the Debate over the District Court's Discretion to Decline Supplemental Jurisdiction*, 69 TENN. L. REV. 111 (2001).

Problem: A Disappointed Ex-Employee

Mark Hartley has brought suit in federal district court against Apex Motor Co., his former employer. Hartley worked as a salesman for Apex for five years before he was discharged. The complaint is in three counts. Count I alleges that Hartley was discharged by Apex solely because of his age and thus in violation of the federal Age Discrimination in Employment Act (ADEA). Hartley seeks to recover his actual and liquidated damages as provided for by ADEA.

Count II of the complaint alleges that plaintiff had an oral contract with Apex by which he was promised that he would "always" have a position with Apex as long as he met certain sales objectives; that Hartley met the sales objectives; and that in firing him Apex violated this oral contract. Count III alleges "willful and tortious misconduct on the part of the Apex in violation of a duty owed the plaintiff of continued employment." This count essentially sounds as a violation of the "duty of fair dealing."

The parties are not diverse, and Apex has moved to dismiss the two state-law counts (Counts II and III) for want of subject matter jurisdiction. Hartley asserts that the district court has supplemental jurisdiction over the state-law claims.

How should the court rule on the motion to dismiss?

Note: Tolling and Supplemental Claims

1. Under section 1367(c), as under *Gibbs*, a district court may decline to exercise jurisdiction over supplemental claims. If the plaintiff wishes to pursue the claims that the district court has dismissed, the plaintiff must file an action in state court. But suppose the statute of limitations has run. Are the claims barred?

Before the enactment of § 1367, the answer to that question depended solely on state law. Now, § 1367 provides a tolling rule that must be applied by state courts:

> (d) The period of limitations for any claim asserted under subsection (a), and for any other claim in the same action that is voluntarily dismissed at the same time as or after the dismissal of the claim under subsection (a), shall be tolled while the claim is pending and for a period of 30 days after it is dismissed unless State law provides for a longer tolling period.

In *Jinks v. Richland County*, 538 U.S. 456 (2003), the Court explained the operation of § 1367(d) and upheld its constitutionality. The Court said:

> [Section 1367(d)] provides an alternative to the unsatisfactory options that federal judges faced when they decided whether to retain jurisdiction over supplemental state-law claims that might be time barred in state court. In the pre-§ 1367(d) world, they had three basic choices: First, they could condition dismissal of the state-law claim on the defendant's waiver of any statute-of-limitations defense in state court. That waiver could be refused, however, in which case one of the remaining two choices would have to be pursued. Second, they could retain jurisdiction over the state-law claim even though it would more appropriately be heard in state court. That would produce an obvious frustration of statutory policy. And third, they could dismiss the state-law claim but allow the plaintiff to reopen the federal case if the state court later held the claim to be time barred. That was obviously inefficient. By providing a straightforward tolling rule in place of this regime, § 1367(d) unquestionably promotes fair and efficient operation of the federal courts and is therefore conducive to the administration of justice.
>
> And it is conducive to the administration of justice for another reason: It eliminates a serious impediment to access to the federal courts on the part of plaintiffs pursuing federal- and state-law claims that "derive from a common nucleus of operative fact." Prior to enactment of § 1367(d), they had the following unattractive options: (1) They could file a single federal-court action, which would run the risk that the federal court would dismiss the state-law claims after the limitations period had expired; (2) they could file a single state-law action, which would abandon their right to a federal

forum; (3) they could file separate, timely actions in federal and state court and ask that the state-court litigation be stayed pending resolution of the federal case, which would increase litigation costs with no guarantee that the state court would oblige. Section 1367(d) replaces this selection of inadequate choices with the assurance that state-law claims asserted under § 1367(a) will not become time barred while pending in federal court.

The Court held that § 1367 is within the power of Congress under Article I and that it does not violate principles of state sovereignty.

2. Section 1367(d) tolls the limitations period for "any claim *asserted* under subsection (a)." (Emphasis added.) Suppose that, as in *Lyon*, the plaintiff "asserts" a claim under § 1367(a), but the court finds that the claim does not come within the statute. Does § 1367(d) still toll the limitations period? The Third Circuit in *Lyon* seems to have assumed that it does not; the court, in discussing the issue, refers only to state law. See footnote 10 in the opinion.

Is there any federal interest in tolling the limitations period for state-law claims that are not "so related to claims [over which the court has jurisdiction] that they form part of the same case or controversy"? Note that the Court in *Jinks* refers to "plaintiffs pursuing federal- and state-law claims *that 'derive from a common nucleus of operative fact.'*" (Emphasis added.) Should that description be read as establishing that the tolling provision applies only to claims that do fall within § 1367(a)?

Chapter 11

Diversity Jurisdiction

From 1789 to the present day, the federal trial courts have had original and removal jurisdiction over suits between citizens of different states, provided that the amount in controversy exceeds a specified sum. In the Judiciary Act of 1789, the sum was set at $500. Since then, Congress raised the amount on five separate occasions; it now stands at $75,000.

Over the years, numerous issues have arisen as to whether particular cases or classes of cases fall within the statutory jurisdiction. Some of these issues have been resolved by legislation. For example, the federal courts long wrestled with the problem of determining citizenship when suits were filed by or against guardians or administrators. In 1988, Congress dealt with the matter by amending § 1332. The statute now provides in section (c):

> For the purposes of this section and section 1441 of this title . . . (2) the legal representative of the estate of a decedent shall be deemed to be a citizen only of the same State as the decedent, and the legal representative of an infant or incompetent shall be deemed to be a citizen only of the same State as the infant or incompetent.

Courts also had difficulties in determining whether diversity existed in suits involving corporations that were incorporated in more than one state. An amendment in 1958, also codified as part of § 1332(c), eliminated that conundrum:

> (c) For the purposes of this section and section 1441 of this title — (1) a corporation shall be deemed to be a citizen of any State by which it has been incorporated and of the State where it has its principal place of business . . . .

The 1958 amendment itself turned out to contain an ambiguity (did "State" include foreign states?), and in 2011 Congress further amended the statute to clarify the point. (See the Note following the *Carden* case *infra* section A.)

Notwithstanding these various amendments, numerous issues remain open to litigation. In recent years the Supreme Court has seldom addressed questions involving diversity jurisdiction, so the law has been developed largely by the lower courts. This law is embodied in a collection of rules, tests, and exceptions that will vary (although often only in details) from one circuit to another.

In this chapter we look at some of the important and recurring issues that determine whether a particular suit falls within the "diversity jurisdiction" conferred by 28 U.S.C. § 1332. We begin by considering suits brought by or against corporations and other artificial entities. Next, we examine some of the problems of determining whether the amount in controversy requirement is satisfied. This leads to an issue that divided the courts of appeals for years until the Supreme Court resolved it in a landmark 5-4 ruling: whether the supplemental jurisdiction statute, 28 U.S.C. § 1367, "allows parties who cannot themselves satisfy § 1332's amount-in-controversy requirement to sue in federal court by joining forces with a plaintiff who can."

Some issues of diversity jurisdiction arise primarily or exclusively in the context of removal. These are addressed in Chapter 12.

A. Corporations and Other Entities as Parties

The 1958 amendment to § 1332 defined the citizenship of a corporation for purposes of diversity jurisdiction. But it said nothing about how federal courts were to deal with suits by or against unincorporated associations or other artificial entities. And it introduced a new subject for litigation at the jurisdictional stage: how should courts determine the "principal place of business" of a corporation that carries out activities in more than one state? We examine these issues in turn.

Carden v. Arkoma Associates

Supreme Court of the United States, 1990.

494 U.S. 185.

JUSTICE SCALIA delivered the opinion of the Court.

The question presented in this case is whether, in a suit brought by a limited partnership, the citizenship of the limited partners must be taken into account to determine diversity of citizenship among the parties.

I

Respondent Arkoma Associates (Arkoma), a limited partnership organized under the laws of Arizona, brought suit on a contract dispute in the United States District Court for the Eastern District of Louisiana, relying upon diversity of citizenship for federal jurisdiction. The defendants, C. Tom Carden and Leonard L. Limes, citizens of Louisiana, moved to dismiss, contending that one of Arkoma's limited partners was also a citizen of Louisiana. The District Court denied the motion but certified the question for interlocutory appeal, which the Fifth Circuit declined. Thereafter Magee Drilling Company intervened in the suit and, together with the original defendants, counterclaimed against Arkoma under Texas law. Following a bench trial, the District Court awarded Arkoma a money judgment plus interest and attorney's fees; it dismissed Carden and Limes' counterclaim as well as Magee's intervention and counterclaim. Carden, Limes, and Magee (petitioners here) appealed, and the Fifth Circuit affirmed. With respect to petitioners' jurisdictional challenge, the Court of Appeals found complete diversity, reasoning that Arkoma's citizenship should be determined by reference to the citizenship of the general, but not the limited, partners. We granted certiorari.

II

Article III of the Constitution provides, in pertinent part, that "the judicial Power shall extend to . . . Controversies . . . between Citizens of different States." Congress first authorized the federal courts to exercise diversity jurisdiction in the Judiciary Act of 1789. In its current form, the diversity statute provides that "the district courts shall have original jurisdiction of all civil actions where the matter in controversy exceeds . . . $ 50,000 . . . , and is between . . . citizens of different States. . . ." 28 U.S.C. § 1332(a). Since its enactment, we have interpreted the diversity statute to require "complete diversity" of citizenship. See *Strawbridge v. Curtiss*, 3 Cranch 267 (1806). The District Court erred in finding complete diversity in this case unless (1) a limited partnership may be considered in its own right a "citizen" of the State that created it, or (2) a federal court must look to the citizenship of only its general, but not its limited, partners to determine whether there is complete diversity of citizenship. We consider these questions in turn.

A

We have often had to consider the status of artificial entities created by state law insofar as that bears upon the existence of federal diversity jurisdiction. The precise question posed under the terms of the diversity statute is whether such an entity may be considered a "citizen" of the State under whose laws it was created.

A corporation is the paradigmatic artificial "person," and the Court has considered its proper characterization under the diversity statute on more than one occasion — not always reaching the same conclusion. Initially, we held that a corporation "is certainly not a citizen," so that to determine the existence of diversity jurisdiction the Court must "look to the character of the individuals who compose [it]." *Bank of United States v. Deveaux*, 5 Cranch 61 (1809). We overruled *Deveaux* 35 years later in *Louisville, C. & C. R. Co. v. Letson*, 2 How. 497 (1844), which held that a corporation is "capable of being treated as a citizen of [the State which created it], as much as a natural person." Ten years later, we reaffirmed the result of *Letson*, though on the somewhat different theory that "those who use the corporate name, and exercise the faculties conferred by it," should be presumed conclusively to be citizens of the corporation's State of incorporation. *Marshall v. Baltimore & Ohio R. Co.*, 16 How. 314 (1854).

While the rule regarding the treatment of corporations as "citizens" has become firmly established, we have (with an exception to be discussed presently) just as firmly resisted extending that treatment to other entities. For example, in *Chapman v. Barney*, 129 U.S. 677 (1889), a case involving an unincorporated "joint stock company," we raised the question of jurisdiction on our own motion, and found it to be lacking:

> On looking into the record we find no satisfactory showing as to the citizenship of the plaintiff. The allegation of the amended petition is, that the United States Express Company is a joint stock company organized under a law of the State of New York, and is a citizen of that State. But the express company cannot be a *citizen* of New York, within the meaning of the statutes regulating jurisdiction, unless it be a corporation. The allegation that the

company was *organized* under the laws of New York is not an allegation that it is a corporation. In fact the allegation is, that the company is *not* a corporation, but a joint stock company—that is, a mere partnership.

Similarly, in *Great Southern Fire Proof Hotel Co. v. Jones*, 177 U.S. 449 (1900), we held that a "limited partnership association"—although possessing "some of the characteristics of a corporation" and deemed a "citizen" by the law creating it—may not be deemed a "citizen" under the jurisdictional rule established for corporations. "That rule must not be extended." As recently as 1965, our unanimous opinion in *Steelworkers v. R. H. Bouligny, Inc.*, 382 U.S. 145, reiterated that "the doctrinal wall of *Chapman v. Barney*" would not be breached.

The one exception to the admirable consistency of our jurisprudence on this matter is *Puerto Rico v. Russell & Co.*, 288 U.S. 476 (1933), which held that the entity known as a *sociedad en comandita*, created under the civil law of Puerto Rico, could be treated as a citizen of Puerto Rico for purposes of determining federal-court jurisdiction. The *sociedad*'s juridical personality, we said, "is so complete in contemplation of the law of Puerto Rico that we see no adequate reason for holding that the *sociedad* has a different status for purposes of federal jurisdiction than a corporation organized under that law."

Arkoma fairly argues that this language, and the outcome of the case, "reflect the Supreme Court's willingness to look beyond the incorporated/unincorporated dichotomy and to study the internal organization, state law requirements, management structure, and capacity or lack thereof to act and/or sue, to determine diversity of citizenship." The problem with this argument lies not in its logic, but in the fact that the approach it espouses was proposed and specifically rejected in *Bouligny*. There, in reaffirming "the doctrinal wall of *Chapman v. Barney*," we explained *Russell* as a case resolving the distinctive problem "of fitting an exotic creation of the civil law . . . into a federal scheme which knew it not." There could be no doubt, after *Bouligny*, that at least common-law entities (and likely all entities beyond the Puerto Rican *sociedad en comandita*) would be treated for purposes of the diversity statute pursuant to what *Russell* called "the tradition of the common law," which is "to treat as legal persons only incorporated groups and to assimilate all others to partnerships."

Arkoma claims to have found another exception to our *Chapman* tradition in *Navarro Savings Assn. v. Lee*, 446 U.S. 458 (1980). That case, however, did not involve the question whether a party that is an artificial entity other than a corporation can be considered a "citizen" of a State, but the quite separate question whether parties that were undoubted "citizens" (viz., natural persons) were the real parties to the controversy. The plaintiffs in *Navarro* were eight individual trustees of a Massachusetts business trust, suing in their own names. The defendant, Navarro Savings Association, disputed the existence of complete diversity, claiming that the trust beneficiaries rather than the trustees were the real parties to the controversy, and that the citizenship of the former and not the latter should therefore control. In the course of rejecting this claim, we did indeed discuss the characteristics of a Massachusetts business trust—not at all, however, for the purpose of determining whether the trust had attributes making it a "citizen," but only for the purpose of establishing that the respondents were "active trustees whose control over the assets held in their names is real and substantial," thereby bringing them under the rule, "more than 150 years" old, which permits such trustees "to sue in their own right, without regard to the citizenship of the trust beneficiaries."

Navarro, in short, has nothing to do with the *Chapman* question, except that it makes available to respondent the argument by analogy that, just as business reality is taken into account for purposes of determining whether a trustee is the real party to the controversy, so also it should be taken into account for purposes of determining whether an artificial entity is a citizen. That argument is, to put it mildly, less than compelling.

B

As an alternative ground for finding complete diversity, Arkoma asserts that the Fifth Circuit correctly determined its citizenship solely by reference to the citizenship of its general partners, without regard to the citizenship of its limited partners. Only the general partners, it points out, "manage the assets, control the litigation, and bear the risk of liability for the limited partnership's debts," and, more broadly, "have exclusive and complete management and control of the operations of the partnership." This approach of looking to the citizenship of only some of the members of the artificial entity finds even less support in our precedent than looking to the State of organization (for which one could at least point to *Russell*). We have never held that an artificial entity, suing or being sued in its own name, can invoke the diversity jurisdiction of the federal courts based on the citizenship of some but not all of its members. No doubt some members of the joint stock company in *Chapman*, the labor union in *Bouligny*, and the limited partnership association in *Great Southern* exercised greater control over their respective entities than other members. But such considerations have played no part in our decisions.

To support its approach, Arkoma seeks to press *Navarro* into service once again, arguing that just as that case looked to the trustees to determine the citizenship of the business trust, so also here we should look to the general partners, who have the management powers, in determining the citizenship of this partnership. As we have already explained, however, *Navarro* had nothing to do with the citizenship of the "trust," since it was a suit by the trustees in their own names.

The dissent supports Arkoma's argument on this point, though [under] the rubric of determining which parties supposedly before the Court are the real parties, rather than under the rubric of determining the citizenship of the limited partnership. The dissent asserts that "the real party to the controversy approach"—by which it means an approach that looks to "control over the conduct of the business and the ability to initiate or control the course of litigation"—"has been implemented by the Court both in its oldest and in its most recent cases examining diversity jurisdiction with respect to business associations." Not a single case the dissent discusses, either old or new, supports that assertion. . . .

[Admittedly, the 1854 decision in *Marshall*] contains language quite clearly adopting a "real party to the controversy" approach, and arguably even adopting a "control" test for that status. ("The court . . . will look behind the corporate or collective name . . . to find the persons who act *as the representatives, curators, or trustees. . . .*" (Emphasis added.) "The presumption arising from the habitat of a corporation in the place of its creation [is] conclusive as to the residence or citizenship *of those who use the corporate name and exercise the faculties conferred by it . . . .*" (Emphasis added.)) But as we have also discussed, and as the last quotation shows, that analysis was a complete fiction; the real citizenship of the shareholders (or the controlling shareholders) was not consulted at all.[3] From the fictional *Marshall*, the dissent must leap almost a century and a third to *Navarro* to find a "real party to the controversy" analysis that discusses "control." That case, as we have said, is irrelevant, since it involved not a juridical person but the distinctive common-law institution of trustees. . . .

In sum, we reject the contention that to determine, for diversity purposes, the citizenship of an artificial entity, the court may consult the citizenship of less than all of the entity's members. We adhere to our oft-repeated rule that diversity jurisdiction in a suit by or against the entity depends on the citizenship of "all the members," *Chapman*, "the several persons composing such association," *Great Southern*, "each of its members," *Bouligny*.

C

The resolutions we have reached above can validly be characterized as technical, precedent-bound, and unresponsive to policy considerations raised by the changing realities of business organization. But, as must be evident from our earlier discussion, that has been the character of our jurisprudence in this field after *Letson*. See Currie, *The Federal Courts and the American Law Institute*, 36 U. Chi. L. Rev. 1, 35 (1968). Arkoma is undoubtedly correct that limited partnerships are functionally similar to "other types of organizations that have access to federal courts," and is perhaps correct that "considerations of basic fairness and substance over form require that limited partnerships receive similar treatment." Similar arguments were made in *Bouligny*. The District Court there had upheld removal because it could divine "no common sense reason for treating an unincorporated national labor union differently from a corporation," and we recognized that that contention had "considerable merit." We concluded, however, that "whether unincorporated labor unions ought to be assimilated to the status of corporations for diversity purposes" is "properly a matter for legislative consideration which cannot adequately or appropriately be dealt with by this Court." In other words, having entered the field of diversity policy with

---

3. *Marshall*'s fictional approach appears to have been abandoned. Later cases revert to the formulation of *Louisville, C. & C. R. Co. v. Letson*, 2 How. 497 (1844), that the corporation has its own citizenship. See *Great Southern Fire Proof Hotel Co. v. Jones*, 177 U.S. 449 (1900) ("For purposes of jurisdiction . . . a corporation was to be deemed a citizen of the State creating it") (citing *Letson*); *Chapman v. Barney*, 129 U.S. 677 (1889) ("express company cannot be a *citizen* of New York, within the meaning of the statutes regulating jurisdiction, unless it be a corporation").

regard to artificial entities once (and forcefully) in *Letson*, we have left further adjustments to be made by Congress.

Congress has not been idle. In 1958 it revised the rule established in *Letson*, providing that a corporation shall be deemed a citizen not only of its State of incorporation but also "of the State where it has its principal place of business." 28 U.S.C. § 1332(c). No provision was made for the treatment of artificial entities other than corporations, although the existence of many new, post-*Letson* forms of commercial enterprises, including at least the sort of joint stock company at issue in *Chapman*, the sort of limited partnership association at issue in *Great Southern*, and the sort of Massachusetts business trust at issue in *Navarro*, must have been obvious.

Thus, the course we take today does not so much disregard the policy of accommodating our diversity jurisdiction to the changing realities of commercial organization, as it honors the more important policy of leaving that to the people's elected representatives. Such accommodation is not only performed more legitimately by Congress than by courts, but it is performed more intelligently by legislation than by interpretation of the statutory word "citizen." The 50 States have created, and will continue to create, a wide assortment of artificial entities possessing different powers and characteristics, and composed of various classes of members with varying degrees of interest and control. Which of them is entitled to be considered a "citizen" for diversity purposes, and which of their members' citizenship is to be consulted, are questions more readily resolved by legislative prescription than by legal reasoning, and questions whose complexity is particularly unwelcome at the threshold stage of determining whether a court has jurisdiction. We have long since decided that, having established special treatment for corporations, we will leave the rest to Congress; we adhere to that decision.

III

Arkoma argues that even if this Court finds complete diversity lacking with respect to Carden and Limes, we should nonetheless affirm the judgment with respect to Magee because complete diversity indisputably exists between Magee and Arkoma. This question was not considered by the Court of Appeals. We decline to decide it in the first instance, and leave it to be resolved by the Court of Appeals on remand.

The judgment of the Court of Appeals is reversed, and the case is remanded for further proceedings consistent with this opinion.

Justice O'Connor, with whom Justice Brennan, Justice Marshall, and Justice Blackmun join, dissenting.

The only potentially nondiverse party in this case is a limited partner. All other parties, including the general partners and the limited partnership itself, assuming it is a citizen, are diverse. Thus, the Court has before it a single question—whether the citizenship of a limited partner must be counted for purposes of diversity jurisdiction. The Court first addresses whether the limited partnership is a "citizen." I do not consider that issue, because even if we were to hold that a limited partnership is a citizen, we are still required to consider which, if any, of the other citizens before the Court as members of Arkoma Associates are real parties to the controversy, *i.e.*, which parties have control over the subject of and litigation over the controversy. See *Marshall v. Baltimore & Ohio R. Co.*, 16 How. 314 (1854). Application of that test leads me to conclude that limited partners are not real parties to the controversy and, therefore, should not be counted for purposes of diversity jurisdiction.

I

The Court asserts that "we have long since decided" to leave to Congress the issue of the proper treatment of unincorporated associations for diversity purposes, because the issue of which business association "is entitled to be considered a 'citizen' for diversity purposes, and which of their members' citizenship is to be consulted, are questions more readily resolved by legislative prescription than by legal reasoning." That assertion is insupportable in light of *Navarro Savings Assn. v. Lee*, 446 U.S. 458 (1980) (determination of which members of unincorporated business trust must be considered for purposes of diversity jurisdiction), and even *Steelworkers v. R. H. Bouligny, Inc.*, 382 U.S. 145 (1965) (determination of proper treatment of union for diversity jurisdiction purposes according to settled law; Congress has power to change result), on which the Court relies. Indeed, the Court in this case does not leave the issue to Congress, but rather decides the issue and then invokes deference to Congress to justify its newly formulated rule that the Court will, without analysis of the particular entity before it, count every member of an unincorporated association for purposes of diversity jurisdiction. In my view, the Court properly tackles the issue, because "application of statutes to situations not anticipated by the legislature is a preeminently judicial function." Currie, *Federal Courts and the American Law Institute*, 36 U. Chi. L. Rev. 1, 35 (1968).

II

. . . Since the early 19th century, one of the benchmarks for determining whether a particular party among those involved in the litigation must be counted for purposes of diversity jurisdiction has been whether the party has a "real interest" in the suit or, in other words, is a "real party" to the controversy. . . .

The real party to the controversy approach has been implemented by the Court both in its oldest and in its most recent cases examining diversity jurisdiction with respect to business associations. . . .

[For example, in *Marshall*,] the determination whether the corporation was a citizen did not signal the end of the diversity jurisdiction inquiry. Rather, the Court engaged in a two-part inquiry: (1) is the corporation a "juridical person" which can serve as a real party to the controversy; and (2) are the shareholders real parties to the controversy. To determine whether the corporation or the shareholders were real parties to the controversy, the Court considered which citizens held control over the business decisions and assets of the corporation and over the initiation and course of litigation involving the corporation. The corporation, as the representative body of the shareholders, itself had such power. The shareholders did not. . . .

Having concluded that the shareholders were not the real parties to the controversy, the Court held that only the State of incorporation of the corporate entity need be counted for purposes of diversity jurisdiction and that the citizenship of the shareholders would be presumed to be that of the State of incorporation. As the Court makes plain in *Marshall*, consideration of whether the shareholders were real parties to the controversy was a necessary prerequisite to the creation of the legal fiction that their citizenship would be deemed that of the corporation. . . .

In the [most recent] case, in which application of the real party to the controversy test was appropriate, the Court unanimously applied it. [This was] *Navarro Savings Assn. v. Lee*, 446 U.S. 458 (1980). In that case, the Court addressed the question whether the beneficiaries' citizenship must be counted when the trustees brought suit involving the assets of the trust. Because the trust beneficiaries lacked both control over the conduct of the business and the ability to initiate or control the course of litigation, the Court held that the citizenship of the trust beneficiaries should not be counted. . . .

The Court attempts to distinguish *Navarro* on the ground that it involved not a juridical person, but rather the "distinctive common-law institution of trustees." Such a view is consonant with the Court's new diversity jurisdiction analysis announced in this case, but fails to take into account the actual language and analysis in *Navarro*. If the nature of the institution of trustees was sufficient to answer the question of which parties to count for diversity jurisdiction purposes in that case, the Court's discussion of whether the trust beneficiaries were real parties to the controversy would have been wholly superfluous. Given that the Court granted certiorari in that case on the very issue whether the citizenship of trust beneficiaries must be counted, and then unanimously applied the real parties to the controversy test, the discussion clearly was not superfluous.

Application of the parties to the controversy test to the limited partnership yields the conclusion that limited partners should not be considered for purposes of diversity jurisdiction. Like the trust beneficiary in *Navarro*, the limited partner "can neither control the disposition of this action nor intervene in the affairs of the trust except in the most extraordinary situations." See, [*e.g.*,] Uniform Limited Partnership Act § 26, 6 U.L.A. 614 (1969) (limited partner "is not a proper party to proceedings by or against a partnership, except where the object is to enforce a limited partner's right against or liability to the partnership"). . . . Without the power to "control . . . the assets" or to initiate or "control the litigation," *Navarro*, the limited partner is not a real party to the controversy and, therefore, should not be counted for purposes of diversity jurisdiction. Because the majority of States have adopted the Uniform Limited Partnership Act, this rule would result in uniform treatment of limited partners for purposes of diversity jurisdiction. . . .

Because there is complete diversity between petitioners and the limited partnership (assuming that it should be considered a citizen) and each of the general partners, the issue presented by this case is fully resolved by application of the parties to the controversy test.

III

. . . It is hardly an answer to the history of the limited partnership in this country and abroad to assert that it appears 25 years after *Steelworkers v. R. H. Bouligny, Inc.*, 382 U.S. 145 (1965). The "admirable consistency of our jurisprudence" is not blemished by distinguishing between unions and limited partnerships. It is, however, severely marred by holding that an association within the continental United States is not afforded the same treatment as its virtually identical Puerto Rican counterpart. The Court's decision today, endorsing treatment of a Puerto Rican business association as an entity while refusing to treat as an entity its virtually identical stateside counterpart, is justified neither by our precedents nor by historical and commercial realities.

For the foregoing reasons, I respectfully dissent.

Note: Artificial Entities as Parties

1. Both the majority and dissent in *Carden* rely on the 1965 decision in *Steelworkers v. R. H. Bouligny, Inc.*, 382 U.S. 145, in which the Court held unanimously that a labor union is not a "juridical person" and therefore is not a "citizen" for purposes of diversity jurisdiction. *Bouligny* was a landmark in the development of the law on the treatment of unincorporated associations, but its practical importance may not have been as great as one would expect. Today, most suits against labor unions would arise under federal law, and § 1331 provides subject-matter jurisdiction. State-law claims that might otherwise be available will often be preempted. Non-preempted claims may fall within supplemental jurisdiction. Indeed, that is what happened in *United Mine Workers v. Gibbs*, 383 U.S. 715 (1966) (Chapter 10).

2. For the majority in *Carden*, the question before the Court is how to define the citizenship of the artificial entity known as "Arkoma Associates." The dissent defines the issue differently. Here (from the Court's footnote 1) is the majority's response to the dissent's mode of analysis:

> The dissent reaches a conclusion different from ours primarily because it poses, and then answers, an entirely different question. It "do[es] not consider" "whether the limited partnership is a 'citizen,'" but simply "assum[es] it is a citizen," because even if we hold that it is, "we are still required to consider which, if any, of the *other citizens before the Court* as members of Arkoma Associates are real parties to the controversy." (Emphasis added.) Furthermore, "the only potentially non-diverse *party* in this case is a limited partner" because "all *other parties*, including the general partners and the limited partnership itself, assuming it is a citizen, are diverse." (Emphasis added.)
>
> That is the central fallacy from which, for the most part, the rest of the dissent's reasoning logically follows. The question presented today is not which of various parties before the Court should be considered for purposes of determining whether there is complete diversity of citizenship, a question that will generally be answered by application of the "real party to the controversy"

test. There are *not*, as the dissent assumes, multiple respondents before the Court, but only *one:* the artificial entity called Arkoma Associates, a limited partnership. And what we must decide is the quite different question of how the citizenship of that single artificial entity is to be determined—which in turn raises the question whether it can (like a corporation) assert its own citizenship, or rather is deemed to possess the citizenship of its members, and, if so, which members. The dissent fails to cite a single case in which the citizenship of an artificial entity, the issue before us today, has been decided by application of the "real party to the controversy" test that it describes.

3. Whatever the validity of the dissent's analysis of the nineteenth-century cases, the opinion in *Bouligny* certainly focused on the labor union as an entity. The Court said: "Certiorari was granted so that we might decide whether an unincorporated labor union is to be treated as a citizen for purposes of federal diversity jurisdiction, without regard to the citizenship of its members." The Court held that the answer was "no."

4. The Court in *Carden* acknowledges that its decisions "can validly be characterized as technical, precedent-bound, and unresponsive to policy considerations raised by the changing realities of business organization." But, says the Court, "having entered the field of diversity policy with regard to artificial entities once [i.e., with respect to corporations], we have left further adjustments to be made by Congress."

Is this persuasive? The Court expressed a similar view in *Bouligny* in 1965, but as of 1990 Congress had made no "further adjustments." Should the Court in *Carden* have reconsidered its position?

5. In the Class Action Fairness Act of 2005 (see Chapter 2), Congress expanded district court jurisdiction over diversity class actions. In addition to providing for jurisdiction based on minimal diversity, Congress accepted the Supreme Court's invitation in *Carden* to "further adjust[]" the "diversity policy with respect to artificial entities." Under § 1332(d)(10), in determining whether a class action may be brought in federal court or removed from state court under the new law, "an unincorporated association shall be deemed to be a citizen of the State where it has its principal place of business and the State under whose laws it is organized." The Senate Report on the bill explains the purpose of § 1332(d)(10):

> This provision is added to ensure that unincorporated associations receive the same treatment as corporations for purposes of diversity jurisdiction. The U.S. Supreme Court has held that "[f]or purposes of diversity jurisdiction, the citizenship of an unincorporated association is the citizenship of the individual members of the association." *Bouligny*. This rule "has been frequently criticized because often * * * an unincorporated association is, as a practical matter, indistinguishable from a corporation in the same business." Some insurance companies, for example, are "inter-insurance exchanges" or "reciprocal insurance associations." For that reason, federal courts have treated them as unincorporated associations for diversity jurisdiction purposes. Since such companies are nationwide companies, they are deemed to be citizens of

any state in which they have insured customers. Consequently, these companies can never be completely or even minimally diverse in any case.

It makes no sense to treat an unincorporated insurance company differently from, say, an incorporated manufacturer for purposes of diversity jurisdiction. New subsection 1332(d)(10) corrects this anomaly.

If this reasoning justifies treating unincorporated associations as entities for class actions, does it also apply to other diversity litigation?

6. The 1958 amendment defined corporate citizenship by reference to the "*State* of incorporation" and "the *State* where [the corporation] it has its principal place of business." Did these references to "State" include foreign states? Lower courts reached different conclusions on that question. A 2011 amendment resolved the issue; section (c) now provides that, for purposes of § 1332 and § 1441, "a corporation shall be deemed to be a citizen of every State *and foreign state* by which it has been incorporated and of the State *or foreign state* where it has its principal place of business."

Note: Carden *Reaffirmed*

1. How should citizenship for diversity purposes be determined for a legal entity that has the same characteristics as a corporation but is nevertheless unincorporated? The Court addressed that issue in *Americold Realty Trust v. Conagra Foods, Inc.*, 136 S. Ct. 1012 (2016), in which a real estate investment trust organized under Maryland law sought to invoke diversity jurisdiction. Under Maryland law, such trusts are similar to corporations—shareholders own the trust, and they have voting rights regarding the trust—but they are considered "unincorporated." Reaffirming *Carden*'s distinction between corporations and other legal entities, the Court held that those trusts are not treated as entities for determining citizenship; instead, the citizenship of these trusts depends on the citizenship of the shareholders.

2. New jurisdictional rules, such as the one announced in *Americold*, can wreak havoc on litigation. Consider *RTP LLC v. ORIX Real Estate Capital, Inc.*, 827 F.3d 689 (7th Cir. 2016). There, two retirement funds (among others) sued ORIX over a loan default in Illinois state court. ORIX removed the suit to federal district court on the basis of diversity jurisdiction and brought its own counterclaims. The two retirement funds are organized as trusts under Michigan law, and ORIX is a citizen of Delaware and Texas. Under then-applicable Seventh Circuit precedent, the citizenship of a trust was that of the trustee, and all of the trustees were citizens of Michigan. The district court awarded $30 million to ORIX.

The Seventh Circuit vacated the judgment. Noting *Americold*'s statement that "while humans and corporations can assert their own citizenship, other entities take the citizenship of their members," the Seventh Circuit concluded that the citizenship of the trusts was not that of the trustees; instead, the "trusts . . . have the citizenships of their own members." Because the trusts had 59 members residing in Delaware or Texas at the time the suit was removed, diversity jurisdiction was likely lacking. The court thus concluded that the district court either had to remand the case for lack of jurisdiction or make a factual finding that those 59 residents were not domiciled in Delaware or Texas.

Is it fair to disrupt judgments such as those in *ORIX* based on new jurisdictional rules? Should it matter that, as the Seventh Circuit acknowledged, the parties had "spent hundreds of thousands of dollars" litigating the case in federal court?

Problem: A Suit Against a "Professional Corporation"

Tamara Blakeley, a citizen of the state of Illiana, has brought a civil action for legal malpractice in federal district court against the law firm that represented her last year in an unsuccessful lawsuit. The law firm, Spencer & Marks, P.C., is a professional corporation incorporated and having its principal place of business in New Harmony, a neighboring state. However, seven of the nine members of the firm (the shareholders in the professional corporation) are citizens of Illiana. Jurisdiction is based on diversity of citizenship.

The defendant has moved to dismiss for lack of subject-matter jurisdiction, arguing that a "professional corporation" under New Harmony law is more like a limited partnership (the entity involved in *Carden*) than like a traditional business corporation. The defendant points out that a principal economic function of corporate organization is separation of ownership from control, but for a professional corporation under New Harmony law, ownership is not separate from control. Moreover, each shareholder of a New Harmony professional corporation must be a current employee licensed to provide the services in which the firm specializes, or another entity consisting solely of such persons.

The defendant also calls attention to the historical origins of the professional corporation. As one court has explained, "Professional corporations were created to permit lawyers, physicians, accountants and others to set up firm-wide tax-advantaged pension plans at a time when federal law restricted that opportunity to corporations. States created entities with the corporate name but the functional features of a professional partnership."

The defendant also points out that some states, including Illiana, do not recognize the "professional corporation"; rather, professionals must call themselves "limited liability partnerships."

Should the court grant the motion to dismiss?

Hertz Corp. v. Friend

Supreme Court of the United States, 2010.

559 U.S. 77.

Justice Breyer delivered the opinion of the Court.

The federal diversity jurisdiction statute provides that "a corporation shall be deemed to be a citizen of any State by which it has been incorporated *and of the State where it has its principal place of business."* 28 U.S.C. § 1332(c)(1) (emphasis added). We seek here to resolve different interpretations that the Circuits have given this phrase. In doing so, we place primary weight upon the need for judicial administration of a jurisdictional statute to remain as simple as possible. And we conclude that the phrase "principal place of business" refers to the place where the corporation's high level officers direct, control, and coordinate the corporation's activities. Lower federal courts have often metaphorically called that place the corporation's "nerve center." See, *e.g., Wisconsin Knife Works v. National Metal Crafters,* 781 F.2d 1280 (C.A. 7 1986); *Scot Typewriter Co. v. Underwood Corp.,* 170 F. Supp. 862 (S.D.N.Y. 1959) (Weinfeld, J.). We believe that the "nerve center" will typically be found at a corporation's headquarters.

I

In September 2007, respondents Melinda Friend and John Nhieu, two California citizens, sued petitioner, the Hertz Corporation, in a California state court. They sought damages for what they claimed were violations of California's wage and hour laws. And they requested relief on behalf of a potential class composed of California citizens who had allegedly suffered similar harms.

Hertz filed a notice seeking removal to a federal court. 28 U.S.C. §§ 1332(d)(2), 1441(a) [*sic* in slip opinion]. Hertz claimed that the plaintiffs and the defendant were citizens of different States. §§ 1332(a)(1), (c)(1). Hence, the federal court possessed diversity-of-citizenship jurisdiction. Friend and Nhieu, however, claimed that the Hertz Corporation was a California citizen, like themselves, and that, hence, diversity jurisdiction was lacking.

To support its position, Hertz submitted a declaration by an employee relations manager that sought to show that Hertz's "principal place of business" was in New Jersey, not in California. The declaration stated, among other things, that Hertz operated facilities in 44 States; and that California—which had about 12% of the Nation's population—accounted for 273 of Hertz's 1,606 car rental locations; about 2,300 of its 11,230 full-time employees; about $811 million of its $4.371 billion in annual revenue; and about 3.8 million of its approximately 21 million annual transactions, i.e., rentals. The declaration also stated that the "leadership of Hertz and its domestic subsidiaries" is located at Hertz's "corporate headquarters" in Park Ridge, New Jersey; that its "core executive and administrative functions . . . are carried out" there and "to a lesser extent" in Oklahoma City, Oklahoma; and that its "major administrative operations . . . are found" at those two locations.

The District Court of the Northern District of California accepted Hertz's statement of the facts as undisputed. But it concluded that, given those facts, Hertz was a citizen of California. In reaching this conclusion, the court applied Ninth Circuit precedent, which instructs courts to identify a corporation's "principal place of business" by first determining the amount of a corporation's business activity State by State. If the amount of activity is "significantly larger" or "substantially predominates" in one State, then that State is the corporation's "principal place of business." If there is no such State, then the "principal place of business" is the corporation's "'nerve center,'" i.e., the place where "'the majority of its executive and administrative functions are performed.'"

Applying this test, the District Court found that the "plurality of each of the relevant business activities" was in California, and that "the differential between the amount of those activities" in California and the amount in "the next closest state" was "significant." Hence, Hertz's "principal place of business" was California, and diversity jurisdiction was thus lacking. The District Court consequently remanded the case to the state courts.

Hertz appealed the District Court's remand order. 28 U.S.C. § 1453(c). The Ninth Circuit affirmed in a brief memorandum opinion. Hertz filed a petition for certiorari. And, in light of differences among the Circuits in the application of the test for corporate citizenship, we granted the writ. . . .

III

We begin our "principal place of business" discussion with a brief review of relevant history. [Omitted. The Court traced the evolution of the law from *Bank of United States v. Deveaux* (1809) through *Marshall v. Baltimore & Ohio R. Co.* (1854). See Justice Scalia's summary of the history in *Carden*.] Whatever the rationale, the practical upshot was that, for diversity purposes, the federal courts considered a corporation to be a citizen of the State of its incorporation. 13F C. WRIGHT, A. MILLER & E. COOPER, FEDERAL PRACTICE AND PROCEDURE § 3623 at 1-7 (3d ed. 2009) [hereinafter WRIGHT & MILLER].

In 1928 this Court made clear that the "state of incorporation" rule was virtually absolute. It held that a corporation closely identified with State A could proceed in a federal court located in that State as long as the corporation had filed its incorporation papers in State B, perhaps a State where the corporation did no business at all. See *Black and White Taxicab & Transfer Co. v. Brown and Yellow Taxicab & Transfer Co.*, 276 U.S. 518 (refusing to question corporation's reincorporation motives and finding diversity jurisdiction). Subsequently, many in Congress and those who testified before it pointed out that this interpretation was at odds with diversity jurisdiction's basic rationale, namely, opening the federal courts' doors to those who might otherwise suffer from local prejudice against out-of-state parties. Through its choice of the State of incorporation, a corporation could manipulate federal-court jurisdiction, for example, opening the federal courts' doors in a State where it conducted nearly all its business by filing incorporation papers elsewhere. Although various legislative proposals to curtail the corporate use of diversity jurisdiction were made, none of these proposals were enacted into law.

At the same time as federal dockets increased in size, many judges began to believe those dockets contained too many diversity cases. A committee of the Judicial Conference of the United States studied the matter. [After a lengthy process, including discussions at circuit conferences, the committee issued a report proposing] that "'a corporation shall be deemed a citizen of the state of its original creation . . . [and] shall also be deemed a citizen of a state where it has its principal place of business.'" [That report is] the source of the present-day statutory language. The committee wrote that [the proposed] new language would provide a "simpler and more practical formula" than the "gross income" test [it had initially suggested]. It added that the language "ha[d] a precedent in the jurisdictional provisions of the Bankruptcy Act." . . .

[The committee report was circulated] to the general public "for the purpose of inviting further suggestions and comments." Subsequently, in 1958, Congress both codified the courts' traditional place of incorporation test and also enacted into law a slightly modified version of the Conference Committee's proposed "principal place of business" language. A corporation was to "be deemed a citizen of any State by which it has been incorporated and of the State where it has its principal place of business." § 2, 72 Stat. 415.

IV

The phrase "principal place of business" has proved more difficult to apply than its originators likely expected. Decisions under the Bankruptcy Act did not provide the firm guidance for which [the Judicial Conference] had hoped because courts interpreting bankruptcy law did not agree about how to determine a corporation's "principal place of business." . . .

After Congress' amendment, courts were similarly uncertain as to where to look to determine a corporation's "principal place of business" for diversity purposes. If a corporation's headquarters and executive offices were in the same State in which it did most of its business, the test seemed straightforward. The "principal place of business" was located in that State.

But suppose those corporate headquarters, including executive offices, are in one State, while the corporation's plants or other centers of business activity are located in other States? In 1959 a distinguished federal district judge, Edward Weinfeld, relied on the Second Circuit's interpretation of the Bankruptcy Act to answer this question in part:

> Where a corporation is engaged in far-flung and varied activities which are carried on in different states, its principal place of business is the nerve center from which it radiates out to its constituent parts and from which its officers direct, control and coordinate all activities without regard to locale, in the furtherance of the corporate objective. The test applied by our Court of Appeals, is that place where the corporation has an "office from which its business was directed and controlled"—the place where "all of its business was under the supreme direction and control of its officers." *Scot Typewriter Co.*, 170 F. Supp. at 865.

Numerous Circuits have since followed this rule, applying the "nerve center" test for corporations with "far-flung" business activities. See, *e.g., Topp v. CompAir Inc.*, 814 F.2d 830 (C.A. 1 1987); see also 15 J. MOORE ET AL., MOORE'S FEDERAL PRACTICE § 102.54[2] at 102-112.1 (3d ed. 2009) [hereinafter MOORE'S].

Scot's analysis, however, did not go far enough. For it did not answer what courts should do when the operations of the corporation are not "far-flung" but rather limited to only a few States. When faced with this question, various courts have focused more heavily on where a corporation's actual business activities are located.

Perhaps because corporations come in many different forms, involve many different kinds of business activities, and locate offices and plants for different reasons in different ways in different regions, a general "business activities" approach has proved unusually difficult to apply. Courts must decide which factors are more important than others: for example, plant location, sales or servicing centers; transactions, payrolls, or revenue generation. [For example, one court emphasized place of sales and advertisement, office, and full-time employees; another looked to place of stores and inventory, employees, income, and sales.]

The number of factors grew as courts explicitly combined aspects of the "nerve center" and "business activity" tests to look to a corporation's "total activities," sometimes to try to determine what treatises have described as the corporation's "center of gravity." See, *e.g.*, 13F WRIGHT & MILLER § 3625 at 100. A major treatise confirms this growing complexity, listing Circuit by Circuit, cases that highlight different factors or emphasize similar factors differently, and reporting that the "federal courts of appeals have employed various tests"—tests which "tend to overlap" and which are sometimes described in "language" that "is imprecise." 15 MOORE's § 102.54[2] at 102-12. See also *id.* §§ 102.54[2], [13] at 102-12 to 102-22 (describing, in 14 pages, major tests as looking to the "nerve center," "locus of operations," or "center of corporate activities"). Not surprisingly, different circuits (and sometimes different courts within a single circuit) have applied these highly general multifactor tests in different ways. . . .

This complexity may reflect an unmediated judicial effort to apply the statutory phrase "principal place of business" in light of the general purpose of diversity jurisdiction, *i.e.*, an effort to find the State where a corporation is least likely to suffer out-of-state prejudice when it is sued in a local court. But, if so, that task seems doomed to failure. After all, the relevant purposive concern—prejudice against an out-of-state party—will often depend upon factors that courts cannot easily measure, for example, a corporation's image, its history, and its advertising, while the factors that courts can more easily measure, for example, its office or plant location, its sales, its employment, or the nature of the goods or services it supplies, will sometimes bear no more than a distant relation to the likelihood of prejudice. At the same time, this approach is at war with administrative simplicity. And it has failed to achieve a nationally uniform interpretation of federal law, an unfortunate consequence in a federal legal system.

V

A

In an effort to find a single, more uniform interpretation of the statutory phrase, we have reviewed the Courts of Appeals' divergent and increasingly complex interpretations. Having done so, we now return to, and expand, Judge Weinfeld's approach, as applied in the Seventh Circuit. See, *e.g., Scot Typewriter Co.*, 170 F. Supp. at 865; *Wisconsin Knife Works*, 781 F.2d at 1282. We conclude that "principal place of business" is best read as referring to the place where a corporation's officers direct, control, and coordinate the corporation's activities. It is the place that Courts of Appeals have called the corporation's "nerve center." And in practice it should normally be the place where the corporation maintains its headquarters—provided that the headquarters is the actual center of direction, control, and coordination, i.e., the "nerve center," and not simply an office where the corporation holds its board meetings (for example, attended by directors and officers who have traveled there for the occasion).

Three sets of considerations, taken together, convince us that this approach, while imperfect, is superior to other possibilities. First, the statute's language supports the approach. The statute's text deems a corporation a citizen of the "State where it has its principal place of business." 28 U.S.C. § 1332(c)(1). The word "place" is in the singular, not the plural. The word "principal" requires us to pick out the "main, prominent" or "leading" place. And the fact that the word "place" follows the words "State where" means that the "place" is a place *within* a State. It is not the State itself.

A corporation's "nerve center," usually its main headquarters, is a single place. The public often (though not always) considers it the corporation's main place of business. And it is a place within a State. By contrast, the application of a more general business activities test has led some courts, as in the present case, to look, not at a particular place within a State, but incorrectly at the State itself, measuring the total amount of business activities that the corporation conducts there and determining whether they are "significantly larger" than in the next-ranking State.

This approach invites greater litigation and can lead to strange results, as the Ninth Circuit has since recognized. Namely, if a "corporation may be deemed a citizen of California on th[e] basis" of "activities [that] roughly reflect California's larger population . . . nearly every national retailer—no matter how far flung its operations—will be deemed a citizen of California for diversity purposes." *Davis v. HSBC Bank Nev., N.A.*, 557 F.3d 1026 (2009). But why award or decline diversity jurisdiction on the basis of a State's population, whether measured directly, indirectly (say proportionately), or with modifications?

Second, administrative simplicity is a major virtue in a jurisdictional statute. Complex jurisdictional tests complicate a case, eating up time and money as the parties litigate, not the merits of their claims, but which court is the right court to decide those claims. Complex tests produce appeals and reversals, encourage gamesmanship, and, again, diminish the likelihood that results and settlements will reflect a claim's legal and factual merits. Judicial resources too are at stake. Courts have an independent obligation to determine whether subject-matter jurisdiction exists, even when no party challenges it. *Arbaugh v. Y & H Corp.* (2006) [Chapter 9]. So courts benefit from straightforward rules under which they can readily assure themselves of their power to hear a case.

Simple jurisdictional rules also promote greater predictability. Predictability is valuable to corporations making business and investment decisions. Predictability also benefits plaintiffs deciding whether to file suit in a state or federal court.

A "nerve center" approach, which ordinarily equates that "center" with a corporation's headquarters, is simple to apply *comparatively speaking*. The metaphor of a corporate "brain," while not precise, suggests a single location. By contrast, a corporation's general business activities more often lack a single principal place where they take place. That is to say, the corporation may have several plants, many sales locations, and employees located in many different places. If so, it will not be as easy to determine which of these different business locales is the "principal" or most important "place."

Third, the statute's legislative history, for those who accept it, offers a simplicity-related interpretive benchmark. The Judicial Conference provided an initial version of its proposal that suggested a numerical test. A corporation would be deemed a citizen of the State that accounted for more than half of its gross income. The Conference changed its mind in light of criticism that such a test would prove too complex and impractical to apply. That history suggests that the words "principal place of business" should be interpreted to be no more complex than the initial "half of gross income" test. A "nerve center" test offers such a possibility. A general business activities test does not.

B

We recognize that there may be no perfect test that satisfies all administrative and purposive criteria. We recognize as well that, under the "nerve center" test we adopt today, there will be hard cases. For example, in this era of telecommuting, some corporations may divide their command and coordinating functions among officers who work at several different locations, perhaps communicating over the Internet. That said, our test nonetheless points courts in a single direction, towards the center of overall direction, control, and coordination. Courts do not have to try to weigh corporate functions, assets, or revenues different in kind, one from the other. Our approach provides a sensible test that is relatively easier to apply, not a test that will, in all instances, automatically generate a result.

We also recognize that the use of a "nerve center" test may in some cases produce results that seem to cut against the basic rationale for 28 U.S.C. § 1332. For example, if the bulk of a company's business activities visible to the public take place in New Jersey, while its top officers direct those activities just across the river in New York, the "principal place of business" is New York. One could argue that members of the public in New Jersey would be *less* likely to be prejudiced against the corporation than persons in New York — yet the corporation will still be entitled to remove a New Jersey state case to federal court. And note too that the same corporation would be unable to remove a New York state case to federal court, despite the New York public's presumed prejudice against the corporation.

We understand that such seeming anomalies will arise. However, in view of the necessity of having a clearer rule, we must accept them. Accepting occasionally counterintuitive results is the price the legal system must pay to avoid overly complex jurisdictional administration while producing the benefits that accompany a more uniform legal system.

The burden of persuasion for establishing diversity jurisdiction, of course, remains on the party asserting it. When challenged on allegations of jurisdictional facts, the parties must support their allegations by competent proof. And when faced with such a challenge, we reject suggestions such as, for example, the one made by petitioner that the mere filing of a form like the Securities and Exchange Commission's Form 10-K listing a corporation's "principal executive offices" would, without more, be sufficient proof to establish a corporation's "nerve center." Such possibilities would readily permit jurisdictional manipulation, thereby subverting a major reason for the insertion of the "principal place of business" language in the diversity statute. Indeed, if the record reveals attempts at manipulation—for example, that the alleged "nerve center" is nothing more than a mail drop box, a bare office with a computer, or the location of an annual executive retreat—the courts should instead take as the "nerve center" the place of actual direction, control, and coordination, in the absence of such manipulation.

VI

Petitioner's unchallenged declaration suggests that Hertz's center of direction, control, and coordination, its "nerve center," and its corporate headquarters are one and the same, and they are located in New Jersey, not in California. Because respondents should have a fair opportunity to litigate their case in light of our holding, however, we vacate the Ninth Circuit's judgment and remand the case for further proceedings consistent with this opinion.

It is so ordered.

Note: Determining a Corporation's "Principal Place of Business"

1. At a single stroke, the decision in *Hertz Corp. v. Friend* wipes out half a century of lower-court case law. For example, the Court notes that the Wright & Miller treatise devoted 73 pages to "describing . . . the 'nerve center,' 'corporate activities,' and 'total activity' tests as part of an effort to locate the corporation's 'center of gravity,' while specifying different ways in which different circuits apply these or other factors." Almost all of that law is now obsolete.

2. Although the Court notes the fact only obliquely (through a reference to the relevant section of Title 28), Hertz removed the case to federal court under the Class Action Fairness Act, 28 U.S.C. § 1332(d)(2). (See Chapter 2.) That explains why the Ninth Circuit Court of Appeals was able to review the district court's remand order notwithstanding the general statutory prohibition of review of such orders. See 28 U.S.C. § 1453(c)(1). However, the Supreme Court's holding also applies to original and removal jurisdiction based on the general diversity statute, 28 U.S.C. § 1332(a).

3. The Court acknowledges that the complex law developed in the lower courts "may reflect an unmediated judicial effort to apply the statutory phrase 'principal place of business' in light of the general purpose of diversity jurisdiction, i.e., an effort to find the State where a corporation is least likely to suffer out-of-state prejudice when it is sued in a local court." But, says the Court, "that task seems doomed to failure." Do you agree? Consider, for example, these comments by the Fifth Circuit, one of the courts that adopted the "total activity" test:

[Local] bias would seem to be most prevalent when a local party sues a foreign corporation that has little if any presence in the district. Any local prejudice is minimized when a corporation, even though incorporated in another state, has significant contact with the district through, for example, a factory that employs local people. In such a situation, the foreign corporation has some identity and familiarity with the people and the courts in the locality. Since the need for diversity jurisdiction is lessened when a foreign corporation has substantial visibility in the community, then our analysis should include consideration of the corporation's contact with the community.

J.A. Olson Co. v. City of Winona, Miss., 818 F.2d 401 (5th Cir. 1987). Would the Supreme Court have done better to give content to "significant contact" and "substantial visibility" rather than using "nerve center" as the exclusive test?

4. "Local bias" can rear its head even in federal court. In *Whitehead v. Food Max of Mississippi, Inc.*, 163 F.3d 265 (5th Cir. 1998), a federal-court jury in Mississippi found that the failure of a Kmart store to provide adequate security for its parking lot was a cause of the abduction of a woman and her daughter "and ensuing heinous criminal acts." The jury awarded damages of $3.4 million. The court of appeals reversed the damages award on the ground that, because of the plaintiffs' closing argument, "the jury was influenced by passion and prejudice." The court placed particular emphasis on statements by the plaintiffs' counsel "that appealed to local bias." The opinion described the lawyer's behavior:

> On numerous occasions, [plaintiffs' counsel] reminded the jury that Kmart is a national, not local, corporation, with its principal place of business in Troy, Michigan. . . . [For example, counsel said:] "The problem is— *way up there in Troy, Michigan—way up there in Troy, Michigan*, where they decide to write a two or three inch thick loss prevention manual, they don't think about the customers' safety and security in the parking lot. Because they are more concerned about profits and not people." (Emphasis added.) . . .
>
> This repeated emphasis on Kmart being a national, not local, corporation was exacerbated by counsel's shameless refusal to abide by the district court's sustaining Kmart's objections to counsel's comments concerning Kmart not presenting proof about its security measures through non-local witnesses. . . .
>
> In his rebuttal closing argument, and notwithstanding the court's having earlier sustained Kmart's objections, the Whiteheads' counsel returned to this improper tactic. [Counsel said:] "Shame on Kmart. *Shame on the corporation for not sending representatives here to testify about why they don't have a policy. Shame on them for having a local man sit here and take the fall. . . .*" (Emphasis added.)

Are lawyers more likely to engage in such behavior in state court than in federal court? If so, do episodes like this one support the Supreme Court's selection of the "nerve center" approach?

5. The Court cautions against "jurisdictional manipulation." By way of illustration, the Court says that "a mail drop box, a bare office with a computer, or the location of an annual executive retreat" will not suffice to establish a corporation's nerve center. How much more activity would be required to put the corporation over the line? Suppose, for example, that the alleged nerve center houses computers and support staff, but the corporation's officers work in other states and communicate with the support office via the Internet and the telephone. Would that suffice? Should it matter whether the officers are located in a single state or multiple states?

6. In contrast to many jurisdictional decisions, *Hertz* may be relevant to lawyers in their work as counselors and advisers. An early commentary suggests that corporations in "selecting a location for their business headquarters may well decide to avoid those states with courts that have a reputation for being less 'business-friendly.'" Stephen Smerek & Ashlea Ramond Pflug, *'Nerve Center' Test Key to Federal Courts*, Daily J. (S.F.), Mar. 8, 2010, at 5. The authors acknowledge that this factor would seldom be dispositive, but they urge companies to consider it.

The American Tort Reform Association publishes a controversial annual list of "judicial hellholes" — "places where judges systematically apply laws and court procedures in an inequitable manner, generally against defendants in civil lawsuits." Tiger Joyce, *And the 2009/2010 Judicial Hellholes Are . . .* , Metropolitan Corporate Counsel, Jan. 2010. See http://www.metrocorpcounsel.com/pdf/2010/January/07.pdf. Under what circumstances, if any, would you advise a client to avoid one of the listed states in selecting a corporate headquarters?

B. The Amount in Controversy Requirement

Diversity suits can be brought in federal court only if "the matter in controversy exceeds the sum or value of $75,000." Often there will be no dispute that this requirement is satisfied. But in other cases the parties may disagree. In this section we examine some of the situations in which a federal court is asked to determine whether the "the matter in controversy" exceeds the amount specified in the jurisdictional statute.

Ericsson GE Mobile Communications, Inc. v. Motorola Communications & Electronics, Inc.

United States Court of Appeals for the Eleventh Circuit, 1997.

120 F.3d 216.

Before ANDERSON, CIRCUIT JUDGE, and FAY and KRAVITCH, SENIOR CIRCUIT JUDGES.

KRAVITCH, SENIOR CIRCUIT JUDGE:

Ericsson GE Communications ("EGE") brought this diversity action pursuant to the Alabama Competitive Bid Law to enjoin the execution of a contract between Motorola Communications & Electronics, Inc. ("Motorola") and the City of Birmingham (the "City") for the purchase of a new public safety communications system.

Because we conclude that the value of an injunction voiding the contract between Motorola and the City, from the perspective of plaintiff-appellee EGE, is too speculative to satisfy the amount in controversy requirement of the diversity statute, 28 U.S.C. § 1332, we remand the case to the district court with instructions to dismiss for lack of subject matter jurisdiction.

I.

This action arises out of the City's purchase of an 800 MHZ trunked simulcast radio communication system for its police and fire departments. In the early 1990's, the Mayor of Birmingham decided that the City needed a new public safety communications system and hired a consultant to research the City's needs and to assist the City in preparing bid specifications and in evaluating competing bids. In May 1993, the City issued a Request for Bids ("RFB") for two different communication technology systems, the APCO 16 and the APCO 25. The APCO 16 and APCO 25 are sets of specifications for public radio systems. The APCO 25, a newer technology, is based on specific technological requirements for the equipment while the APCO 16 is based on functional standards. The RFB provided that a vendor could submit bids for either or both of these technology systems.

Only EGE and Motorola submitted bids in response to the City's request; EGE bid on the APCO 16 system for $9,758,053 and Motorola bid on the APCO 25 system for $11,336,282. After the submission of bids, the Mayor concluded that the APCO 25 system technology would better serve the City's needs. The City then rejected the bids of both EGE and Motorola, and negotiated a new contract with Motorola.

Alleging among other things that the consultant hired by the City was biased in favor of Motorola and that he skewed the decision-making process in that company's favor, EGE brought this action to enjoin the enforcement of the contract between Motorola and the City and to have itself declared the lowest responsible bidder. Motorola and the City moved unsuccessfully to dismiss EGE's claim for lack of subject matter jurisdiction.

[The district court certified questions of state law to the Alabama Supreme Court. That court held, among other things, that EGE could prove a violation of Alabama bid law by demonstrating that the City's selection of the APCO 25 system was based on "ignorance through lack of inquiry, or was the result of improper influence, or was otherwise arbitrary and capricious." The district court then conducted a trial before an advisory jury.] Adopting that jury's verdict, the district court concluded that the City's decision to purchase the APCO 25 technology was the result of improper influence exerted by Motorola on the City's decision makers and, therefore, violated the competitive bid law. Accordingly, the district court voided the contract.[4] Motorola and the City appeal this judgment, as well as the district court's order denying their motion to dismiss.

---

4. In a subsequent order, the district court articulated an additional alternative ground for finding a violation of the Alabama Competitive Bid Law. The district court concluded that the Mayor had violated § 6.09 of the Mayor-Council Act of 1955 by negotiating a contract directly with Motorola

II.

As a threshold matter, we must determine whether this action properly was brought in federal court. EGE alleged jurisdiction under the diversity statute, 28 U.S.C. § 1332, which, at the time this action was filed, provided for federal subject matter jurisdiction over actions between citizens of different states in which the matter in controversy exceeds $50,000. Because EGE sought only declaratory and injunctive relief, "it is well established that the amount in controversy is measured by the value of the object of the litigation." *Hunt v. Washington State Apple Advertising Comm'n*, 432 U.S. 333 (1977).

A. Governing Perspective

Whether courts, in determining the amount in controversy, are to measure the value of the object of the litigation solely from the plaintiff's perspective or whether they may also consider the value of the object from the defendant's perspective is considerably less well-established. The Supreme Court has provided no clear guidance on this question, and, as a result, federal courts are divided as to the proper perspective to use in determining the amount in controversy.

Moreover, district courts in this circuit, reading our prior cases to conflict, have expressed uncertainty as to whether the plaintiff-viewpoint rule governs in this circuit or whether courts are free to consider the value of the object of the litigation to either party. After carefully reviewing this circuit's precedents, however, we find no conflict, and we conclude that this court's predecessor purposefully and conspicuously adopted the plaintiff-viewpoint rule.[10]

In our view, several cases from the former Fifth Circuit establish the plaintiff-viewpoint rule. [For example, in] *Vraney v. County of Pinellas*, a non-resident property owner and taxpayer brought a diversity action to enjoin a county waterworks program. 250 F.2d 617 (5th Cir. 1958) (*per curiam*). Even though the complaint clearly alleged that the value of the waterworks program to the defendant county exceeded the amount in controversy, the court dismissed the action for lack of jurisdiction because "there is no averment showing or tending to show that the *value to the plaintiff* of the object or right sought to be enforced exceeds the sum or value" required by the diversity statute. (Emphasis added.) The court reiterated that "[u]nder the decisions in taxpayers' actions, as well as others, the *value of the plaintiff's* right sought to be enforced must exceed the jurisdictional amount in order to confer federal jurisdiction." (Emphasis added.) . . .

In our view, these cases firmly establish that this circuit has adopted the plaintiff-viewpoint rule. Commentators and other courts likewise have read these cases as endorsing the plaintiff-viewpoint approach. . . .

Although we recognize that there are persuasive arguments to support the adoption of the either-viewpoint rule, as a panel of this court, we remain bound to follow

---

after having rejected the bids of both EGE and Motorola and without first having readvertised for the bids.

10. In *Bonner v. City of Prichard*, 661 F.2d 1206 (11th Cir. 1981) (*en banc*), we adopted as binding precedent decisions of the former Fifth Circuit rendered prior to October 1, 1981.

the plaintiff-viewpoint rule regardless of the wisdom we may attach to it. Only an en banc decision of this court or an intervening decision of the Supreme Court can alter the controlling law of this circuit.

B. Value of the Object of the Litigation

Having determined that the plaintiff-viewpoint rule governs, we now consider whether EGE has alleged an amount in controversy sufficient to satisfy the diversity statute. We first must determine the remedies available to EGE under Alabama law, and then consider the monetary value of the available relief.

The Alabama Competitive Bid Law provides that certain municipal expenditures such as the purchase of a public safety communications system "shall be made under contractual agreement entered into by free and open competitive bidding, on sealed bids, to the lowest responsible bidder." It further states that "[a]ny taxpayer of the area within the jurisdiction of the awarding authority and any bona fide unsuccessful bidder on a particular contract shall be empowered to bring a civil action in the appropriate court to enjoin execution of any contract entered into in violation of the provisions of this article."

Although EGE originally sought a declaration that it was the lowest responsible bidder (and thus entitled to the contract with the City), the district court refused to grant such relief. More importantly, we find no basis in Alabama law for such an award. Rather, under Alabama law, the sole remedy available to EGE in an action challenging a contract under the competitive bid law is an injunction voiding the contract between Motorola and the City.

Simply put, the Alabama Competitive Bid Law, which was designed to benefit the public, "creates no enforceable rights in the bidders." "There is no indication in this statute [] that an unsuccessful bidder has any right or expectancy to insist upon the award of a contract. To the contrary, the statute is carefully crafted to limit the remedy 'to enjoin[ing] execution of any contract entered into in violation of the provisions of this article.'"

Based on these cases, it appears to a legal certainty that EGE can obtain only an injunction voiding the contract entered into by the City and Motorola. We must now determine whether the value of this injunctive relief to EGE is sufficiently measurable and certain to satisfy the $50,000 amount in controversy requirement of the diversity statute. EGE points to no authority to suggest that, in the event of an injunction, the City would be required to rebid the project. Moreover, in the event that the City did decide to rebid the contract, it appears that the City would be free to submit an alternative bid proposal for both the APCO 16 and APCO 25 systems, and absent improper influence, would be free to conclude again that the APCO 25 technology is best suited for serving its needs. It is important to remember that on rebid, as always, the City's "determination of the lowest responsible bidder and its formation of bid specifications may be exercised with a wide margin of discretion."

Any benefit that EGE could receive from the injunctive relief awardable by the district court-namely, the chance to rebid for the contract-is, in our view, too speculative and immeasurable to satisfy the amount in controversy requirement. Because EGE cannot reduce the speculative benefit resulting from a rebid "to a monetary standard, [] there is no pecuniary amount in controversy." We therefore hold that EGE has failed to satisfy the $50,000 amount in controversy requirement of 28 U.S.C. § 1332.

III.

Accordingly, the district court's order is reversed, and this case is remanded with instructions to dismiss for lack of subject matter jurisdiction.

Note: Whose Viewpoint?

1. In the principal case, the district court, at the behest of an unsuccessful bidder, voided a contract that called for the payment of several million dollars. The court of appeals holds that diversity jurisdiction was lacking because the "matter in controversy" did not exceed "the sum or value" of $50,000. It therefore sends the case back to the district court with directions to dismiss the action. This Note explores the law that underlies this seemingly anomalous result.

2. As the court of appeals points out, the lower federal courts "are divided as to the proper perspective to use in determining the amount in controversy." Several circuits have adopted the plaintiff-viewpoint rule; others follow the either-viewpoint approach. Courts on both sides have cited various Supreme Court opinions in support of their position. But the Supreme Court "never has expressly embraced either position in a case in which the value differed depending on the perspective from which it was measured." The Eleventh Circuit therefore does not read "any of [the Court's] apparently conflicting opinions to have resolved this issue." Commentators generally agree with this assessment.

3. The court of appeals acknowledges that "there are persuasive arguments to support the adoption of the either-viewpoint rule." The court quotes from prominent commentators:

> "[The either-viewpoint rule] seems to be the desirable rule, since the purpose of a jurisdictional amount requirement — to keep trivial cases away from the court — is satisfied when the case is worth a large sum to either party." [Wright & Miller.]

> "[T]he jurisdictional-amount requirement reflects a congressional judgment that federal judicial resources should be devoted only to those diversity cases in which the financial stakes rise to a predetermined level. It is difficult to understand why those financial stakes are not implicated when *either* party stands to gain or lose the statutorily determined amount or its equivalent." [Moore's Federal Practice.]

The court offers no arguments (apart from precedent) in support of the plaintiff-viewpoint approach. Can you see any? One district court has stated that "strong policy considerations favor the plaintiff's viewpoint rule; federal courts are courts of limited jurisdiction. To extend jurisdiction beyond the limits firmly established without Congressional approval is beyond this Court's province." *Bernard v. Gerber Food*

Products Co., 938 F. Supp. 218 (S.D.N.Y. 1996). Is this a persuasive rebuttal to the arguments made in the commentaries quoted by the Eleventh Circuit?

4. When the *EGE* case returned to the district court, the district judge rejected an attempt by defendants to tax all costs against the plaintiff. The judge expressed regret that he had not "taken seriously defendants' initial cursory challenge of this court's jurisdiction pursuant to § 1332," and he belatedly wrote an opinion explaining why the amount-in-controversy requirement was satisfied:

> The courts which have limited § 1332 to cases in which a plaintiff can obtain the jurisdiction amount have ignored obvious legislative history and the rules of statutory construction. [Discussion of legislative history omitted.]
>
> The sequence of legislative events is not all that stands in the way of defendants' argument. The primary, if not the only, Congressional rationale for providing diversity jurisdiction to a federal court is to give a non-resident litigant like EGE some protection in controversies involving significant monetary value from the preferential treatment likely to be given a powerful resident litigant in its state forum. This is a very good reason why, in this case, EGE brought its action in this court rather than in the court in the Alabama county in which the defendant City is located. This is why Congress chose the broad phrase "matter in controversy."

Ericsson GE Mobile Communications, Inc. v. Motorola Communications, 179 F.R.D. 328 (N.D. Ala. 1998).

5. In 2002, the Supreme Court granted certiorari in a case presenting the viewpoint issue (among others), but after oral argument the writ was dismissed without decision. *Ford Motor Co. v. McCauley*, 537 U.S. 1 (2002). Thus, the plaintiff-viewpoint approach remains the law in some circuits (including the Eleventh), while others follow the either-viewpoint rule.

6. The either-viewpoint rule has its most direct application in cases where a single plaintiff seeks injunctive relief against a single defendant. A good example is *Grotzke v. Kurz*, 887 F. Supp. 53 (D. R.I. 1995). Plaintiffs had sold their business to the defendants. The parties executed closing documents that provided for certain payments to plaintiffs. Defendants failed to make payments totaling $28,500.00. Plaintiffs brought suit in state court seeking a declaration that defendants were in violation of the closing documents and an injunction enjoining defendants from continuing to use a trade name and other intangible rights that were part of the sale. Defendants removed the suit to federal court on the basis of diversity.

At that time the jurisdictional minimum was $50,000. The plaintiffs argued that because defendants had failed to make payments totaling $28,500, the value of the injunction to the plaintiffs, and thus the amount in controversy, was $28,500. The defendants countered that if the plaintiffs obtained the injunction they sought, the defendants would be forced out of a business worth more than $50,000. The district court agreed with the defendants, saying, "This [is] a bipolar action seeking equitable relief. The pecuniary burden on the defendants would be well in excess of the amount in controversy requirement should the plaintiffs prevail." The court thus upheld the removal.

The picture becomes considerably murkier, however, in class actions and other suits involving multiple plaintiffs. This is because of the "non-aggregation rule" established by the Supreme Court and discussed in the Note that follows.

Note: The "Non-Aggregation Rule"

1. In *Snyder v. Harris*, 394 U.S. 332 (1969), Justice Black, writing for the Court, summarized the Court's interpretation of the amount-in-controversy requirement of the statutes authorizing diversity of citizenship jurisdiction:

> The traditional judicial interpretation under all of these statutes has been from the beginning that the separate and distinct claims of two or more plaintiffs cannot be aggregated in order to satisfy the jurisdictional amount requirement. Aggregation has been permitted only (1) in cases in which a single plaintiff seeks to aggregate two or more of his own claims against a single defendant and (2) in cases in which two or more plaintiffs unite to enforce a single title or right in which they have a common and undivided interest.

In *Snyder*, the Court reaffirmed this interpretation in the context of class actions. The Court quoted with approval from a 1911 decision: "When two or more plaintiffs, having separate and distinct demands, unite for convenience and economy in a single suit, it is essential that the demand of each be of the requisite jurisdictional amount. . . ."

2. As the *Snyder* opinion acknowledged, the courts had recognized two exceptions to the non-aggregation rule. First, a single plaintiff can satisfy the jurisdictional amount requirement by joining two claims against a single defendant. Note that, in that situation, aggregation is permitted even if the claims are totally unrelated. Does it make sense to allow aggregation in that setting but not when two plaintiffs assert claims that are closely related factually but "separate and distinct" as a legal matter?

Second, aggregation is permitted when multiple plaintiffs assert "a single title or right in which they have a common and undivided interest." Justice Black insisted that "lower courts have developed largely workable standards for determining when claims are joint and common, and therefore entitled to be aggregated, and when they are separate and distinct and therefore not aggregable." Professor Wright wryly commented: "It would have been helpful if the Court had indicated what these standards are or where they are to be found." WRIGHT & KANE, FEDERAL COURTS § 36 (6th ed. 2002).

3. Suppose that multiple plaintiffs bring suit against a single defendant, asserting claims that are "separate and distinct." The individual claims are for less than $75,000, but the relief sought would cost the defendant more than $75,000. In a circuit that follows the either-viewpoint rule, does the suit satisfy the amount in controversy requirement?

That is the question that the Ninth Circuit confronted in *Snow v. Ford Motor Co.*, 561 F.2d 787 (9th Cir. 1977). Plaintiff, on behalf of himself and others similarly situated, filed suit in state court against Ford Motor Co. seeking damages and injunctive relief under the California consumer protection statute. The complaint alleged that, contrary to specific representations contained in advertising materials, Ford manufactured and marketed "trailering special packages" that were incomplete in that they did not contain a wiring kit for the connection of the trailer's electrical system to that of the towing vehicle. The actual damages sought were almost embarrassingly trivial— approximately $11.00 for each plaintiff. But the suit also asked the court to enjoin Ford from continuing to sell the trailering special packages without a wiring connector kit.

Ford removed the case to federal district court, alleging diversity jurisdiction. The district court denied plaintiff's motion to remand on the basis that the requisite amount in controversy—at that time $10,000—was met by the value to Ford of the business right which the Snows sought to enjoin. The Ninth Circuit disagreed and directed that the case be remanded to the state court. The court explained:

> We are presented here with two conflicting lines of precedent, each providing a method by which to measure the amount in controversy. One line sets out an area where the amount may be determined from the defendant's point of view. This approach is exemplified by *Ridder Bros., Inc. v. Blethen*, 142 F.2d 395 (9th Cir. 1944). In suits involving equitable relief, the dollar value of the object in controversy may be minimal to the plaintiff, but costly to the defendant. The court in *Ridder Bros.* stated that, in such cases, "if the value of the thing to be accomplished [is] equal to the dollar minimum of the jurisdictional requirement to anyone concerned in the action, then jurisdiction [is] satisfied." Ford maintains that this doctrine is applicable here, and that the injunction sought would have an impact on it far greater than the $10,000 requirement of the diversity statute.
>
> On the other side is *Snyder v. Harris*. . . . While the Court [in *Snyder*] did not speak about "the plaintiff's viewpoint" or "the defendant's viewpoint" in measuring the amount in controversy, it is clear that the Court applied the plaintiff's viewpoint rule at least for a Rule 23(b)(3) class action not involving a request for injunctive relief. And, if a plaintiff cannot aggregate to fulfill the jurisdictional amount requirement of §1332, then neither can a defendant who invokes federal jurisdiction under the removal provisions of §1441. . . .
>
> We agree that *Snyder* is controlling. "Total detriment" is basically the same as aggregation. The only reason the injunction is worth more than $10,000 to Ford is that it would affect all of Ford's future trailer package sales to thousands of other individual consumers. In short, we hold that, where "the equitable relief sought is but a means through which the individual claims may be satisfied, the ban on aggregation [applies] with equal force to the equitable as well as the monetary relief."

Ford, nevertheless, contends that aggregation is not at issue because the right sought to be enjoined is a single right of a single defendant, namely, its right to market its packages. The argument misses the mark. Given *Snyder*, the proper focus in this case is not influenced by the type of relief requested, but rather continues to depend upon the nature and value of the right asserted. The right asserted by plaintiffs is the right of individual future consumers to be protected from Ford's allegedly deceptive advertising which is said to injure them in the amount of $11.00 each. That figure is far below the jurisdictional minimum.

A finding of jurisdiction in this case would provide plaintiffs with a means by which to evade the impact of *Snyder* and *Zahn v. International Paper Co.*, 414 U.S. 291 (1973).

As the *Snow* court acknowledges, *Snyder* involved only claims for damages. Is the court persuasive in explaining why *Snyder* should control cases in which the plaintiff also seeks injunctive relief, and compliance with the injunction would cost the defendant more than the jurisdictional minimum?

4. In *In re Ford Motor Co./Citibank (South Dakota) N.A. Cardholder Rebate Program Litigation*, 264 F.3d 952 (9th Cir. 2001), the Ninth Circuit took *Snow* one step further. This was another state-law class action removed to federal court on the basis of diversity. The defendants conceded that no plaintiff had an individual damages claim exceeding $75,000, but they pointed out that the plaintiffs were seeking an injunction requiring the defendants to reinstate and maintain a rebate program that the defendants had discontinued. This, the defendants argued, was sufficient to distinguish the case from *Snow*. The Ninth Circuit disagreed, saying:

> [The defendants seek to overcome *Snow* by arguing] that because the cost of an injunction running in favor of one plaintiff would exceed $75,000, aggregating the cost of compliance is unnecessary to satisfy the amount in controversy requirement. In other words, while the monetary benefit to an individual plaintiff of reinstating the rebate accrual program would be relatively insubstantial, the fixed costs to Ford and Citibank of reinstating and maintaining the program would be the same whether it is done for one plaintiff or for six million. Thus, Ford and Citibank assert that because the non-aggregation rule would not be violated if their fixed administrative costs were used to establish the amount in controversy requirement, we may look to the "either viewpoint" rule to establish the jurisdictional amount.

> At first blush, this argument appears consistent with *Snow*. However, it is fundamentally violative of the principle underlying the jurisdictional amount requirement—to keep small diversity suits out of federal court. If the argument were accepted, and the administrative costs of complying with an injunction were permitted to count as the amount in controversy, "then every case, however trivial, against a large company would cross the threshold." "It would be an invitation to file state-law nuisance suits in federal court." Therefore, we hold that the amount in controversy requirement

cannot be satisfied by showing that the fixed administrative costs of compliance exceed $75,000.

The court seems to assume that if jurisdiction is allowed based on the "fixed costs" to the defendants of maintaining the rebate program, jurisdiction would also have to be allowed in any case in which the "administrative costs" of complying with an injunction would exceed the statutory minimum. Is that argument persuasive?

The *Ford/Citibank* case is the one that the Supreme Court agreed to hear but dismissed after oral argument.

5. Today, cases like *Ford/Citibank* could probably be removed to federal court under the Class Action Fairness Act of 2005. See Chapter 2. However, disputes over the amount in controversy can still arise in other kinds of cases, particularly when the plaintiff seeks injunctive or declaratory relief. Here is an example.

Problem: A Pipeline across Blackacre

For safety reasons, Acme Energy Co. decided to reroute a small segment of a pipeline it operates in the state of New Harmony. Under state law, companies like Acme are authorized to exercise the power of eminent domain in order to enable them to transport "petroleum" products to the public. The new route would cross several parcels of land, including one owned by Paula Penmarric.

Penmarric has filed suit in federal district court seeking to enjoin Acme from using her land for the pipeline. Jurisdiction is based on diversity. The complaint asserts that under state law Acme is authorized to appropriate her property only for "public use," and that the proposed rerouting does not satisfy this standard. In support of this claim, Penmarric states that the pipeline's termini are located at subsidiary plants owned by the same corporate entity that owns Acme, that no entry or exit pipes exist apart from the termini, and that the pipeline transports a substance known as xylene "which may or may not be 'petroleum' as contemplated by the legislature."

Acme moves to dismiss the action for want of subject-matter jurisdiction. Acme acknowledges that the parties are of diverse citizenship, but asserts that the amount in controversy requirement is not met. In support of its motion, Acme attaches the record of a condemnation proceeding in state court that concluded just a few weeks ago. That suit was filed by Acme against Hanson, the owner of a similar neighboring property, seeking to condemn an easement across Hanson's land. Hanson filed no objection to the complaint, and the state court entered an order condemning the easement sought by Acme and appointing three appraisers to assess the value of the easement. The appraisers ordered compensation of $45,000, and no appeal was taken. The easement Acme seeks from Penmarric involves a smaller parcel of land than Hanson's, so Acme asserts that the matter in controversy in Penmarric's suit cannot exceed $75,000.

In response, Penmarric points out that rerouting the pipeline to avoid crossing her property would cost Acme considerably in excess of $75,000. She therefore argues that the amount in controversy requirement is easily satisfied.

Should the district court grant the motion to dismiss? Is there any other information you might want in order to answer that question?

Note: Indexing the Amount in Controversy

As noted in the introduction to this chapter, Congress has raised the minimum amount in controversy for diversity cases only five times since 1789. The proposed Federal Courts Jurisdiction Clarification Act of 2006, drafted by the Judicial Conference of the United States, would have amended Title 28 to provide for indexing the amount to keep pace with inflation. Judge Janet Hall, testifying on behalf of the Judicial Conference in 2005, explained the rationale of the proposal:

> [This] automatic adjustment would avoid the need to periodically revisit the underlying amount specified in the statute and then to enact large increases. This change would also preserve the monetary amount as a meaningful threshold for diversity jurisdiction....
>
> The formula [in the bill] specifies that effective on January 1 of each year immediately following a year evenly divisible by 5, the jurisdictional amount shall be adjusted according to a formula tied to the Consumer Price Index for All Urban Consumers (CPI-U).

Judge Hall said that if the formula had been applicable beginning in 2000, the amount in controversy would have been increased to $85,000 in 2001 and $95,000 in 2006.

A revised version of the 2006 bill became law in 2011, but the indexing provision had been deleted. Is the idea a good one? Where might opposition have come from?

Note: Supplemental Jurisdiction in Diversity Cases

1. As discussed in Chapter 10, before 1990, the Supreme Court held that if a federal district court had original jurisdiction under §1331 over at least one claim, that court could exercise jurisdiction over all other claims between the same parties arising out of the same Article III case or controversy. This doctrine was called "pendent jurisdiction." A parallel doctrine called "ancillary jurisdiction" was developed in diversity cases. At the same time, however, courts held that ancillary jurisdiction could not be used to effect an end run around the complete diversity requirement of §1332. Thus, if §1332 was the basis for federal jurisdiction in federal court, a court could not exercise ancillary jurisdiction over a party whose presence in the suit would destroy complete diversity. A similar restriction applied to the amount-in-controversy requirement. A party with a claim that did not satisfy the amount-in-controversy requirement could not rely on ancillary jurisdiction to sue in federal court by joining forces with another plaintiff whose claim did meet the amount-in-controversy requirement. Instead, each plaintiff had to satisfy the amount-in-controversy requirement separately.

2. In 1990, Congress enacted the supplemental jurisdiction statute, 28 U.S.C. §1367. That statute codified the doctrine of pendent jurisdiction and merged it with the

doctrine of ancillary jurisdiction. Under § 1367, if a federal district court has original jurisdiction over one claim, irrespective of the basis of the jurisdiction, that court can exercise jurisdiction over other claims that form part of the same case or controversy. Section 1367(a) provides:

> [I]n any civil action of which the district courts have original jurisdiction, the district courts shall have supplemental jurisdiction over all other claims that are so related to claims in the action within such original jurisdiction that they form part of the same case or controversy under Article III of the United States Constitution.

Section 1367(a) also made clear that supplemental jurisdiction generally could be exercised over additional parties, stating that "[s]uch supplemental jurisdiction shall include claims that involve the joinder or intervention of additional parties."

Despite generally extending supplemental jurisdiction over additional claims by other parties, the statute retained the restriction on using supplemental jurisdiction to avoid the restrictions on diversity jurisdiction under 28 U.S.C. § 1332. Section 1367(b) provides:

> In any civil action of which the district courts have original jurisdiction founded solely on section 1332 of this title, the district courts shall not have supplemental jurisdiction . . . over claims by plaintiffs against persons made parties under Rule 14, 19, 20, or 24 of the Federal Rules of Civil Procedure, or over claims by persons proposed to be joined as plaintiffs under Rule 19 of such rules, or seeking to intervene as plaintiffs under Rule 24 of such rules, when exercising supplemental jurisdiction over such claims would be inconsistent with the jurisdictional requirements of section 1332.

For many years, courts agreed that nothing in the 1990 Act allows the exercise of supplemental jurisdiction over a party whose presence in the suit would destroy complete diversity, but they disagreed whether the statute now permits the exercise of supplemental jurisdiction over claims by additional plaintiffs who do not meet the amount-in-controversy requirement.

In *Exxon Mobil Corp. v. Allapattah Services Inc.*, 545 U.S. 546 (2005), the Supreme Court resolved the dispute. In a 5-4 decision written by Justice Kennedy, the Court held that "a federal court in a diversity action may exercise supplemental jurisdiction over additional plaintiffs whose claims do not satisfy the minimum amount-in-controversy requirement, provided the claims are part of the same case or controversy as the claims of plaintiffs who do allege a sufficient amount in controversy."

In reaching that conclusion, the Court drew a sharp distinction between the complete-diversity requirement and the amount-in-controversy requirement. The Court wrote:

> [Refusing to use supplemental jurisdiction to abrogate the complete diversity requirement makes] some sense . . . because the presence of nondiverse parties on both sides of a lawsuit eliminates the justification for providing a federal forum. [A similar limitation], however, makes little sense with respect

to the amount-in-controversy requirement, which is meant to ensure that a dispute is sufficiently important to warrant federal-court attention. The presence of a single nondiverse party may eliminate the fear of bias with respect to all claims, but the presence of a claim that falls short of the minimum amount in controversy does nothing to reduce the importance of the claims that do meet this requirement.

It is fallacious to suppose, simply from the proposition that § 1332 imposes both the diversity requirement and the amount-in-controversy requirement, that [a limitation on] the former is also relevant to the latter. There is no inherent logical connection between the amount-in-controversy requirement and § 1332 diversity jurisdiction. After all, federal-question jurisdiction once had an amount-in-controversy requirement as well. If such a requirement were revived under § 1331, it is clear beyond peradventure that § 1367(a) provides supplemental jurisdiction over federal-question cases where some, but not all, of the federal-law claims involve a sufficient amount in controversy.

Is this distinction between the complete diversity requirement and the amount-in-controversy requirement persuasive? In her dissenting opinion, Justice Ginsburg argued that the diversity statute itself "does not rank order the two requirements."

3. Prior to the enactment of § 1367, some courts held that "ancillary jurisdiction" extended to compulsory counterclaims, but not to permissive counterclaims. *See, e.g., McCaffrey v. Rex Motor Transp., Inc.*, 672 F.2d 246 (1st Cir. 1982). Under § 1367 as interpreted in *Allapattah*, is that still the line of demarcation?

Chapter 12

Special Problems of Removal Jurisdiction

A. Introduction

The plaintiff controls the initial selection of a forum. Within limits, removal jurisdiction levels the playing field. It does so by permitting a defendant to override a plaintiff's initial selection of a state forum in most cases that could have been brought in federal court initially. The governing statute is 28 U.S.C. § 1441(a):

> Except as otherwise expressly provided by Act of Congress, any civil action brought in a State court of which the district courts of the United States have original jurisdiction, may be removed by the defendant or the defendants, to the district court of the United States for the district and division embracing the place where such action is pending.

Removal has become a major battleground in civil litigation today. But the law of removal presents special challenges for plaintiffs and defendants alike. Plaintiffs may discover, too late, that because of litigation decisions made in ignorance of that law, they must litigate in a federal court rather than the state court. Defendants may find that they have lost an opportunity to remove that was open to them earlier in the litigation. Missteps and disputes involving removal proceedings can add to the cost of a lawsuit and delay its ultimate resolution.

In this chapter we examine some of the major issues affecting removal. After a brief introduction, we consider the procedural maneuvering that may follow when the plaintiff files suit in state court asserting both federal and state claims and the defendant removes the case to federal court on the basis of the federal claims. The discussion will encompass not only the familiar supplemental jurisdiction statute, but also 28 U.S.C. § 1441(c), a jurisdictional provision that bedeviled removal practice until 2011, when it was completely rewritten. Next, we examine the major statutes and doctrines that govern removal based on diversity jurisdiction, with particular emphasis on the opportunities for "gamesmanship" that they create. Finally, we look at some of the important procedural aspects of removal.

The aim of this chapter is not to enable you to navigate the many shoals of removal jurisdiction; that would require a book. The purpose, rather, is to give you a sampling of the issues that arise in removal practice, so that you can see the techniques that judges and lawyers use in dealing with the many gaps and ambiguities in the removal statutes.

Note: The Statutory Framework

Congress has provided for some form of removal jurisdiction since the Judiciary Act of 1789. Starting in the late nineteenth century, Congress has tied jurisdiction under the general removal statute to the requirements of original jurisdiction. This means that a defendant seeking removal must ordinarily consider whether the case as presented by the plaintiff might have been filed in federal court in the first place. Chapters 11 and 12 present numerous illustrations of this proposition; for example, in *Grable & Sons Metal Products, Inc. v. Darue Eng'g & Mfg.*, 545 U.S. 308 (2005), the Court upheld removal by reaffirming the doctrine that "arising under" jurisdiction can be based on an "incorporated" federal question.

The most important exception to the equivalency of removal and original jurisdiction is found in 28 U.S.C. § 1441(b). That statute prohibits removal in diversity cases when any defendant who has been "properly joined and served" is a citizen of the state in which the lawsuit is brought.

In addition, Congress has provided that certain kinds of cases may not be removed irrespective of whether they fall within the district courts' original jurisdiction. Under 28 U.S.C. § 1445, nonremovable actions include, among others, those arising under "the workmen's compensation laws of [any] State" and civil actions under § 40302 of the Violence Against Women Act. Prohibitions on removal may also be found in other titles of the United States Code. For example, 15 U.S.C. § 77v(a) provides that no case arising under "this subchapter"—the subchapter dealing with securities regulation— may be removed to federal district court.

At the other end of the spectrum, there are a number of statutes that allow removal of cases involving particular subject-matter or defendants even though the requirements for original jurisdiction might *not* be met. These include 28 U.S.C. §§ 1442 (federal officers or armed forces defendants); 1443 (civil rights actions); 1444 (foreclosure actions against the United States); and 1454 (patent, plant variety protection, and copyright cases).

In the past, some courts of appeals held that the All Writs Act, 28 U.S.C. § 1651, "gives a federal court the authority to remove a state-court case in order to prevent the frustration of orders the federal court has previously issued." The Supreme Court rejected that line of authority in *Syngenta Crop Protection, Inc. v. Henson*, 537 U.S. 28 (2002). The Court held that the All Writs Act does not furnish removal jurisdiction at all. Thus authority for removal must be found in some other statute.

In 2011, Congress substantially revised the provisions of the Judicial Code dealing with removal. These changes were the product of three separate enactments: the "Holmes Group fix" that was part of the Leahy-Smith America Invents Act, the Removal Clarification Act of 2011, and the Federal Courts Jurisdiction and Venue Clarification Act of 2011 (JVCA). Of the three statutes, only the JVCA affects the general run of civil litigation, but the amendments are quite significant. The Act's provisions will be treated throughout this chapter.

Note: A Presumption Against Removability?

1. In *Shamrock Oil & Gas Co. v. Sheets*, 313 U.S. 100 (1941), the Supreme Court held that the removal statute does not allow a plaintiff to remove a case on the basis of a counterclaim filed by the defendant, even if the counterclaim, if filed as an original action, would fall within the jurisdiction of the district court. The Court relied on the language of the removal statute as revised in 1887. Toward the end of its opinion, the Court added the following comment:

> Not only does the language of the Act of 1887 evidence the Congressional purpose to restrict the jurisdiction of the federal courts on removal, but the policy of the successive acts of Congress regulating the jurisdiction of federal courts is one calling for the strict construction of such legislation.

This language—particularly the reference to a congressional policy "calling for the strict construction of [removal] legislation"—has in turn been relied on by many federal courts as requiring that "all doubts about jurisdiction should be resolved in favor of remand to state court." Indeed, these courts sometimes speak of a "presumption in favor of remand." See *University of South Alabama v. American Tobacco Co.*, 168 F.3d 405, 411 (11th Cir. 1999). Two decisions in the twenty-first century may call this approach into question.

2. Under 28 U.S.C. §1447(c), when a district court orders remand of a removed case, the court may award costs, including attorney's fees, to the plaintiff. In *Martin v. Franklin Capital Corp.*, 546 U.S. 132 (2005), the Court granted review "to resolve a conflict among the Circuits concerning when attorney's fees should be awarded under §1447(c)." The Court unanimously held that "absent unusual circumstances, attorney's fees should not be awarded when the removing party has an objectively reasonable basis for removal." In the course of his opinion, Chief Justice Roberts outlined the view of removal that shaped the Court's decision:

> By enacting the removal statute, Congress granted a right to a federal forum to a limited class of state-court defendants. If fee shifting were automatic, defendants might choose to exercise this right only in cases where the right to remove was obvious. But there is no reason to suppose Congress meant to confer a right to remove, while at the same time discouraging its exercise in all but obvious cases.

> Congress, however, would not have enacted §1447(c) if its only concern were avoiding deterrence of proper removals. Instead, Congress thought fee shifting appropriate in some cases. The process of removing a case to federal court and then having it remanded back to state court delays resolution of the case, imposes additional costs on both parties, and wastes judicial resources. Assessing costs and fees on remand reduces the attractiveness of removal as a method for delaying litigation and imposing costs on the plaintiff.

> The appropriate test for awarding fees under §1447(c) should recognize the desire to deter removals sought for the purpose of prolonging litigation and imposing costs on the opposing party, while not undermining Congress'

basic decision to afford defendants a right to remove as a general matter, when the statutory criteria are satisfied.

3. In *Dart Cherokee Basin Operating Co. v. Owens*, 135 S. Ct. 547 (2014), the defendant removed a putative class action under the Class Action Fairness Act of 2005 (CAFA). (See Chapter 2 for a brief description of CAFA.) The district court remanded the case, holding that the notice of removal was deficient because it failed to show that the amount in controversy exceeded the statutory minimum ($5,000,000) and that post-removal evidence could not cure the deficiency.

The Supreme Court reversed, holding that, "as specified in § 1446(a), a defendant's notice of removal need include only a plausible allegation that the amount in controversy exceeds the jurisdictional threshold. Evidence establishing the amount is required by § 1446(c)(2)(B) only when the plaintiff contests, or the court questions, the defendant's allegation." The Court noted that in remanding the case to state court, the district court "relied, in part, on a purported 'presumption' against removal." The Court continued:

> We need not here decide whether such a presumption is proper in mine-run diversity cases. It suffices to point out that no antiremoval presumption attends cases invoking CAFA, which Congress enacted to facilitate adjudication of certain class actions in federal court. See . . . S. Rep. No. 109-14, at 43 (2005) (CAFA's "provisions should be read broadly, with a strong preference that interstate class actions should be heard in a federal court if properly removed by any defendant.").

One district court has said that in non-CAFA lawsuits after *Dart Cherokee*, "the rule of construing removal statutes strictly and resolving doubts in favor of remand," is "still in place."[1] Should it be? Note that the *Martin* opinion refers repeatedly to the defendant's "right" to remove, and the Court rejects the idea that Congress intended to discourage defendants from removing "in all but obvious cases." Do these comments cast doubt on the propriety of an "antiremoval presumption" in "mine-run" diversity cases?

4. Even after *Martin*, courts continue to follow "the traditional rule that the removing party bears the burden of proof with regard to establishing federal court jurisdiction." *Miedema v. Maytag Corp.*, 450 F.3d 1322 (11th Cir. 2006). The *Miediema* opinion does not cite *Martin*. Does *Martin* cast doubt on the "traditional rule" about burden of proof?

B. Federal-Question Removal and State-Law Claims

When a plaintiff's claims are potentially redressable under both federal and state law, the stage is set for procedural maneuvering that may affect not only the selection

---

1. *Erby v. Pride*, 2016 WL 3548792 (N.D. Ala. June 30, 2016).

of the forum, but also other aspects of litigation. If the plaintiff sues in state court, the defendant can generally remove the case to federal court as long as the complaint includes at least one claim arising under federal law. Thereafter, the course of litigation will depend on the relationship between the state and federal claims and on the parties' tactical decisions within the framework established by Title 28. The governing law includes not only the familiar supplemental jurisdiction statute, 28 U.S.C. § 1367, but also a statutory provision uniquely applicable in the context of removal, 28 U.S.C. § 1441(c). We turn first to § 1367.

[1] Supplemental Jurisdiction

City of Chicago v. International College of Surgeons

Supreme Court of the United States, 1997.

522 U.S. 156.

[For the report of this case, see Chapter 10, section E.]

Note: Authority to Remand State-Law Claims

1. The opinion in *City of Chicago v. International College of Surgeons* (*ICS*) outlines the foundational law. When a plaintiff files suit in state court asserting both federal and state claims, § 1441(a) allows the defendant to remove the case to federal court on the basis of the federal claims. Section 1367(a) then permits the district court to adjudicate the state claims as long as the state and federal claims are part of the same constitutional case under Article III. But under § 1367(c) the district court may "decline to exercise" jurisdiction over supplemental claims if one or more of the circumstances specified in that subsection are present. In removed cases, this means that the district court would remand the supplemental claims to the state court from which the case was removed.

2. Two years before § 1367(c) was added to the Judicial Code, a divided Supreme Court recognized a non-statutory basis for remand in cases with pendent claims (as they were then called). In *Carnegie-Mellon University v. Cohill*, 484 U.S. 343 (1988), the Court held that "when all federal-law claims have dropped out of the action and only pendent state-law claims remain," the district court has discretion to remand the case to state court rather than dismissing the suit without prejudice. The Court said:

> *Gibbs* establishes that the pendent jurisdiction doctrine is designed to enable courts to handle cases involving state-law claims in the way that will best accommodate the values of economy, convenience, fairness, and comity, and *Gibbs* further establishes that the Judicial Branch is to shape and apply the doctrine in that light. Because in some circumstances a remand of a removed case involving pendent claims will better accommodate these values than will dismissal of the case, the animating principle behind the pendent jurisdiction doctrine supports giving a district court discretion to remand when the exercise of pendent jurisdiction is inappropriate.

As many lower courts have noted, a remand generally will be preferable to a dismissal when the statute of limitations on the plaintiff's state-law claims has expired before the federal court has determined that it should relinquish jurisdiction over the case. . . .

Even when the applicable statute of limitations has not expired, a remand may best promote the values of economy, convenience, fairness, and comity. . . . Any time a district court dismisses, rather than remands, a removed case involving pendent claims, the parties will have to refile their papers in state court, at some expense of time and money. Moreover, the state court will have to reprocess the case, and this procedure will involve similar costs. Under the analysis set forth in *Gibbs*, this consequence, even taken alone, provides good reason to grant federal courts wide discretion to remand cases involving pendent claims when the exercise of pendent jurisdiction over such cases would be inappropriate. . . .

Petitioners also argue that giving district courts discretion to remand cases involving pendent state-law claims will allow plaintiffs to secure a state forum through the use of manipulative tactics. Petitioners' concern appears to be that a plaintiff whose suit has been removed to federal court will be able to regain a state forum simply by deleting all federal-law claims from the complaint and requesting that the district court remand the case. This concern, however, hardly justifies a categorical prohibition on the remand of cases involving state-law claims regardless of whether the plaintiff has attempted to manipulate the forum and regardless of the other circumstances in the case. A district court can consider whether the plaintiff has engaged in any manipulative tactics when it decides whether to remand a case. If the plaintiff has attempted to manipulate the forum, the court should take this behavior into account in determining whether the balance of factors to be considered under the pendent jurisdiction doctrine support a remand in the case.

3. The Court emphasized in *Cohill* that Congress had not set any limitations on "the federal courts' administration of the doctrine of pendent jurisdiction." With the enactment of 28 U.S.C. § 1367, of course, that is no longer true. But in *Carlsbad Technology, Inc. v. HIF Bio, Inc.*, 556 U.S. 635 (2009), the Court granted certiorari to resolve the question whether the courts of appeals are permitted to review "*Cohill* remands," thus implicitly confirming that *Cohill* is good law.

4. The Court in *Cohill* acknowledged the concern that "a plaintiff whose suit has been removed to federal court will be able to regain a state forum simply by deleting all federal-law claims from the complaint and requesting that the district court remand the case." The Court responded by saying that a district court "can consider whether the plaintiff has engaged in any manipulative tactics." But the Court did not say that the tactic of dropping the federal claims would necessarily be impermissible. Lower courts have taken different approaches to this ploy, as the next case explains.

Payne v. Parkchester North Condominiums

United States District Court for the Southern District of New York, 2001.

134 F. Supp. 2d 582.

WHITMAN KNAPP, SENIOR DISTRICT JUDGE.

Plaintiffs Cardell and Dahlia Payne (hereinafter, the "plaintiffs") move to amend their complaint to strike all federal claims and then to remand the case back to state court. For the reasons stated below, we deny both motions.

Background

Plaintiffs are husband and wife and residents of an apartment located in the Parkchester North Condominiums in the Bronx. According to plaintiffs, Cardell was beaten, pepper-sprayed, handcuffed and arrested by the building's security guards, some of whom have "Special Patrol Officer" status granted by the New York City Police Department. Dahlia also claims that one or more of these guards struck her. The defendants include Parkchester North Condominiums Associates, The Parkchester South Condominium, Inc., Parkchester Preservation Management, LLC, and several security officers (hereinafter, collectively, the "defendants").

In August 1999, plaintiffs sued in the Supreme Court of New York, Bronx County. In their original complaint, and in three places in their October 1999 amended complaint, plaintiffs expressly claim violations of specific federal constitutional rights. They also allege assault and battery, false arrest and imprisonment, malicious prosecution, negligence, and other state torts. In July 2000, defendants served interrogatories. Plaintiffs did not answer the discovery requests until late February 2001, but the parties have taken and/or scheduled depositions.

At about the same time that plaintiffs filed their amended complaint in Supreme Court, defendants attempted unsuccessfully to remove the case to this Court, and at least some of the parties' lawyers labored under confusion about the lawsuit's status. In April 2000, counsel for defendants ascertained that the Clerk of this Court had not assigned a docket number. Accordingly, in June, defendants again tried to file for removal, this time successfully.

Over seven months after such removal, on January 24, 2001, we held a pre-motion conference (requested by defendants) during which we and they learned for the first time that plaintiffs challenged our jurisdiction. Plaintiffs now move (as urged in their reply brief) again to amend their complaint, deleting all references to the United States Constitution. Further, they ask us to remand the case.

Plaintiffs' opening motion papers fashion a very weak argument for remand, namely, that their federal claims represent "nothing more than state court claim[s] recloaked in constitutional garb." In two pages of opposition, defendants vanquish plaintiffs' effort. But then, in their reply papers, plaintiffs take a new stance, asking for leave to drop their explicitly federal causes of action and to substitute state and local analogues.

Discussion

Ordinarily, we should "freely" grant leave to amend the complaint and dismiss causes of action "when justice so requires." FED. R. CIV. P. 15(a). Yet in deciding whether to approve amendment, we must consider not only any substantial prejudice to defendants, undue delay, or bad faith, but also whether such action implicates our subject matter jurisdiction. If we authorize plaintiffs to drop their federal claims, then in our discretion we can remand the case or, under extraordinary circumstances, retain the state claims under supplemental jurisdiction. 28 U.S.C. § 1367(c). In making the determination whether to remand, we must weigh "the values of judicial economy, convenience, fairness, and comity." *Carnegie-Mellon Univ. v. Cohill*, 484 U.S. 343, 350 (1988).

Crucially, we must also take into account whether the plaintiffs have tried to manipulate the forum. [Here the court quoted from *Cohill*.]

Over the years, several courts have confronted the question now before us, namely, whether to permit a plaintiff voluntarily to strike his federal claims after removal and, if so permitted, whether thereafter to remand. Several of these cases adopt one of two opposing rules or directions. Curiously, most of the opinions acknowledge only whichever rule is adopted therein and do not address the counterarguments. On the one hand, courts disposed to reject remand when a plaintiff clearly and intentionally attempts to engage in forum manipulation typically cite three rationales for their rejection—time and resource conservation, Congressional intent, and a sense of fair play. *See, e.g., Boelens v. Redman Homes, Inc.*, 759 F.2d 504, 507 & n.2 (5th Cir. 1985) (citing cases).

We transcribe here an oft-quoted articulation of these reasons [in *Boelens*]:

> "When a plaintiff chooses a state forum, yet also elects to press federal claims, he runs the risk of removal. A federal forum for federal claims is certainly a defendant's right. If a state forum is more important to the plaintiff than his federal claims, he should have to make that assessment before the case is jockeyed from state court to federal court and back to state court. The jockeying is a drain on the resources of the state judiciary, the federal judiciary and the parties involved; tactical manipulation [by the] plaintiff . . . cannot be condoned." The rule that a plaintiff cannot oust removal jurisdiction by voluntarily amending the complaint to drop all federal questions [also] serves the salutary purpose of preventing the plaintiff from being able to destroy the jurisdictional choice that Congress intended to afford a defendant in the removal statute.

In contrast, other courts [including the Ninth Circuit] justify forum manipulation as "a legitimate tactical decision":

> The defendant is not obligated to remove; rather, he has the choice either to submit to state court resolution of his claims, or to assert his right to a federal forum. If the defendant rejects the plaintiff's offer to litigate in state court and removes the action, the plaintiff must then choose between federal

claims and a state forum. Plaintiffs in this case chose the state forum. They dismissed their federal claims and moved for remand with all due speed after removal. There was nothing manipulative about that straightforward tactical decision, and there would be little to be gained in judicial economy by forcing plaintiffs to abandon their federal causes of action before filing in state court.

Baddie v. Berkeley Farms, Inc., 64 F.3d 487, 491 (9th Cir. 1995).

We are not obligated by any Second Circuit precedent to observe either of the two competing general policies. We may use our discretion. . . .

Since both general rules contain flaws,[1] we believe that, rather than fixate upon a bright-line rule, we should glean from the full range of cases the circumstances upon which to focus a fact-intensive inquiry. Applying this approach, we find that, in the atypical case before us, the balance of factors weighs against remand even if we permitted the complaint to be amended.

Intentional Manipulation

It makes more sense to remand if the particular plaintiffs did not intentionally maneuver the forum. *See Cohill.* Even the remand-friendly *Baddie* Court expressed concern about malicious forum-shopping, and thus it suggested that the state court, after remand, can consider sanctioning plaintiffs who acted in "bad faith" or "for the sole purpose of putting defendants through the removal-remand procedure." However, a serious inquiry in the first instance by the federal court into possible bad faith seems more efficient and more apt to discourage plaintiffs from testing the boundaries of ethical advocacy.

The most innocent request to strike federal claims materializes when a plaintiff did not initially realize that his complaint would be construed as containing federal subject matter. *See, e.g., Moscovitch v. Danbury Hosp.*, 25 F. Supp. 2d 74 (D. Conn. 1998) ("it does not appear that the plaintiff intended his original claims . . . to be federal in character and he did not seek relief under a federal statute").

Less innocently but still relatively acceptably, a particular plaintiff may seek to avoid a federal venue but *also* have *other, substantive* reasons to alter his pleadings. [For example, in *Kimsey v. Snap-On Tools Corp.*, 752 F. Supp. 693 (M.D.N.C. 1990),] the court could "envision a host of reasons" why plaintiffs no longer wanted to pursue federal RICO claims, "including the expense and complexity" of such claims.

In the case at bar, this factor tends to persuade us to deny plaintiffs' motion to remand, for plaintiffs have manifestly resolved to manipulate their forum without any reasonable or fair justification. First, plaintiffs must have known that they were advancing federal claims, for they invoked the United States Constitution in three logical

---

1. For example, with regard to one of the three underlying rationales for the "no remand" rule, the legislative intent argument, Congress has crafted a statutory scheme whereby plaintiffs (and not just defendants) have a choice: Plaintiffs may opt to replead and return to state court at the discretion of the federal district courts.

places in their complaint. In so doing, they risked removal. Moreover, they waited months and then surprised their opponents and us with their motion when threatened with potential motions to compel and for summary judgment. This timing suggests unreasonable delay[2] and perhaps even a kind of retaliatory intent.

Also, the instant plaintiffs proffered very weak arguments for remand and installed them in reply papers. Finally, plaintiffs candidly admitted at oral argument that they had no additional reason beyond forum-shopping for now seeking to hinge their case on state law.

Prejudice, Resource-Wasting, & Untimeliness

We must also contemplate other variables, and we now turn to the three interrelated factors of prejudice, resources, and time. When plaintiffs promptly request amendment and remand, less chance exists that the federal court or the defendants have expended significant time or assets on motions, conferences, or other aspects of federal procedure. In fact, in many of the cases condoning remand, the plaintiff had moved within *days* after removal, before discovery and before any attempt at resolution on the merits. . . .

In contrast, in the current case, plaintiffs waited over seven *months* to file for remand, some discovery has already occurred under the Federal Rules, and this Court has become quite familiar with the case through pre-motion conferences. Thus, remand would postpone the litigation, waste judicial resources, and perhaps cause inconsistences in discovery procedure. Similarly, we find that defendants would suffer appreciable prejudice and inconvenience in having to file their summary judgment motion weeks later than they anticipated in front of a judge unfamiliar with the case.

Finally, we deny not only plaintiffs' motion to remand but also their motion for leave to amend their complaint. Plaintiffs admit that they asked for amendment solely to induce remand, and we have decided not to remand in any event. If within twenty days plaintiffs can (and choose to) provide a legitimate reason to revise their complaint, we will consider that request, but only if such revision will not significantly delay the proceedings before us or prejudice their adversaries. Barring such a showing, this litigation will move ahead with the federal and state claims as alleged in the October 1999 amended complaint.

Conclusion

For the foregoing reasons, we DENY plaintiffs' motion for leave to amend their complaint and DENY their motion to remand.

Note: Removal and "Manipulative Tactics"

1. As the *Payne* opinion notes, the lower-court decisions reflect two diametrically opposed views of plaintiffs' attempts to delete federal claims and get their cases

---

2. Granted, plaintiffs' counsel understandably became confused in early 2000 about where this suit was then pending, given that defendants thought that they had filed for removal by that time. Still, plaintiffs' lawyer received service of a notice of removal in June 2000, and he could easily have verified the effectiveness of the removal filing at any time thereafter.

remanded to state court. On one side is the Fifth Circuit's *Boelens* decision. The *Boelens* court believed that "[a] federal forum for federal claims is . . . the defendant's right." To preserve that right, the plaintiff must be required to decide before filing the lawsuit whether the state forum "is more important . . . than his federal claims." On the other side is the Ninth Circuit's *Baddie.* In the Ninth Circuit's view, only if the defendant rejects the plaintiff's "offer" to litigate in state court must the plaintiff be put to the choice between the state forum and the federal claims. Which of these positions is more persuasive?

2. *Payne* is an easy case because all of the circumstances pointed in one direction. Suppose that the plaintiffs had moved immediately to delete their federal claims. Should the court have allowed the amendment and granted the motion to remand?

3. The defendants in *Payne* invoked the "artful pleading" doctrine. (See Chapter 10.) The court responded by saying (in a footnote) that the doctrine "does not apply here [because] federal law is not intrinsic or necessary to a police brutality case. State and local statutes regulate the behavior of police officers, and plaintiffs could have sued under those statutes as well as under New York state common law." Did the court interpret the doctrine correctly?

4. The court is correct in suggesting that a plaintiff in a police brutality case can generally sue under state law rather than pursuing claims under the Fourth and Fourteenth Amendments. But there is a big difference between the two types of suits. A complaint asserting a violation of federal constitutional rights states a cause of action under 42 U.S.C. § 1983. And under the Civil Rights Attorney's Fees Awards Act of 1976 (codified in 42 U.S.C. § 1988), the prevailing plaintiff in a § 1983 case can generally obtain attorney's fees. In a pure state-law case, attorney's fees would seldom be available.

Why would a plaintiff like Payne be so desirous of litigating in state court that he would seek to delete his federal claims and thereby give up the possibility of securing attorney's fees if he prevails?

Problem: Discord in the Police Department

Discord has been simmering in the Bayport Police Department, and on February 10 of last year, four current and former police officers filed suit in Oceana state court against the City of Bayport and Police Chief Ezra Collig. The plaintiffs alleged many forms of wrongful conduct by the defendants, including wrongful termination, alteration of personnel files, favoritism, retaliation, and harassment. The complaint asserted 17 causes of action, including three claims arising under federal law: "violation of First Amendment," "violation of Fourteenth Amendment due process," and "violation of section 1983."

On February 16, the defendants filed a notice of removal based on federal question and supplemental jurisdiction. On March 1, the plaintiffs filed a motion to remand. The rationale for their request was that the Oceana state court "is authorized and is capable of adjudicating and providing remedies to Plaintiffs on all claims asserted by Plaintiffs in this action." The motion did not attack the removal procedurally or substantively. On March 15, the plaintiffs filed an amended complaint that continued to assert the federal claims.

Two weeks after the filing of the amended complaint, the defendants filed an answer and a motion for partial judgment on the pleadings. They also filed their opposition to the motion to remand. The supporting memorandum stated: "The existence of concurrent jurisdiction in the state court does not justify remand if, as here, the case has been properly removed."

The plaintiffs did not respond to the defendants' motion for partial judgment on the pleadings. However, on March 30, the plaintiffs filed a Motion to Expedite Discovery seeking an order allowing them to take a deposition of a witness and issue a subpoena duces tecum prior to the parties' Rule 26(f) conference. Before the district court could rule on the motion, the parties reached an agreement on their discovery dispute.

On April 29, plaintiffs filed a motion to further amend the complaint to dismiss all of the federal claims. The plaintiffs gave no express reason why they wanted to dismiss the federal claims, but the memorandum in support of the motion makes clear their purpose: they want the court to (1) allow them to dismiss the federal claims, (2) decline to assert jurisdiction over the remaining state-law claims, and (3) remand the matter back to state court as requested in the March 1 motion.

Should the court grant the plaintiffs' motions? What might the plaintiffs' lawyer have done to strengthen his argument for sending the case back to state court?

[2] Unrelated State-Law Claims and Federal-Question Removal

Note: Goodbye to the "Separate and Independent Claim" Provision

1. In *Lyon v. Whisman*, 45 F.3d 758 (3d Cir. 1995), the plaintiff sued her employer in federal court, charging that it failed to pay her overtime wages as required by the Fair Labor Standards Act (FLSA). (See Chapter 10.) Her complaint also included state-law contract and tort claims charging that the defendant failed to pay her a promised bonus on time or in full. The Third Circuit held that the state claims did not share a "common nucleus of operative fact" with the FLSA claim, and thus the district court lacked subject matter jurisdiction over them under 28 U.S.C. § 1367.

Suppose the plaintiff brought the same suit in state court and the defendant removed it to federal district court. Could the district court adjudicate the state as well as the federal claims? You might think that the answer must be "No." After all, as the Supreme Court said in *City of Chicago v. International College of Surgeons* (also in Chapter 10), § 1367 "applies with equal force to cases removed to federal court as to cases initially filed there."

There is a catch, however—a statutory provision that applies only in the context of removal. It is 28 U.S.C. § 1441(c), and from 1990 until 2011 it provided:

Whenever a separate and independent claim or cause of action within the jurisdiction conferred by section 1331 of this title is joined with one or more otherwise non-removable claims or causes of action, the entire case may be removed and the district court may determine all issues therein, or, in its discretion, may remand all matters in which State law predominates.

Might the district court have been able to hear Lyon's state-law claims under this version of § 1441(c)? The opaque language of this provision appeared to allow that outcome. But if so, would that exercise of jurisdiction be constitutional?

Recall that in *United Mine Workers v. Gibbs* (1966) (Chapter 10), the Supreme Court held that supplemental jurisdiction (then called "pendent jurisdiction") exists whenever the state and federal claims "derive from a common nucleus of operative fact," such that one would typically expect them to be tried in one judicial proceeding. There is then "*power* in federal courts to hear the whole [of the case]," including the state claims. (Emphasis in original.) In a later decision, the Court noted that the *Gibbs* standard "delineated the constitutional limits of federal judicial power." *Owen Equip. & Erection v. Kroger*, 437 U.S. 365 (1978).

If supplemental jurisdiction extends to the full measure of federal judicial power, and if Lyon's state-law claims do not fall within supplemental jurisdiction (as the Third Circuit held), would it not follow that the district lacked power to hear those claims? Yet § 1441(c) provided that the district court "may determine all issues" in the case.

2. The many problems of interpretation and constitutionality raised by the "separate and independent claim" provision were swept away in late 2011 when Congress, as part of the Federal Courts Jurisdiction and Venue Clarification Act of 2011 (JVCA), completely rewrote § 1441(c). The subsection now provides:

(c) Joinder of Federal law claims and State law claims. —

(1) If a civil action includes —

(A) a claim arising under the Constitution, laws, or treaties of the United States (within the meaning of section 1331 of this title), and

(B) a claim not within the original or supplemental jurisdiction of the district court or a claim that has been made nonremovable by statute, the entire action may be removed if the action would be removable without the inclusion of the claim described in subparagraph (B).

(2) Upon removal of an action described in paragraph (1), the district court shall sever from the action all claims described in paragraph (1)(B) and shall remand the severed claims to the State court from which the action was removed. Only defendants against whom a claim described in paragraph (1)(A) has been asserted are required to join in or consent to the removal under paragraph (1).

3. Under the rewritten version of § 1441(c), how should the district court deal with the state-law claims in *Lyon*?

4. Assume that a plaintiff has both federal and state claims against a defendant, and that the plaintiff has a strong preference for litigating in state court. How might the rewritten § 1441(c) affect the plaintiff's litigation strategy? Consider the pre-JVCA cases discussed in the Problem below.

Problems: Applying Rewritten § 1441(c)

Here are some decisions by lower federal courts applying the pre-JVCA version of § 1441(c). How should the cases be decided under the rewritten law?

1. *Eastus v. Blue Bell Creameries, L.P.*, 97 F.3d 100 (5th Cir. 1996). The case arose out of the following facts, as stated in the court's opinion:

> Greg Eastus worked for Blue Bell for over ten years, mostly as a route sales-man. On July 12, 1994, Eastus asked for time off because he expected his wife, Paige Eastus, to give birth. According to Greg Eastus, his immediate supervisor told him two days later that the branch manager had threatened to fire him if he took the time off. This "resulted" in Eastus's termination on August 5. Eastus complains that this was a violation of section 105 of the Family and Medical Leave Act ("FMLA"). [The FMLA, a federal statute, requires employers to provide leave for "the birth of a son or daughter of the employee and in order to care for such son or daughter."]

> Eastus further complains that Blue Bell knew at that time that he was under considerable stress and that his wife was pregnant and overdue, and thus fir-ing him exceeded "all possible bounds of decency." Consequently, Greg and Paige Eastus sue for intentional infliction of emotional distress under Texas law.

> Greg Eastus further alleges that, when he was interviewing for other jobs, Blue Bell falsely told his potential employers that he was hard to work with and disloyal. Eastus asserts that Blue Bell did so in retaliation for complaints he made on August 1, the day he returned from his vacation, to senior man-agement about the condition of his truck and equipment. Eastus alleges that this was tortious interference with prospective contractual relations under Texas law. Blue Bell denies all of these allegations and asserts that Eastus was a troublesome employee who was fired for insubordination and for making profane statements to his supervisors and managers.

> The Eastuses filed a civil action against Blue Bell in Texas state court for the FMLA violation, tortious interference with prospective contractual relations, and intentional infliction of emotional distress. Blue Bell filed an answer and then removed the case to federal court on the ground that it raised a federal question.

> The Eastuses then moved for remand on the ground that . . . the state law claims predominate and are "separate and independent" from the federal question. The district court [remanded] the two state law claims under 28 U.S.C. § 1441(c).

The Fifth Circuit held that the pre-JVCA § 1441(c) permitted a district court "to remand the entire action, federal claims and all, if the state law claims predominate." Does the district court still have that discretion under the rewritten law?

As for the state-law claims in that case, the Fifth Circuit held that the district court abused its discretion in remanding the intentional infliction claim, but that there was no abuse of discretion in remanding the tortious interference claim. How should the district court deal with the two state-law claims under current law?

2. *Moralez v. Meat Cutters Local 539*, 778 F. Supp. 368 (E.D. Mich. 1991). The plaintiff, a former employee of Kroger, filed suit in state court against Kroger and his union. His complaint asserted that Kroger and the union breached the collective bargaining agreement (CBA), a federal claim under § 301 of the Labor-Management Relations Act. He also asserted various state-law tort claims. The defendants removed the case to federal court; the plaintiff moved to remand.

The district first held that the state claims and federal claims did not "derive from a common nucleus of operative fact." As the court explained, plaintiff's federal claim, "that his employment was terminated by Kroger contrary to a CBA, arises out of a factual scenario separate and distinct from that which brought about his battery claim. Different parties, dates and elements of proof compel this conclusion."

The court then found that plaintiff's state law claims predominated. "Clearly, plaintiff's state law claims are more complex and would require more judicial resources to adjudicate than their federal counterparts. Moreover, the majority of claims in this case are based on state law." The court therefore remanded the entire case, including the federal claims, to state court.

Assume that the district court was correct in holding that the state and federal claims did not "derive from a common nucleus of operative fact." Would the court's remand order be permissible under the revised statute? If not, what should the court do?

3. *Battle v. Park Geriatric Village Nursing Facility*, 948 F. Supp. 33 (E.D. Mich. 1996). The plaintiff filed a civil action in the Circuit Court for the County of Wayne, Michigan, alleging 14 counts against the defendants based on a series of events that allegedly resulted in her termination on May 29, 1994, and a criminal bench trial thereafter. None of the counts made any reference to federal law. However, the workplace was unionized, and the district court found that four of the plaintiff's claims required the interpretation of the collective bargaining agreement. Those claims were thus subject to complete preemption and "necessarily raise[d] questions of federal law." They therefore provided a basis for removal. See Chapter 9, section C. However, the other 10 claims were premised entirely on Michigan law, and they were not subject to complete preemption. The district court found that the state law claims thus predominated, and it remanded the entire action to state court.

How should the court handle the case under the revised § 1441(c)?

4. *Adams v. Unarco Industries*, 2012 U.S. Dist. LEXIS 13840 (E.D. Okla. Feb. 6, 2012). Plaintiff was employed by the defendant. On May 11, 2011, plaintiff was terminated.

On June 27, 2011, plaintiff filed a civil action in state court asserting a state-law claim of wrongful termination in retaliation for plaintiff's filing of a worker's compensation claim. On October 12, 2011, plaintiff filed another action in the same court against the same defendants alleging disparate treatment based on sex in violation of Title VII, age discrimination in violation of the Age Discrimination in Employment Act of 1972 (ADEA), and intentional infliction of emotional distress.

Plaintiff then filed an unopposed motion to consolidate the two actions. The basis for consolidation was that both cases arose out of the same nucleus of facts: the termination of plaintiff on May 11, 2011. The state judge immediately granted the motion, and five days later the defendant removed the case to federal court based on the two federal claims (Title VII and ADEA). Plaintiff filed a timely motion to remand, arguing that removal of the wrongful termination claim was barred by 28 U.S.C. § 1445(c); the federal claims were not separate and independent from the state court claims; and therefore the entire case should be remanded to the state court under (pre-JVCA) 28 U.S.C. § 1441(c).

The district court granted the motion to remand. The court noted that under Tenth Circuit precedent, a wrongful termination claim based on retaliation for filing a workers' compensation claim is treated as one "arising under the workmen's compensation laws" of the state within the meaning of § 1445(c). The court was "persuaded" that § 1445(c) "must trump federal question jurisdiction where all claims are part of one case or controversy." This meant that the entire case was not removable.

Assume that the district court was correct in holding that the wrongful termination claim was made non-removable by § 1445(c). Under the current version of § 1441(c), may the district court remand the entire case? May—or must—the court remand some of the claims?

C. Diversity Jurisdiction, Removal, and Litigation Strategy

[1] The Amount-in-Controversy Requirement

Note: Removal and the Amount in Controversy

1. In the absence of a federal question, a case filed in state court can ordinarily be removed to federal court only if the parties are diverse and the amount in controversy exceeds the amount specified in § 1332(a). We have already examined some of the case law developed by the courts for determining whether the amount in controversy requirement is satisfied. (Chapter 11.) Today, however, the issue rarely arises when the party seeking entry to federal court is the plaintiff invoking original jurisdiction. After all, even a routine slip-and-fall case may plausibly be portrayed as justifying a damages award of $75,000.

Removal presents a very different picture. As we saw in our study of federal-question removal, plaintiffs in civil litigation today often have a strong preference for keeping their cases in state court. When the defendant removes and the amount in controversy is in issue, the plaintiff will be in the anomalous position of seeking to minimize the value of the claim, while the defendant will argue for the higher amount.

State practice rules often create additional complications. These rules may prohibit the plaintiff from asserting a specific demand for money relief in the complaint. They may *permit* the plaintiff to assert a specific amount, but not *require* it. Or state law (following the model of Rule 54(c) of the Federal Rules of Civil Procedure) may allow the plaintiff to recover more than the amount pleaded. Under any of these regimes, the plaintiff can file a civil complaint that describes the alleged injuries only in general terms and provides no dollar amounts for any of the elements of damages that the law might allow (or only a minimum for all damages).

These practices have created great difficulties for courts — and opportunities for manipulation by litigants. Until 2011, the starting-point for analysis was the Supreme Court's decision in *St. Paul Mercury Indemnity Co. v. Red Cab Co.*, 303 U.S. 283 (1938). There the Court used the oft-quoted language:

> The rule governing dismissal for want of jurisdiction in cases brought in federal court is that, unless the law gives a different rule, the sum claimed by the plaintiff controls if the claim is apparently made in good faith. It must appear to a legal certainty that the claim is really for less than the jurisdictional amount to justify dismissal.

As is evident even from a superficial reading, this formulation is of only limited utility in the context of removal. The Court referred to "cases *brought* in federal court." Moreover, by its own terms, the "rule" applies only when the plaintiff's complaint specifies a particular amount of damages. It has nothing to say about situations where the plaintiff does not claim any particular "sum."

2. With minimal guidance from the Supreme Court, the lower courts were in disarray. Finally, Congress stepped in. After a lengthy gestation period, the Federal Courts Jurisdiction and Venue Clarification Act of 2011 (JVCA) became law, applicable to cases commenced in state court on or after January 6, 2012.

Three provisions of the JVCA specifically address the problem of determining the amount in controversy in cases removed on the basis of diversity. The centerpiece of the reform is contained in new paragraph (2) of 28 U.S.C. § 1446(c). Paragraph (2) reads:

> (2) If removal of a civil action is sought on the basis of the jurisdiction conferred by section 1332(a), the sum demanded in good faith in the initial pleading shall be deemed to be the amount in controversy, except that—
>
>> (A) the notice of removal may assert the amount in controversy if the initial pleading seeks—
>>
>>> (i) nonmonetary relief; or

> (ii) a money judgment, but the State practice either does not permit demand for a specific sum or permits recovery of damages in excess of the amount demanded; and
>
> (B) removal of the action is proper on the basis of an amount in controversy asserted under subparagraph (A) if the district court finds, by the preponderance of the evidence, that the amount in controversy exceeds the amount specified in section 1332(a).

Two other provisions deal with cases that are not removable on the basis of the initial pleading because the amount in controversy requirement is not satisfied (or does not appear to be satisfied). Both are contained in new § 1446(c)(3):

> (A) If the case stated by the initial pleading is not removable solely because the amount in controversy does not exceed the amount specified in section 1332(a), information relating to the amount in controversy in the record of the State proceeding, or in responses to discovery, shall be treated as an "other paper" under subsection (b)(3) [which provides a second window for removal after the initial 30-day period].
>
> (B) If the notice of removal is filed more than 1 year after commencement of the action and the district court finds that the plaintiff deliberately failed to disclose the actual amount in controversy to prevent removal, that finding shall be deemed bad faith under paragraph (1) [and will permit removal that would otherwise be untimely].

The last-quoted provision will be discussed in subsection C-3 of this chapter.

3. Note that the JVCA provides a set of rules for situations where state practice "does not permit demand for a specific sum" or where state practice "permits recovery of damages in excess of the amount demanded." In some states, however, the rules *permit* the plaintiff to assert a specific amount, but they do not *require* it. The JVCA does not address this situation. Should courts follow their pre-JVCA practice? Or should they adopt the JVCA's rules?

Nothing in the legislative history addresses this question. Can you think of any reasons why Congress might want one set of procedures for removal in states like Colorado, where the rules prohibit a plaintiff from stating a dollar amount in the complaint, see Colo. R. Civ. Pro. 8(a), and another set of procedures for states like Florida, where the rules leave the matter to the plaintiff's choice, see Fla. R. Civ. Pro. 1.110(b)?

Note: Litigating the "Preponderance" Standard

1. The JVCA provides that when the notice of removal asserts the amount in controversy under § 1446(c)(2)(A), removal is proper "if the district court finds, by the preponderance of the evidence, that the amount in controversy exceeds the amount specified in section 1332(a)." This seemingly straightforward formulation raises several questions.

2. Prior to the enactment of the JVCA, several courts of appeals had adopted the "preponderance" standard, but they formulated it in somewhat different ways. How is the standard to be applied today? The authoritative legislative history of the JVCA, the House Judiciary Committee Report, notes that in adopting the preponderance standard, the new law follows the lead of recent cases. The Report cites two such cases: *McPhail v. Deere & Co.*, 529 F.3d 947 (10th Cir. 2008); and *Meridian Security Ins. Co. v. Sadowski*, 441 F.3d 536 (7th Cir. 2006).

A key point made in both opinions was that the "preponderance of the evidence" standard applies to "jurisdictional facts," not to "jurisdiction itself." Judge Frank Easterbrook, writing for the court in *Meridian*, explained:

> What the proponent of jurisdiction must "prove" is contested factual assertions . . . Jurisdiction itself is a legal conclusion, a consequence of facts rather than a provable "fact." . . .

> To recap: a proponent of federal jurisdiction must, if material factual allegations are contested, prove those jurisdictional facts by a preponderance of the evidence. Once the facts have been established, uncertainty about whether the plaintiff can prove its substantive claim, and whether damages (if the plaintiff prevails on the merits) will exceed the threshold, does not justify dismissal. Only if it is "legally certain" that the recovery (from plaintiff's perspective) or cost of complying with the judgment (from defendant's) will be less than the jurisdictional floor may the case be dismissed.

The House Report summed up the thrust of the decisions in this language:

> In case of a dispute, the district court must make findings of jurisdictional fact to which the preponderance standard applies. If the defendant establishes by a preponderance of the evidence that the amount exceeds $75,000, the defendant, as proponent of Federal jurisdiction, will have met the burden of establishing jurisdictional facts.

H.R. Rep. 112-10 at 16 (2011). Nevertheless, a commentator has expressed concern that the *statute* fails to explain what is meant by the "preponderance" standard. William Baude, *Clarification Needed: Fixing the Jurisdiction and Venue Clarification Act*, 110 Mich. L. Rev. First Impressions 33, 35 (2012). But is there any reason not to read the statute with the gloss supplied by the House Report?

3. In a typical personal injury case, the plaintiff files a barebones complaint that describes the injuries only in vague or general terms. Suppose that the injuries sound serious enough that the defendant removes in a good-faith belief that amount in controversy is greater than $75,000. But a good-faith belief will not carry the day if the plaintiff moves to remand on the ground that the amount in controversy is less than the statutory minimum. How can the defendant satisfy the burden of proof mandated by the new law?

One obvious possibility would be to use the tools of discovery. But when, and where? Keep in mind that the notice of removal must be filed within 30 days after service of the complaint, as long as the case is removable on the basis of that complaint. (See section D of this chapter.) That means that there will often be no opportunity for discovery in the state court. Does the defendant have a right to engage in discovery in *federal* court after filing the notice of removal?

Prior to enactment of the JVCA, several courts held that a defendant could *not* use discovery after removal to show that the amount-in-controversy requirement was satisfied. For example, in *Lowery v. Alabama Power Co.*, 483 F.3d 1184, 1215-16 (11th Cir. 2007), the Eleventh Circuit said:

> Post-removal discovery for the purpose of establishing jurisdiction in diversity cases cannot be squared with the delicate balance struck by Federal Rules of Civil Procedure 8(a) and 11 and the policy and assumptions that flow from and underlie them. . . .

> Just as a plaintiff bringing an original action is bound to assert jurisdictional bases under Rule 8(a), a removing defendant must also allege the factual bases for federal jurisdiction in its notice of removal under § 1446(a). Though the defendant in a diversity case, unlike the plaintiff, may have no actual knowledge of the value of the claims, the defendant is not excused from the duty to show by fact, and not mere conclusory allegation, that federal jurisdiction exists. Indeed, the defendant, by removing the action, has represented to the court that the case belongs before it. Having made this representation, the defendant is no less subject to Rule 11 than a plaintiff who files a claim originally.

> Thus, a defendant that files a notice of removal prior to receiving clear evidence that the action satisfies the jurisdictional requirements, and then later faces a motion to remand, is in the same position as a plaintiff in an original action facing a motion to dismiss. The court should not reserve ruling on a motion to remand in order to allow the defendant to discover the potential factual basis of jurisdiction. Such fishing expeditions would clog the federal judicial machinery, frustrating the limited nature of federal jurisdiction by encouraging defendants to remove, at best, prematurely, and at worst, in cases in which they will never be able to establish jurisdiction.

Does the JVCA overrule cases like *Lowery*? The House Report states unequivocally that "defendants may simply allege or assert that the jurisdictional threshold has been met. *Discovery may be taken with regard to that question.*" (Emphasis added.) But is that a necessary reading of the statute itself?

And what does it mean to say that discovery "may be taken"? Does the defendant have an absolute right to engage in discovery with respect to the amount in controversy, no matter how implausible the assertion that "the jurisdictional threshold has been met"? Does the district court have discretion to remand without allowing discovery?

4. With or without discovery, how would a defendant go about showing that the amount in controversy is greater than the statutory minimum when the plaintiff disputes the assertion? Would it be enough, for example, to point to the damages awarded in other similar cases? How about settlement demands made by the plaintiff prior to removal?

5. Section 1446(b)(3) provides a second window for removal: if—but only if—"the case stated by the initial pleading is not removable," another 30-day period begins when the defendant receives, "through service or otherwise, [a] copy of an amended pleading, motion, order or other paper from which it may first be ascertained that the case is one which is or has become removable." New § 1446(c)(3)(A) adds a special rule for situations where "the case stated by the initial pleading is not removable solely because the amount in controversy does not exceed the amount specified in section 1332(a)." Under those circumstances, "information relating to the amount in controversy in the record of the State proceeding, or in responses to discovery, shall be treated as an 'other paper' under subsection (b)(3)."

Although the second window provided by § 1446(b)(3) can help defendants, it does not eliminate the difficulties that defendants may face in deciding whether to remove based on the complaint as initially filed. Consider again the barebones personal-injury complaint that describes the injuries only in vague or general terms. If the defendant files the notice of removal but cannot satisfy the preponderance standard, the case will be remanded, and the defendant might even have to pay the plaintiff's attorney's fees under § 1447(c).

6. One court has said that "recent changes to the removal statute"—specifically, new 28 U.S.C. § 1446(b)(3)(A) and (B)—"make it clear that defendants should pursue state-court discovery *before* removal." *Ramsey v. Kearns*, 2012 U.S. Dist. LEXIS 22970 (E.D. Ky. Feb. 23, 2012). (Emphasis added.) Is that a correct interpretation of the statute?

7. Suppose that after the case is removed, the plaintiff counters the defendant's arguments by stipulating in writing that the damages are less than $75,000. Should such a stipulation be conclusive to require remand? *Rogers v. Wal-Mart Stores, Inc.*, the next principal case, deals with that question.

Problem: "Disabling" Injuries from a Television Set

1. Mary and Frank Parker (citizens of Illiana) filed suit in West Fremont state court on February 8, 2017, alleging that Mary Parker was injured during a stay at the Westminster Inn in Monroe, the capital city of West Fremont, when a television set fell off the dresser in the hotel room. The complaint named only one defendant, Euclid Properties, Inc., the owner and operator of the hotel. Euclid is incorporated in the state of Oceana, where it has its principal place of business.

The complaint provided few details. It alleged that the hotel room—which the Parkers occupied with one of their grandchildren—was furnished with a dresser, and a television set was on top of the dresser. Mrs. Parker opened a drawer of the dresser to put clothing in the drawer, the dresser tilted forward, and the television fell forward off the dresser. Mrs. Parker grabbed the television as it fell to keep it from falling on her grandchild. Mr. Parker helped her to put the television back on the dresser.

The complaint alleged that Mrs. Parker was "seriously injured." She claimed "permanent and disabling injuries" to both arms, both shoulders, her neck, and her back. She asserted that for three weeks after the accident she was not able to return to her employment as a supermarket cashier; since then, she has been able to work only part-time. In accordance with state law, the complaint did not pray for any particular amount of damages.

You represent defendant Euclid, and you would strongly prefer to litigate in federal court. Is the case as stated in the initial pleading removable?

2. You decide not to remove based on the original complaint, in part because one of the district judges in the district has endorsed the approach taken by a district judge in Louisiana:

> Plaintiff's petition did not directly allege that he sought more than $75,000 in damages, and the nonspecific description of his alleged injuries and treatment did not rise to the level that the petition affirmatively revealed on its face that such an amount was at controversy. Plaintiff did allege that he suffered "disabling" and "severe and debilitating personal injuries," but this court has recognized that such strong adjectives are found in virtually every personal injury petition filed in state and city courts, even when only mild soft tissue injuries are at stake.

> A term like disabling may suggest to some a serious case, but the court knows from experience that it is not a good indicator of the underlying injury or damages. The term is used by some attorneys routinely in their petitions, no matter the kind or extent of damages their client suffered. And a disability (in a case where there really is one at issue) may be partial (20% loss of use of left thumb) or temporary. The bare term itself, without particular facts to describe the alleged nature and duration of the disability, does not trigger the removal period.

> Finally, a list of categories of damages (lost wages, medical expenses, pain and suffering, etc.), without any facts to indicate the possible amounts at issue, is of little weight in determining the amount in controversy. Almost every personal injury petition filed in this state will include a similar boilerplate list of damage categories. Even when these characteristics (use of terms disability and severe injuries; list of categories of damages) are found together in a petition, they do not make it facially apparent that more than $75,000 is in controversy. If that were the case, it would be the extraordinarily rare Louisiana petition, no matter the underlying injuries, that would not trigger the removal period.

Nordman v. Kansas City Southern Ry. Co., 2009 U.S. Dist. LEXIS 29980 (W.D. La. Apr. 9, 2009).

3. Your cautious approach is vindicated in April, when you serve plaintiffs with a request for admission as to whether they are seeking damages in excess of $50,000, which is the threshold for obtaining a jury trial in state court. Plaintiffs respond: "Denied. At this time, plaintiffs do not believe that their damages exceed $50,000."

4. The situation changes in August, when you take Mary Parker's deposition. Mrs. Parker describes her medical treatment, which has included physical therapy, injections, and an MRI. She explains that one week earlier, she made a follow-up visit to her physician, which she recounts as follows:

> He told me there was definitely a problem in my shoulders, in my right shoulder, which is what he was looking at that day. And that I had done physical therapy, I had had the shots, and it still wasn't improving. And he explained to me on a picture why, and then he told me the next step would be surgery.

Mrs. Parker says that she has agreed to surgery on her right shoulder and will be seeing her physician on September 24 to discuss scheduling the procedure. She adds that her physician wants to operate on her left shoulder after the right shoulder surgery.

Two days after the deposition, counsel for plaintiffs serves a supplemental response to your request for admission. He admits that plaintiffs are seeking damages in excess of $50,000, explaining, "at this time, plaintiffs believe that their damages will exceed $50,000, as plaintiff may undergo shoulder surgery because of the injuries she received in this matter."

Based on the deposition testimony and the supplemental response to the request for admissions, is the case now removable on the basis of diversity?

5. You do not remove based on the deposition testimony and supplemental responses. In December, plaintiffs serve answers to your interrogatories. The answers outline the dates and places Mrs. Parker received medical treatment, list a total of more than $14,000 in medical bills, state that Mrs. Parker is still receiving treatment, and assert that she is scheduled for surgery on her right shoulder at the end of the month. Plaintiffs decline to list an amount of general damages sought, saying they could not do so at the time because of the continuing nature of the injuries.

Is the case now removable? If you are not sure, what might you do to get the necessary information? Keep in mind that under § 1446 as amended by the JVCA, a case cannot be removed based on diversity more than one year after commencement of the action, "unless the plaintiff has acted in bad faith in order to prevent [the] defendant from removing the action." If you do not get the necessary information by February, do you think you might have an argument that plaintiffs have acted in bad faith?

Rogers v. Wal-Mart Stores, Inc.

United States Court of Appeals for the Sixth Circuit, 2000.

230 F.3d 868.

Before Guy and Moore, Circuit Judges; Dowd, District Judge.*

Dowd, District Judge.

I. Introduction

This case arises out of injuries suffered by Shirley K. Rogers when she tripped and fell on a wooden pallet located in the aisle of a Wal-Mart store in Memphis, Tennessee. Rogers contends that employees of Wal-Mart acted negligently in leaving the pallet in a shopping area.

On October 17, 1997, Rogers filed a complaint in Tennessee state court asserting her negligence claims and seeking approximately $950,000 in damages. On November 18, 1997, Wal-Mart answered and removed to the United States District Court for the Western District of Tennessee on the grounds of complete diversity among the parties and an amount in controversy exceeding $75,000. On October 9, 1998, the parties stipulated to dismissal, and on October 14, 1998, the district court entered an order dismissing the case without prejudice.

On February 4, 1999, Rogers filed a new complaint in Tennessee state court. The second complaint, arising out of the same occurrence, specified that Rogers sought to recover an amount "not exceeding $75,000."

Wal-Mart filed another notice of removal based on answers to interrogatories in the first case in which Rogers estimated her damages at $447,000. Rogers filed a motion to remand on May 14, 1999, asserting that the amount-in-controversy requirement for diversity jurisdiction had not been met. Along with her motion to remand, Rogers submitted an affidavit stating that she "had no intention of seeking additional damages against Wal-Mart Stores, Inc." and that she had "instructed [her] attorney to stipulate that [her] demand for damages will not exceed $75,000 at any time in the future." Rogers also attached a stipulation admitting that her total damages did not exceed $75,000 and stating that she would not seek leave of court to amend her complaint for additional damages. Meanwhile, Wal-Mart moved the district court, pursuant to Fed. R. Civ. P. 41(d), to award costs and fees for the previously dismissed action.

The district court denied Rogers' motion to remand on June 23, 1999. On the same day, the district court granted Wal-Mart's Rule 41(d) motion and ordered Rogers to pay costs and attorney fees from the original action representing work that would not benefit Wal-Mart in the second action. The district court also stayed the proceedings and gave Rogers fourteen days to pay Wal-Mart the costs and fees. On September 2, 1999, the district court dismissed the case without prejudice due to Rogers' non-payment of Wal-Mart's costs and fees from the first action.

---

* The Honorable David D. Dowd, Jr., United States District Judge for the Northern District of Ohio, sitting by designation.

Rogers has appealed the district court's June 23, 1999 Order denying her motion to remand; its Order of June 23, 1999 granting costs under Fed. R. Civ. P. 41(d); and its Order and Judgment entered on September 2, 1999 dismissing the case without prejudice with costs taxed to the plaintiff.

II. Removal

. . . Generally, a civil case brought in a state court may be removed by a defendant to federal court if it could have been brought there originally. 28 U.S.C. § 1441(a). A federal district court has original "diversity" jurisdiction where the suit is between citizens of different states and the amount in controversy exceeds $75,000, exclusive of costs and interest. 28 U.S.C. 1332(a). A defendant removing a case has the burden of proving the diversity jurisdiction requirements.

A problem arises where, as here, a plaintiff alleges an amount in controversy below the jurisdictional amount. Generally, because the plaintiff is "master of the claim," a claim specifically less than the federal requirement should preclude removal. *See Gafford v. General Elec. Co.*, 997 F.2d 150, 157 (6th Cir. 1993). State counterparts to Fed. R. Civ. P. 54(c) might enable a plaintiff to claim in her complaint an amount lower than the federal amount in controversy but nevertheless seek and recover damages exceeding the amount prayed for. Tennessee has one such rule. Its Civil Procedure Rule 54.03 provides that, except in the case of default, "every final judgment shall grant relief to which the party in whose favor it is rendered is entitled, even if the party has not demanded such relief in the party's pleadings." In such situations, the removing defendant must show that it is "more likely than not" that the plaintiff's claims meet the amount in controversy requirement. *Gafford.*

To meet its burden for removal, the defendant in this case relied on the fact that plaintiff's first action sought nearly $1 million and that plaintiff made sworn responses to discovery requests stating that her amount of damages exceeded $447,000. The district court cited these facts in finding that it was more likely than not that the amount in controversy exceeded $75,000. Rogers, however, argues that the district court should have granted her motion to remand because she (1) filed a complaint in the second action seeking damages under the jurisdictional amount; and (2) stipulated that her damages were under the required amount in controversy for diversity jurisdiction.

Neither of these facts suffices to require a remand to state court. This circuit has recognized a rule that the determination of federal jurisdiction in a diversity case is made as of the time of removal. *See Ahearn v. Charter Twp. of Bloomfield*, 100 F.3d 451, 453 (6th Cir. 1996). Hence, in reviewing the denial of a motion to remand, a court looks to "whether the action was properly removed in the first place." If one does not take into account plaintiff's post-removal stipulation, then there is no question that the district court was correct to deny the motion to remand because defendant showed that, at the time of removal, the amount in controversy was "more likely than not" above the $75,000 pleaded in plaintiff's complaint.[1]

---

1. Plaintiff argues that if the amount prayed for in a complaint may be disregarded in determining the amount in controversy, it would "open the floodgates" to federal jurisdiction over any cases filed

Therefore, the main issue here is the effect, if any, of plaintiff's stipulation. The Seventh Circuit has held that a post-removal stipulation reducing the amount in controversy to below the required jurisdictional amount is ineffective to deprive a district court of jurisdiction. *See In re Shell Oil Co.*, 970 F.2d 355, 356 (7th Cir. 1992). The court based its decision on *St. Paul Mercury Indem. Co. v. Red Cab Co.*, 303 U.S. 283 (1938), in which the Supreme Court considered whether a post-removal amendment of a complaint could destroy diversity jurisdiction. In ruling that it could not, the *St. Paul* Court stated that "[e]vents occurring subsequent to the institution of suit which reduce the amount recoverable below the statutory limit do not oust jurisdiction." On the strength of this rule, the *Shell Oil* court reasoned that "because jurisdiction is determined as of the instant of removal, a post-removal affidavit or stipulation is no more effective than a post-removal amendment of the complaint." . . .

We conclude that post-removal stipulations do not create an exception to the rule articulated in *St. Paul*. Because jurisdiction is determined as of the time of removal, events occurring after removal that reduce the amount in controversy do not oust jurisdiction. Therefore, consistent with *St. Paul* and previous unpublished Sixth Circuit opinions, we hold that a post-removal stipulation reducing the amount in controversy to below the jurisdictional limit does not require remand to state court. This rule is grounded not only in precedent, but also in sound policy. If plaintiffs were able to defeat jurisdiction by way of a post-removal stipulation, they could unfairly manipulate proceedings merely because their federal case begins to look unfavorable. Moreover, the interests of simplicity and uniformity dictate that post-removal stipulations be treated just like any other post-removal event.

Several district courts have given effect to binding, post-removal stipulations; however, we do not see merit in their reasoning. In *Moss v. Voyager Ins. Cos.*, 43 F. Supp. 2d 1298 (M.D. Ala. 1999), the court distinguished cases from the Fifth, Sixth and Seventh Circuits on the ground that the stipulations in those cases had "failed to specifically bind the plaintiffs to accept no more in damages than the requisite jurisdictional amount." Reaching the same result with different reasoning, the courts in *Bailey v. Wal-Mart Stores, Inc.*, 981 F. Supp. 1415 (N.D. Ala. 1997) and *Goodman v. Wal-Mart Stores, Inc.*, 981 F. Supp. 1083 (M.D. Tenn. 1997) ruled that the 1988 amendments to 28 U.S.C. §1447(c) superseded the *St. Paul* rule that post-removal actions by the plaintiff cannot deprive a court of diversity jurisdiction.[2] Those courts reasoned that in changing §1447(c), Congress was responding to *St. Paul*. Further, they interpreted the word "shall" in the newer version to mandate remand—even where the plaintiff reduces his demand three days before trial or merely amends his complaint rather than submits a stipulation.

---

in state court. This argument has long since been settled by cases like *Gafford*, which establish tests for determining when a court can find jurisdiction despite a pleading that states an amount below the required level.

2. The older version of §1447(c) called for remand whenever the judge realized "that the case was removed improvidently and without jurisdiction." This subsection was changed to read: "If at any time before final judgment it appears that the district court lacks subject matter jurisdiction, the case shall be remanded."

Although these cases are interesting for their result, this circuit has already rejected the notion that the 1988 amendment to § 1447(c) directs district courts to look beyond the time of removal in deciding remand motions based on lack of jurisdiction. *Baldridge v. Kentucky-Ohio Transp., Inc.*, 983 F.2d 1341, 1348 & n.11 (6th Cir. 1993). In addition, the fact that a stipulation might be binding should not determine whether it is effective to deprive the federal court of diversity jurisdiction. The same potential for forum shopping and manipulation exists whether or not a stipulation is binding. The same interests in efficiency and simplicity also exist where there is a binding stipulation. Hence, the reasoning that leads us to deny effect to post-removal stipulations generally, also leads us to deny effect to post-removal stipulations that are binding.

Because state law would have allowed plaintiff to recover damages in excess of what she prayed for, it was "more likely than not" that her damages would exceed $75,000 given her previous demands and representations. Plaintiff's post-removal stipulation has no effect because jurisdiction is decided as of the time of removal. The district court did not err in denying plaintiff's motion to remand.

III. The Award of Costs, Including Attorney Fees

[The court held that attorney fees are not available under Rule 41(d), because "the rule does not explicitly provide for them."]

. . . [That] portion of the district court's order which awarded Wal-Mart $1581.55 in attorney fees cannot stand.

IV. Conclusion

We affirm the district court's denial of the motion to remand and we vacate the district court's award of costs insofar as it awarded attorney fees. Further, we remand with instructions for the district court to enter an order that, upon payment of costs in the sum of $185 within thirty (30) days of the date of the district court's order, plaintiff's case will be reinstated on the district court docket.

Note: Stipulations and the Amount in Controversy

1. In *Rogers*, the Sixth Circuit joins the Seventh in holding that a post-removal stipulation by the plaintiff reducing the amount in controversy below the statutory minimum does not destroy removal jurisdiction. Both courts rely on the Supreme Court decision in *St. Paul Mercury Indem. Co. v. Red Cab Co.*, 303 U.S. 283 (1938). There the Court said:

> If the plaintiff could, no matter how bona fide his original claim in the state court, reduce the amount of his demand to defeat federal jurisdiction the defendant's supposed statutory right of removal would be subject to the plaintiff's caprice. The claim, whether well or ill founded in fact, fixes the right of the defendant to remove, and the plaintiff ought not to be able to defeat that right and bring the cause back to the state court at his election. If he does not desire to try his case in the federal court he may resort to the expedient of suing for less than the jurisdictional amount, and though he would be justly entitled to more, the defendant cannot remove.

Does *St. Paul Mercury* stand for the proposition that a plaintiff may *never* secure remand based on a post-removal stipulation? Not necessarily, at least for some federal judges.

2. Note first that the Sixth Circuit holds that "a post-removal stipulation reducing the amount in controversy to below the jurisdictional limit does not *require* remand to state court." (Emphasis added.) Several district courts in the Sixth Circuit have concluded that *Rogers* does not *prevent* the court from remanding on the basis of a post-removal stipulation.

For example, in *Egan v. Premier Scales & Systems*, 237 F. Supp. 2d 774 (W.D. Ky. 2002), the court held that "where a plaintiff provides specific information about the amount in controversy for the first time [after removal], it should be deemed a *clarification* rather than a change." This in turn meant that remand would be permissible. The court emphasized that under Kentucky law, the plaintiff was prohibited from making a specific monetary demand (above the state's minimum amount in controversy) in the complaint.

More recently, the same court gave effect to a stipulation in which the plaintiff "expressly assert[ed] ... that Plaintiff will not seek *or accept* an award of damages in excess of $74,999.00 inclusive of punitive damages, attorney's fees, and the fair value of any injunctive relief." In *Spence v. Centerplate*, 931 F. Supp. 2d 779 (W.D. Ky. 2013), the court said:

> A plain reading of the stipulation leaves Plaintiff no room to escape the bounds of its restrictions. ... Plaintiff's actual damages, if proven, might exceed $75,000, so state courts will be forced to rely on this stipulation to prevent the award of excess damages. The United States Supreme Court determined [in a different context] that factual stipulations are "binding and conclusive ... and the facts stated are not subject to subsequent variation." ...
>
> While the Court may be concerned that a dishonest party may simply use the stipulation mechanism as a ploy to retain a more favorable state court jurisdiction over the claim for whatever reason, the Court is convinced that Plaintiff will be constrained to recovering an amount that is not to exceed $74,999. If a jury were to award Plaintiff that amount, or some award close to that amount, Plaintiff cannot seek attorney's fees in an amount that will inure to Plaintiff's benefit an award greater than $75,000.

Other district judges in the Sixth Circuit have rejected this approach. For example, in *Driscoll v. Wal-Mart Stores East, Inc.*, 2009 WL 4730709 (S.D. Ohio 2009), the plaintiff urged the court to follow Egan and hold that "where a state law prohibits a precise demand for relief, ... a post-removal stipulation is a proper basis for remand." The district court rejected the argument, holding that *Rogers* controlled.

Which is the better reading of *Rogers*? Apart from *Rogers*, does *St. Paul Mercury* allow district courts to give effect to post-removal stipulations in cases like *Egan* and *Spence*? Review the Supreme Court's language quoted above.

3. The *Rogers* decision was severely criticized in *Brooks v. Pre-paid Legal Services, Inc.*, 153 F. Supp. 2d 1299 (M.D. Ala. 2001). In *Brooks*, the plaintiffs brought suit against the defendant and its agents, alleging fraud in connection with the sale of legal insurance. The complaint sought compensatory damages of $74,500 and unspecified punitive damages. The defendants removed on the basis of diversity, asserting that the amount in controversy exceeded $75,000. Shortly thereafter, the plaintiffs filed an affidavit stating that: (1) they did not intend to seek recovery of more than $74,500 when they filed their complaint; (2) they will never claim or accept more than $74,500; and (3) they agreed to a court order capping their damages at $74,500. Based on these representations, the plaintiffs moved to remand. The court granted the motion, saying:

> The court is aware of opinions from other jurisdictions that have retained cases even after a plaintiff limited his or her damages. . . . The court believes that these unpersuasive decisions have improvidently expanded the holding of *St. Paul* and have given unduly narrow consideration to basic principles of federal jurisdiction.

> Initially, the court stresses that *St. Paul* did not hold that post-removal stipulations are unallowable *per se*. . . . A crucial fact [in *St. Paul*] is that the plaintiffs acknowledged that their complaints triggered the amount in controversy at the moment of removal. In this case, on the other hand, Plaintiffs have submitted affidavits bearing on their initial demand and showing that federal jurisdiction has never properly attached. . . .

> Moreover, four bedrock principles of federal jurisdiction require courts to effectuate post-removal stipulations. First, federal courts are tribunals of limited jurisdiction. Second, the diversity statute is strictly construed because of the significant federalism concerns raised by federal courts passing on matters of state law. Third, a plaintiff is the master of her complaint, and a plaintiff suing diverse defendants can avoid federal court by limiting her prayer for damages to less than $75,000. Fourth, a plaintiff is charged with knowledge of her complaint, and the amount of damages that she seeks. None of these interests are furthered when a federal court keeps a diversity case because of some doctrinaire reading of judicial dicta that is divorced from congressional will and any legitimate policy interests.

> Accordingly, the court [considers] Plaintiffs' affidavit and finds that Defendants have not met their burden of showing that the amount in controversy exceeds $74,500.

Note, though, that although the judge in *Brooks* criticized the *Rogers* court's reasoning, he also said that he "shares the concerns expressed [in *Rogers*] about plaintiffs who devilishly move to limit their damages and return to state court only after litigation has taken an unfavorable turn." And he sounded a warning to plaintiffs' counsel:

> The court emphasizes that, while it does not call into question the integrity of Plaintiffs' damages stipulation, should Plaintiffs disregard their demand

and pursue or accept damages in excess of $75,000, then upon motion by opposing counsel, sanctions will be swift in coming and painful upon arrival.

4. If the *Brooks* court's approach is accepted, what kind of stipulation will suffice? For example, suppose that plaintiff files an affidavit after removal stating: "I will accept a sum of $74,990 exclusive of interest and costs as a judgment regardless of what any court finds in excess of that amount." Should that affidavit require remand to state court?

5. *Rogers* refuses to give effect to a stipulation filed *after* the case had been removed. Should a stipulation filed *before* removal be given effect? In *Workman v. United Parcel Service, Inc.*, 234 F.3d 998 (7th Cir. 2000), the court said:

> [The] plaintiff who has a modest claim that he does not want to be forced to litigate in federal court [can] can avoid that fate, in a case in which only monetary relief is sought, simply by stipulating that he is not seeking and will neither demand nor accept any recovery in excess of $75,000 exclusive of costs and interest, though the stipulation must be made at the time the suit is filed since jurisdiction is determined as of then and not later. If he doesn't make such a stipulation, the inference arises that he thinks his claim may be worth more.

6. The cases cited in this Note are only a sample of those in which plaintiffs have stipulated to damages in an amount less than $75,000 so that the district court will be required to grant their motion to remand. Why do plaintiffs find the prospect of litigating in federal court to be so objectionable that they are willing to cap their damages in order to avoid the federal forum?

Note: Authorizing Recovery-Limiting "Declarations"

1. When the Federal Courts Jurisdiction and Venue Clarification Act of 2011 (JVCA) was initially introduced in the 111th Congress (as H.R. 4113), it included two provisions that would have explicitly authorized the use of stipulations to reduce the amount in controversy below the minimum specified in § 1332(a). The legislation, drafted by the Judicial Conference of the United States, referred to these stipulations as "declarations." One provision would have applied in state courts to forestall removal; the other would have applied in federal courts to encourage remand.

2. The state-court provision consisted of two sentences that would have been added at the end of 28 U.S.C. § 1441(a), the basic removal statute. The proposed new language was as follows:

> If the plaintiff has filed a declaration in State court, as part of or in addition to the initial pleading, providing that the plaintiff will neither seek nor accept an award of damages or entry of other relief exceeding the amount specified in section 1332(a), the case may not be removed on the basis of the jurisdiction under section 1332(a) as long as the plaintiff abides by the declaration and the declaration is binding under the laws and practice of the

State. If the plaintiff has filed such a declaration in State court but thereafter fails to abide by that declaration, the defendant or defendants may file a notice of removal within 30 days after receiving, through service or otherwise, a copy of an amended pleading, motion, order or other paper from which it may first be ascertained that the plaintiff seeks or is willing to accept an award of damages or other relief exceeding the amount specified in section 1332(a).

3. Assume that this proposal had been enacted. Suppose that you have filed a personal injury suit in state court against a diverse defendant, and you would prefer—other things being equal—to keep the case out of federal court. What considerations would you take into account in deciding whether to file a "declaration" limiting the plaintiff's recovery to less than $75,000?

4. The most innovative element of the JVCA in its original form was the provision that would have authorized the filing of a recovery-limiting declaration in *federal* court *after* the defendant has removed the case. As you have seen, some courts (like the Sixth Circuit in *Rogers*) interpret the Supreme Court decision in *St. Paul Mercury Ins. Co.* as precluding them from giving any effect to a post-removal stipulation as to the amount in controversy. Other courts (like the district court in *Egan*) recognize an exception for stipulations that "clarify" rather than "amend" the original pleading. But, at best, post-removal stipulations are disfavored. The original version of the JVCA would have changed the law by adding the following new subsection to 28 U.S.C. § 1447:

> (f) Within 30 days after the filing of a notice of removal of a civil action in which the district court's removal jurisdiction rests solely on original jurisdiction under section 1332(a), the plaintiff may file a declaration with the district court providing that the plaintiff will neither seek nor accept an award of damages or entry of other relief exceeding the amount specified in section 1332(a) of this title. Upon the filing of such a declaration, the district court shall remand the action to State court unless equitable circumstances warrant retaining the case.

5. Assume that this proposal had become law. Suppose that the plaintiff files a declaration under § 1447(f) and moves to remand the case to state court. What kinds of "equitable circumstances" might the defendant invoke as a basis for denying the motion and keeping the case in federal court?

6. When the JVCA was reintroduced in the 112th Congress, both of the provisions authorizing "declarations" had disappeared. The House Report on the bill did not specifically explain the omissions, but it noted that an "informal vetting process" had been used "to identify and delete those provisions that were considered controversial by prominent legal experts and advocacy groups." Why might the "declaration" provisions have proved "controversial?" Who might have opposed them?

[2] The Complete-Diversity Requirement

The amount-in-controversy cases discussed in the preceding subsection leave no doubt that plaintiffs in civil litigation today often have a strong preference for avoiding federal district court. But stipulating to a cap on damages is a drastic measure that few plaintiffs will be willing to take. Another possibility is to take advantage of the "complete diversity" rule established by Chief Justice Marshall's opinion in *Strawbridge v. Curtiss*, 3 Cranch (7 U.S.) 267 (1806). As long as the plaintiff can validly name one or more co-citizens as defendants, complete diversity will be destroyed and the defendant will not be able to remove the case to federal court. What are the limits on the plaintiff's ability to use this tactic? We look now at that question.

Filla v. Norfolk Southern Railway Company

United States Court of Appeals for the Eighth Circuit, 2003.

336 F.3d 806.

Before BOWMAN, RILEY, and SMITH, CIRCUIT JUDGES.

SMITH, CIRCUIT JUDGE.

Norfolk Railroad, Darlene March, and Skyline Motors, Inc. ("Skyline") appeal the district court's order remanding this case to state court. Petitioners seek a writ of mandamus directing the district court to rescind its remand order. Respondent, Mark Filla, argues that we lack jurisdiction to review the district court's remand order and that even if subject-matter jurisdiction is present, the district court correctly remanded the case to state court. For the reasons stated below, we dismiss.

I.

Procedural Background

Filla filed an action against the petitioners in Missouri state court seeking damages for injuries received in a collision with a train at a private railroad-track crossing. He later amended his petition adding three individual defendants—Richard March, Darlene March, and Patrick Connaughton—all Missouri citizens. Petitioners removed the action to district court based on the parties' diversity of citizenship. Petitioners noted that Filla is a citizen of Missouri, and that Norfolk is a corporation with Virginia citizenship. Alleging fraudulent joinder, petitioners claimed that Filla joined the additional Missouri defendants merely to defeat federal diversity jurisdiction.

Filla filed a motion to remand to state court. He contended that viable actions existed under Missouri law against Skyline and Darlene March as alleged owners of property adjacent to the private railroad crossing. He also asserted that he had a legitimate complaint against Connaughton, the owner of a nearby "paintball" business.[7] According to Filla's theory, Connaughton was partially liable for the injuries

---

7. "Paintball" typically refers to a game of simulated combat played in a rural setting where the combatants fire paint-filled balls at each other.

Filla sustained because Connaughton failed to warn approaching business invitees of the alleged dangerous conditions near the railroad crossing. [The] district court remanded the case to state court. In its evaluation of the petitioners' fraudulent joinder allegation, the court agreed that Filla's claim against Connaughton had no reasonable basis under Missouri law. However, with respect to Darlene March and Skyline, the district court concluded:

> This Court, and apparently the parties, have been unable to locate any case determining whether there is a cause of action against an owner of property for failure to maintain that property when the road in question was private and the setting was rural. It is not for this Court to speculate how the Missouri courts would decide such an issue. The burden is upon the removing party to demonstrate that the facts pled by Plaintiff cannot possibly create liability to March or Skyline. Norfolk has not met this burden. The Court finds that Skyline and March were not fraudulently joined to defeat diversity.

This appeal asserts that the existence of diversity jurisdiction should have prevented the district court from remanding the remaining state-court claims. Specifically, petitioners argue that the district court failed to reach the question of its own jurisdiction and in so doing failed to perform one of its essential functions.

II.

Discussion

As an initial matter, we must determine whether we have jurisdiction to review the district court's remand order. . . . Our ability to review the order depends on the district court's basis for remand. A remand order based upon lack of subject-matter jurisdiction is not reviewable on appeal. 28 U.S.C. § 1447(d). The language of section 1447(c) mandates a remand of the case (to the state court from which it was removed) whenever the district court concludes that subject-matter jurisdiction is nonexistent. If a district court's order is based upon a lack of subject-matter jurisdiction, the order—whether erroneous or not and whether review is sought by appeal or by extraordinary writ—must stand.

Here, the district court did not explicitly cite 28 U.S.C. § 1447(c)—lack of subject-matter jurisdiction—as its basis for remand. However, such a statement by the district court is not required. "This court reviews a lower court's reasoning for remand independently and determines from the record the district court's basis for remand." We note that on its face petitioners' removal complaint lacks complete diversity—the basis for federal subject-matter jurisdiction.

When, as here, the respondent has joined a non-diverse party as a defendant in its state case, the petitioner may avoid remand—in the absence of a substantial federal question—only by demonstrating that the non-diverse party was fraudulently joined. *Wiles v. Capitol Indemnity Corp.*, 280 F.3d 868, 871 (8th Cir. 2002). Therefore, the petitioners were required to show fraudulent joinder to eliminate the non-diverse parties.

While fraudulent joinder—the filing of a frivolous or otherwise illegitimate claim against a non-diverse defendant solely to prevent removal—is rather easily defined, it is much more difficultly applied. As the Fifth Circuit recently noted, "Neither our circuit nor other circuits have been clear in describing the fraudulent joinder standard."[9] Within our own circuit the fraudulent-joinder standard has been stated in varying ways. In *Wiles*, we looked for a "reasonable basis in fact and law" in the claim alleged. In *Anderson v. Home Ins. Co.*, 724 F.2d 82, 84 (8th Cir. 1983), we articulated something close to a dismissal standard, approving a removal to federal court if, "on the face of plaintiff's state court pleadings, no cause of action lies against the resident defendant." As might be expected, our district courts have used standards that run the gamut—from requiring plaintiff to actually state a cause of action, to a more lenient threshold requiring a removing party to show that there is *no possibility* that the plaintiff will be able to state a cause of action against the resident defendant.

The district court's remand order in this case contains similarly confusing language. At one point the district court concludes that Filla's claim against Connaughton has "*no reasonable basis*" under Missouri law. Later in the order the court states that the "burden is upon the removing party to demonstrate that the facts pled by Plaintiff "*cannot possibly create liability*." (Emphasis added.)

We believe that, despite the semantical differences, there is a common thread in the legal fabric guiding fraudulent-joinder review. It is reason. Thus, a proper review should give paramount consideration to the reasonableness of the basis underlying the state claim. Where applicable state precedent precludes the existence of a cause of action against a defendant, joinder is fraudulent. "It is well established that if it is *clear* under governing state law that the complaint does not state a cause of action against the non-diverse defendant, the joinder is fraudulent and federal jurisdiction of the case should be retained." *Iowa Public Service Co. v. Medicine Bow Coal Co.*, 556 F.2d 400, 406 (8th Cir. 1977) (emphasis added). However, if there is a "colorable"[10] cause of action—that is, if the state law *might* impose liability on the resident defendant under the facts alleged—then there is no fraudulent joinder. As we recently stated in *Wiles*, "... joinder is fraudulent when there exists no reasonable basis in fact and law supporting a claim against the resident defendants." Conversely, if there is a reasonable basis in fact and law supporting the claim, the joinder is not fraudulent.

Petitioners argue that the district court never actually reached the question of its own jurisdiction because it declined to rule on the key underlying issue supporting

---

9. See *Travis v. Irby*, 326 F.3d 644, 647 (5th Cir. 2003), for an in-depth discussion of the various mutations of the fraudulent-joinder standard throughout the circuits. Relevant treatises have not been entirely consistent either. *Moore's Federal Practice* states: "To establish fraudulent joinder, a party must demonstrate ... the absence of *any possibility* that the opposing party has stated a claim under state law." 16 JAMES WM. MOORE ET AL., MOORE'S FEDERAL PRACTICE, P 107.14[2][c][iv][A] (3d ed. 2000) (emphasis added). It then comments: "The ultimate question is whether there is arguably a *reasonable basis* for predicting that state law might impose liability on the facts involved."

10. The "colorable" euphemism has been used by both the Fifth and Sixth Circuits to describe an alleged cause of action that is reasonable, but speculative. See *Jerome-Duncan, Inc. v. Auto-By-Tel, L.L.C.*, 176 F.3d 904, 907 (6th Cir. 1999); *Delgado v. Shell Oil Co.*, 231 F.3d 165, 180 (5th Cir. 2000).

the claim of fraudulent joinder—whether Missouri law would impose a duty upon rural land owners adjacent to a private road and private-railroad crossing to modify the contours of their land or remove vegetation from their land or the railroad's right-of-way. A determination of the current status of the state law, according to petitioners, is an essential court function, and a court cannot simply decide that it will refrain from deciding or interpreting the state's law.

Petitioners' argument is supported by an *Erie* foundation. However, as noted by the Fifth Circuit, fraudulent joinder "is an *Erie* problem in part, but only part." *Badon v. RJR Nabisco Inc.*, 236 F.3d 282, 285–86 (5th Cir. 2000). Unlike most diversity cases (where a federal court is required to ascertain and apply state law no matter how onerous the task), here, the district court's task is limited to determining whether there is arguably a reasonable basis for predicting that the state law might impose liability based upon the facts involved. In making such a prediction, the district court should resolve all facts and ambiguities in the current controlling substantive law in the plaintiff's favor. However, in its review of a fraudulent-joinder claim, the court has no responsibility to definitively settle the ambiguous question of state law.

Instead, the court must simply determine whether there is a reasonable basis for predicting that the state's law might impose liability against the defendant. This determination is the essential function required of the district court in a fraudulent-joinder setting. As we discussed in *Iowa Public Service Co.*, in situations where the sufficiency of the complaint against the non-diverse defendant is questionable, "the better practice is for the federal court not to decide the doubtful question in connection with a motion to remand but simply to remand the case and leave the question for the state courts to decide." Here, the district court—by remanding the case to the state court—did all that was required of it.

We agree that under Missouri law a reasonable basis exists for predicting that liability might be imposed upon petitioners, and the ultimate success—or failure—of Filla's claims is best left to the Missouri courts. By ordering remand of the case to Missouri state court, the district court inevitably *did* reach the question of its own jurisdiction. The fact that § 1447 or "subject-matter jurisdiction" was not mentioned by the district court in its remand order is not determinative.

As it stands, the state defendants' presence destroys complete diversity. Consequently, the district court lacked subject-matter jurisdiction to consider the claim, and remand to the state court was proper. Like the district court, we have no power to decide the merits of a case over which we have no jurisdiction. For the foregoing reasons, the appeal is dismissed.

Note: "Fraudulent Joinder"

1. The court in *Filla* holds that "joinder is fraudulent when applicable state precedent *precludes* the existence of a cause of action against a defendant." (Emphasis added.) Conversely, as long as state law "*might* impose liability on the resident defendant under the facts alleged, then there is no fraudulent joinder." Here, the court says that "under Missouri law a reasonable basis exists for predicting that liability might be imposed upon petitioners." But the court cites no statute or case law in support of that proposition. Does this approach give plaintiffs too much leeway to invent claims against non-diverse defendants?

2. How might the defendants meet the burden established by the Eighth Circuit? Would it be enough, for example, to show that no published decision in the relevant jurisdiction has allowed liability to be imposed under the facts alleged in the complaint with respect to the non-diverse defendant?

3. In *Poulos v. Naas Foods, Inc.*, 959 F.2d 69 (7th Cir. 1992), the Seventh Circuit discussed the purpose of the "fraudulent joinder" doctrine:

> When speaking of jurisdiction, "fraudulent" is a term of art. Although false allegations of jurisdictional fact may make joinder fraudulent, in most cases fraudulent joinder involves a claim against an in-state defendant that simply has no chance of success, whatever the plaintiff's motives. This definition of "fraudulent" accords with the purpose of the doctrine. No matter what the plaintiff's intentions are, an out-of-state defendant may need access to federal court when the plaintiff's suit presents a local court with a clear opportunity to express its presumed bias — when the insubstantiality of the claim against the in-state defendant makes it easy to give judgment for the in-state plaintiff against the out-of-state defendant while sparing the in-state defendant.

Does the Eighth Circuit's approach in *Filla* sufficiently protect the out-of-state defendant from the local bias described by the Seventh Circuit?

4. Can the defendants show fraudulent joinder by pointing to the plaintiffs' failure to substantiate the *factual* basis of the claim against the co-citizen defendant? In *Travis v. Irby*, 326 F.3d 644 (5th Cir. 2003), the plaintiff's decedent was killed when his car was struck by a train. A wrongful death action was brought in state court naming as defendants the railroad that owned the train and the engineer who was operating it. The engineer, Irby, was a co-citizen of the plaintiff. The defendants removed the action to federal court; the plaintiffs moved to remand on the ground that diversity was incomplete. The railroad argued that Irby had been fraudulently joined.

All of the parties acknowledged that the plaintiff stated a claim against Irby as a matter of law. However, the district court found that the plaintiff's responses to the defendants' interrogatories had negated any possibility that Irby could actually be found liable. For example, one interrogatory asked:

> List all facts indicating that Irby failed to keep a proper and reasonable lookout and state the name and address of all witnesses having discoverable knowledge supporting your answer.

The plaintiff responded:

> Plaintiff does not possess the facts supporting said allegations at this time nor has a determination been made as to who may be called to provide expert witness testimony. At such time a determination is made, Plaintiff will

promptly supplement this request in accordance with [the state rules of civil procedure].

The district court said: "While Plaintiff clearly seeks the chance to engage in further discovery, she has failed to present any evidence in support of a claim against Defendant Irby. She fails to provide even cursory evidence which gives the Court reason to believe that there is a potential that Irby may be found liable." This led the district court to find that Irby was fraudulently joined.

The court of appeals reversed. The court concluded that "the district court relied too heavily on the interrogatory responses [without] considering them in the context of the entire record, the status of discovery, and without resolving all ambiguities in [the plaintiff's] favor." The court explained:

> It is [clear from the record that] discovery was continuing. The district court acknowledged that both sides had engaged in dilatory tactics and found that "neither Plaintiff nor Defendants have presented any substantive evidence regarding Defendant Irby. Defendants merely point to Plaintiff's lack of evidence, while Plaintiff apparently clings to the need for further discovery."
>
> In this circumstance, in which the defendant has the burden of establishing fraudulent joinder and the plaintiff can clearly state a claim upon which relief can be granted as to the non-diverse defendant, the lack of substantive evidence as to the non-diverse defendant does not support a conclusion that he was fraudulently joined. In order to establish that Irby was fraudulently joined, the defendant must put forward evidence that would negate a possibility of liability on the part of Irby. As the defendants cannot do so, simply pointing to the plaintiff's lack of evidence at this stage of the case is insufficient to show that there is no possibility for Travis to establish Irby's liability at trial.

If, at the close of discovery in state court, the plaintiff still has not come up with any evidence in support of the claim against Irby, could the defendants then remove? Study 28 U.S.C. § 1446(c) (amended 2011).

Note: The "Fraudulent Joinder Prevention Act"

1. In February 2016, the United States House of Representatives passed H.R. 3624, the Fraudulent Joinder Prevention Act of 2016. The purpose of the bill is to establish "a somewhat more robust version of the fraudulent joinder doctrine" than the one generally applied by the courts today. H.R. REP. No. 114-422 at 5 (2016). To that end, the central provision of the bill would replace standards such as those discussed in *Filla* with a uniform standard of "plausibility" drawn from the Supreme Court's *Twombly* and *Iqbal* decisions that redefined the federal pleading standard under Rule 8 of the Federal Rules of Civil Procedure.[1] Specifically, the bill provides that joinder of a non-diverse or in-state defendant is fraudulent if, "based on the complaint and [other

---

1. *See Bell Atlantic Corp. v. Twombly*, 550 U.S. 544 (2007); *Ashcroft v. Iqbal*, 556 U.S. 662 (2009).

materials submitted by the parties], it is *not plausible* to conclude that applicable state law would impose liability on that defendant." (Emphasis added.)

The Supreme Court's decisions give some content to the meaning of "plausibility." Those decisions make clear that "plausibility" requires more than "possibility," but it is not tantamount to a requirement of "probability." Rather, a claim lacks plausibility when "there is *no reasonable likelihood* that the plaintiffs can construct a claim from the events related in the complaint."

Would application of the FJPA's plausibility standard change the result in *Filla*?

2. Another provision of the FJPA would establish that a plainly meritorious affirmative *defense*, whether under state or federal law, can be the basis for finding fraudulent joinder. Some courts already take that position. Other courts, however, have held that affirmative defenses cannot be considered as a basis for finding fraudulent joinder. There seems to be a particular resistance to considering *federal* defenses, notably the defense of preemption.

Suppose the court finds that the plaintiff's tort claim against the in-state defendant is unquestionably preempted by a federal statute. Is there any reason why that should not be a ground for holding that the joinder of the in-state defendant is fraudulent? Should it make a difference if the same preemption defense would also defeat the plaintiff's claim against the non-citizen defendant? Compare *Smallwood v. Illinois Central R. Co.*, 385 F.3d 568 (5th Cir. 2004) (en banc) (joinder is not fraudulent because preemption is a "common defense"), with *Johnson v. American Towers, LLC*, 781 F.3d 693 (4th Cir. 2015) (finding joinder fraudulent based on preemption defense that also defeated claim against out-of-state defendant).

3. The senior author of this casebook, who participated in the drafting of the bill, offered the following argument in support of the legislation:

> [Even] if it is wrong to presume that state-court judges and juries are biased against out-of-state defendants because they are from *out of state*, it is still possible that litigation practices in state systems reflect an institutional bias against out-of-state defendants as *defendants*. Over the last three decades, the Supreme Court, through rulemaking and adjudication, has substantially dismantled the elements of federal practice that put pressure on defendants "to settle even anemic cases." [These elements include the scope of discovery, the availability of summary judgment, and the qualifications for expert witness testimony.] But state systems may have retained or even strengthened those elements. To the extent that they have done so, defendants sued in state court may legitimately believe they will receive a "juster justice" in the federal court.

Arthur D. Hellman, *The "Fraudulent Joinder Prevention Act of 2016": A New Standard and a New Rationale for an Old Doctrine*, 17 Fed. Soc. L. Rev. 42 (2016). The quoted language about "juster justice" comes from an article by Professor Henry Hart, who posed the question: "Why is it an offense to the ideals of federalism for federal courts to administer, between citizens of different states, a juster justice than state courts, so long as they accept the same premises of underlying, primary obligation and so avoid creating uncertainty in the basic rules which govern the great mass of affairs in the ordinary processes of daily living? Was Hamilton wrong in saying that the assurance of the due administration of justice to out-of-state citizens is one of the great bonds of federal union?" Henry M. Hart, *The Relations Between State and Federal Law*, 54 COLUM. L. REV. 489, 513 (1954).

Congress has not preempted the bulk of the substantive law applied in civil actions in state courts, nor has it required the states to adopt federal procedural rules in cases involving out-of-state defendants. When the local plaintiff chooses to sue both a co-citizen and an out-of-state party on a state claim, why should the out-of-state party be able to escape the burdens of state procedural rules, even if those rules do put pressure on defendants "to settle even anemic cases"?

Problem: An End Run Around the Forum Defendant Rule?

The complete-diversity requirement — which of course applies to original as well as removal jurisdiction — is not the only weapon available to plaintiffs who wish to keep their state-law claims in state court. Plaintiffs can also take advantage of a statutory provision uniquely applicable in removal cases, the forum defendant rule. Section 1441(b), as revised in 2011, provides: "A civil action otherwise removable solely on the basis of the jurisdiction under section 1332(a) of this title may not be removed if any of the parties in interest properly joined and served as defendants is a citizen of the State in which such action is brought."

Anthony Argan, a citizen of West Fremont, has brought a state-law tort suit in the state court of Illiana against a single defendant, Pharmacium Inc. The defendant is a multinational pharmaceutical manufacturer; its state of incorporation is Illiana. The complaint asserts that the plaintiff was seriously injured as a direct result of taking certain drugs made by Pharmacium.

Pharmacium's legal department routinely monitors the electronic docketing systems of state courts. Pharmacium thus learned of Argan's suit before being served with process or receiving any other official notification. Ten days after the filing of the lawsuit, Pharmacium removed the action to federal district court. The notice of removal asserted that the parties were diverse and that the amount in controversy exceeded $75,000.

Argan promptly filed a motion to remand, asserting that removal was barred by § 1441(b). Pharmacium has asked the court to deny the motion, arguing that removal was permissible because § 1441(b) applies only when the in-state defendant has been "properly joined *and served*." (Emphasis added.)

Should the district judge accept the defendant's argument?

[3] The One-Year Limitation and the New "Bad Faith" Exception

Note: Modifying the One-Year Rule

1. Recall that in *Travis v. Irby*, 326 F.3d 644 (5th Cir. 2003), discussed in the preceding subsection, the Fifth Circuit held that the district court erred in finding that the in-state defendant was fraudulently joined, in part because discovery was continuing. Suppose that at the close of discovery in state court the plaintiff still has not come up with any evidence in support of the claim against the in-state defendant, so the plaintiff dismisses that defendant. The dismissal is undoubtedly voluntary. May the out-of-state defendant then remove? Not necessarily, thanks to a statutory provision uniquely applicable to removal based on diversity.

Ordinarily, if a case is not removable based on the initial pleading, the defendant gets another 30-day period that begins when the defendant receives, "through service or otherwise, [a] copy of an amended pleading, motion, order or other paper from which it may first be ascertained that the case is one which is or has become removable." In 1988, however, Congress enacted an exception to that rule: "a case may not be removed on the basis of jurisdiction conferred by section 1332 of this title more than 1 year after commencement of the action."

The one-year limit was added as "a means of reducing the opportunity for removal after substantial progress has been made in state court." H.R. REP. No. 100-889 at 72 (1988). But it also had the effect of opening the door to manipulation and gamesmanship. Sometimes plaintiffs held back information that would reveal that the amount in controversy requirement of § 1332(a) was satisfied — disclosing the information only after the one year had passed. Plaintiffs also used removal-defeating strategies involving joinder. The latter phenomenon was noted by several courts, including a district judge in Virginia, who wrote:

> As numerous courts have acknowledged, and both plaintiffs and defendants recognize, many plaintiffs' attorneys include in diversity cases a non-diverse defendant only to non-suit that very defendant after one year has passed in order to avoid the federal forum.... The result is that diversity jurisdiction — a concept important enough to be included in Article III of the United States Constitution and given to courts by Congress — has become nothing more than a game: defendants are deprived of the opportunity to exercise their right to removal and litigate in federal court not by a genuine lack of diversity in the case but by means of clever pleading. No one can pretend otherwise.

Linnen v. Michielsens, 372 F. Supp. 2d 811, 824-825 (E.D. Va. 2005).

2. Some courts, unwilling to believe that Congress intended to allow such manipulation, found that the one-year limitation was subject to an equitable exception. The leading case was *Tedford v. Warner-Lambert Co.*, 327 F.3d 423 (5th Cir. 2003). The *Tedford* court explained its holding as follows:

Section 1446(b) is not inflexible, and the conduct of the parties may affect whether it is equitable to strictly apply the one-year limit. . . . In enacting § 1446(b), Congress intended to "reduc[e] opportunity for removal after substantial progress has been made in state court." Congress may have intended to limit diversity jurisdiction, but it did not intend to allow plaintiffs to circumvent it altogether. Strict application of the one-year limit would encourage plaintiffs to join nondiverse defendants for 366 days simply to avoid federal court, thereby undermining the very purpose of diversity jurisdiction. . . .

Where a plaintiff has attempted to manipulate the statutory rules for determining federal removal jurisdiction, thereby preventing the defendant from exercising its rights, equity may require that the one-year limit in § 1446(b) be extended.

The court said that the facts of the *Tedford* case demonstrated the point:

Tedford, a resident of Eastland County, filed a complaint with [co-plaintiff] Castro in Johnson County, despite the fact that neither plaintiff could state a cognizable claim under Texas law against the sole nondiverse defendant, [Dr. Johnson]. She amended her complaint to add her own physician [Dr. DeLuca] hours after learning of Warner-Lambert's intent to remove. Then, Tedford signed and post-dated [a] Notice of Nonsuit of Dr. DeLuca prior to the expiration of the one-year period, but did not file the document with the court or notify Warner-Lambert until after the one-year anniversary of the filing of the complaint. Equity demands Tedford be estopped from seeking to remand the case on the basis of the one-year limit in § 1466(b).

Conversely, the defendants have vigilantly sought to try this case in federal court. Each time it became apparent that the right to remove existed, Warner-Lambert sought to exercise that right. In fact, the first time Warner-Lambert sought to remove the case it notified Tedford as a professional courtesy. Tedford, knowing that the motion would be successful if Johnson remained the sole nondiverse defendant, quickly acted to thwart Warner-Lambert's efforts.

However, many district courts and two courts of appeals held that the one-year limitation was jurisdictional or otherwise absolute.

3. In the Federal Jurisdiction and Venue Clarification Act of 2011 (JVCA), Congress established a "bad faith" exception to the one-year limitation. The revised statute (codified as 28 U.S.C. § 1446(c)(1)) provides:

A case [that is not removable based on the initial pleading] may not be removed [based on a later-received pleading or other paper] on the basis of jurisdiction conferred by section 1332 more than 1 year after commencement of the action, unless the district court finds that the plaintiff has acted in bad faith in order to prevent a defendant from removing the action.

The authoritative legislative history of the JVC—the House Judiciary Committee Report—provides only limited guidance on the meaning of the new exception. It cites the *Tedford* case as a decision viewing the one-year limit as "subject to equitable tolling." It adds:

> [The new provision] grants district court judges discretion to allow removal after the 1-year limit if they find that the plaintiff has acted in bad faith in order to prevent a defendant from removing the action. The inclusion in the new standard of the phrase "in order to prevent a defendant from removing the action" makes clear that the exception to the bar of removal after one year is limited in scope.

There can be no doubt that the new law forecloses any argument that the one-year limitation is jurisdictional or absolute. But how far beyond that does it go? Does § 1446(c)(1) codify *Tedford*? If not, where should courts look to determine whether a diversity case may be removed more than a year after commencement of the action? Federal district courts have begun to answer these questions, as illustrated by the decision of the South Carolina District Court in the case that follows.

Shorraw v. Bell

United States District Court for the District of South Carolina, 2016.

2016 WL 3586675.

J. MICHELLE CHILDS, United States District Judge.

This matter is before the court on the Motion to Remand of Plaintiff Georgette Shorraw and Defendant and Cross-Plaintiff Frederick J. Bell (collectively, "Plaintiffs"). Defendant St. Jude Medical S.C., Inc. opposes Plaintiffs' Motion to Remand and asks the court to retain jurisdiction. For the reasons set forth herein, the court **GRANTS** Plaintiffs' Motion to Remand.

I. Relevant Factual and Procedural

Background

Plaintiff Shorraw, a South Carolina resident, initially filed this personal injury and products liability action in the Circuit Court of Horry County, South Carolina, on April 3, 2013. [The complaint named St. Jude Medical, a non-citizen, and Mr. Bell, a citizen of South Carolina, as defendants. Plaintiff alleged that she and Mr. Bell were in a car coming home from dinner when Mr. Bell, the driver, lost consciousness due to a defective condition in his Riata Automatic Implantable Cardioverter-Defibrillator ("AICD") Lead. The car struck another vehicle, resulting in injuries to plaintiff. The complaint asserted claims of negligence, strict liability, and breach of express and implied warranty against St. Jude Medical.]

[St. Jude Medical removed the case to federal court. Plaintiff moved to remand, but the district court denied the motion,] concluding that Mr. Bell faced no financial liability, making him a nominal defendant whose citizenship would not be considered for purposes of diversity jurisdiction.

[Shortly after the court denied the plaintiff's motion to remand, plaintiff moved to amend her complaint to add Scott Kramer, a South Carolina citizen, as a defendant. Kramer was a Technical Services Specialist employed by St. Jude Medical. The amended complaint asserted that Kramer was negligent in failing to either (1) properly conduct testing on Mr. Bell's implanted St. Jude Atlas II+DR AICD and Riata AICD Leads or (2) warn Mr. Bell about the need to replace his AICD, resulting in the AICD's battery failure.

[Plaintiff relied on certain allegations and affidavits from Robert G. Dismukes (a non-physician who has served as a technical service representative for medical device companies) as the basis for bringing claims against Mr. Kramer. Specifically, the amended complaint asserted that (1) Mr. Bell experienced syncopal episodes (loss of consciousness, dizziness, or fainting) prior to the January 2013 car accident; (2) Mr. Bell notified Mr. Kramer that he experienced syncopal episodes (loss of consciousness, dizziness, or fainting) prior to the January 2013 car accident; (3) Mr. Kramer had decision-making power over whether or when to replace Mr. Bell's ICD; and (4) Mr. Bell was "pacemaker dependent" (*i.e.*, Mr. Bell could not survive without the pacemaker).

[Over St. Jude Medical's objection, the court granted plaintiff's motion to add Kramer as a defendant. The court then remanded the case to state court.]

[About one year later, St. Jude Medical filed a second notice of removal,] claiming therein that Plaintiffs' recent depositions, as well as the depositions of Mr. Bell's treating physicians, demonstrate that adding Defendant Kramer was a sham to destroy diversity between the parties. Defendant asserts that removal is proper under the "safe-harbor" provision of 28 U.S.C. § 1446(c)(1) (2012), which allows an action to be removed to federal court more than one year after its commencement if a plaintiff acted in bad faith to prevent removal. . . .

III. Analysis

A. *Plaintiffs' Motion to Remand*

. . . Plaintiffs contend that pursuing a claim against Defendant Kramer was a strategic decision that Plaintiff Shorraw was entitled to make and is, thus, "not inherently bad faith." . . . .

With regard to the four false allegations Defendant specifically describes as evidence of bad faith in its Notice of Removal, Plaintiffs argue in their Motion to Remand that these, too, are insufficient to demonstrate forum manipulation. Specifically, Plaintiffs assert that whether or not Mr. Bell's episodes are labeled as syncopal, record evidence shows that Mr. Bell suffered from dizziness prior to the accident. And while Plaintiffs yield to the fact that Mr. Bell was not pacemaker dependent, they allege that whether he was pacemaker dependent or not is immaterial to Plaintiff Shorraw's cause of action against Defendant Kramer. Finally, Plaintiffs contend that whether Defendant Kramer owed a "duty to inform the treating physician and patient of recalls on St. Jude devices" and whether the treating physician relied on Defendant Kramer are key disputed issues in this action that should be decided by a court with jurisdiction, rather than on a notice of removal or motion to remand.

B. Defendant's Opposition to Plaintiffs' Motion to Remand

. . . Defendant alleges that they learned that this action was removable on or about August 26, 2015 based on Plaintiff Shorraw's deposition testimony, which established that the claims against Defendant Kramer were false. Depositions of Mr. Bell and two treating physicians related to this case were taken after Plaintiff Shorraw's deposition. Defendant alleges that the testimony in those later depositions also support removal. Defendant removed this action on September 25, 2015, within 30 days of the earliest deposition. Defendant thus states that its removal was timely under 28 U.S.C. § 1446(b)(3) because it was within 30 days of receiving notice that the case was removable. . . .

Defendant argues that despite continuing to pursue a cause of action against Defendant Kramer, Plaintiff Shorraw's addition of Defendant Kramer to the litigation was based on a sham affidavit and false allegations intended to destroy diversity. Defendant specifically identifies four false allegations that Plaintiff Shorraw relied on to bring claims against Defendant Kramer. Defendant argues that because deposition testimony specifically refutes these four allegations, Defendant Kramer's addition to this action demonstrates Plaintiff Shorraw's bad faith attempt to prevent Defendant from seeking a federal venue.

Defendant avers that because Defendant Kramer was joined under the pretense of "false allegations propped up by sham affidavits," this court should find that Defendant Kramer was fraudulently joined, and thus his citizenship should not be considered in determining diversity jurisdiction.

C. Court's Review

Upon review of the record, this court finds that removal was untimely, and thus remand is necessary.

1. Defendant's Removal Was Appropriate Under § 1446(b)(3)

Deposition testimony may be construed to fall within the "other paper" designation in 28 U.S.C. § 1446(b)(3), which allows defendants to remove actions when they become aware after parties' initial pleadings that a case is removable. Defendant filed its Notice of Removal within thirty days of the first deposition testimony that indicated that this action was removable. However, this case is beyond the one-year time period that limits removals under § 1446(b)(3) where the basis of jurisdiction is 28 U.S.C. § 1332. Neither party disputes these facts. Therefore, this court must consider whether removal was timely under 28 U.S.C. § 1446(c)(1)'s bad faith exception.

2. Defendant's Removal Fails to Meet the Bad Faith Exception for Removals Beyond the One-Year Time Limit Under § 1446(c)(1)

Courts have not settled on a clear standard for determining bad faith under 28 U.S.C. § 1446(c)(1).

In the Court of Appeals for the Fourth Circuit, what constitutes bad faith under § 1446(c)(1) is a developing standard. This court follows its fellow district courts and considers whether Plaintiff Shorraw's actions demonstrate forum manipulation to determine if removal was timely under § 1446(c)(1)'s bad faith exception.

Defendant argues that to determine whether Plaintiff Shorraw engaged in forum manipulation, this court should look to "whether Plaintiff intentionally took actions to prevent Defendants from removing the case to federal court." However, as Plaintiffs note in their Motion to Remand, "it is not inherently bad faith to use strategy to defeat federal jurisdiction."

In determining the boundary between forum manipulation and litigation strategy, this court considers other cases that contemplate forum manipulation. In *Tedford v. Warner-Lambert Co.*, for example, a precursor to the bad faith exception now codified at § 1446(c)(1), the Court of Appeals for the Fifth Circuit found that the plaintiffs engaged in forum manipulation where, despite signing a Notice of Nonsuit for a nondiverse defendant prior to the expiration of the one-year anniversary of the action's commencement, the plaintiffs failed to timely notify the defendants or the court of the nonsuit, thereby denying the defendants the opportunity to remove the action. Similarly, other courts considering whether a party acted in bad faith to prevent removal evaluate whether the plaintiff's actions specifically consider the one-year limit on removal. *See, e.g., Hiser v. Seay*, 2014 WL 6885433, at *4 (W.D. Ky. Dec. 5, 2014) (denying remand where the plaintiff intentionally chose to delay accepting a settlement offer with a nondiverse defendant until after the one-year time period elapsed); *Brown v. Wal-Mart Stores, Inc.*, 2014 WL 60044, at *2 (W.D. Va. Jan. 7, 2014) (collecting cases where the plaintiffs' actions in delaying disclosure of the amount in controversy until after the one-year time period were found to be in bad faith).

The facts in the instant action do not rise to the same degree of bad faith forum manipulation as in these cases. Here, Plaintiff Shorraw moved to include Defendant Kramer as a defendant in this case prior to Defendant's first removal of this case, and continues to prosecute claims against Defendant Kramer. For example, Plaintiff Shorraw hired an expert in Defendant Kramer's field to review Mr. Bell's medical records and provide information regarding industry standards for checking the battery voltage on an AICD, and defended against a motion to dismiss. Such actions indicate to this court that, even if Defendant Kramer's joinder was convenient for defeating federal diversity jurisdiction, Plaintiff Shorraw believes she has a cause of action against Defendant Kramer and that she intends to pursue it sincerely. Indeed, at least one court considers active litigation of a claim, including "[a]ny non-token amount of discovery," sufficient to create a rebuttable presumption of good faith when evaluating bad faith under § 1446(c)(1). *Aguayo v. AMCO Ins. Co.*, 59 F. Supp. 3d 1225, (D.N.M. 2014). While this court does not go so far as to extend Plaintiff Shorraw a rebuttable presumption of good faith, it does assign significant weight to her continued litigation against Defendant Kramer in its analysis of bad faith.

Plaintiffs characterize the allegedly false statements that Defendant relies on for its bad faith argument as statements that can be reasonably inferred from facts in the record, material disputes that should be litigated by a court with jurisdiction, or statements irrelevant to the claim against Defendant Kramer. This court agrees with

Plaintiffs' characterization that its actions do not rise to the standard of bad faith forum manipulation. Therefore, Defendant's removal must be deemed untimely under § 1446(c)(1).

3. Defendant Fails to Establish Federal Diversity Jurisdiction

Even if Defendant's removal was timely, to remain in federal court Defendant would still need to persuade this court to disregard Defendant Kramer's citizenship to maintain party diversity under 28 U.S.C. § 1332(a). Although this court's ruling renders unnecessary a conclusion on this issue, it does not appear that Defendant successfully argued fraudulent joinder or presented any other reasoning for why this court could disregard Defendant Kramer's citizenship and grant federal diversity jurisdiction under § 1332.

IV. Conclusion

Based on the aforementioned reasons, the court hereby **GRANTS** Plaintiffs' Motion to Remand and **REMANDS** this action to the Court of Common Pleas for Horry County, South Carolina, for further proceedings and rulings on the remaining motions. The court denies Plaintiffs' request for costs and attorneys' fees related to this order. [The court found that under *Martin v. Franklin Capital Corp.*, 546 U.S. 132 (2005), defendant's arguments "were grounded in a reasonable perception of the factual record and the applicable law. Therefore, fees are not appropriate."]

Note: Applying the "Bad Faith" Exception

1. The district court in *Shorraw*, following the lead of some other courts, takes the position that bad faith can be found only if the plaintiff "engaged in forum manipulation specifically to prevent removal." Is that test consistent with *Tedford*? Does it adequately reflect the legislative history set forth in the Note preceding *Shorraw*?

2. Another district court has construed the bad faith exception to require a two-step test. In *Aguayo v. AMCO Ins. Co.*, 59 F. Supp. 2d 1225, 1262-63 (D.N.M. 2014), the court said:

> First, the Court inquires whether the plaintiff actively litigated against the removal spoiler in state court: asserting valid claims, taking discovery, negotiating settlement, seeking default judgments if the defendant does not answer the complaint, et cetera. Failure to actively litigate against the removal spoiler will be deemed bad faith; actively litigating against the removal spoiler, however, will create a rebuttable presumption of good faith.

> Second, the defendant may attempt to rebut this presumption with evidence already in the defendant's possession that establishes that, despite the plaintiff's active litigation against the removal spoiler, the plaintiff would not have named the removal spoiler or would have dropped the spoiler before the one-year mark but for the plaintiff's desire to keep the case in state court. The defendant may introduce direct evidence of the plaintiff's bad faith at this stage—*e.g.*, electronic mail transmissions in which the plaintiff states that he or she is only keeping the removal spoiler joined to defeat removal—but will

not receive discovery or an evidentiary hearing in federal court to obtain such evidence.

Is this a preferable approach? Note that the court excludes the possibility of allowing the defendant to engage in discovery on the issue of bad faith. The House Report on the JVCA, quoted earlier in this chapter, said that if the plaintiff disputes the removing defendant's assertion that the amount-in-controversy requirement is satisfied, discovery may be taken. Is there any reason why discovery should not be allowed on the question of bad faith?

3. When a predecessor bill to the JVCA was introduced in the 109th Congress (2006), the exception to the one-year limitation was written very differently. It provided that a diversity case could not be removed after one year "unless equitable considerations warrant removal. Such equitable considerations include whether the plaintiff has engaged in manipulative behavior, whether the defendant has acted diligently in seeking to remove the action, and whether the case has progressed in State court to a point where removal would be disruptive." Compare that wording to that of the JVCA as enacted. Does the change in language offer any clues as to the proper interpretation of the bad faith exception?

4. Some of the decisions applying *Tedford* declined to allow removal on the ground that the defendant failed to act expeditiously when it learned of the facts supporting jurisdiction. Is that consideration relevant under the JVCA? For example, suppose that the district court were to find that the plaintiff did act in bad faith in order to prevent removal. May the district court nevertheless order remand if the defendant did not seek removal at the first opportunity?

5. The JVCA specifies one circumstance that will satisfy the "bad faith" standard: if "the district court finds that the plaintiff deliberately failed to disclose the actual amount in controversy to prevent removal." What sort of evidence would be necessary to support such a finding? Consider the facts of *Foster v. Landon*, summarized in the Problems below.

6. Prior to the enactment of the JVCA, there was disagreement in the lower courts as to whether the one-year limitation applied to all cases removed on the basis of diversity, or only to those in which a case becomes removable some time after the initial pleading is filed. The JVCA resolves that conflict; the one-year limitation applies only to cases removed "under subsection (b)(3)" — the paragraph that governs removal of cases that are not removable based on the initial pleading.

Problems: Is This "Bad Faith" Under § 1446(c)(1)?

Here are two cases in which district courts in the Fifth Circuit applied the *Tedford* equitable exception. In both cases the court found that the doctrine did not allow removal. How should the cases be decided under the JVCA?

1. *Foster v. Landon* (E.D. La. 2004). In his state court petition, filed on July 3, 2003, plaintiff asserted that the amount in controversy did not exceed $75,000. On August 24, 2004, after the one-year period, plaintiff sent a settlement demand letter to the defendant. The letter estimated that past medical expenses totaled almost $60,000, and that the plaintiff would need $5,000 for future medical expenses. It also claimed lost wages of $3,500 up to that point, and estimated that future wage loss would total $25,000. Attached to the letter were medical records which established that on April 13, 2004, Dr. Kenneth Vogel diagnosed the plaintiff as having a herniated disc. Another attachment showed that on that same date, Dr. Vogel recommended that the plaintiff be admitted to the hospital for further testing. The plaintiff did not go to the hospital until June 23, 2004, when he was admitted to Doctor's Hospital. The plaintiff was released from the hospital on the next day; tests indicated that he had a degenerative disc disease, and he was restricted from returning to work.

The district court found that the plaintiff's activities gave rise to "an aroma of manipulation," but concluded that the record did not present "the egregious, clear pattern of forum manipulation" as in cases where the *Tedford* standard was satisfied. Would the result be different under the new statute?

2. *Tran v. Citibank* (N.D. Tex. 2010). Plaintiff filed suit against Citibank and GC Services in state court on November 13, 2008. His original petition alleged breach of contract, unspecified violations of law with regard to credit reporting, and violations of the Fair Debt Collection Practices Act (FDCPA). Defendants timely removed on the basis of the federal claims. Plaintiff moved to dismiss the federal claims and to remand the case to state court. The district court granted both motions.

Following remand, the state court, by order of March 25, 2009, set a mediation deadline of September 3, 2009. The plaintiff asked Citibank to join in a motion for continuance. Citibank agreed, and the state court signed an agreed order of continuance on August 6, 2009, which extended the mediation deadline to December 31, 2009.

During a mediation session on December 17, 2009, plaintiff made a settlement demand of more than $87,000. Within 30 days after receiving that demand, defendants removed the action.

Quoting *Foster v. Landon*, the district court ordered remand. The court said it was "not convinced that [the plaintiff's] conduct [was] tantamount to 'manipulation' that would call into play *Tedford*'s equitable exception." How should the court rule under the new statute?

[4] Joinder of Parties After Removal

Note: Applying 28 U.S.C. § 1447(e)

1. The "fraudulent joinder" doctrine, discussed in subsection B[2], deals with situations where a plaintiff names both diverse and non-diverse defendants in the initial complaint. But suppose the plaintiff files a complaint naming only diverse defendants, the defendant removes based on diversity, and the plaintiff then seeks to amend the complaint to add one or more non-diverse defendants. Section 1447(e) of Title 28 appears to provide the answer:

If after removal the plaintiff seeks to join additional defendants whose joinder would destroy subject matter jurisdiction, the court may deny joinder,
or permit joinder and remand the action to the State court.

The Fifth Circuit has said that this language gives the district court only two options:
it may permit the joinder of non-diverse defendants or it may remand the case, but it
"may not permit joinder of non-diverse defendants [and] then decline to remand."
Cobb v. Delta Exports, Inc., 186 F.3d 675 (5th Cir. 1999).

Suppose, though, that the defendant does not object to the joinder because the
defendant does not realize that the proposed new defendant is a co-citizen of the plaintiff. In a later case, the Fifth Circuit acknowledged that "*Cobb* seems to create a trap
for the unwary diverse defendant, or a device exploitable by a clever plaintiff." *Borden
v. Allstate Ins. Co.*, 589 F.3d 168 (5th Cir. 2009).

2. Other courts have read the statute more flexibly. In *Bailey v. Bayer Cropscience L.P.*,
563 F.3d 302 (8th Cir. 2009), the plaintiff filed suit against Bayer CropScience (BCS) in
Missouri state court, alleging intentional infliction of emotional distress (IIED). BCS
removed the case to federal court. Bailey subsequently moved to amend the complaint
by adding two BCS employees, Moerer and Jackson, as additional defendants. The
district court permitted joinder, and Bailey then moved to remand due to lack of
jurisdiction. Upon learning that the joinder destroyed diversity, the district court
reconsidered its prior decision and dismissed the joined defendants. The Eighth Circuit found no abuse of discretion:

> Several courts hold, when a trial court grants a plaintiff leave to amend
> the complaint by naming additional defendants, and the plaintiff fails to
> inform the court that one or more of those defendants will destroy diversity,
> the trial court may reconsider its earlier decision. [We agree.] In the present
> case, the district court granted Bailey's motion to amend his complaint and
> permitted Bailey to name two additional defendants without the court real-
> izing such joinder destroyed the court's diversity jurisdiction. When the dis-
> trict court discovered the joinder defeated diversity jurisdiction, the court
> had discretionary authority to reconsider and reverse its previous joinder
> decision. . . .

In the present case, the district court accurately considered the relevant
factors and held the balancing test weighed against the addition of the
nondiverse defendant. First, Bailey waited a year before filing his motion to
amend. When he finally filed the motion, Bailey failed to inform the court
such joinder would destroy diversity. Less than a month after the joinder
order, Bailey filed a motion for remand, suggesting he had known about the
jurisdictional issues. These facts and reasonable inferences support the district court's conclusion the defendants were joined primarily for the purpose
of defeating federal jurisdiction.

Second, Bailey knew all of the involved parties before he filed the action.
Despite knowing all the parties, Bailey originally filed suit only against BCS,

waiting over a year before submitting a motion to join Moerer and Jackson. Bailey claims this delay resulted from his lack of knowledge as to the residences of the two putative defendants. Yet, no evidence in the record suggests Bailey previously made unsuccessful attempts to determine the residences of Moerer and Jackson. The record sufficiently supports the district court's conclusion Bailey was dilatory in filing his motion to name additional defendants.

Finally, because Bailey alleged the parties were joint tortfeasors, Bailey will not be significantly injured if amendment is not allowed. Thus, the district court did not abuse its discretion in first reconsidering, and then in denying Bailey's motion to amend his complaint. Upon denying Bailey's motion, diversity jurisdiction was restored, and the district court properly denied Bailey's motion to remand.

Is this result consistent with the language of § 1447(e)?

3. The court in *Bailey* noted that "Bailey failed to inform the court [that the joinder of *Moerer* and *Jackson*] would destroy diversity." Moerer and Jackson were employees of BCS. If BCS knew their citizenship—as seems likely—should the burden be on BCS to inform the court at the time plaintiff moved to amend the complaint?

Problem: Joining the Insurance Agent

Marilyn Brent brought suit in Oceana state court against Greatlife Insurance Co. (Greatlife), alleging that Greatlife failed to pay benefits owed under a long term care policy it issued to her in 1995. Brent is a citizen of Oceana and Greatlife is incorporated in New Harmony, so Greatlife timely removed the case to federal district court. Greatlife then filed an answer and a counterclaim for declaratory judgment. The district court notified the parties that a Rule 16 scheduling conference would be held two months later.

One month after receiving the notification of the Rule 16 conference, Brent filed an amended complaint. The amended complaint included all of the allegations of the initial complaint, but it also added two defendants, Delta Insurance Associates (DIA), an insurance agency, and its agent, Gerry Lamb. The gist of the new claim is that these defendants misrepresented the terms of the policy they sold her. In particular, Brent asserts that they gave her a booklet describing coverage, and the booklet implied that she would be covered for "all levels of care" rather than merely the specific, state-licensed nursing homes that Greatlife now asserts its coverage is limited to. The amended complaint notes that DIA and Lamb are both citizens of Oceana. Simultaneously with the motion to amend, Brent filed a motion to remand the case to state court.

Greatlife opposes both motions, and the district court holds the status conference to hear argument on the motions. Here are extracts.

Dacer (counsel for Greatlife): This is a transparent effort to destroy diversity jurisdiction. The claim against DIA and Lamb is completely baseless. The language in the booklet *is* consistent with the policy language. In any event, neither DIA nor Lamb published the booklet in question, and neither DIA nor Lamb had any obligation to advise Brent about the terms of the policy.

Park (counsel for Brent): Greatlife's arguments might defeat the claim against DIA and Lamb on the merits, but that doesn't mean it's without foundation. It's true that we would prefer to litigate in state court, but there's nothing improper about that.

Dacer: If plaintiff really believed that she had a claim against DIA and Lamb, she would have included it in her initial state-court complaint. The court shouldn't reward this belated attempt to keep the case out of federal court.

Park: Well, we never thought that DIA and Lamb would still be in business more than 20 years after they sold the policy to our client. It was only after the case was removed to federal court that we decided to search for them. When we discovered that they are still active, we added the claim against them.

Should the court allow the plaintiff to amend the complaint and secure a remand to state court?

D. Some Procedural Aspects of Removal

[1] The Timing of Removal

The timing of removal in the general run of civil cases is governed by 28 U.S.C. § 1446(b). That subsection was extensively revised by the Federal Courts Jurisdiction and Venue Clarification Act of 2011 (JVCA), signed by President Obama on December 7, 2011, and applicable to cases commenced in state court on or after January 6, 2012. The amended provision eliminates some of the difficulties that bedeviled judges and litigants under the pre-2011 law, particularly in cases involving multiple defendants who are served at different times. Yet even with the revisions, subsection (b) continues to be a minefield, particularly for defendants. The statute now provides:

(1) The notice of removal of a civil action or proceeding shall be filed within 30 days after the receipt by the defendant, through service or otherwise, of a copy of the initial pleading setting forth the claim for relief upon which such action or proceeding is based, or within 30 days after the service of summons upon the defendant if such initial pleading has then been filed in court and is not required to be served on the defendant, whichever period is shorter.

(2) (A) When a civil action is removed solely under section 1441(a), all defendants who have been properly joined and served must join in or consent to the removal of the action.

(B) Each defendant shall have 30 days after receipt by or service on that defendant of the initial pleading or summons described in paragraph (1) to file the notice of removal.

(C) If defendants are served at different times, and a later-served defendant files a notice of removal, any earlier-served defendant may consent to the removal even though that earlier-served defendant did not previously initiate or consent to removal.

(3) Except as provided in subsection (c), if the case stated by the initial pleading is not removable, a notice of removal may be filed within thirty days after receipt by the defendant, through service or otherwise, of a copy of an amended pleading, motion, order or other paper from which it may first be ascertained that the case is one which is or has become removable.

As we have seen, § 1446 also includes a special timing rule for diversity cases—the one-year limitation, now qualified by the "bad faith" exception. We have already considered the one-year limit. Here we look at some of the issues that arise in both diversity and federal-question cases. Our study will be illustrative rather than comprehensive.

Preliminarily, one point of nomenclature deserves attention. Under § 1446, a case is removed by filing a *notice* of removal. Until 1988, the document was referred to as a *petition* for removal. Older cases—and even some decided after 1988—use the superseded language.

Note: The Deadline for Removal

1. Subsection 1446(b) provides that the notice of removal must be filed "within 30 days after the receipt by the defendant, through service *or otherwise*, of a copy of the [complaint]." Read literally, the phrase "or otherwise" might suggest that the 30-day clock begins to run the moment the defendant receives a copy of the initial pleading "through *any* means, not just service of process." That is what the Fifth Circuit held in *Reece v. Wal-Mart Stores, Inc.*, 98 F.3d 839 (5th Cir. 1996). Other circuits agreed, but the Supreme Court rejected that interpretation of the statute.

In *Murphy Bros. v. Michetti Pipe Stringing, Inc.*, 526 U.S. 344 (1999), the plaintiff filed a complaint in state court. Three days later, without serving the defendant corporation, the plaintiff's counsel faxed to one of the corporation's officers a "courtesy copy" of the file-stamped complaint. The Supreme Court held that receipt of the file-stamped complaint did not start the 30-day period. Justice Ginsburg wrote for the Court:

> We read Congress' provisions for removal in light of a bedrock principle: An individual or entity named as a defendant is not obliged to engage in litigation unless notified of the action, and brought under a court's authority, by formal process. Accordingly, we hold that a named defendant's time to remove is triggered by simultaneous service of the summons and complaint, or receipt of the complaint, "through service or otherwise," after and apart from service of the summons, but not by mere receipt of the complaint unattended by any formal service.

2. In *Murphy Bros.* the Court held that the defendant's time to remove was triggered by formal service of the *complaint*. However, some states have unusual procedures for commencing an action. How does the *Murphy Bros.* rule apply in those states? In *Whitaker v. American Telecasting, Inc.*, 261 F.3d 196 (2d Cir. 2001), the court held that, in New York, the defendant's receipt of a "summons with notice" can be the triggering event as long as it contains "sufficient information to enable the defendant to intelligently ascertain the basis for removal."

Unusual state procedures can be a trap for the unwary. How can a defendant — who often will be a resident of another state — avoid losing the opportunity to remove?

3. Paragraph (b)(2) provides a second window for removal if — but only if — "the case stated by the initial pleading is not removable," another 30-day period begins when the defendant receives, "through service or otherwise, [a] copy of an amended pleading, motion, order or other paper from which it may first be ascertained that the case is one which is or has become removable."

Suppose that the case stated by the initial pleading is not removable because the plaintiff has joined a co-citizen as defendant along with a non-citizen defendant. Six months after the filing of the action, the non-citizen defendant takes the plaintiff's deposition. In the course of responding to the defendant's questions, the plaintiff mentions that he is no longer seeking relief from the citizen defendant. But the complaint has not been amended. Is the case now removable? If so, when does the 30-day period start? On the day the plaintiff gives his testimony? Or when the defendant receives the transcript of the deposition?

For that matter, is it clear that responses to discovery can constitute an "other paper" in this situation? Note that new § 1446(c)(3)(A) provides expressly that "information relating to the amount in controversy . . . in responses to discovery" shall be treated as an "other paper" when the case as stated by the initial pleading is not removable solely because the amount in controversy requirement is not met. Should we infer from this that responses to discovery should *not* be treated as an "other paper" in other contexts?

Rossetto v. Oaktree Capital Management, LLC

United States District Court for the District of Hawaii, 2009.

664 F. Supp. 2d 1122.

Alan C. Kay, Senior District Judge.

Before this Court is [the objection filed by Defendants Oaktree Capital Management and others] to Magistrate Judge Leslie E. Kobayashi's Findings and Recommendations to Grant Plaintiff Gustavo Rossetto's Motion for Remand.

Background

[According to the complaint,] Plaintiff was employed at the Turtle Bay Resort ("Resort") from December 5, 2003 until November 2007, as a food server in the Resort's banquet department. At these banquets, the Resort typically charged a "service charge" of fifteen to twenty percent of the total cost of the food and beverage purchased in connection with the functions. As a food server at these functions, Plaintiff received only a portion of the "service charge" the Resort received from the function customers.

On January 27, 2009, Plaintiff, on behalf of himself and all persons similarly situated, filed a complaint against Defendants in the Circuit Court of the First Circuit, State of Hawaii. In the Complaint, Plaintiff alleges that under Hawaii Revised Statutes section 481B-14, the Resort was required to either pay the Plaintiff Class 100% of the "service charge" or to disclose to the customers that the Resort was retaining all or a portion of the "service charge." Plaintiff contends that Defendants did neither of these, which constitutes unfair methods of competition in violation of Hawaii law.

This case was removed by Defendants on April 3, 2009. Defendants assert that federal subject matter jurisdiction is appropriate because the case requires the Court to interpret the Collective Bargaining Agreement ("CBA"), between the Resort and an employee union known as UNITE HERE! Local 5 ("Union"), thus preempting state law claims pursuant to Section 301 of the Labor Management Relations Act.

On May 1, 2009, Plaintiff filed a motion for remand to state court ("Motion for Remand") on the ground that removal was untimely. Both parties agree that if the Complaint provided the grounds for removal, Defendants' removal would be untimely pursuant to 28 U.S.C. § 1446(b). Defendants contend, however, that removal was timely because the Complaint failed to affirmatively reveal Plaintiff's membership in the Union and the existence of the CBA governing the employee-employer relationship. Accordingly, the thirty-day removal period would only be triggered by a motion or some other paper which provides the grounds for removal. *See* 28 U.S.C. § 1446(b).

Plaintiff, however, contends that the facts that gave rise to Defendants' defense of complete preemption under Section 301 of the LMRA, i.e., that Plaintiff and the Plaintiff Class were employees covered by the CBA, were known to the Defendants at the time they were served the Complaint, thus making removal untimely. In the alternative, Plaintiff asserts if the Complaint did not provide grounds for removal, then likewise no other paper subsequently has sufficed to establish such grounds. Plaintiff further argues that the Court lacks subject matter jurisdiction over the claims because resolution of the state law claims does not require the Court to interpret the terms of the CBA. To dispute this, Defendants have submitted a copy of the CBA to this Court in their Memorandum in Opposition to the Motion for Remand, which Defendants argue contains several provisions concerning wages, tips, and service charges that act to waive Plaintiff's right to maintain an action against the Resort.

On June 1, 2009, Defendants filed their Second Notice of Removal ("Second Notice"). Defendants first argue that their answer filed on March 9, 2009 ("Answer"), served as the "other paper" triggering the thirty-day removal period. In the alternative, Defendants contend that Plaintiff's Motion for Remand, which mentions Plaintiff's union membership and the CBA, commenced the thirty-day removal period, thus making the Second Notice both necessary and timely.

On July 1, 2009, Plaintiff filed a Second Motion for Remand ("Second Motion"). The memorandum in support of the Second Motion simply incorporates by reference the first Motion for Remand and supporting memorandum, declaration and exhibits, as support for the Second Motion.

On August 28, 2009, Magistrate Judge Leslie E. Kobayashi issued a findings and recommendation to grant Plaintiff's motion for a remand and to award attorneys costs and fees. She concluded that the thirty-day period for removal began with the filing of the Complaint, thus making Defendants' April 4 notice of removal untimely. She reasoned that Defendants' actual knowledge of Plaintiff's membership in a union, combined with the fact the complaint was based on Plaintiff's employment, provided sufficient notice of grounds for removal. Judge Kobayashi took note that Defendants must have known of the existence of a union and CBA because Defendants' Answer contains several references to these facts. Accordingly, Judge Kobayashi found that the removal period began with Defendants' receipt of the Complaint and removal on April 4, 2009, therefore was beyond the thirty-day period allotted under 28 U.S.C. § 1446(b). With regard to attorney's fees, Judge Kobayashi found that Defendants decision to file a notice of removal was not objectively reasonable, thus warranting an award of attorneys' fees and costs to Plaintiff. . . .

[Defendants filed an objection to Judge Kobayashi's findings and recommendation. Review by the district court is *de novo*.]

Discussion

This Court begins its analysis by recognizing the canon in the Ninth Circuit which instructs that "[r]emoval statutes are to be strictly construed, and any doubts as to the right of removal must be resolved in favor of remanding to state court." This Court reaches the same conclusions as Judge Kobayashi, but with a different analysis.

I. *Removal*

At issue in this case is whether removal was evident from the face of the Complaint and if not, whether any additional filings by the parties permit Defendants to remove the matter to federal court.

A. *Face of the Complaint*

Section 1446 provides two thirty-day periods during which a defendant may remove an action. The first thirty-day requirement "only applies if the case stated by the initial pleading is removable on its face." [In *Harris v. Bankers Life & Cas. Co.*, 425 F.3d 689 (9th Cir. 2005), the Ninth Circuit Court of Appeals adopted] a bright line rule that [the] facts establishing [the] grounds for removal must be included in the initial complaint in order to start the initial thirty-day period. Further, "notice of removability under § 1446(b) is determined through examination of the four corners of the applicable pleadings, not through subjective knowledge or a duty to make further inquiry." The second thirty-day requirement, which applies where no grounds for removal are evident from the initial pleading, occurs "thirty days after receipt by the defendant of a copy of an amended pleading, motion, order or other paper from which it may first be ascertained that the case is one which is or has become removable."

In *Harris*, the Ninth Circuit rejected the duty to investigate approach, [saying:] "We join with the other circuits that have adopted the same approach to indeterminate pleadings—the grounds for removal must be revealed affirmatively in the initial pleading in order for the first thirty-day clock under § 1446(b) to begin." In the context of LMRA preemption, the Ninth Circuit has noted that until acknowledgment of a CBA is contained within a pleading or other paper, the thirty-day deadline for removal does not commence. *See Rose v. Beverly Health and Rehab. Servs., Inc.*, 295 Fed. Appx. 142 (9th Cir. 2008) (unpublished mem. decision) (holding that notice of removal was timely because the complaint did not disclose that the suit was one for breach of a CBA even though defendant had subjective knowledge of this).[4] The initial thirty-day clock does not run even where the removing party has possession of documents that provide grounds for preemption.

In this case, the initial thirty-day removal period never began because Plaintiff's complaint did not indicate that Plaintiff was a member of a union, or that a CBA existed governing the payment of service charges. Although it is true, as Judge Kobayashi indicates, that Defendants had independent knowledge of these facts, the only relevant question is whether this information was included in the Complaint. *See Chapman v. Powermatic, Inc.*, 969 F.2d 160 (5th Cir. 1992) (holding that a court may only examine the face of the initial pleading, and may not consider other matters the defendant knew, or could have known through investigation). ([As one district court has said,] "the time period to remove cannot depend on defendant's actual knowledge, because the statute expressly allows a defendant to rely on papers presented to it." *Jong v. General Motors Corp.*, 359 F. Supp. 223 (N.D. Cal. 1973).

Upon reviewing the Complaint, no [facts about the CBA] are included. Accordingly, pursuant to 28 U.S.C. § 1446(b), the thirty-day period begins "within thirty days after receipt by the defendant, through service or otherwise, of a copy of an amended pleading, motion, order or other paper from which it may first be ascertained that the case is one which is or has become removable."

B. *Other Filings*

Defendant claims that one of two documents triggered the thirty-day removal period: (1) the Defendants' Answer; or (2) Plaintiff's Motion for Remand to state court. The Court holds that neither of these documents satisfy 28 U.S.C. § 1446(b).

The document that triggers the thirty-day removal period cannot be one created by the defendant. *See S.W.S. Erectors, Inc. v. Infax, Inc.*, 72 F.3d 489 (5th Cir. 1996) (holding that an affidavit executed by the defendant's attorney did not commence the removal period because it did not arise from a voluntary act by the plaintiff). As stated by the Fifth Circuit, "The 'other paper' must result from the voluntary act of a plaintiff which gives the defendant notice of the changes circumstances which now support federal jurisdiction." *Addo v. Globe Life & Accident Ins. Co.*, 230 F.3d 759 (5th Cir. 2000). In the Ninth Circuit, the document providing grounds for removal must

---

4. Pursuant to U.S. Ct. of App. 9th Cir. Rule 36-3, this Court does not rely on *Rose* as precedent, but it does find the opinion illustrative.

be one filed in state court. "The record of the state court is considered the sole source from which to ascertain whether a case originally not removable has since become removable." *Peabody v. Maud Van Cortland Hill Schroll Trust*, 892 F.2d 772 (9th Cir. 1989).

In this case, Defendants' answer does not provide the grounds for removal because it was not voluntarily submitted by the Plaintiff. Further, Plaintiff's Motion for Remand does not provide the grounds for removal because the motion was filed in *federal* court. As indicated in *Peabody*, a motion in federal court cannot trigger a right to remove to federal court. Accordingly, neither Defendants' Answer nor Plaintiff's Motion for Remand triggered commencement of the removal period. Therefore, the Court finds that Defendants' Second Notice of Removal filed on June 1, 2009, is improper because Defendants have not been presented a paper providing grounds for removal pursuant to 28 U.S.C. § 1446(b).

In sum, as Plaintiff argues in the alternative, Defendants' request for removal was premature rather than untimely. The thirty-day removal period has not yet begun because Plaintiff's Complaint did not contain adequate grounds to trigger removal and no additional pleadings or papers, as defined by 28 U.S.C. § 1446(b), have provided subsequent grounds for removal. Accordingly, the Court grants both of Plaintiff's motions for remand.

II. *Attorney's Fees*

When a federal court remands a case, it "may require payment of just costs and any actual expenses, including attorney fees, incurred as a result of the removal." 28 U.S.C. § 1447(c). Further, "absent unusual circumstances, courts may award attorney's fees under § 1447(c) only where the removing party lacked an objectively reasonable basis for removal." *Martin v. Franklin Capital Corp.*, 546 U.S. 132 (2005). . . .

As discussed earlier, Defendants have asserted three different grounds for removal: (1) the receipt of the Complaint, (2) Defendants' Answer, and (3) Plaintiff's Motion for Remand. The Court finds that none of these grounds was objectively reasonable.

First, as Defendants adamantly assert, the Complaint did not mention the existence of a Union or a CBA. Consistent with Defendants' arguments, it would be objectively unreasonable to believe that this document provided grounds for removal. Nevertheless, Defendants sought removal based on this document *beyond* the initial thirty-day period. The Court finds that the Complaint did not provide objectively reasonable grounds for removal because it did not mention a Union or a CBA, and Defendants removed beyond the initial thirty-period.

Second, upon a review of the statute and case law, Defendants would have learned that . . . . a defendant's own filings, including an answer, cannot begin the second thirty-day period. Given the plain language of the statute and the aforementioned case law in the Ninth Circuit, this Court finds Defendants' position objectively unreasonable.

Finally, Defendants' argument that Plaintiff's Motion for Remand satisfies 28 U.S.C. § 1446(b) is clearly not reasonable because the Ninth Circuit in *Peabody* clearly stated that the document triggering commencement of the removal must be filed in state court. Plaintiff's Motion for Remand is a product of Defendant's removal to federal court and thus cannot provide grounds for removal.

Therefore, the Court finds that Defendants did not have an objectively reasonable basis to seek removal in this case and that an award of attorneys' fees and costs incurred in connection with the improper removal is appropriate and warranted in this case.

III. *Section 301 Preemption*

Finally, the Court finds it need not address the issue of preemption under Section 301 of the LMRA in light of this case being remanded to state court on other grounds.

Conclusion

In view of the foregoing findings, the Court adopts, as modified, Judge Kobayashi's recommendation and grants both of Plaintiff's Motions for Remand and awards attorney's fees and costs.

It is so ordered.

Note: Untimely or Premature?

1. In *Rossetto*, the magistrate judge found that the removal was untimely (too late); the district judge found that it was premature (too early). But they both conclude that the defendants "did not have an objectively reasonable basis to seek removal" and thus would be required to pay the plaintiffs' attorneys fees under 28 U.S.C. § 1447(c). Could both judges have been justified in imposing attorney's fees on the defendants?

2. Most courts agree with the Ninth Circuit's decision in *Harris v. Bankers Life & Cas. Co.*, 425 F.3d 689 (9th Cir. 2005) (quoted in *Rossetto*), that "the grounds for removal must be revealed affirmatively in the initial pleading in order for the first thirty-day clock under § 1446(b) to begin." But this "four corners" rule may not provide the "bright line" that the Ninth Circuit envisaged. For example, in *KDY, Inc. v. Hydroslotter Corp.*, 2008 U.S. Dist. LEXIS 95698 (N.D. Cal. 2008), the court acknowledged that the complaint did not specify the citizenship of each defendant. The court nevertheless found that service of the complaint triggered the initial 30-day period, because "the facts giving rise to diversity jurisdiction [were] Defendants' own places of citizenship." The notice of removal, filed more than 30 days after defendants were served, was thus untimely. The court insisted that this reasoning was "not contrary to the holding of *Harris*." The court explained:

> [Although] courts are not to look to the subjective knowledge of a defendant, Defendants here admit that they did not learn their own geographical location from any of Plaintiff's papers. This is not surprising, as courts surely can presume that a defendant is aware of various basic personal facts, including the location of one's citizenship, without delving into the prohibited area of a defendant's subjective knowledge.

Do you agree that this reasoning is consistent with *Harris*?

3. If the court's approach in *KDY* is correct, does the reasoning apply to "facts" other than the defendants' own citizenship? In *Rossetto*, the magistrate judge thought that it did:

> The lack of any specific reference [in the complaint] to the CBA or Plaintiff's membership in the Union is of no moment. Although Defendants are not required to make a *subjective* inquiry in order to determine whether an action is removable, they cannot disavow themselves of *objective* knowledge and information squarely within their possession.

(Emphasis in original.) On that basis, the magistrate judge found that the defendants should have removed within 30 days of receiving the complaint. The district court rejected this rationale, saying: "While some would feel this reasoning makes good common sense, nevertheless it does not comport with case law." Do you agree that the magistrate judge's reasoning comports with "good common sense"?

4. Assume that the defendants in a case like *Rossetto* have at least a good-faith argument that the plaintiff's claim is completely preempted under the *Avco* doctrine and thus is removable. (See Chapter 10.) But when? If removal must be based on the record in the state court (as the Ninth Circuit holds) and the complaint omits any reference to the CBA, is there any way the defendants can remove during the initial 30-day period? If not, what, if anything, can the defendants do to trigger the second 30-day period?

Note: Removal in Multiple-Defendant Cases

1. Before enactment of the JVCA, § 1446 provided simply that the notice of removal must be filed "within thirty days after the receipt by *the defendant* . . . . of a copy of the [complaint]." (Emphasis added.) How did this rule apply when the plaintiff sued multiple defendants? And suppose different defendants were served at different times. When did the 30-day period begin?

Early on, the Supreme Court answered the first question by establishing a "rule of unanimity." Under that rule, which is generally traced to the Court's decision in *Chicago, Rock Island & Pac. Ry. v. Martin*, 178 U.S. 245 (1900), all defendants who have been properly joined and served must join in or consent to removal. The "rule of unanimity" has now been codified by the JVCA; see 28 U.S.C. § 1446(b)(1). Note that the codification is limited to cases removed solely under § 1441(a); it has no application to other statutes that authorize removal.

However, no Supreme Court decision answered the second question: when does the 30-day period begin when different defendants are served at different times? Without guidance from the Supreme Court, lower courts reached sharply different conclusions. Some courts adopted the "first-served" rule, holding that "the thirty-day period begins to run as soon as the first defendant is served (provided the case is then removable)" and that "all served defendants must join in the petition no later than thirty days from the day on which the first defendant was served." See *Getty Oil Corp. v. Insurance Co. of North America*, 841 F.2d 1254 (5th Cir. 1988). Other courts—ultimately including a majority of the courts of appeals that addressed the question—concluded that the 30-day period runs from the date of service on the last-served defendant, and that earlier-served defendants who failed to act during their own 30-day periods could join in, or consent to, the later-served defendant's timely removal. *E.g., Bailey v. Janssen Pharmaceutica, Inc.*, 536 F.3d 1202 (11th Cir. 2008).

The JVCA codifies the last-served rule as explicated in cases like *Bailey*. The House Report (H.R. REP. 112-10) summarizes the revision and outlines the policy justifications:

> New subparagraph 1446(b)(2)(B) provides that each defendant will have 30 days from his or her own date of service (or receipt of initial pleading) to seek removal. Subparagraph (b)(2)(C) would also allow earlier-served defendants to join in or consent to removal by a later-served defendant. Fairness to later-served defendants, whether they are brought in by the initial complaint or an amended complaint, necessitates that they be given their own opportunity to remove, even if the earlier-served defendants chose not to remove initially. Such an approach does not allow an indefinite period for removal; plaintiffs could still choose to serve all defendants at the outset of the case, thereby requiring all defendants to act within the initial 30-day period.

> This new paragraph clarifies the rule of timeliness and provides for equal treatment of all defendants in their ability to obtain Federal jurisdiction over the case against them without undermining the Federal interest in ensuring that defendants act with reasonable promptness in invoking Federal jurisdiction.

2. The JVCA makes clear that if earlier-served defendants do not remove, but a later-served defendant does remove, the earlier-served defendants may consent to the removal. Indeed, under the now-codified rule of unanimity, they must do so if the removal is to be effective. What is the deadline for the earlier-served defendants to join in or consent to the removal?

3. What about the situation where an earlier-served defendant files a timely notice of removal and other defendants are not served until sometime after the removing defendant's 30-day period? The amended statute does not explicitly address this situation beyond stating that "all defendants who have been properly joined and served must join in or consent to the removal of the action." What is the deadline for later-served defendants to join in or consent to the removal?

[2] Motions to Remand

Several provisions of the Judicial Code authorize district courts to remand cases—or parts of cases—to the state court from which they were removed. We have already encountered three of them. First, we saw that § 1367(c), as applied in removed cases, gives district courts discretion to remand claims falling with supplemental jurisdiction.

Next, we discussed the 2011 revision of § 1441(c), which authorizes (and indeed requires) remand of claims that the court has severed because it lacks jurisdiction over them. Finally, we briefly considered § 1447(e), which authorizes remand if, after removal, "the plaintiff seeks to join additional defendants whose joinder would destroy subject matter jurisdiction."

The most important statutory authorization for remand, however, is found in 28 U.S.C. § 1447(c). That section provides in part:

> A motion to remand the case on the basis of any defect other than lack of subject matter jurisdiction must be made within 30 days after the filing of the notice of removal under section 1446(a). If at any time before final judgment it appears that the district court lacks subject matter jurisdiction, the case shall be remanded.

Here we look briefly at the timing of motions to remand.

Note: The Timing of Motions to Remand

1. The language of § 1447(c) might be read to say that all remand motions fall into one of two categories: either they rely on lack of subject matter jurisdiction or they rely on some other "defect." The former may be made at any time; the latter must be made within 30 days after filing the notice of removal. But that is not the way courts read the statute.

In the leading case of *Kamm v. Itex Corp.*, 568 F.3d 752 (9th Cir. 2009), the Ninth Circuit held that there are not two categories of remand motions, but three: motions based on lack of subject matter jurisdiction, which may be made at any time; motions based on a "defect"—defined as "failure to comply with removal requirements in [Chapter 89]"—which must be made within 30 days after the filing of the notice of removal; and other motions, which may be denied if not raised "on a timely basis." The court held that a motion to remand based on a forum selection clause is not a "defect" within the meaning of § 1447(c), so that the 30-day limit did not apply.

2. The opinion in *Kamm* listed three specific "defects" that fall within the 30-day rule: failure to comply with the time limits in § 1446(b) for filing the notice of removal; violation of the "forum defendant" rule of § 1441(b); and violation of the prohibition against removal of workers' compensation claims in § 1445. Only the first of these is non-controversial.

3. Four circuits including the Ninth have held that the forum defendant rule is a "defect" that is waived if not raised within 30 days of removal. The Eighth Circuit, in contrast, takes the position that the rule is a jurisdictional limitation that may be raised at any time before judgment. The court explained:

> [Section 1441(b)] makes diversity jurisdiction in removal cases narrower than if the case were originally filed in federal court by the plaintiff. . . . The fact that [the plaintiff] could have invoked the original jurisdiction of the federal court initially is irrelevant. She did not. The jurisdiction of the lower federal courts, both original and removal, is entirely a creature of statute. If

one of the statutory requirements is not met, the district court has no jurisdiction.

Hurt v. Dow Chemical Co., 963 F.2d 1142 (8th Cir. 1992). Is this a good reason for allowing plaintiff to raise the objection at any time before final judgment? Are there better arguments for treating the forum defendant rule as jurisdictional? In *Horton v. Conklin*, 431 F.3d 602 (8th Cir. 2005), the Eighth Circuit acknowledged the contrary view of other circuits, but adhered to its position.

4. At least one circuit has held, without extended discussion, that § 1445's bar on removal of workers' compensation claims is jurisdictional. See *Reed v. Heil Co.*, 206 F.3d 1055 (11th Cir. 2006). If the forum defendant rule is not jurisdictional, as most circuit to consider the question have held, is there any basis for treating § 1445 differently?

5. Section 1447(c) establishes a 30-day deadline for "[a] motion to remand" based on a non-jurisdictional defect. Suppose that the district court discovers a non-jurisdictional defect more than 30 days after a case has been removed. May the district court sua sponte order remand?

[3] Appellate Review of Remand Orders

Note: Thermtron *and Its Discontents*

A. The "*Thermtron* exception"

1. Appellate review of remand orders, the Supreme Court has said, is "limited" by 28 U.S.C. § 1447(d), which now provides:

> An order remanding a case to the State court from which it was removed is not reviewable on appeal or otherwise, except that an order remanding a case to the State court from which it was removed pursuant to section 1442 or 1443 of this title shall be reviewable by appeal or otherwise.

A literal reading would suggest that appellate review of remand orders (other than those issued in cases removed under § 1442 or § 1443) is not only "limited" by § 1447(d), but completely prohibited. However, that is not the way the Court has read the statute. In *Thermtron Products, Inc. v. Hermansdorfer*, 423 U.S. 336 (1976), the Court held that notwithstanding its language, 28 U.S.C. § 1447(d) does not bar appellate review of all remand orders. Rather, § 1447(d) "must be read *in pari materia* with § 1447(c)," thus limiting the remands barred from appellate review by § 1447(d) to those that are based on a ground specified in § 1447(c).

2. In the years since *Thermtron*, the Supreme Court and the courts of appeals have struggled to determine which kinds of remand orders are reviewable and which are not. One of the most important precedents is *Quackenbush v. Allstate Ins. Co.*, 517 U.S. 706 (1996) [Chapter 16]. The Court held in *Quackenbush* that a remand order based on abstention does not fall within the scope of § 1447(c) and thus is reviewable notwithstanding § 1447(d). More recently, in *Carlsbad Technology, Inc. v. HIF BIO, Inc.*,

556 U.S. 635 (2009), the Court held that a district court order remanding a case to state court after declining to exercise supplemental jurisdiction over state-law claims under 28 U.S.C. § 1367(c) is also reviewable because not within the scope of § 1447(c).

On the other side of the divide is *Powerex Corp. v. Reliant Energy Services*, Inc., 551 U.S. 224 (2007). Justice Breyer described *Powerex* in a concurring opinion in *Carlsbad Technology*:

> In [*Powerex,*] we considered a District Court's decision to remand a case in which a Canadian province-owned power company had sought removal— a matter that the Foreign Sovereign Immunities Act of 1976 specifically authorizes federal judges (in certain instances) to decide. See §§ 1441(d); 1603(a). The case presented a difficult legal question involving the commercial activities of a foreign sovereign; and the District Court's decision (if wrong) had potentially serious adverse consequences, namely preventing a sovereign power from obtaining the federal trial to which the law (in its view) entitled it. We nonetheless held that § 1447 forbids appellate courts from reviewing a district court decision of this kind.

3. When the Supreme Court announced the "*Thermtron* exception" to the statutory bar to review of remand orders, it also held that the proper means for obtaining review was the petition for mandamus. However, in *Quackenbush*, the Court repudiated that aspect of *Thermtron* and ruled that remand orders—if reviewable at all— are appealable as "final decision[s]" under 28 U.S.C. § 1291 and the collateral order doctrine. (See Chapter 14.)

4. One consequence of the *Thermtron* decision is that when the district court remands a case, the issue of whether the remand order was authorized often becomes inseparable from the question of whether the court of appeals has jurisdiction to review the order. Thus, in *Kamm v. ITEX, Inc.*, 568 F.3d 752 (9th Cir. 2009), described briefly in section D[2], the Ninth Circuit noted that if a forum selection clause is a "defect" within the meaning of § 1447(c), the court would have no jurisdiction to review the remand order issued 31 days after the filing of the notice of removal.

Consider the issue of whether the forum defendant rule of § 1441(b) is jurisdictional. Most of the courts of appeals have not yet decided the question. Suppose that a district court in the Fourth Circuit remands a case for violation of the forum defendant rule. If the Fourth Circuit holds, in agreement with the Eighth, that violation of the rule is a jurisdictional defect, what is the proper disposition of the appeal?

5. What if the district court *denies* a motion to remand? The statutory ban on appellate review is inapplicable, but of course such an order is not final. If removability depends on a controlling question of law, the district court may certify an interlocutory appeal under 28 U.S.C. § 1292(b). And if the case proceeds to final judgment in the federal court and the losing party appeals from that judgment, the court of appeals may review the order denying remand. That is what happened in the *Felix* case (Chapter 10).

B. The Future of *Thermtron*

1. All members of the Court joined Justice Thomas's opinion in *Carlsbad Technology*, but the case generated a lively debate among the Justices about the future of *Thermtron*. Justice Stevens acknowledged that the holdings in both *Thermtron* and *Carlsbad* conflict with the "unambiguous . . . command" of § 1447(d), but this did not bother him. On the contrary: "The Court's adherence to precedent in this case," he said, "represents a welcome departure from its sometimes single-minded focus on literal text."

Justice Stevens' comment brought an expression of incredulity from Justice Scalia: "Over the years, the Court has replaced the statute's clear bar on appellate review with a hodgepodge of jurisdictional rules that have no evident basis even in common sense . . . If this muddle represents a *welcome* departure from the literal text, the world is mad." Justice Scalia cited some examples; he also called attention to other anomalies highlighted by Justice Breyer. The latter, in a concurring opinion joined by Justice Souter, wrote:

> In this case, we consider a District Court's decision not to retain on its docket a case that once contained federal law issues but now contains only state law issues. All agree that the law grants the District Court broad discretion to determine whether it should keep such cases on its docket, that a decision to do so (or not to do so) rarely involves major legal questions, and that (even if wrong) a district court decision of this kind will not often have major adverse consequences. We now hold that § 1447 permits appellate courts to review a district court decision of this kind, even if only for abuse of discretion.

> Contrast today's decision with our decision two Terms ago in *Powerex Corp. v. Reliant Energy Services*, Inc., 551 U.S. 224 (2007) [discussed above]. . . .

> Thus, we have held that § 1447 *permits* review of a district court decision in an instance where that decision is unlikely to be wrong and where a wrong decision is unlikely to work serious harm. And we have held that § 1447 *forbids* review of a district court decision in an instance where that decision may well be wrong and where a wrong decision could work considerable harm. Unless the circumstances I describe are unusual, something is wrong. And the fact that we have read other exceptions in the statute's absolute-sounding language suggests that such circumstances are not all that unusual.

To deal with these anomalies, Justice Breyer suggested that "experts in this area of the law [should] reexamine the matter with an eye toward determining whether statutory revision is appropriate." Justice Scalia responded: "This mess—entirely of our own making—does not in my view require expert reexamination of this area of the law. It requires only the reconsideration of our decision in *Thermtron*—and a welcome return to the Court's focus on congressionally enacted text."

2. Justice Scalia noted in his opinion in *Carlsbad* that § 1447(d) "provides a single exception . . . for certain civil rights cases removed under § 1443." In the Removal Clarification Act of 2011, Congress added a second exception, for cases removed under the federal officer removal statute, 28 U.S.C. § 1442. Additionally, the Class Action Fairness Act of 2005 included an elaborate provision allowing for review of orders granting or denying a motion to remand a class action to the state court from which it was removed. See 28 U.S.C. § 1453(c). Do these Congressional enactments have any bearing on the three-cornered debate among Justices Stevens, Scalia, and Breyer?

3. Consider the array of issues raised by the remand motions in the cases in this and the preceding two chapters. Can you identify categories of cases in which remand orders should, as a policy matter, be reviewable?

4. Whatever your answer to that question, what should be done with *Thermtron*, and who should do it? Should "experts" study the decisions and recommend a statutory revision to Congress, as Justice Breyer suggests? Is the Court in a better position to determine which remand orders should be reviewable notwithstanding § 1447(d), as Justice Stevens implies? Or should the Court adopt Justice Scalia's solution and overrule *Thermtron*, so that no remand orders would be reviewable under any circumstances (except those specified in other statutes)?

Note: Merits-Related Jurisdictional Rulings

1. As *Carlsbad* illustrates, the Supreme Court has carved out what is, in substance, an exception to § 1447(d)'s seemingly absolute ban on review of remand orders. But the Court has also emphasized that the prohibition applies in full force to remand orders that are authorized by statute. Of particular importance, there is no review of orders that remand for "lack of subject matter jurisdiction" under § 1447(c).

What happens, though, when the district court's ruling that subject-matter jurisdiction is lacking depends on the court's interpretation or application of substantive law? In *Kircher v. Putnam Funds Trust*, 547 U.S. 633 (2006), the Supreme Court indicated that the substantive underpinning does not make the order reviewable.

Kircher involved the Securities Litigation Uniform Standards Act of 1998 (SLUSA). One provision of the Act—the "preclusion" provision—specifies that certain "covered" class actions under state securities laws may not "be maintained in any State or Federal court." Another provision—the removal provision—authorizes removal of "[a]ny covered class action brought in any State court." In *Kircher*, the district court concluded that the plaintiffs' claims were not covered by the preclusion provision; it therefore remanded the case to the state court. The Seventh Circuit found that it had appellate jurisdiction notwithstanding § 1447(d), but the Supreme Court unanimously reversed:

> Once removal jurisdiction under subsection (c) is understood to be restricted to precluded actions defined by subsection (b), a motion to remand claiming the action is not precluded must be seen as posing a jurisdictional

issue. . . . The work done is jurisdictional, as is the conclusion reached and the [remand] order implementing it.*

2. As the Supreme Court explained in *Beneficial National Bank v. Anderson* (Chapter 10), "when a federal statute wholly displaces the state-law cause of action through complete preemption," a case may be removed "even if pleaded in terms of state law." Suppose that the defendant removes a case on the ground that the plaintiff's claim is "completely preempted" by ERISA, but the district court disagrees, concluding that the claim does not "fall within the scope of" ERISA's civil remedy. It therefore remands the case to state court. Is that remand order reviewable?

3. Assume that a remand order based on a rejection of the defendant's "complete preemption" argument is *not* reviewable. Should the findings and conclusions underlying the district court's determination be given preclusive effect in the state court?

---

* The *Kircher* decision referred to the codification of SLUSA in the Securities Act of 1933. The Judicial Code Supplement includes the amendments to the Securities Exchange Act of 1934. Subsection (c) in the 1933 Act corresponds to paragraph (f)(2) in the 1934 Act, and subsection (b) corresponds to paragraph (f)(1).

Part Five

Challenging State Official Action

Chapter 13

State Sovereign Immunity

Introductory Note

For much of the nation's history, a person who wanted to challenge official action by a state almost invariably had to pursue the challenge in the courts of the state, with the opportunity for review by the Supreme Court if the state court rejected a federal claim. In the aftermath of the Civil War, legislation of the Reconstruction Congress opened up the possibility that the federal courts would be available as an original forum for the litigation of such disputes. But from the first, special restrictions have limited the power of federal courts to entertain suits seeking redress from the state or its officials.

In this and the next two chapters we examine the various bodies of law that govern the availability of the federal district courts as a forum for challenges to state official action. We begin with the Eleventh Amendment and the doctrine of state sovereign immunity. In Chapter 14, we consider claims and defenses under 42 U.S.C. § 1983, the cause of action created by the Reconstruction Congress for persons who believe they have been deprived of federal rights under color of state law. Finally, we consider federal-court review of state judgments of conviction through the law of habeas corpus.

Other statutory and court-created rules that constrain the authority of federal courts to hear cases or grant relief, including some rules affecting suits in which state action is the target of the plaintiff's claim, are considered in Chapter 16. Of particular importance is the doctrine of *Younger v. Harris*, 401 U.S. 37 (1971), which prohibits federal courts from issuing injunctions against pending state criminal proceedings, as well as certain state civil proceedings, except in narrow circumstances.

A. Origins and Early Interpretation of the Eleventh Amendment

The Eleventh Amendment to the United States Constitution provides:

> The Judicial power of the United States shall not be construed to extend to any suit in law or equity, commenced or prosecuted against one of the United States by Citizens of another State, or by Citizens or Subjects of any Foreign State.

The Amendment tracks the opening text of Article III of the Constitution, which describes "[t]he judicial Power of the United States." It was adopted in reaction to

Chisholm v. Georgia, 2 U.S. 419 (1793), in which the Supreme Court held that it had jurisdiction to hear a lawsuit between a citizen of South Carolina and the state of Georgia to collect on the proceeds of a contract, over Georgia's objection that it had immunity from suit as a sovereign state.

Both the Amendment's text and the context of its enactment show that it was intended to protect the states from certain lawsuits, but beyond that starting-point, the Amendment has given rise to enormous controversy. Moreover, the Supreme Court now takes the position that

> the sovereign immunity of the States neither derives from, nor is limited by, the terms of the Eleventh Amendment. Rather, [the] States' immunity from suit is a fundamental aspect of the sovereignty which the States enjoyed before the ratification of the Constitution, and which they retain today ... except as altered by the plan of the Convention or certain constitutional Amendments.

Alden v. Maine, 527 U.S. 706, 713 (1999). In this chapter, we explore the varied understandings of state sovereign immunity, the defendants who can claim its protection, and the circumstances under which plaintiffs can avoid the immunity.

Note: Chisholm *and Its Aftermath*

1. *Chisholm* involved (in the language of the later-adopted Eleventh Amendment) a "suit in law ... commenced ... against one of the United States by Citizens of another State. . . ." The lawsuit was a simple action in assumpsit, but the plaintiff was able to invoke the original jurisdiction of the Supreme Court based on Article III's grant of jurisdiction over controversies "between a State and Citizens of another State." The lawsuit was brought only five years after Article III's ratification, and it was the first case decided under the new Constitution. *See* William A. Fletcher, *Historical Interpretation of the Eleventh Amendment: A Narrow Construction of an Affirmative Grant of Jurisdiction Rather Than a Prohibition Against Jurisdiction*, 35 Stan. L. Rev. 1033, 1055 (1983). Nevertheless, members of the Court disagreed about whether Article III extended jurisdiction over a nonconsenting state. Justice Wilson framed the issue thus:

> This is a case of uncommon magnitude. One of the parties to it is a State ... claiming to be sovereign. The question to be determined is, whether this State, so respectable, and whose claim soars so high, is amenable to the jurisdiction of the Supreme Court of the United States? This question, important in itself, will depend on others, more important still; and, may, perhaps, be ultimately resolved into one, no less radical than this: do the people of the United States form a Nation?

Wilson concluded that Article III granted jurisdiction over nonconsenting states. His opinion reviewed conceptions of popular sovereignty that distinguished the new country from the monarchies that preceded it, the text of Article III itself, and the need for such jurisdiction to enforce Article I, § 10, which prohibits laws impairing contracts. Justices Blair and Cushing and Chief Justice Jay agreed. The Chief Justice saw in the extension of jurisdiction over states an affirmation of the core principles of the Constitution:

> The extension of the judiciary power of the United States to such controversies, appears to me to be wise, because it is honest, and because it is useful. It is honest, because it provides for doing justice without respect of persons, and by securing individual citizens as well as States, in their respective rights, performs the promise which every free Government makes to every free citizen, of equal justice and protection. It is useful, because it is honest, because it leaves not even the most obscure and friendless citizen without means of obtaining justice from a neighbouring State; because it obviates occasions of quarrels between States on account of the claims of their respective citizens; because it recognizes and strongly rests on this great moral truth, that justice is the same whether due from one man or a million, or from a million to one man; because it teaches and greatly appreciates the value of our free republican national Government, which places all our citizens on an equal footing, and enables each and every of them to obtain justice without any danger of being overborne by the weight and number of their opponents; and, because it brings into action, and enforces this great and glorious principle, that the people are the sovereign of this country, and consequently that fellow citizens and joint sovereigns cannot be degraded by appearing with each other in their own Courts to have their controversies determined. The people have reason to prize and rejoice in such valuable privileges; and they ought not to forget, that nothing but the free course of Constitutional law and Government can ensure the continuance and enjoyment of them.

> For the reasons before given, I am clearly of opinion, that a State is suable by citizens of another State. . . .

Justice Iredell dissented. In his view, Article III was not self-executing. To effect jurisdiction, Congress was required affirmatively to provide jurisdiction over lawsuits such as Chisholm's by statute, and it had not done so. Nor, in his view, was such jurisdiction supported by prior practice under the common law.

Within days after *Chisholm*, proposals to amend the Constitution to overrule it appeared in the House of Representatives.[1] Reaction in many states, burdened by debts from the Revolutionary War and concerned about the effect of the decision on their treasuries, was negative. The Eleventh Amendment was ratified within two years of the *Chisholm* decision.

2. Two decisions authored by Chief Justice Marshall were significant early interpretations of the Amendment. The first, *Cohens v. Virginia*, 19 U.S. 264 (1821), held the Amendment inapplicable in cases involving review of state decisions in the Supreme

---

1. As Professor Fletcher notes, the proposed amendments were considerably broader than the one that ultimately passed. Proposals included:

> That no state shall be liable to be made a party defendant in any of the judicial courts, established, or which shall be established under the authority of the United States, at the suit of any person or persons whether a citizen or citizens, or a foreigner or foreigners, of any body politic or corporate, whether within or without the United States.

Court. As more fully described in Chapter 2, the defendants in a state criminal case sought a writ of error in the Supreme Court, arguing that the Supremacy Clause prevented their prosecution for selling lottery tickets authorized by Congress. Chief Justice Marshall rejected an Eleventh Amendment argument by Virginia, stating that "a case arising under the constitution or laws of the United States is cognizable in the Courts of the Union, whoever may be the parties to that case" and that a writ of error was not a "suit" within the meaning of the Amendment. Note that *Cohens*, unlike *Chisholm*, involved a federal question.

Osborn v. Bank of the United States, 22 U.S. 738 (1824), limited the Amendment's effect considerably. *Osborn* held that the Amendment was limited to situations where the state was named as a party; it did not bar suits against state officers. Thus, the Court upheld a decree directly against state officials ordering them to return monies seized from the Bank.

3. As a result of *Osborn*, the Amendment had little practical significance until events after the Civil War again placed the Southern states in considerable fiscal difficulty and brought a new set of cases in which states had defaulted on their debts to the Court. JOHN V. ORTH, THE JUDICIAL POWER OF THE UNITED STATES: THE ELEVENTH AMENDMENT IN AMERICAN HISTORY 34–42 (1987). The most significant of these follows.

Hans v. Louisiana

Supreme Court of the United States, 1890.

134 U.S. 1.

MR. JUSTICE BRADLEY delivered the opinion of the Court.

This is an action brought in the circuit court of the United States . . . against the state of Louisiana, by Hans, a citizen of that state, to recover the amount of certain coupons annexed to bonds of the state, issued under the provisions of an act of the legislature. . . . [After Louisiana issued the bonds in 1874, it amended its state constitution to avoid paying the interest due in 1880. Hans claimed that the effect of the amendment was to impair the validity of his contract in violation of Article I, § 10 of the U.S. Constitution. Hans sought the unpaid interest in the sum of $87,500.]

[T]he present writ of error is brought; and the question is presented whether a state can be sued in a circuit court of the United States by one of its own citizens upon a suggestion that the case is one that arises under the constitution or laws of the United States.

The ground taken is that under the constitution, as well as under the act of congress passed to carry it into effect, a case is within the jurisdiction of the federal courts, without regard to the character of the parties, if it arises under the constitution or laws of the United States. . . . The language relied on is that clause of the third article of the constitution, which declares that "the judicial power of the United States shall extend to all cases in law and equity arising under this constitution, the laws of the United States, and treaties made, or which shall be made, under their authority;" and the corresponding clause of the act conferring jurisdiction upon the circuit court. . . . It is said that these jurisdictional clauses make no exception arising from the character of the parties, and therefore that a state can claim no exemption from suit, if the case is really one arising under the constitution, laws, or treaties of the United States.

It is conceded that, where the jurisdiction depends alone upon the character of the parties, a controversy between a state and its own citizens is not embraced within it; but it is contended that, though jurisdiction does not exist on that ground, it nevertheless does exist if the case itself is one which necessarily involves a federal question; and, with regard to ordinary parties, this is undoubtedly true. The question now to be decided is whether it is true where one of the parties is a state, and is sued as a defendant by one of its own citizens.

That a state cannot be sued by a citizen of another state, or of a foreign state, on the mere ground that the case is one arising under the constitution or laws of the United States, is clearly established by the decisions of this court in several recent cases. . . . Those were cases arising under the constitution of the United States, upon laws complained of as impairing the obligation of contracts, one of which was the constitutional amendment of Louisiana, complained of in the present case. Relief was sought against state officers who professed to act in obedience to those laws. This court held that the suits were virtually against the states themselves, and were consequently violative of the eleventh amendment of the constitution, and could not be maintained. It was not denied that they presented cases arising under the constitution; but, notwithstanding that, they were held to be prohibited by the amendment referred to.

In the present case the plaintiff in error contends that he, being a citizen of Louisiana, is not embarrassed by the obstacle of the eleventh amendment, inasmuch as that amendment only prohibits suits against a state which are brought by the citizens of another state, or by citizens or subjects of a foreign state. It is true the amendment does so read, and, if there were no other reason or ground for abating his suit, it might be maintainable; and then we should have this anomalous result, that, in cases arising under the constitution or laws of the United States, a state may be sued in the federal courts by its own citizens, though it cannot be sued for a like cause of action by the citizens of other states, or of a foreign state; and may be thus sued in the federal courts, although not allowing itself to be sued in its own courts. If this is the necessary consequence of the language of the constitution and the law, the result is no less startling and unexpected than was the original decision of this court, that, under the language of the constitution and of the judiciary act of 1789, a state was liable to be sued by a citizen of another state or of a foreign country. That decision was made in the case of *Chisholm v. Georgia*, 2 Dall. 419 (1793), and created such a shock of surprise throughout the country that, at the first meeting of congress thereafter, the eleventh amendment to the constitution was almost unanimously proposed, and was in due course adopted by the legislatures of the states. This amendment, expressing the will of the ultimate sovereignty of the whole country, superior to all legislatures and all courts, actually reversed the decision of the supreme court. It did not in terms prohibit suits by individuals against the states, but declared that the constitution should not be construed to import any power to authorize the bringing of such suits.

The language of the amendment is that "the judicial power of the United States shall not be construed to extend to any suit, in law or equity, commenced or prosecuted against one of the United States by citizens of another state, or by citizens or subjects of any foreign state." The supreme court had construed the judicial power as extending to such a suit, and its decision was thus overruled. . . . Looking back from our present stand-point at the decision in *Chisholm v. Georgia*, we do not greatly wonder at the effect which it had upon the country. Any such power as that of authorizing the federal judiciary to entertain suits by individuals against the states had been expressly disclaimed, and even resented, by the great defenders of the constitution while it was on its trial before the American people. . . .

Can we suppose that, when the eleventh amendment was adopted, it was understood to be left open for citizens of a state to sue their own state in the federal courts, while the idea of suits by citizens of other states, or of foreign states, was indignantly repelled? Suppose that congress, when proposing the eleventh amendment, had appended to it a proviso that nothing therein contained should prevent a state from being sued by its own citizens in cases arising under the constitution or laws of the United States, can we imagine that it would have been adopted by the states? The supposition that it would is almost an absurdity on its face. . . .

The suability of a state, without its consent, was a thing unknown to the law. This has been so often laid down and acknowledged by courts and jurists that it is hardly necessary to be formally asserted. . . .

But besides the presumption that no anomalous and unheard-of proceedings or suits were intended to be raised up by the constitution—anomalous and unheard of when the constitution was adopted—an additional reason why the jurisdiction claimed for the circuit court does not exist is the language of the act of congress by which its jurisdiction is conferred. The words are these: "The circuit courts of the United States shall have original cognizance, concurrent with the courts of the several states, of all suits of a civil nature, at common law or in equity,* * * arising under the constitution or laws of the United States, or treaties," etc. "Concurrent with the courts of the several states." Does not this qualification show that congress, in legislating to carry the constitution into effect, did not intend to invest its courts with any new and strange jurisdictions? The state courts have no power to entertain suits by individuals against a state without its consent. Then how does the circuit court, having only concurrent jurisdiction, acquire any such power? It is true that the same qualification existed in the judiciary act of 1789, which was before the court in *Chisholm v. Georgia*, and the majority of the court did not think that it was sufficient to limit the jurisdiction of the circuit court. Justice Iredell thought differently. In view of the manner in which that decision was received by the country, the adoption of the eleventh amendment, the light of history, and the reason of the thing, we think we are at liberty to prefer Justice Iredell's views in this regard.

Some reliance is placed by the plaintiff upon the observations of Chief Justice Marshall in *Cohens v. Virginia*, 6 Wheat. 264 (1821). The chief justice was there considering the power of review exercisable by this court over the judgments of a state court, wherein it might be necessary to make the state itself a defendant in error. He showed that this power was absolutely necessary in order to enable the judiciary of the United States to take cognizance of all cases arising under the constitution and laws of the United States. He also showed that making a state a defendant in error was entirely different from suing a state in an original action in prosecution of a demand against it, and was not within the meaning of the eleventh amendment; that the prosecution of a writ of error against a state was not the prosecution of a suit in the sense of that amendment, which had reference to the prosecution by suit of claims against a state. "Where," said the chief justice, "a state obtains a judgment against an individual, and the court rendering such judgment overrules a defense set up under the constitution or laws of the United States, the transfer of this record into the supreme court, for the sole purpose of inquiring whether the judgment violates the constitution or laws of the United States, can, with no propriety, we think, be denominated a suit commenced or prosecuted against the state whose judgment is so far re-examined. Nothing is demanded from the state. No claim against it of any description is asserted or prosecuted. The party is not to be restored to the possession of anything. * * * He only asserts the constitutional right to have his defense examined by that tribunal whose province it is to construe the constitution and laws of the Union."

... The legislative department of a state represents its polity and its will, and is called upon by the highest demands of natural and political law to preserve justice and judgment, and to hold inviolate the public obligations. Any departure from this rule, except for reasons most cogent, (of which the legislature, and not the courts, is the judge,) never fails in the end to incur the odium of the world, and to bring lasting injury upon the state itself. But to deprive the legislature of the power of judging what the honor and safety of the state may require, even at the expense of a temporary failure to discharge the public debts, would be attended with greater evils than such failure can cause.

The judgment of the circuit court is affirmed.

Mr. Justice Harlan concurring.

I concur with the court in holding that a suit directly against a state by one of its own citizens is not one to which the judicial power of the United States extends, unless the state itself consents to be sued. Upon this ground alone I assent to the judgment. But I cannot give my assent to many things said in the opinion. The comments made upon the decision in *Chisholm v. Georgia* do not meet my approval. They are not necessary to the determination of the present case. Besides, I am of opinion that the decision in that case was based upon a sound interpretation of the constitution as that instrument then was.

Note: Hans v. Louisiana

1. As Chief Justice Marshall observed in *Cohens v. Virginia* (Chapter 2), Article III extends the judicial power of the United States to two "classes" of cases. In the first class, the jurisdiction depends on the subject-matter of the lawsuit. In the second class, the jurisdiction depends on the identity of the parties. *Chisholm* was an example of the latter kind of jurisdiction, and one reading of the Eleventh Amendment is that it simply abolished a particular form of diversity jurisdiction, that between a state and a non-citizen of the state when the non-citizen is the plaintiff. *Hans* sees the Amendment quite differently.

2. Note that the Amendment does not by its terms apply: Hans was a citizen of Louisiana. Moreover, the lawsuit was based, not on diversity, but on federal-question jurisdiction. Recall that Congress did not extend general federal-question jurisdiction to the federal courts until 1875, in the aftermath of the Civil War. *Hans* was the first case to hold that the Eleventh Amendment prohibited jurisdiction over a case raising a federal question against a state by a citizen of that state.

3. *Hans* reads the Amendment as recognizing a broad-based immunity from suit for states based on their status as sovereign entities. But what is the source of that immunity? Is it the Eleventh Amendment itself? Or is it a pre-existing common-law understanding that is restored by the Eleventh Amendment? What difference would it make which view one adopted?

4. *Hans*'s reading of the Amendment has been enormously influential. By separating the interpretation of the Amendment from its text, *Hans* freed future Courts to apply state sovereign immunity in the context of admiralty suits, *Ex parte New York*, 256 U.S. 490 (1921); to suits by foreign countries, *Monaco v. Mississippi*, 292 U.S. 313 (1934), and eventually, as we shall see, to suits against states brought in state courts, *Alden v. Maine*, 527 U.S. 706 (1999). *But see Rhode Island v. Massachusetts*, 37 U.S. 657 (1838) (Amendment does not bar suits by one state against another); *United States v. Texas*, 143 U.S. 621 (1892) (Amendment does not bar suit by United States against a state).

5. The last paragraph of the *Hans* opinion states a policy underlying the holding: that legislative bodies are responsible to the people for allocating the fiscal resources of the state. The Court thus suggests that determining whether to respond to the claims of an individual as against the myriad other demands on a state treasury is ultimately a political decision. States have responded to this tension by gradually abolishing the reach of immunity, at least with respect to state-law claims in state courts. *See* Lauren K. Robel, *Sovereignty and Democracy: The States' Obligations to Their Citizens Under Federal Statutory Law*, 78 IND. L.J. 543 (2003).

6. By explicitly including federal questions within the scope of the Eleventh Amendment, *Hans* creates a serious problem: how to enforce the provisions of the Constitution against the states? The next case begins to provide an answer to this question.

B. Enforcing the Constitution Through Suits Against State Officers

[1] Suits for Injunctions

Ex parte Young

Supreme Court of the United States, 1908.

209 U.S. 123.

[When the state of Minnesota passed legislation regulating railroad rates, shareholders of nine railroads brought derivative actions in federal court, challenging the regulations as a violation of the Fourteenth Amendment. Edward T. Young, the Attorney General of Minnesota, was named as a defendant, and the federal court enjoined him from enforcing the legislation over his objection that the lawsuit was barred by the Eleventh Amendment. Young then filed a mandamus action in state court seeking to force the railroads to publish the new rates, in violation of the federal court's injunction. The federal court held Young in contempt, fined him $100, and ordered him held until he complied with the court's injunction. Young then filed an original action for writs of habeas corpus and certiorari in the United States Supreme Court.]

MR. JUSTICE PECKHAM ... delivered the opinion of the court:

We recognize and appreciate to the fullest extent the very great importance of this case, not only to the parties now before the court, but also to the great mass of the citizens of this country, all of whom are interested in the practical working of the courts of justice throughout the land, both Federal and state, and in the proper exercise of the jurisdiction of the Federal courts, as limited and controlled by the Federal Constitution and the laws of Congress. . . .

The question of jurisdiction, whether of the circuit court or of this court, is frequently a delicate matter to deal with, and it is especially so in this case, where the material and most important objection to the jurisdiction of the circuit court is the assertion that the suit is, in effect, against one of the states of the Union. It is a question, however, which we are called upon, and which it is our duty to decide. . . .

[The Court determined that the lower federal court had jurisdiction over the case, "because it involved the decision of [several] Federal questions arising under the Constitution of the United States."]

Coming to the inquiry regarding the alleged invalidity of these acts, we take up the contention that they are invalid on their face on account of the penalties. For disobedience to the freight act the officers, directors, agents, and employees of the company are made guilty of a misdemeanor, and upon conviction each may be punished by imprisonment in the county jail for a period not exceeding ninety days. Each violation would be a separate offense, and, therefore, might result in imprisonment of the various agents of the company who would dare disobey for a term of ninety days each for each offense. Disobedience to the passenger-rate act renders the party guilty of a felony and subject to a fine not exceeding $5,000 or imprisonment in the state prison for a period not exceeding five years, or both fine and imprisonment. The sale of each ticket above the price permitted by the act would be a violation thereof. It would be difficult, if not impossible, for the company to obtain officers, agents, or employees willing to carry on its affairs except in obedience to the act and orders in question. The company itself would also, in case of disobedience, be liable to the immense fines provided for in violating orders of the commission. The company, in order to test the validity of the acts, must find some agent or employee to disobey them at the risk stated. The necessary effect and result of such legislation must be to preclude a resort to the courts (either state or Federal) for the purpose of testing its validity. The officers and employees could not be expected to disobey any of the provisions of the acts or orders at the risk of such fines and penalties being imposed upon them, in case the court should decide that the law was valid. The result would be a denial of any hearing to the company. . . .

We hold, therefore, that the provisions of the acts relating to the enforcement of the rates, either for freight or passengers, by imposing such enormous fines and possible imprisonment as a result of an unsuccessful effort to test the validity of the laws themselves, are unconstitutional on their face, without regard to the question of the insufficiency of those rates. . . . Various affidavits were received upon the hearing before the court prior to the granting of the temporary injunction, and the hearing itself was, as appears from the opinion, full and deliberate, and the fact was found that the rates fixed by the commodity act, under the circumstances existing with reference to the passenger-rate act and the orders of the commission, were not sufficient to be compensatory, and were in fact confiscatory, and the act was therefore unconstitutional. The injunction was thereupon granted. . . .

We have, therefore, upon this record, the case of an unconstitutional act of the state legislature and an intention by the attorney general of the state to endeavor to enforce its provisions, to the injury of the company, in compelling it, at great expense, to defend legal proceedings of a complicated and unusual character, and involving questions of vast importance to all employees and officers of the company, as well as to the company itself. The question that arises is whether there is a remedy that the parties interested may resort to, by going into a Federal court of equity, in a case involving a violation of the Federal Constitution, and obtaining a judicial investigation of the problem, and, pending its solution, obtain freedom from suits, civil or criminal, by a temporary injunction, and, if the question be finally decided favorably to the contention of the company, a permanent injunction restraining all such actions or proceedings.

This inquiry necessitates an examination of the most material and important objection made to the jurisdiction of the circuit court, the objection being that the suit is, in effect, one against the state of Minnesota, and that the injunction issued against the attorney general illegally prohibits state action, either criminal or civil, to enforce obedience to the statutes of the state. This objection is to be considered with reference to the Eleventh and Fourteenth Amendments to the Federal Constitution. The Eleventh Amendment prohibits the commencement or prosecution of any suit against one of the United States by citizens of another state or citizens or subjects of any foreign state. The Fourteenth Amendment provides that no state shall deprive any person of life, liberty, or property without due process of law, nor shall it deny to any person within its jurisdiction the equal protection of the laws.

The case before the circuit court proceeded upon the theory that the orders and acts heretofore mentioned would, if enforced, violate rights of the complainants protected by the latter amendment. We think that whatever the rights of complainants may be, they are largely founded upon that Amendment, but a decision of this case does not require an examination or decision of the question whether its adoption in any way altered or limited the effect of the earlier Amendment. We may assume that each exists in full force, and that we must give to the Eleventh Amendment all the effect it naturally would have, without cutting it down or rendering its meaning any more narrow than the language, fairly interpreted, would warrant. It applies to a suit brought against a state by one of its own citizens, as well as to a suit brought by a citizen of another state. *Hans v. Louisiana*, 134 U.S. 1 (1890). . . .

The various authorities we have referred to furnish ample justification for the assertion that individuals who, as officers of the state, are clothed with some duty in regard to the enforcement of the laws of the state, and who threaten and are about to commence proceedings, either of a civil or criminal nature, to enforce against parties affected an unconstitutional act, violating the Federal Constitution, may be enjoined by a Federal court of equity from such action. . . .

It is also argued that the only proceeding which the attorney general could take to enforce the statute, so far as his office is concerned, was one by mandamus, which would be commenced by the state, in its sovereign and governmental character, and that the right to bring such action is a necessary attribute of a sovereign government. It is contended that the complainants do not complain and they care nothing about any action which Mr. Young might take or bring as an ordinary individual, but that he was complained of as an officer, to whose discretion is confided the use of the name of the state of Minnesota so far as litigation is concerned, and that when or how he shall use it is a matter resting in his discretion and cannot be controlled by any court.

The answer to all this is the same as made in every case where an official claims to be acting under the authority of the state. The act to be enforced is alleged to be unconstitutional; and if it be so, the use of the name of the state to enforce an unconstitutional act to the injury of complainants is a proceeding without the authority of, and one which does not affect, the state in its sovereign or governmental capacity. It is simply an illegal act upon the part of a state official in attempting, by the use of the name of the state, to enforce a legislative enactment which is void because unconstitutional. If the act which the state attorney general seeks to enforce be a violation of the Federal Constitution, the officer, in proceeding under such enactment, comes into conflict with the superior authority of that Constitution, and he is in that case stripped of his official or representative character and is subjected in his person to the consequences of his individual conduct. The state has no power to impart to him any immunity from responsibility to the supreme authority of the United States. It would be an injury to complainant to harass it with a multiplicity of suits or litigation generally in an endeavor to enforce penalties under an unconstitutional enactment, and to prevent it ought to be within the jurisdiction of a court of equity. If the question of unconstitutionality, with reference, at least, to the Federal Constitution, be first raised in a Federal court, that court, as we think is shown by the authorities cited hereafter, has the right to decide it, to the exclusion of all other courts.

It is further objected (and the objection really forms part of the contention that the state cannot be sued) that a court of equity has no jurisdiction to enjoin criminal proceedings, by indictment or otherwise, under the state law. This, as a general rule, is true. But there are exceptions. When such indictment or proceeding is brought to enforce an alleged unconstitutional statute, which is the subject-matter of inquiry in a suit already pending in a Federal court, the latter court, having first obtained jurisdiction over the subject-matter, has the right, in both civil and criminal cases, to hold and maintain such jurisdiction, to the exclusion of all other courts, until its duty is fully performed. But the Federal court cannot, of course, interfere in a case where the proceedings were already pending in a state court. . . .

It is proper to add that the right to enjoin an individual, even though a state official, from commencing suits under circumstances already stated, does not include the power to restrain a court from acting in any case brought before it, either of a civil or criminal nature, nor does it include power to prevent any investigation or action by a grand jury. The latter body is part of the machinery of a criminal court, and an injunction against a state court would be a violation of the whole scheme of our government. If an injunction against an individual is disobeyed, and he commences proceedings before a grand jury or in a court, such disobedience is personal only, and the court or jury can proceed without incurring any penalty on that account.

The difference between the power to enjoin an individual from doing certain things, and the power to enjoin courts from proceeding in their own way to exercise jurisdiction, is plain, and no power to do the latter exists because of a power to do the former.

It is further objected that there is a plain and adequate remedy at law open to the complainants, and that a court of equity, therefore, has no jurisdiction in such case. It has been suggested that the proper way to test the constitutionality of the act is to disobey it, at least once, after which the company might obey the act pending subsequent proceedings to test its validity. But in the event of a single violation the prosecutor might not avail himself of the opportunity to make the test, as obedience to the law was thereafter continued, and he might think it unnecessary to start an inquiry. If, however, he should do so while the company was thereafter obeying the law, several years might elapse before there was a final determination of the question, and, if it should be determined that the law was invalid, the property of the company would have been taken during that time without due process of law, and there would be no possibility of its recovery.

Another obstacle to making the test on the part of the company might be to find an agent or employee who would disobey the law, with a possible fine and imprisonment staring him in the face if the act should be held valid. Take the passenger-rate act, for instance: A sale of a single ticket above the price mentioned in that act might subject the ticket agent to a charge of felony, and, upon conviction, to a fine of $5,000 and imprisonment for five years. It is true the company might pay the fine, but the imprisonment the agent would have to suffer personally. It would not be wonderful if, under such circumstances, there would not be a crowd of agents offering to disobey the law. The wonder would be that a single agent should be found ready to take the risk. . . .

To await proceedings against the company in a state court, grounded upon a disobedience of the act, and then, if necessary, obtain a review in this court by writ of error to the highest state court, would place the company in peril of large loss and its agents in great risk of fines and imprisonment if it should be finally determined that the act was valid. This risk the company ought not to be required to take. Over eleven thousand millions of dollars, it is estimated, are invested in railroad property, owned by many thousands of people, who are scattered over the whole country, from ocean to ocean, and they are entitled to equal protection from the laws and from the courts, with the owners of all other kinds of property, no more, no less. The courts having jurisdiction, Federal or state, should, at all times, be opened to them as well as to others, for the purpose of protecting their property and their legal rights. . . .

Finally, it is objected that the necessary result of upholding this suit in the circuit court will be to draw to the lower Federal courts a great flood of litigation of this character, where one Federal judge would have it in his power to enjoin proceedings by state officials to enforce the legislative acts of the state, either by criminal or civil actions. To this it may be answered, in the first place, that no injunction ought to be granted unless in a case reasonably free from doubt. We think such rule is, and will be, followed by all the judges of the Federal courts. . . .

[The supreme authority of the United States,] which arises from the specific provisions of the Constitution itself, is nowhere more fully illustrated than in the series of decisions under the Federal *habeas corpus* statute, in some of which cases persons in the custody of state officers for alleged crimes against the state have been taken from that custody and discharged by a Federal court or judge, because the imprisonment was adjudged to be in violation of the Federal Constitution. The right to so discharge has not been doubted by this court, and it has never been supposed there was any suit against the state by reason of serving the writ upon one of the officers of the state in whose custody the person was found. . . .

It is somewhat difficult to appreciate the distinction which, while admitting that the taking of such a person from the custody of the state by virtue of service of the writ on the state officer in whose custody he is found is not a suit against the state, and yet service of a writ on the attorney general, to prevent his enforcing an unconstitutional enactment of a state legislature, is a suit against the state.

There is nothing in the case before us that ought properly to breed hostility to the customary operation of Federal courts of justice in cases of this character.

The rule to show cause is discharged and the petition for writs of habeas corpus and certiorari is dismissed.

Mr. Justice Harlan, dissenting:

. . . Let it be observed that the suit instituted . . . in the circuit court of the United States was, as to the defendant Young, one against him *as, and only because he was*, attorney general of Minnesota. No relief was sought against him individually, but only in his capacity *as* attorney general. And the manifest, indeed the avowed and admitted, object of seeking such relief, was *to tie the hands* of the *state* so that it could not in any manner or by any mode of proceeding, *in its own courts*, test the validity of the statutes and orders in question. It would therefore seem clear that within the true meaning of the Eleventh Amendment the suit brought in the Federal court was one, in legal effect, against the state,—as much so as if the state had been formally named on the record as a party,—and therefore it was a suit to which, under the Amendment, so far as the state or its attorney general was concerned, the judicial power of the United States did not and could not extend. If this proposition be sound it will follow— indeed, it is conceded that if, so far as relief is sought against the attorney general of Minnesota, this be a suit against the state—then, the order of the Federal court enjoining that officer from taking any action, suit, step, or proceeding to compel the railway company to obey the Minnesota statute was beyond the jurisdiction of that court and wholly void; in which case, that officer was at liberty to proceed in the discharge of his official duties as defined by the laws of the state, and the order adjudging him to be in contempt for bringing the mandamus proceeding in the state court was a nullity.

The fact that the Federal circuit court had, prior to the institution of the mandamus suit in the state court, preliminarily (but not finally) held the statutes of Minnesota and the orders of its railroad and warehouse commission in question to be in violation of the Constitution of the United States, was no reason why that court should have laid violent hands upon the attorney general of Minnesota, and by its orders have deprived the state of the services of its constitutional law officer in its own courts. Yet that is what was done by the Federal circuit court; for the intangible thing called a state, however extensive its powers, can never appear or be represented or known in any court in a litigated case, except by and through its officers. When, therefore, the Federal court forbade the defendant Young, as attorney general of Minnesota, from taking any action, suit, step, or proceeding whatever looking to the enforcement of the statutes in question, it said in effect to the state of Minnesota: "It is true that the powers not delegated to the United States by the Constitution, nor prohibited by it to the states, are reserved to the states respectively or to its people, and it is true that, under the Constitution, the judicial power of the United States does not extend to any suit brought against a state by a citizen of another state or by a citizen or subject of a foreign state, yet the Federal court adjudges that you, the state, although a sovereign for many important governmental purposes, shall not appear in your own courts, by your law officer, with the view of enforcing, or even for determining the validity of, the state enactments which the Federal court has, upon a preliminary hearing, declared to be in violation of the Constitution of the United States."

This principle, if firmly established, would work a radical change in our governmental system. It would inaugurate a new era in the American judicial system and in the relations of the national and state governments. It would enable the subordinate Federal courts to supervise and control the official action of the states as if they were "dependencies" or provinces. It would place the states of the Union in a condition of inferiority never dreamed of when the Constitution was adopted or when the Eleventh Amendment was made a part of the Supreme Law of the Land. I cannot suppose that the great men who framed the Constitution ever thought the time would come when a subordinate Federal court, having no power to compel a state, in its corporate capacity, to appear before it as a litigant, would yet assume to deprive a state of the right to be represented in its own courts by its regular law officer. That is what the court below did, as to Minnesota, when it adjudged that the appearance of the defendant Young *in the state court*, as the attorney general of Minnesota, representing his state as its chief law officer, was a contempt of the authority of the Federal court, punishable by fine and imprisonment.

Too little consequence has been attached to the fact that the courts of the states are under an obligation equally strong with that resting upon the courts of the Union to respect and enforce the provisions of the Federal Constitution as the supreme law of the land, and to guard rights secured or guaranteed by that instrument. We must assume—a decent respect for the states requires us to assume—that the state courts will enforce every right secured by the Constitution. If they fail to do so, the party complaining has a clear remedy for the protection of his rights; for he can come by writ of error, in an orderly, judicial way, from the highest court of the state to this tribunal for redress in respect of every right granted or secured by that instrument and denied by the state court. . . .

It is to be observed that when the state was, in effect, prohibited by the order of the Federal court from appearing in its own courts, there was no danger, absolutely none whatever, from anything that the attorney general had ever done or proposed to do, that the property of the railway company would be confiscated and its officers and agents imprisoned, beyond the power of that company to stay any wrong done *by bringing to this court, in regular order, any final judgment of the state court, in the mandamus suit, which may have been in derogation of a Federal right*. When the attorney general instituted the mandamus proceeding in the state court against the railway company there was in force, it must not be forgotten, an order of injunction by the Federal court which prevented that company from obeying the state law. . . .

. . . I am justified, by what this court has heretofore declared, in now saying that the men who framed the Constitution, and who caused the adoption of the Eleventh Amendment, would have been amazed by the suggestion that a state of the Union can be prevented, by an order of a subordinate Federal court, from being represented by its attorney general in a suit brought by it in one of its own courts; and that such an order would be inconsistent with the dignity of the states as involved in their constitutional immunity from the judicial process of the Federal courts (except in the limited cases in which they may constitutionally be made parties in this court), and would be attended by most pernicious results.

I dissent from the opinion and judgment.

Note: The Significance of Ex parte Young

1. *Ex parte Young* is an enormously important case. It permits suits for prospective enforcement of federal constitutional requirements against state officers to proceed in federal court without the bar of the Eleventh Amendment. Of course, as Justice Harlan insists in dissent, states can only act through their officers. *Ex parte Young* avoids treating an officer of the state as synonymous with the state itself through treating the act of enforcing an unconstitutional statute as one that the state may never authorize:

> The act to be enforced is alleged to be unconstitutional; and if it be so, the use of the name of the state to enforce an unconstitutional act to the injury of complainants is a proceeding without the authority of, and one which does not affect, the state in its sovereign or governmental capacity. . . . If the act which the state attorney general seeks to enforce be a violation of the Federal Constitution, the officer, in proceeding under such enactment, comes into conflict with the superior authority of that Constitution, and he is in that case stripped of his official or representative character and is subjected in his person to the consequences of his individual conduct. The state has no power to impart to him any immunity from responsibility to the supreme authority of the United States.

2. By "stripping" the state officer of his official status, the Court avoids the bar of the Eleventh Amendment: under *Ex parte Young*, a suit challenging the constitutionality of a state official's action is not a suit against the state. Remember, however, that a suit under the Fourteenth Amendment, such as this one, requires state action. As the Court said in *Shelley v. Kramer*, 334 U.S. 1 (1948), "the action inhibited by . . . the Fourteenth Amendment is only such action as may fairly be said to be that of the States. That Amendment erects no shield against merely private conduct, however discriminatory or wrongful."

If Young is stripped of his character as a state actor for purposes of the Eleventh Amendment, does he nonetheless remain a state actor for purposes of the Fourteenth? The answer is yes: the treatment of Young as a non-state actor for purposes of immunity is a convenient fiction to permit the enforcement of federal rights.

3. To add to the complexity, actions against state officers for injunctive relief are brought against the officers in their official capacity, not their personal capacity. As the court explained in *Ameritech v. McCann*, 297 F.3d 582 (7th Cir. 2002):

> [A] case may proceed under the *Young* exception only when a state official is sued in his official capacity. The twin goals served by the *Young* exception to Eleventh Amendment immunity — vindicating federal rights and holding state officials responsible to federal law — cannot be achieved by a lawsuit against a state official in his or her individual capacity. The reason is that individual (or personal) capacity suits do not seek to conform the State's conduct to federal law; rather, such suits seek recovery from the defendant

personally. [As the Court said in *Kentucky v. Graham*, 473 U.S. 159 (1985),] "a victory in a personal-capacity action is a victory against the individual defendant, rather than against the entity that employs him." As a consequence, individual capacity suits do not implicate the Eleventh Amendment's protections, making an *exception* to Eleventh Amendment immunity obviously unnecessary.

4. In *Ex parte Young*, the Court states:

[I]ndividuals who, as officers of the state, are clothed with some duty in regard to the enforcement of the laws of the state, and who threaten and are about to commence proceedings, either of a civil or criminal nature, to enforce against parties affected an unconstitutional act, violating the Federal Constitution, may be enjoined by a Federal court of equity from such action.

Lower federal courts have read this language to require that the officers sued must be those with enforcement authority for the statute or action being challenged. *See, e.g., Los Angeles Branch NAACP v. Los Angeles Unified School District*, 714 F.2d 946 (9th Cir. 1983) (governor lacked power to remedy alleged violation); *Okpalobi v. Foster*, 244 F.3d 405 (5th Cir. 2001) (en banc) (attorney general and governor not responsible for enforcing abortion statute); *Children's Healthcare is a Legal Duty, Inc. v. Deters*, 92 F.3d 1412 (6th Cir. 1996) (finding that the attorney general "has no connection to enforcement of the statute").

Does the quoted language also suggest that plaintiffs must demonstrate an actual threat that the state official will in fact enforce the statute at issue? *Compare National Audubon Society, Inc. v. Davis*, 307 F.3d 835 (9th Cir. 2002) ("We decline to read additional 'ripeness' or 'imminence' requirements into the *Ex parte Young* exception to Eleventh Amendment immunity in actions for declaratory relief beyond those already imposed by a general Article III and prudential ripeness analysis."), *with Children's Healthcare is a Legal Duty, Inc.* (holding that "*Ex parte Young* does not apply when a defendant state official has neither enforced nor threatened to enforce the allegedly unconstitutional state statute").

5. In *Pennhurst State School and Hospital v. Halderman*, 465 U.S. 89 (1984), the Supreme Court held that federal courts are barred from ordering states to comply with the commands of *state* law. The lower federal court had avoided a federal constitutional question by basing its injunction on state law. The Supreme Court reversed:

[T]he *Young* doctrine has been accepted as necessary to permit the federal courts to vindicate federal rights and hold state officials responsible to "the supreme authority of the United States." . . . The Court also has recognized, however, that the need to promote the supremacy of federal law must be accommodated to the constitutional immunity of the States. . . . This need to reconcile competing interests is wholly absent, however, when a plaintiff alleges that a state official has violated *state* law. In such a case the entire basis for the doctrine of *Young* . . . disappears. A federal court's grant of relief against state officials on the basis of state law . . . does not vindicate the supreme authority of federal law. On the contrary, it is difficult to think of a greater intrusion on state sovereignty than when a federal court instructs state officials on how to conform their conduct to state law. Such a result conflicts directly with the principles of federalism that underlie the Eleventh Amendment.

The Court also rejected the argument that the state-law claims could be heard as pendent claims within the supplemental jurisdiction of the federal courts.

6. What exactly is the source of the cause of action recognized in *Ex parte Young*? Does it emanate from the Constitution, either from the Supremacy Clause, which compels state officials to comply with federal law, or from the particular provisions that state officials have threatened to violate? Is it merely a judge-made remedy, subject to congressional alteration or abrogation? *Cf. Bivens v. Six Unknown Named Agents of Federal Bureau of Narcotics*, 403 U.S. 388 (1971) (discussed in Chapter 8).

Although it took some time for the Court to provide clear answers to those questions, today the *Ex parte Young* action is not understood to derive from the Constitution itself. In *Armstrong v. Exceptional Child Center*, 135 S. Ct. 1378 (2015), the Supreme Court explained that, although the Supremacy Clause obligates state officials to comply with federal law, the Clause "does not create a cause of action." Instead, the Clause simply "creates a rule of decision" under which courts "must not give effect to state laws that conflict with federal law."

So what is the source of an *Ex parte Young* action? The equitable powers of the court. As the *Armstrong* Court explained,

> The ability to sue to enjoin unconstitutional actions by state and federal officers is the creation of courts of equity, and reflects a long history of judicial review of illegal executive action, tracing back to England. It is a judge-made remedy, and we have never held or even suggested that, in its application to state officers, it rests upon an implied right of action contained in the Supremacy Clause.

Four Justices dissented, but they agreed with the majority that neither the Supremacy Clause nor any other provision of the Constitution serves as the basis for *Ex parte Young. See Armstrong* (Sotomayor, J., dissenting) ("Congress may, if it so chooses, either expressly or implicitly preclude *Ex parte Young* enforcement actions with respect to a particular statute or category of lawsuit.").

At the same time, however, the Court has held that the doctrine of *Ex parte Young* also applies with full force in *state* courts. In *General Oil Co. v. Crain*, 209 U.S. 211 (1908), a case decided on the same day as *Ex parte Young*, a corporation brought suit in Tennessee state court against the state's inspector of oils, seeking an injunction against "the collection of a tax for the inspection of certain of its oils in Tennessee." The trial court granted the injunction, but the state supreme court reversed, holding that the suit was one against the state and thus barred by sovereign immunity.

When the plaintiff brought the case to the United States Supreme Court, the defendant argued that the state court's holding "involved no Federal question, but only the powers and jurisdiction of the courts of the State of Tennessee." The Supreme Court disagreed. The opinion said:

> It seems to be an obvious consequence that, as a state can only perform its functions through its officers, a restraint upon them is a restraint upon its sovereignty from which it is exempt, without its consent, in the state tribunals, and exempt by the 11th Amendment of the Constitution of the United States in the national tribunals. The error is in the universality of the conclusion, as we have seen. Necessarily, to give adequate protection to constitutional rights a distinction must be made between valid and invalid state laws, as determining the character of the suit against state officers. And the suit at bar illustrates the necessity. If a suit against state officers is precluded in the national courts by the 11th Amendment to the Constitution, and may be forbidden by a state to its courts, as it is contended in the case at bar that it may be, without power of review by this court, it must be evident that an easy way is open to prevent the enforcement of many provisions of the Constitution; and the 14th Amendment, which is directed at state action, could be nullified as to much of its operation. . . . See *Ex parte Young*, ante, where this subject is fully discussed and the cases reviewed.

Is the Court saying only that the Tennessee court's holding is not an adequate state ground that bars review by the Supreme Court of the underlying federal question? Or is the Court saying that the Constitution requires the state court to hear the suit in the first instance? The Court's description of the state's argument suggests the former, but the reference to *Ex parte Young* suggests the latter.

Does the extension of *Ex parte Young* to state courts cast doubt on the Court's characterization of the doctrine in *Armstrong*?

[2] Suits for Damages

Edelman v. Jordan

Supreme Court of the United States, 1974.

415 U.S. 651.

MR. JUSTICE REHNQUIST delivered the opinion of the Court.

Respondent John Jordan filed a complaint in the United States District Court for the Northern District of Illinois, individually and as a representative of a class, seeking declaratory and injunctive relief against two former directors of the Illinois Department of Public Aid, the director of the Cook County Department of Public Aid, and the comptroller of Cook County. Respondent alleged that these state officials were administering the federal-state programs of Aid to the Aged, Blind, or Disabled (AABD) in a manner inconsistent with various federal regulations and with the Fourteenth Amendment to the Constitution.

AABD is one of the categorical aid programs administered by the Illinois Department of Public Aid pursuant to the Illinois Public Aid Code. Under the Social Security Act, the program is funded by the State and the Federal Governments. The Department of Health, Education, and Welfare (HEW), which administers these payments for the Federal Government, issued regulations prescribing maximum permissible time standards within which States participating in the program had to process AABD applications. Those regulations . . . required, at the time of the institution of this suit, that eligibility determinations must be made by the States within 30 days of receipt of applications for aid to the aged and blind, and within 45 days of receipt of applications for aid to the disabled. For those persons found eligible, the assistance check was required to be received by them within the applicable time period.

During the period in which the federal regulations went into effect, Illinois public aid officials were administering the benefits pursuant to their own regulations. . . . Respondent's complaint charged that the Illinois defendants, operating under those regulations, were improperly authorizing grants to commence only with the month in which an application was approved and not including prior eligibility months for which an applicant was entitled to aid under federal law. The complaint also alleged that the Illinois defendants were not processing the applications within the applicable time requirements of the federal regulations; specifically, respondent alleged that his own application for disability benefits was not acted on by the Illinois Department of Public Aid for almost four months. Such actions of the Illinois officials were alleged to violate federal law and deny the equal protection of the laws. Respondent's prayer requested declaratory and injunctive relief, and specifically requested "a permanent injunction enjoining the defendants to award to the entire class of plaintiffs all AABD benefits wrongfully withheld."

[The District Court declared the Illinois regulation] to be invalid insofar as it was inconsistent with the federal regulations . . . and granted a permanent injunction requiring compliance with the federal time limits for processing and paying AABD applicants. The District Court . . . also ordered the state officials to "release and remit AABD benefits wrongfully withheld to all applicants for AABD in the State of Illinois who applied between July 1, 1968 (the date of the federal regulations) and April 16, 1971 (the date of the preliminary injunction issued by the District Court) and were determined eligible. . . ."

On appeal to the United States Court of Appeals for the Seventh Circuit, the Illinois officials contended . . . that the Eleventh Amendment barred the award of retroactive benefits, that the judgment of inconsistency between the federal regulations and the provisions of the Illinois [regulation] could be given prospective effect only, and that the federal regulations in question were inconsistent with the Social Security Act itself. The Court of Appeals rejected these contentions and affirmed the judgment of the District Court.

. . . Because we believe the Court of Appeals erred in its disposition of the Eleventh Amendment claim, we reverse that portion of the Court of Appeals decision which affirmed the District Court's order that retroactive benefits be paid by the Illinois state officials.

... While the Amendment by its terms does not bar suits against a State by its own citizens, this Court has consistently held that an unconsenting State is immune from suits brought in federal courts by her own citizens as well as by citizens of another State. *Hans v. Louisiana*, 134 U.S. 1 (1890). It is also well established that even though a State is not named a party to the action, the suit may nonetheless be barred by the Eleventh Amendment. In *Ford Motor Co. v. Department of Treasury*, 323 U.S. 459 (1945), the Court said:

> [W]hen the action is in essence one for the recovery of money from the state, the state is the real, substantial party in interest and is entitled to invoke its sovereign immunity from suit even though individual officials are nominal defendants.

Thus the rule has evolved that a suit by private parties seeking to impose a liability which must be paid from public funds in the state treasury is barred by the Eleventh Amendment.

The Court of Appeals in this case, while recognizing that the *Hans* line of cases permitted the State to raise the Eleventh Amendment as a defense to suit by its own citizens, nevertheless concluded that the Amendment did not bar the award of retroactive payments of the statutory benefits found to have been wrongfully withheld. The Court of Appeals held that the above-cited cases, when read in light of this Court's landmark decision in *Ex parte Young*, 209 U.S. 123 (1908), do not preclude the grant of such a monetary award in the nature of equitable restitution.

Petitioner concedes that *Ex parte Young* is no bar to that part of the District Court's judgment that prospectively enjoined petitioner's predecessors from failing to process applications within the time limits established by the federal regulations. Petitioner argues, however, that *Ex parte Young* does not extend so far as to permit a suit which seeks the award of an accrued monetary liability which must be met from the general revenues of a State, absent consent or waiver by the State of its Eleventh Amendment immunity, and that therefore the award of retroactive benefits by the District Court was improper.

Ex parte Young was a watershed case in which this Court held that the Eleventh Amendment did not bar an action in the federal courts seeking to enjoin the Attorney General of Minnesota from enforcing a statute claimed to violate the Fourteenth Amendment of the United States Constitution. This holding has permitted the Civil War Amendments to the Constitution to serve as a sword, rather than merely as a shield, for those whom they were designed to protect. But the relief awarded in *Ex parte Young* was prospective only; the Attorney General of Minnesota was enjoined to conform his future conduct of that office to the requirement of the Fourteenth Amendment. Such relief is analogous to that awarded by the District Court in the prospective portion of its order under review in this case.

But the retroactive position of the District Court's order here, which requires the payment of a very substantial amount of money which that court held should have been paid, but was not, stands on quite a different footing. These funds will obviously not be paid out of the pocket of petitioner Edelman.... The funds to satisfy the award in this case must inevitably come from the general revenues of the State of Illinois, and thus the award resembles far more closely the monetary award against the State itself than it does the prospective injunctive relief awarded in *Ex parte Young*.

The Court of Appeals, in upholding the award in this case, held that it was permissible because it was in the form of "equitable restitution" instead of damages, and therefore capable of being tailored in such a way as to minimize disruptions of the state program of categorical assistance. But we must judge the award actually made in this case, and not one which might have been differently tailored in a different case, and we must judge it in the context of the important constitutional principle embodied in the Eleventh Amendment.[11]

We do not read *Ex parte Young* or subsequent holdings of this Court to indicate that any form of relief may be awarded against a state officer, no matter how closely it may in practice resemble a money judgment payable out of the state treasury, so long as the relief may be labeled "equitable" in nature. The Court's opinion in *Ex parte Young* hewed to no such line....

As in most areas of the law, the difference between the type of relief barred by the Eleventh Amendment and that permitted under *Ex parte Young* will not in many instances be that between day and night. The injunction issued in *Ex parte Young* was not totally without effect on the State's revenues, since the state law which the Attorney General was enjoined from enforcing provided substantial monetary penalties against railroads which did not conform to its provisions. Later cases from this Court have authorized equitable relief which has probably had greater impact on state treasuries than did that awarded in *Ex parte Young*. In *Graham v. Richardson*, 403 U.S. 365 (1971), Arizona and Pennsylvania welfare officials were prohibited from denying welfare benefits to otherwise qualified recipients who were aliens. In *Goldberg v. Kelly*, 397 U.S. 254 (1970), New York City welfare officials were enjoined from following New York State procedures which authorized the termination of benefits paid to welfare recipients without prior hearing. But the fiscal consequences to state treasuries in these cases were the necessary result of compliance with decrees which by their terms

---

11. It may be true, as stated by our Brother Douglas in dissent, that "most welfare decisions by federal courts have a financial impact on the States." But we cannot agree that such a financial impact is the same where a federal court applies *Ex parte Young* to grant prospective declaratory and injunctive relief, as opposed to an order of retroactive payments as was made in the instant case. It is not necessarily true that "whether the decree is prospective only or requires payments for the weeks or months wrongfully skipped over by the state officials, the nature of the impact on the state treasury is precisely the same." This argument neglects the fact that where the State has a definable allocation to be used in the payment of public aid benefits, and pursues a certain course of action such as the processing of applications within certain time periods as did Illinois here, the subsequent ordering by a federal court of retroactive payments to correct delays in such processing will invariably mean there is less money available for payments for the continuing obligations of the public aid system.

were prospective in nature. State officials, in order to shape their official conduct to the mandate of the Court's decrees, would more likely have to spend money from the state treasury than if they had been left free to pursue their previous course of conduct. Such an ancillary effect on the state treasury is a permissible and often an inevitable consequence of the principle announced in *Ex parte Young*.

But that portion of the District Court's decree which petitioner challenges on Eleventh Amendment grounds goes much further than any of the cases cited. It requires payment of state funds, not as a necessary consequence of compliance in the future with a substantive federal-question determination, but as a form of compensation to those whose applications were processed on the slower time schedule at a time when petitioner was under no court-imposed obligation to conform to a different standard. While the Court of Appeals described this retroactive award of monetary relief as a form of "equitable restitution," it is in practical effect indistinguishable in many aspects from an award of damages against the State. It will to a virtual certainty be paid from state funds, and not from the pockets of the individual state officials who were the defendants in the action. It is measured in terms of a monetary loss resulting from a past breach of a legal duty on the part of the defendant state officials.

Were we to uphold this portion of the District Court's decree, we would be obligated to overrule the Court's holding in *Ford Motor Co. v. Department of Treasury*, 323 U.S. 459 (1945). There a taxpayer, who had, under protest, paid taxes to the State of Indiana, sought a refund of those taxes from the Indiana state officials who were charged with their collection. The taxpayer claimed that the tax had been imposed in violation of the United States Constitution. The term "equitable restitution" would seem even more applicable to the relief sought in that case, since the taxpayer had at one time had the money, and paid it over to the State pursuant to an allegedly unconstitutional tax exaction. Yet this Court had no hesitation in holding that the taxpayer's action was a suit against the State, and barred by the Eleventh Amendment. We reach a similar conclusion with respect to the retroactive portion of the relief awarded by the District Court in this case.

The Court of Appeals held in the alternative that even if the Eleventh Amendment be deemed a bar to the retroactive relief awarded respondent in this case, the State of Illinois had waived its Eleventh Amendment immunity and consented to the bringing of such a suit by participating in the federal AABD program. . . .

[The Court of Appeals reasoned] that as a matter of federal law Illinois had "constructively consented" to this suit by participating in the federal AABD program and agreeing to administer federal and state funds in compliance with federal law. Constructive consent is not a doctrine commonly associated with the surrender of constitutional rights, and we see no place for it here. In deciding whether a State has waived its constitutional protection under the Eleventh Amendment, we will find waiver only where stated "by the most express language or by such overwhelming implications from the text as [will] leave no room for any other reasonable construction." *Murray v. Wilson Distilling Co.*, 213 U.S. 151 (1909). We see no reason to retreat from the Court's statement in *Great Northern Life Insurance Co. v. Read*, 322 U.S. 47 (1944):

> [W]hen we are dealing with the sovereign exemption from judicial interference in the vital field of financial administration a clear declaration of the state's intention to submit its fiscal problems to other courts than those of its own creation must be found.

The mere fact that a State participates in a program through which the Federal Government provides assistance for the operation by the State of a system of public aid is not sufficient to establish consent on the part of the State to be sued in the federal courts. And while this Court has, in cases such as *J. I. Case Co. v. Borak*, 377 U.S. 426 (1964) [Chapter 8], authorized suits by one private party against another in order to effectuate a statutory purpose, it has never done so in the context of the Eleventh Amendment and a state defendant. . . .

For the foregoing reasons we decide that the Court of Appeals was wrong in holding that the Eleventh Amendment did not constitute a bar to that portion of the District Court decree which ordered retroactive payment of benefits found to have been wrongfully withheld. The judgment of the Court of Appeals is therefore reversed and the cause remanded for further proceedings consistent with this opinion.

MR. JUSTICE DOUGLAS, dissenting.

. . . As the complaint in the instant case alleges violations by officials of Illinois of the Equal Protections Clause of the Fourteenth Amendment, it seems that the case is governed by *Ex parte Young* so far as injunctive relief is concerned. The main thrust of the argument is that the instant case asks for relief which if granted would affect the treasury of the State.

Most welfare decisions by federal courts have a financial impact on the States. Under the existing federal-state cooperative system, a state desiring to participate, submits a "state plan" to HEW for approval; once HEW approves the plan the State is locked into the cooperative scheme until it withdraws. . . . The welfare cases coming here have involved ultimately the financial responsibility of the State to beneficiaries claiming they were deprived of federal rights. . . . *Rosado v. Wyman*, 397 U.S. 397 (1970), held that under this state-federal cooperative program a State could not reduce its standard of need in conflict with the federal standard. It is true that *Rosado* did not involve retroactive payments as are involved here. But the distinction is not relevant or material because the result in every welfare case coming here is to increase or reduce the financial responsibility of the participating State. In no case when the responsibility of the State is increased to meet the lawful demand of the beneficiary, is there any levy on state funds. Whether the decree is prospective only or requires payments for the weeks or months wrongfully skipped over by the state officials, the nature of the impact on the state treasury is precisely the same. . . . Yet petitioner asserts that money damages may not be awarded against state offenses, as such a judgment will expend itself on the state treasury. But we are unable to say that Illinois on entering the federal-state welfare program waived its immunity to suit for injunctions but did not waive its immunity for compensatory awards which remedy its willful defaults of obligations undertaken when it joined the cooperative venture. . . . I would affirm the judgment of the Court of Appeals.

MR. JUSTICE BRENNAN, dissenting.

This suit is brought by Illinois citizens against Illinois officials. In that circumstance, Illinois may not invoke the Eleventh Amendment, since that Amendment bars only federal court suits against States by citizens of other States. Rather, the question is whether Illinois may avail itself of the nonconstitutional but ancient doctrine of sovereign immunity as a bar to respondent's claim for retroactive AABD payments. In my view Illinois may not assert sovereign immunity for the reason I expressed in dissent in *Employees v. Department of Public Health and Welfare*, 411 U.S. 279 (1973): the States surrendered that immunity in Hamilton's words, "that formed the Union, at least insofar as the States granted Congress specifically enumerated powers." *Parden v. Terminal R. Co.*, 377 U.S. 184 (1964). Congressional authority to enact the Social Security Act, of which AABD is a part, is to be found in Art. I, §8, cl. 1, one of the enumerated powers granted Congress by the States in the Constitution. I remain of the opinion that "because of its surrender, no immunity exists that can be the subject of a congressional declaration or a voluntary waiver," and thus have no occasion to inquire whether or not Congress authorized an action for AABD retroactive benefits, or whether or not Illinois voluntarily waived the immunity by its continued participation in the program against the background of precedents which sustained judgments ordering retroactive payments.

I would affirm the judgment of the Court of Appeals.

MR. JUSTICE MARSHALL, with whom MR. JUSTICE BLACKMUN joins, dissenting.

The Social Security Act's categorical assistance programs, including the Aid to the Aged, Blind, or Disabled (AADB) program involved here, are fundamentally different from most federal legislation. Unlike the Fair Labor Standards Act involved in last Term's decision in *Employees v. Department of Public Health and Welfare*, 411 U.S. 279 (1973), or the Federal Employers' Liability Act at issue in *Parden v. Terminal R. Co.*, 377 U.S. 184 (1964), the Social Security Act does not impose federal standards and liability upon all who engage in certain regulated activities, including often-unwilling state agencies. Instead, the Act seeks to induce state participation in the federal welfare programs by offering federal matching funds in exchange for the State's voluntary assumption of the Act's requirements. I find this basic distinction crucial: it leads me to conclude that by participation in the programs, the States waive whatever immunity they might otherwise have from federal court orders requiring retroactive payment of welfare benefits.

In its contacts with the Social Security Act's assistance programs in recent years, the Court has frequently described the Act as a "scheme of cooperative federalism." While this phrase captures a number of the unique characteristics of these programs, for present purposes it serves to emphasize that the States' decision to participate in the programs is a voluntary one. In deciding to participate, however, the States necessarily give up their freedom to operate assistance programs for the needy as they see fit, and bind themselves to conform their programs to the requirements of the federal statute and regulations.

So here, Illinois elected to participate in the AABD program, and received and expended substantial federal funds in the years at issue. It thereby obligated itself to comply with federal law, including the requirement . . . that "such aid or assistance shall be furnished with reasonable promptness to all eligible individuals."

In agreeing to comply with the requirements of the Social Security Act and HEW regulations, I believe that Illinois has also agreed to subject itself to suit in the federal courts to enforce these obligations. . . . In particular, I am firmly convinced that Congress intended the restitution of wrongfully withheld assistance payments to be a remedy available to the federal courts in these suits. Benefits under the categorical assistance programs "are a matter of statutory entitlement for persons qualified to receive them." *Goldberg v. Kelly.* Retroactive payment of benefits secures for recipients this entitlement which was withheld in violation of federal law. Equally important, the courts' power to order retroactive payments is an essential remedy to insure future state compliance with federal requirements. No other remedy can effectively deter States from the strong temptation to cut welfare budgets by circumventing the stringent requirements of federal law. The funding cutoff is a drastic sanction, one which HEW has proved unwilling or unable to employ to compel strict compliance with the Act and regulations. Moreover, the cutoff operates only prospectively; it in no way deters the States from even a flagrant violation of the Act's requirements for as long as HEW does not discover the violation and threaten to take such action.

Absent any remedy which may act with retroactive effect, state welfare officials have everything to gain and nothing to lose by failing to comply with the congressional mandate that assistance be paid with reasonable promptness to all eligible individuals. This is not idle speculation without basis in practical experience. In this very case, for example, Illinois officials have knowingly violated since 1968 federal regulations on the strength of an argument as to its invalidity which even the majority deems unworthy of discussion. Without a retroactive-payment remedy, we are indeed faced with the spectre of a state, perhaps calculatingly, defying federal law and thereby depriving welfare recipients of the financial assistance Congress thought it was giving them. Like the Court of Appeals, I cannot believe that Congress could possibly have intended any such result.

. . . Illinois chose to participate in the AABD program with its eyes wide open. Drawn by the lure of federal funds, it voluntarily obligated itself to comply with the Social Security Act and HEW regulations, with full knowledge that Congress had authorized assistance recipients to go into federal court to enforce these obligations and to recover benefits wrongfully denied. . . . I cannot avoid the conclusion that, by virtue of its knowing and voluntary decision to nevertheless participate in the program, the State necessarily consented to subject itself to these suits. I have no quarrel with the Court's view that waiver of constitutional rights should not lightly be inferred. But I simply cannot believe that the State could have entered into this essentially contractual agreement with the Federal Government without recognizing that it was subjecting itself to the full scope of the § 1983 remedy provided by Congress to enforce the terms of the agreement.

I respectfully dissent.

Note: Ex parte Young *and* Edelman

1. After *Ex parte Young*, one might have thought that the dividing line between those remedies permitted by the Eleventh Amendment and those barred was the line between equitable and legal relief. In *Edelman*, however, the Court states that the labels attached to federal judicial remedies against the states do not, by themselves, tell us whether a particular remedy is permitted by *Ex parte Young*. Calling the remedy in *Edelman* "equitable restitution," for instance, did not permit the remedy to stand. As the Court explained, the "retroactive" part of the remedy in that case was "indistinguishable in many aspects from an award of damages against the State. It will to a virtual certainty be paid from state funds, and not from the pockets of the individual state officials who were the defendants in the action. It is measured in terms of a monetary loss resulting from a past breach of a legal duty on the part of the defendant state officials."

2. The distinction between forward-looking, prospective relief and backward-looking, retroactive relief is not, as the Court itself noted, always one between "day and night." In *Milliken v. Bradley*, 433 U.S. 267 (1977), the Court upheld a desegregation decree as a remedy for past racial discrimination in the Detroit school system that was estimated to cost the state around $6 million. The decree included requirements to institute remedial learning programs to ameliorate the effects of discrimination in the past. The Court found that the costs associated with the decree fit within *Edelman*'s "prospective-compliance exception":

> That exception, which had its genesis in *Ex parte Young*, permits federal courts to enjoin state officials to conform their conduct to requirements of federal law, notwithstanding a direct and substantial impact on the state treasury. . . . The decree [challenged here] requires state officials, held responsible for unconstitutional conduct, . . . to eliminate a *de jure* segregated school system. . . . The educational components, which the District Court ordered into effect *prospectively*, are plainly designed to wipe out continuing conditions of inequality produced by the inherently unequal dual school system long maintained by [the city].

3. Once a federal court issues an injunction (or enters a consent decree) under *Ex parte Young*, the Eleventh Amendment does not stand as a bar to enforcing the decree. In *Hutto v. Finney*, 437 U.S. 678 (1978), the Court upheld a District Court's award of attorney's fees designed to encourage state compliance with an existing court order. State prisoners had sued state prison officials claiming that the conditions of their confinement violated the Eighth Amendment, and the District Court had ordered the officials to improve prison conditions. When the officials refused to comply in good faith with the order, the District Court awarded attorney's fees to the prisoners' lawyers to be paid from the state treasury. The state officials objected, arguing that the relief was not valid under the Eleventh Amendment because it exceeded the scope of *Ex parte Young*. The Court rejected this argument:

> In exercising their prospective powers under *Ex parte Young* and *Edelman v. Jordan*, federal courts are not reduced to issuing injunctions against state officers and hoping for compliance. Once issued, an injunction may be enforced. . . . If a state agency refuses to adhere to a court order, a financial penalty may be the most effective means of insuring compliance. The principles of federalism that inform Eleventh Amendment doctrine surely do not require federal courts to enforce their decrees only by sending high state officials to jail. The less intrusive power to impose a fine is properly treated as ancillary to the federal court's power to impose injunctive relief.

The award of attorney's fees "vindicated the District Court's authority over a recalcitrant litigant," the Court continued. "We see no reason to distinguish this award from any other penalty imposed to enforce a prospective injunction."

In *Frew v. Hawkins*, 540 U.S. 431 (2004), a unanimous Court found the Eleventh Amendment no bar to enforcement of a consent decree. Officials for the state of Texas entered a consent decree to settle a class action suit alleging violations of the state's obligations under a federal statute that required the state to provide health screening services to children. When the district court later found that the state had failed to comply with the decree, the state argued that the decree was unenforceable on Eleventh Amendment grounds unless the violation of the decree was also a violation of the underlying federal law. The Supreme Court disagreed:

> Consent decrees have elements of both contracts and judicial decrees. A consent decree "embodies an agreement of the parties" and is also "an agreement that the parties desire and expect will be reflected in, and be enforceable as, a judicial decree that is subject to the rules generally applicable to other judgments and decrees." *Rufo v. Inmates of Suffolk County Jail*, 502 U.S. 367 (1992). Consent decrees entered in federal court must be directed to protecting federal interests. . . . [A] consent decree must spring from, and serve to resolve, a dispute within the court's subject-matter jurisdiction; must come within the general scope of the case made by the pleadings; and must further the objectives of the law upon which the complaint was based.

Relying on *Hutto v. Finney*, the Court stated, "While *Finney* is somewhat different from the present case in that it involved the scope of remedies for violation of a prior order rather than the antecedent question whether remedies are permitted in the first instance, a similar principle applies. Federal courts are not reduced to approving consent decrees and hoping for compliance. Once entered, a consent decree may be enforced."

4. In *Quern v. Jordan*, 440 U.S. 332 (1979), the Court upheld a district court order requiring state officials "to send a mere explanatory notice to members of the plaintiff class advising them that there are state administrative procedures available by

which they may receive a determination of whether they are entitled to past benefits." Such notice was permissible under the Eleventh Amendment because it was "ancillary to the prospective relief already ordered by the court."

Problems: The Eleventh Amendment and Permissible Remedies

1. Student members of a campus political organization sue State University arguing that provisions of the university's election code for student government positions violate the First Amendment rights of the organization. They ask the federal court to hold the provisions invalid, and to invalidate the previous election and order new elections held. Is this relief permissible? *injunctive relief→yes ; retroactive→no*

2. Recipients of federal welfare benefits under Aid to Families with Dependent Children (AFDC), a federal welfare program administered by the states, bring a class action against officials of the state, arguing (as in *Edelman*) that the state's calculation of benefits violated federal law. While the lawsuit is pending, Congress terminates the AFDC program. Plaintiffs amend their lawsuit to seek (1) a declaration that the state's policy was in violation of AFDC, and (2) notice, as in *Quern v. Jordan*, that "there are state administrative procedures available by which they may receive a determination of whether they are entitled to past benefits." Is this relief permissible?

3. All states have statutes that "escheat" unclaimed property to the state after a certain period of time. Most of these statutes apply to situations where the owner of the property is dead or has been missing for long periods and the trustee of the property is a third party, such as a bank.

A few years ago, the Illiana legislature enacted a new escheat law. Under the new law, the owners of shares of stock in Illiana public companies will be deemed lost or unknown, and their shares will be treated as abandoned property, if the shareholder failed to file a change of address form, vote a proxy, or cash a dividend check for three years. The state comptroller, who is responsible for enforcing the statute, has not asked public companies whether these shareholders are actually lost or unknown, and his office did not follow the state's own statute for providing notice to lost or unknown shareholders.

Anna Weigand is a shareholder in an Illiana public company. She has been living at the same address for many years, but she throws away her proxy statements and has never cashed the tiny dividend checks she receives. As a result, the company included her, as required, on a list of shareholders who failed to meet the statutory requirements, and it issued duplicate stock certificates to the state. Without notice to Weigand or asking whether the company actually knew where she was, Illiana's comptroller sold Weigand's stock and put the money it received in the state's general fund. Under the statute, the comptroller is required to hold unclaimed property in trust and to maintain an unclaimed property fund until he receives a judgment from a court that the property has been "permanently escheated" to the state.

When Weigand found out what had happened, she sued the state comptroller for the return of her stock, or alternatively for the money. Is this lawsuit barred by sovereign immunity?

C. Congressional Power and State Sovereign Immunity

Seminole Tribe of Florida v. Florida

Supreme Court of the United States, 1996.

517 U.S. 44.

CHIEF JUSTICE REHNQUIST delivered the opinion of the Court.

The Indian Gaming Regulatory Act provides that an Indian tribe may conduct certain gaming activities only in conformance with a valid compact between the tribe and the State in which the gaming activities are located. The Act, passed by Congress under the Indian Commerce Clause, imposes upon the States a duty to negotiate in good faith with an Indian tribe toward the formation of a compact, and authorizes a tribe to bring suit in federal court against a State in order to compel performance of that duty. We hold that notwithstanding Congress' clear intent to abrogate the States' sovereign immunity, the Indian Commerce Clause does not grant Congress that power, and therefore [the Act] cannot grant jurisdiction over a State that does not consent to be sued. We further hold that the doctrine of *Ex parte Young*, 209 U.S. 123 (1908), may not be used to enforce [the Act] against a state official.

Congress passed the Indian Gaming Regulatory Act in 1988 in order to provide a statutory basis for the operation and regulation of gaming by Indian tribes. See 25 U.S.C. § 2702. The Act divides gaming on Indian lands into three classes—I, II, and III—and provides a different regulatory scheme for each class. Class III gaming—the type with which we are here concerned— . . . includes such things as slot machines, casino games, banking card games, dog racing, and lotteries. It is the most heavily regulated of the three classes. The Act provides that class III gaming is lawful only where it is: (1) authorized by an ordinance or resolution that (a) is adopted by the governing body of the Indian tribe, (b) satisfies certain statutorily prescribed requirements, and (c) is approved by the National Indian Gaming Commission; (2) located in a State that permits such gaming for any purpose by any person, organization, or entity; and (3) "conducted in conformance with a Tribal-State compact entered into by the Indian tribe and the State under paragraph (3) that is in effect." § 2710(d)(1).

. . . [Significant for our purposes is] that § 2710(d)(3) describes the process by which a State and an Indian tribe begin negotiations toward a Tribal-State compact:

> (A) Any Indian tribe having jurisdiction over the Indian lands upon which a class III gaming activity is being conducted, or is to be conducted, shall request the State in which such lands are located to enter into negotiations

for the purpose of entering into a Tribal-State compact governing the conduct of gaming activities. Upon receiving such a request, the State shall negotiate with the Indian tribe in good faith to enter into such a compact.

The State's obligation to "negotiate with the Indian tribe in good faith" is made judicially enforceable. . . .

In September 1991, the Seminole Tribe of Florida, petitioner, sued the State of Florida and its Governor, Lawton Chiles. . . . Petitioner alleged that respondents had "refused to enter into any negotiation for inclusion of [certain gaming activities] in a tribal-state compact," thereby violating the "requirement of good faith negotiation" . . . . Respondents moved to dismiss the complaint, arguing that the suit violated the State's sovereign immunity from suit in federal court. The District Court denied respondents' motion, and respondents took an interlocutory appeal of that decision. *See Puerto Rico Aqueduct and Sewer Authority v. Metcalf & Eddy, Inc.*, 506 U.S. 139 (1993) (collateral order doctrine allows immediate appellate review of order denying claim of Eleventh Amendment immunity).

The Court of Appeals for the Eleventh Circuit reversed the decision of the District Court, holding that the Eleventh Amendment barred petitioner's suit against respondents. . . . [W]e granted certiorari in order to consider two questions: (1) Does the Eleventh Amendment prevent Congress from authorizing suits by Indian tribes against States for prospective injunctive relief to enforce legislation enacted pursuant to the Indian Commerce Clause?; and (2) Does the doctrine of *Ex parte Young* permit suits against a State's Governor for prospective injunctive relief to enforce the good-faith bargaining requirement of the Act? We answer the first question in the affirmative, the second in the negative, and we therefore affirm the Eleventh Circuit's dismissal of petitioner's suit.

The Eleventh Amendment provides: "The Judicial power of the United States shall not be construed to extend to any suit in law or equity, commenced or prosecuted against one of the United States by Citizens of another State, or by Citizens or Subjects of any Foreign State." Although the text of the Amendment would appear to restrict only the Article III diversity jurisdiction of the federal courts, "we have understood the Eleventh Amendment to stand not so much for what it says, but for the presupposition . . . which it confirms." *Blatchford v. Native Village of Noatak*, 501 U.S. 775 (1991). That presupposition, first observed over a century ago in *Hans v. Louisiana*, 134 U.S. 1 (1890), has two parts: first, that each State is a sovereign entity in our federal system; and second, that "'[i]t is inherent in the nature of sovereignty not to be amenable to the suit of an individual without its consent,'" *id.*, quoting The Federalist No. 81, 487 (Rossiter ed., 1961) (A. Hamilton). For over a century we have reaffirmed that federal jurisdiction over suits against unconsenting States "was not contemplated by the Constitution when establishing the judicial power of the United States." *Hans*. Here, petitioner has sued the State of Florida and it is undisputed that Florida has not consented to the suit. Petitioner nevertheless contends that its suit is not barred by state sovereign immunity. First, it argues that Congress through the Act abrogated the States' sovereign immunity. Alternatively, petitioner maintains that its suit against the Governor may go forward under *Ex parte Young*. We consider each of those arguments in turn.

II

Petitioner argues that Congress through the Act abrogated the States' immunity from suit. In order to determine whether Congress has abrogated the States' sovereign immunity, we ask two questions: first, whether Congress has "unequivocally expresse[d] its intent to abrogate the immunity," *Green v. Mansour*, 474 U.S. 64 (1985); and second, whether Congress has acted "pursuant to a valid exercise of power."

A

Congress' intent to abrogate the States' immunity from suit must be obvious from "a clear legislative statement." *Blatchford*. This rule arises from a recognition of the important role played by the Eleventh Amendment and the broader principles that it reflects. *See Atascadero State Hospital v. Scanlon*, 473 U.S. 234 (1985); *Quern v. Jordan*, 440 U.S. 332 (1979). . . . Here, we agree with the parties, with the Eleventh Circuit in the decision below, and with virtually every other court that has confronted the question that Congress has in § 2710(d)(7) provided an "unmistakably clear" statement of its intent to abrogate. . . .

B

[W]e turn now to consider whether the Act was passed "pursuant to a valid exercise of power." *Green v. Mansour*. Before we address that question here, however, we think it necessary first to define the scope of our inquiry.

Petitioner suggests that one consideration weighing in favor of finding the power to abrogate here is that the Act authorizes only prospective injunctive relief rather than retroactive monetary relief. But we have often made it clear that the relief sought by a plaintiff suing a State is irrelevant to the question whether the suit is barred by the Eleventh Amendment. We think it follows *a fortiori* from this proposition that the type of relief sought is irrelevant to whether Congress has power to abrogate States' immunity. The Eleventh Amendment does not exist solely in order to "preven[t] federal-court judgments that must be paid out of a State's treasury," *Hess v. Port Authority Trans-Hudson Corporation*, 513 U.S. 30 (1994); it also serves to avoid "the indignity of subjecting a State to the coercive process of judicial tribunals at the instance of private parties," *Puerto Rico Aqueduct and Sewer Authority*.

Similarly, petitioner argues that the abrogation power is validly exercised here because the Act grants the States a power that they would not otherwise have, viz., some measure of authority over gaming on Indian lands. It is true enough that the Act extends to the States a power withheld from them by the Constitution. Nevertheless, we do not see how that consideration is relevant to the question whether Congress may abrogate state sovereign immunity. The Eleventh Amendment immunity may not be lifted by Congress unilaterally deciding that it will be replaced by grant of some other authority. . . . *Cf. Atascadero* ("[T]he mere receipt of federal funds cannot establish that a State has consented to suit in federal court").

Thus our inquiry into whether Congress has the power to abrogate unilaterally the States' immunity from suit is narrowly focused on one question: Was the Act in question passed pursuant to a constitutional provision granting Congress the power to abrogate? Previously, in conducting that inquiry, we have found authority to abrogate under only two provisions of the Constitution. In *Fitzpatrick v. Bitzer*, 427 U.S. 445 (1976), we recognized that the Fourteenth Amendment, by expanding federal power at the expense of state autonomy, had fundamentally altered the balance of state and federal power struck by the Constitution. We noted that § 1 of the Fourteenth Amendment contained prohibitions expressly directed at the States and that § 5 of the Amendment expressly provided that "The Congress shall have power to enforce, by appropriate legislation, the provisions of this article." We held that through the Fourteenth Amendment, federal power extended to intrude upon the province of the Eleventh Amendment and therefore that § 5 of the Fourteenth Amendment allowed Congress to abrogate the immunity from suit guaranteed by that Amendment.

In only one other case has congressional abrogation of the States' Eleventh Amendment immunity been upheld. In *Pennsylvania v. Union Gas Co.*, 491 U.S. 1 (1989), a plurality of the Court found that the Interstate Commerce Clause, Art. I, § 8, cl. 3, granted Congress the power to abrogate state sovereign immunity, stating that the power to regulate interstate commerce would be "incomplete without the authority to render States liable in damages." Justice White added the fifth vote necessary to the result in that case, but wrote separately in order to express that he "[did] not agree with much of [the plurality's] reasoning."

In arguing that Congress through the Act abrogated the States' sovereign immunity, petitioner does not challenge the Eleventh Circuit's conclusion that the Act was passed pursuant to neither the Fourteenth Amendment nor the Interstate Commerce Clause. Instead, accepting the lower court's conclusion that the Act was passed pursuant to Congress' power under the Indian Commerce Clause, petitioner now asks us to consider whether that Clause grants Congress the power to abrogate the States' sovereign immunity. . . . We agree with petitioner that the plurality opinion in *Union Gas* allows no principled distinction in favor of the States to be drawn between the Indian Commerce Clause and the Interstate Commerce Clause.

Respondents argue, however, that . . . "*Union Gas* should be reconsidered and overruled." Generally, the principle of *stare decisis*, and the interests that it serves, viz., "the evenhanded, predictable, and consistent development of legal principles, . . . reliance on judicial decisions, and . . . the actual and perceived integrity of the judicial process," counsel strongly against reconsideration of our precedent. Nevertheless, we always have treated *stare decisis* as a "principle of policy," and not as an "inexorable command." "[W]hen governing decisions are unworkable or are badly reasoned, 'this Court has never felt constrained to follow precedent.'"

The Court in *Union Gas* reached a result without an expressed rationale agreed upon by a majority of the Court. . . . Since it was issued, *Union Gas* has created confusion among the lower courts that have sought to understand and apply the deeply fractured decision.

The plurality's rationale also deviated sharply from our established federalism jurisprudence and essentially eviscerated our decision in *Hans*. [As Justice Scalia said in his dissent in *Union Gas*,] "If *Hans* means only that federal-question suits for money damages against the States cannot be brought in federal court unless Congress clearly says so, it means nothing at all." It was well established in 1989 when *Union Gas* was decided that the Eleventh Amendment stood for the constitutional principle that state sovereign immunity limited the federal courts' jurisdiction under Article III. The text of the Amendment itself is clear enough on this point: "The Judicial power of the United States shall not be construed to extend to any suit. . . ." And our decisions since *Hans* had been equally clear that the Eleventh Amendment reflects "the fundamental principle of sovereign immunity [that] limits the grant of judicial authority in Art. III," *Pennhurst State School and Hospital v. Halderman*, 465 U.S. 89 (1984); see *Union Gas* ("'[T]he entire judicial power granted by the Constitution does not embrace authority to entertain a suit brought by private parties against a State without consent given . . .'") (Scalia, J., dissenting). As the dissent in *Union Gas* recognized, the plurality's conclusion — that Congress could under Article I expand the scope of the federal courts' jurisdiction under Article III — "contradict[ed] our unvarying approach to Article III as setting forth the *exclusive* catalog of permissible federal-court jurisdiction."

Never before the decision in *Union Gas* had we suggested that the bounds of Article III could be expanded by Congress operating pursuant to any constitutional provision other than the Fourteenth Amendment. Indeed, it had seemed fundamental that Congress could not expand the jurisdiction of the federal courts beyond the bounds of Article III. *Marbury v. Madison*, 1 Cranch 137 (1803). . . .

The plurality's extended reliance upon our decision in *Fitzpatrick v. Bitzer*, 427 U.S. 445 (1976), that Congress could under the Fourteenth Amendment abrogate the States' sovereign immunity was also . . . misplaced. *Fitzpatrick* was based upon a rationale wholly inapplicable to the Interstate Commerce Clause, viz., that the Fourteenth Amendment, adopted well after the adoption of the Eleventh Amendment and the ratification of the Constitution, operated to alter the pre-existing balance between state and federal power achieved by Article III and the Eleventh Amendment. As the dissent in *Union Gas* made clear, *Fitzpatrick* cannot be read to justify "limitation of the principle embodied in the Eleventh Amendment through appeal to antecedent provisions of the Constitution."

. . . Reconsidering the decision in *Union Gas*, we conclude that none of the policies underlying *stare decisis* require our continuing adherence to its holding. The decision has, since its issuance, been of questionable precedential value, largely because a majority of the Court expressly disagreed with the rationale of the plurality. The case involved the interpretation of the Constitution and therefore may be altered only by constitutional amendment or revision by this Court. Finally, both the result in *Union Gas* and the plurality's rationale depart from our established understanding of the Eleventh Amendment and undermine the accepted function of Article III. We feel bound to conclude that *Union Gas* was wrongly decided and that it should be, and now is, overruled.

The dissent makes no effort to defend the decision in *Union Gas*, but nonetheless would find congressional power to abrogate in this case[11]. . . . For over a century, we have grounded our decisions in the oft-repeated understanding of state sovereign immunity as an essential part of the Eleventh Amendment. In *Principality of Monaco v. Mississippi*, 292 U.S. 313 (1934), the Court held that the Eleventh Amendment barred a suit brought against a State by a foreign state. Chief Justice Hughes wrote for a unanimous Court:

> [N]either the literal sweep of the words of Clause one of §2 of Article III, nor the absence of restriction in the letter of the Eleventh Amendment, permits the conclusion that in all controversies of the sort described in Clause one, and omitted from the words of the Eleventh Amendment, a State may be sued without her consent. Thus Clause one specifically provides that the judicial Power shall extend "to *all* Cases, in Law and Equity, arising under this Constitution, the Laws of the United States, and Treaties made, or which shall be made, under their Authority." But, although a case may arise under the Constitution and laws of the United States, the judicial power does not extend to it if the suit is sought to be prosecuted against a State, without her consent, by one of her own citizens. . . .

> Manifestly, we cannot rest with a mere literal application of the words of §2 of Article III, or assume that the letter of the Eleventh Amendment exhausts the restrictions upon suits against non-consenting States. Behind the words of the constitutional provisions are postulates which limit and control. There is the essential postulate that the controversies, as contemplated, shall be found to be of a justiciable character. There is also the postulate that States of the Union, still possessing attributes of sovereignty, shall be immune from suits, without their consent, save where there has been a "surrender of this immunity in the plan of the convention."

It is true that we have not had occasion previously to apply established Eleventh Amendment principles to the question whether Congress has the power to abrogate state sovereign immunity (save in *Union Gas*). But consideration of that question must proceed with fidelity to this century-old doctrine.

The dissent, to the contrary, disregards our case law in favor of a theory cobbled together from law review articles and its own version of historical events. The dissent cites not a single decision since *Hans* (other than *Union Gas*) that supports its view of state sovereign immunity, instead relying upon the now-discredited decision in *Chisholm v. Georgia*, 2 Dall. 419 (1793). Its undocumented and highly speculative extralegal explanation of the decision in *Hans* is a disservice to the Court's traditional method of adjudication.

The dissent mischaracterizes the *Hans* opinion. That decision found its roots not solely in the common law of England, but in the much more fundamental

---

11. Unless otherwise indicated, all references to the dissent are to the dissenting opinion authored by Justice Souter.

"'jurisprudence in all civilized nations.'" *Hans.* . . . It also is noteworthy that the principle of state sovereign immunity stands distinct from other principles of the common law in that only the former prompted a specific constitutional amendment.

Hans— with a much closer vantage point than the dissent—recognized that the decision in *Chisholm* was contrary to the well-understood meaning of the Constitution. . . . The dissent's lengthy analysis of the text of the Eleventh Amendment is directed at a straw man—we long have recognized that blind reliance upon the text of the Eleventh Amendment is "to strain the Constitution and the law to a construction never imagined or dreamed of." *Hans.* The text dealt in terms only with the problem presented by the decision in *Chisholm*; in light of the fact that the federal courts did not have federal question jurisdiction at the time the Amendment was passed (and would not have it until 1875), it seems unlikely that much thought was given to the prospect of federal-question jurisdiction over the States.

That same consideration causes the dissent's criticism of the views of Marshall, Madison, and Hamilton to ring hollow. The dissent cites statements made by those three influential Framers, the most natural reading of which would preclude all federal jurisdiction over an unconsenting State. Struggling against this reading, however, the dissent finds significant the absence of any contention that sovereign immunity would affect the new federal-question jurisdiction. But the lack of any statute vesting general federal-question jurisdiction in the federal courts until much later makes the dissent's demand for greater specificity about a then-dormant jurisdiction overly exacting.[13]

In putting forward a new theory of state sovereign immunity, the dissent develops its own vision of the political system created by the Framers, concluding with the statement that "[t]he Framers' principal objectives in rejecting English theories of unitary sovereignty . . . would have been impeded if a new concept of sovereign immunity had taken its place in federal-question cases, and would have been substantially thwarted if that new immunity had been held untouchable by any congressional effort to abrogate it."[14] This sweeping statement ignores the fact that the Nation survived for nearly two centuries without the question of the existence of such power ever being presented to this Court. And Congress itself waited nearly a century before even conferring federal-question jurisdiction on the lower federal courts.

---

13. Although the absence of any discussion dealing with federal-question jurisdiction is therefore unremarkable, what is notably lacking in the Framers' statements is any mention of Congress' power to abrogate the States' immunity. The absence of any discussion of that power is particularly striking in light of the fact that the Framers virtually always were very specific about the exception to state sovereign immunity arising from a State's consent to suit. . . .

14. This argument wholly disregards other methods of ensuring the States' compliance with federal law: The Federal Government can bring suit in federal court against a State, *see, e.g., United States v. Texas*, 143 U.S. 621 (1892) (finding such power necessary to the "permanence of the Union"); an individual can bring suit against a state officer in order to ensure that the officer's conduct is in compliance with federal law, *see, e.g., Ex parte Young*, 209 U.S. 123 (1908); and this Court is empowered to review a question of federal law arising from a state-court decision where a State has consented to suit, *see, e.g., Cohens v. Virginia*, 6 Wheat. 264 (1821).

In overruling *Union Gas* today, we reconfirm that the background principle of state sovereign immunity embodied in the Eleventh Amendment is not so ephemeral as to dissipate when the subject of the suit is an area, like the regulation of Indian commerce, that is under the exclusive control of the Federal Government. Even when the Constitution vests in Congress complete law-making authority over a particular area, the Eleventh Amendment prevents congressional authorization of suits by private parties against unconsenting States.[16] The Eleventh Amendment restricts the judicial power under Article III, and Article I cannot be used to circumvent the constitutional limitations placed upon federal jurisdiction. Petitioner's suit against the State of Florida must be dismissed for a lack of jurisdiction.

III

Petitioner argues that we may exercise jurisdiction over its suit to enforce § 2710(d)(3) against the Governor notwithstanding the jurisdictional bar of the Eleventh Amendment. Petitioner notes that since our decision in *Ex parte Young*, 209 U.S. 123 (1908), we often have found federal jurisdiction over a suit against a state official when that suit seeks only prospective injunctive relief in order to "end a continuing violation of federal law." *Green v. Mansour*. The situation presented here, however, is sufficiently different from that giving rise to the traditional *Ex parte Young* action so as to preclude the availability of that doctrine.

Here, the "continuing violation of federal law" alleged by petitioner is the Governor's failure to bring the State into compliance with § 2710(d)(3). But the duty to negotiate imposed upon the State by that statutory provision does not stand alone. Rather, as we have seen, Congress passed § 2710(d)(3) in conjunction with the carefully crafted and intricate remedial scheme set forth in § 2710(d)(7).

Where Congress has created a remedial scheme for the enforcement of a particular federal right, we have, in suits against federal officers, refused to supplement that scheme with one created by the judiciary. *Schweiker v. Chilicky*, 487 U.S. 412 (1988). Here, of course, the question is not whether a remedy should be created, but instead is whether the Eleventh Amendment bar should be lifted, as it was in *Ex parte Young*, in order to allow a suit against a state officer. Nevertheless, we think that the same general principle applies: Therefore, where Congress has prescribed a detailed remedial scheme for the enforcement against a State of a statutorily created right, a court should hesitate before casting aside those limitations and permitting an action against a state officer based upon *Ex parte Young*.

---

16. Justice Stevens understands our opinion to prohibit federal jurisdiction over suits to enforce the bankruptcy, copyright, and antitrust laws against the States. He notes that federal jurisdiction over those statutory schemes is exclusive, and therefore concludes that there is "no remedy" for state violations of those federal statutes. That conclusion is exaggerated both in its substance and in its significance. First, Justice Stevens' statement is misleadingly overbroad. We have already seen that several avenues remain open for ensuring state compliance with federal law. See n.14, *supra*. Most notably, an individual may obtain injunctive relief under *Ex parte Young* in order to remedy a state officer's ongoing violation of federal law. Second, . . . it has not been widely thought that the federal antitrust, bankruptcy, or copyright statutes abrogated the States' sovereign immunity. This Court never has awarded relief against a State under any of those statutory schemes. . . .

Here, Congress intended §2710(d)(3) to be enforced against the State in an action brought under §2710(d)(7); the intricate procedures set forth in that provision show that Congress intended therein not only to define, but also to limit significantly, the duty imposed by §2710(d)(3). For example, where the court finds that the State has failed to negotiate in good faith, the only remedy prescribed is an order directing the State and the Indian tribe to conclude a compact within 60 days. And if the parties disregard the court's order and fail to conclude a compact within the 60-day period, the only sanction is that each party then must submit a proposed compact to a mediator who selects the one which best embodies the terms of the Act. Finally, if the State fails to accept the compact selected by the mediator, the only sanction against it is that the mediator shall notify the Secretary of the Interior who then must prescribe regulations governing class III gaming on the tribal lands at issue. By contrast with this quite modest set of sanctions, an action brought against a state official under *Ex parte Young* would expose that official to the full remedial powers of a federal court, including, presumably, contempt sanctions. If §2710(d)(3) could be enforced in a suit under *Ex parte Young*, §2710(d)(7) would have been superfluous; it is difficult to see why an Indian tribe would suffer through the intricate scheme of §2710(d)(7) when more complete and more immediate relief would be available under *Ex parte Young*.[17]

Here, of course, we have found that Congress does not have authority under the Constitution to make the State suable in federal court under §2710(d)(7). Nevertheless, the fact that Congress chose to impose upon the State a liability that is significantly more limited than would be the liability imposed upon the state officer under *Ex parte Young* strongly indicates that Congress had no wish to create the latter under §2710(d)(3). Nor are we free to rewrite the statutory scheme in order to approximate what we think Congress might have wanted had it known that §2710(d)(7) was beyond its authority. If that effort is to be made, it should be made by Congress, and not by the federal courts. We hold that *Ex parte Young* is inapplicable to petitioner's suit against the Governor of Florida, and therefore that suit is barred by the Eleventh Amendment and must be dismissed for a lack of jurisdiction.

IV

The Eleventh Amendment prohibits Congress from making the State of Florida capable of being sued in federal court. The narrow exception to the Eleventh Amendment provided by the *Ex parte Young* doctrine cannot be used to enforce §2710(d)(3) because Congress enacted a remedial scheme, §2710(d)(7), specifically designed for the enforcement of that right. The Eleventh Circuit's dismissal of petitioner's suit is hereby affirmed.

Justice Stevens, dissenting.

This case is about power—the power of the Congress of the United States to create a private federal cause of action against a State, or its Governor, for the violation

---

17. Contrary to the claims of the dissent, we do not hold that Congress *cannot* authorize federal jurisdiction under *Ex parte Young* over a cause of action with a limited remedial scheme. We find only that Congress did not intend that result in the Indian Gaming Regulatory Act....

of a federal right. In *Chisholm v. Georgia*, 2 Dall. 419 (1793), the entire Court—including Justice Iredell whose dissent provided the blueprint for the Eleventh Amendment—assumed that Congress had such power. In *Hans v. Louisiana*, 134 U.S. 1 (1890)—a case the Court purports to follow today—the Court again assumed that Congress had such power. In *Fitzpatrick v. Bitzer*, 427 U.S. 445 (1976), and *Pennsylvania v. Union Gas Co.*, 491 U.S. 1 (1989) (Stevens, J., concurring), the Court squarely held that Congress has such power. In a series of cases beginning with *Atascadero State Hospital v. Scanlon*, 473 U.S. 234 (1985), the Court formulated a special "clear statement rule" to determine whether specific Acts of Congress contained an effective exercise of that power. Nevertheless, in a sharp break with the past, today the Court holds that with the narrow and illogical exception of statutes enacted pursuant to the Enforcement Clause of the Fourteenth Amendment, Congress has no such power.

The importance of the majority's decision to overrule the Court's holding in *Pennsylvania v. Union Gas Co.* cannot be overstated. The majority's opinion does not simply preclude Congress from establishing the rather curious statutory scheme under which Indian tribes may seek the aid of a federal court to secure a State's good-faith negotiations over gaming regulations. Rather, it prevents Congress from providing a federal forum for a broad range of actions against States, from those sounding in copyright and patent law, to those concerning bankruptcy, environmental law, and the regulation of our vast national economy.[1]

There may be room for debate over whether, in light of the Eleventh Amendment, Congress has the power to ensure that such a cause of action may be enforced in federal court by a citizen of another State or a foreign citizen. There can be no serious debate, however, over whether Congress has the power to ensure that such a cause of action may be brought by a citizen of the State being sued. Congress' authority in that regard is clear. . . .

Justice Souter, with whom Justice Ginsburg and Justice Breyer join, dissenting.

In holding the State of Florida immune to suit under the Indian Gaming Regulatory Act, the Court today holds for the first time since the founding of the Republic that Congress has no authority to subject a State to the jurisdiction of a federal court at the behest of an individual asserting a federal right. Although the Court invokes the Eleventh Amendment as authority for this proposition, the only sense in which that amendment might be claimed as pertinent here was tolerantly phrased by Justice Stevens in his concurring opinion in *Pennsylvania v. Union Gas Co.* There, he explained how it has come about that we have two Eleventh Amendments, the one ratified in 1795, the other (so-called) invented by the Court nearly a century later in *Hans v. Louisiana*.

---

1. . . . As federal courts have exclusive jurisdiction over cases arising under [some] federal laws, the majority's conclusion that the Eleventh Amendment shields States from being sued under them in federal court suggests that persons harmed by state violations of federal copyright, bankruptcy, and antitrust laws have no remedy. See Harris & Kenny, *Eleventh Amendment Jurisprudence After Atascadero: The Coming Clash With Antitrust, Copyright, and Other Causes of Action Over Which the Federal Courts Have Exclusive Jurisdiction*, 37 Emory L.J. 645 (1988).

. . . I part company from the Court because I am convinced that its decision is fundamentally mistaken, and for that reason I respectfully dissent.

I

It is useful to separate three questions: (1) whether the States enjoyed sovereign immunity if sued in their own courts in the period prior to ratification of the National Constitution; (2) if so, whether after ratification the States were entitled to claim some such immunity when sued in a federal court exercising jurisdiction either because the suit was between a State and a nonstate litigant who was not its citizen, or because the issue in the case raised a federal question; and (3) whether any state sovereign immunity recognized in federal court may be abrogated by Congress.

The answer to the first question is not clear, although some of the Framers assumed that States did enjoy immunity in their own courts. The second question was not debated at the time of ratification, except as to citizen-state diversity jurisdiction;[1] there was no unanimity, but in due course the Court in *Chisholm v. Georgia*, 2 Dall. 419 (1793), answered that a state defendant enjoyed no such immunity. As to federal-question jurisdiction, state sovereign immunity seems not to have been debated prior to ratification, the silence probably showing a general understanding at the time that the States would have no immunity in such cases.

The adoption of the Eleventh Amendment soon changed the result in *Chisholm*, not by mentioning sovereign immunity, but by eliminating citizen-state diversity jurisdiction over cases with state defendants. . . . The *Hans* Court erroneously assumed that a State could plead sovereign immunity against a noncitizen suing under federal-question jurisdiction, and for that reason held that a State must enjoy the same protection in a suit by one of its citizens. The error of *Hans*'s reasoning is underscored by its clear inconsistency with the Founders' hostility to the implicit reception of common-law doctrine as federal law, and with the Founders' conception of sovereign power as divided between the States and the National Government for the sake of very practical objectives.

The Court's answer today to the third question is likewise at odds with the Founders' view that common law, when it was received into the new American legal system, was always subject to legislative amendment. In ignoring the reasons for this pervasive understanding at the time of the ratification, and in holding that a nontextual common-law rule limits a clear grant of congressional power under Article I, the Court follows a course that has brought it to grief before in our history, and promises to do so again. . . .

[Justice Souter's discussion of the history of the Constitution's ratification, the opinion in *Chisholm*, and the adoption of the Eleventh Amendment is omitted.]

---

1. The two Citizen-State Diversity Clauses provide as follows: "The judicial Power shall extend . . . to Controversies . . . between a State and Citizens of another State; . . . and between a State, or the Citizens thereof, and foreign States, Citizens or Subjects." U.S. Const., Art. III, § 2. . . . I have grouped the two as "Citizen-State Diversity Clauses" for ease in frequent repetition here.

The Eleventh Amendment, of course, repudiated *Chisholm* and clearly divested federal courts of some jurisdiction as to cases against state parties. . . .

There are two plausible readings of this provision's text. Under the first, it simply repeals the Citizen-State Diversity Clauses of Article III for all cases in which the State appears as a defendant. Under the second, it strips the federal courts of jurisdiction in any case in which a state defendant is sued by a citizen not its own, even if jurisdiction might otherwise rest on the existence of a federal question in the suit. Neither reading of the Amendment, of course, furnishes authority for the Court's view in today's case, but we need to choose between the competing readings for the light that will be shed on the *Hans* doctrine and the legitimacy of inflating that doctrine to the point of constitutional immutability as the Court has chosen to do.

The history and structure of the Eleventh Amendment convincingly show that it reaches only to suits subject to federal jurisdiction exclusively under the Citizen-State Diversity Clauses.[8] In precisely tracking the language in Article III providing for citizen-state diversity jurisdiction, the text of the Amendment does, after all, suggest to common sense that only the Diversity Clauses are being addressed. . . .

In sum, reading the Eleventh Amendment solely as a limit on citizen-state diversity jurisdiction has the virtue of coherence with this Court's practice, with the views of John Marshall, with the history of the Amendment's drafting, and with its allusive language. . . .

Thus, regardless of which of the two plausible readings one adopts, the further point to note here is that there is no possible argument that the Eleventh Amendment, by its terms, deprives federal courts of jurisdiction over all citizen lawsuits against the States. Not even the Court advances that proposition, and there would be no textual basis for doing so. Because the plaintiffs in today's case are citizens of the State that they are suing, the Eleventh Amendment simply does not apply to them. We must therefore look elsewhere for the source of that immunity by which the Court says their suit is barred from a federal court.[13]

---

8. The great weight of scholarly commentary agrees. *See, e.g.,* Jackson, *The Supreme Court, the Eleventh Amendment, and State Sovereign Immunity,* 98 YALE L.J. 1 (1988); Amar, *Of Sovereignty and Federalism,* 96 YALE L.J. 1425 (1987); Fletcher, *A Historical Interpretation of the Eleventh Amendment: A Narrow Construction of an Affirmative Grant of Jurisdiction Rather than a Prohibition Against Jurisdiction,* 35 STAN. L. REV. 1033 (1983); Gibbons, *The Eleventh Amendment and State Sovereign Immunity: A Reinterpretation,* 83 COLUM. L. REV. 1889 (1983); Field, *The Eleventh Amendment and Other Sovereign Immunity Doctrines: Congressional Imposition of Suit Upon the States,* 126 U. PA. L. REV. 1203 (1978). While a minority has adopted the second view set out above, *see, e.g.,* Marshall, *Fighting the Words of the Eleventh Amendment,* 102 HARV. L. REV. 1342 (1989); Massey, *State Sovereignty and the Tenth and Eleventh Amendments,* 56 U. CHI. L. REV. 61 (1989), and others have criticized the diversity theory, *see, e.g.,* Marshall, *The Diversity Theory of the Eleventh Amendment: A Critical Evaluation,* 102 HARV. L. REV. 1372 (1989), I have discovered no commentator affirmatively advocating the position taken by the Court today. As one scholar has observed, the literature is "remarkably consistent in its evaluation of the historical evidence and text of the amendment as not supporting a broad rule of constitutional immunity for states." Jackson, *supra.*

13. The majority chides me that the "lengthy analysis of the text of the Eleventh Amendment is directed at a straw man." But plain text is the Man of Steel in a confrontation with "background

II

The obvious place to look elsewhere, of course, is *Hans v. Louisiana*, and *Hans* was indeed a leap in the direction of today's holding, even though it does not take the Court all the way. The parties in *Hans* raised, and the Court in that case answered, only what I have called the second question, that is, whether the Constitution, without more, permits a State to plead sovereign immunity to bar the exercise of federal-question jurisdiction. Although the Court invoked a principle of sovereign immunity to cure what it took to be the Eleventh Amendment's anomaly of barring only those state suits brought by noncitizen plaintiffs, the *Hans* Court had no occasion to consider whether Congress could abrogate that background immunity by statute. . . . In deciding how to [resolve that question,] the place to begin is with *Hans*'s holding that a principle of sovereign immunity derived from the common law insulates a State from federal-question jurisdiction at the suit of its own citizen. A critical examination of that case will show that it was wrongly decided, as virtually every recent commentator has concluded. It follows that the Court's further step today of constitutionalizing *Hans*'s rule against abrogation by Congress compounds and immensely magnifies the century-old mistake of *Hans* itself and takes its place with other historic examples of textually untethered elevations of judicially derived rules to the status of inviolable constitutional law.

[Justice Souter's extended critique of *Hans* is omitted.]

III

A

There is and could be no dispute that the doctrine of sovereign immunity that *Hans* purported to apply had its origins in the "familiar doctrine of the common law," *The Siren*, 7 Wall. 152 (1869), "derived from the laws and practices of our English ancestors," *United States v. Lee*, 106 U.S. 196 (1882). . . .

This fact of the doctrine's common-law status in the period covering the founding and the later adoption of the Eleventh Amendment should have raised a warning flag to the *Hans* Court and it should do the same for the Court today. For although the Court has persistently assumed that the common law's presence in the minds of the early Framers must have functioned as a limitation on their understanding of the new Nation's constitutional powers, this turns out not to be so at all. One of the characteristics of the founding generation, on the contrary, was its joinder of an appreciation of its immediate and powerful common-law heritage with caution in settling that inheritance on the political systems of the new Republic. . . .

[Justice Souter reviewed the history of the reception of the common law in the United States. He concluded:] The consequence of this anti-English hostility and awareness of changed circumstances was that the independent States continued the colonists' practice of adopting only so much of the common law as they thought

principle[s]" and "'postulates which limit and control.'" An argument rooted in the text of a constitutional provision may not be guaranteed of carrying the day, but insubstantiality is not its failing. . . .

applicable to their local conditions. . . . Accordingly, in the period following independence, "[l]egislatures and courts and doctrinal writers had to test the common law at every point with respect to its applicability to America."

While the States had limited their reception of English common law to principles appropriate to American conditions, the 1787 draft Constitution contained no provision for adopting the common law at all. This omission stood in sharp contrast to the state constitutions then extant, virtually all of which contained explicit provisions dealing with common-law reception. Since the experience in the States set the stage for thinking at the national level, *see generally* G. Wood, Creation of the American Republic, 1776–1787 (1969) (Wood), this failure to address the notion of common-law reception could not have been inadvertent. . . .

B

Given the refusal to entertain any wholesale reception of common law, given the failure of the new Constitution to make any provision for adoption of common law as such, and given the protests already quoted that no general reception had occurred, the *Hans* Court and the Court today cannot reasonably argue that something like the old immunity doctrine somehow slipped in as a tacit but enforceable background principle. The evidence is even more specific, however, that there was no pervasive understanding that sovereign immunity had limited federal-question jurisdiction. . . .

1

[The] Framers and their contemporaries did not agree about the place of common-law state sovereign immunity even as to federal jurisdiction resting on the Citizen-State Diversity Clauses. . . . [Justice Souter's discussion of materials in *The Federalist Papers* is omitted.]

2

We said in *Blatchford v. Native Village of Noatak*, 501 U.S. 775 (1991) that "the States entered the federal system with their sovereignty intact," but we surely did not mean that they entered that system with the sovereignty they would have claimed if each State had assumed independent existence in the community of nations, for even the Articles of Confederation allowed for less than that. . . . While there is no need here to calculate exactly how close the American States came to sovereignty in the classic sense prior to ratification of the Constitution, it is clear that the act of ratification affected their sovereignty in a way different from any previous political event in America or anywhere else. For the adoption of the Constitution made them members of a novel federal system that sought to balance the States' exercise of some sovereign prerogatives delegated from their own people with the principle of a limited but centralizing federal supremacy. . . .

Given [the] metamorphosis of the idea of sovereignty in the years leading up to 1789, the question whether the old immunity doctrine might have been received as something suitable for the new world of federal-question jurisdiction is a crucial one. The answer is that sovereign immunity as it would have been known to the Framers before ratification thereafter became inapplicable as a matter of logic in a federal suit raising a federal question. The old doctrine, after all, barred the involuntary subjection of a sovereign to the system of justice and law of which it was itself the font, since to do otherwise would have struck the common-law mind from the Middle Ages onward as both impractical and absurd. But the ratification demonstrated that state governments were subject to a superior regime of law in a judicial system established, not by the State, but by the people through a specific delegation of their sovereign power to a National Government that was paramount within its delegated sphere. When individuals sued States to enforce federal rights, the Government that corresponded to the "sovereign" in the traditional common-law sense was not the State but the National Government, and any state immunity from the jurisdiction of the Nation's courts would have required a grant from the true sovereign, the people, in their Constitution, or from the Congress that the Constitution had empowered. . . . Subjecting States to federal jurisdiction in federal-question cases brought by individuals thus reflected nothing more than Professor Amar's apt summary that "[w]here governments are acting within the bounds of their delegated 'sovereign' power, they may partake of sovereign immunity; where not, not." Amar, *Of Sovereignty and Federalism*, 96 YALE L.J. 1425 (1987).

Given the Framers' general concern with curbing abuses by state governments, it would be amazing if the scheme of delegated powers embodied in the Constitution had left the National Government powerless to render the States judicially accountable for violations of federal rights. . . .

. . . Without citing a single source to the contrary, the Court dismisses the historical evidence regarding the Framers' vision of the relationship between national and state sovereignty, and reassures us that "the Nation survived for nearly two centuries without the question of the existence of [the abrogation] power ever being presented to this Court." But we are concerned here not with the survival of the Nation but the opportunity of its citizens to enforce federal rights in a way that Congress provides. The absence of any general federal-question statute for nearly a century following ratification of Article III (with a brief exception in 1800) hardly counts against the importance of that jurisdiction either in the Framers' conception or in current reality; likewise, the fact that Congress has not often seen fit to use its power of abrogation (outside the Fourteenth Amendment context, at least) does not compel a conclusion that the power is not important to the federal scheme. In the end, is it plausible to contend that the plan of the convention was meant to leave the National Government without any way to render individuals capable of enforcing their federal rights directly against an intransigent State?

C

The considerations expressed so far, based on text, *Chisholm*, caution in common-law reception, and sovereignty theory, have pointed both to the mistakes inherent in *Hans* and, even more strongly, to the error of today's holding. Although for reasons of *stare decisis* I would not today disturb the century-old precedent, I surely would not extend its error by placing the common-law immunity it mistakenly recognized beyond the power of Congress to abrogate. . . .

1

[T]he views of the Framers reflected the caution of state constitutionalists and legislators over reception of common-law rules, a caution that the Framers exalted to the point of vigorous resistance to any idea that English common-law rules might be imported wholesale through the new Constitution. The state politicians also took pains to guarantee that once a common-law rule had been received, it would always be subject to legislative alteration, and again the state experience was reflected in the Framers' thought. Indeed, the Framers' very insistence that no common-law doctrine would be received by virtue of ratification was focused in their fear that elements of the common law might thereby have been placed beyond the power of Congress to alter by legislation. . . .

Virtually every state reception provision, be it constitutional or statutory, explicitly provided that the common law was subject to alteration by statute. . . .

2

History confirms the wisdom of Madison's abhorrence of constitutionalizing common-law rules to place them beyond the reach of congressional amendment. The Framers feared judicial power over substantive policy and the ossification of law that would result from transforming common law into constitutional law, and their fears have been borne out every time the Court has ignored Madison's counsel on subjects that we generally group under economic and social policy. It is, in fact, remarkable that as we near the end of this century the Court should choose to open a new constitutional chapter in confining legislative judgments on these matters by resort to textually unwarranted common-law rules, for it was just this practice in the century's early decades that brought this Court to the nadir of competence that we identify with *Lochner v. New York*, 198 U.S. 45 (1905). . . .

The majority today, indeed, seems to be going *Lochner* one better. When the Court has previously constrained the express Article I powers by resort to common-law or background principles, it has done so at least in an ostensible effort to give content to some other written provision of the Constitution, like the Due Process Clause, the very object of which is to limit the exercise of governmental power. Some textual argument, at least, could be made that the Court was doing no more than defining one provision that happened to be at odds with another. Today, however, the Court is not struggling to fulfill a responsibility to reconcile two arguably conflicting and Delphic constitutional provisions, nor is it struggling with any Delphic text at all. For even the Court concedes that the Constitution's grant to Congress of plenary power over relations with Indian tribes at the expense of any state claim to the contrary is unmistakably clear, and this case does not even arguably implicate a textual trump to the grant of federal-question jurisdiction.

I know of only one other occasion on which the Court has spoken of extending its reach so far as to declare that the plain text of the Constitution is subordinate to judicially discoverable principles untethered to any written provision. Justice Chase once took such a position almost 200 years ago:

There are certain vital principles in our free Republican governments, which will determine and over-rule an apparent and flagrant abuse of legislative power. . . . An act of the Legislature (for I cannot call it a law) contrary to the great first principles of the social compact, cannot be considered a rightful exercise of legislative authority." *Calder v. Bull*, 3 Dall. 386 (1798).

This position was no less in conflict with American constitutionalism in 1798 than it is today, being inconsistent with the Framers' view of the Constitution as fundamental law. Justice Iredell understood this, and dissented (again) in an opinion that still answers the position that "vital" or "background" principles, without more, may be used to confine a clear constitutional provision:

[S]ome speculative jurists have held, that a legislative act against natural justice must, in itself, be void; but I cannot think that, under such a government, any Court of Justice would possess a power to declare it so. . . .

. . . [I]t has been the policy of the American states, . . . and of the people of the United States . . . to define with precision the objects of the legislative power, and to restrain its exercise within marked and settled boundaries. If any act of Congress, or of the Legislature of a state, violates those constitutional provisions, it is unquestionably void. . . . If, on the other hand, the Legislature of the Union, or the Legislature of any member of the Union, shall pass a law, within the general scope of their constitutional power, the Court cannot pronounce it to be void, merely because it is, in their judgment, contrary to the principles of natural justice. The ideas of natural justice are regulated by no fixed standard: the ablest and the purest men have differed upon the subject; and all that the Court could properly say, in such an event, would be, that the Legislature (possessed of an equal right of opinion) had passed an act which, in the opinion of the judges, was inconsistent with the abstract principles of natural justice." *Id.* (opinion dissenting in part).

Later jurisprudence vindicated Justice Iredell's view, and the idea that "first principles" or concepts of "natural justice" might take precedence over the Constitution or other positive law "all but disappeared in American discourse." J. ELY, DEMOCRACY AND DISTRUST 52 (1980). It should take more than references to "background principle[s]" and "implicit limitation[s]" to revive the judicial power to overcome clear text unopposed to any other provision, when that clear text is in harmony with an almost equally clear intent on the part of the Framers and the constitutionalists of their generation.

IV

The Court's holding that the States' *Hans* immunity may not be abrogated by Congress leads to the final question in this case, whether federal-question jurisdiction exists to order prospective relief enforcing IGRA against a state officer . . . who is said to be authorized to take the action required by the federal law. . . . The answer to this question is an easy yes, the officer is subject to suit under the rule in *Ex parte Young*, 209 U.S. 123 (1908), and the case could, and should, readily be decided on this point alone.

No clear statement of intent to displace the doctrine of *Ex parte Young* occurs in IGRA, and the Court is instead constrained to rest its effort to skirt *Ex parte Young* on a series of suggestions thought to be apparent in Congress's provision of "intricate procedures" for enforcing a State's obligation under the Act. . . .

. . . But there is no basis in law for this suggestion, and the strongest authority to reject it. . . . IGRA's jurisdictional provision reads as though it had been drafted with the specific intent to apply to officer liability under *Ex parte Young*. It provides that "[t]he United States district courts shall have jurisdiction over . . . any cause of action . . . *arising from the failure of a State* to enter into negotiations . . . or to conduct such negotiations in good faith." 25 U.S.C. § 2710(d)(7)(A)(i) (emphasis added). This language does not limit the possible defendants to States and is quite literally consistent with the possibility that a tribe could sue an appropriate state official for a State's failure to negotiate. . . .

But even if the jurisdictional provision had spoken narrowly of an action against the State itself (as it subsequently speaks in terms of the State's obligation), that would be no indication that Congress had rejected the application of *Ex parte Young*. An order requiring a "State" to comply with federal law can, of course, take the form of an order directed to the State in its sovereign capacity. But as *Ex parte Young* and innumerable other cases show, there is nothing incongruous about a duty imposed on a "State" that Congress intended to be effectuated by an order directed to an appropriate state official. . . .

There is, finally, a response to the Court's rejection of *Young* that ought to go without saying. Our longstanding practice is to read ambiguous statutes to avoid constitutional infirmity, *Edward J. DeBartolo Corp. v. Florida Gulf Coast Building & Constr. Trades Council*, 485 U.S. 568 (1988). This practice alone (without any need for a clear statement to displace *Ex parte Young*) would be enough to require *Young*'s application. So, too, would the application of another rule, requiring courts to choose any reasonable construction of a statute that would eliminate the need to confront a contested constitutional issue (in this case, the place of state sovereign immunity in federal-question cases and the status of Union Gas). *NLRB v. Catholic Bishop of Chicago*, 440 U.S. 490 (1979). Construing the statute to harmonize with *Young*, as it readily does, would have saved an Act of Congress and rendered a discussion on constitutional grounds wholly unnecessary. This case should be decided on this basis alone.

V

Absent the application of *Ex parte Young*, I would, of course, follow *Union Gas* in recognizing congressional power under Article I to abrogate *Hans* immunity. Since the reasons for this position tend to unsettle *Hans* as well as support *Union Gas*, I should add a word about my reasons for continuing to accept *Hans*'s holding as a matter of *stare decisis*.

The *Hans* doctrine was erroneous, but it has not previously proven to be unworkable or to conflict with later doctrine or to suffer from the effects of facts developed since its decision (apart from those indicating its original errors). I would therefore treat *Hans* as it has always been treated in fact until today, as a doctrine of federal common law. For, as so understood, it has formed one of the strands of the federal relationship for over a century now, and the stability of that relationship is itself a value that *stare decisis* aims to respect.

. . . Because neither text, precedent, nor history supports the majority's abdication of our responsibility to exercise the jurisdiction entrusted to us in Article III, I would reverse the judgment of the Court of Appeals.

Note: The Source of State Sovereign Immunity After Seminole Tribe

1. In *Edelman v. Jordan*, Justice Brennan in dissent took the position that the Eleventh Amendment's text controlled its application. For Justice Brennan, then, the Amendment limited only the form of diversity jurisdiction that the text prohibited. In *Seminole Tribe*, as in *Hans*, the Court looks past the text of the Amendment to a principle of state sovereign immunity. Justice Souter in dissent believes that state sovereign immunity is a common-law doctrine, and therefore defeasible by Congress. What view does the majority hold? If not the Eleventh Amendment, where does state sovereign immunity come from?

2. Seminole Tribe was followed by *Alden v. Maine*, 527 U.S. 706 (1999), which held that Congress lacks power under Article I to abrogate a state's sovereign immunity in the *state* courts. A group of probation officers brought suit initially in federal court against Maine to recover overtime pay under the Fair Labor Standards Act. After *Seminole Tribe* was decided, their federal suit was dismissed, and they refiled in Maine state courts. The Maine courts held that the state was immune from liability, despite Congress's abrogation of state sovereign immunity in the statute. The Supreme Court affirmed. The majority opinion by Justice Kennedy sheds more light on the source of state sovereign immunity and the policies it enforces:

> The Eleventh Amendment makes explicit reference to the States' immunity from suits "commenced or prosecuted against one of the United States by Citizens of another State, or by Citizens or Subjects of any Foreign State." U.S. Const., Amdt. 11. We have, as a result, sometimes referred to the States' immunity from suit as "Eleventh Amendment immunity." The phrase is convenient shorthand but something of a misnomer, for the sovereign immunity of the States neither derives from, nor is limited by, the terms of the Eleventh Amendment. Rather, as the Constitution's structure, its history, and the authoritative interpretations by this Court make clear, the States' immunity from suit is a fundamental aspect of the sovereignty which the States enjoyed before the ratification of the Constitution, and which they retain today (either literally or by virtue of their admission into the Union upon an equal footing with the other States) except as altered by the plan of the Convention or certain constitutional Amendments.

In the majority's view, state sovereign immunity was central to the constitutional design:

Any doubt regarding the constitutional role of the States as sovereign entities is removed by the Tenth Amendment, which, like the other provisions of the Bill of Rights, was enacted to allay lingering concerns about the extent of the national power. The Amendment confirms the promise implicit in the original document: "The powers not delegated to the United States by the Constitution, nor prohibited by it to the States, are reserved to the States respectively, or to the people." U.S. Const., Amdt. 10; *see also New York v. United States*, 505 U.S. 144 (1992).

The federal system established by our Constitution preserves the sovereign status of the States in two ways. First, it reserves to them a substantial portion of the Nation's primary sovereignty, together with the dignity and essential attributes inhering in that status. The States "form distinct and independent portions of the supremacy, no more subject, within their respective spheres, to the general authority than the general authority is subject to them, within its own sphere." The Federalist No. 39 (C. Rossiter ed., 1961) (J. Madison).

Second, even as to matters within the competence of the National Government, the constitutional design secures the founding generation's rejection of "the concept of a central government that would act upon and through the States" in favor of "a system in which the State and Federal Governments would exercise concurrent authority over the people—who were, in Hamilton's words, 'the only proper objects of government.'" . . . The States thus retain "a residuary and inviolable sovereignty." The Federalist No. 39. They are not relegated to the role of mere provinces or political corporations, but retain the dignity, though not the full authority, of sovereignty.

. . . The generation that designed and adopted our federal system considered immunity from private suits central to sovereign dignity. . . . Although the American people had rejected other aspects of English political theory, the doctrine that a sovereign could not be sued without its consent was universal in the States when the Constitution was drafted and ratified.

. . . The text and history of the Eleventh Amendment also suggest that Congress acted not to change but to restore the original constitutional design. Although earlier drafts of the Amendment had been phrased as express limits on the judicial power granted in Article III, *see, e.g.*, 3 Annals of Congress 651–52 (1793) ("The Judicial Power of the United States shall not extend to any suits in law or equity, commenced or prosecuted against one of the United States . . ."), the adopted text addressed the proper interpretation of that provision of the original Constitution, see U.S. Const., Amdt. 11 ("The Judicial power of the United States shall not be construed to extend to any suit in law or equity, commenced or prosecuted against one of the United States . . ."). By its terms, then, the Eleventh Amendment did not redefine the federal judicial power but instead overruled the Court.

In response to the argument that state courts are required by the Constitution to hear federal claims such as the plaintiffs', the Court said:

The Supremacy Clause does impose specific obligations on state judges. There can be no serious contention, however, that the Supremacy Clause imposes greater obligations on state-court judges than on the Judiciary of the United States itself. The text of Article III, § 1, which extends federal judicial power to enumerated classes of suits but grants Congress discretion whether to establish inferior federal courts, does give strong support to the inference that state courts may be opened to suits falling within the federal judicial power. The Article in no way suggests, however, that state courts may be required to assume jurisdiction that could not be vested in the federal courts and forms no part of the judicial power of the United States.

We have recognized that Congress may require state courts to hear only "matters appropriate for the judicial power," *Printz v. United States*, 521 U.S. 898 (1997). Our sovereign immunity precedents establish that suits against nonconsenting States are not "properly susceptible of litigation in courts," *Hans*, and, as a result, that "[t]he 'entire judicial power granted by the Constitution' does not embrace authority to entertain such suits in the absence of the State's consent," *Principality of Monaco*. We are aware of no constitutional precept that would admit of a congressional power to require state courts to entertain federal suits which are not within the judicial power of the United States and could not be heard in federal courts.

The Court also considered the policies enforced by sovereign immunity:

Underlying constitutional form are considerations of great substance. Private suits against nonconsenting States—especially suits for money damages—may threaten the financial integrity of the States. It is indisputable that, at the time of the founding, many of the States could have been forced into insolvency but for their immunity from private suits for money damages. Even today, an unlimited congressional power to authorize suits in state court to levy upon the treasuries of the States for compensatory damages, attorney's fees, and even punitive damages could create staggering burdens, giving Congress a power and a leverage over the States that is not contemplated by our constitutional design. The potential national power would pose a severe and notorious danger to the States and their resources.

A congressional power to strip the States of their immunity from private suits in their own courts would pose more subtle risks as well. "The principle of immunity from litigation assures the states and the nation from unanticipated intervention in the processes of government." *Great Northern Life Ins. Co. v. Read*, 322 U.S. 43 (1944). When the States' immunity from private suits is disregarded, "the course of their public policy and the administration of their public affairs" may become "subject to and controlled by the mandates of judicial tribunals without their consent, and in favor of individual interests." *In re Ayers*, 123 U.S. 443 (1887). While the States have relinquished their immunity from suit in some special contexts — at least as a practical matter — this surrender carries with it substantial costs to the autonomy, the decisionmaking ability, and the sovereign capacity of the States.

A general federal power to authorize private suits for money damages would place unwarranted strain on the States' ability to govern in accordance with the will of their citizens. Today, as at the time of the founding, the allocation of scarce resources among competing needs and interests lies at the heart of the political process. While the judgment creditor of a State may have a legitimate claim for compensation, other important needs and worthwhile ends compete for access to the public fisc. Since all cannot be satisfied in full, it is inevitable that difficult decisions involving the most sensitive and political of judgments must be made. If the principle of representative government is to be preserved to the States, the balance between competing interests must be reached after deliberation by the political process established by the citizens of the State, not by judicial decree mandated by the Federal Government and invoked by the private citizen. "It needs no argument to show that the political power cannot be thus ousted of its jurisdiction and the judiciary set in its place." *Louisiana v. Jumel*, 107 U.S. 711 (1883).

The Court concluded: "In light of history, practice, precedent, and the structure of the Constitution, we hold that the States retain immunity from private suit in their own courts, an immunity beyond the congressional power to abrogate by Article I legislation."

Justice Souter, writing for himself and Justices Stevens, Ginsburg, and Breyer dissented:

The Court holds that the Constitution bars an individual suit against a State to enforce a federal statutory right under the Fair Labor Standards Act, when brought in the State's courts over its objection. In thus complementing its earlier decision [in *Seminole Tribe*], the Court of course confronts the fact that the state forum renders the Eleventh Amendment beside the point, and it has responded by discerning a simpler and more straightforward theory of state sovereign immunity than it found in *Seminole Tribe*: a State's sovereign immunity from all individual suits is a "fundamental aspect" of state sovereignty "confirm[ed]" by the Tenth Amendment. As a consequence, *Seminole Tribe*'s contorted reliance on the Eleventh Amendment and its background was presumably unnecessary; the Tenth would have done the work with an economy that the majority in *Seminole Tribe* would have welcomed.

Indeed, if the Court's current reasoning is correct, the Eleventh Amendment itself was unnecessary. Whatever Article III may originally have said about the federal judicial power, the embarrassment to the State of Georgia occasioned by attempts in federal court to enforce the State's war debt could easily have been avoided if only the Court that decided *Chisholm v. Georgia*,

2 Dall. 419 (1793), had understood a State's inherent, Tenth Amendment right to be free of any judicial power, whether the court be state or federal, and whether the cause of action arise under state or federal law.

Justice Souter's lengthy dissent focused on the history of sovereign immunity in the United States and in England. He concluded that the majority's approach was mistaken. He also considered the policies identified by the majority in support of a broad state immunity:

> It is symptomatic of the weakness of the structural notion proffered by the Court that it seeks to buttress the argument by relying on "the dignity and respect afforded a State, which the immunity is designed to protect," and by invoking the many demands on a State's fisc. Apparently beguiled by Gilded Era language describing private suits against States as "'neither becoming nor convenient,'" (quoting *In re Ayers*, 123 U.S. 443 (1887)), the Court calls "immunity from private suits central to sovereign dignity," and assumes that this "dignity" is a quality easily translated from the person of the King to the participatory abstraction of a republican State. The thoroughly anomalous character of this appeal to dignity is obvious from a reading of Blackstone's description of royal dignity, which he sets out as a premise of his discussion of sovereignty:

> > First, then, of the royal dignity. Under every monarchical establishment, it is necessary to distinguish the prince from his subjects. . . . The law therefore ascribes to the king . . . certain attributes of a great and transcendent nature; by which the people are led to consider him in the light of a superior being, and to pay him that awful respect, which may enable him with greater ease to carry on the business of government. This is what I understand by the royal dignity, the several branches of which we will now proceed to examine. 1 Blackstone 241.

> It would be hard to imagine anything more inimical to the republican conception, which rests on the understanding of its citizens precisely that the government is not above them, but of them, its actions being governed by law just like their own. Whatever justification there may be for an American government's immunity from private suit, it is not dignity.

> It is equally puzzling to hear the Court say that "federal power to authorize private suits for money damages would place unwarranted strain on the States' ability to govern in accordance with the will of their citizens." So long as the citizens' will, expressed through state legislation, does not violate valid federal law, the strain will not be felt; and to the extent that state action does violate federal law, the will of the citizens of the United States already trumps that of the citizens of the State: the strain then is not only expected, but necessarily intended.

> Least of all does the Court persuade by observing that "other important needs" than that of the "judgment creditor" compete for public money. The

"judgment creditor" in question is not a dunning bill collector, but a citizen whose federal rights have been violated, and a constitutional structure that stints on enforcing federal rights out of an abundance of delicacy toward the States has substituted politesse in place of respect for the rule of law.[36]

Justice Souter concluded:

> The Court has swung back and forth with regrettable disruption on the enforceability of the FLSA against the States, but if the present majority had a defensible position one could at least accept its decision with an expectation of stability ahead. As it is, any such expectation would be naïve. The resemblance of today's state sovereign immunity to the *Lochner* era's industrial due process is striking. The Court began this century by imputing immutable constitutional status to a conception of economic self-reliance that was never true to industrial life and grew insistently fictional with the years, and the Court has chosen to close the century by conferring like status on a conception of state sovereign immunity that is true neither to history nor to the structure of the Constitution. I expect the Court's late essay into immunity doctrine will prove the equal of its earlier experiment in laissez-faire, the one being as unrealistic as the other, as indefensible, and probably as fleeting.

3. In *College Savings Bank v. Florida Prepaid Postsecondary Education Expense Bd.*, 527 U.S. 666 (1999) (discussed *infra*), Justice Breyer in dissent (joined by Justices Stevens, Souter, and Ginsburg), elaborated on the dissenters' criticism in *Alden*:

> The similarity to *Lochner* lies in the risk that *Seminole Tribe* and the Court's subsequent cases will deprive Congress of necessary legislative flexibility. Their rules will make it more difficult for Congress to create, for example, a decentralized system of individual private remedies, say a private remedial system needed to protect intellectual property, including computer-related educational materials, irrespective of the need for, or importance of, such a system in a 21st-century advanced economy. Similarly, those rules will inhibit the creation of innovative legal regimes, say, incentive-based or decentralized regulatory systems, that deliberately take account of local differences by assigning roles, powers, or responsibility, not just to federal administrators, but to citizens, at least if such a regime must incorporate a private remedy against a State (*e.g.*, a State as water polluter) to work effectively. Yet, ironically, Congress needs this kind of flexibility if it is to achieve one of federalism's basic objectives. . . .

> [Our Nation's changing federalist] doctrines reflect at least one unchanging goal: the protection of liberty. Federalism helps to protect liberty not simply in our modern sense of helping the individual remain free of restraints imposed by a distant government, but more directly by promoting the

---

36. The Court also claims that subjecting States to suit puts power in the hands of state courts that the State may wish to assign to its legislature, thus assigning the state judiciary a role "foreign to its experience but beyond its competence. . . ." This comes perilously close to legitimizing political defiance of valid federal law.

sharing among citizens of governmental decisionmaking authority. The ancient world understood the need to divide sovereign power among a nation's citizens, thereby creating government in which all would exercise that power; and they called "free" the citizens who exercised that power so divided. Our Nation's Founders understood the same, for they wrote a Constitution that divided governmental authority, that retained great power at state and local levels, and which foresaw, indeed assumed, democratic citizen participation in government at all levels, including levels that facilitated citizen participation closer to a citizen's home.

In today's world, legislative flexibility is necessary if we are to protect this kind of liberty. Modern commerce and the technology upon which it rests need large markets and seek government large enough to secure trading rules that permit industry to compete in the global marketplace, to prevent pollution that crosses borders, and to assure adequate protection of health and safety by discouraging a regulatory "race to the bottom." Yet local control over local decisions remains necessary. Uniform regulatory decisions about, for example, chemical waste disposal, pesticides, or food labeling, will directly affect daily life in every locality. But they may reflect differing views among localities about the relative importance of the wage levels or environmental preferences that underlie them. Local control can take account of such concerns and help to maintain a sense of community despite global forces that threaten it. Federalism matters to ordinary citizens seeking to maintain a degree of control, a sense of community, in an increasingly interrelated and complex world.

Note: Congressional Abrogation of State Sovereign Immunity After Seminole Tribe and Alden

Seminole Tribe holds that Congress cannot use its Article I commerce clause (or Indian commerce clause) powers to abrogate the states' sovereign immunity in federal court; *Alden* extends that holding to lawsuits brought in state court. The opinion leaves intact, however, Congress's power to subject the states to suits under section 5 of the Fourteenth Amendment. Congress had passed many statutes in which it had clearly expressed its intent to abrogate the states' immunity before *Seminole Tribe* and *Alden* were decided. Since *Seminole Tribe*, the federal courts have repeatedly been asked to determine whether an attempted congressional abrogation is valid. All such questions begin by asking whether Congress has clearly expressed its intent to subject the states to damages. If so, the answer to whether it has effectively done so depends first on identifying the constitutional authority for abrogation on which Congress relied.

A. Abrogation Under Article I

1. After *Seminole Tribe*, numerous circuits held that no Article I power gives Congress the authority to abrogate state sovereign immunity. For example, the Seventh Circuit declared: "The unequivocal language of these cases demonstrates that the Supreme Court's holding in *Seminole Tribe* was not limited to Article I's Indian Commerce Clause, but applies equally to Congress' attempt to abrogate sovereign immunity under any other Article I legislative power." *Nelson v. LaCrosse County District Attorney*, 301 F.3d 820 (7th Cir. 2002).

For the most part, this broad reading of *Seminole Tribe* has been vindicated by the Supreme Court. Thus, in *Florida Prepaid Postsecondary Education Expense Bd. v. College Savings Bank*, 527 U.S. 627 (1999), the Court stated that *Seminole Tribe* "makes clear that Congress may not abrogate state sovereign immunity pursuant to its Article I powers." The Court went on to hold that neither the Patent Clause, Art. I, § 8, cl. 8 nor the Commerce Clause, Art. I, § 8, cl. 3 provided authorization for the abrogation at issue in that case.

2. Notwithstanding statements such as the one just quoted, different majorities of the Supreme Court have avoided *Seminole Tribe*'s application to bankruptcy proceedings without relying on the concept of Congressional abrogation. Article I, § 8, cl. 4, of the Constitution provides that Congress shall have the power "[t]o establish uniform Laws on the subject of Bankruptcies throughout the United States." In *Tennessee Student Assistance Corp. v. Hood*, 541 U.S. 440 (2004), the Court granted certiorari to determine whether Congress had the authority under the Bankruptcy Clause to abrogate state sovereign immunity. When the case was decided, however, the Court, in an opinion authored by Chief Justice Rehnquist, avoided the question, holding instead that a debtor's action in federal bankruptcy court to discharge her debts is an *in rem* proceeding to which the Eleventh Amendment does not apply. Justice Thomas, joined by Justice Scalia, dissented.

In *Central Virginia Community College v. Katz*, 546 U.S. 356 (2006), a more closely divided Court held that the state could not assert sovereign immunity to resist a bankruptcy trustee's efforts to set aside a debtor's preferential transfers to state agencies. The majority opinion, by Justice Stevens, extended *Hood*'s rationale to "orders ancillary to the bankruptcy courts' *in rem* jurisdiction, like orders directing turnover of preferential transfers." The majority noted the text of the Bankruptcy Clause, which specifically authorizes Congress to establish *uniform* laws, although the Court chose "not to rest [its] analysis on the peculiar text of the Bankruptcy Clause as compared to other clauses of Article I." More importantly, after an extensive review of the history of bankruptcy and the imperatives of national uniformity in the area, the majority found that to the extent such orders "implicate States' sovereign immunity from suit, the States agreed in the plan of the Convention not to assert that immunity. So much is evidenced not only by the history of the Bankruptcy Clause, which shows that the Framers' primary goal was to prevent competing sovereigns' interference with the debtor's discharge . . . but also by legislation considered and enacted in the immediate wake of the Constitution's ratification." The opinion continued:

> The scope of this consent was limited; the jurisdiction exercised in bankruptcy proceedings was chiefly *in rem* —a narrow jurisdiction that does not implicate state sovereignty to nearly the same degree as other kinds of jurisdiction. But while the principal focus of the bankruptcy proceedings is and was always the res, some exercises of bankruptcy courts' powers—issuance of writs of habeas corpus included—unquestionably involved more than

mere adjudication of rights in a res. In ratifying the Bankruptcy Clause, the States acquiesced in a subordination of whatever sovereign immunity they might otherwise have asserted in proceedings necessary to effectuate the in rem jurisdiction of the bankruptcy courts. . . .

The relevant question is not whether Congress has "abrogated" States' immunity in proceedings to recover preferential transfers. The question, rather, is whether Congress' determination that States should be amenable to such proceedings is within the scope of its power to enact "Laws on the subject of Bankruptcies." We think it beyond peradventure that it is.

Congress may, at its option, either treat States in the same way as other creditors insofar as concerns "Laws on the subject of Bankruptcies" or exempt them from operation of such laws. Its power to do so arises from the Bankruptcy Clause itself; the relevant "abrogation" is the one effected in the plan of the Convention, not by statute.

Justice Thomas, joined by Chief Justice Roberts and Justices Scalia and Kennedy, dissented. He wrote:

The majority maintains that the States' consent to suit can be ascertained from the history of the Bankruptcy Clause. But history confirms that the adoption of the Constitution merely established federal power to legislate in the area of bankruptcy law, and did not manifest an additional intention to waive the States' sovereign immunity against suit. . . .

The majority finds a surrender of the States' immunity from suit in Article I of the Constitution, which authorizes Congress "[t]o establish . . . uniform Laws on the subject of Bankruptcies throughout the United States." § 8, cl. 4. But nothing in the text of the Bankruptcy Clause suggests an abrogation or limitation of the States' sovereign immunity. Indeed, as this Court has noted on numerous occasions, "[t]he Eleventh Amendment restricts the judicial power under Article III, and Article I cannot be used to circumvent the constitutional limitations placed upon federal jurisdiction." *Seminole Tribe.*

In contending that the States waived their immunity from suit by adopting the Bankruptcy Clause, the majority conflates two distinct attributes of sovereignty: the authority of a sovereign to enact legislation regulating its own citizens, and sovereign immunity against suit by private citizens. Nothing in the history of the Bankruptcy Clause suggests that, by including that clause in Article I, the founding generation intended to waive the latter aspect of sovereignty. These two attributes of sovereignty often do not run together—and for purposes of enacting a uniform law of bankruptcy, they need not run together.

For example, Article I also empowers Congress to regulate interstate commerce and to protect copyrights and patents. These provisions, no less than the Bankruptcy Clause, were motivated by the Framers' desire for nationally uniform legislation. Thus, we have recognized that "[t]he need for uniformity in the construction of patent law is undoubtedly important." *Florida Prepaid.*

Nonetheless, we have refused, in addressing patent law, to give the need for uniformity the weight the majority today assigns it in the context of bankruptcy, instead recognizing that this need "is a factor which belongs to the Article I patent-power calculus, rather than to any determination of whether a state plea of sovereign immunity deprives a patentee of property without due process of law."

3. The plurality decision in *Pennsylvania v. Union Gas*, overruled by *Seminole Tribe*, also relied on the "plan of the convention" in finding that the Congress could use its Article I commerce clause power to abrogate immunity:

> We have recognized that the States enjoy no immunity where there has been "'a surrender of this immunity in the plan of the convention.'" *Monaco v. Mississippi*, 292 U.S. 313 (1934), quoting *The Federalist No. 81* (H. Dawson ed., 1876) (A. Hamilton). Because the Commerce Clause withholds power from the States at the same time as it confers it on Congress, and because the congressional power thus conferred would be incomplete without the authority to render States liable in damages, it must be that, to the extent that the States gave Congress the authority to regulate commerce, they also relinquished their immunity where Congress found it necessary, in exercising this authority, to render them liable. The States held liable under such a congressional enactment are thus not "unconsenting"; they gave their consent all at once, in ratifying the Constitution containing the Commerce Clause, rather than on a case-by-case basis.

The plurality in *Union Gas* also relied on the "breadth and depth" of the commerce power and the fact that it limited "state authority even where Congress has chosen not to act."

How does the reasoning in *Katz* differ from *Union Gas*? Or is *Katz* simply the revenge of the *Seminole Tribe* dissenters? If so, why did Justice O'Connor join the majority in *Katz*?

4. The *Katz* majority also noted, "Of course, the Bankruptcy Clause, located as it is in Article I, is 'intimately connected' . . . with the Commerce Clause. That does not mean, however, that the state sovereign immunity implications of the Bankruptcy Clause necessarily mirror those of the Commerce Clause. Indeed, the Bankruptcy Clause's unique history, combined with the singular nature of bankruptcy courts' jurisdiction . . . have persuaded us that the ratification of the Bankruptcy Clause does represent a surrender by the States of their sovereign immunity in certain federal proceedings."

Does this language suggest that the sweeping language of earlier Article I abrogation decisions might have been premature? What other avenues for avoiding sovereign immunity might it suggest to Congress?

B. Abrogation Under the Fourteenth Amendment's Section 5

Seminole Tribe reaffirmed the Court's prior holding, in *Fitzpatrick v. Bitzer*, 427 U.S. 445 (1976), that Congress may abrogate state sovereign immunity as part of the proper exercise of its powers under §5 of the Fourteenth Amendment. In *Fitzpatrick* the Court went on to hold that Title VII of the Civil Rights Act of 1964 validly abrogated state sovereign immunity. The Court said:

> [W]e think that the Eleventh Amendment, and the principle of state sovereignty which it embodies, are necessarily limited by the enforcement provisions of §5 of the Fourteenth Amendment. In that section Congress is expressly granted authority to enforce "by appropriate legislation" the substantive provisions of the Fourteenth Amendment, which themselves embody significant limitations on state authority. When Congress acts pursuant to §5, not only is it exercising legislative authority that is plenary within the terms of the constitutional grant, it is exercising that authority under one section of a constitutional Amendment whose other sections by their own terms embody limitations on state authority. We think that Congress may, in determining what is "appropriate legislation" for the purpose of enforcing the provisions of the Fourteenth Amendment, provide for private suits against States or state officials which are constitutionally impermissible in other contexts. . . .

Not all legislation enacted pursuant to §5 of the Fourteenth Amendment has the effect of abrogating state sovereign immunity. To the contrary, the Court has adopted a "clear statement" rule requiring that any abrogation must be explicit to be effective. In *Dellmuth v. Muth*, 491 U.S. 223 (1989), the Court articulated that rule as a "simple but stringent test": "Congress may abrogate the States' constitutionally secured immunity from suit in federal court only by making its intention unmistakably clear in the language of the statute."

Nonetheless, Section 5's enforcement power is potentially quite broad. Recall that the Fourteenth Amendment is directed at the states, and includes not only the prohibitions within the Amendment's terms, such as due process, equal protection, and privileges and immunities, but also all of the Bill of Rights amendments that have been "incorporated" against the states, which include all the Bill of Rights except the Third, the Fifth Amendment's grand jury requirement, and the Seventh Amendment. Thus, the entire range of issues under the First, Second, Fourth, other parts of the Fifth, Sixth, and Eighth Amendments, such as freedom of speech, self-incrimination, confrontation of witnesses, and cruel and unusual punishment fall within the abrogation power.

What must Congress do to effectively abrogate state immunity under §5 of the Fourteenth Amendment? The Supreme Court established the basic framework for analysis of the constitutionality of all §5 legislation in *City of Boerne v. Flores*, 521 U.S. 507 (1997), a case that did not involve abrogation. First, Congress must be acting to enforce a recognized constitutional right—but that does not mean that Congress is limited to regulating conduct that is itself unconstitutional: "Legislation which deters or remedies constitutional violations can fall within the sweep of Congress' enforcement power even if in the process it prohibits conduct which is not itself unconstitutional and intrudes into legislative spheres of autonomy previously reserved to the States." Second, the remedy chosen must be adapted to the constitutional injury Congress has identified: "There must be a congruence and proportionality between the injury to be prevented or remedied and the means adopted to that end." Third, the injury to be prevented must be supported by an adequate Congressional record, in order to assess "[t]he appropriateness of remedial measures . . . in light of the evil presented."

The validity of legislation invoking § 5 is analyzed differently depending on whether the conduct Congress intends to reach independently violates the Amendment or whether Congress has instead prohibited conduct that is itself constitutional but that threatens to impinge on constitutional guarantees. The legislation at issue in *Nevada Dept. of Human Resources v. Hibbs*, 538 U.S. 721 (2003), presents a good example of the difference. The Equal Protection Clause prohibits intentional discrimination by states against members of so-called "suspect classes," but it does not prohibit, without more, state action that negatively affects members of suspect classes more severely than it affects others—i.e., "disparate impact." Gender is one such suspect class, and the Family and Medical Leave Act, 29 U.S.C. § 2601 *et seq.* (FMLA) "aims to protect the right to be free from gender-based discrimination in the workplace."

Hibbs involved the FMLA provision requiring employers to provide their employees with unpaid leave to care for ill family members. The question was whether Congress had validly abrogated state immunity when it created a private right of action that allowed state employees to recover money damages in the event of a state's failure to comply with the family care provision. The Court upheld Congress's exercise of its § 5 power, even though, as the Court later acknowledged, "there was no suggestion that the State's leave policy was adopted or applied with a discriminatory purpose that would render it unconstitutional under" the Court's previous Equal Protection jurisprudence. Thus, while under *City of Boerne* Congress has no independent power "to decree the substance of the Fourteenth Amendment's restrictions on the States"—that is, to expand the definition of the Constitution—it may sometimes use its § 5 power to proscribe conduct that would be constitutional and otherwise lawful. As the Court added in *Hibbs*: "In other words, Congress may enact so-called prophylactic legislation that proscribes facially constitutional conduct, in order to prevent and deter unconstitutional conduct."

In other cases, however, the Court has struck down attempts to abrogate state sovereign immunity, holding that Congress exceeded its underlying power under § 5. *See, e.g., Coleman v. Court of Appeals of Maryland*, 132 S. Ct. 1327 (2012) (funding a different section of Family and Medical Leave Act not a valid abrogation); *Kimel v. Florida Board of Regents*, 528 U.S. 62 (2000) (Title I of Age Discrimination in Employment Act not valid § 5 legislation; abrogation invalid); *Florida Prepaid Secondary Expense Board v. College Savings Bank*, 527 U.S. 627 (1999) (Patent Act not valid § 5 legislation; abrogation invalid).

C. Conclusion: A "Curious" Resting Place?

Remember that all of the cases discussed in this section are concerned with whether the states can be sued for damages, not with the underlying validity or constitutionality of the substantive statutes. Every statute found improper as an exercise of Congressional power under § 5 could likely be sustained as proper exercise of Congress's

Article I powers. Thus, the substantive commands of the statutes (like those of the FLSA in *Alden*) still apply to the states. However, private parties are forbidden to enforce them through lawsuits against a state for money damages.

Not long after *Seminole Tribe*, one scholar suggested that "a freedom from unconsented federal court suit by private individuals seeking retrospective relief—and then only if the statute cannot be viewed as enforcing one of the Reconstruction amendments—is a curious and unstable place for the last stand of state sovereignty." Daniel J. Meltzer, *State Sovereign Immunity: Five Authors in Search of a Theory*, 75 Notre Dame L. Rev. 1011 (2000). Do you agree? Why might states be especially concerned about having to face damage suits by private individuals, as compared with other methods for enforcing federal statutory duties? Is there something different about the Fourteenth Amendment?

D. Consent and Waiver by the State

The Supreme Court has often referred to state sovereign immunity as jurisdictional. For example, in *Edelman v. Jordan*, the Court said: "Eleventh Amendment defense sufficiently partakes of the nature of a jurisdictional bar so that it need not be raised in the trial court."[1] But if this is so, immunity shares aspects of both personal and subject-matter jurisdiction. As with subject-matter jurisdiction, a claim that a lawsuit is barred by sovereign immunity can be raised at any time, even on appeal. But like personal jurisdiction, the defense of sovereign immunity can be waived, and a state defendant can consent to jurisdiction. We look briefly at the doctrines of waiver and consent.

Note: State Consent and State Waiver of Immunity

1. In *College Savings Bank v. Florida Prepaid Postsecondary Education Expense Bd.*, 527 U.S. 666 (1999), the Court discussed the circumstances that would lead to a determination that the state had waived its immunity:

> We have long recognized that a State's sovereign immunity is "a personal privilege which it may waive at pleasure." *Clark v. Barnard*, 108 U.S. 436 (1883). The decision to waive that immunity, however, "is altogether voluntary on the part of the sovereignty." *Beers v. Arkansas*, 20 How. 527 (1858). Accordingly, our "test for determining whether a State has waived its immunity from federal-court jurisdiction is a stringent one." *Atascadero State Hospital v. Scanlon*, 473 U.S. 234 (1985). Generally, we will find a waiver either if the State voluntarily invokes our jurisdiction, *Gunter v. Atlantic Coast Line R. Co.*, 200 U.S. 273 (1906), or else if the State makes a "clear declaration" that it intends to submit itself to our jurisdiction, *Great Northern Life Ins. Co. v. Read*, 322 U.S.

---

1. Most recently, the Court retreated from the jurisdictional language of previous opinions: "The Amendment . . . enacts a sovereign immunity from suit, rather than a nonwaivable limit on the Federal Judiciary's subject-matter jurisdiction." *Idaho v. Coeur d'Alene Tribe of Idaho*, 521 U.S. 261 (1997).

47 (1944). See also *Pennhurst State School and Hospital v. Halderman*, 465 U.S. 89 (1984) (State's consent to suit must be "unequivocally expressed"). Thus, a State does not consent to suit in federal court merely by consenting to suit in the courts of its own creation. *Smith v. Reeves*, 178 U.S. 436 (1900). Nor does it consent to suit in federal court merely by stating its intention to "sue and be sued," *Florida Dept. of Health and Rehabilitative Servs. v. Florida Nursing Home Assn.*, 450 U.S. 147 (1981) (*per curiam*), or even by authorizing suits against it "'in any court of competent jurisdiction,'" *Kennecott Copper Corp. v. State Tax Comm'n*, 327 U.S. 573 (1946). We have even held that a State may, absent any contractual commitment to the contrary, alter the conditions of its waiver and apply those changes to a pending suit.

2. Waiver may occur through the state's litigation conduct. In *Lapides v. Board of Regents of the University System of Georgia*, 535 U.S. 613 (2002), the Supreme Court unanimously held that a state waives its sovereign immunity by voluntarily removing a case to federal court:

> It would seem anomalous or inconsistent for a State both (1) invoke federal jurisdiction, thereby contending that the "Judicial power of the United States" extends to the case at hand, and (2) to claim Eleventh Amendment immunity, thereby denying that the "Judicial power of the United States" extends to the case at hand. And a Constitution that permitted States to follow their litigation interests by freely asserting both claims in the same case could generate seriously unfair results.

What unfair results is the Court anticipating?

3. A state can, then, consent to federal jurisdiction (through voluntarily invoking the jurisdiction of the federal court, for instance), or explicitly waive its immunity to federal suit (through a state statutory provision, for instance). May a federal court find that the state has *constructively* waived its immunity to federal court suit? Justice Marshall argued as much in dissent in *Edelman*, where Illinois had agreed to participate in a federal-state cooperative program. But the Supreme Court has consistently held that it will not construe the state's non-litigation activities as the constructive waiver of its immunity to suit. In *College Savings*, for instance, a federal statute — the Lanham Act — purported to subject the states to lawsuits for engaging in false and misleading advertising. Florida had marketed a college tuition prepayment program; the plaintiff, a competitor, argued that in doing so, Florida had misrepresented its program in a manner that violated the Lanham Act. The plaintiff brought a damages action under the Act. The Court found Congress's attempted abrogation of immunity invalid, whether it was viewed through the lens of Article I's Commerce Clause power or the Fourteenth Amendment's section 5 power.

Florida had neither consented to jurisdiction nor explicitly waived immunity. But the plaintiff argued that Florida had constructively waived its immunity through engaging in voluntary conduct regulated by the Lanham Act with clear notice that Congress intended to subject states' violations of the Act to federal lawsuits. The Court, in an opinion by Justice Scalia, rejected the argument, noting that the concept of constructive waiver was "simply unheard of in the context of *other* constitutionally-protected principles":

> Recognizing a congressional power to exact constructive waivers of sovereign immunity through the exercise of Article I powers would . . . as a practical matter permit Congress to circumvent the antiabrogation holding of *Seminole Tribe*. Forced waiver and abrogation are not even different sides of the same coin—they are the same side of the same coin.

4. The Court in *College Savings* did find "fundamentally different" Congress's use of its Article I Spending Clause powers to disburse funds to the states; "such funds are gifts." However, in *Sossamon v. Texas*, 563 U.S. 277 (2011), the Court stated that it would not assume the availability of a damages remedy against states every time Congress enacts legislation pursuant to the Spending Clause.

The action in *Sossamon* arose under the Religious Land Use and Institutionalized Persons Act (RLUIPA), which granted heightened statutory protection to religious exercise and included an "express private cause of action that is taken from RFRA: 'A person may assert a violation of [RLUIPA] as a claim or defense in a judicial proceeding and obtain appropriate relief against a government,'" including, specifically, states, counties, municipalities, and their officers. The Act expressly limited the United States to seeking only injunctive or declaratory relief.

The majority opinion by Justice Thomas found that the term "appropriate relief" did not "so clearly and unambiguously waive sovereign immunity to private suits for damages that we can be certain that the State in fact consents to such a suit." Justice Thomas noted that the word "appropriate" is "inherently context-dependent, [and] the context here—where the defendant is a sovereign—suggests, if anything, that monetary damages are not suitable or proper." Nor was the narrower language that applied to the United States, as opposed to private litigants, instructive. Since "the State has no immunity defense to a suit brought by the Federal Government, Congress needed to exclude damages affirmatively in that context but not in the context of private suits."

Having found that the statute failed the clear-statement rule, the Court then rejected a rule that would generally assume the availability of a damages remedy against states for violations of Spending clause legislation:

> It would be bizarre to create an "unequivocal statement" rule and then find that every Spending Clause enactment, no matter what its text, satisfies that rule because it includes unexpressed, implied remedies against the States. The requirement of a clear statement in the text of the statute ensures that Congress has specifically considered state sovereign immunity and has intentionally legislated on the matter.

In Section E, we will explore what conditions Congress would have to meet to use the Spending Clause as a source of power to exact agreement from States to be subject to damages liability in exchange for the "gift" of federal funds.

E. The Future of the Immunity

[1] Injunctive Relief: The Scope of the *Ex parte Young* Exception

One surprising aspect of *Seminole Tribe* was its treatment of the request for injunctive relief under *Ex parte Young*. *Seminole Tribe* refused to permit that relief because, in the Court's view, such relief might be incompatible with the "intricate procedures" Congress had adopted for enforcing the requirements of the statute at issue in that case. Presumably, Congress was free to reinstate the remedy authorized by *Ex parte Young* through clarifying its intentions.

Seminole Tribe was followed by *Idaho v. Coeur d'Alene Tribe of Idaho*, 521 U.S. 261 (1997), a case that many commentators believed signaled a significant shift in the Court's approach to injunctive relief. In that case, a divided Supreme Court held that the *Ex parte Young* doctrine did not authorize injunctive relief against state officials that would "diminish, even extinguish, the State's control over a vast reach of lands and waters long deemed by the State to be an integral part of its territory." Justice Kennedy announced the judgment of the Court. In an opinion joined only by Chief Justice Rehnquist, he suggested that the application of *Ex parte Young* should turn on a case-by-case analysis. This analysis would consider, among other things, the availability of relief in a state forum, the importance of the federal interest involved, whether there were especially sensitive sovereignty issues involved, and whether any "special factors counsel hesitation" in the exercise of jurisdiction. Justice O'Connor, joined by Justice Scalia and Justice Thomas, concurred in the result but not in the broader discussion of *Ex parte Young*. In her view, the relief the Tribe sought was indistinguishable from an action to quiet title, and might have resulted in divesting Idaho's control and title over significant lands. She therefore found *Ex parte Young* inapplicable. Justice Souter, joined by Justices Stevens, Breyer, and Ginsburg, dissented.

In 2002, in a case involving an alleged conflict between federal and state regulation of the telecommunications industry, the Supreme Court unanimously reaffirmed its traditional articulation of the doctrine: "In determining whether the doctrine of *Ex parte Young* avoids an Eleventh Amendment bar to suit, a court need only conduct a straightforward inquiry into whether the complaint alleges an ongoing violation of federal law and seeks relief properly characterized as prospective." *Verizon Md., Inc. v. Pub. Serv. Comm'n*, 535 U.S. 635 (2002). Nine years later, however, the unanimity disappeared, and the Justices engaged in a three-cornered debate over the "straightforward inquiry" suggested by *Verizon Md*.

Virginia Office for Protection and Advocacy v. Stewart

Supreme Court of the United States, 2011.

563 U.S. 247.

JUSTICE SCALIA delivered the opinion of the Court.

We consider whether *Ex parte Young*, 209 U.S. 123 (1908), allows a federal court to hear a lawsuit for prospective relief against state officials brought by another agency of the same State.

I

A

The Developmental Disabilities Assistance and Bill of Rights Act of 2000 (DD Act), 42 U.S.C. § 15001 *et seq.*, offers States federal money to improve community services, such as medical care and job training, for individuals with developmental disabilities. As a condition of that funding, a State must establish a protection and advocacy (P & A) system "to protect and advocate the rights of individuals with developmental disabilities." . . . The P & A system receives separate federal funds, paid to it directly. A second federal law, the Protection and Advocacy for Individuals with Mental Illness Act (PAIMI Act), 42 U.S.C. § 10801 *et seq.*, increases that separate funding and extends the mission of P & A systems to include the mentally ill. At present, every State accepts funds under these statutes.

Under the DD and PAIMI Acts, a P & A system must have certain powers. The system "shall . . . have the authority to investigate incidents of abuse and neglect . . . if the incidents are reported to the system or if there is probable cause to believe that the incidents occurred." Subject to certain statutory requirements, it must be given access to "all records" of individuals who may have been abused, as well as "other records that are relevant to conducting an investigation." The Acts also require that a P & A system have authority to "pursue legal, administrative, and other appropriate remedies or approaches to ensure the protection of" its charges. And in addition to pressing its own rights, a P & A system may "pursue administrative, legal, and other remedies on behalf of" those it protects.

A participating State is free to appoint either a state agency or a private nonprofit entity as its P & A system. But in either case, the designated entity must have certain structural features that ensure its independence from the State's government. The DD Act prohibits the Governor from appointing more than one-third of the members of the system's governing board, and restricts the State's ability to impose hiring freezes or other measures that would impair the system's ability to carry out its mission. Once a State designates an entity as its P & A system, it may not change its selection without "good cause."

Virginia is one of just eight States that have designated a government entity as their P & A system. The Virginia Office for Protection and Advocacy (VOPA) is an "independent state agency." Its board consists of eleven "nonlegislative citizen members," of whom only three are appointed by the Governor. The remaining eight are appointed by components of the legislature: five by the Speaker of the House of Delegates, and three by the Senate Committee on Rules. VOPA itself nominates candidates for consideration, and the statute instructs the appointing officials that they "shall seriously consider the persons nominated and appoint such persons whenever feasible." Board members serve for fixed terms and are removable only by a court and only for specified reasons.

VOPA enjoys authority to litigate free of executive-branch oversight. It operates independently of the Attorney General of Virginia and employs its own lawyers, who are statutorily authorized to sue on VOPA's behalf. And Virginia law specifically empowers VOPA to "initiate any proceedings to secure the rights" of disabled individuals.

B

In 2006, VOPA opened an investigation into the deaths of two patients and injuries to a third at state-run mental hospitals. It asked respondents—state officials in charge of those institutions—to produce any records related to risk-management or mortality reviews conducted by the hospitals with respect to those patients. Respondents refused, asserting that the records were protected by a state-law privilege shielding medical peer-review materials from disclosure.

VOPA then brought this action in the United States District Court for the Eastern District of Virginia, alleging that the DD and PAIMI Acts entitled it to the peer-review records, notwithstanding any state-law privilege that might apply. It sought a declaration that respondents' refusal to produce the records violated the DD and PAIMI Acts, along with an injunction requiring respondents to provide access to the records and refrain in the future from interfering with VOPA's right of access to them. Respondents moved to dismiss the action on the grounds that they are immune from suit under the Eleventh Amendment. The District Court denied the motion. In its view, the suit was permitted by the doctrine of *Ex parte Young*, which normally allows federal courts to award prospective relief against state officials for violations of federal law.

The Court of Appeals reversed. Believing VOPA's lawsuit to be an "intramural contest" that "encroaches more severely on the dignity and sovereignty of the states than an *Ex parte Young* action brought by a private plaintiff," the Court of Appeals concluded it was not authorized by that case.

We granted certiorari.

II

[In Parts A and B, Justice Scalia reviewed the history of *Ex parte Young*.]

C

This case requires us to decide how to apply the *Ex parte Young* doctrine to a suit brought by an independent state agency claiming to possess federal rights. Although we have never encountered such a suit before, we are satisfied that entertaining VOPA's action is consistent with our precedents and does not offend the distinctive interests protected by sovereign immunity.

1

In *Verizon Md. Inc. v. Public Serv. Comm'n of Md.*, 535 U.S. 635 (2002), we held that "[i]n determining whether the doctrine of *Ex parte Young* avoids an Eleventh Amendment bar to suit, a court need only conduct a 'straightforward inquiry into whether [the] complaint alleges an ongoing violation of federal law and seeks relief properly characterized as prospective.'" There is no doubt VOPA's suit satisfies that straightforward inquiry. It alleges that respondents' refusal to produce the requested medical records violates federal law; and it seeks an injunction requiring the production of the records, which would prospectively abate the alleged violation. Respondents concede that were VOPA a private organization rather than a state agency, the doctrine would permit this action to proceed.[3]

We see no reason for a different result here. Although respondents argue that VOPA's status as a state agency changes the calculus, there is no warrant in our cases for making the validity of an *Ex parte Young* action turn on the identity of the plaintiff. To be sure, we have been willing to police abuses of the doctrine that threaten to evade sovereign immunity. To do otherwise "would be to adhere to an empty formalism." *Idaho v. Coeur d'Alene Tribe of Idaho*, 521 U.S. 261 (1997). But (as the dissent concedes) the limits we have recognized reflect the principle that the "general criterion for determining when a suit is in fact against the sovereign is the *effect* of the relief sought," *Pennhurst State School and Hospital v. Halderman*, 465 U.S. 89 (1984), not who is bringing the lawsuit. Thus, *Ex parte Young* cannot be used to obtain an injunction requiring the payment of funds from the State's treasury, or an order for specific performance of a State's contract.

Coeur d'Alene Tribe, on which respondents heavily rely, is an application of this principle. There we refused to allow an Indian Tribe to use *Ex parte Young* to obtain injunctive and declaratory relief establishing its exclusive right to the use and enjoyment of certain submerged lands in Idaho and the invalidity of all state statutes and regulations governing that land. We determined that the suit was "the functional equivalent of a quiet title suit against Idaho," would "extinguish . . . the State's control over a vast reach of lands and waters long deemed by the State to be an integral part of its territory," and thus was barred by sovereign immunity.

---

3. The dissent is mistaken when it claims that applying the *Verizon Maryland* test would mean two of our cases were "wrongly decided." We discuss the first of those cases, *Coeur d'Alene Tribe*, below. As for the second, *Seminole Tribe*, it is inapposite. The reason we refused to permit suit to proceed in that case was that the Indian Gaming Regulatory Act created an alternative remedial scheme that would be undermined by permitting *Ex parte Young* suits; Congress, we said, had foreclosed recourse to the doctrine.

Respondents now argue—for the first time in this litigation—that the DD and PAIMI Acts have the same effect here. We reject that suggestion. The fact that the Federal Government can exercise oversight of a federal spending program and even withhold or withdraw funds—which are the chief statutory features respondents point to—does not demonstrate that Congress has "displayed an intent not to provide the 'more complete and more immediate relief' that would otherwise be available under *Ex parte Young.*" *Verizon Maryland* (quoting *Seminole Tribe*).

Respondents have advanced no argument that the relief sought in this case threatens any similar invasion of Virginia's sovereignty. Indeed, they concede that the very injunction VOPA requests could properly be awarded by a federal court at the instance of a private P & A system.

2

Respondents and the dissent argue that entertaining VOPA's lawsuit in a federal forum would nevertheless infringe Virginia's sovereign interests because it diminishes the dignity of a State for a federal court to adjudicate a dispute between its components. We disagree. As an initial matter, we do not understand how a State's stature could be diminished to any greater degree when *its own agency* polices its officers' compliance with their federal obligations, than when *a private person* hales those officers into federal court for that same purpose—something everyone agrees is proper.[4] And in this case, of course, VOPA's power to sue state officials is a consequence of Virginia's own decision to establish a public, rather than a private, P & A system. We fail to perceive what Eleventh Amendment indignity is visited on the Commonwealth when, by operation of its own laws, VOPA is admitted to federal court as a plaintiff.[5]

But even if it were true that the State's dignity were offended in some way by the maintenance of this action in federal court, that would not prove respondents' case. Denial of sovereign immunity, to be sure, offends the dignity of a State; but not every offense to the dignity of a State constitutes a denial of sovereign immunity. The specific indignity against which sovereign immunity protects is the insult to a State of being haled into court without its consent. That effectively occurs, our cases reasonably conclude, when (for example) the object of the suit against a state officer is to reach funds in the state treasury or acquire state lands; it does not occur just because the suit happens to be brought by another state agency. Respondents' asserted dignitary harm is simply unconnected to the sovereign-immunity interest.

The dissent complains that applying *Ex parte Young* to this lawsuit divides Virginia against itself, since the opposing parties are both creatures of the Commonwealth. Even if that were a distinctive consequence of letting this suit proceed in federal court, it would have nothing to do with the concern of sovereign-immunity—whether the suit is against an unconsenting State, rather than against its officers. But it is *not* a consequence of the

---

4. The dissent compares VOPA's lawsuit to such indignities as "cannibalism" and "patricide," since it is a greater "affront to someone's dignity to be sued by a brother than to be sued by a stranger." We think the dissent's principle of familial affront less than universally applicable, even with respect to real families, never mind governmental siblings. Most of us would probably prefer contesting a testamentary disposition with a relative to contesting it with a stranger. And confining one's child to his room is called grounding, while confining a stranger's child is called kidnaping. Jurisdiction over this case does not depend on which is the most apt comparison.

5. The dissent accuses us of circular reasoning, because we "wrongly assum[e] [that] Virginia knew in advance the answer to the question presented in this case." That would be true if we were relying on the Commonwealth's waiver of sovereign immunity. We are not. We rely upon *Ex parte Young*. We say that Virginia has only itself to blame for the position in which it finds itself, not because it consented to suit, but because it created a state entity to sue, instead of leaving the task to a private entity. It did not have to know that this would allow suit in federal court. Know or not know, *Ex parte Young* produces that result.

federal nature of the forum. The same result will follow if the federal claim is sued upon in state court, as the dissent would require. There also, "[w]hatever the decision in the litigation, . . . [t]he Commonwealth will win[, a]nd the Commonwealth will lose." Nor would sending the matter to state court even avoid the prospect that "a federal judge will resolve which part of the Commonwealth will prevail," since the state-court loser could always ask *this* Court to review the matter by certiorari. (Or is that appeal also to be disallowed on grounds of sovereign immunity? But see *Cohens v. Virginia*, 19 U.S. 264 (1821).) And of course precisely the same thing would happen if respondents specifically waived their sovereign-immunity objections *in this very case*. Yet no one would contend that despite the waiver, sovereign immunity forbade the suit. So also here: If, by reason of *Ex parte Young*, there has been no violation of sovereign immunity, the prospect of a federal judge's resolving VOPA's dispute with respondents does not make it so.

We do not doubt, of course, that there are limits on the Federal Government's power to affect the internal operations of a State. But those limits must be found in some textual provision or structural premise of the Constitution. Additional limits cannot be smuggled in under the Eleventh Amendment by barring a suit in federal court that does not violate the State's sovereign immunity.[7]

3

A weightier objection, perhaps, is the relative novelty of this lawsuit. Respondents rightly observe that federal courts have not often encountered lawsuits brought by state agencies against other state officials. That does give us pause. Lack of historical precedent can indicate a constitutional infirmity, and our sovereign-immunity decisions have traditionally warned against "'anomalous and unheard-of proceedings or suits,'" *Alden v. Maine*, 527 U.S. 706 (1999) (quoting *Hans v. Louisiana*, 134 U.S. 1 (1890)).

Novelty, however, is often the consequence of past constitutional doubts, but we have no reason to believe that is the case here. In order to invoke the *Ex parte Young* exception to sovereign immunity, a state agency needs two things: first, a federal right that it possesses against its parent State; and second, authority to sue other state officials to enforce that right, free from any internal veto wielded by the state government. These conditions will rarely coincide—and at least the latter of them cannot exist without the consent of the State that created the agency and defined its powers. We are unaware that the necessary conditions have ever presented themselves except in connection with the DD and PAIMI Acts, and the parties have referred us to no examples.[8] Thus, the apparent novelty of this sort of suit does not at all suggest its unconstitutionality. In any event, we are satisfied, for the reasons we have explained,

---

7. We have no occasion to pass on other questions of federalism lurking in this case, such as whether the DD or PAIMI Acts are a proper exercise of Congress's enumerated powers. As Justice Kennedy observes, whether the Acts run afoul of some *other* constitutional provision (*i.e.*, besides the Eleventh Amendment) "cannot be permitted to distort the antecedent question of jurisdiction."

8. We think greatly exaggerated the dissent's concern that, "[g]iven the number of state agencies across the country that enjoy independent litigating authority," today's decision "could potentially lead to all sorts of litigation in federal courts addressing internal state government disputes." Such litigation cannot occur unless the state agency has been given a federal right of its own to vindicate (as VOPA alleges it has been given under the highly unusual statute at issue here).

that—novelty notwithstanding—the principles undergirding the *Ex parte Young* doctrine support its application to actions of this kind.

* * *

Like the Court of Appeals, we are mindful of the central role autonomous States play in our federal system, and wary of approving new encroachments on their sovereignty. But we conclude no such encroachment is occasioned by straightforwardly applying *Ex parte Young* to allow this suit. It was Virginia law that created VOPA and gave it the power to sue state officials. In that circumstance, the Eleventh Amendment presents no obstacle to VOPA's ability to invoke federal jurisdiction on the same terms as any other litigant.

We reverse the judgment of the Court of Appeals and remand the case for further proceedings consistent with this opinion.

Justice Kagan took no part in the consideration or decision of this case.

Justice Kennedy, with whom Justice Thomas joins, concurring.

Ex parte Young recognized a narrow limitation on state sovereign immunity, permitting railroad stockholders to enjoin enforcement of unconstitutional rate regulations. That negative injunction was nothing more than the pre-emptive assertion in equity of a defense that would otherwise have been available in the State's enforcement proceedings at law.

The Court has expanded the *Ex parte Young* exception far beyond its original office in order "to vindicate the federal interest in assuring the supremacy of [federal] law," *Green v. Mansour*, 474 U.S. 64 (1985), but not without careful attention in each case to the sovereign interests of the State. See *Verizon Md.* (Kennedy, J., concurring). In *Edelman v. Jordan*, 415 U.S. 651 (1974), for example, the Court applied the exception to an affirmative prospective order but not to equitable restitution, for the latter was too similar to an award of damages against the State. And *Pennhurst* declined to extend *Ex parte Young* to suits alleging a state-law violation, for without the need to ensure the supremacy of federal law there was no justification for restricting state sovereignty.

The "straightforward inquiry" of *Verizon Md.* derives from *Edelman* and *Pennhurst*, both of which defined important limits on *Ex parte Young* in order to respect state sovereignty while still adhering to principles necessary to implement the Supremacy Clause. As a result, *Verizon Md.* incorporates the very balancing it might at first seem to reject. *Verizon Md.* itself was an easy case, for it involved the same kind of preenforcement assertion of a defense that was at issue in *Ex parte Young*. But when *Ex parte Young*'s application is explored in novel contexts, as in *Coeur d'Alene Tribe*, and also in this case, the inquiry "proves more complex," *Verizon Md.* (Kennedy, J., concurring).

In this case, in my view, the Virginia Office for Protection and Advocacy may rely on *Ex parte Young*, despite the somewhat striking novelty of permitting a state agency to sue officials of the same State in federal court. In the posture of the case as it comes before the Court, it must be assumed that VOPA has a federal right to the records it seeks, and so the extension of *Ex parte Young* would vindicate the Supremacy Clause. To be balanced against this important interest is the need to preserve "the dignity and respect afforded a State, which the immunity is designed to protect." *Coeur d'Alene Tribe.* Permitting a state agency like VOPA to sue officials of the same State does implicate the State's important sovereign interest in using its own courts to control the distribution of power among its own agents. But the affront to the State's dignity is diminished to some extent when it is noted that if the State had elected the alternate course of designating a private protection and advocacy system it then would have avoided any risk of internal conflict while still participating in the federal program. The availability of that alternate course does not, in my view, weigh much in favor of the validity of the underlying federal scheme, but the only question here is the reach of the *Ex parte Young* exception.

Virginia's concern that the holding here upsets the federal balance is further mitigated by the various protections built into the structure of federal litigation to ensure that state officials do not too often call upon the federal courts to resolve their intramural disputes. . . .

All this is simply to underscore that the program at issue may present constitutional questions but that the parties do not raise them in this litigation. . . . Assuming, as the Court must, that the statutes here are constitutional, the narrow question is whether VOPA may rely on *Ex parte Young* to avoid the sovereign immunity bar. . . .

With these observations, I join the Court's opinion.

Chief Justice Roberts, with whom Justice Alito joins, dissenting.

Today the Court holds that a state agency may sue officials acting on behalf of the State in federal court. This has never happened before. In order to reach this unsettling result, the Court extends the fiction of *Ex parte Young* — what we have called an "empty formalism" — well beyond the circumstances of that case. Because I cannot subscribe to such a substantial and novel expansion of what we have also called "a narrow exception" to a State's sovereign immunity, I respectfully dissent.

I

A

"The federal system established by our Constitution preserves the sovereign status of the States." *Alden v. Maine,* 527 U.S. 706 (1999). As confirmed by the Eleventh Amendment, "[a]n integral component of that residuary and inviolable sovereignty" is the States' "immunity from private suits. . . ."

Because of the key role state sovereign immunity plays in our federal system, the Court has recognized only a few exceptions to that immunity. The sole one relevant here is the "narrow exception," *Seminole Tribe of Fla. v. Florida,* 517 U.S. 44 (1996), established by our decision in *Ex parte Young.* In *Ex parte Young,* the Court held that private litigants could seek an injunction in federal court against a state official, prohibiting him from enforcing a state law claimed to violate the Federal Constitution. . . .

While we have consistently acknowledged the important role *Ex parte Young* plays in "promot[ing] the vindication of federal rights," we have been cautious not to give that decision "an expansive interpretation." *Pennhurst.* Indeed, the history of our *Ex parte Young* jurisprudence has largely been focused on ensuring that this narrow exception is "narrowly construed." We have, for example, held that the fiction of *Ex parte Young* does not extend to suits where the plaintiff seeks retroactive relief, *Edelman*, where the claimed violations are based on state law, *Pennhurst*, where the federal law violation is no longer "ongoing," *Green v. Mansour*, "where Congress has prescribed a detailed remedial scheme for the enforcement against a State" of the claimed federal right, *Seminole Tribe*, and where "special sovereignty interests" are implicated, *Coeur d'Alene Tribe*.

We recently stated that when "determining whether the doctrine of *Ex parte Young* avoids an Eleventh Amendment bar to suit, a court need only conduct a straightforward inquiry into whether [the] complaint alleges an ongoing violation of federal law and seeks relief properly characterized as prospective." *Verizon Md.* But not every plaintiff who complies with these prerequisites will be able to bring suit under *Ex parte Young*. . . .

If *Verizon*'s formulation set forth the only requirements for bringing an action under *Ex parte Young*, two of our recent precedents were wrongly decided. In *Seminole Tribe*, the Court acknowledged that it had often "found federal jurisdiction over a suit against a state official when that suit seeks only prospective injunctive relief in order to end a continuing violation of federal law." The Court held, however, that the "situation presented" there was "sufficiently different from that giving rise to the traditional *Ex parte Young* action so as to preclude the availability of that doctrine."[2]

In *Coeur d'Alene Tribe*, the Court recognized that an "allegation of an ongoing violation of federal law where the requested relief is prospective is *ordinarily* sufficient to invoke the *Ex parte Young* fiction." The Court held, however, that the action could not proceed under *Ex parte Young* because it implicated "special sovereignty interests"— in that case, the State's property rights in certain submerged lands.

As we explained in *Papasan v. Allain*, 478 U.S. 265 (1986), there are "certain types of cases that formally meet the *Ex parte Young* requirements of a state official acting inconsistently with federal law but that stretch that case too far and would upset the balance of federal and state interests that it embodies." This is one of those cases. . . .

B

It is undisputed that petitioner's complaint alleges an ongoing violation of federal law by a state official and seeks only prospective relief. If this were a "traditional *Ex parte Young* action," petitioner might very well be able to pursue its claims under that case. This, however, is anything but a traditional case—and petitioner is anything but a typical *Ex parte Young* plaintiff.

---

2. While I agree that in *Seminole Tribe* "we refused to permit suit to proceed" under *Ex parte Young* because Congress "had foreclosed recourse to the doctrine," that simply confirms my point that the availability of *Ex parte Young* depends on more than just whether *Verizon*'s prescribed inquiry is satisfied. In short, *Seminole Tribe* makes clear that a plaintiff who files a "complaint alleg[ing] an ongoing violation of federal law and seeks relief properly characterized as prospective," *Verizon*, may nonetheless be barred from pursuing an action under *Ex parte Young*.

Unlike the plaintiffs in *Ex parte Young*—and, for that matter, unlike any other plaintiff that has ever sought to invoke *Ex parte Young* before this Court—petitioner is a state agency seeking to sue officials of the same State in federal court. The Court is troubled by this novelty, but not enough. This is especially true in light of the "presumption" we articulated more than 120 years ago in *Hans v. Louisiana* that States are immune from suits that would have been "anomalous and unheard of when the Constitution was adopted." . . .

In addition to its novel character, petitioner's complaint "conflicts directly with the principles of federalism that underlie the Eleventh Amendment." In *Alden*, we held that state sovereign immunity prohibited Congress from authorizing "private suits against nonconsenting States in their own courts." We explained that such power would permit one branch of state government, the "State's own courts," "to coerce the other branches of the State" and "to turn the State against itself."

Here the Court goes further: this suit features a state agency on one side, and state executive officials on the other. The objection in *Alden* was that the Federal Government could force the State to defend itself before itself. Here extending *Ex parte Young* forces the State to defend itself *against* itself in federal court.

Both sides in this case exercise the sovereign power of the Commonwealth of Virginia. Petitioner claims the title of "The Commonwealth of Virginia" in its complaint, respondents are state officials acting in an official capacity. Whatever the decision in the litigation, one thing is clear: The Commonwealth will win. And the Commonwealth will lose. Because of today's holding, a federal judge will resolve which part of the Commonwealth will prevail.

Virginia has not consented to such a suit in federal court; rather, petitioner has unilaterally determined that this intramural dispute should be resolved in that forum. This is precisely what sovereign immunity is supposed to guard against. That indignity is compounded when the State is haled into federal court so that a federal judge can decide an internal state dispute.

The Court is wrong to suggest that Virginia has no sovereign interest in determining *where* such disputes will be resolved. It is one thing for a State to decide that its components may sue one another in its own courts (as Virginia did here); it is quite another thing for such a dispute to be resolved in federal court against the State's wishes. For this reason, the Court's examples of other suits pitting state entities against one another are inapposite. In each of those hypotheticals, the State consented to having a particular forum resolve its internal conflict. That is not true here.

In sum, the "special sovereignty interests" implicated here make this case "sufficiently different from that giving rise to the traditional *Ex parte Young* action so as to preclude the availability of that doctrine." I would cling to reality and not extend the fiction of *Ex parte Young* to cover petitioner's suit.

II

. . . Contrary to the Court's suggestion, there is indeed a real difference between a suit against the State brought by a private party and one brought by a state agency. It is the difference between eating and cannibalism; between murder and patricide. While the ultimate results may be the same—a full stomach and a dead body—it is the means of getting there that attracts notice. I would think it more an affront to someone's dignity to be sued by a brother than to be sued by a stranger. While neither may be welcomed, that does not mean they would be equally received.

The Court also contends that petitioner's ability to sue state officials in federal court "is a consequence of Virginia's own decision to establish a public [protection and advocacy] system." This cannot mean that Virginia has consented to an infringement on its sovereignty. . . .

Instead the Court claims that "Virginia has only itself to blame"—if it wanted to avoid its current predicament, it could have chosen to establish a private entity instead. But I am aware of no doctrine to the effect that an unconstitutional establishment is insulated from challenge simply because a constitutional alternative is available. And here the public and private systems are not interchangeable alternatives in any event.

The Court's analysis is also circular; it wrongly assumes Virginia knew in advance the answer to the question presented in this case. Only after concluding that *Ex parte Young* applies to this arrangement—that for the first time in history a state agency may sue an unwilling State in federal court—can the Court suggest that Virginia knowingly exposed its officers to suit in federal court. . . .

The Court is wrong to suggest that simply because petitioner possesses independent litigating authority, it may sue state officials in federal court. There is more to this case than merely whether petitioner needs the approval of the Attorney General to sue, and the Virginia Code provisions cited by the Court say nothing about actions against the State in federal court.

If independent litigating authority is all that it takes, then scores of state entities now suddenly possess the authority to pursue *Ex parte Young* actions against other state officials in federal court. There would be no Eleventh Amendment impediment to such suits. Given the number of state agencies across the country that enjoy independent litigating authority, the Court's decision today could potentially lead to all sorts of litigation in federal courts addressing internal state government disputes.

And there is also no reason to think that the Court's holding is limited to state *agency* plaintiffs. According to the Court's basic rationale, state officials who enjoy some level of independence could as a matter of federal law bring suit against other state officials in federal court. Disputes that were formerly resolved in state cabinet rooms may now appear on the dockets of federal courts.

* * *

No one questions the continued vitality or importance of the doctrine announced in *Ex parte Young*. But *Ex parte Young* was about affording relief to a private party against unconstitutional state action. It was not about resolving a dispute between two different state actors. That is a matter for the State to sort out, not a federal judge. . . .

Because I believe the Court's novel expansion of *Ex parte Young* is inconsistent with the federal system established by our Constitution, I respectfully dissent.

Note: VOPA v. Stewart *and the Future of* Ex parte Young

1. This case features an unusual line-up of authoring Justices, particularly for a case involving sovereign immunity. Can you precisely articulate why Justices Scalia and Roberts disagree? Why Justice Kennedy (joined by Justice Thomas) writes separately? Is there some possibility that the sovereign immunity discussion is a stalking horse for a set of questions about the constitutionality of the underlying statutory schemes?

2. What is the nature of the disagreement between the majority and the dissent over the role of *Seminole Tribe* in analyzing *Ex parte Young*'s applicability? Whose role—Congress's or the Court's—is it to decide whether to displace this remedy? Or is the role a shared one? If so, in what circumstances?

3. The majority's description of sovereign immunity's role in protecting the states' dignity is precise and concrete:

> The specific indignity against which sovereign immunity protects is the insult to a State of being haled into court without its consent. That effectively occurs ... when (for example) the object of the suit against a state officer is to reach funds in the state treasury or acquire state lands. ...

The dissent's description of the nature of the state dignity interest imperiled by these federal statutes is visceral and metaphoric:

> [T]here is a real difference between a suit against the State brought by a private party and one brought by a state agency. It is the difference between eating and cannibalism; between murder and patricide. ... I would think it more an affront to someone's dignity to be sued by a brother than to be sued by a stranger.

What accounts for Justice Scalia's uncharacteristically mild defense of Virginia's dignity? Virginia's election of a public agency as opposed to a private one under the statute? What, if anything, prevents Virginia from simply changing its mind about that election? Would there be any point in doing so?

[2] Damages Actions and Congress's Spending Power

Seminole Tribe, *Alden*, and cases interpreting the scope of Congress's power under § 5 of the Fourteenth Amendment have severely constrained Congress's ability to subject states to private damages actions for violations of federal law. However, as already noted, the Court suggested in *College Savings* that "Congress may, in the exercise of its spending power, condition its grant of funds to the States upon their taking certain actions that Congress could not require them to take, and that acceptance of the funds entails an agreement to the actions."

At the same time, however, the Court reiterated in dictum that, at some point, "the financial inducement offered by Congress might be so coercive as to pass the point at which pressure turns into compulsion." *College Savings* (quoting *South Dakota v. Dole*, 483 U.S. 203 (1987)). Based on that description, lower courts have struggled to determine when Congress's offer of funding conditioned on a waiver of state sovereign immunity becomes unconstitutionally coercive. *Compare Garcia v. S.U.N.Y. Health Sciences Ctr. of Brooklyn*, 280 F.3d 98 (2d Cir. 2001) (holding that New York did not waive state sovereign immunity for claims under § 504 of the Rehabilitation Act of 1973, because it accepted funds before *Seminole Tribe*, believing that Congress had the power to abrogate state sovereign immunity under the Commerce Clause); *with Barbour v. Wash. Metro. Area Transit Auth.*, 374 F.3d 1161 (D.C. Cir. 2004) (finding that accepting funds under the Rehabilitation Act does waive state sovereign immunity, and that the condition is within Congress's power under the Spending Clause); *Jim C. v. Arkansas Dept. of Educ.*, 235 F.3d 1079 (8th Cir. 2000) (en banc) (reaching the same conclusion, and reasoning: "We do not consider such a choice unconstitutionally 'coercive.' The State may take the money or leave it.").

Why might it be "coercive" for Congress to offer money to States on the condition that they waive state sovereign immunity? Objections to the imposition of state monetary liability under federal statutes have two components. The first is the concern that the states will lose their ability to direct their funds (and thus assure they are responding to, and maintaining the loyalty of, their citizens) if they are required to compensate individual plaintiffs at the will of Congress. The second is that requiring the states to respond to private lawsuits injures their dignity interests as sovereigns. Does Congress's use of the Spending Power to abrogate immunity answer these objections? How does that use differ from abrogation under other Article I powers?

The cases looking at Congress's ability to subject states to lawsuits through the Spending Clause necessarily rely on their understanding of the reach of that power. The Supreme Court has not spoken frequently about the scope of Congress's Spending Clause power, but in *National Federation of Independent Business v. Sebelius*, 132 S. Ct. 2566 (2012), the Court took up the Spending Clause in the context of the Affordable Care Act (ACA) and, for the first time, found an exercise of the Spending Clause unconstitutional. A majority concluded, albeit through slightly different paths, that Congress could not use the Spending Clause to condition States' *continuing* receipt of already-existing Medicaid funds on their willingness to accept the Act's broad expansion of the Medicaid program to new classes of recipients. Plaintiff States argued that Congress had "crossed the line [into] coercion . . . in the way it has structured funding: Instead of simply refusing to grant the new funds to States that will not accept the new conditions, Congress has also threated to withhold those States' existing Medicaid funds." For some of the plaintiff States, the funding cut would amount to a significant percentage of the State's entire budget.

Writing for himself, Justice Breyer, and Justice Kagan, Chief Justice Roberts agreed. Comparing the potential loss of as much as ten percent of some states' overall budgets to the loss, in *South Dakota v. Dole*, of five percent of a State's federal highway funding, Chief Justice Roberts found two distinctions that militated against the ACA. The first was the sheer magnitude of the potential cut: "In this case, the financial 'inducement' Congress has chosen is much more than 'relatively mild encouragement'—it is a gun to the head." The second was the retroactive nature of the cuts to existing funding unrelated to the new healthcare program. He noted that Spending Clause legislation is "much in the nature of a *contract*," which requires the States to understand the terms and conditions they are accepting when they accept federal funds.

> We have upheld Congress's authority to condition the receipt of funds on the States' complying with restrictions on the use of those funds, because that is the means by which Congress ensures that the funds are spent according to its view of the "general Welfare." Conditions that do not here govern the use of the funds, however, cannot be justified on that basis. When, for example, such conditions take the form of threats to terminate other significant independent grants, the conditions are properly viewed as a means of pressuring the States to accept policy changes.

Four Justices (Scalia, Kennedy, Thomas and Alito) in a joint opinion agreed with the Chief Justice that the Spending Clause did not authorize the conditions Congress attempted to place on existing Medicaid funding. In addition to the coercive magnitude of the potential cut, the joint opinion found relevant the size of the federal tax burden imposed on citizens:

> When a heavy federal tax is levied to support a federal program that offers large grants to the States, States may, as a practical matter, be unable to refuse to participate in the federal program and to substitute a state alternative. Even if a State believes that the federal program is ineffective and inefficient, withdrawal would likely force the State to impose a huge tax increase on its residents, and this new state tax would come on top of the federal taxes already paid by residents to support subsidies to participating States.

Justice Ginsburg, writing only for herself and Justice Sotomayor on this point, found the approaches of both the Chief Justice and Justice Scalia unmanageable:

> When future Spending Clause challenges arise, as they likely will in the wake of [this] decision, how will litigants and judges assess whether "a State has a legitimate choice whether to accept the federal conditions in exchange for federal funds"? Are courts to measure the number of dollars the Federal Government might withhold for noncompliance? The portion of the State's budget at stake? And which State's—or States'—budget is determinative: the lead plaintiff, all challenging States (26 in this case, many with quite different fiscal situations), or some national median? Does it matter that Florida, unlike most States, imposes no state income tax, and therefore might be able to replace foregone federal funds with new state revenue? Or that the coercion state officials in fact fear is punishment at the ballot box for turning down a politically popular federal grant?

Recall the history of abrogation under the Commerce Clause and the Fourteenth Amendment and also the history of the Court's struggles with the scope of the Tenth Amendment that preceded *Alden*. In those areas, it is arguable that restrictions on Congress's power to subject states to lawsuits for damages were proxies for disagreements about the scope of the underlying constitutional provisions. Is the Spending Clause a different situation because of the contract-like nature of the relationship between the federal government and the states under Spending Clause legislation? Or do you predict we will see a new proxy fight?

[3] Recap: Exceptions to State Sovereign Immunity

In responding to the dissent's concern that the effect of *Alden* and *Seminole Tribe* would be to eviscerate the effective enforcement of federal law, Justice Kennedy in *Alden* offered the following list of methods for enforcing federal commands:

> [S]overeign immunity bars suits only in the absence of consent. Many States, on their own initiative, have enacted statutes consenting to a wide variety of suits. The rigors of sovereign immunity are thus "mitigated by a sense of justice which has continually expanded by consent the suability of the sovereign." *Great Northern Life Ins. Co. v. Read*, 322 U.S. 47 (1944). Nor, subject to constitutional limitations, does the Federal Government lack the authority or means to seek the States' voluntary consent to private suits. Cf. *South Dakota v. Dole*, 483 U.S. 203 (1987).
>
> The States have consented, moreover, to some suits pursuant to the plan of the Convention or to subsequent constitutional Amendments. In ratifying the Constitution, the States consented to suits brought by other States or by the Federal Government. A suit which is commenced and prosecuted against a State in the name of the United States by those who are entrusted with the constitutional duty to "take Care that the Laws be faithfully executed," U.S. Const., Art. II, § 3, differs in kind from the suit of an individual: While the Constitution contemplates suits among the members of the federal system as an alternative to extralegal measures, the fear of private suits against nonconsenting States was the central reason given by the Founders who chose to preserve the States' sovereign immunity. Suits brought by the United States itself require the exercise of political responsibility for each suit prosecuted against a State, a control which is absent from a broad delegation to private persons to sue nonconsenting States.
>
> We have held also that in adopting the Fourteenth Amendment, the people required the States to surrender a portion of the sovereignty that had been preserved to them by the original Constitution, so that Congress may authorize private suits against nonconsenting States pursuant to its § 5 enforcement power. . . .
>
> The second important limit to the principle of sovereign immunity is that it bars suits against States but not lesser entities. The immunity does not extend to suits prosecuted against a municipal corporation or other governmental entity which is not an arm of the State. *See, e.g., Mt. Healthy City Bd. of Ed. v. Doyle*, 429 U.S. 274 (1977); *Lincoln County v. Luning*, 133 U.S. 529 (1890). Nor does sovereign immunity bar all suits against state officers. Some suits against state officers are barred by the rule that sovereign immunity is not limited to suits which name the State as a party if the suits are, in fact, against

the State. *See, e.g., In re Ayers,* 123 U.S. 443 (1887); *Coeur d'Alene Tribe* ("The real interests served by the Eleventh Amendment are not to be sacrificed to elementary mechanics of captions and pleading"). The rule, however, does not bar certain actions against state officers for injunctive or declaratory relief. Even a suit for money damages may be prosecuted against a state officer in his individual capacity for unconstitutional or wrongful conduct fairly attributable to the officer himself, so long as the relief is sought not from the state treasury but from the officer personally. *Scheuer v. Rhodes,* 416 U.S. 232 (1974); *Ford Motor Co. v. Department of Treasury of Ind.,* 323 U.S. 459 (1945).

Consider the array of federal statutory commands referenced in this chapter. For example, Congress has prohibited discrimination in employment on the basis of age; has required additional compensation for overtime work by employees; and has prescribed penalties for infringement of patents and copyrights. Do the exceptions listed by Justice Kennedy provide an adequate substitute for private damages suits as a means of enforcing these commands against the states? (Recall the discussion of private rights of action in Chapter 8.)

F. Sovereign Immunity in Litigation

[1] Sovereign Immunity and Jurisdictional Doctrines

As Justice Kennedy once observed, sovereign immunity has a "hybrid nature." He explained:

> In certain respects, the immunity bears substantial similarity to personal jurisdiction requirements, since it can be waived and courts need not raise the issue sua sponte. Permitting the immunity to be raised at any stage of the proceedings, in contrast, is more consistent with regarding the Eleventh Amendment as a limit on the federal courts' subject-matter jurisdiction. We have noted the inconsistency. Although the text is framed in terms of the extent of the "Judicial power of the United States," our precedents have treated the Eleventh Amendment as "enact[ing] a sovereign immunity from suit, rather than a nonwaivable limit on the federal judiciary's subject-matter jurisdiction." *Coeur d'Alene Tribe.*

Wisconsin Dept. of Corrections v. Schacht, 524 U.S. 381 (1998) (concurring opinion).

As briefly noted earlier, this "hybrid nature" has multiple consequences. For instance, as Justice Kennedy notes, like subject-matter jurisdiction, sovereign immunity may be raised for the first time on appeal, so "a State which is sued in federal court does not waive [sovereign immunity] simply by appearing and defending on the merits." But, like personal jurisdiction, immunity can be waived: indeed, the Court has consistently held not only that a state can consent to federal-court jurisdiction despite sovereign immunity, but that a State's voluntary appearance in federal court effects a waiver of immunity.

[2] Sovereign Immunity and Removal

The "hybrid nature" noted above explains *Schacht*'s holding: the existence of claims that might be barred by immunity is not ordinarily a *jurisdictional* bar to a state's voluntary removal of a case to federal court (although the voluntary invocation of the federal court's jurisdiction might lead to waiver of these claims). But may plaintiff states be *involuntarily* forced into federal court through removal?

The Eleventh Amendment speaks of actions "commenced or prosecuted against one of the United States." The constitutional immunity discussed in *Seminole Tribe* and *Alden* protects the states as defendants. Are the concerns addressed by sovereign immunity also relevant when plaintiff states are involuntarily removed to federal court? And should it matter whether the underlying action is based on federal or state law?

Cohens v. Virginia (Chapter 2) held that the Eleventh Amendment does not bar Supreme Court review of a judgment obtained by a state in state court against an individual. Does this aspect of *Cohens* resolve the question whether sovereign immunity bars removal of actions brought by states, particularly in light of the reach of *Seminole Tribe* and *Alden*?

Most federal courts that have considered the question conclude that it does, and that removal is not barred. For example, the Ninth Circuit has held that "a state that voluntarily brings suit as a plaintiff in state court cannot invoke the Eleventh Amendment when the defendant seeks removal to federal court of competent jurisdiction." *California ex rel. Lockyer v. Dynegy, Inc.*, 375 F.3d 831 (9th Cir. 2004).

But at least one thoughtful opinion questions whether the issue is settled. In the wake of Hurricanes Katrina and Rita, the Attorney General of Louisiana filed a class action against a number of insurance companies, naming the State and numerous Louisiana citizens as plaintiffs. The claims were based on state law, and the action was brought in state court. The Class Action Fairness Act (CAFA), discussed in Chapter 2, permits removal of class actions to federal court on the basis of minimal diversity. On the basis of the CAFA, the insurance companies removed the case to federal court. Louisiana moved to remand, arguing *inter alia* that it enjoyed sovereign immunity from involuntary removal to federal court under CAFA.

Judge Higginbotham, for the court, wrote that Louisiana's argument against removal stated the question in its "strongest form," and noted that it had so far "eluded answer for the practical reason that it has been long settled that a State is not a person for purposes of diversity jurisdiction. This, with the long time companion insistence upon complete diversity, made the presence of additional parties aligned with the State irrelevant to federal diversity jurisdiction. CAFA, with its grant of jurisdiction to the federal district courts of qualifying class actions with minimal diversity of parties, pushes the question forward . . . ." Thus, the case raised a "constitutional concern: . . . whether a state as plaintiff suing defendants over whom it has regulatory authority in state court under its own *state laws* may be removed to federal court on diversity grounds under CAFA, rather than federal question jurisdiction."

The court ultimately avoided the question by noting that Louisiana had joined private parties as plaintiffs. It held that by doing so, the state had waived any immunity it might otherwise have had: "[W]e are persuaded . . . that any immunity the State may have cannot be conferred by the State upon the prosecution of suits by private citizens under its claimed umbrella of protection in frustration of a congressional decision to give access to federal district courts to defendants exposed to these private claims, presumably for reasons not far removed from those that led the first Congress to confer diversity jurisdiction . . . ." *In re Katrina Canal Litigation Breaches*, 524 F.3d 700 (5th Cir. 2008).

(a) Is the court correct in its view that removal under CAFA presents constitutional concerns in the context of states as plaintiffs? What are the strongest arguments from *Seminole Tribe* and *Alden* on the State's behalf in this case? On the insurers' behalf?

(b) Had the court been forced to address the question of the state's immunity, what would have been the next logical question it would have faced? And how would it have been resolved?

Chapter 14

The Section 1983 Cause of Action

Ex parte Young established that, notwithstanding the Eleventh Amendment and *Hans v. Louisiana*, a citizen could bring suit in federal court to challenge official action by his own state. The holding of that case provides plaintiffs with a means of avoiding the defense of state sovereign immunity. But *Ex parte Young* is subject to important limits. It applies to a limited range of defendants: the complaint must name a state official, not the state itself. It permits a limited range of claims: the plaintiff must allege that the state official is enforcing, or has threatened to enforce, state law in a manner that violates the federal Constitution. It authorizes limited forms of relief: the action must seek an injunction or other prospective relief to prevent enforcement of state law, rather than money damages or other retrospective relief. And, as the Court explained in *Armstrong v. Exceptional Child Center*, 135 S. Ct. 1378 (2015), "The ability to sue to enjoin unconstitutional actions by state and federal officers is the creation of courts of equity." Thus, like any "judge-made remedy," the *Ex parte Young* cause of action may be limited or entirely abrogated by Congress. *See Seminole Tribe of Florida v. Florida*, 517 U.S. 44 (1996) (Chapter 13).

Today, for those reasons, a plaintiff seeking to challenge state official action will seldom invoke the implied cause of action under *Ex parte Young*. Rather, the plaintiff will sue under the cause of action created by Congress as part of the Civil Rights Act of 1871 and now codified as 42 U.S.C. § 1983. Section 1983 provides:

> Every person who, under color of any statute, ordinance, regulation, custom, or usage, of any State or Territory or the District of Columbia, subjects, or causes to be subjected, any citizen of the United States or other person within the jurisdiction thereof to the deprivation of any rights, privileges, or immunities secured by the Constitution and laws, shall be liable to the party injured in an action at law, suit in equity, or other proper proceeding for redress. . . .

Section 1983 was on the books at the time of *Ex parte Young*, but the statute remained in obscurity until it was revived and reinvigorated by the landmark decision in *Monroe v. Pape* in 1961. Since then, § 1983 has become the subject of an enormous body of law. In this chapter we look first at *Monroe*, then at some of the important lines of precedent that determine whether a plaintiff can secure relief under the statute.

A. Conduct "Under Color of" State Law

Monroe v. Pape

Supreme Court of the United States, 1961.

365 U.S. 167.

MR. JUSTICE DOUGLAS delivered the opinion of the Court.

This case presents important questions concerning the construction of R.S. § 1979, 42 U.S.C. § 1983 . . . .

[*Editorial note.* Justice Douglas and Justice Frankfurter (in the dissent) refer to § 1983 as "R.S. § 1979," a usage that was an anachronism even in 1961. These references have been replaced with the modern citation throughout.]

The complaint alleges that 13 Chicago police officers broke into petitioners' home in the early morning, routed them from bed, made them stand naked in the living room, and ransacked every room, emptying drawers and ripping mattress covers. It further alleges that Mr. Monroe was then taken to the police station and detained on "open" charges for 10 hours, while he was interrogated about a two-day-old murder, that he was not taken before a magistrate, though one was accessible, that he was not permitted to call his family or attorney, that he was subsequently released without criminal charges being preferred against him. It is alleged that the officers had no search warrant and no arrest warrant and that they acted "under color of the statutes, ordinances, regulations, customs and usages" of Illinois and of the City of Chicago. Federal jurisdiction was asserted under § 1983 and 28 U.S.C. § 1343 and 28 U.S.C. § 1331.

The City of Chicago moved to dismiss the complaint on the ground that it is not liable under the Civil Rights Acts nor for acts committed in performance of its governmental functions. All defendants moved to dismiss, alleging that the complaint alleged no cause of action under those Acts or under the Federal Constitution. The District Court dismissed the complaint. The Court of Appeals affirmed. The case is here on a writ of certiorari which we granted because of a seeming conflict of that ruling with our prior cases.

I

Petitioners claim that the invasion of their home and the subsequent search without a warrant and the arrest and detention of Mr. Monroe without a warrant and without arraignment constituted a deprivation of their "rights, privileges, or immunities secured by the Constitution" within the meaning of § 1983. . . .

Section 1983 came onto the books as § 1 of the Ku Klux Act of April 20, 1871. It was one of the means whereby Congress exercised the power vested in it by § 5 of the Fourteenth Amendment to enforce the provisions of that Amendment. Senator Edmunds, Chairman of the Senate Committee on the Judiciary, said concerning this section:

"The first section is one that I believe nobody objects to, as defining the rights secured by the Constitution of the United States when they are assailed by any State law or under color of any State law, and it is merely carrying out the principles of the civil rights bill, which has since become a part of the Constitution," *viz.*, the Fourteenth Amendment.

. . . Allegation of facts constituting a deprivation under color of state authority of a right guaranteed by the Fourteenth Amendment satisfies to that extent the requirement of § 1983. So far petitioners are on solid ground. For the guarantee against unreasonable searches and seizures contained in the Fourth Amendment has been made applicable to the States by reason of the Due Process Clause of the Fourteenth Amendment. *Wolf v. Colorado*, 338 U.S. 25 (1949).

II

There can be no doubt at least since *Ex parte Virginia*, 100 U.S. 339 (1879), that Congress has the power to enforce provisions of the Fourteenth Amendment against those who carry a badge of authority of a State and represent it in some capacity, whether they act in accordance with their authority or misuse it. See *Home Tel. & Tel. Co. v. Los Angeles*, 227 U.S. 278 (1913). The question with which we now deal is the narrower one of whether Congress, in enacting § 1983, meant to give a remedy to parties deprived of constitutional rights, privileges and immunities by an official's abuse of his position. We conclude that it did so intend.

It is argued that "under color of" enumerated state authority excludes acts of an official or policeman who can show no authority under state law, state custom, or state usage to do what he did. In this case it is said that these policemen, in breaking into petitioners' apartment, violated the Constitution and laws of Illinois. It is pointed out that under Illinois law a simple remedy is offered for that violation and that, so far as it appears, the courts of Illinois are available to give petitioners that full redress which the common law affords for violence done to a person; and it is earnestly argued that no "statute, ordinance, regulation, custom or usage" of Illinois bars that redress.

[The Ku Klux Act] — in particular the section with which we are now concerned — had several purposes. There are threads of many thoughts running through the debates. One who reads them in their entirety sees that the present section had three main aims.

First, it might, of course, override certain kinds of state laws. . . .

Second, it provided a remedy where state law was inadequate. . . .

But the purposes were much broader. The *third* aim was to provide a federal remedy where the state remedy, though adequate in theory, was not available in practice. The opposition to the measure complained that "It overrides the reserved powers of the States," just as they argued that the second section of the bill "absorb[ed] the entire jurisdiction of the States over their local and domestic affairs."

This Act of April 20, 1871, sometimes called "the third 'force bill,'" was passed by a Congress that had the Klan "particularly in mind." [Here the Court cited RANDALL, THE CIVIL WAR AND RECONSTRUCTION 857 (1937).] The debates are replete with references to the lawless conditions existing in the South in 1871. There was available to the Congress during these debates a report, nearly 600 pages in length, dealing with the activities of the Klan and the inability of the state governments to cope with it. This report was drawn on by many of the speakers. It was not the unavailability of state remedies but the failure of certain States to enforce the laws with an equal hand that furnished the powerful momentum behind this "force bill." . . .

While one main scourge of the evil—perhaps the leading one—was the Ku Klux Klan, the remedy created was not a remedy against it or its members but against those who representing a State in some capacity were *unable* or *unwilling* to enforce a state law. . . .

There was, it was said, no quarrel with the state laws on the books. It was their lack of enforcement that was the nub of the difficulty. . . .

The debates were long and extensive. It is abundantly clear that one reason the legislation was passed was to afford a federal right in federal courts because, by reason of prejudice, passion, neglect, intolerance or otherwise, state laws might not be enforced and the claims of citizens to the enjoyment of rights, privileges, and immunities guaranteed by the Fourteenth Amendment might be denied by the state agencies. . . .

Although the legislation was enacted because of the conditions that existed in the South at that time, it is cast in general language and is as applicable to Illinois as it is to the States whose names were mentioned over and again in the debates. It is no answer that the State has a law which if enforced would give relief. The federal remedy is supplementary to the state remedy, and the latter need not be first sought and refused before the federal one is invoked. Hence the fact that Illinois by its constitution and laws outlaws unreasonable searches and seizures is no barrier to the present suit in the federal court.

We had before us in *United States v. Classic*, 313 U.S. 299 (1941), 18 U.S.C. § 242, which provides a criminal punishment for anyone who "under color of any law, statute, ordinance, regulation, or custom" subjects any inhabitant of a State to the deprivation of "any rights, privileges, or immunities secured or protected by the Constitution or laws of the United States." Section 242 first came into the law as § 2 of the Civil Rights Act, Act of April 9, 1866. After passage of the Fourteenth Amendment, this provision was re-enacted and amended by [the] Act of May 31, 1870. The right involved in the *Classic* case was the right of voters in a primary to have their votes counted. The laws of Louisiana required the defendants "to count the ballots, to record the result of the count, and to certify the result of the election." But according to the indictment they did not perform their duty. In an opinion written by Mr. Justice (later Chief Justice) Stone, in which Mr. Justice Roberts, Mr. Justice Reed, and Mr. Justice Frankfurter joined, the Court ruled, "Misuse of power, possessed by virtue of state law and made possible only because the wrongdoer is clothed with the authority of state law, is action taken 'under color of' state law." There was a dissenting opinion; but the ruling as to the meaning of "under color of" state law was not questioned.

That view of the meaning of the words "under color of" state law, 18 U.S.C. § 242, was reaffirmed in *Screws v. United States*, 325 U.S. 91 (1945). The acts there complained of were committed by state officers in performance of their duties, *viz.*, making an arrest effective. It was urged there, as it is here, that "under color of" state law should not be construed to duplicate in federal law what was an offense under state law. *Id.* (dissenting opinion). It was said there, as it is here, that the ruling in the *Classic* case as to the meaning of "under color of" state law was not in focus and was ill-advised. *Id.* (dissenting opinion). It was argued there, as it is here, that "under color of" state law included only action taken by officials pursuant to state law. *Id.* (dissenting opinion). We rejected that view. We stated:

> The construction given § 20 [18 U.S.C. § 242] in the *Classic* case formulated a rule of law which has become the basis of federal enforcement in this important field. The rule adopted in that case was formulated after mature consideration. . . . The *Classic* case was not the product of hasty action or inadvertence. It was not out of line with the cases which preceded. It was designed to fashion the governing rule of law in this important field. We are not dealing with constitutional interpretations which throughout the history of the Court have wisely remained flexible and subject to frequent re-examination. The meaning which the *Classic* case gave to the phrase "under color of any law" involved only a construction of the statute. Hence if it states a rule undesirable in its consequences, Congress can change it. We add only to the instability and uncertainty of the law if we revise the meaning of [18 U.S.C. § 242] to meet the exigencies of each case coming before us.

We adhered to that view in *Williams v. United States*, 341 U.S. 97 (1951).

Mr. Shellabarger, reporting out the bill which became the Ku Klux Act, said of the provision with which we now deal:

> The model for it will be found in the second section of the act of April 9, 1866, known as the "civil rights act." . . . This section of this bill, on the same state of facts, not only provides a civil remedy for persons whose former condition may have been that of slaves, but also to all people where, under color of State law, they or any of them may be deprived of rights. . . .

Thus, it is beyond doubt that this phrase should be accorded the same construction in both statutes—in § 1983 and in 18 U.S.C. § 242.

Since the *Screws* and *Williams* decisions, Congress has had several pieces of civil rights legislation before it. In 1956 one bill reached the floor of the House. This measure had at least one provision in it penalizing actions taken "under color of law or otherwise." A vigorous minority report was filed attacking, *inter alia*, the words "or otherwise." But not a word of criticism of the phrase "under color of" state law as previously construed by the Court is to be found in that report. [Other examples omitted.]

If the results of our construction of "under color of" law were as horrendous as now claimed, if they were as disruptive of our federal scheme as now urged, if they were such an unwarranted invasion of States' rights as pretended, surely the voice of the opposition would have been heard in those Committee reports. Their silence and the new uses to which "under color of" law have recently been given reinforce our conclusion that our prior decisions were correct on this matter of construction.

We conclude that the meaning given "under color of" law in the *Classic* case and in the *Screws* and *Williams* cases was the correct one; and we adhere to it.

In the *Screws* case we dealt with a statute that imposed criminal penalties for acts "wilfully" done. We construed that word in its setting to mean the doing of an act with "a specific intent to deprive a person of a federal right." We do not think that gloss should be placed on § 1983 which we have here. The word "wilfully" does not appear in § 1983. Moreover, § 1983 provides a civil remedy, while in the *Screws* case we dealt with a criminal law challenged on the ground of vagueness. Section 1983 should be read against the background of tort liability that makes a man responsible for the natural consequences of his actions.

So far, then, the complaint states a cause of action. There remains to consider only a defense peculiar to the City of Chicago.

III

The City of Chicago asserts that it is not liable under § 1983. We do not stop to explore the whole range of questions tendered us on this issue at oral argument and in the briefs. For we are of the opinion that Congress did not undertake to bring municipal corporations within the ambit of § 1983. [Discussion omitted. The holding of *Monroe* on this point was overruled in *Monell v. Department of Social Services of City of New York*, 436 U.S. 658 (1978), *infra* Section D.]

[We] hold that the motion to dismiss the complaint against the City of Chicago was properly granted. But since the complaint should not have been dismissed against the officials the judgment must be and is

Reversed.

MR. JUSTICE HARLAN, whom MR. JUSTICE STEWART joins, concurring.

Were this case here as one of first impression, I would find the "under color of any statute" issue very close indeed. However, in *Classic* and *Screws* this Court considered a substantially identical statutory phrase to have a meaning which, unless we now retreat from it, requires that issue to go for the petitioners here.

From my point of view, the policy of *stare decisis*, as it should be applied in matters of statutory construction, and, to a lesser extent, the indications of congressional acceptance of this Court's earlier interpretation, require that it appear beyond doubt from the legislative history of the 1871 statute that *Classic* and *Screws* misapprehended the meaning of the controlling provision, before a departure from what was decided in those cases would be justified. Since I can find no such justifying indication in that legislative history, I join the opinion of the Court. However, what has been written on both sides of the matter makes some additional observations appropriate.

Those aspects of Congress' purpose which are quite clear in the earlier congressional debates, as quoted by my Brothers Douglas and Frankfurter in turn, seem to me to be inherently ambiguous when applied to the case of an isolated abuse of state authority by an official. . . . If attention is directed at the rare specific references to isolated abuses of state authority, one finds them neither so clear nor so disproportionately divided between favoring the positions of the majority or the dissent as to make either position seem plainly correct.

Besides the inconclusiveness I find in the legislative history, it seems to me by no means evident that a position favoring departure from *Classic* and *Screws* fits better that with which the enacting Congress was concerned than does the position the Court adopted 20 years ago. There are apparent incongruities in the view of the dissent which may be more easily reconciled in terms of the earlier holding in *Classic*.

The dissent considers that the "under color of" provision of § 1983 distinguishes between unconstitutional actions taken without state authority, which only the State should remedy, and unconstitutional actions authorized by the State, which the Federal Act was to reach. If so, then the controlling difference for the enacting legislature must have been either that the state remedy was more adequate for unauthorized actions than for authorized ones or that there was, in some sense, greater harm from unconstitutional actions authorized by the full panoply of state power and approval than from unconstitutional actions not so authorized or acquiesced in by the State. I find less than compelling the evidence that either distinction was important to that Congress. . . .

I

Since the suggested narrow construction of § 1983 presupposes that state measures were adequate to remedy unauthorized deprivations of constitutional rights and since the identical state relief could be obtained for state-authorized acts with the aid of Supreme Court review, this narrow construction would reduce the statute to having merely a jurisdictional function, shifting the load of federal supervision from the Supreme Court to the lower courts and providing a federal tribunal for fact findings in cases involving authorized action. Such a function could be justified on various grounds. It could, for example, be argued that the state courts would be less willing to find a constitutional violation in cases involving "authorized action" and that therefore the victim of such action would bear a greater burden in that he would more likely have to carry his case to this Court, and once here, might be bound by unfavorable state court findings. But the legislative debates do not disclose congressional concern about the burdens of litigation placed upon the victims of "authorized" constitutional violations contrasted to the victims of unauthorized violations. Neither did Congress indicate an interest in relieving the burden placed on this Court in reviewing such cases.

The statute becomes more than a jurisdictional provision only if one attributes to the enacting legislature the view that a deprivation of a constitutional right is significantly different from and more serious than a violation of a state right and therefore deserves a different remedy even though the same act may constitute both a state tort and the deprivation of a constitutional right. This view, by no means unrealistic as a common-sense matter,[5] is, I believe, more consistent with the flavor of the legislative

---

5. There will be many cases in which the relief provided by the state to the victim of a use of state power which the state either did not or could not constitutionally authorize will be far less than what

history than is a view that the primary purpose of the statute was to grant a lower court forum for fact findings. . . .

In my view, these considerations put in serious doubt the conclusion that § 1983 was limited to state-authorized unconstitutional acts, on the premise that state remedies respecting them were considered less adequate than those available for unauthorized acts.

II

I think this limited interpretation of § 1983 fares no better when viewed from the other possible premise for it, namely that state-approved constitutional deprivations were considered more offensive than those not so approved. For one thing, the enacting Congress was not unaware of the fact that there was a substantial overlap between the protections granted by state constitutional provisions and those granted by the Fourteenth Amendment. . . .

These difficulties in explaining the basis of a distinction between authorized and unauthorized deprivations of constitutional rights fortify my view that the legislative history does not bear the burden which *stare decisis* casts upon it. For this reason and for those stated in the opinion of the Court, I agree that we should not now depart from the holdings of the *Classic* and *Screws* cases.

MR. JUSTICE FRANKFURTER, dissenting except insofar as the Court holds that this action cannot be maintained against the City of Chicago. . . .

[After discussing the arguments and opinions in *Classic, Screws,* and *Williams,* Justice Frankfurter concluded:] Thus, although this Court has three times found that conduct of state officials which is forbidden by state law may be "under color" of state law for purposes of the Civil Rights Acts, it is accurate to say that that question has never received here the consideration which its importance merits. That regard for controlling legislative history which is conventionally observed by this Court in determining the true meaning of important legislation that does not construe itself has never been applied to the "under color" provisions; particularly, there has never been canvassed the full record of the debates preceding passage of the 1871 Act with which we are concerned in this case. Neither *Classic* nor *Screws* nor *Williams* warrants refusal now to take account of those debates and the illumination they afford. . . .

[The] relevant demands of *stare decisis* do not preclude considering, for the first time thoroughly and in the light of the best available evidence of congressional purpose, a statutory interpretation which started as an unexamined assumption on the

---

Congress may have thought would be fair reimbursement for deprivation of a constitutional right. I will venture only a few examples. There may be no damage remedy for the loss of voting rights or for the harm from psychological coercion leading to a confession. And what is the dollar value of the right to go to unsegregated schools? Even the remedy for such an unauthorized search and seizure as Monroe was allegedly subjected to may be only the nominal amount of damages to physical property allowable in an action for trespass to land. It would indeed be the purest coincidence if the state remedies for violations of common-law rights by private citizens were fully appropriate to redress those injuries which only a state official can cause and against which the Constitution provides protection.

basis of inapplicable citations and has the claim of a dogma solely through reiteration. Particularly is this so when that interpretation, only recently made, was at its inception a silent reversal of the judicial history of the Civil Rights Acts for three quarters of a century. . . .

IV

This case squarely presents the question whether the intrusion of a city policeman for which that policeman can show no such authority at state law as could be successfully interposed in defense to a state-law action against him, is nonetheless to be regarded as "under color" of state authority within the meaning of § 1983. Respondents, in breaking into the Monroe apartment, violated the laws of the State of Illinois. Illinois law appears to offer a civil remedy for unlawful searches; petitioners do not claim that none is available. Rather they assert that they have been deprived of due process of law and of equal protection of the laws under color of state law, although from all that appears the courts of Illinois are available to give them the fullest redress which the common law affords for the violence done them, nor does any "statute, ordinance, regulation, custom, or usage" of the State of Illinois bar that redress. Did the enactment by Congress of § 1 of the Ku Klux Act of 1871 encompass such a situation?

[Justice Frankfurter's lengthy account of the legislative history is omitted.]

[All] the evidence converges to the conclusion that Congress by § 1983 created a civil liability enforceable in the federal courts only in instances of injury for which redress was barred in the state courts because some "statute, ordinance, regulation, custom, or usage" sanctioned the grievance complained of. This purpose, manifested even by the so-called "Radical" Reconstruction Congress in 1871, accords with the presuppositions of our federal system. The jurisdiction which Article III of the Constitution conferred on the national judiciary reflected the assumption that the state courts, not the federal courts, would remain the primary guardians of that fundamental security of person and property which the long evolution of the common law had secured to one individual as against other individuals. The Fourteenth Amendment did not alter this basic aspect of our federalism.

Its commands were addressed to the States. Only when the States, through their responsible organs for the formulation and administration of local policy, sought to deny or impede access by the individual to the central government in connection with those enumerated functions assigned to it, or to deprive the individual of a certain minimal fairness in the exercise of the coercive forces of the State, or without reasonable justification to treat him differently than other persons subject to their jurisdiction, was an overriding federal sanction imposed. As between individuals, no corpus of substantive rights was guaranteed by the Fourteenth Amendment, but only "due process of law" in the ascertainment and enforcement of rights and equality in the enjoyment of rights and safeguards that the States afford. This was the base of the distinction between federal citizenship and state citizenship drawn by the *Slaughter-House Cases*, 16 Wall. (83 U.S.) 36 (1872). This conception begot the "State action" principle on which, from the time of the *Civil Rights Cases*, 109 U.S. 3 (1883), this Court has relied in its application of Fourteenth Amendment guarantees. . . .

But, of course, in the present case petitioners argue that the wrongs done them were committed not by individuals but by the police as state officials. . . . Certainly the night-time intrusion of the man with a star and a police revolver is a different phenomenon than the night-time intrusion of a burglar. The aura of power which a show of authority carries with it has been created by state government. For this reason the national legislature, exercising its power to implement the Fourteenth Amendment, might well attribute responsibility for the intrusion to the State and legislate to protect against such intrusion. . . .

Should an unlawful intrusion by a policeman in Chicago entail different consequences than an unlawful intrusion by a hoodlum? These are matters of policy in its strictly legislative sense, not for determination by this Court. And if it be, as it is, a matter for congressional choice, the legislative evidence is overwhelming that § 1983 is not expressive of that choice. . . .

. . . [Respect] for principles which this Court has long regarded as critical to the most effective functioning of our federalism should avoid extension of a statute beyond its manifest area of operation into applications which invite conflict with the administration of local policies. Such an extension makes the extreme limits of federal constitutional power a law to regulate the quotidian business of every traffic policeman, every registrar of elections, every city inspector or investigator, every clerk in every municipal licensing bureau in this country. The text of the statute, reinforced by its history, precludes such a reading. . . .

. . . Federal intervention, which must at best be limited to securing those minimal guarantees afforded by the evolving concepts of due process and equal protection, may in the long run do the individual a disservice by deflecting responsibility from the state lawmakers, who hold the power of providing a far more comprehensive scope of protection. Local society, also, may well be the loser, by relaxing its sense of responsibility and, indeed, perhaps resenting what may appear to it to be outside interference where local authority is ample and more appropriate to supply needed remedies.

Note: The Impact of Monroe v. Pape

1. It is doubtful that any single Supreme Court decision has had a more far-reaching effect on the work of the federal courts — or indeed the work of lawyers — than *Monroe v. Pape*. Before *Monroe*, § 1983 suits were rare. Today, they constitute a major component of the federal court docket. Some § 1983 actions present momentous issues of constitutional law; others involve individual grievances that seem to belong in a small-claims court, if anywhere.

2. To state a claim under § 1983, a plaintiff must allege only two elements: first, conduct committed by a person acting under color of state law; second, that the conduct deprived the plaintiff of rights, privileges, or immunities secured by the Constitution or laws of the United States. Doctrinally, the importance of *Monroe* lies in its holding that conduct by state officials could be "under color of" state law notwithstanding the fact that the conduct was unauthorized by the state or even forbidden by it. The Court rejects the position "that 'under color of' enumerated state authority excludes acts of an official or policeman who can show no authority under state law, state custom, or state usage to do what he did."

3. The Court had reached a similar conclusion half a century earlier in considering the scope of the due process clause of the Fourteenth Amendment. In *Home Telephone & Telegraph Co. v. City of Los Angeles*, 227 U.S. 278 (1913), the plaintiff filed suit in federal court seeking to enjoin the enforcement of the city's telephone rate ordinance on the ground that "the rates fixed were so unreasonably low that their enforcement would bring about the confiscation of the property of the corporation" and thus deny due process. The city pointed out that the state constitution had its own due process clause. That being so, the city argued, the acts of its officials "could not be treated as acts of the state within the 14th Amendment . . . until, by final action of an appropriate state court, it was decided that such acts were authorized by the state, and were therefore not repugnant to the state Constitution."

The Supreme Court emphatically rejected this argument. In a unanimous opinion by Chief Justice White, the Court said:

> To speak broadly, the difference between the proposition insisted upon and the true meaning of the Amendment is this: that the one assumes that the Amendment virtually contemplates alone wrongs authorized by a state, and gives only power accordingly, while in truth the Amendment contemplates the possibility of state officers abusing the powers lawfully conferred upon them by doing wrongs prohibited by the Amendment. In other words, the Amendment, looking to the enforcement of the rights which it guarantees and to the prevention of the wrongs which it prohibits, proceeds not merely upon the assumption that states, acting in their governmental capacity, in a complete sense, may do acts which conflict with its provisions, but, also conceiving [that] state powers might be abused by those who possessed them, and as a result might be used as the instrument for doing wrongs, provided against all and every such possible contingency. . . .

> Under these circumstances it may not be doubted that where a state officer, under an assertion of power from the state, is doing an act which could only be done upon the predicate that there was such power, the inquiry as to the repugnancy of the act to the 14th Amendment cannot be avoided by insisting that there is a want of power. That is to say, a state officer cannot, on the one hand, as a means of doing a wrong forbidden by the Amendment, proceed upon the assumption of the possession of state power, and at the same time, for the purpose of avoiding the application of the Amendment, deny the power, and thus accomplish the wrong.

> To repeat: for the purpose of enforcing the rights guaranteed by the Amendment when it is alleged that a state officer, in virtue of state power, is doing an act which, if permitted to be done, prima facie would violate the Amendment, the subject must be tested by assuming that the officer possessed power if the act be one which there would not be opportunity to perform but for the possession of some state authority.

The decision in *Home Telephone & Telegraph* announced, in essence, a requirement of "but-for" causation to determine whether a state official's action is attributable to the state for purposes of the Fourteenth Amendment.

As the Court notes in *Monroe*, the decision in *Home Telephone & Telegraph* confirmed that "Congress has the power to enforce provisions of the Fourteenth Amendment against those who carry a badge of authority of a State and represent it in some capacity, whether they act in accordance with their authority or misuse it." Would the Court have done better to leave to Congress the task of defining the circumstances under which misuse of authority by state officers would be actionable as a matter of federal law? Reconsider this question as you study the cases in the remaining sections of this chapter.

4. There is one significant difference between the implied right of action under *Ex parte Young* and the statutory right of action under § 1983. The *Young* remedy is limited to equitable relief, typically the injunction. But § 1983 provides that a person who violates federally protected rights "shall be liable to the party injured in an *action at law*." An action at law would, of course, ordinarily include the remedy of money damages.

The distinction is important in at least two ways. First, unlike the implied remedy, the § 1983 cause of action can be invoked in instances of isolated wrongdoing. Second, the availability of damages will attract plaintiffs who seek only compensation for past injuries, not a change in the governing legal rules. Thus, the universe of potential § 1983 plaintiffs is much larger than the universe of potential *Ex parte Young* claimants.

5. The Court in *Monroe* seems to agree with Justice Frankfurter that a state-law remedy would generally be available to victims of unlawful searches and other wrongful acts by state officials. But even if that is so, the state-law claim could be brought only in state court. The § 1983 claim, of course, can be brought in federal court. Why might a plaintiff like Monroe have a strong preference for the federal over the state forum?

6. Fifteen years after *Monroe*, Congress created a substantial additional incentive for preferring the § 1983 cause of action over the state tort claim. It enacted the Civil Rights Attorney's Fees Awards Act of 1976, codified at 42 U.S.C. § 1988, which provides that in any action to enforce § 1983 or other civil rights statutes, "the court, in its discretion, may allow the prevailing party, other than the United States, a reasonable attorney's fee as part of the costs." The Supreme Court has said that "a prevailing plaintiff should *ordinarily* recover an attorney's fee unless special circumstances would render such an award unjust." *Hensley v. Eckerhart*, 461 U.S. 424 (1983) (emphasis added). In contrast, a plaintiff in ordinary tort litigation would rarely be able to recover attorney's fees from his adversary.

The implications and consequences of these developments are explored in the remaining sections of this chapter.

B. Section 1983 and Constitutional Claims

Justice Frankfurter, dissenting in *Monroe v. Pape*, predicted that under the Court's interpretation, § 1983 would become "a law to regulate the quotidian business of every traffic policeman, every registrar of elections, every city inspector or investigator, every clerk in every municipal licensing bureau in this country." Nothing in the Court's opinion offered reason to dispute this assertion, and in the years that followed, § 1983 suits proliferated. Even before attorney's fees became routinely available to prevailing plaintiffs, concern was expressed that § 1983 would provide a federal cause of action for "every legally cognizable injury" inflicted by a state official acting under color of state law. *Paul v. Davis*, 424 U.S. 693 (1975).

The Court might have averted this consequence through interpretation (or re-interpretation) of the elements of the § 1983 cause of action, but it did not. Instead, the Court adopted a series of narrow constructions of the Constitution, particularly the due process clause. The Court also developed doctrines of official immunity that shield individual government officials from monetary liability "as long as their actions could reasonably have been thought consistent with the rights they are alleged to have violated." *Anderson v. Creighton*, 483 U.S. 635 (1986). In this section, we look at some of the constitutional decisions that effectively limit the availability of relief under § 1983. The immunity doctrines are considered briefly in section E, *infra*.

[1] State Tort Law, State of Mind, and Section 1983

Section 1983's primary purpose is to vindicate federal constitutional rights violated by state and local officials. Nothing in the statute itself limits the kind of constitutional rights that may properly be the subject of an action under § 1983. It therefore includes deprivations of rights secured by the Fourteenth Amendment's Due Process Clause, which (in its "procedural" form) protects life, liberty, and property from state deprivation without proper procedure. That provision has been the source of a large number of § 1983 claims.

Nor does § 1983 limit relief to cases involving "intentional," "malicious," or "knowing" violations. Unlike 18 U.S.C. § 242, which criminalizes only "willful[]" deprivations of federal rights, § 1983 by its terms imposes no state-of-mind requirement. Instead, according to the Court in *Monroe v. Pape*, § 1983 "should be read against the background of tort liability that makes a man responsible for the natural consequences of his actions." Consistent with that approach, in *Parratt v. Taylor*, 451 U.S. 527 (1981), the Court concluded that "mere negligence" can support a claim for relief under § 1983. The statute "affords a 'civil remedy' for deprivations of federally protected rights caused by persons acting under color of state law without any express requirement of a particular state of mind."

Consider, however, the expansion of the role of the state and the pervasive relationship between the state and its citizens. State actors — school boards, prison guards, police officers, welfare and social services providers — all engage with the citizenry daily in ways that could be the subject of state law tort or other claims. Slip-and-fall cases, automobile accidents, and various forms of negligence by state officials unquestionably affect citizens' "liberty" or "property." Does § 1983, with its broad remedies and lack of any state-of-mind requirement, effectively transform those actions into constitutional claims? Does it federalize the field of tort law whenever the defendant is a state actor?

The Court has avoided that result, not by interpreting § 1983, but through a narrow understanding of the interests protected by due process. In *Paul v. Davis*, 424 U.S. 693 (1976), for example, the plaintiff sued the chief of police in Louisville, Kentucky, who had distributed to merchants throughout the city hundreds of fliers displaying the plaintiff's mug shot and describing him as an "ACTIVE SHOPLIFTER." The plaintiff had in fact never been convicted of shoplifting, and shortly after the fliers were distributed, the charge against him was dismissed. His complaint sought money damages, alleging that the distribution of the flier had damaged his reputation and threatened his employment at a major newspaper. He could have sought relief under state tort law, and he would have had a strong case for defamation *per se* given the nature of the statement. Instead, he brought an action under § 1983 alleging that the fliers had deprived him of rights secured by the Due Process Clause of the Fourteenth Amendment.

The Court rejected that claim on the merits, citing concerns about the effects of § 1983. In an opinion by then-Justice Rehnquist, joined by four other Justices, the Court relied heavily on slippery-slope arguments about the implications of the plaintiff's legal theory:

> If respondent's view is to prevail, a person arrested by law enforcement officers who announce that they believe such person to be responsible for a particular crime in order to calm the fears of an aroused populace, presumably obtains a claim against such officers under § 1983. And since it is surely far more clear from the language of the Fourteenth Amendment that "life" is protected against state deprivation than it is that reputation is protected against state injury, it would be difficult to see why the survivors of an innocent bystander mistakenly shot by a policeman or negligently killed by a sheriff driving a government vehicle, would not have claims equally cognizable under 1983.

> It is hard to perceive any logical stopping place to such a line of reasoning. Respondent's construction would seem almost necessarily to result in every legally cognizable injury which may have been inflicted by a state official acting under "color of law" establishing a violation of the Fourteenth Amendment. We think it would come as a great surprise to those who drafted and shepherded the adoption of that Amendment to learn that it worked such a result, and a study of our decisions convinces us they do not support the construction urged by respondent. . . .

> [As we explained in *Screws v. United States*, 325 U.S. 91 (1945) (plurality opinion)], "violation of local law does not necessarily mean that federal rights have been invaded. The fact that a prisoner is assaulted, injured, or even

murdered by state officials does not necessarily mean that he is deprived of any right protected or secured by the Constitution or laws of the United States." . . . Congress should not be understood to have attempted "to make all torts of state officials federal crimes. It brought within [the criminal provision] only specified acts 'under color' of law and then only those acts which deprived a person of some right secured by the Constitution or laws of the United States." *Screws*.

. . . Respondent, however, has pointed to no specific constitutional guarantee safeguarding the interest he asserts has been invaded. Rather, he apparently believes that the Fourteenth Amendment's Due Process Clause should *ex proprio vigore* extend to him a right to be free of injury wherever the State may be characterized as the tortfeasor. But such a reading would make of the Fourteenth Amendment a font of tort law to be superimposed upon whatever systems may already be administered by the States. We have noted the "constitutional shoals" that confront any attempt to derive from congressional civil rights statutes a body of general federal tort law, *Griffin v. Breckenridge*, 403 U.S. 88 (1971); a fortiori, the procedural guarantees of the Due Process Clause cannot be the source for such law.

The Court ultimately held that "liberty" and "property" interests protected by the Fourteenth Amendment "attain this constitutional status by virtue of the fact that they have been initially recognized and protected by state law." Reputation does not fit that description, and instead "is simply one of a number [of interests] which the State may protect against injury by virtue of its tort law."

Justice Brennan, joined by Justices Marshall and White, dissented. In an action under § 1983, he noted, the existence of a state tort-law remedy—whether against private parties or state officials—is wholly irrelevant. He quoted language from *Monroe v. Pape*: "It is no answer that the State has a law which if enforced would give relief. The federal remedy is supplementary to the state remedy, and the latter need not be first sought and refused before the federal one is invoked." Justice Brennan dismissed concerns about displacing state tort law in state-action cases as "groundless" in light of the § 1983 requirement that the defendant act "under color of" state law:

An official's actions are not "under color of" law merely because he is an official; an off-duty policeman's discipline of his own children, for example, would not constitute conduct "under color of" law. The essential element of this type of § 1983 action is *abuse* of his *official* position. "Congress, in enacting [§ 1983], meant to give a remedy to parties deprived of constitutional rights, privileges and immunities by an official's *abuse of his position*." *Monroe v. Pape* (emphasis supplied). Section 1983 focuses on "[m]isuse of power, possessed by virtue of state law and *made possible only because the wrongdoer is clothed with the authority of state law*." *United States v. Classic*, 313 U.S. 299 (1941) (emphasis supplied). Moreover, whether or not mere negligent official conduct in the course of duty can ever constitute such abuse of power, the police officials here concede that their conduct was intentional and was undertaken in their official capacities. Therefore, beyond peradventure, it is action taken under color of law, and it is disingenuous for the Court to argue that respondent is seeking to convert § 1983 into a generalized font of tort law.

On the merits, Justice Brennan faulted the majority for excluding interests in reputation from the scope of life, liberty, and property "by mere fiat and with no analysis." It is "inexplicable," he argued, to recognize due process violations when the state "suspends [a person] from school, revokes his driver's license, fires him from a job, or denies him the right to purchase a drink of alcohol"—all holdings of previous due process cases—but to refuse due process protection for a person's good name and reputation, "among the most cherished of rights enjoyed by a free people." The decision, he concluded, "must surely be a short-lived aberration."

That prediction proved incorrect, as the Court has reaffirmed its decision in *Paul*. In *Siegert v. Gilley*, 500 U.S. 226 (1991), the Court again confirmed that there is no constitutionally protected interest in avoiding government defamation. The plaintiff sued after learning that he had failed to receive a government position as a result of his previous government employer's bad reference. Characterizing the reference as "defamatory per se," the plaintiff claimed that a constitutionally protected liberty interest in his reputation had been violated, and that as a result he had lost government employment opportunities. Relying on *Paul*, the Court disagreed. Justice Marshall objected: "It is a perverse jurisprudence that recognizes the loss of a 'legal' right to buy liquor as a serious deprivation but fails to accord equal significance to the foreclosure of opportunities for government employment." Setting aside concerns about § 1983 for a moment, is the due process holding of *Paul* coherent? Or is Justice Marshall right in calling it "perverse"?

Concerns about the implications of § 1983 for state tort law seem central to the majority's reasoning in *Paul*. Would Justice Rehnquist's concerns have been better addressed by an interpretation of the statute that limited its reach, rather than by limiting the scope of the Constitution? Recall that Justice Frankfurter cited many of the same concerns in his dissent in *Monroe v. Pape*, urging a narrower interpretation of the phrase "under color of" state law.

It is important to remember that while § 1983 does not require that a state defendant act with a specific state of mind, it does require a showing that the defendant has violated a federal right. Many violations of federal constitutional rights do require a showing of intent or another form of heightened culpability. Consider a few examples:

- A claim of race discrimination in violation of the Equal Protection Clause of the Fourteenth Amendment requires proof that the defendant acted with a "racially discriminatory purpose." *Washington v. Davis*, 426 U.S. 229 (1976).

- A claim challenging conditions of confinement as cruel and unusual punishment in violation of the Eighth Amendment requires proof that prison officials acted with "deliberate indifference" to the prisoner's suffering. *Farmer v. Brennan*, 511 U.S. 825 (1994).

- A claim of an unreasonable seizure in violation of the Fourth Amendment requires proof that the police officer intended to restrain the plaintiff. *Brower v. County of Inyo*, 489 U.S. 593 (1989).

- A claim that a police officer's conduct during a high-speed chase "shocks the conscience" in violation of the Due Process Clause of the Fourteenth Amendment requires proof that the officer intended to physically harm the suspect or worsen his legal plight. *County of Sacramento v. Lewis*, 523 U.S. 833 (1998).

Indeed, the Court has since addressed precisely the kind of negligence action to which it alluded in *Paul v. Davis* and found no liability based on a *constitutional* state-of-mind requirement. In *Daniels v. Williams*, 474 U.S. 327 (1986), the plaintiff was a prisoner who was injured when he tripped on a pillow that a guard negligently left in a stairwell. The Court held that the guard had not "deprive[d]" the prisoner of liberty or property without due process of law, as required by the Fourteenth Amendment, because "a *negligent* act of an official causing unintended loss or injury" does not amount to a "deprivation." The decision "adhere[d] to" the Court's conclusion in *Parratt v. Taylor* that § 1983 itself imposes no state-of-mind requirement. But it overruled *Parratt* "to the extent that it states that mere lack of due care by a state official may 'deprive' an individual of life, liberty, or property under the Fourteenth Amendment."

Return to Justice Rehnquist's hypotheticals in *Paul*. Under the line of cases discussed above, would the "survivors of an innocent bystander mistakenly shot by a policeman or negligently killed by a sheriff driving a government vehicle" have a constitutional claim under § 1983? How about "the person arrested by law enforcement officers who announce that they believe such person to be responsible for a particular crime"?

[2] Exhaustion and Section 1983

The Court's opinion in *Monroe v. Pape* announced, in sweeping terms, that the availability of a state judicial remedy for the defendant's conduct does not defeat the claim under § 1983: "It is no answer that the State has a law which if enforced would give relief. The federal remedy is supplementary to the state remedy, and the latter need not be first sought and refused before the federal one is invoked."

How broadly should this statement be read? Does it foreclose any requirement that a person challenging state official action pursue state *administrative* remedies before filing suit under § 1983? The Supreme Court gave its emphatic answer in *Patsy v. Board of Regents of State of Florida*, 457 U.S. 496 (1982). The Court held that unless Congress requires otherwise, "exhaustion of state administrative remedies is not a prerequisite to an action under § 1983."

Even though § 1983 itself does not require exhaustion of state remedies, however, proving the deprivation of a constitutional right may require exhaustion. Indeed, the Constitution may require that plaintiffs first resort to state procedures that become available only *after* a deprivation of a protected interest has occurred ("postdeprivation" procedures).

In *Parratt v. Taylor*, 451 U.S. 527 (1981), a Nebraska prisoner sued under § 1983 for deprivation of his property—described by the Court as "hobby materials valued at $23.50." The Court held that the Due Process clause does not always require that the state provide procedures before a deprivation occurs. Indeed, because the prisoner alleged that the prison had lost his property, it made little sense to require procedures before a loss that the state could not anticipate would occur. The Court therefore recognized that "the necessity of quick action by the State or the impracticality of providing any meaningful predeprivation process, when coupled with the availability of some meaningful means by which to assess the propriety of the State's action at some time after the initial taking, can satisfy the requirements of procedural due process."

The Court concluded that the prisoner failed to allege a due process violation:

> Although he has been deprived of property under color of state law, the deprivation did not occur as a result of some established state procedure. Indeed, the deprivation occurred as a result of the unauthorized failure of agents of the State to follow established state procedure. There is no contention that the procedures themselves are inadequate nor is there any contention that it was practicable for the State to provide a predeprivation hearing. Moreover, the State of Nebraska has provided respondent with the means by which he can receive redress for the deprivation. The State provides a remedy to persons who believe they have suffered a tortious loss at the hands of the State. Through this tort claims procedure the State hears and pays claims of prisoners housed in its penal institutions.

Expanding on *Parratt* in *Hudson v. Palmer*, 468 U.S. 517 (1984), the Court reasoned that if the state actor's conduct was "random and unauthorized," the state could not be expected to anticipate the loss and provide procedures to protect against it before the deprivation occurred. Thus, in *Hudson*, the Court found that a prison guard's "random and unauthorized" act of destroying inmate property did not violate the inmate's procedural rights unless he could demonstrate that the state did not provide "adequate postdeprivation remedies," such as tort claims, to compensate him for his lost property.

On the other hand, if the deprivation occurs through established state procedures, rather than unauthorized acts, the due process violation is complete when the protected interest is harmed, and no inquiry into postdeprivation remedies is required. *Logan v. Zimmerman Brush Co.*, 455 U.S. 422 (1982).

Outside the context of constitutional claims that require exhaustion of state remedies, Congress by statute has added exhaustion requirements for a few categories of claims where exhaustion otherwise would not be required under § 1983. For example, Congress has adopted a limited exhaustion requirement for adult prisoners bringing actions under § 1983. In 1996, as part of the Prison Litigation Reform Act (PLRA), Congress enacted a broad mandatory exhaustion requirement for prisoner suits. Codified at 42 U.S.C. § 1997e(a), the statute provides:

> No action shall be brought with respect to prison conditions under section 1983 of this title, or any other Federal law, by a prisoner confined in any

jail, prison, or other correctional facility until such administrative remedies as are available are exhausted.

The Supreme Court has held that "the PLRA's exhaustion requirement applies to all inmate suits about prison life, whether they involve general circumstances or particular episodes, and whether they allege excessive force or some other wrong." *Porter v. Nussle*, 534 U.S. 516 (2002). Moreover, the Act "mandates initial recourse to the prison grievance process even when a prisoner seeks only money damages, a remedy not available in that process."

Should Congress adopt an exhaustion requirement for other types of § 1983 suits — suits claiming police brutality, for example? Or employment discrimination cases? Consider this question in light of the § 1983 cases not only in this chapter, but elsewhere in this book.

C. Section 1983 and Statutory Claims

Section 1983 provides a remedy for the deprivation under color of state law of any right "secured by "the Constitution *and laws* of the United States." If this language is read literally, it would embrace all claims asserting a violation of a federal statute by a state actor. In *Maine v. Thiboutot*, the Court held that the literal meaning is the correct one, but later decisions have qualified that holding. We look now at the precedents governing the availability of § 1983 for federal statutory claims.

Maine v. Thiboutot

Supreme Court of the United States, 1980.

448 U.S. 1.

Mr. Justice Brennan delivered the opinion of the Court.

The case presents two related questions arising under 42 U.S.C. § 1983 and 1988. Respondents brought this suit in the Maine Superior Court alleging that petitioners, the State of Maine and its Commissioner of Human Services, violated § 1983 by depriving respondents of welfare benefits to which they were entitled under the federal Social Security Act, specifically 42 U.S.C. § 602(a)(7). The petitioners present two issues: (1) whether § 1983 encompasses claims based on purely statutory violations of federal law, and (2) if so, whether attorney's fees under § 1988 may be awarded to the prevailing party in such an action.

Respondents, Lionel and Joline Thiboutot, are married and have eight children, three of whom are Lionel's by a previous marriage. The Maine Department of Human Services notified Lionel that, in computing the Aid to Families with Dependent Children (AFDC) benefits to which he was entitled for the three children exclusively his, it would no longer make allowance for the money spent to support the other five children, even though Lionel is legally obligated to support them. Respondents, challenging the State's interpretation of 42 U.S.C. § 602(a)(7), exhausted their state administrative remedies and then sought judicial review of the administrative action in the State Superior Court. By amended complaint, respondents also claimed relief under § 1983 for themselves and others similarly situated. The Superior Court's judgment enjoined petitioners from enforcing the challenged rule and ordered them to adopt new regulations, to notify class members of the new regulations, and to pay the correct amounts retroactively to respondents and prospectively to eligible class members. The court, however, denied respondents' motion for attorney's fees. The Supreme Judicial Court of Maine concluded that respondents had no entitlement to attorney's fees under state law, but were eligible for attorney's fees pursuant to the Civil Rights Attorney's Fees Awards Act of 1976. [We affirm.]

II

. . . The question before us is whether the phrase "and laws," as used in § 1983, means what it says, or whether it should be limited to some subset of laws. Given that Congress attached no modifiers to the phrase, the plain language of the statute undoubtedly embraces respondents' claim that petitioners violated the Social Security Act.

Even were the language ambiguous, however, any doubt as to its meaning has been resolved by our several cases suggesting, explicitly or implicitly, that the § 1983 remedy broadly encompasses violations of federal statutory as well as constitutional law. *Rosado v. Wyman*, 397 U.S. 397 (1970), for example, "held that suits in federal court under § 1983 are proper to secure compliance with the provisions of the Social Security Act on the part of participating States." *Edelman v. Jordan*, 415 U.S. 651 (1974). [Other citations omitted.]

While some might dismiss as dictum the foregoing statements, numerous and specific as they are, our analysis in several § 1983 cases involving Social Security Act (SSA) claims has relied on the availability of a § 1983 cause of action for statutory claims. Constitutional claims were also raised in these cases, providing a jurisdictional base, but the statutory claims were allowed to go forward, and were decided on the merits, under the court's pendent jurisdiction. . . .

In the face of the plain language of § 1983 and our consistent treatment of that provision, petitioners nevertheless persist in suggesting that the phrase "and laws" should be read as limited to civil rights or equal protection laws. Petitioners suggest that when § 1 of the Civil Rights Act of 1871, which accorded jurisdiction and a remedy for deprivations of rights secured by "the Constitution of the United States," was divided by the 1874 statutory revision into a remedial section, Rev. Stat. § 1979, and jurisdictional sections, Rev. Stat. § 563(12) and 629(16), Congress intended that the same change made in § 629(16) be made as to each of the new sections as well. Section 629(16), the jurisdictional provision for the circuit courts and the model for the current jurisdictional provision, 28 U.S.C. § 1343(3), applied to deprivations of rights secured by "the Constitution of the United States, or of any right secured by any law providing for equal rights." On the other hand, the remedial provision, the predecessor of § 1983, was expanded to apply to deprivations of rights secured by "the Constitution and laws," and § 563(12), the provision granting jurisdiction to the district courts, to deprivations of rights secured by "the Constitution of the United States, or of any right secured by any law of the United States."

We need not repeat at length the detailed debate over the meaning of the scanty legislative history concerning the addition of the phrase "and laws." See *Chapman v. Houston Welfare Rights Organization*, 441 U.S. 600 (1979). One conclusion which emerges clearly is that the legislative history does not permit a definitive answer. There is no express explanation offered for the insertion of the phrase "and laws." On the one hand, a principal purpose of the added language was to "ensure that federal legislation providing specifically for equality of rights would be brought within the ambit of the civil action authorized by that statute." *Chapman* (Powell, J., concurring). On the other hand, there are no indications that that was the only purpose, and Congress' attention was specifically directed to this new language. Representative Lawrence, in a speech to the House of Representatives that began by observing that the revisers had very often changed the meaning of existing statutes, referred to the civil rights statutes as "possibly [showing] verbal modifications bordering on legislation." He went on to read to Congress the original and revised versions.

In short, Congress was aware of what it was doing, and the legislative history does not demonstrate that the plain language was not intended. Petitioners' arguments amount to the claim that had Congress been more careful, and had it fully thought out the relationship among the various sections, it might have acted differently. That argument, however, can best be addressed to Congress, which, it is important to note, has remained quiet in the face of our many pronouncements on the scope of § 1983.

III

Petitioners next argue that, even if this claim is within § 1983, Congress did not intend statutory claims to be covered by the Civil Rights Attorney's Fees Awards Act of 1976, which added the following sentence to 42 U.S.C. § 1988 (emphasis added):

> In *any action* or proceeding *to enforce* a provision of sections 1981, 1982, *1983*, 1985, and 1986 of this title, [. . .] the court, in its discretion, may allow the prevailing party, other than the United States, a reasonable attorney's fee as part of the costs.

Once again, given our holding in Part II, *supra*, the plain language provides an answer. The statute states that fees are available in *any* § 1983 action. Since we hold that this statutory action is properly brought under § 1983, and since § 1988 makes no exception for statutory § 1983 actions, § 1988 plainly applies to this suit.

The legislative history is entirely consistent with the plain language. As was true with § 1983, a major purpose of the Civil Rights Attorney's Fees Awards Act was to benefit those claiming deprivations of constitutional and civil rights. Principal sponsors of the measure in both the House and the Senate, however, explicitly stated during the floor debates that the statute would make fees available more broadly. Representative Drinan explained that the Act would apply to § 1983 and that § 1983 "authorizes suits against State and local officials based upon Federal statutory as well as constitutional rights. . . ." Senator Kennedy also included an SSA case as an example of the cases "enforc[ing] the rights promised by Congress or the Constitution" which the Act would embrace. In short, there can be no question that Congress passed the Fees Act anticipating that it would apply to statutory § 1983 claims. . . .

Affirmed.

MR. JUSTICE POWELL, with whom THE CHIEF JUSTICE and MR. JUSTICE REHNQUIST join, dissenting.

The Court holds today, almost casually, that 42 U.S.C. § 1983 creates a cause of action for deprivations under color of state law of any federal statutory right. Having transformed purely statutory claims into "civil rights" actions under § 1983, the Court concludes that 42 U.S.C. § 1988 permits the "prevailing party" to recover his attorney's fees. These two holdings dramatically expand the liability of state and local officials and may virtually eliminate the "American Rule" in suits against those officials.

. . . [Until] today this Court never had held that § 1983 encompasses all purely statutory claims. Past treatment of the subject has been incidental and far from consistent. The only firm basis for decision is the historical evidence, which convincingly shows that the phrase the Court now finds so clear was—and remains—nothing more than a shorthand reference to equal rights legislation enacted by Congress. To read "and laws" more broadly is to ignore the lessons of history, logic, and policy.

Part I of this opinion examines the Court's claim that it only construes the "plain meaning" of § 1983, while Part II reviews the historical evidence on the enactment. Part III considers the practical consequences of today's decision. The final substantive section demonstrates that this Court's precedents do not support the Court's ruling today.

I

. . . If we were forbidden to look behind the language in legislative enactments, there might be some force to the suggestion that "and laws" must be read to include all federal statutes. But the "plain meaning" rule is not as inflexible as the Court imagines. . . .

Blind reliance on plain meaning is particularly inappropriate where, as here, Congress inserted the critical language without explicit discussion when it revised the statutes in 1874. Indeed, not a single shred of evidence in the legislative history of the adoption of the 1874 revision mentions this change. Since the legislative history also shows that the revision generally was not intended to alter the meaning of existing law, this Court previously has insisted that apparent changes be scrutinized with some care. . . .

In my view, the legislative history unmistakably shows that the variations in phrasing introduced in the 1874 revision were inadvertent, and that each section was intended to have precisely the same scope. Moreover, the only defensible interpretation of the contemporaneous legislative record is that the reference to "laws" in each section was intended "to do no more than ensure that federal legislation providing specifically for equality of rights would be brought within the ambit of the civil action authorized by [§ 1983]." Careful study of the available materials leaves no serious doubt that the Court's contrary conclusion is completely at odds with the intent of Congress in 1874. [Justice Powell's detailed account is omitted.]

III

The legislative history alone refutes the Court's assertion that the 43d Congress intended to alter the meaning of § 1983. But there are other compelling reasons to reject the Court's interpretation of the phrase "and laws." . . .

The Court's opinion does not consider the nature or scope of the litigation it has authorized. In practical effect, today's decision means that state and local governments, officers, and employees now may face liability whenever a person believes he has been injured by the administration of *any* federal-state cooperative program, whether or not that program is related to equal or civil rights.[11]

Even a cursory survey of the United States Code reveals that literally hundreds of cooperative regulatory and social welfare enactments may be affected. The States now participate in the enforcement of federal laws governing migrant labor, noxious weeds, historic preservation, wildlife conservation, anadromous fisheries, scenic trails, and strip mining. Various statutes authorize federal-state cooperative agreements in most aspects of federal land management. In addition, federal grants administered by state and local governments now are available in virtually every area of public administration. Unemployment, Medicaid, school lunch subsidies, food stamps, and other welfare benefits may provide particularly inviting subjects of litigation. Federal assistance also includes a variety of subsidies for education, housing, health care, transportation, public works, and law enforcement. Those who might benefit from these grants now will be potential § 1983 plaintiffs. . . .

Moreover, state and local governments will bear the entire burden of liability for violations of statutory "civil rights" even when federal officials are involved equally in the administration of the affected program. Section 1983 grants no right of action against the United States, and few of the foregoing cooperative programs provide expressly for private actions to enforce their terms. Thus, private litigants may sue responsible federal officials only in the relatively rare case in which a cause of action may be implied from the governing substantive statute. *Cf. Transamerica Mortgage Advisors, Inc. v. Lewis*, 444 U.S. 11 (1979); *Touche Ross & Co. v. Redington*, 442 U.S. 560 (1979) [Chapter 8 Note]. It defies reason to believe that Congress intended — without discussion — to impose such a burden only upon state defendants.

1

Even when a cause of action against federal officials is available, litigants are likely to focus efforts upon state defendants in order to obtain attorney's fees under the liberal standard of 42 U.S.C. § 1988. There is some evidence that § 1983 claims already are being appended to complaints solely for the purpose of obtaining fees in actions

---

11. The only exception will be in cases where the governing statute provides an exclusive remedy for violations of its terms.

where "civil rights" of any kind are at best an afterthought. In this case, for example, the respondents added a § 1983 count to their complaint some years after the action was initiated, apparently in response to the enactment of the Civil Rights Attorney's Fees Awards Act of 1976. The uses of this technique have not been explored fully. But the rules of pendent jurisdiction are quite liberal, and plaintiffs who prevail on pendent claims may win awards under § 1988. Consequently, ingenious pleaders may find ways to recover attorney's fees in almost any suit against a state defendant. Nothing in the legislative history of the Civil Rights Attorney's Fees Awards Act of 1976 suggests that Congress intended to remove so completely the protection of the "American Rule" in suits against state defendants.

2

When Congress revised the statutes in 1874, it hardly could have anticipated the subsequent proliferation of federal statutes. Yet, congressional power to enact laws under the Spending and Commerce Clauses was well known in 1874. Congress need not have foreseen the ultimate scope of those powers to have understood that the expansion of § 1983 to statutory claims would have serious consequences. . . . It is simply inconceivable that Congress, while professing a firm intention not to make substantive changes in the law, nevertheless intended to enact a major new remedial program by approving—without discussion—the addition of two words to a statute adopted only three years earlier.

IV

The Court finally insists that its interpretation of § 1983 is foreordained by a line of precedent so strong that further analysis is unnecessary. [But far] from being a long-accepted fact, purely statutory § 1983 actions are an invention of the last 20 years. . . . Yet, until last Term, neither this Court nor any Justice ever had undertaken—directly and thoroughly—a consideration of the question presented in this case. [Justice Powell's detailed discussion of the precedents is omitted.]

V

In my view, the Court's decision today significantly expands the concept of "civil rights" and creates a major new intrusion into state sovereignty under our federal system. There is no probative evidence that Congress intended to authorize the pervasive judicial oversight of state officials that will flow from the Court's construction of § 1983. Although today's decision makes new law with far-reaching consequences, the Court brushes aside the critical issues of congressional intent, national policy, and the force of past decisions as precedent. I would reverse the judgment of the Supreme Judicial Court of Maine.

Note: The Aftermath of Thiboutot

1. The Court in *Thiboutot* relies on "the plain language" of § 1983. Justice Powell, in dissent, insists that "the critical language" was inserted inadvertently when Congress revised the federal statutes in 1874. Whether or not Justice Powell had the better of this argument, no one on the Court has shown any interest in reopening the

issue. Thus it is settled that § 1983 provides a cause of action for state deprivations of "rights secured" by "the laws" of the United States.

2. One year after *Thiboutot*, the Court described two qualifications to the rule laid down by that decision. The case was *Pennhurst State School & Hospital v. Halderman*, 451 U.S. 1 (1981), and the opinion was written by Justice Powell. First, the Court indicated that a federal statute that imposes obligations on the states does not necessarily create a "right secured" by the laws of the United States within the meaning of § 1983. Second, the Court noted with apparent approval Justice Powell's suggestion in *Thiboutot* (footnote 11 of his opinion) that § 1983 would not be available where the "governing statute provides an exclusive remedy for violations of its terms." Both of these propositions have generated an extensive body of law.

Gonzaga University v. Doe

Supreme Court of the United States, 2002.

536 U.S. 273.

CHIEF JUSTICE REHNQUIST delivered the opinion of the Court.

The question presented is whether a student may sue a private university for damages under 42 U.S.C. § 1983, to enforce provisions of the Family Educational Rights and Privacy Act of 1974 (FERPA or Act) which prohibit the federal funding of educational institutions that have a policy or practice of releasing education records to unauthorized persons. We hold such an action foreclosed because the relevant provisions of FERPA create no personal rights to enforce under 42 U.S.C. § 1983.

Respondent John Doe is a former undergraduate in the School of Education at Gonzaga University, a private university in Spokane, Washington. He planned to graduate and teach at a Washington public elementary school. Washington at the time required all of its new teachers to obtain an affidavit of good moral character from a dean of their graduating college or university. In October 1993, Roberta League, Gonzaga's "teacher certification specialist," overheard one student tell another that respondent engaged in acts of sexual misconduct against Jane Doe, a female undergraduate. League launched an investigation and contacted the state agency responsible for teacher certification, identifying respondent by name and discussing the allegations against him. Respondent did not learn of the investigation, or that information about him had been disclosed, until March 1994, when he was told by League and others that he would not receive the affidavit required for certification as a Washington schoolteacher.

Respondent then sued Gonzaga and League (petitioners) in state court. He alleged violations of Washington tort and contract law, as well as a pendent violation of § 1983 for the release of personal information to an "unauthorized person" in violation of FERPA.[1] A jury found for respondent on all counts, awarding him $1,155,000,

---

1. The Washington [appellate courts] found petitioners to have acted "under color of state law" for purposes of § 1983 when they disclosed respondent's personal information to state officials in connection with state-law teacher certification requirements. Although the petition for certiorari

including $150,000 in compensatory damages and $300,000 in punitive damages on the FERPA claim.

The Washington Court of Appeals reversed in relevant part, concluding that FERPA does not create individual rights and thus cannot be enforced under § 1983. The Washington Supreme Court reversed that decision, and ordered the FERPA damages reinstated. The court acknowledged that "FERPA itself does not give rise to a private cause of action," but reasoned that FERPA's nondisclosure provision "gives rise to a federal right enforceable under section 1983."

Like the Washington Supreme Court and the state court of appeals below, other state and federal courts have divided on the question of FERPA's enforceability under § 1983. The fact that all of these courts have relied on the same set of opinions from this Court suggests that our opinions in this area may not be models of clarity. We therefore granted certiorari to resolve the conflict among the lower courts and in the process resolve any ambiguity in our own opinions.

Congress enacted FERPA under its spending power to condition the receipt of federal funds on certain requirements relating to the access and disclosure of student educational records. The Act directs the Secretary of Education to withhold federal funds from any public or private "educational agency or institution" that fails to comply with these conditions. As relevant here, the Act provides:

> No funds shall be made available under any applicable program to any educational agency or institution which has a policy or practice of permitting the release of education records (or personally identifiable information contained therein . . .) of students without the written consent of their parents to any individual, agency, or organization. 20 U.S.C. § 1232g(b)(1).

The Act directs the Secretary of Education to enforce this and other of the Act's spending conditions. § 1232g(f). The Secretary is required to establish an office and review board within the Department of Education for "investigating, processing, reviewing, and adjudicating violations of [the Act]." § 1232g(g). Funds may be terminated only if the Secretary determines that a recipient institution "is failing to comply substantially with any requirement of [the Act]" and that such compliance "cannot be secured by voluntary means." § 1234c(a), 1232g(f).

Respondent contends that this statutory regime confers upon any student enrolled at a covered school or institution a federal right, enforceable in suits for damages under § 1983, not to have "education records" disclosed to unauthorized persons without the student's express written consent. But we have never before held, and decline to do so here, that spending legislation drafted in terms resembling those of FERPA can confer enforceable rights.

In *Maine v. Thiboutot*, 448 U.S. 1 (1980), six years after Congress enacted FERPA, we recognized for the first time that § 1983 actions may be brought against state

---

challenged this holding, we agreed to review only the question posed in the first paragraph of this opinion. . . . We therefore assume without deciding that the relevant disclosures occurred under color of state law.

actors to enforce rights created by federal statutes as well as by the Constitution. There we held that plaintiffs could recover payments wrongfully withheld by a state agency in violation of the Social Security Act. A year later, in *Pennhurst State School and Hospital v. Halderman*, 451 U.S. 1 (1981), we rejected a claim that the Developmentally Disabled Assistance and Bill of Rights Act of 1975 conferred enforceable rights, saying:

> In legislation enacted pursuant to the spending power, the typical remedy for state noncompliance with federally imposed conditions is not a private cause of action for noncompliance but rather action by the Federal Government to terminate funds to the State.

We made clear that unless Congress "speaks with a clear voice," and manifests an "unambiguous" intent to confer individual rights, federal funding provisions provide no basis for private enforcement by § 1983.

Since *Pennhurst*, only twice have we found spending legislation to give rise to enforceable rights. [The Court briefly summarized *Wright v. Roanoke Redevelopment and Housing Authority*, 479 U.S. 418 (1987), and *Wilder v. Virginia Hosp. Ass'n*, 496 U.S. 498 (1990).]

Our more recent decisions, however, have rejected attempts to infer enforceable rights from Spending Clause statutes. [The Court briefly summarized *Suter v. Artist M.*, 503 U.S. 347 (1992).]

Similarly, in *Blessing v. Freestone*, 520 U.S. 329 (1997), Title IV-D of the Social Security Act required States receiving federal child-welfare funds to "substantially comply" with requirements designed to ensure timely payment of child support. Five Arizona mothers invoked § 1983 against state officials on grounds that state child-welfare agencies consistently failed to meet these requirements. We found no basis for the suit, saying,

> Far from creating an *individual* entitlement to services, the standard is simply a yardstick for the Secretary to measure the *systemwide* performance of a State's Title IV-D program. Thus, the Secretary must look to the aggregate services provided by the State, not to whether the needs of any particular person have been satisfied. (Emphases in original.)

Because the provision focused on "the aggregate services provided by the State," rather than "the needs of any particular person," it conferred no individual rights and thus could not be enforced by § 1983. We emphasized: "To seek redress through § 1983, . . . a plaintiff must assert the violation of a federal *right*, not merely a violation of federal *law*." (Emphases in original.)

Respondent reads this line of cases to establish a relatively loose standard for finding rights enforceable by § 1983. He claims that a federal statute confers such rights so long as Congress intended that the statute "benefit" putative plaintiffs. He further contends that a more "rigorous" inquiry would conflate the standard for inferring a private right of action under § 1983 with the standard for inferring a private right of action directly from the statute itself, which he admits would not exist under FERPA.

As authority, respondent points to *Blessing* and *Wilder*, which, he says, used the term "benefit" to define the sort of statutory interest enforceable by § 1983.

Some language in our opinions might be read to suggest that something less than an unambiguously conferred right is enforceable by § 1983. *Blessing*, for example, set forth three "factors" to guide judicial inquiry into whether or not a statute confers a right: "Congress must have intended that the provision in question benefit the plaintiff," "the plaintiff must demonstrate that the right assertedly protected by the statute is not so 'vague and amorphous' that its enforcement would strain judicial resources," and "the provision giving rise to the asserted right must be couched in mandatory, rather than precatory, terms." In the same paragraph, however, *Blessing* emphasizes that it is only violations of *rights*, not *laws*, which give rise to § 1983 actions. This confusion has led some courts to interpret *Blessing* as allowing plaintiffs to enforce a statute under § 1983 so long as the plaintiff falls within the general zone of interest that the statute is intended to protect; something less than what is required for a statute to create rights enforceable directly from the statute itself under an implied private right of action. Fueling this uncertainty is the notion that our implied private right of action cases have no bearing on the standards for discerning whether a statute creates rights enforceable by § 1983. *Wilder* appears to support this notion while *Suter* and *Pennhurst* appear to disavow it.

We now reject the notion that our cases permit anything short of an unambiguously conferred right to support a cause of action brought under § 1983. Section 1983 provides a remedy only for the deprivation of "rights, privileges, or immunities secured by the Constitution and laws" of the United States. Accordingly, it is *rights*, not the broader or vaguer "benefits" or "interests," that may be enforced under the authority of that section. This being so, we further reject the notion that our implied right of action cases are separate and distinct from our § 1983 cases. To the contrary, our implied right of action cases should guide the determination of whether a statute confers rights enforceable under § 1983.

We have recognized that whether a statutory violation may be enforced through § 1983 "is a different inquiry than that involved in determining whether a private right of action can be implied from a particular statute." *Wilder*. But the inquiries overlap in one meaningful respect — in either case we must first determine whether Congress *intended to create a federal right*. . . .

Plaintiffs suing under § 1983 do not have the burden of showing an intent to create a private remedy because § 1983 generally supplies a remedy for the vindication of rights secured by federal statutes. Once a plaintiff demonstrates that a statute confers an individual right, the right is presumptively enforceable by § 1983.[4] But the initial inquiry — determining whether a statute confers any right at all — is no different

---

4. The State may rebut this presumption by showing that Congress "specifically foreclosed a remedy under § 1983." *Smith v. Robinson*, 468 U.S. 992 (1984). The State's burden is to demonstrate that Congress shut the door to private enforcement either expressly, through "specific evidence from the statute itself," *Wright*, or "impliedly, by creating a comprehensive enforcement scheme that is incompatible with individual enforcement under § 1983," *Blessing*. See also *Middlesex County Sewerage Authority v. National Sea Clammers Assn.*, 453 U.S. 1 (1981) [*Sea Clammers*]. These questions do not

from the initial inquiry in an implied right of action case, the express purpose of which is to determine whether or not a statute "confers rights on a particular class of persons." *California v. Sierra Club*, 451 U.S. 287 (1981). This makes obvious sense, since § 1983 merely provides a mechanism for enforcing individual rights "secured" elsewhere, *i.e.*, rights independently "secured by the Constitution and laws" of the United States. "One cannot go into court and claim a 'violation of § 1983'— for § 1983 by itself does not protect anyone against anything." *Chapman v. Houston Welfare Rights Organization*, 441 U.S. 600 (1979).

A court's role in discerning whether personal rights exist in the § 1983 context should therefore not differ from its role in discerning whether personal rights exist in the implied right of action context. . . . Both inquiries simply require a determination as to whether or not Congress intended to confer individual rights upon a class of beneficiaries. . . . Accordingly, where the text and structure of a statute provide no indication that Congress intends to create new individual rights, there is no basis for a private suit, whether under § 1983 or under an implied right of action.

Justice Stevens disagrees with this conclusion principally because separation-of-powers concerns are, in his view, more pronounced in the implied right of action context as opposed to the § 1983 context. But we fail to see how relations between the branches are served by having courts apply a multi-factor balancing test to pick and choose which federal requirements may be enforced by § 1983 and which may not. Nor are separation-of-powers concerns within the Federal Government the only guideposts in this sort of analysis. [As we said in] *Will v. Michigan Dep't of State Police*, 491 U.S. 58 (1989), "If Congress intends to alter the 'usual constitutional balance between the States and the Federal Government,' it must make its intention to do so 'unmistakably clear in the language of the statute.'"[5]

With this principle in mind, there is no question that FERPA's nondisclosure provisions fail to confer enforceable rights. To begin with, the provisions entirely lack the sort of "rights-creating" language critical to showing the requisite congressional intent to create new rights. Unlike the individually focused terminology of Titles VI and IX ("no person shall be subjected to discrimination"), FERPA's provisions speak only to the Secretary of Education, directing that "no funds shall be made available" to any "educational agency or institution" which has a prohibited "policy or practice." 20 U.S.C. § 1232g(b)(1). This focus is two steps removed from the interests of individual students and parents and clearly does not confer the sort of "*individual* entitlement" that is enforceable under § 1983. *Blessing* (emphasis in original). As we said in *Cannon v. University of Chicago*, 441 U.S. 677 (1979):

---

arise in this case due to our conclusion that FERPA confers no individual rights and thus cannot give rise to a presumption of enforceability under § 1983.

    5. This case illustrates the point well. Justice Stevens would conclude that Congress intended FERPA's nondisclosure provisions to confer individual rights on millions of school students from kindergarten through graduate school without having ever said so explicitly. This conclusion entails a judicial assumption, with no basis in statutory text, that Congress intended to set itself resolutely against a tradition of deference to state and local school officials by subjecting them to private suits for money damages whenever they fail to comply with a federal funding condition.

> There would be far less reason to infer a private remedy in favor of individual persons if Congress, instead of drafting Title IX with an unmistakable focus on the benefited class, had written it simply as a ban on discriminatory conduct by recipients of federal funds or as a prohibition against the disbursement of public funds to educational institutions engaged in discriminatory practices.

See also *Alexander v. Sandoval*, 532 U.S. 275 (2001) ("Statutes that focus on the person regulated rather than the individuals protected create 'no implication of an intent to confer rights on a particular class of persons'").

FERPA's nondisclosure provisions further speak only in terms of institutional policy and practice, not individual instances of disclosure. See 1232g(b)(1)-(2) (prohibiting the funding of "any educational agency or institution which has a *policy or practice* of permitting the release of education records" (emphasis added)). Therefore, as in *Blessing*, they have an "aggregate" focus, they are not concerned with "whether the needs of any particular person have been satisfied," and they cannot "give rise to individual rights." Recipient institutions can further avoid termination of funding so long as they "comply substantially" with the Act's requirements. § 1234c(a). This, too, is not unlike *Blessing*, which found that Title IV-D failed to support a § 1983 suit in part because it only required "substantial compliance" with federal regulations. . . . For reasons expressed repeatedly in our prior cases, [such] provisions cannot make out the requisite congressional intent to confer individual rights enforceable by § 1983.

Our conclusion that FERPA's nondisclosure provisions fail to confer enforceable rights is buttressed by the mechanism that Congress chose to provide for enforcing those provisions. Congress expressly authorized the Secretary of Education to "*deal with violations*" of the Act, § 1232g(f) (emphasis added), and required the Secretary to "establish or designate [a] review board" for investigating and adjudicating such violations, § 1232g(g). Pursuant to these provisions, the Secretary created the Family Policy Compliance Office (FPCO) "to act as the Review Board required under the Act and to enforce the Act with respect to all applicable programs." The FPCO permits students and parents who suspect a violation of the Act to file individual written complaints. If a complaint is timely and contains required information, the FPCO will initiate an investigation, notify the educational institution of the charge, and request a written response. If a violation is found, the FPCO distributes a notice of factual findings and a "statement of the specific steps that the agency or institution must take to comply" with FERPA. These administrative procedures squarely distinguish this case from *Wright* and *Wilder*, where an aggrieved individual lacked any federal review mechanism and further counsel against our finding a congressional intent to create individually enforceable private rights.[8]

---

8. We need not determine whether FERPA's procedures are "sufficiently comprehensive" to offer an independent basis for precluding private enforcement [under *Sea Clammers*], due to our finding that FERPA creates no private right to enforce.

Congress finally provided that "except for the conduct of hearings, none of the functions of the Secretary under this section shall be carried out in any of the regional offices" of the Department of Education. This centralized review provision was added just four months after FERPA's enactment due to "concern that regionalizing the enforcement of [FERPA] may lead to multiple interpretations of it, and possibly work a hardship on parents, students, and institutions." 120 Cong. Rec. 39863 (1974) (joint statement). It is implausible to presume that the same Congress nonetheless intended private suits to be brought before thousands of federal- and state-court judges, which could only result in the sort of "multiple interpretations" the Act explicitly sought to avoid.

In sum, if Congress wishes to create new rights enforceable under § 1983, it must do so in clear and unambiguous terms — no less and no more than what is required for Congress to create new rights enforceable under an implied private right of action. FERPA's nondisclosure provisions contain no rights-creating language, they have an aggregate, not individual, focus, and they serve primarily to direct the Secretary of Education's distribution of public funds to educational institutions. They therefore create no rights enforceable under § 1983. Accordingly, the judgment of the Supreme Court of Washington is reversed, and the case is remanded for further proceedings not inconsistent with this opinion.

JUSTICE BREYER, with whom JUSTICE SOUTER joins, concurring in the judgment.

The ultimate question, in respect to whether private individuals may bring a lawsuit to enforce a federal statute, through 42 U.S.C. § 1983 or otherwise, is a question of congressional intent. In my view, the factors set forth in this Court's § 1983 cases are helpful indications of that intent. See, *e.g., Blessing; Suter; Wilder; Wright.* But the statute books are too many, the laws too diverse, and their purposes too complex, for any single legal formula to offer more than general guidance. I would not, in effect, pre-determine an outcome through the use of a presumption — such as the majority's presumption that a right is conferred only if set forth "unambiguously" in the statute's "text and structure."

At the same time, I do not believe that Congress intended private judicial enforcement of this statute's "school record privacy" provisions. The Court mentions most of the considerations I find persuasive: The phrasing of the relevant prohibition (stating that "no funds shall be made available" to institutions with a "policy or practice" of permitting the release of "education records"); the total absence (in the relevant statutory provision) of any reference to individual "rights" or the like; the related provisions that make clear, by creating administrative enforcement processes, that the Spending Clause was not simply a device to obtain federal jurisdiction; and later statutory insistence upon centralized federal enforcement at the national, not the regional, level.

I would add one further reason. Much of the statute's key language is broad and nonspecific. The statute, for example, defines its key term, "education records," as (with certain enumerated exceptions) "those records, files, documents, and other materials which (i) contain information directly related to a student; and (ii) are maintained by an educational . . . institution." This kind of language leaves schools uncertain as to just when they can, or cannot, reveal various kinds of information. It has led, or could lead, to legal claims that would limit, or forbid, such practices as peer grading, see *Owasso Independent School Dist. No. I-011 v. Falvo*, 534 U.S. 426 (2002), teacher evaluations, see *Moore v. Hyche*, 761 F. Supp. 112 (N.D. Ala. 1991), school "honor society" recommendations, see *Price v. Young*, 580 F. Supp. 1 (E.D. Ark. 1983), or even roll call responses and "bad conduct" marks written down in class, see Tr. of Oral Arg. in *Falvo*. And it is open to interpretations that invariably favor confidentiality almost irrespective of conflicting educational needs or the importance, or common sense, of limited disclosures in certain circumstances, say, where individuals are being considered for work with young children or other positions of trust.

Under these circumstances, Congress may well have wanted to make the agency remedy that it provided exclusive—both to achieve the expertise, uniformity, widespread consultation, and resulting administrative guidance that can accompany agency decisionmaking and to avoid the comparative risk of inconsistent interpretations and misincentives that can arise out of an occasional inappropriate application of the statute in a private action for damages. This factor, together with the others to which the majority refers, convinces me that Congress did not intend private judicial enforcement actions here.

JUSTICE STEVENS, with whom JUSTICE GINSBURG joins, dissenting.

The Court's *ratio decidendi* in this case has a "now you see it, now you don't" character. At times, the Court seems to hold that FERPA simply does not create any federal rights, thereby disposing of the case with a negative answer to the question "whether Congress *intended to create a federal right*." This interpretation would explain the Court's studious avoidance of the rights-creating language in the title and the text of the Act. Alternatively, its opinion may be read as accepting the proposition that FERPA does indeed create both parental rights of access to student records and student rights of privacy in such records, but that those federal rights are of a lesser value because Congress did not intend them to be enforceable by their owners. I shall first explain why the statute does, indeed, create federal rights, and then explain why the Court's novel attempt to craft a new category of second-class statutory rights is misguided.

I

Title 20 U.S.C. § 1232g, which embodies FERPA in its entirety, includes 10 subsections, which create rights for both students and their parents, and describe the procedures for enforcing and protecting those rights. . . .

Of course, as we have stated previously, a "blanket approach" to determining whether a statute creates rights enforceable under 42 U.S.C. § 1983 is inappropriate. *Blessing v. Freestone*. The precise statutory provision at issue in this case is § 1232g(b). Although the rights-creating language in this subsection is not as explicit as it is in other parts of the statute, it is clear that, in substance, § 1232g(b) formulates an individual right: in respondent's words, the "right of parents to withhold consent and prevent the unauthorized release of education record information by an educational institution . . . that has a policy or practice of releasing such information."

The Court claims that § 1232g(b), because it references a "policy or practice," has an aggregate focus and thus cannot qualify as an individual right. But § 1232g(b) does not simply ban an institution from having a policy or practice—which would be a more systemic requirement. Rather, it permits a policy or practice of releasing information, *so long as* "there is written consent from the student's parents specifying records to be released, the reasons for such release, and to whom, and with a copy of the records to be released to the student's parents and the student if desired by the parents." The provision speaks of the individual "student," not students generally....

The Court also claims that "we have never before held . . . that spending legislation drafted in terms resembling those of FERPA can confer enforceable rights." In making this claim, the Court contrasts FERPA's "no funds shall be made available" language with "individually focused terminology" characteristic of federal antidiscrimination statutes, such as "no person shall be subjected to discrimination." But the sort of rights-creating language idealized by the Court has *never* been present in our § 1983 cases; rather, such language ordinarily gives rise to an implied cause of action. See *Cannon v. University of Chicago*, 441 U.S. 677 (1979). None of our four most recent cases involving whether a Spending Clause statute created rights enforceable under § 1983—*Wright, Wilder, Suter*, and *Blessing* —involved the sort of "no person shall" rights-creating language envisioned by the Court. And in two of those cases—*Wright* and *Wilder*—we concluded that individual rights enforceable under § 1983 existed....

II

Since FERPA was enacted in 1974, all of the Federal Courts of Appeals expressly deciding the question have concluded that FERPA creates federal rights enforceable under § 1983. . . . [The] Court departs from over a quarter century of settled law in concluding that FERPA creates no enforceable rights. Perhaps more pernicious than its disturbing of the settled status of FERPA rights, though, is the Court's novel use of our implied right of action cases in determining whether a federal right exists for § 1983 purposes....

A requirement that Congress intend a "right to support a cause of action," as opposed to simply the creation of an individual federal right, makes sense in the implied right of action context. As we have explained, our implied right of action cases "reflect a concern, grounded in separation of powers, that Congress rather than the courts controls the availability of remedies for violations of statutes." *Wilder*. However, imposing the implied right of action framework upon the § 1983 inquiry is not necessary: The separation-of-powers concerns present in the implied right of action context "are not present in a § 1983 case," because Congress expressly authorized private suits in § 1983 itself....

Note: "Unambiguously Conferred Rights"

1. The Court in *Gonzaga University* lays down a stringent standard for determining whether a federal statute confers rights enforceable under § 1983. Henceforth, nothing short of an "unambiguously conferred right" will suffice.

2. One might think that the *Gonzaga University* standard will be impossible to meet, and that the only statutory rights that can be enforced under § 1983 will be those that were held enforceable in *Wright* and *Wilder*, the cases that the *Gonzaga University* Court distinguishes. In fact, several lower court decisions since *Gonzaga University* have upheld statutory claims under § 1983. A particularly interesting example is *Sabree v. Richman*, 367 F.3d 180 (3d Cir. 2004). The court explained the origins of the case:

> Plaintiffs are a class of mentally retarded adults in need of medical services from an intermediate care facility for persons with mental retardation ("ICF/MR services"). Although they qualify for state assistance to obtain these services under the Medicaid Act, that assistance has not been forthcoming. In an effort to force Pennsylvania to provide the needed services, plaintiffs, pursuant to 42 U.S.C. § 1983, sued the Secretary of the Pennsylvania Department of Public Welfare. Pennsylvania argues that it would provide assistance if it could but that it cannot, and that, in any event, the sole remedy for its non-compliance with the Medicaid Act is the suspension or revocation of funding from Congress. . . .

> The District Court, relying heavily on *Gonzaga University*, concluded that Congress had not unambiguously conferred the rights that plaintiffs sought to vindicate under § 1983, and dismissed the suit. At first blush, language in *Gonzaga University* would appear to support that conclusion. . . . The Court, no doubt, has set a high bar for plaintiffs. Nonetheless, after having considered the relevant provisions of the Medicaid Act against the backdrop of *Gonzaga University*, we are convinced that Congress unambiguously conferred the rights which plaintiffs here seek to enforce.

In explaining how it reached this conclusion, the court began with the language of the statute. The plaintiffs relied on three provisions of the Medicaid Act. The court said:

> Plaintiffs seek to enforce the right to acquire ICF/MR services, by virtue of 42 U.S.C. § 1396a(a)(10) and 1396d(a)(15). The language of the statute requires that a state "must provide . . . medical assistance . . . to . . . all [eligible] individuals," and includes intermediate care facilities in the definition of "medical assistance." Plaintiffs also seek to enforce the right to acquire ICF/MR services with "reasonable promptness," as required by 42 U.S.C. § 1396a(a)(8). The language of the statute declares that a state "must provide . . . assistance . . . with reasonable promptness to all eligible individuals."

> In each of these provisions, the statutory language is clear and unambiguous. Indeed, we can hardly imagine anyone disputing that a state must provide the assistance necessary to obtain ICF/MR services, and that it must do so with "reasonable promptness," and the government does not do so. Our inquiry, however, does not end there. Indisputably, these provisions create law, binding on those states choosing to accept Medicaid funding. Whether the same provisions confer rights, enforceable by individuals, is another question, and is the question we are called upon to answer.

To determine whether these provisions provide plaintiffs with unambiguously conferred rights, we begin with what has come to be called the "*Blessing* Test." As discussed above, the plain language of the statute clearly conveys that a state "must provide" plaintiffs with "medical assistance," including ICF/MR services, with "reasonable promptness." Without difficulty, we conclude that these provisions satisfy the *Blessing* Test because: (1) plaintiffs were the intended beneficiaries of [the three statutory provisions]; (2) the rights sought to be enforced by them are specific and enumerated, not "vague and amorphous"; and (3) the obligation imposed on the states is unambiguous and binding.

But, again, our inquiry does not end there because, as is explained in *Gonzaga University*, the *Blessing* Test may only indicate that plaintiffs "fall[] within the general zone of interest that the statute is intended to protect; something less than what is required for a statute to create rights enforceable directly from the statute itself. . . ." To ensure that Congress unambiguously conferred the rights asserted, we must determine whether Congress used "rights-creating terms."

The Court identified the text of Titles VI and IX as exemplars of rights-creating language. Viewing Titles VI and IX, we find it difficult, if not impossible, as a linguistic matter, to distinguish the import of the relevant Title XIX language—"A State plan must provide"—from the "No person shall" language of Titles VI and IX. Just as in Titles VI and IX, the relevant terms used in Title XIX are "mandatory rather than precatory." Further, the "individual focus" of [the three provisions] is unmistakable. The relevant Title XIX provisions enumerate the entitlements available to "all eligible individuals." The provisions do not focus on "the [entity] . . . regulated rather than the individuals protected." Neither do the statutory references to the individual appear "in the context of describing the type of 'policy or practice' that triggers a funding prohibition."

In requiring states which accept Medicaid funding to provide ICF/MR services with reasonable promptness, Congress conferred specific entitlements on individuals "in terms that 'could not be clearer.'" There is no ambiguity. Where, as here, the plain meaning of the text is evident, we need not look further to determine congressional intent.

The court conceded that the appropriations and general introductory statement of the Medicaid Act does not contain the rights-creating language required by *Gonzaga University*. But that section of the statute, the court said, "cannot neutralize the right-creating language" in the three specific provisions.

Do you agree that the relevant Title XIX language—"A State plan must provide"—is linguistically indistinguishable from the "No person shall" language of Titles VI and IX? Another court reached a different result with respect to the "reasonable promptness" provision of 42 U.S.C. § 1396a(a)(8). The court said that this provision "does not contain the explicit rights-creating language described in *Gonzaga University* and merely places certain conditions upon a state seeking Medicaid funding." *M.A.C. v. Betit*, 284 F. Supp. 2d 1298 (D. Utah 2003). Is this a more persuasive application of *Gonzaga University*?

3. The Third Circuit in *Sabree* repeatedly refers to the "*Blessing* test." The reference is to the following passage from *Blessing*:

> We have traditionally looked at three factors when determining whether a particular statutory provision gives rise to a federal right. First, Congress must have intended that the provision in question benefit the plaintiff. Second, the plaintiff must demonstrate that the right assertedly protected by the statute is not so "vague and amorphous" that its enforcement would strain judicial competence. Third, the statute must unambiguously impose a binding obligation on the States. In other words, the provision giving rise to the asserted right must be couched in mandatory, rather than precatory, terms.

Other courts of appeals also rely on the "*Blessing* test" to determine whether a federal statute confers a right enforceable through § 1983. *See, e.g., Henry A. v. Wilden*, 678 F.3d 991 (9th Cir. 2012) ("If a statute satisfies the *Blessing* test, it is presumptively enforceable through § 1983."); *Ctr. for Special Needs Trust Admin., Inc. v. Olson*, 676 F.3d 688 (8th Cir. 2012) (same).

Should federal courts continue to apply *Blessing*'s three-part "test" to identify enforceable federal rights? Or did *Gonzaga University* fundamentally change the rights-creation inquiry? *See Doe v. Kidd*, 501 F.3d 348 (4th Cir. 2007) (Whitney, J., dissenting in part) (arguing that "the three-factor test of *Blessing*" is no longer controlling after *Gonzaga University*, "which was explicitly intended to resolve considerable uncertainty stemming from the Court's prior opinions on the subject").

How do those "factors" play out in other contexts? Consider the Problem that follows.

Problem: A "Right" to Transport Firearms?

William Cody is a resident of West Fremont, where he is legally authorized to carry a handgun or rifle without a license. Last year, after visiting family in the state of Illiana, Cody drove to Oceana International Airport (OAI or Airport) in the neighboring state of Oceana to catch a flight home. The airport is operated by the Oceana Airport Authority, a state agency.

Cody brought three items of luggage: a suitcase, a garment bag, and a carrying case that contained a Ruger pistol, purchased by his grandfather and given to him by his father. The pistol was properly unloaded and packaged according to federal Transportation Security Administration (TSA) regulations. Upon his arrival at the airport, Cody informed the airline ticket agent that he had a gun in a carrying case, which he wanted to check through. The agent tagged the firearm with an orange firearms declaration tag and advised Cody that it was standard operating procedure to notify the Airport Police when a passenger declares a weapon. She did so.

Officer Jones responded to the agent's call. He took the position that Cody needed to first establish that his possession of the gun was lawful, before the question of whether he could legally possess the gun in Oceana or West Fremont became relevant. A TSA supervisor arrived and took the position that under the Firearms Owners' Protection Act of 1986 (FOPA), Cody was permitted to transport the weapon without regard to local law. Ultimately Officer Jones and other Airport Police officers arrested Cody for violating Oceana Penal Law § 3456, which makes it a crime to possess any firearm without an Oceana firearms license. Cody was held for 28 hours. All charges were later dropped.

Cody has now brought suit against the officers in federal district court under 42 U.S.C. § 1983. He asserts violation of his rights under the Fourth Amendment and also violation of 18 U.S.C. § 926A, enacted as part of FOPA. Section 926A provides in part:

> Notwithstanding any other provision of any law . . . of a State or any political subdivision thereof, any person who is not otherwise prohibited by [the Firearms Chapter of Title 18] from transporting, shipping, or receiving a firearm shall be entitled to transport a firearm for any lawful purpose from any place where he may lawfully possess and carry such firearm to any other place where he may lawfully possess and carry such firearm if, during such transportation the firearm is unloaded, and neither the firearm nor any ammunition being transported is readily accessible or is directly accessible from the passenger compartment of such transporting vehicle. . . .

The defendants move to dismiss the FOPA claim on the ground that a violation of § 926A cannot be enforced through § 1983. Should the district court grant the motion? Does the *Sea Clammers* doctrine, discussed in the next Note, shed any light on the question?

Note: The "Sea Clammers" Doctrine

1. Justice Powell, in a footnote to his dissent in *Thiboutot*, expressed the belief that the § 1983 remedy would not be available for federal statutory claims "where the governing statute provides an exclusive remedy for violations of its terms." This comment became law one year later in *Middlesex County Sewerage Authority v. National Sea Clammers Ass'n*, 453 U.S. 1 (1981). Justice Powell wrote the Court's opinion.

The plaintiffs in *Sea Clammers* alleged damage to fishing grounds caused by discharges and ocean dumping of sewage and other waste. They sued various state governmental entities, basing their claims on the Federal Water Pollution Control Act (FWPCA) and the Marine Protection, Research, and Sanctuaries Act of 1972 (MPRSA), along with other legal theories.

The Supreme Court first held that there is no private right of action for damages under FWPCA or the MPRSA. The Court noted the "unusually elaborate enforcement provisions" in the two statutes, and it rejected the argument that "Congress intended to authorize by implication additional judicial remedies for private citizens suing under" either of the laws. The Court then considered the possible applicability of *Maine v. Thiboutot*:

> Last Term, in *Maine v. Thiboutot*, the Court construed 42 U.S.C. § 1983 as authorizing suits to redress violations by state officials of rights created by federal statutes. Accordingly, it could be argued that [the plaintiffs] may sue the municipalities and sewerage boards among the [defendants] under the FWPCA and MPRSA by virtue of a right of action created by § 1983.

> The claim brought here arguably falls within the scope of *Maine v. Thiboutot* because it involves a suit by a private party claiming that a federal statute has been violated under color of state law, causing an injury.... [However, there is an exception where Congress has] foreclosed private enforcement of that statute in the enactment itself....

> When the remedial devices provided in a particular Act are sufficiently comprehensive, they may suffice to demonstrate congressional intent to preclude the remedy of suits under § 1983.... As Justice Stewart, who later joined the majority in *Maine v. Thiboutot*, stated in [a predecessor case], when "a state official is alleged to have violated a federal statute which provides its own comprehensive enforcement scheme, the requirements of that enforcement procedure may not be bypassed by bringing suit directly under § 1983." As discussed above, the FWPCA and MPRSA do provide quite comprehensive enforcement mechanisms. It is hard to believe that Congress intended to preserve the § 1983 right of action when it created so many specific statutory remedies, including the two citizen-suit provisions.

2. How "comprehensive" must statutory remedies be in order to foreclose an otherwise available § 1983 remedy? In *City of Rancho Palos Verdes v. Abrams*, 544 U.S. 113 (2005), the Court considered whether limitations on local zoning authority set forth in the Telecommunications Act of 1996 (TCA), 47 U.S.C. § 332(c)(7), could be enforced through an action under § 1983. The TCA provides, *inter alia*, that local government decisions denying a request for authorization to locate wireless facilities must "be in writing and supported by substantial evidence." § 332(c)(7)(B). It also creates an express private cause of action:

> Any person adversely affected by any final action or failure to act by a State or local government or any instrumentality thereof that is inconsistent with this subparagraph may, within 30 days after such action or failure to act, commence an action in any court of competent jurisdiction.

§ 332(c)(7)(B)(v). The case involved a homeowner who installed a 52-foot antenna on his property in a high-elevation residential neighborhood. When the City denied his request for a conditional-use permit for the antenna, he filed suit in federal district court, citing both the TCA's express right of action and § 1983. The district court agreed that the denial of the permit was not supported by substantial evidence, calling it "an act of spite by the community," and ordered the City to grant a permit pursuant to the right of action in § 332(c)(7). On appeal, the Ninth Circuit went further, concluding that the homeowner was also entitled to money damages and attorney's fees because his rights under the TCA were enforceable through § 1983.

The Supreme Court reversed, and its judgment was unanimous. All nine Justices agreed, based on the *Sea Clammers* doctrine, that Congress did not intend to authorize the enforcement of § 332(c)(7) rights through actions under § 1983. Writing for the Court, in an opinion joined by seven other Justices, Justice Scalia explained:

> We have found § 1983 unavailable to remedy violations of federal statutory rights in two cases: *Sea Clammers* and *Smith v. Robinson*, 468 U.S. 992 (1984). Both of those decisions rested upon the existence of more restrictive remedies provided in the violated statute itself. . . .
>
> The Government as *amicus*, joined by the City, urges us to hold that the availability of a private judicial remedy is not merely indicative of, but conclusively establishes, a congressional intent to preclude § 1983 relief. We decline to do so. The ordinary inference that the remedy provided in the statute is exclusive can surely be overcome by textual indication, express or implicit, that the remedy is to complement, rather than supplant, § 1983.
>
> There is, however, no such indication in the TCA, which adds no remedies to those available under § 1983, and limits relief in ways that § 1983 does not. Judicial review of zoning decisions under § 332(c)(7)(B)(v) must be sought within 30 days after the governmental entity has taken "final action," and, once the action is filed, the court must "hear and decide" it "on an expedited basis." The remedies available, moreover, perhaps do not include compensatory damages (the lower courts are seemingly in disagreement on this point), and certainly do not include attorney's fees and costs. A § 1983 action, by contrast, can be brought much later than 30 days after the final action, and need not be heard and decided on an expedited basis. [In a footnote, the Court explained: "The statute of limitations for a § 1983 claim is generally the applicable state-law period for personal-injury torts," *Wilson v. Garcia*, 471 U.S. 261 (1985), which in this case presumably would be one year.] And the successful plaintiff may recover not only damages but reasonable attorney's fees and costs under 42 U.S.C. § 1988. Liability for attorney's fees would have a particularly severe impact in the § 332(c)(7) context, making local governments liable for the (often substantial) legal expenses of large commercial interests for the misapplication of a complex and novel statutory scheme.
>
> Respondent's only response to the attorney's-fees point is that it is a "policy argumen[t]," properly left to Congress. That response assumes, however, that Congress's refusal to attach attorney's fees to the remedy that it created in the TCA does not itself represent a congressional choice. *Sea Clammers* and *Smith* adopt the opposite assumption—that limitations upon the remedy contained in the statute are deliberate and are not to be evaded through § 1983. . . .
>
> Enforcement of § 332(c)(7) through § 1983 would distort the scheme of expedited judicial review and limited remedies created by § 332(c)(7)(B)(v).

We therefore hold that the TCA—by providing a judicial remedy different from § 1983 in § 332(c)(7) itself—precluded resort to § 1983.

Justice Breyer joined the opinion of the Court, but also filed a concurrence—joined by three other Justices in the majority—endorsing the Court's "general guidance in the form of an 'ordinary inference' that when Congress creates a specific judicial remedy, it does so to the exclusion of § 1983." He wrote separately to add that "context, not just literal text, will often lead a court to Congress' intent in respect to a particular statute." In his view, the TCA reflected a congressional compromise between a single national solution for choosing wireless communication sites and the patchwork of state and local siting laws that threatened the development of wireless systems. "To permit § 1983 actions here," he concluded, "would undermine the compromise—between purely federal and purely local siting policies—that the statute reflects."

Justice Stevens concurred only in the judgment. He agreed that the structure of § 332(c)(7) was "fundamentally incompatible with the private remedy offered by § 1983," but he identified "flaws in the Court's approach" that persuaded him to write separately. Foremost among them:

> I do not believe that the Court has properly acknowledged the strength of our normal presumption that Congress intended to preserve, rather than preclude, the availability of § 1983 as a remedy for the enforcement of federal statutory rights. Title 42 U.S.C. § 1983 was "intended to provide a remedy, to be broadly construed, against all forms of official violation of federally protected rights." *Monell v. New York City Dept. of Social Servs.*, 436 U.S. 658 (1978). "We do not lightly conclude that Congress intended to preclude reliance on § 1983 as a remedy . . . . Since 1871, when it was passed by Congress, § 1983 has stood as an independent safeguard against deprivations of federal constitutional and statutory rights." *Smith*. Although the Court is correct to point out that this presumption is rebuttable, it remains true that only an exceptional case—such as one involving an unusually comprehensive and exclusive statutory scheme—will lead us to conclude that a given statute impliedly forecloses a § 1983 remedy. While I find it easy to conclude that petitioners have met that heavy burden here, there will be many instances in which § 1983 will be available even though Congress has not explicitly so provided in the text of the statute in question.

Do the separate opinions in *City of Rancho Palos Verdes* suggest deeper disagreements among the Justices about the relationship between § 1983 and specific congressional remedies?

3. Perhaps not, if the Court's most recent *Sea Clammers* case is any indication. That decision involved Title IX of the Education Amendments of 1972, which provides:

> No person in the United States shall, on the basis of sex, be excluded from participation in, be denied the benefits of, or be subjected to discrimination under any education program or activity receiving Federal financial assistance.

In *Cannon v. University of Chicago* (Chapter 8), the Court held that Title IX provides an implied private cause of action for discrimination "on the basis of sex" by educational institutions that receive federal funding. Obviously, Title IX was enacted long after § 1983. Does Title IX preclude an action under § 1983 for gender discrimination by *state* schools that receive federal funds?

This question generated a long-standing conflict in the courts of appeals, with three allowing the § 1983 action and four finding it precluded. Finally, in *Fitzgerald v. Barnstable School Committee*, 555 U.S. 246 (2009), a unanimous Supreme Court gave its answer: Title IX does not preclude the § 1983 action. In an opinion by Justice Alito, the Court explained:

> In determining whether a subsequent statute precludes the enforcement of a federal right under § 1983, we have placed primary emphasis on the nature and extent of that statute's remedial scheme. See *Sea Clammers*. . . . [Title IX's] only express enforcement mechanism. . . . is an administrative procedure resulting in the withdrawal of federal funding from institutions that are not in compliance. In addition, this Court has recognized an implied private right of action [under Title IX]. *Cannon v. University of Chicago.* In a suit brought pursuant to this private right, both injunctive relief and damages are available.

> These remedies — withdrawal of federal funds and an implied cause of action — stand in stark contrast to the "unusually elaborate," "carefully tailored," and "restrictive" enforcement schemes of the statutes at issue in *Sea Clammers*, *Smith v. Robinson*, and *Rancho Palos Verdes*. Unlike those statutes, Title IX has no administrative exhaustion requirement and no notice provisions. Under its implied private right of action, plaintiffs can file directly in court, and can obtain the full range of remedies. As a result, parallel and concurrent § 1983 claims will neither circumvent required procedures, nor allow access to new remedies.

> Moreover, this Court explained in *Rancho Palos Verdes* that "[t]he provision of an express, private means of redress in the statute itself" is a key consideration in determining congressional intent, and that "the existence of a more restrictive private remedy for statutory violations has been the dividing line between those cases in which we have held that an action would lie under § 1983 and those in which we have held that it would not." As noted, Title IX contains no express private remedy, much less a more restrictive one. This Court has never held that an implied right of action had the effect of precluding suit under § 1983, likely because of the difficulty of discerning congressional intent in such a situation. Mindful that we should "not lightly conclude that Congress intended to preclude reliance on § 1983 as a remedy for a substantial equal protection claim," *Smith*, we see no basis for doing so here.

> A comparison of the substantive rights and protections guaranteed under Title IX and under the Equal Protection Clause lends further support to the

conclusion that Congress did not intend Title IX to preclude § 1983 constitutional suits. Title IX's protections are narrower in some respects and broader in others. Because the protections guaranteed by the two sources of law diverge in this way, we cannot agree ... that "Congress saw Title IX as the sole means of vindicating the constitutional right to be free from gender discrimination perpetrated by educational institutions."

The Court also considered Title IX's "context and history," noting that the statute was modeled on the Title VI of the Civil Rights Act of 1964, which had been consistently held to permit concurrent claims under § 1983.

4. The Court in *Gonzaga University* said that because it found that "FERPA creates no private right to enforce," it "need not determine whether FERPA's procedures are 'sufficiently comprehensive' to offer an independent basis for precluding private enforcement" under the *Sea Clammers* doctrine. But one of the reasons the Court gave for finding that FERPA creates no private right is that Congress has established an enforcement mechanism through administrative procedures. Justice Stevens, in dissent, says: "Folding such considerations into the rights question renders the rebuttal inquiry superfluous." Is he correct in this assessment?

D. Governmental Liability

Monroe v. Pape inaugurated a new era in civil rights litigation with its holding that persons claiming injury by state officials could sue under 42 U.S.C. § 1983 notwithstanding the fact that the challenged conduct was unauthorized by the state or even forbidden by it. But the Court also held that "Congress did not undertake to bring municipal corporations within the ambit of" § 1983. In 1978, the Court reconsidered that question and once again transformed civil rights litigation.

Monell v. Department of Social Services of the City of New York

Supreme Court of the United States, 1978.

436 U.S. 658.

Mr. Justice Brennan delivered the opinion of the Court.

Petitioners, a class of female employees of the Department of Social Services and of the Board of Education of the city of New York, commenced this action under 42 U.S.C. § 1983 in July 1971. The gravamen of the complaint was that the Board and the Department had as a matter of official policy compelled pregnant employees to take unpaid leaves of absence before such leaves were required for medical reasons. *Cf. Cleveland Board of Education v. LaFleur*, 414 U.S. 632 (1974). The suit sought injunctive relief and backpay for periods of unlawful forced leave. Named as defendants in the action were the Department and its Commissioner, the Board and its Chancellor, and the city of New York and its Mayor. In each case, the individual defendants were sued solely in their official capacities.

On cross-motions for summary judgment, the District Court for the Southern District of New York held moot petitioners' claims for injunctive and declaratory relief since the city of New York and the Board, after the filing of the complaint, had changed their policies relating to maternity leaves so that no pregnant employee would have to take leave unless she was medically unable to continue to perform her job. No one now challenges this conclusion. The court did conclude, however, that the acts complained of were unconstitutional under *LaFleur*. Nonetheless plaintiffs' prayers for backpay were denied because any such damages would come ultimately from the city of New York and, therefore, to hold otherwise would be to "[circumvent]" the immunity conferred on municipalities by *Monroe v. Pape*, 365 U.S. 167 (1961).

On appeal, petitioners renewed their arguments that the Board of Education[4] was not a "municipality" within the meaning of *Monroe v. Pape*, and that, in any event, the District Court had erred in barring a damages award against the individual defendants. The Court of Appeals for the Second Circuit rejected both contentions . . . We granted certiorari [to consider]

> Whether local governmental officials and/or local independent school boards are "persons" within the meaning of 42 U.S.C. § 1983 when equitable relief in the nature of back pay is sought against them in their official capacities?

Although, after plenary consideration, we have decided the merits of over a score of cases brought under § 1983 in which the principal defendant was a school board, [we] indicated in *Mt. Healthy City Board of Education v. Doyle*, 429 U.S. 274 (1977), last Term that the question presented here was open and would be decided "another day." That other day has come and we now overrule *Monroe v. Pape* insofar as it holds that local governments are wholly immune from suit under § 1983.

I

In *Monroe* v. *Pape*, we held that "Congress did not undertake to bring municipal corporations within the ambit of [§ 1983]." The sole basis for this conclusion was an inference drawn from Congress' rejection of the "Sherman amendment" to the bill which became the Civil Rights Act of 1871, the precursor of § 1983. The amendment would have held a municipal corporation liable for damage done to the person or property of its inhabitants by *private* persons "riotously and tumultuously assembled." Cong. Globe, 42d Cong., 1st Sess., 749 (1871) (hereinafter Globe). Although the Sherman amendment did not seek to amend § 1 of the Act, which is now § 1983, and although the nature of the obligation created by that amendment was vastly different from that created by § 1, the Court nonetheless concluded in *Monroe* that Congress must have meant to exclude municipal corporations from the coverage of § 1 because "'the House [in voting against the Sherman amendment] had solemnly decided that in their judgment Congress had no constitutional power to impose any *obligation* upon county and town organizations, the mere instrumentality for the administration

---

4. Petitioners conceded that the Department of Social Services enjoys the same status as New York City for *Monroe* purposes.

of state law.'" *Monroe* (emphasis added), quoting Globe 804 (Rep. Poland). This statement, we thought, showed that Congress doubted its "constitutional power . . . to impose *civil liability* on municipalities," *id.*, (emphasis added), and that such doubt would have extended to any type of civil liability.

A fresh analysis of the debate on the Civil Rights Act of 1871, and particularly of the case law which each side mustered in its support, shows, however, that *Monroe* incorrectly equated the "obligation" of which Representative Poland spoke with "civil liability." [The Court's detailed analysis, which extends over 25 pages in the United States Reports, is omitted.]

II

Our analysis of the legislative history of the Civil Rights Act of 1871 compels the conclusion that Congress *did* intend municipalities and other local government units to be included among those persons to whom § 1983 applies. Local governing bodies,[5] therefore, can be sued directly under § 1983 for monetary, declaratory, or injunctive relief where, as here, the action that is alleged to be unconstitutional implements or executes a policy statement, ordinance, regulation, or decision officially adopted and promulgated by that body's officers. Moreover, although the touchstone of the § 1983 action against a government body is an allegation that official policy is responsible for a deprivation of rights protected by the Constitution, local governments, like every other § 1983 "person," by the very terms of the statute, may be sued for constitutional deprivations visited pursuant to governmental "custom" even though such a custom has not received formal approval through the body's official decisionmaking channels. As Mr. Justice Harlan, writing for the Court, said in *Adickes v. S. H. Kress & Co.*, 398 U.S. 144 (1970): "Congress included customs and usages [in § 1983] because of the persistent and widespread discriminatory practices of state officials. . . . Although not authorized by written law, such practices of state officials could well be so permanent and well settled as to constitute a 'custom or usage' with the force of law."

On the other hand, the language of § 1983, read against the background of the same legislative history, compels the conclusion that Congress did not intend municipalities to be held liable unless action pursuant to official municipal policy of some nature caused a constitutional tort. In particular, we conclude that a municipality cannot be held liable *solely* because it employs a tortfeasor — or, in other words, a municipality cannot be held liable under § 1983 on a *respondeat superior* theory.

We begin with the language of § 1983 as originally passed:

> [*Any*] *person who*, under color of any law, statute, ordinance, regulation, custom, or usage of any State, *shall subject, or cause to be subjected*, any person . . . to the deprivation of any rights, privileges, or immunities secured

---

5. Since official-capacity suits generally represent only another way of pleading an action against an entity of which an officer is an agent — at least where Eleventh Amendment considerations do not control analysis — our holding today that local governments can be sued under § 1983 necessarily decides that local government officials sued in their official capacities are "persons" under § 1983 in those cases in which, as here, a local government would be suable in its own name.

by the Constitution of the United States, shall, any such law, statute, ordinance, regulation, custom, or usage of the State to the contrary notwithstanding, be liable to the party injured in any action at law, suit in equity, or other proper proceeding for redress. . . . 17 Stat. 13 (emphasis added).

The italicized language plainly imposes liability on a government that, under color of some official policy, "causes" an employee to violate another's constitutional rights. At the same time, that language cannot be easily read to impose liability vicariously on governing bodies solely on the basis of the existence of an employer-employee relationship with a tortfeasor. Indeed, the fact that Congress did specifically provide that A's tort became B's liability if B "caused" A to subject another to a tort suggests that Congress did not intend § 1983 liability to attach where such causation was absent.

Equally important, creation of a federal law of *respondeat superior* would have raised all the constitutional problems associated with the obligation to keep the peace, an obligation Congress chose not to impose because it thought imposition of such an obligation unconstitutional. To this day, there is disagreement about the basis for imposing liability on an employer for the torts of an employee when the sole nexus between the employer and the tort is the fact of the employer-employee relationship. See W. Prosser, Law of Torts § 69, at 459 (4th ed. 1971). Nonetheless, two justifications tend to stand out. First is the common-sense notion that no matter how blameless an employer appears to be in an individual case, accidents might nonetheless be reduced if employers had to bear the cost of accidents. Second is the argument that the cost of accidents should be spread to the community as a whole on an insurance theory.

The first justification is of the same sort that was offered for statutes like the Sherman amendment: "The obligation to make compensation for injury resulting from riot is, by arbitrary enactment of statutes, affirmatory law, and the reason of passing the statute is to secure a more perfect police regulation." Globe 777 (Sen. Frelinghuysen). This justification was obviously insufficient to sustain the amendment against perceived constitutional difficulties and there is no reason to suppose that a more general liability imposed for a similar reason would have been thought less constitutionally objectionable. The second justification was similarly put forward as a justification for the Sherman amendment: "we do not look upon [the Sherman amendment] as a punishment. . . . It is a mutual insurance." *Id.* at 792 (Rep. Butler). Again, this justification was insufficient to sustain the amendment.

We conclude, therefore, that a local government may not be sued under § 1983 for an injury inflicted solely by its employees or agents. Instead, it is when execution of a government's policy or custom, whether made by its lawmakers or by those whose edicts or acts may fairly be said to represent official policy, inflicts the injury that the government as an entity is responsible under § 1983. Since this case unquestionably involves official policy as the moving force of the constitutional violation found by the District Court, we must reverse the judgment below. In so doing, we have no occasion to address, and do not address, what the full contours of municipal liability under § 1983 may be. We have attempted only to sketch so much of the § 1983 cause of action against a local government as is apparent from the history of the 1871 Act and our prior cases, and we expressly leave further development of this action to another day.

III

[The Court held that "*stare decisis* does not bar our overruling of *Monroe* insofar as it is inconsistent with Parts I and II of this opinion."]

IV

Since the question whether local government bodies should be afforded some form of official immunity was not presented as a question to be decided on this petition and was not briefed by the parties or addressed by the courts below, we express no views on the scope of any municipal immunity beyond holding that municipal bodies sued under § 1983 cannot be entitled to an absolute immunity, lest our decision that such bodies are subject to suit under § 1983 "be drained of meaning."

V

For the reasons stated above, the judgment of the Court of Appeals is

Reversed.

MR. JUSTICE POWELL, concurring.

I join the opinion of the Court, and express these additional views.

Few cases in the history of the Court have been cited more frequently than *Monroe v. Pape*, 365 U.S. 167 (1961), decided less than two decades ago. Focusing new light on 42 U.S.C. § 1983, that decision widened access to the federal courts and permitted expansive interpretations of the reach of the 1871 measure. But *Monroe* exempted local governments from liability at the same time it opened wide the courthouse door to suits against officers and employees of those entities—even when they act pursuant to express authorization. The oddness of this result, and the weakness of the historical evidence relied on by the *Monroe* Court in support of it, are well demonstrated by the Court's opinion today. Yet the gravity of overruling a part of so important a decision prompts me to write. . . .

The Court correctly rejects a view of the legislative history that would produce the anomalous result of immunizing local government units from monetary liability for action directly causing a constitutional deprivation, even though such actions may be fully consistent with, and thus not remediable under, state law. No conduct of government comes more clearly within the "under color of" state law language of § 1983. It is most unlikely that Congress intended public officials acting under the command or the specific authorization of the government employer to be *exclusively* liable for resulting constitutional injury. . . .

Difficult questions nevertheless remain for another day. There are substantial line-drawing problems in determining "when execution of a government's policy or custom" can be said to inflict constitutional injury such that "government as an entity is responsible under § 1983." This case, however, involves formal, written policies of a municipal department and school board; it is the clear case. The Court also reserves decision on the availability of a qualified municipal immunity. Initial resolution of the question whether the protection available at common law for municipal corporations or other principles support a qualified municipal immunity in the context of the § 1983 damages action, is left to the lower federal courts.

MR. JUSTICE STEVENS, concurring in part.

Since Parts II and IV of the opinion of the Court are merely advisory and are not necessary to explain the Court's decision, I join only Parts I, III, and V.

MR. JUSTICE REHNQUIST, with whom THE CHIEF JUSTICE joins, dissenting.

Seventeen years ago, in *Monroe v. Pape*, 365 U.S. 167 (1961), this Court held that the 42d Congress did not intend to subject a municipal corporation to liability as a "person" within the meaning of 42 U.S.C. § 1983. Since then, the Congress has remained silent, but this Court has reaffirmed that holding on at least three separate occasions. [Justice Rehnquist cited cases decided in 1973 and 1976.] *See also Mt. Healthy City Board of Ed. v. Doyle*, 429 U.S. 274 (1977). Today, the Court abandons this long and consistent line of precedents, offering in justification only an elaborate canvass of the same legislative history which was before the Court in 1961. Because I cannot agree that this Court is "free to disregard these precedents," which have been "considered maturely and recently" by this Court, *Runyon v. McCrary*, 427 U.S. 160 (1976) (Powell, J., concurring), I am compelled to dissent. . . .

I

[Our] only task is to discern the intent of the 42d Congress. That intent was first expounded in *Monroe*, and it has been followed consistently ever since. This is not some esoteric branch of the law in which congressional silence might reasonably be equated with congressional indifference. Indeed, this very year, the Senate has been holding hearings on a bill which would remove the municipal immunity recognized by *Monroe*. In these circumstances, it cannot be disputed that established principles of *stare decisis* require this Court to pay the highest degree of deference to its prior holdings. *Monroe* may not be overruled unless it has been demonstrated "beyond doubt from the legislative history of the 1871 statute that [*Monroe*] misapprehended the meaning of the controlling provision." The Court must show not only that Congress, in rejecting the Sherman amendment, concluded that municipal liability was not unconstitutional, but also that, in enacting § 1, it intended to impose that liability. I am satisfied that no such showing has been made.

II

[Most of Justice Rehnquist's account of the legislative history is omitted.]

. . . [The] fact remains that Congress rejected the concept of municipal tort liability on the only occasion in which the question was explicitly presented. Admittedly this fact is not conclusive as to whether Congress intended § 1 to embrace a municipal corporation within the meaning of "person," and thus the reasoning of *Monroe* on this point is subject to challenge. The meaning of § 1 of the Act of 1871 has been subjected in this case to a more searching and careful analysis than it was in *Monroe*, and it may well be that on the basis of this closer analysis of the legislative debates a conclusion contrary to the *Monroe* holding could have been reached when that case was decided 17 years ago. But the rejection of the Sherman amendment remains instructive in that here alone did the legislative debates squarely focus on the liability of municipal corporations, and that liability was rejected. . . . Errors such as the Court may have fallen into in *Monroe* do not end the inquiry as to *stare decisis*; they merely begin it. I would adhere to the holding of *Monroe* as to the liability of a municipal corporation under § 1983.

III

The decision in *Monroe* v. *Pape* was the fountainhead of the torrent of civil rights litigation of the last 17 years. Using § 1983 as a vehicle, the courts have articulated new and previously unforeseeable interpretations of the Fourteenth Amendment. At the same time, the doctrine of municipal immunity enunciated in *Monroe* has protected municipalities and their limited treasuries from the consequences of their officials' failure to predict the course of this Court's constitutional jurisprudence. None of the Members of this Court can foresee the practical consequences of today's removal of that protection. Only the Congress, which has the benefit of the advice of every segment of this diverse Nation, is equipped to consider the results of such a drastic change in the law. It seems all but inevitable that it will find it necessary to do so after today's decision.

I would affirm the judgment of the Court of Appeals.

Note: The Aftermath of Monell

1. *Monell* holds that a municipality is a "person" subject to liability under § 1983. That holding extends to all local government units, including school boards and counties. But what about the state itself?

In *Will v. Michigan Dept. of State Police*, 491 U.S. 58 (1989), the Court concluded that neither a state nor its officials acting in their official capacities are "persons" within the meaning of § 1983. The Court noted that the Eleventh Amendment bars suits against a state unless the state has waived the immunity or Congress has exercised its power under § 5 of the Fourteenth Amendment to override the immunity. But the Court said prior cases had established that "Congress, in passing § 1983, had no intention to disturb the States' Eleventh Amendment immunity and so to alter the federal-state balance in that respect." The Court also cited cases, discussed briefly in section E, *infra*, holding that Congress did not intend to override well-established immunities through the general language of the statute.

The Court emphasized, however, that a state official, when sued for injunctive relief in his or her official capacity, *would* be a person under § 1983 because "official-capacity actions for prospective relief are not treated as actions against the State." The Court cited *Ex parte Young*. And state officers sued in their individual capacities for damages are also persons within the meaning of the statute. *Hafer v. Melo*, 502 U.S. 21 (1991).

2. Although Justice Rehnquist, in his dissent in *Monell*, challenges the majority's reading of the legislative history, he does so half-heartedly. In any event, *Monell*'s holding on the availability of municipal liability is now established law. But the nature and scope of that liability are highly controversial issues that generate extensive litigation.

3. The *Monell* opinion itself called attention to one of the issues: immunity. By 1978, the Court's decisions had established that individual state and local officials would generally be able to assert some form of immunity from liability for damages under § 1983. Legislators, judges, and prosecutors enjoyed absolute immunity. Other officials could claim qualified immunity: they would be shielded from liability as long as they acted in good faith and did not violate the plaintiff's clearly established constitutional rights. (This body of law is briefly examined in section E, *infra*.)

Would local government defendants also enjoy at least qualified immunity? Two years after *Monell*, the Court gave its answer. In *Owen v. City of Independence, Missouri*, 445 U.S. 622 (1980), the Court rejected any form of immunity for local government defendants, holding that a municipality "may not assert the good faith of its officers or agents as a defense to liability under § 1983." The Court said: "[T]here is no tradition of immunity for municipal corporations, and neither history nor policy supports a construction of § 1983 that would justify the qualified immunity accorded the city of Independence by the Court of Appeals." The opinion concluded with the following summary and explanation of its decision:

> [Our] decision holding that municipalities have no immunity from damages liability flowing from their constitutional violations harmonizes well with developments in the common law and our own pronouncements on official immunities under § 1983. Doctrines of tort law have changed significantly over the past century, and our notions of governmental responsibility should properly reflect that evolution. No longer is individual "blameworthiness" the acid test of liability; the principle of equitable loss-spreading has joined fault as a factor in distributing the costs of official misconduct.
>
> We believe that today's decision, together with prior precedents in this area, properly allocates these costs among the three principals in the scenario of the § 1983 cause of action: the victim of the constitutional deprivation; the officer whose conduct caused the injury; and the public, as represented by the municipal entity. The innocent individual who is harmed by an abuse of governmental authority is assured that he will be compensated for his injury. The offending official, so long as he conducts himself in good faith, may go about his business secure in the knowledge that a qualified immunity will protect him from personal liability for damages that are more appropriately chargeable to the populace as a whole. And the public will be forced to bear only the costs of injury inflicted by the "execution of a government's policy or custom, whether made by its lawmakers or by those whose edicts or acts may fairly be said to represent official policy." [The quoted language is from *Monell*.]

municipal

Justice Powell, joined by Chief Justice Burger, Justice Stewart, and Justice Rehnquist, dissented. He said:

> After today's decision, municipalities will have gone in two short years from absolute immunity under § 1983 to strict liability. As a policy matter, I believe that strict municipal liability unreasonably subjects local governments to damages judgments for actions that were reasonable when performed. It converts municipal governance into a hazardous slalom through constitutional obstacles that often are unknown and unknowable.
>
> The Court's decision also impinges seriously on the prerogatives of municipal entities created and regulated primarily by the States. At the very least, this Court should not initiate a federal intrusion of this magnitude in the absence of explicit congressional action. Yet today's decision is supported by nothing in the text of § 1983. Indeed, it conflicts with the apparent intent of the drafters of the statute, with the common law of municipal tort liability, and with the current state law of municipal immunities. . . .
>
> The Court turns a blind eye to [the] overwhelming evidence that municipalities have enjoyed a qualified immunity and to the policy considerations that for the life of this Republic have justified its retention. This disregard of precedent and policy is especially unfortunate because suits under § 1983 typically implicate evolving constitutional standards. A good-faith defense is much more important for those actions than in those involving ordinary tort liability. The duty not to run over a pedestrian with a municipal bus is far less likely to change than is the rule as to what process, if any, is due the bus-driver if he claims the right to a hearing after discharge.
>
> The right of a discharged government employee to a "name clearing" hearing was not recognized until our decision in *Board of Regents v. Roth*, 408 U.S. 564 (1972). That ruling was handed down 10 weeks after Owen was discharged and 8 weeks after the city denied his request for a hearing. By stripping the city of any immunity, the Court punishes it for failing to predict our decision in *Roth*. As a result, local governments and their officials will face the unnerving prospect of crushing damages judgments whenever a policy valid under current law is later found to be unconstitutional. I can see no justice or wisdom in that outcome.

4. *Owen* remains good law. But on the other side of the ledger, the Court has also adhered to *Monell*'s dictum that "a local government may not be sued under § 1983 for an injury inflicted solely by its employees or agents." The Court thus distinguishes between *respondeat superior* liability, which is not permissible, and liability based on a municipal "policy" or "custom" that caused the plaintiff's injury. That distinction has proved to be a difficult one to apply, as the materials that follow illustrate.

Note: Identifying a Municipal "Policy"

1. In *Monell*, there could be no doubt that the municipality had an established "policy"—a general rule—that required pregnant employees to take unpaid leaves of absence before such leaves were required for medical reasons. But in the more commonplace § 1983 suit, the plaintiff will not be challenging a rule; rather, the plaintiff will be asserting that conduct by lower-level officials violated his constitutional rights. In this respect, *Monroe v. Pape* —which today would be classified as an "excessive force" case—is far more representative of § 1983 litigation than *Monell*. Under what circumstances may liability be imposed on the municipality for such conduct?

The Court has had great difficulty answering this question. In *Pembaur v. City of Cincinnati*, 475 U.S. 469 (1986), the Court held that "municipal liability may be imposed for a single decision by municipal policymakers under appropriate circumstances" and that the power to establish policy is not the exclusive province of the legislature. Further, "where action is directed by those who establish governmental policy, the municipality is equally responsible whether that action is to be taken only once or to be taken repeatedly." Beyond those propositions, however, the Court could not agree on the standard to be applied in determining whether liability could be imposed on the basis of a single incident.

2. A decade later, in *Board of County Commissioners of Bryan County, Oklahoma v. Brown*, 520 U.S. 397 (1997), the Court summarized the standard that it believed had been established by *Pembaur* and other cases: liability may not be imposed on a municipality "unless *deliberate* action attributable to the municipality itself is the 'moving force' behind the plaintiff's deprivation of federal rights." Further, courts must apply stringent requirements of "culpability and causation" in order to assure that municipal liability does not collapse into *respondeat superior* liability.

3. The *Brown* litigation illustrates the fine distinctions that must be drawn in order to apply this standard. The litigation grew out of the following incident, as described by the Court:

> In the early morning hours of May 12, 1991, [respondent] Jill Brown and her husband were driving from Grayson County, Texas, to their home in Bryan County, Oklahoma. After crossing into Oklahoma, they approached a police checkpoint. Mr. Brown, who was driving, decided to avoid the checkpoint and return to Texas. After seeing the Browns' truck turn away from the checkpoint, Bryan County Deputy Sheriff Robert Morrison and Reserve Deputy Stacy Burns pursued the vehicle. Although the parties' versions of events differ, at trial both deputies claimed that their patrol car reached speeds in excess of 100 miles per hour. Mr. Brown testified that he was unaware of the deputies' attempts to overtake him. The chase finally ended four miles south of the police checkpoint.
>
> After he got out of the squad car, Deputy Sheriff Morrison pointed his gun toward the Browns' vehicle and ordered the Browns to raise their hands. Reserve Deputy Burns, who was unarmed, rounded the corner of the vehicle

on the passenger's side. Burns twice ordered respondent from the vehicle. When she did not exit, he used an "arm bar" technique, grabbing respondent's arm at the wrist and elbow, pulling her from the vehicle, and spinning her to the ground. Respondent's knees were severely injured, and she later underwent corrective surgery. Ultimately, she may need knee replacements.

Brown filed suit under 42 U.S.C. § 1983 seeking compensation for her injuries from Burns, Bryan County Sheriff B.J. Moore, and the county itself. The case went to the jury, and the jury concluded that Burns had arrested Brown without probable cause and had used excessive force. It therefore found Burns liable for Brown's injuries. Brown also prevailed at trial in her claim against the county. It is that claim that interests us here.

In order to succeed on that claim, Brown had to identify a municipal "policy" or "custom" that caused her injury. The county stipulated that Sheriff Moore "was the policy maker for Bryan County regarding the Sheriff's Department." With that hurdle overcome, Brown's claim against the county was based on two theories. The first was grounded in Sheriff Moore's decision to hire Burns. The second was based on inadequate training.

4. In support of the hiring claim, Brown asserted that Sheriff Moore had failed to adequately review Burns' background. Burns was the son of the sheriff's nephew. He had a record of driving infractions and had pleaded guilty to various driving-related and other misdemeanors, including assault and battery, resisting arrest, and public drunkenness. Moore's own testimony indicated that that he did not inquire into the underlying conduct or the disposition of any of the misdemeanor charges reflected on Burns' record before hiring him.

The Fifth Circuit upheld liability on the basis of the hiring claim, but the Supreme Court reversed by a vote of 5 to 4. The Court said:

> We assume that a jury could properly find in this case that Sheriff Moore's assessment of Burns' background was inadequate. . . . But this showing of an instance of inadequate screening is not enough to establish "deliberate indifference." In layman's terms, inadequate screening of an applicant's record may reflect "indifference" to the applicant's background. For purposes of a legal inquiry into municipal liability under § 1983, however, that is not the *relevant* "indifference." A plaintiff must demonstrate that a municipal decision reflects deliberate indifference to the risk that a violation of a particular constitutional or statutory right will follow the decision. . . .
>
> [A] finding of culpability simply cannot depend on the mere probability that any officer inadequately screened will inflict any constitutional injury. Rather, it must depend on a finding that *this* officer was highly likely to inflict the *particular* injury suffered by the plaintiff. The connection between the background of the particular applicant and the specific constitutional violation alleged must be strong. What the District Court's instructions on culpability, and therefore the jury's finding of municipal liability, failed to capture

is whether Burns' background made his use of excessive force in making an arrest a plainly obvious consequence of the hiring decision.

The fact that Burns had pleaded guilty to traffic offenses and other misdemeanors may well have made him an extremely poor candidate for reserve deputy. Had Sheriff Moore fully reviewed Burns' record, he might have come to precisely that conclusion. But unless he would necessarily have reached that decision *because* Burns' use of excessive force would have been a plainly obvious consequence of the hiring decision, Sheriff Moore's inadequate scrutiny of Burns' record cannot constitute "deliberate indifference" to respondent's federally protected right to be free from a use of excessive force. . . .

Cases involving constitutional injuries allegedly traceable to an ill-considered hiring decision pose the greatest risk that a municipality will be held liable for an injury that it did not cause. In the broadest sense, every injury is traceable to a hiring decision. Where a court fails to adhere to rigorous requirements of culpability and causation, municipal liability collapses into *respondeat superior* liability.

Justice Souter, in a dissent joined by Justices Stevens and Breyer, objected both to the majority's standard and to its application:

The Court's formulation that deliberate indifference exists only when the risk of the subsequent, particular constitutional violation is a plainly obvious consequence of the hiring decision, while derived from [precedent, is] a new standard. . . .

While the Court should rightly be skeptical about predicating municipal or individual liability merely on a failure to adopt a crime-free personnel policy or on a particular decision to [hire, for example, someone who once drove an overweight truck], why does it extend that valid skepticism to the quite unsound point of doubting liability for hiring [a scofflaw who had recently engaged in criminal violence]? The Court says it fears that the latter sort of case raises a danger of liability without fault. But if the Court means fault generally (as distinct from the blame imputed on classic *respondeat superior* doctrine), it need only recall that whether a particular violent scofflaw is violent enough or scoffing enough to implicate deliberate indifference will depend on applying the highly demanding standard the Court announces: plainly obvious consequence of particular injury.

It is the high threshold of deliberate indifference that will ensure that municipalities be held liable only for considered acts with substantial risks. That standard will distinguish single-act cases with only a mild portent of injury from single-act cases with a plainly obvious portent, and from cases in which the harm is only the latest in a series of injuries known to have followed from the policymaker's action. . . .

[In this case,] the jury could readily have found that the sheriff knew his nephew's proven propensities, that he thought the thrust of the evidence was

so damaging that he would lie to protect his reputation and the county treasury, and that he simply chose to put a family member on the payroll (the
third relative, in fact) disregarding the risk to the public. . . .

[The] jury could have found that the string of arrests and convictions
revealed "that Burns had [such] a propensity for violence and a disregard for
the law," that his subsequent resort to excessive force was the plainly obvious
consequence of hiring him as a law enforcement officer authorized to employ
force in performing his duties.

The county escapes from liability through the Court's untoward application of an enhanced fault standard to a record of inculpatory evidence showing a contempt for constitutional obligations as blatant as the nepotism that
apparently occasioned it.

5. The majority and the principal dissent in *Brown* agreed on many points. Both
rejected liability based on *respondeat superior*. Both acknowledged that Sheriff Moore
was an authorized decision-maker for the county. And both assumed that to recover
from the county, the plaintiff would have to show "deliberate indifference" by Moore.
But the majority held that it is not enough that Moore's actions reflected deliberate
indifference to Burns' record, or even deliberate indifference to the prospect that
Burns would violate constitutional rights generally. Rather, the plaintiff must show
that the policy maker acted with deliberate indifference to the *particular constitutional right* that the plaintiff asserts was violated. The Court said that this rule is
necessary unless municipalities are to be held liable for injuries they "did not cause."
Do you agree?

6. In a separate dissent to the Supreme Court's decision in *Brown*, Justice Breyer,
joined by Justice Ginsburg, called for a re-examination of *Monell*'s "no vicarious liability" principle. After questioning the soundness of *Monell*'s "original reasoning," he
continued by arguing that the distinction between vicarious liability and liability based
on policy or custom "has generated a body of interpretive law that is so complex that
the law has become difficult to apply." He elaborated:

Today's case provides a good example. The District Court in this case
told the jury it must find (1) Sheriff Moore's screening "*so likely* to result in
violations of constitutional rights" that he could "*reasonably [be] said to have
been deliberately indifferent* to the constitutional needs of the Plaintiff" and
(2) that the "inadequate hiring . . . policy *directly caused* the Plaintiff's injury."
(Emphasis added.) This instruction comes close to repeating this Court's
language in *Canton v. Harris*, 489 U.S. 378 (1989). In *Canton*, the Court said
(of the city's failure to train officers in the use of deadly force):

In light of the duties assigned to specific officers or employees the need
for more or different training is so obvious, and the inadequacy *so likely*
to result in the violation of constitutional rights, that the policymakers of
the city can *reasonably be said to have been deliberately indifferent* to the
need. (Emphasis added.)

The majority says that the District Court and the Court of Appeals did not look closely enough at the specific facts of this case. It also adds that the harm must be a "*plainly obvious consequence*" of the "decision to hire" Burns. But why elaborate *Canton*'s instruction in this way? [Those] words, while adding complexity, do not seem to reflect a difference that significantly helps one understand the difference between "vicarious" liability and "policy."

Consider some of the other distinctions that this Court has had to make as it has sought to distinguish liability based upon policymaking from liability that is "vicarious." It has proved necessary, for example, to distinguish further, between an exercise of *policymaking authority* and an exercise of *delegated discretionary policy-implementing authority*. See *St. Louis v. Praprotnik*, 485 U.S. 112 (1988) (plurality opinion). Without some such distinction, "municipal liability [might] collapse into *respondeat superior*," for the law would treat similarly (and hold municipalities responsible for) both a police officer's decision about how much force to use when making a particular arrest and a police chief's decision about how much force to use when making a particular *kind* of arrest. But the distinction is not a clear one. It requires federal courts to explore state and municipal law that distributes different state powers among different local officials and local entities. That law is highly specialized; it may or may not say just where policymaking authority lies, and it can prove particularly difficult to apply in light of the Court's determination that a decision can be "policymaking" even though it applies only to a single instance.

It is not surprising that results have sometimes proved inconsistent. Nor does the location of "policymaking" authority pose the only conceptually difficult problem. Lower courts must also ask decide whether a failure to make policy was "deliberately indifferent," rather than "grossly negligent." And they must decide, for example, whether it matters that some such failure occurred in the officer-training, rather than the officer-hiring, process.

Given the basic *Monell* principle, these distinctions may be necessary, for without them, the Court cannot easily avoid a "municipal liability" that "collapses into *respondeat superior*." But a basic legal principle that requires so many such distinctions to maintain its legal life may not deserve such longevity.

Note: Canton *and Failure to Train*

1. The plaintiff in *Brown* had prevailed before the jury on a second theory: that the county was liable because it had failed to train its officers in the use of force. The failure-to-train theory was supported by <u>*City of Canton v. Harris*</u>, 489 U.S. 378 (1989), in which a mentally ill woman sued the city alleging that police officers denied her necessary medical treatment when she was arrested and detained. She did not allege that the city had adopted a policy to deny medical treatment to detainees. Rather, her position was that it had failed to train police officers to recognize their constitutional obligations, and that the failure to do so was a policy that had caused the violation of her constitutional rights.

The Court in *Canton* agreed that "the inadequacy of police training may serve as a basis for § 1983 liability [against municipalities]." But it held that "only where the failure to train amounts to deliberate indifference to the rights of persons with whom the police come into contact" could it serve as a "policy" within the meaning of *Monell*:

> The issue in a case like this one . . . is whether that training program is adequate; and if it is not, the question becomes whether such inadequate training can justifiably be said to represent "city policy." It may seem contrary to common sense to assert that a municipality will actually have a policy of not taking reasonable steps to train its employees. But it may happen that in light of the duties assigned to specific officers or employees the need for more or different training is so obvious, and the inadequacy so likely to result in the violation of constitutional rights, that the policymakers of the city can reasonably be said to have been deliberately indifferent to the need.

In a footnote (footnote 10), the Court posed the following hypothetical:

> For example, city policymakers know to a moral certainty that their police officers will be required to arrest fleeing felons. The city has armed its officers with firearms, in part to allow them to accomplish this task. Thus, the need to train officers in the constitutional limitations on the use of deadly force can be said to be "so obvious" that the failure to do so could properly be characterized as "deliberate indifference" to constitutional rights.

> It could also be that the police, in exercising their discretion, so often violate constitutional rights that the need for further training must have been plainly obvious to the city policymakers, who, nevertheless, are "deliberately indifferent" to the need.

2. The footnote 10 hypothetical took center stage in another 5-4 decision more than a decade later. The case was *Connick v. Thompson*, 563 U.S. 51 (2011). Justice Thomas, writing for the Court, summarized the facts and the holding:

> The Orleans Parish District Attorney's Office now concedes that, in prosecuting respondent John Thompson for attempted armed robbery, prosecutors failed to disclose evidence that should have been turned over to the defense under *Brady v. Maryland*, 373 U.S. 83 (1963). Thompson was convicted. Because of that conviction Thompson elected not to testify in his own defense in his later trial for murder, and he was again convicted. Thompson spent 18 years in prison, including 14 years on death row. One month before Thompson's scheduled execution, his investigator discovered the undisclosed evidence from his armed robbery trial. The reviewing court determined that the evidence was exculpatory, and both of Thompson's convictions were vacated.

> After his release from prison, Thompson sued petitioner Harry Connick, in his official capacity as the Orleans Parish District Attorney, for damages

under 42 U.S.C. § 1983. Thompson alleged that Connick had failed to train his prosecutors adequately about their duty to produce exculpatory evidence and that the lack of training had caused the nondisclosure in Thompson's robbery case. The jury awarded Thompson $14 million, and the Court of Appeals for the Fifth Circuit affirmed by an evenly divided en banc court. We granted certiorari to decide whether a district attorney's office may be held liable under § 1983 for failure to train based on a single *Brady* violation. We hold that it cannot.

The Court explained why the jury verdict could not be upheld:

> A pattern of similar constitutional violations by untrained employees is "ordinarily necessary" to demonstrate deliberate indifference for purposes of failure to train. . . . [But instead] of relying on a pattern of similar *Brady* violations, Thompson relies on the "single-incident" liability that this Court hypothesized in *Canton*. He contends that the *Brady* violation in his case was the "obvious" consequence of failing to provide specific *Brady* training, and that this showing of "obviousness" can substitute for the pattern of violations ordinarily necessary to establish municipal culpability. . . .
>
> Failure to train prosecutors in their *Brady* obligations does not fall within the narrow range of *Canton*'s hypothesized single-incident liability. The obvious need for specific legal training that was present in the *Canton* scenario is absent here. Armed police must sometimes make split-second decisions with life-or-death consequences. There is no reason to assume that police academy applicants are familiar with the constitutional constraints on the use of deadly force. And, in the absence of training, there is no way for novice officers to obtain the legal knowledge they require. Under those circumstances there is an obvious need for some form of training. In stark contrast, legal "[t]raining is what differentiates attorneys from average public employees." . . .
>
> In light of [the] regime of legal training and professional responsibility [described by the Court], recurring constitutional violations are not the "obvious consequence" of failing to provide prosecutors with formal in-house training about how to obey the law. . . .

Justice Ginsburg, in a lengthy dissent joined by Justices Breyer, Sotomayor, and Kagan, relied on *Canton* as establishing that "a municipality's failure to provide training may be so egregious that, even without notice of prior constitutional violations, the failure could properly be characterized as deliberate indifference to constitutional rights." Thompson, she said, "presented convincing evidence to satisfy this standard." In particular:

> Abundant evidence supported the jury's finding that additional *Brady* training was obviously necessary to ensure that *Brady* violations would not occur: (1) Connick, the Office's sole policymaker, misunderstood *Brady*. (2) Other leaders in the Office, who bore direct responsibility for training less experienced prosecutors, were similarly uninformed about *Brady*.

(3) Prosecutors in the Office received no *Brady* training. (4) The Office shirked its responsibility to keep prosecutors abreast of relevant legal developments concerning *Brady* requirements. As a result of these multiple shortfalls, it was hardly surprising that *Brady* violations in fact occurred, severely undermining the integrity of Thompson's trials.

The majority insisted that the dissent "misses the point":

> The dissent rejects our holding that *Canton*'s hypothesized single-incident liability does not, as a legal matter, encompass failure to train prosecutors in their *Brady* obligation. It would instead apply the *Canton* hypothetical to this case, and thus devotes almost all of its opinion to explaining why the evidence supports liability under that theory. But the dissent's attempt to address our holding—by pointing out that not all prosecutors will necessarily have enrolled in criminal procedure class—misses the point. The reason why the *Canton* hypothetical is inapplicable is that attorneys, unlike police officers, are equipped with the tools to find, interpret, and apply legal principles. . . .

Does *Connick v. Thompson* put an end to the possibility of establishing "single-incident" municipal liability beyond the precise facts hypothesized in the *Canton* footnote?

3. In *Connick*, all of the Justices agreed that the prosecutors in this case behaved badly: at the least, some were incompetent, and two were clearly in violation of their ethical responsibilities. Why did Thompson hang his hopes on his suit against the city, rather than the prosecutors individually? Consider the materials in section E, *infra*.

Note: Iqbal *and "Supervisory Liability"*

1. In the *Brown* litigation, the plaintiffs sought to recover monetary damages from the county for the actions of Deputy Burns. Could they also have sought recovery from Sheriff Moore as an individual? In other words, does § 1983 allow for supervisory liability and, if so, under what circumstances?

Clearly, supervisory liability cannot be based on a theory of *respondeat superior*. That much is established by *Monell* itself, which relied in part on the "causation" requirement in the language of § 1983. But does the rejection of *respondeat superior* liability necessarily exclude any form of supervisory liability?

The Supreme Court has never answered that question directly, but as of 2008, all of the circuits had endorsed some form of supervisory liability. For example, the Fifth Circuit held that "supervisors may be liable for constitutional violations committed by subordinate employees when supervisors act, or fail to act, with *deliberate indifference* to violations of others' constitutional rights committed by their subordinates." *Atteberry v. Nocona General Hosp.*, 430 F.3d 245 (5th Cir. 2005) (emphasis in original).[1]

---

1. For a good brief summary of the standards applied in the various circuits before *Iqbal*, see Martin A. Schwartz & Kathryn R. Urbonya, Section 1983 Litigation 120–22 (2d ed. 2008).

However, that body of law has now been called into question by the Supreme Court's decision in *Ashcroft v. Iqbal*, 556 U.S. 662 (2009).

2. In *Iqbal*, the plaintiff brought suit against former officials of the federal government, invoking the judicially created counterpart to § 1983, the *Bivens* action. (See Chapter 8.) The Supreme Court summarized the case as follows:

> Respondent Javaid Iqbal is a citizen of Pakistan and a Muslim. In the wake of the September 11, 2001, terrorist attacks he was arrested in the United States on criminal charges and detained by federal officials. Respondent claims he was deprived of various constitutional protections while in federal custody. To redress the alleged deprivations, respondent filed a complaint against numerous federal officials, including John Ashcroft, the former Attorney General of the United States, and Robert Mueller, the Director of the Federal Bureau of Investigation (FBI).

> Ashcroft and Mueller are the petitioners in the case now before us. As to these two petitioners, the complaint alleges that they adopted an unconstitutional policy that subjected respondent to harsh conditions of confinement on account of his race, religion, or national origin. . . . [Specifically,] the complaint posits that petitioners "each knew of, condoned, and willfully and maliciously agreed to subject" respondent to harsh conditions of confinement "as a matter of policy, solely on account of [his] religion, race, and/or national origin and for no legitimate penological interest." The pleading names Ashcroft as the "principal architect" of the policy and identifies Mueller as "instrumental in [its] adoption, promulgation, and implementation."

The Court held that the complaint "fail[ed] to plead sufficient facts to state a claim for purposeful and unlawful discrimination against petitioners." Justice Kennedy, writing for a majority of five, considered "the elements a plaintiff must plead to state a claim of unconstitutional discrimination against officials entitled to assert the defense of qualified immunity." He wrote:

> In the limited settings where *Bivens* [applies], the implied cause of action is the "federal analog to suits brought against state officials under 42 U.S.C. § 1983." Based on the rules our precedents establish, respondent correctly concedes that Government officials may not be held liable for the unconstitutional conduct of their subordinates under a theory of *respondeat superior*. Because vicarious liability is inapplicable to *Bivens* and § 1983 suits, a plaintiff must plead that each Government-official defendant, through the official's own individual actions, has violated the Constitution.

> The factors necessary to establish a *Bivens* violation will vary with the constitutional provision at issue. Where the claim is invidious discrimination in contravention of the First and Fifth Amendments, our decisions make clear that the plaintiff must plead and prove that the defendant acted with discriminatory purpose. . . .

> Respondent [argues] that, under a theory of "supervisory liability," petition-
> ers can be liable for "knowledge and acquiescence in their subordinates' use of
> discriminatory criteria to make classification decisions among detainees." . . .
> We reject this argument. . . . In a § 1983 suit or a *Bivens* action—where masters
> do not answer for the torts of their servants—the term "supervisory liability" is
> a misnomer. Absent vicarious liability, each Government official, his or her title
> notwithstanding, is only liable for his or her own misconduct. In the context of
> determining whether there is a violation of clearly established right to over-
> come qualified immunity, purpose rather than knowledge is required to impose
> *Bivens* liability on the subordinate for unconstitutional discrimination; the
> same holds true for an official charged with violations arising from his or her
> superintendent responsibilities.

Turning to the complaint before it, the Court applied its decision in *Bell Atlantic
Corp. v. Twombly*, 550 U.S. 544 (2007), an antitrust case. Quoting from *Twombly*, the
Court held that Iqbal's complaint "has not 'nudged [his] claims' of invidious discrim-
ination 'across the line from conceivable to plausible.'" The Court explained:

> We begin our analysis by identifying the allegations in the complaint that
> are not entitled to the assumption of truth. Respondent pleads that petition-
> ers "knew of, condoned, and willfully and maliciously agreed to subject [him]"
> to harsh conditions of confinement "as a matter of policy, solely on account
> of [his] religion, race, and/or national origin and for no legitimate penologi-
> cal interest." The complaint alleges that Ashcroft was the "principal architect"
> of this invidious policy and that Mueller was "instrumental" in adopting and
> executing it. These bare assertions, much like the pleading of conspiracy in
> *Twombly*, amount to nothing more than a "formulaic recitation of the ele-
> ments" of a constitutional discrimination claim, namely, that petitioners
> adopted a policy "'because of,' not merely 'in spite of,' its adverse effects upon
> an identifiable group." As such, the allegations are conclusory and not enti-
> tled to be assumed true. *Twombly*.

The Court continued by reemphasizing the need to show unconstitutional conduct by the defendants themselves:

> Unlike in *Twombly*, where the doctrine of *respondeat superior* could
> bind the corporate defendant, here, as we have noted, petitioners cannot be
> held liable unless they themselves acted on account of a constitutionally pro-
> tected characteristic. Yet respondent's complaint does not contain any fac-
> tual allegation sufficient to plausibly suggest petitioners' discriminatory state
> of mind. His pleadings thus do not meet the standard necessary to comply
> with Rule 8 [of the Federal Rules of Civil Procedure].

3. Justice Souter, joined by Justices Stevens, Ginsburg, and Breyer, dissented strongly:

> The majority says that in a *Bivens* action, "where masters do not answer
> for the torts of their servants," "the term 'supervisory liability' is a misnomer,"
> and that "[a]bsent vicarious liability, each Government official, his or her title

notwithstanding, is only liable for his or her own misconduct." Lest there be any mistake, in these words the majority is not narrowing the scope of supervisory liability; it is eliminating *Bivens* supervisory liability entirely. The nature of a supervisory liability theory is that the supervisor may be liable, under certain conditions, for the wrongdoing of his subordinates, and it is this very principle that the majority rejects.

... [The majority's] cursory analysis ... rests on the assumption that only two outcomes are possible here: *respondeat superior* liability, in which "an employer is subject to liability for torts committed by employees while acting within the scope of their employment," or no supervisory liability at all. The dichotomy is false. Even if an employer is not liable for the actions of his employee solely because the employee was acting within the scope of employment, there still might be conditions to render a supervisor liable for the conduct of his subordinate.

In fact, there is quite a spectrum of possible tests for supervisory liability: it could be imposed where a supervisor has actual knowledge of a subordinate's constitutional violation and acquiesces; or where supervisors "know about the conduct and facilitate it, approve it, condone it, or turn a blind eye for fear of what they might see"; or where the supervisor has no actual knowledge of the violation but was reckless in his supervision of the subordinate; or where the supervisor was grossly negligent. [In this paragraph Justice Souter cited decisions from six circuits.]

The dissent also disagreed with the majority's assessment of the complaint.

4. Does *Iqbal* eliminate any possibility of imposing "supervisory liability" under § 1983? Consider the Problems that follow.

Problem: Conditions of Confinement

In *Hydrick v. Hunter*, 500 F. 3d 978 (9th Cir. 2007), a class of approximately 600 persons convicted under California's Sexually Violent Predator (SVP) Act brought suit in federal court under § 1983, alleging that the conditions of their confinement violated their federal constitutional rights. The plaintiffs sought monetary damages from several defendants, including the Director of the California Department of Mental Health and the Director of the California Department of Corrections. A divided panel of the Ninth Circuit held that several of the claims sufficiently pleaded violations of clearly established law. Among them: claims that "the amount of force used is often a gross overreaction to the situation" (in violation of due process) and that plaintiffs have been subjected to unreasonable searches and seizures (in violation of the Fourth Amendment). The Court also rejected the defendants' argument that they were not proper defendants for a § 1983 suit.

Although there is no pure *respondeat superior* liability under § 1983, a supervisor is liable for the constitutional violations of subordinates "if the supervisor participated in or directed the violations, or knew of the violations and failed to act to prevent them." *Taylor v. List*, 880 F.2d 1040 (9th Cir. 1989).

The Plaintiffs proceed on two theories: (a) that the Defendants created policies and procedures that violated the Plaintiffs' constitutional rights; and (b) that the Defendants were willfully blind to constitutional violations committed by their subordinates. Because the Defendants were directors and policy-makers for Atascadero State Hospital, the Plaintiffs have sufficiently alleged that the constitutional violations they suffered were "set in motion" by the Defendants' policy decisions or, at the very least, that the Defendants knew of these abuses and demonstrated a deliberate indifference to the Plaintiffs' plight.

Under *Leer v. Murphy*, 844 F.2d 628 (9th Cir. 1988), the Plaintiffs will need to show how the deliberate indifference or affirmative actions of each Defendant caused a constitutional violation before they can seek monetary damages against any individual Defendant. At this stage of pleading, however, the Plaintiffs need not specifically delineate how each Defendant contributed to the violation of their constitutional rights. Indeed, we do not see how, prior to discovery, they *could* plead the individual roles of each state officer with any more specificity. Taking the statements in the complaint in the light most favorable to the Plaintiffs, the Plaintiffs may be able to state a claim against all of the named Defendants, each of whom played an instrumental role in policymaking and enforcement at Atascadero State Hospital. Therefore, we hold the Plaintiffs have sufficiently alleged the Defendants' role in the alleged constitutional violations against SVPs to survive this motion to dismiss.

The Supreme Court vacated the Ninth Circuit decision and remanded for reconsideration in light of *Iqbal*. Does *Iqbal* require the court to order dismissal of the action, or can *Iqbal* be distinguished?

Problem: A Nurse with a Deadly Touch

Ten plaintiffs have brought a § 1983 action as representatives of ten deceased patients at Cumberland County Hospital. The Plaintiffs allege that Florence Maybrick ("Nurse Maybrick"), a nurse at the Hospital, willfully deprived the patients of life and liberty interests by injecting them with a paralytic drug named Norcavon. The plaintiffs claim that Nurse Maybrick repeatedly stole Norcavon from a hospital dispensary and used it to kill as many as 22 patients between November 2014 and February 2015.

In addition to Maybrick, the plaintiffs have sued Adelaide Bartlett and Madeline Smith. Defendant Bartlett is alleged to have been the Hospital Administrator at Cumberland during the relevant period, with general administrative and supervisory authority over the hospital staff and policymaking authority over drug storage and medical care. Defendant Smith is alleged to have been the Director of Nursing at Cumberland during the relevant time period, with supervisory and training authority over Nurse Maybrick.

Defendants Bartlett and Smith do not dispute that the Hospital is a municipal-government entity. However, they have moved to dismiss the claims against them on the ground that the complaint does not sufficiently allege that they may be held liable based on any constitutional violations Nurse Maybrick may have committed. In response, the plaintiffs point out that the complaint alleges that: (1) in a two-month period, Norcavon was found missing ten different times from the hospital dispensary; (2) Norcavon was wrongfully administered to Cumberland patients, including the plaintiffs' decedents; (3) the death rate at Cumberland was at least double the death rate during the same two-month period in the preceding year; and (4) the defendants knew all of these facts before they took any action to investigate a possible connection between the deaths and the missing drugs.

Should the district court grant the motion to dismiss?

E. Official Immunities

Section 1983 is broadly written to impose liability on "every person" who, under color of state law, deprives another person of rights secured by federal law. However, over time, the Supreme Court has developed an extensive body of immunity law that protects many state and local officials from damages actions under the statute. It has done so by interpreting § 1983 against the common-law background of immunity law that existed when the statute was adopted in 1871. Justice Frankfurter's analysis in *Tenney v. Brandhove*, 341 U.S. 367 (1951), evaluating whether legislators could be held liable for violations of federal constitutional rights, is illustrative. After recounting the long common-law history of legislative immunity and the policies of frank and open debate that support it, he asked:

> Did Congress by the general language of [section 1983] mean to overturn the tradition of legislative freedom achieved in England by Civil War and carefully preserved in the formation of State and National Governments here? Did it mean to subject legislators to civil liability for acts done within the sphere of legislative activity? ... We cannot believe that Congress — itself a staunch advocate of legislative freedom — would impinge on a tradition so well grounded in history and reason by covert inclusion in the general language before us.

Tenney's methodology — a review of the common-law history of an immunity and its policy rationale, followed by a rejection of the argument that § 1983's broad language encompassed an abrogation of that immunity — has led the Court to find that most state and local officers who perform discretionary functions are entitled to some form of immunity defense from damages actions under § 1983.

Immunity defenses seek to balance conflicting policies. On the one hand, § 1983 exists to deter violations of federal law and to ensure that government actors have incentives to know and to consider the constitutional and other federal rights of citizens. On the other hand, the government provides important — indeed, crucial — services, and its employees often act in contexts of factual and legal uncertainty. A system of liability that forces those employees to make fear of personal liability a central consideration in their decisionmaking has considerable costs. Imagine for a moment the myriad ways, all fraught with constitutional concerns, in which police officers interact with suspects, and one can readily imagine the costs of overdeterrence.

There are two categories of immunity defenses. Absolute immunity is available to many of the actors in the judicial process (judges, witnesses, and prosecutors when they are in court) and to legislators. Qualified immunity is available to many executive officers, including police officers, state governors, school board members, and others.

Both absolute and qualified immunity provide immunity both from suit and from damages liability. And both protect defendants who have admittedly violated a plaintiff's constitutional rights and caused otherwise-compensable harm. The defenses differ primarily in how they are established.

One final note. Because the Supreme Court's immunity jurisprudence is, at bottom, a matter of statutory interpretation, it can be altered by Congress. Thus, in *Pulliam v. Allen*, 466 U.S. 522 (1984), the Court held that judicial immunity did not prohibit declaratory and injunctive relief against a judicial officer acting in his or her judicial capacity. In 1996 Congress amended 42 U.S.C. § 1983 to provide that "in any action brought against a judicial officer for an act or omission taken in such officer's judicial capacity, injunctive relief shall not be granted unless a declaratory decree was violated or declaratory relief was unavailable." The Senate Report states that the amendment "restores the doctrine of judicial immunity to the status it occupied prior to [*Pulliam*]" because *Pulliam* had departed from "400 years of common law tradition and weakened judicial immunity protections." S. Rep. 104–366 at 36–37.

[1] Absolute Immunity

Absolute immunity protects entire classes of defendants—judges, legislators, witnesses, and in some cases prosecutors—but *only* when they are acting in certain ways. Judges, for instance, are protected when they act in their "judicial capacity," such as when they are ruling on a case or holding a witness in contempt, but are not protected when they are acting as employers. Compare *Stump v. Sparkman*, 435 U.S. 349 (1978) (holding that a judge was absolutely immune for ordering the sterilization of an adolescent girl, despite the lack of authority to do so), with *Forrester v. White*, 484 U.S. 219 (1988) (holding that a judge was not protected by immunity when he fired a probation officer for discriminatory reasons). The Court has reasoned that the immunity should extend only as far as its rationale. Thus, judges are protected because considerations of personal liability should not infect their decision-making, and because disgruntled litigants could be expected to sue with regularity, taking vast amounts of judicial time. These policies do not extend to the judge as an employer. Similarly, prosecutors are expected to conduct their activities as officers of the court fearlessly, and are given absolute immunity when they are acting as advocates. When they are involved in investigations, however, they are more like police officers—and the immunity they receive, like the immunity accorded to police officers, is qualified.

Because absolute immunity exists to protect certain functions, it can extend to executive officers when they are performing those functions, and even to members of one otherwise-protected group, such as judges, if they are performing the function of another protected group, such as legislators. For instance, the Court has held that administrative agency officials at the Department of Agriculture are entitled to absolute immunity when they are acting in a judicial capacity, even though as executive-branch officers they would ordinarily be entitled to qualified rather than absolute immunity. *Butz v. Economou*, 438 U.S. 478 (1978).

In *Supreme Court of Virginia v. Consumers Union*, 446 U.S. 719 (1980), a consumer group brought a §1983 action against the Virginia Supreme Court, arguing that its disciplinary rule prohibiting attorney advertising violated the First Amendment. Virginia had delegated its entire power to regulate attorneys to its Supreme Court, and that court had promulgated the challenged regulation. In issuing the regulation, the Supreme Court held, the members of the Virginia court were acting in a legislative capacity, and were absolutely immune from suit. The Virginia court also had enforcement authority against attorneys under the regulation: it could initiate proceedings for violations of the disciplinary rules, and it heard appeals from disciplinary adjudications in the lower courts. The Virginia judges were entitled to judicial immunity in their adjudicatory role, but in their role in independent enforcement actions, the Supreme Court held, the Virginia court was entitled to the same absolute immunity as prosecutors.

While judges, legislators, and prosecutors all enjoy absolute immunity from damages, the different roles are relevant when considering injunctive relief. The Supreme Court has held that legislators are immune from both damages and injunctive relief, but that prosecutors may be enjoined. *See, e.g., Ex parte Young*. Thus, while the members of the Virginia court were immune from damages, they could be enjoined from enforcing the challenged rule.

Finally, those who work closely with absolutely-immune officials may share in that immunity derivatively. In *Gravel v. United States*, 408 U.S. 606 (1972), for instance, the Court held that legislative aides share in absolute immunity when they are engaged in acts for which the legislator they serve would be immune. The Court noted that "it is literally impossible . . . for Members of Congress to perform their legislative tasks without the help of aides and assistants" and that "the day-to-day work of such aides is so critical to the Members' performance that they must be treated as the latter's alter egos. . . ."

In summary, absolute immunity applies to judges, witnesses, prosecutors (acting as advocates) and legislators when they are performing the core functions of those positions. It can also extend to officers performing legislative, or judicial functions. Finally, it can extend derivatively to aides of these officers.

[2] Qualified Immunity

Qualified immunity is the default defense for executive-branch officers performing discretionary functions. The following case outlines the scope of qualified immunity and raises numerous practical questions about its application.

Harlow v. Fitzgerald

Supreme Court of the United States, 1982.

457 U.S. 800.

JUSTICE POWELL delivered the opinion of the Court.

The issue in this case is the scope of the immunity available to the senior aides and advisers of the President of the United States in a suit for damages based upon their official acts. [Fitzgerald brought a *Bivens* action against aides of President Nixon, alleging that they conspired to fire him for being a whistle-blower. He claimed that their actions violated federal statutory law and the First Amendment. The aides claimed immunity from suit.]

II

. . . [Our] decisions consistently have held that government officials are entitled to some form of immunity from suits for damages. As recognized at common law, public officers require this protection to shield them from undue interference with their duties and from potentially disabling threats of liability.

Our decisions have recognized immunity defenses of two kinds. For officials whose special functions or constitutional status requires complete protection from suit, we have recognized the defense of "absolute immunity." The absolute immunity of legislators, in their legislative functions, and of judges, in their judicial functions now is well settled. Our decisions also have extended absolute immunity to certain officials of the Executive Branch. These include prosecutors and similar officials, executive officers engaged in adjudicative functions, and the President of the United States, see *Nixon v. Fitzgerald*, 457 U.S. 731 (1982).

For executive officials in general, however, our cases make plain that qualified immunity represents the norm. In *Scheuer v. Rhodes*, 416 U.S. 232 (1974), we acknowledged that high officials require greater protection than those with less complex discretionary responsibilities. Nonetheless, we held that a governor and his aides could receive the requisite protection from qualified or good-faith immunity. In *Butz v. Economou*, 438 U.S. 478 (1978), we extended the approach of *Scheuer* to high federal officials of the Executive Branch. Discussing in detail the considerations that also had underlain our decision in *Scheuer*, we explained that the recognition of a qualified immunity defense for high executives reflected an attempt to balance competing values: not only the importance of a damages remedy to protect the rights of citizens, but also "the need to protect officials who are required to exercise their discretion and the related public interest in encouraging the vigorous exercise of official authority." Without discounting the adverse consequences of denying high officials an absolute immunity from private lawsuits alleging constitutional violations . . . ., we emphasized our expectation that insubstantial suits need not proceed to trial:

> Insubstantial lawsuits can be quickly terminated by federal courts alert to the possibilities of artful pleading. Unless the complaint states a compensable claim for relief . . . , it should not survive a motion to dismiss. Moreover, . . .

damages suits concerning constitutional violations need not proceed to trial, but can be terminated on a properly supported motion for summary judgment based on the defense of immunity. . . . In responding to such a motion, plaintiffs may not play dog in the manger; and firm application of the Federal Rules of Civil Procedure will ensure that federal officials are not harassed by frivolous lawsuits.

Butz continued to acknowledge that the special functions of some officials might require absolute immunity. But the Court held that "federal officials who seek absolute exemption from personal liability for unconstitutional conduct must bear the burden of showing that public policy requires an exemption of that scope."

III

Petitioners argue that they are entitled to a blanket protection of absolute immunity as an incident of their offices as Presidential aides. In deciding this claim we do not write on an empty page. . . . Having decided in *Butz* that Members of the Cabinet ordinarily enjoy only qualified immunity from suit, we conclude today that it would be equally untenable to hold absolute immunity an incident of the office of every Presidential subordinate based in the White House. . . .

[Petitioners also argued that they were entitled to share in the President's absolute immunity, as the Senate aides in *Gravel* shared in legislative immunity.] Petitioners' argument is not without force. Ultimately, however, it sweeps too far. If the President's aides are derivatively immune because they are essential to the functioning of the Presidency, so should the Members of the Cabinet—Presidential subordinates some of whose essential roles are acknowledged by the Constitution itself—be absolutely immune. Yet we implicitly rejected such derivative immunity in *Butz*. Moreover, in general our cases have followed a "functional" approach to immunity law. We have recognized that the judicial, prosecutorial, and legislative functions require absolute immunity. But this protection has extended no further than its justification would warrant. In *Gravel*, for example, we emphasized that Senators and their aides were absolutely immune only when performing "acts legislative in nature," and not when taking other acts even "in their official capacity." Our cases involving judges and prosecutors have followed a similar line. The undifferentiated extension of absolute "derivative" immunity to the President's aides therefore could not be reconciled with the "functional" approach that has characterized the immunity decisions of this Court. . . .

IV

Even if they cannot establish that their official functions require absolute immunity, petitioners assert that public policy at least mandates an application of the qualified immunity standard that would permit the defeat of insubstantial claims without resort to trial. We agree.

A

The resolution of immunity questions inherently requires a balance between the evils inevitable in any available alternative. In situations of abuse of office, an action for damages may offer the only realistic avenue for vindication of constitutional guarantees. *Butz*; *see Bivens v. Six Unknown Named Agents of Fed. Bur. of Narcotics*, 403 U.S. 388 (1971) [Chapter 8]. It is this recognition that has required the denial of absolute immunity to most public officers. At the same time, however, it cannot be disputed seriously that claims frequently run against the innocent as well as the guilty — at a cost not only to the defendant officials, but to society as a whole. These social costs include the expenses of litigation, the diversion of official energy from pressing public issues, and the deterrence of able citizens from acceptance of public office. Finally, there is the danger that fear of being sued will "dampen the ardor of all but the most resolute, or the most irresponsible [public officials], in the unflinching discharge of their duties." *Gregoire v. Biddle*, 177 F.2d 579 (CA2 1949).

In identifying qualified immunity as the best attainable accommodation of competing values, . . . we relied on the assumption that this standard would permit "[i]nsubstantial lawsuits [to] be quickly terminated." Yet petitioners advance persuasive arguments that the dismissal of insubstantial lawsuits without trial — a factor presupposed in the balance of competing interests struck by our prior cases — requires an adjustment of the "good faith" standard established by our decisions.

B

Qualified or "good faith" immunity is an affirmative defense that must be pleaded by a defendant official. *Gomez v. Toledo*, 446 U.S. 635 (1980). Decisions of this Court have established that the "good faith" defense has both an "objective" and a "subjective" aspect. The objective element involves a presumptive knowledge of and respect for "basic, unquestioned constitutional rights." *Wood v. Strickland*, 420 U.S. 308 (1975). The subjective component refers to "permissible intentions." Characteristically the Court has defined these elements by identifying the circumstances in which qualified immunity would not be available. Referring both to the objective and subjective elements, we have held that qualified immunity would be defeated if an official "*knew or reasonably should have known* that the action he took within his sphere of official responsibility would violate the constitutional rights of the [plaintiff], or if he took the action *with the malicious intention* to cause a deprivation of constitutional rights or other injury. . . ." *Ibid*. (emphasis added).

The subjective element of the good-faith defense frequently has proved incompatible with our admonition in *Butz* that insubstantial claims should not proceed to trial. Rule 56 of the Federal Rules of Civil Procedure provides that disputed questions of fact ordinarily may not be decided on motions for summary judgment. And an official's subjective good faith has been considered to be a question of fact that some courts have regarded as inherently requiring resolution by a jury.

In the context of *Butz'* attempted balancing of competing values, it now is clear that substantial costs attend the litigation of the subjective good faith of government officials. Not only are there the general costs of subjecting officials to the risks of trial — distraction of officials from their governmental duties, inhibition of discretionary action, and deterrence of able people from public service. There are special costs to "subjective" inquiries of this kind. Immunity generally is available only to officials performing discretionary functions. In contrast with the thought processes accompanying "ministerial" tasks, the judgments surrounding discretionary action almost inevitably are influenced by the decisionmaker's experiences, values, and emotions. These variables explain in part why questions of subjective intent so rarely can be decided by summary judgment. Yet they also frame a background in which there often is no clear end to the relevant evidence. Judicial inquiry into subjective motivation therefore may entail broad-ranging discovery and the deposing of numerous persons, including an official's professional colleagues. Inquiries of this kind can be peculiarly disruptive of effective government. [In a footnote, the Court quoted a concurring opinion written by Judge Gesell of the D.C. Circuit:]

> We should not close our eyes to the fact that with increasing frequency in this jurisdiction and throughout the country plaintiffs are filing suits seeking damage awards against high government officials in their personal capacities based on alleged constitutional torts. Each such suit almost invariably results in these officials and their colleagues being subjected to extensive discovery into traditionally protected areas, such as their deliberations preparatory to the formulation of government policy and their intimate thought processes and communications at the presidential and cabinet levels. . . . It is not difficult for ingenious plaintiff's counsel to create a material issue of fact on some element of the immunity defense where subtle questions of constitutional law and a decisionmaker's mental processes are involved. A sentence from a casual document or a difference in recollection with regard to a particular policy conversation held long ago would usually, under the normal summary judgment standards, be sufficient [to force a trial]. . . . The effect of this development upon the willingness of individuals to serve their country is obvious.

. . . [We] conclude today that bare allegations of malice should not suffice to subject government officials either to the costs of trial or to the burdens of broad-reaching discovery. We therefore hold that government officials performing discretionary functions generally are shielded from liability for civil damages insofar as their conduct does not violate clearly established statutory or constitutional rights of which a reasonable person would have known.

Reliance on the objective reasonableness of an official's conduct, as measured by reference to clearly established law, should avoid excessive disruption of government and permit the resolution of many insubstantial claims on summary judgment. On summary judgment, the judge appropriately may determine, not only the currently applicable law, but whether that law was clearly established at the time an action occurred. If the law at that time was not clearly established, an official could not reasonably be expected to anticipate subsequent legal developments, nor could he fairly be said to "know" that the law forbade conduct not previously identified as unlawful. Until this threshold immunity question is resolved, discovery should not be allowed. If the law was clearly established, the immunity defense ordinarily should fail, since a reasonably competent public official should know the law governing his conduct. Nevertheless, if the official pleading the defense claims extraordinary circumstances and can prove that he neither knew nor should have known of the relevant legal standard, the defense should be sustained. But again, the defense would turn primarily on objective factors.

By defining the limits of qualified immunity essentially in objective terms, we provide no license to lawless conduct. The public interest in deterrence of unlawful conduct and in compensation of victims remains protected by a test that focuses on the objective legal reasonableness of an official's acts. Where an official could be expected to know that certain conduct would violate statutory or constitutional rights, he should be made to hesitate; and a person who suffers injury caused by such conduct may have a cause of action. But where an official's duties legitimately require action in which clearly established rights are not implicated, the public interest may be better served by action taken "with independence and without fear of consequences." *Pierson v. Ray*, 386 U.S. 547 (1967).

C

In this case petitioners have asked us to hold that the respondent's pretrial showings were insufficient to survive their motion for summary judgment. We think it appropriate, however, to remand the case to the District Court for its reconsideration of this issue in light of this opinion. The trial court is more familiar with the record so far developed and also is better situated to make any such further findings as may be necessary. In *Butz*, we admonished that "insubstantial" suits against high public officials should not be allowed to proceed to trial. We reiterate this admonition. Insubstantial lawsuits undermine the effectiveness of government as contemplated by our constitutional structure. . . .

V

The judgment of the Court of Appeals is vacated, and the case is remanded for further action consistent with this opinion.

[Justice Brennan's concurring opinion on the qualified immunity issue is omitted. Justice Rehnquist's concurring opinion and Chief Justice Burger's dissenting opinion on the absolute immunity issue are also omitted.]

Note: Qualified Immunity after Harlow

1. Harlow was a landmark in the development of immunity doctrine. It made clear that qualified immunity generally should be considered whenever an officer has discretionary authority. It provided a unitary standard for executive-branch officers, from the police officer on the beat to the governor in the mansion. As a practical matter, it also eliminated much of the difference between qualified and absolute immunity, by noting that when an officer is entitled to qualified immunity, that immunity acts to protect the officer both from damages and from having to stand trial.

2. Harlow involved a *Bivens* action against officials of the federal government (see Chapter 8). However, the Court twice quoted its statement in *Butz* that it would be "untenable to draw a distinction for purposes of immunity law between suits brought against state officials under [42 U.S.C.] § 1983 and suits brought directly under the Constitution against federal officials." The Court has never wavered from that position; thus the *Harlow* standard applies to § 1983 suits as well as to *Bivens* actions.

3. *Harlow* eliminates investigation into an official's subjective intentions and focuses the inquiry on whether the law the officer is charged with violating was clearly established at the time the officer took action. The Court hoped especially to avoid the costs of discovery: if immunity hinges on the state of the law, presumably immunity questions can be settled by investigating the state of decisional law when the Constitution allegedly was violated.

4. Several difficulties with this approach quickly emerged. First, many constitutional rights involve the application of standards, rather than rules. When courts employ a balancing test to determine whether the Constitution has been offended, the underlying facts are important—and if they are disputed, it may be impossible to avoid discovery. A variant of this difficulty involves the level of generality at which one describes a right in determining whether it is clearly established. For instance, it has been established for many years that an unreasonable search violates the Fourth Amendment. Is the right to avoid unreasonable searches clearly established, or must that right be evaluated in the context of the facts of a given case?

Finally, application of some constitutional principles, notably in the common area of Fourth Amendment searches and seizures, involves an inquiry into the objective reasonableness of an officer's actions. Lower courts quickly became entangled in the similarity between the substantive constitutional standard and the immunity standard. In *Llaguno v. Mingey*, 763 F.2d 1560 (7th Cir. 1985) (en banc), for example, the court stated:

> The question whether [police officers] had probable cause depends upon what they reasonably believed with respect to the facts that confronted them. To go on and instruct the jury [as to immunity] . . . that even if the police acted without probable cause, they should be exonerated if they reasonably though erroneously) believed that they were acting reasonably is . . . to give the defendants two bites of the apple.

5. In *Anderson v. Creighton*, 483 U.S. 635 (1987), the Court attempted to address several of these difficulties. The question presented was whether a police officer who "participates in a search that violates the Fourth Amendment may be held . . . liable for money damages if a reasonable officer could have believed that the search complied with the Fourth Amendment."

Justice Scalia, writing for the Court, stated:

> [W]hether an official protected by qualified immunity may be held personally liable for an allegedly unlawful official action generally turns on the "objective legal reasonableness" of the action, *Harlow*, assessed in light of the legal rules that were "clearly established" at the time it was taken.

The operation of this standard, however, depends substantially upon the level of generality at which the relevant "legal rule" is to be identified. For example, the right to due process of law is quite clearly established by the Due Process Clause, and thus there is a sense in which any action that violates that Clause (no matter how unclear it may be that the particular action is a violation) violates a clearly established right. Much the same could be said of any other constitutional or statutory violation. But if the test of "clearly established law" were to be applied at this level of generality, it would bear no relationship to the "objective legal reasonableness" that is the touchstone of *Harlow*. Plaintiffs would be able to convert the rule of qualified immunity that our cases plainly establish into a rule of virtually unqualified liability simply by alleging violation of extremely abstract rights. *Harlow* would be transformed from a guarantee of immunity into a rule of pleading. . . .

[O]ur cases establish that the right the official is alleged to have violated must have been "clearly established" in a more particularized, and hence more relevant, sense: The contours of the right must be sufficiently clear that a reasonable official would understand that what he is doing violates that right. This is not to say that an official action is protected by qualified immunity unless the very action in question has previously been held unlawful, but it is to say that in the light of pre-existing law the unlawfulness must be apparent.

Applying this discussion to the case at hand, Justice Scalia continued:

The Court of Appeals' brief discussion of qualified immunity consisted of little more than an assertion that a general right Anderson was alleged to have violated—the right to be free from warrantless searches of one's home unless the searching officers have probable cause and there are exigent circumstances—was clearly established. The Court of Appeals specifically refused to consider the argument that it was not clearly established that the circumstances with which Anderson was confronted did not constitute probable cause and exigent circumstances. The previous discussion should make clear that this refusal was erroneous. It simply does not follow immediately from the conclusion that it was firmly established that warrantless searches not supported by probable cause and exigent circumstances violate the Fourth Amendment that Anderson's search was objectively legally unreasonable. We have recognized that it is inevitable that law enforcement officials will in some cases reasonably but mistakenly conclude that probable cause is present, and we have indicated that in such cases those officials—like other officials who act in ways they reasonably believe to be lawful—should not be held personally liable. The same is true of their conclusions regarding exigent circumstances.

It follows from what we have said that the determination whether it was objectively legally reasonable to conclude that a given search was supported by probable cause or exigent circumstances will often require examination of the information possessed by the searching officials. [T]his does not reintroduce into qualified immunity analysis the inquiry into officials' subjective intent that *Harlow* sought to minimize. The relevant question in this case, for example, is the objective (albeit fact-specific) question whether a reasonable officer could have believed Anderson's warrantless search to be lawful, in light of clearly established law and the information the searching officers possessed. Anderson's subjective beliefs about the search are irrelevant.

> The principles of qualified immunity that we reaffirm today require that Anderson be permitted to argue that he is entitled to summary judgment on the ground that, in light of the clearly established principles governing warrantless searches, he could, as a matter of law, reasonably have believed that the search . . . was lawful.

Justice Scalia noted that this inquiry might require some discovery:

> [O]n remand, it should first be determined whether the actions the Creightons allege Anderson to have taken are actions that a reasonable officer could have believed lawful. If they are, then Anderson is entitled to dismissal prior to discovery. If they are not, and if the actions Anderson claims he took are different from those the Creightons allege (and are actions that a reasonable officer could have believed lawful), then discovery may be necessary before Anderson's motion for summary judgment on qualified immunity grounds can be resolved. Of course, any such discovery should be tailored specifically to the question of Anderson's qualified immunity.

Is it clear what a district court should do in this situation? How is the judge to resolve factual disputes, for instance?

Note: Qualified Immunity, General Standards, and "Unique Facts"

1. As a striking illustration of qualified immunity in action, consider the Supreme Court's decision in *White v. Pauly*, 137 S. Ct. 548 (2017). Two police officers investigating a complaint of drunk driving approached the isolated rural home where the driver, Daniel Pauly, lived with his brother Samuel. It was nighttime. The officers were on foot, using flashlights intermittently but no other lights. The men inside shouted, "Who are you?" and "What do you want?" The officers laughed and responded: "Hey, motherf**kers, we got you surrounded. Come out or we're coming in." The men inside never heard the officers identify themselves as police, so they armed themselves and shouted back: "We have guns."

Meanwhile, a third officer, White, arrived late to the scene. He was approaching the house just as one of the brothers said, "We have guns." When he heard that statement, he drew his gun and took cover behind a stone wall 50 feet from the front of the house. Seconds later, Daniel stepped partway out of the back door, screamed wildly, and fired two blasts from a shotgun. A few seconds after those shots, Samuel opened the front window and pointed a handgun in Officer White's direction. One of the officers near the house fired at Samuel, but missed. Officer White then fired as well, hitting and killing Samuel.

Daniel Pauly and Samuel Pauly's estates filed a § 1983 action against the officers, arguing that their actions amounted to excessive force in violation of the Fourth Amendment. The district court and court of appeals denied the officers' motion for qualified immunity. As to Officer White, the lower courts "relied on general statements from [the Supreme] Court's case law that (1) 'the reasonableness of an officer's use of force depends, in part, on whether the officer was in danger at the precise moment that he used force' and (2) 'if the suspect threatens the officer with a weapon, deadly force may be used if necessary to prevent escape, and if, where feasible, some warning has been given.'" (The quoted language is from *Tennessee v. Garner*, 471 U.S. 1 (1985), and *Graham v. Connor*, 490 U.S. 386 (1989).)

The Supreme Court unanimously reversed in a *per curiam* opinion without oral argument, noting that "[i]n the last five years, this Court has issued a number of opinions reversing federal courts in qualified immunity cases" because "qualified immunity is important to society as a whole," and it is "effectively lost if a case is erroneously permitted to go to trial." The Court explained:

> Qualified immunity attaches when an official's conduct "does not violate clearly established statutory or constitutional rights of which a reasonable person would have known." While this Court's case law "do[es] not require a case directly on point" for a right to be clearly established, "existing precedent must have placed the statutory or constitutional question beyond debate." *Anderson*. In other words, immunity protects "'all but the plainly incompetent or those who knowingly violate the law.'" [That passage, which the Court has repeated many times, originated 30 years ago in *Malley v. Briggs*, 475 U.S. 475 U.S. 335 (1986).] ...

> The [Court of Appeals] misunderstood the "clearly established" analysis: It failed to identify a case where an officer acting under similar circumstances as Officer White was held to have violated the Fourth Amendment. Instead, the majority relied on *Graham*, *Garner*, and their Court of Appeals progeny, which—as noted above—lay out excessive-force principles at only a general level. Of course, "general statements of the law are not inherently incapable of giving fair and clear warning" to officers, *United States v. Lanier*, 520 U. S. 259 (1997), but "in the light of pre-existing law the unlawfulness must be apparent," *Anderson*. For that reason, we have held that *Garner* and *Graham* do not by themselves create clearly established law outside "an obvious case." *Brosseau v. Haugen*, 543 U. S. 194 (2004) (per curiam).

> This is not a case where it is obvious that there was a violation of clearly established law under *Garner* and *Graham*. Of note, the [Tenth Circuit] majority did not conclude that White's conduct—such as his failure to shout a warning—constituted a run-of-the-mill Fourth Amendment violation. Indeed, it recognized that "this case presents a unique set of facts and

circumstances" in light of White's late arrival on the scene. This alone should have been an important indication to the majority that White's conduct did not violate a "clearly established" right. Clearly established federal law does not prohibit a reasonable officer who arrives late to an ongoing police action in circumstances like this from assuming that proper procedures, such as officer identification, have already been followed. No settled Fourth Amendment principle requires that officer to second-guess the earlier steps already taken by his or her fellow officers in instances like the one White confronted here.

The Court noted, however, that its decision was limited to Officer White. Its decision did not preclude the Court of Appeals on remand from concluding that the first two officers on the scene had violated clearly established Fourth Amendment law. The Court also held open the possibility that Officer White might be denied qualified immunity on the theory, not passed upon by the Court of Appeals, that he in fact had observed the other officers' failure to identify themselves while threatening to enter the home.

2. When a constitutional right is governed by a standard defined "only at a general level," will it ever be possible for plaintiffs to overcome qualified immunity? How can any deprivation of rights be "obvious" when the relevant legal test takes into consideration the "unique . . . facts" and the totality of the circumstances?

On the other hand, in the absence of a case holding that an officer in the same situation must give a warning before firing, how could Officer White reasonably have known that his actions violated the Constitution—especially when a suspect literally had a gun pointed at him? Is it fair to hold him personally liable for money damages in these circumstances? What effects might a judgment against Officer White have on police conduct? Would the benefits, on balance, outweigh the costs?

3. In many excessive force cases, all of the participating officers will be protected by qualified immunity, while the plaintiff will not be able to recover from the government department that employed them because of the "rigorous requirements of culpability and causation" imposed by the Court's decisions on municipal liability. See section D of this chapter. Should the Court reconsider its municipal liability doctrine? Or is that a task for Congress? If so, what sort of compensation or liability system would best serve the competing interests in situations like those in *White v. Pauly*?

Note: Litigating Qualified Immunity and the "Order of Battle"

1. Almost as important as the objective standard established by *Harlow* is the procedural ruling in *Mitchell v. Forsyth*, 472 U.S. 511 (1985). There the Court held that when a district court denies qualified immunity on the ground that facts alleged by the plaintiff show a violation of clearly established law, the defendant may obtain immediate appellate review under the "collateral order" doctrine. See Chapter 18. But immediate appeal is available only when the denial "turns on an issue of law." The collateral order doctrine does not apply if the district court denies the

defendant's motion for summary judgment on the ground that the evidence in the pretrial record is sufficient to show a genuine issue of fact. *Johnson v. Jones*, 515 U.S. 304 (1995).

Note, too, that in *Johnson v. Fankell* (1997), the Court held that state courts are not obliged to provide any interlocutory appeals from trial-court orders denying qualified immunity. See Chapter 6.

2. *Harlow v. Fitzgerald* holds that officials are liable only for violating "clearly established statutory or constitutional rights of which a reasonable person would have known." When an official asserts the defense of qualified immunity, the court faces two questions: (1) has the plaintiff established the existence of the constitutional right that the defendant has allegedly violated? and (2) was the right clearly established at the time the defendant acted?

Does it matter which of these questions a court answers first? In *Saucier v. Katz*, 533 U.S. 194 (2001), the Supreme Court held that lower courts were required to answer the first question before moving on to the second. The *Saucier* rule was grounded in a concern that constitutional standards would otherwise remain vague and undefined:

> In the course of determining whether a constitutional right was violated on the premises alleged, a court might find it necessary to set forth principles which will become the basis for a holding that a right is clearly established. This is the process for the law's elaboration from case to case, and it is one reason for our insisting upon turning to the existence or nonexistence of a constitutional right as the first inquiry. The law might be deprived of this explanation were a court simply to skip ahead to the question whether the law clearly established that the officer's conduct was unlawful in the circumstances of the case.

The Court adopted the *Saucier* procedure with barely a hint of disagreement. In the years after *Saucier*, however, the "rigid order of battle" adopted there came under sustained criticism from its own members. *E.g., Brosseau v. Haugen*, 543 U.S. 194 (Breyer, J., joined by Ginsburg and Scalia, JJ., concurring).

3. In *Pearson v. Callahan*, 555 U.S. 223 (2009), the Court *sua sponte* asked the parties to address the question whether *Saucier* should be overruled. After a full briefing, it unanimously held that the *Saucier v. Katz* sequence "should no longer be regarded as mandatory." In an opinion by Justice Alito, the Court explained:

> [Although the *Saucier* procedure is often appropriate,] the rigid *Saucier* procedure comes with a price. The procedure sometimes results in a substantial expenditure of scarce judicial resources on difficult questions that have no effect on the outcome of the case. There are cases in which it is plain that a constitutional right is not clearly established but far from obvious whether in fact there is such a right. District courts and courts of appeals with heavy caseloads are often understandably unenthusiastic about what may seem to be an essentially academic exercise.

Unnecessary litigation of constitutional issues also wastes the parties' resources. Qualified immunity is "an immunity from suit rather than a mere defense to liability." *Mitchell v. Forsyth*, 472 U.S. 511 (1985). *Saucier*'s two-step protocol "disserve[s] the purpose of qualified immunity" when it "forces the parties to endure additional burdens of suit—such as the costs of litigating constitutional questions and delays attributable to resolving them—when the suit otherwise could be disposed of more readily." Brief for Nat. Assn. of Criminal Defense Lawyers as *Amicus Curiae*.

Although the first prong of the *Saucier* procedure is intended to further the development of constitutional precedent, opinions following that procedure often fail to make a meaningful contribution to such development.

[As examples, the Court pointed to cases in which the constitutional question is highly fact-bound, will soon be decided by a higher court, or depends on an uncertain interpretation of state law. Also, in some cases, the basis for the claims may be difficult to identify, or "the briefing of constitutional questions is woefully inadequate" even though qualified immunity is clear.]

Rigid adherence to the *Saucier* rule may make it hard for affected parties to obtain appellate review of constitutional decisions that may have a serious prospective effect on their operations. Where a court holds that a defendant committed a constitutional violation but that the violation was not clearly established, the defendant may face a difficult situation. As the winning party, the defendant's right to appeal the adverse holding on the constitutional question may be contested. In [such] cases . . . the "prevailing" defendant faces an unenviable choice: "compl[y] with the lower court's advisory dictum without opportunity to seek appellate [or certiorari] review," or "def[y] the views of the lower court, adher[e] to practices that have been declared illegal, and thus invit[e] new suits" and potential "punitive damages."

Adherence to *Saucier*'s two-step protocol departs from the general rule of constitutional avoidance and runs counter to the "older, wiser judicial counsel 'not to pass on questions of constitutionality . . . unless such adjudication is unavoidable,'" see *Ashwander v. TVA*, 297 U.S. 288 (1936) (Brandeis, J., concurring). . . .

The decision in *Pearson* leaves lower-court judges free "to exercise their sound discretion in deciding which of the two prongs of the qualified immunity analysis should be addressed first in light of the circumstances in the particular case at hand." Affording that kind of flexibility was appropriate, the Court explained, because "the judges of the district courts and the courts of appeals are in the best position to determine the order of decisionmaking that will best facilitate the fair and efficient disposition of each case."

4. The concern that led to the holding in *Saucier* is real enough: if a court decides only the immunity question, it leaves the contours of the law unclear for the future and provides no guidance for executive officers. The Court in *Pearson* minimized those concerns:

The development of constitutional law is by no means entirely dependent on cases in which the defendant may seek qualified immunity. Most of the constitutional issues that are presented in § 1983 damages actions and *Bivens* cases also arise in cases in which that defense is not available, such as criminal cases and § 1983 cases against a municipality, as well as § 1983 cases against individuals where injunctive relief is sought instead of or in addition to damages.

Are the alternative routes for constitutional elaboration identified by the Court sufficient? In all constitutional contexts?

5. While the *Pearson* Court abandons the "rigid order of battle," it notes that there are cases in which it might still be appropriate to determine the scope of the constitutional norm before tackling the qualified immunity question. How should the lower court approach the ordering of questions in the Problem below?

6. As the Court acknowledges, the "order of battle" required by *Saucier* (and permitted by *Pearson*) can put the defendant in a "difficult situation": if a court decides that the defendant violated a constitutional norm but then holds that the defendant is entitled to qualified immunity, the result may be to leave the defendant protected from damages but exposed to an unappealable decision declaring some of the agency's practices unlawful. Two years after *Pearson*, the Supreme Court took unusual steps to address this situation.

In *Camreta v. Greene*, 563 U.S. 692 (2011), the Ninth Circuit Court of Appeals held that state officials infringed the Fourth Amendment by failing to obtain a warrant before interviewing a girl about allegations that her father had sexually abused her. But the court went on to hold that qualified immunity shielded the officials from monetary liability because the constitutional right at issue was not clearly established at the time of the interview. The Supreme Court granted certiorari to consider whether government officials who prevail on grounds of qualified immunity may obtain Supreme Court review of a court of appeals' decision that their conduct violated the Constitution. The Court held that in that situation, review is "generally" available.

In an opinion by Justice Kagan for five Justices, the Court first rejected the argument that "Article III bars us from adjudicating any and all challenges brought by government officials who have received immunity below." The Court explained:

> [The] Article III standard often will be met when immunized officials seek to challenge a ruling that their conduct violated the Constitution. That is not because a court has made a retrospective judgment about the lawfulness of the officials' behavior, for that judgment is unaccompanied by any personal liability. Rather, it is because the judgment may have prospective effect on the parties. The court in such a case says: "Although this official is immune from damages today, what he did violates the Constitution and he or anyone else who does that thing again will be personally liable."

If the official regularly engages in that conduct as part of his job (as Camreta does), he suffers injury caused by the adverse constitutional ruling. So long as it continues in effect, he must either change the way he performs his duties or risk a meritorious damages action. Only by overturning the ruling on appeal can the official gain clearance to engage in the conduct in the future. He thus can demonstrate, as we demand, injury, causation, and redressability. [See Chapter 3.] And conversely, if the person who initially brought the suit may again be subject to the challenged conduct, she has a stake in preserving the court's holding.

The Court next addressed the "important question of judicial policy" governing its exercise of the certiorari jurisdiction. Again the Court found no obstacle to review:

[When a court of appeals settles a question of constitutional law and thereby guides the conduct of officials,] its decision is reviewable in this Court at the behest of an immunized official. No mere dictum, a constitutional ruling preparatory to a grant of immunity creates law that governs the official's behavior. If our usual rule pertaining to prevailing parties applied, the official would "face an unenviable choice": He must either acquiesce in a ruling he had no opportunity to contest in this Court, or "defy the views of the lower court, adhere to practices that have been declared illegal, and thus invite new suits and potential punitive damages." *Pearson.* And if our usual bar on review applied, it would undermine the very purpose served by the two-step process, "which is to clarify constitutional rights without undue delay."

The Court then noted two limitations on its holding. First, the Court's rationale would not necessarily allow a *court of appeals* to hear an appeal from a party who prevailed on immunity grounds in the *district court.* This is because "district court decisions—unlike those from the courts of appeals—do not necessarily settle constitutional standards or prevent repeated claims of qualified immunity." Second, the holding "concern[ed] only what this Court *may* review; what we actually will choose to review is a different matter."

Finally, the Court found that notwithstanding all it had just said, the case before it was moot, because the plaintiff no longer had any interest in the court of appeals ruling; she had moved to another state and was about to turn 18.

Justice Sotomayor, joined by Justice Breyer, concurred only in the judgment. She said that there was "no warrant for reaching [the question whether Camreta, as a prevailing party, can obtain our review of the Ninth Circuit's constitutional ruling] when there is clearly no longer a genuine case or controversy between the parties before us." Justice Kennedy, joined by Justice Thomas, dissented. He found it "most doubtful that Article III permits appeals by [an] officer to whom the reasoning of a judicial decision might be applied in a later suit." He said that "the Court might find it necessary to reconsider its special permission that the Courts of Appeals may issue unnecessary merits determinations in qualified immunity cases with binding precedential effect."

How effective is the *Camreta* rule likely to be in mitigating the consequences of allowing courts of appeals to find constitutional violations before concluding that the defendant is entitled to qualified immunity? Even if the defendant has an interest in reversing the constitutional holding, when would the plaintiff care about establishing a constitutional right that will not result in an award of damages?

Problem: A Taser Too Far?

Roy Smith was playing his car stereo loudly while driving through town. Two police officers on patrol, noting a possible violation of the town's noise ordinance, turned on the siren and lights, signaling Smith to pull over. Smith continued to his home, less than a mile away. Both the patrol car and Smith pulled into the driveway, and Smith got out of his car. The officers' and Smith's accounts differ as to what happened next. The officers claimed they asked Smith for his license and he bolted for the house, saying he was not giving them anything. Smith claims that he asked why he was being pulled over, while walking toward his house. He also told the officers that he would be right back, but wanted to let his wife know what was going on. Witnesses corroborated Smith's account; the officers corroborated each other. All agreed, however, that the officers followed Smith into his home and applied a taser to incapacitate him, and that the officers knocked him to the floor after he tried to get up. The witnesses and Smith claimed that the officers used a racial slur while applying the taser.

The use of excessive force in arrest can violate the Fourth Amendment. In the circuit in which Smith brings his constitutional damages claim, a court deciding whether the police violated the constitution through the use of excessive force is required to consider multiple factors: (1) the need for the application of force, (2) the relationship between the need and the amount of force used, (3) the extent of the injury inflicted, (4) whether the force was applied in good faith or maliciously and sadistically, (5) the severity of the crime, (6) whether the suspect posed an immediate threat, and (7) whether the suspect was resisting or fleeing. A police officer is entitled to qualified immunity if the officer reasonably believed that these factors required the application of the force used.

Under *Pearson*, where should the court begin by analyzing the constitutional claim or the qualified immunity question?

Note: Qualified Immunity and Intercircuit Conflicts

1. In *Pearson*, the Court unanimously held that the defendants were protected by qualified immunity. The Court emphasized that police officers (and presumably other government employees) "are entitled to rely on existing lower court cases without facing personal liability for their actions." Justice Alito quoted from its decision in *Wilson v. Layne*, 526 U.S. 603 (1997), noting that in that case, as in *Pearson*, "a Circuit split on the relevant issue had developed after the events that gave rise to suit." The Court reiterated *Wilson*'s conclusion: "If judges thus disagree on a constitutional question, it is

unfair to subject police to money damages for picking the losing side of the controversy."

Does this mean that government employees will always be entitled to qualified immunity as long as at least one court of appeals has found no constitutional violation on similar facts? Not necessarily.

Only six months after deciding *Pearson*, the Court considered qualified immunity in another Fourth Amendment context. This time the defendants were school officials rather than police officers. The case was *Safford Unified School District #1 v. Redding*, 557 U.S. 364 (2009), and it arose when a 13-year-old student was subjected to a search of her bra and underpants based on "reasonable suspicion that she had brought forbidden prescription and over-the-counter drugs to school." The Court held (over one dissent) that "[b]ecause there were no reasons to suspect that the drugs presented a danger or were concealed in [the student's] underwear," the search violated the Fourth Amendment. The majority went on to hold that the school officials were entitled to qualified immunity, but it stopped short of endorsing a bright-line rule.

The immunity question turned on the interpretation of the Court's decision in *New Jersey v. T.L.O.*, 469 U.S. 325 (1985). That decision directed school officials to limit the intrusiveness of a search "in light of the age and sex of the student and the nature of the infraction." In *Redding*, the Court acknowledged that "the lower courts have reached divergent conclusions" about how the *T.L.O.* standard applies to strip searches. The Court briefly summarized three court of appeals decisions that read *T.L.O.* not to bar searches such as the one in the case before it. The Court continued:

> We think these differences of opinion from our own are substantial enough to require immunity for the school officials in this case. We would not suggest that entitlement to qualified immunity is the guaranteed product of disuniform views of the law in the other federal, or state, courts, and the fact that a single judge, or even a group of judges, disagrees about the contours of a right does not automatically render the law unclear if we have been clear. That said, however, the cases viewing school strip searches differently from the way we see them are numerous enough, with well-reasoned majority and dissenting opinions, to counsel doubt that we were sufficiently clear in the prior statement of law. We conclude that qualified immunity is warranted.

Justice Stevens, joined by Justice Ginsburg, dissented from the holding on qualified immunity. In his view, "[t]he strip search of Savana Redding in this case was both more intrusive and less justified than the search of the student's purse in *T.L.O.*" The search thus violated clearly established law. Responding to the majority's citation of "divergent conclusions" in the circuits, Justice Stevens insisted that "the clarity of a well-established right should not depend on whether jurists have misread our precedents."

2. The Court says that even if "a group of judges" disagrees about the contours of a right, that "does not automatically render the law unclear if we have been clear." But how can police officers, school administrators, and other government employees (most of whom are not trained in the law) determine that the Supreme Court "has been clear" when federal appellate judges disagree about what the Court has held? Should the Court reaffirm the simpler standard suggested by *Wilson* and *Pearson*—that as long as judges disagree over the applicable law, the right cannot be clearly established for purposes of determining whether officials are entitled to qualified immunity?

Chapter 15

Federal Habeas Corpus

A. Introduction to Federal Habeas Corpus

[1] History and Purposes of the Writ

The writ of habeas corpus predates the United States; it was first codified in England in 1679. In its oldest form, *habeas corpus ad subjiciendum*, it permitted courts to inquire into the legality of imprisonment and required the crown's agents to produce the prisoner. Blackstone captured its significance by describing habeas corpus as "a second magna carta, and stable bulwark of our liberties," 1 BLACKSTONE 133. The Supreme Court has often referred to habeas as simply "the Great Writ."

Rasul v. Bush, 542 U.S. 466 (2004), offers a short history of the writ:

> Congress has granted federal district courts, "within their respective jurisdictions," the authority to hear applications for habeas corpus by any person who claims to be held "in custody in violation of the Constitution or laws or treaties of the United States." 28 U.S.C. §§ 2241(a), (c)(3). The statute traces its ancestry to the first grant of federal court jurisdiction: Section 14 of the Judiciary Act of 1789 authorized federal courts to issue the writ of habeas corpus to prisoners "in custody, under or by colour of the authority of the United States, or committed for trial before some court of the same." Act of Sept. 24, 1789, § 14. In 1867, Congress extended the protections of the writ to "all cases where any person may be restrained of his or her liberty in violation of the constitution, or of any treaty or law of the United States." Act of Feb. 5, 1867.
>
> Habeas corpus is, however, "a writ antecedent to statute, . . . throwing its root deep into the genius of our common law." *Williams v. Kaiser*, 323 U.S. 471 (1945). The writ appeared in English law several centuries ago, became "an integral part of our common-law heritage" by the time the Colonies achieved independence, *Preiser v. Rodriguez*, 411 U.S. 475 (1973), and received explicit recognition in the Constitution, which forbids suspension of "[t]he Privilege of the Writ of Habeas Corpus . . . unless when in Cases of Rebellion or Invasion the public Safety may require it," Art. I, § 9, cl. 2.

Rasul's historical description suggests the long-standing interplay among the legislature, the executive, and the judiciary that is at the core of an understanding of the purposes and significance of habeas corpus. For example, in a companion case to *Rasul*, the Supreme Court said: "[U]nless Congress acts to suspend it, the Great Writ of habeas corpus allows the Judicial Branch to play a necessary role in maintaining this delicate balance of governance, serving as an important judicial check on the Executive's discretion in the realm of detentions." *Hamdi v. Rumsfeld*, 542 U.S. 507 (2004). Habeas corpus is the only common-law writ recognized by the Constitution, Art. I § 9 cl. 2, and it has been available by statute since 1789. However, as the Court notes in *Rasul*, the writ is "antecedent to statute," and the law governing the writ is a product of both statutory evolution and judicial decisions.

No statute gave the federal courts jurisdiction over writs of habeas corpus alleging illegal detention by *state* authorities until 1867, when the Reconstruction Congress expanded the scope of habeas corpus to include "all cases where any person may be restrained of his or her liberty in violation of the constitution, or of any treaty or law of the United States." Act of Feb. 5, 1867, ch. 28. As currently codified, the writ of habeas corpus continues to extend to state prisoners "in custody in violation of the Constitution or laws or treaties of the United States." 28 U.S.C. §§ 2241(c)(3), 2254(a).

Federal prisoners are also covered by statute, 28 U.S.C. § 2255, although technically that section is an alternative to habeas corpus. It permits federal prisoners to challenge their custody in the federal district court in which they were sentenced, and it provides the same relief that would be available through the writ of habeas corpus.

[2] Federal-Court Review of State Court Judgments of Conviction

As the Supreme Court made clear in *Rooker v. Fidelity Trust Co.*, 263 U.S. 413 (1913) (Chapter 17), the lower federal courts are not empowered to review and correct state civil judgments on the ground that they are inconsistent with federal law. Quite the opposite, federal law requires that those civil judgments be given preclusive effect in federal court. See 28 U.S.C. § 1738. The statutes authorizing review of state criminal convictions through federal habeas corpus qualify these rules. The typical habeas petitioner is a state prisoner challenging an existing criminal conviction on the ground that it was obtained in violation of federal law, usually the federal Constitution. Because federal habeas proceedings typically occur after state avenues of relief are exhausted, they are considered collateral proceedings. In order to consider such claims, the federal courts must suspend ordinary rules of res judicata and preclusion. Thus, the lower federal courts are required to reevaluate the substantive validity of an applicant's conviction, often after several state courts have already done so.

Federal-court review of state judgments of conviction is now the most common, and also the most controversial, application of the writ of habeas corpus. The controversy is a function of the competing state and federal interests at stake in habeas corpus in this context.

The state interests involved in such review are formidable. State courts, like federal courts, are bound to enforce the provisions of the United States Constitution, and habeas review risks offending comity by suggesting that state courts shirk that duty. Moreover, state regulation and punishment of crime is at the core of state sovereignty.

The states thus have strong interests in the finality of criminal convictions. But federal habeas proceedings usually take place years after a state conviction has become final, and the decision by a federal judge to issue a writ often makes retrying a criminal defendant difficult or impossible: witnesses may have disappeared or died, or their memories may have faded. Other evidence may no longer be available. The costs of issuing a writ, then, can be high.

On the other hand, habeas corpus proceedings have been crucially important in assuring the supremacy of federal law. Particularly important has been habeas's role in ensuring that federal constitutional requirements in the area of criminal procedure are followed by the states, and that they are uniformly applied. Habeas was a central mechanism for bringing about the federal constitutional criminal procedure revolution that occurred during the 1960s and 1970s, during which the right to counsel, the right against compelled self-incrimination, and many of the due process guarantees of trial were elaborated. *See* Robert M. Cover & Alexander Aleinikoff, *Dialectical Federalism: Habeas Corpus and the Court*, 86 YALE L.J. 1035, 1041 (1977) (discussing Supreme Court's use of habeas corpus to enforce constitutional criminal procedure rules).

Nor is it clear that state courts today uniformly protect federal constitutional rights. As numerous commentators have noted in this context, state court judges are often elected, and they may be subject to political pressure as a result. Several recent studies have demonstrated that this pressure is particularly strong in criminal cases. *See, e.g.,* Amanda Frost, *Countering the Majoritarian Difficulty*, 96 VA. L. REV. 719, 749 (2010) (noting several empirical studies that demonstrate the effect of elections on sentences and arguing for the importance of federal habeas review). It is easy to find cases in which it appears that state courts have been unreceptive to federal constitutional guarantees. *See* John H. Blume, *In Defense of Noncapital Habeas: A Response to Hoffmann and King*, 96 CORNELL L. REV. 435 (2011) (collecting cases).

But while it is undoubtedly true that not every state criminal trial comports with federal constitutional guarantees, it is also costly to provide a federal forum for every state criminal defendant with a possible constitutional claim. The incentives for prisoners to seek federal review of their convictions are quite high. Habeas petitions from state prisoners account for seven percent of the federal civil docket nationwide, and in districts with prisons, as much as 17 percent of that docket.[1] And at least one recent study suggests that all of this activity yields few results. For complex reasons that we will explore in the pages that follow, only a tiny percentage — estimated at 0.35 percent of filed federal noncapital habeas cases — results in relief for the petitioner. Thus, "[f]or all but a very small proportion of the millions of those convicted of crime every year in the United States, the Great Writ is a pipe dream." NANCY J. KING & JOSEPH L. HOFFMANN, HABEAS FOR THE TWENTY-FIRST CENTURY: USES, ABUSES, AND THE FUTURE OF THE GREAT WRIT 75, 81 (2011) (arguing for eliminating habeas review in most noncapital habeas cases).

---

1. Administrative Office of the United States Courts, http://www.uscourts.gov/Statistics/Judicial.

The tensions among the states' interests in finality, federal interests in the supremacy and uniformity of federal law, and prisoners' interests in the protection of their federal constitutional rights have been the source of much debate over the proper role of habeas corpus. In 1996, Congress stepped in with the Anti-Terrorism and Effective Death Penalty Act (AEDPA). As the Conference Report on the bill explained, AEDPA was adopted "to curb the abuse of the statutory writ of habeas corpus and to address the acute problems of unnecessary delay and abuse in capital cases."[2] AEDPA revised federal law on many of the issues that arise in habeas proceedings—among them, when federal courts can provide evidentiary hearings; how they must view the state courts' determinations on matters of federal law; and whether they may hear successive petitions from the same prisoner.

Even before AEDPA, collateral proceedings in habeas were procedurally complex. AEDPA increased that complexity. But stripping away the details, for each of the federal claims that a state prisoner wishes to present as a ground for federal habeas relief, there are basically three possible scenarios. First, the state courts may have rejected the claim on its merits. Second, the state courts may never have considered the claim because the prisoner did not raise it in the state proceedings. Third, the state courts may have refused to consider the claim because the prisoner failed to raise or preserve it in accordance with state procedures.

Each of these scenarios has different consequences for the course of the federal habeas proceeding. The first raises issues as to the scope and standard of review. Perhaps surprisingly, the Supreme Court has held that not all constitutional claims or violations of federal law may be considered by the federal habeas court. Congress has imposed further restrictions. As a result, collateral review by the federal district court on habeas is considerably narrower than direct review by the Supreme Court under its appellate jurisdiction.

The second scenario raises issues that fall under the rubric of exhaustion of state remedies. The Supreme Court and Congress have taken the position that state defendants must first present their federal claims to the state tribunals, and all remedies available there must be attempted, before a claim will be heard by a federal habeas court.

The third scenario brings into play the doctrine of state procedural default. This doctrine severely limits the situations in which procedurally defaulted claims—those that the original tribunals refused to hear or are no longer available to hear—will be considered by the federal courts.

In this chapter, we first consider the substantive scope of habeas review, examining some basic prerequisites, limits on the types of claim that afford a basis for relief, rules concerning retroactivity, and standards of review for claims rejected on the merits by state courts. Next, we consider procedural aspects of habeas review with a discussion of the doctrines of exhaustion, procedural default, and harmless error. We then turn

---

2. Other sections of AEDPA provide incentives for the states to improve the quality of legal representation in state proceedings in death-penalty cases by offering procedural advantages to states that meet specified requirements. These aspects of the law will not be discussed here.

to the question raised by Judge Henry J. Friendly early in the development of modern habeas law: "Is Innocent Irrelevant?" Finally, we consider the limits that the Writ Suspension Clause places on Congress's power to alter the scope of habeas corpus.

The purpose of the chapter is not to prepare you to litigate a habeas claim; that would require a large treatise. Rather, the purpose is to examine the regime of collateral review in criminal cases against the background of section 25 and the history of direct review of state-court judgments rejecting federal claims. How well do the current rules serve the competing imperatives of supremacy and federalism?

B. The Scope and Standard of Review on Collateral Attack

Habeas corpus can be seen as a jurisdictional arrangement that provides a form of federal lower court review for state prisoners whose federal claims have been rejected by the state courts. Yet even if that characterization is accepted, it only leads to more particularized questions about the purpose of habeas review. Is it to assure that *every* state prisoner has access to a federal court for review of a federal claim? To free the innocent? To assure that state courts comply with federal constitutional and statutory requirements, or that state courts give a full and fair hearing on all federal claims? To deter constitutional abuses by state actors?

All of these theories have informed the Supreme Court's habeas jurisprudence over the years, and they can be in tension with each other. We will explore the ramifications of these approaches in three contexts. First, should the federal courts hear all federal claims raised by state prisoners, or only a subset? Second, under what circumstances should prisoners gain the benefit of constitutional rules that were announced after their convictions became final? Third, to what extent should the federal habeas court defer to the state court's conclusion that the prisoner's conviction was not tainted by federal constitutional error? The answers to these questions depend in large part on the underlying theory that one adopts about the purpose of habeas corpus.

[1] Cognizable Claims

The common-law writ of habeas corpus was not designed as a mechanism for review of criminal convictions. Instead, it took the form of a civil action to challenge unlawful confinement, principally by the Executive. The "essence of habeas corpus," the Court has explained, "is an attack by a person in custody upon the legality of that custody," and the writ's "traditional function" was "to secure release from illegal custody." *Preiser v. Rodriguez*, 411 U.S. 475, 484 (1973). The writ compels the defendant, a prison warden or whoever holds the petitioner in custody, to produce the body (the *corpus*) and to defend the legality of continued detention. Originally, a court order authorizing the detention operated as a complete defense to the writ, so long as the issuing court had proper jurisdiction. In a series of decisions in the 20th century, the

Supreme Court moved away from that rule; the Court did so by broadly interpreting the 1867 statute that authorized federal courts to grant writs of habeas corpus to persons in state custody. But even as the function of habeas has expanded, many traditional prerequisites to relief remain.

First, federal courts may grant habeas relief only to persons who are "in custody," 28 U.S.C. § 2254(a), and habeas actions typically are filed by individuals incarcerated in state prisons. The use of habeas corpus is not restricted to situations in which the applicant is in actual physical custody. A person is "in custody" for purposes of the habeas statute if he is "subject to restraints not shared by the public generally." *Hensley v. Municipal Court*, 411 U.S. 345 (1973) (prisoner released on own recognizance "in custody"); *Justices of Boston Municipal Court v. Lydon*, 466 U.S. 294 (1983) (prisoner "in custody" even though his conviction was vacated when he applied for a trial de novo and had been released on personal recognizance).

On the other hand, habeas may not be used to attack a criminal conviction after the sentence has been fully served, even if it rests on an obvious error of federal law. *Maleng v. Cook*, 490 U.S. 488 (1989) ("[O]nce the sentence imposed for a conviction has completely expired, the collateral consequences of that conviction are not themselves sufficient to render an individual 'in custody' for the purposes of a habeas attack upon it"). The custody requirement thus sets important practical limits on the availability of habeas relief. *See* Nancy J. King et al., Final Technical Report: Habeas Litigation in U.S. District Courts 54 (2007) (finding that "[n]on-capital habeas filers continue to be predominantly those inmates serving lengthy sentences" because it may take years to exhaust state-court remedies and then file and fully litigate a habeas claim in federal court).

Second, habeas is available only to correct errors of *federal* law. Section 2254(a) (courts may "entertain" habeas petitions "only on the ground that [the petitioner] is in custody in violation of the Constitution or laws or treaties of the United States"). Neither violations of state law, nor erroneous factual determinations by a state court— no matter how egregious—afford a basis for habeas relief. *See Wilson v. Corcoran*, 562 U.S. 1 (2010) (per curiam) (summarily reversing a habeas order directing a new capital sentencing hearing "to prevent non-compliance with Indiana law" and to correct an "unreasonable determination of the facts").

Third, the traditional remedy provided by the writ of habeas corpus is release from custody—nothing more, and nothing less. When a federal court grants habeas relief to a state-court prisoner, it typically enters a "conditional release" order directing the warden to release the prisoner, but allowing the State a period within which to commence a new proceeding that complies with federal law. *See Boumediene v. Bush*, 553 U.S. 723 (2008) (holding that, as a constitutional matter, habeas courts "must have the power to order the conditional release of an individual unlawfully detained"). A habeas court may also grant equitable relief that speeds up a prisoner's release, such as the modification of a sentence or the recalculation of good-time credits. But "[i]f a state prisoner is seeking damages, he is attacking something other than the fact or length of his confinement, and he is seeking something other than immediate or more speedy release—the traditional purpose of habeas corpus." *Prieser*. Other remedies must be pursued by other means, such as an action under 42 U.S.C. § 1983 (see Chapter 14).

Beyond those basic prerequisites, do the courts have any role to play in defining the substantive scope of habeas? As the following case explains, the Court believes the answer is yes.

Withrow v. Williams

Supreme Court of the United States, 1993.

507 U.S. 680.

JUSTICE SOUTER delivered the opinion of the Court.

In *Stone v. Powell*, 428 U.S. 465 (1976), we held that when a State has given a full and fair chance to litigate a Fourth Amendment claim, federal habeas review is not available to a state prisoner alleging that his conviction rests on evidence obtained through an unconstitutional search or seizure. Today we hold that *Stone*'s restriction on the exercise of federal habeas jurisdiction does not extend to a state prisoner's claim that his conviction rests on statements obtained in violation of the safeguards mandated by *Miranda v. Arizona*, 384 U.S. 436 (1966).

I

[Investigating a double murder, police officers took Williams to the police station, where they questioned him for forty minutes before he implicated himself in the murders. Only at that point did the officers advise him of his *Miranda* rights to remain silent and to have an attorney present. Williams waived those rights and eventually confessed. He was convicted of both murders and sentenced to life in prison. Those convictions were affirmed on appeal. Finding that the failure to provide *Miranda* warnings compromised Williams' constitutional rights, the federal district court issued a writ of habeas corpus. The Court of Appeals for the Sixth Circuit affirmed, rejecting the argument that the rule in *Stone v. Powell* should apply to bar petitioner's *Miranda* claim.]

II

We have made it clear that *Stone*'s limitation on federal habeas relief was not jurisdictional in nature, but rested on prudential concerns counseling against the application of the Fourth Amendment exclusionary rule on collateral review. We simply concluded in *Stone* that the costs of applying the exclusionary rule on collateral review outweighed any potential advantage to be gained by applying it there.

We recognized that the exclusionary rule, held applicable to the States in *Mapp v. Ohio*, 367 U.S. 643 (1961), "is not a personal constitutional right"; it fails to redress "the injury to the privacy of the victim of the search or seizure" at issue, "for any '[r]eparation comes too late.'" *Stone*. The rule serves instead to deter future Fourth Amendment violations, and we reasoned that its application on collateral review would only marginally advance this interest in deterrence. On the other side of the ledger, the costs of applying the exclusionary rule on habeas were comparatively great. We reasoned that doing so would not only exclude reliable evidence and divert attention from the central question of guilt, but would also intrude upon the public interest in "(i) the most effective utilization of limited judicial resources, (ii) the necessity of finality in criminal trials, (iii) the minimization of friction between our federal and state systems of justice, and (iv) the maintenance of the constitutional balance upon which the doctrine of federalism is founded."

Over the years, we have repeatedly declined to extend the rule in *Stone* beyond its original bounds. . . . [The Court cited *Jackson v. Virginia*, 443 U.S. 307 (1979) (insufficiency of the evidence to support a criminal conviction); *Rose v. Mitchell*, 443 U.S. 545 (1979) (race discrimination in selection of grand-jury foreman); and *Kimmelman v. Morrison*, 477 U.S. 365 (1986) (ineffective assistance of counsel).]

In this case, the argument for extending *Stone* again falls short. To understand why, a brief review of the derivation of the *Miranda* safeguards, and the purposes they were designed to serve, is in order.

The Self-Incrimination Clause of the Fifth Amendment guarantees that no person "shall be compelled in any criminal case to be a witness against himself." . . .

In *Miranda*, we spoke of the privilege as guaranteeing a person under interrogation "the right 'to remain silent unless he chooses to speak in the unfettered exercise of his own will,'" and held that "without proper safeguards the process of in-custody interrogation . . . contains inherently compelling pressures which work to undermine the individual's will to resist and to compel him to speak where he would not otherwise do so freely." To counter these pressures we prescribed, absent "other fully effective means," the now-familiar measures in aid of a defendant's Fifth Amendment privilege:

> He must be warned prior to any questioning that he has the right to remain silent, that anything he says can be used against him in a court of law, that he has the right to the presence of an attorney, and that if he cannot afford an attorney one will be appointed for him prior to any questioning if he so desires. . . .

Unless the prosecution can demonstrate the warnings and waiver as threshold matters, we held, it may not overcome an objection to the use at trial of statements obtained from the person in any ensuing custodial interrogation.

Petitioner, supported by the United States as *amicus curiae*, argues that *Miranda*'s safeguards are not constitutional in character, but merely "prophylactic," and that in consequence habeas review should not extend to a claim that a state conviction rests on statements obtained in the absence of those safeguards. We accept petitioner's premise for purposes of this case, but not her conclusion.

The *Miranda* Court did [indeed acknowledge] that, in barring introduction of a statement obtained without the required warnings, *Miranda* might exclude a confession that we would not condemn as "involuntary in traditional terms," and for this reason we have sometimes called the *Miranda* safeguards "prophylactic" in nature.

Calling the *Miranda* safeguards "prophylactic," however, is a far cry from putting *Miranda* on all fours with *Mapp*, or from rendering *Miranda* subject to *Stone*.

As we explained in *Stone*, the *Mapp* rule "is not a personal constitutional right," but serves to deter future constitutional violations; although it mitigates the juridical consequences of invading the defendant's privacy, the exclusion of evidence at trial can do nothing to remedy the completed and wholly extrajudicial Fourth Amendment violation. Nor can the *Mapp* rule be thought to enhance the soundness of the criminal process by improving the reliability of evidence introduced at trial. Quite the contrary, as we explained in *Stone*, the evidence excluded under *Mapp* "is typically reliable and often the most probative information bearing on the guilt or innocence of the defendant."

Miranda differs from *Mapp* in both respects. "Prophylactic" though it may be, in protecting a defendant's Fifth Amendment privilege against self-incrimination, *Miranda* safeguards "a fundamental *trial* right." The privilege [reflects] "many of our fundamental values and most noble aspirations." *Murphy v. Waterfront Comm'n of New York Harbor*, 378 U.S. 52 (1964).

Nor does the Fifth Amendment "trial right" protected by *Miranda* serve some value necessarily divorced from the correct ascertainment of guilt. . . . By bracing against "the possibility of unreliable statements in every instance of in-custody interrogation," *Miranda* serves to guard against "the use of unreliable statements at trial." *Johnson v. New Jersey*, 384 U.S. 719 (1966).

Finally, and most importantly, eliminating review of *Miranda* claims would not significantly benefit the federal courts in their exercise of habeas jurisdiction, or advance the cause of federalism in any substantial way. [It would not] prevent a state prisoner from simply converting his barred *Miranda* claim into a due process claim that his conviction rested on an involuntary confession. Indeed . . . it seems reasonable to suppose that virtually all *Miranda* claims would simply be recast in this way.[5] . . .

We thus fail to see how abdicating *Miranda*'s bright-line (or, at least, brighter-line) rules in favor of an exhaustive totality-of-circumstances approach on habeas would do much of anything to lighten the burdens placed on busy federal courts. We likewise fail to see how purporting to eliminate *Miranda* issues from federal habeas would go very far to relieve such tensions as *Miranda* may now raise between the two judicial systems.

One might argue that tension results between the two judicial systems whenever a federal habeas court overturns a state conviction on finding that the state court let in a voluntary confession obtained by the police without the *Miranda* safeguards. And one would have to concede that this has occurred in the past, and doubtless will occur again. It is not reasonable, however, to expect such occurrences to be frequent enough to amount to a substantial cost of reviewing *Miranda* claims on habeas or to raise federal-state tensions to an appreciable degree. We must remember in this regard that

---

5. Justice O'Connor is confident that many such claims would be unjustified, but that is beside the point. Justifiability is not much of a gatekeeper on habeas.

Miranda came down some 27 years ago. In that time, law enforcement has grown in constitutional as well as technological sophistication, and there is little reason to believe that the police today are unable, or even generally unwilling, to satisfy *Miranda*'s requirements. And if, finally, one should question the need for federal collateral review of requirements that merit such respect, the answer simply is that the respect is sustained in no small part by the existence of such review. "It is the occasional abuse that the federal writ of habeas corpus stands ready to correct." *Jackson*. . . .

IV

The judgment of the Court of Appeals is [affirmed].

JUSTICE O'CONNOR, with whom THE CHIEF JUSTICE joins, [dissenting].

Today the Court permits the federal courts to overturn on habeas the conviction of a double murderer, not on the basis of an inexorable constitutional or statutory command, but because it believes the result desirable from the standpoint of equity and judicial administration. Because the principles that inform our habeas jurisprudence — finality, federalism, and fairness — counsel decisively against the result the Court reaches, I respectfully dissent from this holding.

I

The Court does not sit today in direct review of a state-court judgment of conviction. Rather, respondent seeks relief by collaterally attacking his conviction through the writ of habeas corpus. While petitions for the writ of habeas corpus are now commonplace — over 12,000 were filed in 1990, compared to 127 in 1941 — their current ubiquity ought not detract from the writ's historic importance. "The Great Writ" can be traced through the common law to well before the founding of this Nation; its role as a "prompt and efficacious remedy for whatever society deems to be intolerable restraints" is beyond question. . . .

Nonetheless, we repeatedly have recognized that collateral attacks raise numerous concerns not present on direct review. Most profound is the effect on finality. It goes without saying that, at some point, judicial proceedings must draw to a close and the matter deemed conclusively resolved; no society can afford forever to question the correctness of its every judgment. "[T]he writ," however, "strikes at finality," *McCleskey v. Zant*, 499 U.S. 467 (1991), depriving the criminal law "of much of its deterrent effect," *Teague v. Lane*, 489 U.S. 288 (1989) (plurality opinion), and sometimes preventing the law's just application altogether. "No one, not criminal defendants, not the judicial system, not society as a whole is benefited by a judgment providing a man shall tentatively go to jail today, but tomorrow and every day thereafter his continued incarceration shall be subject to fresh litigation." *Mackey v. United States*, 401 U.S. 667 (1971) (Harlan, J., concurring in part and dissenting in part).

In our federal system, state courts have primary responsibility for enforcing constitutional rules in their own criminal trials. When a case comes before the federal courts on habeas rather than on direct review, the judicial role is "significantly different." *Mackey* (Harlan, J.). Most important here, federal courts on direct review adjudicate every issue of federal law properly presented; in contrast, "federal courts have never had a similar obligation on habeas corpus." *Id.* As the Court explains today, federal courts exercising their habeas powers may refuse to grant relief on certain claims because of "prudential concerns" such as equity and federalism. This follows not only from the express language of the habeas statute, which directs the federal courts to "dispose of [habeas petitions] as law and justice require," 28 U.S.C. § 2243, but from our precedents as well.

Concerns for equity and federalism resonate throughout our habeas jurisprudence. . . . Most telling of all, this Court continuously has recognized that the ultimate equity on the prisoner's side — a sufficient showing of actual innocence — is normally sufficient, standing alone, to outweigh other concerns and justify adjudication of the prisoner's constitutional claim. . . .

Today we face the question whether *Stone v. Powell* should extend to bar claims on habeas that alleged violations of the prophylactic rule of *Miranda v. Arizona* had been violated. . . . In my view, the "prudential concerns" that inform our habeas jurisprudence counsel the exclusion of *Miranda* claims just as strongly as they did the exclusionary rule claims at issue in *Stone* itself.

II

[I believe that the considerations underlying *Stone*] apply to *Miranda* claims with equal, if not greater, force. Like the suppression of the fruits of an illegal search or seizure, the exclusion of statements obtained in violation of *Miranda* is not constitutionally required. This Court repeatedly has held that *Miranda*'s warning requirement is not a dictate of the Fifth Amendment itself, but a prophylactic rule. Because *Miranda* "sweeps more broadly than the Fifth Amendment itself," it excludes some confessions even though the Constitution would not. *Oregon v. Elstad*, 470 U.S. 298 (1985). Indeed, "in the individual case, *Miranda*'s preventive medicine [often] provides a remedy even to the defendant who has suffered no identifiable constitutional harm."

Miranda's overbreadth, of course, is not without justification. The exclusion of unwarned statements provides a strong incentive for the police to adopt "procedural safeguards" against the exaction of compelled or involuntary statements. It also promotes institutional respect for constitutional values. But, like the exclusionary rule for illegally seized evidence, *Miranda*'s prophylactic rule does so at a substantial cost. Unlike involuntary or compelled statements — which are of dubious reliability and are therefore inadmissible for any purpose — confessions obtained in violation of *Miranda* are not necessarily untrustworthy. In fact, because *voluntary* statements are "trustworthy" even when obtained without proper warnings, *Johnson v. New Jersey*, 384 U.S. 719 (1966), their suppression actually *impairs* the pursuit of truth by concealing probative information from the trier of fact.

When the case is on direct review, that damage to the truth-seeking function is deemed an acceptable sacrifice for the deterrence and respect for constitutional values that the *Miranda* rule brings. But once a case is on collateral review, the balance between the costs and benefits shifts; the interests of federalism, finality, and fairness compel *Miranda*'s exclusion from habeas. The benefit of enforcing *Miranda* through habeas is marginal at best. To the extent *Miranda* ensures the exclusion of involuntary statements, that task can be performed more accurately by adjudicating the voluntariness question directly. And, to the extent exclusion of voluntary but unwarned confessions serves a deterrent function, "the awarding of habeas relief years after conviction will often strike like lightning, and it is absurd to think that this added possibility . . . will have any appreciable effect on police training or behavior." . . .

Despite its meager benefits, the relitigation of *Miranda* claims on habeas imposes substantial costs. Just like the application of the exclusionary rule, application of *Miranda*'s prophylactic rule on habeas consumes scarce judicial resources on an issue unrelated to guilt or innocence. No less than the exclusionary rule, it undercuts finality. It creates tension between the state and federal courts. And it upsets the division of responsibilities that underlies our federal system. But most troubling of all, *Miranda*'s application on habeas sometimes precludes the just application of law altogether. The order excluding the statement will often be issued "years after trial, when a new trial may be a practical impossibility." Whether the Court admits it or not, the grim result of applying *Miranda* on habeas will be, time and time again, "the release of an admittedly guilty individual who may pose a continuing threat to society." . . .

III

The Court identifies a number of differences that, in its view, distinguish this case from *Stone v. Powell.* I am sympathetic to the Court's concerns but find them misplaced nonetheless. . . .

To say that the Fifth Amendment is a "fundamental *trial* right," is [both] correct and irrelevant. Long before *Miranda* was decided, it was well established that the Fifth Amendment prohibited the introduction of compelled or involuntary confessions at trial. . . . Excluding *Miranda* claims from habeas [denies] collateral relief only in those cases in which the prisoner's statement was neither compelled nor involuntary but merely obtained without the benefit of *Miranda*'s prophylactic warnings. The availability of a suppression remedy in such cases cannot be labeled a "fundamental trial right," for there is no constitutional right to the suppression of *voluntary* statements. . . .

Similarly unpersuasive is the Court's related argument that the Fifth Amendment trial right is not "necessarily divorced" from the interest of reliability. Whatever the Fifth Amendment's relationship to reliability, *Miranda*'s prophylactic rule is not merely "divorced" from the quest for truth but at war with it as well. The absence of *Miranda* warnings does not by some mysterious alchemy convert a voluntary and trustworthy statement into an involuntary and unreliable one. . . .

The consideration the Court identifies as being "most importan[t]" of all is an entirely pragmatic one. Specifically, the Court "project[s]" that excluding *Miranda* questions from habeas will not significantly promote efficiency or federalism because some *Miranda* issues are relevant to a statement's voluntariness. It is true that barring *Miranda* claims from habeas poses no barrier to the adjudication of voluntariness questions. But that does not make it "reasonable to suppose that virtually all *Miranda* claims [will] simply be recast" and litigated as voluntariness claims.

Involuntariness requires coercive state action, such as trickery, psychological pressure, or mistreatment. A *Miranda* claim, by contrast, requires no evidence of police over-reaching whatsoever; it is enough that law enforcement officers commit a technical error. Even the forgetful failure to issue warnings to the most wary, knowledgeable, and seasoned of criminals will do. Given the Court's unqualified trust in the willing-ness of police officers to satisfy *Miranda*'s requirements, its suggestion that their every failure to do so involves coercion seems to me ironic. . . .

The Court's final rationale is that, because the federal courts rarely issue writs for *Miranda* violations, eliminating *Miranda* claims from habeas will not decrease state-federal tensions to an appreciable degree. The relative infrequency of relief, however, does not diminish the intrusion on state sovereignty; it diminishes only our justification for intruding in the first place. After all, even if relief is denied at the end of the day, the State still must divert its scarce prosecutorial resources to defend an otherwise final conviction. If relief is truly rare, efficiency counsels in favor of dispensing with the search for the prophylactic rule violation in a haystack; instead, the federal courts should concentrate on the search for true Fifth Amend-ment violations by adjudicating the questions of voluntariness and compulsion directly. . . .

The Court's response, that perhaps the police respect the *Miranda* rule as a result of "the existence of [habeas] review," is contrary to both case law and common sense. As explained above, there is simply no reason to think that habeas relief, which often "strike[s] like lightning" years after conviction, contributes much additional deterrence beyond the threat of exclusion during state proceedings. . . .

Justice Scalia, with whom Justice Thomas joins, [dissenting].

The issue in this case—whether the extraordinary remedy of federal habeas cor-pus should routinely be available for claimed violations of *Miranda* rights—involves not *jurisdiction* to issue the writ, but the *equity* of doing so. In my view, both the Court and Justice O'Connor disregard the most powerful equitable consideration: that Wil-liams has already had full and fair opportunity to litigate this claim. He had the oppor-tunity to raise it in the Michigan trial court; he did so and lost. He had the opportunity to seek review of the trial court's judgment in the Michigan Court of Appeals; he did so and lost. Finally, he had the opportunity to seek discretionary review of that Court of Appeals judgment in both the Michigan Supreme Court and this Court; he did so and review was denied. The question at this stage is whether, given all that, a federal habeas court should now reopen the issue and adjudicate the *Miranda* claim anew. The answer seems to me obvious: it should not. That would be the course followed by a federal habeas court reviewing a *federal* conviction; it mocks our federal system to accord state convictions less respect.

I

By statute, a federal habeas court has jurisdiction over any claim that a prisoner is "in custody in violation of the Constitution or laws" of the United States. See 28 U.S.C. §§ 2241(c)(3), 2254(a), 2255. While that jurisdiction does require a claim of legal error in the original proceedings, *cf. Herrera v. Collins*, 506 U.S. 390 (1993), it is otherwise sweeping in its breadth. . . .

But with great power comes great responsibility. Habeas jurisdiction is tempered by the restraints that accompany the exercise of equitable discretion. This is evident from the text of the federal habeas statute, which provides that writs of habeas corpus "*may* be granted"—not that they *shall* be granted—and enjoins the court to "dispose of the matter as law *and justice* require." That acknowledgment of discretion is merely the continuation of a long historic tradition. In English law, habeas corpus was one of the so-called "prerogative" writs, which included the writs of mandamus, certiorari, and prohibition. 3 W. BLACKSTONE, COMMENTARIES 132 (1768). "[A]s in the case of all other prerogative writs," habeas would not issue "as of mere course," but rather required a showing "why the extraordinary power of the crown is called in to the party's assistance." And even where the writ was issued to compel production of the prisoner in court, the standard applied to determine whether relief would be accorded was equitable: The court was to "determine whether the case of [the prisoner's] commitment be just, and thereupon do as to justice shall appertain." . . .

This doctrine continues to be reflected in our modern cases. . . . [Indeed,] this Court's jurisprudence has defined the scope of habeas corpus largely by means of such equitable principles. The use of these principles, which serve as "gateway[s]" through which a habeas petitioner must pass before proceeding to the merits of a constitutional claim, "is grounded in the 'equitable discretion' of habeas courts." *Herrera v. Collins.*

II

As the Court today acknowledges, the rule of *Stone v. Powell* is simply one application of equitable discretion. It does not deny a federal habeas court jurisdiction over Fourth Amendment claims, but merely holds that the court ought not to entertain them when the petitioner has already had an opportunity to litigate them fully and fairly. [I]t is therefore unnecessary to discuss at length the value of *Miranda* rights, as though it has been proposed that since they are particularly worthless they deserve specially disfavored treatment. The proposed rule would treat *Miranda* claims no differently from *all other claims*, taking account of all equitable factors, including the opportunity for full and fair litigation, in determining whether to provide habeas review. . . .

At common law, the opportunity for full and fair litigation of an issue at trial and (if available) direct appeal was not only *a* factor weighing against reaching the merits of an issue on habeas; it was a *conclusive* factor, unless the issue was a legal issue going to the jurisdiction of the trial court. . . .

But to say that prior opportunity for full and fair litigation no longer *automatically* precludes from consideration even nonjurisdictional issues is not to say that such prior opportunity is no longer a relevant equitable factor. Reason would suggest that it must be, and *Stone v. Powell* establishes that it is. Thus, the question before us is not whether a holding unique to Fourth Amendment claims (and resting upon nothing more principled than our estimation that Fourth Amendment exclusion claims are not very important) should be expanded to some other arbitrary category beyond that; but rather, whether the general principle that is the only valid justification for *Stone v. Powell* should for some reason *not* be applied to *Miranda* claims. I think the answer to that question is clear: Prior opportunity to litigate an issue should be an important equitable consideration in *any* habeas case, and should ordinarily preclude the court from reaching the merits of a claim, unless it goes to the fairness of the trial process or to the accuracy of the ultimate result. . . .

III

The rule described above—or indeed a rule even somewhat more limiting of habeas review than that—is followed in federal postconviction review of *federal* convictions under 28 U.S.C. § 2255. In *Kaufman v. United States*, 394 U.S. 217 (1969), which held that res judicata does not bar § 2255 habeas review of constitutional issues, we stated that a district court had "discretion" to refuse to reach the merits of a constitutional claim that had already been raised and resolved against the prisoner at trial and on direct review. Since *Kaufman*, federal courts have uniformly held that, absent countervailing considerations, district courts may refuse to reach the merits of a constitutional claim previously raised and rejected on direct appeal. . . .

Because lower federal courts have not generally recognized their discretion to deny habeas relief in state cases where opportunity for full and fair litigation was accorded, the peculiar state of current federal habeas practice is this: State courts routinely see their criminal convictions vacated by federal district judges, but federal courts see their criminal convictions afforded a substantial measure of finality and respect. Only one theory can possibly justify this disparity—the theory advanced in *Fay v. Noia*, 372 U.S. 391 (1963), that a federal forum must be afforded for every federal claim of a state criminal defendant.*

[The federal right/federal forum theory] misperceives the basic structure of our national system. That structure establishes this Court as the supreme judicial interpreter of the Federal Constitution and laws, but gives other federal courts no higher or more respected a role than state courts in applying that "Law of the Land"—which it says all state courts are bound by, and all state judges must be sworn to uphold. U.S. Const., Art. VI. It would be a strange constitution that regards state courts as second-rate instruments for the vindication of federal rights and yet makes no mandatory provision for lower federal courts (as our Constitution does not). And it would be an unworkable constitution that requires redetermination in federal courts of all issues of pervasive federal constitutional law that arise in state-court litigation.

Absent indication to the contrary, state courts should be presumed to have applied federal law as faithfully as federal courts. A federal court entertaining collateral attack against a state criminal conviction should accord the same measure of respect and finality as it would to a federal criminal conviction. As it exercises equitable discretion

---

* Of course, a federal forum is theoretically available in this Court, by writ of certiorari. Quite obviously, however, this mode of review cannot be generally applied due to practical limitations.

to determine whether the merits of constitutional claims will be reached in the one, it should exercise a similar discretion for the other. The distinction that has arisen in lower court practice is unsupported in law, utterly impractical and demeaning to the States in its consequences, and must be eliminated.

* * *

. . . I would reverse the judgment of the Court of Appeals and remand the case for a determination whether, given that respondent has already been afforded an opportunity for full and fair litigation in the courts of Michigan, any unusual equitable factors counsel in favor of readjudicating the merits of his *Miranda* claim on habeas corpus.

Note: Constitutional Claims Cognizable in Habeas

1. *Stone v. Powell*, 428 U.S. 465 (1976), remains the only example of a substantive limitation on the constitutional claims that may be presented in federal habeas corpus review. As a result of *Stone*, federal courts may not consider Fourth Amendment claims in habeas cases unless the petitioner demonstrates that the state did not provide a full and fair opportunity to litigate his constitutional challenge.

2. What theories of habeas explain the various approaches taken by the Justices in *Withrow*? Is Justice Scalia correct when he states that "[o]nly one theory can possibly justify [the majority's approach]: the theory . . . that a federal forum must be afforded for every federal claim of a state criminal defendant"? When the Court discusses the costs and benefits of reviewing various constitutional violations in habeas proceedings, what is the implicit view of the purpose of habeas corpus it is adopting? And what view of the purpose of habeas supports Justice Scalia's position that "[p]rior opportunity to litigate an issue should be an important equitable consideration in *any* habeas case, and should ordinarily preclude the court from reaching the merits of a claim, unless it goes to the fairness of the trial process or to the accuracy of the ultimate result"?

3. Note that in neither *Withrow* nor *Stone* does the language of the habeas corpus statute play a serious role in determining the outcome. As Justice O'Connor states, equitable considerations and the Court's views about comity and federalism have played a major role in shaping habeas law. As Justice Scalia correctly notes in *Withrow*, "Discretion is implicit in the statutory command that the judge . . . 'dispose of the matter as law and justice require,' 28 U.S.C. § 2243." That broad statutory language would be a slender reed to support the substantial doctrinal developments outlined in Justice O'Connor's opinion without an underlying understanding that the Court has a significant role to play in shaping habeas law that goes beyond statutory language.

4. Justice O'Connor, in her dissent joined by Chief Justice Rehnquist, emphasizes that "*Miranda*'s warning requirement is not a dictate of the Fifth Amendment itself, but a prophylactic rule." However, seven years later, in *Dickerson v. United States*, 530 U.S. 428 (2000), the Court held that *Miranda* was "a constitutional decision of [the

Supreme Court that] may not be in effect overruled by an Act of Congress." The Court relied in part on the decision in *Withrow*:

> Our conclusion regarding *Miranda*'s constitutional basis is further buttressed by the fact that we have allowed prisoners to bring alleged *Miranda* violations before the federal courts in habeas corpus proceedings. Habeas corpus proceedings are available only for claims that a person "is in custody in violation of the Constitution or laws or treaties of the United States." 28 U.S.C. § 2254(a). Since the *Miranda* rule is clearly not based on federal laws or treaties, our decision allowing habeas review for *Miranda* claims obviously assumes that *Miranda* is of constitutional origin.

The opinion was by Chief Justice Rehnquist; Justice O'Connor joined it in full. To what extent does *Dickerson* undermine Justice O'Connor's dissent in *Withrow*?

5. As Justice Souter recounts, the Court held in *Jackson v. Virginia*, 443 U.S. 307 (1979), that habeas review encompasses "a Fourteenth Amendment due process claim of insufficient evidence to support a state conviction." Justice Stevens (joined by Chief Justice Burger and Justice Rehnquist) disagreed with this holding. He posited that one of the principal justifications for collateral review of state proceedings is that federal judges "are less susceptible than state judges to political pressures against applying constitutional rules to overturn convictions." But that justification, he said, has no force in the context of evaluating sufficiency claims:

> [Of] all decisions overturning convictions, the least likely to be unpopular and thus to distort state decisionmaking processes are ones based on the inadequacy of the evidence. Indeed, once federal courts were divested of authority to second-guess state courts on Fourth Amendment issues, which are far more likely to generate politically motivated state-court decisions, see *Stone v. Powell*, a like result in this case would seem to be a fortiori.

As you read the cases in this chapter, consider whether the Court and Congress share Justice Stevens's assumption about the purpose of collateral review.

6. Justice Scalia notes, but does not develop, two exceptions to his "full and fair" standard: he would allow relitigation of claims that go "to the fairness of the trial process or to the accuracy of the ultimate result." How far would these exceptions carry?

7. The habeas statute permits a federal court to review a claim that custody violates the Constitution *or laws* of the United States. In *Stone*, the Court stated:

> Despite the expansion of the scope of the writ, there has been no change in the established rule with respect to nonconstitutional claims. The writ of habeas corpus and its federal counterpart, 28 U.S.C. § 2255, "will not be allowed to do service for an appeal." *Sunal v. Large*, 332 U.S. 174 (1947). For this reason, nonconstitutional claims that could have been raised on appeal, but were not, may not be asserted in collateral proceedings. Even those nonconstitutional claims that could not have been asserted on direct appeal can be raised on collateral review only if the alleged error constituted "a fundamental defect which inherently results in a complete miscarriage of justice."

This language would appear to prohibit most statutory claims in habeas. In *Reed v. Farley*, 512 U.S. 339 (1994), the Court confirmed that a state's failure to comply with a federal statute is cognizable in habeas only if it resulted "in a complete miscarriage of justice or in a proceeding inconsistent with the rudimentary demands of fair procedure."

[2] Retroactivity of New Rules of Constitutional Law

Teague v. Lane

Supreme Court of the United States, 1989.

489 U.S. 288.

JUSTICE O'CONNOR announced the judgment of the Court and delivered the opinion of the Court with respect to Parts I, II, and III, and an opinion with respect to Parts IV and V, in which THE CHIEF JUSTICE, JUSTICE SCALIA, and JUSTICE KENNEDY join.

In *Taylor v. Louisiana*, 419 U.S. 522 (1975), this Court held that the Sixth Amendment required that the jury venire be drawn from a fair cross section of the community. The Court stated, however, that "in holding that petit juries must be drawn from a source fairly representative of the community we impose no requirement that petit juries actually chosen must mirror the community and reflect the various distinctive groups in the population. Defendants are not entitled to a jury of any particular composition." The principal question presented in this case is whether the Sixth Amendment's fair cross section requirement should now be extended to the petit jury. Because we adopt Justice Harlan's approach to retroactivity for cases on collateral review, we leave the resolution of that question for another day.

I

Petitioner, a black man, was convicted by an all-white Illinois jury of three counts of attempted murder, two counts of armed robbery, and one count of aggravated battery. During jury selection for petitioner's trial, the prosecutor used all 10 of his peremptory challenges to exclude blacks. Petitioner's counsel used one of his 10 peremptory challenges to exclude a black woman who was married to a police officer. After the prosecutor had struck six blacks, petitioner's counsel moved for a mistrial. The trial court denied the motion. When the prosecutor struck four more blacks, petitioner's counsel again moved for a mistrial, arguing that petitioner was "entitled to a jury of his peers." The prosecutor defended the challenges by stating that he was trying to achieve a balance of men and women on the jury. The trial court denied the motion, reasoning that the jury "appear[ed] to be a fair [one]."

On appeal, petitioner argued that the prosecutor's use of peremptory challenges denied him the right to be tried by a jury that was representative of the community. The Illinois Appellate Court rejected petitioner's fair cross section claim. The Illinois Supreme Court denied leave to appeal, and we denied certiorari.

Petitioner then filed a petition for a writ of habeas corpus in the United States District Court for the Northern District of Illinois. Petitioner repeated his fair cross section claim, [along with several Equal Protection claims]. The District Court, though sympathetic to petitioner's arguments, held that it was bound by [Supreme Court] and Circuit precedent.

On appeal, petitioner repeated his fair cross section claim and his [other claims]. A panel of the Court of Appeals agreed with petitioner that the Sixth Amendment's fair cross section requirement applied to the petit jury and held that petitioner had made out a prima facie case of discrimination. A majority of the judges on the Court of Appeals voted to rehear the case en banc, and the panel opinion was vacated. Rehearing was postponed until after our decision in *Batson v. Kentucky*, 476 U.S. 79 (1986). . . . After *Batson* was decided, the Court of Appeals held that petitioner could not benefit from the rule in that case because *Allen v. Hardy*, 478 U.S. 255 (1986) (*per curiam*), had held that *Batson* would not be applied retroactively to cases on collateral review. . . . The Court of Appeals rejected petitioner's fair cross section claim, holding that the fair cross section requirement was limited to the jury venire. Judge Cudahy dissented, arguing that the fair cross section requirement should be extended to the petit jury.

II

. . . In *Batson*, the Court . . . held that a defendant can establish a prima facie case [of racial discrimination under the Equal Protection Clause] by showing that he is a "member of a cognizable racial group," that the prosecutor exercised "peremptory challenges to remove from the venire members of the defendant's race," and that those "facts and any other relevant circumstances raise an inference that the prosecutor used that practice to exclude the veniremen from the petit jury on account of their race." Once the defendant makes out a prima facie case of discrimination, the burden shifts to the prosecutor "to come forward with a neutral explanation for challenging black jurors."

In *Allen v. Hardy*, the Court held that *Batson* constituted an "explicit and substantial break with prior precedent" because it overruled [portions of the Court's prior decisions]. Employing the retroactivity standard of *Linkletter v. Walker*, 381 U.S. 618 (1965), the Court concluded that the rule announced in *Batson* should not be applied retroactively on collateral review of convictions that became final before *Batson* was announced. The Court defined final to mean a case "'where the judgment of conviction was rendered, the availability of appeal exhausted, and the time for petition for certiorari had elapsed before our decision in' *Batson*. . . .'"

Petitioner's conviction became final 2 years prior to *Batson*, thus depriving petitioner of any benefit from the rule announced in that case. . . .

IV

Petitioner's third and final contention is that the Sixth Amendment's fair cross section requirement applies to the petit jury. As we noted at the outset, *Taylor* expressly stated that the fair cross section requirement does not apply to the petit jury. Petitioner nevertheless contends that the *ratio decidendi* of *Taylor* cannot be limited to the jury venire, and he urges adoption of a new rule. Because we hold that the rule urged by petitioner should not be applied retroactively to cases on collateral review, we decline to address petitioner's contention.

A

In the past, the Court has, without discussion, often applied a new constitutional rule of criminal procedure to the defendant in the case announcing the new rule, and has confronted the question of retroactivity later when a different defendant sought the benefit of that rule. . . .

In our view, the question "whether a decision [announcing a new rule should] be given prospective or retroactive effect should be faced at the time of [that] decision." Mishkin, *Foreword: the High Court, the Great Writ, and the Due Process of Time and Law*, 79 HARV. L. REV. 56, 64 (1965). Retroactivity is properly treated as a threshold question, for, once a new rule is applied to the defendant in the case announcing the rule, evenhanded justice requires that it be applied retroactively to all who are similarly situated. Thus, before deciding whether the fair cross section requirement should be extended to the petit jury, we should ask whether such a rule would be applied retroactively to the case at issue. This retroactivity determination would normally entail application of the *Linkletter* standard, but we believe that our approach to retroactivity for cases on collateral review requires modification.

It is admittedly often difficult to determine when a case announces a new rule, and we do not attempt to define the spectrum of what may or may not constitute a new rule for retroactivity purposes. In general, however, a case announces a new rule when it breaks new ground or imposes a new obligation on the States or the Federal Government. To put it differently, a case announces a new rule if the result was not *dictated* by precedent existing at the time the defendant's conviction became final. Given the strong language in *Taylor* and our statement in *Akins v. Texas*, 325 U.S. 398 (1945), that "[f]airness in [jury] selection has never been held to require proportional representation of races upon a jury," application of the fair cross section requirement to the petit jury would be a new rule.

Not all new rules have been uniformly treated for retroactivity purposes. Nearly a quarter of a century ago, in *Linkletter*, the Court . . . determined that the retroactivity of [a new rule of constitutional procedure] should be determined by examining the purpose of the [new] rule, the reliance of the States on prior law, and the effect on the administration of justice of a retroactive application of the [new] rule.

The *Linkletter* retroactivity standard has not led to consistent results. Instead, it has been used to limit application of certain new rules to cases on direct review, other new rules only to the defendants in the cases announcing such rules, and still other new rules to cases in which trials have not yet commenced. See *Desist v. United States*, 394 U.S. 244 (1969) (Harlan, J., dissenting).

Application of the *Linkletter* standard led to the disparate treatment of similarly situated defendants on direct review. . . . This inequity also generated vehement criticism.

Dissatisfied with the *Linkletter* standard, Justice Harlan advocated a different approach to retroactivity. He argued that new rules should always be applied retroactively to cases on direct review, but that generally they should not be applied retroactively to criminal cases on collateral review. See *Mackey v. United States*, 401 U.S. 667 (1971) (opinion concurring in judgments in part and dissenting in part); *Desist* (dissenting opinion).

In *Griffith v. Kentucky*, 479 U.S. 314 (1987), we rejected as unprincipled and inequitable the *Linkletter* standard for cases pending on direct review at the time a new rule is announced, and adopted the first part of the retroactivity approach advocated by Justice Harlan. We agreed with Justice Harlan that "failure to apply a newly declared constitutional rule to criminal cases pending on direct review violates basic norms of constitutional adjudication." We gave two reasons for our decision. First, because we can only promulgate new rules in specific cases and cannot possibly decide all cases in which review is sought, "the integrity of judicial review" requires the application of the new rule to "all similar cases pending on direct review." We quoted approvingly from Justice Harlan's separate opinion in *Mackey*:

> If we do not resolve all cases before us on direct review in light of our best understanding of governing constitutional principles, it is difficult to see why we should so adjudicate any case at all. . . . In truth, the Court's assertion of power to disregard current law in adjudicating cases before us that have not already run the full course of appellate review is quite simply an assertion that our constitutional function is not one of adjudication but in effect of legislation.

Second, because "selective application of new rules violates the principle of treating similarly situated defendants the same," we refused to continue to tolerate the inequity that resulted from not applying new rules retroactively to defendants whose cases had not yet become final. Although new rules that constituted clear breaks with the past generally were not given retroactive effect under the *Linkletter* standard, we held that "a new rule for the conduct of criminal prosecutions is to be applied retroactively to all cases, state or federal, pending on direct review or not yet final, with no exception for cases in which the new rule constitutes a 'clear break' with the past." . . .

B

Justice Harlan believed that new rules generally should not be applied retroactively to cases on collateral review. He argued that retroactivity for cases on collateral review could "be responsibly [determined] only by focusing, in the first instance, on the nature, function, and scope of the adjudicatory process in which such cases arise. The relevant frame of reference, in other words, is not the purpose of the new rule whose benefit the [defendant] seeks, but instead the purposes for which the writ of habeas corpus is made available." With regard to the nature of habeas corpus, Justice Harlan wrote:

> Habeas corpus always has been a *collateral* remedy, providing an avenue for upsetting judgments that have become otherwise final. It is not designed as a substitute for direct review. The interest in leaving concluded litigation in a state of repose, that is, reducing the controversy to a final judgment not

subject to further judicial revision, may quite legitimately be found by those responsible for defining the scope of the writ to outweigh in some, many, or most instances the competing interest in readjudicating convictions according to all legal standards in effect when a habeas petition is filed.

Given the "broad scope of constitutional issues cognizable on habeas," Justice Harlan argued that it is "sounder, in adjudicating habeas petitions, generally to apply the law prevailing at the time a conviction became final than it is to seek to dispose of [habeas] cases on the basis of intervening changes in constitutional interpretation." As he had explained in *Desist*, "the threat of habeas serves as a necessary additional incentive for trial and appellate courts throughout the land to conduct their proceedings in a manner consistent with established constitutional standards. In order to perform this deterrence function, . . . the habeas court need only apply the constitutional standards that prevailed at the time the original proceedings took place." . . .

Justice Harlan identified only two exceptions to his general rule of nonretroactivity for cases on collateral review. First, a new rule should be applied retroactively if it places "certain kinds of primary, private individual conduct beyond the power of the criminal law-making authority to proscribe." Second, a new rule should be applied retroactively if it requires the observance of "those procedures that . . . are 'implicit in the concept of ordered liberty.'" *Mackey* (quoting *Palko v. Connecticut*, 302 U.S. 319 (1937) (Cardozo, J.)). . . .

We agree with Justice Harlan's description of the function of habeas corpus. "[T]he Court never has defined the scope of the writ simply by reference to a perceived need to assure that an individual accused of crime is afforded a trial free of constitutional error." *Kuhlmann v. Wilson*, 477 U.S. 436 (1986) (plurality opinion). Rather, we have recognized that interests of comity and finality must also be considered in determining the proper scope of habeas review. . . .

This Court has not "always followed an unwavering line in its conclusions as to the availability of the Great Writ." . . . Nevertheless, it has long been established that a final civil judgment entered under a given rule of law may withstand subsequent judicial change in that rule. . . .

These underlying considerations of finality find significant and compelling parallels in the criminal context. Application of constitutional rules not in existence at the time a conviction became final seriously undermines the principle of finality which is essential to the operation of our criminal justice system. Without finality, the criminal law is deprived of much of its deterrent effect. The fact that life and liberty are at stake in criminal prosecutions "shows only that 'conventional notions of finality' should not have *as much* place in criminal as in civil litigation, not that they should have *none*." Friendly, *Is Innocence Irrelevant? Collateral Attacks on Criminal Judgments*, 38 U. Chi. L. Rev. 142, 150 (1970). "[I]f a criminal judgment is ever to be final, the notion of legality must at some point include the assignment of final competence to determine legality." Bator, *Finality in Criminal Law and Federal Habeas Corpus for State Prisoners*, 76 Harv. L. Rev. 441, 450-451 (1963). [As Justice Harlan said in *Mackey*,] "No one, not criminal defendants, not the judicial system, not society as a whole is benefited by a judgment providing that a man shall tentatively go to jail today, but tomorrow and every day thereafter his continued incarceration shall be subject to fresh litigation." . . .

The "costs imposed upon the State[s] by retroactive application of new rules of constitutional law on habeas corpus . . . generally far outweigh the benefits of this application." *Stumes* (Powell, J., concurring in judgment). In many ways the application of new rules to cases on collateral review may be more intrusive than the enjoining of criminal prosecutions, *cf. Younger v. Harris*, 401 U.S. 37 (1971), for it *continually* forces the States to marshal resources in order to keep in prison defendants whose trials and appeals conformed to then-existing constitutional standards. Furthermore, as we recognized in *Engle v. Isaac*, "[s]tate courts are understandably frustrated when they faithfully apply existing constitutional law only to have a federal court discover, during a [habeas] proceeding, new constitutional commands."

We find these criticisms to be persuasive, and we now adopt Justice Harlan's view of retroactivity for cases on collateral review. Unless they fall within an exception to the general rule, new constitutional rules of criminal procedure will not be applicable to those cases which have become final before the new rules are announced.

V

Petitioner's conviction became final in 1983. As a result, the rule petitioner urges would not be applicable to this case, which is on collateral review, unless it would fall within an exception.

The first exception suggested by Justice Harlan — that a new rule should be applied retroactively if it places "certain kinds of primary, private individual conduct beyond the power of the criminal law-making authority to proscribe," is not relevant here. Application of the fair cross section requirement to the petit jury would not accord constitutional protection to any primary activity whatsoever.

The second exception suggested by Justice Harlan — that a new rule should be applied retroactively if it requires the observance of "those procedures that . . . are 'implicit in the concept of ordered liberty,'" we apply with a modification. The language used by Justice Harlan in *Mackey* leaves no doubt that he meant the second exception to be reserved for watershed rules of criminal procedure:

> Typically, it should be the case that any conviction free from federal constitutional error at the time it became final, will be found, upon reflection, to have been fundamentally fair and conducted under those procedures essential to the substance of a full hearing. However, in some situations it might be that time and growth in social capacity, as well as judicial perceptions of what we can rightly demand of the adjudicatory process, will properly alter our understanding of the *bedrock procedural elements* that must be found to vitiate the fairness of a particular conviction. For example, such, in my view, is the case with the right to counsel at trial now held a necessary condition precedent to any conviction for a serious crime. [Here Justice Harlan cited *Gideon v. Wainwright*, 372 U.S. 335 (1963).]

In *Desist*, Justice Harlan had reasoned that one of the two principal functions of habeas corpus was "to assure that no man has been incarcerated under a procedure which creates an impermissibly large risk that the innocent will be convicted," and concluded "from this that all 'new' constitutional rules which significantly improve the pre-existing fact-finding procedures are to be retroactively applied on habeas." . . .

We believe it desirable to combine the accuracy element of the *Desist* version of the second exception with the *Mackey* requirement that the procedure at issue must implicate the fundamental fairness of the trial. . . . [Since] *Mackey* was decided, our cases have moved in the direction of reaffirming the relevance of the likely accuracy of convictions in determining the available scope of habeas review. . . . Finally, we believe that Justice Harlan's concerns about the difficulty in identifying both the existence and the value of accuracy-enhancing procedural rules can be addressed by limiting the scope of the second exception to those new procedures without which the likelihood of an accurate conviction is seriously diminished.

Because we operate from the premise that such procedures would be so central to an accurate determination of innocence or guilt, we believe it unlikely that many such components of basic due process have yet to emerge. We are also of the view that such rules are "best illustrated by recalling the classic grounds for the issuance of a writ of habeas corpus—that the proceeding was dominated by mob violence; that the prosecutor knowingly made use of perjured testimony; or that the conviction was based on a confession extorted from the defendant by brutal methods." *Rose v. Lundy*, 455 U.S. 509 (1982) (Stevens, J., dissenting).[2]

An examination of our decision in *Taylor* applying the fair cross section requirement to the jury venire leads inexorably to the conclusion that adoption of the rule petitioner urges would be a far cry from the kind of absolute prerequisite to fundamental fairness that is "implicit in the concept of ordered liberty." . . . [As] we stated in *Daniel v. Louisiana*, 420 U.S. 31 (1975), which held that *Taylor* was not to be given retroactive effect, the fair cross section requirement "[does] not rest on the premise that every criminal trial, or any particular trial, [is] necessarily unfair because it [is] not conducted in accordance with what we determined to be the requirements of the Sixth Amendment." Because the absence of a fair cross section on the jury venire does not undermine the fundamental fairness that must underlie a conviction or seriously diminish the likelihood of obtaining an accurate conviction, we conclude that a rule requiring that petit juries be composed of a fair cross section of the community would

---

2. Because petitioner is not under sentence of death, we need not, and do not, express any views as to how the retroactivity approach we adopt today is to be applied in the capital sentencing context. We do, however, disagree with Justice Stevens' suggestion that the finality concerns underlying Justice Harlan's approach to retroactivity are limited to "making convictions final," and are therefore "wholly inapplicable to the capital sentencing context." As we have often stated, a criminal judgment necessarily includes the sentence imposed upon the defendant. Collateral challenges to the sentence in a capital case, like collateral challenges to the sentence in a noncapital case, delay the enforcement of the judgment at issue and decrease the possibility that "there will at some point be the certainty that comes with an end to litigation." *Sanders v. United States*, 373 U.S. 1 (1963) (Harlan, J., dissenting).

not be a "bedrock procedural element" that would be retroactively applied under the second exception we have articulated. . . .

[I]mplicit in the retroactivity approach we adopt today, is the principle that habeas corpus cannot be used as a vehicle to create new constitutional rules of criminal procedure unless those rules would be applied retroactively to *all* defendants on collateral review through one of the two exceptions we have articulated. Because a decision extending the fair cross section requirement to the petit jury would not be applied retroactively to cases on collateral review under the approach we adopt today, we do not address petitioner's claim.

For the reasons set forth above, the judgment of the Court of Appeals is affirmed.

JUSTICE WHITE, concurring in part and concurring in the judgment.

I join Parts I, II, and III of Justice O'Connor's opinion. Otherwise, I concur only in the judgment.

. . . In a series of cases . . . the Court has departed from *Stovall v. Denno*, 388 U.S. 293 (1967) and has held that decisions changing the governing rules in criminal cases will be applied retroactively to all cases then pending on direct review. I dissented in those cases, believing that *Stovall* was the sounder approach.

I regret the course the Court has taken to this point, but . . . I have insufficient reason to continue to object to them. In light of those decisions, the result reached in Parts IV and V of Justice O'Connor's opinion is an acceptable application in collateral proceedings of the theories embraced by the Court in cases dealing with direct review, and I concur in that result. If we are wrong in construing the reach of the habeas corpus statutes, Congress can of course correct us; but because the Court's recent decisions dealing with direct review appear to have constitutional underpinnings, correction of our error, if error there is, perhaps lies with us, not Congress.

[Justice Blackmun's opinion, concurring in part of Justice Stevens' opinion, and concurring in the judgment is omitted.]

[Justice Stevens' opinion, concurring in part and concurring in the judgment is omitted.]

JUSTICE BRENNAN, with whom JUSTICE MARSHALL joins, dissenting.

. . . Out of an exaggerated concern for treating similarly situated habeas petitioners the same, the plurality would for the first time preclude the federal courts from considering on collateral review a vast range of important constitutional challenges; where those challenges have merit, it would bar the vindication of personal constitutional rights and deny society a check against further violations until the same claim is presented on direct review. In my view, the plurality's "blind adherence to the principle of treating like cases alike" amounts to "letting the tail wag the dog" when it stymies the resolution of substantial and unheralded constitutional questions. Because I cannot acquiesce in this unprecedented curtailment of the reach of the Great Writ, particularly in the absence of any discussion of these momentous changes by the parties or the lower courts, I dissent. . . .

II

C

... [From] the plurality's exposition of its new rule, one might infer that its novel fabrication will work no great change in the availability of federal collateral review of state convictions. Nothing could be further from the truth. Although the plurality declines to "define the spectrum of what may or may not constitute a new rule for retroactivity purposes," it does say that generally "a case announces a new rule when it breaks new ground or imposes a new obligation on the States or the Federal Government." Otherwise phrased, "a case announces a new rule if the result was not *dictated* by precedent existing at the time the defendant's conviction became final." This account is extremely broad. Few decisions on appeal or collateral review are "*dictated*" by what came before. Most such cases involve a question of law that is at least debatable, permitting a rational judge to resolve the case in more than one way. Virtually no case that prompts a dissent on the relevant legal point, for example, could be said to be "*dictated*" by prior decisions. By the plurality's test, therefore, a great many cases could only be heard on habeas if the rule urged by the petitioner fell within one of the two exceptions the plurality has sketched. Those exceptions, however, are narrow. Rules that place "'certain kinds of primary, private individual conduct beyond the power of the criminal law-making authority to proscribe,'" are rare. And rules that would require "new procedures without which the likelihood of an accurate conviction is seriously diminished," are not appreciably more common. The plurality admits, in fact, that it "believe[s] it unlikely that many such components of basic due process have yet to emerge." The plurality's approach today can thus be expected to contract substantially the Great Writ's sweep.

Its impact is perhaps best illustrated by noting the abundance and variety of habeas cases we have decided in recent years that could never have been adjudicated had the plurality's new rule been in effect. Although "history reveals no exact tie of the writ of habeas corpus to a constitutional claim relating to innocence or guilt," the plurality's decision to ignore history and to link the availability of relief to guilt or innocence when the outcome of a case is not "*dictated*" by precedent would apparently prevent a great many Fifth, Sixth, and Fourteenth Amendment cases from being brought on federal habeas. . . .

D

These are massive changes, unsupported by precedent. They also lack a reasonable foundation. By exaggerating the importance of treating like cases alike and granting relief to all identically positioned habeas petitioners or none, "the Court acts as if it has no choice but to follow a mechanical notion of fairness without pausing to consider 'sound principles of decisionmaking.'" Certainly it is desirable, in the interest of fairness, to accord the same treatment to all habeas petitioners with the same claims. Given a choice between deciding an issue on direct or collateral review that might result in a new rule of law that would not warrant retroactive application to persons on collateral review other than the petitioner who brought the claim, we should ordinarily grant certiorari and decide the question on direct review. . . . Taking cases on direct review ahead of those on habeas is especially attractive because the retrial of habeas petitioners usually places a heavier burden on the States than the retrial of persons on direct review. Other things being equal, our concern for fairness and finality ought to therefore lead us to render our decision in a case that comes to us on direct review.

Other things are not always equal, however. Sometimes a claim which, if successful, would create a new rule not appropriate for retroactive application on collateral review is better presented by a habeas case than by one on direct review. In fact, sometimes the claim is *only* presented on collateral review. In that case, while we could forgo deciding the issue in the hope that it would eventually be presented squarely on direct review, that hope might be misplaced, and even if it were in time fulfilled, the opportunity to check constitutional violations and to further the evolution of our thinking in some area of the law would in the meanwhile have been lost. In addition, by preserving our right and that of the lower federal courts to hear such claims on collateral review, we would not discourage their litigation on federal habeas corpus and thus not deprive ourselves and society of the benefit of decisions by the lower federal courts when we must resolve these issues ourselves.

. . . In my view, the uniform treatment of habeas petitioners is not worth the price the plurality is willing to pay. Permitting the federal courts to decide novel habeas claims not substantially related to guilt or innocence has profited our society immensely. Congress has not seen fit to withdraw those benefits by amending the statute that provides for them. And although a favorable decision for a petitioner might not extend to another prisoner whose identical claim has become final, it is at least arguably better that the wrong done to one person be righted than that none of the injuries inflicted on those whose convictions have become final be redressed, despite the resulting inequality in treatment. . . .

Perfectly even-handed treatment of habeas petitioners can by no means justify the plurality's *sua sponte* renunciation of the ample benefits of adjudicating novel constitutional claims on habeas corpus that do not bear substantially on guilt or innocence.

[Part III, analyzing Teague's claim, is omitted.]

Note: Teague *and "New Rules"*

1. On the surface, *Teague* is a case about the Supreme Court's exercise of its law-making responsibility. In fact, it is much more than that, but the significance of the decision is easy to miss. The "sting" comes only in the last paragraph of Justice O'Connor's opinion, and even there the point is obscured by the passive voice. The Court holds that "habeas corpus cannot be used as a vehicle to create new constitutional rules of criminal procedure unless those rules would be applied retroactively to *all* defendants on collateral review through one of the two exceptions we have articulated." What this means is that *no* federal court can grant habeas relief based on a "new rule" without finding that one of the exceptions applies. By the same token, retroactivity is a "threshold question" in *every* habeas case.

Later decisions made these points explicit. In *Caspari v. Bohlen*, 510 U.S. 383 (1994), the Court, again speaking through Justice O'Connor, said:

> The nonretroactivity principle *prevents* a federal court from granting habeas corpus relief to a state prisoner based on a rule announced after his conviction and sentence became final. A threshold question in every habeas case, therefore, is whether the court is obligated to apply the *Teague* rule to the defendant's claim. We have recognized that the nonretroactivity principle "is not 'jurisdictional' in the sense that [federal courts] . . . must raise and decide the issue *sua sponte*." Thus, a federal court may, but need not, decline to apply *Teague* if the State does not argue it. But if the State does argue that the defendant seeks the benefit of a new rule of constitutional law, the court *must* apply *Teague* before considering the merits of the claim.

2. Most of the *Teague* opinion is devoted to the problem of determining which litigants will get the benefit of new rules of federal constitutional law. This issue is particularly acute in habeas corpus, where thousands of convicted criminals might bring claims based on any given innovation in criminal constitutional procedure. *Teague* holds that, ordinarily, only those prisoners whose claims are pending on direct review will get the benefit of new rules. Prisoners are barred from presenting claims based on new constitutional theories in habeas unless those claims "undermine the fundamental fairness that must underlie a conviction or seriously diminish the likelihood of obtaining an accurate conviction."

Because the habeas statute provides that relief is available to any prisoner in custody in violation of the Constitution, the Court's resolution of the retroactivity issue is based, not on the statute, but on its underlying views of the costs and benefits of retroactivity in habeas, and its understanding of habeas's purposes. If habeas is primarily a method of assuring that state-court judges comply with constitutional commands, then it would not further that purpose to grant the writ in situations where the state court could not have known it was violating a constitutional norm. The Court summarized its view in *Butler v. McKellar*, 494 U.S. 407 (1990): "The 'new rule' principle [validates] reasonable, good-faith interpretations of existing precedents made by state courts even though they are shown to be contrary to later decisions."

Justice Brennan clearly has a different view of the writ's purposes. Can you articulate it?

3. Justice O'Connor acknowledges that it will often be difficult "to determine when a case announces a new rule." This proved to be a massive understatement. The decision in *Teague* has generated an enormous body of law as courts, including the Supreme Court, struggle to distinguish between new rules and the application of existing rules to new factual situations. Illustrative is *Beard v. Banks*, 542 U.S. 406 (2004). *Banks* concerned the retroactivity of two Supreme Court decisions, *Mills v. Maryland*, 486 U.S. 367 (1988), and *McKoy v. North Carolina*, 494 U.S. 433 (1990). As the Court explained, these cases "held invalid capital sentencing schemes that require juries to disregard mitigating factors not found unanimously."

A bare majority, in an opinion by Justice Thomas, held that *Mills* and *McKoy* announced a new rule. The Court acknowledged that its earlier decision in *Lockett v. Ohio*, 438 U.S. 586 (1978) stood for the proposition that "the sentencer must be allowed to consider any mitigating evidence." But that was not enough:

> The generalized *Lockett* rule . . . could be thought to support the Court's conclusion in *Mills* and *McKoy*. But what is essential here is that it does not mandate the *Mills* rule. Each of the cases relied on by *Mills* (and *McKoy*) specifically considered only obstructions to the *sentencer's* ability to consider mitigating evidence. *Mills*'s innovation rests with its shift in focus to individual jurors. We think it clear that reasonable jurists could have differed as to whether the *Lockett* principle compelled *Mills*.

Justice Stevens, writing for four dissenters, focused on a different body of precedents:

> In my opinion . . . *Mills* simply represented a straightforward application of our longstanding view that "the Eighth and Fourteenth Amendments cannot tolerate the infliction of a sentence of death under [a] legal system that permits this unique penalty to be . . . wantonly and . . . freakishly imposed." . . . When *Mills* was decided, there was nothing novel about acknowledging that permitting one death-prone juror to control the entire jury's sentencing decision would be arbitrary. That acknowledgment was a natural outgrowth of our cases condemning mandatory imposition of the death penalty, recognizing that arbitrary imposition of that penalty violates the Eighth Amendment, and mandating procedures that guarantee full consideration of mitigating evidence.

Note: The Teague *Exceptions*

1. The practical effects of *Teague* depend, in large measure, on the scope of the two exceptions that the Court announced. The first allows for retroactive application of substantive rules that place "certain kinds of primary, private individual conduct beyond the power of the criminal law-making authority to proscribe." The second allows for retroactive application of "watershed rules" of criminal procedure that are "central to an accurate determination of innocence or guilt."

2. Subsequent decisions have done much to clarify the second *Teague* exception, for watershed rules, if only by confirming that it is exceedingly narrow. The plurality in *Teague* itself considered it "unlikely" that many new watershed rules of criminal procedure had yet to emerge. Since then, "[i]n providing guidance as to what might fall within this exception," the Court has "repeatedly referred to the rule of *Gideon v. Wainwright*, 372 U.S. 335 (1963) (right to counsel), and *only* to this rule." *Beard v. Banks* (emphasis added). Indeed, since *Teague,* the Court has never identified a new criminal procedure rule that qualifies as "watershed" and therefore must be given retroactive effect. *See O'Dell v. Netherland*, 521 U.S. 151 (1997) (new rule that a capital defendant must be allowed to inform the sentencer that he would be ineligible for parole, not "watershed"); *Graham v. Collins*, 506 U.S. 461 (1993) (new rule requiring special jury instructions on mitigating factors at capital sentencing, not "watershed"); *Sawyer v. Smith*, 497 U.S. 227 (1990) (new rule that the Eighth Amendment prohibits instructions that lead a capital jury to believe responsibility for the ultimate decision rested elsewhere, not "watershed").

3. The first *Teague* exception for new "substantive" rules, by contrast, is far broader — and its importance appears to be growing. Writing for the Court in *Montgomery v. Louisiana*, 136 S. Ct. 718 (2016), Justice Kennedy explained how the Justices' understanding of the exception has evolved over time:

> Under *Teague*, a new constitutional rule of criminal procedure does not apply, as a general matter, to convictions that were final when the new rule was announced. *Teague* recognized, however, two categories of rules that are not subject to its general retroactivity bar. First, courts must give retroactive effect to new substantive rules of constitutional law. Substantive rules include "rules forbidding criminal punishment of certain primary conduct," as well as "rules prohibiting a certain category of punishment for a class of defendants because of their status or offense." *Penry v. Lynaugh*, 492 U.S. 302 (1989). Although *Teague* describes new substantive rules as an exception to the bar on retroactive application of procedural rules, this Court has recognized that substantive rules "are more accurately characterized as . . . not subject to the bar." *Schriro v. Summerlin*, 542 U.S. 348 (2004).

The Court in *Montgomery* then broke significant new ground (announcing a "new rule" about new rules) by reconceptualizing the exception for substantive rules as grounded in the Constitution, rather than the Court's discretionary power under the habeas statutes. Technically, *Montgomery* was not a habeas case at all; the prisoner sought direct review in the Supreme Court following *state* postconviction proceedings in which the state courts had declined to give retroactive effect to a new rule. That prompted serious questions as to the Court's jurisdiction out of concern that state retroactivity rules might operate as an independent and adequate state-law ground for the judgment (discussed in Chapter 5). Indeed, only a few years earlier, in *Danforth v. Minnesota*, 552 U.S. 264 (2008), the Court had described *Teague* as "an exercise of this Court's power to interpret the federal habeas statute" and thus as "limit[ing] only the scope of *federal* habeas relief." Nonetheless, in *Montgomery*, the Court concluded that its jurisdiction was proper: "[W]hen a new substantive rule of constitutional law controls the outcome of a case, the Constitution requires state collateral review courts to give retroactive effect to that rule." That is because "*Teague's* conclusion establishing the retroactivity of new substantive rules is best understood as resting upon constitutional premises," and is thus "like all federal law, binding on state courts." The Court reasoned:

> [In *Ex parte Siebold*, 100 U.S. 371 (1880),] the Court explained that "[a]n unconstitutional law is void, and is as no law." A penalty imposed pursuant to an unconstitutional law is no less void because the prisoner's sentence became final before the law was held unconstitutional. There is no grandfather clause that permits States to enforce punishments the Constitution forbids. To conclude otherwise would undercut the Constitution's substantive guarantees.

Writing for the Court in *United States Coin & Currency*, Justice Harlan made this point when he declared that "[n]o circumstances call more for the invocation of a rule of complete retroactivity" than when "the conduct being penalized is constitutionally immune from punishment." . . .

If a State may not constitutionally insist that a prisoner remain in jail on federal habeas review, it may not constitutionally insist on the same result in its own postconviction proceedings. Under the Supremacy Clause of the Constitution, state collateral review courts have no greater power than federal habeas courts to mandate that a prisoner continue to suffer punishment barred by the Constitution.

The Court also noted that "the retroactive application of substantive rules does not implicate a State's weighty interests in ensuring the finality of convictions and sentences," because "no resources marshaled by a State could preserve a conviction or sentence that the Constitution deprives the State of power to impose." The Court again quoted Justice Harlan's opinion in *Mackey*: "There is little societal interest in permitting the criminal process to rest at a point where it ought properly never to repose."

Justice Scalia (joined by Justices Thomas and Alito) dissented, arguing that the Court lacked jurisdiction because "[n]either *Teague* nor its exceptions are constitutionally compelled":

[The majority writes that] "*Teague's* conclusion establishing the retroactivity of new substantive rules is best understood as resting upon constitutional premises" binding in both federal and state courts. "Best understood." Because of what? Surely not because of its history and derivation.

Because of the Supremacy Clause, says the majority. But the Supremacy Clause cannot possibly answer the question before us here. It only elicits another question: What federal law is supreme? Old or new? . . .

All that remains to support the majority's conclusion is that all-purpose Latin canon: *ipse dixit*. The majority opines that because a substantive rule eliminates a State's power to proscribe certain conduct or impose a certain punishment, it has "the automatic consequence of invalidating a defendant's conviction or sentence." What provision of the Constitution could conceivably produce such a result? The Due Process Clause? It surely cannot be a denial of due process for a court to pronounce a final judgment which, though fully in accord with federal constitutional law at the time, fails to anticipate a change to be made by this Court half a century into the future. The Equal Protection Clause? Both statutory and (increasingly) constitutional laws change. If it were a denial of equal protection to hold an earlier defendant to a law more stringent than what exists today, it would also be a denial of equal protection to hold a later defendant to a law more stringent than what existed 50 years ago. No principle of equal protection requires the criminal law of all ages to be the same.

The majority grandly asserts that "[t]here is no grandfather clause that permits States to enforce *punishments the Constitution forbids*." Of course the italicized phrase begs the question. There most certainly is a grandfather clause—one we have called *finality*—which says that the Constitution does not require States to revise punishments that were lawful when they were imposed. Once a conviction has become final, whether new rules or old ones will be applied to revisit the conviction is a matter entirely within the State's control; the Constitution has nothing to say about that choice. The majority says that there is no "possibility of a valid result" when a new substantive rule is not applied retroactively. But the whole controversy here arises because many think there *is* a valid result when a defendant has been convicted under the law that existed when his conviction became final. And the States are unquestionably entitled to take that view of things.

Who has the better of the argument concerning the source of the *Teague* exception for new substantive rules? Can you articulate an answer to Justice Scalia's question: "What provision of the Constitution could conceivably produce such a result?"

As a practical matter, does the availability of Supreme Court direct review at an earlier stage make any difference? Justice Scalia's dissent calls the Court's "conscription into federal service" of state postconviction procedures "nothing short of astonishing." But haven't states elected to create those procedures, and to dedicate them to federal service?

4. Quite apart from its holding as to the *source* of the *Teague* exception for new substantive rules, *Montgomery* also offers the Court's most thorough effort to clarify the rationale and scope of the exception:

> Substantive rules . . . set forth categorical constitutional guarantees that place certain criminal laws and punishments altogether beyond the State's power to impose. It follows that when a State enforces a proscription or penalty barred by the Constitution, the resulting conviction or sentence is, by definition, unlawful. Procedural rules, in contrast, are designed to enhance the accuracy of a conviction or sentence by regulating "the manner of determining the defendant's culpability." Those rules "merely raise the possibility that someone convicted with use of the invalidated procedure might have been acquitted otherwise." *Schriro*. Even where procedural error has infected a trial, the resulting conviction or sentence may still be accurate; and, by extension, the defendant's continued confinement may still be lawful. For this reason, a trial conducted under a procedure found to be unconstitutional in a later case does not, as a general matter, have the automatic consequence of invalidating a defendant's conviction or sentence.

> The same possibility of a valid result does not exist where a substantive rule has eliminated a State's power to proscribe the defendant's conduct or impose a given punishment. "[E]ven the use of impeccable factfinding procedures could not legitimate a verdict" where "the conduct being penalized is constitutionally immune from punishment." *United States v. United States Coin & Currency*, 401 U.S. 715 (1971). Nor could the use of flawless sentencing procedures legitimate a punishment where the Constitution immunizes

the defendant from the sentence imposed. "No circumstances call more for the invocation of a rule of complete retroactivity."

If the distinction between procedural and substantive rules sounds clear enough, consider the "new rule" at issue in *Montgomery*. Petitioner Henry Montgomery murdered a deputy sheriff in 1963, when he was 17 years old. He was convicted and received a mandatory sentence of life imprisonment without parole. Nearly 50 years later, in *Miller v. Alabama*, 567 U.S. 460 (2012), the Court held that "the Eighth Amendment forbids a sentencing scheme that mandates life in prison without possibility of parole for juvenile offenders." The Court explained that the constitutional defect was the mandatory nature of the sentence: "Our decision does not categorically bar a penalty for a class of offenders or type of crime .... Instead, it mandates only that a sentencer follow a certain process—considering an offender's youth and attendant characteristics—before imposing a particular penalty." Montgomery sought the protection of that new rule on collateral review in habeas. Does the rule of *Miller* sound procedural, and thus barred by *Teague*? Or substantive, and thus within the exception?

Remarkably, the Court held that the rule of *Miller* was substantive—but only after substantially rewriting it. On Justice Kennedy's account, "*Miller* determined that sentencing a child to life without parole is excessive for all but the rare juvenile offender whose crime reflects irreparable corruption," and thus "rendered life without parole an unconstitutional penalty for 'a class of defendants because of their status.'" The rule of *Miller* qualifies as substantive, he explained, because it "necessarily carr[ies] a *significant risk* that a defendant—here, the *vast majority* of juvenile offenders—faces a punishment that the law cannot impose upon him." *Montgomery* (emphasis added). *Miller*'s insistence on a discretionary process that allows a sentencer to consider the offender's youth and related characteristics was not a procedural rule, but merely "a procedural requirement necessary to implement a substantive guarantee."

After *Montgomery*, is there a coherent difference between procedural and substantive rules? Or does the refusal to give retroactive application of *every* new procedural rule "designed to enhance the accuracy of a conviction or sentence" carry a "significant risk" that the defendant "faces a punishment that the law cannot impose on him"? If the key to *Montgomery* is that the rule casts doubt on the constitutionality of the punishment in the "vast majority" of cases affected, is the *Teague* exception just a glorified form of harmless-error review?

[3] The Effect of AEDPA

The Antiterrorism and Effective Death Penalty Act of 1996 made many changes in the law of federal habeas corpus, but probably none was more important than the adoption of an amended version of 28 U.S.C. § 2254(d). That section now provides in part:

> (d) An application for a writ of habeas corpus on behalf of a person in custody pursuant to the judgment of a State court shall not be granted with

respect to any claim that was adjudicated on the merits in State court proceedings unless the adjudication of the claim—

(1) resulted in a decision that was contrary to, or involved an unreasonable application of, clearly established Federal law, as determined by the Supreme Court of the United States . . .

For more than a decade, the Court divided sharply on the application of § 2254(d)'s standard of review, producing a number of 5-4 opinions on the question whether state courts had reasonably applied law that was clearly established. More recently, the Court has coalesced around a more unified vision of § 2254(d). The following case is illustrative.

Harrington v. Richter

Supreme Court of the United States, 2011.

562 U.S. 86.

JUSTICE KENNEDY delivered the opinion of the Court.

The writ of habeas corpus stands as a safeguard against imprisonment of those held in violation of the law. Judges must be vigilant and independent in reviewing petitions for the writ, a commitment that entails substantial judicial resources. Those resources are diminished and misspent, however, and confidence in the writ and the law it vindicates undermined, if there is judicial disregard for the sound and established principles that inform its proper issuance. That judicial disregard is inherent in the opinion of the Court of Appeals for the Ninth Circuit here under review. The Court of Appeals, in disagreement with the contrary conclusions of the Supreme Court of the State of California and of a United States District Court, ordered habeas corpus relief granted to set aside the conviction of Joshua Richter. . . . This was clear error.

Under 28 U.S.C. § 2254(d), the availability of federal habeas relief is limited with respect to claims previously "adjudicated on the merits" in state-court proceedings. The first inquiry this case presents is whether that provision applies when state-court relief is denied without an accompanying statement of reasons. If it does, the question is whether the Court of Appeals adhered to the statute's terms, in this case as it relates to ineffective-assistance claims judged by the standard set forth in *Strickland v. Washington*, 466 U.S. 668 (1984). [I]t is necessary to reverse the Court of Appeals for failing to accord required deference to the decision of a state court.

I

It is necessary to begin by discussing the details of a crime committed more than a decade and a half ago.

[Richter was charged with murder, attempted murder, burglary, and robbery in connection with a 1994 shooting at the home of a drug dealer in Sacramento, California, that left one man dead and the homeowner critically injured. The prosecution built a strong case against Richter and an accomplice based on the eyewitness testimony of the owner, shell casings that tended to corroborate his account, the discovery of a stolen gun safe and pistol in Richter's home, and Richter's admission that he had disposed of the murder weapon. Investigators had taken a few samples of blood spatter and pools of blood at the scene, but the prosecution initially did not intend to introduce that evidence at trial.

[In his opening statement at trial, Richter's attorney surprised prosecutors by outlining a theory that the shooting of the homeowner was justified in self-defense. The man who was killed, counsel suggested, was caught in the crossfire in the bedroom hallway, not killed in cold blood on the living room couch as the owner had testified. Richter's lawyer emphasized deficiencies in the investigation, including the absence of forensic evidence to support the prosecution's theory.

[The prosecution responded by introducing expert testimony to rebut the self-defense theory. Based on the blood spatter patterns at the crime scene, one detective testified, it was unlikely the man who died had been shot outside the living room and then moved to the couch. An expert serologist also testified that the blood sample near the pool by the bedroom door could have come from the owner, but not the man who was killed. Defense counsel cross-examined both witnesses, probing weaknesses in their testimony, but did not call any blood experts of his own.]

The jury returned a verdict of guilty on all charges. Richter was sentenced to life without parole. On appeal, his conviction was affirmed. The California Supreme Court denied a petition for review, and Richter did not file a petition for certiorari with this Court. His conviction became final. . . .

Richter later petitioned the California Supreme Court for a writ of habeas corpus. He asserted a number of grounds for relief, including ineffective assistance of counsel. As relevant here, he claimed his counsel was deficient for failing to present expert testimony on serology, pathology, and blood spatter patterns, testimony that, he argued, would disclose the source of the blood pool in the bedroom doorway. This, he contended, would bolster his theory . . . . He offered affidavits from three types of forensic experts [who presented their own analyses of the blood evidence] and argued this evidence established the possibility that the blood in the bedroom doorway came from [the dead man], not [the owner]. If that were true, he argued, it would confirm his account . . . . The California Supreme Court denied Richter's petition in a one-sentence summary order. Richter did not seek certiorari from this Court.

After the California Supreme Court issued its summary order denying relief, Richter filed a petition for habeas corpus in United States District Court for the Eastern District of California. He reasserted the claims in his state petition. The District Court denied his petition, and a three-judge panel of the Court of Appeals for the Ninth Circuit affirmed. The Court of Appeals granted rehearing en banc and reversed the District Court's decision.

As a preliminary matter, the Court of Appeals questioned whether 28 U.S.C. § 2254(d) was applicable to Richter's petition, since the California Supreme Court issued only a summary denial when it rejected his *Strickland* claims; but it determined the California decision was unreasonable in any event and that Richter was entitled to relief. The court held Richter's trial counsel was deficient for failing to consult experts on blood evidence in determining and pursuing a trial strategy and in preparing to rebut expert evidence the prosecution might—and later did—offer. Four judges dissented from the en banc decision.

We granted certiorari.

II

The statutory authority of federal courts to issue habeas corpus relief for persons in state custody is provided by 28 U.S.C. § 2254, as amended by the Antiterrorism and Effective Death Penalty Act of 1996 (AEDPA). The text of § 2254(d) states:

> An application for a writ of habeas corpus on behalf of a person in custody pursuant to the judgment of a State court shall not be granted with respect to any claim that was adjudicated on the merits in State court proceedings unless the adjudication of the claim—

> (1) resulted in a decision that was contrary to, or involved an unreasonable application of, clearly established Federal law, as determined by the Supreme Court of the United States; or

> (2) resulted in a decision that was based on an unreasonable determination of the facts in light of the evidence presented in the State court proceeding.

As an initial matter, it is necessary to decide whether § 2254(d) applies when a state court's order is unaccompanied by an opinion explaining the reasons relief has been denied.

By its terms § 2254(d) bars relitigation of any claim "adjudicated on the merits" in state court, subject only to the exceptions in §§ 2254(d)(1) and (d)(2). There is no text in the statute requiring a statement of reasons. The statute refers only to a "decision," which resulted from an "adjudication." As every Court of Appeals to consider the issue has recognized, determining whether a state court's decision resulted from an unreasonable legal or factual conclusion does not require that there be an opinion from the state court explaining the state court's reasoning. And as this Court has observed, a state court need not cite or even be aware of our cases under § 2254(d). *Early v. Packer*, 537 U.S. 3 (2002) (per curiam). Where a state court's decision is unaccompanied by an explanation, the habeas petitioner's burden still must be met by showing there was no reasonable basis for the state court to deny relief. This is so whether or not the state court reveals which of the elements in a multipart claim it found insufficient, for § 2254(d) applies when a "claim," not a component of one, has been adjudicated.

There is no merit to the assertion that compliance with § 2254(d) should be excused when state courts issue summary rulings because applying § 2254(d) in those cases will encourage state courts to withhold explanations for their decisions. Opinion-writing practices in state courts are influenced by considerations other than avoiding scrutiny by collateral attack in federal court. At the same time, requiring a statement of reasons could undercut state practices designed to preserve the integrity of the case-law tradition. The issuance of summary dispositions in many collateral attack cases can enable a state judiciary to concentrate its resources on the cases where opinions are most needed.

There is no merit either in Richter's argument that § 2254(d) is inapplicable because the California Supreme Court did not say it was adjudicating his claim "on the merits." The state court did not say it was denying the claim for any other reason. When a federal claim has been presented to a state court and the state court has denied relief, it may be presumed that the state court adjudicated the claim on the merits in the absence of any indication or state-law procedural principles to the contrary. *Cf. Harris v. Reed*, 489 U.S. 255 (1989) (presumption of a merits determination when it is unclear whether a decision appearing to rest on federal grounds was decided on another basis).

The presumption may be overcome when there is reason to think some other explanation for the state court's decision is more likely. Richter, however, does not make that showing. He mentions the theoretical possibility that the members of the California Supreme Court may not have agreed on the reasons for denying his petition. It is pure speculation, however, to suppose that happened in this case. And Richter's assertion that the mere possibility of a lack of agreement prevents any attribution of reasons to the state court's decision is foreclosed by precedent. . . .

[T]he California courts or Legislature can alter the State's practices or elaborate more fully on their import. But that has not occurred here. This Court now holds and reconfirms that § 2254(d) does not require a state court to give reasons before its decision can be deemed to have been "adjudicated on the merits." Richter has failed to show that the California Supreme Court's decision did not involve a determination of the merits of his claim. Section 2254(d) applies to his petition.

III

Federal habeas relief may not be granted for claims subject to § 2254(d) unless it is shown that the earlier state court's decision "was contrary to" federal law then clearly established in the holdings of this Court, § 2254(d)(1); *Williams v. Taylor*, 529 U.S. 362 (2000); or that it "involved an unreasonable application of" such law, § 2254(d)(1); or that it "was based on an unreasonable determination of the facts" in light of the record before the state court, § 2254(d)(2).

The Court of Appeals relied on the second of these exceptions to § 2254(d)'s relitigation bar, the exception in § 2254(d)(1) permitting relitigation where the earlier state decision resulted from an "unreasonable application of" clearly established federal law. In the view of the Court of Appeals, the California Supreme Court's decision on Richter's ineffective-assistance claim unreasonably applied the holding in *Strickland*. The Court of Appeals' lengthy opinion, however, discloses an improper understanding of § 2254(d)'s unreasonableness standard and of its operation in the context of a *Strickland* claim.

The pivotal question is whether the state court's application of the *Strickland* standard was unreasonable. This is different from asking whether defense counsel's performance fell below *Strickland*'s standard. Were that the inquiry, the analysis would be no different than if, for example, this Court were adjudicating a *Strickland* claim on direct review of a criminal conviction in a United States district court. Under AEDPA, though, it is a necessary premise that the two questions are different. For purposes of § 2254(d)(1), "an unreasonable application of federal law is different from an incorrect application of federal law." *Williams*. A state court must be granted a deference and latitude that are not in operation when the case involves review under the *Strickland* standard itself.

A state court's determination that a claim lacks merit precludes federal habeas relief so long as "fairminded jurists could disagree" on the correctness of the state court's decision. *Yarborough v. Alvarado*, 541 U.S. 652 (2004). And as this Court has explained, "[E]valuating whether a rule application was unreasonable requires considering the rule's specificity. The more general the rule, the more leeway courts have in reaching outcomes in case-by-case determinations." "[I]t is not an unreasonable application of clearly established Federal law for a state court to decline to apply a specific legal rule that has not been squarely established by this Court." *Knowles v. Mirzayance*, 556 U.S. 111 (2009).

Here it is not apparent how the Court of Appeals' analysis would have been any different without AEDPA. The court explicitly conducted a de novo review, and after finding a *Strickland* violation, it declared, without further explanation, that the "state court's decision to the contrary constituted an unreasonable application of *Strickland*." AEDPA demands more. Under § 2254(d), a habeas court must determine what arguments or theories supported or, as here, could have supported, the state court's decision; and then it must ask whether it is possible fairminded jurists could disagree that those arguments or theories are inconsistent with the holding in a prior decision of this Court. The opinion of the Court of Appeals all but ignored "the only question that matters under § 2254(d)(1)." *Lockyer v. Andrade*, 538 U.S. 63 (2003).

The Court of Appeals appears to have treated the unreasonableness question as a test of its confidence in the result it would reach under de novo review: Because the Court of Appeals had little doubt that Richter's *Strickland* claim had merit, the Court of Appeals concluded the state court must have been unreasonable in rejecting it. This analysis overlooks arguments that would otherwise justify the state court's result and ignores further limitations of § 2254(d), including its requirement that the state court's decision be evaluated according to the precedents of this Court. *See Renico v. Lett*, 559 U.S. 766 (2010). It bears repeating that even a strong case for relief does not mean the state court's contrary conclusion was unreasonable.

If this standard is difficult to meet, that is because it was meant to be. As amended by AEDPA, § 2254(d) stops short of imposing a complete bar on federal court relitigation of claims already rejected in state proceedings. It preserves authority to issue the writ in cases where there is no possibility fairminded jurists could disagree that the state court's decision conflicts with this Court's precedents. It goes no farther. Section 2254(d) reflects the view that habeas corpus is a "guard against extreme malfunctions in the state criminal justice systems," not a substitute for ordinary error correction through appeal. *Jackson v. Virginia*, 443 U.S. 307 (1979) (Stevens, J., concurring in judgment). As a condition for obtaining habeas corpus from a federal court, a state prisoner must show that the state court's ruling on the claim being presented in federal court was so lacking in justification that there was an error well understood and comprehended in existing law beyond any possibility for fairminded disagreement.

The reasons for this approach are familiar. "Federal habeas review of state convictions frustrates both the States' sovereign power to punish offenders and their good-faith attempts to honor constitutional rights." *Calderon v. Thompson*, 523 U.S. 538 (1998). It "disturbs the State's significant interest in repose for concluded litigation, denies society the right to punish some admitted offenders, and intrudes on state sovereignty to a degree matched by few exercises of federal judicial authority." *Reed* (Kennedy, J., dissenting).

Section 2254(d) is part of the basic structure of federal habeas jurisdiction, designed to confirm that state courts are the principal forum for asserting constitutional challenges to state convictions. . . . Here, however, the Court of Appeals gave § 2254(d) no operation or function in its reasoning. Its analysis illustrates a lack of deference to the state court's determination and an improper intervention in state criminal processes, contrary to the purpose and mandate of AEDPA and to the now well-settled meaning and function of habeas corpus in the federal system.

IV

The conclusion of the Court of Appeals that Richter demonstrated an unreasonable application by the state court of the *Strickland* standard now must be discussed. To have been entitled to relief from the California Supreme Court, Richter had to show both that his counsel provided deficient assistance and that there was prejudice as a result. . . . "Surmounting *Strickland*'s high bar is never an easy task." *Padilla v. Kentucky*, 559 U.S. 356 (2010). An ineffective-assistance claim can function as a way to escape rules of waiver and forfeiture and raise issues not presented at trial, and so the *Strickland* standard must be applied with scrupulous care, lest "intrusive post-trial inquiry" threaten the integrity of the very adversary process the right to counsel is meant to serve. Even under de novo review, the standard for judging counsel's representation is a most deferential one. Unlike a later reviewing court, the attorney observed the relevant proceedings, knew of materials outside the record, and interacted with the client, with opposing counsel, and with the judge. It is "all too tempting" to "second-guess counsel's assistance after conviction or adverse sentence." The question is whether an attorney's representation amounted to incompetence under "prevailing professional norms," not whether it deviated from best practices or most common custom.

Establishing that a state court's application of *Strickland* was unreasonable under § 2254(d) is all the more difficult. The standards created by *Strickland* and § 2254(d) are both "highly deferential," and when the two apply in tandem, review is "doubly" so, *Knowles*. The *Strickland* standard is a general one, so the range of reasonable applications is substantial. Federal habeas courts must guard against the danger of equating unreasonableness under *Strickland* with unreasonableness under § 2254(d). When § 2254(d) applies, the question is not whether counsel's actions were reasonable. The question is whether there is any reasonable argument that counsel satisfied *Strickland*'s deferential standard.

A

With respect to defense counsel's performance, the Court of Appeals held that because Richter's attorney had not consulted forensic blood experts or introduced expert evidence, the California Supreme Court could not reasonably have concluded counsel provided adequate representation. This conclusion was erroneous. . . .

[*Strickland*] permits counsel to "make a reasonable decision that makes particular investigations unnecessary." It was at least arguable that a reasonable attorney could decide to forgo inquiry into the blood evidence in the circumstances here.

Criminal cases will arise where the only reasonable and available defense strategy requires consultation with experts or introduction of expert evidence, whether pre-trial, at trial, or both. There are, however, "countless ways to provide effective assistance in any given case. Even the best criminal defense attorneys would not defend a particular client in the same way." Rare are the situations in which the "wide latitude counsel must have in making tactical decisions" will be limited to any one technique or approach. . . .

[In the Court of Appeals' view, the dead man's] location was "the single most critical issue in the case" given the differing theories of the prosecution and the defense, and the source of the blood in the doorway was therefore of central concern. But it was far from a necessary conclusion that this was evident at the time of the trial. There were many factual differences between prosecution and defense versions of the events on the night of the shootings. It is only because forensic evidence has emerged concerning the source of the blood pool that the issue could with any plausibility be said to stand apart. Reliance on "the harsh light of hindsight" to cast doubt on a trial that took place now more than 15 years ago is precisely what *Strickland* and AEDPA seek to prevent.

Even if it had been apparent that expert blood testimony could support Richter's defense, . . . [t]his theory overlooks the fact that concentrating on the blood pool carried its own serious risks. If serological analysis or other forensic evidence demonstrated that the blood came from [the owner] alone, Richter's story would be exposed as an invention. An attorney need not pursue an investigation that would be fruitless, much less one that might be harmful to the defense. Here Richter's attorney had reason to question the truth of his client's account . . . . It would have been altogether reasonable to conclude that this concern justified the course Richter's counsel pursued.

True, it appears that defense counsel's opening statement itself inspired the prosecution to introduce expert forensic evidence. But the prosecution's evidence may well have been weakened by the fact that it was assembled late in the process; and in any event the prosecution's response shows merely that the defense strategy did not work out as well as counsel had hoped, not that counsel was incompetent.

To support a defense argument that the prosecution has not proved its case it sometimes is better to try to cast pervasive suspicion of doubt than to strive to prove a certainty that exonerates. All that happened here is that counsel pursued a course that conformed to the first option. If this case presented a de novo review of *Strickland*, the foregoing might well suffice to reject the claim of inadequate counsel, but that is an unnecessary step. The Court of Appeals must be reversed if there was a reasonable justification for the state court's decision. In light of the record here there was no basis to rule that the state court's determination was unreasonable. . . .

The Court of Appeals also found that Richter's attorney was constitutionally deficient because he had not expected the prosecution to offer expert testimony and therefore was unable to offer expert testimony of his own in response. The Court of Appeals erred in suggesting counsel had to be prepared for "any contingency." *Strickland* does not guarantee perfect representation, only a "reasonably competent attorney." Representation is constitutionally ineffective only if it "so undermined the proper functioning of the adversarial process" that the defendant was denied a fair trial. Just as there is no expectation that competent counsel will be a flawless strategist or tactician, an attorney may not be faulted for a reasonable miscalculation or lack of foresight or for failing to prepare for what appear to be remote possibilities. Here, Richter's attorney was mistaken in thinking the prosecution would not present forensic testimony. But the prosecution itself did not expect to make that presentation and had made no preparations for doing so on the eve of trial. For this reason alone, it is at least debatable whether counsel's error was so fundamental as to call the fairness of the trial into doubt.

Even if counsel should have foreseen that the prosecution would offer expert evidence, Richter would still need to show it was indisputable that *Strickland* required his attorney to [offer] expert testimony to rebut the evidence from the prosecution. But *Strickland* does not enact Newton's third law for the presentation of evidence, requiring for every prosecution expert an equal and opposite expert from the defense. . . .

Here Richter's attorney represented him with vigor and conducted a skillful cross-examination. As noted, defense counsel elicited concessions from the State's experts and was able to draw attention to weaknesses in their conclusions stemming from the fact that their analyses were conducted long after investigators had left the crime scene. For all of these reasons, it would have been reasonable to find that Richter had not shown his attorney was deficient under *Strickland*.

B

The Court of Appeals further concluded that Richter had established prejudice under *Strickland* given the expert evidence his attorney could have introduced. It held that the California Supreme Court would have been unreasonable in concluding otherwise. This too was error.

In assessing prejudice under *Strickland*, the question is not whether a court can be certain counsel's performance had no effect on the outcome or whether it is possible a reasonable doubt might have been established if counsel acted differently. Instead, *Strickland* asks whether it is "reasonably likely" the result would have been different. This does not require a showing that counsel's actions "more likely than not altered the outcome," but the difference between *Strickland*'s prejudice standard and a more-probable-than-not standard is slight and matters "only in the rarest case." The likelihood of a different result must be substantial, not just conceivable.

It would not have been unreasonable for the California Supreme Court to conclude Richter's evidence of prejudice fell short of this standard. His expert serology evidence established nothing more than a theoretical possibility that, in addition to blood of [the owner's] type, [the dead man's blood] may also have been present in a blood sample taken near the bedroom doorway pool. At trial, defense counsel extracted a concession along these lines from the prosecution's expert. . . .

It was also reasonable to find Richter had not established prejudice given that he offered no evidence directly challenging other conclusions reached by the prosecution's experts. . . .

There was, furthermore, sufficient conventional circumstantial evidence pointing to Richter's guilt. . . . There was ample basis for the California Supreme Court to think any real possibility of Richter's being acquitted was eclipsed by the remaining evidence pointing to guilt.

The California Supreme Court's decision on the merits of Richter's *Strickland* claim required more deference than it received. Richter was not entitled to the relief ordered by the Court of Appeals. The judgment is reversed, and the case is remanded for further proceedings consistent with this opinion.

It is so ordered.

JUSTICE KAGAN took no part in the consideration or decision of this case.

JUSTICE GINSBURG, concurring. [Omitted.]

Note: Unreasonable Applications of Clearly Established Federal Law Under AEDPA

1. From 2010 to 2016, the Supreme Court issued a remarkable string of 25 reversals of decisions granting writs of habeas corpus, many of them through per curiam decisions. Fourteen summary reversals came after *Richter*, and all reflected the Supreme Court's view that the lower federal courts had been insufficiently deferential to the state courts under § 2254(d). *See, e.g.*, *Kernan v. Hinojosa*, 136 S. Ct. 1603 (2016) (per curiam) (Ex Post Facto Clause); *White v. Wheeler*, 136 S. Ct. 456 (2015) (per curiam) (juror impartiality at capital sentencing); *Glebe v. Frost*, 135 S. Ct. 429 (2014) (per curiam) (structural error); *Felker v. Jackson*, 562 U.S. 594 (2011) (*Batson* claim). Along the way, the Court has repeatedly strengthened the degree of deference owed under § 2254(d)(1). In *Johnson v. Williams*, 133 S. Ct. 1088 (2013), for example, the Court held that a state court's adjudication is presumed to be "on the merits" as to *all* claims, when its opinion rejects some claims on the merits, but ignores others entirely. And in *Parker v. Matthews*, 567 U.S. 37 (2012) (per curiam), the Court held that the decisions of circuit courts of appeals do not constitute, and may not even be relied upon as *evidence* of, "clearly established federal law, as determined by the Supreme Court." These cases led one judge to observe, "No one who has followed the law of federal post-conviction relief for state prisoners since 1996, when the Anti–Terrorism and Effective Death Penalty Act (AEDPA) went into effect, is under the impression that this is a readily available remedy. Indeed, the real question is whether its promise is anything more than an illusion. Success in obtaining relief under 28 U.S.C. §2254 sometimes seems just as difficult as the rich man's quest to enter the Kingdom of Heaven, compared in the Bible to a camel's passing through the eye of a needle." *Overstreet v. Wilson*, 686 F.3d 404 (7th Cir. 2012) (Wood, J., dissenting from denial of rehearing *en banc*).

2. It was not immediately obvious that §2254(d)(1) would have such a profound effect. In the Court's first decision interpreting the provision, Justice Stevens and three other Justices took the position that it made no meaningful change to the standard of review. *Williams v. Taylor*, 529 U.S. 362 (2000) (opinion of Stevens, J.). Neither the statute nor the legislative history uses the word "deference," they noted, and it would be shocking for Congress to intend "that federal courts actually defer to a state-court application of the federal law." Instead, they argued, the statute merely codified existing retroactivity rules while "express[ing] a 'mood' that the Federal Judiciary must respect" by "attend[ing] with the utmost care to state-court decisions."

A majority of the Court disagreed, stressing that through AEDPA "Congress wished to bring change to the field," and holding that §2254(d)(1) indeed requires deference to reasonable state-court decisions on federal constitutional questions. *Williams* (opinion of O'Connor, J.). Yet the Court's initial description of the standard was quite mild: habeas courts "simply . . . should ask whether the state court's application of clearly established federal law was objectively unreasonable," bearing in mind that "an *unreasonable* application of federal law is different from an *incorrect* application of federal law." And the Court specifically rejected a standard, proposed by the court of appeals, by which §2254(d)(1) is satisfied only if "reasonable jurists would *all agree* [that the state-court's application of federal law] is unreasonable."

In *Richter*, the Court states:

> Under §2254(d), a habeas court must determine what arguments or theories supported or, as here, could have supported, the state court's decision; and then it must ask whether it is possible fairminded jurists could disagree that those arguments or theories are inconsistent with the holding in a prior decision of this Court.

Can you explain the distinction? What might explain the Court's shift in the treatment of §2254(d)(1)?

3. In the first part of the opinion, *Richter* holds that a state court need not write an opinion explaining its application of federal law for its decision to be entitled to deference under AEDPA. Consider, however, the Court's decision in *Lafler v. Cooper*, 566 U.S. 156 (2012). On advice of his attorney that all involved conceded was constitutionally ineffective, Cooper rejected a plea deal and went to trial. The result was a sentence 3½ times longer than would have resulted from the plea. While the Michigan courts recited the by-now familiar two-prong *Strickland* test, they applied the constitutional test for the voluntariness of plea agreements. A five-member majority of the Supreme Court upheld the lower federal courts' grant of the writ, finding this decision "contrary to" *Strickland*. In an opinion by Justice Kennedy, who also authored *Richter*, the Court stated, "Rather than applying *Strickland*, the state court simply found that the respondent's rejection of the plea was knowing and voluntary. An inquiry into whether the rejection of a plea is knowing and voluntary, however, is not the correct means by which to address a claim of ineffective assistance of counsel." If the state court had not written an opinion, would the Court have reversed?

4. The Supreme Court's docket is necessarily constrained. In the 2014–2015 Term, the Court announced just 71 decisions on the merits — its lowest tally in decades — of which only a tiny fraction addressed the kind of criminal law and procedure issues relevant to habeas litigation. By contrast, lower federal courts address tens of thousands of habeas petitions, and state courts conduct hundreds of thousands of criminal trials and guilty pleas, appeals, petitions for post-conviction relief, and other criminal proceedings. Yet AEDPA specifies that habeas relief may be granted only when a state-court decision is "contrary to, or involve[s] an unreasonable application of, clearly established Federal law, *as determined by the Supreme Court of the United States*." 28 U.S.C. §2254(d)(1) (emphasis added). As a result, federal courts routinely confront the following question: does a state court "unreasonabl[y] appl[y]" clearly established law when its decision contravenes a broad rule or principle articulated by the Supreme Court, but the facts of the case could plausibly be distinguished from Supreme Court precedent?

Consider the Court's decision in *White v. Woodall*, 134 S. Ct. 1697 (2014). The Justices agreed on the relevant body of "clearly established" law. The Court had held in *Carter v. Kentucky*, 450 U.S. 288 (1981), that the Fifth Amendment's privilege against self-incrimination entitles a defendant in a criminal trial to an "adverse inference" instruction directing the jury that a failure to testify cannot be used as evidence of guilt. It had further held that the Fifth Amendment prohibits both the admission of compulsory statements in a capital sentencing proceeding, *Estelle v. Smith*, 451 U.S. 454 (1981), and an adverse inference at sentencing from a defendant's silence with respect to the facts and circumstances of the crime, *Mitchell v. United States*, 526 U.S. 314 (1999). But the Court had never confronted a case exactly like *Woodall*, in which the defendant requested a blanket instruction prohibiting any adverse inference at sentencing, including an inference that silence indicated a lack of remorse. The question, as Justice Breyer put it in dissent, is whether "two (or more) legal rules read together would dictate a particular outcome."

The Justices also agreed on many ground rules for determining whether the state-court decision was an unreasonable application of "clearly established federal law, as determined by the Supreme Court of the United States." They agreed that the statutory phrase "refers to the holdings, as opposed to the dicta, of th[e Supreme] Court's decisions." *Williams* (opinion of O'Connor, J.). They agreed that habeas courts must measure state-court decisions against the body of Supreme Court precedent "as of the time the state court renders its decision," ignoring any subsequent developments.

Cullen v. Pinholster, 563 U.S. 170 (2011). The Court also expressly rejected the suggestion that a state court's decision can be "unreasonable" by "refusing to extend the governing legal principle to a context in which the principle should have controlled." As the Court explained, "Section 2254(d)(1) provides a remedy for instances in which a state court unreasonably *applies* this Court's precedent; it does not require state courts to extend that precedent or license federal courts to treat the failure to do so as error."

Yet in *Woodall*, the Justices nonetheless sharply divided, by a 6-to-3 vote, over the application of those principles. In part they clashed over what counts as a holding, rather than dictum. In *Estelle*, the Court had stated that it could "discern no basis to distinguish between the guilt and penalty phases of [a] capital murder trial so far as the protection of the Fifth Amendment privilege is concerned." The dissent viewed that passage as essential to the rationale of the decision, and therefore part of the holding. The Court, by contrast, characterized that passage as dictum, noting that *Estelle* involved only the admission of compelled statements, not an adverse inference from silence. The Justices also disagreed over the import of a footnote in *Mitchell* that had expressly reserved the "separate question" whether the Fifth Amendment prohibits an adverse inference from silence as to remorse or acceptance of responsibility. In the majority's view, that reservation served as strong evidence that there was room for "fair-minded disagreement."

Isn't it always possible to find *some* basis for distinguishing precedent? Does the standard applied by the majority in *Woodall* require, in effect, an "identical factual pattern" in a Supreme Court case before deeming a state-court decision unreasonable? In *Yarborough v. Alvarado*, 541 U.S. 652 (2004), the Court commented that "the difference between applying a rule and extending it is not always clear," but "[c]ertain principles are fundamental enough that when new factual permutations arise, the necessity to apply the earlier rule will be beyond doubt."

On the other hand, aren't all *erroneous* decisions in conflict with clearly established "principles" embodied in prior Supreme Court decisions? If a state-court decision may be deemed "unreasonable" for failing to combine previously articulated rules or principles in a novel way, as the dissent in *Woodall* reasoned, how is the inquiry on habeas any different from *de novo* review? *See Lopez v. Smith*, 135 S. Ct. 1 (2014) (per curiam) (summarily reversing the court of appeals for relying on legal principles "far too abstract to establish clearly the specific rule respondent needs," and cautioning the lower courts against "framing our precedents at such a high level of generality").

5. The Supreme Court had never confronted a case quite like *Woodall* before, but many lower federal courts and state courts had. Indeed, at least three federal courts of appeals had reached the same conclusion as the state court, reasoning that the logic of *Estelle* and *Mitchell* did not extend to adverse inferences about facts unrelated to the circumstances of the crime, such as a lack of remorse. Does that kind of circuit conflict prove that there is room for "fairminded disagreement" within the meaning of *Harrington*, and thus effectively foreclose habeas relief? For a discussion of how the Court has addressed similar questions in the qualified immunity context, see Chapter 14.

6. *Richter* assumes that *Teague v. Lane* survives the enactment of AEDPA. But do *Teague* and AEDPA require distinct analyses? In *Horn v. Banks*, 536 U.S. 266 (2002), the Court reversed a grant of the writ where the Third Circuit had found the Pennsylvania Supreme Court's application of a United States Supreme Court precedent unreasonable. The Pennsylvania court had applied a Supreme Court decision without asking whether it applied retroactively to Banks's claim. Because the state court had not considered retroactivity, the Third Circuit did not, either. In a per curiam opinion without oral argument, the Supreme Court reversed:

> While it is of course a necessary prerequisite to federal habeas relief that a prisoner satisfy the AEDPA standard of review set forth in 28 U.S.C. § 2254(d) ("[a]n application . . . shall not be granted . . . *unless*" the AEDPA standard of review is satisfied (emphasis added)), none of our post-AEDPA cases have suggested that a writ of habeas corpus should automatically issue if a prisoner satisfies the AEDPA standard, or that AEDPA relieves courts of the responsibility for addressing properly raised *Teague* arguments. To the contrary, if our post-AEDPA cases suggest anything about AEDPA's relationship to *Teague*, it is that the AEDPA and *Teague* inquiries are distinct.

7. We have now encountered several contexts in which federal courts are asked to decide, not merely whether the defendant violated the law, but whether the violation was objectively unreasonable. The law of qualified immunity (Chapter 14) affords defendants in § 1983 and *Bivens* actions a defense to liability where their actions, although unlawful, did not violate "clearly established" law. That objective inquiry turns on whether the defendant's actions were unreasonable in light of existing law and precedent. Similarly, the retroactivity rules announced in *Teague* foreclose habeas relief when a prisoner's claim depends on a "new rule" of criminal procedure. Distinguishing between new rules and old rules requires an objective assessment of whether the state-court decision was unreasonable based on law and precedent in effect at the time the conviction and sentence became final.

Are there meaningful differences in the Court's approach to "unreasonable applications" of federal law under § 2254(d)(1), its objective standard in evaluating qualified immunity, and its standard for identifying "new rules" under *Teague*? Does each of these inquiries, at bottom, ask essentially the same question about the range of reasonable interpretations of existing precedent? Or does the Court's approach in some contexts strike you as more deferential than in others?

One important difference concerns the source of precedent that may be consulted in assessing the state of the law at the time of the defendant's actions. Section 2254(d)(1) explicitly limits the body of relevant federal law to determinations by "the Supreme Court of the United States." In qualified immunity cases, by contrast, officials' actions may be deemed objectively unreasonable based on the decisions of federal circuit courts of appeals. *See, e.g., Lane v. Franks*, 134 S. Ct. 2369 (2014), in which the Court's ruling on qualified immunity turned principally on the state of Eleventh Circuit precedent at the time of the defendant's actions.

Should there be meaningful differences in the Court's approach in each of those contexts? Should it matter, for example, that qualified immunity and *Teague*'s retroactivity rules were developed by judges in a common-law fashion, whereas § 2254(d)(1) was enacted by Congress? Should it matter that *Teague* and § 2254(d)(1) evaluate decisions by state-court judges, who have extensive legal training and ample time to consider their judgments, whereas qualified immunity evaluates decisions by executive officials such as police officers, who have less legal training and sometimes must make swift decisions on the fly? Should *Teague*'s exceptions for "watershed rules" and substantive rules be extended to qualified immunity and § 2254(d)(1) cases?

[4] Successive and Abusive Petitions

Consider this scenario: State prisoner files a habeas petition in federal court challenging his conviction. The petition is denied. Prisoner then files another petition challenging the same conviction. How should the new petition be treated?

At a minimum, the habeas court will apply the full array of restrictive doctrines and rules described in the preceding sections of this chapter. But is that enough? Should a second—or third, or fourth, or fifth—petition be denied on the ground of res judicata? Should the court be able to consider the petitioner's claims, but with limitations or constraints beyond those applied to an initial petition?

With the enactment of AEDPA, Congress substantially modified the applicable standards for abusive and successive petitions. In successive petitions, claims that have been previously denied will be dismissed without exception. 28 U.S.C. § 2244(b)(1). New claims *not* presented in an earlier application also must be denied, with two exceptions: (1) claims that rely "on a new rule of constitutional law, made retroactive to cases on collateral review by the Supreme Court," a clear reference to *Teague* and its exceptions; and (2) claims based on newly discovered evidence that, if proven, would establish a strong likelihood of actual innocence ("clear and convincing evidence" that, but for the error, "no reasonable factfinder would have found the applicant guilty"). Finally, before the district court can accept a successive or abusive petition, the court of appeals must determine that the petitioner has met the standard required by AEDPA. 28 U.S.C. § 2244(a).

Although they are beyond the scope of this chapter, these provisions of AEDPA raise numerous and intricate issues of construction and application, especially when they interact with other aspects of habeas law.

C. State Processes and Federal Habeas Review

As the preceding cases illustrate, the Supreme Court and Congress have developed doctrines and rules that attempt to mitigate the tensions that arise between the state and federal systems when a state-court judgment is evaluated by a lower federal court. Some of those rules require respect for the substantive decisions of state courts. The standard of review in §2254(d)(1) is a good example: it requires that, before issuing the writ, the federal court must determine that the state court's application of a Supreme Court precedent was not simply erroneous, but *unreasonable*.

Other doctrines require respect for the *processes* of state courts. These doctrines take several forms. First, both the habeas statute and the Supreme Court insist that the habeas petitioner first present his constitutional claims to the state courts before they will be considered by the federal courts. Accordingly, the petitioner is required to exhaust all available state remedies before filing a habeas petition. Second, petitioners are required to comply with state procedural rules in presenting their claims in state court. If a petitioner fails to follow a state procedural rule and, as a consequence, the state court finds that his claims are forfeited, the federal court ordinarily will also refuse to consider the claims. Third, even claims that have been perfectly preserved and exhausted must be dismissed if the federal court deems the error harmless. Fourth, the habeas statute requires that federal habeas courts give special deference to state-court factfinding.

As we examine each of these areas, consider whether the doctrines enforcing respect for state courts strike the correct balance between that concern and the underlying purposes of the habeas remedy.

[1] Exhaustion of State Remedies

A state prisoner who wishes to challenge his conviction through federal habeas corpus must exhaust all available state remedies before seeking relief in federal court. This requirement originated in the Supreme Court's decision in *Ex parte Royall*, 117 U.S. 241 (1886); it was codified by Congress in 1948. Today the statutory rules are set forth in 28 U.S.C. §§2254(b) and (c).

The law of exhaustion is complex and evolving. Here we look at the broad outlines of the requirement.

1. The exhaustion requirement is grounded in comity concerns. It exists to assure that the state courts have "a meaningful opportunity to consider allegations of legal error without interference from the federal judiciary." *Vasquez v. Hillery*, 474 U.S. 254 (1986). The Court elaborated on this point in *Rose v. Lundy*, 455 U.S. 509 (1982):

> The exhaustion doctrine is principally designed to protect the state court's role in the enforcement of federal law and prevent disruption of state judicial proceedings. Under our federal system, the federal and state "courts [are] equally bound to guard and protect rights secured by the Constitution." *Ex parte Royall*. Because "it would be unseemly in our dual system of government for a federal district court to upset a state-court conviction without an opportunity to the state courts to correct a constitutional violation," federal courts apply the doctrine of comity, which "teaches that one court should defer action on causes properly within its jurisdiction until the courts of another sovereignty with concurrent powers, and already cognizant of the

litigation, have had an opportunity to pass upon the matter." *Darr v. Burford*, 339 U.S. 200 (1950). [T]he exhaustion requirement "serves to minimize friction between our federal and state systems of justice by allowing the State an initial opportunity to pass upon and correct alleged violations of prisoners' federal rights."

2. In AEDPA, Congress made substantial changes to the statutory provisions governing exhaustion. The basic rule remains the same: the federal habeas court may not grant the writ unless the applicant "has exhausted the remedies available in the courts of the State." § 2254(b)(1)(A). And the statute continues to specify two exceptions. The bar will be excused if "there is an absence of available State corrective process" or if "circumstances exist that render such process ineffective to protect the rights of the applicant." § 2254(b)(1)(B).

AEDPA added two provisions. First, the statute limits the circumstances in which the habeas court may find that the state has waived the exhaustion requirement. Waiver may be found only if "the State, through counsel, expressly waives the requirement." § 2254(b)(3). Second, and more important, the statute permits a federal habeas court to *deny* (but not to grant) a petition on the merits despite the petitioner's failure to exhaust state remedies. § 2254(b)(2). Under the prior law, the habeas court was required to send the petitioner on a futile journey back to the state court even when the claims in the petition were plainly without merit. Moreover, in some cases the merits question will be easy (i.e., easily resolved against the petitioner), while the exhaustion issue will implicate murky areas of state procedure. The new law enables the habeas court to bypass the procedural morass and deny relief when it is clear that the petitioner's claims must fail.

3. What happens if the prisoner files a "mixed" petition—a petition that contains some claims that have been presented to the state courts and some that have not? In *Rose v. Lundy*, the Court adopted a "total exhaustion" rule. Under that rule, a federal district court must dismiss a habeas petition as long as it contains *any* claims "that have not been exhausted in the state courts." The Court explained the policy behind the rule:

> A rigorously enforced total exhaustion rule will encourage state prisoners to seek full relief first from the state courts, thus giving those courts the first opportunity to review all claims of constitutional error. As the number of prisoners who exhaust all of their federal claims increases, state courts may become increasingly familiar with and hospitable toward federal constitutional issues. Equally as important, federal claims that have been fully exhausted in state courts will more often be accompanied by a complete factual record to aid the federal courts in their review.

Habeas petitioners who file mixed petitions have two choices under *Rose*: "Those prisoners who misunderstand this requirement and submit mixed petitions nevertheless are entitled to resubmit a petition with only exhausted claims or to exhaust the remainder of their claims."

4. Subsequent to the Court's decision in *Rose*, Congress enacted AEDPA, which imposes a one-year statute of limitations for filing a federal habeas corpus petition.

See 28 U.S.C. § 2244(d)(1). The combined effect of *Rose* and AEDPA's limitations period is that if a petitioner comes to federal court with a mixed petition toward the end of the limitations period, a dismissal of his mixed petition could result in the loss of all of his claims—including those already exhausted—because the limitations period could expire during the time a petitioner returns to state court to exhaust his unexhausted claims.

In *Rhines v. Weber*, 544 U.S. 269 (2005), the Court upheld the validity of a procedure designed to overcome this problem. The Court began by explaining the background of the question before it:

> As a result of the interplay between AEDPA's 1-year statute of limitations and [*Rose v.*] *Lundy*'s dismissal requirement, petitioners who come to federal court with "mixed" petitions run the risk of forever losing their opportunity for any federal review of their unexhausted claims. If a petitioner files a timely but mixed petition in federal district court, and the district court dismisses it under *Lundy* after the limitations period has expired, this will likely mean the termination of any federal review. . . . The problem is not limited to petitioners who file close to the AEDPA deadline. Even a petitioner who files early will have no way of controlling when the district court will resolve the question of exhaustion. Thus, whether a petitioner ever receives federal review of his claims may turn on which district court happens to hear his case.
>
> We recognize the gravity of this problem and the difficulty it has posed for petitioners and federal district courts alike. In an attempt to solve the problem, some district courts have adopted a version of the "stay-and-abeyance" procedure. . . . Under this procedure, rather than dismiss the mixed petition pursuant to *Lundy*, a district court might stay the petition and hold it in abeyance while the petitioner returns to state court to exhaust his previously unexhausted claims. Once the petitioner exhausts his state remedies, the district court will lift the stay and allow the petitioner to proceed in federal court.

The Court then held that district courts have the discretion to hold a "mixed" petition on their dockets while the habeas petitioner returns to state court to exhaust his unexhausted claims. However, in order to assure that AEDPA's "twin purposes" of encouraging finality and streamlining habeas proceedings, the Court held that the stay-and-abeyance procedure "is only appropriate when the district court determines there was good cause for the petitioner's failure to exhaust his claims first in state court. Moreover, even if a petitioner had good cause for that failure, the district court would abuse its discretion if it were to grant him a stay when his unexhausted claims are plainly meritless." Finally, "a mixed petition should not be stayed indefinitely. In particular, capital petitioners might deliberately engage in dilatory tactics to prolong their incarceration and avoid execution of the sentence of death. Without time limits, petitioners could frustrate AEDPA's goal of finality by dragging out indefinitely their federal habeas review. Thus, district courts should place reasonable time limits on a petitioner's trip to state court and back. And if a petitioner engages in abusive litigation tactics or intentional delay, the district court should not grant him a stay at all."

[2] Effect of State Procedural Default

Wainwright v. Sykes

Supreme Court of the United States, 1977.

433 U.S. 72.

Mr. Justice Rehnquist delivered the opinion of the Court.

We granted certiorari to consider the availability of federal habeas corpus to review a state convict's claim that testimony was admitted at his trial in violation of his rights under *Miranda v. Arizona*, 384 U.S. 436 (1966), a claim which the Florida courts have previously refused to consider on the merits because of noncompliance with a state contemporaneous-objection rule. Petitioner Wainwright, on behalf of the State of Florida, here challenges a decision of the Court of Appeals for the Fifth Circuit ordering a hearing in state court on the merits of respondent's contention.

Respondent Sykes was convicted of third-degree murder after a jury trial in the Circuit Court of DeSoto County. He testified at trial that on the evening of January 8, 1972, he told his wife to summon the police because he had just shot Willie Gilbert. Other evidence indicated that when the police arrived at respondent's trailer home, they found Gilbert dead of a shotgun wound, lying a few feet from the front porch. Shortly after their arrival, respondent came from across the road and volunteered that he had shot Gilbert, and a few minutes later respondent's wife approached the police and told them the same thing. Sykes was immediately arrested and taken to the police station.

Once there, it is conceded that he was read his *Miranda* rights, and that he declined to seek the aid of counsel and indicated a desire to talk. He then made a statement, which was admitted into evidence at trial through the testimony of the two officers who heard it, to the effect that he had shot Gilbert from the front porch of his trailer home. There were several references during the trial to respondent's consumption of alcohol during the preceding day and to his apparent state of intoxication, facts which were acknowledged by the officers who arrived at the scene. At no time during the trial, however, was the admissibility of any of respondent's statements challenged by his counsel on the ground that respondent had not understood the *Miranda* warnings. Nor did the trial judge question their admissibility on his own motion or hold a factfinding hearing bearing on that issue.

Respondent appealed his conviction, but apparently did not challenge the admissibility of the inculpatory statements. He later filed in the trial court a motion to vacate the conviction and, in the State District Court of Appeals and Supreme Court, petitions for habeas corpus. These filings, apparently for the first time, challenged the statements made to police on grounds of involuntariness. In all of these efforts respondent was unsuccessful.

Having failed in the Florida courts, respondent initiated the present action under 28 U.S.C. § 2254, asserting the inadmissibility of his statements by reason of his lack of understanding of the *Miranda* warnings. The United States District Court for the

Middle District of Florida ruled that [the *Miranda* claim was meritorious]. It held further that respondent had not lost his right to assert such a claim by failing to object at trial or on direct appeal, since only "exceptional circumstances" of "strategic decisions at trial" can create such a bar to raising federal constitutional claims in a federal habeas action. The court stayed issuance of the writ to allow the state court to hold a hearing on the "voluntariness" of the statements.

Petitioner warden appealed this decision to the United States Court of Appeals for the Fifth Circuit. That court first considered the nature of the right to exclusion of statements made without a knowing waiver of the right to counsel and the right not to incriminate oneself. . . .

The court then directed its attention to the effect on respondent's right of Florida Rule Crim. Proc. 3.190(i),[5] which it described as "a contemporaneous objection rule" applying to motions to suppress a defendant's inculpatory statements. It focused on this Court's decisions in *Henry v. Mississippi*, 379 U.S. 443 (1965); *Davis v. United States*, 411 U.S. 233 (1973); and *Fay v. Noia*, 372 U.S. 391 (1963), and concluded that the failure to comply with the rule requiring objection at the trial would only bar review of the suppression claim where the right to object was deliberately bypassed for reasons relating to trial tactics. . . .

. . . Where [a] habeas petitioner challenges a final judgment of conviction rendered by a state court, this Court has been called upon to decide no fewer than four different questions, all to a degree interrelated with one another: (1) What types of federal claims may a federal habeas court properly consider? (2) Where a federal claim is cognizable by a federal habeas court, to what extent must that court defer to a resolution of the claim in prior state proceedings? (3) To what extent must the petitioner who seeks federal habeas exhaust state remedies before resorting to the federal court? (4) In what instances will an adequate and independent state ground bar consideration of otherwise cognizable federal issues on federal habeas review?

Each of these four issues has spawned its share of litigation. [Justice Rehnquist summarized the development of the law on the first three questions.]

As to the role of adequate and independent state grounds, it is a well-established principle of federalism that a state decision resting on an adequate foundation of state substantive law is immune from review in the federal courts. *Fox Film Corp. v. Muller*, 296 U.S. 207 (1935) [Chapter 5]; *Murdock v. Memphis*, 20 Wall. 590 (1875) [Chapter 4]. The application of this principle in the context of a federal habeas proceeding

---

5. Rule 3.190(i):

Motion to Suppress a Confession or Admissions Illegally Obtained.

    (1) Grounds. Upon motion of the defendant or upon its own motion, the court shall suppress any confession or admission obtained illegally from the defendant.

    (2) Time for Filing. The motion to suppress shall be made prior to trial unless opportunity therefor did not exist or the defendant was not aware of the grounds for the motion, but the court in its discretion may entertain the motion or an appropriate objection at the trial.

    (3) Hearing. The court shall receive evidence on any issue of fact necessary to be decided in order to rule on the motion.

has therefore excluded from consideration any questions of state substantive law, and thus effectively barred federal habeas review where questions of that sort are either the only ones raised by a petitioner or are in themselves dispositive of his case. The area of controversy which has developed has concerned the reviewability of federal claims which the state court has declined to pass on because not presented in the manner prescribed by its procedural rules. The adequacy of such an independent state procedural ground to prevent federal habeas review of the underlying federal issue has been treated very differently than where the state-law ground is substantive. . . .

In *Fay v. Noia*, respondent Noia sought federal habeas to review a claim that his state-court conviction had resulted from the introduction of a coerced confession in violation of the Fifth Amendment to the United States Constitution. While the convictions of his two codefendants were reversed on that ground in collateral proceedings following their appeals, Noia did not appeal and the New York courts ruled that his subsequent coram nobis action was barred on account of that failure. This Court held that petitioner was nonetheless entitled to raise the claim in federal habeas[:]

> [T]he doctrine under which state procedural defaults are held to constitute an adequate and independent state law ground barring direct Supreme Court review is not to be extended to limit the power granted the federal courts under the federal habeas statute.

As a matter of comity but not of federal power, the Court acknowledged "a limited discretion in the federal judge to deny relief . . . to an applicant who had deliberately by-passed the orderly procedure of the state courts and in so doing has forfeited his state court remedies." In so stating, the Court made clear that the waiver must be knowing and actual—"'an intentional relinquishment or abandonment of a known right or privilege.'" Noting petitioner's "grisly choice" between acceptance of his life sentence and pursuit of an appeal which might culminate in a sentence of death, the Court concluded that there had been no deliberate bypass of the right to have the federal issues reviewed through a state appeal.

A decade later we decided *Davis v. United States*, in which a federal prisoner's application under 28 U.S.C. § 2255 sought for the first time to challenge the makeup of the grand jury which indicted him. The Government contended that he was barred by the requirement of Fed. Rule Crim. Proc. 12(b)(2) providing that such challenges must be raised "by motion before trial." The Rule further provides that failure to so object constitutes a waiver of the objection, but that "the court for cause shown may grant relief from the waiver." We noted that the Rule "promulgated by this Court and . . . 'adopted' by Congress, governs by its terms the manner in which the claims of defects in the institution of criminal proceedings may be waived," and held that this standard contained in the Rule, rather than the *Fay v. Noia* concept of waiver, should pertain in federal habeas as on direct review. Referring to previous constructions of Rule 12(b)(2), we concluded that review of the claim should be barred on habeas, as on direct appeal, absent a showing of cause for the noncompliance and some showing of actual prejudice resulting from the alleged constitutional violation.

Last Term, in *Francis v. Henderson*, 425 U.S. 536 (1976), the rule of *Davis* was applied to the parallel case of a state procedural requirement that challenges to grand jury composition be raised before trial. [The Court concluded that] "[t]here is no reason to . . . give greater preclusive effect to procedural defaults by federal defendants than to similar defaults by state defendants." As applied to the federal petitions of state convicts, the *Davis* cause-and-prejudice standard was thus incorporated directly into the body of law governing the availability of federal habeas corpus review.

To the extent that the dicta of *Fay v. Noia* may be thought to have laid down an all-inclusive rule rendering state contemporaneous-objection rules ineffective to bar review of underlying federal claims in federal habeas proceedings absent a "knowing waiver" or a "deliberate bypass" of the right to so object its effect was limited by *Francis*, which applied a different rule and barred a habeas challenge to the makeup of a grand jury. Petitioner Wainwright in this case urges that we further confine its effect by applying the principle enunciated in *Francis* to a claimed error in the admission of a defendant's confession. . . .

[The Court rejected petitioner's claim that Florida did not have a contemporaneous objection rule.]

We therefore conclude that Florida procedure did, consistently with the United States Constitution, require that respondents' confession be challenged at trial or not at all, and thus his failure to timely object to its admission amounted to an independent and adequate state procedural ground which would have prevented direct review here. See *Henry v. Mississippi*, 379 U.S. 443 (1965). We thus come to the crux of this case. Shall the rule of *Francis v. Henderson*, barring federal habeas review absent a showing of "cause" and "prejudice" attendant to a state procedural waiver, be applied to a waived objection to the admission of a confession at trial? We answer that question in the affirmative.

[S]ince *Brown v. Allen*, 344 U.S. 443 (1953), it has been the rule that the federal habeas petitioner who claims he is detained pursuant to a final judgment of a state court in violation of the United States Constitution is entitled to have the federal habeas court make its own independent determination of his federal claim, without being bound by the determination on the merits of that claim reached in the state proceedings. This rule of *Brown v. Allen* is in no way changed by our holding today. Rather, we deal only with contentions of federal law which were not resolved on the merits in the state proceeding due to respondent's failure to raise them there as required by state procedure. We leave open for resolution in future decisions the precise definition of the "cause"-and-"prejudice" standard, and note here only that it is narrower than the standard set forth in dicta in *Fay v. Noia*, which would make federal habeas review generally available to state convicts absent a knowing and deliberate waiver of the federal constitutional contention. It is the sweeping language of *Fay v. Noia*, going far beyond the facts of the case eliciting it, which we today reject.

The reasons for our rejection of it are several. The contemporaneous-objection rule itself is by no means peculiar to Florida, and deserves greater respect than *Fay* gives it, both for the fact that it is employed by a coordinate jurisdiction within the federal system and for the many interests which it serves in its own right. A contemporaneous objection enables the record to be made with respect to the constitutional claim when the recollections of witnesses are freshest, not years later in a federal habeas proceeding. It enables the judge who observed the demeanor of those witnesses to make the factual determinations necessary for properly deciding the federal constitutional question. While the 1966 amendment to § 2254 requires deference to be given to such determinations made by state courts, the determinations themselves are less apt to be made in the first instance if there is no contemporaneous objection to the admission of the evidence on federal constitutional grounds.

A contemporaneous-objection rule may lead to the exclusion of the evidence objected to, thereby making a major contribution to finality in criminal litigation. Without the evidence claimed to be vulnerable on federal constitutional grounds, the jury may acquit the defendant, and that will be the end of the case; or it may nonetheless convict the defendant, and he will have one less federal constitutional claim to assert in his federal habeas petition. If the state trial judge admits the evidence in question after a full hearing, the federal habeas court ... will gain significant guidance from the state ruling in this regard. Subtler considerations as well militate in favor of honoring a state contemporaneous-objection rule. An objection on the spot may force the prosecution to take a hard look at its whole card, and even if the prosecutor thinks that the state trial judge will admit the evidence he must contemplate the possibility of reversal by the state appellate courts or the ultimate issuance of a federal writ of habeas corpus based on the impropriety of the state court's rejection of the federal constitutional claim.

We think that the rule of *Fay v. Noia*, broadly stated, may encourage "sandbagging" on the part of defense lawyers, who may take their chances on a verdict of not guilty in a state trial court with the intent to raise their constitutional claims in a federal habeas court if their initial gamble does not pay off. The refusal of federal habeas courts to honor contemporaneous-objection rules may also make state courts themselves less stringent in their enforcement. Under the rule of *Fay v. Noia*, state appellate courts know that a federal constitutional issue raised for the first time in the proceeding before them may well be decided in any event by a federal habeas tribunal. Thus, their choice is between addressing the issue notwithstanding the petitioner's failure to timely object, or else face the prospect that the federal habeas court will decide the question without the benefit of their views.

The failure of the federal habeas courts generally to require compliance with a contemporaneous-objection rule tends to detract from the perception of the trial of a criminal case in state court as a decisive and portentous event. A defendant has been accused of a serious crime, and this is the time and place set for him to be tried by a jury of his peers and found either guilty or not guilty by that jury. To the greatest extent possible all issues which bear on this charge should be determined in this proceeding: the accused is in the court-room, the jury is in the box, the judge is on the bench, and the witnesses, having been subpoenaed and duly sworn, await their turn to testify. Society's resources have been concentrated at that time and place in order to decide, within the limits of human fallibility, the question of guilt or innocence of one of its citizens. Any procedural rule which encourages the result that those proceedings be as free of error as possible is thoroughly desirable, and the contemporaneous-objection rule surely falls within this classification.

We believe the adoption of the *Francis* rule in this situation will have the salutary effect of making the state trial on the merits the "main event," so to speak, rather than a "tryout on the road" for what will later be the determinative federal habeas hearing. There is nothing in the Constitution or in the language of § 2254 which requires that the state trial on the issue of guilt or innocence be devoted largely to the testimony of fact witnesses directed to the elements of the state crime, while only later will there occur in a federal habeas hearing a full airing of the federal constitutional claims which were not raised in the state proceedings. If a criminal defendant thinks that an action of the state trial court is about to deprive him of a federal constitutional right there is every reason for his following state procedure in making known his objection.

The "cause"-and-"prejudice" exception . . . will afford an adequate guarantee, we think, that the rule will not prevent a federal habeas court from adjudicating for the first time the federal constitutional claim of a defendant who in the absence of such an adjudication will be the victim of a miscarriage of justice. Whatever precise content may be given those terms by later cases, we feel confident in holding without further elaboration that they do not exist here. Respondent has advanced no explanation whatever for his failure to object at trial,[14] and, as the proceeding unfolded, the trial judge is certainly not to be faulted for failing to question the admission of the confession himself. The other evidence of guilt presented at trial, moreover, was substantial to a degree that would negate any possibility of actual prejudice resulting to the respondent from the admission of his inculpatory statement.

We accordingly conclude that the judgment of the Court of Appeals for the Fifth Circuit must be reversed, and the cause remanded to the United States District Court for the Middle District of Florida with instructions to dismiss respondent's petition for a writ of habeas corpus.

MR. CHIEF JUSTICE BURGER, concurring.

I concur fully in the judgment and in the Court's opinion. I write separately to emphasize one point which, to me, seems of critical importance to this case. In my view, the "deliberate bypass" standard enunciated in *Fay v. Noia* was never designed for, and is inapplicable to, errors even of constitutional dimension alleged to have been committed during trial.

---

14. In *Henry v. Mississippi*, the Court noted that decisions of counsel relating to trial strategy, even when made without the consultation of the defendant, would bar direct federal review of claims thereby forgone, except where "the circumstances are exceptional." Last Term in *Estelle v. Williams*, the Court reiterated the burden on a defendant to be bound by the trial judgments of his lawyer:

> Under our adversary system, once a defendant has the assistance of counsel the vast array of trial decisions, strategic and tactical, which must be made before and during trial rests with the accused and his attorney.

The touchstone of *Fay* . . . is the exercise of volition by the defendant himself with respect to his own federal constitutional rights. In contrast, the claim in the case before us relates to events during the trial itself. . . .

Once counsel is appointed, the day-to-day conduct of the defense rests with the attorney. He, not the client, has the immediate and ultimate responsibility of deciding if and when to object, which witnesses, if any, to call, and what defenses to develop. Not only do these decisions rest with the attorney, but such decisions must, as a practical matter, be made without consulting the client. The trial process simply does not permit the type of frequent and protracted interruptions which would be necessary if it were required that clients give knowing and intelligent approval to each of the myriad tactical decisions as a trial proceeds.

Since trial decisions are of necessity entrusted to the accused's attorney, the [*Fay v. Noia*] standard of "knowing and intelligent waiver" is simply inapplicable. The dissent in this case, written by the author of *Fay v. Noia*, implicitly recognizes as much . . . I would leave the core holding of *Fay* where it began, and reject this illogical uprooting of an otherwise defensible doctrine.

MR. JUSTICE STEVENS, concurring.

Although the Court's decision today may be read as a significant departure from the "deliberate bypass" standard announced in *Fay v. Noia*, I am persuaded that the holding is consistent with the way other federal courts have actually been applying *Fay*. The notion that a client must always consent to a tactical decision not to assert a constitutional objection to a proffer of evidence has always seemed unrealistic to me. Conversely, if the constitutional issue is sufficiently grave, even an express waiver by the defendant himself may sometimes be excused. Matters such as the competence of counsel, the procedural context in which the asserted waiver occurred, the character of the constitutional right at stake, and the overall fairness of the entire proceeding, may be more significant than the language of the test the Court purports to apply. I therefore believe the Court has wisely refrained from attempting to give precise content to its "cause"-and-"prejudice" exception. . . .

MR. JUSTICE WHITE, concurring in the judgment. [Omitted.]

MR. JUSTICE BRENNAN, with whom MR. JUSTICE MARSHALL joins, dissenting.

Over the course of the last decade, the deliberate-bypass standard announced in *Fay v. Noia* has played a central role in efforts by the federal judiciary to accommodate the constitutional rights of the individual with the States' interests in the integrity of their judicial procedural regimes. The Court today decides that this standard should no longer apply with respect to procedural defaults occurring during the trial of a criminal defendant. In its place, the Court adopts the two-part "cause"-and-"prejudice" test originally developed in *Davis v. United States* and *Francis v. Henderson*. As was true with these earlier cases, however, today's decision makes no effort to provide concrete guidance as to the content of those terms. More particularly, left unanswered is the thorny question that must be recognized to be central to a realistic rationalization of this area of law: How should the federal habeas court treat a procedural default in a state court that is attributable purely and simply to the error or negligence of a defendant's trial counsel? . . .

I

I begin with the threshold question: What is the meaning and import of a procedural default? If it could be assumed that a procedural default more often than not is the product of a defendant's conscious refusal to abide by the duly constituted, legitimate processes of the state courts, then I might agree that a regime of collateral review weighted in favor of a State's procedural rules would be warranted. *Fay*, however, recognized that such rarely is the case; and therein lies *Fay*'s basic unwillingness to embrace a view of habeas jurisdiction that results in "an airtight system of [procedural] forfeitures."

This, of course, is not to deny that there are times when the failure to heed a state procedural requirement stems from an intentional decision to avoid the presentation of constitutional claims to the state forum. . . . [But in] the ordinary case, litigants simply have no incentive to slight the state tribunal, since constitutional adjudication on the state and federal levels are not mutually exclusive. Under the regime of collateral review . . . enforced by the *Fay* bypass test, no rational lawyer would risk the "sandbagging" feared by the Court.[5] If a constitutional challenge is not properly raised on the state level, the explanation generally will be found elsewhere than in an intentional tactical decision.

In brief then, any realistic system of federal habeas corpus jurisdiction must be premised on the reality that the ordinary procedural default is born of the inadvertence, negligence, inexperience, or incompetence of trial counsel. The case under consideration today is typical. The Court makes no effort to identify a tactical motive for the failure of Sykes' attorney to challenge the admissibility or reliability of a highly inculpatory statement. . . . Indeed, there is no basis for inferring that Sykes or his state trial lawyer was even aware of the existence of his claim under the Fifth Amendment; for this is not a case where the trial judge expressly drew the attention of the defense to a possible constitutional contention or procedural requirement, or where the defense signals its knowledge of a constitutional claim by abandoning a challenge previously raised. Rather, any realistic reading of the record demonstrates that we are faced here with a lawyer's simple error.

---

5. . . . This presumably means, first, that [the defense lawyer] would hold back the presentation of his constitutional claim to the trial court, thereby increasing the likelihood of a conviction since the prosecution would be able to present evidence that, while arguably constitutionally deficient, may be highly prejudicial to the defense. Second, he would thereby have forfeited all state review and remedies with respect to these claims (subject to whatever "plain error" rule is available). Third, to carry out his scheme he would now be compelled to deceive the federal habeas court and to convince the judge that he did not "deliberately bypass" the state procedures. If he loses on this gamble, all federal review would be barred, and his "sandbagging" would have resulted in nothing but the forfeiture of all judicial review of his client's claims. The Court, without substantiation, apparently believes that a meaningful number of lawyers are induced into [this behavior] by *Fay*. I do not. That belief simply offends common sense.

Fay's answer thus is plain: the bypass test simply refuses to credit what is essentially a lawyer's mistake as a forfeiture of constitutional rights. I persist in the belief that the interests of Sykes and the State of Florida are best rationalized by adherence to this test, and by declining to react to inadvertent defaults through the creation of an "airtight system of forfeitures."

II

What are the interests that Sykes can assert in preserving the availability of federal collateral relief in the face of his inadvertent state procedural default? Two are paramount....

With respect to federal habeas corpus jurisdiction, Congress explicitly chose to effectuate the federal court's primary responsibility for preserving federal rights and privileges by authorizing the litigation of constitutional claims and defenses in a district court after the State vindicates its own interest through trial of the substantive criminal offense in the state courts....

... If the standard adopted today is later construed to require that the simple mistakes of attorneys are to be treated as binding forfeitures, it would serve to subordinate the fundamental rights contained in our constitutional charter to inadvertent defaults of rules promulgated by state agencies, and would essentially leave it to the States, through the enactment of procedure and the certification of the competence of local attorneys, to determine whether a habeas applicant will be permitted the access to the federal forum that is guaranteed him by Congress.

... [Federal] review is not the full measure of Sykes' interest, for there is another of even greater immediacy: assuring that his constitutional claims can be addressed to some court. For the obvious consequence of barring Sykes from the federal courthouse is to insulate Florida's alleged constitutional violation from any and all judicial review because of a lawyer's mistake. From the standpoint of the habeas petitioner, it is a harsh rule indeed that denies him "any review at all where the state has granted none," *Brown v. Allen* (Black, J., dissenting), particularly when he would have enjoyed both state and federal consideration had his attorney not erred....

III

A regime of federal habeas corpus jurisdiction that permits the reopening of state procedural defaults does not invalidate any state procedural rule as such; Florida's courts remain entirely free to enforce their own rules as they choose, and to deny any and all state rights and remedies to a defendant who fails to comply with applicable state procedure. The relevant inquiry is whether more is required—specifically, whether the fulfillment of important interests of the State necessitates that federal courts be called upon to impose additional sanctions for inadvertent noncompliance with state procedural requirements such as the contemporaneous-objection rule involved here....

Punishing a lawyer's unintentional errors by closing the federal courthouse door to his client is both a senseless and misdirected method of deterring the slighting of state rules. It is senseless because unplanned and unintentional action of any kind generally is not subject to deterrence; and, to the extent that it is hoped that a threatened sanction addressed to the defense will induce greater care and caution on the part of trial lawyers, thereby forestalling negligent conduct or error, the potential loss of all valuable state remedies would be sufficient to this end. And it is a misdirected sanction because even if the penalization of incompetence or carelessness will encourage more thorough legal training and trial preparation, the habeas applicant, as opposed to his lawyer, hardly is the proper recipient of such a penalty.

Especially with fundamental constitutional rights at stake, no fictional relationship of principal-agent or the like can justify holding the criminal defendant accountable for the naked errors of his attorney. This is especially true when so many indigent defendants are without any realistic choice in selecting who ultimately represents them at trial. Indeed, if responsibility for error must be apportioned between the parties, it is the State, through its attorney's admissions and certification policies, that is more fairly held to blame for the fact that practicing lawyers too often are ill-prepared or ill-equipped to act carefully and knowledgeably when faced with decisions governed by state procedural requirements. . . .

In short, I believe that the demands of our criminal justice system warrant visiting the mistakes of a trial attorney on the head of a habeas corpus applicant only when we are convinced that the lawyer actually exercised his expertise and judgment in his client's service, and with his client's knowing and intelligent participation where possible. This, of course, is the precise system of habeas review established by *Fay v. Noia*. . . .

Note: Procedural Foreclosure of Constitutional Claims and the "Cause and Prejudice" Standard

1. The *Wainwright v. Sykes* Court treats a state court's reliance on a procedural ground to avoid deciding a constitutional claim as an independent and adequate state ground that would ordinarily preclude review of that claim by a federal habeas court. In *Coleman v. Thompson*, 501 U.S. 722 (1991), Justice O'Connor, writing for the Court, explained the difference between the ordinary application of that doctrine and its application in habeas:

> This Court will not review a question of federal law decided by a state court if the decision of that court rests on a state law ground that is independent of the federal question and adequate to support the judgment. *See, e.g., Fox Film Corp. v. Muller*, 296 U.S. 207 (1935) [Chapter 5]. This rule applies whether the state law ground is substantive or procedural. In the context of direct review of a state court judgment, the independent and adequate state ground doctrine is jurisdictional. Because this Court has no power to review a state law determination that is sufficient to support the judgment, resolution of any independent federal ground for the decision could not affect the judgment and would therefore be advisory. . . .

> The basis for application of the independent and adequate state ground doctrine in federal habeas is somewhat different than on direct review by this Court. When this Court reviews a state court decision on direct review

pursuant to 28 U.S.C. § 1257, it is reviewing the *judgment*; if resolution of a federal question cannot affect the judgment, there is nothing for the Court to do. This is not the case in habeas. When a federal district court reviews a state prisoner's habeas corpus petition pursuant to 28 U.S.C. § 2254, it must decide whether the petitioner is "in custody in violation of the Constitution or laws or treaties of the United States." The court does not review a judgment, but the lawfulness of the petitioner's custody *simpliciter*.

Nonetheless, a state prisoner is in custody *pursuant* to a judgment. When a federal habeas court releases a prisoner held pursuant to a state court judgment that rests on an independent and adequate state ground, it renders ineffective the state rule just as completely as if this Court had reversed the state judgment on direct review. In such a case, the habeas court ignores the State's legitimate reasons for holding the prisoner.

In the habeas context, the application of the independent and adequate state ground doctrine is grounded in concerns of comity and federalism. Without the rule, a federal district court would be able to do in habeas what this Court could not do on direct review; habeas would offer state prisoners whose custody was supported by independent and adequate state grounds an end run around the limits of this Court's jurisdiction and a means to undermine the State's interest in enforcing its laws.

When the independent and adequate state ground supporting a habeas petitioner's custody is a state procedural default, an additional concern comes into play. This Court has long held that a state prisoner's federal habeas petition should be dismissed if the prisoner has not exhausted available state remedies as to any of his federal claims. This exhaustion requirement is also grounded in principles of comity; in a federal system, the States should have the first opportunity to address and correct alleged violations of state prisoner's federal rights.

The [same concerns that apply to exhaustion] apply to federal claims that have been procedurally defaulted in state court. Just as in those cases in which a state prisoner fails to exhaust state remedies, a habeas petitioner who has failed to meet the State's procedural requirements for presenting his federal claims has deprived the state courts of an opportunity to address those claims in the first instance. A habeas petitioner who has defaulted his federal claims in state court meets the technical requirements for exhaustion; there are no state remedies any longer "available" to him. In the absence of the independent and adequate state ground doctrine in federal habeas, habeas petitioners would be able to avoid the exhaustion requirement by defaulting their federal claims in state court. The independent and adequate state ground doctrine ensures that the States' interest in correcting their own mistakes is respected in all federal habeas cases.

2. In *Michigan v. Long*, 463 U.S. 1032 (1983) (Chapter 5), the Court held that "when the adequacy and independence of any possible state law ground is not clear from the

face of the opinion," the Court will presume that the state court rested its decision on federal law. But in *Coleman*, the Court reversed this presumption for habeas cases, stating that unless "the decision of the last state court to which the petitioner presented his federal claims . . . fairly appears to rest primarily on federal law or to be interwoven with federal law," the Court will presume that the decision rests on state law. What differences between habeas and direct review would justify this approach?

3. *Coleman* confirmed what was only implicit in *Wainwright v. Sykes*: that state procedural default will bar federal habeas review only if the state-court ruling on the procedural ground satisfies both the "independence" and "adequacy" prongs of the test applied on direct review. The Court applied this rule in *Lee v. Kemna*, 534 U.S. 362 (2002). See Chapter 5 for a brief summary of *Lee*.

4. In *Coleman*, the Supreme Court explicitly overruled *Fay v. Noia* and held that the "cause and prejudice" standard applies to all procedural defaults. This included the default in that case, through which the petitioner lost his right to appeal in state court.

5. After *Wainwright v. Sykes*, a procedurally defaulted claim—one that the state courts refused to hear because the habeas petitioner failed to comply with a procedural rule—may be considered by a federal court in habeas only if the petitioner can demonstrate "cause for the noncompliance and some showing of actual prejudice resulting from the alleged constitutional violation."

6. What constitutes "cause"? As *Wainwright v. Sykes* suggested, many procedural defaults occur because of attorney conduct. In *Murray v. Carrier*, 477 U.S. 478 (1986), the Court held that attorney mistakes that do not constitute constitutionally ineffective assistance of counsel under the standards of *Strickland v. Washington*, 466 U.S. 668 (1984) are not "cause" for a procedural default. In an opinion by Justice O'Connor, the Court reasoned:

> [T]he mere fact that counsel failed to recognize the factual or legal basis for a claim, or failed to raise the claim despite recognizing it, does not constitute cause for a procedural default. At least with respect to defaults that occur at trial, [a] holding that ignorant or inadvertent attorney error is cause for any resulting procedural default is plainly inconsistent with . . . the purposes served by the cause and prejudice standard. That standard rests not only on the need to deter intentional defaults but on a judgment that the costs of federal habeas review "are particularly high when a trial default has barred a prisoner from obtaining adjudication of his constitutional claim in the state courts." *Engle v. Isaac*, 456 U.S. 107 (1982). Those costs, which include a reduction in the finality of litigation and the frustration of "both the States' sovereign power to punish offenders and their good-faith attempts to honor constitutional rights," *ibid.*, are heightened in several respects when a trial default occurs: the default deprives the trial court of an opportunity to correct any error without retrial, detracts from the importance of the trial itself, gives state appellate courts no chance to review trial errors, and "exacts an extra charge by undercutting the State's ability to enforce its procedural rules." Clearly, these considerable costs do not disappear when the default stems from

counsel's ignorance or inadvertence rather than from a deliberate decision, for whatever reason, to withhold a claim. . . .

We think, then, that the question of cause for a procedural default does not turn on whether counsel erred or on the kind of error counsel may have made. So long as a defendant is represented by counsel whose performance is not constitutionally ineffective under the standard established in *Strickland v. Washington*, we discern no inequity in requiring him to bear the risk of attorney error that results in a procedural default. Instead, we think that the existence of cause for a procedural default must ordinarily turn on whether the prisoner can show that some objective factor external to the defense impeded counsel's efforts to comply with the State's procedural rule. Without attempting an exhaustive catalog of such objective impediments to compliance with a procedural rule, we note that a showing that the factual or legal basis for a claim was not reasonably available to counsel, or that some interference by officials made compliance impracticable, would constitute cause under this standard.

7. In *Edwards v. Carpenter*, 529 U.S. 446 (2000), the Court held that ineffective assistance of counsel could be "cause" that excuses a procedural default so long as counsel's error in failing properly to preserve a federal constitutional claim for review in state court rose to the level of a violation of the Sixth Amendment. But because ineffective assistance adequate to establish cause for the procedural default is itself an independent constitutional claim, it must be presented first to the state courts and can also be procedurally defaulted. As Justice O'Connor had explained in *Carrier*, "if a petitioner could raise his ineffective assistance claim for the first time on federal habeas in order to show cause for a procedural default, the federal habeas court would find itself in the anomalous position of adjudicating an unexhausted constitutional claim for which state court review might still be available," a result that could "ill serve[]" the "principle of comity that underlies the exhaustion doctrine."

Justice Breyer, joined by Justice Stevens, concurred only in the judgment. He expressed dismay at "the added complexity resulting from the Court's opinion":

> Consider a prisoner who wants to assert a federal constitutional claim (call it FCC). Suppose the State asserts as a claimed "adequate and independent state ground" the prisoner's failure to raise the matter on his first state-court appeal. Suppose further that the prisoner replies by alleging that he had "cause" for not raising the matter on appeal (call it C). After *Carrier*, if that alleged "cause" (C) consists of the claim "my attorney was constitutionally ineffective," the prisoner must have exhausted C in the state courts first. And after today, if he did not follow state rules for presenting C to the state courts, he will have lost his basic claim, FCC, forever. But, I overstate. According to the opinion of the Court, he will not necessarily have lost FCC forever if he had "cause" for not having followed those state rules (i.e., the rules for determining the existence of "cause" for not having followed the state rules governing the basic claim, FCC) (call this "cause" C*). The prisoner could

therefore still obtain relief if he could demonstrate the merits of C*, C, and FCC.

I concede that this system of rules has a certain logic, indeed an attractive power for those who like difficult puzzles. But I believe it must succumb to this question: Why should a prisoner, who may well be proceeding pro se, lose his basic claim because he runs afoul of state procedural rules governing the presentation to state courts of the "cause" for his not having followed state procedural rules for the presentation of his basic federal claim? And, in particular, why should that special default rule apply when the "cause" at issue is an "ineffective-assistance-of-counsel" claim, but not when it is any of the many other "causes" or circumstances that might excuse a failure to comply with state rules? I can find no satisfactory answer to these questions.

8. In *United States v. Frady*, 456 U.S. 152 (1982), the Court defined "prejudice" as a showing that the claimed constitutional error "worked to [the petitioner's] *actual* and substantial disadvantage, infecting the entire trial with error of constitutional dimension."

[3] Harmless Error

Even if a state prisoner advances a meritorious constitutional claim, properly exhausts available state-court remedies, preserves the objection to avoid procedural default, and files a timely habeas petition, a federal court may refuse to issue the writ. That is because some errors, even if proven, are deemed "harmless" and thus an insufficient basis for relief.

In one sense, that proposition should be unsurprising. Appellate courts routinely apply harmless-error standards in other contexts. *See* Fed. R. Crim. P. 52(a) ("Any error, defect, irregularity, or variance that does not affect substantial rights must be disregarded."). Indeed, all 50 states have adopted harmless-error statutes or rules, which "serve a very useful purpose insofar as they block setting aside convictions for small errors or defects that have little, if any, likelihood of having changed the result of the trial." *Chapman v. California*, 386 U.S. 18 (1967). In *Chapman*, the Court held that even constitutional errors may be "so unimportant and insignificant" as to not require the automatic reversal of the conviction. But for criminal cases on *direct* review, the Court announced a demanding standard: the appellate court may set aside a constitutional error as harmless only if the government proves that the error was "harmless beyond a reasonable doubt."

For cases on collateral review, however, a less stringent standard applies. In *Brecht v. Abrahamson*, 507 U.S. 619 (1993), the Court held that habeas petitioners are not entitled to relief "unless they can establish that it resulted in 'actual prejudice,'" meaning that the error "had substantial and injurious effect or influence" in determining the outcome. Shortly thereafter, in *O'Neal v. McAninch*, 513 U.S. 432 (1995), the Court clarified that habeas relief is warranted if the federal court has "grave doubt about whether a trial error of federal law had 'substantial and injurious effect.'" That reduced threshold for harmlessness, the Court explained, reflects states' interest in the finality of convictions, state courts' ability to identify the prejudicial effects of errors, and principles of comity and federalism.

What theories about the purpose of habeas review best explain the standard announced in *Brecht*? Are there any theories that cut in the opposite direction, suggesting that the harmlessness standard should be just as demanding on collateral review as it is on direct review? Or even that constitutional errors should not be deemed harmless at all?

AEDPA introduced a few wrinkles to harmless error questions in habeas. Recall that, under § 2254(d)(1), a federal court may grant habeas relief for claims adjudicated on the merits in state court only if the "decision resulted in a decision that was contrary to, or involved an unreasonable application of, clearly established federal law, as determined by the United States." What happens if a state court finds a constitutional error, but deems the error harmless under *Chapman*? On habeas, is the harmlessness determination *itself* an adjudication "on the merits" entitled to deference under § 2254(d)(1)? Yes, as a formal matter. *Davis v. Ayala*, 135 S. Ct. 2187 (2015) (rejecting the suggestion "that *Brecht* somehow abrogates the limitation on federal habeas relief that § 2254(d) plainly sets out"). But in *Fry v. Pliler*, 551 U.S. 112 (2007), the Court held that the *Brecht* standard makes a formal discussion of the § 2254(d)(1) standard unnecessary. Although AEDPA did not replace *Brecht*, "it certainly makes no sense to require formal application of both tests (AEDPA/*Chapman* and *Brecht*) when the latter obviously subsumes the former." *See Ayala* (Sotomayor, J., dissenting) ("If a trial error is prejudicial under *Brecht*'s standard, a state court's determination that the error was harmless beyond a reasonable doubt is necessarily unreasonable.").

[4] State-Court Factfinding

The Supreme Court has long held that federal habeas courts should give special deference to state-court findings of fact. In 1966, Congress codified a presumption of correctness for state-court factfinding, but included a series of exceptions, including where the state's fact-finding process was inadequate to provide a full and fair hearing; where the merits of the factual dispute were not resolved at the state-court level; and where the petitioner was not afforded due process.

AEDPA modified habeas practice with respect to facts found in state-court proceedings in several ways. First, it specified that "a determination of a factual issue made by a State court shall be presumed to be correct [and] the applicant shall have the burden of rebutting the presumption of correctness by clear and convincing evidence." § 2254(e)(1). Second, if a petitioner has "failed to develop the factual basis of a claim in State court proceedings, the [habeas] court shall not hold an evidentiary hearing on the claim unless the applicant" meets one of three requirements: that the claim relies on a "new rule of constitutional law, made retroactive to cases on collateral review by the Supreme Court, that was previously unavailable"; or that the "factual predicate [for the claim] could not have been previously discovered through the exercise of due diligence"; or that "the facts underlying the claim would be sufficient to establish by clear and convincing evidence that but for constitutional error, no reasonable factfinder would have found the applicant guilty of the underlying offense." §2254(e)(2).

In *Michael Williams v. Taylor*, 529 U.S. 420 (2000), the Court held that §2254(e)(2) forecloses an evidentiary hearing only if the habeas petitioner's failure to develop the record appropriately in state court was due to the petitioner's lack of diligence or some larger fault attributable to the petitioner or his counsel.

Note, though, that the possibility of a federal-court evidentiary hearing applies only to those claims that were not adjudicated on the merits in state court. *Cullen v. Pinholster*, 563 U.S. 170 (2011), explained that if the claim had been adjudicated on the merits in state court, §2254(d)'s deference applies:

> Under §2254(d), [a habeas petition] "shall not be granted with respect to [such a] claim . . . unless the adjudication of the claim":
>
> "(1) resulted in a decision that was contrary to, or involved an unreasonable application of, clearly established Federal law, as determined by the Supreme Court of the United States; or
>
> "(2) resulted in a decision that was based on an unreasonable determination of the facts in light of the evidence presented in the State court proceeding."

Citing *Harrington v. Richter*'s "highly deferential standard for evaluating state-court rulings, which demands that state-court decisions be given the benefit of the doubt," the Court held that review under §2254(d)(1) is limited to the record that was before the state court that adjudicated the claim on the merits. The Court said:

> Section 2254(d)(1) refers, in the past tense, to a state-court adjudication that "resulted in" a decision that was contrary to, or "involved" an unreasonable application of, established law. This backward-looking language requires an examination of the state-court decision at the time it was made. It follows that the record under review is limited to the record in existence at that same time *i.e.*, the record before the state court.

D. The Relevance of Innocence

Herrera v. Collins

Supreme Court of the United States, 1993.

506 U.S. 390.

Chief Justice Rehnquist delivered the opinion of the Court.

Petitioner Leonel Torres Herrera was convicted of capital murder and sentenced to death in January 1982. He unsuccessfully challenged the conviction on direct appeal and state collateral proceedings in the Texas state courts, and in a federal habeas petition. In February 1992 — 10 years after his conviction — he urged in a second federal habeas petition that he was "actually innocent" of the murder for which he was sentenced to death, and that the Eighth Amendment's prohibition against cruel and unusual punishment and the Fourteenth Amendment's guarantee of due process of law therefore forbid his execution. [In support of his claim he introduced affidavits from several sources, including an attorney who had represented his brother. This affidavit asserted that the brother had confessed to the murder.] Petitioner urges us to hold that this showing of innocence entitles him to relief in this federal habeas proceeding. We hold that it does not. . . .

Petitioner asserts that the Eighth and Fourteenth Amendments to the United States Constitution prohibit the execution of a person who is innocent of the crime for which he was convicted. This proposition has an elemental appeal, as would the similar proposition that the Constitution prohibits the imprisonment of one who is innocent of the crime for which he was convicted. After all, the central purpose of any system of criminal justice is to convict the guilty and free the innocent. But the evidence upon which petitioner's claim of innocence rests was not produced at his trial, but rather eight years later. In any system of criminal justice, "innocence" or "guilt" must be determined in some sort of a judicial proceeding. Petitioner's showing of innocence, and indeed his constitutional claim for relief based upon that showing, must be evaluated in the light of the previous proceedings in this case, which have stretched over a span of 10 years.

A person when first charged with a crime is entitled to a presumption of innocence, and may insist that his guilt be established beyond a reasonable doubt. *In re Winship*, 397 U.S. 358 (1970). Other constitutional provisions also have the effect of ensuring against the risk of convicting an innocent person. In capital cases, we have required additional protections because of the nature of the penalty at stake. All of these constitutional safeguards, of course, make it more difficult for the State to rebut and finally overturn the presumption of innocence which attaches to every criminal defendant. But we have also observed that "[d]ue process does not require that every conceivable step be taken, at whatever cost, to eliminate the possibility of convicting an innocent person." *Patterson v. New York*, 432 U.S. 197 (1977). To conclude otherwise would all but paralyze our system for enforcement of the criminal law.

Once a defendant has been afforded a fair trial and convicted of the offense for which he was charged, the presumption of innocence disappears. Here, it is not disputed that the State met its burden of proving at trial that petitioner was guilty of [capital murder] . . . beyond a reasonable doubt. Thus, in the eyes of the law, petitioner does not come before the Court as one who is "innocent," but, on the contrary, as one who has been convicted by due process of law of two brutal murders. . . .

Claims of actual innocence based on newly discovered evidence have never been held to state a ground for federal habeas relief absent an independent constitutional violation occurring in the underlying state criminal proceeding. Chief Justice Warren made this clear in *Townsend v. Sain, supra*, 372 U.S. 293 (1963).

> Where newly discovered evidence is alleged in a habeas application, evidence which could not reasonably have been presented to the state trier of facts, the federal court must grant an evidentiary hearing. Of course, such evidence must bear upon the constitutionality of the applicant's detention; *the existence merely of newly discovered evidence relevant to the guilt of a state prisoner is not a ground for relief on federal habeas corpus.*

This rule is grounded in the principle that federal habeas courts sit to ensure that individuals are not imprisoned in violation of the Constitution — not to correct errors of fact. . . . "Federal courts are not forums in which to relitigate state trials." *Barefoot v. Estelle*, 463 U.S. 880 (1983). The guilt or innocence determination in state criminal trials is "a decisive and portentous event." *Wainwright v. Sykes*, 433 U.S. 72 (1977). "Society's resources have been concentrated at that time and place in order to decide, within the limits of human fallibility, the question of guilt or innocence of one of its citizens." Few rulings would be more disruptive of our federal system than to provide for federal habeas review of freestanding claims of actual innocence.

Our decision in *Jackson v. Virginia*, 443 U.S. 307 (1979), comes as close to authorizing evidentiary review of a state-court conviction on federal habeas as any of our cases. There, we held that a federal habeas court may review a claim that the evidence adduced at a state trial was not sufficient to convict a criminal defendant beyond a reasonable doubt. But in so holding, we emphasized:

> [T]his inquiry does not require a court to "ask itself whether *it* believes that the evidence at the trial established guilt beyond a reasonable doubt." Instead, the relevant question is whether, after viewing the evidence in the light most favorable to the prosecution, *any* rational trier of fact could have found the essential elements of the crime beyond a reasonable doubt. This familiar standard gives full play to the responsibility of the trier of fact fairly to resolve conflicts in the testimony, to weigh the evidence, and to draw reasonable inferences from basic facts to ultimate facts.

We specifically noted that "the standard announced . . . does not permit a court to make its own subjective determination of guilt or innocence."

The type of federal habeas review sought by petitioner here is different in critical respects than that authorized by *Jackson.* First, the *Jackson* inquiry is aimed at determining whether there has been an independent constitutional violation — *i.e.*, a conviction based on evidence that fails to meet the *Winship* standard. Thus, federal habeas courts act in their historic capacity — to assure that the habeas petitioner is not being held in violation of his or her federal constitutional rights. Second, the sufficiency of the evidence review authorized by *Jackson* is limited to "record evidence." *Jackson* does not extend to nonrecord evidence, including newly discovered evidence. Finally, the *Jackson* inquiry does not focus on whether the trier of fact made the *correct* guilt or innocence determination, but rather whether it made a *rational* decision to convict or acquit. . . .

The dissent would place the burden on petitioner to show that he is "probably" innocent. . . . [But it] fails to articulate the relief that would be available if petitioner were to meets its "probable innocence" standard. Would it be commutation of petitioner's death sentence, new trial, or unconditional release from imprisonment? The typical relief granted in federal habeas corpus is a conditional order of release unless the State elects to retry the successful habeas petitioner, or in a capital case a similar conditional order vacating the death sentence. Were petitioner to satisfy the dissent's "probable innocence" standard, therefore, the District Court would presumably be required to grant a conditional order of relief, which would in effect require the State to retry petitioner 10 years after his first trial, not because of any constitutional violation which had occurred at the first trial, but simply because of a belief that in light of petitioner's new-found evidence a jury might find him not guilty at a second trial.

Yet there is no guarantee that the guilt or innocence determination would be any more exact. To the contrary, the passage of time only diminishes the reliability of criminal adjudications. Under the dissent's approach, the District Court would be placed in the even more difficult position of having to weigh the probative value of "hot" and "cold" evidence on petitioner's guilt or innocence.

This is not to say that our habeas jurisprudence casts a blind eye toward innocence. In a series of cases culminating with *Sawyer v. Whitley*, 505 U.S. 333 (1992), . . . we have held that a petitioner otherwise subject to defenses of abusive or successive use of the writ may have his federal constitutional claim considered on the merits if he makes a proper showing of actual innocence. This rule, or fundamental miscarriage of justice exception, is grounded in the "equitable discretion" of habeas courts to see that federal constitutional errors do not result in the incarceration of innocent persons. But this body of our habeas jurisprudence makes clear that a claim of "actual innocence" is not itself a constitutional claim, but instead a gateway through which a habeas petitioner must pass to have his otherwise barred constitutional claim considered on the merits.

Petitioner in this case is simply not entitled to habeas relief based on the reasoning of this line of cases. For he does not seek excusal of a procedural error so that he may bring an independent constitutional claim challenging his conviction or sentence, but rather argues that he is entitled to habeas relief because newly discovered evidence shows that his conviction is factually incorrect. The fundamental miscarriage of justice exception is available "only where the prisoner *supplements* his constitutional claim with a colorable showing of factual innocence." *Kuhlmann v. Wilson*, 477 U.S. 436 (1986). We have never held that it extends to freestanding claims of actual innocence. Therefore, the exception is inapplicable here.

Petitioner asserts that this case is different because he has been sentenced to death. But we have "refused to hold that the fact that a death sentence has been imposed requires a different standard of review on federal habeas corpus." *Murray v. Giarratano*, 492 U.S. 1 (1989). We have, of course, held that the Eighth Amendment requires increased reliability of the process by which capital punishment may be imposed. But petitioner's claim does not fit well into the doctrine of these cases, since, as we have pointed out, it is far from clear that a second trial 10 years after the first trial would produce a more reliable result.

Perhaps mindful of this, petitioner urges not that he necessarily receive a new trial, but that his death sentence simply be vacated if a federal habeas court deems that a satisfactory showing of "actual innocence" has been made. But such a result is scarcely logical; petitioner's claim is not that some error was made in imposing a capital sentence upon him, but that a fundamental error was made in finding him guilty of the underlying murder in the first place. It would be a rather strange jurisprudence, in these circumstances, which held that under our Constitution he could not be executed, but that he could spend the rest of his life in prison. . . .

Alternatively, petitioner invokes the Fourteenth Amendment's guarantee of due process of law in support of his claim that his showing of actual innocence entitles him to a new trial, or at least to a vacation of his death sentence. [Here the Court reviewed the history of the grant of new trials and the availability of new trials in the states.]

[In light of history and contemporary practice, we] cannot say that Texas' refusal to entertain petitioner's newly discovered evidence eight years after his conviction transgresses a principle of fundamental fairness "rooted in the traditions and conscience of our people." *Patterson v. New York*, 432 U.S. 197 (1997). This is not to say, however, that petitioner is left without a forum to raise his actual innocence claim. For under Texas law, petitioner may file a request for executive clemency. See TEX. CONST., art. IV, § 11; TEX. CODE CRIM. PROC. ANN., art. 48.01 (Vernon 1979). Clemency is deeply rooted in our Anglo-American tradition of law, and is the historic remedy for preventing miscarriages of justice where judicial process has been exhausted. . . .

[In] state criminal proceedings the trial is the paramount event for determining the guilt or innocence of the defendant. Federal habeas review of state convictions has traditionally been limited to claims of constitutional violations occurring in the course of the underlying state criminal proceedings. Our federal habeas cases have treated claims of "actual innocence," not as an independent constitutional claim, but as a basis upon which a habeas petitioner may have an independent constitutional claim considered on the merits, even though his habeas petition would otherwise be regarded as successive or abusive. History shows that the traditional remedy for claims of innocence based on new evidence, discovered too late in the day to file a new trial motion, has been executive clemency.

We may assume, for the sake of argument in deciding this case, that in a capital case a truly persuasive demonstration of "actual innocence" made after trial would render the execution of a defendant unconstitutional, and warrant federal habeas relief if there were no state avenue open to process such a claim. But because of the very disruptive effect that entertaining claims of actual innocence would have on the need for finality in capital cases, and the enormous burden that having to retry cases based on often stale evidence would place on the States, the threshold showing for such an assumed right would necessarily be extraordinarily high. The showing made by petitioner in this case falls far short of any such threshold.

[Here the Court reviewed in detail the affidavits Herrera offered in support of his innocence claim. The Court found that they were based primarily on hearsay and contained inconsistencies.]

Finally, the affidavits must be considered in light of the proof of petitioner's guilt at trial — proof which included two eyewitness identifications, numerous pieces of circumstantial evidence, and a handwritten letter in which petitioner apologized for killing the officers and offered to turn himself in under certain conditions. That proof, even when considered alongside petitioner's belated affidavits, points strongly to petitioner's guilt.

This is not to say that petitioner's affidavits are without probative value. Had this sort of testimony been offered at trial, it could have been weighed by the jury, along with the evidence offered by the State and petitioner, in deliberating upon its verdict. Since the statements in the affidavits contradict the evidence received at trial, the jury would have had to decide important issues of credibility. But coming 10 years after petitioner's trial, this showing of innocence falls far short of that which would have to be made in order to trigger the sort of constitutional claim which we have assumed, *arguendo*, to exist.

The judgment of the Court of Appeals is

Affirmed.

JUSTICE O'CONNOR, with whom JUSTICE KENNEDY joins, concurring.

I cannot disagree with the fundamental legal principle that executing the innocent is inconsistent with the Constitution. Regardless of the verbal formula employed — "contrary to contemporary standards of decency," "shocking to the conscience," or offensive to a "principle of justice so rooted in the traditions and conscience of our people as to be ranked as fundamental" — the execution of a legally and factually innocent person would be a constitutionally intolerable event. Dispositive to this case, however, is an equally fundamental fact: Petitioner is not innocent, in any sense of the word.

As the Court explains, petitioner is not innocent in the eyes of the law because, in our system of justice, "the trial is the paramount event for determining the guilt or innocence of the defendant." In petitioner's case, that paramount event occurred 10 years ago. He was tried before a jury of his peers, with the full panoply of protections that our Constitution affords criminal defendants. At the conclusion of that trial, the jury found petitioner guilty beyond a reasonable doubt. Petitioner therefore does not appear before us as an innocent man on the verge of execution. He is instead a legally guilty one who, refusing to accept the jury's verdict, demands a hearing in which to have his culpability determined once again.

Consequently, the issue before us is not whether a State can execute the innocent. It is, as the Court notes, whether a fairly convicted and therefore legally guilty person is constitutionally entitled to yet another judicial proceeding in which to adjudicate his guilt anew, 10 years after conviction, notwithstanding his failure to demonstrate that constitutional error infected his trial. In most circumstances, that question would answer itself in the negative. Our society has a high degree of confidence in its criminal trials, in no small part because the Constitution offers unparalleled protections against convicting the innocent. The question similarly would be answered in the negative today, except for the disturbing nature of the claim before us. Petitioner contends not only that the Constitution's protections "sometimes fail," but that their failure in his case will result in his execution—even though he is factually innocent and has evidence to prove it.

Exercising restraint, the Court and Justice White assume for the sake of argument that, if a prisoner were to make an exceptionally strong showing of actual innocence, the execution could not go forward. Justice Blackmun, in contrast, would expressly so hold; he would also announce the precise burden of proof. Resolving the issue is neither necessary nor advisable in this case. The question is a sensitive and, to say the least, troubling one. It implicates not just the life of a single individual, but also the State's powerful and legitimate interest in punishing the guilty, and the nature of state-federal relations. Indeed, as the Court persuasively demonstrates, throughout our history the federal courts have assumed that they should not and could not intervene to prevent an execution so long as the prisoner had been convicted after a constitutionally adequate trial. The prisoner's sole remedy was a pardon or clemency.

Nonetheless, the proper disposition of this case is neither difficult nor troubling. No matter what the Court might say about claims of actual innocence today, petitioner could not obtain relief. The record overwhelmingly demonstrates that petitioner deliberately shot and killed Officers Rucker and Carrisalez the night of September 29, 1981; petitioner's new evidence is bereft of credibility. Indeed, despite its stinging criticism of the Court's decision, not even the dissent expresses a belief that petitioner might possibly be actually innocent. Nor could it: The record makes it abundantly clear that petitioner is not somehow the future victim of "simple murder," but instead himself the established perpetrator of two brutal and tragic ones.

[Justice O'Connor here reviewed the evidence against Herrera in detail.]

Now, 10 years after being convicted on that seemingly dispositive evidence, petitioner has collected four affidavits that he claims prove his innocence. The affidavits allege that petitioner's brother, who died six years before the affidavits were executed, was the killer—and that petitioner was not. Affidavits like these are not uncommon, especially in capital cases. They are an unfortunate although understandable occurrence. It seems that, when a prisoner's life is at stake, he often can find someone new to vouch for him. Experience has shown, however, that such affidavits are to be treated with a fair degree of skepticism.

These affidavits are no exception. They are suspect, produced as they were at the 11th hour with no reasonable explanation for the nearly decade-long delay. Worse, they conveniently blame a dead man—someone who will neither contest the allegations nor suffer punishment as a result of them. Moreover, they contradict each other on numerous points. . . . Most critical of all, however, the affidavits pale when compared to the proof at trial.

The conclusion seems inescapable: Petitioner is guilty. . . .

If the federal courts are to entertain claims of actual innocence, their attention, efforts, and energy must be reserved for the truly extraordinary case; they ought not be forced to sort through the insubstantial and the incredible as well.

* * *

Ultimately, two things about this case are clear. First is what the Court does *not* hold. Nowhere does the Court state that the Constitution permits the execution of an actually innocent person. Instead, the Court assumes for the sake of argument that a truly persuasive demonstration of actual innocence would render any such execution unconstitutional and that federal habeas relief would be warranted if no state avenue were open to process the claim. Second is what petitioner has not demonstrated. Petitioner has failed to make a persuasive showing of actual innocence. Not one judge—no state court judge, not the District Court Judge, none of the three judges of the Court of Appeals, and none of the Justices of this Court—has expressed doubt about petitioner's guilt. Accordingly, the Court has no reason to pass on, and appropriately reserves, the question whether federal courts may entertain convincing claims of actual innocence. That difficult question remains open. If the Constitution's guarantees of fair procedure and the safeguards of clemency and pardon fulfill their historical mission, it may never require resolution at all.

Justice Scalia, with whom Justice Thomas joins, concurring.

We granted certiorari on the question whether it violates due process or constitutes cruel and unusual punishment for a State to execute a person who, having been convicted of murder after a full and fair trial, later alleges that newly discovered evidence shows him to be "actually innocent." I would have preferred to decide that question, particularly since, as the Court's discussion shows, it is perfectly clear what the answer is: There is no basis in text, tradition, or even in contemporary practice (if that were enough) for finding in the Constitution a right to demand judicial consideration of newly discovered evidence of innocence brought forward after conviction. In saying that such a right exists, the dissenters apply nothing but their personal opinions to invalidate the rules of more than two-thirds of the States, and a Federal Rule of Criminal Procedure for which this Court itself is responsible. If the system that has been in place for 200 years (and remains widely approved) "shock[s]" the dissenters' consciences, perhaps they should doubt the calibration of their consciences, or, better still, the usefulness of "conscience shocking" as a legal test.

I nonetheless join the entirety of the Court's opinion, including the final portion, because there is no legal error in deciding a case by assuming, *arguendo*, that an asserted constitutional right exists, and because I can understand, or at least am accustomed to, the reluctance of the present Court to admit publicly that Our Perfect

Constitution* lets stand any injustice, much less the execution of an innocent man who has received, though to no avail, all the process that our society has traditionally deemed adequate. With any luck, we shall avoid ever having to face this embarrassing question again, since it is improbable that evidence of innocence as convincing as today's opinion requires would fail to produce an executive pardon.

My concern is that in making life easier for ourselves we not appear to make it harder for the lower federal courts, imposing upon them the burden of regularly analyzing newly-discovered-evidence-of-innocence claims in capital cases (in which event such federal claims, it can confidently be predicted, will become routine and even repetitive). A number of Courts of Appeals have hitherto held, largely in reliance on our unelaborated statement in *Townsend v. Sain*, 372 U.S. 293 (1963), that newly discovered evidence relevant only to a state prisoner's guilt or innocence is not a basis for federal habeas corpus relief. I do not understand it to be the import of today's decision that those holdings are to be replaced with a strange regime that assumes permanently, though only "*arguendo*," that a constitutional right exists, and expends substantial judicial resources on that assumption. The Court's extensive and scholarly discussion of the question presented in the present case does nothing but support our statement in *Townsend* and strengthen the validity of the holdings based upon it.

JUSTICE WHITE, concurring in the judgment.

In voting to affirm, I assume that a persuasive showing of "actual innocence" made after trial, even though made after the expiration of the time provided by law for the presentation of newly discovered evidence, would render unconstitutional the execution of petitioner in this case. To be entitled to relief, however, petitioner would at the very least be required to show that based on proffered newly discovered evidence and the entire record before the jury that convicted him, "no rational trier of fact could [find] proof of guilt beyond a reasonable doubt." *Jackson v. Virginia*, 443 U.S. 307 (1979). For the reasons stated in the Court's opinion, petitioner's showing falls far short of satisfying even that standard, and I therefore concur in the judgment.

JUSTICE BLACKMUN, with whom JUSTICE STEVENS and JUSTICE SOUTER join with respect to Parts I-IV, dissenting.

Nothing could be more contrary to contemporary standards of decency, see *Ford v. Wainwright*, 477 U.S. 399 (1986), or more shocking to the conscience, see *Rochin v. California*, 342 U.S. 165 (1952), than to execute a person who is actually innocent.

I therefore must disagree with the long and general discussion that precedes the Court's disposition of this case. That discussion, of course, is dictum because the Court assumes, "for the sake of argument in deciding this case, that in a capital case a truly persuasive demonstration of 'actual innocence' made after trial would render the execution of a defendant unconstitutional." Without articulating the standard it is

---

* My reference is to an article by Professor Monaghan, which discusses the unhappy truth that not every problem was meant to be solved by the United States Constitution, nor can be. See Monaghan, *Our Perfect Constitution*, 56 N.Y.U. L. REV. 353 (1981).

applying, however, the Court then decides that this petitioner has not made a sufficiently persuasive case. Because I believe that in the first instance the District Court
should decide whether petitioner is entitled to a hearing and whether he is entitled to
relief on the merits of his claim, I would reverse the order of the Court of Appeals
and remand this case for further proceedings in the District Court.

I

[We are] being asked to decide whether the Constitution forbids the execution of
a person who has been validly convicted and sentenced but who, nonetheless, can
prove his innocence with newly discovered evidence. Despite the State of Texas' astonishing protestation to the contrary, I do not see how the answer can be anything but
"yes."

A

The Eighth Amendment prohibits "cruel and unusual punishments." This proscription is not static but rather reflects evolving standards of decency. I think it is crystal
clear that the execution of an innocent person is "at odds with contemporary standards of fairness and decency." *Spaziano v. Florida*, 468 U.S. 447 (1984). Indeed, it is
at odds with any standard of decency that I can imagine.

This Court has ruled that punishment is excessive and unconstitutional if it is
"nothing more than the purposeless and needless imposition of pain and suffering,"
or if it is "grossly out of proportion to the severity of the crime." *Coker v. Georgia*, 433
U.S. 584 (1977) (plurality opinion); *Gregg v. Georgia*, 428 U.S. 153 (1976) (opinion of
Stewart, Powell, and Stevens, JJ.). It has held that death is an excessive punishment
for rape, *Coker*, and for mere participation in a robbery during which a killing takes
place, *Enmund v. Florida*, 458 U.S. 782 (1982). If it is violative of the Eighth Amendment to execute someone who is guilty of those crimes, then it plainly is violative of
the Eighth Amendment to execute a person who is actually innocent. Executing an
innocent person epitomizes "the purposeless and needless imposition of pain and suffering." *Coker*. . . .

The Court [suggests] that allowing petitioner to raise his claim of innocence would
not serve society's interest in the reliable imposition of the death penalty because it
might require a new trial that would be less accurate than the first. This suggestion
misses the point entirely. The question is not whether a second trial would be more
reliable than the first but whether, in light of new evidence, the result of the first trial
is sufficiently reliable for the State to carry out a death sentence. Furthermore, it is far
from clear that a State will seek to retry the rare prisoner who prevails on a claim of
actual innocence. As explained in Part III, *infra*, I believe a prisoner must show not
just that there was probably a reasonable doubt about his guilt but that he is probably
actually innocent. I find it difficult to believe that any State would choose to retry a
person who meets this standard.

I believe it contrary to any standard of decency to execute someone who is actually
innocent. Because the Eighth Amendment applies to questions of guilt or innocence,
and to persons upon whom a valid sentence of death has been imposed, I also believe

that petitioner may raise an Eighth Amendment challenge to his punishment on the ground that he is actually innocent.

B

Execution of the innocent is equally offensive to the Due Process Clause of the Fourteenth Amendment. The [majority] misinterprets petitioner's Fourteenth Amendment claim as raising a procedural, rather than a substantive, due process challenge. . . . This Court has held that the Due Process Clause protects individuals against two types of government action. So-called "substantive due process" prevents the government from engaging in conduct that "shocks the conscience," *Rochin v. California*, 342 U.S. 165 (1952), or interferes with rights "implicit in the concept of ordered liberty," *Palko v. Connecticut*, 302 U.S. 319 (1937). When government action depriving a person of life, liberty, or property survives substantive due process scrutiny, it must still be implemented in a fair manner. *Mathews v. Eldridge*, 424 U.S. 319 (1976).

Petitioner's claim falls within our [substantive] due process precedents. . . . The lethal injection that petitioner faces as an allegedly innocent person is certainly closer to the rack and the screw than the stomach pump condemned in *Rochin*. Execution of an innocent person is the ultimate "arbitrary impositio[n]." It is an imposition from which one never recovers and for which one can never be compensated. Thus, I also believe that petitioner may raise a substantive due process challenge to his punishment on the ground that he is actually innocent. . . .

II

Having adopted an "actual-innocence" requirement for review of abusive, successive, or defaulted claims, however, the majority would now take the position that "a claim of 'actual innocence' is not itself a constitutional claim, but instead a gateway through which a habeas petitioner must pass to have his otherwise barred constitutional claim considered on the merits." In other words, having held that a prisoner who is incarcerated in violation of the Constitution must show he is actually innocent to obtain relief, the majority would now hold that a prisoner who is actually innocent must show a constitutional violation to obtain relief. The only principle that would appear to reconcile these two positions is the principle that habeas relief should be denied whenever possible.

III

The Eighth and Fourteenth Amendments, of course, are binding on the States, and one would normally expect the States to adopt procedures to consider claims of actual innocence based on newly discovered evidence. The majority's disposition of this case, however, leaves the States uncertain of their constitutional obligations.

A

Whatever procedures a State might adopt to hear actual-innocence claims, one thing is certain: The possibility of executive clemency is *not* sufficient to satisfy the requirements of the Eighth and Fourteenth Amendments. The vindication of rights guaranteed by the Constitution has never been made to turn on the unreviewable discretion of an executive official or administrative tribunal. . . .

C

The question that remains is what showing should be required to obtain relief on the merits of an Eighth or Fourteenth Amendment claim of actual innocence. I agree with the majority that "in state criminal proceedings the trial is the paramount event for determining the guilt or innocence of the defendant." I also think that "a truly persuasive demonstration of 'actual innocence' made after trial would render the execution of a defendant unconstitutional." The question is what "a truly persuasive demonstration" entails, a question the majority's disposition of this case leaves open.

In articulating the "actual-innocence" exception in our habeas jurisprudence, this Court has adopted a standard requiring the petitioner to show a "fair probability that, in light of all the evidence . . . , the trier of the facts would have entertained a reasonable doubt of his guilt." *Kuhlmann v. Wilson*. In other words, the habeas petitioner must show that there probably would be a reasonable doubt.

I think the standard for relief on the merits of an actual-innocence claim must be higher than the threshold standard for merely reaching that claim or any other claim that has been procedurally defaulted or is successive or abusive. I would hold that, to obtain relief on a claim of actual innocence, the petitioner must show that he probably is innocent. This standard is supported by several considerations. First, new evidence of innocence may be discovered long after the defendant's conviction. Given the passage of time, it may be difficult for the State to retry a defendant who obtains relief from his conviction or sentence on an actual-innocence claim. The actual-innocence proceeding thus may constitute the final word on whether the defendant may be punished. In light of this fact, an otherwise constitutionally valid conviction or sentence should not be set aside lightly. Second, conviction after a constitutionally adequate trial strips the defendant of the presumption of innocence. The government bears the burden of proving the defendant's guilt beyond a reasonable doubt, but once the government has done so, the burden of proving innocence must shift to the convicted defendant. The actual-innocence inquiry is therefore distinguishable from review for sufficiency of the evidence, where the question is not whether the defendant is innocent but whether the government has met its constitutional burden of proving the defendant's guilt beyond a reasonable doubt. When a defendant seeks to challenge the determination of guilt after he has been validly convicted and sentenced, it is fair to place on him the burden of proving his innocence, not just raising doubt about his guilt. . . .

It should be clear that the standard I would adopt would not convert the federal courts into "forums in which to relitigate state trials." It would not "require the habeas court to hear testimony from the witnesses who testified at trial," though, if the petition warrants a hearing, it may require the habeas court to hear the testimony of "those who made the statements in the affidavits which petitioner has presented." I believe that if a prisoner can show that he is probably actually innocent, in light of all the evidence, then he has made "a truly persuasive demonstration," and his execution would violate the Constitution. I would so hold.

IV

In this case, the District Court determined that petitioner's newly discovered evidence warranted further consideration. Because the District Court doubted its own authority to consider the new evidence, it thought that petitioner's claim of actual innocence should be brought in state court, but it clearly did not think that petitioner's evidence was so insubstantial that it could be dismissed without any hearing at all. I would reverse the order of the Court of Appeals and remand the case to the District Court to consider whether petitioner has shown, in light of all the evidence, that he is probably actually innocent. . . .

V

I have voiced disappointment over this Court's obvious eagerness to do away with any restriction on the States' power to execute whomever and however they please. I have also expressed doubts about whether, in the absence of such restrictions, capital punishment remains constitutional at all. Of one thing, however, I am certain. Just as an execution without adequate safeguards is unacceptable, so too is an execution when the condemned prisoner can prove that he is innocent. The execution of a person who can show that he is innocent comes perilously close to simple murder.

Note: The Role of Innocence

1. Chief Justice Rehnquist states that the view that a claim of innocence is not itself cognizable in habeas "is grounded in the principle that federal habeas courts sit to ensure that individuals are not imprisoned in violation of the Constitution—not to correct errors of fact." Does the dissent disagree with this assessment of the purpose of habeas review, or only with the assessment that the execution of an innocent person might violate the Constitution?

2. Ultimately, the Court never reaches the question whether the Eighth Amendment prohibits the execution of a defendant who makes an adequate showing, based on newly discovered evidence, of "actual innocence." Six of the Justices conclude that, no matter what standard might be used to define such an "adequate showing," the defendant in *Herrera* could not possibly meet the standard. While Chief Justice Rehnquist, writing for five of the six Justices, identifies some of the problems that would follow the adoption of an "actual innocence" Eighth Amendment rule, he disposes of the case based on the "assum[ption], for the sake of argument," that "a truly persuasive demonstration of 'actual innocence' made after trial would render the execution of a defendant unconstitutional, and warrant federal habeas relief if there were no state avenue open to process such a claim." Justice White, concurring in the judgment, makes the same assumption.

Is there a theory of habeas corpus that would support relief in a case of actual innocence without a demonstrated constitutional violation?

Note: "Innocence" and Procedural Default

1. While the question of whether the execution of an innocent person violates the Constitution divides the Court in *Herrera*, actual innocence plays another role, discussed by several of the Justices: it can excuse a failure to comply with state procedural rules, and it may excuse a failure to exhaust state remedies.

2. In *Schlup v. Delo*, 513 U.S. 298 (1995), the Court considered the role that evidence of actual innocence plays in excusing procedural defaults. Schlup was sentenced to death for the murder of a fellow inmate. He claimed constitutional violations in his trial and also presented compelling evidence, including both affidavits and a videotape, that he had not committed the murder. The district court found his claims procedurally barred, and also found that Schlup could not meet the cause-and-prejudice standard for excusing procedural default. The court also refused to find that Schlup met the "miscarriage of justice" standard for excusing a procedural default, because it held that Schlup could not demonstrate "by clear and convincing evidence that, but for a constitutional error, no reasonable person would have found [Schlup] guilty." The court of appeals affirmed.

The Supreme Court reversed. The Court distinguished Schlup's claim from Herrera's in two ways. First, Schlup, unlike Herrera, claimed that his trial was infected by constitutional error (specifically, attorney ineffectiveness and withholding of evidence by the prosecutor). Second, "a court's assumptions about the validity of the proceedings that resulted in conviction [were] fundamentally different in" the two cases. Because Schlup accompanied his claim of innocence with a claim of constitutional trial error, his conviction "might not be entitled to the same degree of respect as one, such as Herrera's, that is the result of an error-free trial." The Court said:

> Without any new evidence of innocence, even the existence of a concededly meritorious constitutional violation is not in itself sufficient to establish a miscarriage of justice that would allow a habeas court to reach the merits of a barred claim. However, if a petitioner such as Schlup presents evidence of innocence so strong that a court cannot have confidence in the outcome of the trial unless the court is also satisfied that the trial was free of nonharmless constitutional error, the petitioner should be allowed to pass through the gateway and argue the merits of his underlying claims.

> Consequently, Schlup's evidence of innocence need carry less of a burden. In *Herrera* (on the assumption that petitioner's claim was, in principle, legally well founded), the evidence of innocence would have had to be strong enough to make his execution "constitutionally intolerable" even if his conviction was the product of a fair trial. For Schlup, the evidence must establish sufficient doubt about his guilt to justify the conclusion that his execution would be a miscarriage of justice unless his conviction was the product of a fair trial.

The Court then announced a precise standard of proof for satisfying the "miscarriage of justice" exception for excusing procedural default:

> To ensure that the fundamental miscarriage of justice exception would remain "rare" and would only be applied in the "extraordinary case," while at

the same time ensuring that the exception would extend relief to those who were truly deserving, this Court explicitly tied the miscarriage of justice exception to the petitioner's innocence. . . . [In order to meet that standard, a petitioner must show that] "a constitutional violation has probably resulted in the conviction of one who is actually innocent." To establish the requisite probability, the petitioner must show that it is more likely than not that no reasonable juror would have convicted him in the light of the new evidence. The petitioner thus is required to make a stronger showing than that needed to establish prejudice. At the same time, the showing of "more likely than not" imposes a lower burden of proof than the "clear and convincing" standard. . . . [The standard] thus ensures that petitioner's case is truly "extraordinary," while still providing petitioner a meaningful avenue by which to avoid a manifest injustice.

Chief Justice Rehnquist, joined by Justice Kennedy and Justice Thomas, dissented. Justice Scalia dissented separately.

3. Actual innocence operates as a "gateway," allowing habeas review of otherwise barred claims — and it opens quite a few gates. The Court has announced "actual innocence" or "miscarriage of justice" exceptions not only for procedural default in state court, *Schlup v. Delo*, 513 U.S. 298 (1995), but also for judge-made rules concerning "successive" petitions, *Kuhlmann v. Wilson*, 477 U.S. 436 (1986) (plurality opinion), and "abusive" petitions, *McClesky v. Zant*, 499 U.S. 467 (1991), and for the failure to develop facts in state court, *Keeney v. Tamayo-Reyes*, 504 U.S. 1 (1992).

All of those decisions, however, predated AEDPA, which altered some judge-made limits on habeas relief while adding a host of new limits. That raises two questions: Did AEDPA slam the actual-innocence gateway shut? Or does actual innocence also open some of AEDPA's new gateways?

The Court offered a partial answer to the first question in *House v. Bell*, 547 U.S. 518 (2006), holding that *Schlup*'s actual-innocence gateway for procedural default survived the enactment of AEDPA. Although the Act modified many aspects of habeas decisions, including successive and abusive petitions, none of its provisions specifically addressed "a first federal habeas petition seeking consideration of defaulted claims based on a showing of actual innocence." Congress must have intended to leave that gateway intact, the Court reasoned. Although three Justices dissented on the ground that the petitioner had not satisfied the *Schlup* standard, no member of the Court expressed doubt that the gateway remained viable.

Addressing the second question, the Court went much further in *McQuiggin v. Perkins*, 133 S. Ct. 1924 (2013). In that case, the prisoner had failed to file his habeas petition within the statute of limitations imposed by AEDPA in §2244(d)(1)(D), which specifically requires a filing within one year of "the date on which the factual predicate of the claim or claims presented could have been discovered through the exercise of due diligence." The petitioner argued that his showing of actual innocence, based on newly discovered evidence, should excuse the failure to comply with that statutory requirement.

The Court agreed, in an opinion by Justice Ginsburg, announcing a new "actual innocence" gateway to avoid AEDPA's one-year limitation period:

> The miscarriage of justice exception, our decisions bear out, survived AEDPA's passage. In *Calderon v. Thompson*, 523 U.S. 538 (1998), we applied the exception to hold that a federal court may, consistent with AEDPA, recall its mandate in order to revisit the merits of a decision. *Id.* ("The miscarriage of justice standard is altogether consistent . . . with AEDPA's central concern that the merits of concluded criminal proceedings not be revisited in the absence of a strong showing of actual innocence."). . . . Most recently, in *House*, we reiterated that a prisoner's proof of actual innocence may provide a gateway for federal habeas review of a procedurally defaulted claim of constitutional error.
>
> These decisions "see[k] to balance the societal interests in finality, comity, and conservation of scarce judicial resources with the individual interest in justice that arises in the extraordinary case." *Schlup*. Sensitivity to the injustice of incarcerating an innocent individual should not abate when the impediment is AEDPA's statute of limitations. As just noted, we have held that the miscarriage of justice exception applies to state procedural rules, including filing deadlines. *Coleman v. Thompson*, 501 U.S. 722 (1991). A federal court may invoke the miscarriage of justice exception to justify consideration of claims defaulted in state court under state timeliness rules. The State's reading of AEDPA's time prescription would thus accord greater force to a federal deadline than to a similarly designed state deadline. It would be passing strange to interpret a statute seeking to promote federalism and comity as requiring stricter enforcement of federal procedural rules than procedural rules established and enforced by the *States*.
>
> The State ties to § 2244(d)'s text its insistence that AEDPA's statute of limitations precludes courts from considering late-filed actual-innocence gateway claims. [In the State's view,] AEDPA prescribes a comprehensive system for determining when its one-year limitations period begins to run[,] [including] a specific trigger for the precise circumstance presented here: a constitutional claim based on new evidence. Section 2244(d)(1)(D) runs the clock from "the date on which the factual predicate of the claim . . . could have been discovered through the exercise of due diligence." In light of that provision, the State urges, "there is no need for the courts to act in equity to provide additional time for persons who allege actual innocence as a gateway to their claims of constitutional error." Perkins' request for an equitable exception to the statute of limitations, the State charges, would "rende[r] superfluous this carefully scripted scheme."
>
> The State's argument in this regard bears blinders. AEDPA's time limitations apply to the typical case in which no allegation of actual innocence is

made. The miscarriage of justice exception, we underscore, applies to a severely confined category: cases in which new evidence shows "it is more likely than not that no reasonable juror would have convicted [the petitioner]." *Schlup*. Section 2244(d)(1)(D) is both modestly more stringent (because it requires diligence) and dramatically less stringent (because it requires no showing of innocence). Many petitions that could not pass through the actual-innocence gateway will be timely or not measured by § 2244(d)(1)(D)'s triggering provision. That provision, in short, will hardly be rendered superfluous by recognition of the miscarriage of justice exception. . . .

Our reading of the statute is supported by the Court's opinion in *Holland v. Florida*, 560 U.S. 631 (2010). "[E]quitable principles have traditionally governed the substantive law of habeas corpus," *Holland* reminded, and affirmed that "we will not construe a statute to displace courts' traditional equitable authority absent the clearest command." The text of § 2244(d)(1) contains no clear command countering the courts' equitable authority to invoke the miscarriage of justice exception to overcome expiration of the statute of limitations governing a first federal habeas petition.

Justice Scalia, joined by Chief Justice Roberts and Justices Thomas and Alito, filed a blistering dissent:

The gaping hole in today's opinion for the Court is its failure to answer the crucial question upon which all else depends: What is the source of the Court's power to fashion what it concedes is an "exception" to this clear statutory command? That question is unanswered because there is no answer. This Court has no such power, and not one of the cases cited by the opinion says otherwise. The Constitution vests legislative power only in Congress, which never enacted the exception the Court creates today. That inconvenient truth resolves this case. . . .

There is nothing inherently inappropriate (as opposed to merely unwise) about judge-created exceptions to judge-made barriers to relief. Procedural default, for example, raises "no question of a federal district court's power to entertain an application for a writ of habeas corpus." Where a petitioner would, but for a judge-made doctrine like procedural default, have a good habeas claim, it offends no command of Congress's for a federal court to consider the petition. But that free-and-easy approach has no place where a statutory bar to habeas relief is at issue. "[T]he power to award the writ by any of the courts of the United States, must be given by written law," *Ex parte Bollman*, 4 Cranch 75 (1807) (Marshall, C.J.), and "judgments about the proper scope of the writ are normally for Congress to make," *Felker v. Turpin*, 518 U.S. 651 (1996). One would have thought it too obvious to mention that this Court is duty bound to enforce AEDPA, not amend it. . . .

Because we have no "equitable" power to discard statutory barriers to habeas relief, we cannot simply extend judge-made exceptions to judge-made barriers into the statutory realm. The Court's insupportable leap from judge-made procedural bars to all procedural bars, including statutory bars, does all the work in its opinion—and there is not a whit of precedential support for it. . . . *House v. Bell* [was an] application[] of the judge-made doctrine of procedural default. *Calderon v. Thompson*, a non-AEDPA case, involved the courts of appeals' "inherent power to recall their mandates, subject to review for an abuse of discretion"; it stands only for the proposition that the miscarriage-of-justice exception is an appropriate "means of channeling" that discretion. . . . Judicially amending a validly enacted statute in this way is a flagrant breach of the separation of powers.

Justice Scalia asks, "What is the source of the Court's power to fashion what it concedes is an 'exception' to [a] clear statutory command?" Can you explain how the majority would answer that question? Or does the majority object to the premise of the question?

Just how broad is the authority claimed by the majority in *Perkins*? In addition to the one-year statute of limitations, AEDPA imposes a host of limitations on the federal courts' power to grant habeas relief. Federal courts "shall entertain" a habeas petition "only on the ground that [the petitioner] is in custody in violation of the Constitution or laws of the United States." 28 U.S.C. §2254(a). A petition "shall not be granted" unless the petitioner "has exhausted the remedies available in the courts of the State." §2254(b)(1). The ineffective assistance of counsel in collateral post-conviction proceedings "shall not be a ground for relief." §2254(i). Does *Perkins* authorize federal courts to create "actual innocence" gateways for those provisions as well?

4. In *Herrera*, the Court purports to leave open the question whether "in a capital case a truly persuasive demonstration of 'actual innocence' made after trial would render the execution of a defendant unconstitutional, and warrant federal habeas relief if there were no state avenue open to process such a claim." In *Schlup*, the Court concludes that innocence has a role in excusing procedural defaults and permitting habeas courts, under the proper showing, to reach an otherwise-barred constitutional claim. What explains these results?

5. Our examination of the issues in habeas administration has focused on underlying tensions between the states' interests in the integrity of their criminal sentences and the federal interest in assuring that states comply with federal law. Professor Joseph Hoffmann suggests that in the area of capital sentencing, the "fundamental miscarriage of justice" standard is better explained by the state of federal constitutional law, particularly the Eighth Amendment law that controls capital punishment:

> The primary practical problem with federal habeas corpus in death penalty cases today is that habeas courts are limited to dealing with procedural issues. Although such issues are important, they should properly be seen as secondary, especially in capital cases, to the overriding importance of ensuring that substantive justice is done. It is intolerable for a habeas court reviewing a state death penalty case to be unable to consider directly the possibility of the defendant's factual innocence or the sense that the

defendant, even though guilty, does not deserve to die for his crime; yet this is the way it is.

But what of those capital cases involving substantive error — where the defendant is, in fact, innocent, or where ([as] measured by the community's moral standards) the defendant, even though guilty, does not deserve to die? Fortunately for the defendant, in some such cases, properly preserved procedural error also clearly exists, perhaps even as the cause of the substantive error. Again, the current habeas system is designed to deal, albeit indirectly, with the substantive problems in these kinds of cases.

The current habeas system provides no solution at all, however, for capital cases involving possible substantive error in the absence of clear and properly preserved procedural error. In cases such as *Herrera v. Collins* . . . only two things can happen — and both of them are bad. One possibility is that the habeas court, faced with a persuasive claim of substantive injustice, strains to find a constitutional procedural error sufficient to reverse the conviction or death sentence, thereby contributing to the subsequent over-reversal of other death penalty cases and perpetuating the cycle of excessive proceduralism described above. The other, more horrific possibility is that the habeas court is compelled, in the absence of clear procedural error, to affirm the defendant's conviction and death sentence, thus allowing a possibly innocent defendant, or one deserving only a life sentence, to be executed.

Hoffmann argues that the solution to the problem he poses is a reinterpretation of the Eighth Amendment to place substantive limits on all capital sentences. Joseph Hoffmann, *Substance and Procedure in Capital Cases: Why Federal Habeas Courts Should Review the Merits of Every Death Sentence*, 78 TEX. L. REV. 1771, 1795-96 (2000).

Justice Scalia disagrees:

It would be marvelously inspiring to be able to boast that we have a criminal-justice system in which a claim of "actual innocence" will always be heard, no matter how late it is brought forward, and no matter how much the failure to bring it forward at the proper time is the defendant's own fault. But, of course, we do not have such a system, and no society unwilling to devote unlimited resources to repetitive criminal litigation ever could.

Bousley v. United States, 523 U.S. 614 (1998) (Scalia, J., dissenting).

6. The empirical study cited at the outset of this chapter noted that the success rate is dramatically different for habeas petitioners in capital cases (33 of 368 cases) as opposed to non-capital cases (1 in 341). Many of the cases in which the Court has had the most difficulty applying reasonableness standards are capital cases. Should Congress and the Court recognize this reality by adopting explicitly different, and less exacting, standards for habeas review of death penalty cases?

E. The Suspension Clause and "Adequate Substitutes" for Habeas Corpus

The Constitution forbids the suspension of the writ of habeas corpus except "when in Cases of Rebellion or Invasion the public Safety may require it," Art. I, §9, cl. 2. Nevertheless, in an early opinion by Chief Justice Marshall, the Supreme Court held that the Suspension Clause does not, of its own force, provide federal jurisdiction to issue writs of habeas corpus. Rather, jurisdiction exists only if Congress has granted it through statute. *Ex parte Bollman*, 8 U.S. (4 Cranch) 75 (1807): "[F]or the meaning of the term habeas corpus, resort may unquestionably be had to the common law; but the power to award the writ by any of the courts of the United States, must be given by written law."

Under *Bollman*, is Congress free to refuse to vest habeas corpus jurisdiction in the federal courts at all? For most of our nation's history, this question has been purely theoretical. Section 14 of the Judiciary Act of 1789 vested federal courts with jurisdiction to hear habeas corpus petitions from federal prisoners, and in 1867, the Reconstruction Congress expanded that jurisdiction to state prisoners. Despite *Bollman*, the Court has repeatedly suggested that a congressional repeal of all power to hear claims of illegal detention would raise serious constitutional questions. *See, e.g., I.N.S. v. St. Cyr*, 533 U.S. 289 (2001); *Felker v. Turpin*, 518 U.S. 651 (1996); *Swain v. Pressley*, 430 U.S. 372 (1977). None of these decisions, however, involved statutes that withdrew the federal courts' jurisdiction over the writ and none provided the opportunity to discuss the contours of the Suspension Clause.

In the wake of the attacks of September 11, 2001, and the wars in Afghanistan and Iraq, the Executive Branch and Congress began to devise methods for dealing with those who were detained both on the battlefield and in other regions of the globe. By legislation in 2005 and 2006, Congress sought to withdraw federal courts' jurisdiction over petitions for habeas corpus brought by aliens imprisoned at Guantanamo Bay, Cuba, and to replace it with proceedings before newly formed Combatant Status Review Tribunals (CSRTs). The aliens challenged that action as a violation of the Suspension Clause.

In *Boumediene v. Bush*, 553 U.S. 723 (2008), the Supreme Court held in a 5-4 decision that Congress had improperly suspended the writ of habeas corpus; it struck down the provisions withdrawing federal courts' jurisdiction to hear habeas claims. The sprawling majority opinion delved deep into the common-law history of the writ to resolve difficult threshold questions, holding *inter alia* that the writ extends to foreign nationals and enemy combatants and that it applies extraterritorially to areas under the complete control of the United States. An extended discussion of *Boumediene* is beyond the scope of this casebook, but one feature of the decision warrants brief discussion. The Court acknowledged that no writ suspension occurs when Congress provides an "adequate substitute" to habeas proceedings. To qualify as adequate, however, the substitute process must at a minimum "entitle[] the prisoner to a meaningful opportunity to demonstrate that he is being held pursuant to the erroneous application or interpretation of relevant law," and afford the habeas court "power to order the conditional release of an individual unlawfully detained." The CSRTs were not adequate, the Court concluded, because constraints on the detainee's ability to rebut the factual basis for the Government's assertion that he is an enemy combatant created "considerable risk of error in the tribunal's findings of fact."

But what is the baseline against which the Court will measure substitute procedures? The writ as it existed at common law? The statutory writ as it is expressed through 28 U.S.C. § 2241? The protections required by the Due Process Clause? Or something else?

Numerous unsuccessful Suspension Clause challenges have been raised to various AEDPA provisions, including its statute of limitations and its requirement that a petitioner seek leave to proceed from the court of appeals before bringing a second or successive petition. In *Felker v. Turpin*, 518 U.S. 651 (1996), for example, the Court acknowledged that AEDPA "further restricts the availability of relief to habeas petitioners." But it noted that, long before AEDPA, the courts themselves had developed an "abuse of the writ" doctrine that limited second and successive petitions through "a complex and evolving body of equitable principles." Because the new restrictions in AEDPA "are well within the compass of this evolutionary process," the Court reasoned, they "do not amount to a 'suspension' of the writ contrary to Article I, § 9."

Given the Court's sharp distinction between executive detention and conviction by a court of record, can you imagine any situation in which a restriction on, rather than elimination of, habeas review could trigger Suspension Clause concerns? Could Congress, for instance, limit the lower federal courts to review of only those state criminal convictions that involve a sentence of death, on the theory that the combination of state appellate and post-conviction review and the possibility of direct review in the Supreme Court for other state convictions is adequate?

Part Six

Systemic Issues in Federal Litigation

Chapter 16

Parallel Proceedings in State and Federal Court

Sections 1331 and 1332 of Title 28 are broad grants of jurisdiction. On their face, they authorize the federal district courts to hear any case either arising under federal law or satisfying the diversity requirements. Further, the Supreme Court has emphasized that if a federal court has jurisdiction over a case, the court's obligation to hear and decide the case is "virtually unflagging."

Although these expansive grants of jurisdiction serve important purposes, their breadth raises several concerns. One concern is the risk of unnecessarily duplicative litigation. Almost all district court jurisdiction is concurrent with the jurisdiction of the state courts. Accordingly, lawsuits involving the same controversy between the same parties can be brought simultaneously in both state and federal court, consuming the resources of both court systems and increasing the expense of litigation. There is also the possibility that the state and federal courts will reach conflicting results. Another concern is the threat of undue federal interference with state court proceedings, especially when the relief requested in federal court is designed to short-circuit proceedings in state court. A fourth worry is that these broad jurisdictional grants raise the possibility that the federal courts will be asked to hear suits involving quintessentially state-law issues.

For these reasons, there are quite a few circumstances in which the pendency or possibility of a parallel state-court proceeding does limit what the federal court can do.

First, Congress itself has enacted various statutes prohibiting federal courts from issuing *injunctions* to stay proceedings in state courts. The most significant of these is the Anti-Injunction Act. That Act bars federal courts from enjoining any proceeding in a state court, but it also includes three significant exceptions. The Act and its exceptions are considered in section A.

Second, notwithstanding its repeated statements about the "virtually unflagging" obligation, the Supreme Court has developed a variety of doctrines under which federal courts may or must abstain from exercising jurisdiction. Under these abstention doctrines, district courts may decline to hear some suits to avoid "needless friction with state policies" when state law is unclear (*Pullman*), to avoid disruption of important state governmental processes (*Burford*), or to avoid interference with pending state criminal proceedings (and some closely related civil proceedings) (*Younger*). These doctrines are discussed in section B.

Third, even when abstention doctrines do not apply, the Court has held that "exceptional circumstances" and "the danger of piecemeal litigation" may sometimes require a federal court to stay its hand in deference to a parallel proceeding already pending in state court. This line of cases is discussed in section C.

Finally, the Court has held that federal district courts do not have jurisdiction over suits that raise certain family matters such as divorce and alimony, or that involve probate. Section D discusses these domestic relations and probate exceptions.

Some of the judicially created doctrines apply broadly to civil litigation otherwise within the jurisdiction under section 1331 or 1332; others are designed for suits challenging state official action. As you read the materials in this chapter, consider: (a) the class of cases to which each doctrine applies; (b) the interests Congress sought to protect when it vested jurisdiction over those cases; and (c) whether the Court has adequately justified the limitations it has placed on the exercise of that jurisdiction.

A. Injunctions Against Suits in State Court

Atlantic Coast Line Railroad Company v. Brotherhood of Locomotive Engineers

Supreme Court of the United States, 1970.

398 U.S. 281.

Mr. Justice Black delivered the opinion of the Court.

Congress in 1793, shortly after the American Colonies became one united Nation, provided that in federal courts "a writ of injunction [shall not] be granted to stay proceedings in any court of a state." Act of March 2, 1793, § 5, 1 Stat. 335. Although certain exceptions to this general prohibition have been added, that statute, directing that state courts shall remain free from interference by federal courts, has remained in effect until this time. Today that amended statute provides:

> A court of the United States may not grant an injunction to stay proceedings in a State court except as expressly authorized by Act of Congress, or where necessary in aid of its jurisdiction, or to protect or effectuate its judgments. 28 U.S.C. § 2283.

Despite the existence of this longstanding prohibition, in this case a federal court did enjoin the petitioner, Atlantic Coast Line Railroad Co. (ACL), from invoking an injunction issued by a Florida state court which prohibited certain picketing by respondent Brotherhood of Locomotive Engineers (BLE). The case arose in the following way.

In 1967 BLE began picketing the Moncrief Yard, a switching yard located near Jacksonville, Florida, and wholly owned and operated by ACL. As soon as this picketing began ACL went into federal court seeking an injunction. When the federal judge denied the request, ACL immediately went into state court and there succeeded in obtaining an injunction. No further legal action was taken in this dispute until two years later in 1969, after this Court's decision in *Brotherhood of Railroad Trainmen v. Jacksonville Terminal Co.*, 394 U.S. 369 (1969). In that case the Court considered the validity of a state injunction against picketing by the BLE and other unions at the Jacksonville Terminal, located immediately next to Moncrief Yard. The Court reviewed the factual situation surrounding the Jacksonville Terminal picketing and concluded that the unions had a federally protected right to picket under the Railway Labor Act, and that that right could not be interfered with by state court injunctions.

Immediately after a petition for rehearing was denied in that case, the respondent BLE filed a motion in state court to dissolve the Moncrief Yard injunction, arguing that under the *Jacksonville Terminal* decision the injunction was improper. The state judge refused to dissolve the injunction, holding that this Court's *Jacksonville Terminal* decision was not controlling. The union did not elect to appeal that decision directly, but instead went back into the federal court and requested an injunction against the enforcement of the state court injunction. The District Judge granted the injunction and upon application a stay of that injunction, pending the filing and disposition of a petition for certiorari, was granted. The Court of Appeals summarily affirmed on the parties' stipulation, and we granted a petition for certiorari to consider the validity of the federal court's injunction against the state court.

In this Court the union contends that the federal injunction was proper either "to protect or effectuate" the District Court's denial of an injunction in 1967, or as "necessary in aid of" the District Court's jurisdiction. Although the questions are by no means simple and clear, and the decision is difficult, we conclude that the injunction against the state court was not justified under either of these two exceptions to the anti-injunction statute. We therefore hold that the federal injunction in this case was improper.

I

. . . While all the reasons that led Congress to adopt [the anti-injunction statute] are not wholly clear, it is certainly likely that one reason stemmed from the essentially federal nature of our national government. When this Nation was established by the Constitution, each State surrendered only a part of its sovereign power to the national government. But those powers that were not surrendered were retained by the States and unless a State was restrained by "the supreme Law of the Land" as expressed in the Constitution, laws, or treaties of the United States, it was free to exercise those retained powers as it saw fit. One of the reserved powers was the maintenance of state judicial systems for the decision of legal controversies. Many of the Framers of the Constitution felt that separate federal courts were unnecessary and that the state courts could be entrusted to protect both state and federal rights. Others felt that a complete system of federal courts to take care of federal legal problems should be provided for in the Constitution itself. This dispute resulted in compromise. One "supreme Court" was created by the Constitution, and Congress was given the power to create other federal courts. In the first Congress this power was exercised and a system of federal trial and appellate courts with limited jurisdiction was created by the Judiciary Act of 1789.

While the lower federal courts were given certain powers in the 1789 Act, they were not given any power to review directly cases from state courts, and they have not been given such powers since that time. . . . Thus from the beginning we have had in this country two essentially separate legal systems. Each system proceeds independently of the other with ultimate review in this Court of the federal questions raised in either system. Understandably this dual court system was bound to lead to conflicts and frictions. Litigants who foresaw the possibility of more favorable treatment in one or the other system would predictably hasten to invoke the powers of whichever court it was believed would present the best chance of success. Obviously this dual system could not function if state and federal courts were free to fight each other for control of a particular case. Thus, in order to make the dual system work and "to prevent needless friction between state and federal courts," it was necessary to work out lines of demarcation between the two systems. Some of these limits were spelled out in the 1789 Act. Others have been added by later statutes as well as judicial decisions. The 1793 anti-injunction Act was at least in part a response to these pressures.

On its face the present Act is an absolute prohibition against enjoining state court proceedings, unless the injunction falls within one of three specifically defined exceptions. The respondents here have intimated that the Act only establishes a "principle of comity," not a binding rule on the power of the federal courts. The argument implies that in certain circumstances a federal court may enjoin state court proceedings even if that action cannot be justified by any of the three exceptions. We cannot accept any such contention. In 1955 when this Court interpreted this statute, it stated: "This is not a statute conveying a broad general policy for appropriate ad hoc application. Legislative policy is here expressed in a clearcut prohibition qualified only by specifically defined exceptions." *Amalgamated Clothing Workers v. Richman Bros.*, 348 U.S. 511 (1955). Since that time Congress has not seen fit to amend the statute and we therefore adhere to that position and hold that any injunction against state court proceedings otherwise proper under general equitable principles must be based on one of the specific statutory exceptions to § 2283 if it is to be upheld. Moreover since the statutory prohibition against such injunctions in part rests on the fundamental constitutional independence of the States and their courts, the exceptions should not be enlarged by loose statutory construction. Proceedings in state courts should normally be allowed to continue unimpaired by intervention of the lower federal courts, with relief from error, if any, through the state appellate courts and ultimately this Court.

II

In this case the Florida Circuit Court enjoined the union's intended picketing, and the United States District Court enjoined the railroad "from giving effect to or availing [itself] of the benefits of that state court order." Both sides agree that although this federal injunction is in terms directed only at the railroad it is an injunction "to stay proceedings in a State court." It is settled that the prohibition of § 2283 cannot be evaded by addressing the order to the parties or prohibiting utilization of the results of a completed state proceeding. *Oklahoma Packing Co. v. Oklahoma Gas & Electric Co.*, 309 U.S. 4, 9 (1940). Thus if the injunction against the Florida court proceedings is to be upheld, it must be "expressly authorized by Act of Congress," "necessary in aid of [the District Court's] jurisdiction," or "to protect or effectuate [that court's] judgments."

Neither party argues that there is any express congressional authorization for injunctions in this situation and we agree with that conclusion. The respondent union does contend that the injunction was proper either as a means to protect or effectuate the District Court's 1967 order, or in aid of that court's jurisdiction. We do not think that either alleged basis can be supported.

A

The argument based on protecting the 1967 order is not clearly expressed, but in essence it appears to run as follows: In 1967 the railroad sought a temporary restraining order which the union opposed. In the course of deciding that request, the United States District Court determined that the union had a federally protected right to picket Moncrief Yard and that this right could not be interfered with by state courts. When the Florida Circuit Court enjoined the picketing, the United States District Court could, in order to protect and effectuate its prior determination, enjoin enforcement of the state court injunction. Although the record on this point is not unambiguously clear, we conclude that no such interpretation of the 1967 order can be supported.

When the railroad initiated the federal suit it filed a complaint with three counts, each based entirely on alleged violations of federal law. The first two counts alleged violations of the Railway Labor Act, and the third alleged a violation of that Act and the Interstate Commerce Act as well. Each of the counts concluded with a prayer for an injunction against the picketing. Although the union had not been formally served with the complaint and had not filed an answer, it appeared at a hearing on a motion for a temporary restraining order and argued against the issuance of such an order. The union argued that it was a party to a labor dispute with the FEC [another railroad, whose cars used the Moncrief Yard], that it had exhausted the administrative remedies required by the Railway Labor Act, and that it was thus free to engage in "self-help," or concerted economic activity. Then the union argued that such activity could not be enjoined by the federal court. . . . At no point during the entire argument did either side refer to state law, the effects of that law on the picketing, or the possible preclusion of state remedies as a result of overriding federal law. The next day the District Court entered an order denying the requested restraining order. In relevant part that order included these conclusions of law:

3. The parties to the BLE-FEC "major dispute," having exhausted the procedures of the Railway Labor Act . . . are now free to engage in self-help. * * *

4. The conduct of the FEC pickets and that of the responding ACL employees are a part of the FEC-BLE major dispute.* * *

7. The Norris-LaGuardia Act, 29 U.S.C. § 101, and the Clayton Act, 29 U.S.C. § 52, are applicable to the conduct of the defendants here involved.

In this Court the union asserts that the determination that it was "free to engage in self-help" was a determination that it had a federally protected right to picket and that state law could not be invoked to negate that right. The railroad, on the other hand, argues that the order merely determined that the federal court could not enjoin the picketing, in large part because of the general prohibition in the Norris-LaGuardia Act against issuance by federal courts of injunctions in labor disputes. Based solely on the state of the record when the order was entered, we are inclined to believe that the District Court did not determine whether federal law precluded an injunction based on state law. Not only was that point never argued to the court, but there is no language in the order that necessarily implies any decision on that question. In short we feel that the District Court in 1967 determined that federal law could not be invoked to enjoin the picketing at Moncrief Yard, and that the union did have a right "to engage in self-help" as far as the federal courts were concerned. But that decision is entirely different from a decision that the Railway Labor Act precludes state regulation of the picketing as well, and this latter decision is an essential prerequisite for upholding the 1969 injunction as necessary "to protect or effectuate" the 1967 order. . . .

Any lingering doubts we might have as to the proper interpretation of the 1967 order are settled by references to the positions adopted by the parties later in the litigation. . . . At no point did the union appear to argue that the federal court had already determined that the railroad was precluded from obtaining an injunction under Florida law.

Similarly the union's arguments in 1969 indicate that the 1967 federal order did not determine whether federal law precluded resort to the state courts. When the union tried to dissolve the state court injunction, the argument was based entirely on the controlling effect of the *Jacksonville Terminal* decision on the picketing at Moncrief Yard. The union argued that this Court's "decision is squarely controlling upon [the Moncrief Yard] case which is identical in all material respects." Although the union again mentioned that the federal District Judge had determined in 1967 that it was free to engage in self-help, it never argued that the 1967 order had in effect held with respect to Moncrief Yard what this Court later held was the law with respect to the Jacksonville Terminal situation. The railroad argued that *Jacksonville Terminal* was not controlling, and the Florida judge agreed.

Our reading of this record is not altered by the District Court's 1969 opinion issued when the injunction was granted two years after the 1967 order was entered. [The opinion is ambiguous, and proper interpretation requires consideration of the arguments presented to the District Court by the union.]

. . . At no point during [the] hearing did the union try to argue, as it now appears to do, that the 1967 order itself had anticipated the *Jacksonville Terminal* decision. . . . On the contrary, we read [language] in the 1969 opinion as an indication that the District Court accepted the union's argument and concluded that the *Jacksonville Terminal* decision had amplified its 1967 order, and it was this amplification, rather than the original order itself, that required protection. Such a modification of an earlier order through an opinion in another case is not a "judgment" that can properly be protected by an injunction against state court proceedings.

This record, we think, conclusively shows that neither the parties themselves nor the District Court construed the 1967 order as the union now contends it should be construed. Rather we are convinced that the union in effect tried to get the Federal District Court to decide that the state court judge was wrong in distinguishing the *Jacksonville Terminal* decision. Such an attempt to seek appellate review of a state decision in the Federal District Court cannot be justified as necessary "to protect or effectuate" the 1967 order. The record simply will not support the union's contention on this point.

B

This brings us to the second prong of the union's argument in which it is suggested that even if the 1967 order did not determine the union's right to picket free from state interference, once the decision in *Jacksonville Terminal* was announced, the District Court was then free to enjoin the state court on the theory that such action was "necessary in aid of [the District Court's] jurisdiction." Again the argument is some-what unclear, but it appears to go in this way: The District Court had acquired juris-diction over the labor controversy in 1967 when the railroad filed its complaint, and it determined at that time that it did have jurisdiction. The dispute involved the legality of picketing by the union and the *Jacksonville Terminal* decision clearly indicated that such activity was not only legal, but was protected from state court interference. The state court had interfered with that right, and thus a federal injunction was "necessary in aid of its jurisdiction." For several reasons we cannot accept the contention.

First, a federal court does not have inherent power to ignore the limitations of § 2283 and to enjoin state court proceedings merely because those proceedings inter-fere with a protected federal right or invade an area preempted by federal law, even when the interference is unmistakably clear. This rule applies regardless of whether the federal court itself has jurisdiction over the controversy, or whether it is ousted from jurisdiction for the same reason that the state court is. This conclusion is required because Congress itself set forth the only exceptions to the statute, and those excep-tions do not include this situation.

Second, if the District Court does have jurisdiction, it is not enough that the requested injunction is related to that jurisdiction, but it must be "necessary in aid of" that jurisdiction. While this language is admittedly broad, we conclude that it implies something similar to the concept of injunctions to "protect or effectuate" judg-ments. Both exceptions to the general prohibition of § 2283 imply that some federal injunctive relief may be necessary to prevent a state court from so interfering with a federal court's consideration or disposition of a case as to seriously impair the federal court's flexibility and authority to decide that case.

Third, no such situation is presented here. Although the federal court did have juris-diction of the railroad's complaint based on federal law, the state court also had juris-diction over the complaint based on state law and the union's asserted federal defense as well. While the railroad could probably have based its federal case on the pendent state law claims as well, *United Mine Workers v. Gibbs*, 383 U.S. 715 (1966) [Chapter 10], it was free to refrain from doing so and leave the state law questions and the related issue concerning preclusion of state remedies by federal law to the state courts. Conversely, although it could have tendered its federal claims to the state court, it was also free to restrict the state complaint to state grounds alone. *Cf. England v. Louisiana State Board of Medical Examiners*, 375 U.S. 411 (1964).

conclusion

In short, the state and federal courts had concurrent jurisdiction in this case, and neither court was free to prevent either party from simultaneously pursuing claims in both courts. *Kline v. Burke Constr. Co.*, 260 U.S. 226 (1922); *cf. Donovan v. City of Dallas*, 377 U.S. 408 (1964). Therefore the state court's assumption of jurisdiction over the state law claims and the federal preclusion issue did not hinder the federal court's jurisdiction so as to make an injunction necessary to aid that jurisdiction. Nor was an injunction necessary because the state court may have taken action which the federal court was certain was improper under the *Jacksonville Terminal* decision. Again, lower federal courts possess no power whatever to sit in direct review of state court decisions. If the union was adversely affected by the state court's decision, it was free to seek vindication of its federal right in the Florida appellate courts and ultimately, if necessary, in this Court. Similarly if, because of the Florida Circuit Court's action, the union faced the threat of immediate irreparable injury sufficient to justify an injunction under usual equitable principles, it was undoubtedly free to seek such relief from the Florida appellate courts, and might possibly in certain emergency circumstances seek such relief from this Court as well. Unlike the Federal District Court, this Court does have potential appellate jurisdiction over federal questions raised in state court proceedings, and that broader jurisdiction allows this Court correspondingly broader authority to issue injunctions "necessary in aid of its jurisdiction."

III

This case is by no means an easy one. The arguments in support of the union's contentions are not insubstantial. But whatever doubts we may have are strongly affected by the general prohibition of § 2283. Any doubts as to the propriety of a federal injunction against state court proceedings should be resolved in favor of permitting the state courts to proceed in an orderly fashion to finally determine the controversy. The explicit wording of § 2283 itself implies as much, and the fundamental principle of a dual system of courts leads inevitably to that conclusion.

The injunction issued by the District Court must be vacated. Since that court has not yet proceeded to a final judgment in the case, the cause is remanded to it for further proceedings in conformity with this opinion.

MR. JUSTICE MARSHALL took no part in the consideration or decision of this case.

MR. JUSTICE HARLAN, concurring. [Omitted.]

MR. JUSTICE BRENNAN, with whom MR. JUSTICE WHITE joins, dissenting.

My disagreement with the Court in this case is a relatively narrow one. I do not disagree with much that is said concerning the history and policies underlying 28 U.S.C. § 2283. Nor do I dispute the Court's holding . . . that federal courts do not have authority to enjoin state proceedings merely because it is asserted that the state court is improperly asserting jurisdiction in an area preempted by federal law or federal procedures. Nevertheless in my view the District Court has discretion to enjoin the state proceedings in the present case because it acted pursuant to an explicit exception to the prohibition of §2283, that is, "to protect or effectuate [the District Court's] judgments." . . .

The thrust of the District Judge's [1967] order is that the procedures prescribed by the Railway Labor Act had been exhausted in relation to the BLE-FEC dispute, that BLE was therefore free to engage in self-help tactics, and that it was properly exercising this federal right when it engaged in the picketing that ACL sought to enjoin. . . . In my view, what the District Court decided in 1967 was that BLE had a federally protected right to picket at the Moncrief Yard and, by necessary implication, that this right could not be subverted by resort to state proceedings. . . .

Note: The Anti-Injunction Act and Its Exceptions

1. As Justice Black notes, the Anti-Injunction Act has existed in some form since the beginning of the nation. The statute as interpreted in *Atlantic Coast Line*, however, is the result of a 1948 revision. The history of the Act, including that revision, is recounted in *Mitchum v. Foster*, 407 U.S. 225 (1972):

> In 1793, Congress enacted a law providing that no "writ of injunction be granted [by any federal court] to stay proceedings in any court of a state." The precise origins of the legislation are shrouded in obscurity, but the consistent understanding has been that its basic purpose is to prevent "needless friction between state and federal courts." The law remained unchanged until 1874, when it was amended to permit a federal court to stay state court proceedings that interfered with the administration of a federal bankruptcy proceeding. The present wording of the legislation was adopted with the enactment of Title 28 of the United States Code in 1948.
>
> Despite the seemingly uncompromising language of the anti-injunction statute prior to 1948, the Court soon recognized that exceptions must be made to its blanket prohibition if the import and purpose of other Acts of Congress were to be given their intended scope. So it was that, in addition to the bankruptcy law exception that Congress explicitly recognized in 1874, the Court through the years found that federal courts were empowered to enjoin state court proceedings, despite the anti-injunction statute, in carrying out the will of Congress under at least six other federal laws. These covered a broad spectrum of congressional action: (1) legislation providing for removal of litigation from state to federal courts, (2) legislation limiting the liability of ship-owners, (3) legislation providing for federal interpleader actions, (4) legislation conferring federal jurisdiction over farm mortgages, (5) legislation governing federal habeas corpus proceedings, and (6) legislation providing for control of prices.

In addition to the exceptions to the anti-injunction statute found to be embodied in these various Acts of Congress, the Court recognized other "implied" exceptions to the blanket prohibition of the anti-injunction statute. One was an "in rem" exception, allowing a federal court to enjoin a state court proceeding in order to protect its jurisdiction of a res over which it had first acquired jurisdiction. Another was a "relitigation" exception, permitting a federal court to enjoin relitigation in a state court of issues already decided in federal litigation. Still a third exception, more recently developed, permits a federal injunction of state court proceedings when the plaintiff in the federal court is the United States itself, or a federal agency asserting "superior federal interests."

In *Toucey v. New York Life Ins. Co.*, 314 U.S. 118, the Court in 1941 issued an opinion casting considerable doubt upon the approach to the anti-injunction statute reflected in its previous decisions. The Court's opinion expressly disavowed the "relitigation" exception to the statute, and emphasized generally the importance of recognizing the statute's basic directive "of 'hands off' by the federal courts in the use of the injunction to stay litigation in a state court." The congressional response to *Toucey* was the enactment in 1948 of the anti-injunction statute in its present form in 28 U.S.C. § 2283, which, as the Reviser's Note makes evident, served not only to overrule the specific holding of *Toucey*, but to restore "the basic law as generally understood and interpreted prior to the *Toucey* decision."

2. The Court in *Atlantic Coast Line Railroad* acknowledges that the union may have a federally protected right to picket free from state-court interference, but it holds that the Act prohibits a federal district court from enforcing that right through an injunction. The union's only recourse is to seek certiorari from the state-court decision in the United States Supreme Court. But the Supreme Court's jurisdiction is entirely discretionary; moreover, before taking the case to the Supreme Court, the union must seek redress from "the highest court of [the] state in which a decision could be had." (See Chapter 5.) Does this arrangement adequately protect federal rights? Note the parallel to the well-pleaded complaint rule, discussed in Chapter 10.

3. *Atlantic Coast Line* recognizes that the Act itself contains three explicit exceptions. First, injunctions against state-court proceedings may be "expressly authorized by Act of Congress." Second, they may be "necessary in aid of [the federal court's] jurisdiction." Finally, they may be necessary "to protect or effectuate [the federal court's] judgments."

Note: "Expressly Authorized" Exceptions

1. The prohibition of § 2283 does not apply when an exception is "expressly authorized by Act of Congress." In *Mitchum v. Foster*, 407 U.S. 225 (1972), the Court held that 42 U.S.C. § 1983 is such an Act. Section 1983 authorizes suits against "[e]very person who, under color of any statute, ordinance, custom, or usage, of any state or territory, subjects . . . any citizen of the United States or other person within the

jurisdiction thereof to the deprivation of any rights, privileges, or immunities secured by the Constitution or laws, shall be liable to the party injured in an action at law, suit in equity, or other proper proceeding for redress." Section 1983 provides a powerful tool for enforcing federal constitutional rights against state officials. For discussion, see Chapter 14.

The *Mitchum* Court reviewed the application of the "expressly authorized" exception:

> In the first place, it is evident that, in order to qualify under the "expressly authorized" exception of the anti-injunction statute, a federal law need not contain an express reference to that statute. . . . Indeed, none of the previously recognized statutory exceptions contains any such reference. Secondly, a federal law need not expressly authorize an injunction of a state court proceeding in order to qualify as an exception. Three of the six previously recognized statutory exceptions contain no such authorization. Thirdly, it is clear that, in order to qualify as an "expressly authorized" exception to the anti-injunction statute, an Act of Congress must have created a specific and uniquely federal right or remedy, enforceable in a federal court of equity, that could be frustrated if the federal court were not empowered to enjoin a state court proceeding.

> This is not to say that in order to come within the exception an Act of Congress must, on its face and in every one of its provisions, be totally incompatible with the prohibition of the anti-injunction statute. The test, rather, is whether an Act of Congress, clearly creating a federal right or remedy enforceable in a federal court of equity, could be given its intended scope only by the stay of a state court proceeding.

After reviewing the legislative history of § 1983, the Court concluded:

> This legislative history makes evident that Congress clearly conceived that it was altering the relationship between the States and the Nation with respect to the protection of federally created rights; it was concerned that state instrumentalities could not protect those rights; it realized that state officers might, in fact, be antipathetic to the vindication of those rights; and it believed that these failings extended to the state courts.

> . . . Section 1983 was thus a product of a vast transformation from the concepts of federalism that had prevailed in the late 18th century when the anti-injunction statute was enacted. The very purpose of § 1983 was to interpose the federal courts between the States and the people, as guardians of the people's federal rights—to protect the people from unconstitutional action under color of state law, "whether that action be executive, legislative, or judicial." *Ex parte Virginia*, 100 U.S. 339 (1880). In carrying out that purpose, Congress plainly authorized the federal courts to issue injunctions in § 1983 actions, by expressly authorizing a "suit in equity" as one of the means of redress. And this Court long ago recognized that federal injunctive relief

against a state court proceeding can in some circumstances be essential to prevent great, immediate, and irreparable loss of a person's constitutional rights. *Ex parte Young*, 209 U.S. 123 (1908) [Chapter 13]. For these reasons we conclude that, under the criteria established in our previous decisions construing the anti-injunction statute, § 1983 is an Act of Congress that falls within the "expressly authorized" exception of that law.

2. The holding in *Mitchum* remains intact, but that does not mean that injunctions against state court proceedings routinely issue in proceedings under § 1983. In section B, *infra*, we will explore the doctrine that prevents federal courts from interfering in pending state criminal proceedings, even when such proceedings are alleged to be unconstitutional and are challenged in federal court through a lawsuit under § 1983. The landmark decision is *Younger v. Harris*, 401 U.S. 37 (1971).

3. While § 1983 was certainly the result of a change in thinking about the role of the federal government after the Civil War, its text does not explicitly state that federal courts may enjoin state court proceedings. Compare, for instance, the federal interpleader statute, 28 U.S.C. § 2361, which states:

> In any civil action of interpleader or in the nature of interpleader . . . , a district court may issue its process for all claimants and enter its order restraining them from instituting or prosecuting any proceeding in any State or United States court affecting the property, instrument or obligation involved in the interpleader action until further order of the court.

On the other hand, several other statutes that do not explicitly state that the federal court can restrain state-court litigation have been held to be within the exception. For example, the federal removal statute, at 28 U.S.C.A. § 1446(d), states:

> Promptly after the filing of . . . notice of removal of a civil action the defendant or defendants shall give written notice thereof to all adverse parties and shall file a copy of the notice with the clerk of such State court, which shall effect the removal and the State court shall proceed no further unless and until the case is remanded.

This language is generally held to be an explicit exception to the Anti-Injunction Act prohibition, although the power of the federal court to enforce this provision by injunction is nowhere stated.

4. Does *Mitchum* mean that any federal statute authorizing equitable relief will be found to be an expressly authorized exception? In *Vendo Co. v. Lectro-Vend Corp.*, 433 U.S. 623 (1977), the Court considered the argument that section 16 of the Clayton Act falls within this category. Section 16 provides in relevant part:

> [A]ny person . . . shall be entitled to sue for and have injunctive relief, in any court of the United States having jurisdiction over the parties, against threatened loss or damage by violation of the antitrust laws . . . when and under the same conditions and principles as injunctive relief against threatened conduct that will cause loss or damage is granted by courts of equity, under the rules governing such proceedings. . . .

The *Vendo* case involved a dispute between competing vending machine companies that led to parallel suits in state and federal court. Vendo sued Lectro-Vend in state court for breach of certain covenants not to compete, while Lectro-Vend sued Vendo in federal district court for antitrust violations. The state-court litigation ran its protracted course; ultimately the Supreme Court of Illinois affirmed a judgment in favor of Vendo in the amount of $7,363,500. The court predicated its judgment on a theory of breach of fiduciary duty rather than upon any breach of the noncompetitive covenants.

Meanwhile, the federal antitrust suit was allowed to lie dormant. However, at the conclusion of the state proceedings Lectro-Vend moved in the federal district court for a preliminary injunction against collection of the Illinois judgment. The district court granted the motion upon finding that Vendo used litigation as a method of harassing and eliminating competition. The court of appeals affirmed.

The Supreme Court reversed, but without a majority opinion. Justice Rehnquist, writing for himself and Justices Stewart and Powell, took the position that section 16 is *not* an expressly authorized exception to the Anti-Injunction Act. He distinguished *Mitchum*:

> [In] *Mitchum*, absence of express language authorization for enjoining state-court proceedings in § 1983 actions was cured by the presence of relevant legislative history. In this case, however, neither the respondents nor the courts below have called to our attention any similar legislative history in connection with the enactment of § 16 of the Clayton Act. . . .

> Section 16 undoubtedly embodies congressional policy favoring private enforcement of the antitrust laws, and undoubtedly there exists a strong national interest in antitrust enforcement. However, the "importance of the federal policy to be protected" by the injunction is not the focus of the inquiry. Presumptively, all federal policies enacted into law by Congress are important, and there will undoubtedly arise particular situations in which a particular policy would be fostered by the granting of an injunction against a pending state-court action. If we were to accept respondents' contention that § 16 could be given its "intended scope" only by allowing such injunctions, then § 2283 would be completely eviscerated since the ultimate logic of this position can mean no less than that virtually *all* federal statutes authorizing injunctive relief are exceptions to § 2283.

Justice Blackmun, joined by Chief Justice Burger, concurred in the result, but on narrow grounds. He said:

> In my opinion, application of the *Mitchum* test for deciding whether a statute is an "expressly authorized" exception to the Anti-Injunction Act shows that § 16 is such an exception under narrowly limited circumstances. Nevertheless, consistently with [a 1972 antitrust decision], I would hold that no injunction may issue against currently pending state-court proceedings unless those proceedings are themselves part of a "pattern of baseless, repetitive

claims" that are being used as an anticompetitive device, all the traditional prerequisites for equitable relief are satisfied, and the only way to give the antitrust laws their intended scope is by staying the state proceedings.

[Here, the trial court] did not find a "pattern of baseless, repetitive claims," nor could it have done so under the circumstances. . . . In my opinion, therefore, it cannot be said on this record that Vendo was using the state-court proceeding as an anticompetitive device in and of itself. Thus, I believe that § 16 itself did not authorize the injunction below, and on this ground I would reverse.

Justice Stevens, joined by Justices Brennan, White, and Marshall, dissented. He said:

In the decades following the formulation of the Rule of Reason in 1911, this Court has made it perfectly clear that the prosecution of litigation in a state court may itself constitute a form of violation of the federal [antitrust laws]. . . . Since the judicial construction of a statute is as much a part of the law as the words written by the legislature, the illegal use of state-court litigation as a method of monopolizing or restraining trade is as plainly a violation of the antitrust laws as if Congress had specifically described each of the [cited] cases as an independent violation. The language in § 16 of the Clayton Act which expressly authorizes injunctions against violations of the antitrust laws is therefore applicable to this species of violation as well as to other kinds of violations.

After *Vendo*, would a district court be justified in enjoining state-court proceedings under § 16 if it found that the conditions set forth in Justice Blackmun's opinion were satisfied?

5. No subsequent Supreme Court decisions have found other federal statutes to be an "expressly authorized" exception to the Anti-Injunction Act. A current subject of controversy is ERISA. The preemption provision of ERISA provides that, with certain exceptions, "the provisions of this subchapter . . . shall supersede any and all State laws insofar as they may now or hereafter relate to any employee benefit plan." In *General Motors Corp. v. Buha*, 623 F.2d 455 (6th Cir. 1980), the court said:

ERISA meets both prongs of the *Mitchum* test. [It confers a uniquely federal right or remedy, and it is an act which "could be given its intended scope only by the stay of a state court proceeding."] When a district court finds that an action in a state court will have the effect of making it impossible for a fiduciary of a pension plan to carry out its responsibilities under ERISA, the anti-injunction provisions of § 2283 do not prohibit it from enjoining the state court proceedings.

However, this is distinctly a minority view. See *Denny's Inc. v. Cake*, 364 F.3d 521, 532–35 (4th Cir. 2004) (Williams, J., concurring), for citations.

Note: "Necessary in Aid of Jurisdiction"

1. When is it necessary to enjoin a state court proceeding to protect the jurisdiction of the federal court? The clearest instance, one recognized before the 1948 amendment to § 2283, is when the federal court has obtained jurisdiction over a res in an action in rem. In *Kline v. Burke Const. Co.*, 260 U.S. 226, 229 (1922), the Court stated:

> It is settled that where a federal court has first acquired jurisdiction of the subject-matter of a cause, it may enjoin the parties from proceeding in a state court of concurrent jurisdiction where the effect of the action would be to defeat or impair the jurisdiction of the federal court. Where the action is in rem the effect is to draw to the federal court the possession or control, actual or potential, of the res, and the exercise by the state court of jurisdiction over the same res necessarily impairs, and may defeat, the jurisdiction of the federal court already attached.

But *Kline* also established that in personam actions may proceed simultaneously in both state and federal court:

> [A] controversy is not a thing, and a controversy over a mere question of personal liability does not involve the possession or control of a thing, and an action brought to enforce such a liability does not tend to impair or defeat the jurisdiction of the court in which a prior action for the same cause is pending. Each court is free to proceed in its own way and in its own time, without reference to the proceedings in the other court. Whenever a judgment is rendered in one of the courts and pleaded in the other, the effect of that judgment is to be determined by the application of the principles of res adjudicata by the court in which the action is still pending in the orderly exercise of its jurisdiction, as it would determine any other question of fact or law arising in the progress of the case. The rule, therefore, has become generally established that where the action first brought is in personam and seeks only a personal judgment, another action for the same cause in another jurisdiction is not precluded.

2. The exception has had other applications, most famously to protect a court's ongoing supervision of a desegregation decree. Thus, in *Swann v. Charlotte-Mecklenburg Board of Education*, 402 U.S. 1 (1971), the Supreme Court upheld the terms of a desegregation decree. In *Swann v. Charlotte-Mecklenburg Board of Education*, 501 F.2d 383 (4th Cir. 1974) (en banc), the court held that the district court acted permissibly in enjoining a private, civil suit in state court in which the plaintiff sought an injunction compelling the government to disregard the federal court's decree.

3. More recently, this exception has been widely debated in the class-action and complex-litigation areas, where the federal courts have felt the need to control the proliferation of state-court suits while negotiating settlements in complicated multi-party or class action cases. *See* Andrew Weinstein, *Avoiding the Race to Res Judicata: Federal Antisuit Injunctions of Competing State Class Actions*, 75 N.Y.U. L. Rev. 1085 (2000) (describing efforts of federal courts to analogize class actions to a "res"); *In re*

Corrugated Container Antitrust Litigation, 659 F.2d 1332 (5th Cir. 1981) (relying on *Atlantic Coast Line*'s statement that injunctions may be issued where "necessary to prevent a state court from so interfering with a federal court's consideration or disposition of a case as to seriously impair the federal court's flexibility and authority to decide that case.").

Note: The "Relitigation" Exception

1. The third exception permits federal courts to enter anti-suit injunctions in order to "protect or effectuate" their judgments. It is known as the "relitigation" exception because its primary application is to prevent relitigation of a court's judgments. The ordinary protections against relitigation are the doctrines of preclusion. In *Smith v. Bayer Corp.*, 564 U.S. 299 (2011), the Supreme Court made clear that the relitigation exception is a way of enforcing the preclusive effects of federal judgments and, accordingly, that the exception applies only if the prerequisites for preclusion are met.

In *Smith*, George McCollins brought a putative class action against Bayer Corporation in West Virginia state court. He alleged that Bayer had violated West Virginia's consumer-protection statute and Bayer's express and implied warranties by selling an allegedly hazardous prescription drug called Baycol. Around the same time, Keith Smith also filed a putative class action against Bayer in West Virginia state court, raising claims similar to those in McCollins' action. Bayer removed McCollins' case to federal court. The federal court refused to certify McCollins' proposed class, concluding that individualized issues would predominate over common ones. Then, to prevent relitigation of the class-certification issue, the federal court granted Bayer's motion for an injunction barring the West Virginia state court from certifying the class in Smith's case.

The Supreme Court held that the injunction was improper. The Supreme Court stated that the relitigation exception is "strict and narrow" and justifies an injunction only "if preclusion is clear beyond peradventure." Accordingly, because Bayer sought to prevent relitigation of an issue resolved by the federal court, it had to establish that the basic requirements of issue preclusion had been met. One of those requirements is "the issue the federal court decided must be the same as the one presented in the state tribunal." A second is that the party in the second suit against whom the injunction is sought "must have been a party to the federal suit, or else must fall within one of a few discrete exceptions to the general rule against binding nonparties."

The Court concluded that neither requirement had been satisfied. The Court began by explaining that the issue before the state court was not the same that had been decided by the federal court. The Court stated that the district court in the federal case "ruled that the proposed class did not meet the requirements of Federal Rule 23 (because individualized issues would predominate over common ones). But the state court was poised to consider whether the proposed class satisfied *West Virginia* Rule 23." And, the Court concluded, West Virginia Rule 23 is not identical to Federal Rule 23. The Court wrote:

> [T]he West Virginia Supreme Court has *disapproved* the approach to Rule 23(b)(3)'s predominance requirement that the Federal District Court

embraced. Recall that the federal court held that the presence of a single individualized issue—injury from the use of [Bayer's drug]—prevented class certification. The court did not identify the common issues in the case; nor did it balance these common issues against the need to prove individual injury to determine which predominated. The court instead applied a strict test barring class treatment when proof of each plaintiff's injury is necessary. By contrast, the West Virginia Supreme Court in *In re Rezulin*, 585 S.E.2d 52 (2003), adopted an all-things-considered, balancing inquiry in interpreting its Rule 23. Rejecting any "rigid test," the state court opined that the predominance requirement "contemplates a review of many factors." Indeed, the court noted, a "'single common issue'" in a case could outweigh "'numerous ... individual questions.'" That meant, the court further explained (quoting what it termed the "leading treatise" on the subject), that even objections to certification "'based on ... causation, or reliance'"—which typically involve showings of individual injury—"'will not bar predominance satisfaction.'" So point for point, the analysis set out in *In re Rezulin* diverged from the District Court's interpretation of Federal Rule 23. A state court using the *In re Rezulin* standard would decide a different question than the one the federal court had earlier resolved.

The Court also concluded that Smith, who was not a party to the federal action, did not fall within one of the exceptions for binding nonparties. Rejecting Bayer's argument that Smith could be bound under the rule that unnamed members of a class action can be bound by a judgment even if they are not parties to the suit, the Court wrote:

> If we know one thing about the McCollins suit, we know that it was *not* a class action. Indeed, the very ruling that Bayer argues ought to be given preclusive effect is the District Court's decision that a class could not properly be certified. ...
>
> McCollins sought class certification, but he failed to obtain that result. Because the District Court found that individual issues predominated, it held that the action did not satisfy Federal Rule 23's requirements for class proceedings. In these circumstances, we cannot say that a properly conducted class action existed at any time in the litigation.

Because these requirements of issue preclusion had not been satisfied, the relitigation exception did not apply.

2. Given that res judicata and collateral estoppel are the usual tools for preventing relitigation in state court of matters already decided by a federal court, when should the relitigation exception apply? In *Laker Airways Ltd. v. Sabena*, 731 F.2d 909 (D.C. Cir. 1981), the D.C. Circuit stated that, for the exception to apply, "a showing of harassment, bad faith, or other strong equitable circumstances should ordinarily be required."

3. What happens if a state court has already determined that res judicata does not apply? (This point is discussed further in the next chapter.) In *Parsons Steel, Inc. v.*

First Alabama Bank, 474 U.S. 518 (1986), the Court held that § 2283 is not an exception to 28 U.S.C. § 1738, which requires federal courts to give preclusive effect to state-court judgments. Accordingly, a federal court may not issue an injunction under the relitigation exception if the state court has already ruled that the federal court's earlier ruling does not have preclusive effect.

4. May state courts enjoin federal proceedings to prevent religitation? In *Donovan v. City of Dallas*, 377 U.S. 408 (1964), losers in a state-court class action brought a new federal-court action for the same relief. The state court enjoined the federal plaintiffs from continuing the federal lawsuit. The Supreme Court reversed, holding that "whether or not a plea of res judicata in the second suit would be good is a question for the federal court to decide. While Congress has seen fit to authorize courts of the United States to restrain state-court proceedings in some special circumstances, it has in no way relaxed the old and well-established judicially declared rule that state courts are completely without power to restrain federal-court proceedings in *in personam* actions like this one."

Note: Other Issues Under the Anti-Injunction Act

1. Other exceptions to the Anti-Injunction Act have been implied, most notably in cases involving the federal government. In *Leiter Minerals, Inc. v. United States*, 352 U.S. 220 (1957), the Court concluded that the statute's prohibition does not reach actions in which the party seeking the stay is the United States. That holding was extended in *NLRB v. Nash-Finch Co.*, 404 U.S. 138 (1971), where the Court decided that the National Labor Relations Board is also excluded from the prohibition:

> The purpose of § 2283 was to avoid unseemly conflict between the state and the federal courts, not to hamstring the federal government and its agencies in the use of federal courts to protect federal rights.

2. What triggers the prohibitions of the Anti-Injunction Act? It is clear from *Atlantic Coast Line* that the Act cannot be avoided by enjoining a party, as opposed to a court. A more difficult question is whether the prohibition applies when the request for an injunction is filed before the state proceedings have been instituted. The Seventh Circuit, in *Barancik v. Investors Funding Corp.*, 489 F.2d 933 (7th Cir. 1973), held that the applicability of § 2283 "must be determined as of the time when the federal court's injunctive powers are invoked." In an opinion by then-Judge Stevens, the court explained:

> Unless the applicability of the statutory bar is determined by the state of the record at the time the motion for an injunction is made, a litigant would have an absolute right to defeat a well-founded motion by taking the very step the federal court was being urged to enjoin. Under defendant's reading of the statute, if a federal court took time for fair consideration of the merits of a request for an injunction, the court would deliberate at its peril; its authority to rule on the pending motion could be terminated by the action of one of the litigants. We consider this possibility unseemly. . . .

It may be argued that the statute requires the federal court to protect its authority by promptly issuing a temporary restraining order. But such a construction might encourage the liberal granting of the kind of protective orders the statute was intended to prevent. Moreover, it might require the court to take action without notice to the opposing party lest the court's power be defeated before it can rule with deliberation.

However, most courts have rejected this position. In *Denny's, Inc. v. Cake*, 364 F.3d 521 (4th Cir. 2004), the Fourth Circuit joined the majority, explaining:

> The plain language of the Act clearly and unequivocally prohibits a federal court from granting "an injunction to stay proceedings in a State court." Of course, in order for the Act's bar to apply, proceedings in state court must have begun. [As the Supreme Court said in *Dombrowski v. Pfister*, 380 U.S. 479, 484 n.2 (1965),] the Act does "not preclude injunctions against the institution of state court proceedings, but only bar[s] stays of suits already instituted." But nothing in the Act confines its bar to situations in which the federal plaintiff requests injunctive relief *after* the state suit has been filed. . . .
>
> The *Barancik* court [suggested] that its ruling had "the salutary advantage of discouraging the unseemly race to the state courthouse . . . while the federal court had under consideration a motion for a status quo order." But by hinging the applicability of § 2283 on whether the state or federal suit is commenced first, the *Barancik* rule creates a race to the courthouse of its own. [As the Sixth Circuit has said,] the *Barancik* rule "merely moves the finish line." Even worse, following *Barancik* would permit a federal court plaintiff who wins this race to "unilaterally . . . nullify the effectiveness of" the Act with the "mere application for injunctive relief."

Under the majority view, is there any way the would-be federal plaintiff can win the race to the courthouse?

Note: Other Acts Prohibiting Federal Injunctions

The Anti-Injunction Act is not the only statute aimed at preventing federal courts from interfering with state proceedings. Under the Tax Injunction Act (TIA), 28 U.S.C. § 1341, for example, federal district courts "shall not enjoin, suspend or restrain the assessment, levy or collection of any tax under State law where a plain, speedy and efficient remedy may be had in the courts of such State." That limitation "shields state tax collections from federal-court restraints" by "stop[ping] taxpayers, with the aid of a federal injunction, from withholding large sums [and] thereby disrupting state government finances." *Hibbs v. Winn*, 542 U.S. 88 (2004).

Similarly, the Johnson Act, 28 U.S.C. § 1342, provides that federal district courts "shall not enjoin, suspend or restrain the operation of, or compliance with, any order affecting rates chargeable by a public utility and made by a State administrative agency or a rate-making body of a State political subdivision" where four specified circumstances are present, including the availability of a "plain, speedy and efficient remedy" in state court.

B. Abstention Doctrines

[1] *Pullman* Abstention

Railroad Commission of Texas v. Pullman Co.

Supreme Court of the United States, 1941.

312 U.S. 496.

MR. JUSTICE FRANKFURTER delivered the opinion of the Court.

In those sections of Texas where the local passenger traffic is slight, trains carry but one sleeping car. These trains, unlike trains having two or more sleepers, are without a Pullman conductor; the sleeper is in charge of a porter who is subject to the train conductor's control. As is well known, porters on Pullmans are colored and conductors are white. Addressing itself to this situation, the Texas Railroad Commission after due hearing ordered that "no sleeping car shall be operated on any line of railroad in the State of Texas * * * unless such cars are continuously in the charge of an employee * * * having the rank and position of Pullman conductor." Thereupon, the Pullman Company and the railroads affected brought this action in a federal district court to enjoin the Commission's order. Pullman porters were permitted to intervene as complainants, and Pullman conductors entered the litigation in support of the order. Three judges having been convened, the court enjoined enforcement of the order. From this decree, the case came here directly.

The Pullman Company and the railroads assailed the order as unauthorized by Texas law as well as violative of the Equal Protection, the Due Process and the Commerce Clauses of the Constitution. The intervening porters adopted these objections but mainly objected to the order as a discrimination against Negroes in violation of the Fourteenth Amendment.

The complaint of the Pullman porters undoubtedly tendered a substantial constitutional issue. It is more than substantial. It touches a sensitive area of social policy upon which the federal courts ought not to enter unless no alternative to its adjudication is open. Such constitutional adjudication plainly can be avoided if a definitive ruling on the state issue would terminate the controversy. It is therefore our duty to turn to a consideration of questions under Texas law.

The Commission found justification for its order in a Texas statute which we quote in the margin.[1] It is common ground that if the order is within the Commission's authority its subject matter must be included in the Commission's power to prevent "unjust discrimination * * * and to prevent any and all other abuses" in the conduct

---

1. Vernon's Ann. Texas Civil Statutes, Article 6445:

   Power and authority are hereby conferred upon the Railroad Commission of Texas over all railroads [. . . ,] and it is hereby made the duty of the said Commission to adopt all necessary rates, charges and regulations, to govern and regulate such railroads, . . . and to correct abuses and prevent unjust discrimination in the rates, charges and tolls of such railroads, . . . and to prevent any and all other abuses in the conduct of their business and to do and perform such other duties and details in connection therewith as may be provided by law.

of railroads. Whether arrangements pertaining to the staffs of Pullman cars are covered by the Texas concept of "discrimination" is far from clear. What practices of the railroads may be deemed to be "abuses" subject to the Commission's correction is equally doubtful. Reading the Texas statutes and the Texas decisions as outsiders without special competence in Texas law, we would have little confidence in our independent judgment regarding the application of that law to the present situation. The lower court did deny that the Texas statutes sustained the Commission's assertion of power. And this represents the view of an able and experienced circuit judge of the circuit which includes Texas and of two capable district judges trained in Texas law. Had we or they no choice in the matter but to decide what is the law of the state, we should hesitate long before rejecting their forecast of Texas law.

But no matter how seasoned the judgment of the district court may be, it cannot escape being a forecast rather than a determination. The last word on the meaning of 6445 of the Texas Civil Statutes, and therefore the last word on the statutory authority of the Railroad Commission in this case, belongs neither to us nor to the district court but to the supreme court of Texas. In this situation a federal court of equity is asked to decide an issue by making a tentative answer which may be displaced tomorrow by a state adjudication. The reign of law is hardly promoted if an unnecessary ruling of a federal court is thus supplanted by a controlling decision of a state court. The resources of equity are equal to an adjustment that will avoid the waste of a tentative decision as well as the friction of a premature constitutional adjudication.

. . . The history of equity jurisdiction is the history of regard for public consequences in employing the extraordinary remedy of the injunction. . . . Few public interests have a higher claim upon the discretion of a federal chancellor than the avoidance of needless friction with state policies, whether the policy relates to the enforcement of the criminal law, *Fenner v. Boykin*, 271 U.S. 240 (1926); *Spielman Motor Co. v. Dodge*, 295 U.S. 89 (1935); or the administration of a specialized scheme for liquidating embarrassed business enterprises, *Pennsylvania v. Williams*, 294 U.S. 176 (1935); or the final authority of a state court to interpret doubtful regulatory laws of the state, *Gilchrist v. Interborough Co.*, 279 U.S. 159 (1929). These cases reflect a doctrine of abstention appropriate to our federal system whereby the federal courts, "exercising a wise discretion," restrain their authority because of "scrupulous regard for the rightful independence of the state governments" and for the smooth working of the federal judiciary. This use of equitable powers is a contribution of the courts in furthering the harmonious relation between state and federal authority without the need of rigorous congressional restriction of those powers.

Regard for these important considerations of policy in the administration of federal equity jurisdiction is decisive here. If there was no warrant in state law for the Commission's assumption of authority there is an end of the litigation; the constitutional issue does not arise. The law of Texas appears to furnish easy and ample means for determining the Commission's authority. Article 6453 of the Texas Civil Statutes gives a review of such an order in the state courts. Or, if there are difficulties in the way of this procedure of which we have not been apprised, the issue of state law may be settled by appropriate action on the part of the State to enforce obedience to the order. In the absence of any showing that these obvious methods for securing a definitive ruling in the state courts cannot be pursued with full protection of the constitutional claim, the district court should exercise its wise discretion by staying its hands.

We therefore remand the cause to the district court, with directions to retain the bill pending a determination of proceedings, to be brought with reasonable promptness, in the state court in conformity with this opinion.

Mr. Justice Roberts took no part in the consideration or decision of this case.

Note: The Rationale of Pullman Abstention

1. Recall Chief Justice Marshall's admonition that "[w]e have no more right to decline the exercise of a jurisdiction than to usurp that which is not given." *Cohens v. Virginia*, 19 U.S. (6 Wheat) 264 (1824). The *Pullman* case was undoubtedly within the federal courts' statutory jurisdiction. What policies does the Court identify that overcome the principle articulated by Marshall? Is there a separation of powers issue in declining to exercise congressionally granted jurisdiction, or does the Court's traditional discretion in equitable cases permit abstention? Is the hope of avoiding a constitutional decision enough to take this case outside of the ordinary obligation to assume jurisdiction? Would it make a difference if the Pullman porters had asked for damages?

2. *Pullman* abstention is predicated on two ideas. First, constitutional rulings should be avoided if possible. *See Ashwander v. TVA*, 297 U.S. 288 (1936) (Brandeis, J., concurring). Second, a constitutional ruling that is based on uncertain state law could be mooted if the state court authoritatively interprets the state law in a way that narrows it or otherwise avoids the constitutional question. One court has summarized yet another reason to abstain:

> We give some attention to the fact that our failure to abstain or certify may "prevent the informed evolution of state policy by state tribunals." *Moore v. Sims*, 442 U.S. 415 (1979). We defer to state primacy in areas of traditional state concern, such as family law, not only out of comity but also because the state is often far more expert than are we at understanding the implications of each decision in its practiced field. The sinews of family law and the complex web of relationships underlying it are delicate indeed. We are loath to interpret the meaning of a state law without the guidance of the New York Court of Appeals, which has a deep understanding of the body of that law and its intersection with the full weave of policy.

Nicholson v. Scoppetta, 344 F.3d 154 (2d Cir. 2003).

3. A court should not abstain if state law is clear, or not amenable to a limiting construction — or if there is no way in which the constitutional question can be avoided. In *City of Houston v. Hill*, 482 U.S. 451 (1987), the Court considered an ordinance that made it "unlawful for any person to . . . in any manner oppose, molest, abuse or interrupt any policeman in the execution of his duty." The Court held that it is rarely appropriate to seek a limiting construction through abstention in cases

involving a facial challenge to a statute on First Amendment grounds. The Court was concerned with the delay in the exercise of First Amendment rights that abstention would require. It also expanded on ways in which state courts might limit a statute to avoid constitutional defects:

> In cases involving a facial challenge to a statute, the pivotal question in determining whether abstention is appropriate is whether the statute is "fairly subject to an interpretation which will render unnecessary or substantially modify the federal constitutional question." *Harman v. Forssenius*, 380 U.S. 528 (1965). If the statute is not obviously susceptible of a limiting construction, then even if the statute has "never [been] interpreted by a state tribunal . . . it is the duty of the federal court to exercise its properly invoked jurisdiction."
>
> This ordinance is not susceptible to a limiting construction because, as both courts below agreed, its language is plain and its meaning unambiguous. Its constitutionality cannot "turn upon a choice between one or several alternative meanings." Nor can the ordinance be limited by severing discrete unconstitutional subsections from the rest.

4. Notice the result in *Pullman*: the lower court is directed to "retain the bill"— stay the proceedings in federal court—while the plaintiffs attempt to receive a determination in state court that authoritatively construes the statute. Then what? The hope, of course, is that the state court's interpretation will narrow the coverage of the statute, or otherwise avoid the necessity of ruling on the constitutional question.

Plaintiffs in *Pullman* abstention cases, however, face a daunting task. First, they must file a new lawsuit in the state court and attempt to get the requested authoritative ruling (from the state's highest court). Second, they must comply with a complicated set of procedures to avoid having the state court adjudicate the federal constitutional claim—for if it does, of course, its adjudication must be accorded preclusive effect under 28 U.S.C. § 1738 (see Chapter 17). However, they must also make the federal constitutional context of their claims apparent, to allow the state courts to consider their interpretation of the contested law in light of those claims. This is required by the Supreme Court's elaboration of the abstention doctrine in *Government and Civic Employees Organizing Committee v. Windsor*, 353 U.S. 364 (1953). There the Court refused to consider a federal constitutional claim because the Alabama Supreme Court was not asked, after federal abstention, to consider the contested statute in light of that claim.

In *England v. Louisiana State Bd. of Medical Examiners*, 375 U.S. 411 (1964), the Court acknowledged that there would be "fundamental objections" to *Pullman* abstention if, in effect, it compelled a plaintiff who had properly invoked the jurisdiction of a federal court to accept a state court's resolution of a federal question. It therefore held that a plaintiff may avoid the preclusive effect of any state-court judgment as to a federal question by making an explicit statement on the state record "reserving" that question. Such a statement, the Court explained, should "inform the state courts that he is exposing his federal claims there only for the purpose of complying with *Windsor*, and that he intends, should the state courts hold against him on the question of state law, to return to the District Court for disposition of his federal contentions."

5. The cost of *Pullman* abstention is increased by the fact that it can be raised at any point, even on appeal, and even *sua sponte* by the court. Thus, cases are sometimes sent to state court after proceedings in the federal district court have been concluded. In *Waldron v. McAtee*, 723 F.2d 1348 (7th Cir. 1983), the court said: "the court has the power and in an appropriate case the duty to order abstention, if necessary for the first time at the appellate level, even though no party is asking for it."

6. It is now possible in almost every jurisdiction for federal courts to certify questions to the state's highest court for an authoritative interpretation of unclear state law. Rebecca A. Cochran, *Federal Court Certification of Questions of State Law to State Courts: A Theoretical and Empirical Study*, 29 J. Legis. 157 (2003) (47 states, District of Columbia, and Puerto Rico permit certification). Given the delay inherent in *Pullman* abstention, should the certification alternative replace abstention? Justice Powell, concurring in *City of Houston v. Hill*, 482 U.S. 451 (1987) noted two advantages of certification over abstention:

> First, certification saves time by sending the question directly to the court that is empowered to provide an authoritative construction of the statute. Second, certification obviates the procedural difficulties that may hinder efforts to obtain declaratory judgments from state trial courts.

Professor Cochran, however, cautions that certification should not be embraced uncritically. In a case study of Ohio certification cases, she concluded that "in practice, certification in Ohio has resulted in advisory opinions, permitted a range of forum shopping, encouraged efforts to avoid the appellate process, and produced opinions so devoid of analysis that for years afterward, courts work to fill in the potholes of missing doctrine." For further discussion of certification, see Chapter 7.

Problem: An Anti-Loitering Ordinance

Shortly before midnight, David Andrew, a law student, was driving in downtown Gas City, State of Illiana, when he noticed a friend of his in an automobile in the next lane. They agreed to meet in a few minutes in front of the Public Library. They drove there, parked their cars, got out, and were chatting on the sidewalk, when several policemen approached and told them to move along. When Andrew asked why, he was told that he and his friends were violating the city's loitering ordinance, that "there are only thieves and police out here at this time of night," and that they would be arrested for loitering if they were ever again found late at night in the vicinity of the Library. Andrew and his friend left; they were not arrested.

The Gas City Code provides:

> No person shall loiter or prowl in a place, at a time or in a manner not usual for law abiding citizens, under circumstances that warrant a justifiable and reasonable alarm or immediate concern for the safety of persons or property in the vicinity, in any public way, street, highway, place, or alley and

refuse to obey the lawful command of a police officer to move on or provide to said police officer a lawful reason for remaining on said public way, street, highway, place or alley if the alleged loitering by said person would create or cause to be created any of the following:

(1) Danger of a breach of the peace;

(2) The unreasonable danger of a disturbance to the comfort and repose of any person acting lawfully on or in a public way, street, highway, place, or alley reserved for pedestrians;

(3) The obstruction or attempted obstruction of the free normal flow of vehicular traffic or the normal passage of pedestrian traffic upon any public way, street, highway, place, or alley;

(4) The obstruction, molestation or interference or attempt to obstruct, molest or interfere with any person lawfully on or in a public way, street, highway, place, or alley to fear for his or her safety.

Violation is punishable by a fine of up to $1000.

Andrew brought suit against the mayor, police chief, and council of Gas City under 42 U.S.C. § 1983, seeking a declaration that the loitering ordinance, both as applied to his conduct and on its face (*i.e.*, as it might be applied to other conduct), is void for vagueness under the First Amendment. The complaint also seeks a permanent injunction against enforcing the ordinance. Andrew submitted an affidavit that states that he is afraid to congregate with his friends at night on the sidewalks of downtown Gas City for fear of being arrested for violating the ordinance. The defendants file a motion suggesting that the district court abstain. The Gas City ordinance has never been interpreted by an Illiana court. How should the federal court rule?

[2] *Burford* Abstention

Quackenbush v. Allstate Insurance Company

Supreme Court of the United States, 1996.

517 U.S. 706.

JUSTICE O'CONNOR delivered the opinion of the Court.

In this case, we consider whether an abstention-based remand order is appealable as a final order under 28 U.S.C. § 1291, and whether the abstention doctrine first recognized in *Burford v. Sun Oil Co.*, 319 U.S. 315 (1943), can be applied in a common-law suit for damages.

I

Petitioner, the Insurance Commissioner for the State of California, was appointed trustee over the assets of the Mission Insurance Company and its affiliates (Mission companies) in 1987, after those companies were ordered into liquidation by a California court. In an effort to gather the assets of the defunct Mission companies, the

Commissioner filed the instant action against respondent Allstate Insurance Company in state court, seeking contract and tort damages for Allstate's alleged breach of certain reinsurance agreements, as well as a general declaration of Allstate's obligations under those agreements.

Allstate removed the action to federal court on diversity grounds and filed a motion to compel arbitration under the Federal Arbitration Act. The Commissioner sought remand to state court, arguing that the District Court should abstain from hearing the case under *Burford*, because its resolution might interfere with California's regulation of the Mission insolvency. Specifically, the Commissioner indicated that Allstate would be asserting its right to set off its own contract claims against the Commissioner's recovery under the contract, that the viability of these setoff claims was a hotly disputed question of state law, and that this question was currently pending before the state courts in another case arising out of the Mission insolvency.

The District Court observed that "California has an overriding interest in regulating insurance insolvencies and liquidations in a uniform and orderly manner," and that in this case "this important state interest could be undermined by inconsistent rulings from the federal and state courts." Based on these observations, and its determination that the setoff question should be resolved in state court, the District Court concluded this case was an appropriate one for the exercise of *Burford* abstention. The District Court did not stay its hand pending the California courts' resolution of the setoff issue, but instead remanded the entire case to state court. The District Court entered this remand order without ruling on Allstate's motion to compel arbitration.

[The Court of Appeals for the Ninth Circuit] vacated the District Court's decision and ordered the case sent to arbitration. The Ninth Circuit concluded that federal courts can abstain from hearing a case under *Burford* only when the relief being sought is equitable in nature, and therefore held that abstention was inappropriate in this case because the Commissioner purported to be seeking only legal relief.

. . . We granted certiorari . . . and now affirm on grounds different from those provided by the Ninth Circuit.

II

We first consider whether the Court of Appeals had jurisdiction to hear Allstate's appeal under 28 U.S.C. § 1291, which confers jurisdiction over appeals from "final decisions" of the district courts, and 28 U.S.C. § 1447(d), which provides that "[a]n order remanding a case to the State court from which it was removed is not reviewable on appeal or otherwise."

We agree with the Ninth Circuit and the parties that § 1447(d) interposes no bar to appellate review of the remand order at issue in this case. . . . [The Court then determined that the abstention order was immediately appealable.]

III

A

. . . We have . . . held that federal courts have the power to refrain from hearing cases that would interfere with a pending state criminal proceeding, see *Younger v. Harris*, 401 U.S. 37 (1971), or with certain types of state civil proceedings, see *Huffman v. Pursue, Ltd.*, 420 U.S. 592 (1975); *Juidice v. Vail*, 430 U.S. 327 (1977); cases in which the resolution of a federal constitutional question might be obviated if the state courts were given the opportunity to interpret ambiguous state law, see *Railroad Comm'n of Tex. v. Pullman Co.*, 312 U.S. 496 (1941); cases raising issues "intimately involved with [the States'] sovereign prerogative," the proper adjudication of which might be impaired by unsettled questions of state law, see *Louisiana Power & Light Co. v. City of Thibodaux*, 360 U.S. 25 (1959); cases whose resolution by a federal court might unnecessarily interfere with a state system for the collection of taxes, see *Great Lakes Dredge & Dock Co. v. Huffman*, 319 U.S. 293 (1943); and cases which are duplicative of a pending state proceeding, see *Colorado River Water Conservation Dist. v. United States*, 424 U.S. 800 (1976).

Our longstanding application of these doctrines reflects "the common-law background against which the statutes conferring jurisdiction were enacted," *New Orleans Public Service, Inc. v. Council of City of New Orleans*, 491 U.S. 350 (1989) *(NOPSI)* (citing Shapiro, *Jurisdiction and Discretion*, 60 N.Y.U. L. Rev. 543 (1985)). And [it] has long been established that a federal court has the authority to decline to exercise its jurisdiction when it "is asked to employ its historic powers as a court of equity." This tradition informs our understanding of the jurisdiction Congress has conferred upon the federal courts, and explains the development of our abstention doctrines. . . .

Though we have thus located the power to abstain in the historic discretion exercised by federal courts "sitting in equity," we have not treated abstention as a "technical rule of equity procedure." Rather, we have recognized that the authority of a federal court to abstain from exercising its jurisdiction extends to all cases in which the court has discretion to grant or deny relief. Accordingly, we have not limited the application of the abstention doctrines to suits for injunctive relief, but have also required federal courts to decline to exercise jurisdiction over certain classes of declaratory judgments, the granting of which is generally committed to the courts' discretion.

Nevertheless, we have not previously addressed whether the principles underlying our abstention cases would support the remand or dismissal of a common-law action for damages. . . .

[We] have applied abstention principles to actions "at law" only to permit a federal court to enter a stay order that *postpones* adjudication of the dispute, not to dismiss the federal suit altogether. *See, e.g., Thibodaux* (approving stay order).

Our decisions in *Thibodaux* and *County of Allegheny v. Frank Mashuda Co.*, 360 U.S. 185 (1959), illustrate the distinction we have drawn between abstention-based remand orders or dismissals and abstention-based decisions merely to stay adjudication of a federal suit. In *Thibodaux*, a city in Louisiana brought an eminent domain proceeding in state court, seeking to condemn for public use certain property owned by a Florida corporation. After the corporation removed the action to federal court on diversity grounds, the Federal District Court decided on its own motion to stay the case, pending a state court's determination whether the city could exercise the power of eminent domain under state law. The case did not arise within the "equity" jurisdiction of the federal courts, because the suit sought compensation for a taking, and the District Court lacked discretion to deny relief on the corporation's claim. Nonetheless, the issues in the suit were "intimately involved with [the State's] sovereign prerogative." We concluded that "[t]he considerations that prevailed in conventional equity suits for avoiding the hazards of serious disruption by federal courts of state government or needless friction between state and federal authorities are similarly appropriate in a state eminent domain proceeding brought in, or removed to, a federal court." And based on that conclusion, we affirmed the District Court's order staying the case.

County of Allegheny was decided the same day as *Thibodaux*, and like *Thibodaux* it involved review of a District Court order abstaining from the exercise of diversity jurisdiction over a state law eminent domain action. Unlike in *Thibodaux*, however, the District Court in *County of Allegheny* had not merely stayed adjudication of the federal action pending the resolution of an issue in state court, but rather had dismissed the federal action altogether. Based in large measure on this distinction, we reversed the District Court's order.

We were careful to note in *Thibodaux* that the District Court had only *stayed* the federal suit pending adjudication of the dispute in state court. Unlike the outright dismissal or remand of a federal suit, we held, an order merely staying the action "does not constitute abnegation of judicial duty. On the contrary, it is a wise and productive discharge of it. There is only postponement of decision for its best fruition." We have thus held that in cases where the relief being sought is equitable in nature or otherwise discretionary, federal courts not only have the power to stay the action based on abstention principles, but can also, in otherwise appropriate circumstances, decline to exercise jurisdiction altogether by either dismissing the suit or remanding it to state court. By contrast, while we have held that federal courts may stay actions for damages based on abstention principles, we have not held that those principles support the outright dismissal or remand of damages actions. . . .

B

With these background principles in mind, we consider the contours of the *Burford* doctrine. The principal issue presented in *Burford* was the "reasonableness" of an order issued by the Texas Railroad Commission, which granted "a permit to drill four oil wells on a small plot of land in the East Texas oil field." Due to the potentially overlapping claims of the many parties who might have an interest in a common pool of oil and the need for uniform regulation of the oil industry, Texas endowed the Railroad Commission with exclusive regulatory authority in the area. Texas also placed the authority to review the Commission's orders in a single set of state courts, "[t]o prevent the confusion of multiple review," and to permit an experienced cadre of state judges to obtain "specialized knowledge" in the field. Though Texas had thus demonstrated its interest in maintaining uniform review of the Commission's orders, the federal courts had, in the years preceding *Burford*, become increasingly involved in reviewing the reasonableness of the Commission's orders, both under a constitutional standard imposed under the Due Process Clause, and under state law, which established a similar standard.

Viewing the case as "a simple proceeding in equity to enjoin the enforcement of the Commissioner's order," we framed the question presented in terms of the power of a federal court of equity to abstain from exercising its jurisdiction:

> Although a federal equity court does have jurisdiction of a particular proceeding, it may, in its sound discretion, whether its jurisdiction is invoked on the ground of diversity of citizenship or otherwise, "refuse to enforce or protect legal rights, the exercise of which may be prejudicial to the public interest," for it "is in the public interest that federal courts of equity should exercise their discretionary power with proper regard for the rightful independence of state governments in carrying out their domestic policy." While many other questions are argued, we find it necessary to decide only one: Assuming that the federal district court had jurisdiction, should it, as a matter of sound equitable discretion, have declined to exercise that jurisdiction here?

Having thus posed the question in terms of the District Court's discretion, as a court sitting "in equity," to decline jurisdiction, we approved the District Court's dismissal of the complaint on a number of grounds that were unique to that case. We noted, for instance, the difficulty of the regulatory issues presented, stating that the "order under consideration is part of the general regulatory system devised for the conservation of oil and gas in Texas, an aspect of 'as thorny a problem as has challenged the ingenuity and wisdom of legislatures.'" We also stressed the demonstrated need for uniform regulation in the area, citing the unified procedures Texas had established to "prevent the confusion of multiple review," and the important state interests this uniform system of review was designed to serve. Most importantly, we also described the detrimental impact of ongoing federal court review of the Commission's orders, which review had already led to contradictory adjudications by the state and federal courts.

We ultimately concluded in *Burford* that dismissal was appropriate because the availability of an alternative, federal forum threatened to frustrate the purpose of the complex administrative system that Texas had established. We have since provided more generalized descriptions of the *Burford* doctrine, *see, e.g., County of Allegheny* ("abstention on grounds of comity with the States where the exercise of jurisdiction by the federal court would disrupt a state administrative process"); *Colorado River* (abstention where "exercise of federal review of the question in a case and in similar cases would be disruptive of state efforts to establish a coherent policy with respect to a matter of substantial public concern"), but with the exception of cases that rest only loosely on the *Burford* rationale, *e.g., Thibodaux*, we have revisited the decision only infrequently in the intervening 50 years. See *NOPSI*.

In *NOPSI*, our most recent exposition of the *Burford* doctrine, we again located the power to dismiss based on abstention principles in the discretionary power of a federal court sitting in equity, and we again illustrated the narrow range of circumstances in which *Burford* can justify the dismissal of a federal action. The issue in *NOPSI* was pre-emption. A New Orleans utility that had been saddled by a decision of the Federal Energy Regulatory Commission (FERC) with part of the cost of building and operating a nuclear reactor sought approval of a rate increase from the Council of the City of New Orleans. The council denied the rate increase on the grounds that "a public hearing was necessary to explore 'the legality and prudency' [*sic*]" of the expenses allocated to the utility under the FERC decision, and the utility brought suit in federal court, seeking an injunction against enforcement of the council's order and a declaration that the utility was entitled to a rate increase. The utility claimed that "federal law required the Council to allow it to recover, through an increase in retail rates, its FERC-allocated share of the [cost of the reactor]." The federal pre-emption question was the only issue raised in the case; there were no state law claims.

In reversing the District Court's decision to dismiss under *Burford*, we recognized "the federal courts' discretion in determining whether to grant certain types of relief," and we indicated, as we had previously in *Alabama Pub. Serv. Comm'n v. Southern R. Co.*, 341 U.S. 341 (1951), that *Burford* permits "a federal court sitting in equity" to dismiss a case only in extraordinary circumstances. We thus indicated that *Burford* allows a federal court to dismiss a case only if it presents "difficult questions of state law bearing on policy problems of substantial public import whose importance transcends the result in the case then at bar," or if its adjudication in a federal forum "would be disruptive of state efforts to establish a coherent policy with respect to a matter of substantial public concern."

We ultimately held that *Burford* did not provide proper grounds for an abstention-based dismissal in *NOPSI* because the "case [did] not involve a state-law claim, nor even an assertion that the federal claims [were] 'in any way entangled in a skein of state law that must be untangled before the federal case can proceed,'" and because there was no serious threat of conflict between the adjudication of the federal claim presented in the case and the State's interest in ensuring uniformity in ratemaking decisions:

> While *Burford* is concerned with protecting complex state administrative processes from undue federal influence, it does not require abstention whenever there exists such a process, or even in all cases where there is a "potential for conflict" with state regulatory law or policy. Here, NOPSI's primary claim is that the Council is prohibited by federal law from refusing to provide reimbursement for FERC-allocated wholesale costs. Unlike a claim that a state agency has misapplied its lawful authority or has failed to take into consideration or properly weigh relevant state-law factors, federal adjudication of this sort of pre-emption claim would not disrupt the State's attempt to ensure uniformity in the treatment of an "essentially local problem."

These cases do not provide a formulaic test for determining when dismissal under *Burford* is appropriate, but they do demonstrate that the power to dismiss under the *Burford* doctrine, as with other abstention doctrines, derives from the discretion historically enjoyed by courts of equity. They further demonstrate that exercise of this discretion must reflect "principles of federalism and comity." Ultimately, what is at stake is a federal court's decision, based on a careful consideration of the federal interests in retaining jurisdiction over the dispute and the competing concern for the "independence of state action," that the State's interests are paramount and that a dispute would best be adjudicated in a state forum. [As we said in *NOPSI*, the] question under *Burford* is whether adjudication in federal court would "unduly intrude into the processes of state government or undermine the State's ability to maintain desired uniformity." This equitable decision balances the strong federal interest in having certain classes of cases, and certain federal rights, adjudicated in federal court, against the State's interests in maintaining "uniformity in the treatment of an 'essentially local problem,'" and retaining local control over "difficult questions of state law bearing on policy problems of substantial public import," *Colorado River*. This balance only rarely favors abstention, and the power to dismiss recognized in *Burford* represents an "extraordinary and narrow exception to the duty of the District Court to adjudicate a controversy properly before it."

C

We turn, finally, to the application of *Burford* in this case. As in *NOPSI*, the federal interests in this case are pronounced, as Allstate's motion to compel arbitration under the Federal Arbitration Act (FAA) implicates a substantial federal concern for the enforcement of arbitration agreements. With regard to the state interests, however, the case appears at first blush to present nothing more than a run-of-the-mill contract dispute. The Commissioner seeks damages from Allstate for Allstate's failure to perform its obligations under a reinsurance agreement. What differentiates this case from other diversity actions seeking damages for breach of contract, if anything, is the impact federal adjudication of the dispute might have on the ongoing liquidation proceedings in state court: The Commissioner claims that any recovery by Allstate on its setoff claims would amount to an illegal "preference" under state law. This question appears now to have been conclusively answered by the California Supreme Court, see *Prudential Reinsurance Co. v. Superior Court of Los Angeles Cty.*, 3 Cal. 4th 1118 (1992) (permitting reinsurers to assert setoff claims in suits filed by the Commissioner in the Mission insolvency), although at the time the District Court ruled this question was still hotly contested.

The Ninth Circuit concluded that the District Court's remand order was inappropriate because "*Burford* abstention does not apply to suits seeking solely legal relief." Addressing our abstention cases, the Ninth Circuit held that the federal courts' power to abstain in certain cases is "locat[ed] . . . in the unique powers of equitable courts," and that it derives from equity courts' "'discretionary power to grant or withhold relief.'" The Ninth Circuit's reversal of the District Court's abstention-based remand order in this case therefore reflects the application of a *per se* rule: "[T]he power of federal courts to abstain from exercising their jurisdiction, at least in *Burford* abstention cases, is founded upon a discretion they possess only in equitable cases."

To the extent the Ninth Circuit held only that a federal court cannot, under *Burford*, dismiss or remand an action when the relief sought is not discretionary, its judgment is consistent with our abstention cases. We have explained the power to dismiss or remand a case under the abstention doctrines in terms of the discretion federal courts have traditionally exercised in deciding whether to provide equitable or discretionary relief, and the Commissioner appears to have conceded that the relief being sought in this case is neither equitable nor otherwise committed to the discretion of the court. In those cases in which we have applied traditional abstention principles to damages actions, we have only permitted a federal court to "withhold action until the state proceedings have concluded"; that is, we have permitted federal courts applying abstention principles in damages actions to enter a stay, but we have not permitted them to dismiss the action altogether.

The *per se* rule described by the Ninth Circuit is, however, more rigid than our precedents require. We have not strictly limited abstention to "equitable cases," but rather have extended the doctrine to all cases in which a federal court is asked to provide some form of discretionary relief. Moreover, as demonstrated by our decision in *Thibodaux*, we have not held that abstention principles are completely inapplicable in damages actions. *Burford* might support a federal court's decision to postpone adjudication of a damages action pending the resolution by the state courts of a disputed question of state law. For example, given the situation the District Court faced in this case, a stay order might have been appropriate: The setoff issue was being decided by the state courts at the time the District Court ruled, and in the interest of avoiding inconsistent adjudications on that point, the District Court might have been justified in entering a stay to await the outcome of the state court litigation.

Like the Ninth Circuit, we review only the remand order which was entered, and find it unnecessary to determine whether a more limited abstention-based stay order would have been warranted on the facts of this case. . . . Nor do we find it necessary to inquire fully as to whether this case presents the sort of "exceptional circumstance" in which *Burford* abstention or other grounds for yielding federal jurisdiction might be appropriate. Under our precedents, federal courts have the power to dismiss or remand cases based on abstention principles only where the relief being sought is equitable or otherwise discretionary. Because this was a damages action, we conclude that the District Court's remand order was an unwarranted application of the *Burford* doctrine. The judgment is affirmed.

JUSTICE SCALIA, concurring.

I join the opinion of the Court. I write separately only to respond to Justice Kennedy's concurrence.

Justice Kennedy, while joining the opinion of the Court, says that he would "not rule out . . . the possibility that a federal court might dismiss a suit for damages in a case where a serious affront to the interests of federalism could be averted in no other way." I would not have joined today's opinion if I believed it left such discretionary dismissal available. Such action is foreclosed, I think, by the Court's holding, clearly summarized in the concluding sentences of the opinion: "Under our precedents, federal courts have the power to dismiss or remand cases based on abstention principles only where the relief being sought is equitable or otherwise discretionary. Because this was a damages action, we conclude that the District Court's remand order was an unwarranted application of the *Burford* doctrine."

Justice Kennedy's projected horrible of a "serious affront to the interests of federalism" cannot possibly materialize under the Court's holding. There *is* no "serious affront to the interests of federalism" when Congress lawfully decides to pre-empt state action—which is what our cases hold (and today's opinion affirms) Congress does whenever it instructs federal courts to assert jurisdiction over matters as to which relief is not discretionary.

If the Court today felt empowered to decide for itself when congressionally decreed jurisdiction constitutes a "serious affront" and when it does not, the opinion would have read much differently. Most pertinently, it would not have found it *unnecessary* "to inquire fully as to whether this case presents the sort of 'exceptional circumstance' in which *Burford* abstention or other grounds for yielding federal jurisdiction might be appropriate." There were certainly grounds for such an inquiry if we thought it relevant. The "[then] unsettled but since resolved question of California law" to which Justice Kennedy refers, was only part of the basis for the District Court's decision to remand to state court; the court also pointed more generally to what it thought was the State's "overriding interest in regulating insurance insolvencies and liquidations in a uniform and orderly manner." As the Court's opinion says, it is not necessary to inquire fully into that matter because this was a damages action.

JUSTICE KENNEDY, concurring.

When this suit first was filed, it raised an unsettled but since resolved question of California law concerning the ability of companies in Allstate's position to set off claims held against Mission. The principal reason for the District Court's decision to dismiss the case was the threat posed to the state proceedings by different state and federal rulings on the question. The court's concern was reasonable. States, as a matter of tradition and express federal consent, have an important interest in maintaining precise and detailed regulatory schemes for the insurance industry. *See, e.g.*, the McCarran-Ferguson Act. The fact that a state court rather than an agency was chosen to implement California's scheme provided more reason, not less, for the federal court to stay its hand.

At the same time, however, we have not considered a case in which dismissal of a suit for damages by extension of the doctrine of *Burford v. Sun Oil Co.*, 319 U.S. 315 (1943), was held to be authorized and necessary. As the Court explains, no doubt the preferred course in such circumstances is to resolve any serious potential for federal intrusion by staying the suit while retaining jurisdiction. We ought not rule out, though, the possibility that a federal court might dismiss a suit for damages in a case where a serious affront to the interests of federalism could be averted in no other way. We need not reach that question here.

Abstention doctrines are a significant contribution to the theory of federalism and to the preservation of the federal system in practice. They allow federal courts to give appropriate and necessary recognition to the role and authority of the States. The duty to take these considerations into account must inform the exercise of federal jurisdiction. Principles of equity thus are not the sole foundation for abstention rules;

obligations of comity, and respect for the appropriate balance between state and federal interests, are an important part of the justification and authority for abstention as well. The traditional role of discretion in the exercise of equity jurisdiction makes abstention easiest to justify in cases where equitable relief is sought, but abstention, including dismissal, is a possibility that may yet be addressed in a suit for damages, if fundamental concerns of federalism require us to face the issue.

With these observations, I join the opinion of the Court.

Note: Burford *Abstention*

1. *Burford* abstention has been described by one court in the following way:

> *Burford* allows courts to "decline to rule on an essentially local issue arising out of a complicated state regulatory scheme." Its application requires first, that the state has chosen to concentrate suits challenging the actions of the agency involved in a particular court; second, that federal issues could not be separated easily from complex state law issues with respect to which state courts might have special competence; and third, that federal review might disrupt state efforts to establish a coherent policy.

United States v. Morros, 268 F.3d 695 (9th Cir. 2001).

Another court stated that "a federal court should refuse to exercise its jurisdiction in a manner that would interfere with a state's efforts to regulate an area of law in which state interests predominate and in which adequate and timely state review of the regulatory scheme is available," and described *Burford* abstention's purpose as "to avoid federal intrusion into matters of local concern and which are within the special competence of local courts." *Chiropractic America v. Lavecchia*, 180 F.3d 99 (3d Cir. 1999).

Are these descriptions consistent with *Quackenbush*? How much of a limitation on federal court power does the doctrine impose?

2. In *Morros*, the court also said that "*Burford* abstention is particularly inappropriate when the plaintiff's claim is based on preemption, because abstaining under *Burford* would be an implicit ruling on the merits." Has the Supreme Court embraced that position?

3. At the other end of the spectrum (and notwithstanding *Quackenbush*), *Burford* abstention is most likely to be found appropriate in the context of insurance insolvency. In *Clark v. Fitzgibbons*, 105 F.3d 1049 (5th Cir. 1997), the court explained why:

> The *Burford* doctrine provides for abstention in deference to complex state administrative procedures. Insurance companies are ineligible for the protections afforded by the federal Bankruptcy Code. 11 U.S.C. § 109. Instead, insolvent insurers are subject to the comprehensive oversight of state administrative agencies and courts. Federal law consigns to the states the primary responsibility for regulating the insurance industry. [Here the court cited the McCarran-Ferguson Act.]
>
> Against this backdrop, allowing a creditor or claimant to proceed against an insolvent insurer in federal court while a state insolvency proceeding is

pending would "usurp [the state's] control over the liquidation proceeding by allowing [the claimant] to preempt others in the distribution of [the insurance company's] assets." This not only would violate the policy of the McCarran-Ferguson Act, but also would undermine "the comity rationale promoted by the *Burford* doctrine."

Would the Court do better to establish categories where *Burford* abstention is presumptively appropriate or inappropriate, rather than leaving the matter open-ended, as the *Quackenbush* opinion does?

[3] *Younger* Abstention

Younger v. Harris

Supreme Court of the United States, 1971.

401 U.S. 37.

MR. JUSTICE BLACK delivered the opinion of the Court.

Appellee, John Harris, Jr., was indicted in a California state court, charged with violation of the California Penal Code §§ 11400 and 11401, known as the California Criminal Syndicalism Act, set out below.[1] He then filed a complaint in the Federal District Court, asking that court to enjoin the appellant, Younger, the District Attorney

---

1. § 11400. Definition
   "Criminal syndicalism" as used in this article means any doctrine or precept advocating, teaching or aiding and abetting the commission of crime, sabotage (which word is hereby defined as meaning wilful and malicious physical damage or injury to physical property), or unlawful acts of force and violence or unlawful methods of terrorism as a means of accomplishing a change in industrial ownership or control, or effecting any political change.
   § 11401. Offense; punishment Any person who:
   1. By spoken or written words or personal conduct advocates, teaches or aids and abets criminal syndicalism or the duty, necessity or propriety of committing crime, sabotage, violence or any unlawful method of terrorism as a means of accomplishing a change in industrial ownership or control, or effecting any political change; or
   2. Wilfully and deliberately by spoken or written words justifies or attempts to justify criminal syndicalism or the commission or attempt to commit crime, sabotage, violence or unlawful methods of terrorism with intent to approve, advocate or further the doctrine of criminal syndicalism; or
   3. Prints, publishes, edits, issues or circulates or publicly displays any book, paper, pamphlet, document, poster or written or printed matter in any other form, containing or carrying written or printed advocacy, teaching, or aid and abetment of, or advising, criminal syndicalism; or
   4. Organizes or assists in organizing, or is or knowingly becomes a member of, any organization, society, group or assemblage of persons organized or assembled to advocate, teach or aid and abet criminal syndicalism; or
   5. Wilfully by personal act or conduct, practices or commits any act advised, advocated, taught or aided and abetted by the doctrine or precept of criminal syndicalism, with intent
   to accomplish a change in industrial ownership or control, or effecting any political change;
   Is guilty of a felony and punishable by imprisonment in the state prison not less than one nor more than 14 years.

of Los Angeles County, from prosecuting him, and alleging that the prosecution and even the presence of the Act inhibited him in the exercise of his rights of free speech and press, rights guaranteed him by the First and Fourteenth Amendments. Appellees Jim Dan and Diane Hirsch intervened as plaintiffs in the suit, claiming that the prosecution of Harris would inhibit them as members of the Progressive Labor Party from peacefully advocating the program of their party, which was to replace capitalism with socialism and to abolish the profit system of production in this country. Appellee Farrell Broslawsky, an instructor in history at Los Angeles Valley College, also intervened claiming that the prosecution of Harris made him uncertain as to whether he could teach about the doctrines of Karl Marx or read from the Communist Manifesto as part of his classwork. All claimed that unless the United States court restrained the state prosecution of Harris each would suffer immediate and irreparable injury. A three-judge Federal District Court [held] that it had jurisdiction and power to restrain the District Attorney from prosecuting, held that the State's Criminal Syndicalism Act was void for vagueness and over breadth in violation of the First and Fourteenth Amendments, and accordingly restrained the District Attorney from "further prosecution of the currently pending action against plaintiff Harris for alleged violation of the Act."

The case is before us on appeal by the State's District Attorney Younger ... In his notice of appeal and his jurisdictional statement appellant presented two questions: (1) whether the decision of this Court in *Whitney v. California*, 274 U.S. 357, holding California's law constitutional in 1927 was binding on the District Court and (2) whether the State's law is constitutional on its face. In this Court the brief for the State of California, filed at our request, also argues that only Harris, who was indicted, has standing to challenge the State's law, and that issuance of the injunction was a violation of a longstanding judicial policy and of 28 U.S.C. § 2283, which provides:

> A court of the United States may not grant an injunction to stay proceedings in a State court except as expressly authorized by Act of Congress, or where necessary in aid of its jurisdiction, or to protect or effectuate its judgments.

See, e.g., Atlantic Coast Line R. Co. v. Engineers, 398 U.S. 281 (1970). Without regard to the questions raised about *Whitney v. California*, since overruled by *Brandenburg v. Ohio*, 395 U.S. 444 (1969), or the constitutionality of the state law, we have concluded that the judgment of the District Court, enjoining appellant Younger from prosecuting under these California statutes, must be reversed as a violation of the national policy forbidding federal courts to stay or enjoin pending state court proceedings except under special circumstances. We express no view about the circumstances under which federal courts may act when there is no prosecution pending in state courts at the time the federal proceeding is begun.

I

Appellee Harris has been indicted, and was actually being prosecuted by California for a violation of its Criminal Syndicalism Act at the time this suit was filed. He thus has an acute, live controversy with the State and its prosecutor. But none of the other parties plaintiff in the District Court, Dan, Hirsch, or Broslawsky, has such a controversy. None has been indicted, arrested, or even threatened by the prosecutor. . . .

Whatever right Harris, who is being prosecuted under the state syndicalism law may have, Dan, Hirsch, and Broslawsky cannot share it with him. If these three had alleged that they would be prosecuted for the conduct they planned to engage in, and if the District Court had found this allegation to be true—either on the admission of the State's district attorney or on any other evidence—then a genuine controversy might be said to exist. But here appellees Dan, Hirsch, and Broslawsky do not claim that they have ever been threatened with prosecution, that a prosecution is likely, or even that a prosecution is remotely possible. They claim the right to bring this suit solely because, in the language of their complaint, they "feel inhibited." We do not think this allegation even if true, is sufficient to bring the equitable jurisdiction of the federal courts into play to enjoin a pending state prosecution. A federal lawsuit to stop a prosecution in a state court is a serious matter. And persons having no fears of state prosecution except those that are imaginary or speculative, are not to be accepted as appropriate plaintiffs in such cases. Since Harris is actually being prosecuted under the challenged laws, however, we proceed with him as a proper party.

II

Since the beginning of this country's history Congress has, subject to few exceptions, manifested a desire to permit state courts to try state cases free from interference by federal courts. In 1793 an Act unconditionally provided: "[N]or shall a writ of injunction be granted to stay proceedings in any court of a state * * *." A comparison of the 1793 Act with 28 U.S.C. § 2283, its present-day successor, graphically illustrates how few and minor have been the exceptions granted from the flat, prohibitory language of the old Act. [See section A.] In addition, a judicial exception to the longstanding policy evidenced by the statute has been made where a person about to be prosecuted in a state court can show that he will, if the proceeding in the state court is not enjoined, suffer irreparable damages. *See Ex parte Young*, 209 U.S. 123 (1908) [Chapter 13].

The precise reasons for this longstanding public policy against federal court interference with state court proceedings have never been specifically identified but the primary sources of the policy are plain. One is the basic doctrine of equity jurisprudence that courts of equity should not act, and particularly should not act to restrain a criminal prosecution, when the moving party has an adequate remedy at law and will not suffer irreparable injury if denied equitable relief. The doctrine may originally have grown out of circumstances peculiar to the English judicial system and not applicable in this country, but its fundamental purpose of restraining equity jurisdiction within narrow limits is equally important under our Constitution, in order to prevent erosion of the role of the jury and avoid a duplication of legal proceedings and legal sanctions where a single suit would be adequate to protect the rights asserted.

This underlying reason for restraining courts of equity from interfering with criminal prosecutions is reinforced by an even more vital consideration, the notion of "comity," that is, a proper respect for state functions, a recognition of the fact that the entire country is made up of a Union of separate state governments, and a continuance of the belief that the National Government will fare best if the States and their institutions are left free to perform their separate functions in their separate ways. This, perhaps for lack of a better and clearer way to describe it, is referred to by many as "Our Federalism." . . . The concept does not mean blind deference to "States' Rights" any more than it means centralization of control over every important issue in our National Government and its courts. The Framers rejected both these courses. What the concept does represent is a system in which there is sensitivity to the legitimate interests of both State and National Governments, and in which the National Government, anxious though it may be to vindicate and protect federal rights and federal interests, always endeavors to do so in ways that will not unduly interfere with the legitimate activities of the States. It should never be forgotten that this slogan, "Our Federalism," born in the early struggling days of our Union of States, occupies a highly important place in our Nation's history and its future.

This brief discussion should be enough to suggest some of the reasons why it has been perfectly natural for our cases to repeat time and time again that the normal thing to do when federal courts are asked to enjoin pending proceedings in state courts is not to issue such injunctions. In *Fenner v. Boykin*, 271 U.S. 240 (1926), suit had been brought in the Federal District Court seeking to enjoin state prosecutions under a recently enacted state law that allegedly interfered with the free flow of interstate commerce. The Court, in a unanimous opinion made clear that such a suit, even with respect to state criminal proceedings not yet formally instituted, could be proper only under very special circumstances:

> *Ex parte Young* and following cases have established the doctrine that, when absolutely necessary for protection of constitutional rights, courts of the United States have power to enjoin state officers from instituting criminal actions. But this may not be done, except under extraordinary circumstances, where the danger of irreparable loss is both great and immediate. Ordinarily, there should be no interference with such officers; primarily, they are charged with the duty of prosecuting offenders against the laws of the state, and must decide when and how this is to be done. The accused should first set up and rely upon his defense in the state courts, even though this involves a challenge of the validity of some statute, unless it plainly appears that this course would not afford adequate protection.

These principles, made clear in the *Fenner* case, have been repeatedly followed and reaffirmed in other cases involving threatened prosecutions. [Citations omitted.]

In all of these cases the Court stressed the importance of showing irreparable injury, the traditional prerequisite to obtaining an injunction. In addition, however, the Court also made clear that in view of the fundamental policy against federal interference with state criminal prosecutions, even irreparable injury is insufficient unless it is "both great and immediate." Certain types of injury, in particular, the cost, anxiety, and inconvenience of having to defend against a single criminal prosecution, could not by themselves be considered "irreparable" in the special legal sense of that term. Instead, the threat to the plaintiff's federally protected rights must be one that cannot be eliminated by his defense against a single criminal prosecution. *See, e.g., Ex parte Young.* Thus, in [*Watson v. Buck*, 313 U.S. 387,] we stressed:

> Federal injunctions against state criminal statutes, either in their entirety or with respect to their separate and distinct prohibitions, are not to be granted as a matter of course, even if such statutes are unconstitutional. "No citizen or member of the community is immune from prosecution, in good faith, for his alleged criminal acts. The imminence of such a prosecution even though alleged to be unauthorized and hence unlawful is not alone ground for relief in equity which exerts its extraordinary powers only to prevent irreparable injury to the plaintiff who seeks its aid."

And similarly, in *Douglas v. City of Jeannette*, 319 U.S. 142 (1943), we made clear, after reaffirming this rule, that:

> It does not appear from the record that petitioners have been threatened with any injury other than that incidental to every criminal proceeding brought lawfully and in good faith * * *.

This is where the law stood when the Court decided *Dombrowski v. Pfister*, 380 U.S. 479 (1965), and held that an injunction against the enforcement of certain state criminal statutes could properly issue under the circumstances presented in that case.[4] In *Dombrowski*, unlike many of the earlier cases denying injunctions, the complaint made substantial allegations that:

> the threats to enforce the statutes against appellants are not made with any expectation of securing valid convictions, but rather are part of a plan to employ arrests, seizures, and threats of prosecution under color of the statutes to harass appellants and discourage them and their supporters from asserting and attempting to vindicate the constitutional rights of Negro citizens of Louisiana.

The appellants in *Dombrowski* had offered to prove that their offices had been raided and all their files and records seized pursuant to search and arrest warrants that were later summarily vacated by a state judge for lack of probable cause. They also offered to prove that despite the state court order quashing the warrants and suppressing the evidence seized, the prosecutor was continuing to threaten to initiate new prosecutions of appellants under the same statutes, was holding public hearings at which photostatic

---

4. Neither the cases dealing with standing to raise claims of vagueness or overbreadth, *e.g., Thornhill v. Alabama*, 310 U.S. 88 (1940), nor the loyalty oath cases, *e.g., Baggett v. Bullitt*, 377 U.S. 360 (1964), changed the basic principles governing the propriety of injunctions against state criminal prosecutions. In the standing cases we allowed attacks on overly broad or vague statutes in the absence of any showing that the defendant's conduct could not be regulated by some properly drawn statute. But in each of these cases the statute was not merely vague or overly broad "on its face"; the statute was held to be vague or overly broad as construed and applied to a particular defendant in a particular case. If the statute had been too vague as written but sufficiently narrow as applied, prosecutions and convictions under it would ordinarily have been permissible. *See Dombrowski. . . .*

copies of the illegally seized documents were being used, and was threatening to use other copies of the illegally seized documents to obtain grand jury indictments against the appellants on charges of violating the same statutes. These circumstances, as viewed by the Court sufficiently establish the kind of irreparable injury, above and beyond that associated with the defense of a single prosecution brought in good faith, that had always been considered sufficient to justify federal intervention. . . .

And the Court made clear that even under these circumstances the District Court issuing the injunction would have continuing power to lift it at any time and remit the plaintiffs to the state courts if circumstances warranted. . . .

It is against the background of these principles that we must judge the propriety of an injunction under the circumstances of the present case. Here a proceeding was already pending in the state court, affording Harris an opportunity to raise his constitutional claims. There is no suggestion that this single prosecution against Harris is brought in bad faith or is only one of a series of repeated prosecutions to which he will be subjected. In other words, the injury that Harris faces is solely "that incidental to every criminal proceeding brought lawfully and in good faith," *Douglas*, and therefore under the settled doctrine we have already described he is not entitled to equitable relief "even if such statutes are unconstitutional," *Buck*.

The District Court, however, thought that the *Dombrowski* decision substantially broadened the availability of injunctions against state criminal prosecutions and that under that decision the federal courts may give equitable relief, without regard to any showing of bad faith or harassment, whenever a state statute is found "on its face" to be vague or overly broad, in violation of the First Amendment. We recognize that there are some statements in the *Dombrowski* opinion that would seem to support this argument. But, as we have already seen, such statements were unnecessary to the decision of that case, because the Court found that the plaintiffs had alleged a basis for equitable relief under the long-established standards. In addition, we do not regard the reasons adduced to support this position as sufficient to justify such a substantial departure from the established doctrines regarding the availability of injunctive relief.

It is undoubtedly true, as the Court stated in *Dombrowski*, that "[a] criminal prosecution under a statute regulating expression usually involves imponderables and contingencies that themselves may inhibit the full exercise of First Amendment freedoms." But this sort of "chilling effect," as the Court called it, should not by itself justify federal intervention. In the first place, the chilling effect cannot be satisfactorily eliminated by federal injunctive relief. . . .

Moreover, the existence of a "chilling effect," even in the area of First Amendment rights, has never been considered a sufficient basis, in and of itself, for prohibiting state action. Where a statute does not directly abridge free speech, but—while regulating a subject within the State's power—tends to have the incidental effect of inhibiting First Amendment rights, it is well settled that the statute can be upheld if the effect on speech is minor in relation to the need for control of the conduct and the lack of alternative means for doing so. *Schneider v. State*, 308 U.S. 147 (1939); *Cantwell v. Connecticut*, 310 U.S. 296 (1940); *United Mine Workers of America, Dist. 12 v. Illinois*

Bar Assn., 389 U.S. 217 (1967). Just as the incidental "chilling effect" of such statutes does not automatically render them unconstitutional, so the chilling effect that admittedly can result from the very existence of certain laws on the statute books does not in itself justify prohibiting the State from carrying out the important and necessary task of enforcing these laws against socially harmful conduct that the State believes in good faith to be punishable under its laws and the Constitution.

Beyond all this is another, more basic consideration. Procedures for testing the constitutionality of a statute "on its face" in the manner apparently contemplated by *Dombrowski*, and for then enjoining all action to enforce the statute until the State can obtain court approval for a modified version, are fundamentally at odds with the function of the federal courts in our constitutional plan. The power and duty of the judiciary to declare laws unconstitutional is in the final analysis derived from its responsibility for resolving concrete disputes brought before the courts for decision; a statute apparently governing a dispute cannot be applied by judges, consistently with their obligations under the Supremacy Clause, when such an application of the statute would conflict with the Constitution. *Marbury v. Madison*, 5 U.S. (1 Cranch) 137 (1803). But this vital responsibility, broad as it is, does not amount to an unlimited power to survey the statute books and pass judgment on laws before the courts are called upon to enforce them.

Ever since the Constitutional Convention rejected a proposal for having members of the Supreme Court render advice concerning pending legislation it has been clear that, even when suits of this kind involve a "case or controversy" sufficient to satisfy the requirements of Article III of the Constitution, the task of analyzing a proposed statute, pinpointing its deficiencies, and requiring correction of these deficiencies before the statute is put into effect, is rarely if ever an appropriate task for the judiciary. The combination of the relative remoteness of the controversy, the impact on the legislative process of the relief sought, and above all the speculative and amorphous nature of the required line-by-line analysis of detailed statutes ordinarily results in a kind of case that is wholly unsatisfactory for deciding constitutional questions, whichever way they might be decided. In light of this fundamental conception of the Framers as to the proper place of the federal courts in the governmental processes of passing and enforcing laws, it can seldom be appropriate for these courts to exercise any such power of prior approval or veto over the legislative process.

For these reasons, fundamental not only to our federal system but also to the basic functions of the Judicial Branch of the National Government under our Constitution, we hold that the *Dombrowski* decision should not be regarded as having upset the settled doctrines that have always confined very narrowly the availability of injunctive relief against state criminal prosecutions. We do not think that opinion stands for the proposition that a federal court can properly enjoin enforcement of a statute solely on the basis of a showing that the statute "on its face" abridges First Amendment rights. There may, of course, be extraordinary circumstances in which the necessary irreparable injury can be shown even in the absence of the usual prerequisites of bad faith and harassment. For example, as long ago as the *Buck* case, we indicated:

It is of course conceivable that a statute might be flagrantly and patently violative of express constitutional prohibitions in every clause, sentence and paragraph, and in whatever manner and against whomever an effort might be made to apply it.

Other unusual situations calling for federal intervention might also arise, but there is no point in our attempting now to specify what they might be. It is sufficient for purposes of the present case to hold, as we do, that the possible unconstitutionality of a statute "on its face" does not in itself justify an injunction against good-faith attempts to enforce it, and that appellee Harris has failed to make any showing of bad faith, harassment, or any other unusual circumstance that would call for equitable relief. Because our holding rests on the absence of the factors necessary under equitable principles to justify federal intervention, we have no occasion to consider whether 28 U.S.C. § 2283, which prohibits an injunction against state court proceedings "except as expressly authorized by Act of Congress" would in and of itself be controlling under the circumstances of this case.

The judgment of the District Court is reversed, and the case is remanded for further proceedings not inconsistent with this opinion.

MR. JUSTICE STEWART, with whom MR. JUSTICE HARLAN joins, concurring.

. . . In basing its decisions on policy grounds, the Court does not reach any questions concerning the independent force of the federal anti-injunction statute, 28 U.S.C. § 2283. Thus we do not decide whether the word "injunction" in § 2283 should be interpreted to include a declaratory judgment, or whether an injunction to stay proceedings in a state court is "expressly authorized" by § 1 of the Civil Rights Act of 1871, now 42 U.S.C. § 1983. . . .

MR. JUSTICE BRENNAN with whom MR. JUSTICE WHITE and MR. JUSTICE MARSHALL join, concurring in the judgment. [Omitted.]

MR. JUSTICE DOUGLAS, dissenting.

. . . The special circumstances when federal intervention in a state criminal proceeding is permissible are not restricted to bad faith on the part of state officials or the threat of multiple prosecutions. They also exist where for any reason the state statute being enforced is unconstitutional on its face. . . .

Harris is charged only with distributing leaflets advocating political action toward his objective. He tried unsuccessfully to have the state court dismiss the indictment on constitutional grounds. He resorted to the state appellate court for writs of prohibition to prevent the trial, but to no avail. He went to the federal court as a matter of last resort in an effort to keep this unconstitutional trial from being saddled on him.

Note: Equitable Restraint and Younger Abstention

1. Consider the rationales for *Younger* abstention. What are the strongest? Comity principles and respect for state courts? Judicial administration issues? Avoiding duplicative proceedings? Imagine what the relationship of the state and federal courts would be if injunctive relief could be granted in the *Younger* context.

2. Compare the impact of *Pullman* and *Younger* abstention on the federal plaintiff. In *Pullman* abstention, the plaintiff may return to federal court to bring his federal claims. In *Younger* abstention, the federal plaintiff is required to litigate federal claims within the context of a state-court criminal proceeding. If he returns to federal court at all, it will be as a petitioner in a habeas corpus proceeding.

3. As the Court notes, Attorney General Younger argued that the injunction issued by the district court was a violation of the Anti-Injunction Act, 28 U.S.C. § 2283. The Court does not consider that argument; instead, it rests its decision on the "longstanding public policy against federal court interference with state court proceedings." One year later, in *Mitchum v. Foster*, 407 U.S. 225 (1972), the Court held that 42 U.S.C. § 1983 is an "expressly authorized" exception to the prohibition in § 2283. See section A. But by the time the Court decided *Mitchum*, the *Younger* doctrine was already on the books to assure that plaintiffs could not use § 1983 to halt state criminal proceedings even if § 2283 did not stand as a barrier.

4. Although Justice Black does not mention it, Harris filed suit in federal district court under 42 U.S.C. § 1983 and invoked the jurisdictional grant in what is today 28 U.S.C. § 1343(a)(3). As Justice Stewart notes in his concurring opinion, section 1983 was first enacted as part of § 1 of the Civil Rights Act of 1871. Section 1 also included what appears to be a grant of exclusive jurisdiction in the federal courts over what are today § 1983 actions. Later codifications separated the remedial and jurisdictional provisions of § 1, and the language suggesting exclusive jurisdiction was dropped. But could the Court properly invoke "equitable principles" or "policy grounds" to bar Harris's suit without considering the implications of the 1871 Act and its vesting of jurisdiction — probably exclusive jurisdiction — in the federal courts over cases like Harris's?

5. In *Younger*, the Court lists several circumstances that might overcome the policies favoring abstention. Noting that the burdens attending all criminal prosecutions are not enough, in and of themselves, to warrant injunctive relief, the Court states that a showing that the criminal proceedings were brought in bad faith, or simply to harass, might warrant federal intervention. In addition, the Court states:

> There may, of course, be extraordinary circumstances in which the necessary irreparable injury can be shown even in the absence of the usual prerequisites of bad faith and harassment. For example, ... a statute might be flagrantly and patently violative of express constitutional prohibitions in every clause, sentence and paragraph, and in whatever manner and against whomever an effort might be made to apply it.

After the *Dombrowski* case, which the Court distinguishes in *Younger*, there are no cases in which the Supreme Court has found any of these exceptions to be applicable. Why did the Court think it necessary to recognize the exceptions? Are there any situations in which a state court would not be capable of addressing the federal constitutional issues that a criminal defendant might wish to raise?

6. At the time the state proceedings were initiated against Harris, the Supreme Court had not yet held the Syndicalism Act unconstitutional. If the state were to initiate such a proceeding today, would the defendant be able to obtain a federal-court injunction against the prosecution?

7. Although *Pullman* and *Burford* are discretionary doctrines, *Younger* is not. "Where a case is properly within [the *Younger*] category of cases, there is no discretion to grant injunctive relief." *Colorado River Water Conservation Dist. v. United States*, 424 U.S. 800, 816 n.22 (1976).

8. In *Samuels v. Mackell*, 401 U.S. 66 (1971), decided on the same day as *Younger*, the Court held that the same principles that bar injunctive relief when a state criminal proceeding is pending against the federal plaintiff also bar declaratory relief. The Court believed the effect of a declaratory judgment on pending state proceedings would be "precisely the same" as an injunction:

> This is true for at least two reasons. In the first place, the Declaratory Judgment Act provides that after a declaratory judgment is issued the district court may enforce it by granting "[f]urther necessary or proper relief," 28 U.S.C. § 2202, and therefore a declaratory judgment issued while state proceedings are pending might serve as the basis for a subsequent injunction against those proceedings to "protect or effectuate" the declaratory judgment, 28 U.S.C. § 2283, and thus result in a clearly improper interference with the state proceedings. Secondly, even if the declaratory judgment is not used as a basis for actually issuing an injunction, the declaratory relief alone has virtually the same practical impact as a formal injunction would. As we said in *Public Service Commission v. Wycoff Co.*, 344 U.S. 237 (1953):
>
> > Is the declaration contemplated here to be res judicata, so that the [state court] can not hear evidence and decide any matter for itself? If so, the federal court has virtually lifted the case out of the State [court] before it could be heard. If not, the federal judgment serves no useful purpose as a final determination of rights.

9. Suppose that the state-court defendant concludes his case and then appeals unsuccessfully through the state system. May he then return to federal court for adjudication of his federal claims? In almost all circumstances, the answer is no.

If the state-court proceedings were civil in nature, the *Rooker-Feldman* doctrine, discussed in Chapter 17, would prevent a lawsuit that challenged the results of a state-court judgment.

If the state-court proceedings were criminal, the defendant is required to pursue federal-court objections to his conviction through habeas corpus proceedings. *Preiser v. Rodriguez*, 411 U.S. 475 (1973). If the former defendant is seeking relief that is not available through habeas corpus, such as damages, his claim may still be barred. In *Heck v. Humphrey*, 512 U.S. 477 (1994), the Court held that where success in a prisoner's § 1983 damages action would implicitly question the validity of either conviction or the duration of sentence, the federal plaintiff must first achieve favorable termination of his available state, or federal habeas, opportunities to challenge the underlying conviction or sentence.

Note: Younger *and Threatened Prosecutions*

Several of the plaintiffs in *Younger* were found not to have standing because they had not yet been threatened with prosecution. In *Steffel v. Thompson*, 415 U.S. 452 (1974), the Court held that abstention was unjustified when the plaintiff made a credible claim that he was threatened with prosecution, but charges had not yet been brought.

The plaintiff in *Steffel* was a war protester who was ordered to leave the sidewalk outside a shopping mall, where he was passing out handbills, on threat of prosecution. He left, but his companion did not, and the companion was arrested and charged with criminal trespass. Plaintiff filed a federal-court action for a declaratory judgment (and an injunction, which he later abandoned) against the prosecutor, the chief of police, and the owner of the shopping center, arguing that the criminal trespass statute could not be constitutionally applied to his activity. The parties stipulated that if plaintiff again passed out handbills at the center, he would be arrested. The Court found standing:

> [Plaintiff] has alleged threats of prosecution that cannot be characterized as "imaginary or speculative." He has been twice warned to stop handbilling that he claims is constitutionally protected and has been told by the police that if he again handbills at the shopping center and disobeys a warning to stop he will likely be prosecuted. The prosecution of petitioner's handbilling companion is ample demonstration that petitioner's concern with arrest has not been "chimerical," *Poe v. Ullman*, 367 U.S. 497 (1961). In these circumstances, it is not necessary that petitioner first expose himself to actual arrest or prosecution to be entitled to challenge a statute that he claims deters the exercise of his constitutional rights. Moreover, petitioner's challenge is to those specific provisions of state law which have provided the basis for threats of criminal prosecution against him.

The Court then turned to *Younger*'s application:

> When no state criminal proceeding is pending at the time the federal complaint is filed, federal intervention does not result in duplicative legal proceedings or disruption of the state criminal justice system; nor can federal intervention, in that circumstance, be interpreted as reflecting negatively upon the state court's ability to enforce constitutional principles. In addition, while a pending state prosecution provides the federal plaintiff with a concrete opportunity to vindicate his constitutional rights, a refusal on the part of the federal courts to intervene when no state proceeding is pending may place the hapless plaintiff between the Scylla of intentionally flouting state law and the Charybdis of forgoing what he believes to be constitutionally protected activity in order to avoid becoming enmeshed in a criminal proceeding.

Finally, the Court considered the role of the Declaratory Judgment Act, which was passed in part to permit courts to answer questions without requiring the issuance of an injunction:

> When no state proceeding is pending and thus considerations of equity, comity, and federalism have little vitality, the propriety of granting federal

declaratory relief may properly be considered independently of a request for injunctive relief. Here, the Court of Appeals held that, because injunctive relief would not be appropriate since petitioner failed to demonstrate irreparable injury—a traditional prerequisite to injunctive relief—it followed that declaratory relief was also inappropriate. [T]he court erred in treating the requests for injunctive and declaratory relief as a single issue. "[W]hen no state prosecution is pending and the only question is whether declaratory relief is appropriate, . . . the congressional scheme that makes the federal courts the primary guardians of constitutional rights, and the express congressional authorization of declaratory relief, afforded because it is a less harsh and abrasive remedy than the injunction, become the factors of primary significance." *Perez v. Ledesma*, 401 U.S. 82 (1971) (separate opinion of Brennan, J.).

. . . In the instant case, principles of federalism not only do not preclude federal intervention, they compel it. Requiring the federal courts totally to step aside when no state criminal prosecution is pending against the federal plaintiff would turn federalism on its head. When federal claims are premised on 42 U.S.C. § 1983 and 28 U.S.C. § 1343(3)—as they are here—we have not required exhaustion of state judicial or administrative remedies, recognizing the paramount role Congress has assigned to the federal courts to protect constitutional rights. *See, e.g., McNeese v. Board of Education*, 373 U.S. 668 (1963); *Monroe v. Pape*, 365 U.S. 167 (1961) [Chapter 14]. But exhaustion of state remedies is precisely what would be required if both federal injunctive and declaratory relief were unavailable in a case where no state prosecution had been commenced.

Justice Stewart joined the opinion of the Court, but he added a cautionary note:

Our decision today must not be understood as authorizing the invocation of federal declaratory judgment jurisdiction by a person who thinks a state criminal law is unconstitutional, even if he genuinely feels "chilled" in his freedom of action by the law's existence, and even if he honestly entertains the subjective belief that he may now or in the future be prosecuted under it.

The petitioner in this case has succeeded in objectively showing that the threat of imminent arrest, corroborated by the actual arrest of his companion, has created an actual concrete controversy between himself and the agents of the State. He has, therefore, demonstrated "a genuine threat of enforcement of a disputed state criminal statute. . . ." Cases where such a "genuine threat" can be demonstrated will, I think, be exceedingly rare.

As Justice Stewart's opinion implicitly suggests, timing is critical: if the would-be federal plaintiff goes into court too soon, the court will find no "actual concrete controversy"; if he waits too long, the proceeding will have been initiated, and *Younger* will apply.

Note: The Timing of the Federal and State Proceedings

Suppose that after the plaintiff in *Steffel* filed his federal-court action, the prosecutor filed the threatened criminal charges in state court. Is the federal court now required to abstain under *Younger*? Possibly, but not necessarily. The Supreme Court addressed this question in *Hicks v. Miranda*, 422 U.S. 332 (1975). The court held that "where state criminal proceedings are begun against the federal plaintiffs after the federal complaint is filed but before any proceedings of substance on the merits have taken place in the federal court, the principles of *Younger v. Harris* should apply in full force."

On the one hand, this admonition means that *Younger* may apply even if the federal suit is instituted before the state criminal prosecution. On the other hand, there does come a point where the state prosecutor can no longer force the plaintiff out of federal court. The Supreme Court has held, for instance, that issuance of a preliminary injunction by a federal court constitutes a proceeding of substance on the merits. In *Hawaii Housing Auth. v. Midkiff*, 467 U.S. 229 (1984), the Court said: "A federal court action in which a preliminary injunction is granted has proceeded well beyond the 'embryonic stage,' and considerations of economy, equity, and federalism counsel against *Younger* abstention at that point." Lower federal courts have found that the *denial* of a preliminary injunction also can constitute a proceeding of substance, when coupled with a thorough evidentiary hearing. *See, e.g., Adultworld Bookstore v. City of Fresno*, 758 F.2d 1348 (9th Cir. 1985). What policies support the rule that a federal plaintiff may not automatically be ousted by the filing of state criminal proceedings?

Sprint Communications, Inc. v. Jacobs

Supreme Court of the United States, 2013.

134 S. Ct. 548.

JUSTICE GINSBURG delivered the opinion of the Court.

This case involves two proceedings, one pending in state court, the other in federal court. Each seeks review of an Iowa Utilities Board (IUB or Board) order. And each presents the question whether Windstream Iowa Communications, Inc. (Windstream), a local telecommunications carrier, may impose on Sprint Communications, Inc. (Sprint), intrastate access charges for telephone calls transported via the Internet. Federal-court jurisdiction over controversies of this kind was confirmed in *Verizon Md., Inc. v. Public Serv. Comm'n of Md.*, 535 U.S. 635 (2002). Invoking *Younger v. Harris*, 401 U.S. 37 (1971), the U.S. District Court for the Southern District of Iowa abstained from adjudicating Sprint's complaint in deference to the parallel state-court proceeding, and the Court of Appeals for the Eighth Circuit affirmed the District Court's abstention decision.

We reverse the judgment of the Court of Appeals. In the main, federal courts are obliged to decide cases within the scope of federal jurisdiction. Abstention is not in order simply because a pending state-court proceeding involves the same subject matter. *New Orleans Public Service, Inc. Council of City of New Orleans*, 491 U.S. 350 (*NOPSI*) ("[T]here is no doctrine that . . . pendency of state judicial proceedings excludes the federal courts."). This Court has recognized, however, certain instances in which the prospect of undue interference with state proceedings counsels against federal relief.

Younger exemplifies one class of cases in which federal-court abstention is required: When there is a parallel, pending state criminal proceeding, federal courts must refrain from enjoining the state prosecution. This Court has extended *Younger* abstention to particular state civil proceedings that are akin to criminal prosecutions, see *Huffman v. Pursue, Ltd.*, 420 U.S. 592 (1975), or that implicate a State's interest in enforcing the orders and judgments of its courts, see *Pennzoil Co. v. Texaco Inc.*, 481 U.S. 1 (1987). We have cautioned, however, that federal courts ordinarily should entertain and resolve on the merits an action within the scope of a jurisdictional grant, and should not "refus[e] to decide a case in deference to the States." *NOPSI*.

Circumstances fitting within the *Younger* doctrine, we have stressed, are "exceptional"; they include, as catalogued in *NOPSI*, "state criminal prosecutions," "civil enforcement proceedings," and "civil proceedings involving certain orders that are uniquely in furtherance of the state courts' ability to perform their judicial functions." Because this case presents none of the circumstances the Court has ranked as "exceptional," the general rule governs: "[T]he pendency of an action in [a] state court is no bar to proceedings concerning the same matter in the Federal court having jurisdiction." *Colorado River Water Conservation Dist. v. United States*, 424 U.S. 800 (1976).

I

Sprint, a national telecommunications service provider, has long paid intercarrier access fees to the Iowa communications company Windstream . . . for certain long distance calls placed by Sprint customers to Windstream's in-state customers. In 2009, however, Sprint decided to withhold payment for a subset of those calls, classified as Voice over Internet Protocol (VoIP), after concluding that the Telecommunications Act of 1996 preempted intrastate regulation of VoIP traffic. In response, Windstream threatened to block all calls to and from Sprint customers.

Sprint filed a complaint against Windstream with the IUB asking the Board to enjoin Windstream from discontinuing service to Sprint. In Sprint's view, Iowa law entitled it to withhold payment while it contested the access charges and prohibited Windstream from carrying out its disconnection threat. In answer to Sprint's complaint, Windstream retracted its threat to discontinue serving Sprint, and Sprint moved, successfully, to withdraw its complaint. Because the conflict between Sprint and Windstream over VoIP calls was "likely to recur," however, the IUB decided to continue the proceedings to resolve the underlying legal question, i.e., whether VoIP calls are subject to intrastate regulation. The question retained by the IUB, Sprint argued, was governed by federal law, and was not within the IUB's adjudicative jurisdiction. The IUB disagreed, ruling that the intrastate fees applied to VoIP calls.[2]

Seeking to overturn the Board's ruling, Sprint commenced two lawsuits. First, Sprint sued the members of the IUB (respondents here) in their official capacities in the United States District Court for the Southern District of Iowa. In its federal-court

---

2. At the conclusion of the IUB proceedings, Sprint paid Windstream all contested fees.

complaint, Sprint sought a declaration that the Telecommunications Act of 1996 preempted the IUB's decision; as relief, Sprint requested an injunction against enforcement of the IUB's order. Second, Sprint petitioned for review of the IUB's order in Iowa state court. The state petition reiterated the preemption argument Sprint made in its federal-court complaint; in addition, Sprint asserted state law and procedural due process claims. Because Eighth Circuit precedent effectively required a plaintiff to exhaust state remedies before proceeding to federal court, see *Alleghany Corp. v. McCartney*, 896 F.2d 1138 (1990), Sprint urges that it filed the state suit as a protective measure. Failing to do so, Sprint explains, risked losing the opportunity to obtain any review, federal or state, should the federal court decide to abstain after the expiration of the Iowa statute of limitations.[4]

As Sprint anticipated, the IUB filed a motion asking the Federal District Court to abstain in light of the state suit, citing *Younger*. The District Court granted the IUB's motion and dismissed the suit. The IUB's decision, and the pending state-court review of it, the District Court said, composed one "uninterruptible process" implicating important state interests. On that ground, the court ruled, *Younger* abstention was in order.

For the most part, the Eighth Circuit agreed with the District Court's judgment. The Court of Appeals rejected the argument, accepted by several of its sister courts, that *Younger* abstention is appropriate only when the parallel state proceedings are "coercive," rather than "remedial," in nature. Instead, the Eighth Circuit read this Court's precedent to require *Younger* abstention whenever "an ongoing state judicial proceeding . . . implicates important state interests, and . . . the state proceedings provide adequate opportunity to raise [federal] challenges" (citing *Middlesex County Ethics Comm. v. Garden State Bar Assn.*, 457 U.S. 423 (1982)). Those criteria were satisfied here, the appeals court held, because the ongoing state-court review of the IUB's decision concerned Iowa's "important state interest in regulating and enforcing its intrastate utility rates." Recognizing the "possibility that the parties [might] return to federal court," however, the Court of Appeals vacated the judgment dismissing Sprint's complaint. In lieu of dismissal, the Eighth Circuit remanded the case, instructing the District Court to enter a stay during the pendency of the state-court action.

We granted certiorari to decide whether, consistent with our delineation of cases encompassed by the *Younger* doctrine, abstention was appropriate here.

II

A

Neither party has questioned the District Court's jurisdiction to decide whether federal law preempted the IUB's decision, and rightly so. In *Verizon Md.*, we reviewed a similar federal-court challenge to a state administrative adjudication. In that case,

---

4. Since we granted certiorari, the Iowa state court issued an opinion rejecting Sprint's preemption claim on the merits. The Iowa court decision does not, in the parties' view, moot this case. Because Sprint intends to appeal the state-court decision, the "controversy . . . remains live." *Exxon Mobil Corp. v. Saudi Basic Industries Corp.*, 544 U.S. 280 (2005).

as here, the party seeking federal-court review of a state agency's decision urged that the Telecommunications Act of 1996 preempted the state action. We had "no doubt that federal courts ha[d federal question] jurisdiction under [28 U.S.C.] § 1331 to entertain such a suit," and nothing in the Telecommunications Act detracted from that conclusion.

Federal courts, it was early and famously said, have "no more right to decline the exercise of jurisdiction which is given, than to usurp that which is not given." *Cohens v. Virginia*, 6 Wheat. 264 (1821). Jurisdiction existing, this Court has cautioned, a federal court's "obligation" to hear and decide a case is "virtually unflagging." *Colorado River*. Parallel state-court proceedings do not detract from that obligation.

In *Younger*, we recognized a "far-from-novel" exception to this general rule. *NOPSI*. The plaintiff in *Younger* sought federal-court adjudication of the constitutionality of the California Criminal Syndicalism Act. Requesting an injunction against the Act's enforcement, the federal-court plaintiff was at the time the defendant in a pending state criminal prosecution under the Act. In those circumstances, we said, the federal court should decline to enjoin the prosecution, absent bad faith, harassment, or a patently invalid state statute. . . .

We have since applied *Younger* to bar federal relief in certain civil actions. *Huffman* is the pathmarking decision. There, Ohio officials brought a civil action in state court to abate the showing of obscene movies in Pursue's theater. Because the State was a party and the proceeding was "in aid of and closely related to [the State's] criminal statutes," the Court held *Younger* abstention appropriate.

More recently, in *NOPSI*, the Court had occasion to review and restate our *Younger* jurisprudence. *NOPSI* addressed and rejected an argument that a federal court should refuse to exercise jurisdiction to review a state council's ratemaking decision. "[O]nly exceptional circumstances," we reaffirmed, "justify a federal court's refusal to decide a case in deference to the States." Those "exceptional circumstances" exist, the Court determined after surveying prior decisions, in three types of proceedings. First, *Younger* precluded federal intrusion into ongoing state criminal prosecutions. Second, certain "civil enforcement proceedings" warranted abstention. Finally, federal courts refrained from interfering with pending "civil proceedings involving certain orders . . . uniquely in furtherance of the state courts' ability to perform their judicial functions." *NOPSI* (citing *Juidice v. Vail*, 430 U.S. 327 (1977), and *Pennzoil Co. v. Texaco Inc.*, 481 U.S. 1 (1987)). We have not applied *Younger* outside these three "exceptional" categories, and today hold, in accord with *NOPSI*, that they define *Younger*'s scope.

B

The IUB does not assert that the Iowa state court's review of the Board decision, considered alone, implicates *Younger*. Rather, the initial administrative proceeding justifies staying any action in federal court, the IUB contends, until the state review process has concluded. The same argument was advanced in *NOPSI*. We will assume without deciding, as the Court did in *NOPSI*, that an administrative adjudication and the subsequent state court's review of it count as a "unitary process" for *Younger* purposes. The question remains, however, whether the initial IUB proceeding is of the "sort . . . entitled to *Younger* treatment."

The IUB proceeding, we conclude, does not fall within any of the three exceptional categories described in *NOPSI* and therefore does not trigger *Younger* abstention. The first and third categories plainly do not accommodate the IUB's proceeding. That proceeding was civil, not criminal in character, and it did not touch on a state court's ability to perform its judicial function. Cf. *Juidice* (civil contempt order); *Pennzoil* (requirement for posting bond pending appeal).

Nor does the IUB's order rank as an act of civil enforcement of the kind to which *Younger* has been extended. Our decisions applying *Younger* to instances of civil enforcement have generally concerned state proceedings "akin to a criminal prosecution" in "important respects." *Huffman*. See also *Middlesex* (*Younger* abstention appropriate where "noncriminal proceedings bear a close relationship to proceedings criminal in nature"). Such enforcement actions are characteristically initiated to sanction the federal plaintiff, i.e., the party challenging the state action, for some wrongful act. *See, e.g., Middlesex* (state-initiated disciplinary proceedings against lawyer for violation of state ethics rules). In cases of this genre, a state actor is routinely a party to the state proceeding and often initiates the action. See, *e.g., Ohio Civil Rights Comm'n v. Dayton Christian Schools, Inc.*, 477 U.S. 619 (1986) (state-initiated administrative proceedings to enforce state civil rights laws); *Moore v. Sims*, 442 U.S. 415 (1979) (state-initiated proceeding to gain custody of children allegedly abused by their parents); *Trainor v. Hernandez*, 431 U.S. 434 (1977) (civil proceeding "brought by the State in its sovereign capacity" to recover welfare payments defendants had allegedly obtained by fraud); *Huffman* (state-initiated proceeding to enforce obscenity laws). Investigations are commonly involved, often culminating in the filing of a formal complaint or charges. See, *e.g., Dayton* (noting preliminary investigation and complaint); *Middlesex* (same).

The IUB proceeding does not resemble the state enforcement actions this Court has found appropriate for *Younger* abstention. It is not "akin to a criminal prosecution." *Huffman*. Nor was it initiated by "the State in its sovereign capacity." *Trainor*. A private corporation, Sprint, initiated the action. No state authority conducted an investigation into Sprint's activities, and no state actor lodged a formal complaint against Sprint.

In its brief, the IUB emphasizes Sprint's decision to withdraw the complaint that commenced proceedings before the Board. At that point, the IUB argues, Sprint was no longer a willing participant, and the proceedings became, essentially, a civil enforcement action.[6] The IUB's adjudicative authority, however, was invoked to settle a civil dispute between two private parties, not to sanction Sprint for commission of a

---

6. To determine whether a state proceeding is an enforcement action under *Younger*, several Courts of Appeals, as noted, inquire whether the underlying state proceeding is "coercive" rather than "remedial." Though we referenced this dichotomy once in a footnote, see *Dayton*, we do not find the inquiry necessary or inevitably helpful, given the susceptibility of the designations to manipulation.

wrongful act. Although Sprint withdrew its complaint, administrative efficiency, not misconduct by Sprint, prompted the IUB to answer the underlying federal question. By determining the intercarrier compensation regime applicable to VoIP calls, the IUB sought to avoid renewed litigation of the parties' dispute. Because the underlying legal question remained unsettled, the Board observed, the controversy was "likely to recur." Nothing here suggests that the IUB proceeding was "more akin to a criminal prosecution than are most civil cases." *Huffman.*

In holding that abstention was the proper course, the Eighth Circuit relied heavily on this Court's decision in *Middlesex. Younger* abstention was warranted, the Court of Appeals read *Middlesex* to say, whenever three conditions are met: There is (1) "an ongoing state judicial proceeding, which (2) implicates important state interests, and (3) ... provide[s] an adequate opportunity to raise [federal] challenges." ...

The Court of Appeals and the IUB attribute to this Court's decision in *Middlesex* extraordinary breadth. We invoked *Younger* in *Middlesex* to bar a federal court from entertaining a lawyer's challenge to a New Jersey state ethics committee's pending investigation of the lawyer. Unlike the IUB proceeding here, the state ethics committee's hearing in *Middlesex* was indeed "akin to a criminal proceeding." As we noted, an investigation and formal complaint preceded the hearing, an agency of the State's Supreme Court initiated the hearing, and the purpose of the hearing was to determine whether the lawyer should be disciplined for his failure to meet the State's standards of professional conduct. The three *Middlesex* conditions recited above were not dispositive; they were, instead, additional factors appropriately considered by the federal court before invoking *Younger*.

Divorced from their quasi-criminal context, the three *Middlesex* conditions would extend *Younger* to virtually all parallel state and federal proceedings, at least where a party could identify a plausibly important state interest. That result is irreconcilable with our dominant instruction that, even in the presence of parallel state proceedings, abstention from the exercise of federal jurisdiction is the "exception, not the rule." *Hawaii Housing Authority v. Midkiff*, 467 U.S. 229 (1984). In short, to guide other federal courts, we today clarify and affirm that *Younger* extends to the three "exceptional circumstances" identified in *NOPSI*, but no further.

* * *

For the reasons stated, the judgment of the United States Court of Appeals for the Eighth Circuit is Reversed.

Note: The Extension of Younger Beyond Criminal Proceedings

1. The Court's unanimous decision in *Sprint* does much to clarify—and to limit—the scope of *Younger* abstention outside the criminal context. Justice Ginsburg's opinion makes clear that ordinary parallel civil litigation in a state court or administrative agency does not trigger *Younger* abstention, even if the case touches on important state interests and the parties have a full opportunity to litigate their federal claims in the state proceedings. Instead, the Court appears to restrict *Younger* to civil enforcement proceedings closely analogous to criminal prosecutions. The Court identifies three key features of such actions: (1) they are initiated by the State in its sovereign capacity; (2) they sanction the federal-court plaintiff for some wrongful act; and (3) they involve an investigation and the filing of a formal complaint or charge.

Yet in describing the kind of "quasi-criminal" civil cases to which *Younger* extends, the Court does not state that all of those features are essential. It uses words like "generally," "characteristically," "routinely," "often," and "common" to describe them. After *Sprint*, should federal district courts insist that all of those features be present in a state civil proceeding before invoking *Younger*? Or has the Court left them some wiggle room?

2. Does a claim that the state proceeding is completely preempted by federal law preclude *Younger* abstention? In *NOPSI*, the Court concluded it does not:

> NOPSI argues that *Younger* does not require abstention in the face of a substantial claim that the challenged state action is completely pre-empted by federal law. Such a claim, NOPSI contends, calls into question the prerequisite of *Younger* abstention that the State have a legitimate, substantial interest in its pending proceedings. . . .

> We disagree. There is no greater federal interest in enforcing the supremacy of federal statutes than in enforcing the supremacy of explicit constitutional guarantees, and constitutional challenges to state action, no less than preemption-based challenges, call into question the legitimacy of the State's interest in its proceedings reviewing or enforcing that action. Yet it is clear that the mere assertion of a substantial constitutional challenge to state action will not alone compel the exercise of federal jurisdiction. That is so because when we inquire into the substantiality of the State's interest in its proceedings we do not look narrowly to its interest in the *outcome* of a particular case—which could arguably be offset by a substantial federal interest in the opposite outcome. Rather, what we look to is the importance of the generic proceedings to the State. . . . [T]he appropriate question here is not whether Louisiana has a substantial, legitimate interest in reducing NOPSI's retail rate below that necessary to recover its wholesale costs, but whether it has a substantial, legitimate interest in regulating intrastate retail rates. It clearly does. "[T]he regulation of utilities is one of the most important of the functions traditionally associated with the police power of the States."

The Court therefore concluded that "NOPSI's challenge must stand or fall upon the answer to the question whether the Louisiana court action is the *type of proceeding* to which *Younger* applies." (Emphasis added.) As explained in the *Sprint* opinion, the Court held that it was not.

C. Deference to State Proceedings

Colorado River Water Conservation District v. United States

Supreme Court of the United States, 1976.

424 U.S. 800.

MR. JUSTICE BRENNAN delivered the opinion of the Court.

The McCarran Amendment, 43 U.S.C. § 666, provides that "consent is hereby given to join the United States as a defendant in any suit (1) for the adjudication of rights to the use of water of a river system or other source, or (2) for the administration of such rights, where it appears that the United States is the owner of or is in the process of acquiring water rights by appropriation under State law, by purchase, by exchange, or otherwise, and the United States is a necessary party to such suit." The questions presented by this case concern the effect of the McCarran Amendment upon the jurisdiction of the federal district courts under 28 U.S.C. § 1345 over suits for determination of water rights brought by the United States as trustee for certain Indian tribes and as owner of various non-Indian Government claims.

I

It is probable that no problem of the Southwest section of the Nation is more critical than that of scarcity of water. As southwestern populations have grown, conflicting claims to this scarce resource have increased. To meet these claims, several Southwestern States have established elaborate procedures for allocation of water and adjudication of conflicting claims to that resource. In 1969, Colorado enacted its Water Rights Determination and Administration Act in an effort to revamp its legal procedures for determining claims to water within the State.

Under the Colorado Act, the State is divided into seven Water Divisions, each Division encompassing one or more entire drainage basins for the larger rivers in Colorado. Adjudication of water claims within each Division occurs on a continuous basis. Each month, Water Referees in each Division rule on applications for water rights filed within the preceding five months or refer those applications to the Water Judge of their Division. Every six months, the Water Judge passes on referred applications and contested decisions by Referees. A State Engineer and engineers for each Division are responsible for the administration and distribution of the waters of the State according to the determinations in each Division.

Colorado applies the doctrine of prior appropriation in establishing rights to the use of water. Under that doctrine, one acquires a right to water by diverting it from its natural source and applying it to some beneficial use. Continued beneficial use of the water is required in order to maintain the right. In periods of shortage, priority among confirmed rights is determined according to the date of initial diversion.

The reserved rights of the United States extend to Indian reservations and other federal lands, such as national parks and forests. The reserved rights claimed by the

United States in this case affect waters within Colorado Water Division No. 7. On November 14, 1972, the Government instituted this suit in the United States District Court for the District of Colorado, invoking the court's jurisdiction under 28 U.S.C. § 1345. The District Court is located in Denver, some 300 miles from Division 7. The suit, against some 1,000 water users, sought declaration of the Government's rights to waters in certain rivers and their tributaries located in Division 7. In the suit, the Government asserted reserved rights on its own behalf and on behalf of certain Indian tribes, as well as rights based on state law. It sought appointment of a water master to administer any waters decreed to the United States. Prior to institution of this suit, the Government had pursued adjudication of non-Indian reserved rights and other water claims based on state law in Water Divisions 4, 5, and 6, and the Government continues to participate fully in those Divisions.

Shortly after the federal suit was commenced, one of the defendants in that suit filed an application in the state court for Division 7, seeking an order directing service of process on the United States in order to make it a party to proceedings in Division 7 for the purpose of adjudicating all of the Government's claims, both state and federal. On January 3, 1973, the United States was served pursuant to authority of the McCarran Amendment. Several defendants and intervenors in the federal proceeding then filed a motion in the District Court to dismiss on the ground that under the Amendment, the court was without jurisdiction to determine federal water rights. Without deciding the jurisdictional question, the District Court, on June 21, 1973, granted the motion . . . stating that the doctrine of abstention required deference to the proceedings in Division 7. On appeal, the Court of Appeals for the Tenth Circuit reversed. . . . We granted certiorari to consider the important questions of whether the McCarran Amendment terminated jurisdiction of federal courts to adjudicate federal water rights and whether, if that jurisdiction was not terminated, the District Court's dismissal in this case was nevertheless appropriate. We reverse.

II

We first consider the question of district-court jurisdiction under 28 U.S.C. § 1345. [The Court concluded that the McCarran Amendment does not constitute an exception to the jurisdiction of district courts under § 1345 to entertain federal water suits.]

III

We turn next to the question whether this suit nevertheless was properly dismissed in view of the concurrent state proceedings in Division 7.

A

First, we consider whether the McCarran Amendment provided consent to determine federal reserved rights held on behalf of Indians in state court. . . . [The Court had previously held that the provisions of the McCarran Amendment, whereby "consent is . . . given to join the United States as a defendant in any suit (1) for the adjudication . . . or (2) for the administration of [water] rights, where it appears that the United States is the owner . . . by appropriation under State law, by purchase, by exchange, or otherwise. . . . ," subject federal reserved rights to general adjudication in state proceedings for the determination of water rights. The Court concluded that reserved Indian water rights were included in the statute.]

B

Next, we consider whether the District Court's dismissal was appropriate under the doctrine of abstention. We hold that the dismissal cannot be supported under that doctrine in any of its forms.

(a) [*Pullman* abstention] is appropriate "in cases presenting a federal constitutional issue which might be mooted or presented in a different posture by a state court determination of pertinent state law." This case, however, presents no federal constitutional issue for decision.

(b) Abstention is also appropriate where there have been presented difficult questions of state law bearing on policy problems of substantial public import whose importance transcends the result in the case then at bar. *Louisiana Power & Light Co. v. City of Thibodaux*, 360 U.S. 25 (1959). [It is also appropriate under *Burford v. Sun Oil Co.*, 319 U.S. 315 (1943), when the] exercise of federal review of the question in a case and in similar cases would be disruptive of state efforts to establish a coherent policy with respect to a matter of substantial public concern.

The present case clearly does not fall within this second category of abstention. While state claims are involved in the case, the state law to be applied appears to be settled. No questions bearing on state policy are presented for decision. Nor will decision of the state claims impair efforts to implement state policy as in *Burford*. To be sure, the federal claims that are involved in the case go to the establishment of water rights which may conflict with similar rights based on state law. But the mere potential for conflict in the results of adjudications, does not, without more, warrant staying exercise of federal jurisdiction. The potential conflict here, involving state claims and federal claims, would not be such as to impair impermissibly the State's effort to effect its policy respecting the allocation of state waters. Nor would exercise of federal jurisdiction here interrupt any such efforts by restraining the exercise of authority vested in state officers.

(c) [*Younger* abstention] is appropriate where, absent bad faith, harassment, or a patently invalid state statute, federal jurisdiction has been invoked for the purpose of restraining state criminal proceedings [or related civil proceedings]. Like the previous two categories, this category also does not include this case. We deal here neither with a criminal proceeding, nor [a covered civil proceeding.] We also do not deal with an attempt to restrain such actions or to seek a declaratory judgment as to the validity of a state criminal law under which criminal proceedings are pending in a state court.

C

Although this case falls within none of the abstention categories, there are principles unrelated to considerations of proper constitutional adjudication and regard for federal-state relations which govern in situations involving the contemporaneous exercise of concurrent jurisdictions, either by federal courts or by state and federal courts.

These principles rest on considerations of "[w]ise judicial administration, giving regard to conservation of judicial resources and comprehensive disposition of litigation." *Kerotest Mfg. Co. v. C-O-Two Fire Equipment Co.*, 342 U.S. 180, 183 (1952). Generally, as between state and federal courts, the rule is that "the pendency of an action in the state court is no bar to proceedings concerning the same matter in the Federal court having jurisdiction. . . ." *See Donovan v. City of Dallas*, 377 U.S. 408 (1964). As between federal district courts, however, though no precise rule has evolved, the general principle is to avoid duplicative litigation. *See Kerotest Mfg. Co. v. C-O-Two Fire Equipment Co.*

This difference in general approach between state-federal concurrent jurisdiction and wholly federal concurrent jurisdiction stems from the virtually unflagging obligation of the federal courts to exercise the jurisdiction given them. *England v. Louisiana State Bd. of Medical Examiners*, 375 U.S. 411, 415 (1964); *Cohens v. Virginia*, 6 Wheat. 264, 404 (1821) (dictum). Given this obligation, and the absence of weightier considerations of constitutional adjudication and state-federal relations, the circumstances permitting the dismissal of a federal suit due to the presence of a concurrent state proceeding for reasons of wise judicial administration are considerably more limited than the circumstances appropriate for abstention. The former circumstances, though exceptional, do nevertheless exist.

It has been held, for example, that the court first assuming jurisdiction over property may exercise that jurisdiction to the exclusion of other courts. *Donovan v. City of Dallas.* . . . In assessing the appropriateness of dismissal in the event of an exercise of concurrent jurisdiction, a federal court may also consider such factors as the inconvenience of the federal forum, *cf. Gulf Oil Corp. v. Gilbert*, 330 U.S. 501 (1947); the desirability of avoiding piecemeal litigation, *cf. Brillhart v. Excess Ins. Co.*, 316 U.S. 491, 495 (1942); and the order in which jurisdiction was obtained by the concurrent forums, *Pacific Live Stock Co. v. Oregon Water Bd.*, 241 U.S. 440, 447 (1916). No one factor is necessarily determinative; a carefully considered judgment taking into account both the obligation to exercise jurisdiction and the combination of factors counselling against that exercise is required. Only the clearest of justifications will warrant dismissal.

Turning to the present case, a number of factors clearly counsel against concurrent federal proceedings. The most important of these is the McCarran Amendment itself. The clear federal policy evinced by that legislation is the avoidance of piecemeal adjudication of water rights in a river system. This policy is akin to that underlying the rule requiring that jurisdiction be yielded to the court first acquiring control of property, for the concern in such instances is with avoiding the generation of additional litigation through permitting inconsistent dispositions of property. This concern is heightened with respect to water rights, the relationships among which are highly interdependent. Indeed, we have recognized that actions seeking the allocation of water essentially involve the disposition of property and are best conducted in unified proceedings. . . .

[T]he Colorado Water Rights Determination and Administration Act established such a [comprehensive] system for the adjudication and management of rights to the use of the State's waters. As the Government concedes, . . . the Act established a single continuous proceeding for water rights adjudication which antedated the suit in District Court. That proceeding "reaches all claims, perhaps month by month but inclusively in the totality." Additionally, the responsibility of managing the State's waters, to the end that they be allocated in accordance with adjudicated water rights, is given to the State Engineer.

Beyond the congressional policy expressed by the McCarran Amendment and consistent with furtherance of that policy, we also find significant (a) the apparent absence of any proceedings in the District Court, other than the filing of the complaint, prior to the motion to dismiss, (b) the extensive involvement of state water rights occasioned by this suit naming 1,000 defendants, (c) the 300-mile distance between the District Court in Denver and the court in Division 7, and (d) the existing participation by the Government in Division 4, 5, and 6 proceedings. We emphasize, however, that we do not overlook the heavy obligation to exercise jurisdiction. We need not decide, for example, whether, despite the McCarran Amendment, dismissal would be warranted if more extensive proceedings had occurred in the District Court prior to dismissal, if the involvement of state water rights were less extensive than it is here, or if the state proceeding were in some respect inadequate to resolve the federal claims. But the opposing factors here, particularly the policy underlying the McCarran Amendment, justify the District Court's dismissal in this particular case.

The judgment of the Court of Appeals is reversed and the judgment of the District Court dismissing the complaint is affirmed for the reasons here stated.

Mr. Justice Stewart, with whom Mr. Justice Blackmun and Mr. Justice Stevens concur, dissenting.

The Court says that the United States District Court for the District of Colorado clearly had jurisdiction over this lawsuit. I agree. The Court further says that the McCarran Amendment "in no way diminished" the District Court's jurisdiction. I agree. The Court also says that federal courts have a "virtually unflagging obligation . . . to exercise the jurisdiction given them." I agree. And finally, the Court says that nothing in the abstention doctrine "in any of its forms" justified the District Court's dismissal of the Government's complaint. I agree. These views would seem to lead ineluctably to the conclusion that the District Court was wrong in dismissing the complaint. Yet the Court holds that the order of dismissal was "appropriate." With that conclusion I must respectfully disagree.

In holding that the United States shall not be allowed to proceed with its lawsuit, the Court relies principally on cases reflecting the rule that where "control of the property which is the subject of the suit [is necessary] in order to proceed with the cause and to grant the relief sought, the jurisdiction of one court must of necessity yield to that of the other." *Penn General Casualty Co. v. Pennsylvania ex rel. Schnader*, 294 U.S. 189. But, as those cases make clear, this rule applies only when exclusive control over the subject matter is necessary to effectuate a court's judgment. Here the federal court did not need to obtain *in rem* . . . jurisdiction in order to decide the issues before it. The court was asked simply to determine as a matter of federal law whether federal reservations of water rights had occurred, and, if so, the date and scope of the reservations. The District Court could make such a determination without having control of the river.

[Here the dissent reviewed the cases cited by the Court.]

The Court's principal reason for deciding to close the doors of the federal courthouse to the United States in this case seems to stem from the view that its decision will avoid piecemeal adjudication of water rights. . . . To the extent that the Court's view is based on the realistic practicalities of this case, it is simply wrong, because the relegation of the Government to the state courts will not avoid piecemeal litigation. [The dissent reviewed the kinds of water proceedings under the state water-rights law, and concluded that the state court would have to "conduct separate proceedings to determine these claims. And only after the state court adjudicates the claims will they be incorporated into the water source tabulations. If this suit were allowed to proceed in federal court the same procedures would be followed, and the federal court decree would be incorporated into the state tabulation, as other federal court decrees have been incorporated in the past. Thus, the same process will occur regardless of which forum considers these claims."]

As the Court says, it is the virtual "unflagging obligation" of a federal court to exercise the jurisdiction that has been conferred upon it. Obedience to that obligation is particularly "appropriate" in this case, for at least two reasons.

First, the issues involved are issues of federal law. A federal court is more likely than a state court to be familiar with federal water law and to have had experience in interpreting the relevant federal statutes, regulations, and Indian treaties. Moreover, if tried in a federal court, these issues of federal law will be reviewable in a federal appellate court, whereas federal judicial review of the state courts' resolution of issues of federal law will be possible only on review by this Court in the exercise of its certiorari jurisdiction.

Second, some of the federal claims in this lawsuit relate to water reserved for Indian reservations. It is not necessary to determine that there is no state-court jurisdiction of these claims to support the proposition that a federal court is a more appropriate forum than a state court for determination of questions of life-and-death importance to Indians. This Court has long recognized that "'[t]he policy of leaving Indians free from state jurisdiction and control is deeply rooted in the Nation's history.'" *McClanahan v. Arizona State Tax Comm'n*, 411 U.S. 164.

The Court says that "[o]nly the clearest of justifications will warrant dismissal" of a lawsuit within the jurisdiction of a federal court. In my opinion there was no justification at all for the District Court's order of dismissal in this case.

I would affirm the judgment of the Court of Appeals.

MR. JUSTICE STEVENS, dissenting.

While I join Mr. Justice Stewart's dissenting opinion, I add three brief comments:

First, I find the holding that the United States may not litigate a federal claim in a federal court having jurisdiction thereof particularly anomalous. I could not join such a disposition unless commanded to do so by an unambiguous statutory mandate or by some other clearly identifiable and applicable rule of law. . . . Second, the Federal Government surely has no lesser right of access to the federal forum than does a private litigant, such as an Indian asserting his own claim. If this be so, today's holding will necessarily restrict the access to federal court of private plaintiffs asserting water rights claims in Colorado. This is a rather surprising byproduct of the McCarran Amendment; for there is no basis for concluding that Congress intended that Amendment to impair the private citizen's right to assert a federal claim in a federal court.

Third, even on the Court's assumption that this case should be decided by balancing the factors weighing for and against the exercise of federal jurisdiction, I believe we should defer to the judgment of the Court of Appeals rather than evaluate those factors in the first instance ourselves. . . . Facts such as the number of parties, the distance between the courthouse and the water in dispute, and the character of the Colorado proceedings are matters which the Court of Appeals sitting in Denver is just as able to evaluate as are we.

Although I agree with Parts I, II, III-A, and III-B of the opinion of the Court, I respectfully dissent from the decision to reverse the judgment of the Court of Appeals for the Tenth Circuit.

Note: Deference to Parallel State Proceedings

1. The Court in *Sprint Communications Inc. v. Jacobs*, 134 S. Ct. 548 (2013) *supra* section B, takes the position that parallel litigation in state and federal courts is a consequence of our federal system, ordinarily one that we tolerate. In *Colorado River*, however, the Court finds "extraordinary circumstances" that permit a federal district court to dismiss a federal action — and here, one that involves the United States government — in deference to pending state court proceedings. What circumstances made this case "extraordinary"? Were all of the factors cited by the Court necessary, or should some be viewed as more important than others?

2. One of the petitioners' arguments in *Colorado River* was that the suit should be dismissed based on *Burford* abstention because allowing the federal court to adjudicate the claims could undermine Colorado's water policies. But the majority in *Colorado River* rejected that argument. Although acknowledging that allowing the federal court to adjudicate the claims could produce results that conflicted with the state's adjudication of those claims, the Court concluded that the "potential conflict . . . would not be such as to impair impermissibly the State's effort to effect its policy respecting the allocation of state waters." Would it have been preferable to expand *Burford* abstention to this situation instead of creating a new doctrine authorizing courts to decline jurisdiction?

3. The most important Supreme Court discussion of *Colorado River* since its decision came in *Moses H. Cone Memorial Hospital v. Mercury Construction Corp.*, 460 U.S. 1 (1983). The hospital and the construction company were involved in a contract dispute, and a critical question was whether the hospital was required to arbitrate the dispute. The hospital brought a declaratory judgment action in state court asking for a declaration that it owed nothing on the contract and was not required to arbitrate; the construction company volleyed with a federal action seeking an order to compel arbitration under the Federal Arbitration Act, 9 U.S.C. § 4. The federal district court stayed the federal suit pending resolution of the state suit, since both involved the central question of arbitrability. The Supreme Court found the stay unsupported by "the consideration that was paramount in *Colorado River* itself — the danger of piecemeal litigation."

> It is true that if [the construction company] obtains an arbitration order, the Hospital will be required to resolve . . . related disputes in different forums. That misfortune, however, is not the result of any choice between the federal and state courts; it occurs because the relevant federal law *requires* piecemeal resolution when necessary to give effect to an arbitration agreement. . . . If the dispute between [the construction company] and the Hospital *is* arbitrable under the [Arbitration] Act, then the Hospital's two disputes will be resolved separately — one in arbitration and the other (if at all) in state-court litigation.

The Court discussed the remaining *Colorado River* factors, noting that several were not present (no res was involved and there were no relative convenience issues), and stating that the priority in which jurisdiction was obtained cut against the federal court retaining the case:

> [T]he Hospital's priority argument gives too mechanical a reading to the "priority" element of the *Colorado River* balance. This factor, as with the other *Colorado River* factors, is to be applied in a pragmatic, flexible manner with a view to the realities of the case at hand. Thus, priority should not be measured exclusively in terms of which complaint was filed first, but rather in terms of how much progress has been made in the two actions.

The Court also discussed the relevance of a factor that was not prominent in *Colorado River*: "the fact that federal law provides the rule of decision on the merits."

> [W]e emphasize that our task in cases such as this is not to find some substantial reason for the *exercise* of federal jurisdiction by the district court; rather, the task is to ascertain whether there exist "exceptional" circumstances, the "clearest of justifications," that can suffice under *Colorado River* to justify the *surrender* of that jurisdiction. Although in some rare circumstances, the presence of state-law issues may weigh in favor of that surrender, the presence of federal-law issues must always be a major consideration weighing against surrender.

Finally, the Court focused on the "probable inadequacy of the state-court proceeding to protect" the construction company's rights, because it was less than clear whether state courts were obliged to compel arbitration under the federal arbitration statute.

4. The *Moses H. Cone* decision is independently important for its holding on the appealability of stays on *Colorado River* grounds. The Court found the stay order immediately appealable as a final order, reasoning that the stay of the federal suit would be the practical end of the litigation, since the state-court judgment would be preclusive of further federal litigation. Alternatively, the Court believed the stay order fit the exception to finality announced in *Cohen v. Beneficial Loan Corp.*, 337 U.S. 541 (1949): the stay "resolve[d] an important issue separate from the merits of the action, and [would be] effectively unreviewable on appeal from a final judgment." For discussion of this point, see Chapter 18.

Note: Federal Declaratory Judgment Suits

1. Congress's creation of the declaratory judgment remedy in 1934 opened up new possibilities for parallel proceedings in state and federal courts. Early in the development of the law, the Supreme Court made clear that a district court has broad discretion to dismiss a declaratory judgment action in favor of a pending proceeding in state court. In *Brillhart v. Excess Insurance Co. of America*, 316 U.S. 491 (1942), the Court said:

> Ordinarily it would be uneconomical as well as vexatious for a federal court to proceed in a declaratory judgment suit where another suit is pending in a state court presenting the same issues, not governed by federal law, between the same parties. Gratuitous interference with the orderly and comprehensive disposition of a state court litigation should be avoided.

> Where a district court is presented with a claim such as was made here, it should ascertain whether the questions in controversy between the parties to the federal suit, and which are not foreclosed under the applicable substantive law, can better be settled in the proceeding pending in the state court. This may entail inquiry into the scope of the pending state court proceeding and the nature of defenses open there. The federal court may have to consider whether the claims of all parties in interest can satisfactorily be adjudicated in that proceeding, whether necessary parties have been joined, whether such parties are amenable to process in that proceeding, etc.

2. The *Brillhart* standard gives the district court considerably more discretion to decline the exercise of jurisdiction than the "exceptional circumstances" test of *Colorado River*. After *Colorado River*, the question arose whether *Brillhart* was still good law. In *Wilton v. Seven Falls Company*, 515 U.S. 277 (1995), the Supreme Court held unanimously that *Brillhart* continues to provide guidance in the declaratory judgment context. The Court said:

> Since its inception, the Declaratory Judgment Act has been understood to confer on federal courts unique and substantial discretion in deciding whether to declare the rights of litigants. . . . In the declaratory judgment context, the normal principle that federal courts should adjudicate claims within their jurisdiction yields to considerations of practicality and wise judicial administration.

3. *Wilton* also clarified the law on two important procedural issues. First, the Court (in a footnote) briefly addressed the question whether the district court should dismiss

the declaratory judgment suit or stay it. The Court said that "where the basis for declining to proceed is the pendency of a state proceeding, a stay will often be the preferable course, because it assures that the federal action can proceed without risk of a time bar if the state case, for any reason, fails to resolve the matter in controversy."

Second, the Court resolved a circuit conflict on the standard of review on appeal. The Court held that district court decisions granting or denying declaratory relief are to be reviewed for abuse of discretion, not de novo. The Court said: "We believe it more consistent with the statute to vest district courts with discretion in the first instance, because facts bearing on the usefulness of the declaratory judgment remedy, and the fitness of the case for resolution, are peculiarly within their grasp." The Court added that "proper application of the abuse of discretion standard on appellate review [can] provide appropriate guidance to district courts."

4. The Court in *Wilton* offered little guidance on the considerations that should guide a district court's exercise of discretion. Most of the circuits use multi-factor tests. In *Sherwin-Williams Co. v. Holmes County*, 343 F.3d 383 (5th Cir. 2003), the court synthesized the decisions:

> Despite the circuits' different expressions of the *Brillhart* factors, each circuit's formulation addresses the same three aspects of the analysis.

> The first is the proper allocation of decision-making between state and federal courts. Each circuit's test emphasizes that if the federal declaratory judgment action raises only issues of state law and a state case involving the same state law issues is pending, generally the state court should decide the case and the federal court should exercise its discretion to dismiss the federal suit.

> The second aspect of the inquiry is fairness. The circuits' varying formulations all distinguish between legitimate and improper reasons for forum selection. Although many federal courts use terms such as "forum selection" and "anticipatory filing" to describe reasons for dismissing a federal declaratory judgment action in favor of related state court litigation, these terms are shorthand for more complex inquiries. The filing of every lawsuit requires forum selection. Federal declaratory judgment suits are routinely filed in anticipation of other litigation. The courts use pejorative terms such as "forum shopping" or "procedural fencing" to identify a narrower category of federal declaratory judgment lawsuits filed for reasons found improper and abusive, other than selecting a forum or anticipating related litigation. Merely filing a declaratory judgment action in a federal court with jurisdiction to hear it, in anticipation of state court litigation, is not in itself improper anticipatory litigation or otherwise abusive "forum shopping."

> The third aspect of the analysis is efficiency. A federal district court should avoid duplicative or piecemeal litigation where possible. A federal court should be less inclined to hear a case if necessary parties are missing from the federal forum, because that leads to piecemeal litigation and duplication of effort in state and federal courts. Duplicative litigation may also raise

federalism or comity concerns because of the potential for inconsistent state and federal court judgments, especially in cases involving state law issues.

5. The Supreme Court's opinion in *Wilton* can easily be read as saying that (a) district courts should readily exercise their discretion to stay declaratory judgment actions in deference to pending state proceedings; and (b) when they do, the courts of appeals should generally respect their decisions. However, the cases in the lower courts are by no means one-sided. For example, in *Penn-America Insurance Co. v. Coffey*, 368 F.3d 409 (4th Cir. 2004), the insurance company brought an action to obtain a declaratory judgment that it had no duty to defend or to indemnify its insured, a sports bar, with respect to a tort action filed by a customer, James Sizemore, in Virginia state court. Sizemore's suit sought damages for injuries he sustained in the bar's parking lot when he was struck by an automobile driven by another customer. The other customer had been involved in a violent altercation with the bar's employees. As he drove away, the employees struck both the automobile and the occupants "with fists and metal pipes," leading the customer to lose control of his vehicle and strike Sizemore.

The liability policy issued to the sports bar excluded from coverage claims "resulting from assault and battery or physical altercations," regardless of whether the claimant's injuries were caused by the bar, its employees, or its patrons. Penn-America asserted that Sizemore's claims fell within this exclusion.

The district court concluded that to decide whether Penn-America was obligated to defend and indemnify the sports bar would require resolution of the same factual issues of causation raised in Sizemore's underlying state court action—i.e., whether Sizemore's injuries resulted from assault and battery. It therefore dismissed the declaratory judgment action. The court of appeals reversed. It said:

> *First*, the duty-to-defend question in this case will not require the district court to resolve factual questions at all. It need only decide such coverage by comparing what Sizemore *has alleged* in the state court action with the language of the Penn-America insurance policy. Under Virginia law, an insurer's duty to defend arises "whenever the complaint against the insured alleges facts and circumstances, some of which, if proved, would fall within the risk covered by the policy." . . . Although an insurer's duty *to indemnify* will depend on resolution of facts alleged in the complaint, no such factfinding is necessary if there is no duty *to defend* because the allegations, even when taken as proved, would fall outside the policy's coverage. . . .

> *Second*, the finding of causation necessary to decide whether Sizemore's injuries "resulted from" a physical altercation [within the meaning of the policy] is distinct in kind from the causation questions that will have to be resolved in deciding whether Sizemore recovers on his tort claims. . . . [The court] need only decide the scope of the *contractual* language, "resulted from," regardless of *who caused* Sizemore's injuries. On the other hand, in the state court proceeding, the fact-finder will have to determine whether Sizemore's injuries were "proximately caused" by any of the defendants during the events on April 5, 2001, assessing responsibility to each.

Note that this analysis requires careful attention to the content of the governing state law as well as careful distinctions between superficially similar issues of law and fact.

6. Neither *Brillhart* nor *Wilton* involved any federal questions. The cases indicate that a district court has less discretion to decline the exercise of jurisdiction when federal questions are present, but there is no firm rule requiring the district court to hear the declaratory judgment suit. In *Verizon Communications, Inc. v. Inverizon International, Inc.*, 295 F.3d 870 (8th Cir. 2002), the district court granted a stay. The court of appeals reversed. Judge Kermit Bye, concurring, said:

> Our reversal and remand is carefully based upon the district court's *failure to consider* the presence of the federal trademark issues, so we avoid directly holding that the district court's stay constituted an abuse of discretion because of the mere *presence* of federal trademark issues. My personal view is that a district court should not stay a federal action when federal questions predominate over state law issues, and for that reason I would not have stayed Verizon's suit if I were the district judge. But my personal disagreement with the district court does not equate to an abuse of discretion because [circuit precedents] prohibit us from finding an abuse of discretion based *solely* upon the presence of a federal issue or claim. (Emphasis added in final sentence.) . . .
>
> I [write] separately to express my disagreement with those decisions, and to suggest that their reconsideration may be in order. Why should a federal action involving federal issues be stayed in favor of a strike suit in state court?

Put aside the reference to a "strike suit." Should it always be deemed an abuse of discretion for a district court to stay a declaratory judgment action presenting federal questions? If your answer is "No," how about declaratory judgment actions in which federal questions *predominate*?

Problem: Parallel Age Discrimination Suits

On April 15, plaintiff Martha Jones filed a complaint in the district court for the Southern District of Indiana in Indianapolis alleging discrimination in employment pursuant to the Age Discrimination in Employment Act. Jones was an elderly cleaning woman in the defendant Big Auto's manufacturing plant. On the same day, Jones filed a petition in the Marion County Superior Court, also in Indianapolis, alleging discrimination in employment under the Indiana Human Rights Act. The parties agree that the two suits contain the same allegations based on the same set of facts. In August, defendant Big Auto filed answers to Jones's state and federal suits.

In September, with knowledge of both actions, the district court entered a scheduling order directing the parties to conduct discovery that could be used in either state or federal court. That same month, the state court also entered a scheduling order. Thereafter, the parties exchanged one set of written discovery for purposes of both the state and federal litigation.

On September 26, Big Auto filed a Motion to Stay Pending State Court Action, in which it asked the district court to stay the state court action until the conclusion of the federal ADEA action pursuant to 29 U.S.C. § 633(a), which states:

> (a) Federal action superseding State action: Nothing in this Act shall affect the jurisdiction of any agency of any State performing like functions with regard to discriminatory employment practices on account of age except that upon commencement of action under this Act such action shall supersede any State action.

Instead, the district court *sua sponte* issued an order staying proceedings in federal court on the basis of *Colorado River* and *Moses H. Cone*.

Was Big Auto correct that the district court could enjoin the state-court proceedings in these circumstances? Was the district court correct that the federal lawsuit should be stayed?

D. Implied Subject-Matter Exclusions from Federal Jurisdiction

In addition to limitations on injunctions directed at state-court proceedings and the various abstention doctrines, the courts have recognized certain subject-matter exclusions from federal jurisdiction. The two most common are the so-called "probate exception" and the "domestic relations exception." The scope of both exceptions has been narrowed considerably by the Supreme Court in recent years, resulting in an expansion of federal jurisdiction over actions that touch on existing domestic relations and probate matters.

[1] The Domestic Relations Exception

The domestic relations exception to federal jurisdiction was first discussed by the Supreme Court in *Barber v. Barber*, 62 U.S. (21 How.) 582 (1858). In that case, Huldah Barber brought a diversity suit in federal court in Wisconsin asking the court to enforce an alimony decree entered by a New York state court against her ex-husband. The lower court granted the request, and the ex-husband appealed to the Supreme Court. Although the Court held that federal jurisdiction existed to adjudicate the dispute, it expressed some doubt about whether federal courts possessed the power to hear other types of domestic relations matters:

> Our first remark is — and we wish it to be remembered — that this is not a suit asking the court for the allowance of alimony. That has been done by a court of competent jurisdiction. The court in Wisconsin was asked to interfere to prevent that decree from being defeated by fraud.

> We disclaim altogether any jurisdiction in the courts of the United States upon the subject of divorce, or for the allowance of alimony . . . .

The *Barber* majority failed to articulate a theoretical justification for its view that alimony decrees fell outside of the jurisdiction of federal courts. In dissent, Justice Daniel pointed to § 11 of the Judiciary Act of 1789—the original statutory grant of diversity jurisdiction—as the source of the limitation. According to the dissent, the Act's grant of diversity jurisdiction to federal courts over "all suits of a civil nature at common law or at equity" was limited to the equitable jurisdiction exercised by the English chancery courts as of 1789. Because alimony decrees were part of the jurisdiction of the ecclesiastical courts rather than the courts of chancery, "all power with respect to those subjects by the courts of the United States *in chancery* [were] excluded." Three decades later, the exception was expanded to include child custody determinations. *See Ex parte Burrus*, 136 U.S. 586 (1890).

In the century following *Barber*, federal courts disagreed about the types of matters that fell within the domestic relations exception. In *Ankenbrandt v. Richards*, 504 U.S. 689 (1992), the Court finally addressed the scope of the exception in the context of whether a federal court could entertain a tort suit by one parent against another for the alleged physical and sexual abuse of their children. Justice White, writing for the Court, held that the action was not barred by the domestic relations exception. The Court began by noting that the exception is not constitutionally required because it is grounded in an interpretation of the diversity jurisdiction statute, 28 U.S.C. § 1332. Without rejecting the reasoning of Justice Daniel's *Barber* dissent entirely, the Court premised the continued vitality of the domestic relations exception on Congress's implied acceptance of the doctrine when it amended the diversity jurisdiction statute in 1948. As the Court explained:

> We have no occasion here to join the historical debate over whether the English court of chancery had jurisdiction to handle certain domestic relations matters . . . . We . . . are content to rest our conclusion that a domestic relation exception exists as a matter of statutory construction not on the accuracy of the historical justifications on which it was seemingly based, but rather on Congress' apparent acceptance of this construction . . . .

The Court also explained that the domestic relations exception is consistent with "sound policy considerations":

> Issuance of decrees of this type not infrequently involves retention of jurisdiction by the court and deployment of social workers to monitor compliance. As a matter of judicial economy, state courts are more eminently suited to work of this type than are federal courts, which lack the close association with state and local government organizations dedicated to handling issues that arise out of conflicts over divorce, alimony, and child custody decrees. Moreover, as a matter of judicial expertise, it makes far more sense to retain the rule that federal courts lack power to issue these types of decrees because of the special proficiency developed by state tribunals over the past century and a half in handling issues that arise in the granting of such decrees.

But the exception that survived *Ankenbrandt* was a sharply limited one. In the Court's view, the domestic relations exception only "divests the federal courts of power to issue divorce, alimony, and child custody decrees." Carol Ankenbrandt's tort claim, therefore, did not fall within the exception.

In a 2004 case, the Court again considered the domestic relations exception in holding that a non-custodial father lacked third-party standing to challenge the constitutionality of the words "under God" in the Pledge of Allegiance on behalf of his daughter. *See Elk Grove Unified School District v. Newdow*, 542 U.S. 1 (2004). Justice Stevens, writing for the Court, noted that "[o]ne of the principal areas in which this Court has customarily declined to intervene is the realm of domestic relations." Though the Court did not strictly rest its decision on the domestic relations exception or abstention doctrine, the Court's decision on prudential standing was "informed" by the exception because "the disputed family law rights [were] inextricably intertwined with the threshold standing inquiry." In other words, the Court held that "[w]hen hard questions of domestic relations are sure to affect the outcome, the prudent course is for the federal court to stay its hand rather than reach out to resolve a weighty question of federal constitutional law" because "it is improper for the federal courts to entertain a claim by a plaintiff whose standing to sue is based solely on family law rights that are in dispute." Accordingly, the Court concluded that the plaintiff lacked prudential standing to bring the suit in federal court.

Although *Newdow* involved the rights of a non-custodial parent under state law, it did not require a federal court to issue a child custody, divorce, or alimony decree. Accordingly, did the Court expand the domestic relations exception in *Newdow*? If *Newdow* had nothing to do with diversity jurisdiction, as Chief Justice Rehnquist argued in dissent, then why did the Court discuss the domestic relations exception? After *Ankenbrandt* and *Newdow*, is the domestic relations exception nothing more than a highly-manipulable doctrine permitting the Supreme Court to avoid difficult questions of federal law, or is it a principled doctrine that limits the scope of federal jurisdiction?

[2] The Probate Exception

Marshall v. Marshall

Supreme Court of the United States, 2006.

547 U.S. 293.

Justice Ginsburg delivered the opinion of the Court.

In *Cohens v. Virginia*, Chief Justice Marshall famously cautioned: "It is most true that this Court will not take jurisdiction if it should not: but it is equally true, that it must take jurisdiction, if it should . . . . We have no more right to decline the exercise of jurisdiction which is given, than to usurp that which is not given." 19 U.S. (6 Wheat.) 264 (1821). Among longstanding limitations on federal jurisdiction otherwise properly exercised are the so-called "domestic relations" and "probate" exceptions. Neither is compelled by the text of the Constitution or federal statute. Both are judicially created doctrines stemming in large measure from misty understandings of English legal history. *See, e.g.*, Winkler, *The Probate Jurisdiction of the Federal Courts*, 14 PROBATE L.J. 77, 125–26, and n.256 (1997) (describing historical explanation for probate exception as "an exercise in mythography"). In the years following Marshall's 1821 pronouncement, courts have sometimes lost sight of his admonition and have rendered decisions expansively interpreting the two exceptions. In *Ankenbrandt v. Richards*, 504 U.S. 689 (1992), this Court reined in the "domestic relations exception." Earlier, in *Markham v. Allen*, 326 U.S. 490 (1946), the Court endeavored similarly to curtail the "probate exception."

I

[Petitioner in this case was Vickie Lynn Marshall, better known as model and television personality Anna Nicole Smith. In 1991, Vickie met oil billionaire J. Howard Marshall ("J. Howard"). In June of 1994, Vickie and J. Howard married; thirteen months later in August of 1995, J. Howard died. The primary beneficiary of his will was one of his sons, E. Pierce Marshall ("Pierce"). While Vickie was not included in J. Howard's will, she maintained that he had intended to provide for her financial security through a trust.

[After J. Howard's will was submitted to probate in Texas state court, Vickie filed for bankruptcy in the United States Bankruptcy Court for the Central District of California. Pierce filed a claim against her in the bankruptcy proceedings alleging that her lawyers had defamed him in the press. Vickie then counterclaimed against Pierce in the Bankruptcy Court, claiming that Pierce had tortiously interfered with the trust J. Howard had wished to create for her. The Bankruptcy Court found in favor of Vickie, and the District Court affirmed, assessing $44.3 million in compensatory damages and the same amount in punitive damages.

[On appeal, however, the Ninth Circuit held that the case fell within the probate exception to federal jurisdiction. According to the Ninth Circuit, in addition to claims seeking probate of a will or the administration of an estate, "a claim falls within the probate exception if it raises 'questions which would ordinarily be decided by a probate court in determining the validity of the decedent's estate planning instrument,' whether those questions involved 'fraud, undue influence[, or] tortious interference with the testator's intent.'" The Ninth Circuit ordered that on remand the case be dismissed for lack of subject matter jurisdiction.]

We granted certiorari to resolve the apparent confusion among federal courts concerning the scope of the probate exception. Satisfied that the instant case does not fall within the ambit of the narrow exception recognized by our decisions, we reverse the Ninth Circuit's judgment.

* * *

III

Decisions of this Court have recognized a "probate exception," to otherwise proper federal jurisdiction. *See*, [*e.g.*], *Markham v. Allen*. The probate exception has been linked to language contained in the Judiciary Act of 1789.

Markham, the Court's most recent and pathmarking pronouncement on the probate exception, stated that "the equity jurisdiction conferred by the Judiciary Act of 1789 . . . , which is that of the English Court of Chancery in 1789, did not extend to probate matters." As in *Ankenbrandt*, so in this case, "we have no occasion . . . to join the historical debate" over the scope of English chancery jurisdiction in 1789, for Vickie Marshall's claim falls far outside the bounds of the probate exception described in *Markham*.

In *Markham*, the plaintiff Alien Property Custodian[4] commenced suit in Federal District Court against an executor and resident heirs to determine the Custodian's asserted rights regarding a decedent's estate. At the time the federal suit commenced, the estate was undergoing probate administration in a state court. The Custodian had issued an order vesting in himself all right, title, and interest of German legatees. He sought and gained in the District Court a judgment determining that the resident heirs had no interest in the estate, and that the Custodian, substituting himself for the German legatees, was entitled to the entire net estate, including specified real estate passing under the will.

Reversing the Ninth Circuit, which had ordered the case dismissed for want of federal subject-matter jurisdiction, this Court held that federal jurisdiction was properly invoked. The Court first stated:

> It is true that a federal court has no jurisdiction to probate a will or administer an estate . . . . But it has been established by a long series of decisions of this Court that federal courts of equity have jurisdiction to entertain suits "in favor of creditors, legatees and heirs" and other claimants against a decedent's estate "to establish their claims" so long as the federal court does not interfere with the probate proceedings or assume general jurisdiction of the probate or control of the property in the custody of the state court.

Next, the Court described a probate exception of distinctly limited scope:

> While a federal court may not exercise its jurisdiction to disturb or affect the possession of property in the custody of a state court, . . . it may exercise its jurisdiction to adjudicate rights in such property where the final judgment does not undertake to interfere with the state court's possession save to the extent that the state court is bound by the judgment to recognize the right adjudicated by the federal court.

The first of the above-quoted passages from *Markham* is not a model of clear statement. The Court observed that federal courts have jurisdiction to entertain suits to determine the rights of creditors, legatees, heirs, and other claimants against a decedent's estate, "so long as the federal court does not *interfere with the probate proceedings*." (Emphasis added.) Lower federal courts have puzzled over the meaning of the

---

4. Section 6 of the Trading with the Enemy Act authorizes the President to appoint an official known as the "alien property custodian," who is responsible for "receiv[ing,] . . . hold[ing], administer[ing], and account[ing] for" "all money and property in the United States due or belonging to an enemy, or ally of enemy. . . ."

words "interfere with the probate proceedings," and some have read those words to block federal jurisdiction over a range of matters well beyond probate of a will or administration of a decedent's estate.

We read *Markham*'s enigmatic words, in sync with the second above-quoted passage, to proscribe "disturbing or affecting the possession of property in the custody of a state court." True, that reading renders the first-quoted passage in part redundant, but redundancy in this context, we do not doubt, is preferable to incoherence. In short, we comprehend the "interference" language in *Markham* as essentially a reiteration of the general principle that, when one court is exercising *in rem* jurisdiction over a *res*, a second court will not assume *in rem* jurisdiction over the same *res*. Thus, the probate exception reserves to state probate courts the probate or annulment of a will and the administration of a decedent's estate; it also precludes federal courts from endeavoring to dispose of property that is in the custody of a state probate court. But it does not bar federal courts from adjudicating matters outside those confines and otherwise within federal jurisdiction.

A

As the Court of Appeals correctly observed, Vickie's claim does not "involve the administration of an estate, the probate of a will, or any other purely probate matter." Provoked by Pierce's claim in the bankruptcy proceedings, Vickie's claim, like Carol Ankenbrandt's, alleges a widely recognized tort. See RESTATEMENT (SECOND) OF TORTS § 774B (1977) ("One who by fraud, duress or other tortious means intentionally prevents another from receiving from a third person an inheritance or gift that she would otherwise have received is subject to liability to the other for loss of the inheritance or gift."). Vickie seeks an *in personam* judgment against Pierce, not the probate or annulment of a will. Nor does she seek to reach a *res* in the custody of a state court.

Furthermore, no "sound policy considerations" militate in favor of extending the probate exception to cover the case at hand. *Cf. Ankenbrandt.* Trial courts, both federal and state, often address conduct of the kind Vickie alleges. State probate courts possess no "special proficiency ... in handling [such] issues."

* * *

For the reasons stated, the judgment of the Court of Appeals for the Ninth Circuit is reversed, and the case is remanded for further proceedings consistent with this opinion.

JUSTICE STEVENS, concurring in part and concurring in the judgment.

... I write separately to explain why I do not believe there is any "probate exception" that ousts a federal court of jurisdiction it otherwise possesses.

The familiar aphorism that hard cases make bad law should extend to easy cases as well. *Markham*, like this case, was an easy case. In *Markham*, as here, it was unnecessary to question the historical or logical underpinnings of the probate exception to federal jurisdiction because, whatever the scope of the supposed exception, it did not extend to the case at hand. But *Markham*'s obiter dicta — dicta that the Court now describes as redundant if not incoherent—generated both confusion and abdication of the obligation Chief Justice Marshall so famously articulated. While the Court today rightly abandons much of that dicta, I would go further.

The Court is content to adopt the approach it followed in *Ankenbrandt*, and to accept as foundation for the probate exception *Markham*'s bald assertion that the English High Court of Chancery's jurisdiction did not "extend to probate matters" in 1789. I would not accept that premise. Not only had the theory *Markham* espoused been only sporadically and tentatively cited as justification for the exception, but the most comprehensive article on the subject has persuasively demonstrated that *Markham*'s assertion is "an exercise in mythography."

Markham's theory apparently is the source of the Court's reformulated exception, which "reserves to state probate courts the probate or annulment of a will and the administration of a decedent's estate." Although undoubtedly narrower in scope than *Markham*'s ill-considered description of the probate carve-out, this description also sweeps too broadly.

To be sure, there are cases that support limitations on federal courts' jurisdiction over the probate and annulment of wills and the administration of decedents' estates. But careful examination reveals that at least most of the limitations so recognized stem not from some *sui generis* exception, but rather from generally applicable jurisdictional rules. Some of those rules, like the rule that diversity jurisdiction will not attach absent an *inter partes* controversy, plainly are still relevant today. Others, like the rule that a bill in equity will lie only where there is no adequate remedy elsewhere, have less straightforward application in the wake of 20th-century jurisdictional developments. Whatever the continuing viability of these individual rules, together they are more than adequate to the task of cabining federal courts' jurisdiction. They require no helping hand from the so-called probate exception.

Rather than preserving whatever vitality that the "exception" has retained as a result of the *Markham* dicta, I would provide the creature with a decent burial in a grave adjacent to the resting place of the *Rooker-Feldman* doctrine [Chapter 17].

Note: Reining in the Probate Exception

1. Prior to *Marshall*, suits brought by the beneficiary of an estate against a trustee or executor for breach of fiduciary duty were often dismissed by federal courts under the probate exception. Under *Markham*, a federal suit by a beneficiary against an administrator—even if the beneficiary did not specifically seek to reach or affect the probate property—seemingly "interfere[d] with probate proceedings." *See, e.g., Golden v. Golden*, 382 F.3d 348 (2d Cir. 2004) (dismissing a breach of fiduciary duty claim against an executor under the probate exception); *Mangieri v. Mangieri*, 226 F.3d 1 (1st Cir. 2000) (same).

After *Marshall*, however, it is less likely that the probate exception limits federal jurisdiction over such cases. In *Lefkowitz v. Bank of New York*, 528 F.3d 102 (2d Cir. 2007), the Second Circuit considered a case in which the beneficiary of an estate sued the Bank of New York as administrator of the estate. Lefkowitz alleged twelve separate counts against the bank, including breach of fiduciary duty, conversion, and fraud. Some counts sought the payment of specific estate funds and property, while others focused on the bank in its role as administrator. The District Court—prior to the release of the *Marshall* opinion—had dismissed all twelve counts under the Second Circuit's expansive interpretation of the probate exception.

The Court of Appeals, in light of *Marshall*, held that eight of Lefkowitz's claims sought, in essence, the disgorgement of estate property. These claims, according to the court, fell within the probate exception. The four remaining claims, by contrast, sought "damages from Defendants personally rather than assets or distributions from [the] estate." According to the court, "[t]he probate exception can no longer be used to dismiss 'widely recognized tort[s]' such as breach of fiduciary duty or fraudulent misrepresentation merely because the issues intertwine with state proceedings in a state court." Because the remaining four counts sought *in personam* judgments against the bank, the probate exception did not apply.

In *Marshall*, it is unlikely that Pierce would have been able to pay the $88 million judgment against him from any funds other than those in the custody of the Texas probate court. But because Vickie did not specifically seek those funds, the Court held that federal jurisdiction was proper over her counterclaim. In light of this interpretation of *Marshall*, can plaintiffs evade the probate exception by artfully pleading their claims?

2. The probate and the domestic relations exceptions are seemingly connected. Both at one time were derived from jurisdictional limitations on the English courts of chancery, both exclude particular subject-matter areas from federal jurisdiction, and both have been narrowed considerably by the Court from expansive beginnings. In fact, Judge Posner has written that the two exceptions are essentially identical: "[t]he fact that they are two rather than one reflects nothing more profound than the legal profession's delight in multiplying entities." *Struck v. Cook County Public Guardian*, 508 F.3d 858 (7th Cir. 2007). Is Judge Posner correct? If not, what are the material differences between the two exceptions? If he is correct, then what explains Justice Stevens's willingness to expand the domestic relations exception in *Newdow*, yet do away with the probate exception in *Marshall*?

3. As Justice Stevens's concurring opinion indicates, the *Marshall* opinion follows in the wake of a decision curtailing the *Rooker-Feldman* doctrine, another judicially-recognized limitation on federal jurisdiction. *See* Chapter 17. In light of the Court's willingness to reevaluate these long-standing jurisdictional doctrines, should the Court consider narrowing the abstention doctrines of *Colorado River* and *Brillhart* too?

Problem: A Quarrel Over Probate Property

At the time of his death, businessman Vincent Gambiano owned A&S Sanitation, the largest waste management company on the east coast. According to the terms of Gambiano's will, all of his property was to be managed for the benefit of his wife and seven children after his death. The will named Gambiano's close friend and business associate, Thomas Hayden, as executor of the estate.

Six months after Gambiano's death, Hayden, acting as executor of the estate, sold 25% of the estate's interest in A&S to Four Doors, Ltd., an entity created and entirely controlled by Hayden. The beneficiaries of the estate filed an action for breach of fiduciary duty and self-dealing against Hayden in the Oceana Probate Court. After a hearing, the Probate Court issued an order removing Hayden as the executor of the Gambiano estate. The order did not address the disposition of the shares of A&S in Four Doors' custody.

Shortly after Hayden was removed as executor of the estate, Four Doors filed an action against Gambiano's widow and children in the United States District Court for the District of Oceana on the basis of the federal diversity jurisdiction statute, 28 U.S.C. § 1332. Count One, styled as a "Declaratory Judgment," requests that the court declare that Four Doors owns the A&S shares transferred by Hayden from the estate. Count Two alleges breach of fiduciary duty against the widow and children, on the theory that they, as majority shareholders and fiduciaries in A&S Sanitation, have prevented Four Doors from accessing and enjoying its interest in A&S. The latter count seeks compensatory damages from Gambiano's widow and children.

Oceana state law provides that "all personal property . . . registered in the name of the decedent . . . at the time of his death" is subject to the jurisdiction of the Oceana Probate Court. Gambiano's widow and children have moved to dismiss Four Doors' complaint on the ground that it falls within the probate exception to federal jurisdiction. Should the court dismiss the complaint?

Chapter 17

Inter-System Preclusion and the *Rooker-Feldman* Doctrine

In the preceding chapter, we considered the doctrines that come into play when a federal court is confronted with a pending or imminent state-court proceeding that involves related issues. What happens when the state court enters a judgment? We turn now to that question.

A. Federal Courts and the Preclusive Effect of State-Court Judgments

Migra v. Warren City School District Board of Education

Supreme Court of the United States, 1984.

465 U.S. 75.

Justice Blackmun delivered the opinion of the Court.

This case raises issues concerning the claim preclusive effect[1] of a state-court judgment in the context of a subsequent suit, under 42 U.S.C. §§ 1983 and 1985, in federal court.

I

Petitioner, Dr. Ethel D. Migra, was employed by the Warren [Ohio] City School District Board of Education from August 1976 to June 1979. She served as supervisor of

---

1. The preclusive effects of former adjudication are discussed in varying and, at times, seemingly conflicting terminology, attributable to the evolution of preclusion concepts over the years. These effects are referred to collectively by most commentators as the doctrine of "res judicata." Res judicata is often analyzed further to consist of two preclusion concepts: "issue preclusion" and "claim preclusion." Issue preclusion refers to the effect of a judgment in foreclosing relitigation of a matter that has been litigated and decided. This effect also is referred to as direct or collateral estoppel. Claim preclusion refers to the effect of a judgment in foreclosing litigation of a matter that never has been litigated, because of a determination that it should have been advanced in an earlier suit. Claim preclusion therefore encompasses the law of merger and bar.

This Court on more than one occasion has used the term "res judicata" in a narrow sense, so as to exclude issue preclusion or collateral estoppel. *See, e.g., Allen v. McCurry*, 449 U.S. 90, 94 (1980); *Brown v. Felsen*, 442 U.S. 127 (1979). When using that formulation, "res judicata" becomes virtually synonymous with "claim preclusion." In order to avoid confusion resulting from the two uses of "res judicata," this opinion utilizes the term "claim preclusion" to refer to the preclusive effect of a judgment in foreclosing relitigation of matters that should have been raised in an earlier suit.

elementary education. Her employment was on an annual basis under written contracts for successive school years.

On April 17, 1979, at a regularly scheduled meeting, the Board, with all five of its members present, unanimously adopted a resolution renewing Dr. Migra's employment as supervisor for the 1979–1980 school year. Being advised of this, she accepted the renewed appointment by letter dated April 18 delivered to a member of the Board on April 23. Early the following morning her letter was passed on to the Superintendent of Schools and to the Board's President.

The Board, however, held a special meeting, called by its President, on the morning of April 24. Although there appear to have been some irregularities about the call, four of the five members of the Board were present. The President first read Dr. Migra's acceptance letter. Then, after disposing of other business, a motion was made and adopted, by a vote of three to one, not to renew petitioner's employment for the 1979–1980 school year. Dr. Migra was given written notice of this nonrenewal and never received a written contract of employment for that year. . . .

Petitioner brought suit in the Court of Common Pleas of Trumbull County, Ohio, against the Board and its three members who had voted not to renew her employment. The complaint, although in five counts, presented what the parties now accept as essentially two causes of action, namely, breach of contract by the Board, and wrongful interference by the individual members with petitioner's contract of employment. . . . [The state court] ruled that under Ohio law petitioner had accepted the employment proffered . . . , that this created a binding contract between her and the Board, and that the Board's subsequent action purporting not to renew the employment relationship had no legal effect. The court awarded Dr. Migra reinstatement to her position and compensatory damages. . . . The Ohio Court of Appeals [affirmed] the judgment of the Court of Common Pleas. Review was denied by the Supreme Court of Ohio.[2]

In July 1980, Dr. Migra filed the present action in the United States District Court for the Northern District of Ohio against the Board, its then individual members, and the Superintendent of Schools. Her complaint alleged that Dr. Migra had become the director of a commission appointed by the Board to fashion a voluntary plan for the desegregation of the District's elementary schools; that she had prepared a social studies curriculum; that the individual defendants objected to and opposed the curriculum and resisted the desegregation plan; that hostility and ill will toward petitioner developed; and that, as a consequence, the individual defendants determined not to renew petitioner's contract of employment. Many of the alleged facts had been proved in the

---

2. It is apparent, from the foregoing recital of facts and of events that took place in the state court litigation, that the cause of action for reinstatement and for damages was brought to a conclusion in the Ohio courts, but that the cause of action sounding in tort, that is, for wrongful interference with petitioner's contract of employment, was not. Instead, that cause of action was "reserved and continued," evidently by the state trial court *sua sponte*, and was eventually dismissed without prejudice upon petitioner's motion. This dismissal was subsequent to the entry of judgment on the breach of contract cause of action.

earlier state-court litigation. Dr. Migra claimed that the Board's actions were intended to punish her for the exercise of her First Amendment rights. She also claimed that the actions deprived her of property without due process and denied her equal protection. Her federal claim thus arose under the First, Fifth and Fourteenth Amendments and 42 U.S.C. §§ 1983 and 1985. She requested injunctive relief and compensatory and punitive damages. Answers were filed in due course and shortly thereafter the defendants moved for summary judgment on the basis of res judicata. . . .

The District Court granted summary judgment for the defendants and dismissed the complaint. The United States Court of Appeals for the Sixth Circuit [affirmed].[3] Because of the importance of the issue, and because of differences among the Courts of Appeals, we granted certiorari.

II

The Constitution's Full Faith and Credit Clause is implemented by the Federal Full Faith and Credit Statute, 28 U.S.C. § 1738. That statute reads in pertinent part:

> Such Acts, records and judicial proceedings or copies thereof, so authenticated, shall have the same full faith and credit in every court within the United States and its Territories and Possessions as they have by law or usage in the courts of such State, Territory or Possession from which they are taken.

It is now settled that a federal court must give to a state-court judgment the same preclusive effect as would be given that judgment under the law of the State in which the judgment was rendered. In *Allen v. McCurry*, 449 U.S. 90 (1980), this Court said:

> Indeed, though the federal courts may look to the common law or to the policies supporting res judicata and collateral estoppel in assessing the preclusive effect of decisions of other federal courts, Congress has specifically required all federal courts to give preclusive effect to state-court judgments whenever the courts of the State from which the judgments emerged would do so. . . .

This principle was restated in *Kremer v. Chemical Construction Corp.*, 456 U.S. 461 (1982):

> Section 1738 requires federal courts to give the same preclusive effect to state court judgments that those judgments would be given in the courts of the State from which the judgments emerged.

Accordingly, in the absence of federal law modifying the operation of § 1738, the preclusive effect in federal court of petitioner's state-court judgment is determined by Ohio law.

In *Allen*, the Court considered whether 42 U.S.C. § 1983 modified the operation of § 1738 so that a state-court judgment was to receive less than normal preclusive effect

---

3. Respondents tell us that after petitioner's favorable judgment in the state court was affirmed by the Ohio Court of Appeals, with review denied by the Supreme Court of Ohio, the Board gave Dr. Migra back pay for the 1979–1980 school year reduced by the amount of unemployment compensation she had received for that period.

in a suit brought in federal court under § 1983. In that case, the respondent had been convicted in a state-court criminal proceeding. In that proceeding, the respondent sought to suppress certain evidence against him on the ground that it had been obtained in violation of the Fourth Amendment. The trial court denied the motion to suppress. The respondent then brought a § 1983 suit in federal court against the officers who had seized the evidence. The District Court held the suit barred by collateral estoppel (issue preclusion) because the issue of a Fourth Amendment violation had been resolved against the respondent by the denial of his suppression motion in the criminal trial. The Court of Appeals reversed. That court concluded that, because a § 1983 suit was the respondent's only route to a federal forum for his constitutional claim,[5] and because one of § 1983's underlying purposes was to provide a federal cause of action in situations where state courts were not adequately protecting individual rights, the respondent should be allowed to proceed to trial in federal court unencumbered by collateral estoppel. This Court, however, reversed the Court of Appeals, explaining:

> [N]othing in the language of § 1983 remotely expresses any congressional intent to contravene the common-law rules of preclusion or to repeal the express statutory requirements of the predecessor of 28 U.S.C. § 1738. . . . Section 1983 creates a new federal cause of action. It says nothing about the preclusive effect of state-court judgments.
>
> Moreover, the legislative history of § 1983 does not in any clear way suggest that Congress intended to repeal or restrict the traditional doctrines of preclusion. . . . [T]he legislative history as a whole . . . lends only the most equivocal support to any argument that, in cases where the state courts have recognized the constitutional claims asserted and provided fair procedures for determining them, Congress intended to override § 1738 or the common-law rules of collateral estoppel and res judicata. Since repeals by implication are disfavored . . . much clearer support than this would be required to hold that § 1738 and the traditional rules of preclusion are not applicable to § 1983 suits.

Allen therefore made clear that issues actually litigated in a state-court proceeding are entitled to the same preclusive effect in a subsequent federal § 1983 suit as they enjoy in the courts of the State where the judgment was rendered.

The Court in *Allen* left open the possibility, however, that the preclusive effect of a state-court judgment might be different as to a federal issue that a § 1983 litigant could have raised but did not raise in the earlier state-court proceeding. That is the central issue to be resolved in the present case. Petitioner did not litigate her § 1983 claim in state court, and she asserts that the state-court judgment should not preclude her suit in federal court simply because her federal claim could have been litigated in the

---

5. The respondent had not asserted that the state courts had denied him a "full and fair opportunity" to litigate his search and seizure claim; he therefore was barred by *Stone v. Powell*, 428 U.S. 465 (1976), from seeking a writ of habeas corpus in federal district court.

state-court proceeding. Thus, petitioner urges this Court to interpret the interplay of § 1738 and § 1983 in such a way as to accord state-court judgments preclusive effect in § 1983 suits only as to issues actually litigated in state court.

It is difficult to see how the policy concerns underlying § 1983 would justify a distinction between the issue preclusive and claim preclusive effects of state-court judgments. The argument that state-court judgments should have less preclusive effect in § 1983 suits than in other federal suits is based on Congress' expressed concern over the adequacy of state courts as protectors of federal rights. *See, e.g., Mitchum v. Foster*, 407 U.S. 225, 241–42 (1972). *Allen* recognized that the enactment of § 1983 was motivated partially out of such concern, but *Allen* nevertheless held that § 1983 did not open the way to relitigation of an issue that had been determined in a state criminal proceeding. Any distrust of state courts that would justify a limitation on the preclusive effect of state judgments in § 1983 suits would presumably apply equally to issues that actually were decided in a state-court as well as to those that could have been. If § 1983 created an exception to the general preclusive effect accorded to state-court judgments, such an exception would seem to require similar treatment of both issue preclusion and claim preclusion. Having rejected in *Allen* the view that state-court judgments have no issue preclusive effect in § 1983 suits, we must reject the view that § 1983 prevents the judgment in petitioner's state-court proceeding from creating a claim preclusion bar in this case.

Petitioner suggests that to give state-court judgments full issue preclusive effect but not claim preclusive effect would enable litigants to bring their state claims in state court and their federal claims in federal court, thereby taking advantage of the relative expertise of both forums. Although such a division may seem attractive from a plaintiff's perspective, it is not the system established by § 1738. That statute embodies the view that it is more important to give full faith and credit to state-court judgments than to ensure separate forums for federal and state claims. This reflects a variety of concerns, including notions of comity, the need to prevent vexatious litigation, and a desire to conserve judicial resources.

In the present litigation, petitioner does not claim that the state court would not have adjudicated her federal claims had she presented them in her original suit in state court. Alternatively, petitioner could have obtained a federal forum for her federal claim by litigating it first in a federal court. Section 1983, however, does not override state preclusion law and guarantee petitioner a right to proceed to judgment in state court on her state claims and then turn to federal court for adjudication of her federal claims. We hold, therefore, that petitioner's state-court judgment in this litigation has the same claim preclusive effect in federal court that the judgment would have in the Ohio state courts. . . .

III

[The Court's discussion of Ohio preclusion law is omitted.]

In reading the opinion of the District Court in the present litigation, we are unable to determine whether that court was applying what it thought was the Ohio law of preclusion. . . . Our holding today makes clear that Ohio state preclusion law is to be applied to this case. Prudence also dictates that it is the District Court, in the first instance, not this Court, that should interpret Ohio preclusion law and apply it.

The judgment of the Court of Appeals, accordingly, is vacated and the case is remanded to that court so that it may instruct the District Court to conduct such further proceedings as are required by, and are consistent with, this opinion.

JUSTICE WHITE, with whom THE CHIEF JUSTICE [BURGER] and JUSTICE POWELL join, concurring.

In *Union & Planters' Bank v. Memphis*, 189 U.S. 71, 75 (1903), this Court held that a federal court "can accord [a state judgment] no greater efficacy" than would the judgment-rendering state. That holding has been adhered to on at least three occasions since that time. The Court has also indicated that the states are bound by a similar rule under the full faith and credit clause. The Court is thus justified in this case to rule that preclusion in this case must be determined under state law, even if there would be preclusion under federal standards.

This construction of § 1738 [is] unfortunate. In terms of the purpose of that section, which is to require federal courts to give effect to state-court judgments, there is no reason to hold that a federal court may not give preclusive effect to a state judgment simply because the judgment would not bar relitigation in the state courts. If the federal courts have developed rules of res judicata and collateral estoppel that prevent relitigation in circumstances that would not be preclusive in state courts, the federal courts should be free to apply them, the parties then being free to relitigate in the state courts. The contrary construction of § 1738 is nevertheless one of long standing, and Congress has not seen fit to disturb it, however justified such an action might have been.

Accordingly, I join the opinion of the Court.

Note: Preclusion in Federal Courts

1. The effect of state-court judgments in federal court is governed by 28 U.S.C. § 1738, quoted in *Migra*. The statute has been interpreted to require federal courts to give a state-court judgment the same preclusive effect as the rendering state would give it—no more and no less. In effect, then, the preclusive effect of a state-court judgment in federal court is a state-law, not a federal-law, question—a point made in Justice White's concurrence.

2. Does § 1738 extend beyond judgments? In *McDonald v. City of West Branch*, 466 U.S. 284 (1984), the Court unanimously declined to apply preclusion rules to an arbitration decision that had not been reviewed by a court.

3. Should the result under § 1738 change when the defendant seeks to preclude a claim that could not have been brought in state court because it fell within the exclusive jurisdiction of the federal courts? In *Marrese v. American Academy of Orthopaedic Surgeons*, 470 U.S. 373 (1985), the Court stated that § 1738 is not necessarily inapplicable to claims within the exclusive jurisdiction of the federal courts. The plaintiffs filed a suit in state court challenging their exclusion from the defendant Academy as a violation of their common-law associational rights. They filed no state-law antitrust claim. They could not add a federal antitrust claim to their state lawsuit, because such claims are within the exclusive jurisdiction of the federal courts. (See Chapter 6.) After losing in state court, the plaintiffs filed a federal antitrust claim. The Court of Appeals found the claim barred by claim preclusion, but the Supreme Court reversed:

> In this case the Court of Appeals should have first referred to Illinois law to determine the preclusive effect of the state judgment. Only if state law indicates that a particular claim or issue would be barred, is it necessary to determine if an exception to § 1738 should apply. Although for purposes of this case, we need not decide if such an exception exists for federal antitrust claims, we observe that the more general question is whether the concerns underlying a particular grant of exclusive jurisdiction justify a finding of an implied partial repeal of § 1738. Resolution of this question will depend on the particular federal statute as well as the nature of the claim or issue involved in the subsequent federal action. Our previous decisions indicate that the primary consideration must be the intent of Congress. *See Kremer v. Chemical Construction Corp.*, 456 U.S. 461 at 470–76 (1982) (finding no congressional intent to depart from § 1738 for purposes of Title VII); *cf. Brown v. Felsen*, 442 U.S. 127, 138 (1979) (finding congressional intent that state judgments would not have claim preclusive effect on dischargeability issue in bankruptcy).

The Court continued:

> If we had a single system of courts and our only concerns were efficiency and finality, it might be desirable to fashion claim preclusion rules that would require a plaintiff to bring suit initially in the forum of most general jurisdiction, thereby resolving as many issues as possible in one proceeding. The decision of the Court of Appeals approximates such a rule inasmuch as it encourages plaintiffs to file suit initially in federal district court and to attempt to bring any state law claims pendent to their federal antitrust claims. Whether this result would reduce the overall burden of litigation is debatable, and we decline to base our interpretation of § 1738 on our opinion on this question.

> More importantly, we have parallel systems of state and federal courts, and the concerns of comity reflected in § 1738 generally allow States to determine the preclusive scope of their own courts' judgments. These concerns certainly are not made less compelling because state courts lack jurisdiction over federal antitrust claims. We therefore reject a judicially created exception to § 1738 that effectively holds as a matter of federal law that a plaintiff can bring state law claims initially in state court only at the cost of forgoing subsequent federal antitrust claims.

The Court remanded the case for determination of what state preclusion law would require.

Justices Blackmun and Stevens did not participate in the case. Chief Justice Burger concurred in the judgment, saying:

> [I]t is likely that the principles of Illinois claim preclusion law do not speak to the preclusive effect that petitioners' state court judgments should have on the present action. In this situation, it may be consistent with § 1738 for a federal court to formulate a federal rule to resolve the matter. If state law is simply indeterminate, the concerns of comity and federalism underlying § 1738 do not come into play. At the same time, the federal courts have direct interests in ensuring that their resources are used efficiently and not as a means of harassing defendants with repetitive lawsuits, as well as in ensuring that parties asserting federal rights have an adequate opportunity to litigate those rights.
>
> Given the insubstantiality of the state interests and the weight of the federal interests, a strong argument could be made that a federal rule would be more appropriate than a creative interpretation of ambiguous state law. When state law is indeterminate or ambiguous, a clear federal rule would promote substantive interests as well: "Uncertainty intrinsically works to defeat the opportunities for repose and reliance sought by the rules of preclusion, and confounds the desire for efficiency by inviting repetitious litigation to test the preclusive effects of the first effort."

On remand, the district court found that state preclusion law did not bar the subsequent federal claim.

In *Matsushita Electrical Industrial Co. v. Epstein*, 516 U.S. 367 (1996), the Court considered "whether a federal court may withhold full faith and credit from a [Delaware] state-court judgment approving a class-action settlement simply because the settlement releases [federal securities] claims within the exclusive jurisdiction of the federal courts." The answer was no. "Absent a partial repeal of the Full Faith and Credit Act by another federal statute, a federal court must give the judgment the same effect that it would have in the courts of the State in which it was rendered." The Court first looked to Delaware preclusion law and found that it would bar a second action under these circumstances. It then asked whether the federal securities laws should be viewed as a partial repeal or modification of § 1738, and determined that there was no evidence that Congress expected such a reading of the securities laws.

Given the Court's approach to preclusion of claims within the exclusive jurisdiction of the federal courts, how should litigants structure lawsuits when both state-law and exclusively federal claims are implicated?

Problem: Section 1983 Damages Following a State Mandamus Action

Oscar Veal applied to the zoning board of the City of Utopia for a liquor license for a proposed restaurant and lounge. When a building inspector testified that Veal's building plan failed to comply with City of Utopia building codes, the board unanimously denied Veal's application. Veal applied to the state trial court for a writ of mandamus ordering the City to grant him a liquor license or to hold a second hearing in which to present his arguments. The trial court denied all relief. On appeal, the Oceana Supreme Court reversed and ordered the state trial court to grant Veal a second hearing on the ground that one of the members of the zoning board owned a local restaurant that would be in direct competition with Veal's lounge if the permit were approved, and that board member did not recuse himself from the proceedings.

Rather than pursuing his license through a second hearing, however, Veal abandoned his state-court lawsuit and instead filed a new lawsuit in the United States District Court for the District of Oceana. In this second suit, he sought damages and attorney's fees from the City of Utopia under 42 U.S.C. § 1983, on the theory that by ruling on his application when one of the zoning board members had a conflict of interest, the zoning board deprived him of his federal constitutional right to procedural due process under the Fourteenth Amendment. According to Veal, another lounge opened in direct competition with his proposed establishment during the pendency of his appeal before the Oceana Supreme Court, causing him to lose profits, revenue, and income. In response, the City has asked the federal district court to dismiss the complaint on the basis of res judicata.

Two aspects of Oceana law are particularly relevant to this question. First, a subsequent lawsuit is barred by res judicata under Oceana state law "when the wrong sought to be redressed is the same in both actions" and the claim or issue was "actually litigated or could have been properly raised and determined in a prior action." Second, had Veal continued to pursue his writ of mandamus on remand and been granted the license, Oceana Rev. Stat. § 45-21 would have authorized him to seek damages against the City caused by the delay in granting him the liquor license.

How should the district court rule on the City's motion to dismiss?

B. The *Rooker-Feldman* Doctrine

Exxon Mobil Corp. v. Saudi Basic Industries Corp.

Supreme Court of the United States, 2005.

544 U.S. 280.

JUSTICE GINSBURG delivered the opinion of the Court.

This case concerns what has come to be known as the *Rooker-Feldman* doctrine, applied by this Court only twice, first in *Rooker v. Fidelity Trust Co.*, 263 U.S. 413 (1923), then, 60 years later, in *District of Columbia Court of Appeals v. Feldman*, 460 U.S. 462 (1983). Variously interpreted in the lower courts, the doctrine has sometimes been construed to extend far beyond the contours of the *Rooker* and *Feldman* cases, overriding Congress' conferral of federal-court jurisdiction concurrent with jurisdiction exercised by state courts, and superseding the ordinary application of preclusion law pursuant to 28 U.S.C. § 1738. . . .

The *Rooker-Feldman* doctrine, we hold today, is confined to cases of the kind from which the doctrine acquired its name: cases brought by state-court losers complaining of injuries caused by state-court judgments rendered before the district court proceedings commenced and inviting district court review and rejection of those judgments. *Rooker-Feldman* does not otherwise override or supplant preclusion doctrine or augment the circumscribed doctrines that allow federal courts to stay or dismiss proceedings in deference to state-court actions.

In the case before us, the Court of Appeals for the Third Circuit misperceived the narrow ground occupied by *Rooker-Feldman*, and consequently erred in ordering the federal action dismissed for lack of subject-matter jurisdiction. We therefore reverse the Third Circuit's judgment.

I

In *Rooker v. Fidelity Trust Co.*, the parties defeated in state court turned to a Federal District Court for relief. Alleging that the adverse state-court judgment was rendered in contravention of the Constitution, they asked the federal court to declare it "null and void." This Court noted preliminarily that the state court had acted within its jurisdiction. If the state-court decision was wrong, the Court explained, "that did not make the judgment void, but merely left it open to reversal or modification in an appropriate and timely appellate proceeding." Federal district courts, the *Rooker* Court recognized, lacked the requisite appellate authority, for their jurisdiction was "strictly original." Among federal courts, the *Rooker* Court clarified, Congress had empowered only this Court to exercise appellate authority "to reverse or modify" a state-court judgment. Accordingly, the Court affirmed a decree dismissing the suit for lack of jurisdiction.

Sixty years later, the Court decided *District of Columbia Court of Appeals v. Feldman*. The two plaintiffs in that case, Hickey and Feldman, neither of whom had graduated from an accredited law school, petitioned the District of Columbia Court of Appeals to waive a court Rule that required D.C. bar applicants to have graduated from a law school approved by the American Bar Association. After the D.C. court denied their waiver requests, Hickey and Feldman filed suits in the United States District Court for the District of Columbia. The District Court and the Court of Appeals for the District of Columbia Circuit disagreed on the question whether the federal suit could be maintained, and we granted certiorari.

Recalling *Rooker*, this Court's opinion in *Feldman* observed first that the District Court lacked authority to review a final judicial determination of the D.C. high court. "Review of such determinations," the *Feldman* opinion reiterated, "can be obtained only in this Court." The "crucial question," the Court next stated, was whether the proceedings in the D.C. court were "judicial in nature." Addressing that question, the Court concluded that the D.C. court had acted both judicially and legislatively.

In applying the accreditation Rule to the Hickey and Feldman waiver petitions, this Court determined, the D.C. court had acted judicially. As to that adjudication, *Feldman* held, this Court alone among federal courts had review authority. Hence, "to the extent that Hickey and Feldman sought review in the District Court of the District of Columbia Court of Appeals' denial of their petitions for waiver, the District Court lacked subject-matter jurisdiction over their complaints." But that determination did not dispose of the entire case, for in promulgating the bar admission rule, this Court said, the D.C. court had acted legislatively, not judicially. "Challenges to the constitutionality of state bar rules," the Court elaborated, "do not necessarily require a United States district court to review a final state-court judgment in a judicial proceeding." Thus, the Court reasoned, 28 U.S.C. § 1257 did not bar District Court proceedings addressed to the validity of the accreditation Rule itself. The Rule could be contested in federal court, this Court held, so long as plaintiffs did not seek review of the Rule's application in a particular case.

The Court endeavored to separate elements of the Hickey and Feldman complaints that failed the jurisdictional threshold from those that survived jurisdictional inspection. Plaintiffs had urged that the District of Columbia Court of Appeals acted arbitrarily in denying the waiver petitions of Hickey and Feldman, given that court's "former policy of granting waivers to graduates of unaccredited law schools." That charge, the Court held, could not be pursued, for it was "inextricably intertwined with the District of Columbia Court of Appeals' decisions, in judicial proceedings, to deny [plaintiffs'] petitions."[1]

On the other hand, the Court said, plaintiffs could maintain "claims that the [bar admission] rule is unconstitutional because it creates an irrebuttable presumption that only graduates of accredited law schools are fit to practice law, discriminates against those who have obtained equivalent legal training by other means, and impermissibly delegates the District of Columbia Court of Appeals' power to regulate the bar to the American Bar Association," for those claims "do not require review of a judicial decision in a particular case." The Court left open the question whether the doctrine of res judicata foreclosed litigation of the elements of the complaints spared from dismissal for want of subject-matter jurisdiction.

Since *Feldman*, this Court has never applied *Rooker-Feldman* to dismiss an action for want of jurisdiction. The few decisions that have mentioned *Rooker* and *Feldman* have done so only in passing or to explain why those cases did not dictate dismissal. . . .

II

In 1980, two subsidiaries of petitioner Exxon Mobil Corporation (then the separate companies Exxon Corp. and Mobil Corp.) formed joint ventures with respondent Saudi Basic Industries Corp. (SABIC) to produce polyethylene in Saudi Arabia. Two decades later, the parties began to dispute royalties that SABIC had charged the joint ventures for sublicenses to a polyethylene manufacturing method.

---

1. Earlier in the opinion the Court had used the same expression. In a footnote, the Court explained that a district court could not entertain constitutional claims attacking a state-court judgment, even if the state court had not passed directly on those claims, when the constitutional attack was "inextricably intertwined" with the state court's judgment.

SABIC preemptively sued the two Exxon Mobil subsidiaries in Delaware Superior Court in July 2000 seeking a declaratory judgment that the royalty charges were proper under the joint venture agreements. About two weeks later, Exxon Mobil and its subsidiaries countersued SABIC in the United States District Court for the District of New Jersey, alleging that SABIC overcharged the joint ventures for the sublicenses. Exxon Mobil invoked subject-matter jurisdiction in the New Jersey action under 28 U.S.C. § 1330, which authorizes district courts to adjudicate actions against foreign states.

In January 2002, the Exxon Mobil subsidiaries answered SABIC's state-court complaint, asserting as counterclaims the same claims Exxon Mobil had made in the federal suit in New Jersey. The state suit went to trial in March 2003, and the jury returned a verdict of over $400 million in favor of the Exxon Mobil subsidiaries. SABIC appealed the judgment entered on the verdict to the Delaware Supreme Court.

Before the state-court trial, SABIC moved to dismiss the federal suit, alleging, *inter alia*, immunity under the Foreign Sovereign Immunities Act of 1976. The Federal District Court denied SABIC's motion to dismiss. SABIC took an interlocutory appeal, and the Court of Appeals heard argument in December 2003, over eight months after the state-court jury verdict.

The Court of Appeals, on its own motion, raised the question whether "subject matter jurisdiction over this case fails under the *Rooker-Feldman* doctrine because Exxon Mobil's claims have already been litigated in state court." The court did not question the District Court's possession of subject-matter jurisdiction at the outset of the suit, but held that federal jurisdiction terminated when the Delaware Superior Court entered judgment on the jury verdict. The court rejected Exxon Mobil's argument that *Rooker-Feldman* could not apply because Exxon Mobil filed its federal complaint well before the state-court judgment. The only relevant consideration, the court stated, "is whether the state judgment precedes a federal judgment on the same claims." If *Rooker-Feldman* did not apply to federal actions filed prior to a state-court judgment, the Court of Appeals worried, "we would be encouraging parties to maintain federal actions as 'insurance policies' while their state court claims were pending." Once Exxon Mobil's claims had been litigated to a judgment in state court, the Court of Appeals held, *Rooker-Feldman* "preclude[d] [the] federal district court from proceeding."

Exxon Mobil, at that point prevailing in Delaware, was not seeking to overturn the state-court judgment. Nevertheless, the Court of Appeals hypothesized that, if SABIC won on appeal in Delaware, Exxon Mobil would be endeavoring in the federal action to "invalidate" the state-court judgment, "the very situation," the court concluded, "contemplated by *Rooker-Feldman*'s 'inextricably intertwined' bar."

We granted certiorari to resolve conflict among the Courts of Appeals over the scope of the *Rooker-Feldman* doctrine. We now reverse the judgment of the Court of Appeals for the Third Circuit.

III

Rooker and *Feldman* exhibit the limited circumstances in which this Court's appellate jurisdiction over state-court judgments, 28 U.S.C. § 1257, precludes a United

States district court from exercising subject-matter jurisdiction in an action it would otherwise be empowered to adjudicate under a congressional grant of authority, *e.g.*, § 1330 (suits against foreign states), § 1331 (federal question), and § 1332 (diversity). In both cases, the losing party in state court filed suit in federal court after the state proceedings ended, complaining of an injury caused by the state-court judgment and seeking review and rejection of that judgment. Plaintiffs in both cases, alleging federal-question jurisdiction, called upon the District Court to overturn an injurious state-court judgment. Because § 1257, as long interpreted, vests authority to review a state court's judgment solely in this Court, the District Courts in *Rooker* and *Feldman* lacked subject-matter jurisdiction. . . . [8]

When there is parallel state and federal litigation, *Rooker-Feldman* is not triggered simply by the entry of judgment in state court. This Court has repeatedly held that "the pendency of an action in the state court is no bar to proceedings concerning the same matter in the Federal court having jurisdiction." *E.g., Atlantic Coast Line R. Co. v. Locomotive Engineers*, 398 U.S. 281 (1970). Comity or abstention doctrines may, in various circumstances, permit or require the federal court to stay or dismiss the federal action in favor of the state-court litigation. *See, e.g., Colorado River Water Conservation Dist. v. United States*, 424 U.S. 800 (1976); *Younger v. Harris*, 401 U.S. 37 (1971); *Burford v. Sun Oil Co.*, 319 U.S. 315 (1943); *Railroad Comm'n of Tex. v. Pullman Co.*, 312 U.S. 496 (1941). But neither *Rooker* nor *Feldman* supports the notion that properly invoked concurrent jurisdiction vanishes if a state court reaches judgment on the same or related question while the case remains *sub judice* in a federal court.

Disposition of the federal action, once the state-court adjudication is complete, would be governed by preclusion law. The Full Faith and Credit Act, 28 U.S.C. § 1738, originally enacted in 1790, requires the federal court to "give the same preclusive effect to a state-court judgment as another court of that State would give." *Parsons Steel, Inc. v. First Alabama Bank*, 474 U.S. 518 (1986). Preclusion, of course, is not a jurisdictional matter. See Fed. Rule Civ. Proc. 8(c) (listing res judicata as an affirmative defense). In parallel litigation, a federal court may be bound to recognize the claim- and issue-preclusive effects of a state-court judgment, but federal jurisdiction over an action does not terminate automatically on the entry of judgment in the state court.

Nor does § 1257 stop a district court from exercising subject-matter jurisdiction simply because a party attempts to litigate in federal court a matter previously litigated in state court. If a federal plaintiff "presents some independent claim, albeit one that denies a legal conclusion that a state court has reached in a case to which he was a party . . . , then there is jurisdiction and state law determines whether the defendant prevails under principles of preclusion." *GASH Assocs. v. Village of Rosemont*, 995 F.2d 726, 728 (C.A. 7 1993).

---

8. Congress, if so minded, may explicitly empower district courts to oversee certain state-court judgments and has done so, most notably, in authorizing federal habeas review of state prisoners' petitions. 28 U.S.C. § 2254(a).

This case surely is not the "paradigm situation in which *Rooker-Feldman* precludes a federal district court from proceeding." Exxon Mobil plainly has not repaired to federal court to undo the Delaware judgment in its favor. Rather, it appears Exxon Mobil filed suit in Federal District Court (only two weeks after SABIC filed in Delaware and well before any judgment in state court) to protect itself in the event it lost in state court on grounds (such as the state statute of limitations) that might not preclude relief in the federal venue.[9] *Rooker-Feldman* did not prevent the District Court from exercising jurisdiction when Exxon Mobil filed the federal action, and it did not emerge to vanquish jurisdiction after Exxon Mobil prevailed in the Delaware courts.

*   *   *

For the reasons stated, the judgment of the Court of Appeals for the Third Circuit is reversed, and the case is remanded for further proceedings consistent with this opinion.

Note: Parties, Preclusion, and the Rooker-Feldman *Doctrine*

1. In the Supreme Court Term following *Saudi Basic*, the Court further narrowed the scope of the *Rooker-Feldman* doctrine in *Lance v. Dennis*, 546 U.S. 459 (2006). *Lance* involved a long-running dispute over the drawing of Colorado's congressional districts after the state gained an additional seat in the House of Representatives following the 2000 Census. The Colorado General Assembly (the state legislature) attempted to enact a consensus redistricting plan in time for the 2002 congressional elections, but it failed to do so. A group of citizens brought suit in state court; that lawsuit led to the creation of a redistricting plan by the Colorado Supreme Court. In 2003, the General Assembly finally created its own plan, but the Colorado Attorney General filed suit in state court to enjoin the legislature's plan as violative of the Colorado Constitution. In *People ex rel. Salazar v. Davidson*, 79 P.3d 1221 (Colo. 2003) (en banc), the Colorado Supreme Court agreed with the Attorney General and entered an injunction requiring the Colorado Secretary of State to use the redistricting plan previously created by the court.

After the United States Supreme Court denied certiorari in *Salazar*, a group of Colorado citizens filed suit in federal district court challenging the court-ordered plan under both the Colorado and United States Constitutions. A three-judge district court held that, under the *Rooker-Feldman* doctrine, it had no subject matter jurisdiction to hear the suit. Relying on two Supreme Court precedents holding that "when a state government litigates a matter of public concern, the state's citizens will be deemed to be in privity with the government for preclusion purposes," the three-judge court reasoned that the privity analysis should also apply in the *Rooker-Feldman* context. Thus, because the citizens were in privity with the state-court loser in *Salazar* and were litigating "inextricably intertwined" claims, the court found that *Rooker-Feldman* barred the suit.

In a short *per curiam* opinion, the Supreme Court reversed and held that the concept of privity has no place in the *Rooker-Feldman* analysis. "Whatever the impact of

---

9. The Court of Appeals criticized Exxon Mobil for pursuing its federal suit as an "insurance policy" against an adverse result in state court. There is nothing necessarily inappropriate, however, about filing a protective action.

privity principles on preclusion rules, *Rooker-Feldman* is not simply preclusion by another name." The Court re-emphasized the narrowness of *Rooker-Feldman* and held that it "does not bar actions by non-parties to the earlier state-court judgment simply because, for the purposes of preclusion law, they could be considered in privity with a party to the judgment." Therefore, because the citizens who filed suit in *Lance* were not parties in *Salazar*, the *Rooker-Feldman* doctrine did not apply and the suit could move forward (although, as Justice Stevens pointed out in dissent, ordinary preclusion principles might justify dismissal of the suit).

The *Lance* Court explained the federalism-based policy considerations underlying the clear division between the *Rooker-Feldman* and preclusion doctrines:

> A more expansive *Rooker-Feldman* rule would tend to supplant Congress' mandate, under the Full Faith and Credit Act, 28 U.S.C. § 1738, that federal courts "'give the same preclusive effect to state court judgments that those judgments would be given in the courts of the State from which the judgments emerged.'" Congress has directed federal courts to look principally to *state* law in deciding what effect to give state-court judgments. Incorporation of preclusion principles into *Rooker-Feldman* risks turning that limited doctrine into a uniform *federal* rule governing the preclusive effect of state-court judgments, contrary to the Full Faith and Credit Act.

However, *Lance* left open a narrow window through which some privity considerations might still creep into the *Rooker-Feldman* analysis. In a footnote, the Court noted that it "need not address whether there are *any* circumstances, however limited, in which *Rooker-Feldman* may be applied against a party not named in an earlier state proceeding — *e.g.*, where an estate takes a *de facto* appeal in a district court of an earlier state decision involving the decedent."

2. As noted disapprovingly by the Court, before *Saudi Basic* several circuits had applied the *Rooker-Feldman* doctrine extremely broadly, using it to create, in effect, a uniform federal law of preclusion. These circuits found the basis for their approach in *Feldman*'s reference to federal claims that are "inextricably intertwined" with state law claims that have already been adjudicated by a state tribunal. *See, e.g., Moccio v. New York State Office of Court Administration*, 95 F.3d 195, 199–200 (2d Cir. 1996). Prior to *Saudi Basic*, therefore, some circuits treated the "inextricably intertwined" element as a threshold question in determining the applicability of the doctrine. In *Saudi Basic*, the Supreme Court repudiated this approach, but it did not explicitly address what force, if any, the "inextricably intertwined" language of *Feldman* might have going forward.

Since *Saudi Basic*, most courts have held that *Feldman*'s "inextricably intertwined" language has no independent force. The Second Circuit, for instance, has held that "describing a federal claim as 'inextricably intertwined' with a state-court judgment only states a conclusion," and that:

> *Rooker-Feldman* bars a federal claim, whether or not raised in state court, that asserts an injury based on a state judgment and seeks review and reversal of that judgment; such a claim is "inextricably intertwined" with the

state judgment. But the phrase "inextricably intertwined" has no independent content. It is simply a descriptive label attached to claims that meet the requirements outlined in [*Saudi Basic*].

Hoblock v. Albany County Bd. of Elections, 422 F.3d 77, 86–87 (2d Cir. 2005).

Take a look at *Feldman*'s original articulation of the "inextricably intertwined" test:

> If the constitutional claims presented to a United States District Court are inextricably intertwined with the state court's denial in a judicial proceeding of a particular plaintiff's application for admission to the state bar, then the District Court is in essence being called upon to review the state court decision. This the District Court may not do. Moreover, the fact that we may not have jurisdiction to review a final state court judgment because of a petitioner's failure to raise his constitutional claims in state court does not mean that a United States District Court should have jurisdiction over the claims. By failing to raise his claims in state court a plaintiff may forfeit his right to obtain review of the state decision in any federal court. *District of Columbia Court of Appeals v. Feldman*, 460 U.S. 462, 483 n.16 (1983).

In his concurrence in *Pennzoil Co. v. Texaco, Inc.*, 481 U.S. 1, 25 (1987), Justice Marshall elaborated on what *Feldman* meant by "inextricably intertwined":

> While the question whether a federal constitutional challenge is inextricably intertwined with the merits of a state-court judgment may sometimes be difficult to answer, it is apparent, as a first step, that the federal claim is inextricably intertwined with the state-court judgment if the federal claim succeeds only to the extent that the state court wrongly decided the issues before it. Where federal relief can only be predicated upon a conviction that the state court was wrong, it is difficult to conceive the federal proceeding as, in substance, anything other than a prohibited appeal of the state-court judgment.

Saudi Basic, however, essentially disavowed Justice Marshall's view of "inextricably intertwined" by holding that a federal claim "that denies a legal conclusion that a state court has reached in a case to which [the federal claimant] was a party" is not necessarily barred by *Rooker-Feldman*.

Which of these interpretations of *Feldman*'s "inextricably intertwined" language seems the most plausible? After *Saudi Basic*, is there anything left of the "inextricably intertwined" footnote from *Feldman*?

3. The relationship (or lack thereof) between preclusion as an affirmative defense and *Rooker-Feldman* as a jurisdictional bar confused the lower courts prior to *Saudi Basic*, but much of that confusion has been eliminated by the Court's insistence in *Saudi Basic* that the two doctrines are to be kept strictly separate. The implications for litigants involve more than mere nomenclature: preclusion is a fact-intensive doctrine that requires courts to carefully examine what was adjudicated in a prior action to determine its preclusive effect, whereas *Rooker-Feldman* is a jurisdictional bar to an entire class of potential cases.

4. In his concurrence in *Marshall v. Marshall*, 547 U.S. 293, 318 (2006), Justice Stevens celebrated the "decent burial" of the probate exception "in a grave adjacent to the resting place of the *Rooker-Feldman* doctrine." After *Saudi Basic* and *Lance*, the question remains: is *Rooker-Feldman* effectively dead?

5. Because the facts in *Saudi Basic* were straightforward, the Court's opinion left some recurring *Rooker-Feldman* questions unanswered. Several courts have attempted to fill that void by addressing such lingering questions as whether the doctrine can ever be applied against non-parties to a state court litigation, when a federal court can adjudicate the same legal issues that were already decided by the state court, and when a state court action has "ended" for purposes of triggering the *Rooker-Feldman* doctrine. The Tenth Circuit attempted to answer some of these questions in the next case.

Mo's Express, LLC v. Sopkin

United States Court of Appeals for the Tenth Circuit, 2006.

441 F.3d 1229.

Before KELLY, HENRY, and McCONNELL, CIRCUIT JUDGES.

McCONNELL, CIRCUIT JUDGE.

Thirteen individuals and companies that provide shuttle service to and from the Denver International Airport filed suit [in federal district court against] the Colorado Public Utilities Commission (PUC) and its three commissioners in their official capacities. The Plaintiffs sought to enjoin the PUC from taking enforcement action against them for failure to obtain a certificate of public convenience and necessity issued by the state. They presented two legal theories: first, that certificates granted to each Plaintiff by the Federal Motor Carrier Safety Administration authorized their provision of transportation services, preempting contrary state law requirements, and that the PUC lacked jurisdiction to determine whether they were in compliance with their federal certificates; and second, that the PUC had threatened enforcement action against the Plaintiffs "because each of them are [sic] minorities or foreign born nationals," in violation of the Equal Protection Clause of the Fourteenth Amendment.

In December 2004, the district court dismissed the Complaint for lack of jurisdiction based on the *Rooker-Feldman* doctrine. [This was before the Supreme Court decisions in *Saudi Basic* and *Lance*.] Based on those decisions as well as our *Rooker-Feldman* case law, we REVERSE the judgment of the district court and REMAND the case for further proceedings.

I. FACTS AND PROCEDURAL HISTORY

Colorado law provides that any carrier operating a motor vehicle for purposes of transporting persons on public highways in *intra*state commerce must first obtain a certificate of public convenience and necessity (CPCN) from the PUC. Although they do not possess a state-issued CPCN, some shuttle operators—including each of the Plaintiffs in this case—provide transportation services to and from the Denver International Airport based on federal certificates, issued by the Federal Motor Carrier Safety Administration. These certificates authorize transportation services along certain *inter* state routes. Each federal certificate contains a "CONDITION" that the carrier is "authorized to provide intrastate passenger transportation service under this certificate *only* if the carrier also provides substantial regularly scheduled inter-state passenger transportation service on the same route."

Beginning in 1999, the PUC issued a series of penalty notices to some of these fed-erally certificated carriers, alleging that they were conducting extensive intrastate business without providing the regularly scheduled interstate services, as required by their federal certificates. While review of those penalty notices was still pending in state court, a group of four carriers consisting of Trans Shuttle, Inc., Hallelujah Shut-tle, Ethio Shuttle, and Galaxy Shuttle—none of which is a party to this action—filed suit in federal court against the PUC and other defendants, seeking declaratory and injunctive relief. The district court declined to exercise jurisdiction on Younger absten-tion grounds, citing the pending proceedings in state court. *See Younger v. Harris*, 401 U.S. 37 (1971) [Chapter 16]. In an unpublished order in November 2001, this Court affirmed the abstention decision.

The state court proceedings culminated in a May 2004 decision of the Colorado Supreme Court, which upheld the PUC's jurisdiction over carriers transporting pas-sengers in intrastate commerce. The court also affirmed the PUC's imposition of fines against the three carriers that were parties to the state-court appeal: Trans Shuttle, Inc., Mo's Express, LLC, and Hallelujah Shuttle. In reaching its decision, the Colorado Supreme Court considered and specifically rejected the federal preemption and juris-diction arguments raised by the Plaintiffs in this action.

On August 16, 2004, the PUC sent a letter to each of the thirteen Plaintiffs in this action. The letters described the Colorado Supreme Court's holding in *Trans Shuttle*, and stated that "the PUC intends to go to court to ask for an injunction to halt the operations of any motor carrier transporting passengers to and from Denver Inter-national Airport (DIA) on an intrastate basis . . . without actual, substantial and bona fide interstate operations in full compliance with the carrier's federal certificate." The letters also announced that the PUC "intends to go to court to ask for an injunction against [the named Plaintiff] unless [the named Plaintiff] provides proof to the PUC of its 2004 for-hire interstate passenger transportation operations . . . [within] 30 days from the date of this letter."

In September 2004, the Plaintiffs commenced this federal action seeking declara-tory and injunctive relief to prevent the PUC from going to court as threatened in its letters. They did not seek money damages. They argued, first, that the PUC lacked jurisdiction to impose penalties because federal law authorized them to provide trans-portation services. According to the Plaintiffs, only a federal authority—not a state agency—has jurisdiction to revoke their certificates for failure to satisfy the condi-tions. Second, they argued that the PUC's actions reflected discrimination against businesses with minority and foreign-born owners and operators.

One of the Plaintiffs in this action, Mo's Express, was also a losing party to the state court judgment in *Trans Shuttle*. With one possible exception, the other twelve Plaintiffs . . . had no involvement in the Trans Shuttle litigation. The district court dismissed the case on jurisdictional grounds, citing the *Rooker-Feldman* doctrine. The Plaintiffs had made it "clear," according to the district court, that "their [intention] in filing in this court [was] to void the ruling of the Colorado Supreme Court" in *Trans Shuttle*, and thus to take a *de facto* appeal in federal district court from a judgment by a state court. Although it acknowledged that Mo's Express is the only Plaintiff in this case that was also party to *Trans Shuttle*, the district court found that the Plaintiffs' claims had been "fully presented" in the state court proceedings "by the shuttle operators who were named in the state action." The court concluded that "the identity of interest of all the operators has remained the same throughout." It also found that the Plaintiffs "have always been in privity with one another in their joint commitment to the same claims and arguments." It therefore applied the jurisdictional bar of *Rooker-Feldman* against all Plaintiffs, even those who were not parties to the state court action.

II. *Rooker-Feldman*

The *Rooker-Feldman* doctrine does not reflect a constitutional limitation on the lower federal courts. Instead, it arises by negative inference from 28 U.S.C. § 1257(a), which allows parties to state court judgments to seek direct review in the Supreme Court of the United States, but not to appeal to the lower federal courts. *Rooker-Feldman* precludes federal district courts from effectively exercising appellate jurisdiction over claims "actually decided by a state court" and claims "'inextricably intertwined' with a prior state-court judgment."

Both *Rooker* and *Feldman* were "cases brought by state-court losers complaining of injuries caused by state-court judgments . . . and inviting district court review and rejection of those judgments." *Exxon Mobil Corp. v. Saudi Basic Industries Corp.* As the Supreme Court observed in *Saudi Basic*, however, lower courts have at times construed the *Rooker-Feldman* doctrine "to extend far beyond the contours of the *Rooker* and *Feldman* cases." In particular, some circuit courts—including this one—have occasionally treated *Rooker-Feldman* as a substitute for ordinary principles of preclusion, or as an extension of the various grounds for abstention by federal courts. In *Saudi Basic*, the Supreme Court sought to curb these excesses and "confined" *Rooker-Feldman* "to cases of the kind from which the doctrine acquired its name." In *Lance v. Dennis*, 546 U.S. 459 (2006), the Court again emphasized "the narrowness of the *Rooker-Feldman* rule."

In two respects, assertion of the *Rooker-Feldman* doctrine in this case epitomizes the expansive view that the Supreme Court repudiated in *Saudi Basic*. First, the district court applied *Rooker-Feldman* against all of the Plaintiffs, despite the fact that most of them were not party to the state-court judgment in *Trans Shuttle*. Second, the district court found *Rooker-Feldman* applicable despite the fact that the Plaintiffs sought only prospective relief challenging the constitutionality of the PUC's jurisdiction to take future action. Under our pre-*Saudi Basic* case law, both holdings were questionable; after *Saudi Basic* and *Lance*, they are incorrect.

A. Applying *Rooker-Feldman* Against Nonparties

This Court has repeatedly held that the *Rooker-Feldman* doctrine "should not be applied against non-parties" to the state-court judgment. *Rooker-Feldman*, after all, bars federal district courts from exercising appellate jurisdiction over state-court judgments, and "a person would generally have no basis (or right) to appeal a judgment to which that person was not a party." The Supreme Court appeared to endorse this view in *Saudi Basic*, characterizing its decision in *Johnson v. De Grandy*, 512 U.S. 997 (1999), as holding that "the doctrine has no application to a federal suit brought by a nonparty to the state suit."

In *Lance*, the Court explicitly held that *Rooker-Feldman* does not apply against nonparties to the prior judgment in state court. . . . [The Court emphasized] that in *De Grandy* it had declined to apply *Rooker-Feldman* when the federal-court plaintiff "'was not a party in the state court,' and 'was in no position to ask this Court to review the state court's judgment.'" By asking whether the citizens were "in privity" with the General Assembly, "[t]he District Court erroneously conflated preclusion law with *Rooker-Feldman*." Although *Lance* leaves room for an extremely limited form of privity analysis—for example, in cases "where an estate takes a *de facto* appeal in a district court of an earlier state decision involving the decedent,"—it broadly rejects the use of preclusion principles in determining the scope of *Rooker-Feldman*.

Saudi Basic and *Lance* make the disposition of this appeal straightforward for almost all of the Plaintiffs. Only one of the Plaintiffs, Mo's Express, was a party to the decision of the Colorado Supreme Court in *Trans Shuttle*. The other Plaintiffs had no connection whatsoever to the *Trans Shuttle* case. They were not parties, they were not bound by the judgment, and they were neither predecessors nor successors in interest to the parties. The other Plaintiffs were nothing more than competitors of the shuttle operators who were party to *Trans Shuttle*. That relationship falls far short of the connection necessary under *Rooker-Feldman* to characterize their action in federal court as an appeal of the state-court judgment.

The district court found that "the identity of interest of all of the operators has remained the same throughout" because "they have always been in privity with one another in their joint commitment to the same claims and arguments." The factual basis for this conclusion is uncertain, as there is no evidence to suggest that the other Plaintiffs actually consulted with the *Trans Shuttle* parties before the state court litigation began to coordinate their claims and arguments. As far as the record discloses, the other Plaintiffs became involved only after receiving letters threatening an injunction against the operation of their businesses. In any case, a "commitment" to the same claims and arguments has no bearing on the applicability of *Rooker-Feldman*.

Because only Mo's Express was a party to the Colorado Supreme Court judgment in *Trans Shuttle*, the district court erred in applying *Rooker-Feldman* against the remaining Plaintiffs.

B. Evaluating the Relief Requested in Federal Court

Even against the parties to a state-court judgment, *Rooker-Feldman* only applies when the injury alleged by the plaintiffs was "caused by [the] state-court judgment[ ]." As we explained in our pre-*Saudi Basic* case law, "we approach the question by asking whether the state-court judgment caused, actually and proximately, the injury for which the federal-court plaintiff seeks redress," paying "close attention to the relief sought" in the federal suit.

As the Supreme Court emphasized in *Saudi Basic*, the *Rooker-Feldman* doctrine does not apply "simply because a party attempts to litigate in federal court a matter previously litigated in state court." To the contrary, a party may lose in state court and then raise precisely the same legal issues in federal court, so long as the *relief sought* in the federal action would not reverse or undo the *relief granted* by the state court: "If a federal plaintiff 'present[s] some independent claim, albeit one that denies a legal conclusion that a state court has reached in a case to which he was a party . . . , then there is jurisdiction. . . .'"

Mo's Express, like the other Plaintiffs, has requested only prospective injunctive and declaratory relief that would prevent the PUC from exercising jurisdiction over them in the future. Both of its claims amount to "general constitutional challenges" to the jurisdiction of the PUC: first, that federal law preempts the state's jurisdiction pursuant to the Supremacy Clause; and second, that the PUC has exercised its jurisdiction in a discriminatory fashion in violation of the Equal Protection Clause of the Fourteenth Amendment. Neither claim would disrupt the judgment of the Colorado Supreme Court. The *Trans Shuttle* decision simply "upheld penalties assessed against [the parties, including Mo's Express,] by the Public Utilities Commission." The Plaintiffs in this action have not requested money damages that would compensate them for the amount of those penalties. Nor have they requested retrospective relief that would invalidate any past action of the PUC. Accordingly, their federal suit would not reverse or otherwise "undo" the relief granted by the Colorado Supreme Court, and *Rooker-Feldman* does not operate to deprive the district court of jurisdiction.

To be sure, Mo's Express has asked the federal courts to accept a legal argument that was specifically rejected in its earlier lawsuit in state court. If the Plaintiffs eventually prevail on the merits, the Colorado courts will have held that the PUC can exercise jurisdiction, while the federal courts will have held that it cannot. That result should not be alarming, however, because state and federal courts enjoy concurrent jurisdiction over questions of federal law, and the possibility of inconsistent rulings on issues of federal law is a predictable, if infrequent, consequence of our dual system. A federal court is free to "den[y] a legal conclusion that a state court has reached," provided it does not exercise *de facto* appellate jurisdiction by entertaining a suit that would disrupt the final judgment entered by the state court. Because the prospective relief requested by the Plaintiffs would not undo the penalties imposed by the state court judgment, the district court erred in applying the *Rooker-Feldman* doctrine, even against Mo's Express.

[The court reversed the judgment of the district court and remanded for consideration of alternate grounds for dismissal urged by the defendants, including preclusion and ripeness.]

Note: Developments in the Rooker-Feldman *Doctrine*
after Saudi Basic *and* Lance

1. Following *Saudi Basic,* many courts now employ a four-part inquiry to determine whether *Rooker-Feldman* applies. The Second Circuit articulated the test in *Hoblock v. Albany County Board of Elections,* 422 F.3d 77, 85 (2d Cir. 2005):

> First, the federal-court plaintiff must have lost in state court. Second, the plaintiff must "complain of injuries caused by [a] state-court judgment." Third, the plaintiff must "invite district court review and rejection of [that] judgment." Fourth, the state-court judgment must have been "rendered before the district court proceedings commenced." . . . The first and fourth of these requirements may be loosely termed procedural; the second and third may be termed substantive.

2. *Saudi Basic* made clear that *Rooker-Feldman* applies only when the state-court judgment was "rendered before the district court proceedings commenced," or as the Court puts it elsewhere in the opinion, when the plaintiff files suit in federal court "after the state proceedings [have] *ended.*" (Emphasis added.) A lingering question after *Saudi Basic* is: when does a state-court action "end" for purposes of applying the doctrine? In *Saudi Basic* itself the Court was not required to answer that question, because Exxon Mobil filed its federal complaints shortly after Saudi Basic's state-court action had begun.

Before *Saudi Basic* many courts had used either the test for finality under 28 U.S.C. § 1257 (setting forth when a state case becomes appealable to the United States Supreme Court) or some version of state preclusion rules to decide whether a state case has become sufficiently complete to trigger *Rooker-Feldman* analysis. However, *Saudi Basic*'s rejection of any identity between the *Rooker-Feldman* and preclusion doctrines has cast doubt on the latter decisions.

In *Federación de Maestros de Puerto Rico v. Junta de Relaciones del Trabajo de Puerto Rico,* 410 F.3d 17, 24–25 (1st Cir. 2005), the First Circuit identified three scenarios in which a state court action has "ended" for the purposes of the *Rooker-Feldman* doctrine: "first, when the highest state court in which review is available has affirmed the judgment below and nothing is left to be resolved"; "second, if the state action has reached a point where neither party seeks further action . . . for example, if a lower state court issues a judgment and the losing party allows the time for appeal to expire"; and third, "if the state proceedings have finally resolved all the federal questions in the litigation, but state law or purely factual questions (whether great or small) remain to be litigated."

The third category from *Federación* would potentially apply the *Rooker-Feldman* doctrine "where the state proceeding has ended *with respect to the issues that the federal plaintiff seeks to have reviewed in federal court,* even if other matters remain to be litigated." As the district court in *Phillips ex rel. Green v. New York,* 453 F. Supp. 2d 690, 714 n.20 (S.D.N.Y. 2006), explained:

> The First Circuit inferred this third [category] of "ended" [state court actions] from a footnote in *Saudi Basic* that provided an example of a federal

suit that would be barred by *Rooker-Feldman* even though state court litigation was ongoing: a federal suit seeking to invalidate a state statute governing mineral leases, brought after a state supreme court reversed a lower state court's determination that such statute was invalid and remanded to the lower court with instructions to enter summary judgment for the plaintiffs and to consider what further relief, if any, might be appropriate. In such a case, state court proceedings would be ongoing, but the proceedings as to the federal issue of invalidation of the state statute would have "ended" for *Rooker-Feldman* purposes.

As *Saudi Basic* and *Mo's Express* make clear, the Supreme Court derived the *Rooker-Feldman* doctrine from the negative implication created by 28 U.S.C. § 1257, which vests the United States Supreme Court with appellate jurisdiction over cases from state courts. Does this mean in determining whether a state-court proceeding has "ended" for purposes of *Rooker-Feldman*, a federal court should apply the doctrines that the Supreme Court has developed for determining whether a state-court judgment is "final" for purposes of 28 U.S.C. § 1257? (See Chapter 5.) If so, is the third category from *Federación* consistent with the cases interpreting § 1257? Does the hypothetical described above fit within any of the four categories of state court decisions that are considered "final" under *Cox Broadcasting Corp. v. Cohn*?

3. *Mo's Express* highlights one of the most restrictive elements of the post-*Saudi Basic Rooker-Feldman* analysis. In order for the doctrine to apply, the state-court loser must complain of injuries caused by the state court judgment. The plaintiffs in *Mo's Express* avoided *Rooker-Feldman* by seeking only prospective relief that did not require the federal court to undo or modify the state court judgment.

Plaintiffs can also avoid the *Rooker-Feldman* bar by complaining only of injuries caused by the original state-court *defendant*, rather than the state court judgment itself. As the Second Circuit stated in *Hoblock, supra*,

> Suppose a state court, based purely on state law, terminates a father's parental rights and orders the state to take custody of his son. If the father sues in federal court for the return of his son on the grounds that the state judgment violates his federal substantive due-process rights as a parent, he is complaining of an injury caused by a state judgment and seeking its reversal. This he may not do, regardless of whether he raised any constitutional claims in state court, because only the Supreme Court may hear appeals from state-court judgments.

Because the father's injury in the Second Circuit's hypothetical derives from the effect of the state court judgment itself, *Rooker-Feldman* bars him from seeking relief from it in a federal district court. But

> suppose a plaintiff sues his employer in state court for violating both state anti-discrimination law and Title VII and loses. If the plaintiff brings the same suit in federal court, he will be seeking a decision from the federal court that denies the state court's conclusion that the employer is not liable, but he will

not be alleging injury from the state court judgment. Instead he will be alleging injury based on the employer's discrimination. The fact that the state court chose not to remedy the injury does not transform the subsequent federal suit on the same matter into an appeal, forbidden by *Rooker-Feldman*, of the state court judgment.

But the court noted that the second hypothetical, while not subject to *Rooker-Feldman*, could be barred by ordinary preclusion principles.

Is the apparent distinction drawn in *Hoblock* between suits that aim to remedy an injury caused by a state court judgment and those that seek merely to deny a legal conclusion reached by a state court a convincing one? Does the "inextricably intertwined" language of *Feldman* support the Second Circuit's analysis?

Problem: Religious Land Use and Rooker-Feldman

In the summer of 2015, the Bet Shalom Synagogue in the City of Utopia, Oceana, applied to the Utopia Planning Board for permits to convert a school building into a synagogue. Bet Shalom also requested a zoning variance permitting it to build a smaller parking lot than would ordinarily be required, because the size of the existing building was too small for large gatherings. The Board approved the plan, but a group of concerned neighbors challenged the Board's decision in the Superior Court of Utopia County. The state court found in favor of Bet Shalom in July 2015, and the conversion went ahead as scheduled.

After the synagogue was completed in 2016, the neighbors filed suit once more in the Superior Court of Utopia County, seeking an injunction against Bet Shalom's practice of holding large, boisterous post-Bar Mitzvah celebrations in tents erected in the synagogue's parking lot. After an evidentiary hearing, the Superior Court determined that: (1) Bet Shalom's celebrations violated the zoning rights that the Planning Board had granted, (2) a temporary injunction against the celebrations was warranted, and (3) the Planning Board was in the best position to determine how to balance the synagogue's desire to use tents against other important safety and neighborhood concerns.

The state judge's order held that "the issue of the possible use of parking areas, traffic lanes and fire lanes in connection with primary or accessory outdoor uses at Bet Shalom Synagogue, is hereby remanded to the Utopia Planning Board for review and consideration." The order gave the Board 90 days to reach a final determination. The Board held public meetings on the subject, and eventually ruled that Bet Shalom could only hold three outdoor Bar Mitzvah celebrations per year. On September 30, 2016, the Superior Court dissolved its temporary injunction in light of the Board's resolution of the issue.

On November 3, 2016, Bet Shalom filed suit in United States District Court for the District of Oceana against the City of Utopia and the Utopia Planning Board. Bet Shalom's suit, under 42 U.S.C. § 1983, alleges that the Board's decision violates the synagogue's constitutional rights under the Free Exercise Clause of the First Amendment, as well as its statutory rights as a religious organization under the Religious Land Use and Institutionalized Persons Act (RLUIPA), 42 U.S.C. § 2000cc.

In response to Bet Shalom's suit, the City and Planning Board have moved to dismiss the complaint under Federal Rule of Civil Procedure 12(b)(1) for lack of subject-matter jurisdiction. The defendants argue that the *Rooker-Feldman* doctrine bars the District Court from entertaining the case. How should the court rule on the motion to dismiss?

Problem: A Section 1983 Suit Challenging a Biased Judge

In early 2012, J. Walter Lizer underwent surgery for a heart-valve repair. In the course of the surgery, Lizer's doctors used a new anesthesia medication, which caused major complications resulting in irreversible brain damage. Lizer's family sued the manufacturer, Zetical, in Oceana state court both on their own behalf and as representatives of a class of all individuals injured by the anesthesia medication. In late 2014, the state-court jury found in favor of the plaintiffs, awarding a total of $30 million in damages. Zetical immediately appealed to the Oceana Supreme Court.

Oceana elects its judges every eight years in contested, partisan elections. In the fall of 2015, a high-profile corporate defense attorney, Michael Ping, challenged an incumbent Justice in a close, highly-contested election. Ping had frequently crusaded against what he considered the outrageously pro-plaintiff Oceana Supreme Court, noting that one national business group had classified the state as a "judicial hell-hole" for its exorbitant jury verdicts. Ping's primary financial supporter in the election was George Jarvis, the CEO and majority shareholder of Zetical, who spent more than $5 million of his own money to ensure Ping's election. Jarvis contributed 75% of the total amount of money spent on Ping's behalf during the election. Ping defeated the incumbent and was seated on the Oceana Supreme Court prior to the briefing and oral argument in the Lizer appeal.

Several months later, the plaintiffs filed a motion requesting Justice Ping's recusal under the Due Process Clause of the Fourteenth Amendment as well as state law. They argued that his public statements in opposition to large jury verdicts in products liability cases, coupled with the size of Jarvis's contribution to Ping's campaign, created a risk of actual bias against them on Ping's part. Justice Ping denied the motion, a decision which is unreviewable under Oceana law. The Oceana Supreme Court heard the appeal, and in a 4-3 decision in which Justice Ping cast the deciding vote, reversed the lower court decision and wiped out the jury verdict. Because the Oceana Supreme Court decision was based entirely on Oceana state law, the Lizer plaintiffs did not seek a writ of certiorari to the United States Supreme Court.

Two months after the Oceana Supreme Court decision, the Lizer plaintiffs filed suit against the Oceana Supreme Court and Justice Ping in the United States District Court for the District of Oceana. They sued under 28 U.S.C. § 1983, claiming that Justice Ping's participation in the case violated their Fourteenth Amendment due process rights, based on the United States Supreme Court's decision in *Caperton v. A.T. Massey Coal Co.*, 556 U.S. 868 (2009). That case held that when extraordinarily large judicial campaign contributions create a serious, objective risk of actual bias on a judge's part, due process may require recusal. In response, the defendants have argued, *inter alia*, that the federal district court lacks jurisdiction under the *Rooker-Feldman* doctrine. Without considering the merits of the underlying *Caperton* claim, does the district court have jurisdiction over the case?

Chapter 18

Appellate Review in the Federal System

In Chapter 5 we examined the doctrines that govern review by the United States Supreme Court of decisions rendered by state courts. We turn now to appellate review within the federal judicial system. Three sections of the Judicial Code provide the framework and the basic law. Section 1291 authorizes review by the courts of appeals of "final decisions" of the district courts. Section 1292 provides that the courts of appeals may also review district court interlocutory orders under specified circumstances. Finally, section 1254 authorizes review by the Supreme Court of cases in the courts of appeals. This chapter examines the doctrines that govern review of district court decisions by the federal courts of appeals.

A. Review of "Final Decisions" of the District Courts

Section 1291 of Title 28 provides:

> The courts of appeals (other than the United States Court of Appeals for the Federal Circuit) shall have jurisdiction of appeals from all final decisions of the district courts of the United States . . . except where a direct review may be had in the Supreme Court.

The statute thus authorizes appeals only from *final* decisions of the district courts. A literal reading might suggest that "final decisions" are limited to judgments that terminate an action. However, in *Cohen v. Beneficial Industrial Loan Co.*, 337 U.S. 541 (1949), the Court rejected that interpretation. It held that § 1291 also authorizes appeals from a "small class [of decisions] which finally determine claims of right separable from, and collateral to, rights asserted in the action, too important to be denied review and too independent of the cause itself to require that appellate consideration be deferred until the whole case is adjudicated." *Cohen* (which we have previously encountered for its *Erie* holding, see Chapter 6) thus gave its name to the "collateral order" doctrine.

It would be possible to read *Cohen* as recognizing an exception to the "final decision" rule of § 1291. However, the Supreme Court has said that the doctrine is best understood as a "practical construction" of the statute. For that reason, it makes sense to consider the doctrine separately from the law that governs appellate review of district-court orders that are acknowledged as interlocutory.

Mohawk Industries, Inc. v. Carpenter

Supreme Court of the United States, 2009.

558 U.S. 100.

JUSTICE SOTOMAYOR delivered the opinion of the Court.

Section 1291 of the Judicial Code confers on federal courts of appeals jurisdiction to review "final decisions of the district courts." 28 U.S.C. § 1291. Although "final decisions" typically are ones that trigger the entry of judgment, they also include a small set of prejudgment orders that are "collateral to" the merits of an action and "too important" to be denied immediate review. *Cohen v. Beneficial Industrial Loan Corp.*, 337 U.S. 541 (1949). In this case, petitioner Mohawk Industries, Inc., attempted to bring a collateral order appeal after the District Court ordered it to disclose certain confidential materials on the ground that Mohawk had waived the attorney-client privilege. The Court of Appeals dismissed the appeal for want of jurisdiction.

The question before us is whether disclosure orders adverse to the attorney-client privilege qualify for immediate appeal under the collateral order doctrine. Agreeing with the Court of Appeals, we hold that they do not. Postjudgment appeals, together with other review mechanisms, suffice to protect the rights of litigants and preserve the vitality of the attorney-client privilege.

I

In 2007, respondent Norman Carpenter, a former shift supervisor at a Mohawk manufacturing facility, filed suit in the United States District Court for the Northern District of Georgia, alleging that Mohawk had terminated him in violation of 42 U.S.C. § 1985(2) and various Georgia laws. According to Carpenter's complaint, his termination came after he informed a member of Mohawk's human resources department in an e-mail that the company was employing undocumented immigrants. At the time, unbeknownst to Carpenter, Mohawk stood accused in a pending class-action lawsuit of conspiring to drive down the wages of its legal employees by knowingly hiring undocumented workers in violation of federal and state racketeering laws. *See Williams v. Mohawk Indus., Inc.*, No. 4:04-cv-00003-HLM (N.D. Ga., Jan. 6, 2004). Company officials directed Carpenter to meet with the company's retained counsel in the *Williams* case, and counsel allegedly pressured Carpenter to recant his statements. When he refused, Carpenter alleges, Mohawk fired him under false pretenses.

. . . According to Mohawk, Carpenter himself had "engaged in blatant and illegal misconduct" by attempting to have Mohawk hire an undocumented worker. Because Carpenter's "efforts to cause Mohawk to circumvent federal immigration law" "blatantly violated Mohawk policy," the company terminated him.

As these events were unfolding in the *Williams* case, discovery was underway in Carpenter's case. Carpenter filed a motion to compel Mohawk to produce information concerning his meeting with retained counsel and the company's termination decision. Mohawk maintained that the requested information was protected by the attorney-client privilege.

The District Court agreed that the privilege applied to the requested information, but it granted Carpenter's motion to compel disclosure after concluding that Mohawk had implicitly waived the privilege through its representations in the *Williams* case. The court declined to certify its order for interlocutory appeal under 28 U.S.C. § 1292(b). But, recognizing "the seriousness of its [waiver] finding," it stayed its ruling to allow Mohawk to explore other potential "avenues to appeal . . . , such as a petition for mandamus or appealing this Order under the collateral order doctrine."

Mohawk filed a notice of appeal and a petition for a writ of mandamus to the Eleventh Circuit. The Court of Appeals dismissed the appeal for lack of jurisdiction under 28 U.S.C. § 1291, holding that the District Court's ruling did not qualify as an immediately appealable collateral order within the meaning of *Cohen*. "Under *Cohen*," the Court of Appeals explained, "an order is appealable if it (1) conclusively determines the disputed question; (2) resolves an important issue completely separate from the merits of the action; and (3) is effectively unreviewable on appeal from a final judgment." According to the court, the District Court's waiver ruling satisfied the first two of these requirements but not the third, because "a discovery order that implicates the attorney-client privilege" can be adequately reviewed "on appeal from a final judgment." The Court of Appeals also rejected Mohawk's mandamus petition, finding no "clear usurpation of power or abuse of discretion" by the District Court. We granted certiorari to resolve a conflict among the Circuits concerning the availability of collateral appeals in the attorney-client privilege context.

II

A

By statute, Courts of Appeals "have jurisdiction of appeals from all final decisions of the district courts of the United States, . . . except where a direct review may be had in the Supreme Court." 28 U.S.C. § 1291. A "final decisio[n]" is typically one "by which a district court disassociates itself from a case." This Court, however, "has long given" § 1291 a "practical rather than a technical construction." As we held in *Cohen*, the statute encompasses not only judgments that "terminate an action," but also a "small class" of collateral rulings that, although they do not end the litigation, are appropriately deemed "final." "That small category includes only decisions that are conclusive, that resolve important questions separate from the merits, and that are effectively unreviewable on appeal from the final judgment in the underlying action."

In applying *Cohen*'s collateral order doctrine, we have stressed that it must "never be allowed to swallow the general rule that a party is entitled to a single appeal, to be deferred until final judgment has been entered." Our admonition reflects a healthy respect for the virtues of the final-judgment rule. Permitting piecemeal, prejudgment appeals, we have recognized, undermines "efficient judicial administration" and encroaches upon the prerogatives of district court judges, who play a "special role" in managing ongoing litigation.

The justification for immediate appeal must therefore be sufficiently strong to overcome the usual benefits of deferring appeal until litigation concludes. This requirement finds expression in two of the three traditional *Cohen* conditions. The second condition insists upon "*important* questions separate from the merits." More significantly, "the third *Cohen* question, whether a right is 'adequately vindicable' or 'effectively reviewable,' simply cannot be answered without a judgment about the value of the interests that would be lost through rigorous application of a final judgment requirement." That a ruling "may burden litigants in ways that are only imperfectly reparable by appellate reversal of a final district court judgment . . . has never sufficed." Instead, the decisive consideration is whether delaying review until the entry of final judgment "would imperil a substantial public interest" or "some particular value of a high order."

In making this determination, we do not engage in an "individualized jurisdictional inquiry." Rather, our focus is on "the entire category to which a claim belongs." As long as the class of claims, taken as a whole, can be adequately vindicated by other means, "the chance that the litigation at hand might be speeded, or a 'particular injustic[e]' averted," does not provide a basis for jurisdiction under § 1291.

B

In the present case, the Court of Appeals concluded that the District Court's privilege-waiver order satisfied the first two conditions of the collateral order doctrine—conclusiveness and separateness—but not the third—effective unreviewability. Because we agree with the Court of Appeals that collateral order appeals are not necessary to ensure effective review of orders adverse to the attorney-client privilege, we do not decide whether the other *Cohen* requirements are met.

Mohawk does not dispute that "we have generally denied review of pretrial discovery orders." Mohawk contends, however, that rulings implicating the attorney-client privilege differ in kind from run-of-the-mill discovery orders because of the important institutional interests at stake. According to Mohawk, the right to maintain attorney-client confidences—the *sine qua non* of a meaningful attorney-client relationship—is "irreparably destroyed absent immediate appeal" of adverse privilege rulings.

We readily acknowledge the importance of the attorney-client privilege, which "is one of the oldest recognized privileges for confidential communications." . . .

The crucial question, however, is not whether an interest is important in the abstract; it is whether deferring review until final judgment so imperils the interest as to justify the cost of allowing immediate appeal of the entire class of relevant orders. . . . In *Digital Equipment Corp. v. Desktop Direct, Inc.*, 511 U.S. 863 (1994), we rejected an assertion that collateral order review was necessary to promote "the public policy favoring voluntary resolution of disputes." "It defies common sense," we explained, "to maintain that parties' readiness to settle will be significantly dampened (or the corresponding public interest impaired) by a rule that a district court's decision to let allegedly barred litigation go forward may be challenged as a matter of right only on appeal from a judgment for the plaintiff's favor."

We reach a similar conclusion here. In our estimation, postjudgment appeals generally suffice to protect the rights of litigants and assure the vitality of the attorney-client privilege. Appellate courts can remedy the improper disclosure of privileged material in the same way they remedy a host of other erroneous evidentiary rulings: by vacating an adverse judgment and remanding for a new trial in which the protected material and its fruits are excluded from evidence.

. . . Mohawk is undoubtedly correct that an order to disclose privileged information intrudes on the confidentiality of attorney-client communications. But deferring review until final judgment does not meaningfully reduce the *ex ante* incentives for full and frank consultations between clients and counsel.

One reason for the lack of a discernible chill is that, in deciding how freely to speak, clients and counsel are unlikely to focus on the remote prospect of an erroneous disclosure order, let alone on the timing of a possible appeal. . . .

Moreover, were attorneys and clients to reflect upon their appellate options, they would find that litigants confronted with a particularly injurious or novel privilege ruling have several potential avenues of review apart from collateral order appeal. First, a party may ask the district court to certify, and the court of appeals to accept, an interlocutory appeal pursuant to 28 U.S.C. § 1292(b). The preconditions for § 1292(b) review — "a controlling question of law," the prompt resolution of which "may materially advance the ultimate termination of the litigation" — are most likely to be satisfied when a privilege ruling involves a new legal question or is of special consequence, and district courts should not hesitate to certify an interlocutory appeal in such cases. Second, in extraordinary circumstances — i.e., when a disclosure order "amount[s] to a judicial usurpation of power or a clear abuse of discretion," or otherwise works a manifest injustice — a party may petition the court of appeals for a writ of mandamus. While these discretionary review mechanisms do not provide relief in every case, they serve as useful "safety valve[s]" for promptly correcting serious errors.

Another long-recognized option is for a party to defy a disclosure order and incur court-imposed sanctions. District courts have a range of sanctions from which to choose, including "directing that the matters embraced in the order or other designated facts be taken as established for purposes of the action," "prohibiting the disobedient party from supporting or opposing designated claims or defenses," or "striking pleadings in whole or in part." FED. RULE CIV. PROC. 37(b)(2)(i)-(iii). Such sanctions allow a party to obtain postjudgment review without having to reveal its privileged information. Alternatively, when the circumstances warrant it, a district court may hold a non-complying party in contempt. The party can then appeal directly from that ruling, at least when the contempt citation can be characterized as a criminal punishment.

These established mechanisms for appellate review not only provide assurances to clients and counsel about the security of their confidential communications; they also go a long way toward addressing Mohawk's concern that, absent collateral order appeals of adverse attorney-client privilege rulings, some litigants may experience severe hardship. . . . That a fraction of orders adverse to the attorney-client privilege may nevertheless harm individual litigants in ways that are "only imperfectly reparable" does not justify making all such orders immediately appealable as of right under § 1291.

In short, the limited benefits of applying "the blunt, categorical instrument of § 1291 collateral order appeal" to privilege-related disclosure orders simply cannot justify the likely institutional costs. Permitting parties to undertake successive, piecemeal appeals of all adverse attorney-client rulings would unduly delay the resolution of district court litigation and needlessly burden the Courts of Appeals.... Attempting to downplay such concerns, Mohawk asserts that the three Circuits in which the collateral order doctrine currently applies to adverse privilege rulings have seen only a trickle of appeals. But this may be due to the fact that the practice in all three Circuits is relatively new and not yet widely known. Were this Court to approve collateral order appeals in the attorney-client privilege context, many more litigants would likely choose that route. They would also likely seek to extend such a ruling to disclosure orders implicating many other categories of sensitive information, raising an array of line-drawing difficulties.

C

In concluding that sufficiently effective review of adverse attorney-client privilege rulings can be had without resort to the *Cohen* doctrine, we reiterate that the class of collaterally appealable orders must remain "narrow and selective in its membership." This admonition has acquired special force in recent years with the enactment of legislation designating rulemaking, "not expansion by court decision," as the preferred means for determining whether and when prejudgment orders should be immediately appealable. Specifically, Congress in 1990 amended the Rules Enabling Act to authorize this Court to adopt rules "defin[ing] when a ruling of a district court is final for the purposes of appeal under section 1291." Shortly thereafter, and along similar lines, Congress empowered this Court to "prescribe rules, in accordance with [§ 2072], to provide for an appeal of an interlocutory decision to the courts of appeals that is not otherwise provided for under [§ 1292]." These provisions, we have recognized, "warran[t] the Judiciary's full respect."

Indeed, the rulemaking process has important virtues. It draws on the collective experience of bench and bar, and it facilitates the adoption of measured, practical solutions. We expect that the combination of standard postjudgment appeals, § 1292(b) appeals, mandamus, and contempt appeals will continue to provide adequate protection to litigants ordered to disclose materials purportedly subject to the attorney-client privilege. Any further avenue for immediate appeal of such rulings should be furnished, if at all, through rulemaking, with the opportunity for full airing it provides.

* * *

In sum, we conclude that the collateral order doctrine does not extend to disclosure orders adverse to the attorney-client privilege. Effective appellate review can be had by other means....

JUSTICE THOMAS, concurring in part and concurring in the judgment.

I concur in the judgment and in Part II-C of the Court's opinion because I wholeheartedly agree that "Congress's designation of the rulemaking process as the way to define or refine when a district court ruling is 'final' and when an interlocutory order is appealable warrants the Judiciary's full respect." It is for that reason that I do not join the remainder of the Court's analysis.

The scope of federal appellate jurisdiction is a matter the Constitution expressly commits to Congress, see Art. I, § 8, cl. 9, and that Congress has addressed not only in 28 U.S.C. §§ 1291 and 1292, but also in the Rules Enabling Act amendments to which the Court refers. The Court recognizes that these amendments "designat[e] rulemaking, 'not expansion by court decision,' as the preferred means of determining whether and when prejudgment orders should be immediately appealable." Because that designation is entitled to our full respect, and because the privilege order here is not on all fours with orders we previously have held to be appealable under the collateral order doctrine, I would affirm the Eleventh Circuit's judgment on the ground that any "avenue for immediate appeal" beyond the three avenues addressed in the Court's opinion must be left to the "rulemaking process."

We need not, and in my view should not, further justify our holding by applying the *Cohen* doctrine, which prompted the rulemaking amendments in the first place. In taking this path, the Court needlessly perpetuates a judicial policy that we for many years have criticized and struggled to limit. The Court's choice of analysis is the more ironic because applying *Cohen* to the facts of this case requires the Court to reach conclusions on, and thus potentially prejudice, the very matters it says would benefit from "the collective experience of bench and bar" and the "opportunity for full airing" that rulemaking provides.

"Finality as a condition of review is an historic characteristic of federal appellate procedure" that was incorporated in the first Judiciary Act and that Congress itself has "departed from only when observance of it would practically defeat the right to any review at all." *Cohen* changed all that when it announced that a "small class" of collateral orders that do not meet the statutory definition of finality nonetheless may be immediately appealable if they satisfy certain criteria that show they are "too important to be denied review."

Cohen and the early decisions applying it allowed § 1291 appeals of interlocutory orders concerning the posting of a bond, the attachment of a vessel in admiralty, and the imposition of notice costs in a class action. As the Court's opinion notes, later decisions sought to narrow *Cohen* lest its exception to § 1291 "'swallow'" the final judgment rule. The Court has adhered to that narrowing approach, principally by raising the bar on what types of interests are "important enough" to justify collateral order appeals. As we recognized last Term, however, our attempts to contain the *Cohen* doctrine have not all been successful or persuasive. In my view, this case presents an opportunity to improve our approach.

The privilege interest at issue here is undoubtedly important, both in its own right and when compared to some of the interests (e.g., in bond and notice-cost rulings) we have held to be appealable under *Cohen*. Accordingly, the Court's *Cohen* analysis does not rest on the privilege order's relative unimportance, but instead on its effective reviewability after final judgment. Although I agree with the Court's ultimate conclusion, I see two difficulties with this approach.

First, the Court emphasizes that the alternative avenues of review it discusses (which did not prove adequate in this case) would be adequate where the privilege ruling at issue is "particularly injurious or novel." If that is right, and it seems to me that it is, then the opinion raises the question why such avenues were not also adequate to address the orders whose unusual importance or particularly injurious nature we have held *justified* immediate appeal under *Cohen*.

Second, the facts of this particular case seem in several respects to undercut the Court's conclusion that the benefits of collateral order review "cannot justify the likely institutional costs." The exercise forces the reviewing court to subordinate the realities of each case before it to generalized conclusions about the "likely" costs and benefits of allowing an exception to the final judgment rule in an entire "class of cases." The Court concedes that Congress, which holds the constitutional reins in this area, has determined that such value judgments are better left to the "collective experience of bench and bar" and the "opportunity for full airing" that rulemaking provides. This determination is entitled to our full respect, in deed as well as in word.

Accordingly, I would leave the value judgments the Court makes in its opinion to the rulemaking process, and in so doing take this opportunity to limit — effectively, predictably, and in a way we should have done long ago — the doctrine that, with a sweep of the Court's pen, subordinated what the appellate jurisdiction statute says to what the Court thinks is a good idea.

Note: The Collateral Order Doctrine

1. Under what circumstances, if any, should the collateral order doctrine be applied? Justice Thomas, in his separate opinion, indicates that the correct answer might be "never." The Court has stated that the "collateral order doctrine is best understood not as an exception to the 'final decision' rule laid down by Congress in § 1291, but as 'practical construction' of it." *See Digital Equipment Corp. v. Desktop Direct, Inc.*, 511 U.S. 863 (1992). Is the collateral order doctrine a reasonable interpretation of 28 U.S.C. § 1291 or is it simply a judge-made rule to alleviate the perceived unfairness of the "final decision" rule? Is it consistent for the Court to extol the virtues of the rulemaking process in defining the scope of "final decisions" in Part II-C of the *Mohawk* opinion, while nonetheless applying the Court-created *Cohen* test to resolve the case?

The Court has used its rulemaking authority only once to create a new class of final decisions: to allow appeals of orders granting or denying class action certification. *See* F.R.C.P. 23(f). The Court has not taken steps to define finality under 28 U.S.C. § 1291, and no proposals of that kind are currently on the agenda of the Appellate Rules Advisory Committee.

2. The majority and concurring opinions in *Mohawk* give a good picture of the current state of the collateral order doctrine. Among other things, both opinions emphasize that the Court has rejected a case-by-case approach to deciding whether an order is sufficiently "collateral" to be immediately appealable. Thus, each new precedent settles the question for "the entire category to which a claim belongs." And the range of uncertainty has been narrowed considerably from what it was a few years ago.

3. Because the Court finds that the district court's privilege-waiver order is not "effectively unreviewable on appeal from a final judgment," it does not consider the other two *Cohen* requirements. In *Cunningham v. Hamilton County, Ohio*, 527 U.S. 198 (1999), the Court addressed the requirement of separateness. The question was whether an order imposing sanctions against an attorney under Rule 37(a) of the Federal Rules of Civil Procedure is immediately appealable under § 1291. The Court held that it is not. Justice Thomas, writing for the Court, explained why the separateness requirement was not satisfied:

> We do not think . . . that appellate review of a sanctions order can remain completely separate from the merits. In *Van Cauwenberghe v. Biard*, 486 U.S. 517 (1988), for example, we held that the denial of a motion to dismiss on the ground of *forum non conveniens* was not a final decision. We reasoned that consideration of the factors underlying that decision such as "the relative ease of access to sources of proof" and "the availability of witnesses" required trial courts to "scrutinize the substance of the dispute between the parties to evaluate what proof is required, and determine whether the pieces of evidence cited by the parties are critical, or even relevant, to the plaintiff's cause of action and to any potential defenses to the action." Similarly, in *Coopers & Lybrand v. Livesay*, 437 U.S. 463 (1978), we held that a determination that an action may not be maintained as a class action also was not a final decision, noting that such a determination was enmeshed in the legal and factual aspects of the case.

> Much like the orders at issue in *Van Cauwenberghe* and *Coopers & Lybrand*, a Rule 37(a) sanctions order often will be inextricably intertwined with the merits of the action. An evaluation of the appropriateness of sanctions may require the reviewing court to inquire into the importance of the information sought or the adequacy or truthfulness of a response. . . . Some of the sanctions in this case were based on the fact that petitioner provided partial responses and objections to some of the defendants' discovery requests. To evaluate whether those sanctions were appropriate, an appellate court would have to assess the completeness of petitioner's responses. Such an inquiry would differ only marginally from an inquiry into the merits and counsels against application of the collateral order doctrine. Perhaps not every discovery sanction will be inextricably intertwined with the merits, but we have consistently eschewed a case-by-case approach to deciding whether an order is sufficiently collateral.

How would this analysis be applied to the disclosure order at issue in *Mohawk*?

4. In declining to apply the collateral order doctrine to disclosure orders relating to the attorney-client privilege, the Court in *Mohawk* focuses on the availability of four other mechanisms for reviewing "particularly injurious or novel privilege ruling[s]," including certification of an issue for appeal under 28 U.S.C. § 1292(b) and the filing of a petition for mandamus. Consider the following analysis of *Mohawk* by Erwin Chemerinsky:

> The Supreme Court outlined options available to the party seeking to protect confidentiality. But none seems realistic. Certification by district courts is relatively rare and mandamus even rarer. Advising lawyers to violate court orders and risk sanctions hardly seems a desirable approach. Nonetheless, the Court was explicit that there could be no interlocutory review of trial court orders requiring the disclosure of material allegedly covered by the attorney-client privilege.

Erwin Chemerinsky, *Court Keeps Tight Limits on Interlocutory Review*, 46 TRIAL 52, 54 (Mar. 2010). Do you think the options mentioned by the Court are viable? If Chemerinsky is right, should largely theoretical bases for review bar an immediate appeal under the collateral order doctrine?

5. A comprehensive analysis of the Court's precedents as of 2001 concluded that recent decisions "effectively preclude expansion of the doctrine." Timothy P. Glynn, *Discontent and Indiscretion: Discretionary Review of Interlocutory Orders*, 77 NOTRE DAME L. REV. 175, 212 (2001). This appears to have been an accurate prediction with respect to civil litigation; however, the Court has recognized one new category in the realm of criminal law. In *Sell v. United States*, 539 U.S. 166 (2003), the Court held that the court of appeals had jurisdiction under § 1291 to review a pretrial order requiring a federal criminal defendant to receive medication in order to render him competent to stand trial. The Court said:

> The order (1) "conclusively determine[s] the disputed question," namely, whether Sell has a legal right to avoid forced medication. The order also (2) "resolve[s] an important issue," for, as this Court's cases make clear, involuntary medical treatment raises questions of clear constitutional importance. At the same time, the basic issue—whether Sell must undergo medication against his will—is "completely separate from the merits of the action," i.e., whether Sell is guilty or innocent of the crimes charged. The issue is wholly separate as well from questions concerning trial procedures. Finally, the issue is (3) "effectively unreviewable on appeal from a final judgment." By the time of trial Sell will have undergone forced medication—the very harm that he seeks to avoid. He cannot undo that harm even if he is acquitted. Indeed, if he is acquitted, there will be no appeal through which he might obtain review. These considerations, particularly those involving the severity of the intrusion and corresponding importance of the constitutional issue, readily distinguish Sell's case from the examples raised by the dissent.

The dissent, in the passage to which the Court responded, said that the Court's analysis "effects a breathtaking expansion of appellate jurisdiction over interlocutory orders." The dissent explained:

> A trial-court order requiring the defendant to wear an electronic bracelet could be attacked as an immediate infringement of the constitutional

right to "bodily integrity"; an order refusing to allow the defendant to wear a T-shirt that says "Black Power" in front of the jury could be attacked as an immediate violation of First Amendment rights; and an order compelling testimony could be attacked as an immediate denial of Fifth Amendment rights. All these orders would be immediately appealable.

Do you agree with the Court that these examples are distinguishable?

6. Notwithstanding *Sell*, the Court has continued to underscore the narrow scope of the collateral order doctrine, emphasizing its reluctance to expand the list of immediately appealable orders. *Mohawk* is illustrative.

7. Prior to *Mohawk*, some circuits held that a *nonparty* subject to a discovery order may invoke the collateral order doctrine to obtain immediate review of a discovery order rejecting a privilege claim. *See, e.g., Dellwood Farms, Inc. v. Cargill, Inc.*, 128 F.3d 1122 (7th Cir. 1997). Do these holdings survive *Mohawk*?

B. Review of Interlocutory Orders of the District Courts

Reading the Supreme Court's opinions in cases like *Mohawk*, one could easily gain the impression that the jurisdiction of the federal courts of appeals is governed by a stringent rule of finality and that review of interlocutory orders is reserved for rare circumstances such as those that fall within the "collateral order" doctrine. This impression would be quite misleading. Although the final decision rule is certainly the norm, there are numerous situations in which interlocutory rulings of the district court can be reviewed by the court of appeals. Here we look briefly at some of the statutes and doctrines that govern the availability of such review.

[1] Appeals as of Right

Several provisions of the United States Code — not all of them in Title 28 — authorize appeals as of right from interlocutory rulings. On the criminal side of the docket, 18 U.S.C. § 3731 permits the United States to appeal in a variety of circumstances, as long as there will be no violation of the Double Jeopardy Clause. On the civil side, the Federal Arbitration Act, codified in Title 9, provides for appeals in a limited class of situations involving arbitration.

From a civil litigation perspective, however, the most important statute authorizing appeals of interlocutory orders is the one that deals with injunctions, 28 U.S.C. § 1292(a)(1). That section provides that the courts of appeals shall have jurisdiction of appeals from —

> Interlocutory orders of the district courts of the United States . . . or of the judges thereof, granting, continuing, modifying, refusing or dissolving injunctions, or refusing to dissolve or modify injunctions, except where a direct review may be had in the Supreme Court.

This language embraces preliminary as well as permanent injunctions—though not temporary restraining orders. We consider now the scope and application of 28 U.S.C. § 1292(a)(1).

Note: Appellate Review of Injunction Orders

1. The standard of review for orders involving preliminary injunctions is quite deferential. Decisions from the Ninth and Third Circuits shed light on what this standard means. In *Cooper v. Rimmer*, 379 F.3d 1029 (9th Cir. 2004), a California death row inmate filed a § 1983 action in federal district court seeking to prevent the state from executing him in accordance with California's lethal injection protocol. He argued that the method of execution violated his Eighth Amendment right to be free from cruel and unusual punishment. The district court denied Cooper's motion for a preliminary injunction, and the court of appeals affirmed. The court said:

> The district court applied the proper standard for deciding whether injunctive relief should be granted, and for determining whether the method of execution infringes the protections of the Eighth Amendment. The Eighth Amendment prohibits punishments that involve the unnecessary and wanton inflictions of pain, or that are inconsistent with evolving standards of decency that mark the progress of a maturing society. . . .

> We have previously upheld the constitutionality of lethal injection as a method of execution. . . . Cooper argues that the debate is not as seen by the district court, over whether sodium pentothal in a 5 gram dose will cause unconsciousness; instead, it is whether the protocol sufficiently assures that this will occur and that the drug will have its intended effect. However, the district court's findings are well-supported in the record. While there can be no guarantee that error will not occur, Cooper falls short of showing that he is subject to an unnecessary risk of unconstitutional pain or suffering such that his execution by lethal injection under California's protocol must be restrained.

Judge James R. Browning, concurring, added these observations about the significance of the procedural posture:

> Appellate review of the grant or denial of preliminary injunctive relief requires consideration of the merits of the underlying issue, but it does not decide them. *Southwest Voter Registration Educ. Project v. Shelley*, 344 F.3d 914, 918 (9th Cir. 2003) (en banc). To obtain such relief, "the moving party must show either (1) a combination of probable success on the merits and the possibility of irreparable injury or (2) that serious questions are raised and the balance of hardships tips in its favor." We review for abuse of discretion the district court's decision to grant or deny a preliminary injunction or temporary restraining order. "Our review is limited and deferential." We determine only whether "the district court employed the appropriate legal standards governing the issuance of a preliminary injunction, and correctly apprehended the law with respect to the issues underlying the litigation."

Here, the district court relied on the correct standards for both issuance of a preliminary injunction and the underlying constitutional issue. We determine only that the district court did not abuse its discretion in applying the law to the factual record before it. Our decision under this standard of review does not necessarily reflect our independent view of the evidence, for we are "not empowered to substitute [our] judgment" for the district court's. *Citizens to Preserve Overton Park, Inc. v. Volpe*, 401 U.S. 402, 416, (1971). If the district court's decision relied on the correct law, its grant or denial of preliminary injunctive relief "will not be reversed simply because the appellate court would have arrived at a different result had it applied the law to the facts of the case. Rather, the appellate court will reverse only if the district court abused its discretion."

Our review of the district court's merits decision — if it is appealed — will be more rigorous. Applying a *de novo* standard of review, we will assess for ourselves whether "the evolving standards of decency that mark the progress of a maturing society," *Trop v. Dulles*, 356 U.S. 86, 101 (1958), require lethal injection procedures different from those California currently employs. Our decision may not reach the same conclusion as today's, "because of the limited scope of our [current] review of the law applied by the district court and because the fully developed factual record may be materially different from that initially before the district court. . . ." Neither the district court nor the parties should read today's decision as more than a preliminary assessment of the merits.

2. Cooper's execution was ultimately stayed by the Ninth Circuit on other grounds. *See Cooper v. Woodford*, 358 F.3d 1117 (9th Cir. 2004) (en banc). Suppose that the Ninth Circuit vacates the stay and the district court enters a final judgment rejecting Cooper's challenge to the lethal injection protocol. Ordinarily, decisions of one panel of a court of appeals are binding on other panels within that circuit unless overruled by the Supreme Court. But Judge Browning seems to be saying that the decision affirming the denial of the preliminary injunction would *not* be binding in later proceedings. Is he correct?

The Third Circuit faced this question in *Pitt News v. Pappert*, 379 F.3d 96 (3d Cir. 2004). A student-run university newspaper brought suit in federal district court challenging the constitutionality of a Pennsylvania law that prohibits advertisers from paying for the dissemination of "alcoholic beverage advertising" by communications media affiliated with a university, college, or other "educational institution." The district court denied the newspaper's motion for a preliminary injunction, and a panel of the court of appeals affirmed. The panel applied a test similar to the one followed in the Ninth Circuit. Under that analysis, the court assesses:

(a) the likelihood that the plaintiff will prevail on the merits at the final hearing; (b) the extent to which the plaintiff is being irreparably harmed by the conduct complained of; (c) the extent to which the defendant will suffer irreparable harm if the preliminary injunction is issued; and (d) the public interest.

The panel held that the newspaper failed to satisfy the first prong: it did not show "a likelihood of succeeding on the merits of its claim that the enforcement of [the statute] has violated its right to free speech."

When the case returned to the district court, the parties filed cross-motions for summary judgment, and the court issued an order granting summary judgment for the defendants. The newspaper appealed once again, and the court of appeals panel began by considering whether the prior panel's resolution of the constitutional issue was binding. The court, in an opinion by then-Judge Samuel A. Alito, held that it was not. The opinion explained:

> When a panel is presented with legal issues that are related to issues previously addressed by another panel in an earlier appeal in the same case at the preliminary injunction stage, three separate rules are relevant. First, it is our Court's tradition that a panel may not overrule "a holding" of a prior panel. 3d Cir. IOP [Internal Operating Procedures] 9.1. Second, it is well established that neither this tradition nor the law-of-the-case doctrine requires a panel hearing an appeal from the entry of a final judgment to follow the legal analysis contained in a prior panel decision addressing the question whether a party that moved for preliminary injunctive relief showed a likelihood of success on the merits. Third, although a panel entertaining a preliminary injunction appeal generally decides only whether the district court abused its discretion in ruling on the request for relief and generally does not go into the merits any farther than is necessary to determine whether the moving party established a likelihood of success, a panel is not always required to take this narrow approach. If a preliminary injunction appeal presents a question of law "and the facts are established or of no controlling relevance," the panel *may* decide the merits of the claim.

> In the typical situation — where the prior panel stopped at the question of likelihood of success — the prior panel's legal analysis must be carefully considered, but it is not binding on the later panel. Indeed, particularly where important First Amendment issues are raised, the later panel has a duty, in the end, to exercise its own best judgment. On the other hand, if the first panel does not stop at the question of likelihood of success and instead addresses the merits, the later panel, in accordance with our Court's traditional practice, should regard itself as bound by the prior panel opinion.

> Here, the [prior] panel did not decide whether [the state statute] is or is not constitutional. Instead, [the] panel was careful to state only that *The Pitt News* "ha[d] not shown *a likelihood of succeeding* on the merits of its claim." (Emphasis added). Had [the] panel gone further and taken an unequivocal position on the merits, we would consider ourselves bound under the tradition expressed in IOP 9.1. But [the] panel did not take that approach.

The court then held that the statute was unconstitutional as applied to the newspaper.

3. If the Ninth Circuit were to take the approach outlined by the Third Circuit, would a later panel hearing Cooper's challenge to the lethal injection protocol be free to reach a different result from the panel that considered the denial of the preliminary injunction?

4. In many circuits, appeals from a final judgment may be heard by a different panel from the one that considered the case at the preliminary injunction stage. Do *Cooper* and *Pitt News* have any bearing on the strategies a lawyer might follow in arguing the initial appeal?

[2] Discretionary Appeals

As the preceding discussion suggests, appeals as of right from interlocutory rulings by district courts are available only in limited circumstances. Discretionary appeals are more broadly available—but the criteria are not easy to meet. Three sources of authority deserve attention.

First, the Interlocutory Appeals Act of 1958, codified as 28 U.S.C. § 1292(b), authorizes interlocutory appeals if both the district court and the court of appeals agree that an order that is not otherwise appealable deserves review. This provision is discussed briefly in the Note below.

Second, 28 U.S.C. § 1292(e) authorizes the Supreme Court to use the rule-making process of 28 U.S.C. § 2072 to provide for appeals of interlocutory decisions beyond those already permitted by § 2072 itself. Thus far, the Supreme Court has made use of this authority only once. Rule 23(f) of the Federal Rules of Civil Procedure now provides:

> A court of appeals may in its discretion permit an appeal from an order of a district court granting or denying class action certification under this rule if application is made to it within ten days after entry of the order.

A majority of the circuits have issued decisions outlining the standards that they apply in deciding whether to permit an appeal under Rule 23(f). For a useful discussion of the factors considered by the various circuits, see *Vallario v. Vandehey*, 554 F.3d 1259 (10th Cir. 2009).

Finally, appellate review of interlocutory rulings may be obtained through mandamus or other extraordinary writs. Mandamus is discussed in the *Cole* case and the Note that follows it.

Note: Discretionary Review Under § 1292(b)

In 1958, at the suggestion of the Judicial Conference of the United States, Congress added what is now 28 U.S.C. § 1292(b). That section provides:

> When a district judge, in making in a civil action an order not otherwise appealable under this section, shall be of the opinion that such order involves a controlling question of law as to which there is substantial ground for difference of opinion and that an immediate appeal from the order may

materially advance the ultimate termination of the litigation, he shall so state in writing in such order. The Court of Appeals which would have jurisdiction of an appeal of such action may thereupon, in its discretion, permit an appeal to be taken from such order, if application is made to it within ten days after the entry of the order. . . .

The Sixth Circuit's divided decision in *In re City of Memphis*, 293 F.3d 345 (6th Cir. 2002), offers some insights into the considerations that come into play in determining whether to allow an appeal under § 1292(b). Plaintiffs brought suit challenging the use of minority preferences by the city in awarding construction contracts. The city sought to use a post-enactment study as evidence to demonstrate a compelling governmental interest. The district court ruled that post-enactment evidence would not be admissible, but it certified the question for interlocutory appeal.

The panel majority held that interlocutory review was not appropriate under § 1292(b). First, the court disagreed with the district court's view that "there is substantial disagreement as to the proper role played by post-enactment evidence" in considering a challenge to a minority preference program. The court found that the issue had been resolved in the Sixth Circuit:

> Although [a circuit precedent] did not directly address the admissibility of post-enactment evidence, it held that a governmental entity must have pre-enactment evidence sufficient to justify a racially conscious statute. It also indicates that this circuit would not favor using post-enactment evidence to make that showing.

The court went on to hold the other two requirements were not met either:

> Even if we concluded that there is a substantial difference of opinion, the issue presented in this case is not a controlling legal issue. A legal issue is controlling if it could materially affect the outcome of the case. . . . An allegation of abuse of discretion on an evidentiary ruling does not create a legal issue under § 1292(b).

> Finally, resolution of the City's challenge to the district court's evidentiary ruling may not materially advance the ultimate termination of the litigation. "When litigation will be conducted in substantially the same manner regardless of [the court's] decision, the appeal cannot be said to materially advance the ultimate termination of the litigation." Under [circuit precedent,] the City must present pre-enactment evidence to show a compelling state interest. The City has pre-enactment evidence. Thus, the City will pursue its defense in substantially the same manner. If the City prevails with its pre-enactment evidence, the exclusion of post-enactment evidence will be moot. If it does not prevail, the City can then appeal on the evidentiary ruling and any other issues that may arise below.

Judge Eric Clay, dissenting, argued for a broader perspective on the "controlling question" requirement. He said:

This Court has previously recognized that the "controlling" nature of a legal question does not depend on whether its resolution will immediately dispose of the litigation. "Rather, all that must be shown in order for a question to be 'controlling' is that resolution of the issue on appeal could materially affect the outcome of the litigation in the district court." [The Wright and Miller treatise recommends] taking a practical view of the "controlling question" requirement, explaining that a question is controlling "if interlocutory reversal might save time for the district court, and time and expense for the litigants."

Under [the] characterization advanced by Wright and Miller, resolution of the admissibility of post-enactment evidence presents a controlling question inasmuch as resolving the admissibility of post-enactment evidence would dictate the course and duration of discovery in this litigation, as well as the content of any dispositive motions or trial. For example, if this Court determined on an interlocutory basis that the City of Memphis may utilize post-enactment evidence, that ruling would fundamentally shape the nature of the case presented in the district court, and would therefore have a material impact on the outcome of the litigation. In addition, upholding [the trial judge's] certification order would ultimately save the parties time and expense, by avoiding the need for additional discovery and court proceedings if our Court determined after final judgment that a decision to permit post-enactment evidence was not erroneous.

Given that the court of appeals always has discretion not to permit an interlocutory appeal, is Judge Clay's approach preferable to the majority's?

Cole v. United States District Court for the District of Idaho

United States Court of Appeals for the Ninth Circuit, 2004.

366 F.3d 813.

Before D.W. Nelson, Fisher, and Gould, Circuit Judges.

Gould, Circuit Judge.

We consider a petition for a writ of mandamus arising from a magistrate judge's sanction of disqualification imposed on petitioners' counsel by revocation of counsel's *pro hac vice* status. Petitioners demonstrate that the magistrate judge clearly erred in imposing this sanction without giving petitioners' counsel notice and an opportunity to be heard on the specific grounds for disqualification and revocation of counsel's *pro hac vice* status. But because mandamus is an extraordinary remedy and petitioners did not take advantage of an available remedy by seeking review of the magistrate judge's decision before the district court, we deny the petition.

I

The request for mandamus relief follows an order disqualifying petitioners' lead counsel, Kenneth D. Simoncini, in a case scheduled for trial. The disqualification order resolved a motion brought by the defendants (captioned here as "Real Parties in Interest") to disqualify Simoncini on grounds not relevant to this appeal.[1]

On May 2, 2003, after a hearing on the motion to disqualify, Magistrate Judge Boyle ordered the plaintiffs and Simoncini to submit affidavits for *in camera* review. The purpose of the ordered affidavits was to provide the magistrate judge with the necessary factual basis on which to rule on the disqualification motion.

Though the petitioners submitted the required affidavits on May 20, 2003, the cover letter to their submission informed the magistrate judge that Simoncini respectfully declined to submit an affidavit. On June 4, 2003, the magistrate judge ordered the three plaintiffs and counsel to state under oath the date or dates the "Conflict of Interest and Client Consent to Representation Waiver of Conflict" forms were executed.

On July 18, 2003, the magistrate judge issued the memorandum decision and order that prompted petitioners to file the mandamus petition now before us. In that decision, the magistrate judge rejected every ground advanced by the defendants to disqualify Simoncini. However, the magistrate judge decided *sua sponte* to sanction Simoncini because he had failed to provide the affidavit that he was ordered, but "declined," to submit. Citing District of Idaho Local Rule 83.5(b), governing discipline, and 18 U.S.C. § 401(3), governing contempt, the court expressed concern that Simoncini might refuse future orders, stated that Simoncini's *pro hac vice* status was a "conditional admission," and decided that it was appropriate to disqualify Simoncini and revoke his *pro hac vice* admission, in light of counsel's knowing disregard of the court's prior order.[2] The magistrate judge then so ordered.

Petitioners, who had formerly been represented by Simoncini, did not move for the magistrate judge to reconsider his order. Petitioners did not file a motion in the district court seeking reconsideration of the magistrate judge's order by the district court, which was a statutorily available remedy under 28 U.S.C. § 636(b)(1)(A). Instead, the petitioners bypassed reconsideration by the district court and immediately filed in our court the petition for a writ of mandamus. We have jurisdiction over this original action seeking a writ of mandamus pursuant to the All Writs Act, 28 U.S.C. § 1651, and we deny the petition.

II

The rule is that a writ of mandamus may be used to review the disqualification of counsel. *See Christensen v. United States Dist. Court*, 844 F.2d 694, 697 & n.5 (9th Cir.

---

1. The facts described in the petition for the writ of mandamus, in the accompanying appendix, and in the motion papers filed under seal in the court below, were sealed pursuant to an order of this court on October 21, 2003. The facts as described in this opinion derive from public sources including the non-sealed orders of the magistrate judge and the facts presented at oral argument. To the extent that our prior order granting the motion to seal might be construed to cover the rationale given by the magistrate judge for its challenged order, we lift the seal to the extent necessary to explain the expressed basis for the magistrate judge's ruling.

2. The magistrate judge noted that, rather than merely declining to comply with a court order, counsel had other options to contest the order including seeking a protective order, moving for reconsideration, or pursuing an appeal.

1988). The reason is because the harm of such disqualification cannot be corrected with an ordinary appeal. Whether a writ of mandamus should be granted is determined case-by-case, weighing the factors outlined in *Bauman v. United States Dist. Court*, 557 F.2d 650 (9th Cir. 1977). These are whether (1) the party seeking the writ has no other means, such as a direct appeal, of attaining the desired relief, (2) the petitioner will be damaged in a way not correctable on appeal, (3) the district court's order is clearly erroneous as a matter of law, (4) the order is an oft-repeated error, or manifests a persistent disregard of the federal rules, and (5) the order raises new and important problems, or issues of law of first impression. The *Bauman* factors should not be mechanically applied. Evidence showing that all the *Bauman* factors are affirmatively presented by a case does not necessarily mandate the issuance of a writ, nor does a showing of less than all, indeed of only one, necessarily mandate denial; instead, the decision whether to issue the writ is within the discretion of the court. *See Kerr v. United States Dist. Court*, 426 U.S. 394, 403 (1976).

A

The first *Bauman* factor highlights the need for mandamus to be used only when no other realistic alternative is (or was) available to a petitioner. *See, e.g., Varsic v. United States Dist. Court*, 607 F.2d 245, 251 (9th Cir. 1979). This factor is affirmatively presented in the context of a disqualification of counsel when the petition arises from the action of a district court. *See Christensen* (noting that an order disqualifying counsel is not a collateral order subject to immediate attack and that the petitioner can never obtain the relief sought, i.e., maintaining the disqualified counsel for pending litigation, through a direct appeal). Parties normally have the right to counsel of their choice, so long as the counsel satisfy required bar admissions, and it is no small thing to disqualify a counsel before trial. Absent mandamus relief, a counsel's wrongful disqualification, which cannot be immediately appealed, can cause great harm to a litigant. This harm cannot be corrected by the ordinary appellate process because that occurs after the trial has been held, when it is too late to replace the counsel. This is why the rule of *Christensen*, permitting mandamus relief after a disqualification of counsel by a district court, makes good sense.

Unlike *Christensen*, however, this case concerns a disqualification order made by a magistrate judge acting on authority delegated by, and subject to the supervision of, the district court. The defendants argue that the petitioners could have appealed the magistrate judge's order to the district court.[4]

---

4. The defendants also argue that the petitioners failed to seek certification of an interlocutory appeal under 28 U.S.C. § 1292(b). Under our established precedent, the possibility of certification does not present a bar to mandamus relief. *See Executive Software N. Am., Inc. v. United States Dist. Court*, 24 F.3d 1545, 1550 (9th Cir. 1994). Moreover, it is questionable whether certification of an interlocutory appeal on the disqualification of counsel was a permissible remedy here. 28 U.S.C. § 1292(b) allows a district judge to certify a "controlling question of law" the immediate appeal of which "may materially advance the ultimate termination of the litigation...." Courts have held that attorney disqualification motions (and orders) are collateral to the ultimate resolution of the litigation, and are thus not generally proper for certification.

Defendants' argument has force. It is uncontested that petitioners could have, but did not, move for reconsideration of the magistrate judge's ruling with the district court pursuant to 28 U.S.C. §636(b)(1)(A). The petitioners cannot now seek reconsideration of the magistrate judge's order pursuant to this statute. *See* Fed. R. Civ. P. 72(a). The *Bauman* factor assessing whether a party has "no other means" to gain the desired relief is not presented here. Petitioners had an absolute right to seek district court reconsideration of the magistrate judge's decision. Were we to ignore this simple and direct route open to petitioners for review of the disqualification order, we would be improperly placing our court, rather than the district court, in the role of supervising the magistrate judge's decisions. Petitioners had a ready remedy with the district court, but did not pursue it.

Petitioners' failure to submit this disqualification issue to the district court, where review was automatic, gravely weakens the petitioners' case for the writ of mandamus. The need to show the lack of an available remedy absent a writ of mandamus goes to the heart of this extraordinary remedy which should be sparingly employed. In the ordinary course, the district courts, and not the courts of appeals, are to be called on, in the first instance, to correct any clear error in the decision of a magistrate judge on non-dispositive matters, for this is the role that Congress has created for district courts.[8]

A consideration of extra-circuit case law reinforces our conclusion. In *Califano v. Moynahan*, 596 F.2d 1320 (6th Cir. 1979), the Sixth Circuit addressed a petition for a writ of mandamus to direct the district court to rescind a permanent order directing social security disability appeals to a magistrate judge. *Califano* required that "the party seeking issuance of the writ have no other adequate means to attain the relief he desires. . . ." *Id.* (quoting *Kerr*, 426 U.S. at 403). The Sixth Circuit noted that, pursuant to 28 U.S.C. §636(b)(1)(A), the petitioner could have, but did not, move for reconsideration of the decision of the magistrate judge. It held that the argument advanced on appeal via the mandamus petition "was the type of argument which ought to have been made to the district court. . . . We decline to employ the extraordinary remedy of mandamus to require a district judge to do that which he was never asked to do in a proper way in the first place." . . .

[In a footnote the Court added:] The only authority perhaps weighing in another direction is the Third Circuit case, *In re U.S. Healthcare*, 159 F.3d 142 (3rd Cir. 1998). There, the magistrate judge had remanded a case to state court under the theory that the remand was a non-dispositive order. This conclusion was based on the district court's local rule. The petitioners sought a writ of mandamus to challenge the remand without first appealing the question to the district court. [The Third Circuit] concluded that this failure was no bar because the petitioner had "no realistic remedy other

---

8. Of course, our conclusion, which relies on the ability of the petitioners to seek review under 28 U.S.C. §636(b)(1)(A), does not apply in cases in which a magistrate judge is exercising "civil jurisdiction" over a case based on the consent of the parties. *See* 28 U.S.C. §636(c). In such a case, there is no route of appeal of the magistrate judge's decision through the district court because the magistrate judge is acting as a district court.

than to seek a writ of mandamus in this court. . . ." The court held that district court review was "inadequa[te]" because the existence of the local rule . . . made it "seem[ ] unlikely that the district court would have granted relief on the ground that the magistrate judge did not have jurisdiction to issue an order of remand." . . . The Third Circuit case is distinguishable from the *Califano* line [on the ground that] a party need not seek district court reconsideration if appeal to the district court would have been futile.

We hold as a general rule that if a petitioner for a writ of mandamus does not seek reconsideration of a magistrate judge's order with the district court pursuant to 28 U.S.C. §636(b)(1)(A), then we will find the first *Bauman* factor has not been affirmatively presented. This general rule may give way to an exception if the petitioner can convincingly demonstrate that reconsideration by the district court would have been futile. Apart from this necessarily narrow exception, failure to seek reconsideration of a magistrate judge's non-dispositive ruling by statutory appeal to the district court under 28 U.S.C. §636(b)(1)(A) will preclude a finding that the first *Bauman* factor is shown, which, in turn, will weigh heavily against the granting of the writ.

At oral argument, petitioners argued that appeal to the district court was futile because the district court assigned the attorney disqualification motion to the magistrate judge. The petitioners argue to us that this assignment implied that the district court was disinterested in the merits of the underlying disqualification motion. That argument has no merit in light of the district court's ability to assign nearly any non-dispositive motion to a magistrate judge, 28 U.S.C. §636(b)(1)(A), and the district court's corresponding statutory duty to reconsider for correction of clear error. The petitioners' argument falls far short of the convincing evidence needed to invoke the futility exception. We hold that the first *Bauman* factor is not presented here, counseling against granting the writ.

B

We next address the second *Bauman* factor: whether petitioners will be damaged in a way not correctable through ordinary appeal. This factor is readily shown under the authority of *Christensen* (holding that attorney disqualification satisfies the second *Bauman* factor). The damage in this case includes the petitioners' loss of a lead counsel who has been on the case for more than six years. And if Simoncini's knowledge could be gained by another counsel, another attorney still may not gain the same quality of attorney-client relationship and rapport that Simoncini evidently had with petitioners. Except for compelling reasons, such as necessary bar admissions, clients should be permitted to have the counsel of their choice. A lost choice of counsel at trial cannot be remedied on direct appeal. These same concerns were expressed in *Christensen*. [We said:] "Theoretically, Christensen could appeal the disqualification of his counsel after trial. He could not, however, obtain the desired relief on direct appeal because he seeks to be represented by his chosen counsel *at trial*. Once a new attorney is brought in, the effect of the order is irreversible."

C

We next analyze the third *Bauman* factor, whether there was clear error. Absence of this factor is often dispositive of the petition. We have said that clear error is, if not necessary, a "highly significant" factor.

This factor weighs on the petitioners' side of the scale. Though we sympathize with the magistrate judge's concern that counsel should not have disregarded a court order, and had alternate ways to challenge the order other than "declin[ing]" to submit the affidavit, nonetheless the process that was due demanded something more. The magistrate judge clearly erred by not affording procedural due process when imposing the sanction on Simoncini, who was not given notice that he might lose representation over his refusal to file an ordered affidavit, and was not given an opportunity to present argument. Ninth Circuit law does not permit a summary disqualification of counsel; for the court to sanction an attorney, procedural due process requires notice and an opportunity to be heard. . . . The disqualification of Simoncini and revocation of his *pro hac vice* status is, as the magistrate judge conceded, a sanction.

The magistrate judge doubtless felt that counsel was on general notice that representation and disqualification were at issue, but the magistrate judge gave no specific notice to Simoncini that the court was considering a sanction for Simoncini's failure to submit the required affidavit, nor that counsel might be disqualified on that ground rather than on the theories asserted by the defendants. . . .

. . . The magistrate judge had cause to consider and perhaps impose the sanction given, but it was clear error for the magistrate judge to order the sanction without providing requisite notice and opportunity to respond. Because the procedural error was so clear, we conclude that the third *Bauman* factor points strongly in favor of granting the petition.

III

Although we have concluded that the third *Bauman* factor favors granting the petition, even the undoubted strength of this factor is undermined by the petitioners' failure to seek reconsideration in the district court. Important to our determination is the Supreme Court's guidance that "the party seeking issuance of the writ [of mandamus] have no other adequate means to attain the relief he [or she] desires." *Kerr*. Mandamus is an extraordinary writ to be sparingly used and the petitioners must demonstrate an entitlement to mandamus relief that is "clear and indisputable." *Will v. Calvert Fire Ins. Co.*, 437 U.S. 655, 662 (1978). Petitioners, in this case, had a ready route and were obligated to travel it in seeking reconsideration before the district court. That petitioners' did not avail themselves of review in the district court strongly counsels against our issuing the writ. When review of a decision of a magistrate judge is available as a matter of right by motion for reconsideration before a district court, the opportunity should be taken before extraordinary review by mandamus is sought. The availability of relief that was forgone by the petitioners and a careful consideration of all the other *Bauman* factors[13] presented do not in sum present a compelling case for the issuance of a writ of mandamus. We will not so lightly interfere in the delicate relationship between the district courts and magistrate judges, where a party has deliberately bypassed a customary means of review. To that end, despite the clear error of the magistrate judge, the availability of relief that was forgone shows that the petitioners' asserted right to mandamus relief is not "clear and indisputable." The petitioners have not carried their burden, and we thus conclude that we should deny, and we hereby deny, the petition for the writ of mandamus.[14]

Note: Mandamus and Appellate Review

1. The court holds that the magistrate judge clearly erred in disqualifying counsel without adequate notice, but it refuses to issue the writ because counsel did not seek review of the magistrate judge's order by the district judge. Can you see any tactical reason why review was not sought, or is this just an example of attorney error?

2. As the court emphasizes, mandamus is "an extraordinary writ to be sparingly used." But the higher the stakes, the more likely it is that the writ will be available. A good illustration is *Cheney v. United States District Court for the District of Columbia*, 542 U.S. 367 (2004). The case arose when the district court entered discovery orders directing the Vice President and other senior officials in the Executive Branch to produce information about a task force established to make recommendations to the President on policies relating to energy. The Government sought a writ of mandamus in the court of appeals asking the court to vacate the discovery orders. The court of appeals declined to issue the writ on the ground that alternative avenues of relief remained available. Specifically, the court said that the Government would have to assert executive privilege if it wanted to guard against intrusion into the President's prerogatives.

The Supreme Court held that the court of appeals erred in concluding it lacked authority to issue mandamus because the Government could protect its rights by asserting executive privilege in the district court. The Court said:

> Were the Vice President not a party in the case, the argument that the Court of Appeals should have entertained an action in mandamus, notwithstanding the District Court's denial of the motion for certification, might present different considerations. Here, however, the Vice President and his co-members on the [energy task force] are the subjects of the discovery

---

13. The fourth factor, oft-repeated error or persistent disregard of the federal rules, does not apply because there is no evidence that this error has been made more than once. Nor has the magistrate judge repeatedly refused to reconsider the disqualification order.

14. The petitioners cannot now seek reconsideration of the magistrate judge's order pursuant to 28 U.S.C. § 636(b)(1)(A). *See* Fed. R. Civ. P. 72(a). However, our rejection of the requested mandamus relief is not intended to prohibit the district court from reconsidering *sua sponte* the magistrate judge's order disqualifying counsel. *See* D. Id. L. Civ. R. 72.1(b)(1) (stating that the district court may "consider sua sponte any [magistrate judge's] order found to be clearly erroneous or contrary to law."). We express no view whether the district court should *sua sponte* reconsider the disqualification; we only note that it is permissible.

orders. The mandamus petition alleges that the orders threaten "substantial intrusions on the process by which those in closest operational proximity to the President advise the President." These facts and allegations remove this case from the category of ordinary discovery orders where interlocutory appellate review is unavailable, through mandamus or otherwise. . . .

[The] public interest requires that a coequal branch of Government "afford Presidential confidentiality the greatest protection consistent with the fair administration of justice" and give recognition to the paramount necessity of protecting the Executive Branch from vexatious litigation that might distract it from the energetic performance of its constitutional duties. These separation-of-powers considerations should inform a court of appeals' evaluation of a mandamus petition involving the President or the Vice President. Accepted mandamus standards are broad enough to allow a court of appeals to prevent a lower court from interfering with a coequal branch's ability to discharge its constitutional responsibilities.

However, the Supreme Court declined to direct the court of appeals to issue the writ against the district court. The Court explained:

[This] is not a case where, after having considered the issues, the Court of Appeals abused its discretion by failing to issue the writ. Instead, the Court of Appeals, relying on its mistaken reading of [Supreme Court precedent], prematurely terminated its inquiry after the Government refused to assert privilege and did so without even reaching the weighty separation-of-powers objections raised in the case, much less exercised its discretion to determine whether "the writ is appropriate under the circumstances." Because the issuance of the writ is a matter vested in the discretion of the court to which the petition is made, and because this Court is not presented with an original writ of mandamus, we leave to the Court of Appeals to address the parties' arguments. . . .

3. An important use of mandamus is to challenge a judge's refusal to recuse himself or herself under 28 U.S.C. § 455(a). That statute provides: "Any justice, judge, or magistrate judge of the United States shall disqualify himself in any proceeding in which his impartiality might reasonably be questioned." (The statute also sets forth some specific situations in which disqualification is required.)

A prominent example is *In re Boston's Children First*, 244 F.3d 164 (1st Cir. 2001). The mandamus proceeding arose out of a suit challenging Boston's elementary school student assignment process on the ground of racial discrimination. A newspaper article compared the trial judge's handling of the school case with her actions in another class action suit. After the publication of the article, the trial judge talked to a reporter over the telephone and said that the school case was "more complex." A follow-up article quoted her comments.

On the basis of the comments in the telephone interview, the plaintiffs in the school case moved that the judge recuse herself because her "impartiality might reasonably be questioned." The trial judge denied the motion, and the plaintiffs filed a writ of mandamus in the court of appeals. The court of appeals began by making clear that the plaintiffs' burden was a heavy one:

> [Disqualification is] appropriate only when the charge is supported by a factual basis, and when the facts asserted "provide what an objective, knowledgeable member of the public would find to be a reasonable basis for doubting the judge's impartiality." [We] allow district court judges a "range of discretion" in the decision not to recuse. . . .

> Moreover, a petition for a writ of mandamus raises additional hurdles for the party seeking recusal. We have held that at least "when the issue of partiality has been broadly publicized, and the claim of bias cannot be labeled as frivolous," judicial disqualification may be one of the "unusual situations" appropriate for the writ. Even when such an unusual situation exists, however, we have counseled that the jurisprudence of mandamus requires that "an applicant for the writ . . . show both that there is a clear entitlement to the relief requested, and that irreparable harm will likely occur if the writ is withheld." Mandamus thus requires "a case not merely close to the line, but clearly over it."

The court found that this was one of the rare cases that met the standard:

> Here, a reasonable person might interpret Judge Gertner's comments as a preview of a ruling on the merits of petitioner's motion for class certification, despite the fact that defendants had not yet filed a response to that motion. . . . Whether counsel for petitioners misrepresented the facts or not [in comments quoted in the first newspaper article] is irrelevant: the issue here is whether a reasonable person could have interpreted Judge Gertner's comments as doing more than correcting those misrepresentations and creating an appearance of partiality. We feel that, on these facts, a reasonable person could do so.

The court therefore granted the writ of mandamus. The trial judge then filed a petition for rehearing en banc. The court denied the motion, but added this statement:

> Those active judges who are not members of the panel are currently of the view that, even if the district court's statement to the reporter comprised a comment on the merits, it does not create an appearance of partiality such as to require mandatory recusal under 28 U.S.C. § 455(a).

Problem: Finality, Mandamus, and the Political Question Doctrine

In 2008, eleven villagers from the Middle Eastern country of Ardistan filed suit in federal district court for the District of Oceana against MegaOil Corp., the largest petroleum company in the United States. The villagers alleged that MegaOil's security forces in Ardistan committed murder, torture, sexual assault, battery, false imprisonment, and numerous other torts against them and their families. These security forces, according to the villagers' complaint, consisted entirely of Ardistani military personnel, but the soldiers were paid, outfitted by, and under the direct control of MegaOil.

In response, MegaOil moved to dismiss the villagers' claims, arguing that because the alleged events involved the Ardistani military, and because Ardistan is a vital ally of the United States in the war on terrorism, the case presented a nonjusticiable political question. In support of its position, MegaOil proffered a letter from the U.S. State Department expressing its concern that the lawsuit could harm U.S. relations with Ardistan as well as discourage international investment in the country. In the State Department's view, the lawsuit "could impair cooperation with the U.S. across the full spectrum of diplomatic initiatives, including counterterrorism, military and police reform, and economic and judicial reform." However, the letter also indicated that the effect of the lawsuit could "not be determined with certainty" because the potential damage to U.S.-Ardistani relations would depend on the eventual outcome of the suit.

The district court denied MegaOil's motion to dismiss, but it did issue a protective order giving Ardistan an effective veto over any documents that MegaOil would be required to produce. MegaOil filed an immediate appeal seeking reversal of the district court's denial of the motion to dismiss. In the alternative, MegaOil asked the Court of Appeals to treat its appeal as a petition for a writ of mandamus directing the district court to dismiss the case.

Does the Court of Appeals have jurisdiction over MegaOil's appeal and, if so, on the basis of what statute? If the court does not have jurisdiction to consider the appeal, is review available via a writ of mandamus? If it is, should the court grant the writ?

Part Seven

The Constitutional
Framework Revisited

Chapter 19

Congressional Power to Curtail the Jurisdiction of the Federal Courts

In the preceding chapters, we have examined the many and varied jurisdictional arrangements that Congress has legislated to implement Article III of the Constitution. Three generalizations stand out.

First, Congress has never vested the full measure of the "judicial power of the United States" that Article III delineates. For example, today as in 1789, "controversies . . . between citizens of different states" can be heard in federal court only if the amount in controversy exceeds a designated sum. Judicial interpretations, such as the complete diversity requirement, have brought the allocation even further below the constitutional maximum.

Second, the dominant trend has been to expand the jurisdiction of the federal courts. Thus, from 1789 to 1914, the Supreme Court could review state-court judgments only if the state court had rejected the right or immunity asserted under federal law; after 1914, state-court judgments were reviewable even if the state court had upheld the federal claim. Until 1875, cases "arising under" federal law could be litigated in federal court only if a special statute conferred jurisdiction; after 1875, federal courts could hear all such cases as long as they involved a minimum amount in controversy. And in 1980 the amount in controversy requirement was eliminated.

Third, notwithstanding the dominant trend, from time to time Congress has cut back on the scope of federal jurisdiction. For example, laws passed in 1915 and 1925 overruled a Supreme Court decision of 1885 that allowed federally chartered corporations to remove suits to federal courts on the ground that they were cases "arising under" federal law. On five occasions Congress has increased the minimum amount in controversy for diversity cases.

We turn now to the question: what limits does the Constitution place on the power of Congress to curtail the jurisdiction of the federal courts?

As a practical matter, this question gives rise to controversy only when Congress acts—or considers acting—in response to particular judicial decisions. When Congress denied federally chartered corporations the right they had enjoyed for more than a third of a century to remove their cases to federal court, no one seriously argued that this was unconstitutional. Nor would anyone contend that Congress oversteps its authority when it raises the jurisdictional amount for diversity cases or prohibits the removal of suits under the Federal Employers Liability Act.

Now consider some bills that were introduced in the 108th Congress (2003–2004). (Some of these measures have been reintroduced in later Congresses; others have not.)

- The "Life-Protecting Judicial Limitation Act of 2003," H.R. 1546, provided that the district courts of the United States "shall not have jurisdiction to hear or determine any abortion-related case."

- The "Pledge Protection Act of 2003," H.R. 2028 (as introduced), provided: "No court established by Act of Congress shall have jurisdiction to hear or determine any claim that the recitation of the Pledge of Allegiance . . . violates the [First Amendment]. A modified version of this bill was passed by the House in September 2004. It is the subject of a Problem at the end of this chapter.

- The "Marriage Protection Act of 2003," H.R. 3313 (as introduced), provided: "No court created by Act of Congress shall have any jurisdiction, and the Supreme Court shall have no appellate jurisdiction, to hear or determine any question pertaining to the interpretation of [the laws enacted as part of the Defense of Marriage Act of 1996]." A modified version of this bill was passed by the House in July 2004. It is discussed in a Note later in this section.

- The "Constitution Restoration Act of 2004," H.R. 3799, provided that neither the Supreme Court nor the district court would have jurisdiction over "any matter to the extent that relief is sought against an element of Federal, State, or local government, or against an officer of Federal, State, or local government (whether or not acting in official personal capacity), by reason of that element's or officer's acknowledgment of God as the sovereign source of law, liberty, or government."

Does the Constitution allow Congress to limit federal-court jurisdiction in the way these bills would do? That is an open question.

We shall consider first the scope of Congress's power over the appellate jurisdiction of the Supreme Court, and then the extent of Congress's power to curtail the jurisdiction of the lower federal courts. Chapter 20 considers a related topic: the power of Congress to control decision-making by federal (and state) judges. In Chapter 21 we examine Congress's power to vest jurisdiction over cases and controversies in courts that are not Article III courts and judges who do not have Article III protections.

A. The Appellate Jurisdiction of the Supreme Court

To give concreteness to the debate over Congress's power to curtail the appellate jurisdiction of the Supreme Court, it is useful to consider a specific piece of legislation. H.R. 3799, the proposed Constitution Restoration Act of 2004, would add a new section to Chapter 81 of the Judicial Code, the chapter that defines the jurisdiction of the Supreme Court. Section 1260 would provide:

> Notwithstanding any other provision of this chapter, the Supreme Court shall not have jurisdiction to review, by appeal, writ of certiorari, or

otherwise, any matter to the extent that relief is sought against an element of Federal, State, or local government, or against an officer of Federal, State, or local government (whether or not acting in official personal capacity), by reason of that element's or officer's acknowledgement of God as the sovereign source of law, liberty, or government.

As the wording of the provision might suggest, the legislation has been proposed by members of Congress who disagree with court decisions interpreting the Establishment Clause, particularly those holding that the Constitution is violated by the display of the Ten Commandments in courthouses and other public places.

Is the proposed section 1260 constitutional? The argument that it is relies heavily on the language and structure of Article III section 2. The first sentence of section 2 defines the "judicial power of the United States" by listing nine categories of "Cases" and "Controversies." The second sentence provides that in two of those classes of cases—"Cases affecting Ambassadors, other public Ministers and Consuls, and those in which a State shall be Party"—the Supreme Court shall have original jurisdiction. Article III continues: "In all the other Cases before mentioned, the supreme Court shall have appellate Jurisdiction, both as to Law and Fact, with such Exceptions, and under such Regulations as the Congress shall make."

The final clause thus authorizes Congress to make "Exceptions" to the Supreme Court's appellate jurisdiction. Nothing in Article III limits that authorization. The proposed section 1260 would simply create an "exception" to the grants of appellate jurisdiction in sections 1254 and 1257. Therefore it is constitutional.

So goes the argument. But perhaps the matter is not so simple. We look first at what the Supreme Court has had to say about the "Exceptions and Regulations" clause, then at some of the academic commentary.

Ex Parte McCardle

Supreme Court of the United States, 1869.

7 Wall. (74 U.S.) 506.

Appeal from the Circuit Court for the Southern District of Mississippi.

[*Editorial note*. The statement of facts that precedes the opinion is by John W. Wallace, the Reporter of Decisions. It conveys a sense of the drama that surrounded the decision, but not all of the relevant background. Material in brackets has been added by the editor.]

The case was this:

... Congress, on the 5th February, 1867, by "An act to amend an act to establish the judicial courts of the United States, approved September 24, 1789," provided that the several courts of the United States, and the several justices and judges of such courts, within their respective jurisdiction, in addition to the authority already conferred by law, should have power to grant writs of *habeas corpus* in all cases where any person may be restrained of his or her liberty in violation of the Constitution, or of any treaty or law of the United States. And that, from the final decision of any judge, justice, or court inferior to the Circuit Court, appeal might be taken to the Circuit Court of the United States for the district in which the cause was heard, and *from the judgment of the said Circuit Court to the Supreme Court of the United States.* [This was section 1 of the Act. Section 2 reenacted, with modifications, section 25 of the Judiciary Act of 1789. Section 2 is the provision that came before the Court in *Murdock v. City of Memphis* (Chapter 4).]

This statute being in force, one McCardle, alleging unlawful restraint by military force, preferred a petition in the court below, for the writ of *habeas corpus.*

The writ was issued, and a return was made by the military commander, admitting the restraint, but denying that it was unlawful.

It appeared that the petitioner was not in the military service of the United States, but was held in custody by military authority for trial before a military commission, upon charges founded upon the publication of articles alleged to be incendiary and libellous, in a newspaper of which he was editor. The custody was alleged to be under the authority of certain acts of Congress.

[The principal Act of Congress invoked by the military commander to support the legality of the detention was the Military Reconstruction Act of March 2, 1867. This law divided the ten "rebel States" of the South into "military districts" that were "subject to the military authority of the United States." The commanding officer of each district was given the authority "to organize military commissions or tribunals" to try "offenders," including "all disturbers of the public peace and criminals."

[McCardle was the editor of the *Vicksburg* (Mississippi) *Times.* He had written and published several editorials attacking Reconstruction in harsh language. On the basis of those editorials, he was charged with disturbing the peace, inciting to insurrection and disorder, libel, and impeding reconstruction. McCardle insisted that trial by a military commission would violate his constitutional rights. He also challenged the constitutionality of the Reconstruction Act itself.]

Upon the hearing, the petitioner was remanded to the military custody; but, upon his prayer, an appeal was allowed him to this court, and upon filing the usual appeal-bond, for costs, he was admitted to bail upon recognizance, with sureties, conditioned for his future appearance in the Circuit Court, to abide by and perform the final judgment of this court. The appeal was taken under the above-mentioned act of February 5, 1867.

A motion to dismiss this appeal was made at the last term, and, after argument, was denied. [The reference is to *Ex Parte McCardle*, 6 Wall. (73 U.S.) 318 (1868). This decision will be referred to as *McCardle I.*]

Subsequently, on the 2d, 3d, 4th, and 9th March [1868], the case was argued very thoroughly and ably upon the merits, and was taken under advisement. While it was thus held, and before conference in regard to the decision proper to be made, an act was passed by Congress,[2] returned with objections by the President, and, on the 27th March, repassed by the constitutional majority, the second section of which was as follows:

> *And be it further enacted,* That so much of the act approved February 5, 1867, entitled "An act to amend an act to establish the judicial courts of the United States, approved September 24, 1789," as authorized an appeal from the judgment of the Circuit Court to the Supreme Court of the United States, or the exercise of any such jurisdiction by said Supreme Court, on appeals which have been, or may hereafter be taken, be, and the same is hereby repealed.

The attention of the court was directed to this statute at the last term, but counsel having expressed a desire to be heard in argument upon its effect, and the Chief Justice being detained from his place here, by his duties in the Court of Impeachment, the cause was continued under advisement. Argument was now heard upon the effect of the repealing act.

The CHIEF JUSTICE delivered the opinion of the court.

The first question necessarily is that of jurisdiction; for, if the act of March, 1868, takes away the jurisdiction defined by the act of February, 1867, it is useless, if not improper, to enter into any discussion of other questions.

It is quite true, as was argued by the counsel for the petitioner, that the appellate jurisdiction of this court is not derived from acts of Congress. It is, strictly speaking, conferred by the Constitution. But it is conferred "with such exceptions and under such regulations as Congress shall make."

It is unnecessary to consider whether, if Congress had made no exceptions and no regulations, this court might not have exercised general appellate jurisdiction under rules prescribed by itself. For among the earliest acts of the first Congress, at its first session, was the act of September 24th, 1789, to establish the judicial courts of the United States. That act provided for the organization of this court, and prescribed regulations for the exercise of its jurisdiction.

The source of that jurisdiction, and the limitations of it by the Constitution and by statute, have been on several occasions subjects of consideration here. In the case of *Durousseau v. The United States*, 6 Cranch, 312, particularly, the whole matter was carefully examined, and the court held, that while "the appellate powers of this court are not given by the judicial act, but are given by the Constitution," they are, nevertheless, "limited and regulated by that act, and by such other acts as have been passed on the subject." The court said, further, that the judicial act was an exercise of the power given by the Constitution to Congress "of making exceptions to the appellate jurisdiction of the Supreme Court." "They have described affirmatively," said the court, "its jurisdiction, and this affirmative description has been understood to imply a negation of the exercise of such appellate power as is not comprehended within it."

---

2. Act of March 27, 1868, 15 Stat. at Large, 44.

The principle that the affirmation of appellate jurisdiction implies the negation of all such jurisdiction not affirmed having been thus established, it was an almost necessary consequence that acts of Congress, providing for the exercise of jurisdiction, should come to be spoken of as acts granting jurisdiction, and not as acts making exceptions to the constitutional grant of it.

The exception to appellate jurisdiction in the case before us, however, is not an inference from the affirmation of other appellate jurisdiction. It is made in terms. The provision of the act of 1867, affirming the appellate jurisdiction of this court in cases of *habeas corpus* is expressly repealed. It is hardly possible to imagine a plainer instance of positive exception.

We are not at liberty to inquire into the motives of the legislature. We can only examine into its power under the Constitution; and the power to make exceptions to the appellate jurisdiction of this court is given by express words.

What, then, is the effect of the repealing act upon the case before us? We cannot doubt as to this. Without jurisdiction the court cannot proceed at all in any cause. Jurisdiction is power to declare the law, and when it ceases to exist, the only function remaining to the court is that of announcing the fact and dismissing the cause. And this is not less clear upon authority than upon principle.

Several cases were cited by the counsel for the petitioner in support of the position that jurisdiction of this case is not affected by the repealing act. But none of them, in our judgment, afford any support to it. They are all cases of the exercise of judicial power by the legislature, or of legislative interference with courts in the exercising of continuing jurisdiction.

On the other hand, the general rule, supported by the best elementary writers, is, that "when an act of the legislature is repealed, it must be considered, except as to transactions past and closed, as if it never existed." And the effect of repealing acts upon suits under acts repealed, has been determined by the adjudications of this court. In [cases decided in 1852 and 1867] it was held that no judgment could be rendered in a suit after the repeal of the act under which it was brought and prosecuted.

It is quite clear, therefore, that this court cannot proceed to pronounce judgment in this case, for it has no longer jurisdiction of the appeal; and judicial duty is not less fitly performed by declining ungranted jurisdiction than in exercising firmly that which the Constitution and the laws confer.

Counsel seem to have supposed, if effect be given to the repealing act in question, that the whole appellate power of the court, in cases of *habeas corpus*, is denied. But this is an error. The act of 1868 does not except from that jurisdiction any cases but appeals from Circuit Courts under the act of 1867. It does not affect the jurisdiction which was previously exercised. [Here the Court cited *McCardle I.*]

The appeal of the petitioner in this case must be

Dismissed for want of jurisdiction.

Note: The Implications of Ex Parte McCardle

1. The case of *Ex Parte McCardle* came to the Supreme Court at a time of national crisis. The Civil War had ended only two years earlier. Vice President Andrew Johnson, a Southern Democrat, had succeeded to the Presidency after the assassination of Abraham Lincoln. By 1867 he was locked in a bitter struggle with the Republican-controlled Congress over the direction of Reconstruction. In February 1868 — one week after the Court denied the motion to dismiss in *McCardle I* — the House voted to impeach the President. The impeachment trial began in the Senate on March 5, with Chief Justice Chase presiding. On May 16, the prosecutors fell one vote short of the two-thirds majority required for conviction.

Simultaneously with the impeachment proceedings, Congress sought to abort McCardle's appeal from the circuit court's denial of habeas corpus. Congress did not want the Supreme Court to consider the constitutionality of the Reconstruction Acts. The President vetoed the repealing legislation, but, as the Reporter explains, "the bill was repassed by the constitutional majority."

The stage was thus set for a confrontation between Congress and the Supreme Court. And Chief Justice Chase later told a friend, "I may say to you that if the merits of the *McCardle* Case had been decided the Court would doubtless have held that his imprisonment for trial before a military commission was illegal."[1] But the confrontation did not occur.

In that era, the Supreme Court term began in December. The Court adjourned its December 1867 term in April 1868, and it did not take up the *McCardle* case again until March 1869. By that time, President Johnson had left office, and there was no longer any threat to Congressional Reconstruction. As for McCardle, he had been released from custody pending appeal, and it appears that the military authority no longer had any interest in imprisoning him.

A concise account of the background, with some commentary on its implications for the significance of the Supreme Court decision, can be found in William W. Van Alstyne, *A Critical Guide to* Ex Parte McCardle, 15 ARIZ. L. REV. 229 (1973).

2. The opinion in *McCardle* acknowledges that the appellate jurisdiction of the Supreme Court "is not derived from acts of Congress"; rather, it is conferred by the Constitution itself. But the Court goes on to emphasize that when Congress affirmatively vests appellate jurisdiction in the Supreme Court, this is understood "to imply a negation of the exercise of such appellate power as is not comprehended within it." This point was established by Chief Justice Marshall's decision in *Durousseau v. United States*, 6 Cranch (10 U.S.) 312 (1810); it continues to be the law today. Does it make a difference in determining the constitutionality of limitations on Supreme Court jurisdiction such as those contained in the Marriage Protection Act and the Constitution Restoration Act?

---

1. *See* CHARLES E. FAIRMAN, RECONSTRUCTION AND REUNION 1986–88, Part One, at 494 (1971).

3. Does the opinion in *McCardle* eliminate any possibility of challenging laws that remove particular classes of cases from the Supreme Court's appellate jurisdiction? Note that in the final paragraph of the opinion, the Court says:

> Counsel seem to have supposed, if effect be given to the repealing act in question, that the whole appellate power of the court, in cases of habeas corpus, is denied. But this is an error. The act of 1868 does not except from that jurisdiction any cases but appeals from Circuit Courts under the act of 1867. It does not affect the jurisdiction which was previously exercised.

The Court then cites *McCardle I*. In that opinion the Court discussed the history of federal habeas corpus legislation and noted that even before the 1867 Act, "this court exercised appellate jurisdiction over the action of inferior courts by *habeas corpus*." The Court cited two decisions of the Marshall Court applying section 14 of the Judiciary Act of 1789. It acknowledged that this mode of appellate review "was attended by some inconvenience and embarrassment. It was necessary to use the writ of *certiorari* in addition to the writ of *habeas corpus*, and there was no regulated and established practice for the guidance of parties invoking the jurisdiction." But the preexisting law did allow for appellate review in habeas cases.

Was the Court in *McCardle II* simply seeking to assuage concerns about the consequences of its decision dismissing the appeal in that case? Or was the Court implying that if the alternate channel of review did not exist, the decision in *McCardle II* might have been different?

4. Only a few months after the decision in *McCardle II*, the Court made clear that it meant what it said in the final paragraph of the opinion. In *Ex Parte Yerger*, 8 Wall. (75 U.S.) 85 (1869), the Court confronted another case in which a newspaper editor was prosecuted by military authorities under the Military Reconstruction Act. This time the offense was murder.

The Circuit Court dismissed Yerger's habeas petition. Yerger "asked for a writ of certiorari [and] a writ of habeas corpus" from the Supreme Court. The Government argued that the Court had no jurisdiction to hear the case, but the Court disagreed. The opinion proceeded in two steps. The Court began by reaffirming previous decisions that found appellate jurisdiction in section 14 of the Judiciary Act of 1789. The Court said:

> [In] all cases where a Circuit Court of the United States has, in the exercise of its original jurisdiction, caused a prisoner to be brought before it, and has, after inquiring into the cause of detention, remanded him to the custody from which he was taken, this court, in the exercise of its appellate jurisdiction, may, by the writ of *habeas corpus*, aided by the writ of *certiorari*, revise the decision of the Circuit Court, and if it be found unwarranted by law, relieve the prisoner from the unlawful restraint to which he has been remanded.

The next question was whether the Act of Mar. 27, 1868—the statute that aborted the proceedings in *McCardle II*—"takes away or affects the appellate jurisdiction of this court under the Constitution and the acts of Congress prior to 1867." The Court said it did not. The opinion explained:

> The effect of the act was to oust the court of its jurisdiction of the particular case then before it on appeal, and it is not to be doubted that such was the effect intended. Nor will it be questioned that legislation of this character is unusual and hardly to be justified except upon some imperious public exigency.

> It was, doubtless, within the constitutional discretion of Congress to determine whether such an exigency existed; but it is not to be presumed that an act, passed under such circumstances, was intended to have any further effect than that plainly apparent from its terms. . . .

> [The words of the act] are not of doubtful interpretation. They repeal only so much of the act of 1867 as authorized appeals, or the exercise of appellate jurisdiction by this court. They affected only appeals and appellate jurisdiction authorized by that act. They do not purport to touch the appellate jurisdiction conferred by the Constitution, or to except from it any cases not excepted by the act of 1789. They reach no act except the act of 1867. . . .

> Our conclusion is, that none of the acts prior to 1867, authorizing this court to exercise appellate jurisdiction by means of the writ of *habeas corpus*, were repealed by the act of that year, and that the repealing section of the act of 1868 is limited in terms, and must be limited in effect to the appellate jurisdiction authorized by the act of 1867.

> We could come to no other conclusion without holding that the whole appellate jurisdiction of this court, in cases of *habeas corpus*, conferred by the Constitution, recognized by law, and exercised from the foundation of the government hitherto, has been taken away, without the expression of such intent, and by mere implication, through the operation of the acts of 1867 and 1868.

5. More than a century after *Yerger*, the Court faced a similar issue—and responded in the same way. The statute in question was Title I of the Antiterrorism and Effective Death Penalty Act of 1996 (AEDPA).

AEDPA made substantial changes in the federal habeas corpus statutes, particularly those governing the availability of the writ as a vehicle for collateral review of state criminal convictions. (See Chapter 15.) One change was to create a "gatekeeping" mechanism for the consideration of second or successive applications in district court. The prospective applicant must seek authorization from the court of appeals to proceed with his case. Section 2244(b)(3)(E) specifies that the denial of authorization by a court of appeals "shall not be the subject of a petition for rehearing or for a writ of certiorari."

In *Felker v. Turpin*, 518 U.S. 651 (1996), the habeas petitioner argued that this latter provision constituted an unconstitutional restriction on the jurisdiction of the

Supreme Court. The Court held that it did not. The unanimous opinion by Chief Justice Rehnquist closely tracked the reasoning of *Yerger*.

The Court began by narrowly construing the statute:

> [We] conclude that Title I of the Act has not repealed our authority to entertain original habeas petitions, for reasons similar to those stated in *Yerger*. No provision of Title I mentions our authority to entertain original habeas petitions; in contrast, § 103 amends the Federal Rules of Appellate Procedure to bar consideration of original habeas petitions in the courts of appeals. Although § 2244(b)(3)(E) precludes us from reviewing, by appeal or petition for certiorari, a judgment on an application for leave to file a second habeas petition in district court, it makes no mention of our authority to hear habeas petitions filed as original matters in this Court. As we declined to find a repeal of § 14 of the Judiciary Act of 1789 as applied to this Court by implication then, we decline to find a similar repeal of § 2241 of Title 28 — its descendant — by implication now.

That interpretation, the Court said, eliminated any basis for challenging the restriction under Article III. The Court explained:

> The Act does remove our authority to entertain an appeal or a petition for a writ of certiorari to review a decision of a court of appeals exercising its "gatekeeping" function over a second petition. But since it does not repeal our authority to entertain a petition for habeas corpus, there can be no plausible argument that the Act has deprived this Court of appellate jurisdiction in violation of Article III, § 2.

6. *McCardle, Yerger*, and *Felker* manifest a consistent pattern: in each case the Court took pains to emphasize that Congress had not cut off all avenues of appellate review. But all three cases involved the writ of habeas corpus. How much light do these cases shed on the Court's view of Congress's power to make exceptions to its appellate jurisdiction?

7. One other major precedent bears on this question. This case too is a product of the Reconstruction era. It does not involve habeas corpus, but it has ambiguities of its own.

United States v. Klein

Supreme Court of the United States, 1871.

13 Wall. (80 U.S.) 128.

[*Editorial note.* During the Civil War, the Federal Government seized property in the Confederate states. In the Abandoned and Captured Property Act of 1863, Congress provided a remedy for owners of such property. They could sue in the Court of Claims and could recover the proceeds of the property — but only if they proved that they had "never given any aid or comfort" to the rebellion. In *United States v. Padelford*, 9 Wall. (76 U.S.) 531 (1870), the Supreme Court considered a suit by a claimant who had participated in the rebellion but had taken an oath of allegiance and received a Presidential pardon. The Court held that Padelford, having been pardoned, was "as innocent as if he had never committed the offence." The proof of pardon was thus "a complete substitute for proof that he gave no aid or comfort to the rebellion," and he was entitled to the proceeds of the seized property.

[Soon after the *Padelford* decision was announced, Congress enacted a proviso as part of an appropriations bill. The proviso stated that "no pardon or amnesty granted by the President . . . shall be admissible in evidence on the part of any claimant in the Court of Claims as evidence in support of any claim against the United States." The proviso continued:

> And in all cases where judgment shall have been heretofore rendered in the Court of Claims in favor of any claimant, on any other proof of loyalty than such as is above required and provided, and which is hereby declared to have been and to be the true intent and meaning of said respective acts, the Supreme Court shall, on appeal, have no further jurisdiction of the cause, and shall dismiss the same for want of jurisdiction.

The law included a similar provision for suits in the Court of Claims: upon proof of the claimant's pardon, "the jurisdiction of the court in the case shall cease, and the court shall forthwith dismiss the suit of such claimant."

[Klein was the administrator of the estate of V. F. Wilson, who had aided the rebellion but, like Padelford, had received a Presidential pardon. Klein sued in the Court of Claims to recover the proceeds of cotton that had been abandoned to agents of the United States. He recovered judgment, and the United States appealed to the Supreme Court.

[The appeal was pending when Congress passed the 1870 proviso. In reliance on the proviso, the Government moved "that the case be remanded to the Court of Claims with a mandate that the same be dismissed for want of jurisdiction, as *now* required by law."]

The CHIEF JUSTICE delivered the opinion of the court.

The general question in this case is whether or not the proviso relating to suits for the proceeds of abandoned and captured property in the Court of Claims, contained in the appropriation act of July 12th, 1870, debars the defendant in error from recovering, as administrator of V. F. Wilson, deceased, the proceeds of certain cotton belonging to the decedent, which came into the possession of the agents of the Treasury Department as captured or abandoned property, and the proceeds of which were paid by them according to law into the Treasury of the United States. . . .

The Court of Claims [is] constituted one of those inferior courts which Congress authorizes, and has jurisdiction of contracts between the government and the citizen, from which appeal regularly lies to this court.

Undoubtedly the legislature has complete control over the organization and existence of that court and may confer or withhold the right of appeal from its decisions. And if this act did nothing more, it would be our duty to give it effect. If it simply denied the right of appeal in a particular class of cases, there could be no doubt that it must be regarded as an exercise of the power of Congress to make "such exceptions from the appellate jurisdiction" as should seem to it expedient.

But the language of the proviso shows plainly that it does not intend to with-hold appellate jurisdiction except as a means to an end. Its great and controlling purpose is to deny to pardons granted by the President the effect which this court had adjudged them to have. The proviso declares that pardons shall not be considered by this court on appeal. We had already decided that it was our duty to consider them and give them effect, in cases like the present, as equivalent to proof of loyalty. It provides that whenever it shall appear that any judgment of the Court of Claims shall have been founded on such pardons, without other proof of loyalty, the Supreme Court shall have no further jurisdiction of the case and shall dismiss the same for want of jurisdiction. The proviso further declares that every pardon granted to any suitor in the Court of Claims and reciting that the person pardoned has been guilty of any act of rebellion or disloyalty, shall, if accepted in writing without disclaimer of the fact recited, be taken as conclusive evidence in that court and on appeal, of the act recited; and on proof of pardon or acceptance, summarily made on motion or otherwise, the jurisdiction of the court shall cease and the suit shall be forthwith dismissed.

It is evident from this statement that the denial of jurisdiction to this court, as well as to the Court of Claims, is founded solely on the application of a rule of decision, in causes pending, prescribed by Congress. The court has jurisdiction of the cause to a given point; but when it ascertains that a certain state of things exists, its jurisdiction is to cease and it is required to dismiss the cause for want of jurisdiction.

It seems to us that this is not an exercise of the acknowledged power of Congress to make exceptions and prescribe regulations to the appellate power.

The court is required to ascertain the existence of certain facts and thereupon to declare that its jurisdiction on appeal has ceased, by dismissing the bill. What is this but to prescribe a rule for the decision of a cause in a particular way? In the case before us, the Court of Claims has rendered judgment for the claimant and an appeal has been taken to this court. We are directed to dismiss the appeal, if we find that the judgment must be affirmed, because of a pardon granted to the intestate of the claimants. Can we do so without allowing one party to the controversy to decide it in its own favor? Can we do so without allowing that the legislature may prescribe rules of decision to the Judicial Department of the government in cases pending before it?

We think not; and thus thinking, we do not at all question what was decided in the case of *Pennsylvania v. Wheeling Bridge Company*, 18 How. 429. In that case, after a decree in this court that the bridge, in the then state of the law, was a nuisance and must be abated as such, Congress passed an act legalizing the structure and making it a post-road; and the court, on a motion for process to enforce the decree, held that the bridge had ceased to be a nuisance by the exercise of the constitutional powers of Congress, and denied the motion. No arbitrary rule of decision was prescribed in that case, but the court was left to apply its ordinary rules to the new circumstances created by the act. In the case before us no new circumstances have been created by legislation. But the court is forbidden to give the effect to evidence which, in its own judgment, such evidence should have, and is directed to give it an effect precisely contrary.

We must think that Congress has inadvertently passed the limit which separates the legislative from the judicial power.

It is of vital importance that these powers be kept distinct. The Constitution provides that the judicial power of the United States shall be vested in one Supreme Court and such inferior courts as the Congress shall from time to time ordain and establish. The same instrument, in the last clause of the same article, provides that in all cases other than those of original jurisdiction, "the Supreme Court shall have appellate jurisdiction both as to law and fact, with such exceptions and under such regulations as the Congress shall make."

Congress has already provided that the Supreme Court shall have jurisdiction of the judgments of the Court of Claims on appeal. Can it prescribe a rule in conformity with which the court must deny to itself the jurisdiction thus conferred, because and only because its decision, in accordance with settled law, must be adverse to the government and favorable to the suitor? This question seems to us to answer itself.

The rule prescribed is also liable to just exception as impairing the effect of a pardon, and thus infringing the constitutional power of the Executive.

It is the intention of the Constitution that each of the great co-ordinate departments of the government—the Legislative, the Executive, and the Judicial—shall be, in its sphere, independent of the others. To the executive alone is intrusted the power of pardon; and it is granted without limit. Pardon includes amnesty. It blots out the offence pardoned and removes all its penal consequences. It may be granted on conditions. In these particular pardons, that no doubt might exist as to their character, restoration of property was expressly pledged, and the pardon was granted on condition that the person who availed himself of it should take and keep a prescribed oath.

Now it is clear that the legislature cannot change the effect of such a pardon any more than the executive can change a law. Yet this is attempted by the provision under consideration. The court is required to receive special pardons as evidence of guilt and to treat them as null and void. It is required to disregard pardons granted by proclamation on condition, though the condition has been fulfilled, and to deny them their legal effect. This certainly impairs the executive authority and directs the court to be instrumental to that end.

We think it unnecessary to enlarge. The simplest statement is the best.

We repeat that it is impossible to believe that this provision was not inserted in the appropriation bill through inadvertence; and that we shall not best fulfil the deliberate will of the legislature by denying the motion to dismiss and affirming the judgment of the Court of Claims; which is

Accordingly done.

MR. JUSTICE MILLER (with whom concurred MR. JUSTICE BRADLEY), dissenting.

I cannot agree to the opinion of the court just delivered in an important matter; and I regret this the more because I do agree to the proposition that the proviso to the act of July 12th, 1870, is unconstitutional, so far as it attempts to prescribe to the judiciary the effect to be given to an act of pardon or amnesty by the President. This power of pardon is confided to the President by the Constitution, and whatever may be its extent or its limits, the legislative branch of the government cannot impair its force or effect in a judicial proceeding in a constitutional court. But I have not been able to bring my mind to concur in the proposition that, under the act concerning captured and abandoned property, there remains in the former owner, who had given aid and comfort to the rebellion, any interest whatever in the property or its proceeds when it had been sold and paid into the treasury or had been converted to the use of the public under that act. . . .

Note: The Import of Klein

1. There appear to be at least two distinct grounds of decision in *Klein*. The Court holds that the 1870 proviso intrudes on the authority of the judicial branch: "Congress has inadvertently passed the limit which separates the legislative from the judicial power." The opinion then says: "The rule prescribed is *also* liable to just exception as impairing the effect of a pardon, and thus infringing the constitutional power of the Executive." (Emphasis added.) If the latter holding is independent of the first, as it seems to be, what is the basis for the holding that Congress has intruded on the judicial power?

2. Why is the 1870 proviso "not an exercise of the acknowledged power of Congress to make exceptions" to the Supreme Court's appellate jurisdiction? Does the holding in *Klein* shed light on the constitutionality of the limitations on that jurisdiction proposed by the Marriage Protection Act or the Constitution Restoration Act?

3. One thread in the opinion is that the 1870 proviso is invalid because it has the effect of "allowing one party to the controversy to decide it in its own favor." That would be a very narrow ground of decision. But is that all that the case stands for?

Note: "External" Limitations

Commentators have sometimes distinguished between "internal" and "external" limitations on Congress's power to limit federal court jurisdiction. "Internal" restraints are those grounded in Article III. "External" restraints are those found in other provisions of the Constitution.

As a general matter, no one is likely to disagree with the proposition that Congress's power over the federal courts is subject to the various limitations that the Constitution imposes on all exercises of Congressional power. Thus, notwithstanding the "exceptions and regulations" clause, a law that prohibited Jews or Republicans from seeking review by the Supreme Court plainly would be unconstitutional under the First Amendment. But of course members of Congress do not propose, let alone pass, laws of that kind. When they seek to limit jurisdiction, they take aim not at classes of *litigants* but at classes of *claims*. And claim-based restrictions present more difficult issues under the substantive provisions of the Constitution.

Consider, for example, the proposed "We the People Act," introduced in the 104th Congress (H.R. 3893). One section of that bill would prohibit the Supreme Court from adjudicating "any claim involving the laws, regulations, or policies of any State or unit of local government relating to the free exercise or establishment of religion." Would such a law itself constitute an establishment of religion? Would it violate the "equal protection component" of the Fifth Amendment? To answer those questions, one would have to analyze the Supreme Court's decisions on establishment and equal protection. Those issues are beyond the scope of this book. We turn, instead, to the "internal" limitations on Congressional power.

Note: The "Essential Functions" Thesis

1. Consideration of Article III constraints on Congress's power to limit the appellate jurisdiction of the Supreme Court generally begins with a classic article by Professor Henry M. Hart. Responding to the argument that "the language of the Constitution must be taken as vesting plenary control in Congress," Hart countered with the proposition that "the exceptions [to appellate jurisdiction] must not be such as will destroy the essential role of the Supreme Court in the constitutional plan." Henry M. Hart, *The Power of Congress to Limit the Jurisdiction of Federal Courts: An Exercise in Dialectic*, 66 HARV. L. REV. 1362, 1364 (1953). But Hart did not elaborate on what this "essential role" might be, or how substantial a restraint on congressional power his theory would impose. That was left to others.

2. Three functions of the Supreme Court could plausibly be identified as "essential." For convenience (and in accord with conventional usage), these can be referred to as "supremacy," "checking," and "uniformity."

"Supremacy" refers to the Court's role in enforcing the command of the Supremacy Clause that requires state judges to decide cases in accordance with the federal constitution and laws, "any Thing in the Constitution or Laws of any State to the Contrary notwithstanding." This function probably has the strongest claim on "essentiality," as even opponents of the thesis acknowledge. The arguments in support of the claim track those made by Justice Story in *Martin v. Hunter's Lessee* (Chapter 4) in defending the constitutionality of section 25 of the Judiciary Act of 1789.

"Checking" refers to the Court's role in reviewing Acts of Congress for consistency with the Constitution. Those who view this function as essential often invoke *Marbury v. Madison* (Chapter 1).

"Uniformity" is a shorthand for the Court's role in providing a definitive resolution of issues of federal law that have given rise to conflicts between or among lower appellate courts. In *Felker v. Turpin*, the decision on the 1996 habeas corpus reform law, three members of the Court seemed to give special prominence to this function. Justice Souter, joined by Justice Stevens and Justice Breyer, joined the Court's opinion, but wrote separately to add that "if it should later turn out that statutory avenues other than certiorari for reviewing a gatekeeping determination were closed, the question whether the statute exceeded Congress's Exceptions Clause power would be open. The question could arise if the courts of appeals adopted divergent interpretations of the gatekeeper standard."

3. Dozens of bills to remove particular classes of cases from the Supreme Court's appellate jurisdiction have been introduced in Congress during the last century, but none have been enacted. Is this relevant to answering the question whether Congress has the power to enact such legislation?

4. Scholars have debated the correctness of the "essential functions" thesis. One leading defense of the thesis by Professor Lawrence Sager argues that an essential function of the Supreme Court is to review the constitutionality of state actions, because the Framers intended the Supreme Court to supervise the states. Lawrence Gene Sager, *The Supreme Court, 1980 Term, Foreword: Constitutional Limitations on Congress' Authority to Regulate the Jurisdiction of the Federal Courts*, 95 HARV. L. REV. 17 (1981). In his view, it is unlikely that the Framers meant to give Congress complete control over Supreme Court jurisdiction because of fears that state interests would dominate Congress. As Professor Sager acknowledges, this argument does not extend to Supreme Court supervision of federal courts, because the Framers did not have the same concerns that lower federal courts would disobey the Constitution.

Professor Gerald Gunther provided a leading account of the opposite view. Gerald Gunther, *Congressional Power to Curtail Federal Court Jurisdiction: An Opinionated Guide to the Ongoing Debate*, 36 STAN. L. REV. 895 (1984). He acknowledged that some statements at the debates at the Constitutional Convention support the notion that Supreme Court review of state court judgments was expected. But he argued that the text of Article III does not adopt the position espoused by the statements because Article III does not specify any limits on Congress's power to create "exceptions" to the Supreme Court's appellate jurisdiction. He further argued that historical practice suggests that Congress has broad power to regulate the Supreme Court's appellate jurisdiction; he noted that the Judiciary Act of 1789 passed by the first Congress provided only limited Supreme Court authority over state court judgments. Under that Act, the Court could review only state court decisions that denied a federal claim; when the state court sustained a federal claim, review was unavailable.

Although arguing that the "exceptions" clause contains no inherent limits on Congress's power to limit the Supreme Court's appellate jurisdiction, Gunther acknowledged the desirability of maintaining Supreme Court jurisdiction to review state court judgments. But in his view, that established only that Congress *should* not limit the Court's appellate jurisdiction, not that it *could* not.

Which side has the better of the argument? If you find the "essential functions" thesis persuasive to at least some degree, how do the various "court-stripping" bills described in the introduction to this chapter measure up?

5. The Supreme Court has developed a number of doctrines limiting the jurisdiction of the federal courts. These include the justiciability doctrines covered in Chapter 3—such as standing, mootness, ripeness, and the political-question doctrine—as well as the abstention doctrines covered in Chapter 16. Do these doctrines affect your view of the persuasiveness of the two sides of the debate?

Note: The "Marriage Protection Act"

1. In July 2004, the House passed a substitute version of H.R. 3313, the "Marriage Protection Act." The bill would amend Title 28 by adding a new section 1632, reading as follows: "No court created by Act of Congress shall have any jurisdiction, and the Supreme Court shall have no appellate jurisdiction, to hear or decide any question pertaining to the interpretation of, or the validity under the Constitution of, section 1738C or this section."

Section 1738C was enacted in 1996 as part of the Defense of Marriage Act. It provides:

> No State, territory, or possession of the United States, or Indian tribe, shall be required to give effect to any public act, record, or judicial proceeding of any other State, territory, possession, or tribe respecting a relationship between persons of the same sex that is treated as a marriage under the laws of such other State, territory, possession, or tribe, or a right or claim arising from such relationship.

Put aside the restriction on district court jurisdiction in H.R. 3313. Is the restriction on Supreme Court jurisdiction constitutional?

2. Note that the Marriage Protection Act eliminates the Supreme Court's jurisdiction to decide not only "any question pertaining to the validity [of] section 1738C," but also any question pertaining to the validity of "this section"—i.e., the provision that withdraws jurisdiction. Does that aspect of the bill raise special problems?

The Supreme Court has said that "a federal court always has jurisdiction to determine its own jurisdiction." *See, e.g., United States v. Ruiz*, 536 U.S. 622, 628 (2002). But is that a principle of constitutional dimension? Consider these comments by Professor Friedman:

> It is true that a court must have some inherent power to determine initially whether it has power to hear a case. But once [the jurisdictional facts are determined], the jurisdictional proscription [would bar] further adjudication. Jurisdiction to determine jurisdiction does not include the power to determine the acceptability of jurisdictional limitations: the limitations themselves preclude the endeavor.

Barry Friedman, *A Different Dialogue: The Supreme Court, Congress, and Federal Jurisdiction*, 85 Nw. U. L. Rev. 1, 50 n.246 (1990). Is this view consistent with *Marbury v. Madison*?

3. The Marriage Protection Act provides that the Supreme Court shall have "no appellate jurisdiction to hear or decide any *question*" of the kind specified. (Emphasis added.) Section 1254 gives the Supreme Court jurisdiction over "Cases" in the federal courts of appeals, and section 1257 authorizes review of "Final judgments" of state courts. Assume that a case is properly brought to the Court under 28 U.S.C. § 1254 or 1257, and that a party raises a "question" within the scope of the Act. Assume further that the Court believes that resolution of the question is necessary to a correct decision of the case under the Constitution. What should the Court do? Is the answer necessarily the same for federal-court cases and state-court judgments?

Problems: The "Constitution Restoration Act"

Return now to the question posed at the start of this section: is the restriction on Supreme Court jurisdiction contained in the Constitution Restoration Act of 2004 constitutional? For convenience, the proposed new section 1260 of the Judicial Code is set forth here:

> Notwithstanding any other provision of this chapter, the Supreme Court shall not have jurisdiction to review, by appeal, writ of certiorari, or otherwise, any matter to the extent that relief is sought against an element of Federal, State, or local government, or against an officer of Federal, State, or local government (whether or not acting in official personal capacity), by reason of that element's or officer's acknowledgement of God as the sovereign source of law, liberty, or government.

Assume that this provision becomes law. The presiding judge of the Calhoun County Circuit Court in the state of New Harmony orders the installation of a large plaque opposite the main entrance to the county courthouse. The plaque has engraved on it the text of the Ten Commandments. The presiding judge explains that "America's founders looked to and relied on the Ten Commandments as a source of absolute moral standards," and that it is appropriate, in an American courthouse, to acknowledge the Ten Commandments as providing "the moral foundation of our law and our legal system."

Two lawyers who regularly visit the courthouse on behalf of clients bring suit in New Harmony state court seeking an injunction requiring the removal of the plaque on the ground that it violates the Establishment Clause. The case is heard by a visiting judge from another county, who rejects the claim.

1. Assume first that the state supreme court affirms the judgment dismissing the plaintiffs' suit. The plaintiffs file a petition for certiorari in the United States Supreme Court. The presiding judge, as respondent, moves to dismiss the petition for want of appellate jurisdiction under section 1260. What issues are raised by the motion, and how should they be resolved?

2. Now assume that the state supreme court *reverses* the trial court and holds that the installation of the plaque does violate the Establishment Clause. This time it is the presiding judge who files the certiorari petition, and the plaintiffs as respondents invoke section 1260. Does this situation present the same constitutional issues?

B. The Jurisdiction of the Federal District Courts

Because of constitutional doubts, practical concerns, or some combination of the two, some court-stripping proposals leave the Supreme Court's jurisdiction untouched and restrict only the jurisdiction of the district courts. One example is H.R. 1546, the "Life-Protecting Judicial Limitation Act of 2003." This bill provided that the district courts of the United States "shall not have jurisdiction to hear or determine any abortion-related case." It defined "abortion-related case" to mean: "any action in which any requirement, prohibition, or other provision relating to abortion that is contained in a State or Federal statute is at issue." But it did not modify the jurisdiction of the United States Supreme Court. Is the bill constitutional? The materials that follow will shed light on that question.

Sheldon v. Sill

Supreme Court of the United States, 1850.

8 How. (49 U.S.) 441.

Mr. Justice Grier delivered the opinion of the Court.

The only question which it will be necessary to notice in this case is, whether the Circuit Court had jurisdiction.

Sill, the complainant below, a citizen of New York, filed his bill in the Circuit Court of the United States for Michigan, against Sheldon, claiming to recover the amount of a bond and mortgage, which had been assigned to him by Hastings, the President of the Bank of Michigan.

Sheldon, in his answer, among other things, pleaded that "the bond and mortgage in controversy, having been originally given by a citizen of Michigan to another citizen of the same state, and the complainant being assignee of them, the Circuit Court had no jurisdiction."

The eleventh section of the Judiciary Act, which defines the jurisdiction of the Circuit Courts, restrains them from taking "cognizance of any suit to recover the contents of any promissory note or other chose in action, in favor of an assignee, unless a suit might have been prosecuted in such court to recover the contents, if no assignment had been made, except in cases of foreign bills of exchange."

The third article of the Constitution declares that "the judicial power of the United States shall be vested in one Supreme Court, and such inferior courts as the Congress may, from time to time, ordain and establish." The second section of the same article enumerates the cases and controversies of which the judicial power shall have cognizance, and, among others, it specifies "controversies between citizens of different states."

It has been alleged, that this restriction of the Judiciary Act, with regard to assignees of choses in action, is in conflict with this provision of the Constitution, and therefore void.

It must be admitted, that if the Constitution had ordained and established the inferior courts, and distributed to them their respective powers, they could not be restricted or divested by Congress. But as it has made no such distribution, one of two consequences must result,—either that each inferior court created by Congress must exercise all the judicial powers not given to the Supreme Court, or that Congress, having the power to establish the courts, must define their respective jurisdictions. The first of these inferences has never been asserted, and could not be defended with any show of reason, and if not, the latter would seem to follow as a necessary consequence. And it would seem to follow, also, that, having a right to prescribe, Congress may withhold from any court of its creation jurisdiction of any of the enumerated controversies. Courts created by statute can have no jurisdiction but such as the statute confers. No one of them can assert a just claim to jurisdiction exclusively conferred on another, or withheld from all.

The Constitution has defined the limits of the judicial power of the United States, but has not prescribed how much of it shall be exercised by the Circuit Court; consequently, the statute which does prescribe the limits of their jurisdiction, cannot be in conflict with the Constitution, unless it confers powers not enumerated therein.

Such has been the doctrine held by this court since its first establishment. To enumerate all the cases in which it has been either directly advanced or tacitly assumed would be tedious and unnecessary.

In the case of *Turner v. Bank of North America*, 4 Dall., 10, it was contended, as in this case, that, as it was a controversy between citizens of different states, the Constitution gave the plaintiff a right to sue in the Circuit Court, notwithstanding he was an assignee within the restriction of the eleventh section of the Judiciary Act. But the court said,—"The political truth is, that the disposal of the judicial power (except in a few specified instances) belongs to Congress; and Congress is not bound to enlarge the jurisdiction of the Federal courts to every subject, in every form which the Constitution might warrant." This decision was made in 1799; since that time, the same doctrine has been frequently asserted by this court, as may be seen in *McIntire v. Wood*, 7 Cranch, 506; *Kendall v. United States*, 12 Pet. 616; *Cary v. Curtis*, 3 How. 245.

The only remaining inquiry is, whether the complainant in this case is the assignee of a "chose in action," within the meaning of the statute. The term "chose in action" is one of comprehensive import. It includes the infinite variety of contracts, covenants, and promises, which confer on one party a right to recover a personal chattel or a sum of money from another, by action. . . .

The complainant in this case is the purchaser and assignee of a sum of money, a debt, a chose in action, not of a tract of land. He seeks to recover by this action a debt assigned to him. He is therefore the "assignee of a chose in action," within the letter and spirit of the act of Congress under consideration, and cannot support this action in the Circuit Court of the United States, where his assignor could not.

The judgment of the Circuit Court must therefore be reversed, for want of jurisdiction.

Order.

This cause came on to be heard on the transcript of the record from the Circuit Court of the United States for the District of Michigan, and was argued by counsel. On consideration whereof, it is now here ordered and decreed by this court, that this cause be, and the same is hereby, reversed, for the want of jurisdiction in that court, and that this cause be, and the same is hereby, remanded to the said Circuit Court, with directions to dismiss the bill of complaint for the want of jurisdiction.

Note: Congress and the Lower Federal Courts

1. In *Martin v. Hunter's Lessee* (Chapter 4), Justice Story expounded at length on the proposition that it is the duty of Congress under the Constitution "to vest the *whole judicial power*" defined by Article III. However, as already noted, Congress did not do so in the Judiciary Act of 1789, nor has it done so since. Moreover, the discussion in *Martin* was only dictum. Does *Sheldon v. Sill* stand as a definitive rejection of the proposition?

2. In *Sheldon*, the Court uses broad language suggesting that the Congress has complete discretion to remove any class of cases from the jurisdiction of the lower federal courts: "Congress may withhold from any court of its creation jurisdiction of any of the enumerated controversies." Not surprisingly, supporters of measures like the "Life-Protecting Judicial Limitation Act" rely heavily on the constitutional holding in *Sheldon*. They also rely on the legislative precedent of the Norris-LaGuardia Act and a Supreme Court decision that sustained its constitutionality, albeit without discussion.

The Norris-LaGuardia Act was enacted in 1932. Section 1 of the Act provided:

> No court of the United States, as defined in this chapter, shall have jurisdiction to issue any restraining order or temporary or permanent injunction in a case involving or growing out of a labor dispute, except in a strict conformity with the provisions of this chapter; nor shall any such restraining order or temporary or permanent injunction be issued contrary to the public policy declared in this chapter.

Other provisions of the Act specified the nature of the hearing required before an injunction could be granted and the limited circumstances under which an injunction would be permitted. In *Lauf v. E. G. Shinner Co.*, 303 U.S. 323 (1938), the Supreme Court summarized the Act, then stated: "There can be no question of the power of Congress thus to define and limit the jurisdiction of the inferior courts of the United States." There was no further discussion or elaboration. A footnote cited a single case— not *Sheldon v. Sill*, as might have been expected, but *Kline v. Burke Construction Co.*, 260 U.S. 226, 233, 234 (1922). In *Kline*, at the pages referenced, the Court quoted Article III sections 1 and 2, then said:

> Only the jurisdiction of the Supreme Court is derived directly from the Constitution. Every other court created by the general government derives its jurisdiction wholly from the authority of Congress. That body may give, withhold or restrict such jurisdiction at its discretion, provided it be not

extended beyond the boundaries fixed by the Constitution. [Here the Court cited *Sheldon v. Sill*, among other cases.] The Constitution simply gives to the inferior courts the capacity to take jurisdiction in the enumerated cases, but it requires an act of Congress to confer it. And the jurisdiction having been conferred may, at the will of Congress, be taken away in whole or in part; and if withdrawn without a saving clause all pending cases though cognizable when commenced must fall.

Do these cases settle the constitutionality of the "Life-Protecting Judicial Limitation Act," at least as far as "internal" restraints are concerned? The language is quite strong, particularly the last-quoted sentence. But none of the cases involved legislation that withdrew jurisdiction over federal constitutional claims. Does that make a difference? Consider *Webster v. Doe*.

Webster v. Doe

Supreme Court of the United States, 1988.

486 U.S. 592.

Chief Justice Rehnquist delivered the opinion of the Court.

Section 102(c) of the National Security Act of 1947, 61 Stat. 498, as amended, provides that:

> [T]he Director of Central Intelligence may, in his discretion, terminate the employment of any officer or employee of the Agency whenever he shall deem such termination necessary or advisable in the interests of the United States. . . . 50 U.S.C. § 403(c).

In this case we decide whether, and to what extent, the termination decisions of the Director under § 102(c) are judicially reviewable.

I

Respondent John Doe was first employed by the Central Intelligence Agency (CIA or Agency) in 1973 as a clerk-typist. He received periodic fitness reports that consistently rated him as an excellent or outstanding employee. By 1977, respondent had been promoted to a position as a covert electronics technician.

In January 1982, respondent voluntarily informed a CIA security officer that he was a homosexual. Almost immediately, the Agency placed respondent on paid administrative leave pending an investigation of his sexual orientation and conduct. On February 12 and again on February 17, respondent was extensively questioned by a polygraph officer concerning his homosexuality and possible security violations. Respondent denied having sexual relations with any foreign nationals and maintained that he had not disclosed classified information to any of his sexual partners. After these interviews, the officer told respondent that the polygraph tests indicated that he had truthfully answered all questions. The polygraph officer then prepared a five-page summary of his interviews with respondent, to which respondent was allowed to attach a two-page addendum.

On April 14, 1982, a CIA security agent informed respondent that the Agency's Office of Security had determined that respondent's homosexuality posed a threat to security, but declined to explain the nature of the danger. Respondent was then asked to resign. When he refused to do so, the Office of Security recommended to the CIA Director (petitioner's predecessor) that respondent be dismissed. After reviewing respondent's records and the evaluations of his subordinates, the Director "deemed it necessary and advisable in the interests of the United States to terminate [respondent's] employment with this Agency pursuant to section 102(c) of the National Security Act. . . ." Respondent was also advised that, while the CIA would give him a positive recommendation in any future job search, if he applied for a job requiring a security clearance the Agency would inform the prospective employer that it had concluded that respondent's homosexuality presented a security threat.

Respondent then filed an action against petitioner in the United States District Court for the District of Columbia. Respondent's amended complaint asserted a variety of statutory and constitutional claims against the Director. Respondent alleged that the Director's decision to terminate his employment violated the Administrative Procedure Act (APA), 5 U.S.C. § 706, because it was arbitrary and capricious, represented an abuse of discretion, and was reached without observing the procedures required by law and CIA regulations. He also complained that the Director's termination of his employment deprived him of constitutionally protected rights to property, liberty, and privacy in violation of the First, Fourth, Fifth, and Ninth Amendments. Finally, he asserted that his dismissal transgressed the procedural due process and equal protection of the laws guaranteed by the Fifth Amendment. Respondent requested a declaratory judgment that the Director had violated the APA and the Constitution, and asked the District Court for an injunction ordering petitioner to reinstate him to the position he held with the CIA prior to his dismissal. As an alternative remedy, he suggested that he be returned to paid administrative leave and that petitioner be ordered to reevaluate respondent's employment termination and provide a statement of the reasons for any adverse final determination. Respondent sought no monetary damages in his amended complaint.

Petitioner moved to dismiss respondent's amended complaint on the ground that § 102(c) of the National Security Act (NSA) precludes judicial review of the Director's termination decisions under the provisions of the APA set forth in 5 U.S.C. §§ 701, 702, and 706. Section 702 provides judicial review to any "person suffering legal wrong because of agency action, or adversely affected or aggrieved by agency action within the meaning of a relevant statute." . . . [However, the availability of judicial review is predicated on satisfying the requirements of § 701, which provides:]

(a) This chapter applies, according to the provisions thereof, except to the extent that—

   (1) statutes preclude judicial review; or

   (2) agency action is committed to agency discretion by law. . . .

. . . We granted certiorari to decide the question whether the Director's decision to discharge a CIA employee under §102(c) of the NSA is judicially reviewable under the APA.

II

[In this part of the opinion, the Court, relying on "the language and structure of §102(c)," found that "Congress meant to commit individual employee discharges to the Director's discretion." The Court therefore concluded that §701(a)(2) "precludes judicial review of these decisions under the APA."]

III

In addition to his claim that the Director failed to abide by the statutory dictates of §102(c), respondent also alleged a number of constitutional violations in his amended complaint. Respondent charged that petitioner's termination of his employment deprived him of property and liberty interests under the Due Process Clause of the Fifth Amendment, denied him equal protection of the laws, and unjustifiably burdened his right to privacy. Respondent asserts that he is entitled, under the APA, to judicial consideration of these claimed violations.

We share the confusion of the Court of Appeals as to the precise nature of respondent's constitutional claims. It is difficult, if not impossible, to ascertain from the amended complaint whether respondent contends that his termination, based on *his* homosexuality, is constitutionally impermissible, or whether he asserts that a more pervasive discrimination policy exists in the CIA's employment practices regarding *all* homosexuals. This ambiguity in the amended complaint is no doubt attributable in part to the inconsistent explanations respondent received from the Agency itself regarding his termination. Prior to his discharge, respondent had been told by two CIA security officers that his homosexual activities themselves violated CIA regulations. In contrast, the Deputy General Counsel of the CIA later informed respondent that homosexuality was merely a security concern that did not inevitably result in termination, but instead was evaluated on a case-by-case basis.

Petitioner maintains that, no matter what the nature of respondent's constitutional claims, judicial review is precluded by the language and intent of §102(c). In petitioner's view, all Agency employment termination decisions, even those based on policies normally repugnant to the Constitution, are given over to the absolute discretion of the Director, and are hence unreviewable under the APA. We do not think §102(c) may be read to exclude review of constitutional claims. We emphasized in *Johnson v. Robison*, 415 U.S. 361 (1974), that where Congress intends to preclude judicial review of constitutional claims its intent to do so must be clear. In *Weinberger v. Salfi*, 422 U.S. 749 (1975), we reaffirmed that view. We require this heightened showing in part to avoid the "serious constitutional question" that would arise if a federal statute were construed to deny any judicial forum for a colorable constitutional claim. See *Bowen v. Michigan Academy of Family Physicians*, 476 U.S. 667, 681 n.12 (1986).

Our review of §102(c) convinces us that it cannot bear the preclusive weight petitioner would have it support. As detailed above, the section does commit employment termination decisions to the Director's discretion, and precludes challenges to these decisions based upon the statutory language of § 102(c). A discharged employee thus cannot complain that his termination was not "necessary or advisable in the interests of the United States," since that assessment is the Director's alone. Subsections (a)(1) and (a)(2) of § 701, however, remove from judicial review only those determinations specifically identified by Congress or "committed to agency discretion by law." Nothing in § 102(c) persuades us that Congress meant to preclude consideration of colorable constitutional claims arising out of the actions of the Director pursuant to that section; we believe that a constitutional claim based on an individual discharge may be reviewed by the District Court. We agree with the Court of Appeals that there must be further proceedings in the District Court on this issue. . . .

Petitioner also contends that even if respondent has raised a colorable constitutional claim arising out of his discharge, Congress in the interest of national security may deny the courts the authority to decide the claim and to order respondent's reinstatement if the claim is upheld. For the reasons previously stated, we do not think Congress meant to impose such restrictions when it enacted § 102(c) of the NSA. Even without such prohibitory legislation from Congress, of course, traditional equitable principles requiring the balancing of public and private interests control the grant of declaratory or injunctive relief in the federal courts. On remand, the District Court should thus address respondent's constitutional claims and the propriety of the equitable remedies sought.

[The] case is remanded for further proceedings consistent with this opinion.

JUSTICE KENNEDY took no part in the consideration or decision of this case.

JUSTICE O'CONNOR, concurring in part and dissenting in part.

I agree that the Administrative Procedure Act (APA) does not authorize judicial review of the employment decisions referred to in § 102(c) of the National Security Act of 1947. Because § 102(c) does not provide a meaningful standard for judicial review, such decisions are clearly "committed to agency discretion by law" within the meaning of the provision of the APA set forth in 5 U.S.C. § 701(a)(2). . . . Accordingly, I join Parts I and II of the Court's opinion.

I disagree, however, with the Court's conclusion that a constitutional claim challenging the validity of an employment decision covered by § 102(c) may nonetheless be brought in a federal district court. Whatever may be the exact scope of Congress' power to close the lower federal courts to constitutional claims in other contexts, I have no doubt about its authority to do so here. The functions performed by the Central Intelligence Agency and the Director of Central Intelligence lie at the core of "the very delicate, plenary and exclusive power of the President as the sole organ of the federal government in the field of international relations." *United States v. Curtiss-Wright Export Corp.*, 299 U.S. 304, 320 (1936). The authority of the Director of Central Intelligence to control access to sensitive national security information by discharging employees deemed to be untrustworthy flows primarily from this constitutional power of the President, and Congress may surely provide that the inferior federal courts are not used to infringe on the President's constitutional authority. *See, e.g., Department of Navy v. Egan*, 484 U.S. 518, 526–30 (1988); *Totten v. United States*, 92 U.S. (2 Otto) 105 (1876). Section 102(c) plainly indicates that Congress has done exactly that, and the Court points to nothing in the structure, purpose, or legislative history of the National Security Act that would suggest a different conclusion. Accordingly, I respectfully dissent from the Court's decision to allow this lawsuit to go forward.

JUSTICE SCALIA, dissenting.

I agree with the Court's apparent holding in Part II of its opinion, that the Director's decision to terminate a CIA employee is "committed to agency discretion by law" within the meaning of 5 U.S.C. § 701(a)(2). But because I do not see how a decision can, either practically or legally, be both unreviewable and yet reviewable for constitutional defect, I regard Part III of the opinion as essentially undoing Part II. I therefore respectfully dissent from the judgment of the Court. . . .

II

Before taking the reader through the terrain of the Court's holding that respondent may assert constitutional claims in this suit, I would like to try to clear some of the underbrush, consisting primarily of the Court's ominous warning that "[a] 'serious constitutional question' . . . would arise if a federal statute were construed to deny any judicial forum for a colorable constitutional claim."

The first response to the Court's grave doubt about the constitutionality of denying all judicial review to a "colorable constitutional claim" is that the denial of all judicial review is not at issue here, but merely the denial of review in United States district courts. As to that, the law is, and has long been, clear. Article III, § 2, of the Constitution extends the judicial power to "all Cases . . . arising under this Constitution." But Article III, § 1, provides that the judicial power shall be vested "in one supreme Court, *and in such inferior Courts as the Congress may from time to time ordain and establish*" (emphasis added). We long ago held that the power not to create any lower federal courts at all includes the power to invest them with less than all of the judicial power.

> The Constitution has defined the limits of the judicial power of the United States, but has not prescribed how much of it shall be exercised by the Circuit Court; consequently, the statute which does prescribe the limits of their jurisdiction, cannot be in conflict with the Constitution, unless it confers powers not enumerated therein. *Sheldon v. Sill*, 8 How. 441 (1850).

Thus, if there is any truth to the proposition that judicial cognizance of constitutional claims cannot be eliminated, it is, at most, that they cannot be eliminated from state courts, and from this Court's appellate jurisdiction over cases from state courts (or cases from federal courts, should there be any) involving such claims. Narrowly viewed, therefore, there is no shadow of a constitutional doubt that we are free to hold that the present suit, whether based on constitutional grounds or not, will not lie.

It can fairly be argued, however, that our interpretation of § 701(a)(2) indirectly implicates the constitutional question whether state courts can be deprived of jurisdiction, because if they cannot, then interpreting § 701(a)(2) to exclude relief here would impute to Congress the peculiar intent to let state courts review Federal Government action that it is unwilling to let federal district courts review—or, alternatively, the peculiar intent to let federal district courts review, upon removal from state courts pursuant to 28 U.S.C. § 1442(a)(1), claims that it is unwilling to let federal district courts review in original actions. I turn, then, to the substance of the Court's warning that judicial review of all "colorable constitutional claims" arising out of the respondent's dismissal may well be constitutionally required. What could possibly be the basis for this fear? Surely not some general principle that *all* constitutional violations must be remediable in the courts. The very text of the Constitution refutes that principle, since it provides that "[e]ach House shall be the Judge of the Elections, Returns and Qualifications of its own Members," Art. I, § 5, and that "for any Speech or Debate in either House, [the Senators and Representatives] shall not be questioned in any other Place," Art. I, § 6. Claims concerning constitutional violations committed in these contexts—for example, the rather grave constitutional claim that an election has been stolen—cannot be addressed to the courts. *See, e.g., Morgan v. United States*, 801 F.2d 445, 255 U.S. App. D.C. 231 (1986). Even apart from the strict text of the Constitution, we have found some constitutional claims to be beyond judicial review because they involve "political questions." *See, e.g., Coleman v. Miller*, 307 U.S. 433, 443–46 (1939). The doctrine of sovereign immunity—not repealed by the Constitution, but to the contrary at least partly reaffirmed as to the States by the Eleventh Amendment— is a monument to the principle that some constitutional claims can go unheard. No one would suggest that, if Congress had not passed the Tucker Act, 28 U.S.C. § 1491(a) (1), the courts would be able to order disbursements from the Treasury to pay for property taken under lawful authority (and subsequently destroyed) without just compensation. See *Schillinger v. United States*, 155 U.S. 163, 166–69 (1894). And finally, the doctrine of equitable discretion, which permits a court to refuse relief, even where no relief at law is available, when that would unduly impair the public interest, does not stand aside simply because the basis for the relief is a constitutional claim. In sum, it is simply untenable that there must be a judicial remedy for every constitutional violation. Members of Congress and the supervising officers of the Executive Branch take the same oath to uphold the Constitution that we do, and sometimes they are left to perform that oath unreviewed, as we always are.

Perhaps, then, the Court means to appeal to a more limited principle, that although there may be areas where judicial review of a constitutional claim will be denied, the scope of those areas is fixed by the Constitution and judicial tradition, and cannot be affected by *Congress*, through the enactment of a statute such as § 102(c). That would be a rather counter-intuitive principle, especially since Congress has in reality been the principal determiner of the scope of review, for constitutional claims as well as all other claims, through its waiver of the pre-existing doctrine of sovereign immunity. On the merits of the point, however: It seems to me clear that courts would not entertain, for example, an action for backpay by a dismissed Secretary of State claiming that the reason he lost his Government job was that the President did not like his religious views—surely a colorable violation of the First Amendment. I am confident we would hold that the President's choice of his Secretary of State is a "political question." But what about a similar suit by the Deputy Secretary of State? Or one of the Under Secretaries? Or an Assistant Secretary? Or the head of the European Desk? Is there really a constitutional line that falls at some immutable point between one and another of these offices at which the principle of unreviewability cuts in, and which cannot be altered by congressional prescription? I think not. I think Congress can prescribe, at least within broad limits, that for certain jobs the dismissal decision will be unreviewable—that is, will be "committed to agency discretion by law."

Once it is acknowledged, as I think it must be, (1) that not all constitutional claims require a judicial remedy, and (2) that the identification of those that do not can, even if only within narrow limits, be determined by Congress, then it is clear that the "serious constitutional question" feared by the Court is an illusion. Indeed, it seems to me that if one is in a mood to worry about serious constitutional questions the one to worry about is not whether Congress can, by enacting § 102(c), give the President, through his Director of Central Intelligence, unreviewable discretion in firing the agents that he employs to gather military and foreign affairs intelligence, but rather whether Congress could constitutionally *permit* the courts to review all such decisions if it wanted to. We have acknowledged that the courts cannot intervene when there is "a textually demonstrable constitutional commitment of the issue to a coordinate political department." *Baker v. Carr*, 369 U.S. 186, 217 (1962). We have recognized "the insistence (evident from the number of Clauses devoted to the subject) with which the Constitution confers authority over the Army, Navy, and militia upon the political branches." *United States v. Stanley*, 483 U.S. 669, 682 (1987). We have also recognized "the very delicate, plenary and exclusive power of the President as the sole organ of the federal government in the field of international relations—a power which does not require as a basis for its exercise an act of Congress." *United States v. Curtiss-Wright Export Corp.*, 299 U.S. 304, 320 (1936). And finally, we have acknowledged that "[i]t is impossible for a government wisely to make critical decisions about foreign policy and national defense without the benefit of dependable foreign intelligence." *Snepp v. United States*, 444 U.S. 507, 512 n.7 (1980) (*per curiam*). We have thus recognized that the "authority to classify and control access to information bearing on national security and to determine whether an individual is sufficiently trustworthy to occupy a position in the Executive Branch that will give that person access to such information flows primarily from this constitutional investment of power in the President *and exists quite apart from any explicit congressional grant*." *Department of Navy v. Egan*, 484 U.S. at 527 (emphasis added).

I think it entirely beyond doubt that if Congress intended, by the APA in 5 U.S.C. § 701(a)(2), to exclude judicial review of the President's decision (through the Director of Central Intelligence) to dismiss an officer of the Central Intelligence Agency, that disposition would be constitutionally permissible.

III

I turn, then, to whether that executive action is, within the meaning of § 701(a)(2), "committed to agency discretion by law." [Discussion omitted.]

Note: Eliminating Jurisdiction over Constitutional Claims

1. Chief Justice Rehnquist, writing for the Court in *Webster v. Doe*, refers to "the 'serious constitutional question' that would arise if a federal statute were construed to deny any judicial forum for a colorable constitutional claim." Justice Scalia, in dissent, insists that "the 'serious constitutional question' feared by the Court is an illusion." Do the examples that he gives persuade you on this point?

2. Does the Court implicitly accept the proposition that denying a judicial forum for *non*-constitutional claims would *not* raise a serious constitutional question? Does that conclusion necessary follow from *Sheldon v. Sill* and other cases in that line?

3. None of the bills quoted at the start of this chapter seek to deny *any* judicial forum for the constitutional claims within their scope; they deny access only to *federal* court. Does this eliminate any potential "serious constitutional question"? After all, the language of Article III does not require Congress to create "inferior" federal courts, and the records of the Constitutional Convention confirm that the Framers reached a compromise (in Madison's words) "giving a discretion to the Legislature to establish or not establish" such courts.

As long as a constitutional claim can be pursued in the state courts, with the possibility of review by the United States Supreme Court, what is the basis for an argument that the Constitution requires that a federal court be made available as an original forum? Consider this question in the context of the Problem that follows.

4. One writer has argued that "the framers intended that national tribunals would hear each case within the federal judicial power. . . . When Supreme Court review of all cases within Article III jurisdiction was possible, lower federal courts were perhaps unnecessary. As federal caseloads grew, however, lower federal courts became necessary components of the national judiciary if the constitutional duty of case-by-case consideration of all federal cases was to be fulfilled. It can now be asserted that their existence in some form is constitutionally required." Theodore Eisenberg, *Congressional Authority to Restrict Lower Federal Court Jurisdiction*, 83 YALE L.J. 498, 507, 513 (1974).

Do you find this persuasive? Professor Gunther responded: "Changed circumstances cannot overcome the unambiguous language of Article III or the clearly expressed intent of the Framers to give Congress broad discretion over lower federal court jurisdiction." Gerald Gunther, *Congressional Power to Curtail Federal Court Jurisdiction: An Opinionated Guide to the Ongoing Debate*, 36 STAN. L. REV. 895, 914 (1984).

Problem: Removing Jurisdiction over "Abortion-Related" Cases

Assume that the proposed "Life-Protecting Judicial Limitation Act of 2003" becomes law. It provides that the district courts of the United States "shall not have jurisdiction to hear or determine any abortion-related case," and it defines "abortion-related case" to mean: "any action in which any requirement, prohibition, or other provision relating to abortion that is contained in a State or Federal statute is at issue." But it makes no change in the Supreme Court's appellate jurisdiction.

The State of New Harmony has adopted a law that requires the licensing and regulation of any medical facility in which five or more first trimester abortions in any month or any second or third trimester abortions are performed. Physicians who provide abortions in their private medical practices have brought suit in federal district court under 42 U.S.C. § 1983 challenging the constitutionality of the law under *Planned Parenthood v. Casey*, 505 U.S. 833 (1992). The defendant state officials have moved to dismiss the suit for want of subject-matter jurisdiction under the "Life-Protecting Judicial Limitation Act." The plaintiffs acknowledge that the case comes within the Act, but they argue that the statute is unconstitutional. How should the court rule?

Problems: The "Pledge Protection Act"

1. As originally introduced, the Pledge Protection Act of 2003 (H.R. 2028) provided as follows:

> No court established by Act of Congress shall have jurisdiction to hear or determine any claim that the recitation of the Pledge of Allegiance, as set forth in section 4 of title 4, violates the first article of amendment to the Constitution of the United States.

When the bill came before the House Judiciary Committee for markup, Chairman Sensenbrenner offered a substitute with the following language:

> No court created by Act of Congress shall have any jurisdiction, and the Supreme Court shall have no appellate jurisdiction, to hear or decide any question pertaining to the interpretation of, or the validity under the Constitution of, the Pledge of Allegiance, as defined in section 4 of title 14, or its recitation.

On September 23, 2004, the House passed the substitute bill. (An amendment on the floor added one sentence: "The limitation in this section shall not apply to the Superior Court of the District of Columbia or the District of Columbia Court of Appeals.")

Is the original version of the bill constitutional? Did the substitute diminish or increase its vulnerability to constitutional challenge?

2. When the House considered the substitute version of H.R. 2028, an amendment was offered to allow jurisdiction over—

> a case in which the claim involved alleges coerced or mandatory recitation of the Pledge of Allegiance, including coercion in violation of the protection of the free exercise of religion, such as that held to be in violation of the First Amendment in *West Virginia State Board of Education v. Barnett*, 319 U.S. 624, 638 (1943) and *Circle Schools v. Pappert* [381 F.3d 172 (3d Cir. 2004)].

The amendment was rejected. Chairman Sensenbrenner, speaking in opposition, said:

> [Nothing] in H.R. 2028 would allow State courts to deviate from Supreme Court precedent prohibiting the coerced recitation of the Pledge of Allegiance. Even when Federal courts are denied jurisdiction to hear certain classes of

cases, and those classes of cases are thereby reserved to the State courts, the previously existing Supreme Court precedents still govern State court determinations. This is required by the Supremacy Clause of the Constitution; and in *West Virginia Board of Education v. Barnette*, the Supreme Court held it is unconstitutional to require individuals to salute the flag. . . . Under H.R. 2028 as written, that decision will preclude State courts from allowing coerced recitations of the Pledge.

State courts are not second-class courts, and they are equally capable of deciding Federal constitutional questions. The Supreme Court has clearly rejected claims that State courts are less competent to decide Federal constitutional issues than Federal courts. . . .

Is this a sufficient answer to concerns about the bill's constitutionality? Would the proposed amendment extending jurisdiction to cases involving coerced or mandatory recitation of the Pledge of Allegiance help the bill pass constitutional muster if it were ever enacted into law?

Chapter 20

Congressional Power to Control Judicial Decision Making

As the examples in the preceding chapter indicate, one reason members of Congress introduce legislation to eliminate federal court jurisdiction over particular classes of cases is that they disagree with the rulings of the courts in that area of the law. (The Marriage Protection Act of 2004 was an exception; that bill was aimed at *forestalling* a decision that would hold the Defense of Marriage Act unconstitutional.) Commentators have sometimes suggested that such legislation would be self-defeating, because the very decisions that the legislators do not like would be frozen into law: when new cases arose presenting the issues, the courts could not hear them and thus could not reverse the rulings that triggered the legislation.

Other observers have been more cynical. They suggest that the sponsors of such legislation fully expect that state courts will disregard the targeted rulings and that, without the possibility of Supreme Court review, these courts will decide cases in accordance with the legislators' preferences.

Some court-stripping measures have taken a more aggressive approach: they seek to limit the precedential effect of the decisions that are the target of the jurisdictional restrictions. Consider a bill that was the subject of a hearing in the 108th Congress (2003–2004)—H.R. 3799, the "Constitution Restoration Act of 2004." Title I of the bill provided that neither the Supreme Court nor the district courts shall have jurisdiction of "any matter to the extent that relief is sought against an element of Federal, State, or local government, or against an officer of Federal, State, or local government (whether or not acting in official personal capacity), by reason of that element's or officer's acknowledgment of God as the sovereign source of law, liberty, or government." Title III added an "enforcement" provision:

> Any decision of a Federal court which has been made prior to or after the effective date of this Act, to the extent that the decision relates to an issue removed from Federal jurisdiction under [this Act], is not binding precedent on any State court.

H.R. 3799 also included a separate, unrelated provision governing the interpretation of the Constitution by federal courts. Title II provided:

> In interpreting and applying the Constitution of the United States, a court of the United States may not rely upon any constitution, law, administrative rule, Executive order, directive, policy, judicial decision, or any other

action of any foreign state or international organization or agency, other than the constitutional law and English common law.

H.R. 3799 thus told *state* courts that certain federal decisions are "not binding precedent," and it further told *federal* courts that they "may not rely upon" certain materials in "interpreting and applying the Constitution of the United States." Were these directives constitutional? What are the limits on Congress's power to control decision making by federal and state courts? This chapter examines those questions.

United States v. Klein

Supreme Court of the United States, 1871.

13 Wall. (80 U.S.) 128.

[The report of this decision appears in Chapter 19, Section A.]

Plaut v. Spendthrift Farm, Inc.

Supreme Court of the United States, 1995.

514 U.S. 211.

JUSTICE SCALIA delivered the opinion of the Court.

The question presented in this case is whether § 27A(b) of the Securities Exchange Act of 1934, to the extent that it requires federal courts to reopen final judgments in private civil actions under § 10(b) of the Act, contravenes the Constitution's separation of powers or the Due Process Clause of the Fifth Amendment.

I

In 1987, petitioners brought a civil action against respondents in the United States District Court for the Eastern District of Kentucky. The complaint alleged that in 1983 and 1984 respondents had committed fraud and deceit in the sale of stock in violation of § 10(b) of the Securities Exchange Act of 1934 and Rule 10b-5 of the Securities and Exchange Commission. The case was mired in pretrial proceedings in the District Court until June 20, 1991, when we decided *Lampf, Pleva, Lipkind, Prupis & Petigrow v. Gilbertson*, 501 U.S. 350. *Lampf* held that "[l]itigation instituted pursuant to § 10(b) and Rule 10b-5 . . . must be commenced within one year after the discovery of the facts constituting the violation and within three years after such violation." We applied that holding to the plaintiff-respondents in *Lampf* itself, found their suit untimely, and reinstated a summary judgment previously entered in favor of the defendant-petitioners.

On the same day we decided *James B. Beam Distilling Co. v. Georgia*, 501 U.S. 529 (1991), in which a majority of the Court held, albeit in different opinions, that a new rule of federal law that is applied to the parties in the case announcing the rule must be applied as well to all cases pending on direct review. See *Harper v. Virginia Dept. of Taxation*, 509 U.S. 86, 92, 113 (1993). The joint effect of *Lampf* and *Beam* was to mandate application of the 1-year/3-year limitations period to petitioners' suit. The District Court, finding that petitioners' claims were untimely under the *Lampf* rule, dismissed their action with prejudice on August 13, 1991. Petitioners filed no appeal; the judgment accordingly became final 30 days later. See 28 U.S.C. § 2107(a).

On December 19, 1991, the President signed the Federal Deposit Insurance Corporation Improvement Act of 1991. Section 476 of the Act—a section that had nothing to do with FDIC improvements—became § 27A of the Securities Exchange Act of 1934, and was later codified as 15 U.S.C. § 78aa-1. It provides:

(a) Effect on pending causes of action

The limitation period for any private civil action implied under section 78j(b) of this title [§ 10(b) of the Securities Exchange Act of 1934] that was commenced on or before June 19, 1991, shall be the limitation period provided by the laws applicable in the jurisdiction, including principles of retroactivity, as such laws existed on June 19, 1991.

(b) Effect on dismissed causes of action

Any private civil action implied under section 78j(b) of this title that was commenced on or before June 19, 1991—

(1) which was dismissed as time barred subsequent to June 19, 1991, and

(2) which would have been timely filed under the limitation period provided by the laws applicable in the jurisdiction, including principles of retroactivity, as such laws existed on June 19, 1991,

shall be reinstated on motion by the plaintiff not later than 60 days after December 19, 1991.

On February 11, 1992, petitioners returned to the District Court and filed a motion to reinstate the action previously dismissed with prejudice. The District Court found that the conditions set out in §§ 27A(b)(1) and (2) were met, so that petitioners' motion was required to be granted by the terms of the statute. It nonetheless denied the motion, agreeing with respondents that § 27A(b) is unconstitutional. The United States Court of Appeals for the Sixth Circuit affirmed. We granted certiorari.

II

Respondents bravely contend that § 27A(b) does not require federal courts to reopen final judgments. . . . [The Court rejected the argument. Its discussion is omitted.]

III

Respondents submit that § 27A(b) violates both the separation of powers and the Due Process Clause of the Fifth Amendment. Because the latter submission, if correct, might dictate a similar result in a challenge to state legislation under the Fourteenth Amendment, the former is the narrower ground for adjudication of the constitutional questions in the case, and we therefore consider it first. We conclude that in § 27A(b) Congress has exceeded its authority by requiring the federal courts to exercise "[t]he judicial Power of the United States," U.S. CONST., art. III, § 1, in a manner repugnant to the text, structure, and traditions of Article III.

Our decisions to date have identified two types of legislation that require federal courts to exercise the judicial power in a manner that Article III forbids. The first appears in *United States v. Klein*, 13 Wall. 128 (1872), where we refused to give effect to a statute that was said "[to] prescribe rules of decision to the Judicial Department of the government in cases pending before it." Whatever the precise scope of *Klein*, however, later decisions have made clear that its prohibition does not take hold when Congress "amend[s] applicable law." *Robertson v. Seattle Audubon Soc.*, 503 U.S. 429, 441 (1992). Section 27A(b) indisputably does set out substantive legal standards for the Judiciary to apply, and in that sense changes the law (even if solely retroactively). The second type of unconstitutional restriction upon the exercise of judicial power identified by past cases is exemplified by *Hayburn's Case*, 2 Dall. 409 (1792), which stands for the principle that Congress cannot vest review of the decisions of Article III courts in officials of the Executive Branch. *See, e.g., Chicago & Southern Air Lines, Inc. v. Waterman S.S. Corp.*, 333 U.S. 103 (1948). Yet under any application of § 27A(b) only courts are involved; no officials of other departments sit in direct review of their decisions. Section 27A(b) therefore offends neither of these previously established prohibitions.

We think, however, that § 27A(b) offends a postulate of Article III just as deeply rooted in our law as those we have mentioned. Article III establishes a "judicial department" with the "province and duty . . . to say what the law is" in particular cases and controversies. *Marbury v. Madison*, 1 Cranch 137, 177 (1803). The record of history shows that the Framers crafted this charter of the judicial department with an expressed understanding that it gives the Federal Judiciary the power, not merely to rule on cases, but to *decide* them, subject to review only by superior courts in the Article III hierarchy—with an understanding, in short, that "a judgment conclusively resolves the case" because "a 'judicial Power' is one to render dispositive judgments." Easterbrook, *Presidential Review*, 40 CASE W. RES. L. REV. 905, 926 (1990). By retroactively commanding the federal courts to reopen final judgments, Congress has violated this fundamental principle.

A

The Framers of our Constitution lived among the ruins of a system of intermingled legislative and judicial powers, which had been prevalent in the colonies long before the Revolution, and which after the Revolution had produced factional strife and partisan oppression. In the 17th and 18th centuries colonial assemblies and legislatures functioned as courts of equity of last resort, hearing original actions or providing appellate review of judicial judgments. G. WOOD, THE CREATION OF THE AMERICAN REPUBLIC 1776–1787, pp. 154–155 (1969). Often, however, they chose to correct the judicial process through special bills or other enacted legislation. It was common for such legislation not to prescribe a resolution of the dispute, but rather simply to set aside the judgment and order a new trial or appeal. M. CLARKE, PARLIAMENTARY PRIVILEGE IN THE AMERICAN COLONIES 49–51 (1943). *See, e.g., Judicial Action by the Provincial Legislature of Massachusetts*, 15 HARV. L. REV. 208 (1902) (collecting documents from 1708–1709). Thus, as described in our discussion of *Hayburn's Case*, such legislation bears not on the problem of interbranch review but on the problem of finality of judicial judgments.

The vigorous, indeed often radical, populism of the revolutionary legislatures and assemblies increased the frequency of legislative correction of judgments. "The period 1780–1787 . . . was a period of 'constitutional reaction'" to these developments, "which . . . leaped suddenly to its climax in the Philadelphia Convention." E. CORWIN, THE DOCTRINE OF JUDICIAL REVIEW 37 (1914). Voices from many quarters, official as well as private, decried the increasing legislative interference with the private-law judgments of the courts. . . .

This sense of a sharp necessity to separate the legislative from the judicial power, prompted by the crescendo of legislative interference with private judgments of the courts, triumphed among the Framers of the new Federal Constitution. See Corwin, *The Progress of Constitutional Theory Between the Declaration of Independence and the Meeting of the Philadelphia Convention*, 30 AM. HIST. REV. 511, 514–517 (1925). The Convention made the critical decision to establish a judicial department independent of the Legislative Branch by providing that "the judicial Power of the United States shall be vested in one supreme Court, and in such inferior Courts as the Congress may from time to time ordain and establish." Before and during the debates on ratification, Madison, Jefferson, and Hamilton each wrote of the factional disorders and disarray that the system of legislative equity had produced in the years before the framing; and each thought that the separation of the legislative from the judicial power in the new Constitution would cure them.

If the need for separation of legislative from judicial power was plain, the principal effect to be accomplished by that separation was even plainer. As Hamilton wrote in his exegesis of Article III, § 1, in THE FEDERALIST No. 81:

> It is not true . . . that the parliament of Great Britain, or the legislatures of the particular states, can rectify the exceptionable decisions of their respective courts, in any other sense than might be done by a future legislature of the United States. The theory neither of the British, nor the state constitutions, authorises the revisal of a judicial sentence, by a legislative act. . . . A legislature without exceeding its province cannot reverse a determination once made, in a particular case; though it may prescribe a new rule for future cases. THE FEDERALIST No. 81, p. 545 (J. Cooke ed., 1961).

The essential balance created by this allocation of authority was a simple one. The Legislature would be possessed of power to "prescrib[e] the rules by which the duties and rights of every citizen are to be regulated," but the power of "[t]he interpretation of the laws" would be "the proper and peculiar province of the courts." THE FEDERALIST No. 78, pp. 523, 525. The Judiciary would be, "from the nature of its functions, . . . the [department] least dangerous to the political rights of the constitution," not because its acts were subject to legislative correction, but because the binding effect of its acts was limited to particular cases and controversies. Thus, "though individual oppression may now and then proceed from the courts of justice, the general liberty of the people can never be endangered from that quarter: . . . so long as the judiciary remains truly distinct from both the legislative and executive." *Id.* No. 78, at 522.

Judicial decisions in the period immediately after ratification of the Constitution confirm the understanding that it forbade interference with the final judgments of courts. In *Calder v. Bull*, 3 Dall. 386 (1798), the Legislature of Connecticut had enacted a statute that set aside the final judgment of a state court in a civil case. Although the issue before this Court was the construction of the *Ex Post Facto* Clause, Art. I, § 10, Justice Iredell (a leading Federalist who had guided the Constitution to ratification in North Carolina) noted that

> the Legislature of [Connecticut] has been in the uniform, uninterrupted, habit of exercising a general superintending power over its courts of law, by granting new trials. It may, indeed, appear strange to some of us, that in any form, there should exist a power to grant, with respect to suits depending or adjudged, new rights of trial, new privileges of proceeding, not previously recognized and regulated by positive institutions. . . . The power . . . is judicial in its nature; and whenever it is exercised, as in the present instance, it is an exercise of judicial, not of legislative, authority.

By the middle of the 19th century, the constitutional equilibrium created by the separation of the legislative power to make general law from the judicial power to apply that law in particular cases was so well understood and accepted that it could survive even *Dred Scott v. Sandford*, 19 How. 393 (1857). In his First Inaugural Address, President Lincoln explained why the political branches could not, and need not, interfere with even that infamous judgment:

> I do not forget the position assumed by some, that constitutional questions are to be decided by the Supreme Court; nor do I deny that such decisions must be binding in any case, upon the parties to a suit, as to the object of that suit. . . . And while it is obviously possible that such decision may be erroneous in any given case, still the evil effect following it, being limited to that particular case, with the chance that it may be over-ruled, and never become a precedent for other cases, can better be borne than could the evils of a different practice. 4 R. Basler, The Collected Works of Abraham Lincoln 268 (1953) (First Inaugural Address 1861).

And the great constitutional scholar Thomas Cooley addressed precisely the question before us in his 1868 treatise:

> If the legislature cannot thus indirectly control the action of the courts, by requiring of them a construction of the law according to its own views, it is very plain it cannot do so directly, by setting aside their judgments, compelling them to grant new trials, ordering the discharge of offenders, or directing what particular steps shall be taken in the progress of a judicial inquiry.

B

Section 27A(b) effects a clear violation of the separation-of-powers principle we have just discussed.

It is, of course, retroactive legislation, that is, legislation that prescribes what the law was at an earlier time, when the act whose effect is controlled by the legislation occurred—in this case, the filing of the initial Rule 10b-5 action in the District Court. When retroactive legislation requires its own application in a case already finally adjudicated, it does no more and no less than "reverse a determination once made, in a particular case." THE FEDERALIST No. 81, at 545. Our decisions stemming from *Hayburn's Case*—although their precise holdings are not strictly applicable here—have uniformly provided fair warning that such an act exceeds the powers of Congress. *See, e.g., Chicago & Southern Air Lines, Inc.*, 333 U.S. at 113 ("Judgments within the powers vested in courts by the Judiciary Article of the Constitution may not lawfully be revised, overturned or refused faith and credit by another Department of Government"). Today those clear statements must either be honored, or else proved false.

It is true, as petitioners contend, that Congress can always revise the judgments of Article III courts in one sense: When a new law makes clear that it is retroactive, an appellate court must apply that law in reviewing judgments still on appeal that were rendered before the law was enacted, and must alter the outcome accordingly. See *United States v. Schooner Peggy*, 1 Cranch 103 (1801); *Landgraf v. USI Film Products*, 511 U.S. 244, 273–80 (1994). Since that is so, petitioners argue, federal courts must apply the "new" law created by §27A(b) in finally adjudicated cases as well; for the line that separates lower court judgments that are pending on appeal (or may still be appealed), from lower-court judgments that are final, is determined by statute, *see, e.g.*, 28 U.S.C. §2107(a) (30-day time limit for appeal to federal court of appeals), and so cannot possibly be a constitutional line. But a distinction between judgments from which all appeals have been forgone or completed, and judgments that remain on appeal (or subject to being appealed), is implicit in what Article III creates: not a batch of unconnected courts, but a judicial *department* composed of "inferior Courts" and "one supreme Court." Within that hierarchy, the decision of an inferior court is not (unless the time for appeal has expired) the final word of the department as a whole. It is the obligation of the last court in the hierarchy that rules on the case to give effect to Congress's latest enactment, even when that has the effect of overturning the judgment of an inferior court, since each court, at every level, must "decide according to existing laws." *Schooner Peggy*. Having achieved finality, however, a judicial decision becomes the last word of the judicial department with regard to a particular case or controversy, and Congress may not declare by retroactive legislation that the law applicable to that very case was something other than what the courts said it was. Finality of a legal judgment is determined by statute, just as entitlement to a government benefit is a statutory creation; but that no more deprives the former of its constitutional significance for separation-of-powers analysis than it deprives the latter of its significance for due process purposes.

To be sure, §27A(b) reopens (or directs the reopening of) final judgments in a whole class of cases rather than in a particular suit. We do not see how that makes any difference. The separation-of-powers violation here, if there is any, consists of depriving judicial judgments of the conclusive effect that they had when they were announced, not of acting in a manner—viz., with particular rather than general effect—that is unusual (though, we must note, not impossible) for a legislature. To be sure, a general statute such as this one may reduce the perception that legislative interference with judicial judgments was prompted by individual favoritism; but it is legislative interference with judicial judgments nonetheless. Not favoritism, nor even corruption, but *power* is the object of the separation-of-powers prohibition. The prohibition is violated when an individual final judgment is legislatively rescinded for even the very best of reasons, such as the legislature's genuine conviction (supported by all the law professors in the land) that the judgment was wrong; and it is violated 40 times over when 40 final judgments are legislatively dissolved.

It is irrelevant as well that the final judgments reopened by §27A(b) rested on the bar of a statute of limitations. The rules of finality, both statutory and judge made, treat a dismissal on statute-of-limitations grounds the same way they treat a dismissal for failure to state a claim, for failure to prove substantive liability, or for failure to prosecute: as a judgment on the merits. *See, e.g.*, FED. RULE CIV. PROC. 41(b).

The dissent maintains that *Lampf* "announced" a new statute of limitations in an act of "judicial . . . lawmaking" that "changed the law." That statement, even if relevant, would be wrong. The point decided in *Lampf* had never before been addressed by this Court, and was therefore an open question, no matter what the lower courts had held at the time. But the more important point is that *Lampf* as such is irrelevant to this case. The dissent itself perceives that "[w]e would have the same issue to decide had Congress enacted the *Lampf* rule," and that the *Lampf* rule's genesis in judicial lawmaking rather than, shall we say, legislative lawmaking, "should not affect the separation-of-powers analysis." Just so. The issue here is not the validity or even the source of the legal rule that produced the Article III judgments, but rather the immunity from legislative abrogation of those judgments themselves. The separation-of-powers question before us has nothing to do with *Lampf*, and the dissent's attack on *Lampf* has nothing to do with the question before us.

C

Apart from the statute we review today, we know of no instance in which Congress has attempted to set aside the final judgment of an Article III court by retroactive legislation. That prolonged reticence would be amazing if such interference were not understood to be constitutionally proscribed. The closest analogue that the Government has been able to put forward is the statute at issue in *United States v. Sioux Nation*, 448 U.S. 371 (1980). That law required the Court of Claims "'[n]otwithstanding any other provision of law . . . [to] review on the merits, without regard to the defense of res judicata or collateral estoppel,'" a Sioux claim for just compensation from the United States—even though the Court of Claims had previously heard and rejected that very claim. We considered and rejected separation-of-powers objections to the statute based upon *Hayburn's Case* and *United States v. Klein*. The basis for our rejection was a line of precedent (starting with *Cherokee Nation v. United States*, 270 U.S. 476 (1926)) that stood, we said, for the proposition that "Congress has the power to waive the res judicata effect of a prior judgment entered in the Government's favor on a claim against the United States." And our holding was as narrow as the precedent on which we had relied: "In sum, . . . Congress' mere waiver of the res judicata effect of a prior judicial decision rejecting the validity of a legal claim against the United States does not violate the doctrine of separation of powers."

Petitioners also rely on a miscellany of decisions upholding legislation that altered rights fixed by the final judgments of non-Article III courts, *see, e.g., Sampeyreac v. United States*, 7 Pet. 222, 238 (1833); *Freeborn v. Smith*, 2 Wall. 160 (1865), or administrative agencies, *Paramino Lumber Co. v. Marshall*, 309 U.S. 370 (1940), or that altered the prospective effect of injunctions entered by Article III courts, *Pennsylvania v. Wheeling & Belmont Bridge Co.*, 18 How. 421 (1856). These cases distinguish themselves; nothing in our holding today calls them into question. Petitioners rely on general statements from some of these cases that legislative annulment of final judgments is not an exercise of judicial power. But even if it were our practice to decide cases by weight of prior dicta, we would find the many dicta that reject congressional power to revise the judgments of Article III courts to be the more instructive authority.

Finally, petitioners liken § 27A(b) to Federal Rule of Civil Procedure 60(b), which authorizes courts to relieve parties from a final judgment for grounds such as excusable neglect, newly discovered evidence, fraud, or "any other reason justifying relief. . . ." We see little resemblance. Rule 60(b), which authorizes discretionary judicial revision of judgments in the listed situations and in other "extraordinary circumstances," *Liljeberg v. Health Services Acquisition Corp.*, 486 U.S. 847, 864 (1988), does not impose any legislative mandate to reopen upon the courts, but merely reflects and confirms the courts' own inherent and discretionary power, "firmly established in English practice long before the foundation of our Republic," to set aside a judgment whose enforcement would work inequity. *Hazel-Atlas Glass Co. v. Hartford-Empire Co.*, 322 U.S. 238, 244 (1944). Thus, Rule 60(b), and the tradition that it embodies, would be relevant refutation of a claim that reopening a final judgment is always a denial of property without due process; but they are irrelevant to the claim that legislative instruction to reopen impinges upon the independent constitutional authority of the courts.

The dissent promises to provide "[a] few contemporary examples" of statutes retroactively requiring final judgments to be reopened, "to demonstrate that [such statutes] are ordinary products of the exercise of legislative power." That promise is not kept. The relevant retroactivity, of course, consists not of the requirement that there be set aside a judgment that has been rendered prior to its being setting aside—for example, a statute passed today which says that all default judgments rendered in the future may be reopened within 90 days after their entry. In that sense, all requirements to reopen are "retroactive," and the designation is superfluous. Nothing we say today precludes a law such as that. The finality that a court can pronounce is no more than what the law in existence at the time of judgment will permit it to pronounce. If the law then applicable says that the judgment may be reopened for certain reasons, that limitation is built into the judgment itself, and its finality is so conditioned. The present case, however, involves a judgment that Congress subjected to a reopening requirement which did not exist when the judgment was pronounced. The dissent provides not a single clear prior instance of such congressional action.

The dissent's perception that retroactive reopening provisions are to be found all about us is perhaps attributable to its inversion of the statutory presumption regarding retroactivity. Thus, it asserts that Rule 60(b) must be retroactive, since "[n]ot a single word in its text suggests that it does not apply to judgments entered prior to its effective date." This reverses the traditional rule, confirmed only last Term, that statutes *do not* apply retroactively *unless* Congress expressly states that they do. See *Landgraf*. The dissent adds that "the traditional construction of remedial measures . . . support[s] construing [Rule 60(b)] to apply to past as well as future judgments." But reliance on the vaguely remedial purpose of a statute to defeat the presumption against retroactivity was rejected in the companion cases of *Landgraf* and *Rivers v. Roadway Express*, 511 U.S. at 309–13.

The dissent sets forth a number of hypothetical horribles flowing from our assertedly "rigid holding"—for example, the inability to set aside a civil judgment that has become final during a period when a natural disaster prevented the timely filing of a certiorari petition. That is horrible not because of our holding, but because the underlying statute *itself* enacts a "rigid" jurisdictional bar to entertaining untimely civil petitions. Congress could undoubtedly enact *prospective* legislation permitting, or indeed requiring, this Court to make equitable exceptions to an otherwise applicable rule of finality, just as district courts do pursuant to Rule 60(b). It is no indication whatever of the invalidity of the constitutional rule which we announce, that it produces unhappy consequences when a legislature lacks foresight, and acts belatedly to remedy a deficiency in the law. That is a routine result of constitutional rules. *See, e.g., Collins v. Youngblood*, 497 U.S. 37 (1990) (*Ex Post Facto* Clause precludes post-offense statutory extension of a criminal sentence); *United States Trust Co. of N.Y. v. New Jersey*, 431 U.S. 1 (1977) (Contract Clause prevents retroactive alteration of contract with state bondholders); *Louisville Joint Stock Land Bank v. Radford*, 295 U.S. 555, 589–90 (1935) (Takings Clause invalidates a bankruptcy law that abrogates a vested property interest).

Finally, we may respond to the suggestion of the concurrence that this case should be decided more narrowly. The concurrence is willing to acknowledge only that "*sometimes* Congress lacks the power under Article I to reopen an otherwise closed court judgment." In the present context, what it considers critical is that § 27A(b) is "exclusively retroactive" and "appli[es] to a limited number of individuals." If Congress had only "provid[ed] some of the assurances against 'singling out' that ordinary legislative activity normally provides—say, prospectivity and general applicability—we might have a different case."

This seems to us wrong in both fact and law. In point of fact, § 27A(b) does not "single out" any defendant for adverse treatment (or any plaintiff for favorable treatment). Rather, it identifies a class of actions (those filed pre-*Lampf*, timely under applicable state law, but dismissed as time barred post-*Lampf*) which embraces many plaintiffs and defendants, the precise number and identities of whom we even now do not know. The concurrence's contention that the number of covered defendants "is too small (*compared with the number of similar, uncovered firms*) to distinguish meaningfully the law before us from a similar law aimed at a single closed case" (emphasis added), renders the concept of "singling out" meaningless.

More importantly, however, the concurrence's point seems to us wrong in law. To be sure, the class of actions identified by § 27A(b) could have been more expansive (*e.g.*, all actions that were *or could have been* filed pre-*Lampf*) and the provision could have been written to have prospective as well as retroactive effect (*e.g.*, "all post-*Lampf* dismissed actions, plus all future actions under Rule 10b-5, shall be timely if brought within 30 years of the injury"). But it escapes us how this could in any way cause the statute to be any less an infringement upon the judicial power. The nub of that infringement consists *not* of the Legislature's acting in a particularized and hence (according to the concurrence) nonlegislative fashion;[1] but rather of the Legislature's nullifying prior, authoritative judicial action. It makes no difference whatever to that separation-of-powers violation that it is in gross rather than particularized (*e.g.*, "we hereby set aside *all* hitherto entered judicial orders"), or that it is not accompanied by an "almost" violation of the Bill of Attainder Clause, or an "almost" violation of any other constitutional provision.

Ultimately, the concurrence agrees with our judgment only "[b]ecause the law before us embodies risks of the very sort that our Constitution's 'separation of powers' prohibition seeks to avoid." But the doctrine of separation of powers is a *structural safeguard* rather than a remedy to be applied only when specific harm, or risk of specific harm, can be identified. In its major features (of which the conclusiveness of judicial judgments is assuredly one) it is a prophylactic device, establishing high walls and clear distinctions because low walls and vague distinctions will not be judicially defensible in the heat of interbranch conflict. It is interesting that the concurrence quotes twice, and cites without quotation a third time, the opinion of Justice Powell in *INS v. Chadha*, 462 U.S. at 959. But Justice Powell wrote only for himself in that case. He alone expressed dismay that "[t]he Court's decision . . . apparently will invalidate every use of the legislative veto," and opined that "[t]he breadth of this holding gives one pause." It did not give pause to the six-Justice majority, which put an end to the long-simmering interbranch dispute that would otherwise have been indefinitely prolonged. We think legislated invalidation of judicial judgments deserves the same categorical treatment accorded by *Chadha* to congressional invalidation of executive action. The delphic alternative suggested by the concurrence (the setting aside of

---

1. The premise that there is something wrong with particularized legislative action is of course questionable. While legislatures usually act through laws of general applicability, that is by no means their only legitimate mode of action. Private bills in Congress are still common, and were even more so in the days before establishment of the Claims Court. Even laws that impose a duty or liability upon a single individual or firm are not on that account invalid—or else we would not have the extensive jurisprudence that we do concerning the Bill of Attainder Clause, including cases which say that it requires not merely "singling out" but also *punishment, see, e.g., United States v. Lovett*, 328 U.S. 303, 315–18 (1946), and a case which says that Congress may legislate "a legitimate class of one," *Nixon v. Administrator of General Services*, 433 U.S. 425, 472 (1977).

judgments is all right so long as Congress does not "impermissibly tr[y] to *apply*, as well as *make*, the law") simply prolongs doubt and multiplies confrontation. Separation of powers, a distinctively American political doctrine, profits from the advice authored by a distinctively American poet: Good fences make good neighbors.

* * *

We know of no previous instance in which Congress has enacted retroactive legislation requiring an Article III court to set aside a final judgment, and for good reason. The Constitution's separation of legislative and judicial powers denies it the authority to do so. Section 27A(b) is unconstitutional to the extent that it requires federal courts to reopen final judgments entered before its enactment. The judgment of the Court of Appeals is affirmed.

JUSTICE BREYER, concurring in the judgment.

I agree with the majority that § 27A(b) of the Securities Exchange Act of 1934 is unconstitutional. In my view, the separation of powers inherent in our Constitution means that at least *sometimes* Congress lacks the power under Article I to reopen an otherwise closed court judgment. And the statutory provision here at issue, § 27A(b), violates a basic "separation-of-powers" principle—one intended to protect individual liberty. Three features of this law—its exclusively retroactive effect, its application to a limited number of individuals, and its reopening of closed judgments—taken together, show that Congress here impermissibly tried to *apply*, as well as *make*, the law. Hence, § 27A(b) falls outside the scope of Article I. But, it is far less clear, and unnecessary for the purposes of this case to decide, that separation of powers "is violated" *whenever* an "individual final judgment is legislatively rescinded" or that it is "violated 40 times over when 40 final judgments are legislatively dissolved." I therefore write separately.

The majority provides strong historical evidence that Congress lacks the power simply to reopen, and to revise, final judgments in individual cases. . . . For one thing, the authoritative application of a general law to a particular case by an independent judge, rather than by the legislature itself, provides an assurance that even an unfair law at least will be applied evenhandedly according to its terms. . . . For another thing, as Justice Powell has pointed out, the Constitution's "separation-of-powers" principles reflect, in part, the Framers' "concern that a legislature should not be able unilaterally to impose a substantial deprivation on one person." *INS v. Chadha*, 462 U.S. 919, 962 (1983) (opinion concurring in judgment). The Framers "expressed" this principle, both in "specific provisions, such as the Bill of Attainder Clause," and in the Constitution's "general allocation of power."

Despite these two important "separation-of-powers" concerns, *sometimes* Congress can enact legislation that focuses upon a small group, or even a single individual. *See, e.g., Nixon v. Administrator of General Services*, 433 U.S. 425 (1977); *Selective Service System v. Minnesota Public Interest Research Group*, 468 U.S. 841 (1984). Congress also sometimes passes private legislation. See *Chadha, supra*, 462 U.S. at 966 n.9 (Powell, J., concurring in judgment) ("When Congress grants particular individuals relief or benefits under its spending power, the danger of oppressive action that the separation of powers was designed to avoid is not implicated"). And, *sometimes* Congress can enact legislation that, as a practical matter, radically changes the effect of an individual, previously entered court decree. See *Pennsylvania v. Wheeling & Belmont Bridge Co.*, 18 How. 421 (1856). Statutes that apply prospectively and (in part because of that prospectivity) to an open-ended class of persons, however, are more than simply an effort to apply, person by person, a previously enacted law, or to single out for oppressive treatment one, or a handful, of particular individuals. Thus, it seems to me, if Congress enacted legislation that reopened an otherwise closed judgment but in a way that mitigated some of the here relevant "separation-of-powers" concerns, by also providing some of the assurances against "singling out" that ordinary legislative activity normally provides — say, prospectivity and general applicability — we might have a different case. Because such legislation, in light of those mitigating circumstances, might well present a different constitutional question, I do not subscribe to the Court's more absolute statement.

The statute before us, however, has no such mitigating features. It reopens previously closed judgments. It is entirely retroactive, applying only to those Rule 10b-5 actions actually filed, on or before (but on which final judgments were entered after) June 19, 1991. It lacks generality, for it applies only to a few individual instances. See [House hearings] (listing, by case name, only 15 cases that had been dismissed on the basis of *Lampf, Pleva, Lipkind, Prupis & Petigrow v. Gilbertson*, 501 U.S. 350 (1991)). And, it is underinclusive, for it excludes from its coverage others who, relying upon pre-*Lampf* limitations law, may have failed to bring timely securities fraud actions against any other of the Nation's hundreds of thousands of businesses. I concede that its coverage extends beyond a single individual to many potential plaintiffs in these class actions. But because the legislation disfavors not plaintiffs but defendants, I should think that the latter number is the more relevant. And, that number is too small (compared with the number of similar, uncovered firms) to distinguish meaningfully the law before us from a similar law aimed at a single closed case. Nor does the existence of § 27A(a), which applies to Rule 10b-5 actions pending at the time of the legislation, change this conclusion. That provision seems aimed at too few additional individuals to mitigate the low level of generality of § 27A(b).

The upshot is that, viewed in light of the relevant, liberty-protecting objectives of the "separation of powers," this case falls directly within the scope of language in this Court's cases suggesting a restriction on Congress' power to reopen closed court judgments. *See, e.g.,* . . . *Hayburn's Case*, 2 Dall. 409, 413 (1792) (letter from Justice Iredell and District Judge Sitgreaves to President Washington) ("[N]o decision of any court of the United States can, under any circumstances, in our opinion, agreeable to the Constitution, be liable to a revision, or even suspension, by the Legislature itself").

JUSTICE STEVENS, with whom JUSTICE GINSBURG joins, dissenting.

On December 19, 1991, Congress enacted § 27A of the Securities Exchange Act of 1934 (hereinafter 1991 amendment), to remedy a flaw in the limitations rule this Court announced on June 20, 1991, in *Lampf, Pleva, Lipkind, Prupis & Petigrow v. Gilbertson*, 501 U.S. 350 (1991). In *Lampf* the Court replaced the array of state statutes of limitations that had governed [10b-5 actions] with a uniform federal limitations rule.

Congress found only one flaw in the Court's new rule: its failure to exempt pending cases from its operation. Accordingly, without altering the prospective effect of the *Lampf* rule, the 1991 amendment remedied its flaw by providing that pre-*Lampf* law should determine the limitations period applicable to all cases that had been pending on June 20, 1991—both those that remained pending on December 19, 1991, when § 27A was enacted, and those that courts dismissed between June 20 and December 19, 1991. Today the Court holds that the 1991 amendment violates the Constitution's separation of powers because, by encompassing the dismissed claims, it requires courts to reopen final judgments in private civil actions.

Section 27A is a statutory amendment to a rule of law announced by this Court. The fact that the new rule announced in *Lampf* was a product of judicial, rather than congressional, lawmaking should not affect the separation-of-powers analysis. We would have the same issue to decide had Congress enacted the *Lampf* rule but, as a result of inadvertence or perhaps a scrivener's error, failed to exempt pending cases, as is customary when limitations periods are shortened. In my opinion, if Congress had retroactively restored rights its own legislation had inadvertently or unfairly impaired, the remedial amendment's failure to exclude dismissed cases from the benefited class would not make it invalid. The Court today faces a materially identical situation and, in my view, reaches the wrong result.

Throughout our history, Congress has passed laws that allow courts to reopen final judgments. Such laws characteristically apply to judgments entered before as well as after their enactment. When they apply retroactively, they may raise serious due process questions, but the Court has never invalidated such a law on separation-of-powers grounds until today.

The familiar history the Court invokes, involving colonial legislatures' ad hoc decisions of individual cases, "'unfettered by rules,'" provides no support for its holding. On the contrary, history and precedent demonstrate that Congress may enact laws that establish both substantive rules and procedures for reopening final judgments. When it enacted the 1991 amendment to the *Lampf* rule, Congress did not encroach on the judicial power. It decided neither the merits of any 10b-5 claim nor even whether any such claim should proceed to decision on the merits. It did provide that the rule governing the timeliness of 10b-5 actions pending on June 19, 1991, should be the pre-*Lampf* statute of limitations, and it also established a procedure for Article III courts to apply in determining whether any dismissed case should be reinstated. Congress' decision to extend that rule and procedure to 10b-5 actions dismissed during the brief period between this Court's law-changing decision in *Lampf* and Congress' remedial action is not a sufficient reason to hold the statute unconstitutional. . . .

II

Aside from § 27A(b), the Court claims to "know of no instance in which Congress has attempted to set aside the final judgment of an Article III court by retroactive legislation." In fact, Congress has done so on several occasions. [The dissent's lengthy discussion of *Sampeyreac v. United States*, 7 Pet. 222 (1833), and *Freeborn v. Smith*, 2 Wall. 160 (1865), is omitted.]

Also apposite is *United States v. Sioux Nation*, 448 U.S. 371 (1980), which involved the Sioux Nation's longstanding claim that the Government had in 1877 improperly abrogated the treaty by which the Sioux had held title to the Black Hills. The Sioux first brought their claim under a special 1920 jurisdictional statute. The Court of Claims dismissed the suit in 1942, holding that the 1920 Act did not give the court jurisdiction to consider the adequacy of the compensation the Government had paid in 1877. Congress passed a new jurisdictional statute in 1946, and in 1950 the Sioux brought a new action. In 1975 the Court of Claims, although acknowledging the merit of the Sioux's claim, held that the res judicata effect of the 1942 dismissal barred the suit. In response, Congress passed a statute in 1978 that authorized the Court of Claims to take new evidence and instructed it to consider the Sioux's claims on the merits, disregarding res judicata. The Sioux finally prevailed. We held that the 1978 Act did not violate the separation of powers.

The Court correctly notes that our opinion in *Sioux Nation* prominently discussed precedents establishing Congress' power to waive the res judicata effect of judgments against the United States. We never suggested, however, that those precedents sufficed to overcome the separation-of-powers objections raised against the 1978 Act. Instead, we made extensive comments about the propriety of Congress' action that were as necessary to our holding then as they are salient to the Court's analysis today. In passing the 1978 Act, we held, Congress

> only was providing a forum so that a new judicial review of the Black Hills claim could take place. This review was to be based on the facts found by the Court of Claims after reviewing all the evidence, and an application of generally controlling legal principles to those facts. For these reasons, Congress was not reviewing the merits of the Court of Claims' decisions, and did not interfere with the finality of its judgments.
>
> Moreover, Congress in no way attempted to prescribe the outcome of the Court of Claims' new review of the merits.

Congress observed the same boundaries in enacting §27A(b).

Our opinions in *Sampeyreac, Freeborn*, and *Sioux Nation* correctly characterize statutes that specify new grounds for the reopening of final judgments as remedial. Moreover, these precedents correctly identify the unremarkable nature of the legislative power to enact remedial statutes. "[A]cts . . . of a remedial character . . . are the peculiar subjects of legislation. They are not liable to the imputation of being assumptions of judicial power." *Freeborn*. A few contemporary examples of such statutes will suffice to demonstrate that they are ordinary products of the exercise of legislative power.

The most familiar remedial measure that provides for reopening of final judgments is Rule 60(b) of the Federal Rules of Civil Procedure. That Rule both codified common-law grounds for relieving a party from a final judgment and added an encompassing reference to "any other reason justifying relief from the operation of the judgment." Not a single word in its text suggests that it does not apply to judgments entered prior to its effective date. On the contrary, the purpose of the Rule, its plain language, and the traditional construction of remedial measures all support construing it to apply to past as well as future judgments. Indeed, because the Rule explicitly abolished the common-law writs it replaced, an unintended gap in the law would have resulted if it did not apply retroactively.[9]

In contrast, in the examples of colonial legislatures' review of trial courts' judgments on which today's holding rests, the legislatures issued directives in individual cases without purporting either to set forth or to apply any legal standard. *See, e.g., INS v. Chadha*, 462 U.S. 919, 961–62 (1983) (Powell, J., concurring in judgment). The principal compendium on which the Court relies accurately describes these legislative directives: "In these records, which are of the first quarter of the 18th century, the provincial legislature will often be found acting in a judicial capacity, sometimes trying causes in equity, sometimes granting equity powers to some court of the common law for a particular temporary purpose, and constantly granting appeals, new trials, and other relief from judgments, on equitable grounds." *Judicial Action by the Provincial Legislature of Massachusetts*, 15 HARV. L. REV. 208 n.1 (1902).

The Framers' disapproval of such a system of ad hoc legislative review of individual trial court judgments has no bearing on remedial measures such as Rule 60(b) or the 1991 amendment at issue today. The history on which the Court relies provides no support for its holding.

III

The lack of precedent for the Court's holding is not, of course, a sufficient reason to reject it. Correct application of separation-of-powers principles, however, confirms that the Court has reached the wrong result. As our most recent major pronouncement on the separation of powers noted, "we have never held that the Constitution requires that the three branches of Government 'operate with absolute independence.'" *Morrison v. Olson*, 487 U.S. 654, 693–94 (1988). Rather, our jurisprudence reflects "Madison's flexible approach to separation of powers." *Mistretta v. United States*, 488 U.S. 361, 380 (1989). In accepting Madison's conception rather than any "hermetic division among the Branches," "we have upheld statutory provisions that to some degree commingle the functions of the Branches, but that pose no danger of either aggrandizement or encroachment." Today's holding does not comport with these ideals.

Section 27A shares several important characteristics with the remedial statutes discussed above. It does not decide the merits of any issue in any litigation but merely removes an impediment to judicial decision on the merits. The impediment it removes would have produced inequity because the statute's beneficiaries did not cause the

---

9. In its criticism of this analysis of Rule 60(b), the majority overstates our holdings on retroactivity in *Landgraf*. Our opinion in *Landgraf* nowhere says "that statutes do *not* apply retroactively *unless* Congress expressly states that they do." To the contrary, it says that, "[w]hen . . . the statute contains no such express command, the court must determine whether the new statute would have retroactive effect," an inquiry that requires "clear congressional *intent* favoring such a result." In the case of Rule 60(b), the factors I have identified, taken together, support a finding of clear congressional intent.

impediment. It requires a party invoking its benefits to file a motion within a specified time and to convince a court that the statute entitles the party to relief. Most
important, § 27A(b) specifies both a substantive rule to govern the reopening of a class
of judgments—the pre-*Lampf* limitations rule—and a procedure for the courts to
apply in determining whether a particular motion to reopen should be granted. These
characteristics are quintessentially legislative. They reflect Congress' fealty to the separation of powers and its intention to avoid the sort of ad hoc excesses the Court rightly
criticizes in colonial legislative practice. In my judgment, all of these elements distinguish § 27A from "judicial" action and confirm its constitutionality. A sensible analysis would at least consider them in the balance.

The majority's rigid holding unnecessarily hinders the Government from addressing difficult issues that inevitably arise in a complex society. This Court, for example,
lacks power to enlarge the time for filing petitions for certiorari in a civil case after 90
days from the entry of final judgment, no matter how strong the equities. See 28 U.S.C.
§ 2101(c). If an Act of God, such as a flood or an earthquake, sufficiently disrupted
communications in a particular area to preclude filing for several days, the majority's
reasoning would appear to bar Congress from addressing the resulting inequity.

Even if the rule the Court announces today were sound, it would not control the
case before us. In order to obtain the benefit of § 27A, petitioners had to file a timely
motion and persuade the District Court they had timely filed their complaint under
pre-*Lampf* law. In the judgment of the District Court, petitioners satisfied those conditions. Congress reasonably could have assumed, indeed must have expected, that
some movants under § 27A(b) would fail to do so. The presence of an important condition that the District Court must find a movant to have satisfied before it may
reopen a judgment distinguishes § 27A from the unconditional congressional directives the Court appears to forbid.

Moreover, unlike the colonial legislative commands on which the Court bases its
holding, § 27A directed action not in "a civil case," *ante* (discussing *Calder v. Bull*, 3
Dall. 386 (1798)), but in a large category of civil cases. The Court declares that a legislative direction to reopen a class of 40 cases is 40 times as bad as a direction to reopen
a single final judgment because "power is the object of the separation-of-powers prohibition." This self-evident observation might be salient if § 27A(b) unconditionally
commanded courts to reopen judgments even absent findings that the complaints
were timely under pre-*Lampf* law. But Congress did not decide—and could not know
how any court would decide—the timeliness issue in any particular case in the
affected category. Congress, therefore, had no way to identify which particular plaintiffs would benefit from § 27A. It merely enacted a law that applied a substantive rule
to a class of litigants, specified a procedure for invoking the rule, and left particular
outcomes to individualized judicial determinations—a classic exercise of legislative
power.

"All we seek," affirmed a sponsor of § 27A, "is to give the victims [of securities fraud]
a fair day in court." A statute, such as § 27A, that removes an unanticipated and unjust
impediment to adjudication of a large class of claims on their merits poses no danger

of "aggrandizement or encroachment."[19] This is particularly true for §27A in light of Congress' historic primacy over statutes of limitations. The statute contains several checks against the danger of congressional overreaching. The Court in *Lampf* undertook a legislative function. Essentially, it supplied a statute of limitations for 10b-5 actions. The Court, however, failed to adopt the transition rules that ordinarily attend alterations shortening the time to sue. Congress, in §27A, has supplied those rules. The statute reflects the ability of two coequal branches to cooperate in providing for the impartial application of legal rules to particular disputes. The Court's mistrust of such cooperation ill serves the separation of powers.

* * *

Accordingly, I respectfully dissent.

Note: Congress and the Exercise of "Judicial Power"

1. The opinion in *Plaut* discusses three kinds of statutes that will be held unconstitutional because they "require federal courts to exercise the judicial power in a manner that Article III forbids."

First, Congress may attempt to "vest review of the decisions of Article III courts in officials of the Executive Branch." This kind of impermissible legislation is exemplified by the statute considered in *Hayburn's Case*, 2 Dall. 409 (1792).

Hayburn's Case involved a 1792 statute that authorized pensions for veterans of the Revolutionary War. Under the statute, the circuit courts initially determined the appropriate amount of each pension, and the Secretary of War had the discretion either to adopt or reject the courts' findings. Although the Supreme Court did not assess the constitutionality of this arrangement, five Justices, acting as circuit judges, determined that the statute was unconstitutional, and the Supreme Court has since recognized that the case "stands for the principle that Congress cannot vest review of the decisions of Article III courts in officials of the Executive Branch."

Second, Congress may attempt "to set aside the final judgment of an Article III court by retroactive legislation." That is the Court's description of the statute held unconstitutional in *Plaut*. Does Justice Stevens, in dissent, disagree with the application of this proposition, or does he dispute the Court's view of what the Constitution forbids?

Finally and most broadly, Congress may attempt to "prescribe rules of decision to the Judicial Department of the government in cases pending before it." That is the *Plaut* Court's description of the statute struck down in *Klein*. However, the Court immediately adds that the prohibition articulated in *Klein* "does not take hold when Congress amends applicable law."

---

19. Today's decision creates a new irony of judicial legislation. A challenge to the constitutionality of §27A(a) could not turn on the sanctity of final judgments. Section 27A(a) benefits litigants who had filed appeals that *Lampf* rendered frivolous; petitioners and other law-abiding litigants whose claims *Lampf* rendered untimely had acquiesced in the dismissal of their actions. By striking down §27A(b) on a ground that would leave §27A(a) intact, the Court indulges litigants who protracted proceedings but shuts the courthouse door to litigants who proceeded with diligence and respect for the *Lampf* judgment.

2. Although the majority in *Plaut* held that Congress cannot alter a judgment entered by an Article III court, it acknowledged that Congress can direct the reopening of a judgment if it specifies before the entry of judgment the grounds for reopening the judgment.

Another exception to the reopening rule was recognized in *Miller v. French*, 530 U.S. 327 (2000). At issue there was the Prison Litigation Reform Act of 1995 (PLRA), which establishes standards for the entry and termination of prospective relief in civil actions challenging prison conditions. Under 18 U.S.C. §3626(b)(2), a prison subject to an existing injunction for prison conditions may move for "the immediate termination of any prospective relief if the relief was approved or granted in the absence of a finding by the court that the relief is narrowly drawn, extends no further than necessary to correct the violation of the Federal right, and is the least intrusive means necessary to correct the violation of the Federal right." Section 3626(e)(2) provides for an automatic stay that is triggered when a motion for termination under §3626(b)(2) is filed and terminates upon the court's ruling on that motion. The question in *Miller* was whether this automatic stay provision impermissibly suspended the judgment of an Article III court in violation of *Plaut*.

The Court held that the provision did not offend the separation of powers. It explained that, although *Plaut* held that Congress cannot modify an award for retrospective relief such as damages, nothing in *Plaut* "call[ed] . . . into question Congress' authority to alter the prospective effect of a previously entered injunction." Thus, the Court said, "[p]rospective relief under a continuing, executory decree remains subject to alteration due to changes in the underlying law." The Court wrote:

> [When] Congress changes the law underlying a judgment awarding prospective relief, that relief is no longer enforceable to the extent it is inconsistent with the new law. Although the remedial injunction . . . is a "final judgment" for purposes of appeal, it is not the "last word of the judicial department." *Plaut*. The provision of prospective relief is subject to the continuing supervisory jurisdiction of the court, and therefore may be altered according to subsequent changes in the law. Prospective relief must be "modified if, as it later turns out, one or more of the obligations placed upon the parties has become impermissible under federal law."

Applying that standard, the Court concluded that the automatic stay provision does "not unconstitutionally suspend or reopen a judgment of an Article III court." The Court explained:

> Section 3626(e)(2) does not by itself "tell judges when, how, or what to do." Instead, §3626(e)(2) merely reflects the change implemented by §3626(b), which does the "heavy lifting" in the statutory scheme by establishing new standards for prospective relief. . . . The PLRA's automatic stay provision assists in the enforcement of [those provisions] by requiring the court to stay any prospective relief that, due to the change in the underlying standard, is no longer enforceable.

Is the distinction between prospective and retrospective relief persuasive? Does Article III impose any limits on Congress's ability to modify an injunction?

3. Given the opaqueness of the opinion in *Klein*, it is not surprising that courts sometimes have difficulty distinguishing between statutes that impermissibly attempt to "prescribe rules of decision" and those that permissibly amend the underlying law. The Court clarified the scope of *Klein* in the next case.

Bank Markazi v. Peterson

Supreme Court of the United States, 2016.

136 S. Ct. 1310.

JUSTICE GINSBURG delivered the opinion of the Court.*

A provision of the Iran Threat Reduction and Syria Human Rights Act of 2012, 22 U.S.C. § 8772, makes available for postjudgment execution a set of assets held at a New York bank for Bank Markazi, the Central Bank of Iran. The assets would partially satisfy judgments gained in separate actions by over 1,000 victims of terrorist acts sponsored by Iran. The judgments remain unpaid. Section 8772 is an unusual statute: It designates a particular set of assets and renders them available to satisfy the liability and damages judgments underlying a consolidated enforcement proceeding that the statute identifies by the District Court's docket number. The question raised by petitioner Bank Markazi: Does § 8772 violate the separation of powers by purporting to change the law for, and directing a particular result in, a single pending case?

Section 8772, we hold, does not transgress constraints placed on Congress and the President by the Constitution. The statute, we point out, is not fairly portrayed as a "one case-only regime." Rather, it covers a category of postjudgment execution claims filed by numerous plaintiffs who, in multiple civil actions, obtained evidence-based judgments against Iran together amounting to billions of dollars. Section 8772 subjects the designated assets to execution "to satisfy *any* judgment" against Iran for damages caused by specified acts of terrorism. § 8772(a)(1). Congress, our decisions make clear, may amend the law and make the change applicable to pending cases, even when the amendment is outcome determinative.

Adding weight to our decision, Congress passed, and the President signed, § 8772 in furtherance of their stance on a matter of foreign policy. Action in that realm warrants respectful review by courts. The Executive has historically made case-specific sovereign-immunity determinations to which courts have deferred. And exercise by Congress and the President of control over claims against foreign governments, as well as foreign-government-owned property in the United States, is hardly a novelty. In accord with the courts below, we perceive in § 8772 no violation of separation-of-powers principles, and no threat to the independence of the Judiciary.

---

* JUSTICE THOMAS joins all but Part II–C of this opinion.

I

A

... American nationals may file suit against state sponsors of terrorism in the courts of the United States. See 28 U.S.C. § 1605A. ...

Victims of state-sponsored terrorism ... may obtain a judgment against a foreign state on "establish[ing] [their] claim[s] ... by evidence satisfactory to the court." § 1608(e). ...

[T]he Terrorism Risk Insurance Act of 2002 (TRIA) authorizes execution of [such] judgments ... against "the blocked assets of [a] terrorist party (including the blocked assets of any agency or instrumentality of that terrorist party)." A "blocked asset" is any asset seized by the Executive Branch pursuant to either the Trading with the Enemy Act (TWEA) or the International Emergency Economic Powers Act (IEEPA). Both measures, TWEA and IEEPA, authorize the President to freeze the assets of "foreign enemy state[s]" and their agencies and instrumentalities. ...

Invoking his authority under the IEEPA, the President, in February 2012, issued an Executive Order blocking "[a]ll property and interests in property of any Iranian financial institution, including the Central Bank of Iran, that are in the United States." Exec. Order No. 13599. The availability of these assets for execution, however, was contested.

To place beyond dispute the availability of some of the Executive Order No. 13599-blocked assets for satisfaction of judgments rendered in terrorism cases, Congress passed the statute at issue here: § 22 U.S.C. § 8772. Enacted as a freestanding measure, not as an amendment to the FSIA or the TRIA, § 8772 provides that, if a court makes specified findings, "a financial asset ... shall be subject to execution ... in order to satisfy any judgment to the extent of any compensatory damages awarded against Iran for damages for personal injury or death caused by" the acts of terrorism enumerated in the FSIA's terrorism exception. § 8772(a)(1). Section 8772(b) defines as available for execution by holders of terrorism judgments against Iran "the financial assets that are identified in and the subject of proceedings in the United States District Court for the Southern District of New York in *Peterson et al. v. Islamic Republic of Iran et al.*, Case No. 10 Civ. 4518 (BSJ) (GWG), that were restrained by restraining notices and levies secured by the plaintiffs in those proceedings."

Before allowing execution against an asset described in § 8772(b), a court must determine that the asset is:

> (A) held in the United States for a foreign securities intermediary doing business in the United States;

> (B) a blocked asset (whether or not subsequently unblocked) ... ; and

> (C) equal in value to a financial asset of Iran, including an asset of the central bank or monetary authority of the Government of Iran .... § 8772(a)(1).

In addition, the court in which execution is sought must determine "whether Iran holds equitable title to, or the beneficial interest in, the assets ... and that no other person possesses a constitutionally protected interest in the assets . . . under the Fifth Amendment to the Constitution of the United States."

B

Respondents are victims of Iran-sponsored acts of terrorism, their estate representatives, and surviving family members. Numbering more than 1,000, respondents [brought lawsuits against Iran]. Upon finding a clear evidentiary basis for Iran's liability to each suitor, the [District Court] entered judgments by default. "Together, [respondents] have obtained billions of dollars in judgments against Iran, the vast majority of which remain unpaid." The validity of those judgments is not in dispute.

To enforce their judgments, [Respondents] moved under Federal Rule of Civil Procedure 69 for turnover of about $1.75 billion in bond assets held in a New York bank account—assets that, respondents alleged, were owned by Bank Markazi. This turnover proceeding began in 2008 when the terrorism judgment holders in *Peterson* filed writs of execution and the District Court restrained the bonds. [*Ed. note*: In other words, the court entered an order attaching the bonds so that they could be used to satisfy judgments against Iran.] Other groups of terrorism judgment holders—some of which had filed their own writs of execution against the bonds—were joined in the *Peterson* enforcement proceeding. . . . It is this judgment-enforcement proceeding and assets restrained in that proceeding that § 8772 addresses.

Although the enforcement proceeding was initiated prior to the issuance of Executive Order No. 13599 and the enactment of § 8772, the judgment holders updated their motions in 2012 to include execution claims under § 8772. Making the findings necessary under § 8772, the District Court ordered the requested turn-over.

In reaching its decision, the court reviewed the financial history of the assets and other record evidence showing that Bank Markazi owned the assets. . . .

[The district court rejected Bank Markazi's argument that] "in passing § 8772, Congress effectively dictated specific factual findings in connection with a specific litigation—invading the province of the courts." The ownership determinations § 8772 required, the court said, "[were] not mere fig leaves," for "it [was] quite possible that the court could have found that defendants raised a triable issue as to whether the blocked assets were owned by Iran, or that Clearstream and/or UBAE had some form of beneficial or equitable interest." . . . The Court of Appeals for the Second Circuit unanimously affirmed.

II

Article III of the Constitution establishes an independent Judiciary, a Third Branch of Government with the "province and duty . . . to say what the law is" in particular cases and controversies. *Marbury v. Madison*, 1 Cranch 137, 177 (1803). Necessarily, that endowment of authority blocks Congress from "requir[ing] federal courts to exercise the judicial power in a manner that Article III forbids." *Plaut v. Spendthrift Farm, Inc.* (1995). Congress, no doubt, "may not usurp a court's power to interpret and apply the law to the [circumstances] before it," for "[t]hose who apply [a] rule to particular cases, must of necessity expound and interpret that rule," *Marbury*.[17] And our decisions place off limits to Congress "vest[ing] review of the decisions of Article III courts in officials of the Executive Branch." Congress, we have also held, may not "retroactively command the federal courts to reopen final judgments." *Plaut*.

A

Citing *United States v. Klein* (1872) [Chapter 19] Bank Markazi urges a further limitation. Congress treads impermissibly on judicial turf, the Bank maintains, when it "prescribe[s] rules of decision to the Judicial Department . . . in [pending] cases." According to the Bank, § 8772 fits that description. *Klein* has been called "a deeply puzzling decision." More recent decisions, however, have made it clear that *Klein* does not inhibit Congress from "amend[ing] applicable law." *Robertson v. Seattle Audubon Soc.*, 503 U.S. 429, 441 (1992). Section 8772, we hold, did just that.

Klein involved Civil War legislation providing that persons whose property had been seized and sold in wartime could recover the proceeds of the sale in the Court of Claims upon proof that they had "never given any aid or comfort to the present rebellion." In 1863, President Lincoln pardoned "persons who . . . participated in the . . . rebellion" if they swore an oath of loyalty to the United States. One of the persons so pardoned was a southerner named Wilson, whose cotton had been seized and sold by Government agents. Klein was the administrator of Wilson's estate. In *United States v. Padelford* this Court held that the recipient of a Presidential pardon must be treated as loyal, *i.e.*, the pardon operated as "a complete substitute for proof that [the recipient] gave no aid or comfort to the rebellion." Thereafter, Klein prevailed in an action in the Court of Claims, yielding an award of $125,300 for Wilson's cotton.

During the pendency of an appeal to this Court from the Court of Claims judgment in *Klein*, Congress enacted a statute providing that no pardon should be admissible as proof of loyalty. Moreover, acceptance of a pardon without disclaiming participation in the rebellion would serve as conclusive evidence of disloyalty. The statute directed the Court of Claims and the Supreme Court to dismiss for want of jurisdiction any claim based on a pardon. Affirming the judgment of the Court of Claims, this Court held that Congress had no authority to "impai[r] the effect of a pardon," for the Constitution entrusted the pardon power "[t]o the executive alone." The Legislature, the Court stated, "cannot change the effect of . . . a pardon any more than the executive can change a law." Lacking authority to impair the pardon power of the Executive, Congress could not "direc[t] [a] court to be instrumental to that end." In other words, the statute in *Klein* infringed the judicial power, not because it left too little for courts to do, but because it attempted to direct the result without altering the legal standards governing the effect of a pardon—standards Congress was powerless to prescribe.

---

17. Consistent with this limitation, respondents rightly acknowledged at oral argument that Congress could not enact a statute directing that, in "Smith v. Jones," "Smith wins." Such a statute would create no new substantive law; it would instead direct the court how pre-existing law applies to particular circumstances.

Bank Markazi, as earlier observed, argues that § 8772 conflicts with *Klein*. The Bank points to a statement in the *Klein* opinion questioning whether "the legislature may prescribe rules of decision to the Judicial Department . . . in cases pending before it." One cannot take this language from *Klein* "at face value," however, "for congressional power to make valid statutes retroactively applicable to pending cases has often been recognized." As we explained in *Landgraf v. USI Film Products*, 511 U.S. 244 (1994), the restrictions that the Constitution places on retroactive legislation "are of limited scope":

> The *Ex Post Facto* Clause flatly prohibits retroactive application of penal legislation. Article I, § 10, cl. 1, prohibits States from passing . . . laws "impairing the Obligation of Contracts." The Fifth Amendment's Takings Clause prevents the Legislature (and other government actors) from depriving private persons of vested property rights except for a "public use" and upon payment of "just compensation." The prohibitions on "Bills of Attainder" in Art. I, §§ 9–10, prohibit legislatures from singling out disfavored persons and meting out summary punishment for past conduct. The Due Process Clause also protects the interests in fair notice and repose that may be compromised by retroactive legislation; a justification sufficient to validate a statute's prospective application under the Clause "may not suffice" to warrant its retroactive application.

"Absent a violation of one of those specific provisions," when a new law makes clear that it is retroactive, the arguable "unfairness of retroactive civil legislation is not a sufficient reason for a court to fail to give [that law] its intended scope." So yes, we have affirmed, Congress may indeed direct courts to apply newly enacted, outcome-altering legislation in pending civil cases.

Bank Markazi argues most strenuously that § 8772 did not simply amend pre-existing law. Because the judicial findings contemplated by § 8772 were "foregone conclusions," the Bank urges, the statute "effectively" directed certain factfindings and specified the outcome under the amended law. Recall that the District Court, closely monitoring the case, disagreed.

In any event, a statute does not impinge on judicial power when it directs courts to apply a new legal standard to undisputed facts. "When a plaintiff brings suit to enforce a legal obligation it is not any less a case or controversy upon which a court possessing the federal judicial power may rightly give judgment, because the plaintiff's claim is uncontested or incontestable." In *Schooner Peggy*, 1 Cranch 103 (1801) for example, this Court applied a newly ratified treaty that, by requiring the return of captured property, effectively permitted only one possible outcome. And in *Robertson* a statute replaced governing environmental-law restraints on timber harvesting with new legislation that permitted harvesting in all but certain designated areas. Without inquiring whether the new statute's application in pending cases was a "foregone conclusio[n]," we upheld the legislation because it left for judicial determination whether any particular actions violated the new prescription. In short, § 8772 changed the law by establishing new substantive standards, entrusting to the District Court application of those standards to the facts (contested or uncontested) found by the court.

Resisting this conclusion, The Chief Justice compares § 8772 to a hypothetical "law directing judgment for Smith if the court finds that Jones was duly served with notice of the proceedings." Of course, the hypothesized law would be invalid—as would a law directing judgment for Smith, for instance, if the court finds that the sun rises in the east. For one thing, a law so cast may well be irrational and, therefore, unconstitutional for reasons distinct from the separation-of-powers issues considered here. For another, the law imagined by the dissent does what *Robertson* says Congress cannot do: Like a statute that directs, in "Smith v. Jones," "Smith wins," it "compel[s] . . . findings or results under old law," for it fails to supply any new legal standard effectuating the lawmakers' reasonable policy judgment.[22] By contrast, § 8772 provides a new standard clarifying that, if Iran owns certain assets, the victims of Iran-sponsored terrorist attacks will be permitted to execute against those assets. Applying laws implementing Congress' policy judgments, with fidelity to those judgments, is commonplace for the Judiciary.

B

Section 8772 remains "unprecedented," Bank Markazi charges, because it "prescribes a rule for a single pending case—identified by caption and docket number." The amended law in *Robertson*, however, also applied to cases identified by caption and docket number and was nonetheless upheld. Moreover, § 8772, as already described facilitates execution of judgments in 16 suits, together encompassing more than 1,000 victims of Iran-sponsored terrorist attacks. Although consolidated for administrative purposes at the execution stage, the judgment-execution claims brought pursuant to Federal Rule of Civil Procedure 69 were not independent of the original actions for damages and each claim retained its separate character.

The Bank's argument is further flawed, for it rests on the assumption that legislation must be generally applicable, that "there is something wrong with particularized legislative action." We have found that assumption suspect:

> While legislatures usually act through laws of general applicability, that is by no means their only legitimate mode of action. Private bills in Congress are still common, and were even more so in the days before establishment of the Claims Court. Even laws that impose a duty or liability upon a single individual or firm are not on that account invalid—or else we would not have the extensive jurisprudence that we do concerning the Bill of Attainder Clause, including cases which say that [the Clause] requires not merely "singling out"

---

22. The dissent also analogizes § 8772 to a law that makes "conclusive" one party's flimsy evidence of a boundary line in a pending property dispute, notwithstanding that the governing law ordinarily provides that an official map establishes the boundary. Section 8772, however, does not restrict the evidence on which a court may rely in making the required findings. A more fitting analogy for depicting § 8772's operation might be: In a pending property dispute, the parties contest whether an ambiguous statute makes a 1990 or 2000 county map the relevant document for establishing boundary lines. To clarify the matter, the legislature enacts a law specifying that the 2000 map supersedes the earlier map.

but also *punishment* [or] a case [holding] that Congress may legislate "a legitimate class of one."

This Court and lower courts have upheld as a valid exercise of Congress' legislative power diverse laws that governed one or a very small number of specific subjects.

C

We stress, finally, that § 8772 is an exercise of congressional authority regarding foreign affairs, a domain in which the controlling role of the political branches is both necessary and proper. In furtherance of their authority over the Nation's foreign relations, Congress and the President have, time and again, as exigencies arose, exercised control over claims against foreign states and the disposition of foreign-state property in the United States. In pursuit of foreign policy objectives, the political branches have regulated specific foreign-state assets by, *inter alia*, blocking them or governing their availability for attachment. Such measures have never been rejected as invasions upon the Article III judicial power.

Particularly pertinent, the Executive, prior to the enactment of the FSIA, regularly made case-specific determinations whether sovereign immunity should be recognized, and courts accepted those determinations as binding. [It] is "not for the courts to deny an immunity which our government has seen fit to allow, or to allow an immunity on new grounds which the government has not seen fit to recognize." This practice, too, was never perceived as an encroachment on the federal courts' jurisdiction.

Enacting the FSIA in 1976, Congress transferred from the Executive to the courts the principal responsibility for determining a foreign state's amenability to suit. But it remains Congress' prerogative to alter a foreign state's immunity and to render the alteration dispositive of judicial proceedings in progress. By altering the law governing the attachment of particular property belonging to Iran, Congress acted comfortably within the political branches' authority over foreign sovereign immunity and foreign-state assets.

* * *

For the reasons stated, we are satisfied that § 8772—a statute designed to aid in the enforcement of federal-court judgments—does not offend "separation of powers principles . . . protecting the role of the independent Judiciary within the constitutional design."

Affirmed.

CHIEF JUSTICE ROBERTS, with whom JUSTICE SOTOMAYOR joins, dissenting.

Imagine your neighbor sues you, claiming that your fence is on his property. His evidence is a letter from the previous owner of your home, accepting your neighbor's version of the facts. Your defense is an official county map, which under state law establishes the boundaries of your land. The map shows the fence on your side of the property line. You also argue that your neighbor's claim is six months outside the statute of limitations.

Now imagine that while the lawsuit is pending, your neighbor persuades the legislature to enact a new statute. The new statute provides that for your case, and your case alone, a letter from one neighbor to another is conclusive of property boundaries, and the statute of limitations is one year longer. Your neighbor wins. Who would you say decided your case: the legislature, which targeted your specific case and eliminated your specific defenses so as to ensure your neighbor's victory, or the court, which presided over the *fait accompli*?

That question lies at the root of the case the Court confronts today. Article III of the Constitution commits the power to decide cases to the Judiciary alone. Yet, in this case, Congress arrogated that power to itself.

Contrary to the majority, I would hold that § 8772 violates the separation of powers. No less than if it had passed a law saying "respondents win," Congress has decided this case by enacting a bespoke statute tailored to this case that resolves the parties' specific legal disputes to guarantee respondents victory.

II

A

* * *

[Our decisions have recognized] three kinds of "unconstitutional restriction[s] upon the exercise of judicial power." Two concern the effect of judgments once they have been rendered: "Congress cannot vest review of the decisions of Article III courts in officials of the Executive Branch," for to do so would make a court's judgment merely "an advisory opinion in its most obnoxious form." And Congress cannot "retroactively command[ ] the federal courts to reopen final judgments," because Article III "gives the Federal Judiciary the power, not merely to rule on cases, but to decide them, subject to review only by superior courts in the Article III hierarchy." Neither of these rules is directly implicated here.

This case is about the third type of unconstitutional interference with the judicial function, whereby Congress assumes the role of judge and decides a particular pending case in the first instance. Section 8772 does precisely that, changing the law—for these proceedings alone—simply to guarantee that respondents win. The law serves no other purpose—a point, indeed, that is hardly in dispute. As the majority acknowledges, the statute "'sweeps away . . . any . . . federal or state law impediments that might otherwise exist'" to bar respondents from obtaining Bank Markazi's assets. In the District Court, Bank Markazi had invoked sovereign immunity under the Foreign Sovereign Immunities Act of 1976. Section 8772(a)(1) eliminates that immunity. Section 8772(d)(3) ensures that the Bank is liable. Section 8772(a)(1) makes its assets subject to execution. And lest there be any doubt that Congress's sole concern was deciding this particular case, rather than establishing any generally applicable rules, § 8772 provided that nothing in the statute "shall be construed . . . to affect the availability, or lack thereof, of a right to satisfy a judgment in any other action against a terrorist party in any proceedings other than" these. § 8772(c).

B

There has never been anything like § 8772 before. Neither the majority nor respondents have identified another statute that changed the law for a pending case in an outcome-determinative way and explicitly limited its effect to particular judicial proceedings. That fact alone is "[p]erhaps the most telling indication of the severe constitutional problem" with the law. Congress's "prolonged reticence would be amazing if such interference were not understood to be constitutionally proscribed." *Plaut.*

Section 8772 violates the bedrock rule of Article III that the judicial power is vested in the Judicial Branch alone. We first enforced that rule against an Act of Congress during the Reconstruction era in *United States v. Klein.* . . .

The majority characterizes *Klein* as a delphic, puzzling decision whose central holding — that Congress may not prescribe the result in pending cases — cannot be taken at face value. It is true that *Klein* can be read too broadly, in a way that would swallow the rule that courts generally must apply a retroactively applicable statute to pending cases. See *United States v. Schooner Peggy.* But *Schooner Peggy* can be read too broadly, too. Applying a retroactive law that says "Smith wins" to the pending case of *Smith v. Jones* implicates profound issues of separation of powers, issues not adequately answered by a citation to *Schooner Peggy.* And just because *Klein* did not set forth clear rules defining the limits on Congress's authority to legislate with respect to a pending case does not mean — as the majority seems to think — that Article III itself imposes no such limits.

The same "record of history" that drove the Framers to adopt Article III to implement the separation of powers ought to compel us to give meaning to their design. The nearly two centuries of experience with legislative assumption of judicial power meant that "[t]he Framers were well acquainted with the danger of subjecting the determination of the rights of one person to the tyranny of shifting majorities." Article III vested the judicial power in the Judiciary alone to protect against that threat to liberty. It defined not only what the Judiciary can do, but also what Congress cannot.

The Court says it would reject a law that says "Smith wins" because such a statute "would create no new substantive law." Of course it would: Prior to the passage of the hypothetical statute, the law did not provide that Smith wins. After the passage of the law, it does. Changing the law is simply how Congress acts. The question is whether its action constitutes an exercise of judicial power. Saying Congress "creates new law" in one case but not another simply expresses a conclusion on that issue; it does not supply a reason.

"Smith wins" is a new law, tailored to one case in the same way as § 8772 and having the same effect. All that both statutes "effectuat[e]," in substance, is lawmakers' "policy judgment" that one side in one case ought to prevail. The cause for concern is that though the statutes are indistinguishable, it is plain that the majority recognizes no limit under the separation of powers beyond the prohibition on statutes as brazen as "Smith wins." . . . .

It is true that some of the precedents cited by the majority have allowed Congress to approach the boundary between legislative and judicial power. None, however, involved statutes comparable to §8772. In *Robertson v. Seattle Audubon Soc.*, for example, the statute at issue referenced particular cases only as a shorthand for describing certain environmental law requirements, not to limit the statute's effect to those cases alone. And in *Plaut*, the Court explicitly distinguished the statute before it—which directed courts to reopen final judgments in an entire class of cases—from one that "'single[s] out' any defendant for adverse treatment (or any plaintiff for favorable treatment)." *Plaut*, in any event, held the statute before it invalid, concluding that it violated Article III based on the same historical understanding of the judicial power outlined above.

I readily concede, without embarrassment, that it can sometimes be difficult to draw the line between legislative and judicial power. That should come as no surprise; Chief Justice Marshall's admonition "that 'it is a *constitution* we are expounding' is especially relevant when the Court is required to give legal sanctions to an underlying principle of the Constitution—that of separation of powers." But however difficult it may be to discern the line between the Legislative and Judicial Branches, the entire constitutional enterprise depends on there being such a line.

C

Finally, the majority suggests that §8772 is analogous to the Executive's historical power to recognize foreign state sovereign immunity on a case-by-case basis. As discussed above, however, §8772 does considerably more than withdraw the Bank's sovereign immunity. It strips the Bank of any protection that federal common law, international law, or New York State law might have offered against respondents' claims. That is without analogue or precedent. In any event, the practice of applying case-specific Executive submissions on sovereign immunity was not judicial acquiescence in an intrusion on the Judiciary's role. It was instead the result of substantive sovereign immunity law, developed and applied by the courts, which treated such a submission as a dispositive fact.

* * *

At issue here is a basic principle, not a technical rule. Section 8772 decides this case no less certainly than if Congress had directed entry of judgment for respondents. As a result, the potential of the decision today "to effect important change in the equilibrium of power" is "immediately evident." Hereafter, with this Court's seal of approval, Congress can unabashedly pick the winners and losers in particular pending cases. Today's decision will indeed become a "blueprint for extensive expansion of the legislative power" at the Judiciary's expense feeding Congress's tendency to "extend[ ] the sphere of its activity and draw[ ] all power into its impetuous vortex."

I respectfully dissent.

Note: Congress's Power to Control Decisionmaking
After Bank Markazi

1. The *Markazi* majority reads *Klein*'s statement that Congress may not "prescribe rules of decision to the Judicial Department . . . in [pending] cases" to mean that Congress may not "attempt[] to direct the result" of a case "without altering the legal standards." Is that all that *Klein*'s statement stands for after *Markazi*? Or can *Klein*'s statement be read to impose broader limitations on Congress?

2. In footnote 17, the *Markazi* majority says that Congress cannot enact a statute directing that "in *Smith v. Jones*, Smith wins," because that statute would "create no new substantive law" but instead would "direct the court how pre-existing law applies to particular circumstances." After *Markazi*, could Congress enact a statute stating that "the statute applicable in Smith v. Jones is hereby amended so that Smith wins"?

3. In his dissent, Chief Justice Roberts says that if Congress enacted a statute stating that "Smith wins" would change the substantive law, reasoning that before the enactment of the statute, the law did not provide that Smith wins, but after the enactment, it does. Is this reasoning persuasive, or does it erase the distinction between changing the law and deciding a case?

4. In upholding § 8772, the *Markazi* majority stresses that the statute relates to foreign policy, an area in which the political branches have broad authority. After *Markazi*, does Congress have broader authority to affect the outcomes in judicial proceedings relating to foreign policy than in other types of proceedings?

Problem: Save Mount Rushmore

In 2011, the National Association to Save Mount Rushmore filed suit in the United States District Court for the District of South Dakota against the Department of the Interior seeking an injunction to prevent the construction of a Presidential Memorabilia building at the base of Mount Rushmore in Keystone, South Dakota. The Association alleged that if the proposed plans went through, the building would violate a number of federal statutes, including the National Environmental Protection Act, 42 U.S.C. § 4321 *et seq.*, and the National Historic Preservation Act, 16 U.S.C. § 470 *et seq.*

In response, Congress passed Public Law No. 112-401. The Act provided in part:

Section 1. Approval of Presidential Memorabilia Building and Design.

> Notwithstanding any other provision of law, the Presidential Memorabilia building described in plans approved by the Secretary of the Interior on March 17, 2010 shall be constructed expeditiously at the base of Mount Rushmore in Keystone, South Dakota, in a manner consistent with such plans and permits, subject to design modifications, if any, approved in accordance with applicable laws and regulations. . . .

Section 3. Judicial Review.

> The decision to locate the Presidential Memorabilia building at the base of Mount Rushmore . . . identified in section 1 shall not be subject to judicial review.

After the passage of the Act, the district court dismissed the Association's suit, holding that it no longer had subject matter jurisdiction over the case.

The Coalition appealed to the Eighth Circuit, arguing that the withdrawal of judicial review in this case violates Article III, particularly the principles set forth in *United States v. Klein* (Chapter 19). How should the court rule?

Note: The Import of Dickerson

Can Congress compel changes in the law when the law is found in Supreme Court decisions interpreting the Constitution? In *Dickerson v. United States*, 530 U.S. 428 (2000), the Supreme Court considered the constitutionality of 18 U.S.C. § 3501, enacted as part of the Omnibus Crime Control and Safe Streets Act of 1968. Section 3501 provides in part: "In any criminal prosecution brought by the United States or by the District of Columbia, a confession . . . shall be admissible in evidence if it is voluntarily given." The statute offers a non-exclusive list of factors that courts should consider in determining voluntariness.

Two years before section 3501 was enacted, the Supreme Court decided *Miranda v. Arizona*, 384 U.S. 436 (1966). In *Miranda*, of course, the Court held that a confession could not be admitted into evidence against a defendant unless it was preceded by the now-familiar warnings. Section 3501 made no mention of any required warnings. In *Dickerson*, Chief Justice Rehnquist, writing for the Court, described the conflict between section 3501 and *Miranda*:

> Given § 3501's express designation of voluntariness as the touchstone of admissibility, its omission of any warning requirement, and the instruction for trial courts to consider a nonexclusive list of factors relevant to the circumstances of a confession, we agree with the Court of Appeals that Congress intended by its enactment to overrule *Miranda*. Because of the obvious conflict between our decision in *Miranda* and § 3501, we must address whether Congress has constitutional authority to thus supersede *Miranda*. If Congress has such authority, § 3501's totality-of-the-circumstances approach must prevail over *Miranda*'s requirement of warnings; if not, that section must yield to *Miranda*'s more specific requirements.

The Chief Justice then laid out the governing rules:

> The law in this area is clear. This Court has supervisory authority over the federal courts, and we may use that authority to prescribe rules of evidence and procedure that are binding in those tribunals. However, the power to judicially create and enforce nonconstitutional "rules of procedure and evidence for the federal courts exists only in the absence of a relevant Act of Congress." Congress retains the ultimate authority to modify or set aside any judicially

created rules of evidence and procedure that are not required by the Constitution.

But *Congress may not legislatively supersede our decisions interpreting and applying the Constitution.* (Emphasis added.)

In support of this last proposition, the Chief Justice cited (with "e.g.") *City of Boerne v. Flores*, 521 U.S. 507, 517–21 (1997). In that case the Court held that Congress exceeded its power under the Fourteenth Amendment when it enacted the Religious Freedom Restoration Act (RFRA). The purpose of RFRA was to overturn the Supreme Court's rejection of the "compelling interest test" for claims under the Free Exercise Clause. In the passage cited in *Dickerson*, the Court said:

> Congress' power under § 5, however, extends only to "enforc[ing]" the provisions of the Fourteenth Amendment.... The design of the Amendment and the text of § 5 are inconsistent with the suggestion that Congress has the power to decree the substance of the Fourteenth Amendment's restrictions on the States. Legislation which alters the meaning of the Free Exercise Clause cannot be said to be enforcing the Clause. Congress does not enforce a constitutional right by changing what the right is. It has been given the power "to enforce," not the power to determine what constitutes a constitutional violation.

As the quoted language makes clear, *City of Boerne* dealt solely with Congress's power under section 5 of the Fourteenth Amendment. *Dickerson* thus articulates a much broader proposition. Is it surprising that the *Dickerson* opinion did not cite any cases more directly on point?

Problem: The Constitution Restoration Act

Consider now the two provisions of the Constitution Restoration Act quoted at the start of this chapter. Section 301 of the Act provides:

> Any decision of a Federal court which has been made prior to or after the effective date of this Act, to the extent that the decision relates to an issue removed from Federal jurisdiction under [this Act], is not binding precedent on any State court.

Is section 301 constitutional insofar as it tells state courts that they are not bound by decisions of the United States Supreme Court on "issues" removed from federal jurisdiction by the other provisions of the bill? Does the answer depend on whether the jurisdictional restrictions are themselves constitutional?

Section 201 provides:

> In interpreting and applying the Constitution of the United States, a court of the United States may not rely upon any constitution, law, administrative rule, Executive order, directive, policy, judicial decision, or any other action of any foreign state or international organization or agency, other than the constitutional law and English common law.

Does Congress have the authority under the Constitution to impose this requirement on the federal courts? Do any of the cases discussed in this chapter directly address the constitutionality of section 201?

Note: The Judicial Conduct Act

In 2007, Representative W. Todd Akin introduced a bill entitled the "Judicial Conduct Act" that is intended to "establish standards for impeachment of judges and justices in the United States." The bill, H.R. 2898, would provide for impeachment in cases of treason, bribery, and other high crimes and misdemeanors as provided by Article II, Section 4 of the United States Constitution. However, more controversially, this bill defines "other high crimes and misdemeanors" expansively to include the following actions:

(b) Definitions — In this section: (3) The term "other high crimes and misdemeanors" means, with respect to a justice or judge, any act of misbehavior or misconduct by such justice or judge, which evidences an unfitness for the bench, including, but not limited to, the following . . . .

(B) Usurpation of power, including the entering or enforcement of orders or decisions based on powers reserved to the Congress under Article I of the United States Constitution. . . .

(G) Entering or enforcement of orders or decisions based on judgments, laws, agreements, or pronouncements of foreign institutions, governments, or multilateral organizations, other than orders or decisions based on the common law of the United Kingdom.

(H) Entering or enforcement of orders or decisions that conflict with or are inconsistent with the text of the United States Constitution.

(I) Entering or enforcement of orders or decisions based on precedent from previous Federal court decisions that conflict with or are inconsistent with the text of the United States Constitution.

Although a bill like H.R. 2898 is unlikely ever to be enacted, it raises interesting questions about the respective roles of Congress and the courts in interpreting the Constitution. Does Congress have power to define "other high crimes and misdemeanors" in such a way as to allow judges to be removed if they rely upon certain legal sources or judicial philosophies in their orders or decisions? Where would you look for answers to that question?

In *Nixon v. United States* (Chapter 3), the Supreme Court held that the Senate has final authority, unreviewable in the Judicial Branch, to determine the meaning of the word "try" in the Impeachment Trial Clause. Does anything in the Court's opinion bear upon the authority of Congress to define impeachable offenses? Does the legislation violate the separation of powers? Why or why not?

Problem: The Constitutionality of AEDPA

As discussed in Chapter 15, the Antiterrorism and Effective Death Penalty Act of 1996 (AEDPA) added an important new restriction on the power of federal courts to grant habeas corpus to state prisoners. Section 2254(d) provides:

> An application for a writ of habeas corpus on behalf of a person in custody pursuant to the judgment of a State court shall not be granted with respect to any claim that was adjudicated on the merits in State court proceedings unless the adjudication of the claim—
>
> (1) resulted in a decision that was contrary to, or involved an unreasonable application of, clearly established Federal law, as determined by the Supreme Court of the United States; or
>
> (2) resulted in a decision that was based on an unreasonable determination of the facts in light of the evidence presented in the State court proceeding.

In *Irons v. Carey*, 408 F.3d 1165 (9th Cir. 2005), a federal court of appeals panel requested supplemental briefing on the constitutionality of the limitation in paragraph (1) of § 2254(d). The panel wrote:

> [The] parties should discuss, in light of *Marbury v. Madison*, 5 U.S. (1 Cranch) 137 (1803), and *City of Boerne v. Flores*, 521 U.S. 507, 536 (1997), whether AEDPA unconstitutionally prescribes the sources of law that the Judicial Branch must use in exercising its jurisdiction or unconstitutionally prescribes the substantive rules of decision by which the federal courts must decide constitutional questions that arise in state habeas cases. The parties should consider whether, under the separation of powers doctrine or for any other reason involving the constitutionality of 28 U.S.C. § 2254(d)(1), this court should decline to apply the AEDPA standards in this case.

The panel handed down its decision in March 2007. *Irons v. Carey*, 479 F.3d 658 (9th Cir. 2007). The lead opinion said that prior circuit precedent foreclosed the panel from considering the constitutionality of § 2254(d). Judge Noonan, concurring specially, said, "I may still ask the question as to constitutionality in the light of governing decisions by the Supreme Court." Citing *Marbury* and *Klein* (among other cases), he wrote:

> AEDPA [operates] over the whole class of cases of habeas corpus. It does not require a result in any particular case. What it does do is to strike at the center of the judge's process of reasoning. It shuts the judge off from the judge's normal sources of law and curbs that use of analogy which is the way the mind of a judge works. In our system of law where precedent prevails and is developed, AEDPA denies the judge the use of circuit precedent, denies development of Supreme Court and circuit precedent, denies the deference due the penumbra and emanations of precedent, and even denies the courts the power to follow the law as now determined by the Supreme Court—the precedent to be applied must have been in existence at the

earlier moment when a state decision occurred. A more blinkered concept of law cannot be imagined—law, particularly constitutional law—is treated as what once was the law. The development of doctrine is despised. That despisal is a direct legislative interference in the independence of the judiciary.

Judge Reinhardt, also concurring specially, added:

> Having granted the courts the authority to review state convictions under our habeas powers, it seems to me inconsistent with our fundamental obligations as judges to require us, except in unusual or exceptional circumstances, to rule for the state regardless of whether it violated the Constitution. Such a mandate appears to me to tell us how to decide a case. That, for the reasons Judge Noonan so well expresses, Congress simply may not do.

In a dissent from denial of rehearing en banc in *Crater v. Galaza*, 508 F.3d 1261 (2007), Judge Reinhardt further developed his argument that §2254(d) is unconstitutional. He stated:

> Section 2254(d)(1) violates the fundamental attributes of the "judicial power," granted exclusively to the federal judiciary in Article III, in two principal ways. First, in dictating that federal courts may grant habeas relief only in cases in which the state proceeding violated clearly established law "as determined by the Supreme Court," §2254(d)(1) prescribes a "rule of decision"— i.e., a limitation on the federal courts' independent adjudicatory process akin to the statute invalidated in *Klein*. The rule of decision prescribed in AEDPA, however, is more egregious than that of *Klein* because it effectively suspends the ordinary doctrine of stare decisis in the federal courts' adjudication of habeas cases. Second, §2254(d)(1) violates Article III by requiring federal courts to defer to, and thereby give effect to, decisions of state courts that the federal courts interpret as violating the Constitution. Both congressionally imposed rules pose a serious threat to the integrity of our nation's separation of powers; neither can be tolerated.

Is 28 U.S.C. §2254(d) unconstitutional? Does Supreme Court precedent support the arguments made by Judges Noonan and Reinhardt?

Chapter 21

Non-Article III Courts and Judges

In a variety of contexts, the Supreme Court has emphasized the special character of Article III courts. An Article III court can adjudicate only actual "cases" and "controversies," and it must confine its adjudications to a sphere defined by a "system of separated powers." (Chapter 3.) It may not hear a case that is outside its statutory jurisdiction even if no party objects. (Chapter 9.) Congress cannot prescribe rules of decision to an Article III court in cases pending before it, nor can Congress authorize review of the court's decisions by officials of the executive branch. (Chapter 20.) In addition, of course, Article III itself provides that the judges have life tenure and that their salary may not be reduced while they hold office.

But is a federal court necessarily an Article III court? Can Congress create adjudicative tribunals outside the framework of Article III and vest them with jurisdiction to hear and decide cases similar to those that an Article III court might hear?

And what about the judges? Can Congress authorize Article III judges to delegate some of the functions that they would otherwise perform to decision-makers who lack the protection of tenure and compensation that Article III requires?

In considering these questions, we confront what the late Professor Paul Bator called a "constitutional puzzle":

> [On the one hand, the text of Article III] seems to adopt a simple, majestic, and powerful model: Congress may leave the initial adjudication of some or all of article III's list of cases to the state courts, but if federal adjudication is felt to be needed, the requirements of article III automatically come into play and specify what sorts of courts Congress must employ for federal adjudication. . . . [Yet for some 200 years,] Congress has consistently acted on the premise that it has the authority, in exercising its various substantive legislative powers, [to] constitute special courts, tribunals and agencies which exercise — or at least seem to exercise — the federal judicial power . . . and yet which are not the inferior courts specified in article III. . . .

Paul M. Bator, *The Constitution as Architecture: Legislative and Administrative Courts Under Article III*, 65 IND. L.J. 233, 234–35 (1989). We look now at the decisions that assess the constitutionality of Congress's departures from the "simple model."

Stern v. Marshall

Supreme Court of the United States, 2011.

564 U.S. 462.

CHIEF JUSTICE ROBERTS delivered the opinion of the Court.

This "suit has, in course of time, become so complicated, that ... no two ... lawyers can talk about it for five minutes, without coming to a total disagreement as to all the premises. Innumerable children have been born into the cause: innumerable young people have married into it;" and, sadly, the original parties "have died out of it." A "long procession of [judges] has come in and gone out" during that time, and still the suit "drags its weary length before the Court."

Those words were not written about this case, see C. Dickens, *Bleak House, in* 1 WORKS OF CHARLES DICKENS 4-5 (1891), but they could have been. This is the second time we have had occasion to weigh in on this long-running dispute between Vickie Lynn Marshall and E. Pierce Marshall over the fortune of J. Howard Marshall II, a man believed to have been one of the richest people in Texas. The Marshalls' litigation has worked its way through state and federal courts in Louisiana, Texas, and California, and two of those courts — a Texas state probate court and the Bankruptcy Court for the Central District of California — have reached contrary decisions on its merits. The Court of Appeals below held that the Texas state decision controlled, after concluding that the Bankruptcy Court lacked the authority to enter final judgment on a counterclaim that Vickie brought against Pierce in her bankruptcy proceeding.[1] To determine whether the Court of Appeals was correct in that regard, we must resolve two issues: (1) whether the Bankruptcy Court had the statutory authority under 28 U.S.C. § 157(b) to issue a final judgment on Vickie's counterclaim; and (2) if so, whether conferring that authority on the Bankruptcy Court is constitutional.

Although the history of this litigation is complicated, its resolution ultimately turns on very basic principles. Article III, § 1, of the Constitution commands that "[t]he judicial Power of the United States, shall be vested in one supreme Court, and in such inferior Courts as the Congress may from time to time ordain and establish." That Article further provides that the judges of those courts shall hold their offices during good behavior, without diminution of salary. Those requirements of Article III were not honored here. The Bankruptcy Court in this case exercised the judicial power of the United States by entering final judgment on a common law tort claim, even though the judges of such courts enjoy neither tenure during good behavior nor salary protection. We conclude that, although the Bankruptcy Court had the statutory authority to enter judgment on Vickie's counterclaim, it lacked the constitutional authority to do so.

I

[This case involves] two claims Vickie filed in an attempt to secure half of J. Howard's fortune. Known to the public as Anna Nicole Smith, Vickie was J. Howard's third

---

1. Because both Vickie and Pierce passed away during this litigation, the parties in this case are Vickie's estate and Pierce's estate. We continue to refer to them as "Vickie" and "Pierce."

wife and married him about a year before his death. Although J. Howard bestowed on Vickie many monetary and other gifts during their courtship and marriage, he did not include her in his will. Before J. Howard passed away, Vickie filed suit in Texas state probate court, asserting that Pierce—J. Howard's younger son—fraudulently induced J. Howard to sign a living trust that did not include her, even though J. Howard meant to give her half his property. Pierce denied any fraudulent activity and defended the validity of J. Howard's trust and, eventually, his will.

After J. Howard's death, Vickie filed a petition for bankruptcy in the Central District of California. Pierce filed a complaint in that bankruptcy proceeding, contending that Vickie had defamed him by inducing her lawyers to tell members of the press that he had engaged in fraud to gain control of his father's assets. The complaint sought a declaration that Pierce's defamation claim was not dischargeable in the bankruptcy proceedings. Pierce subsequently filed a proof of claim for the defamation action, meaning that he sought to recover damages for it from Vickie's bankruptcy estate. Vickie responded to Pierce's initial complaint by asserting truth as a defense to the alleged defamation and by filing a counterclaim for tortious interference with the gift she expected from J. Howard. As she had in state court, Vickie alleged that Pierce had wrongfully prevented J. Howard from taking the legal steps necessary to provide her with half his property.

On November 5, 1999, the Bankruptcy Court issued an order granting Vickie summary judgment on Pierce's claim for defamation. On September 27, 2000, after a bench trial, the Bankruptcy Court issued a judgment on Vickie's counterclaim in her favor. The court later awarded Vickie over $400 million in compensatory damages and $25 million in punitive damages.

In post-trial proceedings, Pierce argued that the Bankruptcy Court lacked jurisdiction over Vickie's counterclaim. In particular, Pierce renewed a claim he had made earlier in the litigation, asserting that the Bankruptcy Court's authority over the counterclaim was limited because Vickie's counterclaim was not a "core proceeding" under 28 U.S.C. § 157(b)(2)(C). As explained below, bankruptcy courts may hear and enter final judgments in "core proceedings" in a bankruptcy case. In non-core proceedings, the bankruptcy courts instead submit proposed findings of fact and conclusions of law to the district court, for that court's review and issuance of final judgment. The Bankruptcy Court in this case concluded that Vickie's counterclaim was "a core proceeding" under § 157(b)(2)(C), and the court therefore had the "power to enter judgment" on the counterclaim under § 157(b)(1).

The District Court disagreed. It recognized that "Vickie's counterclaim for tortious interference falls within the literal language" of the statute designating certain proceedings as "core," see § 157(b)(2)(C), but understood this Court's precedent to "suggest[ ] that it would be unconstitutional to hold that any and all counterclaims are core." The District Court accordingly concluded that a "counterclaim should not be characterized as core" when it "is only somewhat related to the claim against which it is asserted, and when the unique characteristics and context of the counterclaim place it outside of the normal type of set-off or other counterclaims that customarily arise."

Because the District Court concluded that Vickie's counterclaim was not core, the court determined that it was required to treat the Bankruptcy Court's judgment as "proposed[,] rather than final," and engage in an "independent review" of the record. Although the Texas state court had by that time conducted a jury trial on the merits of the parties' dispute and entered a judgment in Pierce's favor, the District Court declined to give that judgment preclusive effect and went on to decide the matter itself. Like the Bankruptcy Court, the District Court found that Pierce had tortiously interfered with Vickie's expectancy of a gift from J. Howard. The District Court awarded Vickie compensatory and punitive damages, each in the amount of $44,292,767.33.

The Court of Appeals reversed the District Court on a different ground, and we — in the first visit of the case to this Court — reversed the Court of Appeals on that issue. On remand from this Court, the Court of Appeals held that § 157 mandated "a two-step approach" under which a bankruptcy judge may issue a final judgment in a proceeding only if the matter both "meets Congress' definition of a core proceeding and arises under or arises in title 11," the Bankruptcy Code. The court also reasoned that allowing a bankruptcy judge to enter final judgments on all counterclaims raised in bankruptcy proceedings "would certainly run afoul" of this Court's decision in *Northern Pipeline v. Constr. Co. v. Marathon Pipe Line Co.*, 458 U.S. 50 (1982). With those concerns in mind, the court concluded that "a counterclaim under § 157(b)(2)(C) is properly a 'core' proceeding 'arising in a case under' the [Bankruptcy] Code only if the counterclaim is so closely related to [a creditor's] proof of claim that the resolution of the counterclaim is necessary to resolve the allowance or disallowance of the claim itself." The court ruled that Vickie's counterclaim did not meet that test. That holding made "the Texas probate court's judgment . . . the earliest final judgment entered on matters relevant to this proceeding," and therefore the Court of Appeals concluded that the District Court should have "afford[ed] preclusive effect" to the Texas "court's determination of relevant legal and factual issues."

We again granted certiorari.

II

[After a detailed analysis of the Bankruptcy Code, the Court concluded that 28 U.S.C. § 157(b) authorized the Bankruptcy Court to enter final judgment on Vickie's counterclaim for tortious interference because it was a "core proceeding" under § 157(b)(2)(C).]

III

Although we conclude that § 157(b)(2)(C) permits the Bankruptcy Court to enter final judgment on Vickie's counterclaim, Article III of the Constitution does not.

A

Article III, § 1, of the Constitution mandates that "[t]he judicial Power of the United States, shall be vested in one supreme Court, and in such inferior Courts as the Congress may from time to time ordain and establish." The same section provides that the judges of those constitutional courts "shall hold their Offices during good

Behaviour" and "receive for their Services[ ] a Compensation[ ] [that] shall not be diminished" during their tenure.

As its text and our precedent confirm, Article III is "an inseparable element of the constitutional system of checks and balances" that "both defines the power and protects the independence of the Judicial Branch." *Northern Pipeline* (plurality opinion). Under "the basic concept of separation of powers . . . that flow[s] from the scheme of a tripartite government" adopted in the Constitution, "the 'judicial Power of the United States' . . . can no more be shared" with another branch than "the Chief Executive, for example, can share with the Judiciary the veto power, or the Congress share with the Judiciary the power to override a Presidential veto."

In establishing the system of divided power in the Constitution, the Framers considered it essential that "the judiciary remain[ ] truly distinct from both the legislature and the executive." THE FEDERALIST No. 78, p. 466 (C. Rossiter ed., 1961) (A. Hamilton). As Hamilton put it, quoting Montesquieu, "'there is no liberty if the power of judging be not separated from the legislative and executive powers.'"

We have recognized that the three branches are not hermetically sealed from one another, but it remains true that Article III imposes some basic limitations that the other branches may not transgress. Those limitations serve two related purposes. "Separation-of-powers principles are intended, in part, to protect each branch of government from incursion by the others. Yet the dynamic between and among the branches is not the only object of the Constitution's concern. The structural principles secured by the separation of powers protect the individual as well." *Bond v. United States*, 564 U.S. 211 (2011).

Article III protects liberty not only through its role in implementing the separation of powers, but also by specifying the defining characteristics of Article III judges. The colonists had been subjected to judicial abuses at the hand of the Crown, and the Framers knew the main reasons why: because the King of Great Britain "made Judges dependent on his Will alone, for the tenure of their offices, and the amount and payment of their salaries." The Declaration of Independence ¶ 11. The Framers undertook in Article III to protect citizens subject to the judicial power of the new Federal Government from a repeat of those abuses. By appointing judges to serve without term limits, and restricting the ability of the other branches to remove judges or diminish their salaries, the Framers sought to ensure that each judicial decision would be rendered, not with an eye toward currying favor with Congress or the Executive, but rather with the "[c]lear heads . . . and honest hearts" deemed "essential to good judges." 1 WORKS OF JAMES WILSON 363 (J. Andrews ed., 1896).

Article III could neither serve its purpose in the system of checks and balances nor preserve the integrity of judicial decisionmaking if the other branches of the Federal Government could confer the Government's "judicial Power" on entities outside Article III. That is why we have long recognized that, in general, Congress may not "withdraw from judicial cognizance any matter which, from its nature, is the subject of a suit at the common law, or in equity, or admiralty." *Murray's Lessee v. Hoboken Land & Improvement Co.*, 18 How. 272, 284 (1856). When a suit is made of "the stuff of the traditional actions at common law tried by the courts at Westminster in 1789," and is brought within the bounds of federal jurisdiction, the responsibility for deciding that suit rests with Article III judges in Article III courts. The Constitution assigns that job—resolution of "the mundane as well as the glamorous, matters of common law and statute as well as constitutional law, issues of fact as well as issues of law"—to the Judiciary.

B

This is not the first time we have faced an Article III challenge to a bankruptcy court's resolution of a debtor's suit. In *Northern Pipeline*, we considered whether bankruptcy judges serving under the Bankruptcy Act of 1978—appointed by the President and confirmed by the Senate, but lacking the tenure and salary guarantees of Article III—could "constitutionally be vested with jurisdiction to decide [a] state-law contract claim" against an entity that was not otherwise part of the bankruptcy proceedings. The Court concluded that assignment of such state law claims for resolution by those judges "violates Art. III of the Constitution."

The plurality in *Northern Pipeline* recognized that there was a category of cases involving "public rights" that Congress could constitutionally assign to "legislative" courts for resolution. That opinion concluded that this "public rights" exception extended "only to matters arising between" individuals and the Government "in connection with the performance of the constitutional functions of the executive or legislative departments . . . that historically could have been determined exclusively by those" branches. A full majority of the Court, while not agreeing on the scope of the exception, concluded that the doctrine did not encompass adjudication of the state law claim at issue in that case. . . . [5]

A full majority of Justices in *Northern Pipeline* also rejected the debtor's argument that the bankruptcy court's exercise of jurisdiction was constitutional because the bankruptcy judge was acting merely as an adjunct of the district court or court of appeals.

After our decision in *Northern Pipeline*, Congress revised the statutes governing bankruptcy jurisdiction and bankruptcy judges. In the 1984 Act, Congress provided that the judges of the new bankruptcy courts would be appointed by the courts of appeals for the circuits in which their districts are located. 28 U.S.C. § 152(a). And . . . Congress permitted the newly constituted bankruptcy courts to enter final judgments only in "core" proceedings.

With respect to such "core" matters, however, the bankruptcy courts under the 1984 Act exercise the same powers they wielded under the Bankruptcy Act of 1978 (1978 Act). As in *Northern Pipeline*, for example, the newly constituted bankruptcy courts are charged under § 157(b)(2)(C) with resolving "[a]ll matters of fact and law in whatever domains of the law to which" a counterclaim may lead. As in *Northern Pipeline*, the new courts in core proceedings "issue final judgments, which are

---

5. The dissent is thus wrong in suggesting that less than a full Court agreed on the points pertinent to this case.

binding and enforceable even in the absence of an appeal." And, as in *Northern Pipeline*, the district courts review the judgments of the bankruptcy courts in core proceedings only under the usual limited appellate standards. That requires marked deference to, among other things, the bankruptcy judges' findings of fact.

C

Vickie and the dissent argue that the Bankruptcy Court's entry of final judgment on her state common law counterclaim was constitutional, despite the similarities between the bankruptcy courts under the 1978 Act and those exercising core jurisdiction under the 1984 Act. We disagree. It is clear that the Bankruptcy Court in this case exercised the "judicial Power of the United States" in purporting to resolve and enter final judgment on a state common law claim, just as the court did in *Northern Pipeline*. No "public right" exception excuses the failure to comply with Article III in doing so, any more than in *Northern Pipeline*. Vickie argues that this case is different because the defendant is a creditor in the bankruptcy. But the debtors' claims in the cases on which she relies were themselves federal claims under bankruptcy law, which would be completely resolved in the bankruptcy process of allowing or disallowing claims. Here Vickie's claim is a state law action independent of the federal bankruptcy law and not necessarily resolvable by a ruling on the creditor's proof of claim in bankruptcy. *Northern Pipeline* and our subsequent decision in *Granfinanciera S.A. v. Nordberg*, 492 U.S. 33 (1989), rejected the application of the "public rights" exception in such cases.

Nor can the bankruptcy courts under the 1984 Act be dismissed as mere adjuncts of Article III courts, any more than could the bankruptcy courts under the 1978 Act. The judicial powers the courts exercise in cases such as this remain the same, and a court exercising such broad powers is no mere adjunct of anyone.

1

Vickie's counterclaim cannot be deemed a matter of "public right" that can be decided outside the Judicial Branch. As explained above, in *Northern Pipeline* we rejected the argument that the public rights doctrine permitted a bankruptcy court to adjudicate a state law suit brought by a debtor against a company that had not filed a claim against the estate. Although our discussion of the public rights exception since that time has not been entirely consistent, and the exception has been the subject of some debate, this case does not fall within any of the various formulations of the concept that appear in this Court's opinions.

We first recognized the category of public rights in *Murray's Lessee v. Hoboken Land & Improvement Co.*, 18 How. 272 (1856). That case involved the Treasury Department's sale of property belonging to a customs collector who had failed to transfer payments to the Federal Government that he had collected on its behalf. The plaintiff, who claimed title to the same land through a different transfer, objected that the Treasury Department's calculation of the deficiency and sale of the property was void, because it was a judicial act that could not be assigned to the Executive under Article III.

"To avoid misconstruction upon so grave a subject," the Court laid out the principles guiding its analysis. It confirmed that Congress cannot "withdraw from judicial cognizance any matter which, from its nature, is the subject of a suit at the common law, or in equity, or admiralty." The Court also recognized that "[a]t the same time there are matters, involving public rights, which may be presented in such form that the judicial power is capable of acting on them, and which are susceptible of judicial determination, but which congress may or may not bring within the cognizance of the courts of the United States, as it may deem proper."

As an example of such matters, the Court referred to "[e]quitable claims to land by the inhabitants of ceded territories" and cited cases in which land issues were conclusively resolved by Executive Branch officials. In those cases "it depends upon the will of congress whether a remedy in the courts shall be allowed at all," so Congress could limit the extent to which a judicial forum was available. The challenge in *Murray's Lessee* to the Treasury Department's sale of the collector's land likewise fell within the "public rights" category of cases, because it could only be brought if the Federal Government chose to allow it by waiving sovereign immunity. The point of *Murray's Lessee* was simply that Congress may set the terms of adjudicating a suit when the suit could not otherwise proceed at all.

Subsequent decisions from this Court contrasted cases within the reach of the public rights exception—those arising "between the Government and persons subject to its authority in connection with the performance of the constitutional functions of the executive or legislative departments"—and those that were instead matters "of private right, that is, of the liability of one individual to another under the law as defined." *Crowell v. Benson*, 285 U.S. 22 (1932).

Shortly after *Northern Pipeline*, the Court rejected the limitation of the public rights exception to actions involving the Government as a party. The Court has continued, however, to limit the exception to cases in which the claim at issue derives from a federal regulatory scheme, or in which resolution of the claim by an expert government agency is deemed essential to a limited regulatory objective within the agency's authority. In other words, it is still the case that what makes a right "public" rather than private is that the right is integrally related to particular federal government action.

Our decision in *Thomas v. Union Carbide Agricultural Products Co.*, 473 U.S. 568 (1985), for example, involved a data-sharing arrangement between companies under a federal statute providing that disputes about compensation between the companies would be decided by binding arbitration. This Court held that the scheme did not violate Article III, explaining that "[a]ny right to compensation . . . results from [the statute] and does not depend on or replace a right to such compensation under state law."

Commodity Futures Trading Commission v. Schor, 478 U.S. 833 (1986), concerned a statutory scheme that created a procedure for customers injured by a broker's violation of the federal commodities law to seek reparations from the broker before the Commodity Futures Trading Commission (CFTC). A customer filed such a claim to recover a debit balance in his account, while the broker filed a lawsuit in Federal District Court to recover the same amount as lawfully due from the customer. The broker later submitted its claim to the CFTC, but after that agency ruled against the customer, the customer argued that agency jurisdiction over the broker's counterclaim violated Article III. This Court disagreed, but only after observing that (1) the claim and the counterclaim concerned a "single dispute"—the same account balance; (2) the CFTC's assertion of authority involved only "a narrow class of common law claims" in a "'particularized area of law'"; (3) the area of law in question was governed by "a specific and limited federal regulatory scheme" as to which the agency had "obvious expertise"; (4) the parties had freely elected to resolve their differences before the CFTC; and (5) CFTC orders were "enforceable only by order of the district court." Most significantly, given that the customer's reparations claim before the agency and the broker's counterclaim were competing claims to the same amount, the Court repeatedly emphasized that it was "necessary" to allow the agency to exercise jurisdiction over the broker's claim, or else "the reparations procedure would have been confounded."

The most recent case in which we considered application of the public rights exception—and the only case in which we have considered that doctrine in the bankruptcy context since *Northern Pipeline* —is *Granfinanciera, S. A. v. Nordberg*, 492 U.S. 33 (1989). In *Granfinanciera* we rejected a bankruptcy trustee's argument that a fraudulent conveyance action filed on behalf of a bankruptcy estate against a noncreditor in a bankruptcy proceeding fell within the "public rights" exception. We explained that, "[i]f a statutory right is not closely intertwined with a federal regulatory program Congress has power to enact, and if that right neither belongs to nor exists against the Federal Government, then it must be adjudicated by an Article III court." We reasoned that fraudulent conveyance suits were "quintessentially suits at common law that more nearly resemble state law contract claims brought by a bankrupt corporation to augment the bankruptcy estate than they do creditors' hierarchically ordered claims to a pro rata share of the bankruptcy res." As a consequence, we concluded that fraudulent conveyance actions were "more accurately characterized as a private rather than a public right as we have used those terms in our Article III decisions."

Vickie's counterclaim—like the fraudulent conveyance claim at issue in *Granfinanciera*—does not fall within any of the varied formulations of the public rights exception in this Court's cases. It is not a matter that can be pursued only by grace of the other branches, as in *Murray's Lessee*, or one that "historically could have been determined exclusively by" those branches, *Northern Pipeline*. The claim is instead one under state common law between two private parties. It does not "depend[ ] on the will of congress," *Murray's Lessee*. Congress has nothing to do with it.

In addition, Vickie's claimed right to relief does not flow from a federal statutory scheme, as in *Thomas*. It is not "completely dependent upon" adjudication of a claim created by federal law, as in *Schor*. And in contrast to the objecting party in *Schor*, Pierce did not truly consent to resolution of Vickie's claim in the bankruptcy court proceedings. He had nowhere else to go if he wished to recover from Vickie's estate.

Furthermore, the asserted authority to decide Vickie's claim is not limited to a "particularized area of the law," as in *Crowell, Thomas,* and *Schor*. We deal here not with an agency but with a court, with substantive jurisdiction reaching any area of the *corpus juris*. This is not a situation in which Congress devised an "expert and inexpensive method for dealing with a class of questions of fact which are particularly suited to examination and determination by an administrative agency specially assigned to that task." *Crowell*; see *Schor*. The "experts" in the federal system at resolving common law counterclaims such as Vickie's are the Article III courts, and it is with those courts that her claim must stay.

The dissent reads our cases differently, and in particular contends that more recent cases view *Northern Pipeline* as "'establish[ing] only that Congress may not vest in a non-Article III court the power to adjudicate, render final judgment, and issue binding orders in a traditional contract action arising under state law, without consent of the litigants, and subject only to ordinary appellate review.'" Just so: Substitute "tort" for "contract," and that statement directly covers this case.

We recognize that there may be instances in which the distinction between public and private rights — at least as framed by some of our recent cases — fails to provide concrete guidance as to whether, for example, a particular agency can adjudicate legal issues under a substantive regulatory scheme. Given the extent to which this case is so markedly distinct from the agency cases discussing the public rights exception in the context of such a regime, however, we do not in this opinion express any view on how the doctrine might apply in that different context.

What is plain here is that this case involves the most prototypical exercise of judicial power: the entry of a final, binding judgment *by a court* with broad substantive jurisdiction, on a common law cause of action, when the action neither derives from nor depends upon any agency regulatory regime. If such an exercise of judicial power may nonetheless be taken from the Article III Judiciary simply by deeming it part of some amorphous "public right," then Article III would be transformed from the guardian of individual liberty and separation of powers we have long recognized into mere wishful thinking.

2

[The Court rejected the argument made by Vickie and the dissent that Pierce's filing of a proof of claim in the bankruptcy proceedings gave the Bankruptcy Court authority to adjudicate Vickie's counterclaim.]

3

Vickie additionally argues that the Bankruptcy Court's final judgment was constitutional because bankruptcy courts under the 1984 Act are properly deemed "adjuncts" of the district courts. We rejected a similar argument in *Northern Pipeline*, and our reasoning there holds true today.

To begin, as explained above, it is still the bankruptcy court itself that exercises the essential attributes of judicial power over a matter such as Vickie's counterclaim. The new bankruptcy courts, like the old, do not "ma[k]e only specialized, narrowly confined factual determinations regarding a particularized area of law" or engage in "statutorily channeled factfinding functions." Instead, bankruptcy courts under the 1984 Act resolve "[a]ll matters of fact and law in whatever domains of the law to which" the parties' counterclaims might lead.

In addition, whereas the adjunct agency in *Crowell v. Benson* "possessed only a limited power to issue compensation orders . . . [that] could be enforced only by order of the district court," *Northern Pipeline*, a bankruptcy court resolving a counterclaim under 28 U.S.C. § 157(b)(2)(C) has the power to enter "appropriate orders and judgments"—including final judgments—subject to review only if a party chooses to appeal. It is thus no less the case here than it was in *Northern Pipeline* that "[t]he authority—and the responsibility—to make an informed, final determination . . . remains with" the bankruptcy judge, not the district court. Given that authority, a bankruptcy court can no more be deemed a mere "adjunct" of the district court than a district court can be deemed such an "adjunct" of the court of appeals. We certainly cannot accept the dissent's notion that judges who have the power to enter final, binding orders are the "functional[ ]" equivalent of "law clerks[ ] and the Judiciary's administrative officials." And even were we wrong in this regard, that would only confirm that such judges should not be in the business of entering final judgments in the first place.

It does not affect our analysis that, as Vickie notes, bankruptcy judges under the current Act are appointed by the Article III courts, rather than the President. If—as we have concluded—the bankruptcy court itself exercises "the essential attributes of judicial power [that] are reserved to Article III courts," it does not matter who appointed the bankruptcy judge or authorized the judge to render final judgments in such proceedings. The constitutional bar remains. See The Federalist No. 78, at 471 ("Periodical appointments, however regulated, or by whomsoever made, would, in some way or other, be fatal to [a judge's] necessary independence").

D

Finally, Vickie and her *amici* predict as a practical matter that restrictions on a bankruptcy court's ability to hear and finally resolve compulsory counterclaims will create significant delays and impose additional costs on the bankruptcy process. It goes without saying that "the fact that a given law or procedure is efficient, convenient, and useful in facilitating functions of government, standing alone, will not save it if it is contrary to the Constitution." *INS v. Chadha*, 462 U.S. 919 (1983).

In addition, we are not convinced that the practical consequences of such limitations on the authority of bankruptcy courts to enter final judgments are as significant as Vickie and the dissent suggest. The dissent asserts that it is important that counterclaims such as Vickie's be resolved "in a bankruptcy court," and that, "to be effective, a single tribunal must have broad authority to restructure [debtor-creditor] relations." But the framework Congress adopted in the 1984 Act already contemplates that certain state law matters in bankruptcy cases will be resolved by judges other than those of the bankruptcy courts. Section 1334(c)(2), for example, requires that bankruptcy courts abstain from hearing specified non-core, state law claims that "can be timely adjudicated[ ] in a State forum of appropriate jurisdiction." Section 1334(c)(1) similarly provides that bankruptcy courts may abstain from hearing any proceeding, including core matters, "in the interest of comity with State courts or respect for State law."

[The] current bankruptcy system also requires the district court to review *de novo* and enter final judgment on any matters that are "related to" the bankruptcy proceedings, § 157(c)(1), and permits the district court to withdraw from the bankruptcy court any referred case, proceeding, or part thereof, § 157(d). Pierce has not argued that the bankruptcy courts "are barred from 'hearing' all counterclaims" or proposing findings of fact and conclusions of law on those matters, but rather that it must be the district court that "finally decide[s]" them. We do not think the removal of counterclaims such as Vickie's from core bankruptcy jurisdiction meaningfully changes the division of labor in the current statute; we agree with the United States that the question presented here is a "narrow" one.

If our decision today does not change all that much, then why the fuss? Is there really a threat to the separation of powers where Congress has conferred the judicial power outside Article III only over certain counterclaims in bankruptcy? The short but emphatic answer is yes. A statute may no more lawfully chip away at the authority of the Judicial Branch than it may eliminate it entirely. "Slight encroachments create new boundaries from which legions of power can seek new territory to capture." *Reid v. Covert*, 354 U.S. 1, 39 (1957) (plurality opinion). Although "[i]t may be that it is the obnoxious thing in its mildest and least repulsive form," we cannot overlook the intrusion: "illegitimate and unconstitutional practices get their first footing in that way, namely, by silent approaches and slight deviations from legal modes of procedure." *Boyd v. United States*, 116 U.S. 616 (1886). We cannot compromise the integrity of the system of separated powers and the role of the Judiciary in that system, even with respect to challenges that may seem innocuous at first blush.

* * *

Article III of the Constitution provides that the judicial power of the United States may be vested only in courts whose judges enjoy the protections set forth in that Article. We conclude today that Congress, in one isolated respect, exceeded that limitation in the Bankruptcy Act of 1984. The Bankruptcy Court below lacked the constitutional authority to enter a final judgment on a state law counterclaim that is not resolved in the process of ruling on a creditor's proof of claim. Accordingly, the judgment of the Court of Appeals is affirmed.

[JUSTICE SCALIA, concurring. Omitted.]

JUSTICE BREYER, with whom JUSTICE GINSBURG, JUSTICE SOTOMAYOR, and JUSTICE KAGAN join, dissenting.

I agree with the Court that the bankruptcy statute, § 157(b)(2)(C), authorizes a bankruptcy court to adjudicate [Vickie's] counterclaim. But I do not agree with the majority about the statute's constitutionality. I believe the statute is consistent with the Constitution's delegation of the "judicial Power of the United States" to the Judicial Branch of Government. Consequently, it is constitutional.

I

My disagreement with the majority's conclusion stems in part from my disagreement about the way in which it interprets, or at least emphasizes, certain precedents. In my view, the majority overstates the current relevance of statements this Court made in an 1856 case, *Murray's Lessee v. Hoboken Land & Improvement Co.*, 18 How. 272 (1856), and it overstates the importance of an analysis that did not command a Court majority in *Northern Pipeline Constr. Co. v. Marathon Pipe Line Co.*, 458 U.S. 50 (1982), and that was subsequently disavowed. At the same time, I fear the Court understates the importance of a watershed opinion widely thought to demonstrate the constitutional basis for the current authority of administrative agencies to adjudicate private disputes, namely, *Crowell v. Benson*, 285 U.S. 22 (1932). And it fails to follow the analysis that this Court more recently has held applicable to the evaluation of claims of a kind before us here, namely, claims that a congressional delegation of adjudicatory authority violates separation-of-powers principles derived from Article III. See *Thomas v. Union Carbide Agricultural Products Co.*, 473 U.S. 568 (1985); *Commodity Futures Trading Comm'n v. Schor*, 478 U.S. 833 (1986).

I shall describe these cases in some detail in order to explain why I believe we should put less weight than does the majority upon the statement in *Murray's Lessee* and the analysis followed by the *Northern Pipeline* plurality and instead should apply the approach this Court has applied in *Crowell, Thomas*, and *Schor*.

A

In *Murray's Lessee*, the Court held that the Constitution permitted an executive official, through summary, nonjudicial proceedings, to attach the assets of a customs collector whose account was deficient. The Court found evidence in common law of "summary method[s] for the recovery of debts due to the crown, and especially those due from receivers of the revenues," and it analogized the Government's summary attachment process to the kind of self-help remedies available to private parties. In the course of its opinion, the Court wrote:

> [W]e do not consider congress can either withdraw from judicial cognizance any matter which, from its nature, is the subject of a suit at the common law, or in equity, or admiralty; nor, on the other hand, can it bring under the judicial power a matter which, from its nature, is not a subject for judicial determination. At the same time there are matters, involving public rights, which may be presented in such form that the judicial power is capable of acting on them, and which are susceptible of judicial determination, but which congress may or may not bring within the cognizance of the courts of the United States, as it may deem proper.

The majority reads the first part of the statement's first sentence as authoritatively defining the boundaries of Article III. I would read the statement in a less absolute way. For one thing, the statement is in effect dictum. For another, it is the remainder of the statement, announcing a distinction between "public rights" and "private rights," that has had the more lasting impact. Later Courts have seized on that distinction when upholding non-Article III adjudication, not when striking it down. The one exception is *Northern Pipeline*, where the Court struck down the Bankruptcy Act of 1978.

But in that case there was no majority. And a plurality, not a majority, read the statement roughly in the way the Court does today.

B

At the same time, I believe the majority places insufficient weight on *Crowell*, a seminal case that clarified the scope of the dictum in *Murray's Lessee*. In that case, the Court considered whether Congress could grant to an Article I administrative agency the power to adjudicate an employee's workers' compensation claim against his employer. The Court assumed that an Article III court would review the agency's decision *de novo* in respect to questions of law but it would conduct a less searching review (looking to see only if the agency's award was "supported by evidence in the record") in respect to questions of fact. The Court pointed out that the case involved a dispute between private persons (a matter of "private rights") and (with one exception not relevant here) it upheld Congress' delegation of primary factfinding authority to the agency....

C

The majority, in my view, overemphasizes the precedential effect of the plurality opinion in *Northern Pipeline*. There, the Court held unconstitutional the jurisdictional provisions of the Bankruptcy Act of 1978 granting adjudicatory authority to bankruptcy judges who lack the protections of tenure and compensation that Article III provides. Four Members of the Court wrote that Congress could grant adjudicatory authority to a non-Article III judge only where (1) the judge sits on a "territorial cour[t]" (2) the judge conducts a "courts-martial," or (3) the case involves a "public right," namely, a "matter" that "at a minimum arise[s] 'between the government and others.'" Two other Members of the Court, without accepting these limitations, agreed with the result because the case involved a breach-of-contract claim brought by the bankruptcy trustee on behalf of the bankruptcy estate against a third party who was not part of the bankruptcy proceeding, and none of the Court's preceding cases (which, the two Members wrote, "do not admit of easy synthesis") had "gone so far as to sanction th[is] type of adjudication."

> Three years later, [in *Thomas*,] the Court held that *Northern Pipeline*
>
> > establishes only that Congress may not vest in a non-Article III court the power to adjudicate, render final judgment, and issue binding orders in a traditional contract action arising under state law, without consent of the litigants, and subject only to ordinary appellate review.

D

Rather than leaning so heavily on the approach taken by the plurality in *Northern Pipeline*, I would look to this Court's more recent Article III cases *Thomas* and *Schor*—cases that commanded a clear majority. In both cases the Court took a more pragmatic approach to the constitutional question. It sought to determine whether, in the particular instance, the challenged delegation of adjudicatory authority posed a genuine and serious threat that one branch of Government sought to aggrandize its own constitutionally delegated authority by encroaching upon a field of authority that the Constitution assigns exclusively to another branch.

1

[In *Thomas*, the Court pointed out] that the right in question was created by a federal statute, it "represent[s] a pragmatic solution to the difficult problem of spreading [certain] costs," and the statute "does not preclude review of the arbitration proceeding by an Article III court."

2

Most recently, in *Schor*, the Court described in greater detail how this Court should analyze this kind of Article III question. The question at issue in *Schor* involved a delegation of authority to an agency to adjudicate a counterclaim. . . .

[The Court] upheld the agency's authority to adjudicate the counterclaim. The Court conceded that the adjudication might be of a kind traditionally decided by a court and that the rights at issue were "private," not "public." But, the Court said, the CFTC deals only with a "'particularized area of law'"; the decision to invoke the CFTC forum is "left entirely to the parties"; Article III courts can review the agency's findings of fact under "the same 'weight of the evidence' standard sustained in *Crowell*" and review its "legal determinations . . . *de novo*"; and the agency's "counterclaim jurisdiction" was necessary to make "workable" a "reparations procedure," which constitutes an important part of a congressionally enacted "regulatory scheme." The Court concluded that for these and other reasons "the magnitude of any intrusion on the Judicial Branch can only be termed *de minimis*."

II

A

This case law, as applied in *Thomas* and *Schor*, requires us to determine pragmatically whether a congressional delegation of adjudicatory authority to a non-Article III judge violates the separation-of-powers principles inherent in Article III. That is to say, we must determine through an examination of certain relevant factors whether that delegation constitutes a significant encroachment by the Legislative or Executive Branches of Government upon the realm of authority that Article III reserves for exercise by the Judicial Branch of Government. Those factors include (1) the nature of the claim to be adjudicated; (2) the nature of the non-Article III tribunal; (3) the extent to which Article III courts exercise control over the proceeding; (4) the presence or absence of the parties' consent; and (5) the nature and importance of the legislative purpose served by the grant of adjudicatory authority to a tribunal with judges who lack Article III's tenure and compensation protections. The presence of "private rights" does not automatically determine the outcome of the question but requires a more "searching" examination of the relevant factors. *Schor*.

Insofar as the majority would apply more formal standards, it simply disregards recent, controlling precedent.

B

Applying *Schor*'s approach here, I conclude that the delegation of adjudicatory authority before us is constitutional. A grant of authority to a bankruptcy court to adjudicate compulsory counterclaims does not violate any constitutional separation-of-powers principle related to Article III.

First, I concede that *the nature of the claim to be adjudicated* argues against my conclusion. Vickie Marshall's counterclaim—a kind of tort suit—resembles "a suit at the common law." *Murray's Lessee.* Although not determinative of the question, a delegation of authority to a non-Article III judge to adjudicate a claim of that kind poses a heightened risk of encroachment on the Federal Judiciary.

At the same time the significance of this factor is mitigated here by the fact that bankruptcy courts often decide claims that similarly resemble various common-law actions. Suppose, for example, that ownership of 40 acres of land in the bankruptcy debtor's possession is disputed by a creditor. If that creditor brings a claim in the bankruptcy court, resolution of that dispute requires the bankruptcy court to apply the same state property law that would govern in a state court proceeding. This kind of dispute arises with regularity in bankruptcy proceedings.

Of course, in this instance the state-law question is embedded in a debtor's counterclaim, not a creditor's claim. But the counterclaim is "compulsory." It "arises out of the transaction or occurrence that is the subject matter of the opposing party's claim." Thus, resolution of the counterclaim will often turn on facts identical to, or at least related to, those at issue in a creditor's claim that is undisputedly proper for the bankruptcy court to decide.

Second, *the nature of the non-Article III tribunal* argues in favor of constitutionality. That is because the tribunal is made up of judges who enjoy considerable protection from improper political influence. Unlike the 1978 Act which provided for the appointment of bankruptcy judges by the President with the advice and consent of the Senate, current law provides that the federal courts of appeals appoint federal bankruptcy judges. Bankruptcy judges are removable by the circuit judicial counsel (made up of federal court of appeals and district court judges) and only for cause. Their salaries are pegged to those of federal district court judges, and the cost of their courthouses and other work-related expenses are paid by the Judiciary. Thus, although Congress technically exercised its Article I power when it created bankruptcy courts, functionally, bankruptcy judges can be compared to magistrate judges, law clerks, and the Judiciary's administrative officials, whose lack of Article III tenure and compensation protections do not endanger the independence of the Judicial Branch.

Third, *the control exercised by Article III judges over bankruptcy proceedings* argues in favor of constitutionality. Article III judges control and supervise the bankruptcy court's determinations—at least to the same degree that Article III judges supervised the agency's determinations in *Crowell*, if not more so. Any party may appeal those determinations to the federal district court, where the federal judge will review all determinations of fact for clear error and will review all determinations of law *de novo*.

FED. RULE BKRTCY. PROC. 8013. But for the here-irrelevant matter of what *Crowell* considered to be special "constitutional" facts, the standard of review for factual findings here ("clearly erroneous") is more stringent than the standard at issue in *Crowell* (whether the agency's factfinding was "supported by evidence in the record"). And, as *Crowell* noted, "there is no requirement that, in order to maintain the essential attributes of the judicial power, all determinations of fact in constitutional courts shall be made by judges."

Moreover, in one important respect Article III judges maintain greater control over the bankruptcy court proceedings at issue here than they did over the relevant proceedings in any of the previous cases in which this Court has upheld a delegation of adjudicatory power. The District Court here may "withdraw, in whole or in part, any case or proceeding referred [to the Bankruptcy Court] . . . on its own motion or on timely motion of any party, for cause shown." 28 U.S.C. § 157(d).

Fourth, the fact that *the parties have consented* to Bankruptcy Court jurisdiction argues in favor of constitutionality, and strongly so. Pierce Marshall, the counterclaim defendant, is not a stranger to the litigation, forced to appear in Bankruptcy Court against his will. Rather, he appeared voluntarily in Bankruptcy Court as one of Vickie Marshall's creditors, seeking a favorable resolution of his claim against Vickie Marshall to the detriment of her other creditors. He need not have filed a claim, perhaps not even at the cost of bringing it in the future, for he says his claim is "nondischargeable," in which case he could have litigated it in a state or federal court after distribution. Thus, Pierce Marshall likely had "an alternative forum to the bankruptcy court in which to pursue [his] clai[m]."

The Court has held, in a highly analogous context, that this type of consent argues strongly in favor of using ordinary bankruptcy court proceedings. In *Granfinanciera*, the Court held that when a bankruptcy trustee seeks to void a transfer of assets from the debtor to an individual on the ground that the transfer to that individual constitutes an unlawful "preference," the question of whether the individual has a right to a jury trial "depends upon whether the creditor has submitted a claim against the estate." . . .

As we have recognized, the jury trial question and the Article III question are highly analogous. And to that extent, *Granfinanciera*'s . . . basic reasoning and conclusion apply here: Even when private rights are at issue, non-Article III adjudication may be appropriate when both parties consent. The majority argues that Pierce Marshall "did not truly consent" to bankruptcy jurisdiction, but filing a proof of claim was sufficient in . . . *Granfinanciera*, and there is no relevant distinction between [the claim filed in that case] and the claim filed here.

Fifth, *the nature and importance of the legislative purpose served* by the grant of adjudicatory authority to bankruptcy tribunals argues strongly in favor of constitutionality. Congress' delegation of adjudicatory powers over counterclaims asserted against bankruptcy claimants constitutes an important means of securing a constitutionally authorized end. Article I, § 8, of the Constitution explicitly grants Congress the "Power To . . . establish . . . uniform Laws on the subject of Bankruptcies throughout the United States."

Congress established the first Bankruptcy Act in 1800. From the beginning, the "core" of federal bankruptcy proceedings has been "the restructuring of debtor-creditor relations." And, to be effective, a single tribunal must have broad authority to restructure those relations, "having jurisdiction of the parties to controversies brought before them," "decid[ing] all matters in dispute," and "decree[ing] complete relief."

The restructuring process requires a creditor to file a proof of claim in the bankruptcy court. In doing so, the creditor "triggers the process of 'allowance and disallowance of claims,' thereby subjecting himself to the bankruptcy court's equitable power." By filing a proof of claim, the creditor agrees to the bankruptcy court's resolution of that claim, and if the creditor wins, the creditor will receive a share of the distribution of the bankruptcy estate. When the bankruptcy estate has a related claim against that creditor, that counterclaim may offset the creditor's claim, or even yield additional damages that augment the estate and may be distributed to the other creditors.

The consequent importance to the total bankruptcy scheme of permitting the trustee in bankruptcy to assert counterclaims against claimants, *and resolving those counterclaims in a bankruptcy court*, is reflected in the fact that Congress included "counterclaims by the estate against persons filing claims against the estate" on its list of "[c]ore proceedings." And it explains the difference, reflected in this Court's opinions, between a claimant's and a nonclaimant's constitutional right to a jury trial.

Consequently a bankruptcy court's determination of such matters has more than "some bearing on a bankruptcy case." It plays a critical role in Congress' constitutionally based effort to create an efficient, effective federal bankruptcy system. At the least, that is what Congress concluded. We owe deference to that determination, which shows the absence of any legislative or executive motive, intent, purpose, or desire to encroach upon areas that Article III reserves to judges to whom it grants tenure and compensation protections.

Considering these factors together, I conclude that, as in *Schor*, "the magnitude of any intrusion on the Judicial Branch can only be termed *de minimis*." I would similarly find the statute before us constitutional.

III

The majority predicts that as a "practical matter" today's decision "does not change all that much." But I doubt that is so. Consider a typical case: A tenant files for bankruptcy. The landlord files a claim for unpaid rent. The tenant asserts a counterclaim for damages suffered by the landlord's (1) failing to fulfill his obligations as lessor, and (2) improperly recovering possession of the premises by misrepresenting the facts in housing court. This state-law counterclaim does not "ste[m] from the bankruptcy itself," it would not "necessarily be resolved in the claims allowance process," and it would require the debtor to prove damages suffered by the lessor's failures, the extent to which the landlord's representations to the housing court were untrue, and damages suffered by improper recovery of possession of the premises. Thus, under the majority's holding, the federal district judge, not the bankruptcy judge, would have to hear and resolve the counterclaim.

Why is that a problem? Because these types of disputes arise in bankruptcy court with some frequency. Because the volume of bankruptcy cases is staggering, involving almost 1.6 million filings last year, compared to a federal district court docket of around 280,000 civil cases and 78,000 criminal cases. Because unlike the "related" non-core state law claims that bankruptcy courts must abstain from hearing, compulsory counterclaims involve the same factual disputes as the claims that may be finally adjudicated by the bankruptcy courts. Because under these circumstances, a constitutionally required game of jurisdictional ping-pong between courts would lead to inefficiency, increased cost, delay, and needless additional suffering among those faced with bankruptcy.

For these reasons, with respect, I dissent.

Note: The Decisions in Northern Pipeline and Stern

1. The *Stern* majority relies heavily on the Court's fractured decision in *Northern Pipeline Construction Co. v. Marathon Pipe Line Co.*, 458 U.S. 50 (1982), which was the first time the Court confronted "an Article III challenge to a bankruptcy court's resolution of the debtor's suit." No opinion commanded a majority of the Court in *Northern Pipeline*. Justice Brennan's plurality opinion emphasized that the Court had historically recognized only three narrow exceptions to the requirement that adjudication occur in Article III courts: territorial courts, military courts-martial, and legislative courts resolving disputes over "public rights." The plurality defined "public rights" disputes as "matters arising 'between the Government and persons subject to its authority in connection with the performance of the constitutional functions of the executive or legislative departments,' and only to matters that historically could have been determined exclusively by those departments." In *Stern*, Chief Justice Roberts acknowledges that the Court's "discussion of the public rights exception since [*Northern Pipeline*] has not been entirely consistent, and the exception has been the subject of some debate," but nonetheless concludes that Vickie's counterclaim "does not fall within any of the various formulations of the [public rights exception] that appear in this Court's opinions." Do you agree with Chief Justice Roberts that the counterclaim in this case does not fit within the "public rights" exception?

2. In a separate concurrence in *Stern*, Justice Scalia expressed doubt about the correctness of some of the Court's precedents, observing: "Article III gives no indication that state-law claims have preferential entitlement to an Article III judge." But the thrust of the precedents certainly tilts in that direction. Justice Brennan in *Northern Pipeline* acknowledged the counter-intuitive quality of the law delineated by his plurality opinion:

> Doubtless it could be argued that the need for independent judicial determination is greatest in cases arising between the Government and an individual. But the rationale for the public-rights line of cases lies not in political theory, but rather in Congress' and this Court's understanding of what power was reserved to the Judiciary by the Constitution as a matter of historical fact.

The *Stern* opinion stresses that the case before it involved "a common law cause of action [that] neither derives from nor depends upon any [federal] agency regime." Does Chief Justice Roberts adequately explain why the cause of action in *Stern* must be heard by an Article III judge, while many cases "arising between the [Federal] Government and an individual" can be adjudicated by a non-Article III tribunal?

3. In *Northern Pipeline*, the concurring Justices emphasized that "the claims of Northern [Pipeline arose] entirely under state law." The plurality likewise noted that the case before it involved the adjudication of a "state-created private right." Similarly, the Court explains in *Stern* that a public right is one that is "integrally related to particular federal government action" and that Vickie's counterclaim is "one under state common law between two private parties. . . . Congress has nothing to do with it." What role do concerns about federalism play in the Court's decisions in *Northern Pipeline* and *Stern*? Is there any reason to believe that life-tenured Article III judges are more likely to respect state law than judges who lack Article III protections?

4. Justice Breyer, in his dissent in *Stern*, identifies a number of practical problems that may arise under the majority's holding. He observes that the "volume of bankruptcy cases is staggering, involving almost 1.6 million filings last year, compared to a federal district court docket of around 280,000 civil cases and 78,000 criminal cases." He fears that a "constitutionally required game of jurisdictional ping-pong between courts would lead to inefficiency, increased cost, delay, and needless additional suffering among those faced with bankruptcy." Are the policy concerns identified by Justice Breyer sufficient to overcome the separation of powers problems discussed in the majority opinion?

5. In *Stern*, the Court did not answer the question of how bankruptcy courts should handle those "core proceedings" over which they lack the constitutional authority to enter final judgment. That question was answered just three years later in *Executive Benefits Insurance Agency v. Arkison*, 134 S. Ct. 2165 (2014). The Court concluded in *Arkison* that, with respect to "core proceedings" that fall within the ambit of *Stern*'s constitutional holding, bankruptcy courts should treat such proceedings as non-core and "submit proposed findings of fact and conclusions of law to the district court for de novo review and entry of judgment" rather than enter final judgment on their own.

Note: Crowell v. Benson *and Administrative Agencies*

One of the most important of the precedents debated by the Court in *Northern Pipeline* and *Stern* is *Crowell v. Benson*, 285 U.S. 22 (1932). The congressional scheme in *Crowell* created an administrative agency and gave it the authority to make initial factual determinations under a federal law requiring employers to compensate their employees for certain work-related maritime injuries.

The plurality in *Northern Pipeline* characterized *Crowell* as a case involving the use of an administrative agency as an "adjunct" to an Article III court. Indeed, the plurality chided the dissent for not accepting this characterization:

Justice White's dissent fails to distinguish between Congress' power to create adjuncts to Art. III courts and Congress' power to create Art. I courts in limited circumstances. Congress' power to create adjuncts and assign them limited adjudicatory functions is in no sense an "exception" to Art. III. Rather, such an assignment is consistent with Art. III, so long as "the essential attributes of the judicial power" are retained in the Art. III court, and so long as Congress' adjustment of the traditional manner of adjudication can be sufficiently linked to its legislative power to define substantive rights.

The majority opinion in *Stern* reads *Crowell* similarly:

Although the Court in *Crowell* [decided] that the facts of the private dispute before it could be determined by a non-Article III tribunal in the first instance, subject to judicial review, the Court did so only after observing that the administrative adjudicator had only limited authority to make specialized, narrowly confined factual determinations regarding a particularized area of law and to issue orders that could be enforced only by action of the District Court. In other words, the agency in *Crowell* functioned as a true "adjunct" of the District Court.

But the agency in *Crowell* was not part of the judicial branch; it was entirely independent of it. In what sense was it an "adjunct" to an Article III court?

Note: The Decisions in Stern and Schor

1. One of the cases discussed in *Stern* is *Commodity Futures Trading Commission v. Schor*, 478 U.S. 833 (1986), which involved a statutory scheme that created a procedure for customers injured by a broker's violation of the federal commodities law to seek reparations from the broker before the Commodity Futures Trading Commission (CFTC). Federal regulations also authorized the CFTC to hear counterclaims brought by brokers against customers who sued those brokers. In *Schor*, a customer filed such a claim in the CFTC against a broker, and the broker filed a state-law counterclaim against the customer in the CFTC relating to the same account.

The Supreme Court held that the CFTC could hear the broker's state-law claim. In doing so, the Court identified two interests served by Article III. First, Article III confers a "personal right" to an "impartial and independent" adjudicator. According to the Court, the broker waived this personal right by filing his claim in the CFTC. Second, Article III creates an independent Judiciary that is integral to "the constitutional system of checks and balances" because it balances the other branches of government. According to the Court, Article III protects this role for the Judiciary by "barring congressional attempts to transfer jurisdiction to non-Article III tribunals for the purpose of emasculating [Article III] courts." The Court explained that, unlike with the personal right, "parties cannot by consent" avoid this structural limitation.

Nevertheless, the Court explained, this structural limitation is not absolute. Instead, in determining whether Congress could assign a claim to an Article I tribunal, the Court "weighed a number of factors, none of which . . . determinative, with an eye to the practical effect that the congressional action will have on the constitutionally assigned role of the federal judiciary." Included among those factors were "the extent to which the essential attributes of judicial power are reserved to Article III courts, and, conversely, the extent to which the non-Article III forum exercises the range of jurisdiction and powers normally vested only in Article III courts, the origins and importance of the right to be adjudicated, and the concerns that drove Congress to depart from the requirements of Article III."

2. In *Stern*, the majority did not apply *Schor*'s balancing test to determine whether allowing a non-Article III court to resolve a claim would violate the structural interests protected by Article III. Instead, *Stern* adopted a presumption against allowing bankruptcy courts to hear state law claims, and it characterized *Schor* as a limited example of a dispute involving a public right that can be decided by non-Article III courts. Based on the summary above, is the *Stern* majority's characterization of *Schor* fair?

3. In *Stern*, the majority opinion noted that the bankruptcy regime invalidated in that case was "markedly distinct from the agency cases discussing the public rights exception." Are *Stern* and *Schor* reconcilable on the ground that *Schor* involved an agency adjudication, while *Stern* involved an adjudication by a bankruptcy judge? If not, how can the two cases be reconciled?

4. If *Stern* and *Schor* are distinguishable based on the type of adjudication involved, then does the Court's distinction between bankruptcy and agency adjudications make sense? Is it counter-intuitive to allow executive branch agencies to adjudicate state-law claims when bankruptcy courts, which are supervised by Article III courts, cannot?

5. In rejecting the balancing approach set forth in *Schor*, the majority in *Stern* explains why a balancing approach threatens the separation of powers: "A statute may no more lawfully chip away at the authority of the Judicial Branch than it may eliminate it entirely. 'Slight encroachments create new boundaries from which legions of power can seek new territory to capture.'" Is Chief Justice Roberts correct that even "de minimis" encroachments on the judiciary violate the separation of powers? Are the concerns about separation of powers as pronounced here as in *Plaut v. Spendthrift Farm, Inc.*, 514 U.S. 211 (1995) (Chapter 20), in which the "conclusiveness of final judgments" was at issue?

Wellness International Network, Ltd. v. Sharif

Supreme Court of the United States, 2015.

135 S. Ct. 1932.

JUSTICE SOTOMAYOR delivered the opinion of the Court.

Article III, § 1, of the Constitution provides that "the judicial Power of the United States, shall be vested in one supreme Court, and in such inferior Courts as the Congress may from time to time ordain and establish." Congress has in turn established 94 District Courts and 13 Courts of Appeals, composed of judges who enjoy the protections of Article III: life tenure and pay that cannot be diminished. Because these protections help to ensure the integrity and independence of the Judiciary, "we have long recognized that, in general, Congress may not withdraw from" the Article III courts "any matter which, from its nature, is the subject of a suit at the common law, or inequity, or in admiralty." *Stern v. Marshall*, 564 U.S. 462 (2011).

Congress has also authorized the appointment of bankruptcy and magistrate judges, who do not enjoy the protections of Article III, to assist Article III courts in their work. The number of magistrate and bankruptcy judgeships exceeds the number of circuit and district judgeships. And it is no exaggeration to say that without the distinguished service of these judicial colleagues, the work of the federal court system would grind nearly to a halt.

Congress' efforts to align the responsibilities of non-Article III judges with the boundaries set by the Constitution have not always been successful. In *Northern Pipeline Constr. Co. v. Marathon Pipe Line Co.*, 458 U.S. 50 (1982), and more recently in *Stern*, this Court held that Congress violated Article III by authorizing bankruptcy judges to decide certain claims for which litigants are constitutionally entitled to an Article III adjudication. This case presents the question whether Article III allows bankruptcy judges to adjudicate such claims with the parties' consent. We hold that Article III is not violated when the parties knowingly and voluntarily consent to adjudication by a bankruptcy judge.

I

A

[Under the Bankruptcy Amendments and Federal Judgeship Act of 1984,] district courts have original jurisdiction over bankruptcy cases and related proceedings. 28 U.S.C. §§ 1334(a), (b). But "each district court may provide that any or all" bankruptcy cases and related proceedings "shall be referred to the bankruptcy judges for the district." Bankruptcy judges are "judicial officers of the United States district court," appointed to 14-year terms by the courts of appeals, and subject to removal for cause. "The district court may withdraw" a reference to the bankruptcy court "on its own motion or on timely motion of any party, for cause shown."

When a district court refers a case to a bankruptcy judge, that judge's statutory authority depends on whether Congress has classified the matter as a "core proceeding" or a "non-core proceeding." . . . Congress identified as "core" a nonexclusive list of 16 types of proceedings, in which it thought bankruptcy courts could constitutionally enter judgment. Congress gave bankruptcy courts the power to "hear and determine" core proceedings and to "enter appropriate orders and judgments," subject to appellate review by the district court. . . .

B

Petitioner Wellness International Network is a manufacturer of health and nutrition products. Wellness and respondent Sharif entered into a contract under which Sharif would distribute Wellness' products. The relationship quickly soured, and in 2005, Sharif sued Wellness in the United States District Court for the Northern District of Texas. Sharif repeatedly ignored Wellness' discovery requests and other litigation obligations, resulting in an entry of default judgment for Wellness. The District Court eventually sanctioned Sharif by awarding Wellness over $650,000 in attorney's fees. This case arises from Wellness' long-running—and so far unsuccessful—efforts to collect on that judgment.

In February 2009, Sharif filed for Chapter 7 bankruptcy in the Northern District of Illinois. The bankruptcy petition listed Wellness as a creditor. Wellness requested documents concerning Sharif's assets, which Sharif did not provide. Wellness later obtained a loan application Sharif had filed in 2002, listing more than $5 million in assets. When confronted, Sharif informed Wellness and the Chapter 7 trustee that he had lied on the loan application. The listed assets, Sharif claimed, were actually owned by the Soad Wattar Living Trust (Trust), an entity Sharif said he administered on behalf of his mother, and for the benefit of his sister. Wellness pressed Sharif for information on the Trust, but Sharif again failed to respond.

Wellness filed a five-count adversary complaint against Sharif in the Bankruptcy Court. . . . Count V of the complaint sought a declaratory judgment that the Trust was Sharif's alter ego and that its assets should therefore be treated as part of Sharif's bankruptcy estate. In his answer, Sharif admitted that the adversary proceeding was a "core proceeding"—*i.e.,* a proceeding in which the Bankruptcy Court could enter final judgment subject to appeal. Indeed, Sharif requested judgment in his favor on all counts of Wellness' complaint and urged the Bankruptcy Court to "find that the Soad Wattar Living Trust is not property of the [bankruptcy] estate." In July 2010, the Bankruptcy Court . . . declared, as requested by count V of Wellness' complaint, that the assets supposedly held by the Trust were in fact property of Sharif's bankruptcy estate because Sharif "treats [the Trust's] assets as his own property."

Sharif appealed to the District Court. Six weeks before Sharif filed his opening brief in the District Court, this Court decided *Stern*. In *Stern*, the Court held that Article III prevents bankruptcy courts from entering final judgment on claims that seek only to "augment" the bankruptcy estate and would otherwise "exist without regard to any bankruptcy proceeding." [The District Court affirmed the Bankruptcy Court's judgment. The Seventh Circuit reversed with respect to count V. It concluded] that count V of the complaint alleged a so-called "*Stern* claim," that is, "a claim designated for final adjudication in the bankruptcy court as a statutory matter, but prohibited from proceeding in that way as a constitutional matter." The Seventh Circuit therefore ruled that the Bankruptcy Court lacked constitutional authority to enter final judgment on count V. . . .

II

Our precedents make clear that litigants may validly consent to adjudication by bankruptcy courts.

A

Adjudication by consent is nothing new. Indeed, "during the early years of the Republic, federal courts, with the consent of the litigants, regularly referred adjudication of entire disputes to non-Article III referees, masters, or arbitrators, for entry of final judgment in accordance with the referee's report." Brubaker, The

Constitutionality of Litigant Consent to Non-Article III Bankruptcy Adjudications, 32 Bkrtcy. L. Letter No. 12, at 6 (Dec. 2012).

The foundational case in the modern era is *Commodity Futures Trading Comm'n v. Schor*, 478 U.S. 833 (1986). The Commodity Futures Trading Commission (CFTC), which Congress had authorized to hear customer complaints against commodities brokers, issued a regulation allowing itself to hear state-law counterclaims as well. William Schor filed a complaint with the CFTC against his broker, and the broker, which had previously filed claims against Schor in federal court, refiled them as counterclaims in the CFTC proceeding. The CFTC ruled against Schor on the counterclaims. This Court upheld that ruling against both statutory and constitutional challenges.

On the constitutional question (the one relevant here) the Court began by holding that Schor had "waived any right he may have possessed to the full trial of [the broker's] counterclaim before an Article III court." The Court then explained why this waiver legitimated the CFTC's exercise of authority: "As a personal right, Article III's guarantee of an impartial and independent federal adjudication is subject to waiver, just as are other personal constitutional rights"—such as the right to a jury—"that dictate the procedures by which civil and criminal matters must be tried."

The Court went on to state that a litigant's waiver of his "personal right" to an Article III court is not always dispositive because Article III "not only preserves to litigants their interest in an impartial and independent federal adjudication of claims . . . , but also serves as 'an inseparable element of the constitutional system of checks and balances.' . . . To the extent that this structural principle is implicated in a given case"—but only to that extent—"the parties cannot by consent cure the constitutional difficulty . . . ."

Leaning heavily on the importance of Schor's consent, the Court found no structural concern implicated by the CFTC's adjudication of the counterclaims against him. While "Congress gave the CFTC the authority to adjudicate such matters," the Court wrote,

> the decision to invoke this forum is left entirely to the parties and the power of the federal judiciary to take jurisdiction of these matters is unaffected. In such circumstances, separation of powers concerns are diminished, for it seems self-evident that just as Congress may encourage parties to settle a dispute out of court or resort to arbitration without impermissible incursions on the separation of powers, Congress may make available a quasi-judicial mechanism through which willing parties may, at their option, elect to resolve their differences.

The option for parties to submit their disputes to a non-Article III adjudicator was at most a "*de minimis*" infringement on the prerogative of the federal courts.

A few years after *Schor*, the Court decided a pair of cases—*Gomez v. United States*, 490 U.S. 858 (1989), and *Peretz v. United States*, 501 U.S. 923 (1991)—that reiterated the importance of consent to the constitutional analysis. Both cases concerned whether the Federal Magistrates Act authorized magistrate judges to preside over jury selection in a felony trial; the difference was that Peretz consented to the practice while Gomez did not. That difference was dispositive.

In *Gomez*, the Court interpreted the statute as not allowing magistrate judges to supervise *voir dire* without consent, emphasizing the constitutional concerns that might otherwise arise. In *Peretz*, the Court upheld the Magistrate Judge's action, stating that "the defendant's consent significantly changes the constitutional analysis." The Court concluded that allowing a magistrate judge to supervise jury selection—with consent—does not violate Article III, explaining that "litigants may waive their personal right to have an Article III judge preside over a civil trial," and that "the most basic rights of criminal defendants are similarly subject to waiver." And "even assuming that a litigant may not waive structural protections provided by Article III," the Court found "no such structural protections . . . implicated by" a magistrate judge's supervision of *voir dire*:

> Magistrates are appointed and subject to removal by Article III judges. The "ultimate decision" whether to invoke the magistrate's assistance is made by the district court, subject to veto by the parties. The decision whether to empanel the jury whose selection a magistrate has supervised also remains entirely with the district court. Because "the entire process takes place under the district court's total control and jurisdiction," there is no danger that use of the magistrate involves a 'congressional attempt "to transfer jurisdiction [to non-Article III tribunals] for the purpose of emasculating" constitutional courts.'[9]

The lesson of *Schor*, *Peretz*, and the history that preceded them is plain: The entitlement to an Article III adjudicator is "a personal right" and thus ordinarily "subject to waiver." Article III also serves a structural purpose, "barring congressional attempts 'to transfer jurisdiction [to non-Article III tribunals] for the purpose of emasculating' constitutional courts and thereby prevent[ing] 'the encroachment or aggrandizement of one branch at the expense of the other.'" But allowing Article I adjudicators to decide claims submitted to them by consent does not offend the separation of powers so long as Article III courts retain supervisory authority over the process.

B

The question here, then, is whether allowing bankruptcy courts to decide *Stern* claims by consent would "impermissibly threaten the institutional integrity of the Judicial Branch." *Schor*. And that question must be decided not by "formalistic and unbending rules," but "with an eye to the practical effect that the" practice "will have on the constitutionally assigned role of the federal judiciary." The Court must weigh

> the extent to which the essential attributes of judicial power are reserved to Article III courts, and, conversely, the extent to which the non-Article III

---

9. Discounting the relevance of *Gomez* and *Peretz*, the principal dissent emphasizes that neither case concerned the entry of final judgment by a non-Article III actor. Here again, the principal dissent's insistence on formalism leads it astray. As we explained in *Peretz*, the "responsibility and importance [of] presiding over *voir dire* at a felony trial" is equivalent to the "supervision of entire civil and misdemeanor trials," tasks in which magistrate judges may "order the entry of judgment" with the parties' consent.

forum exercises the range of jurisdiction and powers normally vested only in Article III courts, the origins and importance of the right to be adjudicated, and the concerns that drove Congress to depart from the requirements of Article III.

Applying these factors, we conclude that allowing bankruptcy litigants to waive the right to Article III adjudication of *Stern* claims does not usurp the constitutional prerogatives of Article III courts. Bankruptcy judges, like magistrate judges, "are appointed and subject to removal by Article III judges," *Peretz*. They "serve as judicial officers of the United States district court," [28 U.S.C. §] 151, and collectively "constitute a unit of the district court" for that district, § 152(a)(1). Just as "the 'ultimate decision' whether to invoke [a] magistrate [judge]'s assistance is made by the district court," *Peretz*, bankruptcy courts hear matters solely on a district court's reference, which the district court may withdraw *sua sponte* or at the request of a party. "Separation of powers concerns are diminished" when, as here, "the decision to invoke [a non-Article III] forum is left entirely to the parties and the power of the federal judiciary to take jurisdiction" remains in place. *Schor*.

Furthermore, like the CFTC in *Schor*, bankruptcy courts possess no free-floating authority to decide claims traditionally heard by Article III courts. Their ability to resolve such matters is limited to "a narrow class of common law claims as an incident to the [bankruptcy courts'] primary, and unchallenged, adjudicative function." "In such circumstances, the magnitude of any intrusion on the Judicial Branch can only be termed *de minimis*."

Finally, there is no indication that Congress gave bankruptcy courts the ability to decide *Stern* claims in an effort to aggrandize itself or humble the Judiciary. As in *Peretz*, "because 'the entire process takes place under the district court's total control and jurisdiction,' there is no danger that use of the [bankruptcy court] involves a 'congressional attempt "to transfer jurisdiction [to non-Article III tribunals] for the purpose of emasculating" constitutional courts.'"[10]

Congress could choose to rest the full share of the Judiciary's labor on the shoulders of Article III judges. But doing so would require a substantial increase in the number of district judgeships. Instead, Congress has supplemented the capacity of district courts through the able assistance of bankruptcy judges. So long as those judges are subject to control by the Article III courts, their work poses no threat to the separation of powers.

C

Our recent decision in *Stern*, on which Sharif and the principal dissent rely heavily, does not compel a different result. That is because *Stern*—like its predecessor, *Northern Pipeline*—turned on the fact that the litigant "did not truly consent to" resolution of the

---

10. The principal dissent accuses us of making Sharif's consent "'dispositive' in curing [a] structural separation of powers violation," contrary to the holding of *Schor*. That argument misapprehends both *Schor* and the nature of our analysis. What *Schor* forbids is using consent to excuse an actual violation of Article III. But *Schor* confirms that consent remains highly relevant when determining, as we do here, whether a particular adjudication in fact raises constitutional concerns. Thus, we do not rely on Sharif's consent to "cur[e]" a violation of Article III. His consent shows, in part, why no such violation has occurred.

claim against it in a non-Article III forum. . . . Because *Stern* was premised on non-consent to adjudication by the Bankruptcy Court, the "constitutional bar" it announced simply does not govern the question whether litigants may validly consent to adjudication by a bankruptcy court. In sum, the cases in which this Court has found a violation of a litigant's right to an Article III decisionmaker have involved an objecting defendant forced to litigate involuntarily before a non-Article III court. The Court has never done what Sharif and the principal dissent would have us do—hold that a litigant who has the right to an Article III court may not waive that right through his consent.

D

The principal dissent warns darkly of the consequences of today's decision. To hear the principal dissent tell it, the world will end not in fire, or ice, but in a bankruptcy court. The response to these ominous predictions is the same now as it was when Justice Brennan, dissenting in *Schor*, first made them nearly 30 years ago:

> This is not to say, of course, that if Congress created a phalanx of non-Article III tribunals equipped to handle the entire business of the Article III courts without any Article III supervision or control and without evidence of valid and specific legislative necessities, the fact that the parties had the election to proceed in their forum of choice would necessarily save the scheme from constitutional attack. But this case obviously bears no resemblance to such a scenario . . . .

Adjudication based on litigant consent has been a consistent feature of the federal court system since its inception. Reaffirming that unremarkable fact, we are confident, poses no great threat to anyone's birthrights, constitutional or otherwise.

III

Sharif contends that to the extent litigants may validly consent to adjudication by a bankruptcy court, such consent must be express. We disagree.

Nothing in the Constitution requires that consent to adjudication by a bankruptcy court be express. Nor does the relevant statute, 28 U.S.C. § 157, mandate express consent; it states only that a bankruptcy court must obtain "the consent"—consent *simpliciter*—"of all parties to the proceeding" before hearing and determining a non-core claim. § 157(c)(2). And a requirement of express consent would be in great tension with our decision in *Roell v. Withrow*, 538 U.S. 580 (2003). That case concerned the interpretation of § 636(c), which authorizes magistrate judges to "conduct any or all proceedings in a jury or non-jury civil matter and order the entry of judgment in the case," with "the consent of the parties." The specific question in *Roell* was whether, as a statutory matter, the "consent" required by § 636(c) had to be express. The dissent argued that "reading § 636(c)(1) to require express consent not only is more consistent with the text of the statute, but also" avoids constitutional concerns by "ensur[ing] that the parties knowingly and voluntarily waive their right to an Article III judge." But the majority—thus placed on notice of the constitutional concern—was untroubled by it, opining that "the Article III right is substantially honored" by permitting waiver based on "actions rather than words."

The implied consent standard articulated in *Roell* supplies the appropriate rule for adjudications by bankruptcy courts under § 157. Applied in the bankruptcy context, that standard possesses the same pragmatic virtues—increasing judicial efficiency and checking gamesmanship—that motivated our adoption of it for consent-based adjudications by magistrate judges. It bears emphasizing, however, that a litigant's consent—whether express or implied—must still be knowing and voluntary. . . .

IV

[The Court remanded to the Seventh Circuit for it to determine whether Sharif consented to adjudication by the Bankruptcy Court.]

It is so ordered.

JUSTICE ALITO, concurring in part and concurring in the judgment.

I join the opinion of the Court insofar as it holds that a bankruptcy judge's resolution of a "*Stern* claim" with the consent of the parties does not violate Article III of the Constitution. The Court faithfully applies *Commodity Futures Trading Comm'n v. Schor*, 478 U.S. 833 (1986). No one believes that an arbitrator exercises "the judicial Power of the United States," Art. III, § 1, in an ordinary, run-of-the mill arbitration. And whatever differences there may be between an arbitrator's "decision" and a bankruptcy court's "judgment," those differences would seem to fall within the Court's previous rejection of "formalistic and unbending rules." Whatever one thinks of *Schor*, it is still the law of this Court, and the parties do not ask us to revisit it.

Unlike the Court, however, I would not decide whether consent may be implied. [Justice Alito asserted that Sharif forfeited the argument that he did not consent.]

CHIEF JUSTICE ROBERTS, with whom JUSTICE SCALIA joins, and with whom JUSTICE THOMAS joins as to Part I, dissenting.

I

. . . The Court granted certiorari on two questions in this case. The first is whether the Bankruptcy Court's entry of final judgment on Wellness's claim violated Article III based on *Stern*. The second is whether an Article III violation of the kind recognized in *Stern* can be cured by consent. Because the first question can be resolved on narrower grounds, I would answer it alone.

B

. . . In my view, Article III likely poses no barrier to the Bankruptcy Court's resolution of Wellness's claim. At its most basic level, bankruptcy is "an adjudication of interests claimed in a *res*." *Katchen v. Landy*, 382 U.S. 323 (1966). Wellness asked the Bankruptcy Court to declare that assets held by Sharif are part of that res. Defining what constitutes the estate is the necessary starting point of every bankruptcy; a court cannot divide up the estate without first knowing what's in it. As the Solicitor General explains, "Identifying the property of the estate is therefore inescapably central to the restructuring of the debtor-creditor relationship."

II

The Court "expresses no view" on whether Wellness's claim was a *Stern* claim. Instead, the Court concludes that the Bankruptcy Court had constitutional authority to enter final judgment on Wellness's claim either way. The majority rests its decision on Sharif's purported consent to the Bankruptcy Court's adjudication. But Sharif has no authority to compromise the structural separation of powers or agree to an exercise of judicial power outside Article III. His consent therefore cannot cure a constitutional violation.

A

"If there is a principle in our Constitution . . . more sacred than another," James Madison said on the floor of the First Congress, "it is that which separates the Legislative, Executive, and Judicial powers." 1 Annals of Cong. 581 (1789). . . . By diffusing federal powers among three different branches, and by protecting each branch against incursions from the others, the Framers devised a structure of government that promotes both liberty and accountability.

We have emphasized that the values of liberty and accountability protected by the separation of powers belong not to any branch of the Government but to the Nation as a whole. A branch's consent to a diminution of its constitutional powers therefore does not mitigate the harm or cure the wrong. . . .

B

If a branch of the Federal Government may not consent to a violation of the separation of powers, surely a private litigant may not do so. Just as a branch of Government may not consent away the individual liberty interest protected by the separation of powers, so too an individual may not consent away the institutional interest protected by the separation of powers. To be sure, a private litigant may consensually relinquish *individual* constitutional rights. A federal criminal defendant, for example, may knowingly and voluntarily waive his Sixth Amendment right to a jury trial by pleading guilty to a charged offense. But that same defendant may not agree to stand trial on federal charges before a state court, a foreign court, or a moot court, because those courts have no constitutional authority to exercise judicial power over his case, and he has no power to confer it. . . .

As the majority recognizes, the Court's most extensive discussion of litigant consent in a separation of powers case occurred in *Commodity Futures Trading Comm'n v. Schor*, 478 U.S. 833 (1986). There the Court held that Article III confers both a "personal right" that can be waived through consent and a structural component that "safeguards the role of the Judicial Branch in our tripartite system." "To the extent that this structural principle is implicated in a given case, the parties cannot by consent cure the constitutional difficulty for the same reason that the parties by consent cannot confer on federal courts subject-matter jurisdiction beyond the limitations imposed by Article III." . . .

. . . Thus, the key inquiry in this case — as the majority puts it — is "whether allowing bankruptcy courts to decide *Stern* claims by consent would 'impermissibly threaten the institutional integrity of the Judicial Branch.'"

One need not search far to find the answer. In *Stern*, this Court applied the analysis from *Schor* to bankruptcy courts and concluded that they lack Article III authority to enter final judgments on matters now known as *Stern* claims. The Court noted that bankruptcy courts, unlike the administrative agency in *Schor*, were endowed by Congress with "substantive jurisdiction reaching any area of the *corpus juris*," power to render final judgments enforceable without any action by Article III courts, and authority to adjudicate counterclaims entirely independent of the bankruptcy itself. The Court concluded that allowing Congress to bestow such authority on non-Article III courts would "compromise the integrity of the system of separated powers and the role of the Judiciary in that system." If there was any room for doubt about the basis for its holding, the Court dispelled it by asking a question: "Is there really a threat to the separation of powers where Congress has conferred the judicial power outside Article III only over certain counterclaims in bankruptcy?" "The short but emphatic answer is yes."

In other words, allowing bankruptcy courts to decide *Stern* claims by consent would "impermissibly threaten the institutional integrity of the Judicial Branch." . . .

The majority also relies heavily on the supervision and control that Article III courts exercise over bankruptcy courts. As the majority notes, court of appeals judges appoint bankruptcy judges, and bankruptcy judges receive cases only on referral from district courts (although every district court in the country has adopted a standing rule automatically referring all bankruptcy filings to bankruptcy judges). The problem is that Congress has also given bankruptcy courts authority to enter final judgments subject only to deferential appellate review, and Article III precludes those judgments when they involve *Stern* claims. The fact that Article III judges played a role in the Article III violation does not remedy the constitutional harm. . . .

C

Eager to change the subject from *Stern*, the majority devotes considerable attention to defending the authority of magistrate judges, who may conduct certain proceedings with the consent of the parties under 28 U.S.C. §636. No one here challenges the constitutionality of magistrate judges or disputes that they, like bankruptcy judges, may issue reports and recommendations that are reviewed *de novo* by Article III judges. The cases about magistrate judges cited by the majority therefore have little bearing on this case, because none of them involved a constitutional challenge to the entry of final judgment by a non-Article III actor.

The majority also points to 19th-century cases in which courts referred disputes to non-Article III referees, masters, or arbitrators. In those cases, however, it was the Article III court that ultimately entered final judgment. *E.g., Thornton v. Carson*, 7 Cranch 596 (1813). Article III courts do refer matters to non-Article III actors for assistance from time to time. This Court does so regularly in original jurisdiction cases. But under the Constitution, the "ultimate responsibility for deciding" the case must remain with the Article III court.

The concurrence's comparison of bankruptcy judges to arbitrators is similarly inapt. Arbitration is "a matter of contract" by which parties agree to resolve their disputes in a private forum. Such an arrangement does not implicate Article III any more than does an agreement between two business partners to submit a difference of opinion to a mutually trusted friend. Arbitration agreements, like most private contracts, can be enforced in court. And Congress, pursuant to its Commerce Clause power, has authorized district courts to enter judgments enforcing arbitration awards under certain circumstances. See 9 U.S.C. § 9. But this ordinary scheme of contract enforcement creates no constitutional concern. As the concurrence acknowledges, only Article III judges — not arbitrators — may enter final judgments enforcing arbitration awards.

In *Stern*, the Court cautioned that Congress "may no more lawfully chip away at the authority of the Judicial Branch than it may eliminate it entirely." The majority sees no reason to fret, however, so long as two private parties consent. But such parties are unlikely to carefully weigh the long-term structural independence of the Article III judiciary against their own short-term priorities. Perhaps the majority's acquiescence in this diminution of constitutional authority will escape notice. Far more likely, however, it will amount to the kind of "blueprint for extensive expansion of the legislative power" that we have resisted in the past.

I respectfully dissent.

Justice Thomas, dissenting. [Omitted]

Note: Consent and Structural Protections

1. The opinions in *Wellness* refer to "*Stern* claims." Recall what is meant by that phrase: claims designated by statute for final adjudication by the bankruptcy courts, but that cannot constitutionally be decided by those courts under the holding in *Stern*. In *Wellness*, the Court created an exception to the restriction on adjudication by bankruptcy courts, stating that *Stern* claims can be adjudicated by bankruptcy courts if the litigants consent.

2. In *Wellness*, the majority stated that when the litigants consent to adjudication by a bankruptcy court, the "separation of powers concerns are diminished." Is litigant consent to adjudication by a non-Article III tribunal necessary for that tribunal to adjudicate the claim? Or are there other circumstances that can diminish the separation-of-powers concerns to a degree that a non-Article III court may adjudicate a claim? Compare *Schor*, Note *supra* this chapter.

3. The *Wellness* majority says not only that a litigant's consent may waive the "personal right" to an Article III tribunal, but also that the litigant's consent is "highly relevant" to determining whether adjudication by a non-Article III court violates the structural protections of Article III. How does a litigant's consent bear on whether adjudication by an Article I tribunal violates Article III's structural protections? Can *Wellness*'s approach be squared with the rule that litigants cannot waive Article III's justiciability doctrines through consent?

Problem: Mandatory Arbitration in Bankruptcy

In 2015, George and Lucille Sitwell purchased a mattress at Consolidated Mattress Outlets, Inc. Over the next two years they both suffered a number of mysterious ailments that their doctor attributed to toxic chemicals seeping out of their mattress. In 2017, the Sitwells sued Consolidated in Oceana state court, alleging a variety of state-law tort claims.

As a result of numerous other lawsuits against Consolidated and declining mattress sales, the company subsequently filed for bankruptcy protection in the United States Bankruptcy Court for the District of Oceana—a court created pursuant to Congress's bankruptcy powers under Article I, § 8 of the Constitution. Under the automatic stay provision of the Bankruptcy Code, the filing of the bankruptcy petition operated as a stay of all pending civil actions against Consolidated. After determining that a global settlement of all personal injury claims was unlikely, the bankruptcy court lifted the automatic stay with respect to pending litigation. As a result, the Sitwells prepared for trial in Oceana state court.

After successfully settling a number of personal injury claims through an Alternative Dispute Resolution (ADR) program, Consolidated petitioned the bankruptcy court to issue an order requiring that all remaining personal injury claims against it be resolved in mandatory, binding arbitration. The court agreed, issuing an order compelling arbitration for the remaining claims, and staying all litigation currently pending against Consolidated. As authority for its actions, the bankruptcy court cited sections 1124(b) and 524(a) of Title 11 of the United States Code, which permit bankruptcy courts to dispose of all of the debtor's property and to enjoin any suits seeking to impose personal liability against the debtor. The court also pointed to 11 U.S.C. § 105, which gives bankruptcy courts the power to issue "any order . . . necessary or appropriate" to the restructuring of the debtor's estate.

Rather than undergo the mandatory ADR process, the Sitwells have appealed the bankruptcy court's order to the United States District Court for the District of Oceana, arguing that, as an Article I court, the bankruptcy court lacks the constitutional power to send their state-law tort claims to mandatory, binding arbitration. Consolidated, on the other hand, argues that Congress has vested exclusive jurisdiction in the bankruptcy courts to resolve such claims, under the authority of Article I, § 8 and Title 11 of the United States Code. Assuming that the bankruptcy court possesses the statutory power under Title 11 to order mandatory, binding arbitration of the Sitwells' state-law claims, how should the district court rule on the constitutional question? In other words, may a bankruptcy court, consistent with the requirements of Article III, order pending state-law claims to be resolved in mandatory, binding arbitration?

Note: Magistrate Judges in the Federal Judicial System

1. In debating whether Wellness's claims could be adjudicated in a bankruptcy court, both the majority and the dissent discuss the constitutionality of allowing federal magistrate judges to resolve cases. Magistrate judges make up the majority of federal judges. According to one commentator, as of 2001, "845 judgeships [were] designated for bankruptcy and magistrate judges in contrast to the 646 authorized for district court judges. [Moreover,] in six federal district courts, the number of magistrate judges was greater than the number of life-tenured judges. In another sixteen districts, their numbers were equal." Judith Resnik, *"Uncle Sam Modernizes His Justice": Inventing the Federal District Courts of the Twentieth Century for the District of Columbia and the Nation*, 90 GEO. L.J. 607, 612 (2002).

What are the consequences of this delegation? And what limits does the Constitution place on Congress's power to authorize magistrate judges to perform adjudicative functions that otherwise would be carried out by life-tenured district judges?

2. According to the majority in *Wellness*, whether the parties have consented to adjudication by a magistrate judge plays a large role in assessing whether a magistrate judge may adjudicate a case consistent with Article III. In *Gomez v. United States*, 490 U.S. 858 (1989), the Court held that a magistrate judge could not conduct jury voir dire in a felony case over the objections of the defendants, but in *Peretz v. United States*, 501 U.S. 923 (1991), the Court held that a defendant's consent obviated any concerns, statutory or constitutional, about a magistrate judge conducting jury selection in a felony trial.

Gomez was unanimous, but *Peretz* was a 5-4 decision. Justice Marshall, joined by Justices White and Blackmun, found *Gomez* indistinguishable: in the dissent's view, Congress did not intend to permit magistrates to conduct jury selection in felony cases, with or without the defendant's consent. Justice Scalia in dissent also agreed that *Gomez*'s statutory conclusion barred the role the magistrate assumed in *Peretz*, even with consent. He then concluded:

> The Court's [constitutional] analysis turns on the fact that courts themselves control the decision whether, and to what extent, magistrates will be used. But the Constitution guarantees not merely that no Branch will be forced by one of the other branches to let someone else exercise its assigned powers—but that none of the branches will itself alienate its assigned powers. Otherwise, the doctrine of unconstitutional delegation of legislative power (which delegation cannot plausibly be compelled by one of the other branches) is a dead letter. . . .

3. Dissenting in *Wellness*, Chief Justice Roberts argues that *Gomez* and *Peretz* do not support allowing bankruptcy judges to decide *Stern* claims, because in neither case did the magistrate judge enter final judgments. Instead, both cases involved jury selection, a preliminary stage in a criminal prosecution. In response, the majority argues in footnote 9 that magistrate judges may enter final judgment in civil and misdemeanor cases—so long as the parties consent. Does this arrangement comport with the Constitution? The Supreme Court has never addressed this question directly, but the courts of appeals have uniformly upheld the procedure.

Appendix A

The Constitution of the United States

(Excerpts)

We the People of the United States, in Order to form a more perfect Union, establish Justice, insure domestic Tranquility, provide for the common defence, promote the general Welfare, and secure the Blessings of Liberty to ourselves and our Posterity, do ordain and establish this Constitution for the United States of America.

Article I

Section 1.

All legislative Powers herein granted shall be vested in a Congress of the United States, which shall consist of a Senate and House of Representatives.

Section 2.

The House of Representatives shall be composed of Members chosen every second Year by the People of the several States, and the Electors in each State shall have the Qualifications requisite for Electors of the most numerous Branch of the State Legislature.

No Person shall be a Representative who shall not have attained to the Age of twenty five Years, and been seven Years a Citizen of the United States, and who shall not, when elected, be an Inhabitant of that State in which he shall be chosen. . . .

When vacancies happen in the Representation from any State, the Executive Authority thereof shall issue Writs of Election to fill such Vacancies.

The House of Representatives shall chuse their Speaker and other Officers; and shall have the sole Power of Impeachment.

Section 3.

[*Editorial note*. The first paragraph of Section 3 is omitted. It has been superseded by the Seventeenth Amendment.]

No Person shall be a Senator who shall not have attained to the Age of thirty Years, and been nine Years a Citizen of the United States, and who shall not, when elected, be an Inhabitant of that State for which he shall be chosen.

The Vice President of the United States shall be President of the Senate, but shall have no Vote, unless they be equally divided.

The Senate shall chuse their other Officers, and also a President pro tempore, in the Absence of the Vice President, or when he shall exercise the Office of President of the United States.

The Senate shall have the sole Power to try all Impeachments. When sitting for that Purpose, they shall be on Oath or Affirmation. When the President of the United States is tried, the Chief Justice shall preside: And no Person shall be convicted without the Concurrence of two thirds of the Members present.

Judgment in Cases of Impeachment shall not extend further than to removal from Office, and disqualification to hold and enjoy any Office of honor, Trust or Profit under the United States: but the Party convicted shall nevertheless be liable and subject to Indictment, Trial, Judgment and Punishment, according to Law.

Section 4.

The Times, Places and Manner of holding Elections for Senators and Representatives, shall be prescribed in each State by the Legislature thereof; but the Congress may at any time by Law make or alter such Regulations, except as to the Places of chusing Senators. . . .

Section 5.

Each House shall be the Judge of the Elections, Returns and Qualifications of its own Members, and a Majority of each shall constitute a Quorum to do Business; but a smaller Number may adjourn from day to day, and may be authorized to compel the Attendance of absent Members, in such Manner, and under such Penalties as each House may provide.

Each House may determine the Rules of its Proceedings, punish its Members for disorderly Behaviour, and, with the Concurrence of two thirds, expel a Member. . . .

Section 6.

The Senators and Representatives shall receive a Compensation for their Services, to be ascertained by Law, and paid out of the Treasury of the United States. They shall in all Cases, except Treason, Felony and Breach of the Peace, beprivileged from Arrest during their Attendance at the Session of their respective Houses, and in going to and returning from the same; and for any Speech or Debate in either House, they shall not be questioned in any other Place.

No Senator or Representative shall, during the Time for which he was elected, be appointed to any civil Office under the Authority of the United States, which shall have been created, or the Emoluments whereof shall have been encreased during such time; and no Person holding any Office under the United States, shall be a Member of either House during his Continuance in Office.

Section 7.

All Bills for raising Revenue shall originate in the House of Representatives; but the Senate may propose or concur with Amendments as on other Bills.

Every Bill which shall have passed the House of Representatives and the Senate, shall, before it become a Law, be presented to the President of the United States; If he approve he shall sign it, but if not he shall return it, with his Objections to that House in which it shall have originated, who shall enter the Objections at large on their Journal, and proceed to reconsider it. If after such Reconsideration two thirds of that House shall agree to pass the Bill, it shall be sent, together with the Objections, to the other House, by which it shall likewise be reconsidered, and if approved by two thirds of that House, it shall become a Law. But in all such Cases the Votes of both Houses shall be determined by yeas and Nays, and the Names of the Persons voting for and against the Bill shall be entered on the Journal of each House respectively. If any Bill shall not be returned by the President within ten Days (Sundays excepted) after it shall have been presented to him, the Same shall be a Law, in like Manner as if he had signed it, unless the Congress by their Adjournment prevent its Return, in which Case it shall not be a Law.

Every Order, Resolution, or Vote to which the Concurrence of the Senate and House of Representatives may be necessary (except on a question of Adjournment) shall be presented to the President of the United States; and before the Same shall take Effect, shall be approved by him, or being disapproved by him, shall be repassed by two thirds of the Senate and House of Representatives, according to the Rules and Limitations prescribed in the Case of a Bill.

Section 8.

The Congress shall have Power To lay and collect Taxes, Duties, Imposts and Excises, to pay the Debts and provide for the common Defence and general Welfare of the United States; but all Duties, Imposts and Excises shall be uniform throughout the United States;

To borrow Money on the credit of the United States;

To regulate Commerce with foreign Nations, and among the several States, and with the Indian Tribes;

To establish an uniform Rule of Naturalization, and uniform Laws on the subject of Bankruptcies throughout the United States;

To coin Money, regulate the Value thereof, and of foreign Coin, and fix the Standard of Weights and Measures;

To provide for the Punishment of counterfeiting the Securities and current Coin of the United States;

To establish Post Offices and post Roads;

To promote the Progress of Science and useful Arts, by securing for limited Times to Authors and Inventors the exclusive Right to their respective Writings and Discoveries;

To constitute Tribunals inferior to the supreme Court;

To define and punish Piracies and Felonies committed on the high Seas, and Offences against the Law of Nations;

To declare War, grant Letters of Marque and Reprisal, and make Rules concerning Captures on Land and Water;

To raise and support Armies, but no Appropriation of Money to that Use shall be for a longer Term than two Years;

To provide and maintain a Navy;

To make Rules for the Government and Regulation of the land and naval Forces;

To provide for calling forth the Militia to execute the Laws of the Union, suppress Insurrections and repel Invasions;

To provide for organizing, arming, and disciplining, the Militia, and for governing such Part of them as may be employed in the Service of the United States, reserving to the States respectively, the Appointment of the Officers, and the Authority of training the Militia according to the discipline prescribed by Congress;

To exercise exclusive Legislation in all Cases whatsoever, over such District (not exceeding ten Miles square) as may, by Cession of particular States, and the Acceptance of Congress, become the Seat of the Government of the United States, and to exercise like Authority over all Places purchased by the Consent of the Legislature of the State in which the Same shall be, for the Erection of Forts, Magazines, Arsenals, dock-Yards, and other needful Buildings;—And

To make all Laws which shall be necessary and proper for carrying into Execution the foregoing Powers, and all other Powers vested by this Constitution in the Government of the United States, or in any Department or Officer thereof.

Section 9.

The Migration or Importation of such Persons as any of the States now existing shall think proper to admit, shall not be prohibited by the Congress prior to the Year one thousand eight hundred and eight, but a Tax or duty may be imposed on such Importation, not exceeding ten dollars for each Person.

The Privilege of the Writ of Habeas Corpus shall not be suspended, unless when in Cases of Rebellion or Invasion the public Safety may require it.

No Bill of Attainder or ex post facto Law shall be passed.

No Capitation, or other direct, Tax shall be laid, unless in Proportion to the Census or Enumeration herein before directed to be taken. [*Editorial note*. This provision has been nullified by the Sixteenth Amendment.]

No Tax or Duty shall be laid on Articles exported from any State.

No Preference shall be given by any Regulation of Commerce or Revenue to the Ports of one State over those of another: nor shall Vessels bound to, or from, one State, be obliged to enter, clear, or pay Duties in another.

No Money shall be drawn from the Treasury, but in Consequence of Appropriations made by Law; and a regular Statement and Account of the Receipts and Expenditures of all public Money shall be published from time to time.

No Title of Nobility shall be granted by the United States: And no Person holding any Office of Profit or Trust under them, shall, without the Consent of the Congress, accept of any present, Emolument, Office, or Title, of any kind whatever, from any King, Prince, or foreign State.

Section 10.

No State shall enter into any Treaty, Alliance, or Confederation; grant Letters of Marque and Reprisal; coin Money; emit Bills of Credit; make any Thing but gold and silver Coin a Tender in Payment of Debts; pass any Bill of Attainder, ex post facto Law, or Law impairing the Obligation of Contracts, or grant any Title of Nobility.

No State shall, without the Consent of the Congress, lay any Imposts or Duties on Imports or Exports, except what may be absolutely necessary for executing it's inspection Laws: and the net Produce of all Duties and Imposts, laid by any State on Imports or Exports, shall be for the Use of the Treasury of the United States; and all such Laws shall be subject to the Revision and Controul of the Congress.

No State shall, without the Consent of Congress, lay any Duty of Tonnage, keep Troops, or Ships of War in time of Peace, enter into any Agreement or Compact with another State, or with a foreign Power, or engage in War, unless actually invaded, or in such imminent Danger as will not admit of delay.

Article II

Section 1.

The executive Power shall be vested in a President of the United States of America. He shall hold his Office during the Term of four Years, and, together with the Vice President, chosen for the same Term, be elected, as follows:

Each State shall appoint, in such Manner as the Legislature thereof may direct, a Number of Electors, equal to the whole Number of Senators and Representatives to which the State may be entitled in the Congress: but no Senator or Representative, or Person holding an Office of Trust or Profit under the United States, shall be appointed an Elector. . . .

The Congress may determine the Time of chusing the Electors, and the Day on which they shall give their Votes; which Day shall be the same throughout the United States.

No Person except a natural born Citizen, or a Citizen of the United States, at the time of the Adoption of this Constitution, shall be eligible to the Office of President; neither shall any Person be eligible to that Office who shall not have attained to the Age of thirty five Years, and been fourteen Years a Resident within the United States. . . .

The President shall, at stated Times, receive for his Services, a Compensation, which shall neither be encreased nor diminished during the Period for which he shall have been elected, and he shall not receive within that Period any other Emolument from the United States, or any of them.

Before he enter on the Execution of his Office, he shall take the following Oath or Affirmation: — "I do solemnly swear (or affirm) that I will faithfully execute the Office of President of the United States, and will to the best of my Ability, preserve, protect and defend the Constitution of the United States."

Section 2.

The President shall be Commander in Chief of the Army and Navy of the United States, and of the Militia of the several States, when called into the actual Service of the United States; he may require the Opinion, in writing, of the principal Officer in each of the executive Departments, upon any Subject relating to the Duties of their respective Offices, and he shall have Power to grant Reprieves and Pardons for Offences against the United States, except in Cases of Impeachment.

He shall have Power, by and with the Advice and Consent of the Senate, to make Treaties, provided two thirds of the Senators present concur; and he shall nominate, and by and with the Advice and Consent of the Senate, shall appoint Ambassadors, other public Ministers and Consuls, Judges of the supreme Court, and all other Officers of the United States, whose Appointments are not herein otherwise provided for, and which shall be established by Law: but the Congress may by Law vest the Appointment of such inferior Officers, as they think proper, in the President alone, in the Courts of Law, or in the Heads of Departments.

The President shall have Power to fill up all Vacancies that may happen during the Recess of the Senate, by granting Commissions which shall expire at the End of their next Session.

Section 3.

He shall from time to time give to the Congress Information of the State of the Union, and recommend to their Consideration such Measures as he shall judge necessary and expedient; he may, on extraordinary Occasions, convene both Houses, or either of them, and in Case of Disagreement between them, with Respect to the Time of Adjournment, he may adjourn them to such Time as he shall think proper; he shall receive Ambassadors and other public Ministers; he shall take Care that the Laws be faithfully executed, and shall Commission all the Officers of the United States.

Section 4.

The President, Vice President and all civil Officers of the United States, shall be removed from Office on Impeachment for, and Conviction of, Treason, Bribery, or other high Crimes and Misdemeanors.

Article III

Section 1.

The judicial Power of the United States, shall be vested in one supreme Court, and in such inferior Courts as the Congress may from time to time ordain and establish. The Judges, both of the supreme and inferior Courts, shall hold their Offices during good Behaviour, and shall, at stated Times, receive for their Services, a Compensation, which shall not be diminished during their Continuance in Office.

Section 2.

The judicial Power shall extend to all Cases, in Law and Equity, arising under this Constitution, the Laws of the United States, and Treaties made, or which shall be made, under their Authority;—to all Cases affecting Ambassadors, other public Ministers and Consuls;—to all Cases of admiralty and maritime Jurisdiction;—to Controversies to which the United States shall be a Party;—to Controversies between two or more States;—between a State and Citizens of another State;—between Citizens of different States,—between Citizens of the same State claiming Lands under Grants of different States, and between a State, or the Citizens thereof, and foreign States, Citizens or Subjects.

In all Cases affecting Ambassadors, other public Ministers and Consuls, and those in which a State shall be Party, the supreme Court shall have original Jurisdiction. In all the other Cases before mentioned, the supreme Court shall have appellate Jurisdiction, both as to Law and Fact, with such Exceptions, and under such Regulations as the Congress shall make.

The Trial of all Crimes, except in Cases of Impeachment, shall be by Jury; and such Trial shall be held in the State where the said Crimes shall have been committed; but when not committed within any State, the Trial shall be at such Place or Places as the Congress may by Law have directed.

Section 3.

Treason against the United States, shall consist only in levying War against them, or in adhering to their Enemies, giving them Aid and Comfort. No Person shall be convicted of Treason unless on the Testimony of two Witnesses to the same overt Act, or on Confession in open Court.

The Congress shall have Power to declare the Punishment of Treason, but no Attainder of Treason shall work Corruption of Blood, or Forfeiture except during the Life of the Person attainted.

Article IV

Section 1.

Full Faith and Credit shall be given in each State to the public Acts, Records, and judicial Proceedings of every other State. And the Congress may by general Laws prescribe the Manner in which such Acts, Records and Proceedings shall be proved, and the Effect thereof.

Section 2.

The Citizens of each State shall be entitled to all Privileges and Immunities of Citizens in the several States.

A Person charged in any State with Treason, Felony, or other Crime, who shall flee from Justice, and be found in another State, shall on Demand of the executive Authority of the State from which he fled, be delivered up, to be removed to the State having Jurisdiction of the Crime.

No Person held to Service or Labour in one State, under the Laws thereof, escaping into another, shall, in Consequence of any Law or Regulation therein, be discharged from such Service or Labour, but shall be delivered up on Claim of the Party to whom such Service or Labour may be due.

Section 3.

New States may be admitted by the Congress into this Union; but no new State shall be formed or erected within the Jurisdiction of any other State; nor any State be formed by the Junction of two or more States, or Parts of States, without the Consent of the Legislatures of the States concerned as well as of the Congress.

The Congress shall have Power to dispose of and make all needful Rules and Regulations respecting the Territory or other Property belonging to the United States; and nothing in this Constitution shall be so construed as to Prejudice any Claims of the United States, or of any particular State.

Section 4.

The United States shall guarantee to every State in this Union a Republican Form of Government, and shall protect each of them against Invasion; and on Application of the Legislature, or of the Executive (when the Legislature cannot be convened) against domestic Violence.

Article V

The Congress, whenever two thirds of both Houses shall deem it necessary, shall propose Amendments to this Constitution, or, on the Application of the Legislatures of two thirds of the several States, shall call a Convention for proposing Amendments, which, in either Case, shall be valid to all Intents and Purposes, as Part of this Constitution, when ratified by the Legislatures of three fourths of the several States, or by Conventions in three fourths thereof, as the one or the other Mode of Ratification may be proposed by the Congress; Provided that no Amendment which may be made prior to the Year One thousand eight hundred and eight shall in any Manner affect the first and fourth Clauses in the Ninth Section of the first Article; and that no State, without its Consent, shall be deprived of its equal Suffrage in the Senate.

Article VI

All Debts contracted and Engagements entered into, before the Adoption of this Constitution, shall be as valid against the United States under this Constitution, as under the Confederation.

This Constitution, and the Laws of the United States which shall be made in Pursuance thereof; and all Treaties made, or which shall be made, under the Authority of the United States, shall be the supreme Law of the Land; and the Judges in every State shall be bound thereby, any Thing in the Constitution or Laws of any State to the Contrary notwithstanding.

The Senators and Representatives before mentioned, and the Members of the several State Legislatures, and all executive and judicial Officers, both of the United States and of the several States, shall be bound by Oath or Affirmation, to support this Constitution; but no religious Test shall ever be required as a Qualification to any Office or public Trust under the United States.

* * *

Amendment I [1791]

Congress shall make no law respecting an establishment of religion, or prohibiting the free exercise thereof; or abridging the freedom of speech, or of the press; or the right of the people peaceably to assemble, and to petition the Government for a redress of grievances.

Amendment II [1791]

A well regulated Militia, being necessary to the security of a free State, the right of the people to keep and bear Arms, shall not be infringed.

Amendment III [1791]

No Soldier shall, in time of peace be quartered in any house, without the consent of the Owner, nor in time of war, but in a manner to be prescribed by law.

Amendment IV [1791]

The right of the people to be secure in their persons, houses, papers, and effects, against unreasonable searches and seizures, shall not be violated, and no Warrants shall issue, but upon probable cause, supported by Oath or affirmation, and particularly describing the place to be searched, and the persons or things to be seized.

Amendment V [1791]

No person shall be held to answer for a capital, or otherwise infamous crime, unless on a presentment or indictment of a Grand Jury, except in cases arising in the land or naval forces, or in the Militia, when in actual service in time of War or public danger; nor shall any person be subject for the same offence to be twice put in jeopardy of life or limb; nor shall be compelled in any criminal case to be a witness against himself, nor be deprived of life, liberty, or property, without due process of law; nor shall private property be taken for public use, without just compensation.

Amendment VI [1791]

In all criminal prosecutions, the accused shall enjoy the right to a speedy and public trial, by an impartial jury of the State and district wherein the crime shall have been committed, which district shall have been previously ascertained by law, and to be informed of the nature and cause of the accusation; to be confronted with the witnesses against him; to have compulsory process for obtaining witnesses in his favor, and to have the Assistance of Counsel for his defence.

Amendment VII [1791]

In Suits at common law, where the value in controversy shall exceed twenty dollars, the right of trial by jury shall be preserved, and no fact tried by a jury, shall be otherwise re-examined in any Court of the United States, than according to the rules of the common law.

Amendment VIII [1791]

Excessive bail shall not be required, nor excessive fines imposed, nor cruel and unusual punishments inflicted.

Amendment IX [1791]

The enumeration in the Constitution, of certain rights, shall not be construed to deny or disparage others retained by the people.

Amendment X [1791]

The powers not delegated to the United States by the Constitution, nor prohibited by it to the States, are reserved to the States respectively, or to the people.

Amendment XI [1798]

The Judicial power of the United States shall not be construed to extend to any suit in law or equity, commenced or prosecuted against one of the United States by Citizens of another State, or by Citizens or Subjects of any Foreign State.

Amendment XIII [1865]

Section 1.

Neither slavery nor involuntary servitude, except as a punishment for crime whereof the party shall have been duly convicted, shall exist within the United States, or any place subject to their jurisdiction.

Section 2.

Congress shall have power to enforce this article by appropriate legislation.

Amendment XIV [1868]

Section 1.

All persons born or naturalized in the United States, and subject to the jurisdiction thereof, are citizens of the United States and of the state wherein they reside. No state shall make or enforce any law which shall abridge the privileges or immunities of citizens of the United States; nor shall any state deprive any person of life, liberty, or property, without due process of law; nor deny to any person within its jurisdiction the equal protection of the laws.

Section 2.

Representatives shall be apportioned among the several states according to their respective numbers, counting the whole number of persons in each state, excluding Indians not taxed. But when the right to vote at any election for the choice of electors for President and Vice President of the United States, Representatives in Congress, the executive and judicial officers of a state, or the members of the legislature thereof, is denied to any of the male inhabitants of such state, being twenty-one years of age, and citizens of the United States, or in any way abridged, except for participation in rebellion, or other crime, the basis of representation therein shall be reduced in the proportion which the number of such male citizens shall bear to the whole number of male citizens twenty-one years of age in such state.

* * *

Section 5.

The Congress shall have power to enforce, by appropriate legislation, the provisions of this article.

Amendment XV [1870]

Section 1.

The right of citizens of the United States to vote shall not be denied or abridged by the United States or by any State on account of race, color, or previous condition of servitude.

Section 2.

The Congress shall have power to enforce this article by appropriate legislation.

Amendment XVI [1913]

The Congress shall have power to lay and collect taxes on incomes, from whatever source derived, without apportionment among the several States, and without regard to any census or enumeration.

Amendment XVII [1913]

[1] The Senate of the United States shall be composed of two Senators from each State, elected by the people thereof, for six years; and each Senator shall have one vote. The electors in each State shall have the qualifications requisite for electors of the most numerous branch of the State legislatures.

[2] When vacancies happen in the representation of any State in the Senate, the executive authority of such State shall issue writs of election to fill such vacancies: *Provided*, That the legislature of any State may empower the executive thereof to make temporary appointments until the people fill the vacancies by election as the legislature may direct. . . .

* * *

Amendment XIX [1920]

[1] The right of citizens of the United States to vote shall not be denied or abridged by the United States or by any State on account of sex.

[2] Congress shall have power to enforce this article by appropriate legislation.

* * *

Amendment XXI [1933]

Section 1.

The eighteenth article of amendment to the Constitution of the United States is hereby repealed.

Section 2.

The transportation or importation into any State, Territory, or possession of the United States for delivery or use therein of intoxicating liquors, in violation of the laws thereof, is hereby prohibited.

Section 3.

This article shall be inoperative unless it shall have been ratified as an amendment to the Constitution by conventions in the several States, as provided in the Constitution, within seven years from the date of the submission hereof to the States by the Congress.

* * *

Amendment XXIV [1964]

Section 1.

The right of citizens of the United States to vote in any primary or other election for President or Vice President, for electors for President or Vice President, or for Senator or Representative in Congress, shall not be denied or abridged by the United States or any state by reason of failure to pay any poll tax or other tax.

Section 2.

The Congress shall have power to enforce this article by appropriate legislation.

* * *

Amendment XXVI [1971]

Section 1.

The right of citizens of the United States, who are 18 years of age or older, to vote, shall not be denied or abridged by the United States or any state on account of age.

Section 2.

The Congress shall have the power to enforce this article by appropriate legislation.

Amendment XXVII [1992]

No law varying the compensation for the services of the Senators and Representatives shall take effect until an election of Representatives shall have intervened.

Appendix B

The Justices of the United States Supreme Court, 1946-2015 Terms

U.S. Reports	Term*	The Court**
329–332[1]	1946	**Vinson**, Black, Reed, Frankfurter, Douglas, Murphy, Jackson, Rutledge, Burton
332[1]–335[2]	1947	"
335[2]–338[3]	1948	"
338[3]–339	1949	Vinson, Black, Reed, Frankfurter, Douglas, Jackson, Burton, Clark, Minton
340–341	1950	"
342–343	1951	"
344–346[4]	1952	"
346[4]–347	1953	**Warren**, Black, Reed, Frankfurter, Douglas, Jackson, Burton, Clark, Minton
348–349	1954	Warren, Black, Reed, Frankfurter, Douglas, Burton, Clark, Minton, Harlan[5]
350–351	1955	"
352–354	1956	Warren, Black, Reed,[6] Frankfurter, Douglas, Burton, Clark, Harlan, Brennan, Whittaker[7]
355–357	1957	Warren, Black, Frankfurter, Douglas, Burton, Clark, Harlan, Brennan, Whittaker

---

* Rule 3 of the Supreme Court's Rules provides in part: "The Court holds a continuous annual Term commencing on the first Monday in October and ending on the day before the first Monday in October of the following year."

** Justices are listed in order of seniority. Boldface indicates a new Chief Justice.

1. The 1947 Term begins at 332 U.S. 371.
2. The 1948 Term begins at 335 U.S. 281.
3. The 1949 Term begins at 338 U.S. 217.
4. The 1953 Term begins at 346 U.S. 325.
5. Participation begins with 349 U.S.
6. Participation ends with 352 U.S. 564.
7. Participation begins with 353 U.S.

U.S. Reports	Term	The Court*
358–360	1958	Warren, Black, Frankfurter, Douglas, Clark, Harlan, Brennan, Whittaker, Stewart
361–364[8]	1959	"
364[8]–367	1960	"
368–370	1961	Warren, Black, Frankfurter,[9] Douglas, Clark, Harlan, Brennan, Whittaker,[10] Stewart, White[11]
371–374	1962	Warren, Black, Douglas, Clark, Harlan, Brennan, Stewart, White, Goldberg
375–378	1963	"
379–381	1964	"
382–384	1965	Warren, Black, Douglas, Clark, Harlan, Brennan, Stewart, White, Fortas
385–388	1966	"
389–392	1967	Warren, Black, Douglas, Harlan, Brennan, Stewart, White, Fortas, Marshall
393–395	1968	Warren, Black, Douglas, Harlan, Brennan, Stewart, White, Fortas,[12] Marshall
396–399	1969	**Burger**, Black, Douglas, Harlan, Brennan, Stewart, White, Marshall, [vacancy]
400–403	1970	Burger, Black, Douglas, Harlan, Brennan, Stewart, White, Marshall, Blackmun
404–408	1971	Burger, Douglas, Brennan, Stewart, White, Marshall, Blackmun, Powell,[13] Rehnquist[13]
409–413	1972	"
414–418	1973	"
419–422	1974	"
423–428	1975	Burger, Brennan, Stewart, White, Marshall, Blackmun, Powell, Rehnquist, Stevens[14]
429–433	1976	"
434–438	1977	"
439–443	1978	"
444–448	1979	"
449–453	1980	"

* Justices are listed in order of seniority. Boldface indicates a new Chief Justice.
8. The 1960 Term begins with 364 U.S. 285.
9. Participation ends with 369 U.S. 422.
10. Participation ends with 369 U.S. 120.
11. Participation begins with 370 U.S.
12. Participation ends with 394 U.S.
13. Participation begins with 405 U.S.
14. Participation begins with 424 U.S.

U.S. Reports	Term	The Court*
454–458	1981	Burger, Brennan, White, Marshall, Blackmun, Powell, Rehnquist, Stevens, O'Connor
459–463	1982	"
464–468	1983	"
469–473	1984	"
474–478	1985	"
479–483	1986	**Rehnquist**, Brennan, White, Marshall, Blackmun, Powell, Stevens, O'Connor, Scalia
484–487	1987	"
488–492	1988	Rehnquist, Brennan, White, Marshall, Blackmun, Stevens, O'Connor, Scalia, Kennedy
493–497	1989	"
498–501	1990	Rehnquist, White, Marshall, Blackmun, Stevens, O'Connor, Scalia, Kennedy, Souter
502–505	1991	Rehnquist, White, Blackmun, Stevens, O'Connor, Scalia, Kennedy, Souter, Thomas
506–509	1992	"
510–512	1993	Rehnquist, Blackmun, Stevens, O'Connor, Scalia, Kennedy, Souter, Thomas, Ginsburg
513–515	1994	Rehnquist, Stevens, O'Connor, Scalia, Kennedy, Souter, Thomas, Ginsburg, Breyer
516–518	1995	"
519–521	1996	"
522–524	1997	"
525–527	1998	"
528–530	1999	"
531–533	2000	"
534–536	2001	"
537–539	2002	"
540–542	2003	"
543–545	2004[15]	Rehnquist, Stevens, O'Connor, Scalia, Kennedy, Souter, Thomas, Ginsburg, Breyer
546–548	2005	**Roberts**, Stevens, O'Connor,[16] Scalia, Kennedy, Souter, Thomas, Ginsburg, Breyer, Alito[17]

---

* Justices are listed in order of seniority. Boldface indicates a new Chief Justice.

15. Chief Justice Rehnquist died on Sept. 3, 2005, shortly before the 2004 Term officially concluded, but after all opinions from that Term had been delivered.

16. Participation ends with 546 U.S. 417.

17. Participation begins with 547 U.S.

U.S. Reports	Term	The Court*
549–551	2006	Roberts, Stevens, Scalia, Kennedy, Souter, Thomas, Ginsburg, Breyer, Alito
552–554	2007	"
555–557	2008	"
558–561	2009	Roberts, Stevens, Scalia, Kennedy, Thomas, Ginsburg, Breyer, Alito, Sotomayor
562–564	2010	Roberts, Scalia, Kennedy, Thomas, Ginsburg, Breyer, Alito, Sotomayor, Kagan
565–567	2011	"
568–570	2012	"
571–573	2013	"
574–576	2014	"
577–579	2015	Roberts, Scalia,[18] Kennedy, Thomas, Ginsburg, Breyer, Alito, Sotomayor, Kagan

---

* Justices are listed in order of seniority. Boldface indicates a new Chief Justice.

18. Justice Scalia died on February 13, 2016, before most of the cases argued in the 2015 Term were decided. His participation ended with 136 S. Ct. 760.

Table of Cases

[References are to page numbers. Boldface indicates principal cases.]

C

Index

[References are to page numbers.]